CHAPTER 11

Degrees of Freedom for an Independent-Samples t Test

$$df_{total} = df_X + df_Y$$

Pooled Variance

$$s^2_{pooled} = \left(\frac{df_X}{df_{total}}\right)s^2_X + \left(\frac{df_Y}{df_{total}}\right)s^2_Y$$

Variance for a Distribution of Means for an Independent-Samples t Test

$$s^2_{M_X} = \frac{s^2_{pooled}}{N_X} \qquad s^2_{M_Y} = \frac{s^2_{pooled}}{N_Y}$$

Variance for a Distribution of Differences Between Means

$$s^2_{difference} = s^2_{M_X} + s^2_{M_Y}$$

Standard Deviation of the Distribution of Differences Between Means

$$s_{difference} = \sqrt{s^2_{difference}}$$

t Statistic for an Independent-Samples t Test

$$t = \frac{(M_X - M_Y) - (\mu_X - \mu_Y)}{s_{difference}}$$

often abbreviated as: $t = \dfrac{(M_X - M_Y)}{s_{difference}}$

Confidence Interval for an Independent-Samples t Test

$$(M_X - M_Y)_{lower} = -t(s_{difference}) + (M_X - M_Y)_{sample}$$
$$(M_X - M_Y)_{upper} = t(s_{difference}) + (M_X - M_Y)_{sample}$$

Pooled Standard Deviation

$$s_{pooled} = \sqrt{s^2_{pooled}}$$

Effect Size for an Independent-Samples t Test

$$\text{Cohen's } d = \frac{(M_X - M_Y) - (\mu_X - \mu_Y)}{s_{pooled}}$$

CHAPTER 12

One-Way Between-Groups ANOVA

$$df_{between} = N_{groups} - 1$$
$$df_{within} = df_1 + df_2 + \cdots + df_{last}$$
(in which df_1 etc. are the degrees of freedom, $N - 1$, for each sample)
$$df_{total} = df_{between} + df_{within}$$
$$\text{or } df_{total} = N_{total} - 1$$
$$GM = \frac{\Sigma(X)}{N_{total}}$$
$$SS_{total} = \Sigma(X - GM)^2 \text{ for each score}$$
$$SS_{within} = \Sigma(X - M)^2 \text{ for each score}$$
$$SS_{between} = \Sigma(M - GM)^2 \text{ for each score}$$
$$SS_{total} = SS_{within} + SS_{between}$$
$$MS_{between} = \frac{SS_{between}}{df_{between}}$$
$$MS_{within} = \frac{SS_{within}}{df_{within}}$$
$$F = \frac{MS_{between}}{MS_{within}}$$

Effect Size for a One-Way Between-Groups ANOVA

$$R^2 = \frac{SS_{between}}{SS_{total}}$$

Tukey HSD post-hoc test

$$s_M = \sqrt{\frac{MS_{within}}{N}}, \text{ if equal sample sizes}$$
$$N' = \frac{N_{groups}}{\Sigma(1/N)}$$
$$s_M = \sqrt{\frac{MS_{within}}{N'}}, \text{ if unequal sample sizes}$$
$$HSD = \frac{(M_1 - M_2)}{s_M}, \text{ for any two sample means}$$

(Formulas continued on inside back cover.)

Statistics
for the
Behavioral
Sciences

fourth
edition

Susan A. Nolan
Seton Hall University

Thomas E. Heinzen
William Paterson University

worth publishers
Macmillan Learning
New York

Vice President, Social Sciences: Charles Linsmeier

Executive Acquisitions Editor: Daniel McDonough

Developmental Editor: Michael Kimball

Assistant Editor: Kimberly Morgan Smith

Senior Marketing Manager: Lindsay Johnson

Marketing Assistant: Morgan Ratner

Director of Content Management Enhancement: Tracey Kuehn

Managing Editor: Lisa Kinne

Media Editor: Anthony Casciano

Media Producer: Joseph Tomasso

Senior Production Supervisor: Paul Rohloff

Project Editor: Kayci Wyatt, MPS North America LLC

Photo Editor: Sheena Goldstein

Director of Design, Content Management: Diana Blume

Interior Designer: Kevin Kall

Cover Designer: Blake Logan

Illustrations: MPS Limited

Composition: MPS Limited

Printing & Binding: King Printing Co., Inc.

Cover Painting: Detail from *Untitled (bluegreensmokestripes)*, oil on panel, 2013 by Leslie Wayne

Library of Congress Control Number: 2016935624

ISBN-13: 978-1-319-29242-3

ISBN-10: 1-319-29242-9

Worth Publishers

One New York Plaza

Suite 4500

New York, NY 10004-1562

www.macmillanhighered.com

FORMULAS

CHAPTER 13 (Formulas continued from inside front cover.)

One-Way Within-Groups ANOVA

$df_{subjects} = n - 1$

$df_{within} = (df_{between})(df_{subjects})$

$df_{total} = df_{between} + df_{subjects} + df_{within}$

$SS_{subjects} = \Sigma(M_{participant} - GM)^2$ for each score

$SS_{within} = SS_{total} - SS_{between} - SS_{subjects}$

$$MS_{subjects} = \frac{SS_{subjects}}{df_{subjects}}$$

$$F_{subjects} = \frac{MS_{subjects}}{MS_{within}}$$

Effect Size for a One-Way Within-Groups ANOVA

$$R^2 = \frac{SS_{between}}{(SS_{total} - SS_{subjects})}$$

CHAPTER 14

Two-Way Between-Groups ANOVA

$df_{rows} = N_{rows} - 1$

$df_{columns} = N_{columns} - 1$

$df_{interaction} = (df_{rows})(df_{columns})$

$SS_{total} = \Sigma(X - GM)^2$ for each score

$SS_{between(rows)} = \Sigma(M_{row} - GM)^2$ for each score

$SS_{between(columns)} = \Sigma(M_{column} - GM)^2$ for each score

$SS_{within} = \Sigma(X - M_{cell})^2$ for each score

$SS_{between(interaction)} = SS_{total} - (SS_{between(rows)} + SS_{between(columns)} + SS_{within})$

Effect Sizes for a Two-Way Between-Groups ANOVA

$$R^2_{rows} = \frac{SS_{rows}}{(SS_{total} - SS_{columns} - SS_{interaction})}$$

$$R^2_{columns} = \frac{SS_{columns}}{(SS_{total} - SS_{rows} - SS_{interaction})}$$

$$R^2_{interaction} = \frac{SS_{interaction}}{(SS_{total} - SS_{rows} - SS_{columns})}$$

CHAPTER 15

Pearson Correlation Coefficient

$$r = \frac{\Sigma[(X - M_X)(Y - M_Y)]}{\sqrt{(SS_X)(SS_Y)}}$$

$df_r = N - 2$

CHAPTER 16

Standardized Regression Equation

$z_{\hat{Y}} = (r_{XY})(z_X)$

Simple Linear Regression Equation

$\hat{Y} = a + b(X)$

Standardized Regression Coefficient

$$\beta = (b)\frac{\sqrt{SS_X}}{\sqrt{SS_Y}}$$

Proportionate Reduction in Error

$$r^2 = \frac{(SS_{total} - SS_{error})}{SS_{total}}$$

For my "chosen family" in Jersey City
and New York

Susan Nolan

To the person who had
the best idea that anyone ever had:
Charles Darwin

Tom Heinzen

ABOUT THE AUTHORS

Ivan Bojanic

SUSAN NOLAN turned to psychology after suffering a career-ending accident on her second workday as a bicycle messenger. A native of Boston, she graduated from the College of Holy Cross and earned her PhD in clinical psychology from Northwestern University. Her research involves experimental investigations of the role of gender in the interpersonal consequences of depression, and studies on gender and mentoring in the fields of science, technology, engineering, and mathematics; her research has been funded by the National Science Foundation. Susan is a professor of psychology at Seton Hall University in New Jersey. She served as a representative from the American Psychological Association (APA) to the United Nations in New York City for 5 years, and is the Vice President for Diversity and International Relations of the Society for the Teaching of Psychology (STP). She also was the chair of the 2012 Society for the Teaching of Psychology (STP) Presidential Task Force on Statistical Literacy. Susan is a past president of the Eastern Psychological Association (EPA) and was a 2015–2016 U.S. Fulbright scholar. She is a fellow of the EPA, the APA, and the Association for Psychological Science.

Susan's academic schedule allows her to pursue one travel adventure per year, a tradition that she relishes. Over the years she has ridden her bicycle across the United States (despite her earlier crash), swapped apartments to live in Montréal (her favorite North American city), and explored the Adriatic coast in an intermittently roadworthy 1985 Volkswagen Scirocco. She writes much of the book on her annual trip to Bosnia and Herzegovina, where she and her husband, Ivan Bojanic, own a small house on the Vrbas River in the city of Banja Luka. They currently reside in Jersey City, New Jersey, where Susan roots feverishly, if quietly, for the Boston Red Sox.

TOM HEINZEN was a 29-year-old college freshman; he began graduate school 8 days after the birth of his fourth daughter, and is still amazed that he and his wife somehow managed to stay married. A magna cum laude graduate of Rockford College, he earned his PhD in social psychology at the State University of New York at Albany in just 3 years.

He published his first book on frustration and creativity in government 2 years later; was a research associate in public policy until he was fired for arguing over the shape of a graph; consulted for the Johns Hopkins Center for Talented Youth; and then began a teaching career at William Paterson University of New Jersey. He founded the psychology club, established an undergraduate research conference, and has been awarded various teaching honors while continuing to write journal articles, books, plays, and two novels that support the teaching of general psychology and statistics. He is also the editor of *Many Things to Tell You*, a volume of poetry by elderly writers.

He has recently become enamored with the potential of game-based designs to influence students at risk for not completing their degrees. He belongs to numerous professional societies, including the APA, the EPA, the APS, and the New York Academy of Science, whose meeting place next to the former Twin Towers offers such a spectacular view of New York City that they have to cover the windows so the speakers don't lose their focus during their talks.

His wife, Donna, is a physician assistant who has volunteered her time in relief work following hurricanes Mitch and Katrina; and their daughters work in public health, teaching, and medicine. Tom is an enthusiastic but mediocre tennis player and, as a Yankees, Cubs, and emerging Pittsburgh Pirates fan, sympathizes with Susan's tortured New England loyalties.

BRIEF CONTENTS

CONTENTS

PREFACE

Statistics is hotter than ever. This is the era of big data. According to an article in the *New York Times*, statistics is perhaps the most promising, adventurous career option you can choose right now—and the field is likely to expand significantly in the future, thanks to the large amounts of information (called *big data*) available to us in this digital age. Gone is the stereotype of boring (but influential) statistics geeks hiding behind their glowing screens. The new reality requires smart, reflective people who have been trained to explore big data, transforming them into something useful, while not losing sight of the people behind the numbers. This book trains you to find and create data, ask tough questions about a data set, interpret the feedback coming from data analysis, and display data in ways that reveal a precise, coherent, data-driven story. Statistical reasoning is not *at* the cutting edge of information; statistical reasoning *is* the cutting edge of information.

Repeat out loud: "I am a statistician." You don't have to love math to become a good statistician. But if you are thinking about variability (and you are), then you already are thinking like a statistician. There are probably some natural boundaries to the benefits of statistical reasoning, such as the power of intuition. But every time we think we have bumped into a boundary, somebody busts through it, wins a Nobel Prize, and challenges the rest of us to become more creative as we learn how to live together on this beautiful planet.

We dare you to love this course.

Principles for Teaching Statistics

In their classic and persuasive article, Marsha Lovett and Joel Greenhouse (2000) present principles to teach statistics more effectively (all based on empirical research from cognitive psychology). And other researchers continue to build on their helpful work (see Benassi, Overson, & Hakala, 2014). We look to this body of research as we create every edition of this statistics text, from designing the pedagogy to deciding what specific examples to include. Six principles emerge from this research on teaching statistics and drive our text:

1. **Practice and participation.** Recent research has shown that active learning, broadly defined, increases student performance and reduces the failure rate in science courses, including psychology courses (Freeman et al., 2013). This principle pertains to work outside the classroom as well (Lovett & Greenhouse, 2000). Based on these findings, we encourage students to actively participate in their learning throughout the text. Students can practice their knowledge through the many applied exercises, especially in the Applying the Concepts and Putting It All Together sections. In these sections, as well as in the examples integrated into the chapters, the source of the original data is often supplied, whether it is YouTube data on viral videos or statistics from the blog of online dating company OkCupid, encouraging students to dig deeper. And students can take advantage of data sets from the General Social Survey and EESEE Case Studies to "play" with statistics beyond the exercises in the book.

2. **Vivid examples.** Researchers have found that students are most likely to remember concepts illustrated with a vivid instructional tool (VanderStoep, Fagerlin, & Feenstra, 2000). So, whenever possible, we use striking, vivid examples to make statistical concepts memorable, including the lengths of great white sharks to explain samples, destructive hurricanes in the discussion of confounding variables, a

Chipotle burrito hack to teach about control groups, a Damien Hirst dot painting to explain randomness, and a house purchase by Beyoncé to highlight celebrity outliers. Vivid examples are often accompanied by photos to enhance their memorability. When such examples are drawn from outside the academic literature, we follow with engaging research examples from the behavioral sciences to increase the memorability of important concepts.

3. **Integrating new knowledge with previous knowledge.** When connecting new material to existing student knowledge, students can more easily embed that new material into "a framework that will enable them to learn, retrieve, and use new knowledge when they need it" (p. 7, Ambrose & Lovett, 2014). Throughout the text, we illustrate new concepts with examples that connect to things most students already know. In Chapter 1, an example from *Britain's Got Talent* uses students' understanding of the ranking systems on reality shows to explain ordinal variables. In Chapter 5, we use students' understanding of the potential fallibility of pregnancy tests to teach the difference between Type I and Type II errors. Chapter 16, uses the predictive abilities of Facebook profiles to teach regression. And Chapter 18 presents common sentences from popular book series like *The Hunger Games* to help students understand nonparametric hypothesis testing. Learning in different contexts helps students to transfer knowledge to new situations, so we use multiple examples for each concept—typically an initial one that is easier to grasp followed by more traditional behavioral science research examples.

4. **Confronting misconceptions.** Conversely, some kinds of prior knowledge can slow students down (Lovett & Greenhouse, 2000). Students know many statistical words—from independent to variability to significant. But they know the "everyday" definitions of these words, and this prior knowledge can impede their learning of the statistical definitions. Throughout the book, we point out students' likely prior understanding of these key terms, and contrast that with the newer statistical definitions. We also include exercises aimed at having students explain the various ways a given word can be understood. Plus, in Chapter 5, we introduce ways in which other types of misconceptions can emerge through illusory correlation, confirmation bias, and coincidence. Throughout the rest of the book, we highlight these types of flawed thinking with examples, and show how statistics can be the antidote to misconceptions—whether it's a belief that holiday weight gain is a serious problem, that cheating is associated with better grades, or that people swear a lot because they have an otherwise limited vocabulary.

5. **Real-time feedback.** It's not uncommon—in fact, it's actually expected—for students to make mistakes when they first try their hand at a new statistical technique. Research demonstrates that one of the best ways to get past these errors is to provide students with immediate feedback (Kornell & Metcalfe, 2014). For this reason, we include solutions at the back of the book for all Check Your Learning exercises that fall after each section of a chapter and for the odd-numbered exercises at the end of each chapter. Importantly, we don't just provide final answers. We offer fully worked-out solutions that show students all of the steps and calculations to arrive at the final answers. That way, students can figure out exactly where they went astray. Learning is simply more efficient when students can immediately correct their mistakes or receive validation that they answered correctly. This learning is also bolstered by other types of feedback embedded in the book that students can use as models. These include worked-out examples in the chapters and additional "How It Works" worked-out examples at the end of each chapter.

As Lovett and Greenhouse (2000) explain "seeing worked examples before solving new problems makes the subsequent problem solving an easier task" (p. 201). Finally, students can gain additional practice by using the LearningCurve adaptive quizzing system in LaunchPad.

6. **Repetition.** There is a growing literature on the role of "desirable difficulty" in learning—that is, students learn better when they struggle with new material with support (Clark & Bjork, 2014). The three techniques of spacing, interleaving, and testing—all based on the central idea of repetition—help to create the right level of difficulty to help students learn more efficiently.

- *Spacing* involves repeated practice sessions with the same material with delays in between. Our book is set up to encourage spacing. For example, the Before You Go On sections at the beginning of each chapter offer students a chance to review previous material. Several sets of Check Your Learning questions are included across each chapter, and more exercises are included at the end of each chapter.

- *Interleaving* refers to the practice of mixing the types of exercises the student is practicing. Rather than practicing each new task in one block of exercises, students mix exercises on a new topic with repeats of exercises on earlier topics. This repetition of practice with earlier concepts increases retention of material. We build in exercises that encourage interleaving in the Putting It All Together sections, which ask students to return to concepts learned in earlier chapters.

- *Testing* is possibly the best way to learn new material. Simply studying does not introduce the desirable difficulty that enhances learning, but testing forces errors and drives efficient retention of new material. The tiered exercises throughout the chapter and at the end of the chapter provide numerous opportunities for testing—and then more testing. The LearningCurve adaptive quizzing system in LaunchPad provides even more opportunities for students to test themselves throughout the course. We encourage students to aim for repeated practice, completing more exercises than assigned, rather than by studying in more traditional, but less effective, ways.

Trends in Statistics: What's Coming Next?

The field of statistics might seem stable, even staid. But there is an exciting statistical revolution afoot and it is taking place on a number of fronts. Here are five trends that we address in this text:

Trend 1: Visual Displays of Data. Data graphics are the hot new way to search for patterns, tell data-driven stories, and gain new insights from the enormous volumes of information available to us. This trend isn't coming; it's here. And the field needs a lot of guidance, without suppressing all the energy and creativity that fuel it. In short, the field needs smart, hard-working, creative, and visually oriented behavioral scientists. We help students to become savvier at visualizing data not only in Chapter 3, but in a number of other chapters that introduce variations on graphing.

Trend 2: Crowdsourcing. Increasingly, researchers are crowdsourcing their data. Whether via Facebook, online games, or other technological tools, some studies now have millions, or even billions, of data points. In Chapter 5, we lay out the pros and cons of analyzing data derived in this way.

Trend 3: Reproducibility. Even the mainstream media have been breathlessly reporting on a "reproducibility crisis" in the behavioral sciences. The problem? A whole lot of studies have failed to replicate the original findings the second (and third and fourth) times they were conducted. In Chapter 7, we outline this high-visibility challenge to the field, but we also consider the possibility that self-correcting science is good for the behavioral sciences and for society.

Trend 4: The "New Statistics." Behavioral science research journals are increasingly demanding the inclusion of the so-called "new statistics"—particularly effect sizes and confidence intervals—in published articles (Cumming, 2012). We explore these recent changes in the reporting of statistics, and why this is a big step in the right direction, in Chapter 8. We also introduce the relevant new statistics alongside every hypothesis test in Chapters 9 through 17.

Trend 5: Bayesian Analysis. Perhaps the biggest part of the statistics revolution is the nascent movement to overthrow traditional hypothesis testing in favor of Bayesian analysis—an approach that takes into account not just the current data but what we already know about the topic being studied (Kruschke, 2010a). In Chapter 11, we introduce basic Bayesian logic, and explore why many researchers prefer this approach. We urge students to watch for a continuing shift in accepted statistical approaches over the next decade.

What's New in the Fourth Edition

In this new edition of *Statistics for the Behavioral Sciences*, we highlight innovations in statistics, including those outlined in the trends section just above. It is an exciting time to be studying statistics, as can be seen through our discussions of crowdsourcing, the replication crisis, the "new statistics," and Bayesian analysis. In addition, throughout the text, we connect students to statistical concepts as efficiently and memorably as possible. We've sharpened the focus of the book on the core concepts and introduce each topic with a vivid, real-world example. Our pedagogy first emphasizes mastering concepts, and then gives students multiple step-by-step examples of the process of each statistical method, including the mathematical calculations. The extensive Check Your Learning exercises at the end of each section of the chapter, along with the end-of-chapter exercises and the new LaunchPad Web site, give students lots of opportunities to practice. Indeed, there are more than twice as many exercises in the fourth edition as in the first. We've also clarified our approach by fine-tuning the following features throughout the book.

Before You Go On

Each chapter opens with a Before You Go On section that highlights the concepts students need to have mastered before they move on to the next chapter.

BEFORE YOU GO ON

- You should understand the difference between a sample and a population (Chapter 1).

- You should know how to measure central tendency, especially the mean (Chapter 4).

Mastering the Formulas and Mastering the Concepts

Some of the most difficult tasks for students new to statistics are identifying the key points and connecting this new knowledge to what they have covered in previous chapters. The unique Mastering the Formula and Mastering the Concept marginal notes provide students with helpful explanations that identify each formula when it is first introduced and each important concept at its point of relevance. Figure E-1 ("Choosing the Appropriate Hypothesis Test") in Appendix E is a terrific summary that shows students how to apply statistical techniques to their research. It's the entire text summarized on a single page; students will learn it quickly and use it for the rest of their careers in statistics.

> **MASTERING THE FORMULA**
>
> **6-2:** The formula to calculate the raw score from a z score is:
>
> $$X = z(\sigma) + \mu.$$
>
> We multiply the z score by the population standard deviation, then add the population mean.

> **MASTERING THE CONCEPT**
>
> **3-1:** Graphs can be misleading. As critical thinkers, we want to know whether a sample represents a population, how the variables were actually measured, and whether a graph tells an accurate data story.

Illustrative, Step-by-Step Examples

The text is filled with real-world examples from a wide variety of sources in the behavioral sciences. Many of these examples are new to the current edition of this text. We outline statistical techniques in a step-by-step fashion, guiding students through each concept by applying the material creatively and effectively.

EXAMPLE 4.4

Here is an example with an even number of scores. We omitted the second highest score, 451, in addition to the extreme outlier, 4586, so there are now 48 scores.

> **STEP 1: Arrange the scores in ascending order.**

The data are now:

```
  5  16  17  48  53  54  55  74  87  87
 88  91  95 100 101 102 114 118 122 123
126 142 143 156 160 168 178 184 190 191
199 213 223 224 225 228 239 241 257 265
270 276 292 302 309 336 345 360
```

> **STEP 2: Find the middle score.**

First, we count the scores. There are 48. We then divide the number of scores by 2: $48/2 = 24$. If we add 0.5 to this result, we get 24.5; therefore, the median is the average of the 24th and 25th scores. The 24th and 25th scores are 156 and 160. The median is their mean—the mean of 156 and 160 is 158. ●

SPSS®

For instructors who integrate SPSS into their course, each chapter includes outlined instructions and screenshots of SPSS output to help students master the program using data from the text.

SPSS®

SPSS is divided into two main screens. The easiest way to move back and forth between these two screens is by using the two tabs located at the lower left labeled "Variable View" and "Data View." When data are collected, each data point should be connected with an identifier unique to each participant. This variable is often noted as the "ID." Every variable that is measured needs to have its own Name and Label, and SPSS needs to know how the variable was measured.

To name the variables, go to "Variable View" (see screenshot A) and select:

Name. Type in a short version of the variable name—for example, BDI for the Beck Depression Inventory, a common measure of depressive symptoms. A second variable to add could be the BAI, short for the Beck Anxiety Inventory. Note that SPSS will not allow spaces in the "Name" of the variable.

To tell SPSS what the variable name means, select:

Label. Type in the full name of the variable, such as Beck Depression Inventory and the Beck Anxiety Inventory.

Now tell SPSS what kind of variables these are by selecting:

Measure. Highlight the type of variable by clicking on the cell in the column labeled "Measure" next to each variable, then clicking on the arrow to access the tool that allows you to identify whether the variable is scale, ordinal, or nominal.

After describing all of the variables in the study in "Variable View," switch over to "Data View" (remember, at the lower left corner of the screen—see screenshot B)). The information you entered was automatically transferred to that screen, but now the variables are displayed across the tops of the columns instead of along the left-hand side of the rows. You can now enter the data in "Data View" under the appropriate heading; each participant's data are entered across one row.

A

SPSS Statistics

How It Works—Chapter-Specific Worked-Out Exercises

Many students have anxiety as they approach end-of-chapter exercises. To ease that anxiety, the How It Works section provides students with step-by-step worked-out exercises representative of those they will see at the end of the chapter. This section appears just before the end-of-chapter exercises and acts as a model for the more challenging Applying the Concepts and Putting It All Together questions. This edition includes a number of new exercises based on actual behavioral sciences findings.

HOW IT WORKS

17.1 CONDUCTING A CHI-SQUARE TEST FOR GOODNESS OF FIT

Have you heard of the Bechdel Test? Allison Bechdel developed a simple rubric to determine if a movie (or other fictional work) was at least trying for gender equality. The test: You have to be able to answer "yes" to three questions: 1) Are there at least two women in the film? 2) Who talk to each other? 3) About something other than a man? It's surprisingly hard to find films that meet these criteria. Researchers examined the effect of the screenwriters' genders on films' gender equality (Friedman, Daniels, & Blinderman, 2016). Of high-earning films written entirely by men, 53% failed the Bechdel Test. What about similarly successful films with at least one female writer? In a sample of 61 top films that had at least one woman on the writing team, 23 failed the Bechdel Test and 38 passed. (For fun, check out the researchers' Bechdel Test simulator on http://poly-graph.co/bechdel/. You can see the likelihood that a film will pass the Bechdel Test given a particular director, producer, and writer. For example, a film directed by Tina Fey, produced by Judd Apatow, and written by Shonda Rimes would only have an 11% chance of failing.) How can we use the Bechdel Test to conduct the six steps of hypothesis testing for a chi-square test for goodness of fit?

Step 1: Population 1: High-earning films with at least one woman on the writing team. Population 2: High-earning films written entirely by men.

The comparison distribution is a chi-square distribution. The hypothesis test will be a chi-square test for goodness of fit because we have one nominal variable only. This study meets three of the four assumptions: (1) The one variable

Building Better Graphs Using Excel

A new appendix reinforces lessons from Chapter 3 on graphing and guides students through the basics of creating a clear, readable graph with Excel. Using an example from the text, students are guided through the steps of creating a graph and then changing Excel's default choices to meet the criteria for an excellent graph.

Game Design and Practice

Like a computer game that uses repetition and small changes to lift its players to higher levels of achievement, *Statistics for the Behavioral Sciences* has increasingly difficult challenges, beginning with confidence-building Check Your Learning sections within each chapter. Many of the more than 1000 exercises in the text, most written by the authors, are based on real data, so professors and students can choose from among the most engaging exercises. Students can develop the ability to conduct, interpret, understand, and report statistics used in scientific journals by selecting from four tiers of exercises:

- **Clarifying the Concepts** questions help students to master the general concepts, the statistical terminology, and the conceptual assumptions of each topic.

- **Calculating the Statistics** exercises provide students a way to practice making the basic calculations for each formula and statistic.

- **Applying the Concepts** exercises apply statistical questions to real-world situations across the behavioral sciences and require students to bridge their knowledge of concepts and calculations.

- **Putting It All Together** exercises encourage interleaving by asking students both to apply the concepts from the chapter to a real-world situation and to connect the chapter's concepts to ideas from previous chapters.

Media and Supplements

LaunchPad with LearningCurve Quizzing

A comprehensive Web resource for teaching and learning statistics

LaunchPad combines Worth Publishers' award-winning media with an innovative platform for easy navigation. For students, it is the ultimate online study guide, with rich interactive tutorials, videos, an e-Book, and the LearningCurve adaptive quizzing system. For instructors, LaunchPad is a full course space where class documents can be posted, quizzes can be easily assigned and graded, and students' progress can be assessed and recorded. Whether you are looking for the most effective study tools or a robust platform for an online course, LaunchPad is a powerful way to enhance your class.

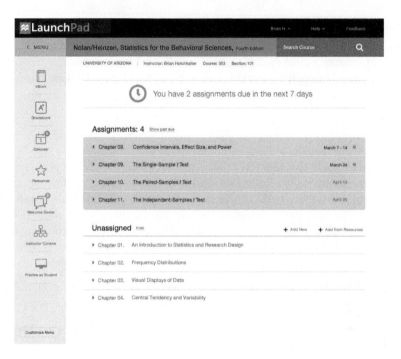

LaunchPad to accompany *Statistics for the Behavioral Sciences*, Fourth Edition, can be previewed and purchased at **launchpadworks.com**.

Statistics for the Behavioral Sciences, Fourth Edition, and LaunchPad can be ordered together (ISBN-10: 1-319-10421-5/ISBN-13: 978-1-319-10421-4).

LaunchPad for *Statistics for the Behavioral Sciences*, Fourth Edition, includes all the following resources:

- The **LearningCurve** quizzing system was designed using the latest findings from learning and memory research. It combines adaptive question selection, immediate and valuable feedback, and a gamelike interface to engage students in a learning experience that is unique to them. Each LearningCurve quiz is fully integrated with other resources in LaunchPad through the Personalized Study Plan, so students can review Worth's library of videos and activities. State-of-the-art question analysis reports allow instructors to track the progress of individual students as well as their class as a whole.

- An **interactive e-Book** allows students to highlight, bookmark, and make their own notes, just as they would with a printed textbook. Students can use Google-style searching and take advantage of in-text glossary definitions.

- The **Statistical Video Series** consists of StatClips, StatClips Examples, and Statistically Speaking "Snapshots." The videos can be used to view animated lecture videos, whiteboard lessons, and documentary-style footage that illustrate key statistical concepts and help students visualize statistics in real-world scenarios.

- **StatClips lecture videos,** created and presented by Alan Dabney, PhD, Texas A&M University, are innovative visual tutorials that illustrate key statistical concepts. In 3 to 5 minutes, each StatClips video combines dynamic animation, data sets, and interesting scenarios to help students understand the concepts in an introductory statistics course.

- In **StatClips Examples,** Alan Dabney walks students through step-by-step examples related to the StatClips lecture videos to reinforce the concepts through problem solving.

- **SnapShots** videos are abbreviated, student-friendly versions of the Statistically Speaking video series, and they bring the world of statistics into the classroom. In the same vein as the successful PBS series *Against All Odds: Inside Statistics*, Statistically Speaking uses new and updated documentary footage and interviews that show real people using data analysis to make important decisions in their careers and in their daily lives. From business to medicine, from the environment to understanding the census, SnapShots help students see why statistics is important for their careers and how statistics can be a powerful tool for understanding their world.

- **Statistical Applets** allow students to master statistical concepts by manipulating data. The applets also can be used to solve problems.

- **EESEE Case Studies**, taken from the *Electronic Encyclopedia of Statistical Exercises and Examples*, offer students additional applied exercises and examples.

- A **data set from the General Social Survey (GSS)** gives students access to data from one of the most trusted sources of sociological information. Since 1972, the GSS has collected data that reflect changing opinions and trends in the United States. A number of exercises in the text use GSS data, and this data set allows students to explore further.

- The **Assignment Center** lets instructors easily construct and administer tests and quizzes from the book's Test Bank and course materials. The Test Bank includes a subset of questions from the end-of-chapter exercises and uses algorithmically generated values so that each student can be assigned a unique version of the question. Assignments can be automatically graded, and the results can be recorded in a customizable gradebook.

Additional Student Supplements

SPSS: A User-Friendly Approach by Jeffery Aspelmeier and Thomas Pierce of Radford University is an accessible introduction to using SPSS. The book uses a proven teaching method, building each section of the text around the storyline from a popular cartoon. Easing anxiety and giving students the necessary support to learn the material, *SPSS: A User-Friendly Approach* provides instructors and students with an informative guide to the basics of SPSS.

- The **iClicker** Classroom Response System is a versatile polling system developed by educators for educators that makes class time more efficient and interactive. iClicker allows instructors to ask questions and instantly record students' responses, gauge students' understanding and opinions, and take attendance. It can help instructors gather data on students that can be used to teach statistics, connecting the concepts to students' lives. iClicker is available at a 10% discount when packaged with *Statistics for the Behavioral Sciences*, Fourth Edition.

Take Advantage of Our Most Popular Combinations!

Worth Publishers is pleased to offer cost-saving packages of *Statistics for the Behavioral Sciences*, Fourth Edition, with our most popular supplements. In addition to LaunchPad access listed below, contact your sales representative for more combinations available for order through your local bookstore.

Statistics for the Behavioral Sciences, Fourth Edition, and LaunchPad Access Card
(ISBN-10: 1-319-10421-5/ ISBN-13: 978-1-319-10421-4)

Instructor Supplements

We understand that one book alone cannot meet the educational needs and teaching expectations of the modern classroom. Therefore, we have engaged our colleagues to create a comprehensive supplements package that makes both teaching and learning statistics much easier.

- **Instructor's Resources** by Jeffrey Henriques, University of Wisconsin-Madison, with contributions by Katherine Makarec, William Paterson University. The contents include "Teaching Tips" and sample course outlines. Each chapter includes a brief overview, discussion questions, classroom activities, handouts, additional reading suggestions, and online resources.

- **Downloadable Test Bank for Diploma** Available for Windows or Macintosh, the Test Bank includes multiple-choice, true/false, fill-in-the-blank, and critical thinking/problem-solving questions for each chapter. Developed by Jennifer Coleman, Western New Mexico University, Kelly M. Goedert, Seton Hall University, and Daniel Cruz, Caldwell College, the downloadable Test Bank allows instructors to add an unlimited number of new questions; edit questions; format a test; scramble questions; and include figures, graphs, and pictures. The downloadable Test Bank also allows instructors to export into a variety of formats compatible with many Internet-based testing products. **macmillanhighered.com/Catalog/**

- Worth Publishers supports multiple **Course Management Systems** with enhanced cartridges that include Test Bank questions and other resources. Cartridges are provided free upon adoption of *Statistics for the Behavioral Sciences*, Fourth Edition, and can be requested through Worth's online catalog at **macmillanhighered.com/Catalog/**.

Acknowledgments

We would like to thank the many people who have contributed directly and indirectly to the writing of this text. We want to thank our students at Seton Hall University and William Paterson University for teaching us how to teach statistics in a way that makes sense and for calling our attention to some of the more fun examples you'll now find in these pages.

Tom: The family members who know me on a daily basis and decide to love me anyway deserve more thanks than words can convey: Donna, Rebekah, Nagesh, Debbie, Anthony, Amy, Elizabeth, Mollie, Jodah, and Benjamin. The close friends, artists, and colleagues who voiced encouragement and timely support also deserve my deep appreciation: Beth, Army, Culley, and Miran Schultz; Laura Cramer-Berness; Ariana DeSimone; J. Allen Suddeth; Nancy Vail; Gerry Esposito; and Sally Ellyson.

My students have always provided a reality check on my teaching methods with the kind of candor that only students engaged in the learning process can bring. And in recent years, our psychology department has made enormous strides by following the "always hire people who are better than you" rule. Some of those "better than you" colleagues have been a steady source of helpful conversation: Michael Gordon, Amy Learmonth, and Natalie Obrecht. Thank you. And Susan, of course, has been as fine a colleague and friend as I could ever have hoped for.

I also want to thank the people at Worth, all of them. They have a vision for quality textbook publishing that is different from that of many publishers. I know I speak for Susan as well when I say how deeply we appreciate their level of close cooperation, timely support, and determination to get every detail right. People with those values are what have made Worth's textbooks so special.

Susan: I am grateful to my Northwestern University professors and classmates for convincing me that statistics can truly be fun. I am also eternally thankful to Beatrix Mellauner for bringing Tom Heinzen and me together as coauthors; it has been a privilege and a pleasure to collaborate with Tom for so many years.

I owe thanks, as well, to my Seton Hall colleagues and students who are the sources for an endless stream of engaging examples. I owe a huge thank you to Emily Dow who contributed ideas, calculations, accuracy checks, and more. The fourth edition is better for her work on it. Finally, Seton Hall Department of Psychology secretary, Willie Yaylaci, has contributed in so many ways through her help, support, and friendship; thank you.

Much of the writing of this book took place during two sabbaticals and numerous summers in Bosnia and Herzegovina; I thank my Bosnian friends and colleagues for their warmth and hospitality every time I visit. I'm particularly grateful to have been welcomed into the Department of Psychology at the University of Banja Luka during my time there in 2015–2016 as a U.S. Fulbright Scholar.

A special thank you to the members of the Bojanic and Nolan clans—especially my parents, Diane and Jim, who have patiently endured the barrage of statistics I often inject into everyday conversation. Finally, I am most grateful to my husband, Ivan Bojanic, for the memorable adventures we've had (and the statistical observations that have grown out of many of them); Ivan has experienced the evolution of this book through countless road-trip conversations and late-night editorial sessions.

We would like to take a moment to highlight the impressive cast of instructors who have joined our team. The contributions of the supplements authors are innumerable, and Katherine Makarec, Robert Weathersby, and Robin Freyberg are all professionals with a deep interest in creating successful classrooms. We appreciate the opportunity to work with people of such commitment.

Throughout the writing of the four editions of this textbook, we relied on the criticism, corrections, encouragement, and thoughtful contributions from reviewers, focus group attendees, survey respondents, and class-testers. We thank them for their expertise and for the time they set aside to help us develop this textbook. We also are grateful to the professors who have used our book and then provided specific and valuable feedback; in particular, we thank Jon Grahe, Harvey H. C. Marmurek, and Patricia A. Smiley. Special thanks go to Jennifer Coleman and Byron Reischl at Western New Mexico University and to Kelly Goedert at Seton Hall University for their tireless work in developing the pedagogy with us, providing a responsible accuracy check, and contributing numerous ideas for us to consider as we continue to make this book even better. Special thanks also go to Melanie Maggard at the University of the Rockies, Sherry L. Serdikoff at James Madison University, and Emily A. A. Dow at Loyola University in Maryland for their invaluable efforts checking the text and exercises.

Caitlin Abar
State University of New York, Brockport

Tsippa Ackerman
John Jay College

Anthony Albano
University of Nebraska

Melissa Atkins
Marshall University

Elizabeth Bauer
New York University

Taunjah Bell
Jackson State University

Kenneth Bonanno
Merrimack College

Danuta Bukatko
College of the Holy Cross

Heidi Burross
Pima Community College

Mary Jo Carnot
Chadron State College

Wilson Chu
California State University, Long Beach

Jennifer Coleman
Western New Mexico University

Melanie Conti
College of Saint Elizabeth

Ken Cramer
University of Windsor

Maria Czyzewska
Texas State University, San Marcos

Melvin Davis
Jackson State University

Betty Dorr
Fort Lewis College

Nancy Dorr
The College of St. Rose

Kevin Eames
Covenant College

Laszlo Erdodi
University of Windsor

Warren Fass
University of Pittsburgh, Bradford

Nancy Gee
State University of New York, Fredonia

Shahram Ghiasinejad
University of Central Florida, Sanford/Lake Mary

Marilyn Gibbons
Texas State University

Nuria Giralt
California State University, Long Beach

Anthony Greene
University of Wisconsin, Milwaukee

Tammy Greer
University of Southern Mississippi

Elizabeth Haines
William Paterson University

Leslie Hawley
University of Nebraska

Roberto Heredia
Texas A&M University

Michael Hurley
George Mason University

Cynthia Ingle
Bluegrass Community and Technical College

E. Jean Johnson
Governors State University

Lauriann Jones-Moore
University of South Florida

Min Ju
State University of New York, New Paltz

Donald Keller
George Washington University

Karl Kelley
North Central College

Shelley Kilpatrick
Southwest Baptist University

Megan Knowles
University of Georgia

Paul Koch
Saint Ambrose University

Marika Lamoreaux
Georgia State University

Jennifer Lancaster
St. Francis College

Jarrod Lewis-Peacock
The University of Texas

Christine MacDonald
Indiana State University

Suzanne Mannes
Widener University

Walter Marcantoni
Bishop's University

Kelly Marin
Manhattan College

Marsha McCartney
University of Kansas

Connie Meinholdt
Ferris State University

William Merriman
Kent State University

Chris Molnar
LaSalle University

Matthew Mulvaney
State University of New York, Brockport

Erin Murdoch
George Mason University

Angela K. Murray
University of Kansas

Aminda O'Hare
University of Kansas

Sue Oliver
Glendale Community College of Arizona

Stephen O'Rourke
The College of New Rochelle

Debra Oswald
Marquette University

Mark Otten
California State University, Northridge

Alison Papdakis
Loyola College in Maryland

John Poggio
University of Kansas

Laura Rabin
City University of New York, Brooklyn

Byron Reischl
Western New Mexico University

Lorena Ruci
Carleton University

Michelle Samuel
Mount St. Mary's College, Chalon

Ken Savitsky
Williams College

Heidi Shaw
Yakima Valley Community College

Julian Smit
College of Southern Nevada, Henderson

Ross B. Steinman
Widener University

Sarah Strand
California State University, Sacramento

Colleen Sullivan
Worcester University

Brian Stults
Florida State University

Melanie Tabak
William Penn University

Mark Tengler
University of Houston, Clear Lake

Cheryl Terrance
University of North Dakota

Patricia Tomich
Kent State University

Bethany Van Vleet
Arizona State University

Alex Varakin
Eastern Kentucky University

Noe Vargas
Grand Canyon University

Laurel Wainwright
University of Massachusetts, Boston

David Wallace
Fayetteville State University

Elizabeth Weiss
The Ohio State University

Erika Wells
Boston University

Charles Woods
Austin Peay State University

Alison Young
Olivet Nazarene University

Tiffany Yip
Fordham University

Widaad Zaman
University of Central Florida, Valencia/Osceola

Accuracy Reviewers

Verne Bacharach
Appalachian State University

Jeffrey Berman
University of Memphis

Dennis Goff
Randolph College

Linda Henkel
Fairfield University

Melanie Maggard
University of the Rockies

Kathy Oleson
Reed College

Christy Porter
College of William and Mary

Sherry L. Serdikoff
James Madison University

Alexander Wilson
University of New Brunswick

Emily A. A. Dow
Loyola University Maryland

It has truly been a pleasure for us to work with everyone at Worth Publishers. From the moment we signed there, we have been impressed with the passionate commitment of everyone we have encountered at Worth at every stage of the publishing process. Charles Linsmeier, vice president, social science; Kevin Feyen, vice president, digital product development; Catherine Woods, vice president, content management; and Rachel Losh, director of personalized learning foster that commitment to quality in the Worth culture.

Our development editor, Michael Kimball, provides an attention to detail that helps us to achieve our vision for this book. As someone without a statistics background who nevertheless "gets" statistics, Michael helps us shape our language in ways that make it more accessible to students. Director of content management enhancement Tracey Kuehn has been enormously important in shaping this edition; we rely heavily on her expert guidance and eternally good-humored encouragement. We are grateful to executive acquisitions editor Daniel McDonough for his humor, skill, and patience in guiding the revision process. Thanks also goes to assistant editor Kimberly Morgan Smith who expertly and cheerfully kept track of countless details, stacks of paper, and electronic files.

Project editor Kayci Wyatt, managing editor Lisa Kinne, and senior production supervisor Paul Rohloff managed the production of the text and worked tirelessly to bring the book to fruition. Designer Kevin Kall united beauty with clarity and content in the interior design. Copyeditor Heather Hutches and her hawk's eye made our prose more consistent, more accurate, and easier to read. Photo editor Sheena Goldstein helped us to select photos that told the stories of statistics. Thanks to each of you for fulfilling Worth's promise to create a book whose aesthetics so beautifully support the specific pedagogical demands of teaching statistics.

Media editor Anthony Casciano guided the development and creation of the supplements package, making life so much better for so many students and instructors. Marketing manager Lindsay Johnson quickly understood why we believe so deeply in this book, and contributed unstinting effort to advocate for this fourth edition with our colleagues across the country. (And we credit Lindsay for finding several of the examples in this book!)

We also want to thank the tremendously dedicated Worth team that consistently champions our book while garnering invaluable accolades and critiques from their professor contacts—information that directly leads to a better book.

An Introduction to Statistics and Research Design

The Two Branches of Statistics
Descriptive Statistics
Inferential Statistics
Distinguishing Between a Sample and a Population

How to Transform Observations into Variables
Discrete Observations
Continuous Observations

Variables and Research
Independent, Dependent, and Confounding Variables
Reliability and Validity

Introduction to Hypothesis Testing
Conducting Experiments to Control for Confounding Variables
Between-Groups Design Versus Within-Groups Design
Correlational Research

Next Steps: Outlier Analysis

BEFORE YOU GO ON

■ **You should be familiar with basic mathematics (see Reference for Basic Mathematics in Appendix A).**

Map 1. Published by C.F. Cheffins, Lith, Southhampton Buildings, London, England, 1854 in Snow, John. *On the Mode of Communication of Cholera*, 2nd Ed, John Churchill, New Burlington Street, London

John Snow's Famous Map By mapping cholera deaths in relation to the Broad Street water well, Dr. John Snow solved the urgent mystery of how cholera could infect so many people so suddenly. The X's are all neighborhood wells. The X in the red circle is the Broad Street well. Each dot indicates that a person living at this address died of cholera, and a cluster of cases is clearly seen around the Broad Street well (but not around the other wells). Snow was careful to include the other X's to demonstrate that the deaths were closer to one specific source of water.

Statistics saves lives.

The London cholera epidemic of 1854 hit with terrifying swiftness and apparent randomness. Some 500 people died during the first 10 days and no one could figure out why. Everyone involved only knew that the disease dehydrated its victims in gruesome ways no matter how much water the sufferer drank. It was as if an angel of death had decided, during that late summer of 1854, to take a random stroll through London's Golden Square neighborhood. A workhouse with 535 inmates had only a few mortalities and a nearby brewery with 70 employees was untouched by the epidemic, yet another nearby factory suffered 18 deaths.

Dr. John Snow had spent years trying to determine how cholera was communicated from one person to another (Vinten-Johansen, Brody, Paneth, Rachman, & Rip, 2003). He was searching for a pattern behind the apparent randomness. He marked the location of each cholera victim's home on a map and then added an X for each neighborhood's water well. The visual presentation of these data revealed a relation between distance from the well and numbers of deaths! The closer a home was to the well on Broad Street (see the red X circled in the accompanying image), the more likely it was that a death from cholera had occurred.

Snow proposed a simple solution: Remove the pump handle—a health intervention that startled the Board of Guardians of St. James's parish. Surprisingly, when the authorities finally removed the Broad Street pump handle, cholera deaths declined dramatically. Nevertheless, Snow still had a statistical problem: The rate of deaths from cholera had started to decline before the handle was removed! How could this happen? Did Snow's intervention really make a difference? The answer is both disturbing and insightful: So many people had died or fled the neighborhood around the Broad Street well that there were fewer people left to be infected.

- A **descriptive statistic** organizes, summarizes, and communicates a group of numerical observations.

- An **inferential statistic** uses sample data to make estimates about the larger population.

- A **sample** is a set of observations drawn from the population of interest.

- The **population** includes all possible observations about which we'd like to know something.

The Two Branches of Statistics

The statistical genius and research of Dr. Snow not only saved lives, it anticipated the two main branches of modern statistics: descriptive statistics and inferential statistics.

Descriptive Statistics

Descriptive statistics organize, summarize, and communicate a group of numerical observations. Descriptive statistics describe large amounts of data in a single number or in just a few numbers. Here's an illustration using a familiar measure: length in feet (or meters). *National Geographic* reported on their Web site that the average adult great white shark is 15 feet long, or 4.6 meters (2015). And that's just the average. Some great white sharks grow to 20 feet, or 6 meters long! Most dorm rooms aren't even that big. The average length of great white sharks is a descriptive statistic because it *describes* the lengths of many sharks in just one number. A single number reporting the average communicates observations more clearly than would a long list of lengths for every shark that researchers have ever studied (National Geographic, 2015).

Inferential Statistics

Inferential statistics use sample data to make estimates about the larger population. Inferential statistics infer, or make an intelligent guess about, the population. For example, the researchers from whom *National Geographic* got their data made inferences about shark length even though they did not actually measure *every* great white shark in the world. Instead, researchers studied a smaller representative group of sharks to make an intelligent guess about the entire population.

Distinguishing Between a Sample and a Population

*A **sample** is a set of observations drawn from the population of interest.* Researchers usually study a sample, but they are really interested in the **population**, which *includes all possible observations about which we'd like to know something.* For example, the average length of the researcher's sample of great white sharks was used to estimate the average length for the entire world population of great white sharks, which was *National Geographic*'s interest.

Samples are used most often because researchers are rarely able to study every person (or shark or organization or laboratory rat) in a population. For one thing, it's far too expensive. In addition, it would take too long. Snow did not want to interview every family in the Broad Street neighborhood—people were dying too fast! Fortunately, what he learned from his sample also applied to the larger population.

Descriptive Statistics Summarize Information It is more useful to use a single number to summarize the lengths of many great white sharks than to provide a long, overwhelming list of every shark's length.

CatPix: The Art of Nature/Moment/Getty Images

CHECK YOUR LEARNING

Reviewing the Concepts

> Descriptive statistics organize, summarize, and communicate large amounts of numerical information.

> Researchers working with sample data use inferential statistics to draw conclusions about larger populations.

> Samples, or selected observations of a population, are intended to be representative of the larger population.

Clarifying the Concepts   1-1   Which are used in inferential statistics: samples or populations?

continued on next page

| Calculating the Statistics | 1-2a | If your professor calculated the average grade for your statistics class, would that be considered a descriptive statistic or an inferential statistic? |
| | 1-2b | If that same class average is used to predict something about how future students might do in statistics, would it be considered a descriptive statistic or an inferential statistic? |

Applying the Concepts	1-3	Researcher Andrew Gelman wrote about his research in the *New York Times* (February 18, 2013): "The average American knows about 600 people. How do we know this? Researchers led by my Columbia colleague Tian Zheng posed a series of questions to a representative sample of 1,500 Americans."
		a. What is the sample?
		b. What is the population?
		c. What is the descriptive statistic?
		d. What is the inferential statistic?

Solutions to these Check Your Learning questions can be found in Appendix D.

- A **variable** is any observation of a physical, attitudinal, or behavioral characteristic that can take on different values.

- A **discrete observation** can take on only specific values (e.g., whole numbers); no other values can exist between these numbers.

- A **continuous observation** can take on a full range of values (e.g., numbers out to several decimal places); an infinite number of potential values exists.

- A **nominal variable** is a variable used for observations that have categories or names as their values.

- An **ordinal variable** is a variable used for observations that have rankings (i.e., 1st, 2nd, 3rd...) as their values.

- An **interval variable** is a variable used for observations that have numbers as their values; the distance (or interval) between pairs of consecutive numbers is assumed to be equal.

How to Transform Observations into Variables

Like John Snow, we begin the research process by making observations and transforming them into a useful format. For example, Snow observed the locations of people who had died of cholera and placed these locations on a map that also showed wells in the area. The numbers of cholera deaths and their distances from the Broad Street well are both variables. *Variables are observations of physical, attitudinal, and behavioral characteristics that can take on different values.* Behavioral scientists often study abstract variables such as motivation and self-esteem; they typically begin the research process by transforming their observations into numbers.

Researchers use both discrete and continuous numerical observations to quantify variables. *Discrete observations can take on only specific values (e.g., whole numbers); no other values can exist between these numbers.* For example, if we measured the number of times study participants get up early in a particular week, the only possible values would be whole numbers. It is reasonable to assume that each participant could get up early 0 to 7 times in any given week but not 1.6 or 5.92 times.

Continuous observations can take on a full range of values (e.g., numbers out to several decimal places); an infinite number of potential values exists. For example, a person might complete a task in 12.83912 seconds, or a shark might be 13.83 feet long. The possible values are continuous, limited only by the number of decimal places we choose to use.

Discrete Observations

Two types of observations are always discrete: nominal variables and ordinal variables. *Nominal variables are used for observations that have categories or names as their values.* For example, when entering data into a statistical computer program, a researcher might code male participants with the number 1 and female participants with the number 2. In this case, the numbers only identify the gender category for each participant. They do not imply any other meaning. For instance, men aren't better than women because they get the first number and women aren't twice as good as men because they happen to be coded as a 2. Note that nominal variables are always discrete (whole numbers).

Ordinal variables are used for observations that have rankings (i.e., 1st, 2nd, 3rd...) as their values. In reality television shows, like *Britain's Got Talent* or *American Idol*, for example, a performer finishes the season in a particular place, or rank. It doesn't matter if the performer was first because she was slightly more talented than the next performer or much more talented. And it doesn't matter if the winning performer was ahead of the next one by one vote or by a million votes. Like nominal variables, ordinal variables are always discrete. A singer could be 1st or 3rd or 12th, but could not be ranked 1.563.

● A **ratio variable** is a variable that meets the criteria for an interval variable but also has a meaningful zero point.

Continuous Observations

Two types of observations can be continuous: interval variables and ratio variables. *Interval variables are used for observations that have numbers as their values; the distance (or interval) between pairs of consecutive numbers is assumed to be equal.* For example, temperature is an interval variable because the interval from one degree to the next is always the same. Some interval variables are also discrete variables, such as the number of times one has to get up early each week. This is an interval variable because the distance between numerical observations is assumed to be equal. The difference between 1 and 2 times is the same as the difference between 5 and 6 times. However, this observation is also discrete because, as noted earlier, the number of days in a week cannot be anything but a whole number. Several behavioral science measures are treated as interval measures but also can be discrete, such as some personality measures and attitude measures.

Ordinal Variables Are Ranked Simone Biles of the United States came in first place, winning the gold medal in the vault at the Rio Olympics. Russia's Maria Paseka captured second place, claiming the silver medal, and Switzerland's Giulia Steingruber was third for the bronze medal. This is an ordinal variable, so they are ranked first, second, and third regardless of how much better Biles did than Paseka and Steingruber.

Sometimes discrete interval observations, such as the number of times one has to get up early each week, are also *ratio variables, variables that meet the criteria for interval variables but also have meaningful zero points.* For example, if someone never has to get up early, then zero is a meaningful observation and could represent a variety of life circumstances. Perhaps the person is unemployed, retired, ill, or merely on vacation. Another example of a discrete ratio variable is the number of times a rat pushes a lever to receive food. This also has a true zero point—the rat might never push the bar (and go hungry). Ratio observations that are not discrete include time running out in a basketball game and crossing the finish line in a race.

Many cognitive studies use the ratio variable of reaction time to measure how quickly people process difficult information. For example, the Stroop test is a ratio measure that assesses how long it takes to read a list of color words printed in ink of the wrong color (Figure 1-1), such as when the word *red* is printed in green or the word *green* is printed in brown. If it takes you 1.264 seconds to press a computer key that accurately identifies that the word *red* printed in green actually reads *red*, then your reaction time is a ratio variable; time always implies a meaningful zero.

red	**white**	**green**	brown
green	red	brown	**white**
white	**brown**	**green**	red
red	white	green	brown
brown	green	**white**	**red**
white	**brown**	red	green
green	white	**brown**	**red**
red	**brown**	green	white

FIGURE 1-1

Reaction Time and the Stroop Test

Read these words out loud to yourself as quickly as possible. Notice what happens in the third line. Your reaction time (how long it takes to read the list) is a ratio variable (also called a *scale variable*). The Stroop test assesses how long it takes to read a list of colored words printed in the wrong color, such as the word *red* printed in the color white.

1-2: The three main types of variables are nominal (or categorical), ordinal (or ranked), and scale. The third type (scale) includes both interval variables and ratio variables; the distances between numbers on the measure are meaningful.

Many statistical computer programs refer to both interval numbers and ratio numbers as *scale observations* because both interval observations and ratio observations are analyzed with the same statistical tests. Specifically, a **scale variable** is a variable that meets the criteria for an interval variable or a ratio variable. Throughout this text, we use the term *scale variable* to refer to variables that are interval or ratio, but it is important to remember the distinction between interval variables and ratio variables. Table 1-1 summarizes the four types of variables.

TABLE 1-1 Quantifying Observations

There are four types of variables that researchers can use to quantify their observations. Two of them, nominal and ordinal, are always discrete. Interval variables can be discrete or continuous; ratio variables are almost always continuous. (Interval variables and ratio variables are often referred to as "scale variables.")

	Discrete	Continuous
Nominal	Always	Never
Ordinal	Always	Never
Interval	Sometimes	Sometimes
Ratio	Seldom	Almost always

CHECK YOUR LEARNING

Reviewing the Concepts

> Variables are quantified with discrete or continuous observations.

> Depending on the study, statisticians select nominal, ordinal, or scale (interval or ratio) variables.

Clarifying the Concepts 1-4 What is the difference between discrete observations and continuous observations?

Calculating the Statistics 1-5 Three students complete a Stroop test. Lorna finishes in 12.67 seconds; Desiree finishes in 14.87 seconds; and Marianne finishes in 9.88 seconds.

a. Are these data discrete or continuous?

b. Is the variable an interval or a ratio observation?

c. On an ordinal scale, what is Lorna's score?

Applying the Concepts 1-6 Uber, the company that offers on-demand car service, measures the performance of their drivers in a variety of ways (Rosenblat, 2015). Below are several ways in which performance is measured. For each, state whether the variable is nominal, ordinal, or scale, and explain your answer.

a. Uber drivers receive ratings from their passengers on a scale of 1–5.

b. Uber notes whether the driver has received a warning from the company regarding their performance.

c. Uber measures hours spent logged in to the Uber app during which the driver is available for passengers.

d. Drivers are sometimes given feedback that they're, for example, among the top Uber drivers.

Solutions to these Check Your Learning questions can be found in Appendix D.

e. Uber sometimes refers drivers to take a particular class to improve their performance, and tracks who has and has not taken the class.

Variables and Research

A major aim of research is to understand the relations among variables with many different values. It is helpful to remember that variables vary. For example, when studying a discrete nominal variable such as gender, we refer to gender as the variable because it can vary—either male or female. The term *level*, along with the terms *value* and *condition*, all refer to the same idea. **Levels** *are the discrete values or conditions that variables can take on.* For example, male is a level of the variable gender. Female is another level of the variable gender. In both cases, gender is the variable. Similarly, when studying a continuous, scale variable, such as how fast a runner completes a marathon, we refer to time as the variable. For example, 3 hours, 42 minutes, 27 seconds is one of an infinite number of possible times it would take to complete a marathon. With this in mind, let's explore the three types of variables: independent, dependent, and confounding.

Independent, Dependent, and Confounding Variables

The three types of variables that we consider in research are independent, dependent, and confounding. Two of these, independent variables and dependent variables, are necessary for good research. But the third type, a confounding variable, is the enemy of good research. We usually conduct research to determine if one or more independent variables predict a dependent variable. *An **independent variable** has at least two levels that we either manipulate or observe to determine its effects on the dependent variable.* For example, if we are studying whether gender predicts one's attitude about politics, then the independent variable is gender.

The **dependent variable** *is the outcome variable that we hypothesize to be related to or caused by changes in the independent variable.* For example, we hypothesize that the dependent variable (attitudes about politics) depends on the independent variable (gender). If in doubt as to which is the independent variable and which is the dependent variable, ask yourself which one depends on the other; that one is the dependent variable.

By contrast, a **confounding variable** *is any variable that systematically varies with the independent variable so that we cannot logically determine which variable is at work.* So how do we decide which is the independent variable and which might be a confounding variable (also called a *confound*)? Well, it all comes down to what *you* decide to study. Let's use an example. Suppose you want to lose weight, so you start using a diet drug *and* begin exercising at the same time. The drug and the exercising are confounded because you cannot logically tell which one is responsible for any weight loss. If we hypothesize that a particular diet drug leads to weight loss, then whether someone uses the diet drug becomes the independent variable, and exercise becomes the potentially confounding variable that we would try to control. On the other hand, if we hypothesize that exercise leads to weight loss, then whether someone exercises or not becomes the independent variable and whether that person uses diet drugs along with it becomes the potentially confounding variable that we would try to control. In both of these cases, the dependent variable would be weight loss. But the researcher has to make some decisions about which variables to treat as independent variables, which variables must be controlled, and which variables to treat as dependent. You, the experimenter, are in control of the experiment.

- A **scale variable** is a variable that meets the criteria for an interval variable or a ratio variable.

- A **level** is a discrete value or condition that a variable can take on.

- An **independent variable** has at least two levels that we either manipulate or observe to determine its effects on the dependent variable.

- A **dependent variable** is the outcome variable that we hypothesize to be related to or caused by changes in the independent variable.

- A **confounding variable** is any variable that systematically varies with the independent variable so that we cannot logically determine which variable is at work; also called a *confound*.

MASTERING THE CONCEPT

1-3: We conduct research to see if the independent variable predicts the dependent variable.

Dan Callister/Rex Features/AP Images

Was the Damage from Wind or Water? During hurricanes, like Hurricane Sandy in 2012, high winds are often confounded with high water so it is not always possible to determine whether property damage was due to wind (insured) or to water (often not insured).

- ● **Reliability** refers to the consistency of a measure.

- ● **Validity** refers to the extent to which a test actually measures what it was intended to measure.

Reliability and Validity

You probably have a lot of experience in assessing variables—at least on the receiving end. You've taken standardized tests when applying to your university; you've taken short surveys to choose the right product for you, whether jeans or smartphones; and you've taken online quizzes (perhaps sent through social networking sites like Facebook) such as the Dogster Breed Quiz, which uses a 10-item scale to assess the breed of dog you are most like (http://www.dogster.com/quizzes/what_dog_breed_are _you/, 2015).

How good is this quiz? One of the authors took the quiz—answering one of the questions by choosing a light chicken salad over alternative choices of heavier fare—and was declared to be a bulldog: "You may look like the troublemaker of the pack, but it turns out your tough guy mug is worse than its bite." To determine whether a measure is a good one, we need to know if it is both reliable and valid.

*A **reliable** measure is consistent.* If you were to weigh yourself on your bathroom scale now, and then again in an hour, you would expect your weight to be almost exactly the same. If your weight, as shown on the scale, remains the same when you haven't done anything to change it, then your bathroom scale is reliable. As for the Dogster Breed Quiz, the bulldog author took it twice two years apart and was a bulldog the second time as well, one indication of reliability.

But a reliable measure is not necessarily a valid measure. *A **valid** measure is one that measures what it was intended to measure.* Your bathroom scale could be incorrect but consistently incorrect—that is, reliable but not valid. A more extreme example is using a ruler when you want to know your weight. You would get a number, and that number might be reliable, but it would not be a valid measure of your weight.

And the Dogster Breed Quiz? It's probably not an accurate measure of personality. The quiz, for example, lists an unlikely mix of celebrities, with seemingly different personalities, as bulldogs—Ellen DeGeneres, Whoopi Goldberg, Jack Black, and George W. Bush! However, we're guessing that no one has done the statistical work to determine whether it is valid or not. When you take such online quizzes, our advice is to view the results as entertaining rather than enlightening.

Reliable and Valid Scoring guidelines have made projective personality tests such as the Rorschach more reliable, but it is still unclear whether they provide a valid measure. A measure must be both reliable (consistent over time) and valid (assesses what it is intended to assess).

A measure with poor reliability cannot have high validity. It is not possible to measure what we intend to measure when the test itself produces varying results. The well-known Rorschach inkblot test is one example of a test whose reliability is questionable, so the validity of the information it produces is difficult to interpret (Wood, Nezworski, Lilienfeld, & Garb, 2003). For instance, two clinicians might analyze the identical set of responses to a Rorschach test and develop quite different interpretations of those responses—meaning it lacks reliability. Reliability can be increased with scoring guidelines, but that doesn't mean validity is increased. Just because two clinicians scoring a Rorschach test designate a person as psychotic, it doesn't necessarily mean the person *is* psychotic. Reliability is necessary, but not sufficient, to create a valid measure. Nevertheless, the idea that ambiguous images somehow invite revealing information remains attractive to many people; as a result, tests such as the Rorschach are still used frequently, even though there is much controversy about them (Wood et al., 2003).

MASTERING THE CONCEPT

1-4: A good measure is both reliable and valid.

CHECK YOUR LEARNING

Reviewing the Concepts

> Independent variables are manipulated or observed by the experimenter.

> Dependent variables are outcomes in response to changes or differences in the independent variable.

> Confounding variables systematically vary with the independent variable, so we cannot logically tell which variable may have influenced the dependent variable.

> Researchers control factors that are not of interest in order to explore the relation between an independent variable and a dependent variable.

> A measure is useful only if it is both reliable (consistent over time) and valid (assesses what it is intended to assess).

Clarifying the Concepts   1-7   The _____ variable predicts the _____ variable.

Calculating the Statistics   1-8   A researcher examines the effects of two variables on memory. One variable is beverage (caffeine or no caffeine) and the other variable is the subject to be remembered (numbers, word lists, aspects of a story).

a. Identify the independent and dependent variables.

b. How many levels do the variables "beverage" and "subject to be remembered" have?

Applying the Concepts   1-9   Kiho Kim and Stevia Morawski (2012) studied 360 students in a university cafeteria, measuring how much food students wasted. The researchers compared waste among students when trays were available to waste among students when trays were not available. They found that students wasted 32% less food when trays were not available.

a. What is the independent variable in this study?

b. What are the levels of the independent variable?

c. What is the dependent variable? Suggest at least one way in which Kim and Morawski might have measured this.

d. What would it mean for the food waste measure to be reliable?

e. What would it mean for the food waste measure to be valid?

Solutions to these Check Your Learning questions can be found in Appendix D.

Introduction to Hypothesis Testing

When John Snow suggested that the pump handle be removed from the Broad Street well, he was testing his idea that an independent variable (contaminated well water) led to a dependent variable (deaths from cholera). Behavioral scientists use research to test ideas through a specific statistics-based process called **hypothesis testing**, *the process of drawing conclusions about whether a particular relation between variables is supported by the evidence.* Typically, researchers examine data from a sample to draw conclusions about a population, but there are many ways to conduct research. In this section, we discuss the process of determining the variables, two ways to approach research, and two experimental designs.

Determining which breed of dog you most resemble might seem silly; however, adopting a dog is a very important decision. Can an online quiz such as the *Animal Planet* "Dog Breed Selector" help (http://animal.discovery.com/breed-selector/dog-breeds.html, 2015)? We could conduct a study by having 30 people choose a

● **Hypothesis testing** is the process of drawing conclusions about whether a particular relation between variables is supported by the evidence.

- An **operational definition** specifies the operations or procedures used to measure or manipulate a variable.

- A **correlation** is an association between two or more variables.

type of dog to adopt and have another 30 people let the selector dictate their choice. We would then have to decide how to measure the outcome.

*An **operational definition** specifies the operations or procedures used to measure or manipulate a variable.* We could operationalize a good outcome with a new dog in several ways. Did you keep the dog for more than a year? On a rating scale of satisfaction with your pet, did you get a high score? Does a veterinarian give a high rating to your dog's health?

Do you think a quiz would lead you to make a better choice in dogs? You might hypothesize that the quiz would lead to better choices because it makes you think about important factors in dog ownership, such as outdoor space, leisure time, and your tolerance for dog hair. You already carry many hypotheses like these in your head. You just haven't bothered to test most of them yet, at least not formally. For example, perhaps you believe that pet owners are happier than other people, or that smokers simply lack the willpower to stop. Maybe you are convinced that the parking problem on your campus is part of a conspiracy by administrators to make your life more difficult.

In each of these cases, as shown in the accompanying table, we frame a hypothesis in terms of an independent variable and a dependent variable. The best way to learn about operationalizing a variable is to experience it for yourself. So propose a way to measure each of the variables identified in Table 1-2. We've given you a start with "pet ownership"—owns a pet versus doesn't own a pet (easy to operationalize)—and "how bad the parking problem is" (more difficult to operationalize).

Conducting Experiments to Control for Confounding Variables

Once we have decided how to operationalize the variables, we can conduct a study and collect data. There are several ways to approach research, including experiments and correlational research. A **correlation** is *an association between two or more variables.* In Snow's cholera research, it was the idea of a systematic co-relation between two variables (the proximity to the Broad Street well and the number of deaths) that saved so many lives. A correlation is one way to test a hypothesis, but it is not the only way. Researchers usually prefer to conduct an experiment rather than a correlational study because it is easier to interpret the results of experiments.

TABLE 1-2	Operationalized Variables	
The Independent Variable...	Predicts...	the Dependent Variable
Pet ownership ◄──────────────────►		level of happiness.
Amount of willpower ◄──────────────────►		level of cigarette smoking.
Level of caring by administrators ◄──────────────────►		how bad the parking problem is.

Conceptual Variable	Operationalized Variable
Pet ownership	Owns a pet versus doesn't own a pet
Level of happiness	_____
Amount of willpower	_____
Level of cigarette smoking	_____
Level of caring by administrators	_____
How bad the parking problem is	Ask students to rate the problem on a scale ranging from 1 (no problem) to 5 (worst problem on campus).

The hallmark of experimental research is random assignment. *With **random assignment**, every participant in the study has an equal chance of being assigned to any of the groups, or experimental conditions, in the study.* And *an **experiment** is a study in which participants are randomly assigned to a condition or level of one or more independent variables.* Random assignment means that neither the participants nor the researchers get to choose the condition. Experiments are the gold standard of hypothesis testing because they are the best way to control confounding variables. Controlling confounding variables allows researchers to infer a cause–effect relation between variables, rather than merely a systematic association between variables. Even when researchers cannot conduct a true experiment, they include as many of the characteristics of an experiment as possible. The critical feature that makes a study worthy of being called an *experiment* is random assignment to groups.

When researchers conduct experiments, they create approximately equivalent groups by randomly assigning participants to different levels, or conditions, of the independent variable. Random assignment controls the effects of personality traits, life experiences, personal biases, and other potential confounds by distributing them evenly across each condition of the experiment. So, if you wanted to study the effects of pet ownership on happiness using an experiment, you'd have to randomly assign people to own a pet or not own a pet. This would be tricky from a practical perspective (and potentially unethical to both the humans and the pets), but it would eliminate possible confounds, such as the fact that pet owners might be more likely to have certain personality traits that lead them to be happier (or unhappier). Let's look at a real-life study to see the problem that confounds can create.

- With **random assignment**, every participant in a study has an equal chance of being assigned to any of the groups, or experimental conditions, in the study.

- An **experiment** is a study in which participants are randomly assigned to a condition or level of one or more independent variables.

EXAMPLE 1.1

You might wonder whether the hours you spend playing Candy Crush or Call of Duty are useful. A team of physicians and a psychologist investigated whether video game playing (the independent variable) leads to superior surgical skills (the dependent variable). They reported that surgeons with more video game playing experience were faster and more accurate, on average, when conducting training drills that mimic laparoscopic surgery (a surgical technique that uses a small incision, a small video camera, and a video monitor) than surgeons with no video game playing experience (Rosser et al., 2007).

In the video game and surgery study, the researchers did not randomly assign surgeons to play video games or not. Rather, they asked surgeons to report their video game playing histories and then measured their laparoscopic surgical skills. Can you spot the confounding variable? People may choose to play video games *because* they already have the fine motor skills and eye–hand coordination necessary for surgery, and they enjoy using their skills by playing video games. If that is the case, then, those who play video games will of course tend to have better surgical skills—they already did before they took up video games!

It would be much more useful to set up an experiment that randomly assigns surgeons to one of the two levels of the independent variable: (1) play video games or (2) do not play video games. Random assignment assures us that our two groups are roughly equal, on average, on all the variables that might contribute to excellent surgical skills, such as fine motor skills, eye–hand coordination, and experience playing other video games. Random assignment diminishes the effects of all these potential confounds. Consequently, random assignment to groups increases our confidence that the two groups were similar, on average, on aptitude for laparoscopic surgery *prior to* this experiment. (Figure 1-2 visually clarifies the difference between self-selection and random assignment. In Chapter 5, we explore more specifically how random

MASTERING THE CONCEPT

1-5: When possible, researchers prefer to use an experiment rather than a correlational study. Experiments use random assignment, which is the only way to determine whether one variable causes another.

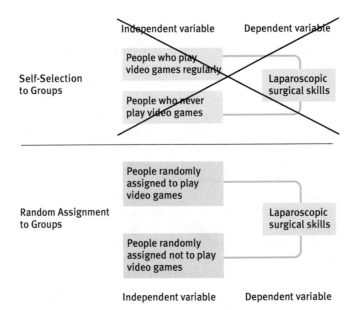

assignment is implemented.) If we use random assignment and the "play video games" group has better average laparoscopic surgical skills after the experiment than the "do not play video games group," then we are more confident in the conclusion that playing video games caused the better surgical skills.

Indeed, many researchers have used experimental designs to explore the causal effects of video game playing. Using random assignment, they have found both positive effects, such as improved spatial skills following action games (Feng, Spence, & Pratt, 2007), and negative effects, such as increased hostility after playing violent games with lots of blood (Bartlett, Harris, & Bruey, 2008). ●

Between-Groups Design Versus Within-Groups Design

Experimenters can create meaningful comparison groups in several ways. However, most studies have either a *between-groups* research design or a *within-groups* (also called a *repeated-measures*) research design.

A **between-groups research design** *is an experiment in which participants experience one and only one level of the independent variable.* An experiment that compares a control group (such as people randomly assigned not to play video games) with an experimental group (such as people randomly assigned to play video games) is an example of a between-groups design.

A **within-groups research design** *is an experiment in which all participants in the study experience the different levels of the independent variable.* An experiment that compares the same group of people before and after they experience a level of an independent variable, such as video game playing, is an example of a within-groups design. The word *within* emphasizes that if you experience one condition of a study, then you remain within the study until you experience all conditions of the study.

Many applied questions in the behavioral sciences are best studied using a within-groups design. This is particularly true of long-term (often called *longitudinal*) studies that examine how individuals and organizations change over time, or studies involving a naturally occurring event that cannot be duplicated in the laboratory. If you participated in a study at your university that followed you over time—say, once a year—then you participated in a longitudinal study. Within-group studies are useful

● With a **between-groups research design**, participants experience one and only one level of the independent variable.

● With a **within-groups research design**, all participants in the study experience the different levels of the independent variable; also called a *repeated-measures design*.

in other contexts. For example, researchers obviously cannot randomly assign people to either experience or not experience a hurricane. However, researchers could use nature's predictability to anticipate hurricane season, collect "before" data, and then collect data once again "after" people experience a hurricane.

Correlational Research

Often, a researcher cannot conduct an experiment because it is unethical or impractical to randomly assign participants to conditions. We can't really assign people to have a pet or not. What would we do with someone who is allergic to animals? What about the poor dog given to the animal hater assigned to have a pet? And what would we do with the pets people already have? And Snow's cholera research could not randomly assign some people to drink water from the Broad Street well. These studies are correlational, not experimental.

In correlational studies, we do not manipulate either variable. We merely assess the two variables as they exist. For example, it would be difficult to randomly assign people to either play or not play video games over several years. However, we could observe people over time to see the effects of their actual video game usage. Möller and Krahé (2009) studied German teenagers over a period of 30 months and found that the amount of video game playing when the study started was related to aggression 30 months later. Although these researchers found that video game playing and aggression are related (as shown in Figure 1-3), they do not have evidence that playing video games *causes* aggression. As we will discuss in Chapter 13, there are always alternative explanations in a correlational study; don't be too eager to infer causality just because two variables are correlated.

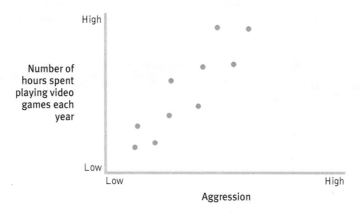

FIGURE 1-3

Correlation Between Aggression and Playing Video Games

This graph depicts a relation between aggression and hours spent playing video games for a study of 10 fictional participants. The more one plays video games, the higher one's level of aggression tends to be.

Outlier Analysis

Next Steps

John Snow wanted to understand the cholera outbreak, in part to prevent another one. So he paid particular attention to outliers, cases that did not fit the pattern that he had observed. *An **outlier** is an extreme score that is either very high or very low in comparison with the rest of the scores in the sample. Some researchers conduct **outlier analysis**, studies examining observations that do not fit the overall pattern of the data, in an effort to understand the factors that influence the dependent variable.*

Snow used outlier analysis when he sought to explain why two Londoners died in the cholera epidemic even though they lived far away from the Broad Street well that transmitted that terrible disease. A woman in West End, Hampstead, died on September 2, 1854; her niece in Islington died the following day. These two women had very high scores on the variable "distance from the Broad Street well," unexpected among those who died of cholera.

- An **outlier** is an extreme score that is either very high or very low in comparison with the rest of the scores in the sample.

- In **outlier analysis**, studies examine observations that do not fit the overall pattern of the data in an effort to understand the factors that influence the dependent variable.

These two cases did not fit the overall pattern, so Snow saddled up his horse and rode up to Hampstead to interview relatives of the two women who should not have died of cholera. His interview revealed that the Hampstead woman had once lived near Broad Street and developed a taste for the wonderful-tasting water that came out of the Broad Street pump. In fact, she had sent for a large container of the water on August 31, 1854, three days before her death and the same day that the cholera outbreak began. She had shared this wonderful-tasting water with her niece.

The outliers on Snow's map allowed him to see other clues about the cholera outbreak, including what may be the only known case in which lives were saved by drinking large amounts of beer. The 535 inmates at the workhouse had their own well; the 70 unaffected men working at the nearby Broad Street brewery were given a free daily allowance of beer; the 18 deaths at a nearby factory occurred because two large tubs of Broad Street well water were always kept available for the thirsty workers.

Outlier analysis would prove to be crucial once again in the 1990s, when researchers were desperately trying to track down effective strategies to fight the ongoing HIV/AIDS epidemic (Kolata, 2001). In this case, the outlier was a man with hemophilia, Robert Massie, who "should" have died but did not (Belluck, 2005). Like many other people with hemophilia, Massie had become infected through repeated exposure to the untested, contaminated blood supply. Oddly, though, Massie didn't show any symptoms of AIDS! His immune system was working so well that it convinced researchers that the immune system could fight off the AIDS virus. Identifying him as an outlier in part led the way to effective, innovative treatments for HIV. Researchers can stumble into critical insights by paying attention to statistical outliers.

CHECK YOUR LEARNING

Reviewing the Concepts

> Hypothesis testing is the process of drawing conclusions about whether a particular relation between variables (the hypothesis) is supported by the evidence.

> All variables must be operationalized—that is, we need to specify how they are to be measured or manipulated.

> Experiments attempt to explain a cause–effect relation between an independent variable and a dependent variable.

> Random assignment to groups to control for confounding variables is the hallmark of an experiment.

> Most studies have either a between-groups design or a within-groups design.

> Correlational studies can be used when it is not possible to conduct an experiment.

> Outliers are extreme scores that are very different from the rest of the observations.

> Outlier analysis refers to studies that examine outliers, those scores that do not fit the overall pattern of the rest of the data.

Clarifying the Concepts

1-10   How do the two types of research discussed in this chapter—experimental and correlational—differ?

1-11   How does random assignment help to address confounding variables?

Calculating the Statistics

1-12   In Check Your Learning 1-6, you saw several ways in which Uber measured the performance of its drivers (Rosenblat, 2015).

   a. Define the term *operational definition* in your own words, using one or more of these examples in your answer. What is Uber trying to operationally define?

b. Another operational definition that Uber uses is a high cancellation rate; that is, drivers who cancel rides a lot are viewed negatively. Rosenblat (2015), points out, however, that "the contexts of … a high cancellation rate are not taken into account. There's no flexibility for when accepting a ride would mean the driver actually loses money, let alone a mechanism for indicating when passengers are behaving badly." In your own words, explain why "cancellation rate" might be a bad operational definition in this case.

Applying the Concepts   **1-13**   Expectations matter. Many researchers have examined how expectations based on stereotypes influence women's math performance (see Steele, 2011). In some studies, women were told that a gender difference was found on a certain math test and that women tended to receive lower scores than men did. Other women were told that no gender differences were evident on the test. In studies like this, women in the first group tend to perform more poorly than men do, on average, whereas women in the second group do not.

a. Briefly outline how researchers could conduct this research as a true experiment using a between-groups design.

b. Why would researchers want to use random assignment?

c. If researchers did not use random assignment but rather chose people who were *already* in those conditions (i.e., who already either believed or did not believe the stereotypes), what might be the possible confounds? Name at least two.

Solutions to these Check Your Learning questions can be found in Appendix D.

d. How is math performance operationalized here?

e. Briefly outline how researchers could conduct this study using a within-groups design.

REVIEW OF CONCEPTS

The Two Branches of Statistics

Statistics is divided into two branches: descriptive statistics and inferential statistics. *Descriptive statistics* organize, summarize, and communicate large amounts of numerical information. *Inferential statistics* draw conclusions about larger populations based on smaller samples of that population. *Samples* are intended to be representative of larger *populations.*

How to Transform Observations into Variables

Observations may be described as either discrete or continuous. *Discrete observations* are those that can take on only certain numbers (for example, whole numbers, such as 1), and *continuous observations* are those that can take on all possible numbers in a range (for example, 1.68792). Two types of *variables*, nominal and ordinal, can only be discrete. *Nominal variables* use numbers simply to give names to scores. *Ordinal variables* are rank-ordered. Two types of variables can be continuous (although both can also be discrete in some cases): interval and ratio. *Interval variables* are those in which the distances between numerical values are assumed to be equal. *Ratio variables* are those that meet the criteria for interval variables but also have a meaningful zero point. *Scale variable* is a term used for both interval variables and ratio variables, particularly in statistical computer programs.

Variables and Research

Independent variables can be manipulated or observed by the experimenter, and they have at least two *levels*, or conditions. *Dependent variables* are outcomes in response to changes or differences in the independent variable. *Confounding variables* systematically vary with the independent variable, so we cannot logically determine which variable may have influenced the dependent variable. The independent and dependent variables allow researchers to test and explore the relations between variables. A measure is useful only if it is both *reliable* and *valid*. A reliable measure is one that is consistent, and a valid measure is one that assesses what it is intended to assess.

Introduction to Hypothesis Testing

Hypothesis testing is the process of drawing conclusions about whether a particular relation between variables is supported by the evidence. *Operational definitions* of the independent variable and the dependent variable are necessary to test a hypothesis. *Experiments* attempt to identify a cause–effect relation between an independent variable and a dependent variable. *Random assignment* to groups to control for confounding variables is the hallmark of an experiment. Most studies have either a *between-groups design* or a *within-groups design*. *Correlational studies* can be used when it is not possible to conduct an experiment; they allow us to determine whether there is a predictable relation between two variables.

Outliers are extreme scores that are either very high or very low compared with the rest of the observed data. Outlier analysis studies outliers to understand how the independent variable affects the dependent variable.

SPSS®

SPSS is divided into two main screens. The easiest way to move back and forth between these two screens is by using the two tabs located at the lower left labeled "Variable View" and "Data View." When data are collected, each data point should be connected with an identifier unique to each participant. This variable is often noted as the "ID." Every variable that is measured needs to have its own Name and Label, and SPSS needs to know how the variable was measured.

To name the variables, go to "Variable View" (see screenshot A) and select:

Name. Type in a short version of the variable name—for example, BDI for the Beck Depression Inventory, a common measure of depressive symptoms. A second variable to add could be the BAI, short for the Beck Anxiety Inventory. Note that SPSS will not allow spaces in the "Name" of the variable.

To tell SPSS what the variable name means, select:

Label. Type in the full name of the variable, such as Beck Depression Inventory and the Beck Anxiety Inventory.

Now tell SPSS what kind of variables these are by selecting:

Measure. Highlight the type of variable by clicking on the cell in the column labeled "Measure" next to each variable, then clicking on the arrow to access the tool that allows you to identify whether the variable is scale, ordinal, or nominal.

After describing all of the variables in the study in "Variable View," switch over to "Data View" (remember, at the lower left corner of the screen—(see screenshot B)). The information you entered was automatically transferred to that screen, but now the variables are displayed across the tops of the columns instead of along the left-hand side of the rows. You can now enter the data in "Data View" under the appropriate heading; each participant's data are entered across one row.

A

Source: SPSS Statistics

B

Source: SPSS Statistics

EXERCISES

The solutions to the odd-numbered exercises can be found in Appendix C.

Clarifying the Concepts

1.1 What is the difference between descriptive statistics and inferential statistics?

1.2 What is the difference between a sample and a population?

1.3 Identify and define the four types of variables that researchers use to quantify their observations.

1.4 Describe two ways that statisticians might use the word *scale*.

1.5 Distinguish between discrete variables and continuous variables.

1.6 What is the relation between an independent variable and a dependent variable?

1.7 What are confounding variables (or simply *confounds*), and how are they controlled using random assignment?

1.8 What is the difference between reliability and validity, and how are the two concepts related?

1.9 To test a hypothesis, we need operational definitions of the independent and dependent variables. What is an operational definition?

1.10 In your own words, define the word *experiment*—first as you would use it in everyday conversation and then as a researcher would use it.

1.11 What is the difference between experimental research and correlational research?

1.12 What is the difference between a between-groups research design and a within-groups research design?

1.13 In statistics, it is important to pay close attention to language. The following statements are wrong but can be corrected by substituting one word or phrase. For example, the sentence "Only correlational studies can tell us something about causality" could be corrected by changing "correlational studies" to "experiments." Identify the incorrect word or phrase in each of the following statements and supply the correct word.

    a. In a study on exam preparation, every participant had an equal chance of being assigned to study alone or with a group. This was a correlational study.

    b. A psychologist was interested in studying the effects of the dependent variable of caffeine on hours of sleep, and she used a scale measure for sleep.

    c. A university assessed the reliability of a commonly used scale—a mathematics placement test—to determine whether it truly measures math ability.

    d. In a within-groups experiment on calcium and osteoporosis, participants were assigned to one of two levels of the independent variable: no change in diet or supplementing the diet with calcium.

1.14 The following statements are wrong but can be corrected by substituting one word or phrase. (See the instructions in Exercise 1.13.) Identify the incorrect word or phrase in each of the following statements and supply the correct word.

    a. A researcher examined the effect of the ordinal variable "gender" on the scale variable "hours of reality television watched per week."

    b. A psychologist used a between-groups design to study the effects of an independent variable (a workout video) on the dependent variable (the weight) of a group of undergraduate students before and after viewing the video.

c. In a study on the effects of the confounding variable of noise level on the dependent variable of memory, researchers were concerned that the memory measure was not valid.

d. A researcher studied a population of 20 rats to determine whether changes in exposure to light would lead to changes in the dependent variable of amount of sleep.

1.15 When John Snow investigated the 1854 outbreak of cholera in London, he paid particular attention to outliers. What is an outlier?

1.16 What are potential benefits of outlier analysis?

Calculating the Statistics

1.17 A researcher studies the number of hours 2500 Canadians work out every week. Identify the sample and the population for this example.

1.18 University bookstore employees asked 225 students to complete a customer satisfaction survey after these customers bought their books. The bookstore manager wanted to find ways to improve the customer experience. Identify the sample and population for this example.

1.19 Over the course of 1 week, a grocery store randomly selected 100 customers to complete a survey about their favorite products. Identify the sample and population for this example.

1.20 A researcher studies the average distance that 130 people living in U.S. urban areas walk each week.

a. What is the size of the sample?

b. Identify the population.

c. Is this "average" a descriptive statistic or an inferential statistic if it is used to describe the 130 people studied?

d. How might you operationalize the average distance walked in 1 week as an ordinal measure?

e. How might you operationalize the average distance walked in 1 week as a scale measure?

1.21 As they leave a popular grocery store, 73 people are stopped and the number of fruit and vegetable items they purchased is counted.

a. What is the size of the sample?

b. Identify the population.

c. If this number of items counted is used to estimate the diets of all shoppers, is it a descriptive statistic or an inferential statistic?

d. How might you operationalize the amount of fruit and vegetable items purchased as a nominal measure?

e. How might you operationalize the amount of fruit and vegetable items purchased as an ordinal measure?

f. How might you operationalize the amount of fruit and vegetable items purchased as a scale measure?

1.22 In the fall of 2008, the U.S. stock market plummeted several times, with grave consequences for the world economy. A researcher might assess the economic effect this situation had by seeing how much money people saved in 2009. That amount could be compared to the amount people saved in more economically stable years. How might you operationalize the economic implications at a national level—that is, across countries?

1.23 A researcher might be interested in evaluating how a person's physical and emotional distance from Manhattan at the time of the 9/11 terrorist attacks relates to the accuracy of memory about the event.

a. Identify the independent variables and the dependent variable.

b. Imagine that physical distance is assessed as within 100 miles or beyond 100 miles; also, imagine that emotional distance is assessed as knowing no one who was affected, knowing people who were affected but lived, and knowing someone who died in the attacks. How many levels do the independent variables have?

c. How might you operationalize the dependent variable (which you identified in part (a) above)?

1.24 A study of the effects of skin tone (light, medium, and dark) on the severity of facial wrinkles in middle age might be of interest to cosmetic surgeons.

a. What would the independent variable be in this study?

b. What would the dependent variable be in this study?

c. How many levels would the independent variable have?

1.25 Since 1980, most of the cyclists who have won the Tour de France have won it just once. Several cyclists have won it two or three times in a row. The Spanish cyclist Miguel Induráin won it five times in a row, and the U.S. cyclist Lance Armstrong won it seven consecutive times (although he was stripped of his medals for violating the drug policy). Identify the outlier or outliers among the cyclists.

1.26 Referring to the previous exercise, what might be the purpose of an outlier analysis in this case? What might it reveal?

Applying the Concepts

1.27 **Average weights in the United States:** The CDC reported very large weight increases for U.S. residents of both genders and all age groups over a period of four decades. Go to the Web site that reports these data (http://www.cdc.gov) and search for the article titled "Americans Slightly Taller, Much Heavier Than Four Decades Ago."

a. What were the average weights of 10-year-old girls in 1963 and in 2002?

b. Do you think the CDC weighed every girl in the United States to get these averages? If not, explain why this would not be feasible.

c. How does the average weight of 10-year-old girls in 2002 or the average weight of 10-year-old boys in 1963 represent both a descriptive and an inferential statistic?

1.28 Sample versus population in Norway: The Nord-Trøndelag health study surveyed more than 60,000 people in a Norwegian county and reported that gastrointestinal symptoms, depression, and anxiety disorders are strongly related (Haug, Mykletun, & Dahl, 2002).

a. What is the sample used by these researchers?

b. What is the population to which the researchers would like to extend their findings?

1.29 Types of variables and Olympic swimming: At the 2012 London Summer Olympics, American Michael Phelps won 4 gold medals, bringing his overall Olympic career total to 18 gold medals, the all-time career record for Olympic gold medals in any sport. One of the events he won was the 100-meter butterfly. For each of the following examples, identify the type of variable—nominal, ordinal, or scale.

a. Phelps of the United States came in first, and Chad le Clos of South Africa and Evgeny Korotyshkin of Russia tied for second place.

b. Phelps finished in 51.21 seconds, and le Clos and Korotyshkin finished in 51.44 seconds.

c. Phelps and Korotyshki live in the Northern Hemisphere, whereas le Clos lives in the Southern Hemisphere.

1.30 Types of variables and the Kentucky Derby: The Kentucky Derby is perhaps the premier event in U.S. horse racing. For each of the following examples from the derby, identify the type of variable—nominal, ordinal, or scale.

a. As racing fans, we would be very interested in the variable finishing position. A horse called Orb won in 2013, followed by Golden Soul in second and Revolutionary in third.

b. We also might be interested in the variable finishing time. Orb won in 2 minutes, 2.89 seconds.

c. Derby attendance was 151,616 in 2013, not as high as the record-setting 165,307 people who attended in 2012.

d. If we were the betting type, we might examine the variable payoffs. For each $2.00 bet on Orb, a gambler won $12.80.

e. We might be interested in the history of the derby and the demographic variables of jockeys, such as gender or race. For example, in the first 28 runnings of the Kentucky Derby, 15 of the winning jockeys were African American.

f. In the luxury boxes, high fashion reigns; we might be curious about the variable of hat wearing, observing how many women wear hats and how many do not.

1.31 Discrete versus continuous variables: For each of the following examples, state whether the scale variable is discrete or continuous.

a. The capacity, in terms of songs, of a smartphone

b. The playing time of an individual song

c. The cost in cents to download a song legally

d. The number of posted reviews that an album has on Amazon.com

1.32 Reliability and validity: Go online and take the personality test found at http://www.outofservice.com/starwars. This test assesses your personality in terms of the characters from the original *Star Wars* movies.

a. What does it mean for a test to be reliable? Take the test a second time. Does it seem to be reliable?

b. What does it mean for a test to be valid? Does this test seem to be valid? Explain.

c. The test asks a number of demographic questions at the end, including "In what country did you spend most of your youth?" Can you think of a hypothesis that might have led the developers of this Web site to ask this question?

d. For your hypothesis in part (c), identify the independent and dependent variables.

1.33 Reliability, validity, and wine ratings: You may have been in a wine store and wondered just how useful those posted wine ratings are. (They are usually rated on a scale from 50 to 100, with 100 being the top score.) After all, aren't ratings subjective? Corsi and Ashenfelter (2001) studied whether wine experts are consistent. Knowing that the weather is the best predictor of price, the researchers wondered how well weather predicted experts' ratings. The variables used for weather included temperature and rainfall, and the variable used for wine experts' ratings was the number they assigned to each wine.

a. Name one independent variable. What type of variable is it? Is it discrete or continuous?

b. Name the dependent variable. What type of variable is it? Is it discrete or continuous?

c. How does this study reflect the concept of reliability?

d. Let's say that you frequently drink wine that has been rated highly by Robert Parker, one of this study's wine experts. His ratings were determined to be reliable, and you find that you usually agree with Parker. How does this observation reflect the concept of validity?

1.34 Operationalizing variables and rap statistics: The Web site Rap Genius analyzes rap music using what they call RapMetrics (http://rapgenius.com/posts/63 -Introducing-rapmetricstm-the-birth-of-statistical -analysis-of-rap-lyrics). It has developed a measure called rhyme density, which is the proportion of all syllables that are part of the rhyme. Eminem's *Without Me*, for example, has a rhyme density of 0.49 (49%) because almost half of the lyrics are part of the rhyme, whereas Notorious B.I.G.'s *Juicy* only has a rhyme density of 0.23 (23%). The people behind Rap Genius say, "Over the course of a career, the rappers with the highest rhyme densities are basically the best technical rappers."

a. How does Rap Genius operationalize the best rapper?

b. List at least three other variables that might be considered in determining the best rapper.

c. Across all songs, MF Doom came in first with an overall rhyme density of 0.44, and Cam'ron came in second with a rhyme density of 0.41. What kind of variable is the ranking, and what kind of variable is the rhyme density?

d. Rap Genius summarized its rhyme density discussion by saying: "MF Doom surprised us a little. First the big *New Yorker* profile and now this… it's too much! Cam'ron is much more culturally relevant and interesting (plus he doesn't need to wear a mask, he's naturally silly), so we at RapMetrics™ consider *him* the G.O.A.T. [greatest of all time] MC [rapper] overall." Rap Genius, therefore, changed its operational definition a bit. What has it added to its operational definition of the overall G.O.A.T. MC?

1.35 Operationalizing the earnings of comedians: In 2013, *Forbes* reported the 10 top-earning comedians, and all 10 were men—Louis C.K., Kevin Hart, and Larry the Cable Guy among them. A number of online journalists wanted to know why there were no women on the list. Erin Gloria Ryan of *Jezebel*, for example, wondered where women like Ellen DeGeneres and Amy Poehler were. Under a "methodology" heading, *Forbes* explained the process of gathering these data. "To compile our earnings numbers, which consist of pretax gross income, we talked to agents, lawyers and other industry insiders to come up with an estimate for what each comedian earned." *Forbes* added a caveat: "In order for comics to make the cut, their primary source of income had to come from concert ticket sales." In response to that caveat, Ryan wrote: "Okay, guys? That's a super weird definition of what constitutes a comedian."

a. Explain how *Forbes* is operationalizing the earnings of comedians.

b. Explain why *Jezebel*'s Ryan might have a problem with this definition.

c. Ryan wrote: "If Dr. Dre doesn't have to record an album or perform a concert to be considered a real 'hip hop artist,' then why does Mindy Kaling need to hold a mic in front of a brick wall to be a real 'comedian'?" Based on Ryan's critique, offer at least one different way of operationalizing the earnings of comedians.

1.36 Between-groups versus within-groups and exercise: Noting marked increases in weight across the population, researchers, nutritionists, and physicians have struggled to find ways to stem the tide of obesity in many Western countries. They have advocated a number of exercise programs, and there has been a flurry of research to determine the effectiveness of these programs. Pretend that you are in charge of a research study to examine the effects of an exercise program on weight loss in comparison with a program that does not involve exercise.

a. Describe how you could study the exercise program using a between-groups research design.

b. Describe how you could study the exercise program using a within-groups design.

c. What is a potential confound of a within-groups design?

1.37 Correlational research and smoking: For decades, researchers, politicians, and tobacco company executives debated the relation between smoking and health problems such as cancer, with tragic consequences.

a. Why was this research necessarily correlational in nature?

b. What confounding variables might make it difficult to isolate the health effects of smoking tobacco?

c. How might the nature of this research and these confounds buy time for the tobacco industry with regard to acknowledging the hazardous effects of smoking?

d. All ethics aside, how could you study the relation between smoking and health problems using a between-groups experiment?

1.38 Experimental versus correlational research and culture: A researcher interested in the cultural values of individualistic and collectivist societies collects data on the rate of relationship conflict experienced by 32 people who test high for individualism and 37 people who test high for collectivism.

a. Is this research experimental or correlational? Explain.

b. What is the sample?

c. Write a possible hypothesis for this researcher.

d. How might we operationalize relationship conflict?

1.39 Experimental versus correlational research and recycling: A study in Argentina concluded that grocery store customers were more likely to bring their own bags when stores charged for plastic bags than when stores did not charge (Jakovcevic et al., 2014). Imagine that you want to design a follow-up study on this topic in a country other than Argentina.

a. Write a hypothesis for this researcher.

b. Describe how you could design a correlational study to test this hypothesis.

c. Describe how you could design an experiment to test this hypothesis.

1.40 Outliers, exercise, and weight gain: Imagine that you conducted the study described in Exercise 1.36 and that one person had gained many, many pounds while in the exercise program.

a. Why would this individual be considered an outlier?

b. Explain why outlier analysis might be useful in this situation.

c. What kinds of things are we looking for in an outlier analysis?

1.41 Outliers and response time: Imagine that a researcher is measuring the time it takes participants to identify whether a string of letters constitutes a word (e.g., duke) or a nonword (e.g., dake). She measures the response time of 40 participants. She finds that most participants took from 0 to 1 second to make their decision but that one participant took 3 minutes to make a decision.

a. Why would the participant who took 3 minutes be considered an outlier?

b. What kinds of things might the researcher look for in an outlier analysis of this situation?

Putting It All Together

1.42 Romantic relationships: Goodman and Greaves (2010) reported findings from the Millennium Cohort Study, a large research project in the United Kingdom. They stated that "while it is true that cohabiting parents are more likely to split up than married ones, there is very little evidence to suggest that this is due to a causal effect of marriage. Instead, it seems simply that different sorts of people choose to get married and have children, rather than to have children as a cohabiting couple, and that those relationships with the best prospects of lasting are the ones that are most likely to lead to marriage" (p. 1).

a. What is the sample in this study?

b. What is the likely population?

c. Is this a correlational study or an experiment? Explain.

d. What is the independent variable?

e. What is the dependent variable?

f. What is one possible confounding variable? Suggest at least one way in which the confounding variable might be operationalized.

1.43 Experiments, HIV, and cholera: Several studies have documented that people who are HIV-positive are susceptible to cholera (likely because of having a weakened immune system). Researchers in Mozambique (Lucas et al., 2005), a country where an estimated 20% to 30% of the population is HIV-positive, wondered whether an oral vaccine for cholera would work among people who are HIV-positive. Cholera immunization was administered to 14,000 people in Mozambique who tested positive for HIV. Soon thereafter, an epidemic of cholera spread through the region, giving the researchers an opportunity to test their hypothesis.

a. Describe a way in which the researchers could have conducted an experiment to examine the effectiveness of the cholera vaccine among people who are HIV-positive.

b. If the researchers did conduct an experiment, would this have been a between-groups or a within-groups experiment? Explain.

c. The researchers did not randomly assign participants to vaccine or no-vaccine conditions; rather, they conducted a general mass immunization. Why does this limit their ability to draw causal conclusions? Include at least one possible confounding variable.

d. The researchers did not use random assignment when conducting this study. List at least one practical reason and at least one ethical reason that they might not have used random assignment.

1.44 Ability and wages: Arcidiacono, Bayer, and Hizmo (2008) analyzed data from a national longitudinal survey called NLSY79, which includes data from more than 12,000 men and women in the United States who were in the 14- to 22-year age range in 1979. The researchers reported that ability is related to wages in early career jobs for university graduates but not for high school graduates. In line with this, research has found that racial discrimination with respect to wages is more prevalent against high school graduates than college graduates, because when ability is not the primary reason for determining wages, other factors irrelevant to ability, such as race, play in. The researchers suggest that their findings might explain why, on average, a black person is more likely to earn a college degree than is a white person of the same ability level.

a. List any independent variables.

b. List any dependent variables.

c. What is the sample in this study?

d. What is the population about which researchers want to draw conclusions?

e. What do the authors mean by "longitudinal" in this study?

f. The researchers used the Armed Forces Qualification Test (AFQT) as their measure of ability. The AFQT combines scores on word knowledge, paragraph comprehension, arithmetic reasoning, and mathematics knowledge subscales. Can you suggest at least one confounding variable in the relation between ability and wages when comparing college graduates to high school graduates?

g. Suggest at least two other ways in which the researchers might have operationalized ability.

1.45 Assessing charitable organizations: Many people do research on charitable organizations before deciding where to donate their money. Tina Rosenberg (2012) reported that traditionally many people have used sources such as Charity Navigator or the Better Business Bureau's Web sites. Both of these sites rate organizations more highly if the organizations use less of their donation money for fundraising or administration and more of it for the cause they are supporting. On Charity Navigator, for example, Doctors Without Borders, a nonprofit focused on health and medical needs, gets a rating of 57.11 out of 70 based on its financial practices, accountability, and transparency; this puts that organization in the second of Charity Navigator's five tiers (http://www.charitynavigator.org/).

a. How does Charity Navigator operationalize a good charity?

b. What kind of variable is the score of 57.11 out of 70—nominal, ordinal, or scale? Explain your answer.

c. What kind of variable is the tier, second out of five—nominal, ordinal, or scale? Explain your answer.

d. There are many types of charities. Doctors Without Borders focuses on health and medical needs. What kind of variable is its type of charity—nominal, ordinal, or scale? Explain your answer.

e. According to Rosenberg (2012), Toby Ord, a moral philosopher from Oxford University, thinks the traditional operational definition of what constitutes a good charity is too limited. He has five criteria that he sees as important for a good charity: It targets the most serious problems (disease over art, for example). It uses evidence-based practices. It uses cost-effective interventions. It is competent and honest. And it "can make good use of each additional dollar." Ord touts an organization called GiveWell as a source for ratings that incorporates many of his criteria (http://www.givewell.org/). Doctors Without Borders fares less well on GiveWell; the site reports: "We believe that the overall cost-effectiveness of [Doctors Without Borders'] activities are unlikely to compare well with those of our top charities." Explain why Web sites like Charity Navigator might look just at measures relating to finances, as opposed to a fuller definition such as that described by Ord.

f. Which is more likely to be reliable, the rating by Charity Navigator or that by GiveWell? Explain your answer.

g. Which is more likely to be valid, the rating by Charity Navigator or that by GiveWell? Explain your answer.

h. If you were to monitor whether increased donation funds led to a lower death rate in a country, would that be an experiment or a correlational study? Explain your answer.

i. If you were to randomly assign some regions to receive more donation funds and other regions to receive fewer, and then track the death rate in both sets of regions, would that be an experiment or a correlational study? Explain your answer.

TERMS

descriptive statistic (p. 2)
inferential statistic (p. 3)
sample (p. 3)
population (p. 3)
variable (p. 4)
discrete observation (p. 4)
continuous observation (p. 4)
nominal variable (p. 4)
ordinal variable (p. 5)
interval variable (p. 5)

ratio variable (p. 5)
scale variable (p. 6)
level (p. 7)
independent variable (p. 7)
dependent variable (p. 7)
confounding variable (p. 7)
reliability (p. 8)
validity (p. 8)
hypothesis testing (p. 9)
operational definition (p. 10)

correlation (p. 10)
random assignment (p. 11)
experiment (p. 11)
between-groups research
    design (p. 12)
within-groups research
    design (p. 12)
outlier (p. 13)
outlier analysis (p. 13)

Frequency Distributions

2

Frequency Distributions

Frequency Tables
Grouped Frequency Tables
Histograms
Frequency Polygons

Shapes of Distributions

Normal Distributions
Skewed Distributions

Next Steps: Stem-and-Leaf Plot

BEFORE YOU GO ON

- You should understand the different types of variables—nominal, ordinal, and scale (Chapter 1).

- You should understand the difference between a discrete variable and a continuous variable (Chapter 1).

John Snow didn't need an algebraic formula to think like a statistician. In fact, counting is the main mathematical skill you will need to understand frequency distributions. But don't let the simplicity of the mathematics fool you: Statistical reasoning is powerful stuff. Counting and then rearranging those numerical observations from the highest to the lowest number (or vice versa) can reveal all sorts of hidden patterns.

For example, YouTube videos that go viral are an advertiser's dream. But what makes a video go viral? In a 2010 article from Time.com, researchers suggested "the 5 elements of a viral video:" (1) cute animals, (2) cute kids, (3) remixes, (4) spontaneity, and (5) cute kids and cute animals (Aneja & Ross, 2015). An undergraduate student at Elon University in North Carolina, Tyler West (2011), followed the hints coming from frequency distributions based on a rating of viral videos from Time.com. One of the factors was the length of the video clip. Table 2-1 shows the list of YouTube's 50 Best Videos, as reported by Time.com.

TABLE 2-1	Viral Videos

This table includes YouTube's 50 Best Videos, as Reported by Time.com in 2010. The data in this table use the longest time, in seconds, from available YouTube clips.

Rank	Title	Seconds	Rank	Title	Seconds
1	Charlie Bit My Finger	55	26	"Yes We Can"	270
2	Evolution of Dance	360	27	Hilary Clinton's 1984	74
3	David After Dentist	118	28	Noah's Daily Photos	345
4	"Here It Goes Again"	184	29	Bank of America's "One"	302
5	Rickroll	213	30	Grape Lady Falls!	87
6	Leave Britney Alone	257	31	Randy Pausch's Last Lecture	4586
7	Don't Tase Me, Bro	143	32	Zinedine Zidane's Head Butt	53
8	Keyboard Cat	54	33	Leprechaun Sighting	123
9	Dramatic Chipmunk	5	34	Justin Bieber	228
10	Hitler's *Downfall*	239	35	Daft Hands	224
11	Flea Market Montgomery	122	36	Auto-Tune the News	160
12	"United Breaks Guitars"	276	37	Fred	191
13	Kittens, Inspired by *Kittens*	91	38	"Chocolate Rain"	292
14	Potter Puppet Pals	126	39	*Will It Blend?*	114
15	Jill and Kevin's Big Day	309	40	"Thriller" in Manila	265
16	Sneezing Panda	16	41	Where the Hell is Matt?	223
17	Otters Holding Hands	101	42	"Lazy Sunday"	142
18	Total Eclipse of the Heart, Literal Video Version	336	43	Diet Coke and Mentos	178
19	OMG, Shoes	241	44	Obama Girl	199
20	Baby Laughing	100	45	Lonelygirl15	95
21	Susan Boyle's Debut	451	46	Guinness T-Shirt Record	87
22	Miss Teen South Carolina	48	47	Tillman, the Skateboarding Dog	88
23	Baby Bobbing to "Single Ladies"	168	48	Christian the Lion	156
24	Zombie Kid Likes Turtles	17	49	Charlie the Unicorn	225
25	"Hey Jude" Kid	102	50	Trapped in an Elevator	190

Rearranging the data from shortest to longest video clip (see Table 2-2) allows us to see something that we could not see in the original data set: Seven of the 13 shortest video clips involve cute animals: a chipmunk, a panda, turtles, a cat, a dog, a kitten, and two otters. Of course, we still don't know whether the combination of "short length" and "cute animals" is more likely to go viral, but we may be a little closer to understanding why that happens. And any summary from these data is only a descriptive statistic. We would need to calculate inferential statistics to know if this is true across all videos.

In this chapter, we learn how to organize individual data points in a table. Then we go one step further and learn how to use two types of graphs—histograms and frequency polygons—to show the overall pattern of data. Finally, we learn to use these graphs to understand the shape of the distribution of the data points. These tools are important steps for using statistics in the behavioral sciences.

TABLE 2-2 YouTube's 50 Best Videos, as Reported by Time.com, Ranked by Length of Video

Rank	Title	Seconds	Rank	Title	Seconds
9	Dramatic Chipmunk	5	43	Diet Coke and Mentos	178
16	Sneezing Panda	16	4	"Here It Goes Again"	184
24	Zombie Kid Likes Turtles	17	50	Trapped in an Elevator	190
22	Miss Teen South Carolina	48	37	Fred	191
32	Zinedine Zidane's Head Butt	53	44	Obama Girl	199
8	Keyboard Cat	54	5	Rickroll	213
1	Charlie Bit My Finger	55	41	Where the Hell is Matt?	223
27	Hilary Clinton's 1984	74	35	Daft Hands	224
30	Grape Lady Falls!	87	49	Charlie the Unicorn	225
46	Guinness T-Shirt Record	87	34	Justin Bieber	228
47	Tillman, the Skateboarding Dog	88	10	Hitler's *Downfall*	239
13	Kittens, Inspired by *Kittens*	91	19	OMG, Shoes	241
45	Lonelygirl15	95	6	Leave Britney Alone	257
20	Baby Laughing	100	40	"Thriller" in Manila	265
17	Otters Holding Hands	101	26	"Yes We Can"	270
25	"Hey Jude" Kid	102	12	"United Breaks Guitars"	276
39	*Will It Blend?*	114	38	"Chocolate Rain"	292
3	David After Dentist	118	29	Bank of America's "One"	302
11	Flea Market Montgomery	122	15	Jill and Kevin's Big Day	309
33	Leprechaun Sighting	123	18	Total Eclipse of the Heart, Literal Video Version	336
14	Potter Puppet Pals	126			
42	"Lazy Sunday"	142	28	Noah's Daily Photos	345
7	Don't Tase Me, Bro	143	2	Evolution of Dance	360
48	Christian the Lion	156	21	Susan Boyle's Debut	451
36	Auto-Tune the News	160	31	Randy Pausch's Last Lecture	4586
23	Baby Bobbing to "Single Ladies"	168			

Frequency Distributions

Researchers are usually most interested in the relations between two or more variables, such as the effect of the length of a video clip (the independent variable) on whether that video will go viral (the dependent variable). But to understand the relation between variables, we must first understand each individual variable's data points. The basic ingredients of a data set are called *raw scores*, *data that have not yet been transformed or analyzed*. In statistics, we organize raw scores into a *frequency distribution*, which *describes the pattern of a set of numbers by displaying a count or proportion for each possible value of a variable*. For example, a frequency distribution can display the pattern of the scores—the length of a video clip—from the list in Table 2-2.

Frequency Tables

There are several different ways to organize the data in terms of a frequency distribution. The first approach, the frequency table, is also the starting point for each of the three other approaches that we will explore. A *frequency table* is a *visual depiction of data that shows how often each value occurred; that is, how many scores were at each value*. Once organized into a frequency table, data can be displayed as a grouped frequency table, a histogram, or a frequency polygon.

EXAMPLE 2.1

- A **raw score** is a data point that has not yet been transformed or analyzed.

- A **frequency distribution** describes the pattern of a set of numbers by displaying a count or proportion for each possible value of a variable.

- A **frequency table** is a visual depiction of data that shows how often each value occurred; that is, how many scores were at each value. Values are listed in one column, and the numbers of individuals with scores at that value are listed in the second column.

Lake Kivu, one of the world's so-called killer lakes, sits between the African countries of Rwanda and the Democratic Republic of Congo (DRC). Activity from the nearby chain of volcanoes causes dangerous gases, including highly explosive methane, to seep into the lake. The upside: The methane is harnessed to power the region. The downside: The methane might lead the lake to explode, something that occurs about every 1000 years and could kill hundreds of thousands of people (Turner, 2015).

So what do volcanoes have to do with psychology and statistics? Clinical and environmental psychologists have focused on responses to natural disasters (see Norris, Stevens, Pfefferbaum, Wyche, & Pfefferbaum, 2008). Psychologists are interested not only in the psychological toll in the aftermath of a disaster but also when a hypothetical disaster quietly, but incessantly, threatens a community.

Imagine that you lived in such a place. Or maybe you already do. The Northwest United States and the southwest of Canada up through Vancouver Island, for example, are overdue for a devastating earthquake (Schulz, 2015). What would you feel? How would you cope? Maybe you'd try to ignore it. When a reporter expressed that Lake Kivu would be better without the methane, Emanuel, a local waiter, responded that "We do not think about that too much," and quickly walked away (Turner, 2015). Maybe you'd become anxious. As lava flow threatened a town in Hawaii, one resident acknowledged that, "everybody, including myself, is quite nervous. We don't know. We can't see the future" (Carroll, 2014).

Volcanoes are perhaps the most visible of these quiet, ongoing environmental threats because they are literally looming over the people who live near them. A psychologist interested in the human psychological damage from the threat of volcanoes might be interested in examining how this threat is dispersed around the world. Oregon State University publishes a fairly comprehensive list of the world's volcanoes (Volcanoes by country, 2016).

Table 2-3 lists the numbers of volcanoes for each of the 55 countries that has at least one volcano. We can use these data to create a frequency table.

At first glance, it is not easy to find a pattern in most lists of numbers. But when we reorder those numbers, a pattern begins to emerge. A frequency table is the best way to create an easy-to-understand distribution of data. In this example, we simply organize the data into a table with two columns, one for the range of responses (the values) and one for the frequencies of each response (the scores).

There are specific steps to create a frequency table. First, we determine the range of raw scores. For each country, we can count how many volcanoes it has. We see that the lowest score is 1 and the highest is 81. Remember, we are only including countries with at least one volcano. Also, for the purposes of this example, we won't use the four outliers—Indonesia, Japan, Russia, and the United States. It would make our frequency table too long. We'll learn how to deal with this situation in the next section. So, for now the top score is 17. Simply noting that the scores range from 1 to 17 brings some clarity to the data set. But we can do even better.

After we identify the lowest and highest scores, we create the two columns that we see in Table 2-4. We examine the raw scores and determine how many countries fall at each value in the range. The appropriate number for each value is recorded in the table. For example, there is one country with 17 volcanoes, so a 1 is marked there. It is important to note that we include *all* numbers in the range; there are no countries with 11, 14, 15, or 16 volcanoes, so we put a 0 next to each one.

Here is a recap of the steps to create a frequency table:

1. Determine the highest score and the lowest score.
2. Create two columns; label the first with the variable name, and label the second "Frequency."

Stressful Volcanoes Psychology researchers study the chronic stress experienced by people living under the threat of a possible natural disaster. Here, people living in Goma, a city on Lake Kivu in the Democractic Republic of Congo, watch the aftermath of a volcanic eruption. People living along the shores of Lake Kivu may experience the stress of two environmental dangers—the potential for a volcanic eruption and the possibility that the lake itself might explode due to the build-up of volcano-induced explosive gases.

TABLE 2-3   Volcanoes Around the World

This table shows the numbers of volcanoes in each country that has at least one volcano. The data were compiled by researchers at Oregon State University.

Country	Number	Country	Number	Country	Number	Country	Number
Antarctica	1	DRC	2	Italy	6	Portugal	3
Argentina	1	Ecuador	12	Japan	40	Russia	55
Australia	4	El Salvador	5	Kenya	7	Solomon Islands	2
Azores	3	Eritrea	2	Lesser Sunda Islands	1	Spain	5
Cameroon	2	Ethiopia	10	Libya	1	St. Kitts and Nevis	2
Canary Islands	1	France	4	Mariana Islands	4	St. Vincent	1
Cape Verde Islands	2	Galápagos Islands	1	Mexico	7	Tanzania	3
Chad	1	Greece	5	Netherlands	2	Tonga	1
Chile	10	Grenada	1	New Zealand	8	Turkey	2
China	1	Guatemala	7	Nicaragua	9	Uganda	1
Colombia	3	Iceland	5	Norway	1	United Kingdom	4
Comoros	1	India	2	Papua New Guinea	17	United States	81
Congo	2	Indonesia	45	Peru	2	Vanuatu	9
Costa Rica	4	Iran	2	Philippines	13		

Data from http://volcano.oregonstate.edu/volcanoes_by_country (2016)

TABLE 2-4	Frequency Tables and Volcanoes

This frequency table depicts the numbers of volcanoes per country for the 51 countries that have between 1 and 17 volcanoes. The four outliers—Indonesia, Japan, Russia, and the United States—have between 40 and 81 volcanoes and would make this frequency table too long to be of much use.

Number of Volcanoes	Frequency
17	1
16	0
15	0
14	0
13	1
12	1
11	0
10	2
9	2
8	1
7	3
6	1
5	4
4	5
3	4
2	12
1	14

Data from http://volcano.oregonstate.edu/volcanoes_by_country (2016).

3. List the full range of values that encompasses all the scores in the data set, from highest to lowest. Include *all* values in the range, even those for which the frequency is 0.

4. Count the number of scores at each value, and write those numbers in the frequency column.

As shown in Table 2-5, we can add a column for percentages. To calculate a percentage, we divide the number of countries at a certain value by the total number of countries, and then multiply by 100. As we observed earlier, 1 out of 51 countries had 17 volcanoes.

$$\frac{1}{51}(100) = 1.961$$

So, for countries with 17 volcanoes, the percentage for 1 of 51 countries is 1.96%. We can see from Table 2-5 that more than 50% of countries have either one or two volcanoes.

Note that when we calculate statistics, we can come up with different answers depending on the number of steps and how we decide to round numbers. In this book, we round off to three decimal places throughout the calculations, but we report the final answers to two decimal places, rounding up or down as appropriate. Sometimes the numbers don't add up to 100% exactly, due to rounding. But if you follow this guideline, then you should get the same answers that we get.

TABLE 2-5	Frequencies and Percentages for Volcanoes by Country

This frequency table is an expansion of Table 2-4, which depicts the number of countries that have varying numbers of volcanoes. Again, it only includes the 51 countries that have between 1 and 17 volcanoes. It now includes percentages, which are often more descriptive than actual counts.

Number of Volcanoes	Frequency	Percentage
17	1	1.96
16	0	0
15	0	0
14	0	0
13	1	1.96
12	1	1.96
11	0	0
10	2	3.92
9	2	3.92
8	1	1.96
7	3	5.88
6	1	1.96
5	4	7.84
4	5	9.80
3	4	7.84
2	12	23.53
1	14	27.45

Data from http://volcano.oregonstate.edu/volcanoes_by_country (2016).

Creating a frequency table for the data gives us more insight into the set of numbers. We can see that countries with volcanoes are most likely to have just one or two, and only a few have dozens. In the next section, we'll see how to handle a data set like this with some outliers, values that are far from the others. ●

Grouped Frequency Tables

In the previous example, we used data that counted the numbers of countries, which are whole numbers. In addition, we limited our range to 1 to 17. But often data are not so easily understood. Consider these two situations:

1. When data can go to many decimal places, such as in reaction times
2. When data cover a wider range, such as the full set of volcano data

In both of these situations, the frequency table could go on for pages and pages. For example, if someone weighed only 0.0003 pound more than the person at the next weight, that first person would belong to a distinctive, unique category. Using such specific values would lead to two problems: We would create an enormous amount of unnecessary work for ourselves, and we wouldn't see trends in the data. Fortunately, we have a technique to deal with these situations: *a **grouped frequency table** allows researchers to depict data visually by reporting the frequencies within a given interval rather than the frequencies for a specific value.*

● A **grouped frequency table** is a visual depiction of data that reports frequencies within a given interval rather than the frequencies for a specific value.

Language Alert! The word *interval* is used in more than one way by statisticians. Here, it refers to a range of values (as opposed to an interval variable, the type of variable that has equal distances between values).

• •

EXAMPLE 2.2

The following data exemplify the second of these two situations in which the data aren't easily conveyed in a standard frequency table. This is the full set of volcano data as depicted in Table 2-3.

1	1	4	3	2	1	2	1
10	1	3	1	2	4	2	12
5	2	10	4	1	5	1	7
5	2	45	2	6	40	7	1
1	4	7	2	8	9	1	17
2	13	3	55	2	5	2	1
3	1	2	1	4	81	9	

You may remember that we omitted four outliers when we created a frequency table. If we included all of these data points, the table would go from 1 to 81. Such a table would be longer than the list of the original raw data.

Instead of reporting every single value in the range, we can report intervals, or ranges of values. Here are the five steps to generate a standard grouped frequency table:

> **STEP 1: Find the lowest and highest scores in the frequency distribution.**

In the volcano example, these scores are 1 and 81.

> **STEP 2: Get the full range of data.**

If there are decimal places, round both the highest and the lowest scores down to the nearest whole numbers. If they already are whole numbers, such as with the volcano example, use those. Subtract the lowest whole number from the highest whole number and add 1 to get the full range of the data. (Why do we add 1? Try it yourself. If we subtract 1 from 81, we get 80—but there are actually 81 values. (This seems obvious when the first number is one, but try it with a range of 3 to 10. $10 - 3 = 7$, but there are 8 values. Count them. When in doubt, always count the individual values.)

In the volcano example, $81 - 1 = 80$, and $80 + 1 = 81$. The scores fall within a range of 81.

> **STEP 3: Determine the number of intervals and the best interval size.**

There is no consensus about the ideal number of intervals, but most researchers recommend between 5 and 10 intervals, unless the data set is enormous and has a huge range. To find the best interval size, we divide the range by the number of intervals we want, then round to the nearest whole number (as long as the numbers are not too small—that is, as long as there are not too many decimal places). For ranges that are wide, the size of intervals could be a multiple of 10 or 100 or 1000; for smaller ranges, it could be as small as 2, 3, or 5, or even less than 1, if the numbers go to many decimal places. Try several interval sizes to determine the best one.

In the volcanoes example, we might choose to have intervals of size 10, which would mean we would have 9 intervals.

STEP 4: Figure out the number that will be the bottom of the lowest interval.

We want the bottom of the lowest interval to be a multiple of the interval size. For example, if we have 9 intervals of size 10, then we want the bottom interval to start at a multiple of 10.

It could start at 0, 10, 80, or 1050, depending on the data. We select the multiple of 10 that is below the lowest score.

In the volcano example, there are 9 intervals of size 10, so the bottom of the lowest interval would be 0. If the lowest score had been, say, 12, we would choose 10. (Note that this process sometimes leads to one more interval than we had planned for; this is perfectly fine.)

STEP 5: Finish the table by listing the intervals from highest to lowest and then counting the numbers of scores in each.

This step is much like creating a frequency table (without intervals), which we discussed earlier. If we decide on intervals of size 10 and the first one begins at 0, then we add 10 to get the bottom of the next interval. So, first interval runs from 0 to 9.9999, the next one from 10 to 19.9999, and so on. With whole numbers, we can just say 0 to 9, 10 to 19, and so on. A good rule of thumb is that the *bottom* of the intervals should jump by the chosen interval size, in this case 10.

TABLE 2-6	Grouped Frequency Table of Number of Volcanoes by Country Around the World

Grouped frequency tables make sense of data sets in which there are many possible values. This grouped frequency table depicts 9 intervals that summarize the numbers of volcanoes in 55 countries—the countries summarized in Table 2-4 along with the four outlier countries. (As before, these are only the countries with at least 1 volcano.)

Interval	Frequency
80–89	1
70–79	0
60–69	0
50–59	1
40–49	2
30–39	0
20–29	0
10–19	5
0–9	46

Data from http://volcano.oregonstate.edu/volcanoes_by_country (2016).

In the volcano example, the lowest interval would be 0-9 (technically 0.00 to 9.99). The next would be 10 to 19, and so on.

Compared to the long list of raw data or a frequency distribution, the grouped frequency table in Table 2-6 is much easier to understand. ●

Histograms

Even more than tables, graphs help us to see data at a glance. The two most common methods for graphing scale data for one variable are the histogram and the frequency polygon. Here we learn to construct and interpret the histogram (more common) and the frequency polygon (less common).

2-2: The data in a frequency table can be viewed in graph form. In a histogram, bars are used to depict frequencies at each score or interval. In a frequency polygon, a dot is placed above each score or interval to indicate the frequency, and the dots are connected.

*A **histogram** is a graph that looks like a bar graph but depicts just one variable, usually based on scale data, with the values of the variable on the x-axis and the frequencies on the y-axis.* Each bar reflects the frequency for a value or an interval. The difference between histograms and bar graphs is that bar graphs typically provide scores for nominal data (e.g., men and women) relative to another variable (e.g., height), whereas histograms typically provide frequencies for one scale variable (e.g., levels of pacing indices). We can construct histograms from frequency tables or from grouped frequency tables. Histograms allow for the many intervals that typically occur with scale data. The bars are stacked one against the next, with the intervals meaningfully arranged from lower numbers (on the left) to higher numbers (on the right). With bar graphs, the categories do not need to be arranged in one particular order and the bars should not touch.

EXAMPLE 2.3

Let's start by constructing a histogram from a frequency table. Table 2-4 depicts a frequency table of countries' numbers of volcanoes, for countries with 17 or fewer volcanoes. We construct a histogram by drawing the x-axis (horizontal) and y-axis (vertical) of a graph. We label the x-axis with the variable of interest—in our case, "Numbers of volcanoes"—and we label the y-axis "Frequency." As with most graphs, the lowest numbers start where the axes intersect and the numbers go up as we go to the right on the x-axis and as we go up on the y-axis. Ideally, the lowest number on each axis is 0, so that the graphs are not misleading. However, if the range of numbers on either axis is far from 0, histograms sometimes use a number other than 0 as the lowest number. Further, if there are negative numbers among the scores (as can be the case in scores for air temperature, for example), the x-axis could have negative numbers.

Once we've created the graph, we draw a bar for each value. Each bar is *centered on* the value for which it provides the frequency. The height of the bars represents the numbers of scores that fall at each value—the frequencies. If no country had a score at a particular value, then we would not draw a bar for that value. So, for the value of 2 on the x-axis, a bar centers on 2 with a height of 12 on the y-axis, indicating that 12 countries had two volcanoes. Figure 2-1 shows the histogram for the volcano data.

● A **histogram** is a graph that looks like a bar graph but depicts just one variable, usually based on scale data, with the values of the variable on the x-axis and the frequencies on the y-axis.

Here is a recap of the steps to construct a histogram from a frequency table:

1. Draw the x-axis and label it with the variable of interest and the full range of values for this variable. (Include 0 unless all of the scores are so far from 0 that this would be impractical.)

FIGURE 2-1

Histogram for the Frequency Table of Number of Volcanoes by Country Around the World

Histograms are graphic depictions of the information in frequency tables or grouped frequency tables. This histogram shows the numbers of volcanoes in the 51 countries that have between 1 and 17 volcanoes.

Data from http://volcano.oregonstate.edu/volcanoes_by_country (2016).

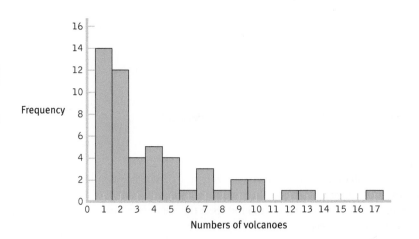

2. Draw the *y*-axis, label it "Frequency," and include the full range of frequencies for this variable. (Include 0 unless it's impractical.)

3. Draw a bar for each value, centering the bar around that value on the *x*-axis and drawing the bar as high as the frequency for that value, as represented on the *y*-axis.

Grouped frequency tables can also be depicted as histograms. Instead of listing values on the *x*-axis, we list the midpoints of intervals. Students commonly make mistakes in determining midpoints. If an interval ranges from 0 to 4, what is the midpoint? If you said 2, you're making a *very* common mistake. Remember, this interval really goes from 0.000000 to 4.999999, or as close as you can get to 5, the bottom of the next interval, without actually being 5. Given that there are 5 numbers in this range (0, 1, 2, 3 and 4), the midpoint would be 2.5 from the bottom. So the midpoint for 0 to 4 is 2.5. A good rule: When determining a midpoint, look at the bottom of the interval that you're interested in and then the bottom of the next interval; then, determine the midpoint of these two numbers. ●

EXAMPLE 2.4

Let's look at the volcano data for which we constructed a grouped frequency table. What are the midpoints of the 9 intervals? Let's calculate the midpoint for the lowest interval, 0 to 9. We should look at the bottom of this interval, 0, and the bottom of the next interval, 10. The midpoint of these numbers is 5, so that is the midpoint of this interval. The remaining midpoints can be calculated the same way. For the highest interval, 80 to 89, it helps to imagine that we had one more interval. If we did, it would start at 90. The midpoint of 80 and 90 is 85. Using these guidelines, we calculate the midpoints as 5, 15, 25, 35, 45, 55, 65, 75, and 85. (A good check is to see if the midpoints jump by the interval size—in this case, 10.) We now can construct the histogram by placing these midpoints on the *x*-axis and drawing bars that center on them and are as high as the frequency for each interval. The histogram for these data is shown in Figure 2-2.

Here is a recap of the steps to construct a histogram from a grouped frequency table:

1. Determine the midpoint for every interval.

2. Draw the *x*-axis and label it with the variable of interest and with the midpoint for each interval on this variable. (Include 0 unless it's impractical.)

FIGURE 2-2

Histogram for the Grouped Frequency Table of Number of Volcanoes by Country Around the World

Histograms can also depict the data in a grouped frequency table. This histogram depicts the data seen in the grouped frequency table for volcanoes in countries that have at least 1 volcano.

- A **frequency polygon** is a line graph, with the *x*-axis representing values (or midpoints of intervals) and the *y*-axis representing frequencies; a dot is placed at the frequency for each value (or midpoint), and the dots are connected.

3. Draw the *y*-axis, label it "Frequency," and include the full range of frequencies for this variable. (Include 0 unless it's impractical.)
4. Draw a bar for each midpoint, centering the bar on that midpoint on the *x*-axis and drawing the bar as high as the frequency for that interval, as represented on the *y*-axis. ●

Frequency Polygons

Frequency polygons are constructed in a similar way to histograms. As the name might imply, polygons are many-sided shapes. Histograms look like city skylines, but polygons look more like mountain landscapes. Specifically, a *frequency polygon is a line graph, with the* x-*axis representing values (or midpoints of intervals) and the* y-*axis representing frequencies; a dot is placed at the frequency for each value (or midpoint), and the dots are connected.*

EXAMPLE 2.5

For the most part, we make frequency polygons exactly as we make histograms. Instead of constructing bars above each value or midpoint, however, we draw dots and connect them. The other difference is that we need to add an appropriate value (or midpoint) on either end of the graph so that we can draw lines down to 0, grounding the shape. In the case of the volcano data, we calculate one more midpoint on each end by subtracting the interval size, 10, from the bottom midpoint ($5 - 10 = -5$) and adding the interval size, 10, to the top midpoint ($85 + 10 = 95$). Because the first new midpoint, -5, is negative, we'll use 0. After all, you can't have -5 volcanoes in a country. We now can construct the frequency polygon by placing these new midpoints, 0 and 95, on the *x*-axis, drawing dots at each midpoint that are as high as the frequency for each interval, and connecting the dots. Figure 2-3 shows the frequency polygon for the grouped frequency distribution of number of countries that have particular numbers of volcanoes that we constructed previously in Figure 2-2.

Here is a recap of the steps to construct a frequency polygon. When basing a frequency polygon on a frequency table, we place the specific values on the *x*-axis. When basing it on a grouped frequency table, we place the midpoints of intervals on the *x*-axis.

FIGURE 2-3

Frequency Polygon as Another Graphing Option for the Volcano Data

Frequency polygons are an alternative to histograms. This frequency polygon depicts the same data that were depicted in the histogram in Figure 2-2. In either case, the graph provides an easily interpreted "picture" of the distribution.

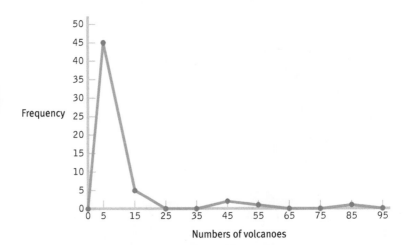

1. If the frequency polygon is based on a grouped frequency table, determine the midpoint for every interval. If it is based on a frequency table, skip this step.
2. Draw the x-axis and label it with the variable of interest and either the values or the midpoints. (Include 0 unless it's impractical.)
3. Draw the y-axis, label it "Frequency," and include the full range of frequencies for this variable. (Include 0 unless it's impractical.)
4. Mark a dot above each value or midpoint depicting the frequency, as represented on the y-axis, for that value or midpoint, and connect the dots.
5. Add an appropriate hypothetical value or midpoint on both ends of the x-axis, and mark a dot to indicate a frequency of 0 for each of these values or midpoints. Connect the existing line to these dots to create a shape rather than a "floating" line. ●

CHECK YOUR LEARNING

Reviewing the Concepts

> The first steps in organizing data for a single variable are to list all the values in order of magnitude and then count how many times each value occurs.

> There are four techniques for organizing information about a single variable: frequency tables, grouped frequency tables, histograms, and frequency polygons.

Clarifying the Concepts   **2-1**   Name four different ways to organize raw scores visually.

2-2   What is the difference between frequencies and grouped frequencies?

Calculating the Statistics   **2-3**   In 2013, *U.S. News & World Report* published a list of the citations per faculty member score for the 400 best universities in the world. As examples, the Massachusetts Institute of Technology is number 1 on the list of best universities and McGill University in Montreal is number 18. The citation score tells us how many times a faculty member's research has been cited by other researchers over the previous 5 years, and is an indicator of research productivity. Here are the data for the top 50 institutions:

100.0 100.0 100.0 100.0 99.8 99.5 99.5 99.3 99.1 98.8

97.9 97.9 97.8 97.2 97.0 96.9 96.4 96.3 94.0 93.3

92.4 92.1 90.7 90.0 89.4 87.3 87.3 86.5 81.6 80.2

79.9 78.3 77.3 77.1 75.7 75.6 74.9 74.8 74.7 73.1

70.8 70.0 69.1 68.9 68.0 64.3 63.1 62.2 62.1 60.2

a. Construct a grouped frequency table of these data.

b. Construct a histogram for this grouped frequency table.

c. Construct a frequency polygon for this grouped frequency table.

Applying the Concepts   **2-4**   Consider the data from Check Your Learning 2-3, as well as the table and graphs that you constructed.

a. What can we tell from the graphs and table that we cannot tell from a quick glance at the list of scores?

Solutions to these Check Your Learning questions can be found in Appendix D.

b. What issues might arise in considering data across countries with a wide range of academic systems?

● **A normal distribution** is a specific frequency distribution that is a bell-shaped, symmetric, unimodal curve.

Shapes of Distributions

We learned how to organize data so that we can better understand the concept of a distribution, a major building block for statistical analysis. We can't get a sense of the overall pattern of data by looking at a list of numbers, but we *can* get a sense of the pattern by looking at a frequency table. We can get an even better sense by creating a graph. Histograms and frequency polygons allow us to see the overall pattern, or shape, of the distribution of data.

The shape of a distribution provides distinctive information. When the U.S.-based General Social Survey (a large data set available to the public via the Internet) asked people about the influence of children's programming—both network television and public television—the responses showed very different patterns for each type of children's programming (Figure 2-4). For example, the most common response for network television shows was that they have a neutral influence, whereas the most common response for public television shows was that they have a positive influence. In this section, we provide you with language that expresses the differences between these patterns. Specifically, you'll learn to describe different shapes of distributions, including normal distributions and skewed distributions.

Normal Distributions

Many, but not all, distributions of variables form a bell-shaped, or *normal*, curve. Statisticians use the word *normal* to describe distributions in a very particular way. *A **normal distribution** is a specific frequency distribution that is a bell-shaped, symmetric, unimodal curve* (Figure 2-5). People's attitudes about the network programming of

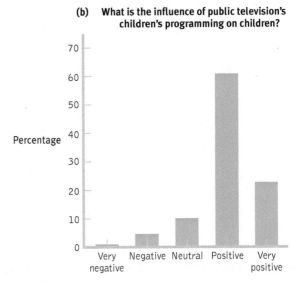

FIGURE 2-4

The Influence of Television Programming on Children

These two histograms tell different stories about the perceptions of the influence of television programming on children. The first histogram (a) describes the influence of network television on children; the second histogram (b) describes the influence of public television on children.

Data from McCollum & Bryant (2003)

children's shows provide an example of a distribution that approaches a normal distribution. There are fewer scores at values that are farther from the center and even fewer scores at the most extreme values (as can be seen in the bar graph in Figure 2-4a). Most scores cluster around the word *neutral* in the middle of the distribution, which would be at the top of the bell.

Skewed Distributions

Reality is often—but not always—normally distributed, which means that the distributions describing some observations are not shaped normally. So we need a new term to help us describe some of the distributions that are not normal—*skew*. **Skewed distributions** *are distributions in which one of the tails of the distribution is pulled away from the center.* Although the technical term for such data is *skewed*, a skewed distribution may also be described as lopsided, off-center, or simply nonsymmetric. Skewed data have an ever-thinning tail in one direction or the other. The distribution of people's attitudes about the children's programming offered by public television (see Figure 2-4b) is an example of a skewed distribution. The scores cluster to the right side of the distribution around the word *positive*, and the tail extends to the left.

When a distribution is **positively skewed**, as in Figure 2-6a, *the tail of the distribution extends to the right, in a positive direction.* Positive skew sometimes occurs when there

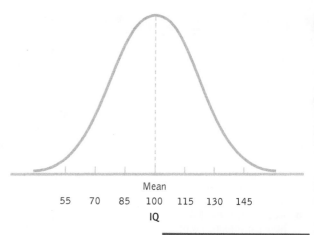

FIGURE 2-5

The Normal Distribution

The normal distribution, shown here for IQ scores, is a frequency distribution that is bell-shaped, symmetric, and unimodal. It is central to many calculations in statistics.

(a) Positive skew

(b) Negative skew

FIGURE 2-6

Two Kinds of Skew

The mnemonic "the tail tells the tale" means that the distribution with the long, thin tail to the right is positively skewed and the distribution with the long, thin tail to the left is negatively skewed.

- A **skewed distribution** is a distribution in which one of the tails of the distribution is pulled away from the center.

- With **positively skewed** data, the distribution's tail extends to the right, in a positive direction.

2-3: If a histogram indicates that the data are symmetric and bell-shaped, then the data are normally distributed. If the data are not symmetric and the tail extends to the right, the data are positively skewed; if the tail extends to the left, the data are negatively skewed.

● A **floor effect** is a situation in which a constraint prevents a variable from taking values below a certain point.

● **Negatively skewed** data have a distribution with a tail that extends to the left, in a negative direction.

● A **ceiling effect** is a situation in which a constraint prevents a variable from taking on values above a given number.

is a *floor effect*, a situation in which a constraint prevents a variable from taking values below a certain point. For example, in the "volcano" data, scores indicating how many countries had particular numbers of volcanoes is an example of a positively skewed distribution with a floor effect. We only included countries with at least one volcano, which means that the data were constrained at the lower end of the distribution, 1 (that is, they can't go below 1).

The distribution in Figure 2-6b shows *negatively skewed* data, which *have a distribution with a tail that extends to the left, in a negative direction.* The distribution of people's attitudes toward public television's programming of children's shows is favorable because it is clustered around the word *positive*, but we describe the shape of that distribution as negatively skewed because the thin tail is to the left side of the distribution. Not surprisingly, negative skew is sometimes the result of a *ceiling effect*, a situation in which a constraint prevents a variable from taking on values above a given number. If a professor gives an extremely easy quiz, then the quiz scores might show a ceiling effect. A number of students would cluster around 100, the highest possible score, with a few stragglers down in the lower end.

Next Steps   Stem-and-Leaf Plot

● A **stem-and-leaf plot** is a graph that displays all the data points of a variable (or of two levels of a variable) both numerically and visually.

Histograms and frequency polygons do not let us view two groups in a single graph very easily, but the stem-and-leaf plot does. A *stem-and-leaf plot* is a graph *that displays all the data points of a variable (or of two levels of a variable) both numerically and visually.*

Every year, the United Nations publishes its Human Development Report, which includes scores for 195 countries that reflect the overall well-being of its people. As part of the report, the UN publishes mean years of education (2015). Table 2.7 shows a randomly selected sample of mean years of education for 26 countries for 2013, the most recent year for which there was available data.

Before we start creating a stem-and-leaf plot for these data, we'll arrange them from highest to lowest:

TABLE 2-7	Mean Years of Education Globally		
Country	Years of education	Country	Years of education
Armenia	10.8	Malawi	4.2
Bahrain	9.4	Mauritius	8.5
Brazil	7.2	Montenegro	10.5
Cameroon	5.9	New Zealand	12.5
Canada	12.3	Norway	12.6
Cyprus	11.6	Poland	11.8
Egypt	6.4	Samoa	10.3
Gambia	2.8	Serbia	9.5
Guinea	1.6	South Africa	9.9
Iceland	10.4	Togo	5.3
Iraq	5.6	Ukraine	11.3
Israel	12.5	United States	12.9
Lesotho	5.9	Vietnam	5.5

Source: United Nations Development Programme (2015a).

12.9 12.6 12.5 12.5

12.3 11.8 11.6 11.3

10.8 10.5 10.4 10.3

 9.9   9.5   9.4   8.5

 7.2   6.4   5.9   5.9

 5.6   5.5   5.3   4.2

 2.8   1.6

STEP 1: Create the stem.

In this example, the stem will consist of the digits to the left of the decimal place arranged from highest to lowest:

12

11

10

9

8

7

6

5

4

3

2

1

TABLE 2-8	Stem-and-Leaf Plot

A stem-and-leaf plot allows us to see the shape of the data, along with the individual scores.

Mean Years of Education Globally
12 35569
11 368
10 3458
9 459
8 5
7 2
6 4
5 35699
4 2
3
2 8
1 6

Note that each category is represented on the stem, even if it has no leaf (e.g., no score with a 3 to the left of the decimal place.

STEP 2: Add the leaves.

The leaves, the digit to the right of the decimal place for each score are added in ascending order for each part of the stem, as shown in Table 2-8. In the education example, the only score that starts with 1 is 1.6, so we add 6 as a leaf next to 1. There is no score starting at 3, so we have no leaf for that part of the stem. There are five scores starting with 12, so we add 5 leaves in ascending order next to 12.

The stem-and-leaf plot displays the same information as a histogram, but in a slightly different way and with a little more detail. In fact, as seen in Figure 2-7, the stem-and-leaf plot looks like a histogram if turned on its side.

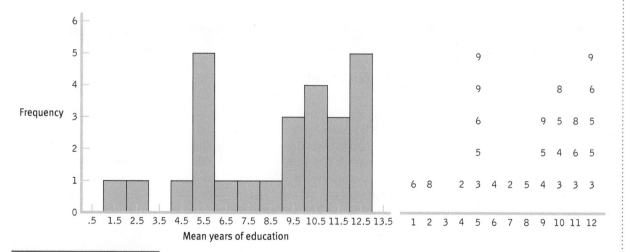

FIGURE 2-7

A Histogram and a Stem-and-Leaf Plot

The stem-and-leaf plot displays the same information as a histogram, but in a slightly different way and with a little more detail. (Note that the histogram on the left uses midpoints on the *x*-axis, whereas the stem-and-leaf plot uses the first digit or digits.)

CHECK YOUR LEARNING

Reviewing the Concepts > A normal distribution is a specific distribution that is unimodal, symmetric, and bell-shaped.

> A skewed distribution "leans" either to the left or to the right. A tail to the right indicates positive skew; a tail to the left indicates negative skew.

> Stem-and-leaf plots allow us to view the shape of a sample's distribution while displaying every single data point in the sample.

Clarifying the Concepts **2-5** Distinguish a normal distribution from a skewed distribution.

2-6 When the bulk of data cluster together but the data trail off to the left, the skew is _____; when data trail off to the right, the skew is _____.

Calculating the Statistics **2-7** In Check Your Learning 2-3, you constructed two visual displays of the distribution of citations per faculty at top universities around the world. How would you describe this distribution? Is there skew evident in your graphs? If there is, what kind of skew is it?

2-8 Alzheimer's disease is typically diagnosed in adults above the age of 70; cases diagnosed sooner are called "early onset."

   a. Assuming that these early-onset cases represent unique trailing off of data on one side, would the skew be positive or negative?

   b. Do these data represent a floor effect or ceiling effect?

Applying the Concepts **2-9** Referring to Check Your Learning 2-8, what implication would identifying such skew have in the screening and treatment process for Alzheimer's disease?

Solutions to these Check Your Learning questions can be found in Appendix D.

REVIEW OF CONCEPTS

Frequency Distributions

There are several ways in which we can depict a *frequency distribution* of a set of *raw scores*. *Frequency tables* are comprised of two columns, one with all possible values and one with a count of how often each value occurs. *Grouped frequency tables* allow us to work with more complicated data. Instead of containing values, the first column consists of intervals. *Histograms* display bars of different heights indicating the frequency of each value (or interval) that the variable can take on. *Frequency polygons* show frequencies with dots at different heights depicting the frequency of each value (or interval) that the variable can take on. The dots in a frequency polygon are connected to form the shape of the data.

Shapes of Distributions

The *normal distribution* is a specific distribution that is unimodal, symmetric, and bell-shaped. Data can also display *skewness*. A distribution that is *positively skewed* has a tail in a positive direction (to the right), indicating more extreme scores above the center. It sometimes results from a *floor effect*, in which scores are constrained and cannot be below a certain number. A distribution that is *negatively skewed* has a tail in a negative direction (to the left), indicating more extreme scores below the center. It sometimes results from a *ceiling effect*, in which scores are constrained and cannot be above a certain number. *Stem-and-leaf plots* allow us to view the shape of a distribution but also display every single score in a sample.

SPSS®

As discussed in the SPSS section of Chapter 1, at the bottom left of your screen, you may choose between "Data View" and "Variable View." The left-hand column in Data View is prenumbered, beginning with 1. Each column to the right of that number contains information about a particular variable; each row represents a unique observation—that is, the data for an individual, whether it's a person, video, or country. The Variable View provides information about the name of the variable, the label for the variable, and the type of variable (e.g., nominal, ordinal, scale).

In this example, data from the YouTube example discussed earlier in this chapter have been entered into an SPSS datafile. Note, there was one extreme outlier— "Randy Pausch's Last Lecture," at 4586 seconds—in the data. Because it is an extreme outlier, it has been removed from this example for teaching purposes (don't worry: outliers will be discussed in Chapter 4). When entering the data, be sure to start with Variable View first, and then move to Data View. To enter the text for the name of each video, be sure to change the "Type" of variable (found in Variable View) to be String instead of Numeric. Enter the YouTube data from Table 2-1 on page 24 (remember to exclude the data for "Randy Pausch's Last Lecture"), and then, from the menu at the top of the screen, select Analyze → Descriptive Statistics → Frequencies. Select the variables you want SPSS to describe by highlighting them and clicking the arrow in the middle. In this case, we'll select the length of each video. We also want to visualize each variable, so after selecting any variables, select Charts → Histograms (click the box next to "show normal curve on histogram") → Continue → OK.

For all of the SPSS functions, an "output" file automatically appears after "OK" is clicked. You can save your output file, and even convert it to a PDF or Word document for access at a later time. The screenshot shown here depicts the part of the SPSS output that includes the histogram. Double-click on the graph to enter the SPSS Chart Editor, and then double-click on each feature in order to make the graph look the way you want it to. For example, you might choose to change the text of the title to be more specific (e.g., Histogram of Top 50 YouTube Videos). You can do this by single-clicking twice to edit the title. Additionally, you may want to change the color of the bars in the chart. You can do this by double-clicking on a bar, and a dialogue box will appear. Under the "Fill & Border" tab, you can chose a color of your liking. Click and change any feature of the graph to let the data speak more clearly.

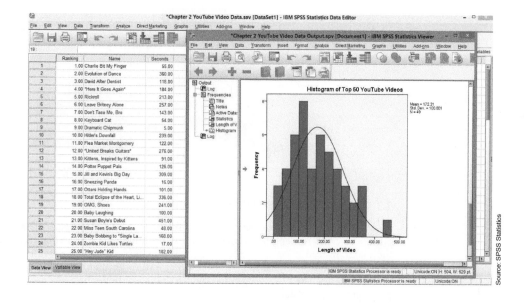

Source: SPSS Statistics

HOW IT WORKS

2.1 CREATING A GROUPED FREQUENCY TABLE

As you may recall, the YouTube data discussed at the beginning of the chapter included the top 50 videos of 2010 according to *Time Magazine*. A grouped frequency table would be an appropriate way to depict the length of each video, as we can report the frequencies within a given interval. For this example, we can use intervals of 50 seconds (e.g., 0–49, 50–99). For teaching purposes the outlier, "Randy Pausch's Last Lecture" (4586 seconds), will not be included in this example.

Seconds	Frequency
400–449	1
350–399	1
300–349	4
250–299	5
200–249	7
150–199	8
100–149	10
50–99	10
0–49	3

2.2 CREATING A GROUPED HISTOGRAM

How can we use these same data to create a grouped histogram? First, we put the intervals for length of video on the x-axis and the frequency for each interval on the y-axis. The bar for each frequency is centered at the midpoint of each interval. The figure below shows the histogram for these data.

2.3 CREATING A FREQUENCY POLYGON

How can we use these same data to create a frequency polygon? As with the histogram, we put the intervals for length of video on the x-axis and the frequency for each interval on the y-axis. Instead of bars, we now place a dot for each frequency above the appropriate interval. We add additional midpoints at either end to ground the polygon. (Because we can't have a negative time, we ground the left at 0.) The figure below shows the frequency polygon for these data.

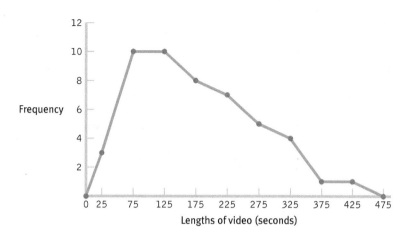

EXERCISES

The solutions to the odd-numbered exercises can be found in Appendix C.

Clarifying the Concepts

2.1 What are raw scores?

2.2 What are the steps to create a frequency table?

2.3 What is the difference between a frequency table and a grouped frequency table?

2.4 Describe two ways that statisticians might use the word *interval*.

2.5 What is the difference between a histogram and a bar graph?

2.6 What are the typical labels for the *x*-axis and the *y*-axis in a histogram?

2.7 What are the differences between a histogram and a frequency polygon?

2.8 What is the benefit of creating a visual distribution of data rather than simply looking at a list of the data?

2.9 In your own words, define the word *distribution*, first as you would use it in everyday conversation and then as a statistician would use it.

2.10 What is a normal distribution?

2.11 How do positively skewed distributions and negatively skewed distributions deviate from a normal distribution?

2.12 What is a floor effect and how does it affect a distribution?

2.13 What is a ceiling effect and how does it affect a distribution?

2.14 What are potential benefits of using a stem-and-leaf plot as opposed to a histogram?

2.15 In what way are stem-and-leaf plots similar to histograms?

Calculating the Statistics

2.16 Convert the following to percentages: 63 out of 1264; 2 out of 88.

2.17 Convert the following to percentages: 7 out of 39; 122 out of 300.

2.18 Counts are often converted to percentages. Convert 817 out of 22,140 into a percentage. Now convert 4009 out of 22,140 into a percentage. What type of variable (nominal, ordinal, or scale) are these data as counts? What kind of variable are they as percentages?

2.19 Convert 2 out of 2000 into a percentage. Now convert 60 out of 62 into a percentage.

2.20 Throughout this book, final answers are reported to two decimal places. Report the following numbers this way: 1888.999, 2.6454, and 0.0833.

2.21 Report the following numbers to two decimal places: 0.0391, 198.2219, and 17.886.

2.22 On a test of marital satisfaction, scores could range from 0 to 27.

a. What is the full range of data, according to the calculation procedure described in this chapter?

b. What would the interval size be if we wanted six intervals?

c. List the six intervals.

2.23 If you have data that range from 2 to 68 and you want seven intervals in a grouped frequency table, what would the intervals be?

2.24 A grouped frequency table has the following intervals: 30–44, 45–59, and 60–74. If converted into a histogram, what would the midpoints be?

2.25 Referring to the grouped frequency table in Table 2-6, how many countries had at least 30 volcanoes?

2.26 Referring to the histogram in Figure 2-1, how many countries had 1 or 2 volcanoes?

2.27 If the average person convicted of murder killed only one person, serial killers would create what kind of skew?

2.28 Would the data for number of murders by those convicted of the crime be an example of a floor effect or ceiling effect?

2.29 A researcher collects data on the ages of college students. As you have probably observed, the distribution of age clusters around 19 to 22 years, but there are extremes on both the low end (high school prodigies) and the high end (nontraditional students returning to school).

    a. What type of skew might you expect for such data?

    b. Do the skewed data represent a floor effect or a ceiling effect?

2.30 If you have a Facebook account, you are allowed to have up to 5000 friends. At that point, Facebook cuts you off, and you have to "unfriend" people to add more. Imagine you collected data from Facebook users at your university about the number of friends each has.

    a. What type of skew might you expect for such data?

    b. Do the skewed data represent a floor effect or ceiling effect?

2.31 a. Using the following set of data, construct a stem-and-leaf plot. For each score, use the first digit for the stem and the second digit for the leaf. For values under 10, use 0 as the stem and single digit for the leaf.

          34   1 16 20 33   31 28

          25 18 29 33 24   34 35

           5 27 30 34 35   27 36

          35 10 28 20 23 387 28

          13 18 30 33 34   24 38

    b. Refer to the stem-and-leaf plot you created for part (a). Does it depict a symmetric or a skewed distribution?

2.32 a. Using the following set of data, construct a stem-and-leaf plot. Follow the model in the Next Steps section of the chapter to set up the stem and add the leaves.

          3.5 2.0 4.0 3.5 2.0 2.5 4.5

          4.0 3.0 3.5 3.0 3.0 4.0 4.5

          2.5 3.5 3.5 3.0 2.5 3.5 3.5

    b. Refer to the stem-and-leaf plot you created for part (a). Does it depict a symmetric or a skewed distribution?

Applying the Concepts

2.33 **Frequency tables, histograms, and the National Survey of Student Engagement:** The National Survey of Student Engagement (NSSE) surveys freshmen and seniors about their level of engagement in campus and classroom activities that enhance learning. Hundreds of thousands of students at almost 1000 schools have completed surveys since 1999, when the NSSE was first administered. Among the many questions, students are asked how often they have been assigned a paper of 20 pages or more during the academic year. For a sample of 19 institutions classified as national universities that made their data publicly available through the *U.S. News & World Report* Web site, here are the percentages of students who said they were assigned between 5 and 10 twenty-page papers:

          0 5 3 3 1 10 2

          2 3 1 2 4   2 1

          1 1 4 3 5

    a. Create a frequency table for these data. Include a third column for percentages.

    b. For what percentage of these schools did exactly 4% of the students report that they wrote between 5 and 10 twenty-page papers that year?

    c. Is this a random sample? Explain your answer.

    d. Create a histogram of grouped data, using six intervals.

    e. In how many schools did 6% or more of the students report that they wrote between 5 and 10 twenty-page papers that year?

    f. How are the data distributed?

2.34 **Frequency tables, histograms, and the Survey of Earned Doctorates:** The Survey of Earned Doctorates regularly assesses the numbers and types of doctorates awarded at U.S. universities. It also provides data on the length of time in years that it takes to complete a doctorate. Each data point is the mean time for one university. Below is a modified list of this completion-time data, truncated to whole numbers and shortened to make your analysis easier. These data have been collected every 5 years since 1982.

        8 88 8 8 87 6 7 7 777

        6 66 6 66 7 8 8 887

        6 67 7 76 11 13 15 15

      14 12 9 10 10 9 9 9

a. Create a frequency table for these data.

b. How many schools have an average completion time of 8 years or less?

c. Is a grouped frequency table necessary? Why or why not?

d. Describe how these data are distributed.

e. Create a histogram for these data.

f. At how many universities did students take, on average, 10 or more years to complete their doctorates?

2.35 Frequency tables, histograms, polygons, and life expectancy rates:

The United Nations Development Programme (2015b) recently published life expectancy rates—the number of years an adult can expect to live—for 195 countries around the world. Below is a randomly selected sample of 30 of them for 2013, the most recent year in which there was available data.

Country	Life Expectancy
Afghanistan	60.95
Armenia	74.56
Australia	82.50
Belarus	69.93
Bosnia and Herzegovina	76.37
Burkina Faso	56.34
Canada	81.48
Côte d'Ivoire	50.72
Cuba	79.26
Ecuador	76.47
Ghana	61.13
Guyana	66.30
Indonesia	70.83
Japan	83.58
Jordan	73.85
Lebanon	80.01
Malaysia	75.02
Mexico	77.50
Namibia	64.48
New Zealand	81.13
Panama	77.56
Saint Lucia	74.80
Slovakia	75.40
Sweden	81.82

Country	Life Expectancy
Tonga	72.67
Trinidad and Tobago	69.87
Tunisia	75.87
United Kingdom	80.55
United States	78.94
Zimbabwe	59.87

a. Create a grouped frequency table for these data.

b. The data have quite a range, with the lowest life expectancy of 50.72 in Côte d'Ivoire and the highest life expectancy of 83.58 in Japan. What research hypotheses come to mind when you examine these data? State at least one research question that these data suggest to you.

c. Create a grouped histogram for these data. As always, be careful when determining the midpoints of the intervals.

d. Create a frequency polygon for these data.

e. Examine these graphs and give a brief description of the distribution. Are there unusual scores? Are the data symmetric, or are they skewed? If they are skewed, in which direction?

2.36 Frequency tables, histograms, and basketball wins: Here are the number of wins for the 30 U.S. National Basketball Association (NBA) teams for the 2012–2013 NBA season.

60 44 39 29 23 57 50 43 37 27
49 42 37 29 19 56 51 40 33 26
48 42 31 25 18 53 44 40 29 23

a. Create a grouped frequency table for these data.

b. Create a histogram based on the grouped frequency table.

c. Write a summary describing the distribution of these data with respect to shape and direction of any skew.

d. Here are the numbers of wins for the 8 teams in the National Basketball League (NBL) of Canada. Explain why we would not necessarily need a grouped frequency table for these data.

26 33
20 22
20 18
19 2

2.37 Types of distributions: Consider these three variables: finishing times in a marathon, number of university dining hall meals eaten in a semester on a three-meal-a-day plan, and scores on a scale of extroversion.

a. Which of these variables is most likely to have a normal distribution? Explain your answer.

b. Which of these variables is most likely to have a positively skewed distribution? Explain your answer, stating the possible contribution of a floor effect.

c. Which of these variables is most likely to have a negatively skewed distribution? Explain your answer, stating the possible contribution of a ceiling effect.

2.38 Type of frequency distribution and type of graph: For each of the types of data described below, first state how you would present individual data values or grouped data when creating a frequency distribution. Then, state which visual display(s) of data would be most appropriate to use. Explain your answers clearly.

a. Eye color observed for 87 people

b. Minutes used on a cell phone by 240 teenagers

c. Time to complete the London Marathon for the more than 35,000 runners who participate

d. Number of siblings for 64 college students

2.39 Number of televisions and a grouped frequency distribution: The Canadian Radio-television and Communications Commission (http://www.crtc.gc.ca/eng/publications/reports/radio/srg.htm) gathers data on the numbers of television sets in Canadian homes. Two percent of homes had no television; 28% had one television; 32% had two televisions; 20% had three televisions; and 18% had four or more televisions. Create a histogram for these percentages. (Treat "four or more televisions" as four for the purposes of this exercise.)

2.40 Skew and surname frequencies: Researchers published a summary of the frequency of surnames based on U.S. Census data (Word, Coleman, Nunziata, & Kominski, 2008). The table lists the frequencies of last names in the left column, the number of last names with that level of frequency in the next column, and then the cumulative number and cumulative percentage in the next two columns. For example, 2.3 million people in the United States have the last name Smith, the most common name in this data set. So, Smith would be one of the seven names listed in the top row—last names that occur more than 1,000,000 times in the population. In another example, more than 72,000 people have the last name Singh. So, Singh is one of the 3012 surnames in the third row—names that occur between 10,000 and 99,999 times in the population.

a. Is this a frequency table or a grouped frequency table? Explain your answer.

b. How is this table different from the tables you created in this chapter? Why do you think the researchers constructed this table differently?

c. Based on this table, does this distribution seem to be normal, negatively skewed, or positively skewed? Explain your answer.

d. Is there a floor effect or a ceiling effect? Explain your answer.

Last Names			
Frequency of Occurrence	Number	Cumulative Number	Cumulative Percentage
1,000,000+	7	7	0.0
100,000–999,999	268	275	0.0
10,000–99,999	3012	3287	0.1
1000–9999	20,369	23,656	0.4
100–999	128,015	151,671	2.4
50–99	105,609	257,280	4.1
25–49	166,059	423,339	6.8
10–24	331,518	754,857	12.1
5–9	395,600	1,150,457	18.4
2–4	1,056,992	2,207,449	35.3
1	4,040,966	6,248,415	100.0

2.41 Skew and movie ratings: IMDb (Internet Movie Database) publishes average ratings of movies worldwide. Anyone can log on and rate a film. What's the worst-rated film of the more than 235,000 that are listed on IMDb? The Bollywood action-romance *Gunday*, which earned a rating of 1.4 on a scale of 1–10 (Goldenburg, 2014). Hardly any other movies even came close to that low rating. In fact, the average film is rated 6.3, and most of the movies garnered ratings between 5.5 and 7.2. Even though *Gunday* got pretty good critical reviews, including three out of four stars from Roger Ebert, it tanked on the crowd-sourced IMDb. Why? Activists in Bangladesh harnessed social media to give it a bad rating. One posted "If you're a Bangladeshi and care enough to not let some Indian crappy movie distort our history of independence, let's unite and boycott this movie!!!"

a. Based on what you know about the typical ratings on IMDb, is a frequency polygon based on these data likely to be normally distributed, negatively skewed, or positively skewed? Explain your answer.

b. Is there more likely to be a floor effect or a ceiling effect for these data? Explain your answer.

c. Based on this story, are audience-generated IMDb ratings a good way to operationalize the quality of a movie? What might be a better way?

2.42 Use the NBL data in Exercise 2.36(d) to create a stem-and-leaf plot. For each score, use the first digit for the stem and the second digit for the leaf. For values under 10, use 0 as the stem and single digit for the leaf.

2.43 Use the NBA data from Exercise 2.36 to create a stem-and-leaf plot. For each score, use the first digit for the stem and the second digit for the leaf.

Putting It All Together

2.44 Frequencies, distributions, and numbers of friends: A college student is interested in how many friends the average person has. She decides to count the number of people who appear in photographs on display in dorm rooms and offices across campus. She collects data on 84 students and 33 faculty members. The data are presented below.

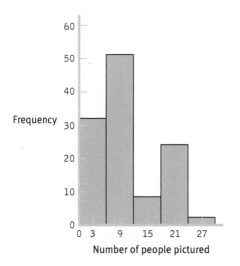

a. What kind of visual display is this?

b. Estimate how many people have fewer than 6 people pictured.

c. Estimate how many people have more than 18 people pictured.

d. Can you think of additional questions you might ask after reviewing the data displayed here?

e. Below is a subset of the data described here. Create a grouped frequency table for these data, using seven groupings.

$$1 \quad 5 \quad 3 \quad 9 \quad 13 \quad 0 \quad 18 \quad 15$$
$$3 \quad 3 \quad 5 \quad 7 \quad 7 \quad 7 \quad 11 \quad 3$$
$$12 \quad 20 \quad 16 \quad 4 \quad 17 \quad 15 \quad 16 \quad 10$$
$$6 \quad 8 \quad 8 \quad 7 \quad 3 \quad 17$$

f. Create a histogram of the grouped data from (e).

g. Describe how the data depicted in the original graph and the histogram you created in part (f) are distributed.

h. Use the data in part (e) to create a stem-and-leaf plot. For each score, use the first digit for the stem and the second digit for the leaf. For values under 10, use 0 as the stem and single digit for the leaf.

i. Refer to the stem-and-leaf plot you created in (h). Do these data reflect a floor effect or a ceiling effect? Explain your answer.

2.45 Frequencies, distributions, and breast-feeding duration: The Centers for Disease Control and other organizations are interested in the health benefits of breast-feeding for infants. The National Immunization Survey includes questions about breast-feeding practices, including: "How long was [your child] breast-fed or fed breast milk?" The data for duration of breast-feeding, in months, for 20 hypothetical mothers are presented below.

$$0 \quad 7 \quad 0 \quad 12 \quad 9 \quad 3 \quad 2 \quad 0 \quad 6 \quad 10$$
$$3 \quad 0 \quad 2 \quad 1 \quad 3 \quad 0 \quad 3 \quad 1 \quad 1 \quad 4$$

a. Create a frequency table for these data. Include a third column for percentages.

b. Create a histogram of these data.

c. Create a frequency polygon of these data.

d. Create a grouped frequency table for these data with three groups (create groupings around the midpoints of 2.5 months, 7.5 months, and 12.5 months).

e. Create a histogram of the grouped data.

f. Create a frequency polygon of the grouped data.

g. Write a summary describing the distribution of these data with respect to shape and direction of any skew.

h. If you wanted the data to be normally distributed around 12 months, how would the data have to shift to fit that goal? How could you use knowledge about the current distribution to target certain women?

2.46 Developing research ideas from frequency distributions: Below are frequency distributions for two sets of the friends data described in Exercise 2.44, one for the students and one for the faculty members studied.

Interval	Faculty Frequency	Student Frequency
24–27	0	2
20–23	0	37
16–19	0	27
12–15	0	2
8–11	1	24
4–7	11	26
0–3	21	0

a. How would you describe the distribution for faculty members?

b. How would you describe the distribution for students?

c. If you were to conduct a study comparing the numbers of friends that faculty members and students have, what would the independent variable be and what would be the levels of the independent variable?

d. In the study described in (c), what would the dependent variable be?

e. What is a confounding variable that might be present in the study described in (c)?

f. Suggest at least two additional ways to operationalize the dependent variable. Would either of these ways reduce the impact of the confounding variable described in (e)?

2.47 Frequencies, distributions, and graduate advising: In a study of mentoring in chemistry fields, a team of chemists and social scientists identified the most successful U.S. mentors—professors whose students were hired by the top 50 chemistry departments in the United States (Kuck et al., 2007). Fifty-four professors had at least three students go on to such jobs. Here are the data for the 54 professors. Each number indicates the number of students successfully mentored by each different professor.

```
3 3 3 4 5  9 5 3 3 5 6
3 4 8 6 3  3 3 4 4 4 7
6 3 5 5 7 13 3 3 3 3 3
4 4 4 5 6  7 6 7 8 8 3
3 3 5 3 3  5 3 5 3 3
```

a. Construct a frequency table for these data. Include a third column for percentages.

b. Construct a histogram for these data.

c. Construct a frequency polygon for these data.

d. Describe the shape of this distribution.

e. How did the researchers operationalize the variable of mentoring success? Suggest at least two other ways in which they might have operationalized mentoring success.

f. Imagine that researchers hypothesized that an independent variable—good mentoring—predicts the dependent variable of mentoring job success. One professor, Dr. Yuan T. Lee from the University of California at Berkeley, trained 13 future top faculty members. Dr. Lee won a Nobel Prize. Explain how such a prestigious and public accomplishment might present a confounding variable to the hypothesis described above.

g. Dr. Lee had many students who went on to top professorships before he won his Nobel Prize. Several other chemistry Nobel Prize winners in the United States serve as graduate advisors but have not had Dr. Lee's level of success as mentors. What are other possible variables that might predict the dependent variable of attaining a top professor position?

TERMS

raw score (p. 26)
frequency distribution (p. 26)
frequency table (p. 26)
grouped frequency table (p. 29)
histogram (p. 32)

frequency polygon (p. 34)
normal distribution (p. 36)
skewed distribution (p. 37)
positively skewed (p. 37)
floor effect (p. 38)

negatively skewed (p. 38)
ceiling effect (p. 38)
stem-and-leaf plot (p. 38)

Visual Displays of Data

3

How to Lie with Visual Statistics

"The Most Misleading Graph Ever Published"
Techniques for Misleading with Graphs

Common Types of Graphs

Scatterplots
Line Graphs
Bar Graphs
Pictorial Graphs
Pie Charts

How to Build a Graph

Choosing the Appropriate Type of Graph
How to Read a Graph
Guidelines for Creating a Graph
The Future of Graphs

Next Steps: Multivariable Graphs

BEFORE YOU GO ON

- **You should understand the different types of variables—nominal, ordinal, and scale (Chapter 1).**

- **You should understand the difference between independent variables and dependent variables (Chapter 1).**

- **You should know how to construct a histogram (Chapter 2).**

The legendary nineteenth-century nurse Florence Nightingale was also known as the "passionate statistician" (Diamond & Stone, 1981). The lens of time has softened the image of this sarcastic, sharp-elbowed infighter (Gill, 2005) who created trouble simply by counting things. She counted supplies in a closet and discovered corruption; she counted physicians' diagnoses and discovered incompetence. She created the visual display in Figure 3-1 after counting the causes of death of British soldiers in Bulgaria and the Crimea. The British army was killing more of its own soldiers through poor hygiene than were dying due to wounds of war—and an outraged public demanded change. That is one powerful graph!

Graphs continue to save lives. Recent research documents the power of graphs to guide decisions about health care and even to reduce risky health-related behaviors (Garcia-Retamero & Cokely, 2013).

This chapter shows you how to create graphs, called *figures* in APA-speak, that tell data stories. We recommend *Displaying Your Findings* by Adelheid Nicol and Penny Pexman (2010) for a more detailed look, but a checklist on pp. 62-63 will answer most of your questions about how to create graphs.

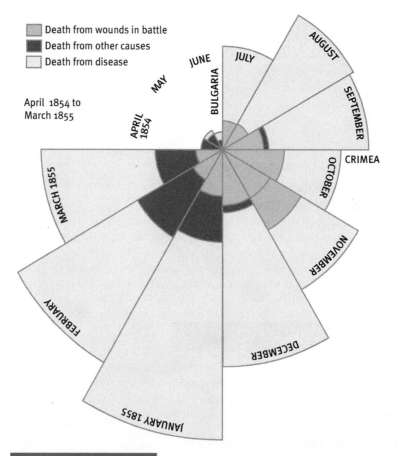

FIGURE 3-1

Graphs That Persuade

This coxcomb graph, based on Florence Nightingale's original coxcomb graph, "Diagram of the Causes of Mortality in the Army in the East," addresses the period from April 1854 to March 1855. It is called a *coxcomb graph* because the data arrangement resembles the shape of a rooster's head. The 12 sections represent the ordinal variable of a year broken into 12 months. The size of the sections representing each month indicates the scale variable of how many people died in that particular month. The colors represent the nominal variable of cause of death.

How to Lie with Visual Statistics

Teaching students how to lie may sound like an odd way to teach statistics, but spotting visual tricks can be empowering. We are indebted to Michael Friendly of York University in Toronto for collecting and managing a Web site (http://www.math.yorku.ca/SCS/Gallery/) that humorously demonstrates the power of graphs both to deceive and to enlighten. He described Figure 3-2 as possibly "the most misleading graph ever published."

"The Most Misleading Graph Ever Published"

The *Ithaca Times* graph in Figure 3-2 appears to answer a simple question: "Why does college have to cost so much?" This graph is chock full of lies.

- Lie 1: The two lines cover different periods of time. The rising line represents rising tuition costs over *35 years*; the falling line represents the ranking of Cornell University over only *11 years*.
- Lie 2: The *y*-axis compares an ordinal observation (university rank) to a scale observation (tuition). These should be two different graphs.
- Lie 3: Cornell's rank arbitrarily begins at a lower point on the *y*-axis than tuition costs, suggesting that an institution already failing to deliver what students are paying for has become dramatically worse.
- Lie 4: The graph *reverses* the implied meaning of up and down. A low number in the world of rankings is a good thing. Over this 11-year period, Cornell's ranking *improved* from 15th place to 6th place!

Techniques for Misleading with Graphs

When you learn a few statistical tricks, you will immediately become a much more critical—and less gullible—consumer of visual statistics:

1. The biased scale lie. *New York* magazine's (see http://nymag.com) reviewers use five stars to indicate that a restaurant's food, service, and ambience are "ethereal; almost perfect"; three stars means "generally excellent"; one means "good." So zero stars must mean bad, right? Wrong. Zero "means our critics don't recommend you go out of your way to eat there." Apparently, you can't buy a bad meal in New York City if a *New York* magazine reviewer has eaten there.

2. The sneaky sample lie. You might pick up some useful information from Web sites that rate professors, but be cautious. The students most likely to supply ratings are those who strongly dislike or strongly approve of a particular professor. A self-selected sample means that the information might not apply to you.

3. The interpolation lie. Interpolation involves assuming that some value between the data points lies on a straight line between those data points. For example, *Statistics Canada* reported that in 2006, Canada had its lowest rate of break-ins (property crime) since the 1970s (Figure 3-3), but you cannot assume a gradual decline over 30 years. In the years leading up to 1991, there was a dramatic increase in property crime. Make sure that a reasonable number of in-between data points have been reported.

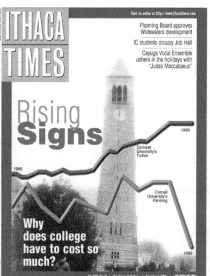

FIGURE 3-2

Graphs That Lie

Michael Friendly describes this graph as a "spectacular example of more graphical sins than I have ever seen in one image" and possibly "the most misleading graph ever published."

FIGURE 3-3

The Perils of Interpolation

Without seeing all of the data, it is easy to draw false conclusions. Although Canada's property crime rate declined from the late 1970s through 2006, there was a peak in the middle, around 1991. If we saw only the data points for the 1970s and 2006, we might falsely conclude that there was a gradual decline during this time. You can search http://statcan.gc.ca for this and many other interesting statistics about Canada.

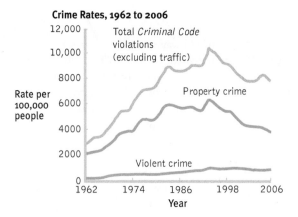

Crime Rates, 1962 to 2006

MASTERING THE CONCEPT

3-1: Graphs can be misleading. As critical thinkers, we want to know whether a sample represents a population, how the variables were actually measured, and whether a graph tells an accurate data story.

4. The extrapolation lie. This lie assumes that values beyond the data points will continue indefinitely. In 1976, *The Complete CB Handbook* assumed that elementary schools would soon have to teach students how to communicate with CB radios, their popularity then growing exponentially. They are now used mostly by long-distance truckers. What happened? Mobile phones. Do not assume that a pattern will continue indefinitely.

5. The inaccurate values lie. This lie tells the truth in one part of the data but visually distorts it in another place. Notice in Figure 3-4 that just four stick figures are meant to represent more than 43,000 nurses in the first three columns. But when only a few thousand more nurses are included, as in the last column, 40 stick figures are used. The proportional change in the number of stick figures is much larger than the proportional change in the size of the data.

There are many more ways to lie with graphs, and we hope you'll keep watch for them. Researchers categorize all of these lies into two groups: (1) lies that exaggerate and (2) lies that reverse the finding (Pandey, Rall, Satterthwaite, Nov, & Bertini, 2015). Lies that exaggerate lead us to think a given difference is bigger or smaller than it really is. Lies that reverse the finding make us think that the opposite finding is occurring. These researchers even conducted a series of studies that demonstrated that visual distortions can affect our perceptions and responses. In one example, only 7 of 38 people who saw a deceptive graph were able to interpret it correctly, whereas 39 out of 40 who saw a clearly designed version were right. For students of psychology and statistics, it is important to learn to create clear graphs and to be alert for visual lies.

FIGURE 3-4

The Inaccurate Values Lie

The visual lie told here is the result of using a representation of a person to have a different value depending on which column it's in. As bloggers Abhimanyu Das and Diana Biller pointed out, "four stick people stand in for 43,000 nurses—but then 28 stick people stand in for an additional 3,000 nurses" (2015). So, a 7% increase over five years is visually depicted as a 7000% increase!

Source: http://static.guim.co.uk/sys -images/Guardian/Pix/pictures/2013/ 8/1/1375343461201/misleading.jpg

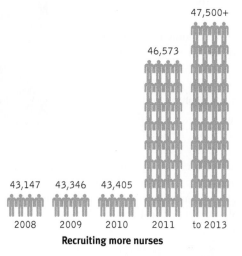

CHECK YOUR LEARNING

Reviewing the Concepts
> Creating and understanding graphs are critical skills in our data-filled society.

> Graphs can reveal or obscure information. To understand what a graph actually conveys, we must examine it and ask critical questions about it.

Clarifying the Concepts   **3-1**   What is the purpose of a graph?

Calculating the Statistics   **3-2**   Referring to Figure 3-4, the inaccurate values lie, calculate how many more nurses there were in 2011–2012 than in 2010–2011. Explain why this is an example of a graphing lie.

Applying the Concepts   **3-3**   Which of the two following graphs is misleading? Which seems to be a more accurate depiction of the data? Explain your answer.

Solutions to these Check Your Learning questions can be found in Appendix D.

Common Types of Graphs

Graphs are powerful because they can display the *relation* between two or more variables in just one image. We first show you how to create scatterplots and line graphs—types of graphs that have two scale variables. Then we learn how to create—and criticize—graphs with just one nominal variable: bar graphs, pictorial graphs, and pie charts.

● A **scatterplot** is a graph that depicts the relation between two scale variables.

Scatterplots

A **scatterplot** *is a graph that depicts the relation between two scale variables.* The values of each variable are marked along the two axes, and a mark is made to indicate the intersection of the two scores for each participant. The mark is above the participant's score on the *x*-axis and across from the score on the *y*-axis. We suggest that you think through your graph by sketching it by hand before creating it on a computer.

•••

Figure 3-5 describes the relation between the number of hours students spent studying and students' grades on a statistics exam. In this example, the independent variable (*x*, on the horizontal axis) is the number of hours spent studying, and the dependent variable (*y*, on the vertical axis) is the grade on the statistics exam.

EXAMPLE 3.1

FIGURE 3-5

Scatterplot of Hours Spent Studying and Statistics Grades

This scatterplot depicts the relation between hours spent studying and grades on a statistics exam. Each dot represents one student's score on the independent variable along the *x*-axis and on the dependent variable along the *y*-axis.

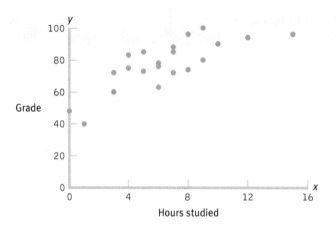

MASTERING THE CONCEPT

3-2: Scatterplots and line graphs are used to depict relations between two scale variables.

The scatterplot in Figure 3-5 suggests that more hours studying is associated with higher grades; it includes each participant's two scores (one for hours spent studying and the other for grade received) that reveal the overall pattern of scores. In this scatterplot, the values on both axes go down to 0, but they don't have to. Sometimes the scores are clustered and the pattern in the data might be clearer by adjusting the range on one or both axes. (If it's not practical for the scores to go down to 0, be sure to indicate this with cut marks. Cut marks are breaks in the axis indicating that the axis starts at a value other than zero.)

To create a scatterplot:

1. Organize the data by participant; each participant will have two scores, one on each scale variable.

2. Label the horizontal *x*-axis with the name of the independent variable and its possible values, starting with 0 if practical.

3. Label the vertical *y*-axis with the name of the dependent variable and its possible values, starting with 0 if practical.

4. Make a mark on the graph above each study participant's score on the *x*-axis and next to his or her score on the *y*-axis.

A scatterplot between two scale variables can tell three possible stories. First, there may be no relation at all; in this case, the scatterplot looks like a jumble of random dots. This is an important scientific story if we previously believed that there was a systematic pattern between the two variables.

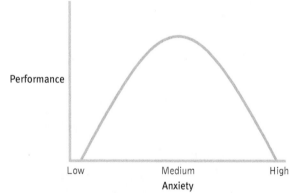

FIGURE 3-6

Nonlinear Relations

The Yerkes–Dodson law predicts that stress/anxiety improves test performance—but only to a point. Too much anxiety leads to an inability to perform at one's best. This inverted U-curve illustrates the concept, but a scatterplot would better clarify the particular relation between these two variables.

Second, *a **linear relation** between variables means that the relation between variables is best described by a straight line.* When the linear relation is positive, the pattern of data points flows upward and to the right. When the linear relation is negative, the pattern of data points flows downward and to the right. The data story about hours studying and statistics grades in Figure 3-5 indicates a positive, linear relation.

*A **nonlinear relation** between variables means that the relation between variables is best described by a line that breaks or curves in some way.* Nonlinear simply means "not straight," so there are many possible nonlinear relations between variables.

For example, the Yerkes–Dodson law described in Figure 3-6 predicts the relation between level of arousal and test performance. As professors, we don't want you so relaxed that you don't even show up for the test, but we also don't want you so stressed out that you have a panic attack. You will maximize your performance somewhere in the happy middle described by a nonlinear relation (in this case, an upside-down U-curve). ●

Line Graphs

*A **line graph** is used to illustrate the relation between two scale variables.* One type of line graph is based on a scatterplot and allows us to construct a line of best fit that represents the predicted *y* score for each *x* value. A second type of line graph allows us to visualize changes in the values on the *y*-axis over time.

- A **linear relation** between variables means that the relation between variables is best described by a straight line.

- A **nonlinear relation** between variables means that the relation between variables is best described by a line that breaks or curves in some way.

- A **line graph** is used to illustrate the relation between two scale variables.

•••

The first type of line graph, based on a scatterplot, is especially useful because the line of best fit minimizes the distances between all the data points from that line. That allows us to use the *x* value to predict the *y* value and make predictions based on only one piece of information. For example, we can use the line of best fit in Figure 3-7 to predict that a student will earn a test score of about 62 if she studies for 2 hours; if she studies for 13 hours, she will earn a score of about 100. For now, we can simply eyeball the scatterplot and draw a line of best fit; in Chapter 16, you will learn how to calculate a line of best fit.

Here is a recap of the steps to create a scatterplot with a line of best fit:

1. Label the *x*-axis with the name of the independent variable and its possible values, starting with 0 if practical.

2. Label the *y*-axis with the name of the dependent variable and its possible values, starting with 0 if practical.

3. Make a mark above each study participant's score on the *x*-axis and next to his or her score on the *y*-axis.

4. Visually estimate and sketch the line of best fit through the points on the scatterplot.

A second situation in which a line graph is more useful than just a scatterplot involves time-related data. A ***time plot***, or ***time series plot***, *is a graph that plots a scale variable on the* y-*axis as it changes over an increment of time (for example, hour, day, century) labeled on the* x-*axis.* As with a scatterplot, marks are placed above each value on the *x*-axis (for example, at a given hour) at the value for that particular time on the *y*-axis (i.e., the score on the dependent variable). These marks are then connected with a line. It is possible to graph several lines on the same graph in a time plot, as long as the lines use the same scale variable on the *y*-axis. With multiple lines, the viewer can compare the trends for different levels of another variable. ●

EXAMPLE 3.2

- A **time plot**, or **time series plot**, is a graph that plots a scale variable on the *y*-axis as it changes over an increment of time (e.g., second, day, century) labeled on the *x*-axis.

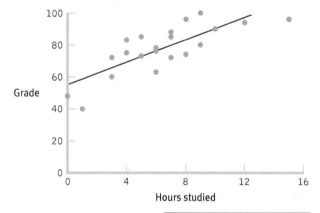

FIGURE 3-7

The Line of Best Fit

The line of best fit allows us to make predictions about a person's value on the *y* variable from his or her value on the *x* variable.

•••

Figure 3-8, for example, shows a time plot for positive attitudes and negative attitudes around the world, as expressed on Twitter. The researchers analyzed more than half a billion tweets over the course of 24 hours (Golder & Macy, 2011) and plotted separate

EXAMPLE 3.3

Time Plots Show Mood Changes on Twitter

Researchers tracked positive attitudes and negative attitudes expressed through Twitter over the course of a day and from around the globe (Golder & Macy, 2011). Time plots allow for multiple scale variables on one graph. In this case, there are separate lines for each day of the week, allowing us to see, for example, that the lines for Saturday and Sunday tend to be highest for positive attitudes and lowest for negative attitudes across the day.

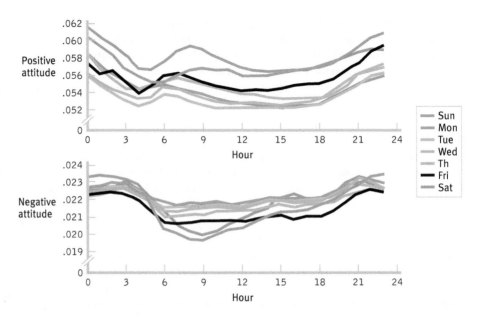

- A **bar graph** is a visual depiction of data in which the independent variable is nominal or ordinal and the dependent variable is scale. The height of each bar typically represents the average value of the dependent variable for each category.

lines for each day of the week. These fascinating data tell many stories. For example, people tend to express more positive attitudes and fewer negative attitudes in the morning than later in the day; people express more positive attitudes on the weekends than during the week; and the weekend morning peak in positive attitudes is later than during the week, perhaps an indication that people are sleeping in.

Here is a recap of the steps to create a time plot:

1. Label the x-axis with the name of the independent variable and its possible values. The independent variable should be an increment of time (e.g., hour, month, year).
2. Label the y-axis with the name of the dependent variable and its possible values, starting with 0 if practical.
3. Make a mark above each value on the x-axis at the value for that time on the y-axis.
4. Connect the dots. ●

3-3: Bar graphs depict data for two or more categories. They tell a data story more precisely than do either pictorial graphs or pie charts.

Bar Graphs

*A **bar graph** is a visual depiction of data in which the independent variable is nominal or ordinal and the dependent variable is scale. The height of each bar typically represents the average value of the dependent variable for each category.* The independent variable on the x-axis could be either nominal (such as gender) or ordinal (such as Olympic medal winners who won gold, silver, or bronze medals). We could even combine two independent variables in a single graph by drawing two separate clusters of bars to compare men's and women's finishing times of the gold, silver, and bronze medalists.

Here is a recap of the variables used to create a bar graph:

1. The x-axis of a bar graph indicates discrete levels of a nominal variable or an ordinal variable.
2. The y-axis of a bar graph may represent counts or percentages. But the y-axis of a bar graph can also indicate many other scale variables, such as average running speeds, scores on a memory task, or reaction times.

Bar graphs are flexible tools for presenting data visually. For example, if there are many categories to be displayed along the horizontal *x*-axis, researchers sometimes create a ***Pareto chart***, *a type of bar graph in which the categories along the* x-*axis are ordered from highest bar on the left to lowest bar on the right.* This ordering allows easier comparisons and easier identification of the most common and least common categories.

● A **Pareto chart** is a type of bar graph in which the categories along the *x*-axis are ordered from highest bar on the left to lowest bar on the right.

EXAMPLE 3.4

Figure 3-9 shows two different ways of depicting the percentage of Internet users in a given country who visited Twitter.com over one recent month. One graph is an alphabetized bar graph; the other is a Pareto chart. Where does Canada's usage fit relative to that of other countries? Which graph makes it is easier to answer that question?

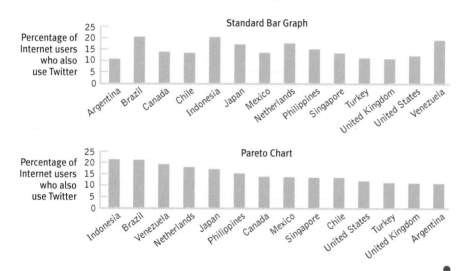

FIGURE 3-9

Pareto Charts Are Easier to Understand

The standard bar graph provides a comparison of Twitter usage among 14 levels of a nominal dependent variable, country. The Pareto chart, a version of a bar graph, orders the countries from highest to lowest along the horizontal axis, which allows us to more easily pick out the highest and lowest bars. We can more easily see that Canada places in the middle of these countries, and that the United States and the United Kingdom are toward the bottom. We have to do more work to draw these conclusions from the original bar graph.

EXAMPLE 3.5

Bar graphs can help us understand the answers to interesting questions. For example, researchers wondered whether piercings and tattoos, once seen as indicators of a "deviant" worldview, had become mainstream (Koch, Roberts, Armstrong, & Owen, 2010). They surveyed 1753 college students with respect to numbers of piercings and tattoos, as well as about a range of destructive behaviors including academic cheating, illegal drug use, and number of arrests (aside from traffic arrests). The bar graph in Figure 3-10 depicts one finding: The likelihood of having been arrested was fairly similar among all groups, except among those with four or more tattoos, 70.6% of whom reported having been arrested at least once. A magazine article about this research advised parents, "So, that butterfly on your sophomore's ankle is not a sign she is hanging out with the wrong crowd. But if she comes home for spring break covered from head to toe, start worrying" (Jacobs, 2010).

Liars' Alert! The small differences among the students with no tattoos, one tattoo, and two or three tattoos could be exaggerated if a reporter wanted to scare parents. Compare Figure 3-11 to the first three bars of Figure 3-10. Notice what happens when the fourth bar for four or more tattoos is eliminated: The values on the *y*-axis do not begin at 0, the intervals change from 10 to 2, and the *y*-axis ends at 20%. The exact same data leave

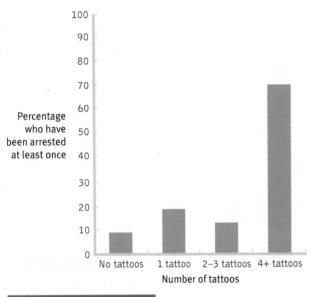

Bar Graphs Highlight
Differences Between Averages
or Percentages

This bar graph depicts the percentages
of university students who have been
arrested at least once (other than
in a traffic arrest). The researchers
measured four groups: those with no
tattoos, one tattoo, two to three tattoos,
or four or more tattoos. A bar graph can
more vividly depict differences between
percentages than just the typed
numbers themselves can: 8.5, 18.7,
12.7, and 70.6.

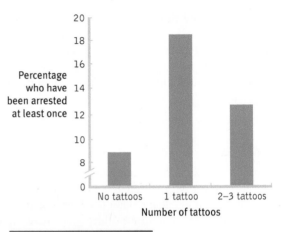

Deceiving with the Scale

To exaggerate a difference between means, graphmakers sometimes
compress the rating scale that they show on their graphs. When
possible, label the axis beginning with 0, and when displaying
percentages, include all values up to 100%.

a very different impression. (*Note:* If the data are very far from 0, and it does not make
sense to have the axis go down to 0, indicate this on the graph by including double
slashes—called cut marks—like those shown in Figure 3-11.)

Here is a recap of the steps to create a bar graph. The critical choice for you, the
graph creator, is in step 2.

1. Label the *x*-axis with the name and levels (i.e., categories) of the nominal or
   ordinal independent variable.
2. Label the *y*-axis with the name of the scale dependent variable and its possible
   values, starting with 0 if practical.
3. For every level of the independent variable, draw a bar with the height of that
   level's value on the dependent variable. ●

Pictorial Graphs

Occasionally, a pictorial graph is acceptable, but such a graph should be used spar-
ingly and only if carefully created. *A **pictorial graph** is a visual depiction of data typically used for an independent variable with very few levels (categories) and a scale dependent
variable. Each level uses a picture or symbol to represent its value on the scale dependent
variable.* Eye-catching pictorial graphs are far more common in the popular media
than in research journals. They tend to direct attention to the clever artwork rather
than to the story that the data tell.

For example, a graphmaker might use stylized drawings of people to indicate population size. Figure 3-12 demonstrates one problem with pictorial graphs. The picture
makes the person three times as tall *and* three times as wide (so that the taller person
won't look so stretched out). But then the total area of the picture is about nine times
larger than the shorter one, even though the population is only three times as big—a
false impression.

Pictorial graphs can work, though, if carefully designed. In the graph in Figure 3-13,
every stick figure is the same size and each represents a single person. These design
features decrease the chances that the graph will be misinterpreted.

● A **pictorial graph** is a visual
depiction of data typically
used for an independent
variable with very few
levels (categories) and a
scale dependent variable.
Each level uses a picture
or symbol to represent
its value on the scale
dependent variable.

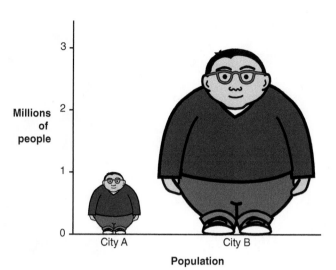

FIGURE 3-12

Distorting the Data with Pictures

In a pictorial graph, tripling the height of a picture is often coupled with tripling the width—which is multiplying by 3 twice. Instead of being three times as big, the picture is *nine times* as big!

An unprecedented death toll in Qatar

🚶 = *1 worker death*

London	**Vancouver**	**South Africa**	**Brazil**	**Sochi**	**Beijing**
2012	2010	2010	2014	2014	2008
Olympics	Olympics	World Cup	World Cup	Olympics	Olympics

Qatar
2022 World Cup (as of 2015)

FIGURE 3-13

A Pictograph of Individual Deaths

Major world sporting events involve the construction of a great deal of infrastructure, including stadiums. This graph shows the enormous death toll for the 2022 World Cup in Qatar as compared to the death toll for sporting events in other countries.

Source: http://www.motherjones.com/mixed -media/2015/05/chart-fifa-deaths-qatar-move -it-to-the-united-states

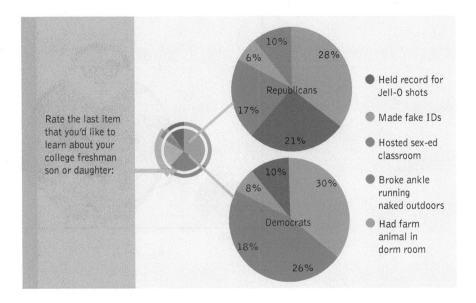

Rate the last item that you'd like to learn about your college freshman son or daughter:

Republicans: 10%, 6%, 28%, 17%, 21%

Democrats: 10%, 30%, 8%, 18%, 26%

● Held record for Jell-O shots
● Made fake IDs
● Hosted sex-ed classroom
● Broke ankle running naked outdoors
● Had farm animal in dorm room

Pie Charts

A **pie chart** *is a graph in the shape of a circle, with a slice for every level (category) of the independent variable. The size of each slice represents the proportion (or percentage) of each category. A pie chart's slices should* always *add up to 100% (or 1.00, if using proportions).* Figure 3-14 demonstrates the difficulty in making comparisons from a pair of pie charts. As suggested by this graph, data can almost always be presented more clearly in a table or bar graph than in a pie chart. Edward R. Tufte is well known for his several beautiful books that demonstrate simple ways to create clearer graphs (1997/2005, 2001/2006b, 2006a). Regarding pie charts, Tufte (2006b) bluntly advises: "A table is nearly always better than a dumb pie chart" (p. 178). Because of the limitations of pie charts and the ready alternatives, we do not outline the steps for creating a pie chart here.

● A **pie chart** is a graph in the shape of a circle, with a slice for every level (category) of the independent variable. The size of each slice represents the proportion (or percentage) of each level.

CHECK YOUR LEARNING

Reviewing the Concepts

> Scatterplots and line graphs allow us to see relations between two scale variables.

> When examining the relations between variables, it is important to consider linear and nonlinear relations, as well as the possibility that no relation is present.

> Bar graphs, pictorial graphs, and pie charts depict summary values (such as means or percentages) on a scale variable for various levels of a nominal or ordinal variable.

> Bar graphs are preferred; pictorial graphs and pie charts can be misleading.

Clarifying the Concepts   3-4   How are scatterplots and line graphs similar?

3-5   Why should we typically avoid using pictorial graphs and pie charts?

Calculating the Statistics   3-6   What type of visual display of data allows us to calculate or evaluate how a variable changes over time?

Applying the Concepts   3-7   What is the best type of common graph to depict each of the following data sets and research questions? Explain your answers.

a. Depression severity and amount of stress for 150 university students. Is depression related to stress level?

b. Number of inpatient mental health facilities in Canada as measured every 10 years between 1890 and 2000. Has the number of facilities declined in recent years?

c. Number of siblings reported by 100 people. What size family is most common?

d. Mean years of education for six regions of the United States. Are education levels higher in some regions than in others?

Solutions to these Check Your Learning questions can be found in Appendix D.

e. Calories consumed in a day and hours slept that night for 85 people. Does the amount of food a person eats predict how long he or she sleeps at night?

How to Build a Graph

In this section, you will learn how to choose the most appropriate type of graph and then use a checklist to ensure that the graph conforms to APA style. We also discuss innovative graphs that highlight the exciting future of graphing. Innovations in graphing can help us to deliver a persuasive message, much like that conveyed by Florence Nightingale's coxcomb graph.

Choosing the Appropriate Type of Graph

When deciding what type of graph to use, first examine the variables. Decide which is the independent variable and which is the dependent variable. Also, identify which type of variable—nominal, ordinal, or scale (interval/ratio)—each is. Most of the time, the independent variable belongs on the horizontal x-axis and the dependent variable goes on the vertical y-axis.

After assessing the types of variables that are in the study, use the following guidelines to select the appropriate graph:

1. If there is one scale variable (with frequencies), use a histogram or a frequency polygon (Chapter 2).

2. If there is one scale independent variable and one scale dependent variable, use a scatterplot or a line graph. (Figure 3-8 on page 56 provides an example of how to use more than one line on a time plot.)

3. If there is one nominal or ordinal independent variable and one scale dependent variable, use a bar graph. Consider using a Pareto chart if the independent variable has many levels.

4. If there are two or more nominal or ordinal independent variables and one scale dependent variable, use a bar graph.

MASTERING THE CONCEPT

3-4: The best way to determine the type of graph to create is to identify the independent variable and the dependent variable, along with the type of variable that each is—nominal, ordinal, or scale.

How to Read a Graph

Let's use the graph in Figure 3-15 to confirm your understanding of independent and dependent variables. This study of jealousy (Maner, Miller, Rouby, & Gailliot, 2009) includes two independent variables: level of jealousy (whether a participant is low or high in chronic jealousy) and how people were primed (whether they were primed to think about infidelity or about a neutral topic). People primed to think about infidelity visualized and wrote about a time when they had infidelity-related concerns. People primed to think about a neutral topic wrote a detailed account of four or five things they had done the previous day. The dependent variable is how long participants looked at photographs of an attractive same-sex person; for a jealous heterosexual person, an attractive person of the same sex would be a potential threat to his or her relationship.

FIGURE 3-15

Two Independent Variables

When graphing a data set that has two independent variables, show one independent variable on the *x*-axis (in this case, chronic jealousy—low or high) and one independent variable in a color-coded key (in this case, type of prime—infidelity or neutral). This graph demonstrates that heterosexual people high in chronic jealousy looked longer at an attractive person of the same sex, a potential threat, when primed by thinking about infidelity than when primed by thinking about a neutral topic. The pattern was reversed for people low in chronic jealousy.

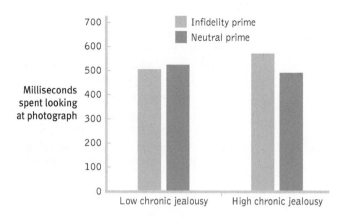

Here are the critical questions you need to ask in order to understand the graph of the findings of the jealousy study. A well-designed graph makes it easy to see the answers; a graph intended to mislead or lie will obscure the answers.

1. What variable are the researchers trying to predict? That is, what is the *dependent variable*?
2. Is the dependent variable nominal, ordinal, or scale?
3. What are the units of measurement on the dependent variable? For example, if the dependent variable is IQ as measured by the Wechsler Adult Intelligence Scale, then the possible scores are the IQ scores themselves, ranging from 0 to 145.
4. What variables did the researchers use to predict this dependent variable? That is, what are the *independent variables*?
5. Are these two independent variables nominal, ordinal, or scale?
6. What are the levels for each of these independent variables?

Now check your answers:

1. The dependent variable is time, in milliseconds.
2. Milliseconds is a scale variable.
3. Milliseconds can range from 0 on up. In this case, no average exceeds 600 milliseconds.
4. The first independent variable is level of jealousy; the second independent variable is priming condition.
5. Level of jealousy is an ordinal variable, but it can be treated as a nominal variable in the graph; priming condition is a nominal variable.
6. The levels for jealousy condition are low chronic jealousy and high chronic jealousy. The levels for priming condition are infidelity and neutral.

Because there are two independent variables—both of which are nominal—and one scale dependent variable, we used a bar graph to depict these data.

Guidelines for Creating a Graph

Here is a helpful checklist of questions to ask when you encounter a graph or when you're creating a graph. Some we've mentioned previously, and all are wise to follow.

- ☐ Does the graph have a clear, specific title?
- ☐ Are both axes labeled with the names of the variables? Do all labels read left to right—even the one on the *y*-axis?
- ☐ Are all terms on the graph the same terms that are used in the text that the graph is to accompany? Have all unnecessary abbreviations been eliminated?

- **Chartjunk** is any unnecessary information or feature in a graph that detracts from a viewer's ability to understand the data.

- **Moiré vibrations** are any visual patterns that create a distracting impression of vibration and movement.

- **Grids** are chartjunk that take the form of a background pattern, almost like graph paper, on which the data representations, such as bars, are superimposed.

- A **duck** is a form of chartjunk in which a feature of the data has been dressed up to be something other than merely data.

- Computer **defaults** are the options that the software designer has preselected; these are the built-in decisions that the software will implement if you do not instruct it otherwise.

FIGURE 3-16

Chartjunk Run Amok

Moiré vibrations, such as those seen in the patterns on these bars, might be fun to use, but they detract from the viewer's ability to glean the story of the data. Moreover, the grid pattern behind the bars might appear scientific, but it serves only to distract. Ducks—like the 3-D shadow effect on the bars and the globe clip-art—add nothing to the data, and the colors are absurdly eye straining. Don't laugh; we've had students submit carefully written research papers accompanied by graphs even more garish than this!

☐ Are the units of measurement (e.g., minutes, percentages) included in the labels?

☐ Do the values on the axes either go down to 0 or have cut marks (double slashes) to indicate that they do not go down to 0?

☐ Are colors used in a simple, clear way—ideally, shades of gray instead of other colors?

☐ Has all chartjunk been eliminated?

The last of these guidelines involves a new term, the graph-corrupting fluff called *chartjunk*, a term coined by Tufte, whom we introduced in the context of pie charts (2001). According to Tufte, **chartjunk** *is any unnecessary information or feature in a graph that detracts from a viewer's ability to understand the data.* Chartjunk can take the form of any of three unnecessary features, all demonstrated in the rather frightening graph in Figure 3-16.

1. ***Moiré vibrations*** *are any visual patterns that create a distracting impression of vibration and movement.* Unfortunately, they are sometimes the default settings for bar graphs in statistical software. Tufte recommends using shades of gray instead of patterns.

2. *A **grid** is a background pattern, almost like graph paper, on which the data representations, such as bars, are superimposed.* Tufte recommends the use of grids only for hand-drawn drafts of graphs. In final versions of graphs, use only very light grids, if necessary.

3. ***Ducks*** *are features of the data that have been dressed up to be something other than merely data.* Think of ducks as data in costume. Named for the Big Duck, a store in Flanders, New York, that was built in the form of a very large duck, graphic ducks can be three-dimensional effects, cutesy pictures, fancy fonts, or any other flawed design features. Avoid chartjunk!

MASTERING THE CONCEPT

3-5: Avoid chartjunk—any unnecessary aspect of a graph that detracts from its clarity.

There are several computer-generated graphing programs that have defaults that correspond to many—but not all—of these guidelines. Computer **defaults** *are the options that the software designer has preselected; these are the built-in decisions that the software will implement if you do not instruct it otherwise.* You cannot assume that these defaults represent the APA guidelines for your particular situation. You can usually point the cursor at a part of the graph and click to view the available options.

The Future of Graphs

Thanks to computer technology, we have entered a second golden age of scientific graphing. We mention only three categories here: interactive graphs, geographic information systems, and word clouds.

Franck Fotos/Alamy

Edward Tufte's Big Duck The graphics theorist Edward Tufte was fascinated by the Big Duck, a store in the form of a duck for which he named a type of chartjunk (graphic clutter). In graphs, ducks are any aspects of the graphed data that are "overdressed," obscuring the message of the data. Think of ducks as data in a ridiculous costume.

Interactive Graphs One informative and haunting graph was published online in the *New York Times* on September 9, 2004, to commemorate the day on which the 1000th U.S. soldier died in Iraq (tinyurl.com/55nlu). Titled "A Look at 1000 Who Died," this beautifully designed tribute is formed by a square representing each of the dead servicemen and women. One can view these squares organized by variables such as last name, where they were from, gender, cause of death, and age. Because the squares are the same size, the stacking of the squares also functions as a bar graph. By clicking on two or more months in a row, or on two or more ages in a row, one can visually compare numbers of deaths among levels of a category.

Yet this interactive graph is even more nuanced because it provides a glimpse into the life stories of these soldiers. By holding the cursor over a square, you can learn, for example, that Spencer T. Karol, regular duty in the U.S. Army, from Woodruff, Arizona, died on October 6, 2003, at the age of 20, from hostility-inflicted wounds. You can even see a photo of him. A thoughtfully designed interactive graph such as this one holds even more power than a traditional flat graph in how it educates, evokes emotion, and provides details that humanize the stories behind the numbers.

Geographic Information Systems (GIS) Many companies have published software that enables computer programmers to link Internet-based data to Internet-based maps (Markoff, 2005). These visual tools are all variations on geographic information systems (GIS). The APA has sponsored advanced workshops on how to apply GIS to the social sciences.

Sociologists, geographers, political scientists, consumer psychologists, and epidemiologists (who use statistics to track patterns of disease) have already become familiar with GIS in their respective fields. Organizational psychologists, social psychologists, and environmental psychologists can use GIS to organize workflow, assess group dynamics, and study the design of classrooms. Ironically, this advance in computerized mapping is pretty much what John Snow did without a computer in 1854 when he studied the Broad Street cholera outbreak.

Word Clouds Word clouds, an increasingly common type of graph, provide information on the most popular words used in a specific text (McKee, 2014). When creating a word cloud, the researcher defines what "most popular" means—the top 50 most frequently used words, the top 25 most frequently used words, or some other quantity. The size of the word usually indicates the frequency of the word (the larger the word, the more frequent).

Remember, though: word clouds are great for visually showcasing frequently used words in a text, but they do not necessarily provide quantitative data for analysis. For example, the Columbus Metropolitan Library in Ohio used Facebook data from users to describe the library of their childhood (word cloud on the left) and versus a library

FIGURE 3-17

Word Clouds

Word clouds provide information on the most popular words used in a specific text. These two word clouds describe people's perceptions of libraries of the past (a) and libraries of the future (b).

Source: http://www.theatlantic.com/national/archive/2014/10/not-your-mothers-library/381119/

(a)

(b)

20 years from now (word cloud on the right). Clearly, the perceptions of the uses and purposes of libraries have changed over the past 50 years—especially with increased access to technology and the Internet—and these two word clouds demonstrate this kind of data. We can also visualize consistent trends in perceptions of libraries, with the use of the words *research*, *information*, and *books* being fairly prominent in both word clouds. However, we are limited in our interpretation: we do not know how often people actually use the library for these purposes, or how important each element is (i.e., do people go to the library primarily to do research, or primarily for the community?).

Multivariable Graphs

Next Steps

As graphing technologies become more advanced, there are increasingly elegant ways to depict multiple variables on a single graph. Using the bubble graph option under "Other Charts" on Microsoft Excel (and even better, downloading Excel templates from sites such as http://juiceanalytics.com/chartchooser), we can create a bubble graph that depicts multiple variables.

In an article titled "Is the Emotion-Health Connection a 'First-World Problem'"?, Sarah Pressman and her colleagues used a more sophisticated version of a bubble graph to display four variables (Figure 3-18; Pressman, Gallagher, & Lopez, 2013):

1. Country. Each bubble is one country. For example, the large yellow bubble toward the upper right corner represents Ireland; the small red bubble toward the lower far left represents Georgia.

2. Self-reported health. The *x*-axis indicates self-reported physical health for a country.

3. Positive emotions. The *y*-axis indicates reported positive emotions for a country.

4. Gross domestic product (GDP). Both the size and the color of the bubbles represent a country's GDP. Smaller and darker red bubbles indicate lower GDP; larger and brighter yellow bubbles indicate higher GDP.

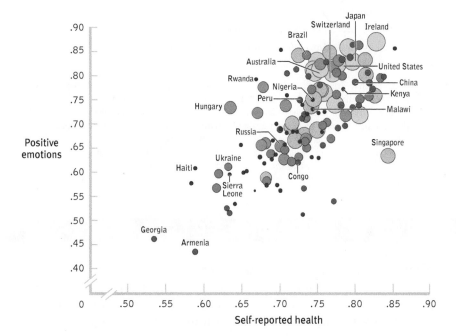

FIGURE 3-18

A Multivariable Graph

Increasingly sophisticated technology allows us to create increasingly sophisticated graphs. This bubble graph from a study by Sarah Pressman and her colleagues (2013) depicts four variables: country (each bubble), self-reported health (*x*-axis), positive emotions (*y*-axis), and gross domestic product (size and color of bubbles). The researchers could have had five variables if they had not used both the size and the color of the bubbles to represent GDP.

The researchers could have chosen to add a fifth variable by using either size or color to represent GDP, rather than both. They might have used size, for example, to represent GDP, and color to represent the continent for each country.

From this graph, we can see a strong relation between physical health and positive emotions. GDP appears to be related to both measures; for countries with higher GDP (larger, brighter yellow dots) and lower GDP (smaller, darker red dots), there is a link between emotions and health.

Some interactive versions of a bubble graph have, amazingly, added a sixth variable to the five that are possible on a printed page. For instance, www.gapminder.org/world has fascinating bubble graphs with data on countries around the world. Gapminder allows you to add the variable year by clicking "Play" in the lower left corner; the graph is then animated and can show the movement of countries with respect to a range of variables since 1800!

CHECK YOUR LEARNING

Reviewing the Concepts

> Graphs should be used when they add information to written text or help to clarify difficult material.

> To decide what kind of graph to use, determine whether the independent variable and the dependent variable are nominal, ordinal, or scale variables.

> A brief checklist will help you create an understandable graph. Label graphs precisely and avoid chartjunk.

> The future of graphs is now! Online interactive graphs, computerized mapping, word clouds, and multivariable graphs are becoming increasingly common.

Clarifying the Concepts 3-8 What is chartjunk?

Calculating the Statistics 3-9 Decisions about which kind of graph to use depend largely on how variables are measured. Imagine a researcher is interested in how "quality of sleep" is related to statistics exam grade (measured by the number of errors made). For each of the measures of sleep below, decide which kind of graph to use.

    a. Total minutes slept

    b. Sleep assessed as sufficient or insufficient

    c. Using a scale from 1 (low-quality sleep) to 7 (excellent sleep)

Applying the Concepts 3-10 Imagine that the graph in Figure 3-16 represents data testing the hypothesis that exposure to the sun can impair IQ. Further imagine that the researcher has recruited groups of people and randomly assigned them to different levels of exposure to the sun: 0, 1, 6, and 12 hours per day (enhanced, in all cases, by artificial sunlight when natural light is not available). The mean IQ scores are 142, 125, 88, and 80, respectively. Redesign this chartjunk graph, either by hand or by using software, paying careful attention to the dos and don'ts outlined in this section.

Solutions to these Check Your Learning questions can be found in Appendix D.

REVIEW OF CONCEPTS

How to Lie with Visual Statistics

Learning how visual displays of statistics can mislead or lie will empower you to spot lies for yourself. Visual displays of data are easily manipulated, so it is important to pay close attention to a graph's details to make sure they aren't conveying false information.

Common Types of Graphs

When developing graphing skills, it is important to begin with the basics. Several types of graphs are commonly used by social scientists. *Scatterplots* depict the relation between two scale variables. They are useful when determining whether the relation between the variables is *linear* or *nonlinear*. Some *line graphs* expand on scatterplots by including a line of best fit. Others, called *time plots* or *time series plots*, show the change in a scale variable over time.

Bar graphs are used to compare two or more categories of a nominal or ordinal independent variable with respect to a scale dependent variable. A bar graph on which the levels of the independent variable are organized from the highest bar to the lowest bar, called a *Pareto chart*, allows for easy comparison of levels. *Pictorial graphs* are like bar graphs except that pictures are used in place of bars. *Pie charts* are used to depict proportions or percentages on one nominal or ordinal variable with just a few levels. Because both pictorial graphs and pie charts are frequently constructed in a misleading way or are misperceived, bar graphs are almost always preferred to pictorial graphs and pie charts.

How to Build a Graph

We first decide which type of graph to create by examining the independent and dependent variables and by identifying each as nominal, ordinal, or scale. We then consider a number of guidelines to develop a clear, persuasive graph. It is important that all graphs be labeled appropriately and given a title that allows the graph to tell its story without additional text. For an unambiguous graph, it is imperative that graph creators avoid *chartjunk*: unnecessary information, such as *moiré vibrations*, *grids*, and *ducks*, that clutters a graph and makes it difficult to interpret. When using software to create graphs, it is important to question the *defaults* built into the software and to override them when necessary to adhere to these guidelines.

Finally, keeping an eye to the future of graphing—including interactive graphs, computer-generated maps, word clouds, and multivariable graphs—helps us stay at the forefront of graph-making in the behavioral sciences. New techniques allow us to make increasingly complex graphs: bubble graphs, for example, allow us to include as many as five variables in a single graph.

SPSS®

We can request visual displays of data from both the "Data View" screen and the "Variable View" screen. Most graphing is done in SPSS using the Chart Builder. This section walks you through the general steps to create a graph, using a scatterplot as an example. But first, enter the data in the screenshot for hours spent studying and exam grades that were used to create the scatterplot in Figure 3-5. You can see the data here in the screenshot.

Select Graphs → Chart Builder. Under the "Gallery" tab, select the type of graph under "Choose From" by clicking on it. For example, to create a scatterplot, click on "Scatter/Dot." Drag a sample graph from the right to the large box above. Usually you'll want the simplest graph, which tends to be the upper-left sample graph.

Drag the appropriate variables from the "Variables" box to the appropriate places on the sample graph (e.g., "x-axis").

For a scatterplot, drag "hours" to the *x*-axis and "grade" to the *y*-axis. Chart Builder then looks like the screenshot shown here. Click "OK;" SPSS then creates the graph.

Remember: You should not rely on the default choices of the software; you are the designer of the graph. Once the graph is created, you can change its appearance by double-clicking on the graph to open the Chart Editor, the tool that allows you to make changes. Then click or double-click on the particular feature of the graph that you want to modify. Clicking once on part of the graph allows you to make some changes. For example, clicking the label of the *y*-axis allows you to change the font using the drop-down menu above; double-clicking allows you to make other changes, such as setting the label horizontal (after double-clicking, select the orientation "Horizontal" under "Text Layout").

HOW IT WORKS

3.1 CREATING A SCATTERPLOT

As mentioned at the end of the chapter, www.gapminder.org/world is a wonderful Web site that allows people to play with a graph and explore the relations between variables over time. We used Gapminder World to find scores for 10 countries on two variables.

Country	Children per Woman (total fertility)	Life Expectancy at Birth (years)
Afghanistan	7.15	43.00
India	2.87	64.00
China	1.72	73.00
Hong Kong	0.96	82.00
France	1.89	80.00
Bolivia	3.59	65.00
Ethiopia	5.39	53.00
Iraq	4.38	59.00
Mali	6.55	54.00
Honduras	3.39	70.00

How can we create a scatterplot to show the relation between these two variables? To create a scatterplot, we put total fertility on the x-axis and life expectancy in years on the *y*-axis. We then add a dot for each country at the intersection of its fertility rate and life expectancy. The scatterplot is shown in the figure below.

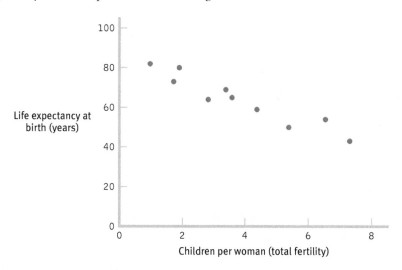

3.2 CREATING A BAR GRAPH

The International Monetary Fund listed the 2012 gross domestic product (GDP) per capita, in U.S. dollars (USD), for each of the world economic powers that make up what is called the Group of Eight, or G8, nations.

Canada: $52,232   Italy: $33,115   United Kingdom: $38,589

France: $41,141   Japan: $46,736   United States: $49,922

Germany: $41,513   Russia: $14,247

How can we create a bar graph for these data? First, we put the countries on the *x*-axis. Then, for each country, we draw a bar in which height corresponds to the country's GDP per capita. The following figure shows a bar graph with bars arranged in alphabetical order by country.

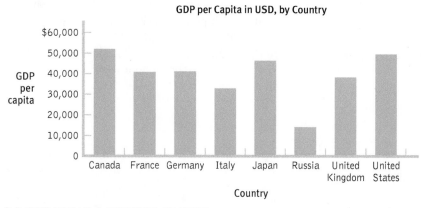

3.3 CREATING A PARETO CHART

How can we use the same G8 data as for the bar graph to create a Pareto chart? A Pareto chart is simply a bar graph in which the bars are arranged from highest value to lowest value. We would rearrange the countries so that they are ordered from the country with the highest GDP per capita to the country with the lowest GDP per capita. The Pareto chart is shown in the figure below.

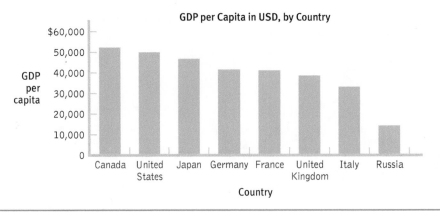

GDP per Capita in USD, by Country

EXERCISES

The solutions to the odd-numbered exercises can be found in Appendix C.

Clarifying the Concepts

3.1 What are the five techniques discussed in this chapter for misleading with graphs?

3.2 What are the steps to create a scatterplot?

3.3 What does an individual dot on a scatterplot represent?

3.4 What does it mean for two variables to be linearly related?

3.5 How can we tell whether two variables are linearly or nonlinearly related?

3.6 What is the difference between a line graph and a time plot?

3.7 What is the difference between a bar graph and a Pareto chart?

3.8 Bar graphs and histograms look very similar. In your own words, what is the difference between the two?

3.9 What are pictorial graphs and pie charts?

3.10 Why are bar graphs preferred over pictorial graphs and pie charts?

3.11 Why is it important to identify the independent variable and the dependent variable before creating a visual display?

3.12 Under what circumstances would the x-axis and y-axis not start at 0?

3.13 Chartjunk comes in many forms. What specifically are moiré vibrations, grids, and ducks?

3.14 Geographic information systems (GIS), such as those provided by computerized graphing technologies, are particularly powerful tools for answering what kinds of research questions?

3.15 How is a bubble graph similar to a traditional scatterplot?

3.16 How does a bubble graph differ from a traditional scatterplot?

Calculating the Statistics

3.17 Alumni giving rates, calculated as the total dollars donated per year from 2006 to 2016, represent which kind of variable—nominal, ordinal, or scale? What would be an appropriate graph to depict these data?

3.18 Alumni giving rates for a number of universities, calculated as the number of alumni who donated and the number who did not donate in a given year, represent which kind of variable—nominal, ordinal, or scale? What would be an appropriate graph to depict these data?

3.19 You are exploring the relation between gender and video game performance, as measured by final scores on a game.

   a. In this study, what are the independent and dependent variables?

   b. Is gender a nominal, ordinal, or scale variable?

   c. Is final score a nominal, ordinal, or scale variable?

   d. Which graph or graphs would be appropriate to depict the data? Explain why.

3.20 Do the data in the graph below show a linear relation, a nonlinear relation, or no relation? Explain.

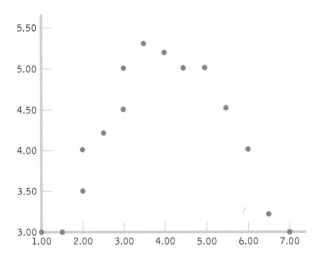

3.21 Do the data in the graph below show a linear relation, a nonlinear relation, or no relation? Explain.

3.22 What elements are missing from the graphs in Exercises 3.20 and 3.21?

3.23 The following figure presents the enrollment of graduate students at a university, across six fall terms, as a percentage of the total student population.

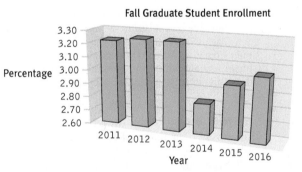

a. What kind of visual display is this?

b. What other type of visual display could have been used?

c. What is missing from the axes?

d. What chartjunk is present?

e. Using this graph, estimate graduate student enrollment, as a percentage of the total student population, in the fall terms of 2011, 2012, and 2014.

f. How would the comparisons between bars change if the *y*-axis started at 0?

3.24 When creating a graph, we need to make a decision about the numbering of the axes. If you had the following range of data for one variable, how might you label the relevant axis?

337 280 279 311 294 301 342 273

3.25 If you had the following range of data for one variable, how might you label the relevant axis?

0.10 0.31 0.27 0.04 0.09 0.22 0.36 0.18

3.26 The scatterplot in How It Works 3.1 depicts the relation between fertility and life expectancy. Each dot represents a country.

a. Approximately, what is the highest life expectancy in years? Approximately, what fertility rate (children per woman) is associated with the highest life expectancy?

b. Does this seem to be a linear relation? Explain why or why not, and explain the relation in plain English.

3.27 Based on the data in the bubble graph in Figure 3-18, what is the relation between physical health and positive emotions?

3.28 The colors and sizes of the bubbles in the bubble graph in Figure 3-18 represent the gross domestic product (GDP) for each country. Using this information, explain what the relation is between positive emotions and GDP.

Applying the Concepts

3.29 **Graphing the relation between international researchers and the impact of research:** Does research from international teams make a bigger splash? Researchers explored whether research conducted by multinational research teams had a bigger impact than research from teams with less international representation (Hsiehchen, Espinoza, & Hsieh, 2015). The graph here shows the relation between two measures: 1) the number of authors on a journal article who are from a different country than the first author, and 2) a measure that assesses the scientific impact of the research with a higher score, indicating more influential research.

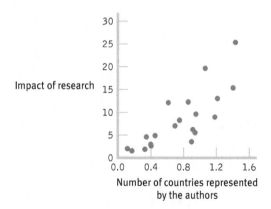

a. In this study, are the independent and dependent variables nominal, ordinal, or scale?

b. What type of graph is this? Why did the researchers choose this type of graph?

c. In your own words, explain what the researchers found.

3.30 Type of graph for the effects of cognitive-behavioral therapy on depression: A social worker tracked the depression levels of clients being treated with cognitive-behavioral therapy for depression. For each client, depression was assessed at weeks 1 to 20 of therapy. She calculated a mean for all of her clients at week 1, week 2, and so on, all the way through week 20.

a. What are the independent and dependent variables in this study?

b. Are the variables nominal, ordinal, or scale?

c. Which graph or graphs would be most appropriate to depict the data? Explain why.

3.31 Type of graph for comparative suicide rates: The World Health Organization tracks suicide rates by gender across countries. For example, in 2011, the rate of suicide per 100,000 men was 17.3 in Canada, 17.7 in the United States, 44.6 in Sri Lanka, 53.9 in the Russian Federation, 1.4 in South Africa, and 2.5 in the Philippines.

a. What are the variables in this study?

b. Are the variables nominal, ordinal, or scale?

c. Which graph would be most appropriate to depict the data? Explain why.

d. If you wanted to track the suicide rates for three of these countries over 50 years, what type of graph might you use to show these data?

3.32 Scatterplot of daily cycling distances and type of climb: Every summer, the touring company America by Bicycle conducts the "Cross Country Challenge," a 7-week bicycle journey across the United States from San Francisco, California, to Portsmouth, New Hampshire. At some point during the trip, the exhausted cyclists usually start to complain that the organizers are purposely planning for days with lots of hill and mountain climbing to coincide with longer distances. The tour staff counter that no relation exists between climbs and mileage and that the route is organized based on practical issues, such as the location of towns in which riders can stay. The organizers who planned the route (these are the company owners who are not on the tour) say that they actually tried to reduce the mileage on the days with the worst climbs. Here are the approximate daily mileages and climbs (in vertical feet), as estimated from one rider's bicycle computer.

a. Construct a scatterplot of the cycling data, putting mileage on the x-axis. Be sure to label everything and include a title.

b. We haven't yet learned to calculate inferential statistics on these data, so we can't estimate what's really going on, but do you think that the amount

Mileage	Climb	Mileage	Climb	Mileage	Climb
83	600	69	2500	102	2600
57	600	63	5100	103	1000
51	2000	66	4200	80	1000
76	8500	96	900	72	900
51	4600	124	600	68	900
91	800	104	600	107	1900
73	1000	52	1300	105	4000
55	2000	85	600	90	1600
72	2500	64	300	87	1100
108	3900	65	300	94	4000
118	300	108	4200	64	1500
65	1800	97	3500	84	1500
76	4100	91	3500	70	1500
66	1200	82	4500	80	5200
97	3200	77	1000	63	5200
92	3900	53	2500		

of vertical climb is related to a day's mileage? If yes, explain the relation in your own words. If no, explain why you think there is no relation.

c. It turns out that inferential statistics do not support the existence of a relation between these variables and that the staff seems to be the most accurate in their appraisal. Why do you think the cyclists and organizers are wrong in opposite directions? What does this say about people's biases and the need for data?

3.33 Scatterplot of gross domestic product and education levels: The Group of Eight (G8) consists of many of the major world economic powers. It meets annually to discuss pressing world problems. In 2013, for example, the G8 met in the United Kingdom with an agenda that included international security. Decisions made by G8 nations can have a global impact; in fact, the eight nations that make up the membership reportedly account for almost two-thirds of the world's economic output. Here are data for seven of the eight G8 nations for gross domestic product (GDP) in 2004 and a measure of education. The measure of education is the percentage of the population between the ages of 25 and 64 that had at least one university degree (Sherman, Honegger, & McGivern, 2003). No data point for education in Russia was available, so Russia is not included.

a. Create a scatterplot of these data, with university degree percentages on the x-axis. Be sure to label everything and to give it a title. Later, we'll use

Country	GDP (in trillions of USD)	Percentage with University Degree
Canada	0.98	19
France	2.00	11
Germany	2.71	13
Italy	1.67	9
Japan	4.62	18
United Kingdom	2.14	17
United States	11.67	27

statistical tools to determine the equation for the line of best fit. For now, draw a line of best fit that represents your best guess as to where it would go.

b. In your own words, describe the relation between the variables that you see in the scatterplot.

c. Education is on the x-axis, indicating that education is the independent variable. Explain why it is possible that education predicts GDP. Now reverse your explanation of the direction of prediction, explaining why it is possible that GDP predicts education.

3.34 Time series plot of organ donations: The Canadian Institute for Health Information (CIHI) is a non-profit organization that compiles data from a range of institutions—from governmental organizations to hospitals to universities. Among the many topics that interest public health specialists is the problem of low levels of organ donation. Medical advances have led to ever-increasing rates of transplantation, but organ donation has not kept up with doctors' ability to perform more sophisticated and more complicated surgeries. Data reported by CIHI (https://secure.cihi .ca/free_products/2011_CORR_Annua_Report_EN .pdf, 2015) provide Canadian transplantation and donation rates for 2001–2010. Here are the donor rates per million in the population; these numbers include only deceased donors.

Year	Donor Rate per Million People	Year	Donor Rate per Million People
2001	13.4	2006	14.1
2002	12.9	2007	14.7
2003	13.3	2008	14.4
2004	12.9	2009	14.4
2005	12.7	2010	13.6

a. Construct a time series plot from these data. Be sure to label and title your graph.

b. What story are these data telling?

c. If you worked in public health and were studying the likelihood that families would agree to donate after a loved one's death, what research question might you ask about the possible reasons for the trend suggested by these data?

3.35 Bar graph of acceptance rates for different types of psychology doctoral programs: The American Psychological Association gathered data from almost 1000 psychology doctoral programs (2015). (Note: If a school offered four different psychology doctorates, each would be counted separately.) The table below includes overall acceptance rates for each of 10 different types of psychology doctorates.

Psychology Subfield	Acceptance Rate
Clinical psychology	12.0%
Cognitive psychology	10.9%
Counseling psychology	11.0%
Developmental psychology	14.1%
Experimental psychology	12.7%
Industrial/organizational psychology	14.6%
Neuroscience	10.7%
School psychology	29.0%
Social psychology	7.0%
Other applied psychology	25.2%

a. What is the independent variable in this example? Is it nominal or scale? If nominal, what are the levels? If scale, what are the units and what are the minimum and maximum values?

b. What is the dependent variable in this example? Is it nominal or scale? If nominal, what are the levels? If scale, what are the units and what are the minimum and maximum values?

c. Construct a bar graph of these data, with one bar for each of the types of psychology doctoral programs, using the default options in your computer software.

d. Construct a second bar graph of these data, but change the defaults to satisfy the guidelines for graphs discussed in this chapter. Aim for simplicity and clarity.

e. Cite at least one research question that you might want to explore next. Your research question should grow out of these data.

f. Explain how these data could be presented as a pictorial graph. (Note that you do not have to construct such a graph.) What kind of picture could you use? What would it look like?

g. What are the potential pitfalls of a pictorial graph? Why is a bar chart usually a better choice?

3.36 Bar graph versus Pareto chart of countries' gross domestic product: In How It Works 3.2, we created a bar graph for the 2012 GDP, in U.S. dollars per capita, for each of the G8 nations. In How It Works 3.3, we created a Pareto chart for these same data.

a. Explain the difference between a Pareto chart and a standard bar graph in which the countries are in alphabetical order along the x-axis.

b. What is the benefit of the Pareto chart over the standard bar graph?

3.37 Bar graph versus time series plot of graduate school mentoring: Johnson, Koch, Fallow, and Huwe (2000) conducted a study of mentoring in two types of psychology doctoral programs: experimental and clinical. Students who graduated from the two types of programs were asked whether they had a faculty mentor while in graduate school. In response, 48% of clinical psychology students who graduated between 1945 and 1950 and 62.31% who graduated between 1996 and 1998 reported having had a mentor; 78.26% of experimental psychology students who graduated between 1945 and 1950 and 78.79% who graduated between 1996 and 1998 reported having had a mentor.

a. What are the two independent variables in this study, and what are their levels?

b. What is the dependent variable?

c. Create a bar graph that depicts the percentages for the two independent variables simultaneously.

d. What story is this graph telling us?

e. Was this a true experiment? Explain your answer.

f. Why would a time series plot be inappropriate for these data? What would a time series plot suggest about the mentoring trend for clinical psychology graduate students and for experimental psychology graduate students?

g. For four time points—1945–1950, 1965, 1985, and 1996–1998—the mentoring rates for clinical psychology graduate students were 48.00, 56.63, 47.50, and 62.31, respectively. For experimental psychology graduate students, the rates were 78.26, 57.14, 57.14, and 78.79, respectively. How does the story

we see here conflict with the one that we developed based on just two time points?

3.38 Bar graph versus pie chart and perceptions of health care advice: The company that makes Fitbit, the wristband that tracks exercise and sleep, commissioned a report that included the pie chart shown here (2013).

a. Explain why a bar graph would be more suitable for these data than a pie chart.

b. What statistical lie appears to be present in these data?

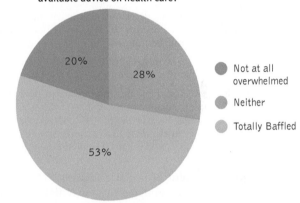

How overwhelmed do people get by the vast array of available advice on health care?

3.39 Software defaults of graphing programs and perceptions of health care advice: For this exercise, use the data in the pie chart from the Fitbit report in the previous exercise.

a. Create a bar graph for these data. Play with the options available to you and make changes so that the graph meets the guidelines in this chapter.

b. List the aspects of the bar graph that you changed when creating your graph in part a. Be specific.

3.40 Software defaults of graphing programs for depicting the "world's deepest" trash bin: The car company Volkswagen has sponsored a "fun theory" campaign in recent years in which ordinary behaviors are given game-like incentives to promote pro-social behaviors such as recycling or obeying the speed limit (http://www.thefuntheory.com/). In one example, Volkswagen created a seemingly super-deep trash bin; when a person would throw something out, a high-pitched whistling sound played for 7 seconds, culminating in a far-off-sounding boom, as if the item had fallen for hundreds of feet! The fun-theory people collected data; in a single day, 72 kilograms of trash were thrown out in their "deep" bin, versus just 31 kilograms in a nearby trash bin.

a. Use a software program that produces graphs (e.g., Excel, SPSS, Minitab) to create a bar graph for these data, using the default options.

b. Play with the options available to you. List aspects of the bar graph that you are able to change to make your graph meet the guidelines listed in this chapter. Be specific, and include the revised graph.

3.41 Multivariable graphs and college rankings by academics and sexiness: Buzzfeed.com published a multivariable graph that purported to rank colleges by academics and "hotness." The data from this graph are represented here.

a. What kind of graph is this? Explain.

b. List the variables that are included in this graph.

c. List at least three ways in which this graph could be redesigned in light of the guidelines in this chapter.

3.42 Types of graph appropriate for behavioral science research: Give an example of a study—real or hypothetical—in the behavioral sciences for which the researchers could use each type of graph. State the independent variable(s) and dependent variable, including levels for any nominal variables.

a. Frequency polygon

b. Line graph (line of best fit)

c. Bar graph (one independent variable)

d. Scatterplot

e. Time series plot

f. Pie chart

g. Bar graph (two independent variables)

3.43 Creating the perfect graph: What advice would you give to the creators of each of the following graphs? Consider the basic guidelines for a clear graph, for avoiding chartjunk, and regarding the ways to mislead through statistics. Give three pieces of advice for each graph. Be specific—don't just say that there is chartjunk; say exactly what you would change.

a. Business and women:

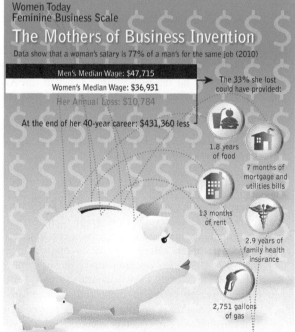

b. Workforce participation:

How many of us work

3.44 **Graphs in the popular media:** Find an article in the popular media (newspaper, magazine, Web site) that includes a graph in addition to the text.

a. Briefly summarize the main point of the article and graph.

b. What are the independent and dependent variables depicted in the graph? What kinds of variables are they? If nominal, what are the levels?

c. What descriptive statistics are included in the article or on the graph?

d. In one or two sentences, what story is the graph (rather than the article) trying to tell?

e. How well do the text and graph match up? Are they telling the same story? Are they using the same terms? Explain.

f. Write a paragraph to the graph's creator with advice for improving the graph. Be specific, citing the guidelines from this chapter.

g. Redo the graph, either by hand or by computer, in line with your suggestions.

3.45 **Interpreting a graph about two kinds of career regrets:** The Yerkes–Dodson graph demonstrates that graphs can be used to describe theoretical relations that can be tested. In a study that could be applied to the career decisions made during college, Gilovich and Medvec (1995) identified two types of regrets—regrets of action and regrets of inaction—and proposed that their intensity changes over time. You can think of these as Type I regrets—things you have done that you wish you had not done (regrets of action)—and Type II regrets—things you have not

done that you wish you had done (regrets of inaction). The researchers suggested a theoretical relation between the variables that might look something like the graph below.

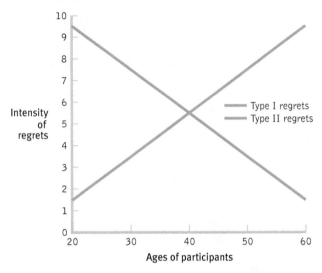

a. Briefly summarize the theoretical relations proposed by the graph.

b. What are the independent and dependent variables depicted in the graph? What kinds of variables are they? If nominal or ordinal, what are the levels?

c. What descriptive statistics are included in the text or on the graph?

d. In one or two sentences, what story is the graph trying to tell?

3.46 **Thinking critically about a graph of the frequency of psychology degrees:** The American Psychological Association (APA) compiles many statistics about training and careers in the field of psychology. The accompanying graph tracks the number of bachelor's, master's, and doctoral degrees conferred between the years 1970 and 2000.

Number of Psychology Degrees Conferred by Level of Degree: 1970–2000

a. What kind of graph is this? Why did the researchers choose this type of graph?

b. Briefly summarize the overall story being told by this graph.

c. What are the independent and dependent variables depicted in the graph? What kind of variables are they? If nominal or ordinal, what are the levels?

d. List at least three things that the graph creators did well (that is, in line with the guidelines for graph construction).

e. List at least one thing that the graph creators should have done differently (that is, not in line with the guidelines for graph construction).

f. Name at least one variable other than number that might be used to track the prevalence of psychology bachelor's, master's, and doctoral degrees over time.

g. The increase in bachelor's degrees over the years is not matched by an increase in doctoral degrees. List at least one research question that this finding suggests to you.

3.47 Thinking critically about a graph about international students: Researchers surveyed Canadian students on their perceptions of the globalization of their campuses (Lambert & Usher, 2013). The 13,000 participants were domestic undergraduate and graduate students—that is, they were not recently from countries outside of Canada. The pie chart here shows the responses to one survey item: "The increasing number of international students attending my institution has led to improvements in the university's reputation and image."

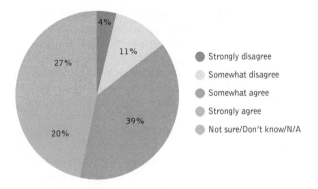

a. What is the story that these data are telling?

b. Why would a bar graph of these data tell this story better than a pie chart does?

c. Create a bar graph of these data, keeping the bars in the order of the labels here—from "Strongly disagree" on the left to "Not sure/Don't know/N/A" on the right.

d. Why would it not make sense to create a Pareto chart in this case?

3.48 Interpreting a graph about traffic flow: Go to http://maps.google.com/. On a map of your country, select "Traffic" from the drop-down menu in the upper left corner.

a. How is the density and flow of traffic represented in this graph?

b. Describe traffic patterns in different regions of your country.

c. What are the benefits of this interactive graph?

3.49 Critiquing a graph about gun deaths: In this chapter, we learned about graphs that include statistical lies and graphs designed to be unclear. Think about the problems in the graph shown here.

a. What is the primary flaw in the presentation of these data?

b. How would you redesign this graph? Be specific and cite at least three ways in which you would change it.

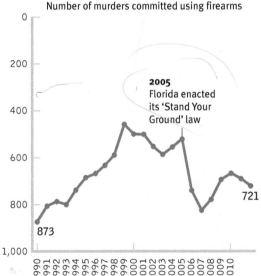

Source: http://io9.com/11-most-useless-and-misleading-infographics-on-the-inte -1688239674?utm_source=recirculation&utm_medium=recirculation&utm_campaign =thursdayPM

3.50 Word clouds and statistics textbooks: The Web site Wordle lets you create your own word clouds (http:// www.wordle.net/create). (There also are a number of other online tools to create word clouds, including TagCrowd and WordItOut.) Here's a word cloud we made with the main text from this chapter. In your own words, explain why ten or so of the most popular words are showing up here. That is, why are these words so important when learning how to create excellent, clear graphs?

3.51 Comparing word clouds and subjective well-being: Social science researchers are increasingly using word clouds to convey their results. A research team from the Netherlands asked 66 older adults to generate a list of what they perceive to be important to their well-being (Douma, Steverink, Hutter, & Meijering, 2015). Based on these lists, the researchers identified fifteen general areas perceived to be related to well-being. They created a version of the word cloud shown here to visualize the frequency that each of these areas was mentioned.

a. In your own words, summarize what the researchers found.

b. What research questions might these findings suggest for psychologists working in communities for older adults?

Social Life
Activities Health
Independence / Mobility
Financial situation / Societal criticism
Space and Place
Political situation
Personal characteristics / Way of Life
Other
Religion / Health care and support / Personal development

3.52 Multivariable graphs and shipwrecks: The cliché "women and children first" originated in part because of the *Titanic* captain's famous directive as his ship was sinking. Yet, the cliché is not grounded in reality. See the following multivariable graph.

a. What kind of graph is this?

b. List the variables that are included in this graph.

c. Are the data on the top and the bottom necessary to tell this story? Explain. Why do you think both sides are included?

d. In your own words, tell the story that this graph is visualizing.

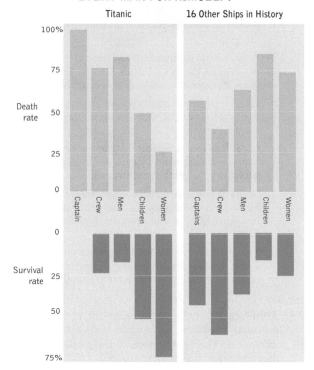

EVERY MAN FOR HIMSELF?

A review of 18 large shipwrecks from 1852 to 2011 suggests that crew members and male passengers survive at higher rates than women and children. Shipwrecks like the Titanic, in which the captain ordered "women and children first," are famous exceptions.

Putting It All Together

3.53 Type of graph describing the effect of romantic songs on ratings of attractiveness: Guéguen, Jacob, and Lamy (2010) wondered if listening to romantic songs would affect the dating behavior of the French heterosexual women who participated in their study. The women were randomly assigned to listen to either a romantic song ("Je l'aime à Mourir," or "I Love Her to Death") or a nonromantic song ("L'heure du Thé," or "Tea Time") while waiting for the study to begin. Later in the study, an attractive male researcher asked each participant for her phone number. Of the women who listened to the romantic song, 52.2% gave their phone number to the researcher, whereas only 27.9% of the women who listened to the nonromantic song gave their phone number to the researcher.

a. What is the independent variable in this study?

b. What is the dependent variable?

c. Is this a between-groups or a within-groups study? Explain your answer.

d. Think back to our discussion of variables in Chapter 1. How did the researcher operationalize "dating behavior" in this study? Do you think this is a valid measure of dating behavior? Explain your answer.

e. What is the best type of graph to depict these results? Explain your answer.

f. Create the graph you described in part (e) using software without changing any of the defaults.

g. Create the graph you described in part (e) a second time, changing the defaults to meet the criteria in the checklist introduced in this chapter.

3.54 Developing research questions from graphs: Graphs not only answer research questions, but can spur new ones. Figure 3-8 on page 56 depicts the pattern of changing attitudes, as expressed through Twitter.

a. On what day and at what time is the highest average positive attitude expressed?

b. On what day and at what time is the lowest average negative attitude expressed?

c. What research question(s) do these observations suggest to you with respect to weekdays versus weekends? (Remember, 0 on Sunday is midnight—or late Saturday night.) Name the independent and dependent variables.

d. How do the researchers operationalize mood? Do you think this is a valid measure of mood? Explain your answer.

e. One of the highest average negative attitudes occurs at midnight on Sunday. How does this fit with the research hypothesis you developed in part (c)? Does this suggest a new research hypothesis?

TERMS

scatterplot (p. 53)
linear relation (p. 54)
nonlinear relation (p. 54)
line graph (p. 55)
time plot, or time series plot (p. 55)

bar graph (p. 56)
Pareto chart (p. 57)
pictorial graph (p. 58)
pie chart (p. 60)
chartjunk (p. 63)

moiré vibration (p. 63)
grid (p. 63)
duck (p. 63)
defaults (p. 63)

Central Tendency and Variability

4

Central Tendency

Mean, the Arithmetic Average
Median, the Middle Score
Mode, the Most Common Score
How Outliers Affect Measures of Central Tendency
Which Measure of Central Tendency Is Best?

Measures of Variability

Range
Variance
Standard Deviation

Next Steps: The Interquartile Range

BEFORE YOU GO ON

■ **You should understand what a distribution is (Chapter 2).**

■ **You should be able to interpret histograms and frequency polygons (Chapter 2).**

High Quality Zippers The Japanese company YKK is known for its high quality zippers. The key is low variability. They have figured out how to ensure that just about every zipper is a good one.

There is big money in understanding statistical variability. Just ask YKK, the Japanese company that runs "the largest zipper factory in the world" and dominates the zipper market (Balzar, 1998).

You read that right: zippers. How do you feel when a zipper snags on material, malfunctions at the bottom, or catches unpredictably? At best, a stuck zipper is annoying, but it could be socially embarrassing or even life threatening. YKK limits product variability by controlling everything about the manufacturing process, from smelting their own brass to fabricating their own cardboard boxes for shipping. The company even builds the machines that make their products (see Balzar, 1998). Controlling every part of the manufacturing process helps YKK to create and sell exceptionally consistent zippers. This low variability leads to a high quality product, which in turn gives clothing manufacturers great confidence in YKK zippers. This is all part of a larger YKK corporate philosophy called "the cycle of goodness" (YKK, 2015).

YKK understands that no retailer wants an expensive dress, bag, or suit to fail because one of the least expensive components, the zipper, did not operate properly. YKK hopes that none of their zippers ever fail, but perfection in manufacturing is essentially impossible. So YKK wants the next best thing: low variability (or deviation) from that standard of perfection. In this chapter, you will learn three common ways to measure how much a distribution varies from its central tendency: range, variance, and standard deviation. But to fully understand variability, we first have to know how to identify the middle, or central tendency of a distribution.

Central Tendency

Central tendency refers to the descriptive statistic that best represents the center of a data set, the particular value that all the other data seem to be gathering around—the "typical" score. Creating a visual representation of the distribution, as we did in Chapter 2, reveals its central tendency. The central tendency is usually at (or near) the highest point in the histogram or the polygon. The way data cluster around their central tendency can be measured in three different ways: mean, median, and mode. For example, Figure 4-1 shows the histogram for the data on the lengths of the top 50 viral videos, which we first considered in Chapter 2 (omitting one extreme score, that for "Randy Pausch's Last Lecture," 4586 seconds). Our guess is that the central tendency for the data is toward the right side of the two tallest bars.

Mean, the Arithmetic Average

The mean is simple to calculate and is the gateway to understanding statistical formulas. The mean is such an important concept in statistics that we provide you with

Estimating Central Tendency with Histograms

Histograms and frequency polygons allow us to see the likely center of a sample's distribution. The arrow points to our guess as to the center of the distribution of the lengths of the top viral videos (Aneja & Ross, 2015). (Note that the extreme outlier of 4586 seconds is not included.)

four distinct ways to think about it: verbally, arithmetically, visually, and symbolically (using statistical notation).

The Mean in Plain English The most commonly reported measure of central tendency is *the **mean**, the arithmetic average of a group of scores.* The mean, often called the *average*, is used to represent the "typical" score in a distribution. This is different from the way we sometimes use the word *average* in everyday conversation, noting that someone is "just" average in athletic ability or that a movie was "only" average. We need to define the mean arithmetically to determine a precise calculation.

The Mean in Plain Arithmetic The mean is calculated by summing all the scores in a data set and then dividing this sum by the total number of scores. You likely have calculated means many times in your life.

● The **mean** is the arithmetic average of a group of scores. It is calculated by summing all the scores in a data set and then dividing this sum by the total number of scores.

EXAMPLE 4.1

For example, the mean viral video length (for all scores except the outlier) is calculated by (a) adding the lengths in seconds for each of the 49 remaining top viral videos, then (b) dividing by the total number of viral videos. We'll do this for the top viral videos.

> **STEP 1: Add all of the scores together.**

55 + 360 + 118 + 184 + 213 + 257 + 143 + 54 + 5 + 239 + 122 + 276 + 91 + 126 + 309 + 16 + 101 + 336 + 241 + 100 + 451 + 48 + 168 + 17 + 102 + 270 + 74 + 345 + 302 + 87 + 53 + 123 + 228 + 224 + 160 + 191 + 292 + 114 + 265 + 223 + 142 + 178 + 199 + 95 + 87 + 88 + 156 + 225 + 190 = 8443

> **STEP 2: Divide the sum of all scores by the total number of scores.**

In this case, we divide 8443, the sum of all scores, by 49, the number of scores in this sample:

$$8443/49 = 172.31 ●$$

Visual Representations of the Mean Think of the mean as the visual point that perfectly balances two sides of a distribution. For example, the mean of 172.31 seconds

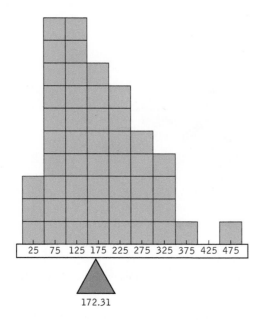

FIGURE 4-2

The Mean as the Fulcrum of the Data

The mean 172.31 is the balancing point for all the scores for the lengths in seconds of the 49 top viral videos (excluding the 50th score, an extreme outlier). Mathematically, the scores always balance around the mean for any sample.

is represented visually as the point that perfectly balances that distribution, as you can see in the Figure 4-2 histogram.

The Mean Expressed by Symbolic Notation Symbolic notation may sound more difficult than it really is. After all, you just calculated a mean without symbolic notation and without a formula. Fortunately, we need to understand only a handful of symbols to express the ideas necessary to understand statistics.

Here are the several symbols that represent the mean. For the mean of a sample, statisticians typically use M or $\bar{X}$. In this text, we use M; many other texts also use M, but some use $\bar{X}$ (pronounced "X bar"). For a population, statisticians use the Greek letter μ (pronounced "mew") to symbolize the mean. (Latin letters such as M tend to refer to numbers based on samples; Greek letters such as μ tend to refer to numbers based on populations.) *The numbers based on samples taken from a population are called* **statistics***;* M *is a statistic. The numbers based on whole populations are called* **parameters***;* μ *is a parameter.* Table 4-1 summarizes how these terms are used, and Figure 4-3 presents a mnemonic, or memory aid, for these terms to help you grow accustomed to using them.

The formula to calculate the mean of a sample uses the symbol M on the left side of the equation; the right side describes how to perform the calculation. A single score is typically symbolized as X. We know that we're summing all the scores—all

● A **statistic** is a number based on a sample taken from a population; statistics are usually symbolized by Latin letters.

● A **parameter** is a number based on the whole population; parameters are usually symbolized by Greek letters.

TABLE 4-I The Mean in Symbols

The mean of a sample is an example of a statistic, whereas the mean of a population is an example of a parameter. The symbols we use depend on whether we are referring to the mean of a sample or of a population.

Number	Used for	Symbol	Pronounced
Statistic	Sample	M or $\bar{X}$	"M" or " X bar"
Parameter	Population	μ	"Mew"

FIGURE 4-3

Samples and Parameters

Use this memory trick to remember the distinction between samples and parameters. The letter *s* means that numbers based on (*s*)amples are called (*s*)tatistics. The letter *p* means that numbers based on (*p*)opulations are called (*p*)arameters.

the *X*'s—so the first step is to use the summation sign, Σ (pronounced "sigma"), to indicate that we're summing a list of scores. As you might guess, the full expression for summing all the scores would be ΣX or "the sum of *X*." This symbol combination instructs us to add up all of the *X*'s in the sample.

Here are step-by-step instructions for constructing the equations:

Step 1: Add up all of the scores in the sample. In statistical notation, this is ΣX.

Step 2: Divide the total of all of the scores by the total number of scores.

The total number of scores in a sample is typically represented by *N*. (Note that the capital letter *N* is typically used when we refer to the number of scores in the entire data set; if we break the sample down into smaller parts, as we'll see in later chapters, we typically use the lowercase letter *n*.) The full equation would be:

$$M = \frac{\Sigma X}{N}$$

MASTERING THE FORMULA

4-1: The formula for the mean is: $M = \dfrac{\Sigma X}{N}$. To calculate the mean, we add up every score, and then divide by the total number of scores.

- -

Let's look at the mean for the viral video data that we considered earlier in Example 4.1.

EXAMPLE 4.2

| STEP 1: Add up every score. |

The sum of all scores, as we calculated previously, is 8443.

| STEP 2: Divide the sum of all scores by the total number of scores. |

In this case, we divide the sum of all scores, 8443 by the total number of scores, 49. The result is 172.31, rounded up from 172.306. Here's how it would look as a formula:

$$M = \frac{\Sigma X}{N} = \frac{8443}{49} = 172.31$$

Language Alert! As demonstrated above, almost all symbols are italicized, but the actual numerical values of the statistics are not italicized. In addition, changing a symbol from uppercase to lowercase often indicates a change in meaning. When you practice calculating means using this formula, be sure to italicize the symbols and use capital letters for *M*, *X*, and *N*. ●

Median, the Middle Score

The second most common measure of central tendency is the median. *The **median** is the middle score of all the scores in a sample when the scores are arranged in ascending order.* We can think of the median as the 50th percentile. The American Psychological Association (APA) suggests abbreviating *median* by writing *Mdn*. APA style, by the way, is used across the social and behavioral sciences in many countries, so this would be a good time to get used to it.

● The **median** is the middle score of all the scores in a sample when the scores are arranged in ascending order. If there is no single middle score, the median is the mean of the two middle scores.

Mean versus Median Hong Kong's skyline is distinctive for its one extremely tall building, the International Finance Center—toward the right in this photo. If we calculated a median height for the buildings in this skyline, the 88-story outlier would pull the mean higher. The median, however, is the middle score and would be unaffected by the outlying International Finance Center. In a situation like this, the median is a safer bet than the mean.

To determine the median, follow these steps:

Step 1: Line up all the scores in ascending order.

Step 2: Find the middle score. With an odd number of scores, there will be an actual middle score. With an even number of scores, there will be no actual middle score. In this case, calculate the mean of the two middle scores.

Don't bother with a formula when a distribution has only a few data points. Just list the numbers from lowest to highest and note which score has the same number of scores above it and below it. The calculation is easy even when a distribution has many data points. Divide the number of scores (N) by 2 and add 1/2—that is, 0.5. That number is the ordinal position (rank) of the median, or middle score. As illustrated below, simply count that many places over from the start of the scores and report that number.

EXAMPLE 4.3

Here is an example with an odd number of scores (representing the lengths in seconds for the viral video data; we omitted the extreme score, "Randy Pausch's Last Lecture," with 4586 seconds). Here are the 49 scores:

```
55 360 118 184 213 257 143   54    5 239 122 276   91
126 309  16 101 336 241 100 451   48 168   17 102 270
 74 345 302  87  53 123 228 224  160 191 292 114 265
223 142 178 199  95  87  87  88  156 225 190
```

> **STEP 1: Arrange the scores in ascending order:**

```
  5  16  17  48  53  54  55  74  87  87
 88  91  95 100 101 102 114 118 122 123
126 142 143 156 160 168 178 184 190 191
199 213 223 224 225 228 239 241 257 265
270 276 292 302 309 336 345 360 451
```

> **STEP 2: Find the middle score.**

To do this, first we count. There are 49 scores: $49/2 = 24.5$. If we add 0.5 to this result, we get 25. Therefore, the median is the 25th score. We now count across to the 25th score. The median is 160. ●

EXAMPLE 4.4

Here is an example with an even number of scores. We omitted the second highest score, 451, in addition to the extreme outlier, 4586, so there are now 48 scores.

STEP 1: Arrange the scores in ascending order.

The data are now:

- The **mode** is the most common score of all the scores in a sample.

```
  5  16  17  48  53  54  55  74  87  87
 88  91  95 100 101 102 114 118 122 123
126 142 143 156 160 168 178 184 190 191
199 213 223 224 225 228 239 241 257 265
270 276 292 302 309 336 345 360
```

STEP 2: Find the middle score.

First, we count the scores. There are 48. We then divide the number of scores by 2: 48/2 = 24. If we add 0.5 to this result, we get 24.5; therefore, the median is the average of the 24th and 25th scores. The 24th and 25th scores are 156 and 160. The median is their mean—the mean of 156 and 160 is 158. ●

Mode, the Most Common Score

The *mode* is perhaps the easiest of the three measures of central tendency to calculate. *The **mode** is the most common score of all the scores in a sample.* It is readily picked out on a frequency table, a histogram, or a frequency polygon. Like the median, the APA style for the mode does not have a symbol—in fact, it doesn't even have an abbreviation. When reporting modes, just write: "The mode is…."

••

Determine the mode for the lengths of viral videos data. Remember that each score represents the length in seconds of one of the top viral videos (excluding the extreme outlier of 4586). The mode can be found either by searching the list of numbers for the most common score or by constructing a frequency table:

EXAMPLE 4.5

Score	Frequency	Score	Frequency	Score	Frequency
5	1	118	1	224	1
16	1	122	1	225	1
17	1	123	1	228	1
48	1	126	1	239	1
53	1	142	1	241	1
54	1	143	1	257	1
55	1	156	1	265	1
74	1	160	1	270	1
87	2	168	1	276	1
88	1	178	1	292	1
91	1	184	1	302	1
95	1	190	1	309	1
100	1	191	1	336	1
101	1	199	1	345	1
102	1	213	1	360	1
114	1	223	1	451	1

FIGURE 4-4

The Bimodal Ages of Women Named Violet

With a bimodal or multimodal distribution, neither the mean nor the median is representative of the data. The ages of girls and women named Violet form a bimodal distribution (Silver & McCann, 2014). If your name is Violet, you're likely to be elderly or a child. One quarter of Violets were born before 1936, and another quarter have been born since 2010. In the intervening years, far fewer babies were named Violet each year, with almost none in the 1970s and 1980s. So, the median age for women named Violet is around 50, but there are almost no 50-year-old women with that name.

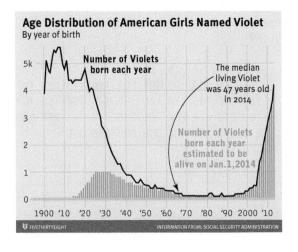

Age Distribution of American Girls Named Violet
By year of birth

The mode is: ____

Did you get 87? If you didn't, you might have made a common mistake. The mode is the score that occurs most frequently, not the frequency of that score. So, in the data set above, the score 87 occurs 2 times. The mode is 87, *not* 2. ●

The mode in this example is particularly easy to determine because it is the only score that is repeated more than once. All other scores only occur once. Sometimes a data set has no specific mode. This is especially true when the scores are reported to several decimal places (and no number occurs twice). When there is no specific mode, we sometimes report the most common interval as the mode; for example, we may say that the mode on a statistics exam is 70–79 (1 interval in the full range of 0–100). When there is more than one mode, we report both, or all, of the most common scores. *When a distribution of scores has one mode, we refer to it as* **unimodal**. *When a distribution has two modes, we call it* **bimodal**. *When a distribution has more than two modes, we call it* **multimodal**. For example, the distribution of ages of girls and women named Violet in the United States is bimodal, as illustrated in Figure 4-4.

As demonstrated in the baby name example, the mode can be used with scale data; however, it is more commonly used with nominal data. For example, the British newspaper the *Guardian* (Rogers, 2013) published maps based on census data that showed how residents of England and Wales typically commute to work. They reported that 3.5% work at home; 10.5% use public transportation; 40.4% commute by car; 0.5% ride a motorcycle; 1.9% ride a bicycle; 0.3% take a taxi; and 6.9% walk. In this data set, the modal commute is by car. (Note that this doesn't add up to 100 because the remaining people are not employed.)

How Outliers Affect Measures of Central Tendency

The mean is not the best measure of central tendency when the data are skewed by one or a few statistical outliers—extreme scores that are either very high or very low in comparison with the other scores. The examples provided in this chapter have removed an outlier from the viral video data: "Randy Pausch's Last Lecture," at 4586 seconds. Figure 4-5 displays the distribution of the top viral videos with "Randy Pausch's Last Lecture." The viral video data are positively skewed because "Randy Pausch's Last Lecture" is a very high score (i.e., a very long video) compared to the rest of the videos. We calculated the mean for this distribution without this outlier earlier. The mean was 172.31. But if we calculate the mean for the distribution with the outlier, we get 260.58—almost 90 seconds longer. The median—the middle score of the distribution—is not affected by outliers in

- A **unimodal** distribution has one mode, or most common score.

- A **bimodal** distribution has two modes, or most common scores.

- A **multimodal** distribution has more than two modes, or most common scores.

such a drastic way. In this example, the median increases from 160 without the outlier to 164 with the outlier—just four seconds longer. To demonstrate the effect of outliers on the mean, as well as the median's resistance to the effect of outliers, let's take a look at the Mundi Index estimates, which compare how many physicians there are per 1000 people in different countries (a statistic called *physician density*). We'll focus on the top five.

San Marino	47.35
Cuba	6.40
Greece	6.04
Monaco	5.81
Belarus	4.87

EXAMPLE 4.6

To get a sense of overall physician density, we might want to calculate a measure of central tendency for these five countries. We'll use the formula to get a little more practice with the symbols of statistics.

$$M = \frac{\Sigma X}{N} = \frac{(47.35 + 6.40 + 6.04 + 5.81 + 4.87)}{5} = \frac{70.47}{5} = 14.09$$

In Figure 4-6, weights are placed to represent each of the scores in the sample, and they demonstrate an important feature of the mean. Like a seesaw, the mean is the point at which all the other scores are perfectly balanced. The physician density

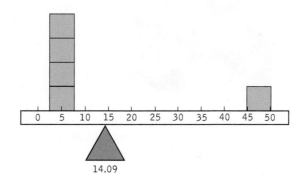

scores range from 4.87 to 47.35 and demonstrate the problem with using the mean when there is an outlier: The mean is not typical for any of the five countries in this sample, even though the seesaw is perfectly balanced if we put its fulcrum at the mean of 14.09.

We can't help but notice that the tiny country of San Marino (an enclave within Italy; population 33,000) is very different from the other countries. Four of the scores are between 4.87 and 6.40 physicians per 1000 people, a much smaller range. But San Marino enjoys 47.35 physicians per 1000 people. When there is an outlier like San Marino, it is important to consider what this score does to the mean, especially if we have only a few observations. ●

EXAMPLE 4.7

When we eliminate San Marino's score, the data are now 6.40, 6.04, 5.81, and 4.87, and the new mean is:

$$M = \frac{\Sigma X}{N} = \frac{23.12}{4} = 5.78$$

FIGURE 4-7

The Mean Without the Outlier

When the outlier—San Marino—is omitted from the physician density data, the mean becomes more representative of the actual scores in the sample.

The new mean of these scores, 5.78, is a good deal lower than the original mean of the scores that included San Marino's outlier. We see from Figure 4-7 that this new mean, like the original mean, marks the point at which all other scores are perfectly balanced around it. However, this new mean is a little more representative of the scores: 5.78 is a more typical score for these four countries. Pay attention to outliers; they usually tell an interesting story! ●

Which Measure of Central Tendency Is Best?

Different measures of central tendency can lead to different conclusions, but when a decision needs to be made, the choice is usually between the mean and the median. The mean usually wins, especially when there are many observations—but doesn't always. When distributions are skewed by outliers such as San Marino, for example, or when there are only a handful of available observations, the median may provide a better sense of a distribution's central tendency.

Celebrity Outliers Reports of the cost of a typical home depend on whether the mean or the median is reported. For example, performing artist Beyoncé bought a $5.9 million home in Houston, Texas, for her mother, Tina Knowles. The 23,562 square foot mansion has eight bedrooms and 12 bathrooms! According to the real estate Web site Trulia.com, the median home price in Houston around the time Beyoncé bought the house was $88,693 and the mean was $318,377. Beyoncé's purchase was an outlier for Houston; such a purchase explains why the mean is much higher than the median for home prices in most cities. Extreme outlier purchases boost the mean, but do not affect the median.

Rex/Rex USA

The mode is generally used in three situations: (1) when one particular score dominates a distribution; (2) when the distribution is bimodal or multimodal; and (3) when the data are nominal. When you are uncertain as to which measure is the best indicator of central tendency, report all three.

Central tendency communicates an enormous amount of information with a single number, so it is not surprising that measures of central tendency are among the most widely reported of descriptive statistics. Unfortunately, consumers can be tricked by reports that use the mean instead of the median.

When you hear a report about the central tendency of housing prices, for example, first notice whether it is reporting an average (mean) or a median. You can see an example of a celebrity outlier in the housing market in the photograph on the previous page.

CHECK YOUR LEARNING

Reviewing the Concepts

> The central tendency of a distribution is the one number that best describes what is typical in that distribution (often its high point).

> The three measures of central tendency are the mean (arithmetic average), the median (middle score), and the mode (most frequently occurring score).

> The mean is the most commonly used measure of central tendency, but the median is preferred when the distribution is skewed.

> The symbols used in statistics have very specific meanings; changing a symbol even slightly can change its meaning a great deal.

Clarifying the Concepts

4-1 What is the difference between statistics and parameters?

4-2 Does an outlier have the greatest effect on the mean, the median, or the mode? Explain your answer.

Calculating the Statistics

4-3 Calculate the mean, median, and mode of the following sets of numbers.

a. 10 8 22 5 6 1 19 8 13 12 8

b. 122.5 123.8 121.2 125.8 120.2 123.8 120.5 119.8 126.3 123.6

c. 0.100 0.866 0.781 0.555 0.222 0.245 0.234

Applying the Concepts

4-4 Let's examine fictional data for 20 seniors in college. Each score represents the number of nights a student spends socializing in one week:

1 0 1 2 5 3 2 3 1 3 1 7 2 3 2 2 2 0 4 6

a. Using the formula, calculate the mean of these scores.

b. If the researcher reported the mean of these scores as an estimate for the whole university population, what symbol would she use for the mean? Why?

c. If the researcher were interested only in the scores of these 20 students, what symbol would she use for the mean? Why?

d. What is the median of these scores?

e. What is the mode of these scores?

f. Are the median and mean similar to or different from each other? What does this similarity or difference tell you about the distribution of scores?

4-5 Savvy companies can use their knowledge of outliers to trick consumers. For example, television networks need high average ratings to attract advertising dollars; the U.S. network NBC aired the Republican presidential primary debate in January 2012, a show that should have been categorized as "special programming." A *New York Times* article explained the trickery: "Careful viewers noticed that the debate was labeled a regular edition of the network's ratings-challenged newsmagazine program, 'Rock Center with Brian Williams'—one that, as it turned out, just happened to double the show's usual audience to just over 7.1 million viewers" (Carter, 2012). In your own words, explain why this labeling would be useful to NBC.

Solutions to these Check Your Learning questions can be found in Appendix D.

Measures of Variability

The zipper company YKK understands that a high-quality product requires low variability. Low variability lets you trust that your car will start, your computer won't crash, and your zipper will work. *Variability is a numerical way of describing how much spread there is in a distribution.* One way to numerically describe the variability of a distribution is by computing its *range*. A second and more common way to describe variability is by computing *variance* and its square root, known as *standard deviation*.

Range

The range is the easiest measure of variability to calculate. *The **range** is a measure of variability calculated by subtracting the lowest score (the minimum) from the highest score (the maximum).* Maximum and minimum are sometimes substituted in this formula to describe the highest and lowest scores, and some statistical computer programs abbreviate these as *max* and *min*. The range is represented in a formula as:

$$\text{range} = X_{highest} - X_{lowest}$$

Here are scores for the lengths of the 49 top viral videos that we discussed earlier in the chapter:

5	16	17	48	53	54	55	74	87	87
88	91	95	100	101	102	114	118	122	123
126	142	143	156	160	168	178	184	190	191
199	213	223	224	225	228	239	241	257	265
270	276	292	302	309	336	345	360	451	

EXAMPLE 4.8

We can determine the highest and lowest scores either by reading through the data or, more easily, by glancing at the frequency table for these data.

> **STEP 1: Determine the highest score.**

In this case, the highest score is 451.

> **STEP 2: Determine the lowest score.**

In this case, the lowest score is 5.

> **STEP 3: Calculate the range by subtracting the lowest score from the highest score:**

$$\text{range} = X_{highest} - X_{lowest} = 451 - 5 = 446$$

- **Variability** is a numerical way of describing how much spread there is in a distribution.

- The **range** is a measure of variability calculated by subtracting the lowest score (the minimum) from the highest score (the maximum).

- **Variance** is the average of the squared deviations from the mean.

The range can be a useful first indicator of variability, but it is influenced only by the highest and lowest scores. All the other scores in between could be clustered near the highest score, huddled near the center, spread out evenly, or have some other unexpected pattern. We can't know based only on the range. ●

Variance

Variance is the average of the squared deviations from the mean. When something varies, it must vary from (or be different from) some standard. That standard is the mean. So when we compute variance, that number describes how far a distribution varies around the mean. A small number indicates a small amount of spread or deviation around the mean, and a larger number indicates a great deal of spread or deviation around the mean. The YKK zipper company, for example, was always aiming at a lower number because it meant high reliability—products you could trust.

• •

Students who seek therapy at university counseling centers often do not attend many sessions. For example, in one study, the median number of therapy sessions was 3 and the mean was 4.6 (Hatchett, 2003). Let's examine the spread of fictional scores for a sample of five students: 1, 2, 4, 4, and 10 therapy sessions, with a mean of 4.2. We find out how far each score deviates from the mean by subtracting the mean from every score. First, we label with an X the column that lists the scores. Here, the second column includes the results we get when we subtract the mean from each score, or $X - M$. We call each of these a **deviation from the mean** (or just a *deviation*)—*the amount that a score in a sample differs from the mean of the sample.*

EXAMPLE 4.9

X	$X - M$
1	−3.2
2	−2.2
4	−0.2
4	−0.2
10	5,8

But we can't just take the mean of the deviations. If we do (and if you try this, don't forget the signs—negative and positive), we get 0—every time. Are you surprised? Remember, the mean is the point at which all scores are perfectly balanced. Mathematically, the scores *have* to balance out. Yet we know that there *is* variability among these scores. The number representing the amount of variability is certainly not 0!

When we ask students for ways to eliminate the negative signs, two suggestions typically come up: (1) Take the absolute value of the deviations, thus making them all positive, or (2) square all the scores, again making them all positive. It turns out that the latter, squaring all the deviations, is how statisticians solve this problem. Once we square the deviations, we can take their average and get a measure of variability. Later (using a beautifully descriptive term created by our students), we will "*un*square" those deviations in order to calculate the standard deviation.

To recap:

STEP 1: Subtract the mean from every score.	We call these *deviations from the mean.*

STEP 2: Square every deviation from the mean.	We call these *squared deviations.*

STEP 3: Sum all of the squared deviations.	This is often called the *sum of squared deviations,* or the *sum of squares* for short.

● A **deviation from the mean** is the amount that a score in a sample differs from the mean of the sample; also called a *deviation.*

TABLE 4-2	Variance and Standard Deviation in Symbols

The variance or standard deviation of a sample is an example of a statistic, whereas the variance or standard deviation of a population is an example of a parameter. The symbols we use depend on whether we are referring to the spread of a sample or of a population.

Number	Used for ...	Standard Deviation Symbol	Pronounced	Variance Symbol	Pronounced
Statistic	Sample	SD or s	As written	SD^2, s^2, or MS	Letters as written; if there is a superscript^2, the term is followed by "squared" (e.g., "ess squared")
Parameter	Population	σ	"Sigma"	σ^2	"Sigma squared"

● The **sum of squares**, symbolized as *SS*, is the sum of each score's squared deviation from the mean.

> **STEP 4: Divide the sum of squares by the total number in the sample (N).**

This number represents the mathematical definition of variance—the average of the squared deviations from the mean.

Let's try it. To calculate the variance for the therapy session data, we add a third column to contain the squares of each of the deviations. Then we add all of these numbers up to compute the ***sum of squares*** *(symbolized as SS), the sum of each score's squared deviation from the mean.* In this case, the sum of the squared deviations is 48.80, so the average squared deviation is $48.80/5 = 9.76$. Thus, the variance equals 9.76.

X	$X - M$	$(X - M)^2$
1	−3.20	10.24
2	−2.20	4.84
4	−0.20	0.04
4	−0.20	0.04
10	5.80	33.64

Language Alert! We need a few more symbols to use symbolic notation to represent the idea of variance. Each of these symbols represents the same idea (variance) applied to slightly different situations. The symbols that represent the variance of a *sample* include SD^2, s^2, and MS. The first two symbols, SD^2 and s^2, both represent the words *standard deviation squared*. The symbolic notation MS comes from the words *mean square* (referring to the average of the squared deviations). We'll use SD^2 at this point, but we will alert you when we switch to other symbols for variance later. The variance of the *sample* uses all three symbolic notations; however, the variance of a *population* uses just one symbol: σ^2 (pronounced "sigma squared"). Table 4-2 summarizes the symbols and language used to describe different versions of the mean and variance, but we will keep reminding you as we go along.

We already know all the other symbols needed to calculate variance: X to indicate the individual scores, M to indicate the mean, and N to indicate the sample size.

MASTERING THE FORMULA

4-3: The formula for variance is: $SD^2 = \dfrac{\Sigma(X - M)^2}{N}$. To calculate variance, subtract the mean (M) from every score (X) to calculate deviations from the mean; then square these deviations, sum them, and divide by the sample size (N). By summing the squared deviations and dividing by sample size, we are taking their mean.

$$SD^2 = \frac{\Sigma(X - M)^2}{N}$$

As you can see, variance is really just a mean—the mean of squared deviations. ●

Standard Deviation

Language Alert! Variance and standard deviation refer to the same core idea. The standard deviation is more useful because it *is the typical amount that each score varies from the mean*. Mathematically, the **standard deviation** is the square root of the average of the squared deviations from the mean, or, more simply, the square root of the variance. The beauty of the standard deviation—compared to the variance—is that we can understand it at a glance.

> ● The **standard deviation** is the square root of the average of the squared deviations from the mean; it is the typical amount that each score varies, or deviates, from the mean.

EXAMPLE 4.10

The numbers of therapy sessions for the five students were 1, 2, 4, 4, and 10, with a mean of 4.2. The typical score does not vary from the mean by 9.76. The variance is based on squared deviations, not deviations, so it is too large. When we ask our students how to solve this problem, they invariably say, "Unsquare it," and that's just what we do. We take the square root of variance to come up with a much more useful number, the standard deviation. The square root of 9.76 is 3.12. Now we have a number that "makes sense" to us. We can now say that the typical number of therapy sessions for students in this sample is 4.2 and the typical amount a student varies from that is 3.12.

As you read journal articles, you often will see the mean and standard deviation reported as: ($M = 4.2$, $SD = 3.12$). A glance at the original data (1, 2, 4, 4, 10) tells us that these numbers make sense: 4.2 does seem to be approximately in the center, and scores do seem to vary from 4.2 by roughly 3.12. The score of 10 is a bit of an outlier—but not so much of one; the mean and the standard deviation are still somewhat representative of the typical score and typical deviation.

We didn't actually need a formula to get the standard deviation. We just took the square root of the variance. Perhaps you guessed the symbols for standard deviation by just taking the square root of those for variance. With a sample, standard deviation is either SD or s. With a population, standard deviation is σ. Table 4-2 presents this information concisely. We can write the formula showing how standard deviation is calculated from variance:

$$SD = \sqrt{SD^2}$$

We can also write the formula showing how standard deviation is calculated from the original X's, M, and N:

$$SD = \sqrt{\frac{\Sigma(X - M)^2}{N}}$$

> **MASTERING THE FORMULA**
>
> **4-4:** The most basic formula for standard deviation is: $SD = \sqrt{SD^2}$. We simply take the square root of the variance.

> **MASTERING THE FORMULA**
>
> **4-5:** The full formula for standard deviation is: $SD = \sqrt{\dfrac{\Sigma(X - M)^2}{N}}$. To determine standard deviation, subtract the mean from every score to calculate deviations from the mean. Then, square the deviations from the mean. Sum the squared deviations, then divide by the sample size. Finally, take the square root of the mean of the squared deviations.

The Interquartile Range

Next Steps

As we noted earlier in the chapter, the range has a major limitation: it is completely dependent on the maximum and minimum scores. For example, the $17 million home at the high end or the shack at the low end of the distribution skew a distribution of home prices. Whenever we have outliers, the range will be an exaggerated measure of the variability. Fortunately, we have an alternative to the range: the interquartile range.

The **interquartile range** *is a measure of the distance between the first and third quartiles.* As we learned earlier, the median marks the 50th percentile of a data set. Similarly, *the* **first quartile** *marks the 25th percentile of a data set*, and *the* **third quartile** *marks the 75th percentile of a data set*. Essentially, the first and third quartiles are the medians of

> ● The **interquartile range** is a measure of the distance between the first and third quartiles.
>
> ● The **first quartile** marks the 25th percentile of a data set.
>
> ● The **third quartile** marks the 75th percentile of a data set.

the two halves of the data—the half below the median and the half above the median. We calculate the first quartile and the third quartile in a similar manner to how we calculate the median.

Here are the steps for finding the interquartile range:

Step 1: Calculate the median.

Step 2: Look at all of the scores below the median. The median of these scores, the lower half of the scores, is the first quartile, often called *Q1* for short.

Step 3: Look at all of the scores above the median. The median of these scores, the upper half of the scores, is the third quartile, often called *Q3* for short.

Step 4: Subtract *Q1* from *Q3*. The interquartile range, often abbreviated as *IQR*, is the difference between the first and third quartiles: $IQR = Q3 - Q1$.

Because the interquartile range is the distance between the 25th and 75th percentile of the data, it can be thought of as the range of the middle 50% of the data.

The interquartile range has an important advantage over the range. Because it is not based on the minimum and maximum—the most extreme scores—it is less susceptible to outliers. Let's look at an example.

EXAMPLE 4.11

Here are the data for the viral video example that we examined earlier in the chapter. As we did before, we omitted the extreme score ("Randy Pausch's Last Lecture," 4586 seconds).

5	16	17	48	53	54	55	74	87	87
88	91	95	100	101	102	114	118	122	123
126	142	143	156	160	168	178	184	190	191
199	213	223	224	225	228	239	241	257	265
270	276	292	302	309	336	345	360	451	

Earlier we calculated the median of these scores as the 25th score, 160. We now take the first 24 scores: 5, 16, 17, 48, 53, 54, 55, 74, 87, 87, 88, 91, 95, 100, 101, 102, 114, 118, 122, 123, 126, 142, 143, 156. If we divide the number of scores, 24, by 2 and add 1/2, we get 12.5. The median of these scores—the first quartile—is the mean of the 12th and 13th scores, 91 and 95, respectively. So, the first quartile is 93.

We'll do the same with the top half of the scores, not including the median: 168, 178, 184, 190, 191, 199, 213, 223, 224, 225, 228, 239, 241, 257, 265, 270, 276, 292, 302, 309, 336, 345, 360, 451. Again, there are 24 scores, so the median of these scores—the third quartile—is also the mean of the 12th and 13th scores. This time the 12th and 13th scores are 239 and 241, respectively, so the third quartile is 240. The range is the maximum minus the minimum: range $= X_{highest} - X_{lowest} = 451 - 5 = 446$. However, the interquartile range is the third quartile minus the first quartile: $IQR = Q3 - Q1 = 240 - 93 = 147$.

Along with the minimum, median, and maximum, the first and third quartiles provide us with an overview of the data. These five numbers—scores at the 0, 25th, 50th, 75th, and 100th percentiles—give a good sense of the overall distribution. As seen in Figure 4-8, the five-number summary includes the minimum (5), first quartile (93), median (160), third quartile (240), and maximum (451). The longer distance between the third quartile and the maximum, as compared to the distance between the first quartile and the minimum, indicates a skewed distribution. Specifically, the whole data set has a width of 446, but the middle 50% only has a width of 147.

FIGURE 4-8

Five-Number Summary

Just five numbers give a good sense of the overall distribution: 5, 93, 160, 240, and 451. These five numbers represent the scores at the 0, 25th, 50th, 75th, and 100th percentiles: the minimum, first quartile, median, third quartile, and maximum.

The interquartile range is not influenced by the most extreme scores (like the minimum and maximum values), so it is a more valid measure of variability for these data than is the range. The interquartile range, unlike the range, is resistant to outliers. Imagine if we included the extreme score for "Randy Pausch's Last Lecture" (4586 seconds). The range would increase dramatically from 446 to 4581, but the interquartile range would be rather unaffected. ●

CHECK YOUR LEARNING

Reviewing the Concepts

> The simplest way to measure variability is to use the range, which is calculated by subtracting the lowest score from the highest score.

> Variance and standard deviation both measure the degree to which scores in a distribution vary from the mean. The standard deviation is simply the square root of the variance: It represents the typical deviation of a score from the mean.

> The interquartile range is calculated by subtracting the score at the 25th percentile from the score at the 75th percentile. It communicates the width of the middle 50% of the data.

Clarifying the Concepts

4-6 In your own words, what is variability?

4-7 Distinguish the range from the standard deviation. What does each tell us about the distribution?

Calculating the Statistics

4-8 Calculate the range, variance, and standard deviation for the following data sets (the same ones from the section on central tendency).

a. 10 8 22 5 6 1 19 8 13 12 8

b. 122.5 123.8 121.2 125.8 120.2 123.8 120.5 119.8 126.3 123.6

c. 0.100 0.866 0.781 0.555 0.222 0.245 0.234

Applying the Concepts

4-9 Final exam week is approaching, and students are not eating as well as usual. Four students were asked how many calories of junk food they had consumed between noon and 10:00 P.M. on the day before an exam. The estimated numbers of empty calories, calculated with the help of a nutritional software program, were 450, 670, 1130, and 1460.

a. Using the formula, calculate the range for these scores.

b. What information can't you glean from the range?

c. Using the formula, calculate variance for these scores.

d. Using the formula, calculate the standard deviation for these scores.

e. If a researcher were interested only in these four students, which symbols would he use for variance and standard deviation, respectively?

Solutions to these Check Your Learning questions can be found in Appendix D.

f. If another researcher hoped to generalize from these four students to all students at the university, which symbols would she use for variance and standard deviation, respectively?

REVIEW OF CONCEPTS

Central Tendency

Three measures of *central tendency* are commonly used in research. When a numeric description, such as a measure of central tendency, describes a sample, it is a *statistic*; when it describes a population, it is a *parameter*. The *mean* is the arithmetic average of the data. The *median* is the midpoint of the data set; 50% of scores fall on either side of the median. The *mode* is the most common score in the data set. When there's one mode, the distribution is *unimodal*; when there are two modes, it's *bimodal*; and when there are three or more modes, it's *multimodal*. The mean is highly influenced by outliers, whereas the median and mode are resistant to outliers.

Measures of Variability

The *range* is the simplest measure of *variability* to calculate. It is calculated by subtracting the minimum score in a data set from the maximum score. Variance and standard deviation are much more common measures of variability. They are used when the preferred measure of central tendency is the mean. *Variance* is the average of the squared deviations from the mean. It is calculated by subtracting the mean from every score to get *deviations from the mean*, then squaring each of the deviations. (In future chapters, we will use the *sum of squares* of the deviations when making inferences about a population based on a sample.) *Standard deviation* is the square root of variance. It is the typical amount that a score deviates from the mean.

When the median is the preferred measure of central tendency, the interquartile range (IQR) is used, as it provides a better measure of variability than does the range. The IQR is the third quartile, or 75th percentile, minus the first quartile, or 25th percentile. The IQR is the width of the middle 50% of the data set and, unlike the range, is resistant to outliers.

SPSS®

Using the viral video data from Chapter 2, we can use SPSS to identify the descriptive statistics discussed in this chapter. First, enter the data as seen in the screenshot here. (Do not include the outlier, 4586 seconds.)

To get a numerical description of a variable—in this case, length of video—select: Analyze → Descriptive Statistics → Frequencies. Then select the variance of interest, "Length of Video," by highlighting it and then clicking the arrow to move it from the left side to the

right side. Then select: Statistics → Mean, Median, Mode, Std deviation, Variance, Range → Continue → OK. As you might have noticed, there are several other descriptive statistics that SPSS can provide (e.g., quartiles, minimum, maximum).

The data and output will look like those in the screenshot shown here. By default, SPSS will also provide a frequency table in the output.

HOW IT WORKS

4.1 CALCULATING THE MEAN

How do we calculate a mean? We looked up the top 15 Vietnamese restaurants in Vancouver on yelp.com. All of these restaurants received very high overall ratings, but from different numbers of reviewers. (Why are these data useful? Well, we might decide that we trust an overall rating more for restaurants with more reviewers who agree that it's great. But of course, we must be cautious because Yelp reviewers are probably not a representative sample.) Below are the numbers of people who reviewed each of these 15 restaurants on Yelp—from Cafe Xu Hue, which has the fewest reviews among these top Vietnamese places, to Phnom Penh, which has the most:

$$423 \ 123 \ 50 \ 78 \ 43 \ 98 \ 139 \ 53 \ 78 \ 69 \ 112 \ 120 \ 74 \ 39 \ 130$$

How can we calculate the mean? First, we add up all of the scores:

$$423 + 123 + 50 + 78 + 43 + 98 + 139 + 53 + 78$$
$$+ \ 69 + 112 + 120 + 74 + 39 + 130 = 1629$$

Then we divide by 15, the number of scores:

$$1629/15 = 108.60$$

With the formula, we calculate:

$$M = \frac{(423 + 123 + 50 + 78 + 43 + 98 + 139 + 53 + 78 + 69 + 112 + 120 + 74 + 39 + 130)}{15} = 108.60$$

4.2 CALCULATING THE MEDIAN

Using the data for numbers of Yelp reviewers for Vietnamese restaurants in Vancouver, how can we calculate the median? The median is either the middle score (for odd numbers of scores) or the average of the two middle scores (for even numbers of scores). We first arrange the data from lowest score to highest score:

$$39 \ 43 \ 50 \ 53 \ 69 \ 74 \ 78 \ 78 \ 98 \ 112 \ 120 \ 123 \ 130 \ 139 \ 423$$

With 15 scores (an odd number), there is one middle score, the 8th score. The 8th score is 78. The median is 78.

4.3 CALCULATING THE MODE

How can we calculate the mode for the "numbers of Yelp reviewer" data? The mode is the most common score. We can determine the mode for these data by looking at the frequency distribution. Two restaurants had 78 reviewers. The mode is 78.

4.4 CALCULATING VARIANCE

How can we calculate variance for the "numbers of Yelp reviewers" data? To calculate variance for these data, we first subtract the mean, 108.60, from every score. We then square these deviations. These calculations are shown in the table below.

Score	$(X - M)$	$(X - M)^2$
39	−69.6	4844.16
43	−65.6	4303.36
50	−58.6	3433.96
53	−55.6	3091.36
69	−39.6	1568.16
74	−34.6	1197.16
78	−30.6	936.36
78	−30.6	936.36
98	−10.6	112.36
112	3.4	11.56
120	11.4	129.96
123	14.4	207.36
130	21.4	457.96
139	30.4	924.16
423	314.4	98847.36

We then add all of the scores in the third column to get the sum of squared deviations, or the sum of squares. This sum is 121001.60.

We can use the formula to complete the calculations:

$$SD^2 = \sqrt{\frac{\Sigma(X - M)^2}{N}} = \frac{121001.60}{15} = 8066.773$$

The variance is 8066.773.

4.5 CALCULATING STANDARD DEVIATION

How can we calculate standard deviation for the data on the "the data on the number of Yelp reviews per restaurant"? The standard deviation is the square root of the variance. For these data, we calculate standard deviation directly from the variance we calculated above using this formula:

$$SD = \sqrt{SD^2} = \sqrt{8066.773} = 89.815$$

The standard deviation is 89.82.

EXERCISES

The solutions to the odd-numbered exercises can be found in Appendix C.

Clarifying the Concepts

4.1 Define the three measures of central tendency: mean, median, and mode.

4.2 The mean can be assessed visually and arithmetically. Describe each method.

4.3 Explain how the mean mathematically balances the distribution.

4.4 Explain what is meant by unimodal, bimodal, and multimodal distributions.

4.5 Explain why the mean might not be useful for a bimodal or multimodal distribution.

4.6 What is an outlier?

4.7 How do outliers affect the mean and median?

4.8 In which situations is the mode typically used?

4.9 Explain the concept of standard deviation in your own words.

4.10 Define the symbols used in the equation for variance:

$$SD^2 = \sqrt{\frac{\Sigma(X - M)^2}{N}}$$

4.11 Why is the standard deviation typically reported, rather than the variance?

4.12 Find the incorrectly used symbol or symbols in each of the following statements or formulas. For each statement or formula, (1) state which symbol(s) is/are used incorrectly, (2) explain why the symbol(s) in the original statement is/are incorrect, and (3) state which symbol(s) *should* be used.

   a. The mean and standard deviation of the sample of reaction times were calculated ($m = 54.2$, $SD^2 = 9.87$).

   b. The mean of the sample of high school student GPAs was $\mu = 3.08$.

   c. range $= X_{highest} - X_{lowest}$

4.13 How does the interquartile range differ from the range?

4.14 Using your knowledge of how to calculate the median, describe how to calculate the first and third quartiles of your data.

4.15 At what percentile is the first quartile?

4.16 At what percentile is the third quartile?

Calculating the Statistics

4.17 Use the following data for this exercise:

      15 34 32 46 22 36 34 28 52 28

   a. Calculate the mean, the median, and the mode.

   b. Add another data point, 112. Calculate the mean, median, and mode again. How does this new data point affect the calculations?

   c. Calculate the range, variance, and standard deviation for the original data.

4.18 Use the following salary data for this exercise:

$44,751	$38,862
$52,000	$51,380
$41,500	$61,774

   a. Calculate the mean, the median, and the mode.

   b. Add another salary, $97,582. Calculate the mean, median, and mode again. How does this new salary affect the calculations?

   c. Calculate the range, variance, and standard deviation for the original salary data.

   d. How does the range change when you include the outlier salary, $97,582?

4.19 The Mount Washington Observatory (MWO) in New Hampshire claims to have the world's worst weather. Below are some data on the weather extremes recorded at the MWO.

Month	Normal Daily Maximum (°F)	Normal Daily Minimum (°F)	Record Low in °F (year)	Peak Wind Gust in Miles per Hour (year)
January	14.0	−3.7	−47 (1934)	173 (1985)
February	14.8	−1.7	−46 (1943)	166 (1972)
March	21.3	5.9	−38 (1950)	180 (1942)
April	29.4	16.4	−20 (1995)	231 (1934)
May	41.6	29.5	−2 (1966)	164 (1945)
June	50.3	38.5	8 (1945)	136 (1949)
July	54.1	43.3	24 (2001)	154 (1996)
August	53.0	42.1	20 (1986)	142 (1954)
September	46.1	34.6	9 (1992)	174 (1979)
October	36.4	24.0	−5 (1939)	161 (1943)
November	27.6	13.6	−20 (1958)	163 (1983)
December	18.5	1.7	−46 (1933)	178 (1980)

   a. Calculate the mean and median normal daily minimum temperature across the year.

   b. Calculate the mean, median, and mode for the record low temperatures.

c. Calculate the mean, median, and mode for the peak wind-gust data.

d. When no mode appears in the raw data, we can compute a mode by breaking the data into intervals. How might you do this for the peak wind-gust data?

e. Calculate the range, variance, and standard deviation for the normal daily minimum temperature across the year.

f. Calculate the range, variance, and standard deviation for the record low temperatures.

g. Calculate the range, variance, and standard deviation for the peak wind-gust data.

4.20 Calculate the range and the interquartile range for the following set of data. Explain why they are so different.

83 99 103   65 66   77   55 82

93 93 108 543 72 109 115 85

92 74 101   98 84

4.21 Calculate the interquartile range for the following set of data:

2 5 1 3 3 4 3 6 7 1 4 3 7 2 2 2 8 3 3 12 1

4.22 Using the data presented in Exercise 4.19, calculate the interquartile range for peak wind gust.

4.23 Why is the interquartile range you calculated for the previous exercise so much smaller than the range you calculated in Exercise 4.19?

4.24 Here are recent *U.S. News & World Report* data on acceptance rates at the top 70 national universities. These are the percentages of accepted students out of all students who applied.

6.3 14.0   8.9   21.6   40.6   51.2   50.5   69.4   42.4   68.3

8.5   12.4   18.0   30.4   31.4   51.3   47.5   49.4   54.6   63.5

7.7   12.8   18.8   25.5   28.0   33.4   38.3   25.0   49.4   56.7

7.0   10.1   24.3   23.0   32.7   46.0   52.4   31.6   44.7   62.8

16.3   18.0   16.4   33.3   40.0   35.5   67.6   43.2   57.9   63.3

9.7   18.4   26.7   39.9   34.6   39.6   46.6   34.5   47.3   61.1

7.1   16.5   18.1   21.9   34.1   45.7   58.4   63.4   63.0   46.6

a. Calculate the mean of these data, showing that you know how to use the symbols and formula.

b. Determine the median of these data.

c. Describe the variability in these data by computing the range.

Applying the Concepts

4.25 Mean versus median for salary data: In Exercises 4.17 and 4.18, we saw how the mean and median changed when an outlier was included in the computations. If you were reporting the "average" salary at a company, how might the mean and median give different impressions to potential applicants?

4.26 Mean versus median for temperature data: For the data in Exercise 4.19, the "normal" daily maximum and minimum temperatures recorded at the Mount Washington Observatory are presented for each month. These are likely to be measures of central tendency for each month over time. Explain why these "normal" temperatures might be calculated as means or medians. What would be the reasoning for using one type of statistic over the other?

4.27 Mean versus median for depression scores: A depression research unit recently assessed seven participants chosen at random from the university population. Is the mean or the median a better indicator of the central tendency of these seven participants? Explain your answer.

4.28 Measures of central tendency for weather data: The "normal" weather data from the Mount Washington Observatory are broken down by month. Why might you not want to average across all months in a year? How else could you summarize the year?

4.29 Outliers, central tendency, and data on wind gusts: There appears to be an outlier in the data for peak wind gust recorded on top of Mount Washington (see the data in Exercise 4.19). Where do you see an outlier and how does excluding this data point affect the different calculations of central tendency?

4.30 Measures of central tendency for measures of baseball performance: Here are winning percentages for 11 baseball players for their best 4-year pitching performances:

0.755 0.721 0.708 0.773 0.782 0.747

0.477 0.817 0.617 0.650 0.651

a. What is the mean of these scores?

b. What is the median of these scores?

c. Compare the mean and the median. Does the difference between them suggest that the data are skewed very much?

4.31 Mean versus median in "real life": Briefly describe a real-life situation in which the median is preferable to the mean. Give hypothetical numbers for the mean and median in your explanation. Be original! (Don't use home prices or another example from the chapter.)

4.32 Descriptive statistics in the media: Find an advertisement for an anti-aging product either online or in the print media—the more unbelievable the claims, the better!

a. What does the ad promise that this product will do for the consumer?

b. What data does it offer for its promised benefits? Does it offer any descriptive statistics or merely testimonials? If it offers descriptive statistics, what are the limitations of what they report?

c. If you were considering this product, what measures of central tendency would you most like to see? Explain your answer, noting why not all measures of central tendency would be helpful.

d. If a friend with no statistical background were considering this product, what would you tell him or her?

4.33 Descriptive statistics in the media: When there is an ad on TV for a body-shaping product (e.g., an abdominal muscle machine), often a person with a wonderful success story is featured in the ad. The statement "Individual results may vary" hints at what kind of data the advertisement may be presenting.

a. What kind of data is being presented in these ads?

b. What statistics could be presented to help inform the public about how much "individual results might vary"?

4.34 Range of data for Canadian TV ratings: Numeris (formerly BBM Canada) collects Canadian television ratings data (http://en.numeris.ca/). The following are the average number of viewers per minute (in thousands) for the top 30 English-language shows for 1 week. The NHL playoffs are listed at 1198, which indicates that an average of 1,198,000 viewers watched per minute. *Big Bang Theory* is in the number 1 position, with *2 Broke Girls* at number 30.

3117 2935 2216 2128 1785 1735 1616 1602 1548 1519
1513 1476 1462 1263 1201 1198 1193 1189 1186 1155
1117 1102 1079 1057 1036 1034 1008 · 925 902 887

a. What is the range of these data?

b. What is the interquartile range of these data?

c. How does the IQR you calculated in part (b) differ from the range you calculated in part (a), and why is it different?

4.35 Descriptive statistics for data from the National Survey of Student Engagement: Every year, the National Survey of Student Engagement (NSSE) asks U.S. university students how many 20-page papers they had been assigned. Here are the percentages, for 1 year, of students who said they had been assigned between 5 and 10 twenty-page papers for a sample of 19 universities.

0 5 3 3 1 10 2
2 3 1 2 4 2 1
1 1 4 3 5

a. Calculate the mean of these data using the symbols and formula.

b. Calculate the variance of these data using the symbols and formula; also use columns to show all calculations.

c. Calculate the standard deviation using the symbols and formula.

d. In your own words, describe what the mean and standard deviation of these data tell us about these scores.

4.36 Statistics versus parameters: For each of the following situations, state whether the mean would be a statistic or a parameter. Explain your answer.

a. According to Canadian census data, the median family income in British Columbia was $66,970, lower than the national average of $69,860.

b. The stadiums of teams in the English Premier League had a mean capacity of 38,391 fans.

c. The General Social Survey (GSS) includes a vocabulary test in which participants are asked to choose the appropriate synonym from a multiple-choice list of five words (e.g., *beast* with the choices *afraid*, *words*, *large*, *animal*, and *separate*). The mean vocabulary test score was 5.98.

d. The National Survey of Student Engagement (NSSE) asks students at participating institutions how often they discuss ideas or readings with professors outside of class. Among the 19 universities that made their data public, the mean percentage of students who responded "Very often" was 8%.

4.37 Central tendency and the shapes of distributions: Consider the many possible distributions of grades on a quiz in a statistics class; imagine that the grades could range from 0 to 100. For each of the following situations, give a hypothetical mean and median (that is, make up a mean and a median that might occur with a distribution that has this shape). Explain your answer.

a. Normal distribution

b. Positively skewed distribution

c. Negatively skewed distribution

4.38 Shapes of distributions, chemistry grades, and first-generation college students: David Laude was a chemistry professor at the University of Texas at Austin (and a former underprepared college student) who developed an intervention that led underprepared students to perform at the same average level as others (Tough, 2014). He started this program because he observed a bimodal distribution of grades, rather than a unimodal distribution with a peak in the middle. Specifically, "in each class of 500 students, there would be 400 or so who did quite well, clustered around the A and high-B range.

They got it. Then there would be a second cluster of perhaps 100 students whose grades were way down at the bottom—D's and F's. They didn't get it."

a. Draw a distribution that ranges from F on the left to A on the right and shows what the chemistry grades would look like if the distribution were unimodal with a peak in the center.

b. Draw the distribution that Laude observed in his chemistry classes.

c. Take a guess as to what the mean would be—in terms of a letter grade—for the distribution in part a and the distribution in part b.

d. For which distribution—the one in part a or the one in part b—is the mean likely to be a better measure of central tendency? Explain your answer.

e. Based on the outcome mentioned above, describe in words what you think the distribution looked like after Laude's intervention.

4.39 Outliers, Hurricane Sandy, and a rat infestation: In a *New York Times* article, reporter Cara Buckley described the influx of rats inland from the New York City shoreline following the flooding caused by Hurricane Sandy (2013). Buckley interviewed pest-control expert Timothy Wong, who noted that rat infestations could lead to citations for buildings that did not address the problem; yet, she reported, violations had decreased across the city in the wake of the hurricane—just 1996 violations versus 2750 for the same time period a year before. Why? Buckley explained: "After Hurricane Sandy, as of Nov. 1, the Health Department said it stopped issuing violations for rodents in Zone A," the parts of New York City most vulnerable to flooding.

a. If you were to create a monthly average of rat violations over the course of the year before and after Hurricane Sandy, why would you not be able to make comparisons?

b. Explain how the removal of Zone A violations led both to the removal of an outlier and to inaccurate data.

4.40 Outliers, H&M, and designer collaborations: The relatively low-cost Swedish fashion retailer H&M occasionally partners with high-end designers. For example, they collaborated with the designer Martin Margiela, and his line quickly sold out. If H&M were to report the average number of sales per item of clothing, why would the designer partnerships, like that with Martin Margiela, inflate the mean number of sales but not the median?

4.41 Central tendency and outliers from growth-chart data: When the average height or average weight of children is plotted to create growth charts, do you think it would be appropriate to use the mean for these data? There are often outliers for height, but

why might we not have to be concerned with their effect on these data?

4.42 Teaching assistants, race, and standard deviations: Researchers reported that the race of the teaching assistants (TAs) for a class had an effect on student outcome (Lusher, Campbell, & Carrell, 2015). They reported that "Asian students receive a 2.3% of a standard deviation increase in course grade when the racial composition of the TAs is entirely Asian. Similarly, non-Asian students see a 3.7% of a standard deviation increase in course grade when enrolled in a class with all non-Asian TAs." They hypothesized several reasons for this effect, including that students may see TAs of a similar race as inspiring or may simply be more comfortable learning from someone of the same race. Knowing what you know about standard deviations, explain this finding in your own words. Also, state whether this is a large effect, and explain your answer.

4.43 Mean versus median for age at first marriage: The mean age at first marriage was 31.1 for men and 29.1 for women in Canada in 2008 (http://www4.hrsdc.gc.ca/.3ndic.1t.4r@-eng.jsp?iid=78). The median age at first marriage was 28.9 for men and 26.9 for women in the United States in 2011 (http://factfinder.census.gov/faces/tableservices/jsf/pages/productview.xhtml?pid=ACS_11_1YR_B12007&prodType=table). Beyond the fact that these data are from slightly different years, explain why we cannot directly compare these measures of central tendency to make cross-national comparisons.

4.44 Median ages and technology companies: In an article titled "Technology Workers Are Young (Really Young)," the *New York Times* reported median ages for a number of companies (Hardy, 2013). The reporter wrote: "The seven companies with the youngest workers, ranked from youngest to highest in median age, were Epic Games (26); Facebook (28); Zynga (28); Google (29); and AOL, Blizzard Entertainment, InfoSys, and Monster.com (all 30). According to the Bureau of Labor Statistics, only shoe stores and restaurants have workers with a median age less than 30."

a. Explain why the reporter provided medians rather than means for employee ages.

b. Why might it be easier to use medians rather than means to compare ages across companies?

4.45 Standard deviation and a texting intervention for parents of preschoolers: Researchers investigated READY4K, a program in which parents received text messages over an 8-month period (York & Loeb, 2014). The goal of the text messages was to help parents prepare their preschool-aged children for reading. The children of parents who received the text messages were compared to a second group of children whose parents did not receive text messages. The researchers reported that the text messages led to "student learning gains in some areas of early literacy, ranging from approximately 0.21 to 0.34 standard deviations."

a. Based on your knowledge of mean and standard deviation, explain what this finding means.

b. Did the researchers use a between-groups design or a within-groups design? Explain your answer.

4.46 Range, world records, and a long chain of friendship bracelets: Guinness World Records reported that, as part of an anti-bullying campaign, elementary school students in Pennsylvania created a chain of friendship bracelets that was a world-record 2678 feet long (http://www.guinnessworldrecords.com/news/2013/5/fan-choice-record-may-17-48702/). Guinness relies on what kind of data for amazing claims like this one? How does this relate to the calculation of ranges?

Putting It All Together

4.47 Descriptive statistics and basketball wins: Here are the numbers of wins for the 30 National Basketball Association teams in the 2012–2013 season.

> 60 44 39 29 23 57 50 43 37 27
>
> 49 42 37 29 19 56 51 40 33 26
>
> 48 42 31 25 18 53 44 40 29 23

a. Create a grouped frequency table for these data.

b. Create a histogram based on the grouped frequency table.

c. Determine the mean, median, and mode of these data. Use symbols and the formula when showing your calculation of the mean.

d. Using software, calculate the range and standard deviation of these data.

e. Write a one- to two-paragraph summary describing the distribution of these data. Mention center, variability, and shape. Be sure to discuss the number

of modes (i.e., unimodal, bimodal, multimodal), any possible outliers, and the presence and direction of any skew.

f. State one research question that might arise from this data set.

4.48 Central tendency and outliers for data on traffic deaths: Below are estimated numbers of annual road traffic deaths for 12 countries based on data from the World Health Organization (http://apps.who.int/gho/data/view.main.51310):

Country	Number of Deaths
United States	35,490
Australia	1363
Canada	2296
Denmark	258
Finland	272
Germany	3830
Italy	4371
Japan	6625
Malaysia	7085
Portugal	1257
Spain	2478
Turkey	8758

a. Compute the mean and the median across these 12 data points.

b. Compute the range for these 12 data points.

c. Recalculate the statistics in part (a) and part (b) without the data point for the United States. How are these statistics affected by including or excluding the United States?

d. How might these numbers be affected by using traffic deaths per 100,000 people instead of using the number of traffic deaths overall?

e. Do you think that traffic deaths might vary by other personal or national characteristics? Could these represent confounds (as discussed in Chapter 1)?

TERMS

FORMULAS

$M = \dfrac{\Sigma X}{N}$ (p. 85)

$SD^2 = \dfrac{\Sigma(X - M)^2}{N}$ (p. 94)

$SD = \sqrt{\dfrac{\Sigma(X - M)^2}{N}}$ (p. 95)

Range $= X_{highest} - X_{lowest}$ (p. 92)

$SD = \sqrt{SD^2}$ (p. 95)

$IQR = Q3 - Q1$ (p. 96)

SYMBOLS

M	(p. 84)	Mdn	(p. 85)	SD	(p. 94)
$\bar{X}$	(p. 84)	SS	(p. 94)	s	(p. 94)
μ	(p. 84)	SD^2	(p. 94)	σ	(p. 94)
X	(p. 84)	s^2	(p. 94)	$Q1$	(p. 96)
Σ	(p. 85)	MS	(p. 94)	$Q3$	(p. 96)
N	(p. 85)	σ^2	(p. 94)	IQR	(p. 96)

Sampling and Probability

5

Samples and Their Populations

Random Sampling
Convenience Sampling
The Problem with a Biased Sample
Random Assignment

Probability

Coincidence and Probability
Expected Relative-Frequency Probability
Independence and Probability

Inferential Statistics

Developing Hypotheses
Making a Decision About a Hypothesis

Type I and Type II Errors

Type I Errors
Type II Errors

Next Steps: The Shocking Prevalence of Type I Errors

BEFORE YOU GO ON

- You should understand the difference between a sample and a population (Chapter 1).

- You should know how to measure central tendency, especially the mean (Chapter 4).

Work Smarter, Not Harder! Sampling is a way to do things more efficiently, based on principles that Lillian Gilbreth—a pioneer in the field of industrial and organizational psychology—and her husband Frank applied to raising a happy, if occasionally chaotic, family. Eleven of their twelve children are pictured here.

Lillian Gilbreth, a pioneer in the field of industrial and organizational psychology, was such an introverted little girl that her parents homeschooled her until she was 9 years old. That home was a busy place, and little Lillian, the eldest of 9 children, often filled in for her ill mother. The hectic pace of life that had begun during Lillian's childhood kept up for the rest of her life. She and her husband Frank Gilbreth, both of them efficiency experts, created a consulting business and had 12 children. The couple pioneered the use of filming people at work in order to analyze the motions needed to perform a task more efficiently, and applied those same principles to helping their children manage their lives more effectively. The family's lifestyle inspired two of the children to later write the book *Cheaper By the Dozen*, which also became a popular film.

After Frank died at a relatively young age, Lillian continued to support her family as an industrial consultant. She did this in an era that allowed only her husband's name to appear on the books they wrote together, out of fear of losing credibility if publishers advertised a female author! Frank had never earned a degree, but Lillian had a master's degree from the University of California, Berkeley, and a PhD from Brown.

The San Diego Supercomputer Center described Lillian Gilbreth as "a genius in the art of living." Her ability to think scientifically also helped her create small and large innovations for the home and workplace. Foot pedals on garbage cans? Thank Lillian Gilbreth. The "work triangle" in efficiency kitchens? Thank Lillian Gilbreth. The driving idea behind all these ideas was human efficiency. Efficiency is the driving idea behind sampling as well. Why work harder when an easier way is readily available? Why study 400,000 people if 400 people, sampled properly, will yield the same information?

- A **random sample** is one in which every member of the population has an equal chance of being selected into the study.

- A **convenience sample** is one that uses participants who are readily available.

5-1: There are two main types of samples in social science research. In the ideal type (a random sample), every member of the population has an equal chance of being selected to participate in a study. In the less ideal but more common type (a convenience sample), researchers use participants who are readily available.

Samples and Their Populations

Almost everything worth evaluating requires a sample, from voting trends to sales patterns to the effectiveness of flu vaccines. The goal of sampling is simple: Collect a sample that represents the population. As Lillian Gilbreth reminds us, efficient living and efficient sampling are both possible—and far easier in theory than they are in practice.

There are two main types of samples: random samples and convenience samples. *A **random sample** is one in which every member of the population has an equal chance of being selected into the study. A **convenience sample** is one that uses participants who are readily available,* such as college students. A random sample remains the ideal and is far more likely to lead to a representative sample, but it is usually expensive and can present a lot of practical problems. It is often almost impossible to get access to every member of the population in order to choose a random sample from among them. Technologies such as Amazon Mechanical Turk, SurveyMonkey, and many other Internet tools offer new ways of obtaining convenience samples from a more diverse sample of participants.

Random Sampling

Imagine that there has recently been a traumatic mass murder in a town and that there are exactly 80 officers in the town's police department. You have been hired to determine whether peer counseling or professional counseling is the more effective way to address the department's concerns in the aftermath of this trauma. Unfortunately, budget constraints dictate that the sample you can recruit must be very small—just 10 people. How do you maximize the probability that 10 officers will accurately represent the larger population of 80 officers?

Here's one way: Assign each of the 80 officers a number, from 01 to 80. Next, use a random numbers table (Table 5-1) to choose a sample of 10 police officers. Then, (a) select any point on the table; (b) go across, back, up, or down to read through the numbers. For example, say you begin with the 6th number of the second row of Table 5-1 and count across. The first 10 numbers read: 97654 64501. (The spaces between sets of five numbers are included solely to make it easier to read the table.) The first pair of digits is 97, but we would ignore this number because we only have 80 people in the population. The next pair is 65. The 65th police officer in the list would be chosen for the sample. The next two pairs, 46 and 45, would also be in the sample, followed by 01. If we come across a number a second time—45, for example—we ignore it, just as we would ignore 00 and anything above 80. Stick to your decision—you can't rule out Officer Diaz because she seems to be adjusting well on her own or rule in Officer McIntyre because you think he needs the help right away.

Were you surprised that random sampling selected both the number 46 and the number 45? *Truly random numbers often have strings of numbers that do not seem to be random.* For example, notice the string of three 3's in the third row of the table.

You can also search online for a "random numbers generator," which is how we came up with the following numbers: 10, 23, 27, 34, 36, 67, 70, 74, 77, and 78. You might be surprised that 4 of the 10 numbers were in the 70s. Don't be. Random numbers are truly random, even if they don't look random.

Random samples are almost never used in the social sciences because we almost never have access to the whole population. For example, if we were interested in studying the eating behavior of voles, we could never list the whole population of voles from which to then select a random sample. If we were interested in studying the effect of video games on the attention span of teenagers in the United Kingdom, we could never identify all U.K. teenagers from which to choose a random sample.

TABLE 5-1	Hypothesis Testing: Hypotheses and Decisions

This is a small section from a random numbers table used to randomly select participants from a population, as well as to randomly assign participants to experimental conditions.

04493	52494	75246	33824	45862	51025	61962
00549	97654	64501	88159	96119	63896	54692
35963	15307	26898	09354	33351	35462	77974
59808	08391	45427	26842	83609	49700	46058

Random Dots? True randomness often does not seem random. British artist Damien Hirst farms out the actual painting of many of his works, such as his famous dot paintings, to assistants. He provides his assistants with instructions, including to arrange the color dots randomly. One assistant painted a series of yellow dots next to each other, which led to a fight with Hirst, who said, "I told him those aren't random.... Now I realize he was right, and I was wrong" (Vogel, 2011).

Matthew Lloyd/Getty Images

Convenience Sampling

It is far more convenient (faster, easier, and cheaper) to use voles that we bought from an animal supply company or to gather teenagers from the local school than to take the time to recruit a representative sample—but there is a significant downside. A convenience sample might not represent the larger population. *Generalizability refers to researchers' ability to apply findings from one sample or in one context to other samples or contexts.* This principle is also called *external validity*, and it is extremely important—why bother doing the study if it doesn't apply to anyone else?

Fortunately, we can increase external validity through **replication,** *the duplication of scientific results, ideally in a different context or with a sample that has different characteristics* (sometimes called *reproducibility*). In other words, do the study again. And again. Then ask someone else to replicate it, too. That's the slow but trustworthy process by which science creates knowledge that is both reliable and valid. That's also why some of the real "scientific breakthroughs" you hear about are really just the tipping point based on many smaller research discoveries.

Liars' Alert! We must be even more cautious when we use a *volunteer sample* (also called a *self-selected sample*), *a convenience sample in which participants actively choose to participate in a study.* Participants volunteer, or self-select, when they respond to recruitment flyers or choose to complete an online survey, such as polls that recruit people to vote for a favorite reality show contestant or hockey team. We see volunteer samples in psychology research more and more as crowdsourcing becomes more popular. Crowdsourcing in research occurs when a research team solicits input from a very large group of people, usually recruited online. In one example, researchers collected data from those who played an online game called Airport Scanner (learn about the app here: https://www.airportscannergame.com/; Mitroff, Biggs, Adamo, Dowd, Winkle, & Clark, 2015). In this study, literally millions of participants searched for dangerous items, like dynamite, that only rarely showed up. The billions—yes, billions—of data points that resulted allowed researchers to understand what affects our ability to visually search for rare occurrences. On the one hand, only with the Internet can we have so many participants and data points. On the other hand, we must be cautious because, as summarized by a journalist, these researchers explained that "collecting data through crowdsourcing means researchers have no control over who is playing" (APA, 2014).

Amazon Mechanical Turk (http://www.MTurk.com; MTurk) is an online network where anyone can recruit people to complete tasks for a small fee. For psychology,

● **Generalizability** refers to researchers' ability to apply findings from one sample or in one context to other samples or contexts; also called *external validity*.

● **Replication** refers to the duplication of scientific results, ideally in a different context or with a sample that has different characteristics (sometimes called *reproducibility*).

● A **volunteer sample**, or *self-selected sample*, is a special kind of convenience sample in which participants actively choose to participate in a study.

MTurk is becoming a common place for researchers to sample a more representative group of research participants. Anyone can sign up for a free account, provide basic demographic information, and participate in online surveys for monetary payment. There has been some discussion about the validity and reliability of sampling participants in this way (e.g., Buhrmester, Kwang, & Gosling, 2011). However, it seems as though sampling using MTurk eliminates the bias of sampling only college students, which is often the convenience sampling option for many psychological researchers. Despite this advantage, MTurk and other tools like it are still volunteer sampling procedures. The Society for Personality and Social Psychology (SPSP) provides a link of other common crowdsourcing tools used for online data collection (http://spsp.org/node/654), including outlets like Reddit and Craigslist.

Are Testimonials Trustworthy Evidence? Does one woman's positive experience with Sephora by OPI nail polish—"made my nails stronger"—provide evidence that this product actually strengthens nails? Testimonials use a volunteer sample of one person, usually a biased person. Data from a larger, representative sample is always more reliable than a sample of one.

Although online recruitment tools are convenient for researchers, the limitations of using an online volunteer sample remain. Volunteer samples may be very different from a randomly selected sample. The information that volunteer participants provide may not represent the larger population that we are really interested in. Think about the crowdsourcing example. How might people who play Airport Scanner online be different from the general population?

The Problem with a Biased Sample

Let's be blunt: If you don't understand sampling, then you make it easy for others to take advantage of you. For example, the Web site Viewpoint provides a forum for consumer reviews of products ranging from laundry detergent to cameras. Viewpoint has a page devoted to Sephora by OPI nail polish, a brand that offers colors with clever names like "I'm with Brad," "Read My Palm," and "Never Enough Shoes." A reviewer from Beverly Hills, California, calling herself catdoganimal, recommended the polish and wrote "It lasts for more than a week without chipping. Made my nails stronger." Let's examine the flaws in this sample of "evidence"—a brief testimonial—for the supposed long-lasting, nail-strengthening nature of the Sephora by OPI polish.

The population of interest is women who use Sephora by OPI nail polish. The sample is the one woman who posted a review. But there are two major problems with this sample. First, one person is not a trustworthy sample size. Second, this is a volunteer sample. The customer who had this experience chose to post a review. Was she likely to do so if she did not feel very strongly about this product? The nail polish may be amazing and catdoganimal likely truly loves it, but a single testimonial from a probable animal lover from California doesn't provide trustworthy evidence. In fact, when we scouted out other testimonials for this product, there was much disagreement about the pros and cons of Sephora by OPI polish.

Self-selection is a major problem, but all is not lost! We could randomly assign a certain number of people to use Sephora by OPI nail polish and an equal number of people to use another product, then see which group had longer-lasting color as well as which group had stronger nails over time. Which do you find more persuasive: a dubious testimonial or a well-designed experiment? If our honest answer is a dubious testimonial, then statistical reasoning once again leads us to ask a better question (nicely answered by social psychologists, by the way) about why anecdotes are sometimes more persuasive than science.

Random Assignment

Random assignment is the distinctive signature of a scientific study. Why? Because it levels the playing field when every participant has an equal chance of being assigned to any level of the independent variable. Random assignment is different from random selection. Random selection is the ideal way to gather a sample from a population; random assignment is what we do with participants once they have been recruited into a study, regardless of how they got there. Practical problems related to getting access to an entire population mean that random *selection* is almost never used; however, random *assignment* is used whenever possible—and solves many of the problems associated with a convenience sample.

Random assignment involves procedures similar to those used for random selection. If a study has two levels of the independent variable, as in the study of police officers, then you would need to assign participants to one of two groups. You could decide, arbitrarily, to number the groups 0 and 1 for the "peer counseling" and "therapist counseling" groups, respectively. Then, (a) select any point on the table; (b) go across, back, up, or down to read through the numbers—and remember to stick to your decision.

For example, if you began at the first number of the last row of Table 5-1 and read the numbers across, ignoring any number but 0 or 1, you would find 0010000. The first two participants would thus be in group 0, the third would be in group 1, and the next four would be in group 0. (Again, notice the seemingly nonrandom pattern and remember that it *is* random.)

An online random numbers generator lets us tell the computer to give us one set of 10 numbers that range from 0 to 1. We would instruct the program that the numbers should *not* remain unique because we want multiple 0's and multiple 1's. In addition, we would request that the numbers not be sorted because we want to assign participants in the order in which the numbers are generated. When we used an online random numbers generator, the 10 numbers were 1110100001. In an experiment, we usually want equal numbers in the groups. If the numbers were not exactly half 1's and half 0's, as they are in this case, we could decide in advance to use only the first five 1's or the first five 0's. Just be sure to establish your rule for random assignment ahead of time and then stick to it!

CHECK YOUR LEARNING

Reviewing the Concepts

> Data from a sample are used to draw conclusions about the larger population.

> In random sampling, every member of the population has an equal chance of being selected for the sample.

> In the behavioral sciences, convenience samples are far more common than random samples.

> Random numbers may not always appear to be all that random; there may appear to be patterns.

> In random assignment, every participant has an equal chance of being assigned to one of the experimental conditions.

> If a study that uses random assignment is replicated in several contexts, we can start to generalize the findings.

Clarifying the Concepts   **5-1**   What are the risks of sampling?

Calculating the Statistics	**5-2**	Use the excerpt from the random numbers table (Table 5-1) on page 109 to select 6 people out of a sample of 80. Start by assigning each person a number from 01 to 80. Then select 6 of these people by starting in the fourth row and going across. List the numbers of the 6 people who were selected.
	5-3	Use the excerpt from Table 5-1 to randomly assign these six people to one of two experimental conditions, numbered 0 and 1. This time, start at the top of the first column (with a 0 on top) and go down. When you get to the bottom of that column, start at the top of the second column (with a 4 on top). Using the numbers (0 and 1), list the order in which these people would be assigned to conditions.

Applying the Concepts	**5-4**	For each of the following scenarios, state whether, from a practical standpoint, random selection could have been used. Explain your answer, including in it a description of the population to which the researcher likely wants to generalize. Then state whether random assignment could have been used, and explain your answer.
		a. A health psychologist examined whether postoperative recovery time was shorter among patients who received counseling prior to surgery than among those who did not.
		b. The head of a school board asked a school psychologist to examine whether children perform better in history classes if they use an online textbook as opposed to a printed textbook.
Solutions to these Check Your Learning questions can be found in Appendix D.		c. A clinical psychologist studied whether people with diagnosed personality disorders were more likely to miss therapy appointments than were people without diagnosed personality disorders.

Probability

You have probably heard phrases such as "the margin of error" or "plus or minus 3 percentage points," especially during an election season. These are another way of saying, "We're not 100% sure that we can believe our own results." This could make you cynical about statistics—you do all this work, and then you still don't know if you can trust your data.

You would be more justified, however, in celebrating statistics for being so truthful—statistics allows us to quantify the uncertainty. And let's be honest—most of life is filled with uncertainty, whether it's the quality of the jacket that has the high quality YKK zipper, the number of days your nail polish lasts without chipping, or the most efficient way for a worker to perform a task. Probability is central to inferential statistics because our conclusions about a population are based on data collected from a sample rather than on anecdotes and testimonials.

Coincidence and Probability

Probability and statistical reasoning can save us from ourselves when, for example, we are confronted with eerie coincidences. Two personal biases get intertwined in our thinking so that we say with genuine astonishment, "Wow! What are the chances of that?" **Confirmation bias** *is our usually unintentional tendency to pay attention to evidence that confirms what we already believe and to ignore evidence that would disconfirm our beliefs.* It is a confirmation bias when an athlete attributes her team's wins to her lucky earrings, ignoring any losses while wearing them or any wins while wearing other earrings. Confirmation biases closely follow illusory correlations. **Illusory correlation** *is the phenomenon of believing one sees an association between variables when no such association exists.* An athlete with a confirmation bias attributing wins to her lucky earrings now believes an illusory correlation. We invite illusory correlations into our lives whenever we ignore the gentle, restraining logic of statistical reasoning.

- **Confirmation bias** is our usually unintentional tendency to pay attention to evidence that confirms what we already believe and to ignore evidence that would disconfirm our beliefs. Confirmation biases closely follow illusory correlations.

- **Illusory correlation** is the phenomenon of believing one sees an association between variables when no such association exists.

Nelly the Elephant Amazingly, an elephant named Nelly seemed to be a star predictor of sports outcomes. One glowing report boasted that "after predicting 30 of 33 [soccer] results correctly…Nelly seems to be nothing short of a football 'pundit'" (NDTV Sports, 2014). Sadly, all of the press went away when neither Nelly nor her rivals—a piranha named Pele, a pair of armadillos, and an otter named Ferret—fared well in predicting the men's World Cup in 2014 (Reuters, 2014). This failure led to just one headline that explained "animals no longer able to predict World Cup correctly" (Reuters, 2014). Almost no one seemed to care about Nelly's prediction failures. Moreover, it's not at all surprising that there will occasionally be an animal with a lucky streak. As University of Cambridge statistics professor David Spiegelharter pointed out such feats are not that remarkable if you consider all of the animals who have tried and failed to predict sports wins over the years (Shenker, 2010).

MASTERING THE CONCEPT

5-3: Human biases result from two closely related concepts. When we notice only evidence that confirms what we already believe and ignore evidence that refutes what we already believe, we're succumbing to the confirmation bias. Confirmation biases often follow illusory correlations—when we believe we see an association between two variables, but no association exists.

● **Personal probability** is a person's own judgment about the likelihood that an event will occur; also called *subjective probability*.

● **Probability** is the likelihood that a particular outcome—out of all possible outcomes—will occur.

● The **expected relative-frequency probability** is the likelihood of an event occurring based on the actual outcome of many, many trials.

For example, the science show *Radiolab* told a remarkable story of coincidence (Abumrad & Krulwich, 2009). A 10-year-old girl named Laura Buxton released a red balloon from her hometown in the north of England. "Almost 10," Laura corrected the host. Laura had written her address on the balloon as well as an entreaty: "Please return to Laura Buxton." The balloon traveled 140 miles to the south of England and was found by a neighbor of another 10-year-old girl, also named Laura Buxton! The second Laura wrote to the first, and they arranged to meet. They both showed up to their meeting wearing jeans and pink sweaters. They were both the same height, had brown hair; and owned a black Labrador retriever, a gray rabbit, and a brown guinea pig with an orange spot. In fact, each brought her guinea pig to the meeting. At the time of the radio broadcast, they were 18 years old and friends. "Maybe we were meant to meet," one of the Laura Buxtons speculated. "If it was just the wind, it was a very, very lucky wind," said the other.

The chances seem unbelievably slim, but confirmation bias and illusory correlations both play a role here—and probability helps us understand why such coincidences happen. The thing is, coincidences are *not* unlikely. We notice and remember strange coincidences, but do not notice the uncountable times in which there are not unlikely occurrences—the background, so to speak. We remember unusual stories of coincidences and luck, like that of the great-grandmother who won the lottery by playing the numbers in the fortune cookie that came with her Chinese take-out (Rosario & Sutherland, 2014). But we forget the many times we bought lottery tickets and lost—and the millions of people who did the same.

The *Radiolab* story described this phenomenon as the "blade of grass paradox." Imagine a golfer hitting a ball that flies way down the fairway and lands on a blade of grass. The radio show imagines the blade of grass saying: "Wow. What are the odds that that ball, out of all the billions of blades of grass … just landed on me?" Yet we know that there's almost a 100% chance that some blade of grass was going to be crushed by that ball. It just seems miraculous to the individual blade of grass—or to the lottery winner.

Let's go back to our story about the Laura Buxtons. A statistician pointed out that the details were "manipulated" to make for a better story. The host had remembered that they were both 10 years old, yet the first Laura reminded him she was still 9 at the time ("almost 10"). The host also admitted there were many discrepancies—one's favorite color was pink and one's was blue, and they had opposite academic interests—biology, chemistry, and geography for one and English, history, and classical civilization for the other. Further, it was not the second Laura Buxton who found the balloon; rather, it was her neighbor. The similarities make a better story. When you add probability to confirmation bias and illusory correlation, they become the WOW! details that we remember—but it's still just another blade of grass. Still not convinced? Read on.

HOLGER HOLLEMANN/AFP/Getty Images

Expected Relative-Frequency Probability

When we discuss probability in everyday conversation, we tend to think of what statisticians call **personal probability**: *a person's own judgment about the likelihood that an event will occur*; also called *subjective probability*. We might say something like "There's a 75% chance I'll finish my paper and go out tonight." We don't mean that the chance we'll go out is precisely 75%. Rather, this is our rating of our confidence that this event will occur. It's really just our best guess.

Mathematicians and statisticians, however, use the word *probability* a bit differently. Statisticians are concerned with a different type of probability, one that is more objective. In a general sense, **probability** *is the likelihood that a particular outcome—out of all possible outcomes—will occur*. For example, we might talk about the likelihood of getting heads (a particular outcome) if we flip a coin 10 times (all possible outcomes). We use probability because we usually have access only to a sample (10 flips of a coin) when we want to know about an entire population (all possible flips of a coin).

Language Alert! In statistics, we are interested in an even more specific definition of probability—**expected relative-frequency probability**, *the likelihood of an event occurring, based on the actual outcome of many, many trials*. When flipping a coin, the expected relative-frequency probability of heads, in the long run, is 0.50. Probability refers to the likelihood that something would take place, and frequency refers to how often a given outcome (e.g., heads or tails) occurs out of a certain number of trials (e.g., coin flips). *Relative* indicates that this number is relative to the overall number of trials, and *expected* indicates that it's what we would anticipate, which might be different from what actually happens.

In reference to probability, the term **trial** *refers to each occasion that a given procedure is carried out*. For example, each time we flip a coin, it is a trial. **Outcome** *refers to the result of a trial*. For coin-flip trials, the outcome is either heads or tails. **Success** *refers to the outcome for which we're trying to determine the probability*. If we are testing for the probability of heads, then success is heads.

MASTERING THE CONCEPT

5-4: In everyday life, we use the word *probability* very loosely—saying how likely a given outcome is, in our subjective judgment. Statisticians are referring to something very particular when they refer to probability. For statisticians, probability is the actual likelihood of a given outcome in the long run.

© Eyebyte/Alamy

Determining Probabilities To determine the probability of heads, we would have to conduct many trials (coin flips), record the outcomes (either heads or tails), and determine the proportion of successes (in this case, heads).

EXAMPLE 5.1

We can think of probability in terms of a formula. We calculate probability by dividing the total number of successes by the total number of trials. So the formula would look like this:

$$\text{probability} = \frac{\text{successes}}{\text{trials}}$$

If we flip a coin 2000 times and get 1000 heads, then:

$$\text{probability} = \frac{1000}{2000} = 0.50$$

Here is a recap of the steps to calculate probability:

> **STEP 1: Determine the total number of trials.**

> **STEP 2: Determine the number of these trials that are considered successful outcomes.**

> **STEP 3: Divide the number of successful outcomes by the number of trials.**

- In reference to probability, a trial refers to each occasion that a given procedure is carried out.

- In reference to probability, outcome refers to the result of a trial.

- In reference to probability, success refers to the outcome for which we're trying to determine the probability.

People often confuse the terms *probability*, *proportion*, and *percentage*. Probability, the concept of most interest to us right now, is the proportion that we expect to see in the long run. Proportion is the number of successes divided by the number of trials. In the short run, in just a few trials, the proportion might not reflect the underlying probability. A coin flipped six times might come up heads more or fewer than three times, leading to a proportion of heads that does not parallel the underlying probability of heads. Both proportions and probabilities are written as decimals.

Percentage is simply probability or proportion multiplied by 100. A flipped coin has a 0.50 probability of coming up heads and a 50% chance of coming up heads. You are probably already familiar with percentages, so simply keep in mind that probabilities are what we would expect in the long run, whereas proportions are what we observe.

One of the central characteristics of expected relative-frequency probability is that it only works in the long run. This is an important aspect of probability, and it is referred to as the *law of large numbers*. Think of the earlier discussion of random assignment in which we used a random numbers generator to create a series of 0's and 1's to assign participants to levels of the independent variable. In the short run, over just a few trials, we can get strings of 0's and 1's and often do not end up with half 0's and half 1's, even though that is the underlying probability. With many trials, however, we're much more likely to get close to 0.50, or 50%, of each, although many strings of 0's or 1's would be generated along the way. In the long run, the results are quite predictable. ●

Independence and Probability

Language Alert! To avoid bias, statistical probability requires that the individual trials be *independent*, one of the favorite words of statisticians. Here we use *independent* to mean that the outcome of each trial must not depend in any way on the outcome of previous trials. If we're flipping a coin, then each coin flip is independent of every other coin flip. If we're generating a random numbers list to select participants, each number must be generated without thought to the previous numbers. In fact, this is exactly why humans can't think randomly. We automatically glance at the previous numbers we have generated in order to best make the next one "random." Chance has no memory, and randomness is, therefore, the only way to assure that there is no bias.

Gambling and Misperceptions of Probability Many people falsely believe that a slot machine that has not paid off in a long time is "due." A person may continue to feed coins into it, expecting an imminent payout. Of course, the slot machine itself, unless rigged, has no memory of its previous outcomes. Each trial is independent of the others.

Sylvia Serrado/Photolibrary/Getty Images

CHECK YOUR LEARNING

Reviewing the Concepts

> Probability theory helps us understand that coincidences might not have an underlying meaning; coincidences *are* probable when we think of the vast number of occurrences in the world (billions of interactions between people daily).

> An illusory correlation refers to perceiving a connection where none exists. It is often followed by a confirmation bias, whereby we notice occurrences that fit with our preconceived ideas and fail to notice those that do not.

> Personal probability refers to a person's own judgment about the likelihood that an event will occur (also called subjective probability).

> Expected relative-frequency probability is the likelihood of an event occurring, based on the actual outcome of many, many trials.

> The probability of an event occurring is defined as the expected number of successes (the number of times the event occurred) out of the total number of trials (or attempts) over the long run.

> Proportions over the short run might have many different outcomes, whereas proportions over the long run are more indicative of the underlying probabilities.

Clarifying the Concepts	5-5	Distinguish the personal probability assessments we perform on a daily basis from the objective probability that statisticians use.

Calculating the Statistics	5-6	Calculate the probability for each of the following instances.

    a. 100 trials, 5 successes

    b. 50 trials, 8 successes

    c. 1044 trials, 130 successes

Applying the Concepts	5-7	Consider a scenario in which a student wonders whether men or women are more likely to use the banking machine (ATM) in the student center. He decides to observe those who use the banking machine. (Assume that there is an equal number of men and women who use the banking machine.)

Solutions to these Check Your Learning questions can be found in Appendix D.

    a. Define success as a woman using the banking machine on a given trial. What proportion of successes might this student expect to observe in the short run?

    b. What might this student expect to observe in the long run?

Inferential Statistics

In Chapter 1, we introduced the two main branches of statistics—descriptive statistics and inferential statistics. The link that connects the two branches is probability. Descriptive statistics allow us to summarize characteristics of the sample, but we must use probability with inferential statistics when we apply what we've learned from the sample, such as in an exit poll, to the larger population. Inferential statistics, calculated through a process called hypothesis testing, helps us to determine the probability of a given outcome.

Developing Hypotheses

We informally develop and test hypotheses all the time. I hypothesize that the traffic will be heavy on Western Avenue, so I take a parallel street to work and keep looking down each block to see if my hypothesis is being supported. In a science blog, *TierneyLab*, reporter John Tierney and his collaborators asked people to estimate the number of calories in a meal pictured in a photograph (Tierney, 2008a, 2008b). One group was shown a photo of an Applebee's Oriental Chicken Salad and a Pepsi. Another group was shown a photo of the same salad and Pepsi, but it also included a third item—Fortt's crackers, with a label that clearly stated "Trans Fat Free." The researchers hypothesized

MASTERING THE CONCEPT

5-5: Many experiments have an experimental group in which participants receive the treatment or intervention of interest and a control group in which participants do not receive the treatment or intervention of interest. Aside from the intervention with the experimental group, the two groups are treated identically.

Craig Warga/Bloomberg via Getty Images

The Control Burrito You can spot control groups in everyday life. Intern Dylan Grosz describes heaven as "one big Chipotle restaurant where the guac and chips are ALWAYS free" (2015). On a budget, he made it his mission to figure out how to get the most Chipotle for the money. He started by identifying his "control burrito." It included rice, beans, chicken, salsa, and cheese. He then ordered 35 burritos over two weeks—five of each variation—and compared these experimental groups to his control burrito. He identified six tricks that, together, increased the average burrito weight by 86%! Among the tricks, order both kinds of rice and both kinds of beans.

- A **control group** is a level of the independent variable that does not receive the treatment of interest in a study. It is designed to match an experimental group in all ways but the experimental manipulation itself.

- An **experimental group** is a level of the independent variable that receives the treatment or intervention of interest in an experiment.

MASTERING THE CONCEPT

5-6: Hypothesis testing allows us to examine two competing hypotheses. The first, the null hypothesis, posits that there is no difference between populations or that any difference is in the opposite direction from what is predicted. The second, the research hypothesis, posits that there is a difference between populations (or that the difference between populations is in a predicted direction—either higher or lower).

that the addition of the "healthy" food item would affect people's calorie estimates of the entire meal. They tested a sample and used probability to apply their findings from the sample to the population.

Let's put this study in the language of sampling and probability. The sample comprised people living in the Park Slope neighborhood of Brooklyn in New York City, an area that Tierney terms "nutritionally correct" because of the abundance of organic food in local stores. The population would include all the residents of Park Slope who could have been part of this study. The driving concern behind this research was the increasing levels of obesity in many wealthier countries (something that Tierney explored in a follow-up study). For now, however, we can only infer that the results may apply to the residents of Park Slope and similar neighborhoods. The independent variable in this case is the presence or absence of the healthy crackers in the photo of the meal. The dependent variable is the number of calories estimated.

The group that viewed the photo *without* the healthy crackers is the **control group**, *a level of the independent variable that does not receive the treatment of interest in a study.* It is designed to match the **experimental group**— *a level of the independent variable that receives the treatment or intervention of interest*—in all ways but the experimental manipulation itself. In this example, the experimental group would be those viewing the photo that included the healthy crackers.

The next step is the development of the hypotheses to be tested. Ideally, this is done before the data from the sample are actually collected; you will see this pattern of developing hypotheses and then collecting data repeated throughout this book. When we calculate inferential statistics, we're actually comparing two hypotheses. One is the **null hypothesis**—*a statement that postulates that there is no difference between populations or that the difference is in a direction opposite to that anticipated by the researcher.* In most circumstances, we can think of the null hypothesis as the boring hypothesis because it proposes that nothing will happen. In the healthy food study, the null hypothesis is that the average (mean) calorie estimate is the same for both populations, which are comprised of all the people in Park Slope who either view or do not view the photo with the healthy crackers.

In contrast to the null hypothesis, the research hypothesis is usually the exciting hypothesis. The **research hypothesis** (also called the *alternative hypothesis*) *is a statement that postulates a difference between populations.* In the healthy food study, the research hypothesis would be that, on average, the calorie estimate is different for those viewing the photo with the healthy crackers than for those viewing the photo without the healthy crackers. It also could specify a direction—that the mean calorie estimate is higher (or lower) for those viewing the photo with the healthy crackers than for those viewing the photo with just the salad and Pepsi. Notice that, for all hypotheses, we are very careful to state the comparison group. We do not say merely that the group viewing the photo with the healthy crackers has a higher (or lower) average calorie estimate. We say that it has a higher (or lower) average calorie estimate *than* the group that views the photo without the healthy crackers.

We formulate the null hypothesis and research hypothesis to set them up against each other. We use statistics to determine the probability that there is a large enough difference between the means of the samples that we can conclude there's likely a difference between the means of the underlying populations. So, probability plays into the decision we make about the hypotheses.

Making a Decision About a Hypothesis

When we make a conclusion at the end of a study, the data lead us to conclude one of two things:

1. We decide to *reject* the null hypothesis.
2. We decide to *fail to reject* the null hypothesis.

We always begin our reasoning about the outcome of an experiment by reminding ourselves that we are testing the (boring) null hypothesis. In terms of the healthy food study, the null hypothesis is that there is no mean difference between groups. In hypothesis testing, we determine the probability that we would see a difference between the means of the samples, given that there is no actual difference between the underlying population means.

- The **null hypothesis** is a statement that postulates that there is no difference between populations or that the difference is in a direction opposite of that anticipated by the researcher.

- The **research hypothesis** is a statement that postulates that there is a difference between populations or sometimes, more specifically, that there is a difference in a certain direction, positive or negative; also called an *alternative hypothesis*.

••

EXAMPLE 5.2

After we analyze the data, we do one of two things:

1. *Reject the null hypothesis.* "I reject the idea that there is no mean difference between populations." When we reject the null hypothesis that there is *no mean difference*, we can even assert what we believe the difference to be, based on the actual findings. We can say that it seems that people who view a photo of a salad, Pepsi, and healthy crackers estimate a lower (or higher, depending on what we found in our study) number of calories, on average, than those who view a photo with only the salad and Pepsi.

2. *Fail to reject the null hypothesis.* "I do not reject the idea that there is no mean difference between populations." In this case, we can only say that we do not have evidence to support our hypothesis.

Let's take the first possible conclusion, to reject the null hypothesis. If the group that viewed the photo that included the healthy crackers has a mean calorie estimate that is a good deal higher (or lower) than the control group's mean calorie estimate, then we might be tempted to say that we *accept* the research hypothesis that there is such a mean difference in the populations—that the addition of the healthy crackers makes a difference. Probability plays a central role in determining that the mean difference is large enough that we're willing to say it's real. But rather than *accept* the *research* hypothesis in this case, we *reject* the *null* hypothesis, the one that suggests there is nothing going on. We repeat: When the data suggest that there *is* a mean difference, we *reject* the idea that there is no mean difference.

The second possible conclusion is failing to reject the null hypothesis. There's a very good reason for thinking about this in terms of failing to reject the null hypothesis rather than accepting the null hypothesis. Let's say there's a small mean difference, and we conclude that we cannot reject the null hypothesis (remember, rejecting the null hypothesis is what we want to do!). We determine that it's just not likely enough—or probable enough—that the difference between means is real. It could be that a real difference between means didn't show up in this particular sample just by chance. There are many ways in which a real mean difference in the population might not get picked up by a sample. We repeat: When the data do not suggest a difference, we *fail to reject* the null hypothesis, which is that there is no mean difference.

TABLE 5-2	Hypothesis Testing: Hypotheses and Decisions

The null hypothesis posits no difference, on average, whereas the research hypothesis posits a difference of some kind. There are only two decisions we can make. We can fail to reject the null hypothesis if the research hypothesis is *not* supported, or we can reject the null hypothesis if the research hypothesis *is* supported.

	Hypothesis	Decision
Null hypothesis	No change or difference	Fail to reject the null hypothesis (if research hypothesis is not supported)
Research hypothesis	Change or difference	Reject the null hypothesis (if research hypothesis is supported)

The way we decide whether to reject the null hypothesis is based directly on probability. We calculate the probability that the data would produce a difference between means this large and in a sample of this size *if* there was nothing going on.

We will be giving you many more opportunities to get comfortable with the logic of formal hypothesis testing before we start applying numbers to it, but here are three easy rules and a table (Table 5-2) that will help keep you on track.

1. Remember: The null hypothesis is that there is no difference between groups, and usually the hypotheses explore the possibility of a *mean* difference.
2. We either *reject* or *fail to reject* the null hypothesis. There are no other options.
3. We never use the word *accept* in reference to formal hypothesis testing.

Hypothesis testing is exciting when you care about the results. You may wonder what happened in Tierney's study. Well, people who saw the photo with just the salad and the Pepsi estimated, on average, that the 934-calorie meal contained 1011 calories. When the 100-calorie crackers were added, the meal actually increased from 934 calories to 1034 calories; however, those who viewed this photo estimated, on average, that the meal contained only 835 calories! Tierney referred to this effect as "a health halo that magically subtracted calories from the rest of the meal." Interestingly, he replicated this study with mostly foreign tourists in New York's Times Square and did not find this effect. He concluded that health-conscious people like those living in Park Slope were more susceptible to the magical health halo bias than were other people. ●

CHECK YOUR LEARNING

Reviewing the Concepts

> In experiments, we typically compare the average of the responses of those who receive the treatment or manipulation (the experimental group) with the average of the responses of similar people who do not receive the manipulation (the control group).

> Researchers develop two hypotheses: a null hypothesis, which theorizes that there is no average difference between levels of an independent variable in the population, and a research hypothesis, which theorizes that there is an average difference of some kind in the population.

> Researchers can draw two conclusions: They can reject the null hypothesis and conclude that they have supported the research hypothesis or they can fail to reject the null hypothesis and conclude that they have not supported the research hypothesis.

Clarifying the Concepts   5-8   At the end of a study, what does it mean to reject the null hypothesis?

Calculating the Statistics	5-9	State the difference that might be expected, based on the null hypothesis, between the average test grades of students who attend review sessions versus those who do not.

Applying the Concepts	5-10	A university lowers the heat during the winter to save money, and professors wonder whether students will perform more poorly, on average, under cold conditions.

a. Cite the likely null hypothesis for this study.

b. Cite the likely research hypothesis.

c. If the cold temperature appears to decrease academic performance, on average, what will the researchers conclude in terms of formal hypothesis-testing language?

Solutions to these Check Your Learning questions can be found in Appendix D.

d. If the researchers do not gather sufficient evidence to conclude that the cold temperature leads to decreased academic performance, on average, what will they conclude in terms of formal hypothesis-testing language?

Type I and Type II Errors

Wrong decisions can be the result of unrepresentative samples. However, even when sampling has been properly conducted, there are still two ways to make a wrong decision: 1) We can reject the null hypothesis when we *should not* have rejected it, or 2) we can fail to reject the null hypothesis when we *should* have rejected it. So let's consider the two types of errors using statistical language.

Type I Errors

If we reject the null hypothesis, but it was a mistake to do so, then we have made a Type I error. Specifically, *we commit a **Type I error** when we reject the null hypothesis but the null hypothesis is correct.* A Type I error is like a false positive in a medical test. For example, if a woman believes she might be pregnant, then she might buy a home pregnancy test. In this case, the null hypothesis would be that she is not pregnant, and the research hypothesis would be that she is pregnant. If the test is positive, the woman rejects the null hypothesis—the one in which she theorizes that she is not pregnant. Based on the test, the woman believes she is pregnant. Pregnancy tests, however, are not perfect. If the woman tests positive and rejects the null hypothesis, it is possible that she is wrong and it is a false positive. Based on the test, the woman believes she is pregnant even though she is not pregnant. A false positive is equivalent to a Type I error.

A Type I error indicates that we rejected the null hypothesis falsely. As you might imagine, the rejection of the null hypothesis typically leads to action, at least until we discover that it is an error. For example, the woman with a false-positive pregnancy test might announce the news to her family and start buying baby clothes. Many researchers consider the consequences of a Type I error to be particularly detrimental because people often take action based on a mistaken finding.

Type II Errors

If we fail to reject the null hypothesis but it was a mistake to fail to do so, then we have made a Type II error. Specifically, *we commit a **Type II error** when we fail to reject the null*

● A **Type I error** involves rejecting the null hypothesis when the null hypothesis is correct.

● A **Type II error** involves failing to reject the null hypothesis when the null hypothesis is false.

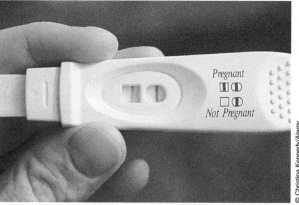

© Christina Kennedy/Alamy

Type I and Type II Errors The results of a home pregnancy test are either positive (indicating pregnancy) or negative (indicating no pregnancy). If the test is positive, but the woman *is not* pregnant, this would be a Type I error. If the test is negative, but the woman *is* pregnant, this would be a Type II error. With pregnancy tests, as with hypothesis testing, people are more likely to act on a Type I error than on a Type II error. In the photo, the pregnancy test seems to indicate that this woman is pregnant, which could be a Type I error.

hypothesis but the null hypothesis is false. A Type II error is like a false negative in medical testing. In the pregnancy example earlier, the woman might get a negative result on the test and fail to reject the null hypothesis, the one that says she's not pregnant. In this case, she would conclude that she's not pregnant when she really is. A false negative is equivalent to a Type II error.

We commit a Type II error when we incorrectly fail to reject the null hypothesis. A failure to reject the null hypothesis typically results in a failure to take action—for instance, a research intervention is not performed or a diagnosis is not given—which is generally less dangerous than incorrectly rejecting the null hypothesis. Yet there are cases in which a Type II error can have serious consequences. For example, the pregnant woman who does not believe she is pregnant because of a Type II error may drink alcohol in a way that unintentionally harms her fetus.

Next Steps   The Shocking Prevalence of Type I Errors

In the *British Medical Journal*, researchers reported that positive outcomes are more likely to be reported than null results (Sterne & Smith, 2001). First, researchers are less likely to want to publish null results, particularly if those results mean that a sponsoring pharmaceutical company's favored drug did not receive support; an article in the *New York Times* described the biased outcome of that practice: "If I toss a coin, but hide the result every time it comes up tails, it looks as if I always throw heads" (Goldacre, 2013). Second, journals tend to publish "exciting" results, rather than "boring" ones (Sterne & Smith, 2001). To translate this into the terms of hypothesis testing, if a researcher rejects the "boring" null hypothesis, thus garnering support for the "exciting" research hypothesis, the editor of a journal is more likely to want to publish these results. Third, the mass media–abetted by us, the general public–compound this problem. As John Oliver, host of *Last Week Tonight*, explained: "We like fun, poppy science that we can share like gossip, and TV news producers know it" (2016).

Using educated estimations, researchers calculated probabilities for 1000 hypothetical studies (Sterne & Smith, 2001). First, based on the literature on coronary heart disease, they assumed that 10% of studies *should* reject the null hypothesis; that is, 10% of studies were on medical techniques that actually worked. Second, based on flaws in methodology such as small sample sizes, as well as the fact that there will be chance findings, they estimated that half of the time the null hypothesis would *not* be rejected when it should be rejected, a Type II error. That is, half of the time, a helpful treatment would not receive empirical support. Finally, when the new treatment does *not* actually work, researchers would falsely reject the null hypothesis 5% of the time; just by chance, studies would lead to a false reportable difference between treatments, a Type I error. (In later chapters, we'll learn more about this 5% cutoff, but for now, it's only important to know that the 5% cutoff is arbitrary yet well established in statistical analyses.) Table 5-3 summarizes the researchers' hypothetical outcomes of 1000 studies.

Of 1000 studies, the exciting research hypothesis would be accurate in only 100; for these studies, we *should* reject the null hypothesis. In the other 900 of these studies, the null hypothesis would be accurate and we *should* not reject the null hypothesis. But remember, we are sometimes incorrect in our conclusions. Given the 5% Type I error rate, we would falsely reject 5%, or 45, of the 900 null hypotheses that we should not reject. Given the 50% Type II error rate, we would incorrectly fail to reject 50 of the 100 studies in which we should reject the null hypothesis.

TABLE 5-3	Estimates of Type I Errors

Sterne and Smith (2001) used educated estimates to calculate the likelihood of Type I errors in published reports of medical findings. Their calculations suggest that almost half of published medical studies exhibit Type I errors!

Result of Study	Null Hypothesis Is True (Treatment Doesn't Work)	Null Hypothesis Is False (Treatment Does Work)	Total
Fail to reject	855	**50**	905
Reject	**45**	50	95
Total	900	100	1000

(Both of the numbers indicating errors are in bold in Table 5-3.) The most important numbers are in the reject row—the row for which we'll have exciting results. Of the 95 total studies for which we would reject the null hypothesis, we would be wrong in 45 of these cases—almost half of the time! These numbers suggest that almost half of published medical studies may be Type I errors.

Let's consider an example. In recent years, there has been a spate of claims about the health benefits of natural substances. Natural health-related products are often less expensive than their manufactured counterparts because they do not have to be invented by large pharmaceutical companies. In addition, they are perceived to be healthy even though natural substances are not always risk-free. (Remember, rattlesnake venom and arsenic are natural substances!) Previous research has supported the use of vitamin E to prevent various maladies, and echinacea has been championed for its alleged ability to prevent the common cold. Yet recent studies that implemented rigorous research designs have largely discredited early, highly publicized accounts of the effectiveness of vitamin E and echinacea.

When the general public reads first of the value of vitamin E or echinacea and then of the health care establishment's dismissal of these treatments, we wonder what to believe and often, sadly, rely even more on our own biased common sense. It would be far better for scientists to improve their research designs from the outset and reduce the Type I errors that so frequently make headlines. Another solution is replication—repeating studies that have important implications for society. You'll learn more about current replication projects in the Next Steps section of Chapter 7.

CHECK YOUR LEARNING

Reviewing the Concepts

> When we draw a conclusion from inferential statistics, there is always a chance that we are wrong.

> When we reject the null hypothesis, but the null hypothesis is true, we have committed a Type I error.

> When we fail to reject the null hypothesis, but the null hypothesis is not true, we have committed a Type II error.

> Because of the flaws inherent in research, numerous null hypotheses are rejected falsely, resulting in Type I errors.

> The educated consumer of research is aware of her or his own biases and how they might affect her or his tendency to abandon critical thinking in favor of illusory correlations and the confirmation bias.

Clarifying the Concepts   5-11

Explain how Type I and Type II errors both relate to the null hypothesis.

continued on next page

Calculating the Statistics	5-12	If 7 out of every 280 people in prison are innocent, what is the rate of Type I errors?
	5-13	If the court system fails to convict 11 out of every 35 guilty people, what is the rate of Type II errors?

| Applying the Concepts | 5-14 | Researchers conduct a study on perception by having participants throw a ball at a target first while wearing virtual-reality glasses and then while wearing glasses that allow normal viewing. The null hypothesis is that there is no difference in performance when wearing the virtual-reality glasses versus when wearing the glasses that allow normal viewing. |

a. The researchers reject the null hypothesis, concluding that the virtual-reality glasses lead to a worse performance than do the normal glasses. What error might the researchers have made? Explain.

b. The researchers fail to reject the null hypothesis, concluding that it is possible that the virtual-reality glasses have no effect on performance. What error might the researchers have made? Explain.

Solutions to these Check Your Learning questions can be found in Appendix D.

REVIEW OF CONCEPTS

Samples and Their Populations

The gold standard of sample selection is *random sampling*, a procedure in which every member of the population has an equal chance of being chosen for study participation. A random numbers table or a computer-based random numbers generator is used to ensure randomness. For practical reasons, random selection is uncommon in social science research. Many behavioral scientists use a *convenience sample*, a sample that is readily available to them. One kind of convenience sample is a *volunteer sample* (also called a *self-selected sample*), in which participants themselves actively choose to participate in a study. With random assignment, every participant in a study has an equal chance of being assigned to any of the experimental conditions. In conjunction with random assignment, *replication*—the duplication of scientific results—can go a long way toward increasing *generalizability*, the ability to generalize findings beyond a given sample.

Probability

Calculating probabilities is essential because human thinking is dangerously biased. Because of *confirmation bias*—the tendency to see patterns that we expect to see—we often see meaning in mere coincidence. A confirmation bias often results from an *illusory correlation*, a relation that appears to be present but does not exist. When we think of probability, many of us think of *personal probability*, a person's own judgment about the likelihood that an event will occur. Statisticians, however, are referring to *expected relative-frequency probability*, or the long-run expected outcome if an experiment or trial were repeated many, many times. A *trial* refers to each occasion that a procedure is carried out, and an *outcome* is the result of a trial. A *success* refers to the outcome for which we're trying to determine the probability. *Probability* is a basic building block of inferential statistics. When we draw a conclusion about a population based on a sample, we can only say that it is probable that our conclusion is accurate, not that it is certain.

Inferential Statistics

Inferential statistics, based on probability, start with a hypothesis. The *null hypothesis* is a statement that usually postulates that there is no average difference between populations. The *research*, or *alternative*, *hypothesis* is a statement that postulates that there is an average difference between populations. After conducting a hypothesis test, we have only two possible conclusions. We can either reject or fail to reject the null hypothesis. When we conduct inferential statistics, we are often comparing an *experimental group*, the group subjected to an intervention, with a *control group*, the group that is the same as the experimental group in every way except the intervention. We use probability to draw conclusions about a population by estimating the probability that we would find a given difference between sample means if there is no underlying difference between population means.

Type I and Type II Errors

Statisticians must always be aware that their conclusions may be wrong. If a researcher rejects the null hypothesis, but the null hypothesis is correct, the researcher is making a *Type I error*. If a researcher fails to reject the null hypothesis, but the null hypothesis is false, the researcher is making a *Type II error*. Scientific and medical journals tend to publish, and the media tend to report on, the most exciting and surprising findings. As such, Type I errors are often overrepresented among reported findings.

SPSS®

There are many ways to look more closely at the independent and dependent variables. You can request a variety of case summaries by selecting Analyze → Reports → Case Summaries. You can then highlight the variable of interest and click the arrow to move it under "Variables."

You also can break down one variable with a second "grouping" variable. For example, you could use the hours studied and exam grade data from the SPSS section of Chapter 3. Select "Score" under "Variables" and "Hours" under "Grouping Variable(s)." Then, click "OK" to see the output screen. The output, part of which is shown in the screenshot here, tells you all the grades for students who studied a given number of hours. This summary, for instance, tells you that the two students who studied for 3 hours earned grades of 50 and 72 on the exam.

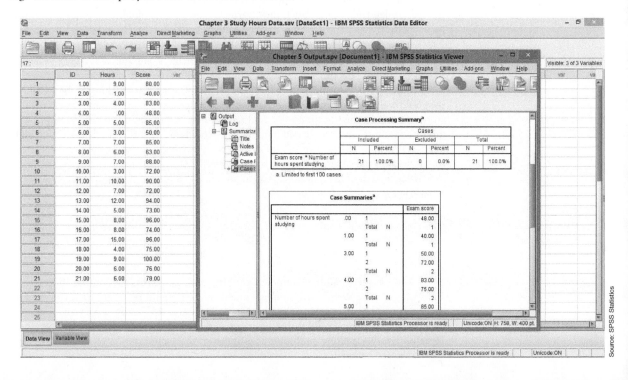

HOW IT WORKS

5.1 UNDERSTANDING RANDOM SELECTION

There are approximately 2000 school psychologists in Australia. A researcher has developed a new diagnostic tool to identify conduct disorder in children and wants to study ways to train school psychologists to administer the tool. How can she recruit a random sample of 30 school psychologists to participate in her study?

She could use an online random numbers generator to randomly select a sample of 30 school psychologists for this study from among the target population of 2000 Australian school psychologists. Let's try it. (You can search for "random numbers generator" on the Internet to find one.) To do so, she would tell the random numbers generator to produce one set of 30 numbers between 0001 and 2000. She would specify that she wants unique numbers, because no school psychologist can be in the study more than once. She can ask the program to sort the numbers, if she wishes, to more easily identify the participants who will comprise her sample. When we generated a set of 30 random numbers, we got the following:

```
 25  48  84  113  159  165  220  312  319  330
337 452 493  562  613  734  822  860  920  924
931 960 983 1290 1305 1462 1502 1515 1675 1994
```

Of course, each time we generate a list of random numbers, the list is different. Notice that the typical list of randomly generated numbers does not necessarily appear random. For example, in this list only 7 out of the 30 numbers are over 1000. There are also several cases in which numbers are close in value (e.g., 920 and 924).

5.2 USING RANDOM ASSIGNMENT

Imagine that the researcher described in How It Works 5.1 has developed two training modules. One is implemented in a classroom setting and requires that school psychologists travel to participate in in-person training. The other is a more cost-effective Web-based training module. She will administer a test to participants after they have received the training to determine how much they learned. How can she randomly assign half of the participants to classroom training and half to Web-based training?

In this case, the independent variable is type of training with two levels: classroom training and Web-based training. The dependent variable is amount of learning as determined by a test. This study is an experiment because participants are randomly assigned to conditions. To determine the condition to which each participant will be assigned, she could use a random numbers generator to produce one set of 30 numbers between 0 and 1. Those assigned to group 0 would receive in-person training and those assigned to group 1 would receive Web-based training. She would not want the numbers to be unique because she wants more than one of each type. She would not want the numbers to be sorted because the order of the numbers matters.

When we used an online random numbers generator, we got the following set of 30 numbers:

11000 01110

01000 00011

01110 01100

Based on these random numbers, the first two participants would be in group 1, and would receive Web-based training. The next four would be in group 0, and receive in-person training. And so on. This set contains 13 ones and 17 zeros. If we wanted exactly 15 in each group, we could stop assigning people to the 0 condition when we reached 15 zeros. Everyone else would then be assigned to the 1 condition.

5.3 CALCULATING PROBABILITY

Let's say that a university provides every student with a laptop computer, but students complain that their computers always crash when they are on the Internet and have at least three other applications open. One student thought this was an exaggeration and decided to calculate the probability that the campus computers would crash under these circumstances. How could he do this?

He could start by randomly selecting 100 different students to participate in his study. On the 100 students' computers, he could open three applications, go online, and record whether each computer crashed.

In this case, the trials would be the 100 instances (one trial on each of the 100 different laptops) in which the student opened three programs and then went online. The outcome would be whether or not the computer crashed. A success in this case would be a computer that crashed, and let's say that happened 55 times. (You might not consider a crashed computer a success, but in probability theory, a success refers to the outcome for which we want to determine the probability.) He could then take the number of successes (55) and divide by the number of trials:

$$55/100 = 0.55$$

So the probability of a computer crashing when three programs are open and the student goes online is 0.55. Of course, to determine the true expected relative-frequency probability, he'd have to conduct many, many more trials.

EXERCISES

The solutions to the odd-numbered exercises can be found in Appendix C.

Clarifying the Concepts

5.1 Why do we study samples rather than populations?

5.2 What is the difference between a random sample and a convenience sample?

5.3 What is generalizability?

5.4 What is a volunteer sample, and what is the main risk associated with it?

5.5 What is the difference between random sampling and random assignment?

5.6 What does it mean to replicate research, and how does replication impact our confidence in the findings?

5.7 Ideally, an experiment would use random sampling so that the data would accurately reflect the larger population. For practical reasons, this is difficult to do. How does random assignment help make up for a lack of random selection?

5.8 What is the confirmation bias?

5.9 What is an illusory correlation?

5.10 How does the confirmation bias lead to the perpetuation of an illusory correlation?

5.11 In your own words, what is personal probability?

5.12 In your own words, what is expected relative-frequency probability?

5.13 Statisticians use terms like *trial*, *outcome*, and *success* in a particular way in reference to probability. What do each of these three terms mean in the context of flipping a coin?

5.14 We distinguish between probabilities and proportions. How does each capture the likelihood of an outcome?

5.15 What are the ways the term *independent* is used by statisticians?

5.16 One step in hypothesis testing is to randomly assign some members of the sample to the control group and some to the experimental group. What is the difference between these two groups?

5.17 What is the difference between a null hypothesis and a research hypothesis?

5.18 What are the two decisions or conclusions we can make about our hypotheses, based on the data?

5.19 What is the difference between a Type I error and a Type II error?

Calculating the Statistics

5.20 Forty-three tractor-trailers are parked for the night in a rest stop along a major highway. You assign each truck a number from 1 to 43. Moving from left to right and using the second line in the random numbers table below, select four trucks to weigh as they leave the rest stop in the morning.

00190 27157 83208 79446 92987 61357

23798 55425 32454 34611 39605 39981

85306 57995 68222 39055 43890 36956

99719 36036 74274 53901 34643 06157

5.21 Airport security makes random checks of passenger bags every day. If 1 in every 10 passengers is checked, use the random numbers table in Exercise 5.20 to determine the first 6 people to be checked. Work from top to bottom, starting in the fourth column (the fourth digit from the left in the top line), and allow the number 0 to represent the 10th person.

5.22 Randomly assign eight people to three conditions of a study, numbered 1, 2, and 3. Use the random numbers table in Exercise 5.20, and read from right to left, starting in the top row. (*Note:* Assign people to conditions without concern for having an equal number of people in each condition.)

5.23 You are running a study with five conditions, numbered 1 through 5. Assign the first seven participants who arrive at your lab to conditions, not worrying about equal assignment across conditions. Use the random numbers table in Exercise 5.20, and read from left to right, starting in the third row from the top.

5.24 Explain why, given the general tendency people have of exhibiting the confirmation bias, it is important to collect objective data.

5.25 Explain why, given the general tendency people have of perceiving illusory correlations, it is important to collect objective data.

5.26 What is the probability of hitting a target if, in the long run, 71 out of every 489 attempts actually hit the target?

5.27 On a game show, 8 people have won the grand prize and a total of 266 people have competed. Estimate the probability of winning the grand prize.

5.28 Convert the following proportions to percentages:

a. 0.0173

b. 0.8

c. 0.3719

5.29 Convert the following percentages to proportions:

a. 62.7%

b. 0.3%

c. 4.2%

5.30 Using the random numbers table in Exercise 5.20, estimate the probability of the number 6 appearing in a random sequence of numbers. Base your answer on the numbers that appear in the first two rows.

5.31 Indicate whether each of the following statements refers to personal probability or to expected relative-frequency probability. Explain your answers.

a. The chance of a die showing an even number is 50%.

b. There is a 1 in 4 chance that I'll be late for class tomorrow.

c. The likelihood that I'll break down and eat ice cream while studying is 80%.

d. PlaneCrashInfo.com reported that the odds of being killed on a single flight on 1 of the top 25 safest airlines is 1 in 9.2 million.

Applying the Concepts

5.32 Coincidence and the lottery: "Woman wins millions from Texas lottery for 4th time" read the headline about Joan Ginther's amazing luck (Baird, 2010). Two of the tickets were from the same store, whose owner, Bob Solis, said, "This is a very lucky store." Citing concepts from the chapter, what would you tell Ginther and Solis about the roles that probability and coincidence played in their fortunate circumstances?

5.33 Random numbers and PINs: How random is your personal identification number or PIN? Your PIN is one of the most important safeguards for the accounts that hold your money and valuable information about you. The BBC reported that, when choosing a four-digit PIN, "people drift towards a small subset of the 10,000 available. In some cases, up to 80% of choices come from just 100 different numbers" (Ward, 2013). Based on what you know about our ability to think randomly, explain this finding.

5.34 Random selection and a school psychologist career survey: The Canadian government reported that there are 7550 psychologists working in Canada (2013). A researcher wants to randomly select 100 of the Canadian psychologists for a survey study regarding aspects of their jobs. Use this excerpt from a random numbers table to answer the following questions:

> 04493 52494 75246 33824 45862 51025
> 00549 97654 64051 88159 96119 63896
> 35963 15307 26898 09354 33351 35462
> 59808 08391 45427 26842 83609 49700

a. What is the population targeted by this study? How large is it?

b. What is the sample desired by this researcher? How large is it?

c. Describe how the researcher would select the sample. Be sure to explain how the members of the population would be numbered and which sets of digits the researcher should ignore when using the random numbers table.

d. Beginning at the left-hand side of the top line and continuing with each succeeding line, list the first 10 participants that this researcher would select for the study.

5.35 Hypotheses and the school psychologist career survey: Continuing with the study described in Exercise 5.34, once the researcher had randomly selected the sample of 100 Canadian psychologists, she decided to randomly assign 50 of them to receive, as part of their survey materials, a (fictional) newspaper article about the improving job market. She assigned the other 50 to receive a (fictional) newspaper article about the declining job market. The participants then responded to questions about their attitudes toward their careers.

   a. What is the independent variable in this experiment, and what are its levels?

   b. What is the dependent variable in this experiment?

   c. Write a null hypothesis and a research hypothesis for this study.

5.36 Random assignment and the school psychologist career survey: Refer to Exercises 5.34 and 5.35 when responding to the following questions.

   a. Describe how the researcher would randomly assign the participants to the levels of the independent variable. Be sure to explain how the levels of the independent variable would be numbered and which sets of digits the researcher should ignore when using the random numbers table.

   b. Beginning at the left-hand side of the bottom line of the random numbers table in Exercise 5.34 and continuing with the left-hand side of the line above it, list the levels of the independent variable to which the first 10 participants would be assigned. Use 0 and 1 to represent the two conditions.

   c. Why do these numbers not appear to be random? Discuss the difference between short-run and long-run proportions.

5.37 Random selection and a survey of psychology majors: Imagine that you have been hired by the psychology department at your school to administer a survey to psychology majors about their experiences in the department. You have been asked to randomly select 60 of these majors from the overall pool of 300. You are working on this project in your dorm room using a random numbers table because the server is down and you cannot use an online random numbers generator. Your roommate offers to write down a list of 60 random numbers between 001 and 300 for you so you can be done quickly. In three to four sentences, explain to your roommate why she is not likely to create a list of random numbers.

5.38 Random selection and random assignment: For each of the following studies, state (1) whether random selection was likely to have been used, and explain whether it would have been possible to use it. Also, describe the population to which the researcher wanted to and could generalize, and state (2) whether random assignment was likely to have been used, and whether it would have been possible to use it.

   a. A developmental psychologist wondered whether children born preterm (prematurely) had different social skills at age 5 than children born full term.

   b. A counseling center director wanted to compare the length of therapy in weeks for students who came in for treatment for depression versus students who came in for treatment for anxiety. She wanted

to report these data to the university administrators to help develop the next year's budget.

   c. An industrial-organizational psychologist wondered whether a new laptop design would affect people's response time when using the computer. He wanted to compare response times when using the new laptop with response times when using two standard versions of laptops, a Mac and a PC.

5.39 Volunteer samples and a college football poll: A volunteer sample is a kind of convenience sample in which participants select themselves to participate. One recent year, *USA Today* published an online poll on its Web site asking this question about U.S. college football: "Who is your pick to win the ACC conference this year?" Eight options—seven universities, including top vote-getters Virginia Tech and Miami, as well as "Other"—were provided.

   a. Describe the typical person who might volunteer to be in this sample. Why might this sample be biased, even with respect to the population of U.S. college football fans?

   b. What is external validity? Why might external validity be limited in this sample?

   c. What other problem can you identify with this poll?

5.40 Samples and *Cosmo* quizzes: *Cosmopolitan* magazine (*Cosmo*, as it's known popularly) publishes many of its well-known quizzes on its Web site. One quiz, aimed at heterosexual women, is titled "Are You Way Too Obsessed with Your Ex?" A question about "your rebound guy" offers these three choices: "Any random guy who will take your mind off the split," "A doppelgänger of your ex," and "The polar opposite of the last guy you dated." Consider whether you want to use the quiz data to determine how obsessed women are with their exes.

   a. Describe the typical person who might respond to this quiz. How might data from such a sample be biased, even with respect to the overall *Cosmo* readership?

   b. What is the danger of relying on volunteer samples in general?

   c. What other problems do you see with this quiz? Comment on the types of questions and responses.

5.41 Samples and a survey on sex education: The Gizmodo blog *Throb,* a Web site focused on the science of sex, released their own sex education survey (Kelly, 2015). The journalist who developed the survey wrote: "I hope that with enough of your answers, we can start to build a picture of what sex ed actually looks like in [the United States]. And then maybe we can start to figure out how it actually affects the students who take it."

   a. Do you think the journalist's results are likely to be representative of the U.S. population? Why or why not?

b. Describe the people most likely to volunteer for this sample. Why might this group be biased in comparison to the overall U.S. population?

c. The blogger says, "Five minutes poking around online forums where teens ask questions about sex can make me weep with rage and despair," an indication that she believes that misinformation is common. How might her perspective, likely one reflected in the blog *Throb* generally, lead to a particular type of survey respondent?

d. Because this survey is posted online, it's likely to get a large number of respondents. Why is it not enough to have a large sample to conduct a study with high external validity? What would we need to change about this sample to increase external validity?

5.42 Random selection or random assignment: For each of the following hypothetical scenarios, state whether selection or assignment is being described. Is the method of selection or assignment random? Explain your answer.

a. A study of the services offered by counseling centers at Canadian universities studied 20 universities; every Canadian university had an equal chance of being in this study.

b. In a study of phobias, 30 rhesus monkeys were either exposed to fearful stimuli or not exposed to fearful stimuli. Every monkey had an equal chance of being placed in either of the exposure conditions.

c. In a study of cell phone usage, participants were recruited by including along with their cell phone bill an invitation to participate in the study.

d. In a study of visual perception, 120 Introduction to Psychology students were recruited to participate.

5.43 Confirmation bias and negative thought patterns: Explain how the general tendency of a confirmation bias might make it difficult to change negative thought patterns that accompany Major Depressive Disorder.

5.44 Probability and coin flips: Short-run proportions are often quite different from long-run probabilities.

a. In your own words, explain why we would expect proportions to fluctuate in the short run, but why long-run probabilities are more predictable.

b. What is the expected long-run probability of heads if a person flips a coin many, many times? Why?

c. Flip a coin 10 times in a row. What proportion is heads? Do this 5 times. *Note:* You will learn more by actually doing it, so don't just write down numbers!

Proportion for the first 10 flips:

Proportion for the second 10 flips:

Proportion for the third 10 flips:

Proportion for the fourth 10 flips:

Proportion for the fifth 10 flips:

d. Do the proportions in part (c) match the expected long-run probability in part (b)? Why or why not?

e. Imagine that a friend flipped a coin 10 times, got 9 out of 10 heads, and complained that the coin was biased. How would you explain to your friend the difference between short-term and long-term probability?

5.45 Probability, proportion, percentage, and *Where's Waldo?*: Salon.com reporter Ben Blatt analyzed the location of Waldo in the game in which you must find Waldo, a cartoon man who always wears a red-and-white-striped sweater and hat, in a highly detailed illustration (2013). Blatt reported that "53 percent of the time Waldo is hiding within one of two 1.5-inch tall bands, one starting three inches from the bottom of the page and another one starting seven inches from the bottom, stretching across the spread." One of Blatt's colleagues used this trick to find Waldo more quickly than another colleague who did not have this information across 11 illustrations.

a. What does the term *probability* refer to? What is the probability of finding Waldo in one of the two 1.5 inch bands that Blatt identified?

b. What does the term *proportion* refer to? What is the proportion of Waldos in one of these two 1.5 inch bands?

c. What does the term *percentage* refer to? What is the percentage of Waldos in one of these two bands?

d. Based on these data, do you have enough information to determine whether the Where's Waldo? game is fixed? Why or why not? (*Note:* Blatt reported that the "probability of any two 1.5-inch bands containing at least 50 percent of all Waldo's is remarkably slim, less than 0.3 percent.")

5.46 Independent trials and Eurovision Song Contest bias: As reported in the *Telegraph* (Highfield, 2005), Oxford University researchers investigated allegations of voting bias in the annual Eurovision Song Contest, which pits pop music acts from across Europe, one per country, against each other. The research team found that neighboring countries tended to vote as a block—Norway with Sweden, Belarus with Russia, and Greece with Cyprus, for example. Explain why one could not consider the votes to be independent of each other in this case.

5.47 Independent trials and the U.S. presidential election: Nate Silver is a statistician and journalist well known for his accurate prediction tools. In an article leading up to the 2012 U.S. presidential election in which Barack Obama bested Mitt Romney, Silver (2012) explained his prediction methods as "principally, an Electoral College simulation, [which] therefore relies more heavily on state-by-state polls." Consider Silver's consolidation of data from polls across the 50 states. In what way are these polls likely to be independent trials? Why could someone argue that they are not truly independent trials?

5.48 Independent or dependent trials and probability: Gamblers often falsely predict the outcome of a future trial based on the outcome of previous trials. When trials are independent, the outcome of a future trial cannot be predicted based on the outcomes of previous trials. For each of the following examples, (1) state whether the trials are independent or dependent and (2) explain why. In addition, (3) state whether it is possible that the quote is accurate or whether it is definitely fallacious, explaining how the independence or dependence of trials influences accuracy.

    a. You are playing Monopoly and have rolled a pair of sixes in 4 out of your last 10 rolls of the dice. You say, "Cool. I'm on a roll and will get sixes again."

    b. You are an Ohio State University football fan and are sad because the team has lost two games in a row. You say, "That is really unusual; the Buckeyes are doomed this season. That's what happens with lots of early-season injuries."

    c. You have a 20-year-old car that has trouble starting from time to time. It has started every day this week, and now it's Friday. You say, "I'm doomed. It's been reliable all week, and even though I did get a tune-up last week, today is bound to be the day it fails me."

5.49 Null hypotheses and research hypotheses: For each of the following studies, cite the likely null hypothesis and the likely research hypothesis.

    a. A forensic cognitive psychologist wondered whether repetition of false information (versus no repetition) would increase the tendency to develop false memories, on average.

    b. A clinical psychologist studied whether ongoing structured assessments of the therapy process (versus no assessment) would lead to better outcomes, on average, among outpatient therapy clients with depression.

    c. A corporation recruited an industrial-organizational psychologist to explore the effects of cubicles (versus enclosed offices) on employee morale.

    d. A team of developmental cognitive psychologists studied whether teaching a second language to children from birth affects children's ability to speak their native language.

5.50 Decision about null hypotheses: For each of the following fictional conclusions, state whether the researcher seems to have rejected or failed to reject the null hypothesis (contingent, of course, on inferential statistics having backed up the statement). Explain the rationale for your decision.

    a. When false information is repeated several times, people seem to be more likely, on average, to develop false memories than when the information is not repeated.

    b. Therapy clients with Major Depressive Disorder who have ongoing structured assessments of therapy seem to have lower post-therapy depression levels, on average, than do clients who do not have ongoing structured assessments.

    c. Employee morale does not seem to be different, on average, whether employees work in cubicles or in enclosed offices.

    d. A child's native language does not seem to be different in strength, on average, whether the child is raised to be bilingual or not.

5.51 Type I versus Type II errors: Examine the statements from Exercise 5.50, repeated here. For each, if this conclusion were incorrect, what type of error would the researcher have made? Explain your answer.

    a. When false information is repeated several times, people seem to be more likely, on average, to develop false memories than when the information is not repeated.

    b. Therapy clients with Major Depressive Disorder who have ongoing structured assessments of therapy seem to have lower post-therapy depression levels, on average, than do clients who do not have ongoing structured assessments.

    c. Employee morale does not seem to be different, on average, whether employees work in cubicles or enclosed offices.

    d. A child's native language does not seem to be different in strength, on average, whether the child is raised to be bilingual or not.

5.52 Rejecting versus failing to reject an invitation: Imagine you have found a new study partner in your statistics class. One day, your study partner asks you to go on a date. This invitation takes you completely by surprise, and you have no idea what to say. You are not attracted to the person in a romantic way, but at the same time you do not want to hurt his or her feelings.

    a. Create two possible responses to the person, one in which you *fail to reject the invitation* and another in which you *reject the invitation.*

    b. How is your failure to reject the invitation different from rejecting or accepting the invitation?

5.53 Confirmation bias, errors, replication, and horoscopes: A horoscope on Astrology.com stated: "A big improvement is in the works, one that you may know nothing about, and today is the day for the big unveiling." A job-seeking recent college graduate might spot some new listings for interesting positions and decide the horoscope was right. If you look for an association, you're likely to find it. Yet, over and over again, careful researchers have failed to find evidence to support the accuracy of astrology (e.g., Dean & Kelly, 2003).

    a. Explain to the college graduate how confirmation bias guides his logic in deciding the horoscope was right.

b. If Dean and Kelly and other researchers were wrong, what kind of error would they have made?

c. Explain why replication (that is, "over and over again") means that this finding is not likely to be an error.

5.54 Probability and sumo wrestling: In their book *Freakonomics*, Levitt and Dubner (2005) describe a study conducted by Duggan and Levitt (2002) that broached the question: Do sumo wrestlers cheat? Sumo wrestlers garner enormous respect in Japan, where sumo wrestling is considered the national sport. The researchers examined the results of 32,000 wrestling matches over an 11-year time span. If a wrestler finishes a tournament with a losing record (7 or fewer wins out of 15 matches), his ranking goes down, as do the money and prestige that come with winning. The researchers wondered whether, going into the last match of the tournament, wrestlers with 7-7 records (needing only 1 more win to rise in the rankings) would have a better-than-expected win record against wrestlers with 8-6 records (those who already are guaranteed to rise in the rankings). Such a phenomenon might indicate cheating. One 7-7 wrestler (wrestler A), based on *past* matches against a given 8-6 opponent (wrestler B), was calculated to have won 48.7% of the time.

a. If there is no cheating, what is the probability that wrestler A will beat wrestler B in any situation, including the one in which A is 7-7 and B is 8-6?

b. If matches tend to be rigged so that 8-6 wrestlers frequently throw matches to help other wrestlers maintain their rankings (and to get payback from 7-7 wrestlers in future matches), what would you expect to happen to the winning percentage when these two wrestlers meet under these exact conditions—that is, the first is 7-7 in the tournament and the second is 8-6?

c. State the null hypothesis and research hypothesis for the study examining whether sumo wrestlers cheat.

d. In this particular real-life example, wrestler A was found to have beaten wrestler B 79.6% of the time when A had a 7-7 record and B had an 8-6 record. If inferential statistics determined that it was very unlikely that this would happen by chance, what would your decision be? Use the language of hypothesis testing.

5.55 Testimonials and Harry Potter: Amazon and other online bookstores offer readers the opportunity to write their own book reviews, and many potential readers scour these reviews to decide which books to buy. Harry Potter books attract a great deal of these reader reviews. One Amazon reviewer, "bel 78," submitted her review of *Harry Potter and the Half-Blood Prince* from Argentina. Of the book, she said, "It's simply outstandingly good," and suggested that readers of her review "run to get your copy." Do these reviews have an impact? In this case, more than 900 people had read bel 78's review, and close to 700 indicated that the review was helpful to them.

a. Imagine that you're deciding whether to buy *Harry Potter and the Half-Blood Prince*, and you want to know what people who had already read the book thought before you invest the money and time. What is the population whose opinion you're interested in?

b. If you read only bel 78's review, what is the sample from which you're gathering your data? What are some of the problems in relying on just this one review?

c. About 5500 readers had reviewed this book on Amazon by 2016. What if all reviewers agreed that this book was amazing? What is the problem with this sample?

d. Given no practical or financial limitations, what would be the best way to gather a sample of Amazon users who had read this Harry Potter book?

e. A friend plans to order a book online to take on spring break. She is reading online reviews of several books to make her decision. Explain to her in just a few sentences why her reliance on testimonials is not likely to provide her with objective information.

Putting It All Together

5.56 Horoscopes and predictions: People remember when their horoscopes had an uncanny prediction—say, the prediction of a problem in love on the exact day of the breakup of a romantic relationship—and decide that horoscopes are accurate. Munro & Munro (2000) are among those who have challenged such a conclusion. They reported that 34% of students chose their own horoscope as the best match for them when the horoscopes were labeled with the signs of the zodiac, whereas only 13% chose their own horoscope when the predictions were labeled only with numbers and in a random order. Thirteen percent is not statistically significantly different from 8.3%, which is the percentage we'd expect by chance.

a. What is the population of interest, and what is the sample in this study?

b. Was random selection used? Explain your answer.

c. Was random assignment used? Explain your answer.

d. What is the independent variable and what are its levels? What is the dependent variable? What type of variables are these?

e. What is the null hypothesis and what is the research hypothesis?

f. What decision did the researchers make? (Respond using the language of inferential statistics.)

g. If the researchers were incorrect in their decision, what kind of error did they make? Explain your answer. What are the consequences of this type of error, both in general and in this situation?

5.57 Alcohol abuse interventions: Sixty-four male students were ordered, after they had violated university alcohol rules, to meet with a school counselor. Borsari and Carey (2005) randomly assigned these students to one of two conditions. Those in the first condition were assigned to undergo a newly developed brief motivational interview (BMI), an intervention in which educational material relates to the students' own experiences; those in the second condition were assigned to attend a standard alcohol education session (AE) in which educational material is presented with no link to students' experiences. Based on inferential statistics, the researchers concluded that those in the BMI group had fewer alcohol-related problems at follow-up, on average, than did those in the AE group.

a. What is the population of interest, and what is the sample in this study?

b. Was random selection likely used? Explain your answer.

c. Was random assignment likely used? Explain your answer.

d. What is the independent variable and what are its levels? What is the dependent variable?

e. What is the null hypothesis and what is the research hypothesis?

f. What decision did the researchers make? (Respond using the language of inferential statistics.)

g. If the researchers were incorrect in their decision, what kind of error did they make? Explain your answer. What are the consequences of this type of error, both in general and in this situation?

5.58 Treatment for depression: Researchers conducted a study of 18 patients whose depression had not responded to treatment (Zarate, 2006). Half received one intravenous dose of ketamine, a hypothesized quick fix for depression; half received one intravenous dose of placebo. Far more of the patients who received ketamine improved, as measured by the Hamilton Depression Rating Scale, usually in less than 2 hours, than patients on placebo.

a. What is the population of interest, and what is the sample in this study?

b. Was random selection likely used? Explain your answer.

c. Was random assignment likely used? Explain your answer.

d. What is the independent variable and what are its levels? What is the dependent variable?

e. What is the null hypothesis and what is the research hypothesis?

f. What decision did the researchers make? (Respond using the language of inferential statistics.)

g. If the researchers were incorrect in their decision, what kind of error did they make? Explain your answer. What are the consequences of this type of error, both in general and in this situation?

TERMS

The Normal Curve, Standardization, and z Scores

6

The Normal Curve

Standardization, z Scores, and the Normal Curve

The Need for Standardization

Transforming Raw Scores into z Scores

Transforming z Scores into Raw Scores

Using z Scores to Make Comparisons

Transforming z Scores into Percentiles

The Central Limit Theorem

Creating a Distribution of Means

Characteristics of the Distribution of Means

Using the Central Limit Theorem to Make Comparisons with z Scores

Next Steps: The Normal Curve and Catching Cheaters

BEFORE YOU GO ON

■ **You should be able to create histograms and frequency polygons (Chapter 2).**

■ **You should be able to describe distributions of scores using measures of central tendency, variability, and skewness (Chapters 2 and 4).**

■ **You should understand that we can have distributions of scores based on samples, as well as distributions of scores based on populations (Chapter 5).**

● A **normal curve** is a specific bell-shaped curve that is unimodal, symmetric, and defined mathematically.

FIGURE 6-1

The Bell Curve Is Born

Daniel Bernoulli (a) created an approximation of the bell-shaped curve in this 1769 sketch "describing the frequency of errors." Augustus De Morgan (b) included this sketch in a letter to astronomer George Airy in 1849.

Abraham De Moivre was still a teenager in the 1680s when he was imprisoned in a French monastery for 2 years because of his religious beliefs. After his release, he found his way to Old Slaughter's Coffee House in London. The political squabbles, hustling artists, local gamblers, and insurance brokers didn't seem to bother the young scholar—he probably scratched out his famous formula on coffee-stained paper. The formula was exactly what gamblers needed to predict throws of the dice. It also helped insurance brokers estimate the probability of ships reaching their destinations.

De Moivre's powerful mathematical idea is far easier to understand as a picture, but that visual insight would take another 200 years. For example, Daniel Bernoulli came close in 1769. Augustus De Morgan came even closer when he mailed a sketch to fellow astronomer George Airy in 1849 (Figure 6-1). They were both trying to draw the **normal curve**, *a specific bell-shaped curve that is unimodal, symmetric, and defined mathematically.*

The astronomers were trying to pinpoint the precise time when a star touched the horizon, but they couldn't get independent observers to agree. Some estimates were probably a little early; others were probably a little late. Nevertheless, the findings revealed (a) that the pattern of errors was symmetric; and (b) that the midpoint represented a reasonable estimate of reality. Only a few estimates were extremely high or extremely low; most errors clustered tightly around the middle. They were starting to understand what seems obvious to us today: Their best estimate was based on a bell-shaped curve—the foundation of inferential statistics (Stigler, 1999).

In this chapter, we learn about the building blocks of inferential statistics: (a) the characteristics of the normal curve; (b) how to use the normal curve to standardize any variable by using a tool called the *z* score; and (c) the central limit theorem, which, coupled with a grasp of standardization, allows us to make comparisons between means.

The Normal Curve

As De Moivre realized, the normal curve is a powerful tool in statistics. It allows us to determine probabilities about data and then draw conclusions that we can apply beyond the data. In this section, we learn more about the normal curve through a real-life example.

EXAMPLE 6.1

Let's examine the heights, in inches, of a sample of 5 students taken from a larger sample of the authors' statistics students:

52 77 63 64 64

Figure 6-2 shows a histogram of those heights, with a normal curve superimposed on the histogram. With so few scores, we can only begin to guess at the emerging shape of a normal distribution. Notice that three of the observations (63 inches, 64 inches, and 64 inches) are represented by the middle bar. This is why it is three times higher than the bars that represent a single observation of 52 inches and another observation of 77 inches.

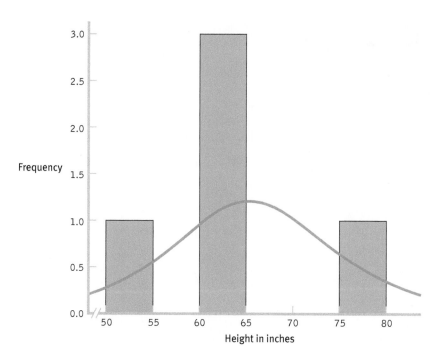

FIGURE 6-2

Sample of 5

Here is a histogram of the heights in inches of 5 students. With so few students, the data are unlikely to closely resemble the normal curve that we would see for an entire population of heights.

Now, here are the heights in inches from a sample of 30 students:

52 77 63 64 64 62 63 64 67 52

67 66 66 63 63 64 62 62 64 65

67 68 74 74 69 71 61 61 66 66

Figure 6-3 shows the histogram for these data. Notice that the heights of 30 students resemble a normal curve more so than do the heights of just 5 students, although certainly they don't match it perfectly.

Table 6-1 gives the heights in inches from a random sample of 140 students. Figure 6-4 shows the histogram for these data.

MASTERING THE CONCEPT

6-1: The distributions of many variables approximate a normal curve, a mathematically defined, bell-shaped curve that is unimodal and symmetric.

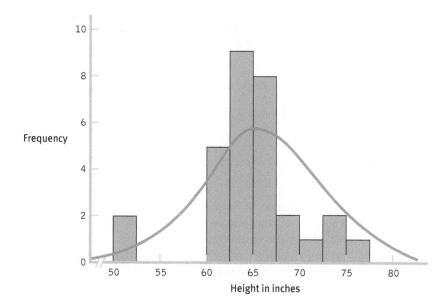

FIGURE 6-3

Sample of 30

Here is a histogram of the heights in inches of 30 students. With a larger sample, the data begin to resemble the normal curve of an entire population of heights.

TABLE 6-1	A Sample of Heights								

These are the heights, in inches, of 140 students.

52	77	63	64	64	62	63	64	67	52
67	66	66	63	63	64	62	62	64	65
67	68	74	74	69	71	61	61	66	66
68	63	63	62	62	63	65	67	73	62
63	63	64	60	69	67	67	63	66	61
65	70	67	57	61	62	63	63	63	64
64	68	63	70	64	60	63	64	66	67
68	68	68	72	73	65	61	72	71	65
60	64	64	66	56	62	65	66	72	69
60	66	73	59	60	60	61	63	63	65
66	69	72	65	62	62	62	66	64	63
65	67	58	60	60	67	68	68	69	63
63	73	60	67	64	67	64	66	64	72
65	67	60	70	60	67	65	67	62	66

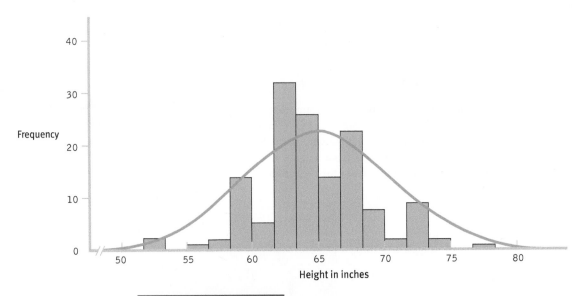

FIGURE 6-4		

Sample of 140

Here is a histogram of the heights in inches of 140 students. As the sample increases, the shape of the distribution becomes more and more like the normal curve we would see for an entire population. Imagine the distribution of the data for a sample of 1000 students or of 1 million.

These three images demonstrate why sample size is so important in relation to the normal curve. As the sample size increases, the distribution more and more closely resembles a normal curve (as long as the underlying population distribution is normal). Imagine even larger samples—of 1000 students or of 1 million. As the size of the sample approaches the size of the population, the shape of the distribution tends to be normally distributed. ●

CHECK YOUR LEARNING

Reviewing the Concepts

> The normal curve is a specific, mathematically defined curve that is bell-shaped, unimodal, and symmetric.

> The normal curve describes the distributions of many variables.

> As the size of a sample approaches the size of the population, the distribution resembles a normal curve (as long as the population is normally distributed).

Clarifying the Concepts   **6-1**   What does it mean to say that the normal curve is unimodal and symmetric?

Calculating the Statistics   **6-2**   A sample of 225 students completed the Consideration of Future Consequences (CFC) scale, a measure that assesses how much people think about the degree to which their current actions affect their future. The scores are means of responses to 12 items. Overall CFC scores range from 1 to 5.

a. Here are CFC scores for 5 students, rounded to the nearest whole or half number: 3.5, 3.5, 3.0, 4.0, and 2.0. Create a histogram for these data, either by hand or by using software.

b. Now create a histogram for these scores of 30 students:

3.5 3.5 3.0 4.0 2.0 4.0 2.0 4.0 3.5 4.5

4.5 4.0 3.5 2.5 3.5 3.5 4.0 3.0 3.0 2.5

3.0 3.5 4.0 3.5 3.5 2.0 3.5 3.0 3.0 2.5

Applying the Concepts   **6-3**   The histogram below uses the actual (not rounded) CFC scores for all 225 students described in 6-2. What do you notice about the shape of this distribution of scores as the size of the sample increases?

Solutions to these Check Your Learning questions can be found in Appendix D.

Standardization, z Scores, and the Normal Curve

De Moivre's discovery of the normal curve meant that scientists could now make meaningful comparisons. Why? When data are normally distributed, we can compare one particular score to an entire distribution of scores. To do this, we convert a raw

● **Standardization** is a way to convert individual scores from different normal distributions to a shared normal distribution with a known mean, standard deviation, and percentiles.

● A *z score* is the number of standard deviations a particular score is from the mean.

score to a standardized score (for which percentiles are already known). *Standardization is a way to convert individual scores from different normal distributions to a shared normal distribution with a known mean, standard deviation, and percentiles.*

In this section, we explain the importance of standardization and introduce the tool that helps us standardize, the *z* score. We show how we can convert raw scores to *z* scores and *z* scores to raw scores. We demonstrate how the distribution of *z* scores allows us to know what percentage of the population falls above or below a given *z* score.

The Need for Standardization

One of the first problems with making meaningful comparisons is that variables are measured on different scales. For example, we might measure height in inches but measure weight in pounds. In order to compare heights and weights, we need a way to put different variables on the same standardized scale. Fortunately, we can standardize different variables by using their means and standard deviations to convert any raw score into a *z* score. *A z score is the number of standard deviations a particular score is from the mean.* A *z* score is part of its own distribution, the *z* distribution, just as a raw score, such as a person's height, is part of its own distribution, a distribution of heights. (Note that as with all statistical symbols, the *z* is italicized.)

EXAMPLE 6.2

Here is a memorable example of standardization: comparing weights of cockroaches. Different countries use different measures of weight. In the United Kingdom and the United States, the pound is typically used, with variants that are fractions or multiples of the pound, such as the dram, ounce, and ton. In most other countries, the metric system is used, with the gram as the basic unit of weight, and variants that are fractions or multiples of the gram, such as the milligram and kilogram.

If we were told that three imaginary species of cockroaches had mean weights of 8.0 drams, 0.25 pound, and 98.0 grams, which one should we most fear? We can answer this question by standardizing the weights and comparing them on the same measure. A dram is 1/256 of a pound, so 8.0 drams is 1/32 = 0.03125 of a pound. One pound equals 453.5924 grams. Based on these conversions, the weights could be standardized into grams as follows:

Standardizing Cockroach Weights
Standardization is a way to create meaningful comparisons by converting different scales to a common, or standardized, scale. We can compare the weights of these cockroaches using different measures of weights—including drams, pounds, and grams.

© Rosanne Tackaberry/Alamy

Cockroach 1 weighs 8.0 drams = 0.03125 pound = 14.17 grams
Cockroach 2 weighs 0.25 pound = 113.40 grams
Cockroach 3 weighs 98.00 grams

Standardizing allows us to determine that the second cockroach species tends to weigh the most: 113.40 grams. Fortunately, the biggest cockroach in the world weighs only about 35 grams and is about 80 millimeters (3.15 inches) long. Cockroaches 2 and 3 exist only in our imaginations. However, not all conversions are as easy as standardizing weights from different units into grams. That's why statisticians developed the *z* distribution. ●

Transforming Raw Scores into z Scores

A desire to make meaningful comparisons forces us to convert raw scores into standardized scores. For example, let's say you know that after taking the midterm examination, you are 1 standard deviation above the mean in your statistics class. Is this good news? What if you are 0.5 standard deviation below the mean? Understanding

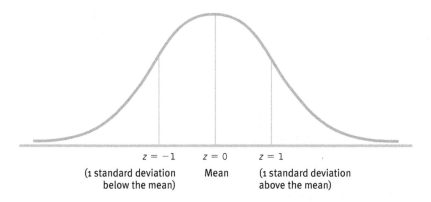

FIGURE 6-5

The z Distribution

The z distribution always has a mean of 0 and a standard deviation of 1.

a score's relation to the mean of its distribution gives us important information. For a statistics test, we know that being above the mean is good; for anxiety levels, we know that being above the mean is usually bad. z scores create an opportunity to make meaningful comparisons.

The only information we need to convert any raw score to a z score is the mean and standard deviation of the population of interest. In the midterm example above, we are probably interested in comparing our grade with the grades of others in this course. In this case, the statistics class is the population of interest. Let's say that your score on the midterm is 2 standard deviations above the mean; your z score is 2.0. Imagine that a friend's score is 1.6 standard deviations below the mean; your friend's z score is −1.6. What would your z score be if you fell exactly at the mean in your statistics class? If you guessed 0, you're correct.

Figure 6-5 illustrates two important features of the z distribution. First, the z distribution always has a mean of 0. So, if you are exactly at the mean, then you are 0 standard deviations from the mean. Second, the z distribution always has a standard deviation of 1. If your raw score is 1 standard deviation above the mean, you have a z score of 1.0.

- -

Let's calculate z scores without a calculator or formula. We'll use the distribution of scores on a statistics exam. (This example is illustrated in Figure 6-6.) If the mean on a statistics exam is 70, the standard deviation is 10, and your score is 80, what is your z score? In this case, you are exactly 10 points, or 1 standard deviation, above the mean, so your z score is 1.0. Now let's say your score is 50, which is 20 points, or 2 standard deviations, below the mean, so your z score is −2.0. What if your score is 85? Now you're 15 points, or 1.5 standard deviations, above the mean, so your z score is 1.5.

EXAMPLE 6.3

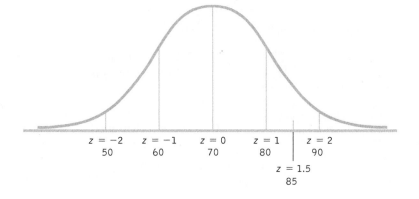

FIGURE 6-6

z Scores Intuitively

With a mean of 70 and a standard deviation of 10, we can calculate many z scores without a formula. A raw score of 50 has a z score of −2.0. A raw score of 60 has a z score of −1.0. A raw score of 70 has a z score of 0. A raw score of 80 has a z score of 1.0. A raw score of 85 has a z score of 1.5.

As you can see, we don't need a formula to calculate a z score when we're working with easy numbers. It is important, however, to learn the notation and language of statistics. So let's also convert z scores using a formula for when the numbers are not easy to work with. To calculate a particular z score, there are just two steps.

> STEP 1: Determine the distance of a particular person's score (X) from the population mean (μ) as part of the calculation: $X - \mu$.

MASTERING THE FORMULA

6-1: The formula for a z score is

$$z = \frac{(X - \mu)}{\sigma}.$$

We calculate the difference between an individual score and the population mean, then divide by the population standard deviation.

> STEP 2: Express this distance in terms of standard deviations by dividing by the population standard deviation, σ.

The formula, therefore, is:

$$z = \frac{(X - \mu)}{\sigma} \quad \bullet$$

EXAMPLE 6.4

Let's take an example that is not so easy to calculate in our heads. The mean height for the population of sophomores at your university is 64.886, with a standard deviation of 4.086. If you are 70 inches tall, what is your z score?

> STEP 1: Subtract the population mean from your score.

In this case, subtract the population mean, 64.886, from your score, 70.

> STEP 2: Divide by the population standard deviation.

The population standard deviation is 4.086. Here are those steps in the context of the formula:

$$z = \frac{(X - \mu)}{\sigma} = \frac{(70 - 64.886)}{4.086} = 1.25$$

You are 1.25 standard deviations above the mean.

We must be careful not to use a formula mindlessly. Always consider whether the answer makes sense. In this case, 1.25 is positive, indicating that the height is just over 1 standard deviation above the mean. This makes sense because the raw score of 70 is also just over 1 standard deviation above the mean. If you do this quick check regularly, then you can correct mistakes before they cost you. ●

EXAMPLE 6.5

Let's take another example: What if you are 62 inches tall?

> STEP 1: Subtract the population mean from your score.

Here, subtract the population mean, 64.886, from your score, 62.

> STEP 2: Divide by the population standard deviation.

The population standard deviation is 4.086. Here are those steps in the context of the formula:

$$z = \frac{(X - \mu)}{\sigma} = \frac{(62 - 64.886)}{4.086} = -0.71$$

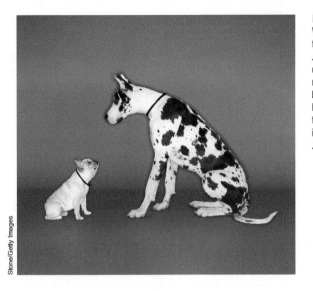

Stone/Getty Images

You are 0.71 standard deviation *below* the mean.

Don't forget the sign of the z score. Changing a z score from negative 0.71 to positive 0.71 makes a big difference! ●

EXAMPLE 6.6

With the height example we've been using, let's now demonstrate that the mean of the z distribution is always 0 and the standard deviation is always 1. The mean is 64.886 and the standard deviation is 4.086. Let's calculate what the z score would be at the mean.

| STEP 1: Subtract the population mean from a score right at the mean. | We subtract the population mean, 64.886, from a score right at the mean, 64.886. |
| STEP 2: Divide by the population standard deviation. | We divide the difference by 4.086. Here are those steps in the context of the formula: |

$$z = \frac{(X - \mu)}{\sigma} = \frac{(64.886 - 64.886)}{4.086} = 0$$

If someone is exactly 1 standard deviation above the mean, his or her score would be $64.886 + 4.086 = 68.972$. Let's calculate what the z score would be for this person.

| STEP 1: Subtract the population mean from a score exactly 1 standard deviation above the mean. | We subtract the population mean, 64.886, from a score exactly 1 standard deviation (4.086) above the mean, 68.972. |
| STEP 2: Divide by the population standard deviation. | We divide the difference by 4.086. Here are those steps in the context of the formula: |

$$z = \frac{(X - \mu)}{\sigma} = \frac{(68.972 - 64.886)}{4.086} = 1 ●$$

Transforming z Scores into Raw Scores

If we already know a z score, then we can reverse the calculations to determine the raw score. The formula is the same; we just plug in all the numbers instead of the X, then solve algebraically. Let's try it with the height example.

EXAMPLE 6.7

The population mean is 64.886, with a standard deviation of 4.086. So, if you have a z score of 1.79, what is your height?

$$z = \frac{(X - \mu)}{\sigma} = 1.79 = \frac{(X - 64.886)}{4.086}$$

6-2: The formula to calculate the raw score from a z score is:

$$X = z(\sigma) + \mu.$$

We multiply the z score by the population standard deviation, then add the population mean.

If we solve for X, we get 72.20. For those who prefer to minimize the use of algebra, we can do the algebra on the equation itself to derive a formula that gets the raw score directly. The formula is derived by multiplying both sides of the equation by σ, then adding μ to both sides of the equation. This isolates the X, as follows:

$$X = z(\sigma) + \mu$$

So, there are two steps to converting a z score to a raw score:

STEP 1: Multiply the z score by the population standard deviation.	Multiply the z score, 1.79, by the population standard deviation, 4.086.
STEP 2: Add the population mean to this product.	Add the population mean, 64.886, to this product.

Here are those steps in the context of the formula:

$$X = 1.79(4.086) + 64.886 = 72.20$$

Regardless of whether we use the original formula or the direct formula, the height is 72.20 inches. As always, think about whether the answer seems accurate. In this case, the answer does make sense because the height is above the mean and the z score is positive. ●

EXAMPLE 6.8

What if your z score is −0.44?

STEP 1: Multiply the z score by the population standard deviation.	Multiply the z score, −0.44, by the population standard deviation, 4.086.
STEP 2: Add the population mean to this product.	Add the population mean, 64.886, to this product.

Here are those steps in the context of the formula:

$$X = -0.44(4.086) + 64.886 = 63.09$$

Your height is 63.09 inches. Don't forget the negative sign when doing this calculation.

As long as we know the mean and standard deviation of the population, we can do two things: (1) calculate the raw score from its *z* score, and (2) calculate the *z* score from its raw score.

Now that you understand *z* scores, let's question the saying that "you can't compare apples and oranges." We can take any apple from a normal distribution of apples, find its *z* score using the mean and standard deviation for the distribution of apples, convert the *z* score to a percentile, and discover that a particular apple is, say, larger than 85% of all apples. Similarly, we can take any orange from a normal distribution of oranges, find its *z* score using the mean and standard deviation for the distribution of oranges, convert the *z* score to a percentile, and discover that this particular orange is, say, larger than 97% of all oranges. The orange (with respect to other oranges) is bigger than the apple (with respect to other apples), and yes, that is an honest comparison. With standardization, we can compare anything, each relative to its own group.

Apples and Oranges Standardization allows us to compare apples with oranges. If we can standardize the raw scores on two different scales, converting both scores to *z* scores, we can then compare the scores directly.

The normal curve also allows us to convert scores to percentiles because 100% of the population is represented under the bell-shaped curve. This means that the midpoint is the 50th percentile. If an individual score on some test is located to the right of the mean, we know that the score lies above the 50th percentile. A score to the left of the mean is below the 50th percentile. To make more specific comparisons, we convert raw scores to *z* scores and *z* scores to percentiles using the *z* distribution. *The **z distribution** is a normal distribution of standardized scores—a distribution of z scores.* And *the **standard normal distribution** is a normal distribution of z scores.*

Most people are not content merely with knowing whether their own score is above or below the average score. After all, there is likely a big difference between scoring at the 51st percentile and scoring at the 99th percentile in height, as shown in Figure 6-7. The standardized *z* distribution allows us to do the following:

1. Transform raw scores into standardized scores called *z* scores
2. Transform *z* scores back into raw scores

- The **z distribution** is a normal distribution of standardized scores.

- The **standard normal distribution** is a normal distribution of *z* scores.

FIGURE 6-7

The All-Encompassing z Distribution

The *z* distribution theoretically includes all possible scores, so when it's based on a normal distribution, we know that 50% of the scores are above the mean and 50% are below the mean. But the 51st percentile and the 99th percentile are still far from each other, so two people making a comparison usually want more precise information than whether or not they are above average.

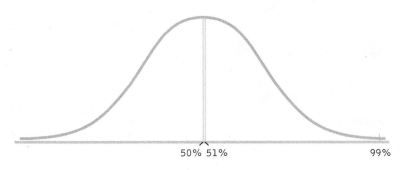

50% 51%   99%

3. Compare *z* scores to each other—even when the underlying raw scores are measured on different scales

4. Transform *z* scores into percentiles that are more easily understood ●

Using z Scores to Make Comparisons

In Figure 6-8, you'll find an example of how researchers use *z* scores as a standardization tool. Using the Google Ngram tool, researchers recorded the numbers of times that different emotion-related words were used in literature since 1900. In order to make direct comparisons, they turned all of the counts into *z* scores. By doing so, even if "fear" words were used more often than "disgust" words, the researchers could directly compare the patterns in the usage of emotion-related words.

Now let's look at an example you may have encountered in your own life. Imagine that a friend is taking a course in statistics at the same time that you are, but with a different professor. Each professor has a different grading scheme, so each class produces a different distribution of scores. Thanks to standardization, we can convert each raw score to a *z* score and compare raw scores from *different* distributions.

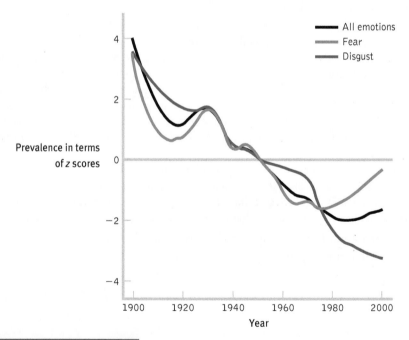

FIGURE 6-8

Using z Scores as a Standardization Tool in Research

Acerbi, Lampos, Garnett, and Bentley (2013) used Google Ngram to look at patterns in the use of emotion-related words in literature over time. They found that, in general, the prevalence of emotion-related words used in the 30 million books catalogued in Google books has decreased over the past century. The one exception was words related to "fear." This graph plots z scores to allow for the comparison of different emotion words. For example, if fear-related words were more common overall than disgust-related words, the lines would be far apart, making comparisons of trend lines difficult.

EXAMPLE 6.9

For example, let's say that you both took a quiz. You earned 92 out of 100; the distribution of your class had a mean of 78.1 and a standard deviation of 12.2. Your friend earned 8.1 out of 10; the distribution of his class had a mean of 6.8 with a standard deviation of 0.74. Again, we're only interested in the classes that took the test, so these are populations. Who did better?

We standardize the scores in terms of their respective distributions.

$$\text{Your score: } z = \frac{(X - \mu)}{\sigma} = \frac{(92 - 78.1)}{12.2} = 1.14$$

$$\text{Your friend's score: } z = \frac{(X - \mu)}{\sigma} = \frac{(8.1 - 6.8)}{0.74} = 1.76$$

First, let's check our work. Do these answers make sense? Yes—both you and your friend scored above the mean and have positive z scores. Second, we compare the z scores. Although you both scored well above the mean in terms of standard deviations, your friend did better with respect to his class than you did with respect to your class. ●

© Corbis

Making Comparisons z scores create a way to compare students taking different exams from different courses. If each exam score can be converted to a z score with respect to the mean and standard deviation for its particular exam, the two scores can then be compared directly.

Transforming z Scores into Percentiles

So z scores are useful because:

1. z scores give us a sense of where a score falls in relation to the mean of its population (in terms of the standard deviation of its population).

2. z scores allow us to compare scores from different distributions.

Yet we can be even more specific about where a score falls. An additional and particularly helpful use of z scores is that they also have this property:

3. z scores can be transformed into percentiles.

Because the shape of a normal curve is standard, we automatically know something about the percentage of any particular area under the curve. Think of the normal curve and the horizontal line below it as forming a shape. (In fact, it *is* a shape; it's essentially a frequency polygon.) Like any shape, the area below the normal curve can be measured. We can quantify the space below a normal curve in terms of percentages.

Remember that the normal curve is, by definition, symmetric. This means that exactly 50% of scores fall below the mean and 50% fall above the mean. But Figure 6-9 demonstrates that we can be even more specific. Approximately 34% of scores fall between the mean and a z score of 1.0; and because of symmetry, 34% of scores also fall between the mean and a z score of −1.0. We also know that approximately 14% of scores fall between the z scores of 1.0 and 2.0, and 14% of scores fall between the z scores of −1.0 and −2.0. Finally, we know that approximately 2% of scores fall between the z scores of 2.0 and 3.0, and 2% of scores fall between the z scores of −2.0 and −3.0.

By simple addition, we can determine that approximately 68% (34 + 34 = 68) of scores fall within 1 standard deviation—or 1 z score—of the mean; that approximately 96% (14 + 34 + 34 + 14 = 96) of scores fall within 2 standard deviations of the mean; and that all or nearly all (2 + 14 + 34 + 34 + 14 + 2 = 100) scores fall within

FIGURE 6-9

The Normal Curve and Percentages

The standard shape of the normal curve allows us to know the approximate percentages under different parts of the curve. For example, about 34% of scores fall between the mean and a z score of 1.0.

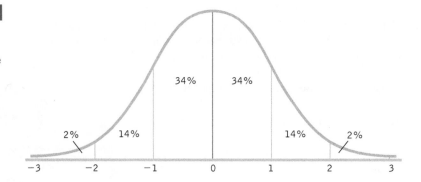

3 standard deviations of the mean. So, if you know you are about 1 standard deviation above the mean on your statistics quiz, then you can add the 50% below the mean to the 34% between the mean and the z score of 1.0 that you earned on your quiz, and know that your score corresponds to approximately the 84th percentile.

If you know that you are about 1 standard deviation below the mean, you know that you are in the lower 50% of scores and that 34% of scores fall between your score and the mean. By subtracting, you can calculate that 50 − 34 = 16% of scores fall below yours. Your score corresponds to approximately the 16th percentile. Scores on standardized tests are often expressed as percentiles.

For now, it's important to understand that the z distribution forms a normal curve with a unimodal, symmetric shape. Because the shape is known and 100% of the population falls beneath the normal curve, we can determine the percentage of any area under the normal curve.

CHECK YOUR LEARNING

Reviewing the Concepts
> Standardization is a way to create meaningful comparisons between observations from different distributions. It can be done by transforming raw scores from different distributions into z scores, also known as standardized scores.

> A z score is the distance that a score is from the mean of its distribution in terms of standard deviations.

> We also can transform z scores to raw scores by reversing the formula for a z score.

> z scores correspond to known percentiles that communicate how an individual score compares with the larger distribution.

Clarifying the Concepts **6-4** Describe the process of standardization.

6-5 What do the numeric value and the sign (negative or positive) of a z score indicate?

Calculating the Statistics **6-6** The mean of a population is 14 and the standard deviation is 2.5. Using the formula, calculate z scores for the following raw scores:

a. 11.5

b. 18

6-7 Using the same population parameters as in Check Your Learning 6-6, calculate raw scores for the following z scores:

a. 2

b. −1.4

| Applying the Concepts | 6-8 | The Consideration of Future Consequences (CFC) scale assesses the degree to which students are future oriented. Researchers believe that a high CFC score is a positive indicator of a student's career potential. One study found a mean CFC score of 3.20, with a standard deviation of 0.70, for the 800 students in the sample (Adams, 2012). |

a. If a student has a CFC score of 2.5, what is her z score? To what percentile does this z score roughly correspond?

b. If a student has a CFC score of 4.6, what is his z score? To what percentile does this z score roughly correspond?

c. If a student has a CFC score at the 84th percentile, what is her z score?

d. What is the raw score of the student at the 84th percentile? Use symbolic notation and the formula. Explain why this answer makes sense.

6-9 Samantha has high blood pressure but exercises; she has a wellness score of 84 on a scale with a mean of 93 and a standard deviation of 4.5 (a higher score indicates better health). Nicole is of normal weight but has high cholesterol; she has a wellness score of 332 on a scale with a mean of 312 and a standard deviation of 20.

a. Without using a formula, who would you say is in better health?

b. Using standardization, determine who is in better health. Provide details using symbolic notation.

Solutions to these Check Your Learning questions can be found in Appendix D.

c. Based on their z scores, what percentage of people are in better health than Samantha and Nicole, respectively?

The Central Limit Theorem

In the early 1900s, W. S. Gossett discovered how the predictability of the normal curve could improve quality control in the Guinness ale factory. One of the practical problems that Gossett faced was related to sampling yeast cultures: too little yeast led to incomplete fermentation, whereas too much yeast led to a bitter-tasting beer. To test whether he could sample both accurately and economically, Gossett averaged samples of four observations to see how well they represented a known population of 3000 (Gossett, 1908, 1942; Stigler, 1999).

This small adjustment (taking the *average* of four samples rather than using just one sample) is possible because of the central limit theorem. *The **central limit theorem** refers to how a distribution of sample means is a more normal distribution than a distribution of scores, even when the population distribution is not normal.* Indeed, as sample size increases, a distribution of sample means more closely approximates a normal curve. More specifically, the central limit theorem demonstrates two important principles:

1. Repeated sampling approximates a normal curve, *even when the original population is not normally distributed.*

2. A distribution of means is less variable than a distribution of individual scores.

Instead of randomly sampling a single data point, Gossett randomly sampled four data points from the population of 3000 and computed the average. He did this repeatedly and used those many averages to create a distribution of means. *A **distribution of means** is a distribution composed of many means that are calculated from all possible samples of a given size, all taken from the same population.* Put another way, the numbers that make up the distribution of means are not individual scores; they are *means* of samples of individual scores. Distributions of means are frequently used to understand data across

MASTERING THE CONCEPT

6-4: The central limit theorem demonstrates that a distribution made up of the means of many samples (rather than individual scores) approximates a normal curve, even if the underlying population is not normally distributed.

● The **central limit theorem** refers to how a distribution of sample means is a more normal distribution than a distribution of scores, even when the population distribution is not normal.

● A **distribution of means** is a distribution composed of many means that are calculated from all possible samples of a given size, all taken from the same population.

A Distribution of Means
A distribution of means reduces the influence of individual outliers such as the length of the fingernails of the woman on the left. When her extreme score is part of a sample that includes smaller, more typical scores, the mean of that sample will be smaller than her individual score. That is why a distribution based on means is less variable than a distribution based on individual scores.

a range of contexts; for example, when a university reports the mean standardized test score of incoming first-year students, that mean would be understood in relation to a distribution of means instead of a distribution of scores.

Gossett experimented with using the average of four data points as his sample, but there is nothing magical about the number four. A mean test score for incoming students would have a far larger sample size. The important outcome is that a distribution of means more consistently produces a normal distribution (although with less variance) *even when the population distribution is not normal*. It might help your understanding to know that the central limit theorem works because a sample of four, for example, will minimize the effect of outliers. When an outlier is just one of four scores being sampled and averaged, the average won't be as extreme as the outlier.

In this section, we learn how to create a distribution of means, as well as how to calculate a z score for a mean (more accurately called a z *statistic* when calculated for means rather than scores). We also learn why the central limit theorem indicates that, when conducting hypothesis testing, a distribution of means is more useful than a distribution of scores.

Creating a Distribution of Means

The central limit theorem underlies many statistical processes that are based on a distribution of means. A distribution of means is more tightly clustered (has a smaller standard deviation) than a distribution of scores.

EXAMPLE 6.10

In class, we conduct an exercise with our students that demonstrates the central limit theorem in action. We start by writing the numbers in Table 6-1 (see page 138) on 140 individual index cards that can be mixed together in a hat. The numbers represent the heights, in inches, of 140 college students from the authors' classes. As before, we treat these 140 students as the entire population.

1. First, we randomly pull one card at a time and record its score by marking it on a histogram. (In class, we create the histograms in this exercise on a white board or smart board.) After recording the score, we return the card to the container representing the population of scores and mix all the cards before pulling the next card. (Not surprisingly, this is known as *sampling with replacement*.) We continue until we have plotted at least 30 scores, drawing a square for each one so

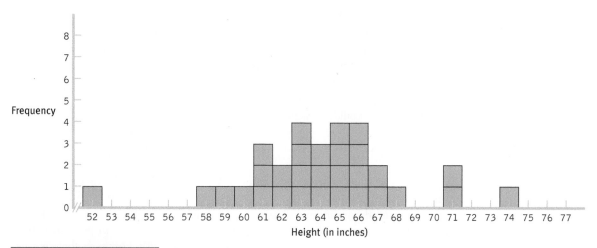

FIGURE 6-10

Creating a Distribution of Scores

This distribution is one of many that could be created by pulling 30 numbers, one at a time, and replacing the numbers between pulls, from the population of 140 heights. If you create a distribution of scores yourself from these data, it should look roughly bell-shaped like this one—that is, unimodal and symmetric.

that bars emerge above each value. This creates the beginning of a *distribution of scores*. Using this method, we created the histogram in Figure 6-10.

2. Now, we randomly pull three cards at a time, compute the mean of these three scores (rounding to the nearest whole number), and record this mean on a different histogram. As before, we draw a square for each mean, with each stack of squares resembling a bar. Again, we return each set of cards to the population and mix before pulling the next set of three. We continue until we have plotted at least 30 values. This is the beginning of a *distribution of means*. Using this method, we created the histogram in Figure 6-11.

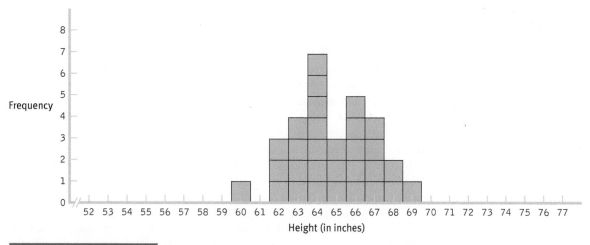

FIGURE 6-11

Creating a Distribution of Means

Compare this distribution of means to the distribution of scores in Figure 6-10. The mean is the same and it is still roughly bell-shaped. The spread is narrower, however, so there is a smaller standard deviation. This particular distribution is one of many similar distributions that could be created by pulling 30 means (the average of three numbers at a time) from the population of 140 heights.

The distribution of scores in Figure 6-10, similar to those we create when we do this exercise in class, ranges from 52 to 77, with a peak in the middle. If we had a larger population, and if we pulled many more numbers, the distribution would become more and more normal. Notice that the distribution is centered roughly around the actual population mean, 64.89. Also notice that all, or nearly all, scores fall within 3 standard deviations of the mean. The population standard deviation of these scores is 4.09. So nearly all scores should fall within this range:

$$64.89 - 3(4.09) = 52.62 \text{ and } 64.89 + 3(4.09) = 77.16$$

In fact, the range of scores—52 through 77—in this population of 140 heights is very close to this range.

Is there anything different about the distribution of means in Figure 6-11? Yes, there are not as many means at the far tails of the distribution as in the distribution of scores—we no longer have any values in the 50s or 70s. However, there are no changes in the center of the distribution. The distribution of means is still centered around the actual mean of 64.89. This makes sense. The means of three scores each come from the same set of scores, so the mean of the individual sample means should be the same as the mean of the whole population of scores.

Why does the spread decrease when we create a distribution of means rather than a distribution of scores? When we plotted individual *scores*, an extreme score was plotted on the distribution. But when we plotted *means*, we averaged that extreme score with two other scores. So each time we pulled a score in the 70s, we tended to pull two lower scores as well; when we pulled a score in the 50s, we tended to pull two higher scores as well.

What do you think would happen if we created a distribution of means of 10 scores rather than 3? As you might guess, the distribution would be even narrower because there would be more scores to balance the occasional extreme score. The mean of each set of 10 scores is likely to be even closer to the actual mean of 64.89. What if we created a distribution of means of 100 scores, or of 10,000 scores? The larger the sample size, the smaller the spread of the distribution of means. ●

Characteristics of the Distribution of Means

Because the distribution of means is less variable than the distribution of scores, the distribution of means needs its own standard deviation—a smaller standard deviation than we used for the distribution of individual scores.

The data presented in Figure 6-12 allow us to visually verify that the distribution of means needs a smaller standard deviation. Using the population mean of 64.886 and standard deviation of 4.086, the z scores for the end scores of 60 and 69 are -1.20 and 1.01, respectively—not even close to 3 standard deviations. These z scores are wrong for this distribution. We need to use a standard deviation of sample *means* rather than a standard deviation of individual *scores*.

Language Alert! We use slightly modified language and symbols when we describe distributions of means instead of distributions of scores. The mean of a distribution of means is the same as the mean of a population of scores, but it uses the symbol μ_M (pronounced "mew sub em"). The μ indicates that it is the mean of a *population*, and the subscript M indicates that the population is composed of *sample means*—the means of all possible samples of a given size from a particular population of individual scores.

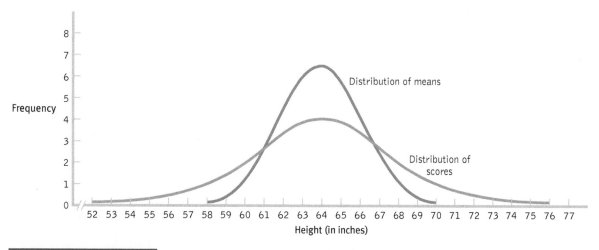

FIGURE 6-12

Using the Appropriate Measure of Spread

Because the distribution of means is narrower than the distribution of scores, it has a smaller standard deviation. This standard deviation has its own name: standard error.

We also need a new symbol and a new name for the standard deviation of the distribution of means—the typical amount that a sample mean varies from the population mean. The symbol is σ_M (pronounced "sigma sub em"). The subscript M again stands for mean; this is the standard deviation of the population of means calculated for *all possible samples* of a given size. The symbol has its own name: **standard error** *is the name for the standard deviation of a distribution of means.* Table 6-2 summarizes the alternative names that describe these related ideas.

Fortunately, there is a simple calculation that lets us know exactly how much smaller the standard error, σ_M, is than the standard deviation, σ. As we've noted, the larger the sample size, the narrower the distribution of means and the smaller the standard deviation of the distribution of means—the standard error. We calculate the standard error by taking into account the sample size used to calculate the means that make up the distribution. The standard error is the standard deviation of the population divided by the square root of the sample size, N. The formula is:

$$\sigma_M = \frac{\sigma}{\sqrt{N}}$$

- **Standard error** is the name for the standard deviation of a distribution of means.

MASTERING THE FORMULA

6-3: The formula for standard error is:
$$\sigma_M = \frac{\sigma}{\sqrt{N}}.$$
We divide the standard deviation for the population by the square root of the sample size.

TABLE 6-2   Parameters for Distributions of Scores Versus Means

When we determine the parameters of a distribution, we must consider whether the distribution is composed of scores or means.

Distribution	Symbol for Mean	Symbol for Spread	Name for Spread
Scores	μ	σ	Standard deviation
Means	μ_M	σ_M	Standard error

EXAMPLE 6.11

Imagine that the standard deviation of the distribution of individual scores is 5 and we have a sample of 10 people. The standard error would be:

$$\sigma_M = \frac{\sigma}{\sqrt{N}} = \frac{5}{\sqrt{10}} = 1.58$$

The spread is smaller when we calculate means for samples of 10 people because any extreme scores are balanced by less extreme scores. With a larger sample size of 200, the spread is even smaller because there are many more scores close to the mean to balance out any extreme scores. The standard error would then be:

$$\sigma_M = \frac{\sigma}{\sqrt{N}} = \frac{5}{\sqrt{200}} = 0.35$$

A distribution of means faithfully obeys the central limit theorem. Even if the population of individual scores is *not* normally distributed, the distribution of means will approximate the normal curve if the samples are composed of at least 30 scores. The three graphs in Figure 6-13 depict (a) a distribution of individual scores that is extremely skewed in the positive direction, (b) the less skewed distribution that results when we create a distribution of means using samples of 2, and (c) the approximately normal curve that results when we create a distribution of means using samples of 25. We have learned three important characteristics of the distribution of means:

1. As sample size increases, the mean of a distribution of means remains the same.
2. The standard deviation of a distribution of means (called the *standard error*) is smaller than the standard deviation of a distribution of scores. As sample size increases, the standard error becomes ever smaller.

A severely skewed distribution of scores in a population

(a)

A less severely skewed distribution of means using samples of 2 from the same population

(b)

A normal distribution of means using samples of 25 from the same population

(c)

FIGURE 6-13

The Mathematical Magic of Large Samples

Even with a population of individual scores that are not normally distributed, the distribution of means approximates a normal curve as the sample gets larger.

3. The shape of the distribution of means approximates the normal curve if the distribution of the population of individual scores has a normal shape or if the size of each sample that makes up the distribution is at least 30 (the central limit theorem). ●

Using the Central Limit Theorem to Make Comparisons with z Scores

z scores are a standardized version of raw scores based on the population. But we seldom have the entire population to work with, so we typically calculate the mean of a sample and calculate a z score based on a distribution of means. When we calculate the z score, we simply use a distribution of means instead of a distribution of scores. The z formula changes only in the symbols it uses:

$$z = \frac{(M - \mu_M)}{\sigma_M}$$

Note that we now use M instead of X because we are calculating a z score for a sample mean rather than for an individual score. Because the z score now represents a mean, not an actual score, it is often referred to as a z *statistic*. Specifically, the z statistic tells us how many standard errors a sample mean is from the population mean.

MASTERING THE FORMULA

6-4: The formula for z based on the mean of a sample is:

$$z = \frac{(M - \mu_M)}{\sigma_M}.$$

We subtract the mean of the distribution of means from the mean of the sample, then we divide by the standard error, the standard deviation of the distribution of means.

EXAMPLE 6.12

Let's consider a distribution for which we know the population mean and standard deviation. Several hundred universities reported data from their counseling centers (Gallagher, 2009). (For this example, we'll treat this sample as the entire population of interest.) The study found that an average of 8.5 students per institution were hospitalized for mental illness over 1 year. For the purposes of this example, we'll assume a standard deviation of 3.8. Let's say we develop a prevention program to reduce the numbers of hospitalizations and we recruit 30 universities to participate. After 1 year, we calculate a mean of 7.1 hospitalizations at these 30 institutions. Is this an extreme sample mean, given the population?

To find out, let's imagine the distribution of means for samples of 30 hospitalization scores. We would collect the means the same way we collected the means of three heights in the earlier example—just with far more means. The average of all those means would have the same mean as the population but the spread would be narrower. The spread of the distribution is skinnier because any extreme hospitalization scores would now be part of a sample that likely included less extreme scores. So, the mean for each sample is less likely to be extreme than is an individual score. The distribution of all of these means, then, would be less variable than the distribution of scores. Here are the mean and standard error of the sample of universities, using proper symbolic notation:

$$\mu_M = \mu = 8.5$$

$$\sigma_M = \frac{\sigma}{\sqrt{N}} = \frac{3.8}{\sqrt{30}} = 0.694$$

At this point, we have all the information we need to calculate the z statistic:

$$z = \frac{(M - \mu_M)}{\sigma_M} = \frac{(7.1 - 8.5)}{0.694} = -2.02$$

From this z statistic, we could determine how extreme the mean number of hospitalizations is in terms of a percentage. Then we could draw a conclusion about whether we would be likely to find a mean number of hospitalizations of 7.1 in a sample of 30 universities if the prevention program did *not* work. The useful combination of a distribution of means and a z statistic has led us to a point where we're prepared for inferential statistics and hypothesis testing. ●

| Next Steps | The Normal Curve and Catching Cheaters |

Cheaters beware! Statisticians have applied principles based on the normal curve to identify patterns of extreme scores. (See Lawrence Stedman's 2011 report on cheating in the Atlanta school system, which led to numerous indictments of teachers and administrators.) In their book *Freakonomics*, Steven Levitt and Stephen Dubner (2009) described alleged cheating among teachers in the Chicago public school system. Certain classrooms had suspiciously strong performances on standardized tests that often mysteriously declined the following year when a new teacher taught the same students. In about 5% of classrooms studied, Levitt and other researchers found blocks of correct answers among most students for the last few questions, an indication that the teacher had changed responses to difficult questions for most students. In one classroom, for example, 15 of 22 students gave identical answers to a string of six questions toward the end of a test, where the questions were more difficult. It did not take a large inferential leap to believe that these teachers were filling in the answers in order to artificially inflate their classes' scores.

In another example, Alan Gerber and Neil Malhotra (2006) looked at all studies published between 1995 and 2004 in two political science journals, *American Political Science Review* and *American Journal of Political Science*, and recorded the z statistics reported in these studies. Gerber and Malhotra combined positive and negative z statistics, so any z statistic above 1.96 indicates that it was among the most extreme 5%. (As we noted in the Chapter 5 Next Steps, a cutoff of 5% is the norm in the social sciences; findings in the most extreme 5% are most likely to be published.) Then Gerber and Malhotra constructed a histogram (Figure 6-14) depicting the frequencies of the z statistics in these articles—and documented an apparent publication bias among researchers!

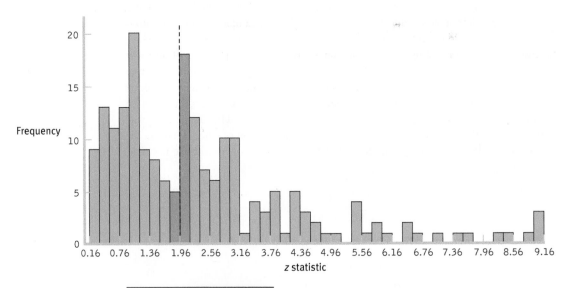

FIGURE 6-14

Identifying Cheaters

An understanding of distributions can help us identify cheaters. This histogram of z statistics for the journals studied by Gerber and Malhotra (2006) shows an unexpectedly short bar for findings with z statistics slightly smaller than 1.96 and an unexpectedly tall bar for findings with z statistics slightly larger than 1.96. This pattern is an indication that researchers might be manipulating their analyses to push their z statistics beyond the cutoffs and into the tails so that they can reject the null hypothesis.

What might be the source of this possible bias? There is nothing magical about the 0.05 (5%) cutoff; it is simply a reasonable standard that gives us a reasonable chance of detecting a real finding while minimizing the likelihood of committing a Type I error. The .05 level is the standard used by journal editors—but guess what? The data don't know about the 0.05 standard, so we would not expect any clustering of reported findings that, for example, just barely achieves that standard (anything less than 0.05). Let's look at the data.

If we think of this histogram as one half of a normal curve, we notice a much lower frequency than would be expected for *z* statistics just below 1.96 (the 5% standard), as seen in the red bar just to the left of the dotted vertical line. And there was a much higher frequency than would be expected for *z* statistics just above 1.96, as seen in the red bar just to the right of the dotted vertical line. Gerber and Malhotra (2006) cite a "1 in 100 million" probability that the patterns they observed occurred just by chance (p. 3). What might account for this?

The authors suggest that the strict 5% cutoff is encouraging researchers to "play" with their data until it beats the cutoff. Some researchers may cheat in this way unwittingly, not realizing that they are biased. However, other researchers might cheat consciously, massaging the data with various analyses until it performs as they hope. The normal curve thus helped to identify a pattern of apparent cheating in social science publishing. Paying attention to the shape of distributions is not a sophisticated form of analysis. Yet such analysis could have flagged the enormous level of corruption at companies such as Enron, Global Crossing, and WorldCom—and prevented thousands of workers from losing their retirement monies. The identification of cheating, and the implementation of reforms that might prevent it, can start with an understanding of the normal, bell-shaped curve.

CHECK YOUR LEARNING

Reviewing the Concepts

> According to the central limit theorem, a distribution of sample means based on 30 or more scores approximates the normal distribution, even if the original population is not normally distributed.

> A distribution of scores has the same mean as a distribution of means. However, a distribution of scores contains more extreme scores and a larger standard deviation than a distribution of means; this is another principle of the central limit theorem.

> *z* scores may be calculated from a distribution of scores or from a distribution of means. When we calculate a *z* score for a mean, we usually call it a *z* statistic.

> For the measure of spread, the two calculations use different terms: *standard deviation* for a distribution of scores and *standard error* for a distribution of means.

> Just as with *z* scores, the *z* statistic tells us about the relative position of a mean within a distribution; this can be expressed as a percentile.

> The normal curve can help identify observations caused by cheating that violate what we would expect by chance.

Clarifying the Concepts **6-10** What are the main ideas behind the central limit theorem?

6-11 Explain what a distribution of means is.

Calculating the Statistics **6-12** The mean of a distribution of scores is 57, with a standard deviation of 11. Calculate the standard error for a distribution of means based on samples of 35 people.

continued on next page

Applying the Concepts   6-13   Let's return to the selection of 30 CFC scores that we considered in Check Your Learning 6-2(b):

$$3.5 \quad 3.5 \quad 3.0 \quad 4.0 \quad 2.0 \quad 4.0 \quad 2.0 \quad 4.0 \quad 3.5 \quad 4.5$$
$$4.5 \quad 4.0 \quad 3.5 \quad 2.5 \quad 3.5 \quad 3.5 \quad 4.0 \quad 3.0 \quad 3.0 \quad 2.5$$
$$3.0 \quad 3.5 \quad 4.0 \quad 3.5 \quad 3.5 \quad 2.0 \quad 3.5 \quad 3.0 \quad 3.0 \quad 2.5$$

a. What is the range of these scores?

b. Take three means of 10 scores each from this sample of scores, one for each row. What is the range of these means?

c. Why is the range smaller for the *means* of samples of 10 scores than for the *individual* scores themselves?

Solutions to these Check Your Learning questions can be found in Appendix D.

d. The mean of these 30 scores is 3.32. The standard deviation is 0.69. Using symbolic notation and formulas (where appropriate), determine the mean and standard error of the distribution of means computed from samples of 10.

REVIEW OF CONCEPTS

The Normal Curve

Three ideas about the normal curve help us to understand inferential statistics. First, the *normal curve* describes the variability of many physical and psychological characteristics. Second, the normal curve may be translated into percentages, allowing us to standardize variables and make direct comparisons of scores on different measures. Third, a distribution of means, rather than a distribution of scores, produces a more normal curve. The last idea is based on the central limit theorem, by which we know that a distribution of means will be normally distributed and less variable as long as the samples from which the means are computed are of a sufficiently large size, usually at least 30.

Standardization, z Scores, and the Normal Curve

The process of *standardization* converts raw scores into *z* scores. Raw scores from any normal distribution can be converted to the *z distribution*. A normal distribution of *z* scores is called the *standard normal distribution*. *z scores* tell us how far a raw score falls from its mean in terms of standard deviation. We can also reverse the formula to convert *z* scores to raw scores. Standardization using *z* scores has two important applications. First, standardized scores—that is, *z* scores—can be converted to percentile ranks (and percentile ranks can be converted to *z* scores and then raw scores). Second, we can directly compare *z* scores from different raw-score distributions. *z* scores work the other way around as well.

The Central Limit Theorem

The *z* distribution can be used with a *distribution of means* in addition to a distribution of scores. Distributions of means have the same mean as the population of individual scores from which they are calculated, but a smaller spread, which means we must adjust for sample size. The standard deviation of a distribution of means is called the *standard error*. The decreased variability is due to the fact that extreme scores are balanced by less extreme scores when means are calculated. Distributions of means are normally distributed if the underlying population of scores is normal, or if the means are computed from sufficiently large samples, usually at least 30 individual scores. This second situation is described by the *central limit theorem*, the principle that a distribution of sample means will be normally distributed even if the underlying distribution of scores is not normally distributed, as long as there are enough scores—usually at least 30—comprising each sample. The characteristics of the normal curve allow us to make inferences from small samples using standardized distributions, such as the *z* distribution. We can use the *z* distribution for means, as well as for individual scores, if we determine the appropriate mean and standard deviation. The bell-shaped curve can also be used to catch cheaters when a pattern of scores violates what we would expect by chance.

SPSS®

SPSS lets us understand each variable, identify its skewness, and explore how well it fits with a normal distribution. Enter the 140 heights from Table 6-1.

We can identify outliers that might skew the normal curve by selecting Analyze → Descriptive Statistics → Explore. In the dialogue box, select Statistics → Outliers. Click "Continue." Choose the variable of interest, "Height," by clicking it on the left and then using the arrow to move it to the right. Click "OK." The screenshot shown here depicts part of the output.

The output provides basic descriptive information for the variable of interest (i.e., mean, standard deviation, median, minimum, maximum, range, etc.), and then provides a description of extreme scores: the top five extreme scores and the bottom five extreme scores. By scrolling farther down in the output, SPSS (by default) will provide both a stem-and-leaf plot and a box plot. Both of these visualizations identify extreme scores using a statistical definition—values more than 1.5 interquartile ranges beyond the 25th or 75th percentiles. (See the Next Steps section of Chapter 4 for more information on interquartile ranges.) In addition to a frequency distribution, the box plot is a useful tool to visualize the shape (or skewness) in a distribution.

We encourage you to explore your data and the many features in SPSS, especially when you are using your own data. SPSS is much easier to learn when you know why every number was included in the study in the first place. It's also much more interesting to test your own ideas!

Source: SPSS Statistics

HOW IT WORKS

6.1 CONVERTING RAW SCORES TO z SCORES

Researchers reported that college students had healthier eating habits, on average, than did those who were neither college students nor college graduates (Georgiou et al., 1997). The researchers found that the 412 college students in the study ate breakfast a mean of 4.1 times per week, with a standard deviation of 2.4. Imagine that this is the entire population of interest.

Using symbolic notation and the formula, how can we calculate the z score for a student who eats breakfast six times per week? We can calculate the z score as follows:

$$z = \frac{(X - \mu)}{\sigma} = \frac{(6 - 4.1)}{2.4} = 0.79$$

Now, how can we calculate the z score for a student who eats breakfast twice a week? We can calculate this z score as follows:

$$z = \frac{(X - \mu)}{\sigma} = \frac{(2 - 4.1)}{2.4} = -0.88$$

6.2 STANDARDIZATION WITH z SCORES AND PERCENTILES

Who is doing better financially—Katy Perry, with respect to the 10 most powerful celebrities, or Tiger Woods, with respect to the 10 golfers with the highest incomes? In 2012, Forbes.com listed the 10 most powerful celebrities in terms of earnings and media exposure, regardless of gender. Katy Perry ranked 8th on this list and earned $45 million that year. In 2012, Golfdigest.com listed the top 10 earners in golf. Woods topped the list, with $86.1 million. In comparison to his top 10 peers, did Woods really do better financially than Perry did in comparison to her top 10 peers?

For celebrities, the mean for the top 10 was $70.3 million, with a standard deviation of $41.4 million. Based on this, Kate Perry's z score is:

$$z = \frac{(X - \mu)}{\sigma} = \frac{(45 - 70.3)}{41.4} = -0.61$$

We can also calculate a range for her percentile rank. Fifty percent of scores fall below the mean. About 34% fall between the mean and a z score of -1.0, so: $50 - 34 = 16$ percent of scores fall below a z score of -1. Therefore, Katy Perry is somewhere between the 16th and 50th percentiles among the top 10 most powerful celebrities.

For golf, the mean for the top 10 was $30.0 million, with a standard deviation of $21.1 million. Based on this, Tiger Woods's z score is:

$$z = \frac{(X - \mu)}{\sigma} = \frac{(86.1 - 30)}{21.1} = 2.66$$

We can also estimate his percentile rank. Fifty percent of scores fall below the mean; about 34% fall between the mean and 1 standard deviation above the mean; and about 14% fall between 1 and 2 standard deviations above the mean: $50 + 34 + 14 = 98$. Woods is above the 98th percentile among the top 10 golfers with the highest incomes.

Tiger Woods outearned Katy Perry when each was compared to the top 10 earners in their respective fields.

EXERCISES

The solutions to the odd-numbered exercises can be found in Appendix C.

Clarifying the Concepts

6.1 Explain how the word *normal* is used in everyday conversation, then explain how statisticians use it.

6.2 What point on the normal curve represents the most commonly occurring observation?

6.3 How does the size of a sample of scores affect the shape of the distribution of data?

6.4 Explain how the word *standardize* is used in everyday conversation, then explain how statisticians use it.

6.5 What is a z score?

6.6 Give three reasons why z scores are useful.

6.7 What are the mean and standard deviation of the z distribution?

6.8 Why is the central limit theorem such an important idea for dealing with a population that is not normally distributed?

6.9 What does the symbol μ_M stand for?

6.10 What does the symbol σ_M stand for?

6.11 What is the difference between standard deviation and standard error?

6.12 Why does the standard error become smaller simply by increasing the sample size?

6.13 What does a z statistic—a z score based on a distribution of means—tell us about a sample mean?

6.14 Each of the following equations has an error. Identify, fix, and explain the error in each of the following equations.

a. $\sigma_M = \dfrac{\mu}{\sqrt{N}}$

b. $z = \dfrac{(\mu - \mu_M)}{\sigma_M}$ (for a distribution of means)

c. $z = \dfrac{(M - \mu_M)}{\sigma}$ (for a distribution of means)

d. $z = \dfrac{(X - \mu)}{\sigma_M}$ (for a distribution of scores)

Calculating the Statistics

6.15 Create a histogram for these three sets of scores. Each set of scores represents a sample taken from the same population.

a. 6 4 11 7 7

b. 6 4 11 7 7 2 10 7 8 6 6 7 5 8

c. 6 4 11 7 7 2 10 7 8 6 6   7   5 8
   7 8   9 7 6 9   3 9 5 6 8 11   8 3
   8 4 10 8 5 5   8 9 9 7 8   7 10 7

d. What do you observe happening across these three distributions?

6.16 A population has a mean of 250 and a standard deviation of 47. Calculate z scores for each of the following raw scores:

a. 391

b. 273

c. 199

d. 160

6.17 A population has a mean of 1179 and a standard deviation of 164. Calculate z scores for each of the following raw scores:

a. 1000

b. 721

c. 1531

d. 1184

6.18 For a population with a mean of 250 and a standard deviation of 47, calculate the z score for 250. Explain the meaning of the value you obtain.

6.19 For a population with a mean of 250 and a standard deviation of 47, calculate the z scores for 203 and 297. Explain the meaning of these values.

6.20 For a population with a mean of 250 and a standard deviation of 47, convert each of the following z scores to raw scores.

a. 0.54

b. −2.66

c. −1.00

d. 1.79

6.21 For a population with a mean of 1179 and a standard deviation of 164, convert each of the following z scores to raw scores.

a. −0.23

b. 1.41

c. 2.06

d. 0.03

6.22 By design, the verbal subtest of the Graduate Record Examination (GRE) has a population mean of 500 and a population standard deviation of 100. Convert the following z scores to raw scores *without* using a formula.

   a. 1.5

   b. −0.5

   c. −2.0

6.23 By design, the verbal subtest of the Graduate Record Examination (GRE) has a population mean of 500 and a population standard deviation of 100. Convert the following z scores to raw scores using symbolic notation and the formula.

   a. 1.5

   b. −0.5

   c. −2.0

6.24 A study of the Consideration of Future Consequences (CFC) scale found a mean score of 3.20, with a standard deviation of 0.70, for the 800 students in the sample (Adams, 2012). (Treat this sample as the entire population of interest.)

   a. If the CFC score is 4.2, what is the z score? Use symbolic notation and the formula. Explain why this answer makes sense.

   b. If the CFC score is 3.0, what is the z score? Use symbolic notation and the formula. Explain why this answer makes sense.

   c. If the z score is 0, what is the CFC score? Explain.

6.25 Using the instructions on p. 145, compare the following "apples and oranges": a score of 45 when the population mean is 51 and the standard deviation is 4, and a score of 732 when the population mean is 765 and the standard deviation is 23.

   a. Convert these scores to standardized scores.

   b. Using the standardized scores, what can you say about how these two scores compare to each other?

6.26 Compare the following scores:

   a. A score of 811 when $\mu = 800$ and $\sigma = 29$ against a score of 4524 when $\mu = 3127$ and $\sigma = 951$

   b. A score of 17 when $\mu = 30$ and $\sigma = 12$ against a score of 67 when $\mu = 88$ and $\sigma = 16$

6.27 Assume a normal distribution when answering the following questions.

   a. What percentage of scores falls below the mean?

   b. What percentage of scores falls between 1 standard deviation below the mean and 2 standard deviations above the mean?

   c. What percentage of scores lies beyond 2 standard deviations away from the mean (on both sides)?

   d. What percentage of scores is between the mean and 2 standard deviations above the mean?

   e. What percentage of scores falls under the normal curve?

6.28 Compute the standard error (σ_M) for each of the following sample sizes, assuming a population mean of 100 and a standard deviation of 20:

   a. 45

   b. 100

   c. 4500

6.29 A population has a mean of 55 and a standard deviation of 8. Compute μ_M and σ_M for each of the following sample sizes:

   a. 30

   b. 300

   c. 3000

6.30 Compute a z statistic for each of the following, assuming the population has a mean of 100 and a standard deviation of 20:

   a. A sample of 43 scores has a mean of 101.

   b. A sample of 60 scores has a mean of 96.

   c. A sample of 29 scores has a mean of 100.

6.31 A sample of 100 people had a mean depression score of 85; the population mean for this depression measure is 80, with a standard deviation of 20. A different sample of 100 people had a mean score of 17 on a different depression measure; the population mean for this measure is 15, with a standard deviation of 5.

   a. Convert these means to z statistics.

   b. Using the z statistics, what can you say about how these two means compare to each other?

Applying the Concepts

6.32 **Normal distributions in real life:** Many variables are normally distributed, but not all are. (Fortunately, the central limit theorem saves us when we conduct research on samples from nonnormal populations if the samples are larger than 30!) Which of the following are likely to be normally distributed, and which are likely to be nonnormal? Explain your answers.

   a. In the population of students admitted to the highly selective University of Toronto, scores on the federal or provincial literacy test (required for university admissions)

   b. In the population of secondary school students in New Zealand, the number of daily calories consumed

   c. In the population of employed adults in San Antonio, Texas, the amount of time spent commuting to work

   d. In the population of North American university students, the number of frequent flyer miles earned in a year

6.33 **Distributions and getting ready for a date:** We asked 150 students in our statistics classes how long, in minutes, they typically spend getting ready for a date. The scores ranged from 1 minute to 120 minutes, and the mean was 51.52 minutes. Here are the data for 40 of these students:

30	90	60	60	5	90	30	40	45	60
60	30	90	60	25	10	90	20	15	60
60	75	45	60	30	75	15	30	45	1
20	25	45	60	90	10	105	90	30	60

a. Construct a histogram for the 10 scores in the first row.

b. Construct a histogram for all 40 of these scores.

c. What happened to the shape of the distribution as you increased the number of scores from 10 to 40? What do you think would happen if the data for all 150 students were included? What if we included 10,000 scores? Explain this phenomenon.

d. Are these distributions of scores or distributions of means? Explain.

e. The data here are self-reported. That is, our students wrote down how many minutes they believe that they typically take to get ready for a date. This accounts for the fact that the data include many "pretty" numbers, such as 30, 60, or 90 minutes. What might have been a better way to operationalize this variable?

f. Do these data suggest any hypotheses that you might like to study? List at least one.

6.34 z scores and the GRE: By design, the verbal subtest of the GRE has a population mean of 500 and a population standard deviation of 100 (the quantitative subtest has the same mean and standard deviation).

a. Use symbolic notation to state the mean and the standard deviation of the GRE verbal test.

b. Convert a GRE score of 700 to a z score *without* using a formula.

c. Convert a GRE score of 550 to a z score *without* using a formula.

d. Convert a GRE score of 400 to a z score *without* using a formula.

6.35 The z distribution and hours slept: A sample of 150 statistics students reported the typical number of hours that they sleep on a weeknight. The mean number of hours was 6.65, and the standard deviation was 1.24. (For this exercise, treat this sample as the entire population of interest.)

a. What is *always* the mean of the z distribution?

b. Using the sleep data, demonstrate that your answer to part (a) is the mean of the z distribution. (*Hint:* Calculate the z score for a student who is exactly at the mean.)

c. What is *always* the standard deviation of the z distribution?

d. Using the sleep data, demonstrate that your answer to part (c) is the standard deviation of the z distribution. (*Hint:* Calculate the z score for a student who is exactly 1 standard deviation above or below the mean.)

e. How many hours of sleep do you typically get on a weeknight? What would your z score be, based on this population?

6.36 The z distribution applied to admiration ratings: A sample of 148 of our statistics students rated their level of admiration for Hillary Clinton on a scale of 1 to 7. The mean rating was 4.06, and the standard deviation was 1.70. (For this exercise, treat this sample as the entire population of interest.)

a. Use these data to demonstrate that the mean of the z distribution is always 0.

b. Use these data to demonstrate that the standard deviation of the z distribution is always 1.

c. Calculate the z score for a student who rated his admiration of Hillary Clinton as 6.1.

d. A student had a z score of −0.55. What rating did she give for her admiration of Hillary Clinton?

6.37 z statistics and CFC scores: We have already discussed summary parameters for CFC scores for the population of participants in a study by Adams (2012). The mean CFC score was 3.20, with a standard deviation of 0.70. (Remember that we treated the sample of 800 participants as the entire population.) Imagine that you randomly selected 40 people from this population and had them watch a series of videos on financial planning after graduation. The mean CFC score after watching the video was 3.62.

a. Why would it not make sense to compare the mean of this sample with the distribution of scores? Be sure to discuss the spread of distributions in your answer.

b. In your own words, what would the null hypothesis predict? What would the research hypothesis predict?

c. Using symbolic notation and formulas, what are the appropriate measures of central tendency and variability for the distribution from which this sample comes?

d. Using symbolic notation and the formula, what is the z statistic for this sample mean?

6.38 Converting z scores to raw CFC scores: A study using the Consideration of Future Consequences scale found a mean CFC score of 3.20, with a standard deviation of 0.70, for the 800 students in the sample (Adams, 2012).

a. Imagine that your *z* score on the CFC score is −1.2. What is your raw score? Use symbolic notation and the formula. Explain why this answer makes sense.

b. Imagine that your *z* score on the CFC score is 0.66. What is your raw score? Use symbolic notation and the formula. Explain why this answer makes sense.

6.39 The normal curve and real-life variables, part I: For each of the following variables, state whether the distribution of scores would likely approximate a normal curve. Explain your answer.

a. Number of movies that a college student watches in a year

b. Number of full-page advertisements in a magazine

c. Human birth weights in Canada

6.40 The normal curve and real-life variables, part II: For each of the following variables, state whether the distribution of scores would likely approximate a normal curve. Explain your answer.

a. Number of minutes that students check Facebook and other social media each week

b. Volume of water that people drink each day

c. The length, in minutes, of YouTube videos

6.41 The normal curve in the media: Statistics geeks rejoiced when the *New York Times* published an article on the normal curve (Dunn, 2013)! Biologist Casey Dunn wrote that "Many real-world observations can be approximated by, and tested against, the same expected pattern: the normal distribution." He described the normal curve as symmetric and bell-shaped with more observations gathered near the mean. He offered several examples: "The size of flowers, the physiological response to a drug, the breaking force in a batch of steel cables," but also noted that there are important exceptions, including household income. In your own words, explain to someone who has never taken statistics why household income, unlike Dunn's other examples, is not normally distributed.

6.42 Percentiles and eating habits: As noted in How It Works 6.1, Georgiou and colleagues (1997) reported that college students had healthier eating habits, on average, than did those who were neither college students nor college graduates. The 412 students in the study ate breakfast a mean of 4.1 times per week, with a standard deviation of 2.4. (For this exercise, again imagine that this is the entire population of interest.)

a. What is the approximate percentile for a student who eats breakfast four times per week?

b. What is the approximate percentile for a student who eats breakfast six times per week?

c. What is the approximate percentile for a student who eats breakfast twice a week?

6.43 *z* scores and comparisons of sports teams: A common quandary faces sports fans who live in the same city but avidly follow different sports. How does one determine whose team did better with respect to its league division? In 2012, the Atlanta Braves baseball team and the Atlanta Falcons football team both did well. The Braves won 94 games and the Falcons won 13. Which team was better in 2012? The question, then, is: Were the Braves better, as compared to the other teams in Major League Baseball (MLB), than the Falcons, as compared to the other teams in the National Football League (NFL)? Some of us could debate this for hours, but it's better to examine some statistics. Let's operationalize performance over the season as the number of wins during regular season play.

a. In 2012, the mean number of wins for MLB teams was 81.00, with a standard deviation of 11.733. Because all teams were included, these are population parameters. What is the Braves' *z* score?

b. In 2012, the mean number of wins for all NFL teams was 7.969, with a standard deviation of 3.036. What is the Falcons' *z* score?

c. Which team did better, according to these data?

d. How many games would the team with the lower *z* score have had to win to beat the team with the higher *z* score?

e. List at least one other way we could have operationalized the outcome variable (i.e., team performance).

6.44 *z* scores and comparisons of admiration ratings: Our statistics students were asked to rate their admiration of Hillary Clinton on a scale of 1 to 7. They also were asked to rate their admiration of actor, singer, and former *American Idol* judge Jennifer Lopez and their admiration of tennis player Venus Williams on a scale of 1 to 7. As noted earlier, the mean rating of Clinton was 4.06, with a standard deviation of 1.70. The mean rating of Lopez was 3.72, with a standard deviation of 1.90. The mean rating of Williams was 4.58, with a standard deviation of 1.46. One of our students rated her admiration of Clinton and Williams at 5 and her admiration of Lopez at 4.

a. What is the student's *z* score for her rating of Clinton?

b. What is the student's *z* score for her rating of Williams?

c. What is the student's *z* score for her rating of Lopez?

d. Compared to the other statistics students in our sample, which celebrity does this student most admire? (We can tell by her raw scores that she prefers

Clinton and Williams to Lopez, but when we take into account the general perception of these celebrities, how does this student feel about each one?)

   e. How do *z* scores allow us to make comparisons that we cannot make with raw scores? That is, describe the benefits of standardization.

6.45 Raw scores, *z* scores, percentiles, and sports teams: Let's look at baseball and football again. We'll look at data for all of the teams in Major League Baseball (MLB) and the National Football League (NFL), respectively.

   a. In 2012, the mean number of wins for MLB teams was 81.00, with a standard deviation of 11.733. The perennial underdogs, the Chicago Cubs, had a *z* score of -1.705. How many games did they win?

   b. In 2012, the mean number of wins for all NFL teams was 7.969, with a standard deviation of 3.036. The New Orleans Saints had a *z* score of -0.319. How many games did they win?

   c. The Indianapolis Colts were just below the 84th percentile in terms of NFL wins. How many games did they win? Explain how you obtained your answer.

   d. Explain how you can examine your answers in parts (a), (b), and (c) to determine whether the numbers make sense.

6.46 Distributions and life expectancy: Researchers have reported that the projected life expectancy for South African men diagnosed with human immunodeficiency virus (HIV) at age 20 who receive antiretroviral therapy (ART) is 27.6 years (Johnson et al., 2013). Imagine that the researchers determined this by following 250 people with HIV who were receiving ART and calculating the mean.

   a. What is the dependent variable of interest?

   b. What is the population?

   c. What is the sample?

   d. For the population, describe what the distribution of *scores* would be.

   e. For the population, describe what the distribution of *means* would be.

   f. If the distribution of the population were skewed, would the distribution of scores likely be skewed or approximately normal? Explain your answer.

   g. Would the distribution of means be skewed or approximately normal? Explain your answer.

6.47 Distributions, personality testing, and depression: The revised version of the Minnesota Multiphasic Personality Inventory (MMPI-2) is the most frequently administered self-report personality measure. Test-takers respond to more than 500 true/false statements, and their responses are scored, typically by a computer, on

a number of scales (e.g., hypochondriasis, depression, psychopathic deviation). Respondents receive a *T* score on each scale that can be compared to norms. (You're likely to encounter *T* scores if you take psychology classes, but it's good to be aware that they are different from the *t* statistic that you will learn about in a few chapters.) *T* scores are another way to standardize scores so that percentiles and cutoffs can be determined. The mean *T* score is always 50, and the standard deviation is always 10. Imagine that you administer the MMPI-2 to 95 respondents who have recently lost a parent; you wonder whether their scores on the depression scale will be, on average, higher than the norms. You find a mean score on the depression scale of 55 in your sample.

   a. Using symbolic notation, report the mean and standard deviation of the population.

   b. Using symbolic notation and formulas (where appropriate), report the mean and standard error for the distribution of means to which your sample will be compared.

   c. In your own words, explain why it makes sense that the standard error is smaller than the standard deviation.

6.48 Distributions, personality testing, and social introversion: See the description of the MMPI-2 in Exercise 6.47. The mean *T* score is always 50, and the standard deviation is always 10. Imagine that you administer the MMPI-2 to 50 respondents who do not use Instagram or any other social media; you wonder whether their scores on the social introversion scale will be, on average, higher than the norms. You find a mean score on the social introversion scale of 60 in your sample.

   a. Using symbolic notation, report the mean and standard deviation of the population.

   b. Using symbolic notation and formulas (where appropriate), report the mean and standard error for the distribution of means to which your sample will be compared.

   c. In your own words, explain why it makes sense that the standard error is smaller than the standard deviation.

6.49 Distributions and the General Social Survey: The General Social Survey (GSS) is a survey of approximately 2000 adults conducted each year since 1972, for a total of more than 38,000 participants. During several years of the GSS, participants were asked how many close friends they have. The mean for this variable is 7.44 friends, with a standard deviation of 10.98. The median is 5.00 and the mode is 4.00.

   a. Are these data for a distribution of scores or a distribution of means? Explain.

   b. What do the mean and standard deviation suggest about the shape of the distribution?

(*Hint:* Compare the sizes of the mean and the standard deviation.)

c. What do the three measures of central tendency suggest about the shape of the distribution?

d. Let's say that these data represent the entire population. Pretend that you randomly selected a person from this population and asked how many close friends she or he had. Would you compare this person to a distribution of scores or to a distribution of means? Explain your answer.

e. Now pretend that you randomly selected a sample of 80 people from this population. Would you compare this sample to a distribution of scores or to a distribution of means? Explain your answer.

f. Using symbolic notation, calculate the mean and standard error of the distribution of means.

g. What is the likely shape of the distribution of means? Explain your answer.

6.50 A distribution of scores and the General Social Survey: Refer to Exercise 6.49. Again, pretend that the GSS sample is the entire population of interest.

a. Imagine that you randomly selected one person from this population who reported that he had 18 close friends. Would you compare his score to a distribution of scores or to a distribution of means? Explain your answer.

b. What is his *z* score? Based on this *z* score, what is his approximate percentile?

c. Does it make sense to calculate a percentile for this person? Explain your answer. (*Hint:* Consider the shape of the distribution.)

6.51 A distribution of means and the General Social Survey: Refer to Exercise 6.49. Again, pretend that the GSS sample is the entire population of interest.

a. Imagine that you randomly selected 80 people from this population, and that they had a mean of 8.7. Would you compare this sample mean to a distribution of scores or to a distribution of means? Explain your answer.

b. What is the *z* statistic for this mean? Based on this *z* statistic, what is the approximate percentile for this sample?

c. Does it make sense to calculate a percentile for this sample? Explain your answer. (*Hint:* Consider the shape of the distribution.)

6.52 Percentiles, raw scores, and credit card theft: Credit card companies will often call cardholders if the pattern of use indicates that the card might have been stolen. Let's say that you charge an average of $280 a month on your credit card, with a standard deviation of $75. The credit card company will call you anytime your purchases for the month exceed the 98th percentile. What is the dollar amount beyond which you'll get a call from your credit card company?

6.53 The *z* distribution and a rogue cardiologist: A cardiologist in Munster, Indiana, has been accused of conducting unnecessary heart surgeries (Creswell, 2015). Investigators found that the rates for one heart procedure were in the top 10% in the country for the city where this doctor worked. Lawyers countered that there were older and sicker people in this part of the country; yet other afflictions of the elderly—for example, treatment for hip fractures—were no higher in this region. In your own words, explain how the *z* distribution might play a role in determining whether this cardiologist was conducting unnecessary surgeries.

6.54 The *z* distribution and a "super recognizer": According to a news article, "Friends call Constable [Gary] Collins Rain Man or Yoda or simply The Oracle. But to Scotland Yard, London's metropolitan police force, he is known as a 'super recognizer'" (Bennhold, 2015). Prosopagnosia, also known as face blindness, is a disorder in which the sufferer cannot recall faces, even of people they know well. About 2% of us experience face blindness. Collins is the opposite; he's among the 1 to 2% of us who recall almost every face they've ever seen. As you can imagine, this gives him an almost superhero ability to help solve crimes— a "Facebook of the mind." A snippet from a security camera, and Collins has a name for the suspect. Most of us, however, fall in between prosopagnosics and super recognizers.

a. Imagine a *z* distribution for face recognition ability. Give an estimate of the *z* score that Collins and other super recognizers are likely to fall above. Explain your answer.

b. Now give an estimate of the *z* score that people with face blindness are likely to fall below. Explain your answer.

c. Between approximately what *z* scores do most of us fall? Explain your answer.

Putting It All Together

6.55 Probability and medical treatments: The three most common treatments for blocked coronary arteries are medication, bypass surgery, and angioplasty, which is a medical procedure that involves clearing out arteries and that leads to higher profits for doctors than do the other two procedures. The highest rate of angioplasty in the United States is in Elyria, a small city in Ohio. A 2006 article in the *New York Times* stated that "the statistics are so far off the charts—Medicare patients in Elyria receive angioplasties at a rate nearly four times the national average—that Medicare and at least one commercial insurer are starting to ask questions." The rate, in fact, is three times as high as that of Cleveland, Ohio, which is located just 30 miles from Elyria.

a. What is the population in this example? What is the sample?

b. How did probability play a role in the decision of Medicare and the commercial insurer to begin investigations?

c. How might the z distribution help the investigators to detect possible fraud in this case?

d. If the insurers determine that physicians in Elyria are committing fraud, but the insurers are wrong, what kind of error would they have made? Explain.

e. Does Elyria's extremely high percentile mean that the doctors in town are committing fraud? Cite two other possible reasons for Elyria's status as an outlier.

6.56 Rural friendships and the General Social Survey: Earlier, we considered data from the GSS on numbers of close friends people reported having. The mean for this variable is 7.44, with a standard deviation of 10.98. Let's say that you decide to use the GSS data to test whether people who live in rural areas have a different mean number of friends than does the overall GSS sample. Again, treat the overall GSS sample as the entire population of interest. Let's say that you select 40 people living in rural areas and find that they have an average of 3.9 friends.

a. What is the independent variable in this study? Is this variable nominal, ordinal, or scale?

b. What is the dependent variable in this study? Is this variable nominal, ordinal, or scale?

c. What is the null hypothesis for this study?

d. What is the research hypothesis for this study?

e. Would we compare the sample data to a distribution of scores or to a distribution of means? Explain.

f. Using symbolic notation and formulas, calculate the mean and standard error for the distribution of means.

g. Using symbolic notation and the formula, calculate the z statistic for this sample.

h. What is the approximate percentile for this sample?

i. Let's say that the researchers concluded that people in rural areas have fewer friends than does the general population (thus rejecting the null hypothesis). If they are incorrect, have they made a Type I or a Type II error? Explain.

6.57 Cheating on standardized tests: In their book *Freakonomics*, Levitt and Dubner (2009) describe alleged cheating among teachers in the Chicago public school system. Certain classrooms had suspiciously strong performances on standardized tests that often mysteriously declined the following year when a new teacher taught the same students. In about 5% of classrooms studied, Levitt and other researchers found blocks of correct answers, among most students, for the last few questions, an indication that the teacher had changed responses to difficult questions for most students. Let's assume cheating in a given classroom if the overall standardized test score for the class showed a surprising change from one year to the next.

a. How are the researchers operationalizing the variable of cheating in this study? Is this a nominal, ordinal, or scale variable?

b. Explain how researchers can use the z distribution to catch cheating teachers.

c. How might a histogram or frequency polygon be useful to researchers who are trying to catch cheating teachers?

d. If researchers falsely conclude that teachers are cheating, what kind of error would they be committing? Explain.

6.58 Which was better, the book or the movie: FiveThirtyEight is a popular blog that uses statistics in creative ways to better understand politics, sports, science and health, economics, and culture. In a recent article (Hickey, 2015), the author uses z scores to standardize book reviews from http://www.goodreads.com (which uses a one to five scale) and movie reviews from http://www.imdb.com (which uses a scale of zero to 100) for the top 500 movies that were based on novels.

a. Explain why converting to z scores would be necessary to find out which story had a better book compared to a movie, or which story had a better movie compared to the book.

b. What might be some sampling biases (think back to Chapter 5) found in using these online ratings?

TERMS

normal curve (p. 136)
standardization (p. 140)
z score (p. 140)

z distribution (p. 145)
standard normal distribution (p. 145)
central limit theorem (p. 149)

distribution of means (p. 149)
standard error (p. 153)

FORMULAS

$z = \dfrac{(X - \mu)}{\sigma}$ (p. 142)

$\sigma_M = \dfrac{\sigma}{\sqrt{N}}$ (p. 153)

$z = \dfrac{(M - \mu_M)}{\sigma_M}$ (p. 155)

$X = z(\sigma) + \mu$ (p. 144)

SYMBOLS

z (p. 136)

μ_M (p. 152)

σ_M (p. 153)

Hypothesis Testing with z Tests

The z Table

Raw Scores, z Scores, and Percentages

The z Table and Distributions of Means

The Assumptions and Steps of Hypothesis Testing

The Three Assumptions for Conducting Analyses

The Six Steps of Hypothesis Testing

An Example of the z Test

Next Steps: Replication

BEFORE YOU GO ON

- ■ You should understand how to calculate a *z* statistic for a distribution of scores and for a distribution of means (Chapter 6).

- ■ You should understand that the *z* distribution allows us to determine the percentage of scores (or means) that fall below a particular *z* statistic (Chapter 6).

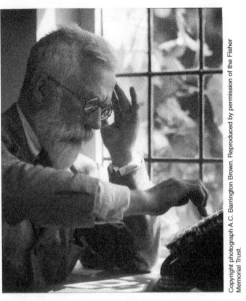

Experimental Design R. A. Fisher was inspired by the "lady drinking tea" who claimed that she could distinguish the taste of a cup of tea that had been poured tea first versus milk first. In his book, *The Design of Experiments*, he demonstrated how statistics become meaningful within the context of an experimental design.

When statistician R. A. Fisher offered a cup of tea to Dr. B. Muriel Bristol, the doctor politely declined, but for a strange reason. She preferred the taste of tea when the milk had been poured into the cup first.

"Nonsense. Surely it makes no difference," Fisher replied.

William Roach (who had witnessed the exchange between his two colleagues and would later marry Dr. Bristol) suggested, "Let's test her." Roach poured cups of tea, some with tea first and others with milk first. But Fisher's mind was awhirl with statistical concerns about how many cups should be used, their order of presentation, and how to control chance variations in temperature or sweetness. The case of the doctor drinking tea connected probability to experimental design and became one chapter's opening story in Fisher's classic textbook, *The Design of Experiments* (Fisher, 1935/1971).

With only two choices, Dr. Bristol had a 50% chance of getting it right—that is, of selecting a milk-first cup of tea. But how often would she need to be above the 50% accuracy level, the expected rate of success for a chance hit, for us to believe in her tea-tasting abilities? Obviously, 100% accuracy would be convincing, but would 55% be enough? 70%? 95%? William Roach reportedly said, "Miss Bristol divined correctly more than enough of those cups into which tea had been poured first to prove her case" (Box, 1978, p. 134). (Her success in divining tea-first cups of tea turned out to be somewhere above the 50% chance rate.) But no one specified what "more than enough" actually meant. Regardless, William Roach was in love, so he might have been biased. The important point here is that Fisher's grand insight from this ordinary event was that probability could be used to test a hypothesis.

We begin our own adventures with hypothesis testing with the *z* test. We learn how the *z* distribution and the *z* test make fair comparisons possible through standardization. Specifically, we learn:

1. How to use a *z* table.
2. How to implement the basic steps of hypothesis testing.
3. How to conduct a *z* test to compare a single sample to a known population.

The *z* Table

In Chapter 6, we learned that (1) about 68% of scores fall within one *z* score of the mean, (2) about 96% of scores fall within two *z* scores of the mean, and (3) nearly all scores fall within three *z* scores of the mean. These guidelines are useful, but the table of *z* statistics and percentages is more specific. The *z* table is printed in its entirety in Appendix B.1 but, for your convenience, we have provided an excerpt in Table 7-1. In this section, we learn how to use the *z* table to calculate percentages when the *z* score is not a whole number.

Raw Scores, *z* Scores, and Percentages

Just as the same person might be called variations of a single name—"Christina," "Christy," or "Tina," for instance—*z* scores are just one of three different ways to identify the same point beneath the normal curve: raw score, *z* score, and percentile ranking.

TABLE 7-1	Excerpt from the z Table

The z table provides the percentage of scores between the mean and a given z value. The full table includes positive z statistics from 0.00 to 4.50. The negative z statistics are not included because all we have to do is change the sign from positive to negative. Remember, the normal curve is symmetric: One side always mirrors the other. See Appendix B.1 for the full table.

z	% Between Mean and z
⋮	⋮
0.97	33.40
0.98	33.65
0.99	33.89
1.00	34.13
1.01	34.38
1.02	34.61
⋮	⋮

The z table is how we transition from one way of naming a score to another. More importantly, the z table gives us a way to state and test hypotheses by standardizing different kinds of observations onto the same scale.

For example, we can determine the percentage associated with a given z statistic by following two steps.

Step 1: Convert a raw score into a z score.

Step 2: Look up a given z score on the z table to find the percentage of scores *between the mean and that z score.*

Note that the z scores displayed in the z table are all positive, but that is just to save space. The normal curve is symmetric, so negative z scores (any scores below the mean) are the mirror image of positive z scores (any scores above the mean) (Figure 7-1).

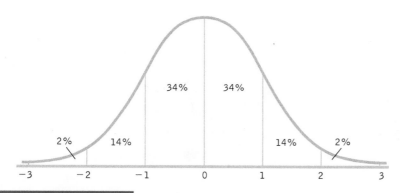

FIGURE 7-1

The Standardized z Distribution

We can use a z table to determine the percentages below and above a particular z score. For example, 34% of scores fall between the mean and a z score of 1.

EXAMPLE 7.1

Here is an interesting way to learn how to use the *z* table: A research team (Sandberg, Bukowski, Fung, & Noll, 2004) wanted to know whether very short children tended to have poorer psychological adjustment than taller children and, therefore, should be treated with growth hormone. They categorized 15-year-old boys and girls into one of three groups—short (bottom 5%), average (middle 90%), or tall (top 5%)—based on published norms for a given age and gender (Centers for Disease Control National Center for Health Statistics, 2000; Sandberg et al., 2004). The mean height for 15-year-old boys was approximately 67.00 inches, with a standard deviation of 3.19. For 15-year-old girls, the mean height was approximately 63.80 inches, with a standard deviation of 2.66. We'll consider two 15-year-olds, one taller than average and the other shorter than average.

Jessica is 66.41 inches tall (just over 5 feet, 6 inches).

> **STEP 1: Convert her raw score to a *z* score, as we learned how to do in Chapter 6.**

We use the mean ($\mu = 63.80$) and standard deviation ($\sigma = 2.66$) for the heights of girls:

$$z = \frac{(X - \mu)}{\sigma} = \frac{(66.41 - 63.80)}{2.66} = 0.98$$

> **STEP 2: Look up 0.98 on the *z* table to find the associated percentage between the mean and Jessica's *z* score.**

Once we know that the associated percentage is 33.65%, we can determine a number of percentages related to her *z* score. Here are three.

1. *Jessica's percentile rank—the percentage of scores below her score:* We add the percentage between the mean and the positive *z* score to 50%, which is the percentage of scores below the mean (50% of scores are on each side of the mean).

Jessica's percentile is 50% + 33.65% = 83.65%

Figure 7-2 shows this visually. As we can do when we are evaluating the calculations of *z* scores, we can run a quick mental check of the likely accuracy of the answer. We're interested in calculating the percentile of a *positive z* score. Because it is above the mean, we know that the answer must be higher than 50%. And it is.

FIGURE 7-2

Calculating the Percentile for a Positive *z* Score

Drawing curves helps us find someone's percentile rank. For Jessica's positive *z* score of 0.98, add the 50% below the mean to the 33.65% between the mean and her *z* score of 0.98; Jessica's percentile rank is 83.65%.

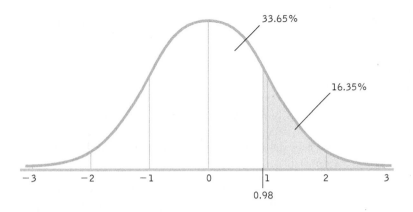

FIGURE 7-3

Calculating the Percentage Above a Positive *z* Score

For a positive *z* score, we subtract the percentage between the mean and that *z* score from 50% (the total percentage above the mean) to get the percentage above that *z* score. Here, we subtract the 33.65% between the mean and the *z* score of 0.98 from 50%, which yields 16.35%.

2. *The percentage of scores above Jessica's score:* We subtract the percentage between the mean and the positive *z* score from 50%, which is the full percentage of scores above the mean:

$$50\% - 33.65\% = 16.35\%$$

So 16.35% of 15-year-old girls' heights are above Jessica's height. Figure 7-3 shows this visually. Here, it makes sense that the percentage would be smaller than 50%; because the *z* score is positive, we could not have more than 50% above it. As an alternative, a simpler method is to subtract Jessica's percentile rank of 83.65% from 100%. This gives us the same 16.35%. We could also look under the "In the tail" column in the *z* table in Appendix B.1.

3. *The scores at least as extreme as Jessica's z score, in both directions:* When we begin hypothesis testing, it will be useful to know the percentage of scores that are at least as extreme as a given *z* score. In this case, 16.35% of heights are extreme enough to have *z* scores above Jessica's *z* score of 0.98. But remember that the curve is symmetric. This means that another 16.35% of the heights are extreme enough to be below a *z* score of −0.98. So we can double 16.35% to find the total percentage of heights that are as far as or farther from the mean than is Jessica's height:

$$16.35\% + 16.35\% = 32.70\%$$

Thus 32.7% of heights are at least as extreme as Jessica's height in either direction. Figure 7-4 shows this visually.

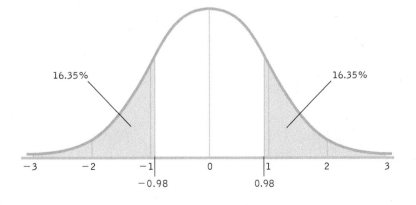

FIGURE 7-4

Calculating the Percentage at Least as Extreme as the *z* Score

For a positive *z* score, we double the percentage above that *z* score to get the percentage of scores that are at least as extreme—that is, at least as far from the mean—as the *z* score is. Here, we double 16.35% to calculate the percentage at least this extreme: 32.70%.

What group would Jessica fall in? Because 16.35% of 15-year-old girls are taller than Jessica, she is not in the top 5%. So she would be classified as being of average height, according to the researchers' definition of average. ●

EXAMPLE 7.2

Now let's repeat this process for a score below the mean. Manuel is 61.20 inches tall (about 5 feet, 1 inch) so we want to know if Manuel can be classified as short. Remember, for boys the mean height is 67.00 inches, and the standard deviation for height is 3.19 inches.

STEP 1: Convert his raw score to a z score.

We use the mean ($\mu = 67.00$) and standard deviation ($\sigma = 3.19$) for the heights of boys:

$$z = \frac{(X - \mu)}{\sigma} = \frac{(61.20 - 67.00)}{3.19} = -1.82$$

STEP 2: Calculate the percentile, the percentage above, and the percentage at least as extreme for the negative z score for Manuel's height.

We can again determine a number of percentages related to the *z* score; however, this time, we need to use the full table in Appendix B. The *z* table includes only positive *z* scores, so we look up 1.82 and find that the percentage between the mean and the *z* score is 46.56%. Of course, percentages are always positive, so don't add a negative sign here!

1. *Manuel's percentile score—the percentage of scores below his score:* For a negative *z* score, we subtract the percentage between the mean and the *z* score from 50% (which is the total percentage below the mean):

   Manuel's percentile is 50% − 46.5% = 3.44% (Figure 7-5).

2. *The percentage of scores above Manuel's score:* We add the percentage between the mean and the negative *z* score to 50%, the percentage above the mean:

   50% + 46.56% = 96.56%

So 96.56% of 15-year-old boys' heights fall above Manuel's height (Figure 7-6).

FIGURE 7-5

Calculating the Percentile for a Negative z Score

As with positive *z* scores, drawing curves helps us to determine the appropriate percentage for negative *z* scores. For a negative *z* score, we subtract the percentage between the mean and that *z* score from 50% (the percentage below the mean) to get the percentage below that negative *z* score, the percentile. Here we subtract the 46.56% between the mean and the *z* score of −1.82 from 50%, which yields 3.44%.

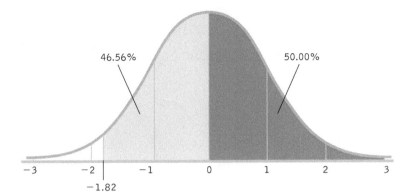

FIGURE 7-6

Calculating the Percentage Above a Negative *z* Score

For a negative *z* score, we add the percentage between the mean and that *z* score to 50% (the percentage above the mean) to get the percentage above that *z* score. Here we add the 46.56% between the mean and the *z* score of −1.82 to the 50% above the mean, which yields 96.56%.

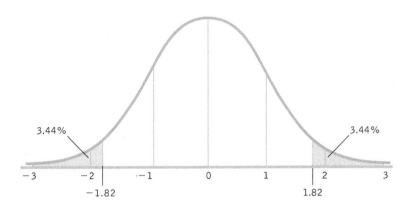

FIGURE 7-7

Calculating the Percentage at Least as Extreme as the *z* Score

With a negative *z* score, we double the percentage below that *z* score to get the percentage of scores that are at least as extreme—that is, at least as far from the mean—as the *z* score is. Here, we double 3.44% to calculate the percentage at least this extreme: 6.88%.

3. *The scores at least as extreme as Manuel's z score, in both directions:* In this case, 3.44% of 15-year-old boys have heights that are extreme enough to have *z* scores below −1.82. And because the curve is symmetric, another 3.44% of heights are extreme enough to be above a *z* score of 1.82. So we can double 3.44% to find the total percentage of heights that are as far as or farther from the mean than is Manuel's height:

$$3.44\% + 3.44\% = 6.88\%$$

So 6.88% of heights are at least as extreme as Manuel's in either direction (Figure 7-7).

In what group would the researchers classify Manuel? Manuel has a percentile rank of 3.44%. He is in the lowest 5% of heights for boys of his age, so he would be classified as short. Now we can get to the question that drives this research. Does Manuel's short stature doom him to a life of few friends and poor social adjustment? Researchers compared the means of the three groups—short, average, and tall—on several measures of peer relations and social adjustment, but they did not find evidence of mean differences among the groups (Sandberg et al., 2004). ●

EXAMPLE 7.3

This example demonstrates (a) how to seamlessly shift among raw scores, *z* scores, and percentile ranks; and (b) why drawing a normal curve makes the calculations much easier to understand.

Christian Rudder, one of the founders of the online dating site OkCupid, writes a blog based on data from their users. The graph in Figure 7-8 shows the attractiveness ratings of heterosexual women and men who have profiles on OkCupid (Rudder,

FIGURE 7-8

Calculating a Score from a Percentile

This graph combines two sets of data presented in an OKCupid article on heterosexual people's ratings of the opposite gender (Rudder, 2009). The *x*-axis represents a five-point scale of attractiveness, from least to most. The *y*-axis represents the percentage of profiles that receive that rating. The orange line represents men's appraisals of women's attractiveness, and the blue line represents women's appraisals of men's attractiveness. Most women rate men as fairly unattractive (note that no male profiles received a perfect score of five), whereas men's ratings of women's attractiveness follow the pattern of a normal distribution.

Source: Rudder (2009, November 17). Your looks and your inbox. *Oktrends*. Retrieved from http://blog.okcupid.com/index.php/ your-looks-and-online-dating/

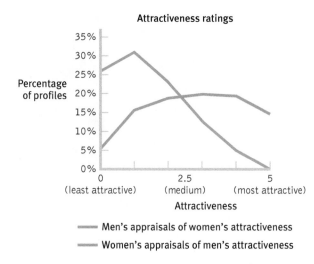

2009). You can see that the distribution of women's ratings of men (the blue line) is positively skewed. Women tend to think men are not all that attractive. Men's ratings of women (the orange line), however, are roughly normally distributed, so we can calculate *z* scores for this distribution. (Women may judge men's looks more harshly, but according to Rudder they're also more likely than men to contact someone they view as less attractive, so it sort of evens out.) Rudder didn't provide the mean and standard deviation, but based on what we know about a normal distribution, we can estimate the mean to be 2.5 and the standard deviation to be 0.833. Let's imagine that Veena's rating is at the 63rd percentile. What was her raw score? Begin by drawing a curve, as in Figure 7-9. Then add a line at the point below which approximately 63% of scores fall. We know that this score is above the mean because 50% of scores fall below the mean, and 63% is larger than 50%.

Using the drawing as a guideline, we see that we have to calculate the percentage between the mean and the *z* score of interest. So, we subtract the 50% below the mean from Veena's rating, 63%:

$$63\% - 50\% = 13\%$$

We look up the closest percentage to 13% in the *z* table (which is 12.93%) and find an associated *z* score of 0.33. This is above the mean, so we do not label it with a

FIGURE 7-9

Calculating a Score from a Percentile

We convert a percentile to a raw score by calculating the percentage between the mean and the *z* score, and looking up that percentage on the *z* table to find the associated *z* score. We then convert the *z* score to a raw score using the formula. Here, we look up 13.00% on the *z* table (12.93% is the closest percentage) and find a *z* score of 0.33, which we can convert to a raw score.

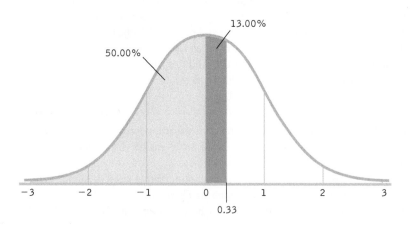

negative sign. We then convert the *z* score to a raw score using the formula we learned in Chapter 6:

$$X = z(\sigma) + \mu = 0.33(0.833) + 2.5 = 2.7749$$

Veena, whose profile rating is at the 63rd percentile, has a raw score of 2.77. Double check! This score is above the mean of 2.5, and the percentage is above 50%. ●

The *z* Table and Distributions of Means

Let's shift our focus from the *z* score of an individual within a group to the *z* statistic for a group. There are a couple changes to the calculations. First, we will use means rather than individual scores because we are now studying a sample of many scores rather than studying one individual score. Fortunately, the *z* table can also be used to determine percentages and *z* statistics for distributions of means calculated from many people. The other change is that we need to calculate the mean and the standard error for the distribution of means before calculating the *z* statistic.

· ·

Let's now imagine that instead of looking at the rating of one person—Veena—we're interested in the average rating of a group. Maybe you wonder how the women at your university who are on OkCupid stack up with the whole population of women on OkCupid. You manage to convince OkCupid to give you the profile ratings for 30 women on your campus. Imagine that the mean rating for these 30 women is 2.84. Before we calculate the *z* statistic, let's use proper symbolic notation to indicate the mean and the standard error of this distribution of means:

EXAMPLE 7.4

$$\mu_M = \mu = 2.5$$

$$\sigma_M = \frac{\sigma}{\sqrt{N}} = \frac{0.833}{\sqrt{30}} = 0.152$$

At this point, we have all the information we need to calculate the percentage using the two steps we learned earlier.

> **STEP 1: We convert to a *z* statistic using the mean and standard error that we just calculated.**

$$z = \frac{(M - \mu_M)}{\sigma_M} = \frac{(2.84 - 2.50)}{0.152} = 2.237$$

> **STEP 2: We determine the percentage below this *z* statistic.**

Draw it! Draw a curve that includes the mean of the *z* distribution, 0, and this *z* statistic, 2.237, rounded to 2.24 (Figure 7-10). Then shade the area in which we are interested: everything below 2.24. Now we look up the percentage between the mean and the *z* statistic of 2.24. The *z* table indicates that this percentage is 48.75, which we write in the section of the curve between the mean and 2.24. We write 50% in the half of the curve below the mean. We add 48.75% to the 50% below the mean to get the percentile rank, 98.75%. (Subtracting from 100%, only 1.25% of mean scores would be higher than the mean if they come from this population.) Based on this percentage, the average rating of a sample of women at your university is quite high. But we still can't arrive at a conclusion about whether these women are rated as significantly more attractive compared to the population average of 2.5 until we conduct a hypothesis test. ●

Percentile for the Mean of a Sample

We can use the z table with sample means in addition to sample scores. The only difference is that we use the mean and standard error of the distribution of means rather than the distribution of scores. Here, the z score of 2.24 is associated with a percentage of 48.75% between the mean and z score. Added to the 50% below the mean, the percentile is 50% + 48.75% = 98.75%.

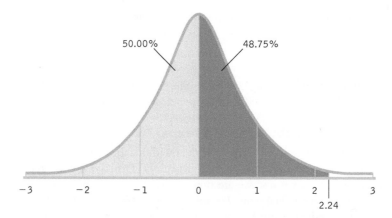

In the next section, we learn (a) the assumptions for conducting hypothesis testing; (b) the six steps of hypothesis testing using the z distribution; and (c) whether to reject or fail to reject the null hypothesis. In the last section, we demonstrate a z test.

CHECK YOUR LEARNING

Reviewing the Concepts

> Raw scores, z scores, and percentile rankings are three ways to describe the same score within a normal distribution.

> If we know the mean and the standard deviation of a population, we can convert a raw score to a z score and then use the z table to determine percentages below, above, or at least as extreme as this z score.

> We can use the z table in reverse as well, taking a percentage and converting it into a z score and then a raw score.

> These same conversions can be conducted on a sample mean instead of on a score. The procedures are identical, but we use the mean and the standard error of the distribution of means, instead of the distribution of scores.

Clarifying the Concepts

7-1 What information do we need to know about a population of interest in order to use the z table?

7-2 How do z scores relate to raw scores and percentile ranks?

Calculating the Statistics

7-3 If the percentage of scores between a z score of 1.37 and the mean is 41.47%, what percentage of scores lies between −1.37 and the mean?

7-4 If 12.93% of scores fall between the mean and a z score of 0.33, what percentage of scores falls below this z score?

Applying the Concepts

7-5 Every year, the Educational Testing Service (ETS) administers the Major Field Test in Psychology (MFTP) to graduating psychology majors. Baylor University wondered how its students compared to the national average. On its Web site, Baylor reported that the mean and the standard deviation of the 18,073 U.S. students who took this exam were 156.8 and 14.6, respectively. Thirty-six students in Baylor's psychology and neuroscience department took the exam; these students had a mean score of 164.6.

a. What is the percentile rank for the sample of students at Baylor? Use symbolic notation and write out your calculations.

b. What percentage of samples of this size scored higher, on average, than the students at Baylor?

Solutions to these Check Your Learning questions can be found in Appendix D.

c. What can you say about how Baylor students compared to students across the nation?

The Assumptions and Steps of Hypothesis Testing

The story of the doctor tasting tea was an informal experiment; however, the formal process of hypothesis testing is based on particular assumptions about the data. At times it might be safe to violate those assumptions and proceed through the six steps of formal hypothesis testing, but it is essential to understand the assumptions before making such a decision.

The Three Assumptions for Conducting Analyses

Think of "statistical assumptions" as the ideal conditions for hypothesis testing. More formally, ***assumptions*** *are the characteristics that we ideally require the population from which we are sampling to have so that we can make accurate inferences.* Why go through all the effort to understand and calculate statistics if you can't believe the story they tell?

The assumptions for the *z* test apply to several other hypothesis tests, especially ***parametric tests***, which are *inferential statistical analyses based on a set of assumptions about the population.* By contrast, ***nonparametric tests*** *are inferential statistical analyses that are not based on a set of assumptions about the population.* Learning the three main assumptions for parametric tests will help you to select the appropriate statistical test for your particular data set.

> ***Assumption 1:*** *The dependent variable is assessed using a scale measure.* If it's clear that the dependent variable is nominal or ordinal, we could not make this first assumption and thus should not use a parametric hypothesis test.
>
> ***Assumption 2:*** *The participants are randomly selected.* Every member of the population of interest must have had an equal chance of being selected for the study. This assumption is often violated; it is more likely that participants are a convenience sample. If we violate this second assumption, we must be cautious when generalizing from a sample to the population.
>
> ***Assumption 3:*** *The distribution of the population of interest must be approximately normal.* Many distributions are approximately normal, but it is important to remember that there are exceptions to this guideline (Micceri, 1989). Because hypothesis tests deal with sample means rather than individual scores, as long as the sample size is at least 30 (recall the discussion about the central limit theorem), it is likely that this third assumption is met.

Many parametric hypothesis tests can be conducted even if some of the assumptions are not met (Table 7-2), and are robust against violations of some of these assumptions. ***Robust*** *hypothesis tests are those that produce fairly accurate results even when the data suggest that the population might not meet some of the assumptions.*

- An **assumption** is a characteristic that we ideally require the population from which we are sampling to have so that we can make accurate inferences.

- A **parametric test** is an inferential statistical analysis based on a set of assumptions about the population.

- A **nonparametric test** is an inferential statistical analysis that is not based on a set of assumptions about the population.

- A **robust** hypothesis test is one that produces fairly accurate results even when the data suggest that the population might not meet some of the assumptions.

MASTERING THE CONCEPT

7-2: When we calculate a parametric statistic, ideally we have met assumptions regarding the population distribution. For a *z* test, there are three assumptions: The dependent variable should be on a scale measure, the sample should be randomly selected, and the underlying population should have an approximately normal distribution.

TABLE 7-2	The Three Assumptions for Hypothesis Testing

We must be aware of the assumptions for the hypothesis test that we choose, and we must be cautious in choosing to proceed with a hypothesis test when the data may not meet all of the assumptions. Note that in addition to these three assumptions, for many hypothesis tests, including the *z* test, the independent variable must be nominal.

The Three Assumptions	Breaking the Assumptions
1. Dependent variable is on a scale measure	Usually OK if the data are not clearly nominal or ordinal
2. Participants are randomly selected	OK if we are cautious about generalizing
3. Population distribution is approximately normal	OK if the sample includes at least 30 scores

These three statistical assumptions represent the ideal conditions and are more likely to produce valid research. *Meeting the assumptions improves the quality of research, but not meeting the assumptions doesn't necessarily invalidate research.*

The Six Steps of Hypothesis Testing

Hypothesis testing can be broken down into six standard steps.

Step 1: Identify the populations, comparison distribution, and assumptions.

When we first approach hypothesis testing, we consider the characteristics of the data in order to determine the distribution to which we will compare the sample. First, we state the populations represented by the groups to be compared. Then we identify the comparison distribution (e.g., a distribution of means). Finally, we review the assumptions of hypothesis testing. The information we gather in this step helps us to choose the appropriate hypothesis test (Appendix E, Figure E-1, provides a quick guide for choosing the appropriate test).

Step 2: State the null and research hypotheses.

Hypotheses are about populations, *not* about samples. The null hypothesis is usually the "boring" one that posits no change or no difference between groups. The research hypothesis is usually the "exciting" one that posits that a given intervention will lead to a change or a difference—for instance, that a particular kind of psychotherapeutic intervention will reduce general anxiety. State the null and research hypotheses in both words and symbolic notation.

Step 3: Determine the characteristics of the comparison distribution.

State the relevant characteristics of the comparison distribution (the distribution based on the null hypothesis). In a later step, we will compare data from the sample (or samples) to the comparison distribution to determine how extreme the sample data are. For *z* tests, we will determine the mean and standard error of the comparison distribution. These numbers describe the distribution represented by the null hypothesis and will be used when we calculate the test statistic.

Step 4: Determine the critical values, or cutoffs.

The critical values, or cutoffs, of the comparison distribution indicate how extreme the data must be, in terms of the *z* statistic, to reject the null hypothesis. Often called simply *cutoffs*, these numbers are more formally called **critical values**, *the test statistic values beyond which we reject the null hypothesis.* In most cases, we determine two cutoffs: one for extreme samples below the mean and one for extreme samples above the mean.

The critical values, or cutoffs, are based on a somewhat arbitrary standard—the most extreme 5% of the comparison distribution curve: 2.5% on either end. At times, cutoffs are based on a less conservative percentage, such as 10%, or a more conservative percentage, such as 1%. Regardless of the chosen cutoff, the area beyond the cutoff, or critical value, is often referred to as the critical region. Specifically, *the **critical region** is the area in the tails of the comparison distribution in which the null hypothesis can be rejected.* These percentages are typically written as probabilities; that is, 5% would be written as 0.05. *The probabilities used to determine the critical values, or cutoffs, in hypothesis testing are* **p levels** (often called *alphas*).

Step 5: Calculate the test statistic.

We use the information from step 3 to calculate the test statistic, in this case the *z* statistic. We can then directly compare the test statistic to the critical values to determine whether the sample is extreme enough to warrant rejecting the null hypothesis.

Step 6: Make a decision.

Using the statistical evidence, we can now decide whether to reject or fail to reject the null hypothesis. Based on the available evidence, we either reject the null hypothesis if the test statistic is beyond the cutoffs, or we fail to reject the null hypothesis if the test statistic is not beyond the cutoffs.

These six steps of hypothesis testing are summarized in Table 7-3.

- A **critical value** is a test statistic value beyond which we reject the null hypothesis; often called a cutoff.

- The **critical region** is the area in the tails of the comparison distribution in which the null hypothesis can be rejected.

- The probability used to determine the critical values, or cutoffs, in hypothesis testing is a *p* **level** (often called *alpha*).

TABLE 7-3	The Six Steps of Hypothesis Testing

We use the same six basic steps with each type of hypothesis test.

1. Identify the populations, distribution, and assumptions, and then choose the appropriate hypothesis test.

2. State the null and research hypotheses, in both words and symbolic notation.

3. Determine the characteristics of the comparison distribution.

4. Determine the critical values, or cutoffs, that indicate the points beyond which we will reject the null hypothesis.

5. Calculate the test statistic.

6. Decide whether to reject or fail to reject the null hypothesis.

Language Alert! When we reject the null hypothesis, we often refer to the results as "statistically significant." A finding is ***statistically significant*** *if the data differ from what we would expect by chance if there were, in fact, no actual difference.* The word *significant* is another one of those statistical terms with a very particular meaning. The phrase *statistically significant* does not necessarily mean that the finding is important or meaningful. A small difference between means could be statistically significant but not practically significant or important.

● A finding is **statistically significant** if the data differ from what we would expect by chance if there were, in fact, no actual difference.

CHECK YOUR LEARNING

Reviewing the Concepts

> When we conduct hypothesis testing, we have to consider the assumptions for that particular test.

> Parametric statistics are those that are based on assumptions about the population distribution; nonparametric statistics have no such assumptions. Parametric statistics are often robust to violations of the assumptions.

> The three assumptions for a *z* test are that the dependent variable is on a scale measure, the sample is randomly selected, and the underlying population distribution is approximately normal.

> There are six standard steps for hypothesis testing. First, we identify the population, comparison distribution, and assumptions, all of which help us to choose the appropriate hypothesis test. Second, we state the null and research hypotheses. Third, we determine the characteristics of the comparison distribution. Fourth, we determine the critical values, or cutoffs, of the comparison distribution. Fifth, we calculate the test statistic. Sixth, we decide whether to reject or fail to reject the null hypothesis.

> The standard practice of statisticians is to consider scores to be statistically significant and to warrant rejection of the null hypothesis if they occur less than 5% of the time based on the null hypothesis; observations that occur more often than 5% of the time do not support this decision, and thus we would fail to reject the null hypothesis in these cases.

Clarifying the Concepts   7-6   Explain the three assumptions made for most parametric hypothesis tests.

7-7   How do critical values help us to make a decision about the hypothesis?

Calculating the Statistics   7-8   If a researcher always sets the critical region as 8% of the distribution, and the null hypothesis is true, how often will he reject the null hypothesis if the null hypothesis is true?

7-9   Rewrite each of these percentages as a probability, or *p* level:

a. 15%

b. 3%

c. 5.5%

continued on next page

| Applying the Concepts | 7-10 | For each of the following scenarios, state whether each of the three basic assumptions for parametric hypothesis tests is met. Explain your answers and label the three assumptions (1) through (3). |

a. Researchers compared the ability of experienced clinical psychologists versus clinical psychology graduate students to diagnose a patient, based on a 1-hour interview. For 2 months, either a psychologist or a student interviewed every outpatient at the local community mental health center who had already received diagnoses based on a number of criteria. For each diagnosis, the psychologists and graduate students were given a score of correct or incorrect.

b. Behavioral scientists wondered whether animals raised in captivity would be healthier with diminished human contact. Twenty large cats (e.g., lions, tigers) were randomly selected from all the wild cats living in zoos in North America. Half were assigned to the control group—no change in human interaction. Half were assigned to the experimental group—no humans entered their cages except when the animals were not in them, one-way mirrors were used so that the animals could not see zoo visitors, and so on. The animals received a score for health over 1 year; points were given for various illnesses; a very few sickly animals had extremely high scores.

Solutions to these Check Your Learning questions can be found in Appendix D.

An Example of the *z* Test

The story of the doctor tasting tea inspired statisticians to use hypothesis testing as a way to understand the many mysteries of human behavior. In this section, we apply what we've learned about hypothesis testing—including the six steps—to a specific example of a *z* test. (The logic of the *z* test is a gateway to understanding all statistical tests; however, in practice, *z* tests are rarely used because researchers seldom have one sample *and* know both the mean and the standard deviation of the population.)

EXAMPLE 7.5

New York City was the first U.S. city to require that chain restaurants post calorie counts for all menu items. Shortly after the new law was implemented, the research team of Bollinger, Leslie, and Sorensen (2010) decided to test the law's effectiveness. For more than a year, they gathered data on every transaction at Starbucks coffee shops in several cities. They determined a population mean of 247 calories in products purchased by customers at stores without calorie postings. Based on the range of 0 to 1208 calories in customer transactions, we estimate a standard deviation of approximately 201 calories, which we'll use as the population standard deviation for this example.

The researchers also recorded calories for a sample in New York City after calories were posted on Starbucks menus. They reported a mean of 232 calories per purchase, a decrease of 6%. For the purposes of this example, we'll assume a sample size of 1000. Here's how to apply hypothesis testing when comparing a sample of customers at Starbucks with calories posted on their menus to the general population of customers at Starbucks without calories posted on their menus.

We'll use the six steps of hypothesis testing to analyze the calorie data. These six steps will tell us if customers visiting a Starbucks with calories listed on the menu consume fewer calories, on average, than customers visiting a Starbucks without

Cold Beverages (Tall—12 fl oz)	
Tazo® Shaken Iced Passion® Tea (Unsweetened)	0 cal
Iced Brewed Coffee (with Classic Syrup)	60 cal
Iced Skinny Latte	60 cal
Caramel Frappuccino® Light Blended Coffee	90 cal
Tazo® Shaken Iced Tea Lemonade	100 cal
Iced Vanilla Latte	140 cal
Nonfat Iced Caramel Macchiato	140 cal
Coffee Frappuccino® Blended Coffee	180 cal

Donna Ranieri

The *z* Test and Starbucks We only use *z* tests when we have one sample and know the population mean and standard deviation, a rare situation. For example, on average, do people consume fewer calories when they know how many calories are in their favorite latte and muffin? We can use the *z* test to compare the average numbers of calories that Starbucks customers consume when calorie counts are either posted or not posted on their menu boards.

calories listed on the menu. In fact, we use the six-step approach so often in this book that it won't be long before it becomes an automatic way of thinking for you. Each step in the example below is followed by a summary that models how to report hypothesis tests.

> **STEP 1: Identify the populations, distribution, and assumptions.**

First, we identify the populations, comparison distribution, and assumptions, which help us to determine the appropriate hypothesis test. The *populations* are (1) all customers at those Starbucks with calories posted on the menu (whether or not the customers are in the sample) and (2) all customers at those Starbucks without calories posted on the menu. Because we are studying a sample rather than an individual, the *comparison distribution* is a distribution of means. We compare the mean of the sample of 1000 people visiting those Starbucks that have calories posted on the menu (selected from the population of all people visiting those Starbucks with calories posted) to a distribution of all possible means of samples of 1000 people (selected from the population of all people visiting those Starbucks that don't have calories posted on the menu). The *hypothesis test* will be a z test because we have only one sample and we know the mean and the standard deviation of the population from the published norms.

Now let's examine the *assumptions* for a z test. (1) The data are on a scale measure, calories. (2) We do not know whether sample participants were selected randomly from among all people visiting those Starbucks with calories posted on the menu. If they were not, the ability to generalize beyond this sample to other Starbucks customers would be limited. (3) The comparison distribution should be normal. The individual data points are likely to be positively skewed because the minimum score of 0 is much closer to the mean of 247 than it is to the maximum score of 1208. However, we have a sample size of 1000, which is greater than 30; so based on the central limit theorem, we know that the comparison distribution—the distribution of means—will be approximately normal.

Summary: Population 1: All customers at those Starbucks that have calories posted on the menu. Population 2: All customers at those Starbucks that don't have calories posted on the menu.

The comparison distribution will be a distribution of means. The hypothesis test will be a z test because we have only one sample and we know the population mean and standard deviation. This study meets two of the three assumptions and may meet the third. The dependent variable is scale. In addition, there are more than 30 participants in the sample, indicating that the comparison distribution will be normal. We do not know whether the sample was randomly selected, however, so we must be cautious when generalizing.

> **STEP 2: State the null and research hypotheses.**

Next we state the null and research hypotheses in words and in symbols. Remember, hypotheses are always about populations, not samples. In most forms of hypothesis testing, there are two possible sets of hypotheses: directional (predicting either an increase or a decrease, but not both) or nondirectional (predicting a difference in either direction).

The first possible set of hypotheses is directional. The null hypothesis is that customers at those Starbucks that have calories posted on the menu do *not* consume fewer mean calories than customers at those Starbucks that don't have calories posted on the menu; in other words, they could consume the same or more mean calories, but not fewer. The research hypothesis is that customers at those Starbucks that have calories

● A **one-tailed test** is a hypothesis test in which the research hypothesis is directional, positing either a mean decrease or a mean increase in the dependent variable, but not both, as a result of the independent variable.

● A **two-tailed test** is a hypothesis test in which the research hypothesis does not indicate a direction of the mean difference or change in the dependent variable, but merely indicates that there will be a mean difference.

posted on the menu consume fewer mean calories than do customers at Starbucks that don't have calories posted on the menu. (Note that the direction of the hypotheses could be reversed.)

The symbol for the null hypothesis is H_0. The symbol for the research hypothesis is H_1. Throughout this text, we use μ for the mean because hypotheses are about populations and their parameters, not about samples and their statistics. So, in symbolic notation, the hypotheses are:

$$H_0: \mu_1 \geq \mu_2$$
$$H_1: \mu_1 < \mu_2$$

For the null hypothesis, the symbolic notation says that the mean calories consumed by those in population 1, customers at those Starbucks with calories posted on the menu, is not lower than the mean calories consumed by those in population 2, customers at those Starbucks without calories posted on the menu. For the research hypothesis, the symbolic notation says that the mean calories consumed by those in population 1 is lower than the mean calories consumed by those in population 2.

This hypothesis test is considered a one-tailed test. *A **one-tailed test** is a hypothesis test in which the research hypothesis is directional, positing either a mean decrease or a mean increase in the dependent variable, but not both, as a result of the independent variable.* One-tailed tests are rarely seen in the research literature; they are used only when the researcher is absolutely certain that the effect cannot go in the other direction or the researcher would not be interested in the result if it did.

The second set of hypotheses is nondirectional. The null hypothesis states that customers at Starbucks with posted calories (whether in the sample or not) consume the same number of calories, on average, as customers at Starbucks without posted calories. The research hypothesis is that customers at Starbucks with posted calories (whether in the sample or not) consume a different average number of calories than do customers at Starbucks without posted calories. The means of the two populations are posited to be different, but neither mean is predicted to be lower or higher.

The hypotheses in symbols would be:

$$H_0: \mu_1 = \mu_2$$
$$H_1: \mu_1 \neq \mu_2$$

For the null hypothesis, the symbolic notation says that the mean number of calories consumed by those in population 1 is the same as the mean number of calories consumed by those in population 2. For the research hypothesis, the symbolic notation says that the mean number of calories consumed by those in population 1 is different from the mean number of calories consumed by those in population 2.

This hypothesis test is considered a two-tailed test. *A **two-tailed test** is a hypothesis test in which the research hypothesis does not indicate a direction of the mean difference or change in the dependent variable, but merely indicates that there will be a mean difference.* Two-tailed tests are much more common than are one-tailed tests. We will use two-tailed tests throughout this book unless we tell you otherwise. If a researcher expects a difference in a certain direction, he or she might have a one-tailed hypothesis; however, if the results are in the opposite direction, the researcher cannot then switch the direction of the hypothesis.

Summary: Null hypothesis: Customers at those Starbucks that have calories posted on the menu consume the same number of calories,

---

MASTERING THE CONCEPT

7-3: We conduct a one-tailed test if we have a directional hypothesis, such as that the sample will have a higher (or lower) mean than the population. We use a two-tailed test if we have a nondirectional hypothesis, such as that the sample will have a different mean than the population does.

on average, as do customers at Starbucks that don't have calories posted on the menu—H_0: $\mu_1 = \mu_2$. Research hypothesis: Customers at those Starbucks that have calories posted on the menu consume a different number of calories, on average, than do customers at those Starbucks that don't have calories posted on the menu—H_1: $\mu_1 \neq \mu_2$.

STEP 3: Determine the characteristics of the comparison distribution.

Now we determine the characteristics that describe the distribution with which we will compare the sample. For z tests, we must know the mean and the standard error of the population of scores; the standard error for samples of this size is calculated from the standard deviation of the population of scores. Here, the population mean for the number of calories consumed by the general population of Starbucks customers is 247, and the standard deviation is 201. The sample size is 1000. Because we use a sample mean in hypothesis testing, rather than a single score, we must use the standard error of the mean instead of the population standard deviation (of the scores). The characteristics of the comparison distribution are determined as follows:

$$\mu_M = \mu = 247$$

$$\sigma_M = \frac{\sigma}{\sqrt{N}} = \frac{201}{\sqrt{1000}} = 6.356$$

Summary: $\mu_M = 247$; $\sigma_M = 6.356$

STEP 4: Determine the critical values, or cutoffs.

Next we determine the critical values, or cutoffs, to which we can compare the test statistic. As stated previously, the research convention is to set the cutoffs to a p level of 0.05. For a two-tailed test, this indicates the most extreme 5%—that is, the 2.5% at the bottom of the comparison distribution and the 2.5% at the top. Because we calculate a test statistic for the sample—specifically a z statistic—we report cutoffs in terms of z statistics. We use the z table to determine the scores for the top and bottom 2.5%.

We know that 50% of the curve falls above the mean, and we know that 2.5% falls above the relevant z statistic. By subtracting (50% − 2.5% = 47.5%), we determine that 47.5% of the curve falls between the mean and the relevant z statistic. When we look up this percentage on the z table, we find a z statistic of 1.96. So the critical values are −1.96 and 1.96 (Figure 7-11).

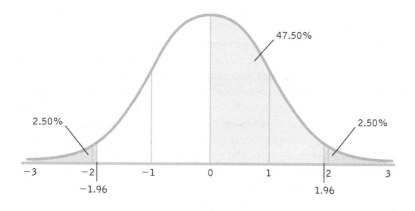

FIGURE 7-11

Determining Critical Values for a z Distribution

We typically determine critical values in terms of z statistics so we can easily compare a test statistic to determine whether it is beyond the critical values. Here, z scores of −1.96 and 1.96 indicate the most extreme 5% of the distribution, 2.5% in each tail.

Making a Decision

To decide whether to reject the null hypothesis, we compare the test statistic to the critical values. In this instance, the *z* score of −2.36 is beyond the critical value of −1.96, so we reject the null hypothesis. Customers at those Starbucks with calories posted on the menu consume fewer calories, on average, than do customers at those Starbucks without posted calories.

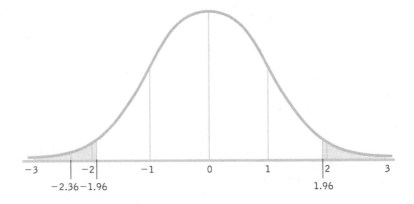

Summary: The cutoff *z* statistics are −1.96 and 1.96.

> **STEP 5: Calculate the test statistic.**

In step 5, we calculate the test statistic, in this case a *z* statistic, to find out what the data really say. We use the mean and standard error calculated in step 3:

$$z = \frac{(M - \mu_M)}{\sigma_M} = \frac{(232 - 247)}{6.356} = -2.36$$

Summary: $z = \dfrac{(232 - 247)}{6.356} = -2.36$

> **STEP 6: Make a decision.**

Finally, we compare the test statistic to the critical values. We add the test statistic to the drawing of the curve that includes the critical *z* statistics (Figure 7-12). If the test statistic is in the critical region, we can reject the null hypothesis. In this example, the test statistic, −2.36, is in the critical region, so we reject the null hypothesis. An examination of the means tells us that the mean number of calories consumed by customers at those Starbucks with calories posted on the menu is lower than the mean number of calories consumed by customers at those Starbucks with no calories posted. So, even though we had nondirectional hypotheses, we can report the direction of the finding—that is, it appears that customers consume fewer calories, on average, at Starbucks that post calories on the menu than at Starbucks that do not post calories on the menu.

If the test statistic is not beyond the cutoffs, we fail to reject the null hypothesis. This means that we can only conclude that there is no evidence from this study to support the research hypothesis. There might be a real mean difference that is not extreme enough to be picked up by the hypothesis test. We just can't know.

Summary: We reject the null hypothesis. It appears that fewer calories are consumed, on average, by customers at Starbucks that post calories on the menus than by customers at Starbucks that do not post calories on the menu.

The researchers who conducted this study concluded that the posting of calories by restaurants does indeed seem to be beneficial. The 6% reduction may seem small, they admit, but they report that the reduction was larger—a 26% decrease in calories—among those consuming 250 or more calories per visit and among those making food purchases. Also, the researchers theorized that given data such as these, chains might respond by adding lower-calorie choices, leading to further reductions in average calories consumed. ●

Replication

Psychologists Ed Diener and Robert Diener-Biswas conjure an interesting thought experiment (n.d.). They ask you to imagine that you're driving to campus and you spot a pirate by the side of the road. Yes, a pirate. You might wonder whether that was *really* a pirate or just someone wearing "an unusual hat and a billowy shirt." But the researchers then ask you to imagine that you keep driving and see another pirate. And then a few blocks later, another pirate. At some point, the researchers guess, you start believing your eyes and wonder why there are so many pirates near your university. Maybe it's "a pirate themed conference" (p. 1)?

Diener and Diener-Biswas admit that it is a silly thought experiment, but nonetheless it's an example of replication—the repetition that gives us confidence that a particular observation is true. Why is replication important? If we conduct the same study with different samples and get the same results each time, it is more likely that the results are accurate. These later studies are then replications of the first study. So, if you think you see a pirate multiple times, then it is more likely that you are actually seeing pirates (or at least people dressed as pirates).

The problem is that, historically, social scientists rarely attempt to replicate (or reproduce) other scientists' findings. Academic scientists need to publish research in order to keep their jobs. But because journals tend to publish only new research, there isn't much incentive to repeat someone else's study. This emphasis on new findings is paralleled among the media where a surprising or unusual finding, often based on a single study, is more likely to show up in the news than a replication of a study.

This is starting to change, however. Increasingly, there's a push to "crowd-source" science (Baranski, 2015). This crowdsourcing of science can involve multiple researchers recruiting participants from their various universities or countries. Perhaps more importantly, though, crowdsourcing can involve researchers sharing their methodology and data online, which allows for more voices and more statistical analyses to contribute to a study's conclusions (Silberzahn & Uhlmann, 2015). It can also lead to other scientists jumping into the research fray via social media, questioning findings and sharing their questions. One journalist observed that "surprisingly high-level critiques of big [scientific] papers happen on Twitter each week," sometimes leading the authors of these papers to issue corrections (White, 2014).

Replicating Pirates If you drove quickly by this man, you might doubt you actually saw a pirate. But if you drove by this man and then another pirate, and then another, you would likely start to believe your eyes. When we conduct hypothesis testing, repeating a finding again and again gives us more confidence that it is a real finding.

The name for this crowdsourcing movement in research is "open science." If you google that term, you'll find lots of examples of projects across different scientific disciplines and around the world. For example, one crowdsourcing example is particularly exciting because it creates new opportunities for undergraduates. Psi Chi (2015), the International Honor Society in Psychology, has partnered with the Open Science Collaboration (2015) to test the reproducibility of well-known experiments. Both faculty and graduate students can serve as mentors in the Reproducibility Project. The Psi Chi faculty advisor in your department can find out how to participate. If you do not have a Psi Chi chapter, you might ask your department chairperson to help you start one. Think of the Reproducibility Project as a way to crowdsource small pieces of important work. You get to play a small part in something big (Yong, 2012).

As open science initiatives play out, we're discovering that many psychology studies have not been replicated by other researchers, which highlights the need for more replication. In one highly publicized study published in the top journal *Science*, more than 100 researchers from more than 100 institutions around the world found that only 36% of a sample of important studies from top academic journals replicated; the remaining 64% of studies did *not* replicate (Open Science Collaboration, 2015). Some believe that failures to replicate may indicate that the original findings were Type I errors—incorrectly rejecting the null hypotheses. For example, one much-discussed study found a link between cleanliness and morality (Schnall, Benton, & Harvey, 2008). Specifically, participants who washed their hands after experiencing the emotion of disgust were less morally judgmental than were participants who did not wash their hands. Other researchers tried and failed to replicate this study (Johnson, Cheung, & Donnellan, 2014a).

The jury is still out, however, on whether the *Science* study really is evidence of a large-scale failure to replicate. In the case of the cleanliness and morality study, the lead author, psychologist Simone Schnall, published a critique of the failure to replicate her work, and the researchers who conducted the replication, in turn, responded to her critique (Bartlett, 2014; Johnson, Cheung, & Donnellan, 2014b; Schnall, 2014).

On a broader scale, Daniel Gilbert and his colleagues reanalyzed the full data set from the *Science* study (Gilbert et al., 2016). Using different statistical techniques, these researchers came to the "opposite conclusion"—a fairly high level of replication of psychological research. Yet, that conclusion hasn't ended the debate. Some of the original researchers wrote a rebuttal saying that Gilbert and colleagues' conclusions are a "very optimistic assessment" and outline the ways in which they disagree with Gilbert and colleagues' statistical methodology (Anderson et al., 2016). These public debates about these findings in particular and replication efforts in general are helpful to making science more transparent.

But let's say that some of the studies really did fail to replicate. Some might think that such outcomes mean that psychological science is a failure itself, but many psychologists do not take this view, including some of the Open Science Collaboration researchers (Samarrai, 2015). Psychologist Lisa Feldman Barrett summarized this viewpoint when she wrote in the *New York Times* about psychological science: The "failure to replicate is not a bug; it is a feature. It is what leads us along the path—the wonderfully twisty path—of scientific discovery" (2015). She pointed out that in some cases, a replication may be different in some ways, and the ways these differences affect the outcome can help scientists understand the exact context under which a finding occurs.

For example, Barrett uses the example of a study in which rats froze at the sound of a tone that had been paired with an electric shock, but only under certain circumstances. In one study, they did not freeze; rather, they ran away. It turned out that the environment—in this case, the layout of the cage—affected whether the rat froze or not. What originally looked like a failure to replicate was in fact the progression toward a better understanding of fear in rats.

Related to Barrett's embrace of replication efforts, some scientists call for more nonexact replications of studies—both to test competing hypotheses and to expand the contexts in which a finding has been tested (Larzelere, Cox, & Swindle, 2015). Other scientists emphasize the need for replication efforts to include new samples of experimental stimuli as well as new samples of participants (Westfall, Judd, & Kenny, 2015). Most social scientists support the movement toward more replication, but a few think it has gone too far. Scientists against the replication movement call it "repligate" and describe replicators as scientific "bullies" (Bartlett, 2014). Most social scientists, however, agree that replication is a good thing, whether it reproduces a finding, uncovers a Type I error, or helps us to tease apart the circumstances in which a finding seems to hold true and those in which it does not (Carey, 2015). And replication is particularly warranted when a finding is new and unexpected.

We'll give Diener and Diener-Biswas the last word. "We are willing to consider unusual ideas if there is evidence to support them: We are open-minded. At the same time, we are critical and believe in replication. Scientists should be willing to consider unusual or risky hypotheses but ultimately allow good evidence to have the final say, not people's opinions" (p. 5, n.d.). We agree.

CHECK YOUR LEARNING

Reviewing the Concepts
> We conduct a z test when we have one sample and we know both the mean and the standard deviation of the population.
> We must decide whether to use a *one-tailed test*, in which the hypothesis is directional, or a *two-tailed test*, in which the hypothesis is nondirectional.
> One-tailed tests are rare in the research literature.
> In the field of psychology, there's a growing push to replicate important research—that is, to repeat the study to see if the findings hold up.

Clarifying the Concepts 7-11 What does it mean to say a test is directional or nondirectional?

Calculating the Statistics 7-12 Calculate the characteristics (μ_M and σ_M) of a comparison distribution for a sample mean based on 53 participants when the population has a mean of 1090 and a standard deviation of 87.

7-13 Calculate the z statistic for a sample mean of 1094 based on the sample of 53 people when $\mu = 1090$ and $\sigma = 87$.

Applying the Concepts 7-14 According to the Web site for the Coffee Research Institute (http://www .coffeeresearch.org/market/usa.htm), the average coffee drinker in the United States consumes 3.1 cups of coffee daily. Let's assume the population standard deviation is 0.9 cup. Jillian decides to study coffee consumption at her local coffee shop. She wants to know if people sitting and working in a coffee shop drink a different amount of coffee from what might be expected in the general U.S. population. Throughout the course of 2 weeks, she collects data on 34 people who spend most of the day at the coffee shop. The average number of cups consumed by this sample is 3.17 cups. Use the six steps of hypothesis testing to determine whether Jillian's sample is statistically significantly different from the population mean.

Solutions to these Check Your Learning questions can be found in Appendix D.

REVIEW OF CONCEPTS

The z Table

The z table has several uses when the data are distributed normally. If we know an individual raw score, we can convert it to a z statistic and then determine percentages above, below, or at least as extreme as this score. Alternatively, if we know a percentage, we can look up a z statistic on the table and then convert it to a raw score. The table can be used in the same way with means instead of scores.

The Assumptions and Steps of Hypothesis Testing

Assumptions are the criteria that are met, ideally, before a hypothesis test is conducted. *Parametric tests* are those that require assumptions about the population, whereas *nonparametric tests* are those that do not. Three basic assumptions apply to many parametric hypothesis tests—the dependent variable should be on a scale measure, the data should be from a randomly selected sample, and the population distribution should be normal (or there should be at least 30 scores in the sample). A *robust* hypothesis test is one that produces valid results even when all assumptions are not met.

There are six steps that apply to every hypothesis test. First, determine the populations, comparison distribution, and assumptions. This step helps us to choose the appropriate hypothesis test from the diagram in Appendix E, Figure E-1. Second, state the null and research hypotheses. Third, determine the characteristics of the comparison distribution to be used to calculate the test statistic. Fourth, determine the *critical values*, or *cutoffs*, usually based on a *p level*, or *alpha*, of 0.05, that demarcate the most extreme 5% of the comparison distribution, the *critical region*. Fifth, calculate the test statistic. Sixth, use that test statistic to decide to reject or fail to reject the null hypothesis. We deem a finding *statistically significant* when we reject the null hypothesis.

An Example of the *z* Test

z tests are conducted in the rare cases in which we have one sample and we know the mean and the standard deviation of the population. We must decide whether to use a *one-tailed test*, in which the hypotheses are directional, or a *two-tailed test*, in which the hypotheses are nondirectional.

When we conduct hypothesis testing and reject the null hypothesis, we can never be sure whether the finding was a Type I error. For this reason, it's important to replicate important findings. There's a growing "open science" movement that is helping to make it easier for scientists to replicate one another's work.

SPSS®

SPSS can be used to transform raw data from different scales into standardized data on one scale based on the *z* distribution. This allows us to look at standardized scores instead of raw scores. We can try this using the length of the top 50 YouTube videos from Chapter 2. To standardize the variable "seconds," select: Analyze → Descriptive Statistics →

Descriptives. Select the relevant variable (i.e., "Length of Video") by clicking it on the left side, then clicking the arrow to move it to the right. Check the "Save standardized values as variables" box and click "OK." Part of the new column of standardized variables under the heading "ZSeconds" is in the accompanying screenshot.

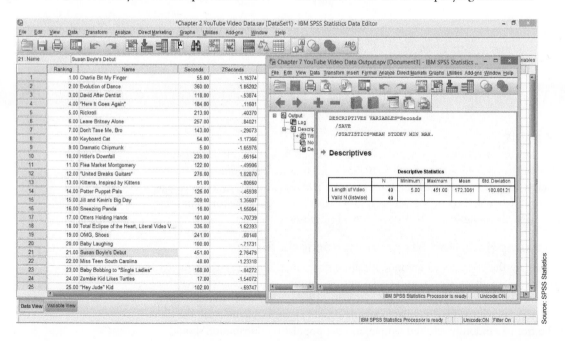

We can now see what videos fall below or above the sample mean by looking at the z score. For example, the video "Susan Boyle's Debut," highlighted in yellow in the screenshot, has a z score of 2.77, indicating that it falls above the mean. The video that follows, "Miss Teen South Carolina," has a z score of −1.23, indicating that it falls below the mean. Now that each video's length has been standardized, we can use the z table to find percentages above or below a certain z score.

HOW IT WORKS

7.1 TRANSITIONING FROM RAW SCORES TO z SCORES AND PERCENTILES

Physician assistants (PAs) are increasingly central to the health care system in many countries. Students who graduated from U.S. PA programs reported their income (American Academy of Physician Assistants, 2005). The incomes of those working in emergency medicine had a mean of $76,553, a standard deviation of $14,001, and a median of $74,044. The incomes of those working in family/general medicine had a mean of $63,521, a standard deviation of $11,554, and a median of $62,935. How can we compare the income of Gabrielle, who earns $75,500 a year in emergency medicine, with that of Colin, who earns $64,300 a year in family/general medicine?

The z distribution should only be used with individual scores if the distribution is approximately normal, as seems to be the case here. For both distributions of incomes, the medians are relatively close to the means of their own distributions, suggesting that the distributions are not skewed. Additionally, the standard deviations are not large compared to the size of the respective means, which suggests that outliers are not inflating the standard deviation, which would also indicate skew.

From the information we have, we can calculate Gabrielle's z score and her percentile on income—that is, the percentage of PAs working in emergency medicine who make less than she does. Her z score is:

$$z = \frac{(X - \mu)}{\sigma} = \frac{(75,500 - 76,553)}{14,001} = -0.08$$

The z table tells us that 3.19% of people fall between Gabrielle's income and the mean. Because her score is below the mean, we calculate 50% − 3.19% = 46.81%. Gabrielle's income is in the 46.81st percentile for PAs working in emergency medicine.

Colin's z score is:

$$z = \frac{(X - \mu)}{\sigma} = \frac{(64,300 - 63,521)}{11,554} = 0.07$$

The z table tells us that 2.79% of people fall between Colin's income and the mean. Because his score is above the mean, we calculate 50% + 2.79% = 52.79%. Colin's income is in the 52.79th percentile for PAs working in general medicine.

Relative to those in their chosen fields, Colin is doing better financially than Gabrielle. Colin's z score of 0.07, which is above the mean for general medicine PAs, is greater than Gabrielle's z score of 20.08, which is below the mean for emergency medicine PAs. Similarly, Colin's income is at about the 53rd percentile, whereas Gabrielle's income is at about the 47th percentile.

7.2 CONDUCTING A z TEST

Summary data from the Consideration of Future Consequences (CFC) scale found a mean CFC score of 3.20 with a standard deviation of 0.70 for a large sample (Adams, 2012). (For the sake of this example, let's assume that this sample comprises the entire population of interest.) You wonder whether students who joined a career discussion group might have different CFC scores compared with those of the population. Forty-five students in your psychology department attended these discussion groups and then completed the CFC scale. The mean for this group is 3.45. From this information, how can we conduct all six steps of a two-tailed z test with a p level of 0.05?

Step 1: Population 1: All students who participated in career discussion groups. Population 2: All students who did not participate in career discussion groups.

The comparison distribution will be a distribution of means. The hypothesis test will be a *z* test because we have only one sample and we know the population mean and standard deviation. This study meets two of the three assumptions but does not seem to meet the third. The dependent variable is on a scale measure. In addition, there are more than 30 participants in the sample, indicating that the comparison distribution will be normal. The data were not randomly selected, however, so we must be cautious when generalizing.

Step 2: Null hypothesis: Students who participated in career discussion groups had the same mean CFC scores as students who did not participate: H_0: $\mu_1 = \mu_2$. Research hypothesis: Students who participated in career discussion groups had mean CFC scores that differed from those of students who did not participate: H_1: $\mu_1 \neq \mu_2$.

Step 3: $\mu_M = \mu = 3.20$; $\sigma_M = \dfrac{\sigma}{\sqrt{N}} = \dfrac{0.70}{\sqrt{45}} = 0.104$

Step 4: The critical *z* statistics are -1.96 and 1.96.

Step 5: $z = \dfrac{(M - \mu_M)}{\sigma_M} = \dfrac{(3.45 - 3.20)}{0.104} = 2.40$

Step 6: Reject the null hypothesis. It appears that students who participate in career discussions have higher mean CFC scores than do students who do not participate.

EXERCISES

The solutions to the odd-numbered exercises can be found in Appendix C.

Clarifying the Concepts

7.1 What is a percentile?

7.2 When we look up a *z* score on the *z* table, what information can we report?

7.3 How do we calculate the percentage of scores below a particular positive *z* score?

7.4 How is calculating a percentile for a mean from a distribution of means different from doing so for a score from a distribution of scores?

7.5 In statistics, what do we mean by *assumptions*?

7.6 What sample size is recommended in order to meet the assumption of a normal distribution of means, even when the underlying population of scores is not normal?

7.7 What is the difference between parametric tests and nonparametric tests?

7.8 What are the six steps of hypothesis testing?

7.9 What are critical values and the critical region?

7.10 What is the standard size of the critical region used by most statisticians?

7.11 What does *statistically significant* mean to statisticians?

7.12 What do these symbolic expressions mean: H_0: $\mu_1 = \mu_2$ and H_1: $\mu_1 \neq \mu_2$?

7.13 Using everyday language rather than statistical language, explain why the words *critical region* might have been

chosen to define the area in which a *z* statistic must fall in order for a researcher to reject the null hypothesis.

7.14 Using everyday language rather than statistical language, explain why the word *cutoff* might have been chosen to define the point beyond which we reject the null hypothesis.

7.15 What is the difference between a one-tailed hypothesis test and a two-tailed hypothesis test in terms of critical regions?

7.16 Why do researchers typically use a two-tailed test rather than a one-tailed test?

7.17 Write the symbols for the null hypothesis and research hypothesis for a one-tailed test.

7.18 What is replication and why is it important for behavioral science research?

7.19 If an effort to replicate a study fails, what are two things that the failure could indicate about the original study?

Calculating the Statistics

7.20 Calculate the following percentages for a *z* score of -1.61, with a tail of 5.37%:

  a. What percentage of scores falls above this *z* score?

  b. What percentage of scores falls between the mean and this *z* score?

  c. What proportion of scores falls above a *z* score of 1.61?

7.21 Calculate the following percentages for a *z* score of 0.74, with a tail of 22.96%:

  a. What percentage of scores falls below this *z* score?

b. What percentage of scores falls between the mean and this z score?

c. What proportion of scores falls below a z score of −0.74?

7.22 Using the z table in Appendix B, calculate the following percentages for a z score of −0.08:

a. Above this z score

b. Below this z score

c. At least as extreme as this z score

7.23 Using the z table in Appendix B, calculate the following percentages for a z score of 1.71:

a. Above this z score

b. Below this z score

c. At least as extreme as this z score

7.24 Rewrite each of the following percentages as probabilities, or p levels:

a. 5%

b. 83%

c. 51%

7.25 Rewrite each of the following probabilities, or p levels, as percentages:

a. 0.19

b. 0.04

c. 0.92

7.26 If the critical values for a hypothesis test occur where 2.5% of the distribution is in each tail, what are the cutoffs for z?

7.27 For each of the following p levels, what percentage of the data will be in each critical region for a two-tailed test?

a. 0.05

b. 0.10

c. 0.01

7.28 State the percentage of scores in a one-tailed critical region for each of the following p levels:

a. 0.05

b. 0.10

c. 0.01

7.29 You are conducting a z test on a sample of 50 people with an average SAT verbal score of 542 (assume we know the population mean to be 500 and the standard deviation to be 100). Calculate the mean and the spread of the comparison distribution (μ_M and σ_M).

7.30 You are conducting a z test on a sample of 132 people for whom you observed a mean SAT verbal score of 490. The population mean is 500, and the standard deviation is 100. Calculate the mean and the spread of the comparison distribution (μ_M and σ_M).

7.31 If the cutoffs for a z test are −1.96 and 1.96, determine whether you would reject or fail to reject the null hypothesis in each of the following cases:

a. $z = 1.06$

b. $z = -2.06$

c. A z score beyond which 7% of the data fall in each tail

7.32 If the cutoffs for a z test are −2.58 and 2.58, determine whether you would reject or fail to reject the null hypothesis in each of the following cases:

a. $z = -0.94$

b. $z = 2.12$

c. A z score for which 49.6% of the data fall between z and the mean

7.33 Use the cutoffs of −1.65 and 1.65 and a p level of approximately 0.10, or 10%. For each of the following values, determine whether you would reject or fail to reject the null hypothesis:

a. $z = 0.95$

b. $z = -1.77$

c. A z statistic that 2% of the scores fall above

7.34 You are conducting a z test on a sample for which you observe a mean weight of 150 pounds. The population mean is 160, and the standard deviation is 100.

a. Calculate a z statistic for a sample of 30 people.

b. Repeat part (a) for a sample of 300 people.

c. Repeat part (a) for a sample of 3000 people.

Applying the Concepts

7.35 **Percentiles and unemployment rates:** The U.S. Bureau of Labor Statistics' annual report published in 2011 provided adjusted unemployment rates for 10 countries. The mean was 7%, and the standard deviation was 1.85. For the following calculations, treat 7% as the population mean and 1.85 as the population standard deviation.

a. Australia's unemployment rate was 5.4. Calculate the percentile for Australia—that is, what percentage is less than that of Australia?

b. The United Kingdom's unemployment rate was 8.5. Calculate its percentile—that is, what percentage is less than that of the United Kingdom?

c. The unemployment rate in the United States was 8.9. Calculate its percentile—that is, what percentage is less than that of the United States?

d. The unemployment rate in Canada was 6.5. Calculate its percentile—that is, what percentage is less than that of Canada?

7.36 Height and the *z* distribution, question 1: Elena, a 15-year-old girl, is 58 inches tall. The Centers for Disease Control (CDC) indicate that the average height for girls at this age is 63.80 inches, with a standard deviation of 2.66 inches.

a. Calculate Elena's *z* score.

b. What percentage of girls are taller than Elena?

c. What percentage of girls are shorter?

d. How much would Elena have to grow to be perfectly average?

e. If Sarah is in the 75th percentile for height at age 15, how tall is she?

f. How much would Elena have to grow in order to be at the 75th percentile with Sarah?

7.37 Height and the *z* distribution, question 2: Kona, a 15-year-old boy, is 72 inches tall. According to the CDC, the average height for boys at this age is 67.00 inches, with a standard deviation of 3.19 inches.

a. Calculate Kona's *z* score.

b. What is Kona's percentile score for height?

c. What percentage of boys this age are shorter than Kona?

d. What percentage of heights are at least as extreme as Kona's, in either direction?

e. If Ian is in the 30th percentile for height as a 15-year-old boy, how tall is he? How does he compare to Kona?

7.38 Height and the *z* statistic, question 1: Imagine a class of thirty-three 15-year-old girls with an average height of 62.6 inches. Remember, $\mu = 63.8$ inches and $\sigma = 2.66$ inches.

a. Calculate the *z* statistic.

b. How does this sample of girls compare to the distribution of sample means?

c. What is the percentile rank for this sample?

7.39 Height and the *z* statistic, question 2: Imagine a basketball team that comprises thirteen 15-year-old boys. The average height of the team is 69.5 inches. Remember, $\mu = 67$ inches and $\sigma = 3.19$ inches.

a. Calculate the *z* statistic.

b. How does this sample of boys compare to the distribution of sample means?

c. What is the percentile rank for this sample?

7.40 The *z* distribution and statistics test scores: Imagine that your statistics professor lost all records of students' raw scores on a recent test. However, she did record students' *z* scores for the test, as well as the class average of 41 out of 50 points and the standard deviation of 3 points (treat these as population parameters). She informs you that your *z* score was 1.10.

a. What was your percentile score on this test?

b. Using what you know about *z* scores and percentiles, how did you do on this test?

c. What was your original test score?

7.41 The *z* statistic, distributions of means, and height, question 1: Using what we know about the height of 15-year-old girls (again, $\mu = 63.8$ inches and $\sigma = 2.66$ inches), imagine that a teacher finds the average height of 14 female students in one of her classes to be 62.4 inches.

a. Calculate the mean and the standard error of the distribution of mean heights.

b. Calculate the *z* statistic for this group.

c. What percentage of mean heights, based on a sample size of 14 students, would we expect to be shorter than this group?

d. How often do mean heights equal to or more extreme than this size occur in this population?

e. If statisticians define sample means that occur less than 5% of the time as "special" or rare, what would you say about this result?

7.42 The *z* statistic, distributions of means, and height, question 2: Another teacher decides to average the heights of all 15-year-old male students in his classes throughout the day. By the end of the day, he has measured the heights of 57 boys and calculated an average of 68.1 inches (remember, for this population $\mu = 67$ inches and $\sigma = 3.19$ inches).

a. Calculate the mean and the standard error of the distribution of mean heights.

b. Calculate the *z* statistic for this group.

c. What percentage of groups of people would we expect to have mean heights taller than this group, based on samples of this size (57)?

d. How often do mean heights equal to or more extreme than 68.1 occur in this population?

e. How does this result compare to the statistical significance cutoff of 5%?

7.43 Directional versus nondirectional hypotheses: For each of the following examples, identify whether the research has expressed a directional or a nondirectional hypothesis:

a. A researcher is interested in studying the relation between the use of antibacterial products and the dryness of people's skin. He thinks these products might alter the moisture in skin differently from other products that are not antibacterial.

b. A student wonders if grades in a class are in any way related to where a student sits in the classroom. In particular, do students who sit in the front row get better grades, on average, than the general population of students?

c. Cell phones are everywhere, and we are now available by phone almost all of the time. Does this translate into a change in the closeness of our long-distance relationships?

7.44 Null hypotheses and research hypotheses: For each of the following examples, state the null hypothesis and the research hypothesis, in both words and symbolic notation:

a. Musician David Teie worked with animal researchers to develop music specifically for cats—music that a typical cat might find relaxing (Stanford, 2015). Imagine that you decided to study whether cat-specific music led to decreased heart rate in feline listeners. Use a one-tailed hypothesis.

b. The National Sleep Foundation encourages U.S. high schools to start later in the morning to improve teenagers' sleep and school performance (2015). Imagine you decide to conduct a study to see if teens who get to sleep an hour later have different grades than those who don't.

c. Smartphones are everywhere, and we are now available to our friends and families almost all of the time. Does this translate into a change in the closeness of our long-distance relationships?

7.45 The *z* distribution and Hurricane Katrina: Hurricane Katrina hit New Orleans on August 29, 2005. The National Weather Service Forecast Office maintains online archives of climate data for all U.S. cities and areas. These archives allow us to find out, for example, how the rainfall in New Orleans that August compared to that in the other months of 2005. The table below shows the National Weather Service data (rainfall in inches) for New Orleans in 2005.

January	4.41
February	8.24
March	4.69
April	3.31
May	4.07
June	2.52
July	10.65
August	3.77
September	4.07
October	0.04
November	0.75
December	3.32

a. Calculate the *z* score for August, the month in which Hurricane Katrina hit. (*Note:* These are raw data for the population, rather than summaries, so

you have to calculate the mean and the standard deviation first.)

b. What is the percentile for the rainfall in August? Does this surprise you? Explain.

c. When results surprise us, it is worthwhile to examine individual data points more closely or even to go beyond the data. The daily climate data as listed by this source for August 2005 shows the code "M" next to August 29, 30, and 31 for all climate statistics. The code says: "[REMARKS] ALL DATA MISSING AUGUST 29, 30, AND 31 DUE TO HURRICANE KATRINA." Pretend you were hired as a consultant to determine the percentile for that August. Write a brief paragraph for your report, explaining why the data you generated are likely to be inaccurate.

d. What raw scores mark the cutoff for the top and bottom 10% for these data? Based on these scores, which months had extreme data for 2005? Why should we not trust these data?

7.46 Steps 1 and 2 of hypothesis testing for a study of the Wechsler Adult Intelligence Scale-Revised: Boone (1992) examined scores on the Wechsler Adult Intelligence Scale-Revised (WAIS-R) for 150 adult psychiatric inpatients. He determined the "intrasubtest scatter" score for each inpatient. Intrasubtest scatter refers to patterns of responses in which respondents are almost as likely to get easy questions wrong as hard ones. In the WAIS-R, we expect more wrong answers near the end, as the questions become more difficult, so high levels of intrasubtest scatter would be an unusual pattern of responses. Boone wondered if psychiatric patients have different response patterns than nonpatients have. He compared the intrasubtest scatter for 150 patients to population data from the WAIS-R standardization group. Assume that he had access both to means and standard deviations for this population. Boone reported that "the standardization group's intrasubtest scatter was significantly greater than those reported for the psychiatric inpatients" and concluded that such scatter is normal.

a. What are the two populations?

b. What would the comparison distribution be? Explain.

c. What hypothesis test would you use? Explain.

d. Check the assumptions for this hypothesis test. Label your answers (1) through (3).

e. What does Boone mean when he says *significantly*?

f. State the null and research hypotheses for a two-tailed test in both words and symbols.

g. Imagine that you wanted to replicate this study. Based on the findings described here, state the null and research hypotheses for a one-tailed test in both words and symbols.

7.47 Passwords, red heads, and a *z* test: The BBC reported that red-haired women were more likely than others to choose strong passwords (Ward, 2013). How might a researcher study this? Computer scientist Cynthia Kuo and her colleagues conducted a study in which they gave passwords a score, with higher scores going to passwords that are not in "password crack dictionaries" that are used by hackers, that are longer, and that use a mix of letters, numbers, and symbols (2006). They found a mean score of 15.7 with a standard deviation of 7.3. For the purposes of this exercise, treat these numbers as the population parameters. Based on your knowledge of the *z* test, explain how you might design a study to test the hypothesis that red-haired women create stronger passwords than others.

Putting It All Together

7.48 The Graded Naming Test and sociocultural differences: Researchers often use *z* tests to compare their samples to known population norms. The Graded Naming Test (GNT) asks respondents to name objects in a set of 30 black-and-white drawings. The test, often used to detect brain damage, starts with easy words like *kangaroo* and gets progressively more difficult, ending with words like *sextant*. The GNT population norm for adults in England is 20.4. Roberts (2003) wondered whether a sample of Canadian adults had different scores than adults in England. If they were different, the English norms would not be valid for use in Canada. The mean for 30 Canadian adults was 17.5. For the purposes of this exercise, assume that the standard deviation of the adults in England is 3.2.

a. Conduct all six steps of a *z* test. Be sure to label all six steps.

b. Some words on the GNT are more commonly used in England. For example, a *mitre*, the headpiece worn by bishops, is worn by the archbishop of Canterbury in public ceremonies in England. No Canadian participant correctly responded to this item, whereas 55% of English adults correctly responded. Explain why we should be cautious about applying norms to people different from those on whom the test was normed.

c. When we conduct a one-tailed test instead of a two-tailed test, there are small changes in steps 2 and 4 of hypothesis testing. (*Note:* For this example, assume that those from populations other than the one on which it was normed will score lower, on average. That is, hypothesize that the Canadians will have a lower mean.) Conduct steps 2, 4, and 6 of hypothesis testing for a one-tailed test.

d. Under which circumstance—a one-tailed or a two-tailed test—is it easier to reject the null hypothesis? Explain.

e. If it becomes easier to reject the null hypothesis under one type of test (one-tailed versus two-tailed), does this mean that there is a bigger difference between the groups with a one-tailed test than with a two-tailed test? Explain.

f. When we change the *p* level that we use as a cutoff, there is a small change in step 4 of hypothesis testing. Although 0.05 is the most commonly used *p* level, other values, such as 0.01, are often used. For this example, conduct steps 4 and 6 of hypothesis testing for a two-tailed test and *p* level of 0.01, determining the cutoff and drawing the curve.

g. With which *p* level—0.05 or 0.01—is it easiest to reject the null hypothesis? Explain.

h. If it is easier to reject the null hypothesis with certain *p* levels, does this mean that there is a bigger difference between the samples with one *p* level versus the other *p* level? Explain.

7.49 Patient adherence and orthodontics: A research report (Behenam & Pooya, 2007) begins, "There is probably no other area of health care that requires… cooperation to the extent that orthodontics does," and explores factors that affected the number of hours per day that Iranian patients wore their orthodontic appliances. The patients in the study reported that they used their appliances, on average, 14.78 hours per day, with a standard deviation of 5.31. We'll treat this group as the population for the purposes of this example. Let's say a researcher wanted to study whether a video with information about orthodontics led to an increase in the amount of time patients wore their appliances, but decided to use a two-tailed test to be conservative. Let's say he studied the next 15 patients at his clinic, asked them to watch the video, and then found that they wore their appliances, on average, 17 hours per day.

a. What is the independent variable? What is the dependent variable?

b. Did the researcher use random selection to choose his sample? Explain your answer.

c. Conduct all six steps of hypothesis testing. Be sure to label all six steps.

d. If the researcher's decision in step 6 were wrong, what type of error would he have made? Explain your answer.

e. Imagine that the researcher had rejected the null hypothesis. Explain how replication might help to determine whether these findings might be a Type I error.

f. Imagine that the researcher had rejected the null hypothesis. If researchers attempted to replicate this study in a different country and failed to replicate it, explain why, other than a Type I error, this might have occurred?

7.50 Radiation levels on Japanese farms: Fackler (2012) reported in the *New York Times* that Japanese farmers have become skeptical of the Japanese government's assurances that radiation levels were within legal limits in the wake of the 2011 tsunami and radiation disaster at Fukushima. After reports of safe levels in Onami, more than 12 concerned farmers tested their crops and found dangerously high levels of cesium.

a. If the farmers wanted to conduct a z test comparing their results to the cesium levels found in areas that had not been exposed to the radiation, what would their sample be? Be specific.

b. Conduct step 1 of hypothesis testing.

c. Conduct step 2 of hypothesis testing.

d. Conduct step 4 of hypothesis testing for a two-tailed test and a p level of 0.05.

e. Imagine that the farmers calculated a z statistic of 3.2 for their sample. Conduct step 6 of hypothesis testing.

f. If the farmers' conclusions were incorrect, what type of error would they have made? Explain your answer.

g. Explain how replication with another set of farmers might help to determine whether these findings might be a Type I error.

TERMS

assumption (p. 179)
parametric test (p. 179)
nonparametric test (p. 179)
robust (p. 179)

critical value (p. 180)
critical region (p. 180)
p level (p. 180)

statistically significant (p. 181)
one-tailed test (p. 184)
two-tailed test (p. 184)

SYMBOLS

H_0 (p. 184)
H_1 (p. 184)

Confidence Intervals, Effect Size, and Statistical Power

The New Statistics

Confidence Intervals

Interval Estimates
Calculating Confidence Intervals
with *z* Distributions

Effect Size

The Effect of Sample Size on
Statistical Significance

What Effect Size Is
Cohen's *d*

Next Steps: Meta-Analysis

Statistical Power

The Importance of Statistical Power
Five Factors That Affect Statistical Power

BEFORE YOU GO ON

- **You should know how to conduct a *z* test (Chapter 7).**

- **You should understand the concept of statistical significance (Chapter 7).**

"Math Class Is Tough" Teen Talk Barbie, with her negative proclamation about math class, was a lightning rod for discussions about gender stereotypes. Some of Barbie's negative press related to the fact that Barbie's message might doom girls to even poorer performances in mathematics. The media tend to play up gender differences instead of the less interesting (and more frequent) realities of gender similarities.

"Want to go shopping? OK, meet me at the mall."

"Math class is tough."

With these and 268 other phrases, Teen Talk Barbie was introduced to the market in July 1992. By September, it was being publicly criticized for its negative message about girls and math. At first the Mattel toy company refused to pull it from store shelves, citing more positive phrases in Barbie's repertoire, such as "I'm studying to be a doctor." But the bad press escalated, and by October Mattel had backed down. The controversy endured, however, and even showed up in a 1994 *Simpsons* episode when Lisa Simpson boycotted the fictional Malibu Stacy doll that had been programmed to say, "Thinking too much gives you wrinkles."

The controversy over gender differences in mathematical reasoning ability began after a study on the topic was published in the prestigious journal *Science*. Participants included about 10,000 male and female students in grades 7 through 10 who were already among the top 2% to 3% on standardized tests of mathematics (Benbow & Stanley, 1980). In this preselected sample, the boys' average score on the mathematics portion of the SAT test was 32 points higher than the girls' average score, a statistically significant difference that gained vast media attention (Jacob & Eccles, 1982). But the danger of reporting such a mean difference is the implication that all or most of the members of one group are different from all or most of the members of the other group. As we see from the overlapping distributions in Figure 8-1, such an assertion is far from the truth.

Language Alert! Part of this misunderstanding is caused by the language of statistics: "Statistically significant" does *not* mean "very important." The misunderstanding about Benbow and Stanley's study (1980) spread from researchers to the media to the general public. The issue gained even more attention when the release of Teen Talk Barbie inspired members of a guerrilla art group. The Barbie Liberation Organization switched the computer chips in talking Barbies and GI Joes and returned them to store shelves. Suddenly, GI Joe was chirping, in a voice uncannily like Barbie's, "Let's plan a great big wedding," as well as complaining that "Math class is tough."

It took a meta-analysis—a study of all the studies about a particular topic—to clarify the story these data were telling. Janet Hyde and colleagues conducted the meta-analysis by compiling the results from 259 mean differences in mathematical reasoning ability (Hyde, Fennema, & Lamon, 1990). These data represented 1,968,846 male participants and 2,016,836 female participants. Here's what the researchers discovered:

☐ The two distributions (one for males; another for females) overlapped almost completely (see Figure 8-1). The dotted-line curve represents male mathematical reasoning ability, and the solid-line curve represents female math reasoning ability.

☐ Mean gender differences in overall mathematical reasoning ability were small.

☐ The difference was smaller and *reversed* (favoring women and girls rather than men and boys) when the extreme tails of the distribution were eliminated (such as scores from participants in remedial or gifted programs).

Are you surprised that a small (but statistically significant) gender difference is almost completely overlapping? This is a case in which hypothesis testing alone inadvertently encouraged a profound misunderstanding (Jacob & Eccles, 1986). Stories like

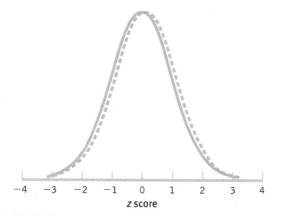

FIGURE 8-1

A Gender Difference in Mathematics Performance

This graph represents the overlap in mathematical performance that would be expected if distributions for males and females differed, on average, by the amount that Hyde and colleagues (1990) reported in their meta-analysis. The solid line represents the distribution for females, and the dotted line represents the distribution for males.

this one have led to an increasing emphasis on what Geoff Cumming calls "the new statistics." In this chapter, we'll talk about the push to use newer statistics, and we'll talk about three ways that statisticians do so. First, we compute confidence intervals, which provide a range of plausible mean differences. Second, we calculate effect sizes, which indicate the size of differences. Finally, we estimate the statistical power of the study to be sure that we have a sufficient sample size to detect a real difference. If we discover that we don't have enough statistical power, then we need to increase statistical power so that we can believe the results of our own study.

The New Statistics

In 2012, Geoff Cumming published *Understanding the New Statistics,* a book that shifted an academic discussion about how statistics is changing into the mainstream. Many researchers have criticized hypothesis testing and the black-and-white thinking it leads to (Nuzzo, 2014). Indeed, the American Statistical Association recently released a statement that carefully defined p values in relation to traditional hypothesis testing, and they offered guidelines for reducing their misuse (Wasserstein, 2016; Wasserstein & Lazar, 2016). What is the problem? In hypothesis testing, a finding is either significant or not significant, which actually tells us very little, as you'll learn in this chapter. Hypothesis testing can also lead researchers to "play" with their data until it edges under the arbitrary criterion of $p < 0.05$. The "new statistics" help us to address these problems, though they are not actually new (Cumming, 2012). Rather, it is the use of these statistics in place of hypothesis testing that would be new for the social sciences.

What are the new statistics? They include effect sizes, confidence intervals, and meta-analysis, all of which are covered in this chapter. Statistical power, which is also covered here, is closely linked to these concepts. All of these new statistics help us to come up with an estimate for the thing that we are observing—the behavior, attitude, emotion, or cognition. Cumming observes that other sciences, like physics, report estimates: "the melting point of the plastic was 85.5 ± 0.2°C," for example (p. ix). The behavioral sciences, on the other hand, tend to report that there is or is not a significant effect, which gives us less information than an estimate would.

● A **point estimate** is a summary statistic from a sample that is just one number used as an estimate of the population parameter.

● An **interval estimate** is based on a sample statistic and provides a range of plausible values for the population parameter.

It is important to note that the estimates that Cumming calls for are intervals rather than a single number. Interval estimates not only give us a range of plausible variables, but they also give us a sense of the uncertainty behind statistics. When we report a single number, it seems like that must be the real number. The interval estimate makes it clearer that we're not all that sure. In fact, researchers who interpreted data based only on the interval estimate tended to be more accurate than researchers who also took hypothesis testing into account (Coulson, Healey, Fidler, & Cumming, 2010).

Beyond the fact that estimates are more useful, journal editors increasingly expect researchers to include the new statistics in their research reports (Cumming, 2013; Funder et al., 2013). For example, the latest edition of the *Publication Manual* of the American Psychological Association (APA) calls for researchers to use the new statistics whenever possible. In addition, the Association for Psychological Science (APS) has added the use of the new statistics to the standards for its flagship journal (APS, 2014; Cumming, 2014). The journal *Basic and Applied Social Psychology* has even gone so far as to ban traditional hypothesis testing in articles that they publish (Trafimow & Marks, 2015).

Researchers increasingly comply with these expectations. For example, in one major journal, 94% of studies published over several years reported effect sizes and 40% reported confidence intervals (Odgaard & Fowler, 2010). The behavioral sciences do continue to use hypothesis testing, which is why it is still helpful to learn it. But the field is shifting, which is why it is also essential to learn the new statistics. If you continue to study and work in the behavioral sciences, one day you may not use hypothesis testing at all. As Cumming puts it, "there's life beyond .05" (2014).

Confidence Intervals

In studies on gender differences in mathematics performance, researchers calculate a mean difference by subtracting a mean score for girls from a mean score for boys. All three summary statistics—the mean for boys, the mean for girls, and the difference between them—are point estimates. *A **point estimate** is a summary statistic from a sample that is just one number used as an estimate of the population parameter.* So, a mean taken from a sample is a point estimate, a single number used as an estimate for a population parameter. A point estimate, however, is rarely exactly accurate. We can increase accuracy by using an interval estimate when possible.

MASTERING THE CONCEPT

8-1: We can use a sample to calculate a point estimate—one plausible number, such as a mean—for the population. More realistically, we also can use a sample to calculate an interval estimate—a range of plausible numbers, such as a range of means—for the population.

Interval Estimates

*An **interval estimate** is based on a sample statistic and provides a range of plausible values for the population parameter.* Interval estimates are frequently used by the media, often when reporting political polls, and are usually constructed by adding and subtracting a margin of error from a point estimate.

EXAMPLE 8.1

For example, a Marist poll asked 938 adult respondents in the United States to select from five choices the word or phrase that they found "most annoying in conversation" (http://maristpoll.marist.edu/-107-whatever-takes-top-honors-as-most-annoying/). "Whatever" was chosen by 47% of respondents, ahead of "you know" (25%), "it is what it is" (11%), "anyway" (7%), and "at the end of the day" (2%). The margin of error was reported to be ±3.2% (plus or minus 3.2%).

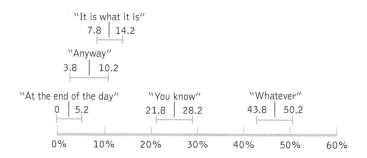

FIGURE 8-2

Intervals and Overlap

When two intervals, like those for "whatever" and "you know," do not overlap, we conclude that the population means are likely different. In the population, it seems that "whatever" really is more annoying than "you know." However, when two intervals do overlap, like those for "it is what it is" and "anyway," then it is plausible that the two phrases are perceived as equal—in this case, equally annoying—in the population.

Because 47 − 3.2 = 43.8 and 47 + 3.2 = 50.2, the interval estimate for "whatever" is 43.8% to 50.2% (Figure 8-2). Interval estimates provide a range of plausible values, not just one statistic.

Pay attention to whether the interval estimates overlap. "You know" came in second, with 25%, giving an interval estimate of 21.8% to 28.2%. There's no overlap with the first-place word, a strong indication that "whatever" really was most annoying in the population as well as in the sample. However, if "you know" had received 42% of the vote, it would have placed only 5% behind "whatever," and it would have had an interval estimate of 38.8% to 45.2%. This range would have overlapped with the one for "whatever" (43.8% to 50.2%), an indication that both expressions could plausibly have been equally annoying in the population.

Language Alert! The terms "margin of error," "interval estimate," and "confidence interval" all represent the same idea. Specifically, *a **confidence interval** is an interval estimate based on a sample statistic; it includes the population mean a certain percentage of the time if the same population is sampled from repeatedly.* (*Note:* We are not saying that we are confident that the population mean falls in the interval; we are merely saying that we expect to find the population mean within a certain interval a certain percentage of the time—usually 95%—when we conduct this same study with the same sample size.)

The confidence interval is centered around the mean of the sample. A 95% confidence level is most commonly used, indicating the 95% that falls *between* the two tails (i.e., 100% − 5% = 95%). Note the terms used here: The confidence *level* is 95%, but the confidence *interval* is the range between the two values that surround the sample mean. ●

Calculating Confidence Intervals with z Distributions

The symmetry of the *z* distribution makes it easy to calculate confidence intervals. We already conducted hypothesis testing in Example 7.5 in Chapter 7 for a study on calories consumed by patrons of different Starbucks stores that either did or did not post the calories on their menus (Bollinger, Leslie, & Sorensen, 2010). Here is how confidence intervals can help us listen more closely to the story these data tell.

> ● A **confidence interval** is an interval estimate based on a sample statistic; it includes the population mean a certain percentage of the time if the same population is sampled from repeatedly.

EXAMPLE 8.2

In the Starbucks study, the population mean was 247 calories, and we considered 201 to be the population standard deviation. The 1000 people in the sample consumed a mean of 232 calories. When we conducted hypothesis testing, we centered the curve around the mean according to the null hypothesis, the population mean of 247. We determined critical values based on this mean and compared the sample mean to these cutoffs. The test statistic (−2.36) was beyond the critical *z* statistic, so we rejected the null hypothesis. The data led us to conclude that people going to those Starbucks that posted calories consumed fewer calories, on average, than people going to those Starbucks that did not post calories.

FIGURE 8-3

A 95% Confidence Interval, Part I

To begin calculating a confidence interval for a *z* distribution, we draw a normal curve, place the sample mean at its center, and indicate the percentages within and beyond the confidence interval.

There are several steps to calculating a confidence interval.

> **STEP 1: Draw a picture of a distribution that will include the confidence interval.**

We draw a normal curve (Figure 8-3) that has the *sample* mean, 232, at its center, instead of the *population* mean, 247.

> **STEP 2: Indicate the bounds of the confidence interval on the drawing.**

We draw a vertical line from the mean to the top of the curve. For a 95% confidence interval, we also draw two small vertical lines to indicate the middle 95% of the normal curve (2.5% in each tail, for a total of 5%).

The curve is symmetric, so half of the 95% falls above and half falls below the mean. Half of 95 is 47.5, so we write 47.5% in the segments on either side of the mean. In the tails beyond the two lines that indicate the end of the middle 95%, we also write the appropriate percentages. You can see these percentages in Figure 8-3.

> **STEP 3: Determine the z statistics that fall at each line marking the middle 95%.**

To do this, we turn back to the versatile *z* table in Appendix B. The percentage between the mean and each of the *z* scores is 47.5%. When we look up this percentage in the *z* table, we find a *z* statistic of 1.96. (Note that this is identical to the cutoffs for the *z* test; this will always be the case because the *p* level of 0.05 corresponds to a confidence level of 95%.) We can now add the *z* statistics of −1.96 and 1.96 to the curve, as seen in Figure 8-4.

FIGURE 8-4

A 95% Confidence Interval, Part II

The next step in calculating a confidence interval is identifying the *z* statistics that indicate each end of the interval. Because the curve is symmetric, the *z* statistics will have the same magnitude—one will be negative and one will be positive (−1.96 and 1.96).

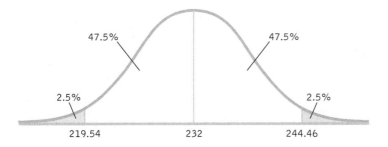

FIGURE 8-5

A 95% Confidence Interval, Part III

The final step in calculating a confidence interval is converting the z statistics that indicate each end of the interval into raw means.

STEP 4: Turn the z statistics back into raw means.

We use the formula for this conversion, but first we identify the appropriate mean and standard deviation. There are two important points to remember. First, we center the interval around the *sample* mean (not the *population* mean). So we use the sample mean of 232 in the calculations. Second, because we have a sample *mean* (rather than an individual *score*), we use a distribution of means. So we calculate standard error as the measure of spread:

$$\sigma_M = \frac{\sigma}{\sqrt{N}} = \frac{201}{\sqrt{1000}} = 6.356$$

Notice that this is the same standard error that we calculated in Example 7.5 in Chapter 7 when we conducted a hypothesis test.

Using this mean and standard error, we calculate the raw mean at each end of the confidence interval, and add them to the curve, as in Figure 8-5:

$$M_{lower} = -z(\sigma_M) + M_{sample} = -1.96(6.356) + 232 = 219.54$$

$$M_{upper} = z(\sigma_M) + M_{sample} = 1.96(6.356) + 232 = 244.46$$

The 95% confidence interval, reported in brackets as is typical, is [219.54, 244.46].

STEP 5: Check that the confidence interval makes sense.

The sample mean should fall exactly in the middle of the two ends of the interval.

$$219.54 - 232 = -12.46 \text{ and } 244.46 - 232 = 12.46$$

We have a match. The confidence interval ranges from 12.46 below the sample mean to 12.46 above the sample mean. We can think of this number, 12.46, as the margin of error.

To recap the steps for the creation of a confidence interval for a z statistic:

1. *Draw* a normal curve with the *sample* mean in the center.
2. *Indicate* the bounds of the confidence interval on either end, and write the percentages under each segment of the curve.
3. *Look up* the z statistics for the lower and upper ends of the confidence interval in the z table. These are always −1.96 and 1.96 for a 95% confidence interval around a z statistic.
4. *Convert* the z statistics to raw means for each end of the confidence interval.
5. *Check* your answer; each end of the confidence interval should be exactly the same distance from the sample mean.

MASTERING THE FORMULA

8-1: The formula for the lower bound of a confidence interval using a z distribution is $M_{lower} = -z(\sigma_M) + M_{sample}$, and the formula for the upper bound is $M_{upper} = z(\sigma_M) + M_{sample}$. The first symbol in each formula refers to the mean at that end of the confidence interval. To calculate each bound, we multiply the z statistic by the standard error, then add the sample mean. The z statistic for the lower bound is negative, and the z statistic for the upper bound is positive.

If we were to sample 1000 customers at the Starbucks that post calories on their menus from the same population over and over, the 95% confidence interval would include the population mean 95% of the time. Note that the population mean for customers at the Starbucks that do not post calories, 247, falls outside of this interval. So, it is not plausible that the sample of customers at Starbucks that post calories comes from the population according to the null hypothesis—customers at Starbucks that do not post calories.

The conclusions from both the z test and the confidence interval are the same, but the confidence interval gives us more information—an interval estimate, not just a point estimate. Moreover, there is some evidence that reporting confidence intervals instead of the results of hypothesis testing can lead to more accurate interpretations of the findings (Coulson, Healey, Fidler, & Cumming, 2010). ●

CHECK YOUR LEARNING

Reviewing the Concepts

> Increasingly, researchers are expected to use the "new statistics"—effect sizes, confidence intervals, meta-analysis, and statistical power—in addition to our instead of traditional hypothesis testing.

> A point estimate is just a single number, such as a mean, that provides a plausible value for the population parameter. An interval estimate provides a range of plausible values for the population parameter.

> A confidence interval is one kind of interval estimate and can be created around a sample mean using a z distribution.

> The confidence interval confirms the results of the hypothesis test while adding more detail.

Clarifying the Concepts   8-1   Why are interval estimates better than point estimates?

Calculating the Statistics   8-2   If 21% of voters want to raise taxes, with a margin of error of 4%, what is the interval estimate? What is the point estimate?

Applying the Concepts   8-3   In How It Works 7.2, we conducted a z test based on the following information adapted from a study by Adams (2012) that used the Consideration of Future Consequences (CFC) scale as the dependent variable. The population mean CFC score was 3.20, with a standard deviation of 0.70. The sample was 45 students who joined a career discussion group, and the study examined whether this might have changed CFC scores. The mean for this group was 3.45.

a. Calculate the 95% confidence interval.

b. Explain what this confidence interval tells us.

Solutions to these Check Your Learning questions can be found in Appendix D.

c. Why is this confidence interval superior to the hypothesis test that we conducted in Chapter 7?

Effect Size

As we learned when we looked at the research on gender differences in mathematical reasoning ability, "statistically significant" does *not* mean that the findings from a study represent a meaningful difference. "Statistically significant" only means that those findings are unlikely to occur if in fact the null hypothesis is true. Geoff Cumming points out that hypothesis testing "relies on strange backward logic and can't give us direct information about what we want to know—the effect itself" (2014). Calculating an effect size moves us a little closer to the question we are most interested in: Is the pattern in a data set meaningful or important?

The Effect of Sample Size on Statistical Significance

The almost completely overlapping curves for mathematics performance in Figure 8-1 were "statistically significant" because the sample size was so big. Increasing sample size always increases the test statistic if all else stays the same. In Example 7.3, we used OkCupid data for men's ratings of women's online dating profiles (Rudder, 2015). Based on the reported distribution, we estimated the mean to be 2.5 and the standard deviation to be 0.833. We used the example of a fictional study in which you compare the mean rating of 2.84 for a sample of 30 women at your university to the overall OkCupid mean rating. Based on the sample size of 30, we reported the mean and standard error for the distribution of means as:

$$\mu_M = \mu = 2.50; \sigma_M = \frac{\sigma}{\sqrt{N}} = \frac{0.833}{\sqrt{30}} = 0.152$$

Misinterpreting Statistical Significance Statistical significance that is achieved by merely collecting a large sample can make a research finding appear to be far more important than it really is, just as a curved mirror can exaggerate a person's size.

The test statistic calculated from these numbers was:

$$z = \frac{(M - \mu_M)}{\sigma_M} = \frac{(2.84 - 2.50)}{0.152} = 2.236$$

What would happen if we increased the sample size to 200? We'd have to recalculate the standard error to reflect the larger sample, and then recalculate the test statistic to reflect the smaller standard error.

$$\mu_M = \mu = 2.50; \sigma_M = \frac{\sigma}{\sqrt{N}} = \frac{0.833}{\sqrt{200}} = 0.059$$

$$z = \frac{(M - \mu_M)}{\sigma_M} = \frac{(2.84 - 2.50)}{0.059} = 5.763$$

What if we increased the sample size to 1000?

$$\mu_M = \mu = 2.50; \sigma_M = \frac{\sigma}{\sqrt{N}} = \frac{0.833}{\sqrt{1000}} = 0.026$$

$$z = \frac{(M - \mu_M)}{\sigma_M} = \frac{(2.84 - 2.50)}{0.026} = 13.077$$

What if we increased it to 100,000?

$$\mu_M = \mu = 2.50; \sigma_M = \frac{\sigma}{\sqrt{N}} = \frac{0.833}{\sqrt{100,000}} = 0.003$$

$$z = \frac{(M - \mu_M)}{\sigma_M} = \frac{(2.84 - 2.50)}{0.003} = 113.333$$

Notice that each time we increased the sample size, the standard error decreased and the test statistic increased. The original test statistic, 2.24, was beyond the critical values of 1.96 and −1.96. And as the sample size increased, the test statistics (5.76, 13.08, and 113.33) were increasingly more extreme than the positive critical value. In their study of gender differences in mathematics performance, researchers studied 10,000 participants, a very large sample (Benbow & Stanley, 1980). It is not surprising, then, that a small difference would be a statistically significant difference.

8-2: As sample size increases, so does the test statistic (if all else stays the same). Because of this, a small difference might not be statistically significant with a small sample but might be statistically significant with a large sample.

Let's consider, logically, why it makes sense that a large sample should allow us to reject the null hypothesis more readily than a small sample. If we randomly selected 5 women at your university and they had a mean score well above the OkCupid average, we might say, "It could be chance." But if we randomly selected 1000 women with a mean rating well above the OkCupid average, it is very unlikely that we just happened to choose 1000 people with high scores.

But just because a real difference exists does not mean it is a large or meaningful difference. The difference we found with 5 people might be the same as the difference we found with 1000 people. As we demonstrated with multiple z tests with different sample sizes, we might fail to reject the null hypothesis with a small sample but then reject the null hypothesis for the same-size difference between means with a large sample.

Cohen (1990) used the small but statistically significant correlation between height and IQ to explain the difference between statistical significance and practical importance. The sample size was big: 14,000 children. Imagining that height and IQ were causally related, Cohen calculated that a person would have to grow by 3.5 feet to increase her IQ by 30 points (two standard deviations). Or, to increase her height by 4 inches, she would have to increase her IQ by 233 points! Height may have been statistically significantly related to IQ, but there was no practical real-world application. A larger sample size should influence the level of confidence that the story is true, but it should not increase our confidence that the story is important.

Language Alert! When you come across the term *statistical significance*, do not interpret this as an indication of practical importance.

What Effect Size Is

Effect size can tell us whether a statistically significant difference might also be an important difference. *Effect size indicates the size of a difference and is unaffected by sample size.* Effect size tells us how much two populations *do not* overlap. Simply put, the less overlap, the bigger the effect size.

● **Effect size** indicates the size of a difference and is unaffected by sample size.

The amount of overlap between two distributions can be decreased in two ways. First, as shown in Figure 8-6, overlap decreases and effect size increases when means

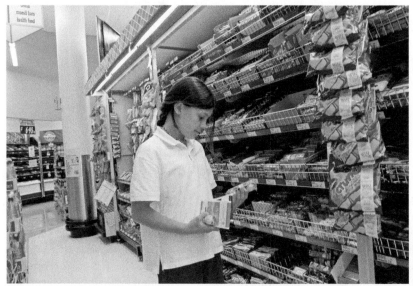

Larger Samples Give Us More Confidence in Our Conclusions Stephen, a British student studying in the United States, is told that he won't be able to find his favorite candy bar, Yorkie. He tests this hypothesis in 3 stores and finds no Yorkie bars. Another British student, Victoria, also warned by her friends, looks for her favorite, Curly Wurly. She tests her hypothesis in 25 U.S. stores and finds no Curly Wurly bars. Both conclude that their friends were right. Do you feel more confident that Stephen or Victoria really won't be able to find their favorite candy bar?

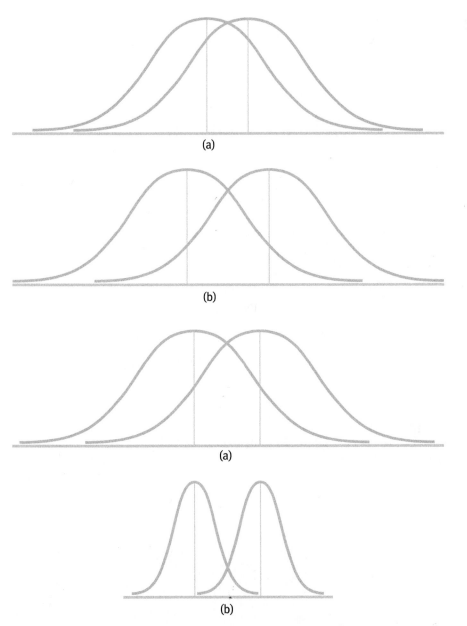

FIGURE 8-6

Effect Size and Mean Differences

When two population means are farther apart, as in (b), the overlap of the distributions is less and the effect size is bigger.

FIGURE 8-7

Effect Size and Standard Deviation

When two population distributions decrease their spread, as in (b), the overlap of the distributions is less and the effect size is bigger.

are further apart. Second, as shown in Figure 8-7, overlap decreases and effect size increases when variability within each distribution of scores is smaller.

When we discussed gender differences in mathematical reasoning ability, you may have noticed that we described the size of the findings as "small" (Hyde, 2005). Because effect size is a standardized measure based on scores rather than means, we can compare the effect sizes of different studies with one another, even when the studies have different sample sizes.

EXAMPLE 8.3

Figure 8-8 demonstrates why we use scores instead of means to calculate effect size. First, assume that each of these distributions is based on the same underlying population. Second, notice that all means represented by the vertical lines are identical. The

Making Fair Comparisons

The top two pairs of curves (a and b) depict two studies, study 1 and study 2. The first study (a) compared two samples with very large sample sizes, so each curve is very narrow. The second study (b) compared two samples with much smaller sample sizes, so each curve is wider. The first study has less overlap, but that doesn't mean it has a bigger effect than study 2; we just can't compare the effects. The bottom two pairs (c and d) depict the same two studies, but used standard deviation for the individual scores. Now they are comparable and we see that they have the same amount of overlap—the same effect sizes.

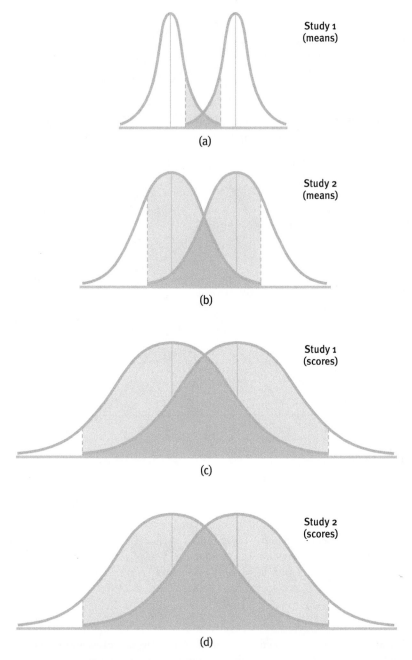

(a) Study 1 (means)

(b) Study 2 (means)

(c) Study 1 (scores)

(d) Study 2 (scores)

differences are due only to the spread of the distributions. The small degree of overlap in the tall, skinny distributions of means in Figure 8-8a is the result of a large sample size. The greater degree of overlap in the somewhat wider distributions of means in Figure 8-8b is the result of a smaller sample size. By contrast, the distributions of scores in Figures 8-8c and 8-8d represent scores rather than means for these two studies. Because these flatter, wider distributions include actual scores, sample size is not an issue in making comparisons.

In this case, the amounts of real overlap in Figures 8-8c and 8-8d are identical. We can directly compare the amount of overlap and see that they have the same effect size. ●

Cohen's *d*

There are many different effect-size statistics, but they all neutralize the influence of sample size. When we conduct a *z* test, the effect-size statistic is typically Cohen's *d*, developed by Jacob Cohen (Cohen, 1988). **Cohen's d** *is a measure of effect size that assesses the difference between two means in terms of standard deviation, not standard error.* In other words, Cohen's *d* allows us to measure the difference between means using standard deviations, much like a *z* statistic. We accomplish this by using standard deviation in the denominator (rather than using standard error).

● **Cohen's *d*** is a measure of effect size that assesses the difference between two means in terms of standard deviation, not standard error.

● ●

Let's calculate Cohen's *d* for the same Starbucks data from Example 8.2 with which we constructed a confidence interval. We simply substitute standard deviation for standard error. When we calculated the test statistic for the 1000 customers at Starbucks with posted calories, we first calculated standard error:

EXAMPLE 8.4

$$\sigma_M = \frac{\sigma}{\sqrt{N}} = \frac{201}{\sqrt{100}} = 6.356$$

We calculated the *z* statistic using the population mean of 247 and the sample mean of 232:

$$z = \frac{(M - \mu_M)}{\sigma_M} = \frac{(232 - 247)}{6.356} = -2.36$$

To calculate Cohen's *d*, we simply use the formula for the *z* statistic, substituting σ for σ_M (and μ for μ_M, even though these means are always the same). So we use 201 instead of 6.356 in the denominator. Cohen's *d* is based on the spread of the distribution of scores, rather than the distribution of means.

$$d = \frac{(M - \mu)}{\sigma} = \frac{(232 - 247)}{201} = -0.07$$

Now that we have the effect size, often written in shorthand as $d = -0.07$, we ask: What does it mean? First, we know that the two sample means are 0.07 standard deviation apart, which doesn't sound like a big difference—and it isn't. Cohen developed guidelines for what constitutes a small effect (0.2), a medium effect (0.5), and a large effect (0.8). Table 8-1 displays these guidelines, along with the amount of overlap between two curves that is indicated by an effect of that size. No sign is provided because it is the magnitude of an effect size that matters; an effect size of −0.5 is the same size as one of 0.5.

MASTERING THE FORMULA

8-2: The formula for Cohen's *d* for a *z* statistic is:

$$d = \frac{(M - \mu)}{\sigma}.$$

It is the same formula as for the *z* statistic, except we divide by the population standard deviation rather than by standard error.

MASTERING THE CONCEPT

8-3: Because a statistically significant effect might not be an important one, we should calculate effect size in addition to conducting a hypothesis test. We can then report whether a statistically significant effect is small, medium, or large.

TABLE 8-1	Cohen's Conventions for Effect Sizes: *d*

Jacob Cohen published guidelines (or conventions) based on the overlap between two distributions to help researchers determine whether an effect is small, medium, or large. These numbers are not cutoffs; they are merely rough guidelines to help researchers interpret results.

Effect Size	Convention	Overlap
Small	0.2	85%
Medium	0.5	67%
Large	0.8	53%

Based on these numbers, the effect size for the study of Starbucks customers (−0.07) is not even at the level of a small effect. As we pointed out in Chapter 7, however, the researchers hypothesized that even a small effect might spur eateries to provide more low-calorie choices. Sometimes a small effect can be meaningful. ●

Next Steps | Meta-Analysis

Many researchers consider meta-analysis to be the most important recent advancement in social science research (e.g., Newton & Rudestam, 1999). *A **meta-analysis** is a study that involves the calculation of a mean effect size from the individual effect sizes of more than one study.* Meta-analysis provides added statistical power by considering multiple studies simultaneously and helps to resolve debates fueled by contradictory research findings (Lam & Kennedy, 2005). Although the goal of meta-analysis, traditionally, has been to combine many studies, researchers are increasingly encouraging the use of meta-analysis with fewer studies—even as few as two (Cumming, 2012). Cumming argues that small meta-analyses can even replace hypothesis testing.

The logic of the meta-analysis process is surprisingly simple. There are just four steps:

1. Select the topic of interest and decide exactly how to proceed *before* beginning to track down studies.

2. Locate every study that has been conducted and meets criteria.

3. Calculate an effect size, often Cohen's *d*, for every study.

4. Calculate statistics—ideally, summary statistics, a hypothesis test, a confidence interval, and a visual display of the effect sizes (Rosenthal, 1995).

> **STEP 1: Select the topic of interest and decide exactly how to proceed *before* beginning to track down studies.**

Here are some of the considerations to keep in mind:

1. Make sure the necessary statistical information, either effect sizes or the summary statistics necessary to calculate effect sizes, is available.

2. Consider selecting only studies in which participants meet certain criteria, such as age, gender, or geographic location.

3. Consider eliminating studies based on the research design—for example, because they were not experimental in nature.

For example, British researcher Fidelma Hanrahan and her colleagues conducted a meta-analysis to examine the effectiveness of cognitive therapy in reducing levels of worrying in people with generalized anxiety disorder (Hanrahan, Field, Jones, & Davey, 2013). Before they began their meta-analysis, they developed criteria for the studies they would include; for example, they decided to include only studies that were true experiments and only studies in which the participants were between the ages of 18 and 65.

> **STEP 2: Locate every study that has been conducted and meets the criteria.**

Obvious places to start are PsycINFO, Google Scholar, and other electronic databases. For example, these researchers searched several databases using terms such as "generalized anxiety disorder," "cognitive," "therapy," and "anxiety" (Hanrahan et al., 2013). A key part of meta-analysis, however, is finding any studies that have been conducted but have not been published (Conn, Valentine, Cooper, & Rantz, 2003).

● A **meta-analysis** is a study that involves the calculation of a mean effect size from the individual effect sizes of more than one study.

Much of this "fugitive literature" (Rosenthal, 1995, p. 184) or "gray literature" (Lam & Kennedy, 2005) is unpublished simply because the studies did not find a significant difference. The effect size seems larger without these studies. We find these studies by using other sources—for example, by reading the proceedings of relevant conferences or contacting the primary researchers in the field to obtain any relevant unpublished findings. Hanrahan and her colleagues emailed the authors of the studies they located by using databases and asked whether they had any unpublished data.

> **STEP 3:** Calculate an effect size, often Cohen's *d*, for every study.

When the effect size has not been reported, the researcher must calculate it from summary statistics that were reported. These researchers were able to calculate 19 effect sizes from the 15 studies that met their criteria (some studies reported more than one effect) (Hanrahan et al., 2013).

> **STEP 4:** Calculate statistics— ideally, summary statistics, a hypothesis test, a confidence interval, and a visual display of the effect sizes (Rosenthal, 1995).

Most importantly, researchers calculate a mean effect size for all studies. In fact, we can apply all of the statistical insights we've learned: means, medians, standard deviations, confidence intervals and hypothesis testing, and visual displays such as box plots or stem-and-leaf plots.

In their meta-analysis of cognitive therapy for worry, Hanrahan and colleagues (2013) calculated several mean effect sizes. For example, the mean Cohen's *d* for the comparison of cognitive therapy with no therapy was 1.81. The confidence interval did not include 0, and the researchers were able to reject the null hypothesis that the effect size was 0. The mean Cohen's *d* for the comparison of cognitive therapy with other types of therapy was 0.63. The researchers were again able to reject the null hypothesis; however, they found an outlier that had a large effect size. The researchers found that when they omitted outliers, the mean dropped from 0.63 to 0.45, a smaller but still statistically significant effect. The researchers also included a graph—a *forest plot, which looks similar to a box plot, that shows the confidence interval for the effect size of every study.* For example, Figure 8-9 shows a forest plot for the studies that compared cognitive therapy with no therapy. Based on this meta-analysis, they concluded that cognitive therapy seems to be an effective treatment for worry.

● A **forest plot** shows the confidence interval for the effect size of every study.

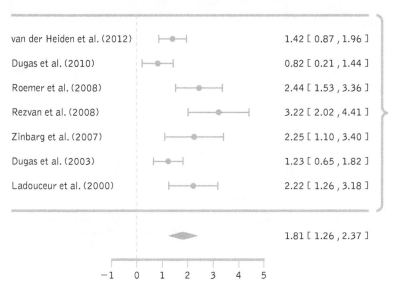

van der Heiden et al. (2012)	1.42 [0.87 , 1.96]
Dugas et al. (2010)	0.82 [0.21 , 1.44]
Roemer et al. (2008)	2.44 [1.53 , 3.36]
Rezvan et al. (2008)	3.22 [2.02 , 4.41]
Zinbarg et al. (2007)	2.25 [1.10 , 3.40]
Dugas et al. (2003)	1.23 [0.65 , 1.82]
Ladouceur et al. (2000)	2.22 [1.26 , 3.18]
	1.81 [1.26 , 2.37]

FIGURE 8-9

Forest Plot

This forest plot shows the effect sizes for the seven studies that compared cognitive therapy with no therapy in the treatment of worry among people with generalized anxiety disorder (Hanrahan et al., 2013). Next to each effect size is the confidence interval for that effect size. The confidence interval for the overall effect size, 1.81, does not include 0. This is not surprising because the confidence intervals for the effect sizes of all seven studies do not include 0. The researchers were able to reject the null hypothesis that the overall effect size is 0.

● A **file drawer analysis** is a statistical calculation, following a meta-analysis, of the number of studies with null results that would have to exist so that a mean effect size would no longer be statistically significant.

Unpublished studies are key to a strong meta-analysis. Much of the fugitive literature of unpublished studies exists because studies with null results are less likely to appear in press (e.g., Begg, 1994). Twenty percent of the studies included in the meta-analysis conducted by Hanrahan and colleagues (2013) were unpublished at the time the meta-analysis was conducted, but there may have been other studies that these researchers were unable to locate. This has been called "the file drawer problem" and we will discuss two solutions to it.

The first solution involves additional analyses. The most common follow-up analysis was proposed by Robert Rosenthal (1991), and became aptly known as a ***file drawer analysis***, *a statistical calculation, following a meta-analysis, of the number of studies with null results that would have to exist so that a mean effect size would no longer be statistically significant.* If just a few studies could render a mean effect size nonsignificant—that is, no longer statistically significantly different from zero—then the mean effect size should be viewed as likely to be an inflated estimate. If it would take several hundred studies in researchers' "file drawers" to render the effect nonsignificant, then it is safe to conclude that there really is a significant effect. For most research topics, it is not likely that there are hundreds of unpublished studies.

There are other variants of the file drawer analysis, including analyses that allow researchers to examine their findings as if there were publication bias—that is, as if there were many studies out there with null results. The meta-analysis described here used a sensitivity analysis developed by Vevea and Woods (2005). Hanrahan and her colleagues concluded that the sensitivity analysis gave them "confidence that the estimated population effect sizes have not been severely inflated by unpublished studies not in the meta-analysis" (p. 126).

A second solution, replication or reproducibility, was discussed in the Next Steps section of Chapter 7. Meta-analysis, despite concerns about the file drawer effect, can work together with replication to help us draw more reliable conclusions. As Geoff Cumming points out, meta-analysis, "even on messy social questions, can give conclusions that are well supported by evidence and have important practical implications" (p. 197). Given the drawbacks of hypothesis testing on its own, meta-analyses are increasingly a gold standard for research.

CHECK YOUR LEARNING

Reviewing the Concepts

> As sample size increases, the test statistic becomes more extreme and it becomes easier to reject the null hypothesis.

> A statistically significant result is not necessarily one with practical importance.

> Effect sizes are calculated with respect to scores, rather than means, so they are not contingent on sample size.

> The size of an effect is based on the difference between two group means and the amount of variability within each group.

> Effect size for a z test is measured with Cohen's d, which is calculated much like a z statistic, but using standard deviation instead of standard error.

> A meta-analysis is a study of studies that provides a more objective measure of an effect size than an individual study does.

> A researcher conducting a meta-analysis chooses a topic, decides on guidelines for a study's inclusion, tracks down every study on a given topic, and calculates an effect size for each. A mean effect size is calculated and reported, often along with a standard deviation, median, significance testing, confidence interval, and appropriate graphs.

Clarifying the Concepts	8-4	Distinguish statistical significance and practical importance.
	8-5	What is effect size?

Calculating the Statistics	8-6	Using IQ as a variable, where we know the mean is 100 and the standard deviation is 15, calculate Cohen's d for an observed mean of 105.

Applying the Concepts	8-7	In Check Your Learning 8-3, you calculated a confidence interval based on CFC data. The population mean CFC score was 3.20, with a standard deviation of 0.70. The mean for the sample of 45 students who joined a career discussion group is 3.45.

a. Calculate the appropriate effect size for this study.

b. Citing Cohen's conventions, explain what this effect size tells us.

c. Based on the effect size, does this finding have any consequences or implications for anyone's life?

Solutions to these Check Your Learning questions can be found in Appendix D.

Statistical Power

The effect size statistic tells us that the public controversy over gender differences in mathematical ability was justified: The observed gender differences had no practical importance. Calculating statistical power is another way to limit such controversies from developing in the first place.

Power is a word that statisticians use in a very specific way. ***Statistical power*** *is a measure of the likelihood that we will reject the null hypothesis, given that the null hypothesis is false.* In other words, statistical power is the probability that we will reject the null hypothesis when we *should* reject the null hypothesis—the probability that we will not make a Type II error.

The calculation of statistical power ranges from a probability of 0.00 to a probability of 1.00 (or from 0% to 100%). Statisticians have historically used a probability of 0.80 as the minimum for conducting a study. If we have an 80% chance of correctly rejecting the null hypothesis, then it is appropriate to conduct the study. Let's look at statistical power for a one-tailed z test. (We use a one-tailed test to simplify calculations.)

● **Statistical power** is a measure of the likelihood that we will reject the null hypothesis, given that the null hypothesis is false.

Statistical Power Statistical power, like the progressive powers of a microscope used to show the fine details of a butterfly's wing, refers to the likelihood that we will detect differences that really exist.

© REUTERS/Daniel Aguilar

James H. Robinson/Science Source

8-4: Statistical power is the likelihood of rejecting the null hypothesis when we should reject the null hypothesis. Researchers consider a probability of 0.80—an 80% chance of rejecting the null hypothesis if we should reject it—to be the minimum for conducting a study.

The Importance of Statistical Power

To understand statistical power, we need to consider several characteristics of the two populations of interest: the population we believe the sample represents (population 1) and the population to which we're comparing the sample (population 2). We represent these two populations visually as two overlapping curves. Let's consider a variation on an example from Chapter 4—a study aimed at determining whether an intervention changes the mean number of sessions attended at university counseling centers (Hatchett, 2003).

EXAMPLE 8.5

> **STEP 1: Determine the information needed to calculate statistical power—the hypothesized mean for the sample, the sample size, the population mean, the population standard deviation, and the standard error based on this sample size.**

In this example, let's say that we hypothesize that a sample of 9 counseling center students will have a mean number of 6.2 sessions after the intervention. The population mean number of sessions attended is 4.6, with a population standard deviation of 3.12. The sample mean of 6.2 is an increase of 1.6 over the population mean, the equivalent of a Cohen's d of about 0.5, a medium effect. Because we have a sample of 9, we need to convert the standard deviation to standard error; to do this, we divide the standard deviation by the square root of the sample size and find that standard error is 1.04. The numbers needed to calculate statistical power are summarized in Table 8-2. We call the population from which the sample comes "population 1" and the population for which we know the mean "population 2."

You might wonder how we came up with the hypothesized sample mean, 6.2. We never know, particularly prior to a study, what the actual effect will be. Researchers typically estimate the mean of population 1 by examining the existing research literature or by deciding how large an effect size would be needed to make the study worthwhile (Murphy & Myors, 2004). Some statisticians recommend erring on the side of using smaller, more conservative effect sizes in power calculations, and others recommend calculating power for a range of effect sizes (Gelman & Carlin, 2014; McShane and Böckenholt, 2014). In this case, we hypothesized a medium effect—a Cohen's d of 0.5—which translated to an increase in the mean of 1.6, from 4.6 to 6.2.

TABLE 8-2   The Ingredients for the Calculation of Statistical Power

To calculate statistical power for a z test, we must know several "ingredients" before beginning.

Ingredients for Calculating Power	Counseling Center Study
Mean of population 1 (expected sample mean)	$M = 6.2$
Planned sample size	$N = 9$
Mean of population 2	$\mu_M = \mu = 4.6$
Standard deviation of the population	$\sigma = 3.12$
Standard error (using the planned sample size)	$\sigma_M = \dfrac{\sigma}{\sqrt{N}} = \dfrac{3.12}{\sqrt{9}} = 1.04$

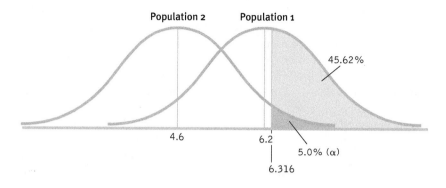

FIGURE 8-10

Statistical Power: The Whole Picture

Now we can visualize statistical power in the context of two populations. Statistical power is the percentage of the distribution of means for population 1 that is above the cutoff. Here the statistical power is 45.62%. Alpha (α) is the percentage of the distribution of means for population 2 that is above the cutoff; alpha is set by the researcher and is usually 0.05, or 5%.

> **STEP 2: Determine a critical value in terms of the z distribution and the raw mean so that statistical power can be calculated.**

For this example, the distribution of means for population 1, centered around 6.2, and the distribution of means for population 2, centered around 4.6, are shown in Figure 8-10. This figure also shows the critical value for a one-tailed test with a p level of 0.05. The critical value as a z statistic is 1.65, which is converted to a raw mean of 6.316.

$$M = 1.65(1.04) + 4.6 = 6.316$$

The p level is shaded in dark purple and marked as 5.0% (α), the percentage version of a proportion of 0.05. The critical value of 6.316 marks off the upper 5% of the distribution based on the null hypothesis, for population 2.

This critical value, 6.316, has the same meaning as it did in hypothesis testing. If the test statistic for a sample falls above this cutoff, then we reject the null hypothesis. Notice that the mean we estimated for population 1 does *not* fall above the cutoff. If the actual difference between the two populations is what we expect, then we can already see that there is a good chance we will not reject the null hypothesis with a sample size of 9. This indicates that we might not have enough statistical power.

> **STEP 3: Calculate the statistical power—the percentage of the distribution of means for population 1 (the distribution centered around the hypothesized sample mean) that falls above the critical value.**

The proportion of the curve above the critical value, shaded in light purple in Figure 8-10, is statistical power, which can be calculated with the use of the z table. Remember, statistical power is the chance that we will reject the null hypothesis if we *should* reject the null hypothesis.

Statistical power in this case is the percentage of the distribution of means for population 1 (the distribution centered around 6.2) that falls above the critical value of 6.316. We convert this critical value to a z statistic based on the hypothesized mean of 6.2.

$$z = \frac{(6.316 - 6.2)}{1.04} = 0.112$$

We look up this z statistic on the z table to determine the percentage above a z statistic of 0.112. That percentage, the area shaded in light purple in Figure 8-10, is 45.62%.

From Figure 8-10, we see the critical value as determined in reference to population 2; in raw score form, it is 6.316. We see that the percentage of the distribution of means for population 2 that falls above 6.316 is 0.05, or 5%, the usual *p* level that was introduced in Chapter 7. The *p* level is the chance of making a Type I error. When we turn to the distribution of means for population 1, the percentage above that same cutoff is the statistical power. Given that population 1 exists, 45.62% of the time that we select a sample of size 9 from this population, we will be able to reject the null hypothesis. This is far below the 80% considered adequate, and we would be wise to increase the sample size.

On a practical level, statistical power calculations tell researchers how many participants are needed to conduct a study whose findings we can trust. Remember, however, that statistical power is based to some degree on hypothetical information, and it is just an estimate. We turn next to several factors that affect statistical power. ●

Five Factors That Affect Statistical Power

Here are five ways to increase the power of a statistical test, from the easiest to the most difficult:

1. Increase alpha. Increasing alpha is like changing the rules by widening the goal posts in football or the goal in soccer. In Figure 8-11, we see how statistical power increases when we increase a *p* level of 0.05 (see Figure 8-11a) to 0.10 (see Figure 8-11b). This has the side effect of increasing the probability of a Type I error from 5% to 10%, however, so researchers rarely choose to increase statistical power in this manner.

2. Turn a two-tailed hypothesis into a one-tailed hypothesis. We have been using a simpler one-tailed test, which provides more statistical power. However, researchers usually begin with the more conservative two-tailed test. In Figure 8-12, we see the difference between the less powerful two-tailed test (part (a)) and the more powerful one-tailed test (part (b)). The curves in part (a), with a two-tailed test, show less statistical power than do the curves in part (b). However, it is usually best to be conservative and use a two-tailed test.

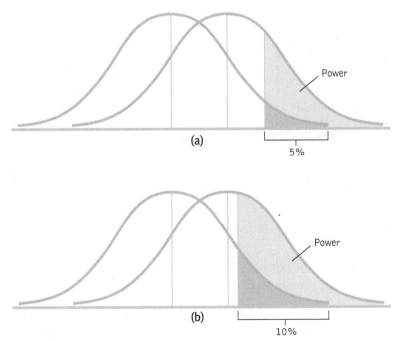

FIGURE 8-11

Increasing Alpha

As we increase alpha from the standard of 0.05 to a larger level, such as 0.10, statistical power increases. Because this also increases the probability of a Type I error, this is not usually a good method for increasing statistical power.

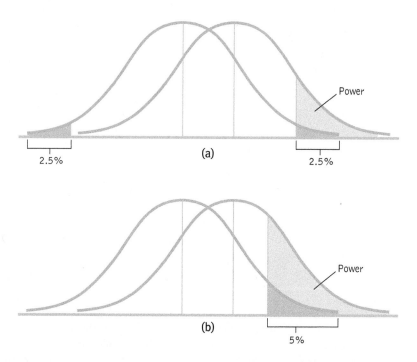

FIGURE 8-12

Two-Tailed Versus One-Tailed Tests

A two-tailed test divides alpha into two tails. When we use a one-tailed test, putting the entire alpha into just one tail, we increase the chances of rejecting the null hypothesis, which translates into an increase in statistical power.

3. Increase N. As we demonstrated earlier in this chapter, increasing sample size leads to an increase in the test statistic, making it easier to reject the null hypothesis. The curves in Figure 8-13a represent a small sample size; those in Figure 8-13b represent a larger sample size. The curves are narrower in part (b) than in part (a) because a larger sample size means smaller standard error. We have direct control over sample size, so simply increasing N is often an easy way to increase statistical power.

4. Exaggerate the mean difference between levels of the independent variable. As seen in Figure 8-14, the mean of population 2 is farther from the mean of

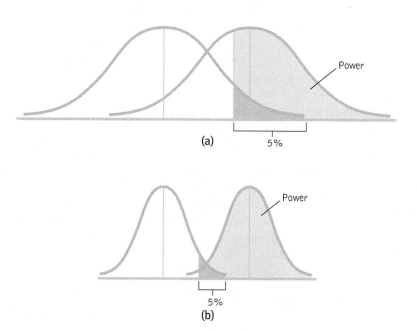

FIGURE 8-13

Increasing Sample Size or Decreasing Standard Deviation

As sample size increases, from part (a) to part (b), the distributions of means become more narrow and there is less overlap. Less overlap means more statistical power. The same effect occurs when we decrease standard deviation. As standard deviation decreases, also reflected from part (a) to part (b), the curves are narrower and there is less overlap—and more statistical power.

Increasing the Difference Between the Means

As the difference between means becomes larger, there is less overlap between curves. Here, the lower pair of curves has less overlap than the upper pair. Less overlap means more statistical power.

(a)

5%

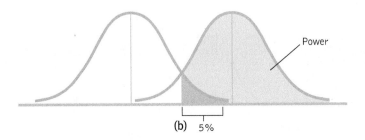

(b) 5%

population 1 in part (b) than it is in part (a). The difference between means is not easily changed, but it can be done. For instance, if we were studying the effectiveness of group therapy for social phobia, we could increase the length of therapy from 12 weeks to 6 months. It is possible that a longer program might lead to a larger change in means than would the shorter program.

5. Decrease standard deviation. We see the same effect on statistical power if we find a way to decrease the standard deviation as when we increase sample size. Look again at Figure 8-13, which reflects an increase in sample size. The curves can become narrower not just because the denominator of the standard error calculation is larger, but also because the numerator is smaller. When standard deviation is smaller, standard error is smaller, and the curves are narrower. We can reduce standard deviation in two ways: (1) by using reliable measures from the beginning of the study, thus reducing error, or (2) by sampling from a more homogeneous group in which participants' responses are more likely to be similar to begin with.

Because statistical power is affected by so many variables, it is important to consider when reading about research. Always ask whether there was sufficient statistical power to detect a real finding. Most importantly, were there enough participants in the sample?

The most practical way to increase statistical power for many behavioral studies is by adding more participants to a study. We can estimate how many participants we need for a particular research design by referring to a table such as that in Jacob Cohen's (1992) article, "A Power Primer." You can also download the free software G★Power, available for Mac or PC (Erdfelder, Faul, & Buchner, 1996; search online for G★Power or find the link on the Web site for this book).

Statistical power calculators like G★Power are versatile tools that are typically used in one of two ways. First, we can calculate power *after* conducting a study from several pieces of information. For most electronic power calculators, including G★Power, we determine power by inputting the effect size and sample size along with some of the information that we outlined earlier in Table 8-2. We calculate power after determining effect size and other characteristics, so G★Power refers to these calculations as *post hoc*, which means "after the fact." Second, we can use them in reverse, *before* conducting a study, by calculating the sample size necessary to achieve a given level of power. In this case, we use a power calculator to determine the sample size necessary to achieve the statistical power that we want *before* we conduct the study. G★Power refers to such calculations as *a priori*, which means "prior to."

The controversy over the 1980 Benbow and Stanley study of gender differences in mathematical ability demonstrates why it is important to go beyond hypothesis testing. The study used 10,000 participants, so it had plenty of statistical power. That means we can trust that the statistically significant difference they found was real. But the effect size informed us that this statistically significant difference was trivial. Combining all four ways of analyzing data (hypothesis testing, confidence intervals, effect size, and power analysis) helps us listen to the data story with all of its wonderful nuances and suggestions for future research.

CHECK YOUR LEARNING

Reviewing the Concepts

> Statistical power is the probability that we will reject the null hypothesis if we should reject it.

> Ideally, a researcher only conducts a study when there is 80% statistical power; that is, at least 80% of the time, the researcher will correctly reject the null hypothesis.

> Statistical power is affected by several factors, but most directly by sample size.

> Before conducting a study, researchers often determine the number of participants they need in order to ensure statistical power of 0.80.

> To get the most complete story about the data, it is best to combine the results of hypothesis testing with information gained from confidence intervals, effect size, and power.

Clarifying the Concepts   **8-8**   What are three ways to increase statistical power?

Calculating the Statistics   **8-9**   Check Your Learning 8-3 and 8-7 discussed a study aimed at changing CFC scores through a career discussion group. Imagine that those in the discussion group of 45 students have a mean CFC score of 3.45. Let's say that you know that the population mean CFC score is 3.20, with a standard deviation of 0.70. Calculate statistical power for this as a one-tailed test.

Applying the Concepts   **8-10**   Refer to Check Your Learning 8-9.

Solutions to these Check Your Learning questions can be found in Appendix D.

    a. Explain what the number obtained in your statistical power calculation means.

    b. Describe how the researchers might increase statistical power.

REVIEW OF CONCEPTS

Confidence Intervals

A summary statistic, such as a mean, is a *point estimate* of the population mean. A more useful estimate is an *interval estimate*, a range of plausible numbers for the population mean. The most commonly used interval estimate is the *confidence interval*, which can be created around a mean using a z distribution. The confidence interval provides the same information as a hypothesis test but also gives us a range of values.

Effect Size

Knowing that a difference is statistically significant does not provide information about the size of the effect. A study with a large sample might find a small effect to be statistically significant, whereas a study with a small sample might fail to detect a large effect. To understand the importance of a finding, we must calculate an *effect size*. Effect sizes are independent of sample size because they are based on distributions of scores rather than distributions of means. One common effect-size measure is *Cohen's d*, which can be used when a *z* test has been conducted.

A *meta-analysis* is a study of studies in which the researcher chooses a topic, decides on guidelines for a study's inclusion, tracks down every study on a given topic, and calculates an effect size for each. A mean effect size is calculated and reported, often along with a standard deviation, median, hypothesis testing, confidence interval, and appropriate graphs. For example, researchers might create a *forest plot*, a graph that shows the confidence intervals for the effect sizes of all studies in the meta-analysis. A *file drawer analysis* can be performed to determine how many unpublished studies that failed to reject the null hypothesis must exist for the effect size to be rendered nonsignificantly different from zero.

Statistical Power

Statistical power is a measure of the likelihood that we will correctly reject the null hypothesis; that is, the chance that we will not commit a Type II error when the research hypothesis is true. Statistical power is affected most directly by sample size, but it is also affected by other factors. Researchers often use a computerized statistical power calculator to determine the appropriate sample size to achieve 0.80 statistical power.

HOW IT WORKS

8.1 CALCULATING CONFIDENCE INTERVALS

The Graded Naming Test (GNT) asks respondents to name objects in a set of 30 black-and-white drawings in order to detect brain damage. The GNT population norm for adults in England is 20.4. Researchers wondered whether a sample of Canadian adults had different scores from adults in England (Roberts, 2003). If the scores were different, the English norms would not be valid for use in Canada. The mean for 30 Canadian adults was 17.5. Assume that the standard deviation of the adults in England is 3.2. How can we calculate a 95% confidence interval for these data?

Given $\mu = 20.4$ and $\sigma = 3.2$, we can start by calculating standard error:

$$\sigma_M = \frac{\sigma}{\sqrt{N}} = \frac{3.2}{\sqrt{30}} = 0.584$$

We then find the *z* values that mark off the most extreme 0.025 in each tail, which are -1.96 and 1.96. We calculate the lower end of the interval as:

$$M_{lower} = -z(\sigma_M) + M_{sample} = -1.96(0.584) + 17.5 = 16.36$$

We calculate the upper end of the interval as:

$$M_{upper} = z(\sigma_M) + M_{sample} = 1.96(0.584) + 17.5 = 18.64$$

The 95% confidence interval around the mean of 17.5 is [16.36, 18.64].

How can we calculate the 90% confidence interval for the same data? In this case, we find the *z* values that mark off the most extreme 0.05 in each tail, which are -1.65 and 1.65. We calculate the lower end of the interval as:

$$M_{lower} = -z(\sigma_M) + M_{sample} = -1.65(0.584) + 17.5 = 16.54$$

We calculate the upper end of the interval as:

$$M_{upper} = z(\sigma_M) + M_{sample} = 1.65(0.584) + 17.5 = 18.46$$

The 90% confidence interval around the mean of 17.5 is [16.54, 18.46].

What can we say about these two confidence intervals in comparison to each other? The range of the 95% confidence interval is larger than that of the 90% confidence interval. When calculating the 95% confidence interval, we are describing where we think a larger portion of our sample means will fall if we repeatedly select samples of this size from the same population (95% as opposed to 90%) so that we have a larger range within which those means are likely to fall.

8.2 CALCULATING EFFECT SIZE

The Graded Naming Test (GNT) study has a population norm for adults in England of 20.4. Researchers found a mean for 30 Canadian adults of 17.5, and we assumed a standard deviation of adults in England of 3.2 (Roberts, 2003). How can we calculate the effect size for these data?

The appropriate measure of effect size for a *z* statistic is Cohen's *d*, which is calculated as:

$$d = \frac{(M - \mu)}{\sigma} = \frac{(17.5 - 20.4)}{3.2} = -0.91$$

Based on Cohen's conventions, this is a large effect size.

EXERCISES

Clarifying the Concepts

8.1 What specific danger exists when reporting a statistically significant difference between two means?

8.2 In your own words, define the word *confidence*—first as you would use it in everyday conversation and then as a statistician would use it in the context of a confidence interval.

8.3 Why do we calculate confidence intervals?

8.4 What are the five steps to create a confidence interval for the mean of a z distribution?

8.5 In your own words, define the word *effect*—first as you would use it in everyday conversation and then as a statistician would use it.

8.6 What effect does increasing the sample size have on standard error and the test statistic?

8.7 Relate effect size to the concept of overlap between distributions.

8.8 What does it mean to say an effect-size statistic neutralizes the influence of sample size?

8.9 What are Cohen's guidelines for small, medium, and large effects?

8.10 How does statistical power relate to Type II errors?

8.11 In your own words, define the word *power*—first as you would use it in everyday conversation and then as a statistician would use it.

8.12 How are statistical power and effect size different but related?

8.13 Traditionally, what minimum percentage chance of correctly rejecting the null hypothesis is suggested in order to proceed with an experiment?

8.14 Explain how increasing alpha increases statistical power.

8.15 List five factors that affect statistical power. For each, indicate how a researcher can leverage that factor to increase power.

8.16 What are the four basic steps of a meta-analysis?

8.17 What is the goal of a meta-analysis?

8.18 Why is it important for a researcher who is conducting a meta-analysis to find not only published studies but also unpublished studies?

8.19 How does a file drawer analysis make the findings from a meta-analysis more persuasive?

8.20 In statistics, concepts are often expressed in symbols and equations. For $M_{lower} = -z(\sigma) + M_{sample}$, (i) identify the incorrect symbol, (ii) state what the correct symbol is, and (iii) explain why the initial symbol was incorrect.

8.21 In statistics, concepts are often expressed in symbols and equations. For $d = \dfrac{(M - \mu)}{\sigma_M}$, (i) identify the incorrect symbol, (ii) state what the correct symbol is, and (iii) explain why the initial symbol was incorrect.

Calculating the Statistics

8.22 In 2008, the Gallup poll asked people whether they were suspicious of steroid use among Olympic athletes. Thirty-five percent of respondents indicated that they were suspicious when they saw an athlete break a track-and-field record, with a 4% margin of error. Calculate an interval estimate.

8.23 In 2008, 22% of Gallup respondents indicated that they were suspicious of steroid use by athletes who broke world records in swimming. Calculate an interval estimate using a margin of error at 3.5%.

8.24 In 2013, the Gallup polling organization and the online publication *Inside Higher Ed* reported the results of a survey of 831 university presidents and chancellors. The report stated: "For results based on the sample size of 831 total respondents, one can say with 95 percent confidence that the margin of error attributable to sampling error is ±3.4 percentage points" (p. 6). Fourteen percent of respondents indicated that they strongly agreed that massive open online courses (MOOCs) could have a positive impact on higher education. Construct an interval estimate for the point estimate of 14%.

8.25 For each of the following confidence levels, indicate how much of the distribution would be placed in the cutoff region for a one-tailed z test.

a. 80%

b. 85%

c. 99%

8.26 For each of the following confidence levels, indicate how much of the distribution would be placed in the cutoff region for a two-tailed z test.

a. 80%

b. 85%

c. 99%

8.27 For each of the following confidence levels, look up the critical z value for a one-tailed z test.

a. 80%

b. 85%

c. 99%

8.28 For each of the following confidence levels, look up the critical z values for a two-tailed z test.

 a. 80%

 b. 85%

 c. 99%

8.29 Calculate the 95% confidence interval for the following fictional data regarding daily TV viewing habits: $\mu = 4.7$ hours; $\sigma = 1.3$ hours; sample of 78 people, with a mean of 4.1 hours.

8.30 Calculate the 80% confidence interval for the same fictional data regarding daily TV viewing habits: $\mu = 4.7$ hours; $\sigma = 1.3$ hours; sample of 78 people, with a mean of 4.1 hours.

8.31 Calculate the 99% confidence interval for the same fictional data regarding daily TV viewing habits: $\mu = 4.7$ hours; $\sigma = 1.3$ hours; sample of 78 people, with a mean of 4.1 hours.

8.32 Calculate the standard error for each of the following sample sizes when $\mu = 1014$ and $\sigma = 136$:

 a. 12

 b. 39

 c. 188

8.33 For a given variable, imagine we know that the population mean is 1014 and the standard deviation is 136. A sample mean of 1057 is obtained. Calculate the z statistic for this mean, using each of the following sample sizes:

 a. 12

 b. 39

 c. 188

8.34 Calculate the effect size for the mean of 1057 observed in Exercise 8.33 where $\mu = 1014$ and $\sigma = 136$.

8.35 Calculate the effect size for each of the following average SAT math scores. Remember, SAT math is standardized such that $\mu = 500$ and $\sigma = 100$.

 a. Sixty-one people sampled have a mean of 480.

 b. Eighty-two people sampled have a mean of 520.

 c. Six people sampled have a mean of 610.

8.36 For each of the effect-size calculations in Exercise 8.35, identify the size of the effect using Cohen's guidelines. Remember, for SAT math, $\mu = 500$ and $\sigma = 100$.

 a. Sixty-one people sampled have a mean of 480.

 b. Eighty-two people sampled have a mean of 520.

 c. Six people sampled have a mean of 610.

8.37 For each of the following d values, identify the size of the effect using Cohen's guidelines.

 a. $d = 0.79$

 b. $d = -0.43$

 c. $d = 0.22$

 d. $d = -0.04$

8.38 For each of the following d values, identify the size of the effect using Cohen's guidelines.

 a. $d = 1.22$

 b. $d = -1.22$

 c. $d = 0.13$

 d. $d = -0.13$

8.39 For each of the following z statistics, calculate the p value for a two-tailed test.

 a. 2.23

 b. −1.82

 c. 0.33

8.40 A meta-analysis reports an average effect size of $d = 0.11$, with a confidence interval of $d = 0.08$ to $d = 0.14$.

 a. Would a hypothesis test (assessing the null hypothesis that the average effect size is 0) lead us to reject the null hypothesis? Explain.

 b. Use Cohen's conventions to describe the average effect size of $d = 0.11$.

8.41 A meta-analysis reports an average effect size of $d = 0.11$, with a confidence interval of $d = -0.06$ to $d = 0.28$. Would a hypothesis test (assessing the null hypothesis that the average effect size is 0) lead us to reject the null hypothesis? Explain.

8.42 Assume you are conducting a meta-analysis over a set of five studies. The effect sizes for each study follow: $d = 0.67$; $d = 0.03$; $d = 0.32$; $d = 0.59$; $d = 0.22$.

 a. Calculate the mean effect size for these studies.

 b. Use Cohen's conventions to describe the mean effect size you calculated in part (a).

8.43 Assume you are conducting a meta-analysis over a set of five studies. The effect sizes for each study follow: $d = 1.23$; $d = 1.08$; $d = -0.35$; $d = 0.88$; $d = 1.69$.

 a. Calculate the mean effect size for these studies.

 b. Use Cohen's conventions to describe the mean effect size you calculated in part (a).

Applying the Concepts

8.44 Margin of error and adult education: According to a report by Public Agenda and the Kresge Foundation, online education is popular among adults planning to return to university (2013). "The majority (73 percent) of adult prospective students want to take at least some classes online, and nearly 4 in 10 (37 percent) say it is absolutely essential for them that their future school offer online classes" (p. 25). The margin of error was reported to be 4.27. Calculate an interval estimate for each of these findings.

8.45 Distributions and the Burakumin: A friend reads in her *Introduction to Psychology* textbook about a minority group in Japan, the Burakumin, who are racially the same as other Japanese people but are viewed as outcasts because their ancestors were employed in positions that involved the handling of dead animals (e.g., butchers). In Japan, the text reported, mean IQ scores of Burakumin were 10 to 15 points below mean IQ scores of other Japanese people. In the United States, where Burakumin experienced no discrimination, there was no mean difference (from Ogbu, 1986, as reported in Hockenbury & Hockenbury, 2013). Your friend says to you: "Wow—when I taught English in Japan last summer, I had a Burakumin student. He seemed smart; perhaps I was fooled." What should your friend consider about the two distributions, the one for Burakumin people and the one for other Japanese people?

8.46 Sample size, z statistics, and the Consideration of Future Consequences scale: Here are summary data from a z test regarding scores on the Consideration of Future Consequences scale (Petrocelli, 2003): The population mean (μ) is 3.20 and the population standard deviation (σ) is 0.70. Imagine that a sample of students had a mean of 3.45.

a. Calculate the test statistic for a sample of 5 students.

b. Calculate the test statistic for a sample of 1000 students.

c. Calculate the test statistic for a sample of 1,000,000 students.

d. Explain why the test statistic varies so much even though the population mean, population standard deviation, and sample mean do not change.

e. Why might sample size pose a problem for hypothesis testing and the conclusions we are able to draw?

8.47 Sample size, z statistics, and the Graded Naming Test: In an exercise in Chapter 7, we asked you to conduct a z test to ascertain whether the Graded Naming Test (GNT) scores for Canadian participants differed from the GNT norms based on adults in England. We also used these data in the How It Works section of this chapter. The mean for a sample of 30 adults in Canada was 17.5. The normative mean for adults in England is 20.4, and we assumed a population standard deviation of 3.2. With 30 participants, the z statistic was −4.97, and we were able to reject the null hypothesis.

a. Calculate the test statistic for 3 participants. How does the test statistic change compared to when N of 30 was used? Conduct step 6 of hypothesis testing. Does your conclusion change? If so, does this mean that the actual difference between groups changed? Explain.

b. Conduct steps 3, 5, and 6 for 100 participants. How does the test statistic change?

c. Conduct steps 3, 5, and 6 for 20,000 participants. How does the test statistic change?

d. What is the effect of sample size on the test statistic?

e. As the test statistic changes, has the underlying difference between groups changed? Why might this present a problem for hypothesis testing?

8.48 Cheating with hypothesis testing: Unsavory researchers know that one can cheat with hypothesis testing. That is, they know that a researcher can stack the deck in her or his favor, making it easier to reject the null hypothesis.

a. If you wanted to make it easier to reject the null hypothesis, what are three specific things you could do?

b. Would it change the actual difference between the samples? Why is this a potential problem with hypothesis testing?

8.49 Overlapping distributions and English-language tests for international students: International students who wish to study at English-speaking universities in Canada or the U.S. are required to take a test, such as the Test of English as a Foreign Language (TOEFL) or the International English Language Testing System (IELTS), if English is not their first language. In a report of mean TOEFL scores by country, people whose first language was Serbian scored a mean of 86 (2015). People whose first language was Portuguese scored a mean of 82. Tijana, from Serbia, and Tomas, from Portugal, both just took the TOEFL.

a. Can we tell which student will do better on the TOEFL? Explain your answer.

b. Draw a picture that represents what the two distributions, that for people whose first language is Serbian and that for people whose first language is Portuguese, might look like with respect to one another. (Note that scores on the TOEFL range from 0 to 120.)

8.50 Confidence intervals, effect sizes, and tennis serves: Let's assume the average speed of a serve in men's tennis is around 135 mph, with a standard deviation of 6.5 mph. Because these statistics are calculated over many years and many players, we will treat them as population parameters. We develop a new training method that will increase arm strength, the force of the tennis swing, and the speed of the serve (we hope). We recruit 9 professional tennis players to use our method. After 6 months, we test the speed of their serves and compute an average of 138 mph.

a. Using a 95% confidence interval, test the hypothesis that our method makes a difference.

b. Compute the effect size and describe its strength.

c. Calculate statistical power using an alpha of 0.05, or 5%, and a one-tailed test.

d. Calculate statistical power using an alpha of 0.10, or 10%, and a one-tailed test.

e. Explain how power is affected by alpha in the calculations in parts (c) and (d).

8.51 Confidence intervals and English-language tests for international students: The International English Language Testing System (IELTS) has six modules, one of which assesses listening skills. IELTS researchers reported that a recent mean for everyone who completed this module in one year was 6.00 and the standard deviation was 1.30 (2013). A sample of 63 international students who were accepted to study at the University of Melbourne in Australia had mean IELTS listening scores of 7.087 with a standard deviation of 0.754 (O'Loughlin & Arkoudis, 2009).

a. Calculate the 95% confidence interval for this sample.

b. State in your own words what we learn from this confidence interval.

c. What information does the confidence interval give us that we also get from a hypothesis test?

d. What additional information does the confidence interval give us that we do not get from a hypothesis test?

8.52 Confidence intervals and English-language tests for international students (continued): Using the IELTS listening data presented in the previous exercise, practice evaluating data using confidence intervals.

a. Compute the 80% confidence interval.

b. How do the conclusion and the confidence interval change as we move from 95% confidence to 80% confidence?

c. Why don't we talk about having 100% confidence?

8.53 Effect size and English-language tests for international students: In the two previous exercises, we considered the IELTS listening module, during which the population of all IELTS takers in a year had a mean score of 6.00 with a standard deviation of 1.30 (2013). A sample of 63 international students at the University of Melbourne had mean IELTS listening scores of 7.087 with a standard deviation of 0.754 (O'Loughlin & Arkoudis, 2009).

a. Calculate the appropriate measure of effect size for this sample.

b. Based on Cohen's conventions, is this a small, medium, or large effect?

c. Why is it useful to have this information in addition to the results of a hypothesis test?

8.54 Effect size and English-language tests for international students (continued): In the previous exercise, you calculated an effect size for data for 63 international students at the University of Melbourne. Imagine that you had a sample of 300 students. How would the effect size change? Explain why it would or would not change.

8.55 Confidence intervals, effect sizes, and Valentine's Day spending: According to the Nielsen Company, Americans spend $345 million on chocolate during the week of Valentine's Day. Let's assume that we know the average married person spends $45, with a population standard deviation of $16. In February 2009, the U.S. economy was in the throes of a recession. Comparing

data for Valentine's Day spending in 2009 with what is generally expected might give us some indication of the attitudes during the recession.

a. Compute the 95% confidence interval for a sample of 18 married people who spent an average of $38.

b. How does the 95% confidence interval change if the sample mean is based on 180 people?

c. If you were testing a hypothesis that things had changed under the financial circumstances of 2009 as compared to previous years, what conclusion would you draw in part (a) versus part (b)?

d. Compute the effect size based on these data and describe the size of the effect.

8.56 More about confidence intervals, effect sizes, and tennis serves: Let's assume the average speed of a serve in women's tennis is around 118 mph, with a standard deviation of 12 mph. We recruit 100 amateur tennis players to use our new training method this time, and after 6 months we calculate a group mean of 123 mph.

a. Using a 95% confidence interval, test the hypothesis that our method makes a difference.

b. Compute the effect size and describe its strength.

8.57 Confidence intervals, effect sizes, and tennis serves (continued): As in the previous exercise, assume the average speed of a serve in women's tennis is around 118 mph, with a standard deviation of 12 mph. But now we recruit only 26 amateur tennis players to use our method. Again, after 6 months we calculate a group mean of 123 mph.

a. Using a 95% confidence interval, test the hypothesis that our method makes a difference.

b. Compute the effect size and describe its strength.

c. How did changing the sample size from 100 (in Exercise 8.56) to 26 affect the confidence interval and effect size? Explain your answer.

8.58 Statistical power and English-language tests for international students: In several exercises in this chapter, we considered scores on the IELTS listening module, during which the population of all IELTS takers in a year had a mean score of 6.00 with a standard deviation of 1.30 (2013). A sample of 63 international students at the University of Melbourne had mean IELTS listening scores of 7.087 with a standard deviation of 0.754 (O'Loughlin & Arkoudis, 2009).

a. Calculate statistical power for this study using a one-tailed test and a p level of 0.05.

b What does the statistical power suggest about how we should view the findings of this study?

c. Using G★Power or an online power calculator, calculate statistical power for this study for a one-tailed test with a p level of 0.05.

8.59 Statistical power and tennis serves: Calculate statistical power based on the data presented in Exercise 8.57 using the following alpha levels in a one-tailed test:

a. Alpha of 0.05, or 5%

b. Alpha of 0.10, or 10%

c. Explain how power is affected by alpha in these calculations.

8.60 Effect size and homeless families: A *New York Times* article reported on the growing problem of homelessness among families (Bellafante, 2013). The reporter wrote that families in a city-run program called Homebase had shorter stays than families not in the program—a difference of about 22.6 fewer nights in a shelter. However, the reporter observed, "Though this is a statistically significant result, it is hardly an impressive one, especially in light of the fact that the average stay for a family in the shelter system is now 13 months, up from 9 months in 2011, and the city is experiencing record levels of homelessness with 50,000 people, including 21,000 children, in shelters every night."

a. How is the reporter's observation about the size of the result—"hardly an impressive one"—related to the concept of effect size?

b. Imagine that a friend who has not taken statistics asks you to explain the difference between a statistically significant result and a large or "impressive" effect. In your own words, how would you explain this difference to your friend?

8.61 Meta-analysis, mental health treatments, and cultural contexts: A meta-analysis examined studies that compared two types of mental health treatments for ethnic and racial minorities—the standard available treatments and treatments that were adapted to the clients' cultures (Griner & Smith, 2006). An excerpt from the abstract follows:

Many previous authors have advocated traditional mental health treatments be modified to better match clients' cultural contexts. Numerous studies evaluating culturally adapted interventions have appeared, and the present study used meta-analytic methodology to summarize these data. Across 76 studies the resulting random effects weighted average effect size was d = .45, indicating a . . . benefit of culturally adapted interventions. (p. 531)

a. What is the topic chosen by the researchers conducting the meta-analysis?

b. What type of effect size statistic did the researchers' calculate for each study in the meta-analysis?

c. What was the mean effect size? According to Cohen's conventions, how large is this effect?

d. If a study chosen for the meta-analysis did not include an effect size, what summary statistics could the researchers use to calculate an effect size?

8.62 Meta-analysis, mental health treatments, and cultural contexts (continued): The research paper on culturally targeted therapy described in the previous exercise reported the following:

Across all 76 studies, the random effects weighted average effect size was d = .45 (SE = .04, p < .0001), with a 95% confidence interval of d = .36 to d = .53. The data consisted of 72 nonzero effect sizes, of which 68 (94%) were positive and 4 (6%) were negative. Effect sizes ranged from d = −48 to d = 2.7. (Griner & Smith, 2006, p. 535)

a. What is the confidence interval for the effect size?

b. Based on the confidence interval, would a hypothesis test lead us to reject the null hypothesis that the effect size is zero? Explain.

c. Why would a graph, such as a histogram, be useful when conducting a meta-analysis like this one? (*Hint:* Consider the problems when using a mean as the measure of central tendency.)

8.63 Meta-analysis and math performance: Below is an excerpt of an abstract from a published meta-analysis by Lindberg, Hyde, Petersen, & Linn (2010). Use this excerpt to describe what is done in each of the four steps of meta-analysis.

In this article, we use meta-analysis to analyze gender differences in recent studies of mathematics performance. First, we meta-analyzed data from 242 studies published between 1990 and 2007, representing the testing of 1,286,350 people. Overall, d = 0.05, indicating no gender difference, and variance ratio = 1.08, indicating nearly equal male and female variances.... These findings support the view that males and females perform similarly in mathematics.

8.64 Meta-analysis and an examination of whether sex and violence sell: Ohio State University researchers conducted a meta-analysis of 53 studies totaling almost 8500 participants (Lull & Bushman, 2015). Their goal was to determine whether advertising that included sex or violence helped to sell products. The researchers reported that "memory for brands and ads was significantly impaired in programs containing sex, violence, or both sex and violence, d = −0.39; 95% CI = −0.55, −0.22" (p. 1029). (They found similar results for participants' reported intention to buy products associated with sex or violence.)

a. What is the confidence interval for the effect size?

b. Based on the confidence interval, would a hypothesis test lead us to reject the null hypothesis that the effect size is zero? Explain.

c. Why would a graph, such as a forest plot, be useful when conducting a meta-analysis like this one? (Hint: Consider the problem when using a mean as the measure of central tendency.)

Putting It All Together

8.65 Fantasy baseball: Your roommate is reading *Fantasyland: A Season on Baseball's Lunatic Fringe* (Walker, 2006) and is intrigued by the statistical methods used by competitors in fantasy baseball leagues (in which competitors select a team of baseball players from across all major league teams, winning in the fantasy league if their eclectic roster of players outperforms the chosen mixes of other fantasy competitors). Among the many statistics reported in the book is a finding that Major League Baseball (MLB) players who have a third child show more of a decline in performance than players who have a first child or a second child. Your friend remembers that Ben Zobrist of the Kansas City Royals recently had his third child and drops him from consideration for his fantasy team.

a. Explain to your friend why a difference between means doesn't provide information about any specific player. Include a drawing of overlapping curves as part of your answer. On the drawing, mark places on the *x*-axis that might represent a player from the distribution of those who recently had a third child (mark with an *X*) scoring *above* a player from the distribution of those who recently had a first or second child (mark with a *Y*).

b. Explain to your friend that a statistically significant difference doesn't necessarily indicate a large effect size. How might a measure of effect size, such as Cohen's *d*, help us understand the importance of these findings and compare them to other predictors of performance that might have larger effects?

c. Given that the reported association is true, can we conclude that having a third child *causes* a decline in performance? Explain your answer. What confounding variables might lead to the difference observed in this study?

d. Given the relatively limited numbers of MLB players (and the relatively limited numbers of those who recently had a child—whether first, second, or third), what general guess would you make about the likely statistical power of this analysis?

8.66 Hours of sleep: The table below provides information about hours of sleep.

Mean of population 1 (from which the sample comes)	14.9 hours of sleep
Sample size	37 infants
Mean of population 2	16 hours of sleep
Standard deviation of the population	1.7 hours of sleep
Standard error	$\sigma_M = \dfrac{\sigma}{\sqrt{N}} = \dfrac{1.7}{\sqrt{37}}$ $= 0.279$

a. Calculate statistical power for a one-tailed test ($a = 0.05$, or 5%) aimed at determining if those in the sample sleep fewer hours, on average, than those in the population.

b. Recalculate statistical power with alpha of 0.01, or 1%. Explain why changing alpha affects power. Explain why we should not use a larger alpha to increase power.

c. Without performing any computations, describe how statistical power is affected by performing a two-tailed test for this example. Why are two-tailed tests recommended over one-tailed tests?

d. The easiest way to affect the outcome of a hypothesis test is to increase sample size. Similarly, true results may sometimes be missed because a sufficient sample was not used in the research. Perform the hypothesis test on these data with a sample of 37. Then perform the same hypothesis test but assume that the mean was based on only 4 infants.

e. The easiest way to increase statistical power is to increase sample size. Similarly, statistical power decreases with a smaller sample size. For these data, compute the statistical power of the one-tailed statistical test with alpha of 0.05 when *N* is 4. How does that value compare to when *N* was 37?

8.67 Effect size and an intervention to increase college applications: Caroline Hoxby and Sarah Turner (2013) conducted an experiment to determine whether a simple intervention could increase the number of college applications among low-income students. The intervention consisted of information about the college application process and about college costs that were specific to the student, along with an easy-to-implement waiver of college application fees. The following is an excerpt from a table. The intervention seemed to work with a statistically significant effect on this variable at a *p* level of 0.01.

Dependent variable	Effect in percentage change	Effect in effect size
Number of applications submitted	19.0%	0.247

a. Describe the sample and population of this study.

b. What is the independent variable and what are its levels?

c. What is the dependent variable?

d. The finding was statistically significant. Why is this not sufficient to determine that this intervention, which costs about $6 per student, is worthwhile?

e. What is the effect size for the dependent variable? How large is it, according to Cohen's conventions?

f. What does this effect size mean in terms of standard deviations in the context of this study?

g. The researchers also included the effect in percentage change. Explain what this means in the context of this study.

TERMS

point estimate	(p. 202)	effect size	(p. 208)	forest plot	(p. 213)
interval estimate	(p. 202)	Cohen's d	(p. 211)	file drawer analysis	(p. 214)
confidence interval	(p. 203)	meta-analysis	(p. 212)	statistical power	(p. 215)

FORMULAS

$M_{lower} = -z(\sigma_M) + M_{sample}$ (p. 205)

$M_{upper} = z(\sigma_M) + M_{sample}$ (p. 205)

Cohen's $d = \dfrac{(M - \mu)}{\sigma}$ for a z distribution   (p. 211)

SYMBOLS

Cohen's d (or just d)   (p. 211)

α (p. 217)

The Single-Sample t Test

9

BEFORE YOU GO ON

- You should know the six steps of hypothesis testing (Chapter 7).

- You should know how to determine a confidence interval for a z statistic (Chapter 8).

- You should understand the concept of effect size and know how to calculate Cohen's d for a z test (Chapter 8).

The Voice of a Stranger Have you ever dated someone you met online? If you did, you probably talked on the phone before meeting in person. Did you form an impression of what your date looked like from the sound of his or her voice? That may not be a bad tactic. Researchers used a single-sample *t* test to determine how much better than chance—50% —people matched voices with attractive or unattractive photos. And they found that people did statistically significantly better than chance, matching 72.6% correctly.

So you've swiped right on Tinder, and after some back and forth messaging you've decided to actually talk to your potential date on the phone. How much of an impression do you form from someone's voice? If you decide to meet in person, would their physical appearance match the impression you had formed from her or his voice? Researchers Susan Hughes and Noelle Miller (2015) found that women tended to perceive high-pitched male voices as unattractive, but men tended to perceive high-pitched female voices as more attractive. Both men and women tended to perceive mid-pitched voices as "sexy." Hughes and Miller (2015) wanted to test whether people could match an attractive voice with an attractive face, so they presented 55 participants with two faces on a screen (one rated as attractive, the other as unattractive). Each participant heard 40 voices counting from one to ten and each voice was paired with two photos. Then participants were asked which photo matched the voice.

The participants had a 50% chance of correctly matching the voice with the photo. But how much above 50% would convince you that participants were really making an association between voice and appearance? In this study, participants matched the voices and photos an average of 72.6% of the time. Is that a big enough difference that it's unlikely to have occurred by chance? Based on a single-sample *t* test, which we'll learn about in this chapter, Hughes and Miller concluded that people did indeed hold a stereotype that "what sounds beautiful looks beautiful." The researchers also found that people were confused when an attractive voice didn't match an attractive face or vice-versa. The researchers had just one sample (the participants in the experiment) and a comparison mean—the baseline expectation of 50% in the population if there were no significant difference. But that's all they needed to use the single-sample *t* test to answer their question. So let's say your potential Tinder date has an attractive voice. Based on this study's results, there's a pretty good chance that she or he will be physically attractive as well.

With a *t* distribution, we can compare one sample to a population when we don't know all the details about the parameters, and we can compare two samples to each other. There are two ways to compare two samples: by using a within-groups design (as when the same people are weighed before and after the holidays) or by using a between-groups design (as when different people are in the preholiday sample than those in the postholiday sample). For a within-groups design, we use a paired-samples *t* test, which we'll learn about in Chapter 10. For a between-groups design, we use an independent-samples *t* test, which we will learn about in Chapter 11.

9-1: There are three types of *t* tests: (1) We use a single-sample *t* test when comparing a sample mean to a population mean but do not know the population standard deviation. (2) We use a paired-samples *t* test, discussed in Chapter 10, when comparing two samples and every participant is in both samples—a within-groups design. (3) We use an independent-samples *t* test, discussed in Chapter 11, when comparing two samples and every participant is in only one sample—a between-groups design.

The *t* Distributions

The *t* distributions (note the plural) help us specify how confident we can be about research findings. We want to know whether we can generalize what we have learned about one sample to a larger population.

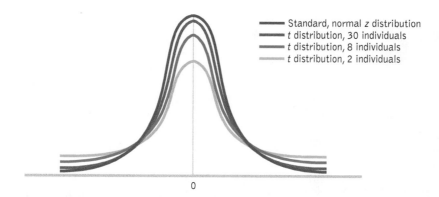

Standard, normal *z* distribution
t distribution, 30 individuals
t distribution, 8 individuals
t distribution, 2 individuals

0

FIGURE 9-1

The Wider and Flatter *t* Distributions

For smaller samples (such as of 2 or 8 individuals), the *t* distributions are wider and flatter than the *z* distribution. However, as the sample size increases (such as to 30 individuals), the *t* distributions look more like the *z* distribution. This makes sense because a larger sample size would be more similar to the entire population than a smaller sample size would.

The *t* test, based on the *t* distributions, tells us how confident we can be that the sample differs from the larger population.

The *t* distributions are more versatile than the *z* distribution because we can use them when (a) we don't know the population standard deviation, and (b) we compare two samples. Figure 9-1 demonstrates that there are many *t* distributions—one for each possible sample size. Just as we are less likely to believe gossip from only one or two people, we are less certain about what the population distribution really looks like when we have a small sample size. The uncertainty of a small sample size means that the *t* distributions become flatter and more spread out. However, as the sample size gets larger, the *t* distributions begin to merge with the *z* distribution because we gain confidence as more participants are added to a study, just as we become increasingly confident in gossip that is repeated by many independent sources.

Estimating Population Standard Deviation from a Sample

Before we conduct a single-sample *t* test, we must estimate the population standard deviation by using the sample standard deviation. Estimating the standard deviation is the only practical difference between conducting a *z* test with the *z* distribution and conducting a *t* test with a *t* distribution. Here is the sample standard deviation formula that we have used up until now:

$$SD = \sqrt{\frac{\Sigma(X - M)^2}{N}}$$

We need to make a correction to this formula to account for the fact that there is likely to be some level of error when we estimate the population standard deviation from a sample. Specifically, any given sample is likely to have somewhat less spread than does the entire population. One tiny alteration of this formula leads to a slightly larger and more accurate standard deviation. Instead of dividing by N, we divide by $(N - 1)$ to get the mean of the squared deviations. Subtraction is the key. For example, if the numerator were 90 and the denominator (N) were 10, the answer would be 9; if we divide by $(N - 1) = (10 - 1) = 9$, the answer would be 10, a slightly larger value. So the formula is:

$$\acute{s} = \sqrt{\frac{\Sigma(X - M)^2}{(N - 1)}}$$

MASTERING THE FORMULA

9-1: The formula for standard deviation when estimating from a sample is:

$$s = \sqrt{\frac{\Sigma(X - M)^2}{(N - 1)}}.$$

We subtract 1 from the sample size in the denominator to correct for the probability that the sample standard deviation slightly underestimates the actual standard deviation in the population.

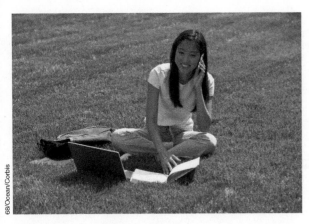

Multitasking If multitasking reduces productivity in a sample, we can estimate the amount by which multitasking reduces productivity in a larger population.

Notice that we call this standard deviation *s* instead of *SD*. We still use Latin rather than Greek letters because it is a statistic (from a sample) rather than a parameter (from a population). From now on, we will calculate the standard deviation in this way because we will be estimating the population standard deviation.

Let's apply the new formula for standard deviation to a familiar activity: multitasking. Employees were observed at one of two high-tech companies for more than 1000 hours (Mark, Gonzalez, & Harris, 2005). The employees spent just 11 minutes, on average, on one project before being interrupted. Moreover, after each interruption, they needed an average of 25 minutes to get back to the original project! So maybe the reality is that multitasking actually reduces overall productivity.

Suppose you were a manager at one of these firms and decided to reserve a period from 1:00 to 3:00 each afternoon during which employees could not interrupt one another, but might still be interrupted by people outside the company. To test the intervention, you observe five employees and develop a score for each—time spent on a selected task before being interrupted. Here are the fictional data: 8, 12, 16, 12, and 14 minutes. In this case, we treat 11 minutes as the population mean, but we do not know the population standard deviation.

EXAMPLE 9.1

To calculate the estimated standard deviation for the population, there are two steps.

STEP 1: Calculate the sample mean.

Even though we know the population mean (11 minutes), we use the sample mean to calculate the corrected sample standard deviation. The mean for these scores is:

$$M = \frac{(8 + 12 + 16 + 12 + 14)}{5} = 12.4$$

STEP 2: Use the sample mean in the corrected formula for the standard deviation.

$$s = \sqrt{\frac{\Sigma(X - M)^2}{(N - 1)}}$$

Remember, the easiest way to calculate the numerator under the square root sign is by first organizing the data into columns, as shown here:

X	X – M	(X – M)²
8	−4.4	19.36
12	−0.4	0.16
16	3.6	12.96
12	−0.4	0.16
14	1.6	2.56

A Simple Correction: *N* − 1 When estimating variability, subtracting one person from a sample of three makes a big difference. Subtracting one person from a sample of thousands makes only a small difference. In this example, you would notice if one of the women disappeared from the photo on the left, but it would be almost impossible to notice if one of the crowd disappeared from the photo on the right.

The numerator is:

$$\Sigma(X - M)^2 = \Sigma(19.36 + 0.16 + 12.96 + 0.16 + 2.56) = 35.2$$

And given a sample size of 5, the corrected standard deviation is:

$$s = \sqrt{\frac{\Sigma(X - M)^2}{(N - 1)}} = \sqrt{\frac{35.2}{(5 - 1)}} = \sqrt{8.8} = 2.97 \ \bullet$$

Calculating Standard Error for the *t* Statistic

We now have an estimate of the standard deviation of the distribution of scores, but not an estimate of the spread of a distribution of means, the standard error. As we did with the z distribution, we make the spread smaller to reflect the fact that a distribution of means is less variable than a distribution of scores. We do this in exactly the same way that we adjusted for the z distribution. We divide s by $\sqrt{N}$. The formula for the standard error as estimated from a sample, therefore, is:

$$s_M = \frac{s}{\sqrt{N}}$$

Notice that we have replaced σ with s because we are using the corrected sample standard deviation rather than the population standard deviation.

MASTERING THE FORMULA

9-2: The formula for standard error when we estimate from a sample is:

$$s_M = \frac{s}{\sqrt{N}}.$$

It only differs from the formula for standard error we learned previously in that we use s instead of σ because we're working from a sample instead of a population.

EXAMPLE 9.2

Here's how we convert the corrected standard deviation of 2.97 to a standard error. The sample size was 5, so we divide by the square root of 5:

$$s_M = \frac{s}{\sqrt{N}} = \frac{2.97}{\sqrt{5}} = 1.33$$

So the standard error is 1.33. Just as the central limit theorem predicts, the standard error for the distribution of sample means is smaller than the standard deviation of sample scores. (*Note:* This step can lead to a common mistake. Because we implemented a correction when calculating s, students often want to implement an extra correction here by dividing by $\sqrt{N - 1}$. Do not do this! We still divide by $\sqrt{N}$ in this step. There is no need for a further correction to the standard error.) ●

● The *t* statistic indicates the distance of a sample mean from a population mean in terms of the estimated standard error.

9-3: The formula for the single-sample *t* statistic is:

$$t = \frac{(M - \mu_M)}{s_M}.$$

It only differs from the formula for the *z* statistic in that we use s_M (estimated from a sample) instead of σ_M (based on the population).

Using Standard Error to Calculate the t Statistic

We now have the tools necessary to conduct the single-sample *t* test. When conducting a single-sample *t* test, we calculate the **t *statistic***, *the distance of a sample mean from a population mean in terms of the estimated standard error.* We introduce the formula for that *t* statistic here, and in the next section we go through all six steps for a single-sample *t* test. The formula is identical to that for the *z* statistic, except that it uses estimated standard error. Here is the formula for the *t* statistic for a distribution of means:

$$t = \frac{(M - \mu_M)}{s_M}$$

Note that the denominator is the only difference between this formula for the *t* statistic and the formula used to compute the *z* statistic for a sample mean. The corrected denominator makes the *t* statistic smaller and thereby reduces the probability of having an extreme *t* statistic. That is, a *t* statistic is not as extreme as a *z* statistic; in scientific terms, it's more conservative.

EXAMPLE 9.3

The *t* statistic for the sample of five scores representing minutes until interruptions is:

$$t = \frac{(M - \mu_M)}{s_M} = \frac{(12.4 - 11)}{1.33} = 1.05$$

As part of the six steps of hypothesis testing, the *t* statistic can help us make an inference about whether the ban on internal interruptions affected the average number of minutes until an interruption. ●

CHECK YOUR LEARNING

Reviewing the Concepts

> We use *t* distributions when we do not know the population standard deviation and are comparing only two groups.

> The two groups may be a sample and a population, or two samples as part of a within-groups design or a between-groups design.

> The formula for the *t* statistic for a single-sample *t* test is the same as the formula for the *z* statistic for a distribution of means, except that we use estimated standard error in the denominator rather than the actual standard error for the population.

> We calculate estimated standard error by dividing by $N - 1$, rather than dividing by N, when calculating standard error.

Clarifying the Concepts   **9-1**   What is the *t* statistic?

Calculating the Statistics   **9-2**   Calculate the standard deviation for a sample (*SD*) and as an estimate of the population (*s*) using the following data: 6, 3, 7, 6, 4, 5.

   9-3   Calculate standard error for *t* for the data given in Check Your Learning 9-2.

Applying the Statistics   **9-4**   In the discussion of a study on multitasking (Mark et al., 2005), we imagined a follow-up study in which we measured time until a task was interrupted. For each of the five employees, let's now examine time until work on the initial task was resumed at 20, 19, 27, 24, and 18 minutes. Remember that the original research showed it took 25 minutes on average for an employee to return to a task after being interrupted.

a. What distribution would be used in this situation? Explain your answer.

b. Determine the appropriate mean and standard deviation (or standard error) for this distribution. Show all your work; use symbolic notation and formulas where appropriate.

c. Calculate the *t* statistic.

Solutions to these Check Your Learning questions can be found in Appendix D.

The Single-Sample *t* Test

To explore whether we can accurately guess how attractive a stranger is just by hearing a voice, researchers compared their sample mean to the population mean that would occur just by chance—50%. To do so, they used a ***single-sample t test*** *is a hypothesis test in which we compare a sample from which we collect data to a population for which we know the mean but not the standard deviation.* The logic of the single-sample *t* test is a model for other *t* tests that allow us to compare two samples—and all of the other more sophisticated statistical tests that will follow. You will soon be able to study just about anything you want.

The *t* Table and Degrees of Freedom

When we use the *t* distributions, we use the *t* table. There are different *t* distributions for every sample size and the *t* table takes sample size into account. However, we do not look up the actual sample size on the table. Rather, we look up ***degrees of freedom***, *the number of scores that are free to vary when we estimate a population parameter from a sample.*

Language Alert! The phrase "free to vary" refers to the number of scores that can take on different values when a given parameter is known.

● A **single-sample *t* test** is a hypothesis test in which we compare a sample from which we collect data to a population for which we know the mean but not the standard deviation.

● **Degrees of freedom** is the number of scores that are free to vary when we estimate a population parameter from a sample.

• •

For example, the manager of a baseball team needs to assign nine players to particular spots in the batting order but only has to make eight decisions ($N - 1$). Why? Because only one option remains after making the first eight decisions. So before the manager makes any decisions, there are $N - 1$, or $9 - 1 = 8$, degrees of freedom. After the second decision, there are $N - 1$, or $8 - 1 = 7$, degrees of freedom, and so on. But after the first 8 players have been assigned, there is no "freedom" when assigning the 9th player. There's only one spot left.

As in the baseball example, there is always one score that cannot vary once all of the others have been determined. For example, if we know that the mean of four scores is 6 and we know that three of the scores are 2, 4, and 8, then the last score must be 10. So the degrees of freedom is the number of scores in the sample minus 1. Degrees of freedom is written in symbolic notation as *df*, which is always italicized. The formula for degrees of freedom for a single-sample *t* test, therefore, is:

$$df = N - 1 ●$$

Table 9-1 is an excerpt from a *t* table; the full table is in Appendix B. Notice the relation between degrees of freedom and the critical value needed to declare statistical significance. As degrees of freedom go up, the critical values go down. In the column corresponding to a one-tailed test at a *p* level of 0.05 with only 1 degree of freedom

EXAMPLE 9.4

MASTERING THE CONCEPT

9-2: *Degrees of freedom* refers to the number of scores that can take on different values when a given parameter is known. For example, if we know that the mean of three scores is 10, only two scores are free to vary. Once we know the values of two scores, we know the value of the third. If we know that two of the scores are 9 and 10, then we know that the third must be 11.

MASTERING THE FORMULA

9-4: The formula for degrees of freedom for a single-sample *t* test is: $df = N - 1$. To calculate degrees of freedom, we subtract 1 from the sample size.

TABLE 9-1	Excerpt from the *t* Table

When conducting hypothesis testing, we use the *t* table to determine critical values for a given *p* level, based on the degrees of freedom and whether the test is one- or two-tailed. The full table is in Appendix B.

	One-Tailed Tests			Two-Tailed Tests		
df	0.10	0.05	0.01	0.10	0.05	0.01
1	3.078	6.314	31.821	6.314	12.706	63.657
2	1.886	2.920	6.965	2.920	4.303	9.925
3	1.638	2.353	4.541	2.353	3.182	5.841
4	1.533	2.132	3.747	2.132	2.776	4.604
5	1.476	2.015	3.365	2.015	2.571	4.032

(two observations), the critical *t* value is 6.314. With only 1 degree of freedom, the two means have to be extremely far apart and/or the standard deviation has to be very small to declare a statistically significant difference. But with 2 degrees of freedom (three observations), the critical *t* value drops to 2.920. It is easier to reach the critical *t* value because we're more confident in making a reliable observation with three observations than with just two, just as we are more confident that a rumor is true when we hear the same story from three independent observers than from just two people.

The pattern continues when we have four observations (with *df* of 3). The critical *t* value needed to declare statistical significance decreases from 2.920 to 2.353. The level of confidence in the observations increases and the critical value decreases.

The *t* distributions become closer to the *z* distribution as sample size increases. After all, if we kept enlarging the sample, we would eventually study the entire population and wouldn't need a pesky *t* test in the first place. But in the real world of research, the corrected standard deviation of a large enough sample is so similar to the actual standard deviation of the population that the *t* distribution is the same as the *z* distribution.

Check it out for yourself by comparing the *z* and *t* tables in Appendix B. For example, the *z* statistic for the 95th percentile—a percentage between the mean and the *z* statistic of 45%—is between 1.64 and 1.65. At a sample size of infinity, the *t* statistic for the 95th percentile is 1.645. Infinity (∞) indicates a very large sample size; a sample size of infinity itself is, of course, impossible.

Let's remind ourselves why the *t* statistic merges with the *z* statistic as sample size increases. More participants in a study—if they are a representative sample—correspond to increased confidence that we are making an accurate observation. So don't think of the *t* distributions as completely separate from the *z* distribution. Rather, think of the *z* statistic as a single-blade Swiss Army knife and the *t* statistic as a multi-blade Swiss Army knife that still includes the single blade that is the *z* statistic.

Let's determine the cutoffs, or critical *t* values, for a research study using the full *t* table in Appendix B.

EXAMPLE 9.5

The study: A researcher knows the mean number of calories lab rats will consume in half an hour if unlimited food is available. She wonders whether a new food will lead rats to consume a different number of calories—either more or fewer. She studies 38 rats and uses a *p* level of 0.05.

The cutoff(s): This is a two-tailed test because the research hypothesis allows for change in either direction. There are 38 rats, so the calculation for the degrees of freedom is:

$$df = N - 1 = 38 - 1 = 37$$

We want to look in the *t* table under two-tailed tests, in the column for 0.05 and in the row for a *df* of 37; however, there is no *df* of 37. In this case, we err on the side of being more conservative and choose the more extreme (i.e., larger) of the two possible critical *t* values, which is always the smaller *df*. Here, we look next to 35, where we see a value of 2.030. Because this is a two-tailed test, we will have critical values of −2.030 and 2.030. ●

The Six Steps of the Single-Sample *t* Test

Now we have all the tools necessary to conduct a single-sample *t* test. So let's consider a hypothetical study and conduct all six steps of hypothesis testing.

EXAMPLE 9.6

Chapter 4 presented data that included the mean number of sessions attended by clients at a university counseling center. We noted that one study reported a mean of 4.6 sessions (Hatchett, 2003). Let's imagine that the counseling center hoped to increase participation rates by having students sign a contract to attend at least 10 sessions. Five students sign the contract and attend 6, 6, 12, 7, and 8 sessions, respectively. The researchers are interested only in their university, so treat the mean of 4.6 sessions as a population mean.

> **STEP 1: Identify the populations, distribution, and assumptions.**

Population 1: All clients at this counseling center who sign a contract to attend at least 10 sessions. Population 2: All clients at this counseling center who do not sign a contract to attend at least 10 sessions.

The comparison distribution will be a distribution of means. The hypothesis test will be a single-sample *t* test because we have only one sample and we know the population mean but not the population standard deviation.

This study meets one of the three assumptions and may meet the other two: (1) The dependent variable is scale. (2) We do not know whether the data were randomly selected, however, so we must be cautious with respect to generalizing to other clients at this university who might sign the contract. (3) We do not know whether the population is normally distributed, and there are not at least 30 participants. However, the data from the sample do not suggest a skewed distribution.

Nonparticipation in Therapy Clients missing appointments can be a problem for both clients and therapists. A *t* test can compare the consequences between those who do and do not sign a contract to attend a set number of sessions.

> **STEP 2: State the null and research hypotheses.**

Null hypothesis: Clients at this university who sign a contract to attend at least 10 sessions attend the same number of sessions, on average, as clients who do not sign such a contract—H_0: $\mu_1 = \mu_2$.

Research hypothesis: Clients at this university who sign a contract to attend at least 10 sessions attend a different number of sessions, on average, than do clients who do not sign such a contract—H_1: $\mu_1 \neq \mu_2$.

STEP 3: Determine the characteristics of the comparison distribution.

$$\mu_M = 4.6; s_M = 1.114$$

Calculations:

$$\mu_M = \mu = 4.6$$

$$M = \frac{\Sigma X}{N} = \frac{(6 + 6 + 12 + 7 + 8)}{5} = 7.8$$

X	$X - M$	$(X - M)^2$
6	−1.8	3.24
6	−1.8	3.24
12	4.2	17.64
7	−0.8	0.64
8	0.2	0.04

The numerator of the standard deviation formula is the sum of squares:

$$\Sigma(X - M)^2 = \Sigma(3.24 + 3.24 + 17.64 + 0.64 + 0.04) = 24.8$$

$$s = \sqrt{\frac{\Sigma(X - M)^2}{(N - 1)}} = \sqrt{\frac{24.8}{(5 - 1)}} = \sqrt{6.2} = 2.490$$

$$s_M = \frac{s}{\sqrt{N}} = \frac{2.490}{\sqrt{5}} = 1.114$$

STEP 4: Determine the critical values, or cutoffs.

$$df = N - 1 = 5 - 1 = 4$$

For a two-tailed test with a *p* level of 0.05 and *df* of 4, the critical values are −2.776 and 2.776 (as seen in the curve in Figure 9-2).

FIGURE 9-2

Determining Cutoffs for a *t* Distribution

As with the *z* distribution, we typically determine critical values in terms of *t* statistics rather than means of raw scores so that we can easily determine whether the test statistic is beyond one of the cutoffs. Here, the cutoffs are −2.776 and 2.776, and they mark off the most extreme 5%, with 2.5% in each tail.

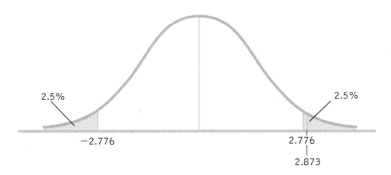

FIGURE 9-3

Making a Decision

To decide whether to reject the null hypothesis, we compare the test statistic to the critical *t* values. In this case, the test statistic, 2.873, is beyond the cutoff of 2.776, so we can reject the null hypothesis.

STEP 5: Calculate the test statistic.

$$t = \frac{(M - \mu_M)}{s_M} = \frac{(7.8 - 4.6)}{1.114} = 2.873$$

STEP 6: Make a decision.

Reject the null hypothesis. It appears that counseling center clients who sign a contract to attend at least 10 sessions do attend more sessions, on average, than do clients who do not sign such a contract (Figure 9-3).

After completing the hypothesis test, we want to present the primary statistical information in a report. There is a standard American Psychological Association (APA) format for the presentation of statistics across the behavioral sciences so that the results are easily understood by the reader.

1. Write the symbol for the test statistic (e.g., *t*).
2. Write the degrees of freedom in parentheses.
3. Write an equal sign and then the value of the test statistic, typically to two decimal places.
4. Write a comma and then indicate the *p* value by writing "*p* =" and then the actual value. (Unless we use software to conduct the hypothesis test, we will not know the actual *p* value associated with the test statistic. In this case, we simply state whether the *p* value is beyond the critical value by saying $p < 0.05$ when we reject the null hypothesis or $p > 0.05$ when we fail to reject the null hypothesis.)

In the counseling center example, the statistics would read:

$$t(4) = 2.87, p < 0.05$$

The statistics typically follow a statement about the finding. For example, "It appears that counseling center clients who sign a contract to attend at least 10 sessions do attend more sessions, on average, than do clients who do not sign such a contract, $t(4) = 2.87$, $p < 0.05$." The report would also include the sample mean and standard deviation (not standard error) to two decimal points. Here, the descriptive statistics would read: ($M = 7.80$, $SD = 2.49$). By convention, we use SD instead of s to symbolize the standard deviation. ●

Calculating a Confidence Interval for a Single-Sample *t* Test

We learned in the previous chapter that hypothesis testing is limited in what it tells us and is often misinterpreted. For these reasons, researchers should report confidence intervals and effect sizes whenever possible. These are reported in addition to hypothesis testing, and increasingly are used in place of hypothesis testing.

EXAMPLE 9.7

MASTERING THE CONCEPT

9-4: Journal editors and psychology research organizations encourage researchers to calculate confidence intervals and effect sizes whenever possible. These can be reported in addition to or instead of hypothesis tests.

We can calculate a confidence interval with the single-sample *t* test data. The population mean was 4.6. We used the sample to estimate the population standard deviation to be 2.490 and the population standard error to be 1.114. The five students in the sample attended a mean of 7.8 sessions.

When we conducted hypothesis testing, we centered the curve around the mean according to the null hypothesis—the population mean of 4.6. Now we can use the same information to calculate the 95% confidence interval around the sample mean of 7.8.

> **STEP 1: Draw a picture of a *t* distribution that includes the confidence interval.**

We draw a normal curve (Figure 9-4) that has the sample mean, 7.8, at its center (instead of the population mean, 4.6).

> **STEP 2: Indicate the bounds of the confidence interval on the drawing.**

We draw a vertical line from the mean to the top of the curve. For a 95% confidence interval, we also draw two much smaller vertical lines that indicate the middle 95% of the *t* distribution (2.5% in each tail, for a total of 5%). We then write the appropriate percentages next to the segments of the curve.

> **STEP 3: Look up the *t* statistics that fall at each line marking the middle 95%.**

For a two-tailed test with a *p* level of 0.05 and a *df* of 4, the critical values are -2.776 and 2.776. We can now add these *t* statistics below the curve, as seen in Figure 9-5.

> **STEP 4: Convert the *t* statistics back into raw means.**

As we did with the *z* test, we can use formulas for this conversion, but first we identify the appropriate mean and measure

---

FIGURE 9-4

A 95% Confidence Interval for a Single-Sample *t* Test, Part I

To begin calculating a confidence interval for a single-sample *t* test, we place the sample mean, 7.8, at the center of a curve and indicate the percentages within and beyond the confidence interval.

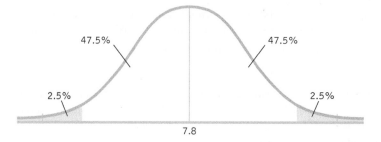

FIGURE 9-5

A 95% Confidence Interval for a Single-Sample *t* Test, Part II

The next step in calculating a confidence interval for a single-sample *t* test is to identify the *t* statistics that indicate each end of the interval. Because the curve is symmetric, the *t* statistics have the same magnitude—one is negative, -2.776, and one is positive, 2.776.

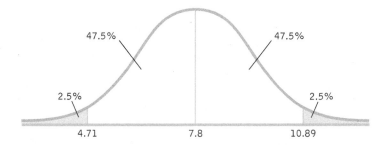

of spread. There are two important points to remember. First, we center the interval around the sample mean, so we use the sample mean of 7.8 in the calculations. Second, because we have a sample mean (rather than an individual score), we use a distribution of means. So we use the standard error of 1.114 as the measure of spread.

Using this mean and standard error, we calculate the raw mean at each end of the confidence interval, and add them below the curve, as in Figure 9-6. The formulas are exactly the same as for the *z* test except that *z* is replaced by *t*, and σ_M is replaced by s_M.

$$M_{lower} = -t(s_M) + M_{sample} = -2.776(1.114) + 7.8 = 4.71$$

$$M_{upper} = t(s_M) + M_{sample} = 2.776(1.114) + 7.8 = 10.89$$

The 95% confidence interval, reported in brackets as is typical, is [4.71, 10.89].

> **STEP 5: Verify that the confidence interval makes sense.**

The sample mean should fall exactly in the middle of the two ends of the interval.

$$4.71 - 7.8 = -3.09; \text{ and } 10.89 - 7.8 = 3.09$$

We have a match. The confidence interval ranges from 3.09 below the sample mean to 3.09 above the sample mean. If we were to sample five students from the same population over and over, the 95% confidence interval would include the population mean 95% of the time. Note that the population mean, 4.6, does not fall within this interval. This means it is not plausible that this sample of students who signed contracts came from the population according to the null hypothesis—students seeking treatment at the counseling center who did not sign a contract. We conclude that the sample comes from a different population, one in which students attend more mean sessions than does the general population. As with the *z* test, the conclusions from the hypothesis test and the confidence interval are the same, but the confidence interval gives us more information—an interval estimate, not just a point estimate. Because the conclusions are the same and the confidence interval gives more information, many researchers are now encouraging others to report *only* confidence intervals and not hypothesis tests. ●

Calculating Effect Size for a Single-Sample *t* Test

As with a *z* test, we can calculate the effect size (Cohen's *d*) for a single-sample *t* test.

Let's calculate the effect size for the counseling center study. Similar to what we did with the *z* test, we simply use the formula for the *t* statistic, substituting *s* for s_M (and μ for μ_M, even though these means are always the same). This means we use 2.490

EXAMPLE 9.8

9-6: The formula for Cohen's *d* for a *t* statistic is:

$$\text{Cohen's } d = \frac{(M - \mu)}{s}.$$

It is the same formula as for the *t* statistic, except that we divide by the population standard deviation (*s*) rather than by the population standard error (s_M).

instead of 1.114 in the denominator. Cohen's *d* is based on the spread of the distribution of individual scores, rather than the distribution of means.

$$\text{Cohen's } d = \frac{(M - \mu)}{s} = \frac{(7.8 - 4.6)}{2.490} = 1.29$$

The effect size, $d = 1.29$, tells us that the sample mean and the population mean are 1.29 standard deviations apart. According to the conventions we learned in Chapter 8 (that 0.2 is a small effect, 0.5 is a medium effect, and 0.8 is a large effect), this is a large effect. We can add the effect size when we report the statistics as follows: $t(4) = 2.87$, $p < 0.05$, $d = 1.29$. ●

Next Steps | Dot Plots

When we conduct hypothesis tests such as the single-sample *t* test, we must be concerned with the shape of the distribution of the underlying populations. When we have a sample size greater than 30, the comparison distribution can be assumed to be normal and we can proceed with hypothesis testings. With smaller samples, however, we often use the shapes of the samples to assess the shapes of the populations from which they are drawn. In earlier chapters, we learned to construct frequency histograms and frequency polygons to examine the shape of the data in a sample, but these graphs do not allow us to see every single data point. In Next Steps in Chapter 2, we explored stem-and-leaf plots. Here, we'll introduce an alternative, the dot plot.

*The **dot plot** is a graph that displays all the data points in a sample, with the range of scores along the x-axis and a dot for each data point above the appropriate value.* Dot plots serve a function similar to that of stem-and-leaf plots. They both allow us to view the overall shape of a sample, and they both retain all of the individual data points. Although we'll demonstrate a dot plot for one sample here, dot plots can include more than one sample. With two samples, for example, the dots for one group would be placed directly above those for the other group, allowing us to view two groups simultaneously, a useful feature for when we compare two groups, as we'll do in chapters 10 and 11.

9-5: A dot plot includes a dot for every score along an *x*-axis, listing the full range of possible values. It allows us to see the overall shape of a sample while also viewing every score. Dot plots also allow us to compare two samples because the dots for one sample are placed directly above the dots for the other.

To demonstrate a dot plot, we'll use the same data we used in the Next Steps section in Chapter 2—the randomly selected sample of mean years of education for 26 countries. You may recall that these data were published by the United Nations in its Human Development Report (2015). Here are the data for the 26 randomly selected countries, already arranged in order from lowest to highest:

1.6	2.8	4.2	5.3	5.5	5.6	5.9	5.9	6.4	7.2	8.5	9.4	9.5
9.9	10.3	10.4	10.5	10.8	11.3	11.6	11.8	12.3	12.5	12.5	12.6	12.9

To create a dot plot, there are three basic steps.

STEP 1: Determine the lowest score and highest score of the sample.

These scores are 1.6 and 12.9.

● The **dot plot** is a graph that displays all the data points in a sample, with the range of scores along the *x*-axis and a dot for each data point above the appropriate value.

STEP 2: Draw an x-axis and label it, including the values from the lowest through highest scores.

If possible, include 0. If it doesn't make sense, include cut marks to indicate that the *x*-axis does not start at 0 (see Figure 9-7).

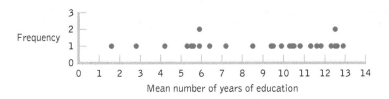

FIGURE 9-7

A Dot Plot for Mean Years of Education

A dot plot allows us to view all the data points in the sample.

STEP 3: Place a dot above the appropriate value for every score (see Figure 9-7).

Figure 9-7 displays the dot plot for the mean years of education for the 26 randomly selected countries. With the dot plot, we can easily observe the central tendency, as well as the potential outlier in the sample.

CHECK YOUR LEARNING

Reviewing the Concepts

> A single-sample *t* test is used to compare data from one sample to a population for which we know the mean but not the standard deviation.

> We consider degrees of freedom, or the number of scores that are free to vary, instead of *N* when we assess estimated *t* statistics against *t* distributions.

> As the sample size increases, confidence in the estimates improves, degrees of freedom increase, and the critical values for *t* drop, making it easier to reach statistical significance. In fact, as sample size grows, the *t* distributions approach the *z* distribution.

> To conduct a single-sample *t* test, we follow the same six steps of hypothesis testing as we do for the *z* test, except that we estimate the standard deviation from the sample before we calculate standard error.

> We can calculate a confidence interval and an effect size, Cohen's *d*, for a single-sample *t* test.

> Dot plots allow us to view the shape of a sample's distribution as well as every single data point in that sample.

Clarifying the Concepts

9-5 Explain the term *degrees of freedom*.

9-6 Why is a single-sample *t* test more useful than a *z* test?

Calculating the Statistics

9-7 Compute degrees of freedom for each of the following:

a. An experimenter times how long it takes 35 rats to run through a maze with eight pathways.

b. Test scores for 14 students are collected and averaged over four semesters.

9-8 Identify the critical *t* value(s) for each of the following tests:

a. A two-tailed test with alpha of 0.05 and 11 degrees of freedom

b. A one-tailed test with alpha of 0.01 and *N* of 17

Applying the Concepts

9-9 Let's assume that according to university summary statistics, the average student misses 3.7 classes during a semester. Imagine that these are the data you have been working with (6, 3, 7, 6, 4, 5) for the number of classes missed by statistics students in your class. Conduct all six steps of hypothesis testing, using a two-tailed test with a *p* level of 0.05. (*Note:* You completed the work for step 3 in Check Your Learning 9-2 and 9-3.)

Solutions to these Check Your Learning questions can be found in Appendix D.

REVIEW OF CONCEPTS

The *t* Distributions

The *t* distributions are similar to the *z* distribution, except that in the former, we must estimate the standard deviation from the sample. When estimating the standard deviation, we make a mathematical correction to adjust for the increased likelihood of error. After estimating the standard deviation, the *t* statistic is calculated like the *z* statistic for a distribution of means. The *t* distributions can be used in three ways: (1) to compare the mean of a sample to a population mean when we don't know the population standard deviation (single-sample *t* test), (2) to compare two samples with a within-groups design (paired-samples *t* test—introduced in Chapter 10), and (3) to compare two samples with a between-groups design (independent-samples *t* test—introduced in Chapter 11).

The Single-Sample *t* Test

Like *z* tests, *single-sample* t *tests* are conducted in the rare cases in which we have one sample that we're comparing to a known population. The difference is that we only have to know the mean of the population to conduct a single-sample *t* test. There are many *t* distributions, one for every possible sample size. We look up the appropriate critical values on the *t* table based on *degrees of freedom*, a number calculated from the sample size. We can calculate a confidence interval and an effect size (Cohen's *d*), for a single-sample *t* test.

Dot plots are graphs that depict the shape of a sample's distribution while also displaying every single data point in the sample. With dot plots, we can also include the scores of two or more samples directly above one another, which allows for comparisons of distributions.

SPSS®

Let's conduct a single-sample *t* test using the data on number of counseling sessions attended that we tested earlier in this chapter. The five scores were: 6, 6, 12, 7, and 8.

Language Alert: The SPSS program uses an uppercase T rather than the lowercase, italicized *t* that you will use to report your results.

Select Analyze → Compare Means → One-Sample T Test. Highlight the dependent variable (Number of sessions attended) and click the arrow in the center to choose it. We have now told SPSS that we're interested in looking at the sample mean for this variable, number of sessions attended. We also need to tell SPSS the population to which we are comparing the sample mean. To do that, type the population mean to which we're comparing the sample, 4.6, next to "Test Value," and click "OK."

If we conduct this test using SPSS, we'll notice that the output presented includes two tables: a table with descriptive statistics for the dependent variable, and a table that includes information used to calculate *t*. Both tables are in the screenshot here. In the second table, we should pay attention to three things: the *t* statistic in the first column, the *p* value in the significance column (in the third column), and the confidence interval (in the fifth and sixth columns). Notice that the *t* statistic, 2.874, is almost identical to the one we calculated earlier, 2.873. The difference is due solely to rounding decisions.

We can also see that the confidence interval is different from the one we calculated previously. This is an interval around the difference between the two means, rather than around the mean of the sample. The *p* value is under "Sig (2-tailed)." The *p* value of .045 is less than the chosen *p* level of .05, an indication that this is a statistically significant finding. All the information we used to hand calculate the *t* statistic should be the same as the information presented in these two SPSS output tables.

HOW IT WORKS

9.1 CONDUCTING A SINGLE-SAMPLE *t* TEST

The Web site Numbeo.com compiles statistics on quality of life issues from countries around the world based on data contributed by visitors to the site (2015). The Numbeo traffic index is calculated by taking into account the typical length of the commute to work, people's unhappiness with the length of their commute, the overall inefficiency of a country's transportation system, and an estimate of commute-related carbon dioxide emissions. The index ranges from 71 for Austria to 284.51 for Egypt, with higher numbers indicating more traffic and related problems. (For comparison, Canada has an index of 161.91 and the United States is 154.2.) The mean for all countries listed in Numbeo is 138.69. For the purposes of this example, we'll treat these numbers as population parameters.

Imagine that 20 countries make a special effort to improve the traffic situation over a five-year period. At the end of this time, the traffic indices are recalculated and these countries now have a mean index of 117.33 with a standard deviation of 45.04. Based on these data, how can we conduct all six steps of hypothesis testing for a two-tailed single-sample *t* test using a *p* level of 0.05? Let's walk through the steps.

Step 1: Population 1: Countries that did not make a special effort to improve the traffic situation over a five-year period.

Population 2: Countries that made a special effort to improve the traffic situation over a five-year period.

The comparison distribution will be a distribution of means. The hypothesis test will be a single-sample *t* test because we have only one sample and we know the population mean, but we do not know the population standard deviation. This study meets one of the three assumptions: the dependent variable is scale. We cannot assume that the countries in this sample were randomly selected from among all countries. In fact, it's likely those countries were self-selected; that is, they may have been motivated by other demands to make improvements. We must be cautious when generalizing. Last, there are fewer than 30 participants (i.e., countries), so we should be concerned about whether the comparison distribution is normal.

Step 2: Null hypothesis: Countries that made an effort to improve traffic conditions over a five-year time frame had the same traffic index score, on average, as countries that did not make explicit improvements—H_0: $\mu_1 = \mu_2$. Research hypothesis: Countries that made an effort to improve traffic conditions over a five-year time frame had different traffic index scores, on average, than countries that did not make explicit improvements—H_1: $\mu_1 \neq \mu_2$.

Step 3: $\mu_M = \mu = 138.69$; $s_M = \dfrac{s}{\sqrt{N}} = \dfrac{45.04}{\sqrt{20}} = 10.072$

Step 4: $df = N - 1 = 20 - 1 = 19$

The critical values, based on 19 degrees of freedom, a p level of 0.05, and a two-tailed test, are −2.093 and 2.093.

Step 5: $t = \dfrac{(M - \mu_M)}{s_M} = \dfrac{(117.33 - 138.69)}{10.072} = -2.121$

Step 6: Reject the null hypothesis. It appears that the countries that made an effort to improve traffic conditions over a five-year time frame had a lower traffic index score, on average, than did countries that did not make explicit improvements.

The statistics, as presented in a journal article, would read:

$$t(19) = -2.12, p < 0.05$$

(*Note:* If we had used software, we would report the actual p value instead of just whether the p value is larger or smaller than the critical p value.)

9.2 CALCULATING THE CONFIDENCE INTERVAL FOR A SINGLE-SAMPLE *t* TEST

How can we calculate a 95% confidence interval for these data?

Given $M = 117.13$ and $s = 45.05$, we can start by calculating standard error:

$$s_M = \frac{s}{\sqrt{N}} = \frac{45.04}{\sqrt{20}} = 10.072$$

We then find the t values that mark off the most extreme 0.025 in each tail and a df of 19, which are −2.093 and 2.093. We calculate the lower end of the interval as:

$$M_{lower} = -t(s_M) + M_{sample} = -2.093(10.072) + 117.13 = 96.049$$

We calculate the upper end of the interval as:

$$M_{upper} = t(s_M) + M_{sample} = 2.093(10.072) + 117.13 = 138.211$$

The 95% confidence interval is [96.05, 138.21].

9.3 CALCULATING EFFECT SIZE FOR A SINGLE-SAMPLE *t* TEST

How can we calculate effect size for these data? The appropriate measure of effect size for a single-sample t test is Cohen's d, which is calculated as:

$$\text{Cohen's } d = t = \frac{(M - \mu)}{s} = \frac{117.13 - 138.69}{45.04} = -0.479$$

Based on Cohen's conventions, this is a medium effect size.

EXERCISES

Clarifying the Concepts

9.1 When should we use a t distribution?

9.2 Why do we modify the formula for calculating standard deviation when using t tests (and divide by $N - 1$)?

9.3 How is the calculation of standard error different for a t test than for a z test?

9.4 Explain why the standard error for the distribution of sample means is smaller than the standard deviation of sample scores.

9.5 Define the symbols in the formula for the t statistic:

$$t = \frac{(M - \mu_M)}{s_M}$$

9.6 When is it appropriate to use a single-sample t test?

9.7 What does the phrase "free to vary," referring to a number of scores in a given sample, mean for statisticians?

9.8 How are the critical t values affected by sample size and degrees of freedom?

9.9 Why do the *t* distributions merge with the *z* distribution as sample size increases?

9.10 Explain what each part of the following statistical phrase means, as it would be reported in APA format: $t(4) = 2.87, p = 0.032$.

9.11 Why is a confidence interval more useful than a single-sample *t* test?

9.12 What is the appropriate effect size for a single-sample *t* test?

9.13 For a single-sample *t* test, how is a Cohen's *d* of 0.5 interpreted, according to Cohen's conventions?

9.14 What information does a dot plot provide?

9.15 How can a dot plot be useful if we're comparing two groups?

Calculating the Statistics

9.16 We use formulas to describe calculations. Find the error in each of the following formulas. Explain why each is incorrect and provide a correction.

a. $s_M = \dfrac{s}{\sqrt{N-1}}$

b. $t = \dfrac{(M - \mu_M)}{\sigma_M}$

9.17 For the data 93, 97, 91, 88, 103, 94, 97, calculate the standard deviation under the conditions in parts a and b. Then, compete parts c and d.

a. For this sample

b. As an estimate of the population

c. Calculate the standard error for *t* using symbolic notation.

d. Calculate the *t* statistic, assuming $\mu = 96$.

9.18 For the data 1.01, 0.99, 1.12, 1.27, 0.82, 1.04, calculate the standard deviation under the conditions in parts a and b. Then, compete parts c and d. (*Note:* You will have to carry some calculations out to the third decimal place to see the difference in calculations.)

a. For the sample

b. As an estimate of the population

c. Calculate the standard error for *t* using symbolic notation.

d. Calculate the *t* statistic, assuming $\mu = 0.96$.

9.19 Identify the critical *t* value in each of the following circumstances:

a. One-tailed test, $df = 73$, *p* level of 0.10

b. Two-tailed test, $df = 108$, *p* level of 0.05

c. One-tailed test, $df = 38$, *p* level of 0.01

9.20 Calculate degrees of freedom and identify the critical *t* value for a single-sample *t* test in each of the following circumstances:

a. Two-tailed test, $N = 8$, *p* level of 0.10

b. One-tailed test, $N = 42$, *p* level of 0.05

c. Two-tailed test, $N = 89$, *p* level of 0.01

9.21 Identify the critical *t* values for each of the following tests:

a. A single-sample *t* test examining scores for 26 participants to see if there is any difference compared to the population, using a *p* level of 0.05

b. A one-tailed, single-sample *t* test performed on scores on the Marital Satisfaction Inventory for 18 people who went through marriage counseling, as compared to the population of people who had not been through marital counseling, using a *p* level of 0.01

c. A two-tailed, single-sample *t* test, using a *p* level of 0.05, with 34 degrees of freedom

9.22 Assume we know the following for a two-tailed, single-sample *t* test, at a *p* level of 0.05: $\mu = 44.3$, $N = 114$, $M = 43$, $s = 5.9$.

a. Calculate the *t* statistic.

b. Calculate a 95% confidence interval.

c. Calculate the effect size using Cohen's *d*.

9.23 Assume we know the following for a two-tailed, single-sample *t* test: $\mu = 7$, $N = 41$, $M = 8.5$, $s = 2.1$.

a. Calculate the *t* statistic.

b. Calculate a 99% confidence interval.

c. Calculate the effect size using Cohen's *d*.

9.24 Using Cohen's conventions, interpret the effect sizes that you calculated in:

a. Exercise 9.22c

b. Exercise 9.23c

9.25 Identify the critical *t* values for each of the following tests:

a. Researchers wanted to know if marriage counseling improved participants' marital satisfaction. Scores were collected on the Marital Satisfaction Inventory for 15 people after a 12-week marriage counseling program. Using a *p* level of .01, identify the critical *t* value(s) for this one-tailed single-sample *t* test.

b. A sample of 4th graders ($N = 44$) participated in a new curriculum for multiplication. A single-sample *t* test (using a *p* level of .05) was conducted to see if there was a significant difference between the scores of the students who participated in the new curriculum, compared to the scores of the all the students attending the same school. Identify the critical *t* value(s) for this two-tailed single-sample t test.

c. Market researchers collected information on smart phone data usage for Uber drivers. They wondered if Uber drivers use a higher amount of smart phone data compared to all other taxi drivers. 31 Uber drivers reported their monthly data usage. Using a *p* level of 0.10, identify the critical *t* value(s) for this one-tailed single-sample *t* test.

9.26 Students in a statistics course reported the number of hours of sleep they get on a typical weeknight. These data appear below.

5	6.5	6	8	6	6	6	7	5
7	6	6.5	7	6	7	4	8	6

a. Create a dot plot of these data.

b. Use the dot plot to describe the distribution of the set of scores.

Applying the Concepts

9.27 The relation between the *z* distribution and the *t* distributions: For the hypothesis tests described below in parts (a) through (c), identify what the critical *z* value would have been if there had been just one sample and we knew the mean and standard deviation of the population:

a. A single-sample *t* test examining scores for 26 participants to see if there is any difference compared to the population, using a *p* level of 0.05

b. A one-tailed, single-sample *t* test performed on scores on the Marital Satisfaction Inventory for 18 people who went through marriage counseling, using a *p* level of 0.01

c. A two-tailed, single-sample *t* test, using a *p* level of 0.05, with 34 degrees of freedom

9.28 *t* statistics and standardized tests: On its Web site, the Princeton Review claims that students who have taken its course improve their Graduate Record Examination (GRE) scores, on average, by 210 points (based on the old scoring system). (No other information is provided about this statistic.) Treating this average gain as a population mean, a researcher wonders whether the far cheaper technique of practicing for the GRE on one's own would lead to a different average gain. She randomly selects five students from the pool of students at her university who plan to take the GRE. The students take a practice test before and after 2 months of self-study. They reported (fictional) gains of 160, 240, 340, 70, and 250 points. (Note that many experts suggest that the results from self-study are similar to those from a structured course for students who have the self-discipline to study on their own. Regardless of the format, preparation has been convincingly demonstrated to lead to increased scores, on average.)

a. Using symbolic notation and formulas (where appropriate), determine the appropriate mean and standard error for the distribution to which we will compare this sample. Show all steps of your calculations.

b. Using symbolic notation and the formula, calculate the *t* statistic for this sample.

c. As an interested consumer, what critical questions would you want to ask about the statistic reported by the Princeton Review? List at least three questions.

9.29 Single-sample *t* test, military training, and anger: Bardwell, Ensign, and Mills (2005) assessed the moods of 60 male U.S. Marines following a month-long training exercise conducted in cold temperatures and at high altitudes. Negative moods, including fatigue and anger, increased substantially during the training and lasted up to 3 months after the training ended. Mean mood scores were compared to population norms for three groups: college men, adult men, and male psychiatric outpatients. Let's examine anger scores for six Marines at the end of training; these scores are fictional, but their mean and standard deviation are very close to the actual descriptive statistics for the sample: 14, 12, 13, 12, 14, 15.

a. The population mean anger score for college men is 8.90. Conduct all six steps of a single-sample *t* test. Report the statistics as you would in a journal article.

b. Now calculate the test statistic to compare this sample mean to the population mean anger score for adult men ($M = 9.20$). You do not have to repeat all the steps from part (a), but conduct step 6 of hypothesis testing and report the statistics as you would in a journal article.

c. Now calculate the test statistic to compare this sample mean to the population mean anger score for male psychiatric outpatients ($M = 13.5$). Do not repeat all the steps from part (a), but conduct step 6 of hypothesis testing and report the statistics as you would in a journal article.

d. What can we conclude overall about Marines' moods following high-altitude, cold-weather training?

9.30 *t* tests and the cost of Levi's jeans and H&M dresses in Halifax: Numbeo is a crowd-sourced Web site that gathers data on cities and countries around the world (http://www.numbeo.com/cost-of-living/). The data are searchable by city or country. For example, when we looked up Halifax, Canada, we discovered that a pair of jeans ("Levis 501 or similar") goes for an average of $62.50 (Numbeo, 2015). The range was $50 to $75. And a summer dress from somewhere like Zara or H&M goes for an average of $48, with a range of $40 to $60. Numbeo also tells us that their Halifax data are based on contributions from 80 different people.

a. Let's say that Levi Strauss & Co. agreed to tell you the mean price (in Canadian dollars) of Levi's 501 jeans around the world. If you wanted to test whether Levi's 501 jeans in Halifax cost a different amount from the world price, what hypothesis test would you use? Explain your answer.

b. What additional information would you need to conduct the hypothesis test that you identified in part (a)?

c. Thinking back to Chapter 5, what kind of sample is this? What concerns might you have about this kind of a sample?

d. Numbeo doesn't tell us how many of the 80 contributors answered each of these questions.

Why might the sample be even smaller than 80 for the average cost of summer dresses?

9.31 Credit card debt and dot plots: Below are the amounts of credit card debt reported by 27 men and 23 women.

Men

0	0	0	0	0	0	0	0	0
0	0	0	0	0	0	0	0	0
0	0	0	0	700	2000	3000	3000	3000

Women

0	0	0	0	0	0	0	0
0	0	0	0	0	0	200	600
900	1700	2000	3000	4000	4500	10,000

a. Construct stacked dot plots for these data.

b. What can we learn about these two distributions from this graph?

9.32 Consideration of Future Consequences and a dot plot: The following data are Consideration of Future Consequences (CFC) scores for 20, already arranged in order from lowest to highest:

2.0, 2.0, 2.5, 2.5, 3.0, 3.0, 3.0, 3.0, 3.5, 3.5,

3.5, 3.5, 3.5, 3.5, 3.5, 4.0, 4.0, 4.0, 4.5, 4.5

a. Construct a dot plot for these data.

b. What can you learn about the shape of this distribution from this plot?

9.33 A single-sample *t* test and Victoria's Secret perfume as an insect repellent: Biology researchers examined the mosquito-repelling effects of a control (no scent), insect repellents that contain DEET, natural insect repellents, and several beauty products (Rodriguez, Drake, Price, Hammond, & Hansen, 2015). In the control condition, on average, 61% of a swarm of mosquitoes chose to enter a chamber with a hand in it. For the purposes of this exercise, we'll treat this as the population mean. When the hand was sprayed with a high concentration of Victoria's Secret Bombshell perfume, only 17% of mosquitoes entered the chamber on average. The standard deviation for the sample of five perfumed hands was 12.052. (Interestingly, the perfume was almost as effective as bug spray with DEET; for example, Cutter Skinsations had a mean of 11%. The perfume worked better than Cutter's natural bug spray, which had a mean of 57% and better than the bug spray based on Avon's Skin So Soft lotion, a long-heralded home remedy, which had a mean of 48%.)

a. Explain why a single-sample *t* test is the appropriate hypothesis test to examine the effect of the perfume against the control.

b. Conduct all six steps of hypothesis testing for the effect of the perfume against the control.

c. Calculate the effect size for this hypothesis test. According to Cohen's conventions, how large is this effect?

d. Calculate the confidence interval for the sample mean for the perfume.

e. Explain how the confidence interval gives us the same information as the hypothesis test.

Putting It All Together

9.34 Paid days off and the single-sample *t* test: The number of paid days off (e.g., vacation, sick leave) taken by eight employees at a small local business is compared to the national average. You are hired as a consultant by the new business owner to help her determine how many paid days off she should provide. In general, she wants to set some standard for her employees and for herself. Let's assume your search on the Internet for data on paid days off leaves you with the impression that the national average is 15 days. The data for the eight local employees during the last fiscal year are: 10, 11, 8, 14, 13, 12, 12, and 27 days.

a. Write hypotheses for your research.

b. Which type of test would be appropriate to analyze these data in order to answer your question?

c. Before doing any computations, do you have any concerns about this research? Are there any questions you might like to ask about the data you have been given?

d. Calculate the appropriate *t* statistic. Show all of your work in detail.

e. Draw a statistical conclusion for this business owner.

f. Calculate the confidence interval.

g. Calculate and interpret the effect size.

h. Consider all the results you have calculated. How would you summarize the situation for this business owner? Identify the limitations of your analyses and discuss the difficulties of making comparisons between populations and samples. Make reference to the assumptions of the statistical test in your answer.

i. After further investigation, you discover that one of the data points, 27 days, was actually the owner's number of paid days off. Calculate the *t* statistic and draw a statistical conclusion, adapting for this new information by deleting that value. What changed in the re-analysis of the data?

j. Calculate and interpret the effect size, adapting for this new information by deleting the outlier of 27 days. What changed in the re-analysis of the data?

9.35 Death row and the single-sample *t* test: The Florida Department of Corrections publishes an online death row fact sheet. It reports the average time on death row prior to execution as 11.72 years but provides no standard deviation. This mean is a parameter because it is calculated from the entire population of executed prisoners in Florida. Did the time spent on death row change over time? According to the execution list linked to the same Web site, the six prisoners executed in Florida during the years 2003, 2004, and 2005 spent 25.62, 13.09, 8.74, 17.63, 2.80, and 4.42 years on death row, respectively. (All were men, although Aileen Wuornos, the serial killer portrayed by Charlize Theron in the 2003 film *Monster*, was among the three prisoners executed by the state of Florida in 2002; Wuornos spent 10.69 years on death row.)

a. Using symbolic notation and formulas (where appropriate), determine the appropriate mean and standard error for the distribution of means. Show all steps of your calculations.

b. Using symbolic notation and the formula, calculate the *t* statistic for time spent on death row for the sample of executed prisoners.

c. The execution list provides data on all prisoners executed since the death penalty was reinstated in Florida in 1976. Included for each prisoner are the name, race, gender, date of birth, date of offense, date sentenced, date arrived on death row, date of execution, number of warrants, and years on death

row. State at least one hypothesis, other than year of execution, that could be examined using a *t* distribution and the comparison mean of 11.72 years on death row. Be specific about your hypothesis (and if you are interested, you can search for the data online).

d. What additional information would you need to calculate a *z* score for the length of time Aileen Wuornos spent on death row?

e. Write hypotheses to address the question "Did the time spent on death row change over time?"

f. Using these data as "over time" and the mean of 11.72 years as the comparison, answer the question based on the *t* statistic calculated in part (b), using alpha of 0.05.

g. Calculate the confidence interval for this statistic based on the data presented.

h. What conclusion would you make about the hypotheses based on this confidence interval? What can you say about the size of this confidence interval?

i. Calculate the effect size using Cohen's *d*.

j. Evaluate the size of this effect.

TERMS

FORMULAS

$$s = \sqrt{\frac{\Sigma(X - M)^2}{(N - 1)}} \quad \text{(p. 233)}$$

$$s_M = \frac{s}{\sqrt{N}} \quad \text{(p. 235)}$$

$$t = \frac{(M - \mu_M)}{s_M} \quad \text{(p. 236)}$$

$$df = N - 1 \quad \text{(p. 237)}$$

$$M_{lower} = -t(s_M) + M_{sample} \quad \text{(p. 243)}$$

$$M_{upper} = t(s_M) + M_{sample} \quad \text{(p. 243)}$$

$$\text{Cohen's } d = \frac{(M - \mu)}{s} \quad \text{(p. 244)}$$

SYMBOLS

t (p. 232)

s_M (p. 235)

df (p. 237)

The Paired-Samples *t* Test

BEFORE YOU GO ON

- You should know how to conduct a single-sample *t* test (Chapter 9).

- You should know how to determine a confidence interval for a single-sample *t* test (Chapter 9).

- You should understand the concept of effect size and know how to calculate Cohen's *d* for a single-sample *t* test (Chapter 9).

Holiday Weight Gain and Two-Group Studies Two-group studies (using before-and-after designs) indicate that the average holiday weight gain by college students is less than many people believe—only about 1 pound.

In many parts of the world, the winter holiday season is a time when family food traditions take center stage. Popular wisdom suggests that during this season, many people put on 5 to 7 pounds. But before-and-after studies suggest a weight gain of just over 1 pound (Hull, Radley, Dinger, & Fields, 2006; Roberts & Mayer, 2000; Yanovski et al., 2000). A 1-pound weight gain over the holidays might not seem so bad, but weight gained over the holidays tends to stay (Yanovski et al., 2000).

The fact that researchers used two groups in their study—students before the holidays and students after the holidays—is important for this chapter. With a *t* distribution, we can compare one sample to a population when we don't know all the details about the parameters, as we did in Chapter 9, and we can compare two samples to each other. There are two ways to compare two samples: by using a within-groups design (as when the same people are weighed before and after the holidays) or by using a between-groups design (as when different people are in the preholiday sample than those in the postholiday sample). For a within-groups design, we use a paired-samples *t* test. The steps for a paired-samples *t* test are similar to those for a single-sample *t* test, which we learned about in Chapter 9. (For a between-groups design, we use an independent-samples *t* test, which we will learn about in Chapter 11.)

The Paired-Samples *t* Test

As we learned in the chapter opening, researchers found that weight gain over the holidays is far less than what folk wisdom had suggested. Guess what? The dreaded "freshman 15" also appears to be a myth. One study found that male university students gained an average of 3.5 pounds between the beginning of the fall semester and November, and female students gained an average of 4.0 pounds (Holm-Denoma, Joiner, Vohs, & Heatherton, 2008). We can use the paired-samples *t* test to make before-and-after comparisons.

The **paired-samples t test** (also called the *dependent-samples* t *test*) *is used to compare two means for a within-groups design, a situation in which every participant is in both samples.* The paired-samples *t* test can be used to analyze the data from many studies. For example, if a participant is in both conditions (such as a memory task before ingesting a caffeinated beverage and again after ingesting a non-caffeinated beverage), then her score in one depends on her score in the other.

● The **paired-samples *t* test** is used to compare two means for a within-groups design, a situation in which every participant is in both samples; also called a *dependent-samples* t *test*.

The steps for the paired-samples *t* test are almost the same as those for the single-sample *t* test. The major difference in the paired-samples *t* test is that we must create difference scores for every participant. Because we'll be working with difference scores, we need to learn about a new distribution—a distribution of the means of these difference scores, or a distribution of *mean differences*.

Distributions of Mean Differences

We already learned about a distribution of scores and a distribution of means. Now we need to develop a distribution of *mean differences* for the pre- and postholiday weight data. The goal is to establish a distribution that specifies the null hypothesis for a within-groups design.

Imagine that many college students' weights were measured before and after the winter holidays and written on individual cards. We begin by gathering data from a sample of three people from among this population of many college students. There are two cards for each person in the population, on which weights are listed—one before the holidays and one after the holidays. We have one pair of cards for each student in the population (which is why one name for this test is the *paired-samples t test*). Let's walk through the steps to create a distribution of mean differences.

Step 1: Randomly choose three pairs of cards, replacing each pair of cards before randomly selecting the next.

Step 2: For each pair, calculate a difference score by subtracting the first weight from the second weight.

Step 3: Calculate the mean of the differences in weights for these three people. Then complete these three steps again. Randomly choose another three people from the population of many college students, calculate their difference scores, and calculate the mean of the three difference scores. And then complete these three steps again, and again, and again.

Let's walk through these steps once again, using an example.

Step 1: We randomly select one pair of cards and find that the first student weighed 140 pounds before the holidays and 144 pounds after the holidays. We replace those cards and randomly select another pair; the second student had before and after scores of 126 and 124, respectively. We replace those cards and randomly select another pair; the third student had before and after scores of 168 and 168, respectively.

Step 2: For the first student, the difference between weights, subtracting the before score from the after score, is $144 - 140 = 4$. She gained 4 pounds. For the second student, the difference between weights is $124 - 126 = -2$. He lost 2 pounds. For the third student, the difference between weights is $168 - 168 = 0$. Her weight did not change.

Step 3: The mean of these three difference scores $(4, -2, 0)$ is 0.667. The mean change in weight is a gain of 0.667 pounds.

We would then choose three more students and calculate the mean of their difference scores. Eventually, we would have many mean differences to plot on a curve of mean differences—some positive, some negative, and some right at 0.

But this would only be the beginning of what this distribution of mean differences would look like. If we were to calculate the whole distribution of mean differences, then we would do this an uncountable number of times. When the authors of this book calculated 30 mean differences for pairs of weights, we got the distribution in Figure 10-1. If no mean difference is found when comparing weights from before and after the holidays, as with the data we used to create Figure 10-1, the distribution would center around 0. According to the null hypothesis, we would expect no mean difference in weight—or a mean difference of 0—from before the holidays to after the holidays.

Before

After

Before and After Don't be fooled by one dramatic before-and-after photo or testimonial. Before you start a potentially dangerous diet or have an expensive cosmetic procedure ask for the results of an independently conducted paired-samples *t* test.

Lucky Business/Shutterstock

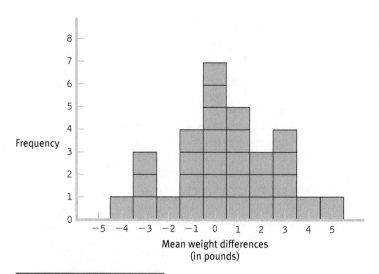

FIGURE 10-1

Creating a Distribution of Mean Differences

This distribution is one of many that could be created by pulling 30 mean differences—the average of three differences between pairs of weights, pulled one at a time from a population of pairs of weights—one preholiday and one postholiday. The population used here is one based on the null hypothesis—that there is no average difference in weight from before the holidays to after the holidays.

The Six Steps of the Paired-Samples *t* Test

In a paired-samples *t* test, each participant has two scores—one in each condition. When we conduct a paired-samples *t* test, we write the pairs of scores in two columns, side by side next to the same participant. We then subtract each score in one column from its paired score in the other column to create difference scores. Ideally, a positive difference score indicates an increase, and a negative difference score indicates a decrease. Typically, we subtract the first score from the second so that the difference scores match this logic. We will now walk through the six steps of hypothesis testing for the paired-samples *t* test.

EXAMPLE 10.1

Let's use an example from the software industry (which employs social scientists to improve the ways in which people interact with their products). For example, behavioral scientists at Microsoft studied how 15 volunteers performed on a set of tasks under two conditions—while using a 15-inch computer monitor and while using a 42-inch monitor (Czerwinski et al., 2003), the latter of which allows the user to have multiple programs in view at the same time.

Here are five participants' fictional data, which reflect the actual means reported by the researchers. Note that a smaller number is good—it indicates a faster time. The first person completed the tasks on the small monitor in 122 seconds and on the large monitor in 111 seconds; the second person in 131 and 116; the third in 127 and 113; the fourth in 123 and 119; and the fifth in 132 and 121.

> **STEP 1:** Identify the populations, distribution, and assumptions.

The paired-samples *t* test is like the single-sample *t* test in that we analyze a single sample of scores. For the paired-samples *t* test, however, we analyze difference scores. For the paired-samples *t* test, one population is reflected by each condition, but the comparison distribution is a

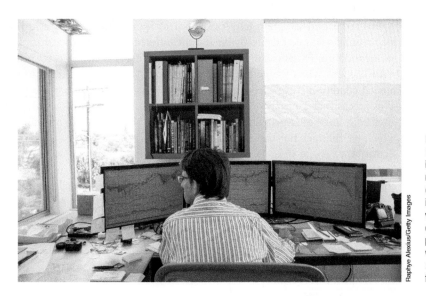

Large Monitors and Productivity Does a large monitor increase your productivity? Microsoft researchers and cognitive psychologists (Czerwinski et al., 2003) reported a 9% increase in productivity when research volunteers used a large 42-inch display versus a 15-inch display. Every participant used both displays and thus was in both samples. A paired-samples *t* test is the appropriate hypothesis test for this two-group design.

distribution of mean difference scores (rather than a distribution of means). The comparison distribution is based on the null hypothesis that posits no mean difference. So the mean of the comparison distribution is 0. For the paired-samples *t* test, the three assumptions are the same as for the single-sample *t* test.

Summary: Population 1: People performing tasks using a 15-inch monitor. Population 2: People performing tasks using a 42-inch monitor.

The comparison distribution is a distribution of mean difference scores based on the null hypothesis. The hypothesis test is a paired-samples *t* test because there are two samples of scores and a within-groups design.

This study meets one of the three assumptions and may meet the other two: (1) The dependent variable is time, which is scale. (2) The participants were not randomly selected, however, so we must be cautious with respect to generalizing the findings. (3) We do not know whether the population is normally distributed, and there are not at least 30 participants. However, the data from this sample do not suggest a skewed distribution.

> **STEP 2: State the null and research hypotheses.**

This step is identical to that for the single-sample *t* test.

Summary: Null hypothesis: People who use a 15-inch screen will complete a set of tasks in the same amount of time, on average, as people who use a 42-inch screen—$H_0: \mu_1 = \mu_2$. Research hypothesis: People who use a 15-inch screen will complete a set of tasks in a different amount of time, on average, than people who use a 42-inch screen—$H_1: \mu_1 \neq \mu_2$.

> **STEP 3: Determine the characteristics of the comparison distribution.**

This step is similar to that for the single-sample *t* test. We determine the appropriate mean and standard error of the comparison distribution—the distribution based on the null hypothesis. With the paired-samples *t* test, however, there is a sample of difference scores and a comparison distribution of mean differences (instead of a sample of individual scores and a comparison distribution of means). According to the null hypothesis, there is no difference. So the mean of the comparison distribution is always 0, as long as the null hypothesis posits no difference.

For the paired-samples *t* test, standard error is calculated exactly as it is calculated for the single-sample *t* test, only we use the difference scores rather than the scores in each condition. To get the difference scores in the current example, we want to know what happens when we go from the control condition (small screen) to the experimental condition (large screen), so we subtract the first score from the second score. This means that a negative difference indicates a decrease in time when the screen goes from small to large. (The test statistic will be the same if we reverse the order in which we subtract, but the sign will change.)

Summary: $\mu_M = 0$; $s_M = 1.924$

Calculations: (Notice that we crossed out the original scores once we created the column of difference scores. We did this to remind ourselves that all remaining calculations involve the differences scores, not the original scores.)

X	Y	Difference	Difference − Mean Difference	Squared Deviation
122	111	−11	0	0
131	116	−15	−4	16
127	113	−14	−3	9
123	119	−4	7	49
132	121	−11	0	0

The mean of the difference scores is calculated by adding up the differences for each participant and dividing by the sample size.

$$M_{difference} = -11$$

The numerator is the sum of squares, SS (which we learned about in Chapter 4):

$$SS = 0 + 16 + 9 + 49 + 0 = 74$$

The standard deviation, *s*, is:

$$s = \sqrt{\frac{74}{(5-1)}} = \sqrt{18.5} = 4.301$$

The standard error, s_M, is:

$$s_M = \frac{4.301}{\sqrt{5}} = 1.924$$

> **STEP 4: Determine the critical values, or cutoffs.**

This step is the same as that for the single-sample *t* test, except that the degrees of freedom is the number of *participants* (not the number of scores) minus 1.

Summary: $df = N - 1 = 5 - 1 = 4$

The critical values, based on a two-tailed test and a *p* level of 0.05, are −2.776 and 2.776, as seen in the curve in Figure 10-2.

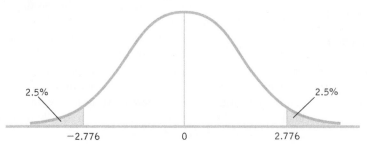

2.5%   2.5%

−2.776   0   2.776

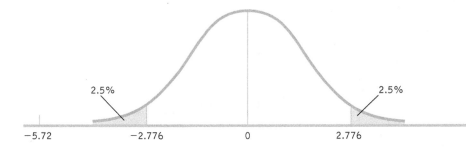

FIGURE 10-3

Making a Decision

To decide whether to reject the null hypothesis, we compare the test statistic to the critical values. In this figure, the test statistic, -5.72, is beyond the cutoff of -2.776, so we can reject the null hypothesis.

STEP 5: Calculate the test statistic. This step is identical to that for the single-sample *t* test, except that we use means of difference scores instead of means of individual scores. We subtract the mean difference score according to the null hypothesis, 0, from the mean difference score calculated for the sample. We then divide by standard error.

Summary: $t = \dfrac{(-11 - 0)}{1.924} = -5.72$

STEP 6: Make a decision. This step is identical to that for the single-sample *t* test.

Summary: Reject the null hypothesis. When we examine the means ($M_X = 127$; $M_Y = 116$), it appears that, on average, people perform faster when using a 42-inch monitor than when using a 15-inch monitor (as shown by the curve in Figure 10-3).

The statistics, as reported in a journal article, follow the same APA format as for a single-sample *t* test. (*Note:* Unless we use software, we can only indicate whether the *p* value is less than or greater than the cutoff *p* level of 0.05.) In the current example, the statistics would read:

$$t(4) = -5.72, p < 0.05$$

We also include the means and the standard deviations for the two samples. We calculated the means in step 6 of hypothesis testing, but we would also have to calculate the standard deviations for the two samples to report them.

The researchers note that the faster time with the large display might not *seem* much faster but that, in their research, they have had great difficulty identifying *any* factors that lead to faster times (Czerwinski et al., 2003). Based on their previous research, therefore, this is an impressive difference. ●

CHECK YOUR LEARNING

Reviewing the Concepts

> The paired-samples *t* test is used when we have data for all participants under two conditions—a within-groups design.

> In the paired-samples *t* test, we calculate a difference score for every individual in the study. The statistic is calculated using those difference scores.

> We use the same six steps of hypothesis testing that we used with the *z* test and with the single-sample *t* test.

Clarifying the Concepts

10-1 How do we conduct a paired-samples *t* test?

10-2 Explain what an individual difference score is, as it is used in a paired-samples *t* test.

continued on next page

Calculating the Statistics 10-3

Below are energy-level data (on a scale of 1 to 7, where 1 = feeling of no energy and 7 = feeling of high energy) for five students before and after lunch. Calculate the mean difference for these people so that loss of energy is a negative value. Assume you are testing the hypothesis that students go into what we call "food comas" after eating, versus lunch giving them added energy.

Before lunch	After lunch
6	3
5	2
4	6
5	4
7	5

Applying the Concepts 10-4

Using the energy-level data presented in Check Your Learning 10-3, test the hypothesis that students have different energy levels before and after lunch. Perform the six steps of hypothesis testing for a two-tailed paired-samples *t* test.

Solutions to these Check Your Learning questions can be found in Appendix D.

Beyond Hypothesis Testing

The APA encourages the use of confidence intervals and effect sizes (as with the *z* test and the single-sample *t* test) for paired-samples *t* tests. We'll calculate both the confidence interval and the effect size for the example of productivity with small versus large computer monitors.

Calculating a Confidence Interval for a Paired-Samples *t* Test

Let's start by determining the confidence interval for the productivity example.

EXAMPLE 10.2

First, let's recap the information we need. The population mean difference according to the null hypothesis was 0, and we used the sample to estimate the population standard deviation to be 4.301 and the standard error to be 1.924. The five participants in the study sample had a mean difference of −11. We will calculate the 95% confidence interval around the sample mean difference of −11.

> **STEP 1: Draw a picture of a *t* distribution that includes the confidence interval.**

We draw a normal curve (Figure 10-4) that has the *sample* mean difference, −11, at its center instead of the *population* mean difference, 0.

FIGURE 10-4

A 95% Confidence Interval for a Paired-Samples *t* Test, Part I

We start the confidence interval for a distribution of mean differences by drawing a curve with the sample mean difference, −11, in the center.

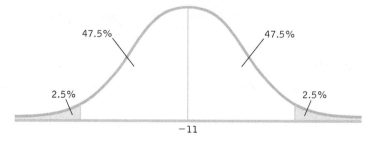

47.5%   47.5%

2.5%   2.5%

−11

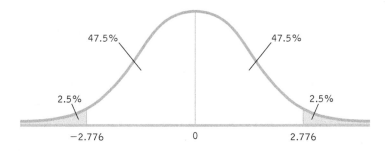

FIGURE 10-5

A 95% Confidence Interval for a Paired-Samples *t* Test, Part II

The next step in calculating a confidence interval for mean differences is identifying the *t* statistics that indicate each end of the interval. Because the curve is symmetric, the *t* statistics have the same magnitude—one is negative, −2.776, and one is positive, 2.776.

STEP 2: Indicate the bounds of the confidence interval on the drawing.	As before, 47.5% fall on each side of the mean between the mean and the cutoff, and 2.5% fall in each tail.

STEP 3: Add the critical *t* statistics to the curve.	For a two-tailed test with a *p* level of 0.05 and 4 *df*, the critical values are −2.776 and 2.776, as seen in Figure 10-5.

STEP 4: Convert the critical *t* statistics back into raw mean differences.	As we do with other confidence intervals, we use the sample mean difference (−11) in the calculations and the standard error (1.924) as the measure of spread. We use the

same formulas as for the single-sample *t* test, recalling that these means and standard errors are calculated from differences between two scores for each participant. We add these raw mean differences to the curve in Figure 10-6.

$$M_{lower} = -t(s_M) + M_{sample} = -2.776(1.924) + (-11) = -16.34$$

$$M_{upper} = t(s_M) + M_{sample} = 2.776(1.924) + (-11) = -5.66$$

The 95% confidence interval, reported in brackets as is typical, is [−16.34, −5.66].

STEP 5: Verify that the confidence interval makes sense.	The sample mean difference should fall exactly in the middle of the two ends of the interval.

$$-11 - (-16.34) = 5.34 \text{ and } -11 - (-5.66) = -5.34$$

We have a match. The confidence interval ranges from 5.34 below the sample mean difference to 5.34 above the sample mean difference. If we were to sample five people from the same population over and over, the 95% confidence interval would include the population mean 95% of the time. Note that the population mean difference according to the null hypothesis, 0, does not fall within this interval. This means it is not plausible that the difference between those using the 15-inch monitor and those using the 42-inch monitor is 0.

MASTERING THE FORMULA

10-1: The formula for the lower bound of a confidence interval for a paired-samples *t* test is: $M_{lower} = -t(s_M) + M_{sample}$. The formula for the upper bound of a confidence interval for a paired-samples *t* test is: $M_{upper} = t(s_M) + M_{sample}$. These are the same as for a single-sample *t* test, but remember that the means and standard errors are calculated from differences between pairs of scores, not individual scores.

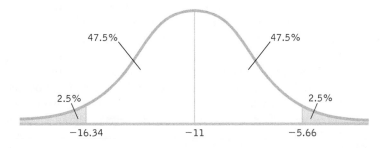

FIGURE 10-6

A 95% Confidence Interval for a Paired-Samples *t* Test, Part III

The final step in calculating a confidence interval for mean differences is converting the *t* statistics that indicate each end of the interval to raw mean differences, −16.34 and −5.66.

As with other hypothesis tests, the conclusions from both the paired-samples *t* test and the confidence interval are the same, but the confidence interval gives us more information—an interval estimate, not just a point estimate. ●

Calculating Effect Size for a Paired-Samples *t* Test

As with a *z* test, we can calculate the effect size (Cohen's *d*) for a paired-samples *t* test.

EXAMPLE 10.3

Let's calculate the effect size for the computer monitor study. Again, we simply use the formula for the *t* statistic, substituting *s* for s_M (and μ for μ_M, even though these means are always the same). This means we use 4.301 instead of 1.924 in the denominator. Cohen's *d* is now based on the spread of the distribution of individual differences between scores, rather than the distribution of mean differences.

$$\text{Cohen's } d = \frac{(M - \mu)}{s} = \frac{(-11 - 0)}{4.301} = -2.56$$

MASTERING THE FORMULA

10-2: The formula for Cohen's *d* for a paired-samples *t* statistic is:

$$\text{Cohen's } d = \frac{(M - \mu)}{s}.$$

It is the same formula as for the single-sample *t* statistic, except that the mean and standard deviation are for difference scores rather than individual scores.

The effect size, $d = -2.56$, tells us that the sample mean difference and the population mean difference are 2.56 standard deviations apart. This is a large effect. Recall that the sign has no effect on the size of an effect: -2.56 and 2.56 are equivalent effect sizes. We can add the effect size when we report the statistics as follows: $t(4) = -5.72$, $p < 0.05$, $d = -2.56$. ●

Next Steps | Order Effects and Counterbalancing

There are particular problems that can occur with a within-groups design (such as the paired-samples *t* test). Specifically, a within-groups design invites a particular kind of confounding variable into a study: order effects. *Order effects refer to how a participant's behavior changes when the dependent variable is presented for a second time.* (They're sometimes called *practice effects.*) Let's consider the computer monitor study for which we conducted a paired-samples *t* test. Remember that the participants completed a series of tasks on a 15-inch computer monitor and also on a 42-inch computer monitor. The time it took them to complete the series of tasks was recorded under each condition. Can you spot the confound? Participants were likely to get faster the second time they completed the tasks. Their responses the second time around would be influenced by the practice of already having completed the tasks once.

Fortunately, we can limit the confounding influence of order effects. *Counterbalancing minimizes order effects by varying the order of presentation of different levels of the independent variable from one participant to the next.* For example, half of the participants could be randomly assigned to complete the tasks on the 15-inch monitor first, then again on the 42-inch monitor. The other half could be randomly assigned to complete the tasks on the 42-inch monitor first, then again on the 15-inch monitor. In this case, any practice effect would be washed out by varying the order of the monitors.

There are other ways to reduce order effects. In the computer monitor example, we might decide to use a different set of tasks in each testing condition. The order in which the two different sets of tasks are given could be counterbalanced along with the order in which participants are assigned to the two different-sized monitors. Measures such as this can reduce order effects in within-groups research designs.

● **Order effects** refer to how a participant's behavior changes when the dependent variable is presented for a second time, sometimes called *practice effects.*

● **Counterbalancing** minimizes order effects by varying the order of presentation of different levels of the independent variable from one participant to the next.

Order Effects You observe that your friends felt exhilarated after riding a roller coaster without loops (which turn riders upside-down), then felt nauseated after riding a roller coaster with loops. You conclude that loops lead to nausea. The problem is that there could be an order effect. Perhaps your friends would have felt nauseated after the second roller coaster ride whether or not it had loops. Counterbalancing would avoid this confound. Half of your friends would be randomly assigned to ride the one without loops first, then the one with loops; half of them would be randomly assigned to ride the one with loops first, then the one without loops. (Your second author gets queasy just thinking about roller coasters and would not participate in this experiment no matter what experimental controls were in place! But your first author would volunteer!)

CHECK YOUR LEARNING

Reviewing the Concepts

> We can calculate a confidence interval for a paired-samples *t* test. This provides us with an interval estimate rather than simply a point estimate. If 0 is *not* in the confidence interval, then it is not plausible that there is no difference between the sample and population mean differences.

> We also can calculate an effect size (Cohen's *d*) for a paired-samples *t* test.

> Order effects occur when participants' behavior is affected when a dependent variable is presented a second time.

> Order effects can be reduced through counterbalancing, a procedure in which the different levels of the independent variable are presented in different orders from one participant to the next.

Clarifying the Concepts   10-5   How does creating a confidence interval for a paired-samples *t* test give us the same information as hypothesis testing with a paired-samples *t* test?

10-6   How do we calculate Cohen's *d* for a paired-samples *t* test?

Calculating the Statistics   10-7   Assume that researchers asked five participants to rate their mood on a scale from 1 to 7 (1 being lowest, 7 being highest) before and after watching a funny video clip. The researchers reported that the average difference between the "before" mood score and the "after" mood score was $M = 1.0$, $s = 1.225$. They calculated a paired-samples *t* test, $t(4) = 1.13$, $p > 0.05$ and, using a two-tailed test with a p level of 0.05, failed to reject the null hypothesis.

a. Calculate the 95% confidence interval for this *t* test and describe how it results in the same conclusion as the hypothesis test.

b. Calculate and interpret Cohen's *d*.

continued on next page

| Applying the Concepts | 10-8 | Using the energy-level data presented in Check Your Learning 10-3 and 10-4, let's go beyond hypothesis testing. |

Solutions to these Check Your Learning questions can be found in Appendix D.

a. Calculate the 95% confidence interval and describe how it results in the same conclusion as the hypothesis test.

b. Calculate and interpret Cohen's *d*.

REVIEW OF CONCEPTS

The Paired-Samples *t* Test

We use a *paired-samples* t *test* when we have two samples and the same participants are in both samples; to conduct the test, we calculate a difference score for every individual in the study. The comparison distribution is a distribution of mean difference scores instead of the distribution of means that we used with a single-sample *t* test. Aside from the comparison distribution, the steps of hypothesis testing are similar to those for a single-sample *t* test.

Beyond Hypothesis Testing

As we can with a *z* test and a single-sample *t* test, we can calculate a confidence interval for a paired-samples *t* test. The confidence interval gives us an interval estimate rather than a point estimate. Its results match that of the hypothesis test. When we reject the null hypothesis, we know that the confidence interval will not include 0. We also can calculate an effect size (Cohen's *d*) for a paired-samples *t* test. This provides information about the size of the observed effect and can let us know if a statistically significant finding is likely to be practically important.

Paired-samples *t* tests are used when we compare two groups using a within-groups design, a situation in which we must be aware of order effects, also called practice effects. Order effects occur when participants' behavior changes when a dependent variable, such as a test or measure, is presented a second time. Researchers use counterbalancing to reduce order effects: They vary the order in which the different levels of the independent variable are presented from one participant to the next.

SPSS®

For the paired-samples *t* test, let's use the data from Example 10.1 on performance using a small monitor versus a large monitor. Enter the data in two columns, with each participant having one score in the first column for his or her performance on the small monitor and one score in the second column for his or her performance on the large monitor.

Select Analyze → Compare Means → Paired-Samples T Test. Choose the dependent variable under the first condition (small) by clicking it, then clicking the center arrow. Choose the dependent variable under the second condition (large) by clicking it, then clicking the center arrow. "Small"

will now appear under the label "Variable 1," and "Large" will now appear under the label "Variable 2." Then click "OK." The data and output are shown in the screenshot. Notice that the *t* statistic and confidence interval match ours (−5.72 and [−16.34, −5.66]) except that the signs are different. This occurs because of the order in which one score was subtracted from the other score—that is, whether the score on the large monitor was subtracted from the score on the small monitor, or vice versa. The outcome is the same in either case. The *p* value is under "Sig. (2-tailed)" and is .005.

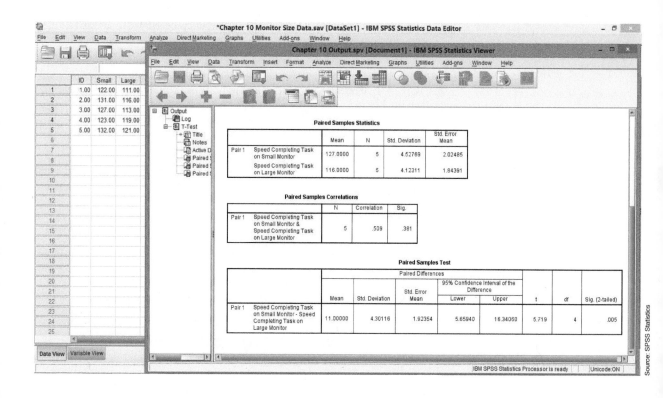

HOW IT WORKS

10.1 CONDUCTING A PAIRED-SAMPLES *t* TEST

Salary Wizard is an online tool that allows you to look up incomes for specific jobs for cities in the United States. We looked up the 25th percentile for income for six jobs in two cities: Boise, Idaho, and Los Angeles, California. The data are below.

	Boise	Los Angeles
Executive chef	$53,047.00	$62,490.00
Genetics counselor	$49,958.00	$58,850.00
Grants/proposal writer	$41,974.00	$49,445.00
Librarian	$44,366.00	$52,263.00
Public schoolteacher	$40,470.00	$47,674.00
Social worker (with bachelor's degree)	$36,963.00	$43,542.00

How can we conduct a paired-samples *t* test to determine whether income in one of these cities differs, on average, from income in the other? We'll use a two-tailed test and a *p* level of 0.05.

Step 1: Population 1: Job types in Boise, Idaho. Population 2: Job types in Los Angeles, California.

The comparison distribution will be a distribution of mean differences. The hypothesis test will be a paired-samples *t* test because we have two samples, and all participants—the job types, in this case—are in both samples.

This study meets the first of the three assumptions and may meet the third. The dependent variable, income, is scale. We do not know whether the population is normally distributed, there are not at least 30 participants, and there is not much variability in the data in the samples, so we should proceed with caution. The data were not randomly selected, so we should be cautious when generalizing beyond this sample of job types.

Step 2: Null hypothesis: Jobs in Boise pay the same, on average, as jobs in Los Angeles—$H_0: \mu_1 = \mu_2$. Research hypothesis: Jobs in Boise pay different incomes, on average, than do jobs in Los Angeles—$H_1: \mu_1 \neq \mu_2$.

Step 3: $\mu_M = \mu = 0; s_M = 438.919$

Boise	Los Angeles	Difference (D)	$(D - M_{difference})$	$(D - M_{difference})^2$
$53,047.00	$62,490.00	9443	1528.667	2,336,822.797
$49,958.00	$58,850.00	8892	977.667	955,832.763
$41,974.00	$49,445.00	7471	−443.333	196,544.149
$44,366.00	$52,263.00	7897	−17.333	300.433
$40,470.00	$47,674.00	7204	−710.333	504,572.971
$36,963.00	$43,542.00	6579	−1335.333	1,783,114.221

$M_{difference} = 7914.333$

$SS = \Sigma(D - M_{difference})^2 = 5{,}777{,}187.334$

$$s = \sqrt{\frac{\Sigma(D - M_{difference})^2}{(N-1)}} = \sqrt{\frac{5{,}777{,}187.334}{(6-1)}} = 1074.913$$

$$s_M = \frac{s}{\sqrt{N}} = \frac{1074.913}{\sqrt{6}} = \frac{1074.913}{2.449} = 438.919$$

Step 4: $df = N - 1 = 6 - 1 = 5$

The critical values, based on 5 degrees of freedom, a *p* level of 0.05, and a two-tailed test, are −2.571 and 2.571.

Step 5: $t = \dfrac{(M_{difference} - \mu_{difference})}{s_M} = \dfrac{(7914.333 - 0)}{438.919} = 18.03$

Step 6: Reject the null hypothesis. It appears that jobs in Los Angeles pay more, on average, than do jobs in Boise.

The statistics, as they would be presented in a journal article, are:

$$t(5) = 18.03, p < 0.05$$

10.2 CALCUATING THE CONFIDENCE INTERVAL FOR A PAIRED-SAMPLES *t* TEST

Given the sample mean difference, $M_{difference} = 7914.333$, and sample variance, $s = 1074.913$, we can start by calculating standard error:

$$s_M = \frac{s}{\sqrt{N}} = \frac{1074.913}{\sqrt{6}} = 438.919$$

We then find the *t* values that mark off the most extreme 0.025 in each tail and a *df* of 5, which are −2.571 and 2.571. We calculate the lower end of the interval as:

$$M_{lower} = -t(s_M) + M_{sample} = -2.571(438.919) + 7914.333 = 6785.872$$

We calculate the upper end of the interval as:

$$M_{upper} = t(s_M) + M_{sample} = 2.571(438.919) + 7914.333 = 9042.794$$

The 95% confidence interval is [6785.87, 9042.79].

10.3 CALCULATING EFFECT SIZE FOR A PAIRED-SAMPLES *t* TEST

How can we calculate effect size for these data? The appropriate measure of effect size for a paired-samples *t* test is Cohen's *d*, which is calculated as:

$$\text{Cohen's } d = \frac{(M_{difference} - \mu_{difference})}{s} = \frac{7914.333 - 0}{1074.913} = 7.363$$

Based on Cohen's conventions, this is a very large effect size.

EXERCISES

Clarifying the Concepts

10.1 What do we mean when we say we have a distribution of mean differences?

10.2 When do we use a paired-samples *t* test?

10.3 Explain the distinction between the terms *independent samples* and *paired samples* as they relate to *t* tests.

10.4 How is a paired-samples *t* test similar to a single-sample *t* test?

10.5 How is a paired-samples *t* test different from a single-sample *t* test?

10.6 Why is the population mean almost always equal to 0 for the null hypothesis in the two-tailed, paired-samples *t* test?

10.7 If we calculate the confidence interval around the sample mean difference used for a paired-samples *t* test, and it includes the value of 0, what can we conclude?

10.8 If we calculate the confidence interval around the sample mean difference used for a paired-samples *t* test, and it does not include the value of 0, what can we conclude?

10.9 Why is a confidence interval more useful than a single-sample *t* test or a paired-samples *t* test?

10.10 What is the appropriate effect size for a paired-samples *t* test? How is the calculation different from the effect size for a single-sample *t* test?

10.11 What are order effects?

10.12 Identify and explain the technique for countering order effects using a within-groups research design.

10.13 Why might order effects lead a researcher to use a between-groups design rather than a within-groups design?

10.14 We introduced confounding variables (or confounds) in Chapter 1. Explain why order effects might be an example of a confound.

Calculating the Statistics

10.15 Identify critical *t* values for each of the following tests:

    a. A one-tailed, paired-samples *t* test performed on before-and-after scores on the Marital Satisfaction Inventory for 18 people who went through marriage counseling, using a *p* level of 0.01.

    b. A two-tailed, paired-samples *t* test performed on before-and-after scores on the Marital Satisfaction Inventory for 64 people who went through marriage counseling, using a *p* level of 0.05.

10.16 Assume 8 participants completed a mood scale before and after watching a funny video clip.

    a. Identify the critical *t* value for a one-tailed, paired-samples *t* test with a *p* level of 0.01.

    b. Identify the critical *t* values for a two-tailed, paired-samples *t* test with a *p* level of 0.01.

10.17 The following are scores for 8 students on two different exams.

Exam I	Exam II
92	84
67	75
95	97
82	87
73	68
59	63
90	88
72	78

    a. Calculate the paired-samples *t* statistic for these exam scores.

    b. Using a two-tailed test and a *p* level of 0.05, identify the critical *t* values and make a decision regarding the null hypothesis.

    c. Assume you instead collected exam scores from 1000 students whose mean difference score and standard deviation were exactly the same as for these 8 students. Using a two-tailed test and a *p* level of 0.05, identify the critical *t* values and make a decision regarding the null hypothesis.

    d. How did changing the sample size affect the decision regarding the null hypothesis?

10.18 The following are mood scores for 12 participants before and after watching a funny video clip (lower values indicate better mood).

Before	After	Before	After
7	2	4	2
5	4	7	3
5	3	4	1
7	5	4	1
6	5	5	3
7	4	4	3

a. Calculate the paired-samples *t* statistic for these mood scores.

b. Using a one-tailed hypothesis test that the video clip improves mood, and a *p* level of 0.05, identify the critical *t* values and make a decision regarding the null hypothesis.

c. Using a two-tailed hypothesis test with a *p* level of 0.05, identify the critical *t* values and make a decision regarding the null hypothesis.

10.19 Consider the following data:

Score 1	Score 2	Score 1	Score 2
45	62	15	26
34	56	51	56
22	40	28	33
45	48		

a. Calculate the paired-samples *t* statistic.

b. Calculate the 95% confidence interval.

c. Calculate the effect size for the mean difference.

10.20 Consider the following data.

Score 1	Score 2
23	16
30	12
28	25
30	27
14	6

a. Calculate the paired-samples *t* statistic.

b. Calculate the 95% confidence interval.

c. Calculate the effect size.

10.21 Assume we know the following for a paired-samples *t* test: $N = 13$, $M_{difference} = -0.77$, $s = 1.42$.

a. Calculate the *t* statistic.

b. Calculate a 95% confidence interval.

c. Calculate the effect size using Cohen's *d*.

10.22 Assume we know the following for a paired-samples *t* test: $N = 32$, $M_{difference} = 1.75$, $s = 4.0$.

a. Calculate the *t* statistic.

b. Calculate a 95% confidence interval for a two-tailed test.

c. Calculate the effect size using Cohen's *d*.

Applying the Concepts

10.23 Brain exercises and a paired-samples *t* test: PowerBrainRx, a Hong Kong–based for–profit company, promises to improve cognition. Their Web site lists testimonials, including one from a parent whose children "seemed to have better working memories, improved problem solving ability like mathematics, more logical thinking and better academic performance" following mental exercise training. There are numerous ads for companies like PowerBrainRx on the Internet and on late-night television, but there does not seem to be a lot of research examining the specific programs these companies are selling. How could you design a study for PowerBrainRx that would use a paired-samples *t* test to analyze the data?

10.24 *t* tests and retail: Many communities worldwide are lamenting the effects of so-called big box retailers (e.g., Walmart) on their local economies, particularly on small, independently owned shops. Do these large stores affect the bottom lines of locally owned retailers? Imagine that you decide to test this premise. You assess earnings at 20 local stores for the month of October, a few months before a big box store opens. You then assess earnings the following October, correcting for inflation.

a. What are the two populations?

b. What is the comparison distribution? Explain.

c. Which hypothesis test would you use? Explain.

d. Check the assumptions for this hypothesis test.

e. What is one flaw in drawing conclusions from this comparison over time?

f. State the null and research hypotheses in both words and symbols.

10.25 Paired-samples *t* tests, confidence intervals, and hockey goals: Below are the numbers of goals scored by the lead scorers of the New Jersey Devils hockey team in the 2007–2008 and 2008–2009 seasons. On average, did the Devils play any differently in 2008–2009 than they did in 2007–2008?

Player	2007–2008	2008–2009
Elias	20	31
Zajac	14	20
Pandolfo	12	5
Langenbrunner	13	29
Gionta	22	20
Parise	32	45

a. Conduct the six steps of hypothesis testing using a two-tailed test and a *p* level of 0.05.

b. Report the test statistic in APA format.

c. Calculate the confidence interval for the paired-samples *t* test you conducted in part (a). Compare the confidence interval to the results of the hypothesis test.

d. Calculate the effect size for the mean difference between the 2007–2008 and 2008–2009 seasons.

10.26 Paired-samples *t* test and graduate admissions: Is it harder to get into graduate programs in psychology or in history? We randomly selected five institutions from among all U.S. institutions with graduate programs. The first number for each is the minimum grade point average (GPA) for applicants to the psychology doctoral program, and the second is for applicants to the history doctoral program. These GPAs were posted on the Web site of the well-known college guide company Peterson's.

Wayne State University:	3.0, 2.75
University of Iowa:	3.0, 3.0
University of Nevada, Reno:	3.0, 2.75
George Washington University:	3.0, 3.0
University of Wyoming:	3.0, 3.0

a. The participants are not people; explain why it is appropriate to use a paired-samples *t* test for this situation.

b. Conduct all six steps of a paired-samples *t* test. Be sure to label all six steps.

c. Calculate the effect size and explain what this adds to your analysis.

d. Report the statistics as you would in a journal article.

10.27 Attitudes toward statistics and the paired-samples *t* test: A professor wanted to know if her students' attitudes toward statistics changed by the end of the course, so she asked them to fill out an "Attitudes Toward Statistics" scale at the beginning of the term and at the end of the term.

a. What kind of *t* test should she use to analyze the data?

b. If the average (mean) at the end of the class was higher than it was at the beginning, is that necessarily a statistically significant improvement?

c. Which situation makes it easier to declare that a certain mean difference is statistically significant: a class with 7 students or a class with 700 students? Explain your answer.

10.28 Paired-samples *t* tests, confidence intervals, and wedding-day weight loss: It seems that 14% of engaged women buy a wedding dress at least one size smaller than their current size. Why? Cornell researchers reported an alarming tendency for women who are engaged to sometimes attempt to lose an unhealthy amount of weight prior to their wedding

(Neighbors & Sobal, 2008). The researchers found that engaged women weighed, on average, 152.1 pounds. The average ideal wedding weight reported by 227 women was 136.0 pounds. The data below represent the fictional weights of 8 women on the day they bought their wedding dress and on the day they got married. Did women lose weight for their wedding day?

Dress Purchase	Wedding Day
163	158
144	139
151	150
120	118
136	132
158	152
155	150
145	146

a. Conduct the six steps of hypothesis testing using a one-tailed test and a *p* level of 0.05.

b. Report the test statistic in APA format.

c. Calculate the confidence interval for the paired-samples *t* test that you conducted in part (a). Compare the confidence interval to the results of the hypothesis test.

d. Calculate the effect size for this example. According to Cohen's conventions, how large is this effect?

10.29 Paired-samples *t* test, decorations in kindergarten classrooms, and science learning: Psychology researcher Anna Fisher and her colleagues studied whether kindergarten students learned better in decorated classrooms or undecorated classrooms, referred to as "sparse classrooms" (Fisher, Godwin, & Seltman, 2014). They wondered whether students would be less distracted and learn better without decorations such as posters, maps, and children's artwork. The same group of children had science lessons in a classroom without decorations and in a classroom with decorations. The students took a test on the material after each condition. Each child received a percentage-correct score, out of 100%, for each condition. In the journal article in which they reported their findings, the researchers wrote that the children's "learning scores were higher in the sparse-classroom condition ($M = 55\%$) than in the decorated-classroom condition ($M = 42\%$), paired-samples $t(22) = 2.95$, $p = .007$; this effect was of medium size, Cohen's $d = 0.65$."

a. What is the independent variable in this study and what are its levels?

b. What is the dependent variable in this study?

c. Why did the researchers analyze their data with a paired-samples *t* test?

d. How many children participated in this study? Explain how you determined your answer.

e. How do you know this result is statistically significant?

f. Using the means, explain the results to someone who has not taken statistics.

g. Why did the researchers report an effect size?

10.30 A paired-samples *t* test and English-language tests for international students: The International English Language Testing System (IELTS) is a test that assesses the English-language skills of international students who wish to study in an English-speaking country. It has six modules, one of which assesses listening skills. Researchers assessed IELTS listening skills for a sample of 63 international students at the University of Melbourne in Australia (O'Loughlin & Arkoudis, 2009). These students were assessed in order to be admitted to the university and then were reassessed during their final semester at the university. Below is a subset of the Australian sample. (The overall pattern of data, including the means and standard errors, are similar to the whole sample of 63 students.)

Time 1	Time 2
5.5	6.5
6.0	7.5
6.5	6.5
6.5	7.5
6.5	7.5
7.0	6.5
7.0	7.5
7.5	8.0
8.0	9.0
8.5	8.5

a. Conduct the six steps of hypothesis testing using a two-tailed test and a *p* level of 0.05.

b. Report the test statistic in APA format.

c. Calculate the confidence interval for the paired-samples t test that you conducted in part (a). Compare the confidence interval to the results of the hypothesis test.

d. Calculate the effect size for this example. According to Cohen's conventions, how large is this effect?

10.31 E-mail, stress, and a paired-samples *t* test: Researchers wondered if frequent checking of email increased stress (Kushlev & Dunn, 2015). They randomly assigned half of their participants to check e-mail just three times a day for a week, and then in the second week, to check e-mail as often as they wanted. The other half of participants checked their e-mail as much

as they wanted in the first week, and just three times a day in the second week. The researchers did find that participants were less stressed, on average, during the limited e-mail week than during the unlimited e-mail week. But they wanted to be sure that it really was limited e-mail that led to this effect, so they conducted a paired-samples *t* test to be sure that participants were doing as they were told. The researchers reported that "confirming the success of our manipulation, people checked their email significantly fewer times per day in the *limited email* condition ($M = 4.70, SD = 4.10$) than in the *unlimited email* condition ($M = 12.54, SD = 8.02$; $t[115] = -10.23, p < .001$)." Was this because those who checked less frequently ended up getting less e-mail or just ignored a lot of potentially stressful e-mail? It doesn't seem like it. The researchers also reported that "there were no significant differences between conditions in how many emails people received ($M_{limited} = 16.64$ vs. $M_{unlimited} = 16.04$, $t(114) = 1.31, p = .19$) or responded to ($M_{limited} = 5.30$ vs. $M_{unlimited} = 5.95$, $t(115) = -1.58$, $p = .12$), suggesting that our manipulation primarily affected how often people checked email rather than the volume of email they managed."

a. Why did the researchers use paired-samples *t* tests to explore their concerns about exactly what might be affecting stress levels in their study?

b. Explain why it would have been useful for the researchers to report confidence intervals in addition to the results of hypothesis testing.

c. Explain why it would have been useful for the researchers to report effect sizes in addition to the results of hypothesis testing.

d. Explain why the researchers assigned half of the participants to start with limited email and the other half to start with unlimited email. In your answer, use the terms *counterbalancing* and *order effects*, showing that you understand both of these terms in the context of this study.

e. Explain how the researchers' additional hypothesis tests, as described here, help them to rule out any potential confounds.

Putting It All Together

10.32 Political bias in academia and a paired-samples *t* test: The following is an excerpt from the abstract (brief opening summary) from a published research study that examined a reported bias against conservatives in American academia (Fosse, Gross, & Ma, 2011).

The American professoriate contains a disproportionate number of people with liberal political views. Is this because of political bias or discrimination?... We sent two emails to directors of graduate study in the leading American departments of sociology, political science, economics, history, and English. The emails came from fictitious students who expressed interest in doing graduate work in the department.... We analyze responses received in terms of frequency, timing, amount of information provided about the department, emotional warmth, and enthusiasm toward the student. (p. 1)

One of the fictional e-mails was from a fictional student who mentioned working on the presidential campaign of John McCain, a well-known conservative, and one was from a fictional student who mentioned working on the presidential campaign of Barack Obama, a well-known liberal. The researchers conducted a series of paired-samples *t* tests but did not find statistically significant differences on the various measures between ratings of the conservative and liberal students.

a. Why is this a within-groups design?

b. What is the independent variable and what are its levels?

c. What are the dependent variables, as listed in the study description, and what kind of variables are they?

d. Explain why it would have been possible to conduct a paired-samples *t* test.

e. Explain why there may have been order effects in this study.

f. How might the researchers have used counterbalancing?

g. Were the *p* values likely to be lower than or higher than 0.05? Explain your answer.

h. Given that the results were not statistically significant, what additional information would you want to know to determine whether there was sufficient statistical power?

10.33 Hypnosis and the Stroop effect: In Chapter 1, you were given an opportunity to complete the Stroop test, in which color words are printed in the wrong color; for example, the word *red* might be printed in the color blue. The conflict that arises when we try to name the color of ink the words are printed in but are distracted when the color word does not match the ink color increases reaction time and decreases accuracy. Several researchers have suggested that the Stroop effect can be decreased by hypnosis. Raz, Fan, and Posner (2005) used brain-imaging techniques to demonstrate that posthypnotic suggestion led highly hypnotizable people to see Stroop words as nonsense words. Imagine that you are working with Raz and colleagues and your assignment is to determine whether reaction times decrease (remember, a decrease is a good thing; it indicates that participants are faster) when highly hypnotizable

people receive a posthypnotic suggestion to view the words as nonsensical. You conduct the experiment on six participants, once in each condition, and receive the following data; the first number is reaction time in seconds without the posthypnotic suggestion, and the second number is reaction time with the posthypnotic suggestion:

Participant 1:	12.6, 8.5
Participant 2:	13.8, 9.6
Participant 3:	11.6, 10.0
Participant 4:	12.2, 9.2
Participant 5:	12.1, 8.9
Participant 6:	13.0, 10.8

a. What is the independent variable and what are its levels? What is the dependent variable?

b. Conduct all six steps of a paired-samples *t* test as a two-tailed test. Be sure to label all six steps.

c. Report the statistics as you would in a journal article.

d. Now let's look at the effect of switching to a one-tailed test. Conduct steps 2, 4, and 6 of hypothesis testing for a one-tailed paired-samples *t* test. Under which circumstance—a one-tailed or a two-tailed test—is it easier to reject the null hypothesis? If it becomes easier to reject the null hypothesis under one type of test (one-tailed versus two-tailed), does this mean that there is a bigger mean difference between the samples? Explain.

e. Now let's look at the effect of *p* level. Conduct steps 4 and 6 of hypothesis testing for a *p* level of 0.01 and a two-tailed test. With which *p* level—0.05 or 0.01—is it easiest to reject the null hypothesis with a two-tailed test? If it is easier to reject the null hypothesis with certain *p* levels, does this mean that there is a bigger mean difference between the samples? Explain.

f. Now let's look at the effect of sample size. Calculate the test statistic using only participants 1–3 and determine the new critical values. Is this test statistic closer to or farther from the cutoff? Does reducing the sample size make it easier or more difficult to reject the null hypothesis? Explain.

g. How might order effects influence the results of this study?

h. Could the researchers use a counterbalanced design? Why or why not? What might they do instead if they think order effects are a problem?

TERMS

paired-samples *t* test (p. 254)   order effects (p. 262)   counterbalancing (p. 262)

The Independent-Samples *t* Test

Conducting an Independent-Samples *t* Test

A Distribution of Differences Between Means
The Six Steps of the Independent-Samples *t* Test
Reporting the Statistics

Beyond Hypothesis Testing

Calculating a Confidence Interval for an Independent-Samples *t* Test
Calculating Effect Size for an Independent-Samples *t* Test

Next Steps: The Bayesian Approach to Data Analysis

BEFORE YOU GO ON

- You should know the six steps of hypothesis testing (Chapter 7).

- You should understand the differences between a distribution of scores (Chapter 2), a distribution of means (Chapter 6), and a distribution of mean differences (Chapter 10).

- You should know how to conduct a single-sample *t* test and a paired-samples *t* test, including the calculations for the corrected versions of standard deviation and variance (Chapter 10).

- You should understand the basics of determining confidence intervals (Chapter 8).

- You should understand the concept of effect size and know the basics of calculating Cohen's *d* (Chapter 8).

Stella Cunliffe Stella Cunliffe created a remarkable career through her statistical reasoning and became the first female president of the Royal Statistical Society. As a statistician, she used hypothesis testing to improve quality control at the Guinness Brewing Company and to shape public policy in the criminology division at the British Home Office.

Stella Cunliffe, the first woman elected president of the Royal Statistical Society, built a path to success through two male-dominated industries: beer making and statistics. After living what she described as "a free and in many ways exciting life," she accepted a job at the Guinness Brewing Company. Cunliffe was a practical statistician whose insights helped her bypass long-standing social norms for gender. In her Royal Statistical Society presidential speech, she reminded her audience that applied "statistics are concerned much more with people than with vague ideas" (1976, p. 4).

For example, maintaining the quality of handmade beer barrels came down to a simple decision by the quality control worker: accept or reject. But that decision was biased because accepting meant kicking a barrel downhill and rejecting required pushing a barrel uphill, clearly the more arduous task. Cunliffe "de-biased" these judgments by moving the quality-control workstation so that it required equal effort either to accept or to reject a barrel—and saved Guinness a great deal of money by reducing the number of false positives (accepting barrels that should have been rejected). We can "de-bias" many experiments in the same way: by equalizing initial conditions through random assignment to independent groups.

In Chapter 9, we learned how to conduct a single-sample *t* test (comparing one sample to a population for which we know the mean but not the standard deviation). In Chapter 10, we learned how to conduct a paired-samples *t* test (such as a before/after design in which the same participants are in both groups). Here is a third situation calling for a *t* test: a two-group study in which each participant is in only one group. The scores for each group are independent of what happens in the other group. We also demonstrate how to determine a confidence interval and calculate an effect size for situations in which we have two independent groups.

Language Alert! The independent-samples *t* test is also called a *between-groups* t *test*.

- An **independent-samples** *t* **test** is used to compare two means for a between-groups design, a situation in which each participant is assigned to only one condition.

Conducting an Independent-Samples *t* Test

The ***independent-samples* t *test*** *is used to compare two means for a between-groups design, a situation in which each participant is assigned to only one condition.* This test uses a distribution of differences between means. This affects the *t* test in a few minor ways, most notably that it takes a bit more work when calculating a *t* test by hand (especially compared to using a computer!). The added calculation is that you have to estimate the appropriate standard error. It's not difficult—just a bit time consuming.

A Distribution of Differences Between Means

Because we have different people in each condition of the study, we cannot create a difference score for each person. We're looking at overall differences between two independent groups, so we need to develop a new type of distribution, a distribution of *differences between means*.

Let's use the Chapter 6 data about heights to demonstrate how to create a distribution of differences between

Your Authors with Stella Cunliffe in 2010 In addition to her accomplishments as a statistician, Ms. Cunliffe was a leader of Britain's Girl Guides, helped in relief work during WWII, and was the first civilian to enter the Bergen-Belsen concentration camp, an experience she recounted for the first time in a BBC interview in 2009.

means. Let's say that we were planning to collect data on two groups of three people each and wanted to determine the comparison distribution for this research scenario. Remember that in Chapter 6, we used the example of a population of 140 college students from the authors' classes. We described writing the height of each student on a card and putting the 140 cards in a bowl.

Let's use that example to create a distribution of differences between means. We'll walk through the steps for this process.

EXAMPLE 11.1

> **STEP 1:** We randomly select three cards, replacing each after selecting it, and calculate the mean of the heights listed on them. This is the first group.

> **STEP 2:** We randomly select three other cards, replacing each after selecting it, and calculate their mean. This is the second group.

> **STEP 3:** We subtract the second mean from the first.

That's really all there is to it—except we repeat these three steps many more times. There are two samples, so there are two sample means, but we're building just *one* distribution of differences between those means.

Here's an example using the three steps.

> **STEP 1:** We randomly select three cards, replacing each after selecting it, and find that the heights are 61, 65, and 72 inches. We calculate a mean of 66 inches. This is the first group.

> **STEP 2:** We randomly select three other cards, replacing each after selecting it, and find that the heights are 62, 65, and 65 inches. We calculate a mean of 64 inches. This is the second group.

> **STEP 3:** We subtract the second mean from the first: 66 − 64 = 2. (Note that it's fine to subtract the first from the second, as long as we're consistent in the arithmetic.)

We repeat the three-step process. Let's say that, this time, we calculate means of 65 and 68 for the two samples. Now the difference between means would be 65 − 68 = −3. We might repeat the three steps a third time and find means of 63 and 63, for a difference of 0. Eventually, we would have many differences between means—some positive, some negative, and some right at 0—and could plot them on a curve. But this would only be the beginning of what this distribution would look like.

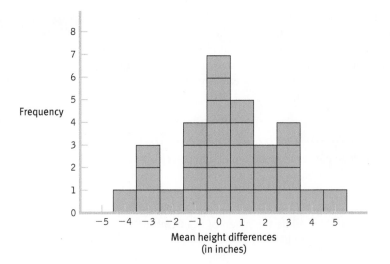

FIGURE 11-1

Distribution of Differences Between Means

This graph represents the beginning of a distribution of differences between means. It includes only 30 differences, whereas the actual distribution would include all possible differences.

If we were to calculate the whole distribution, then we would do this many, many more times. When creating the beginning of a distribution of differences between means, the authors calculated 30 differences between means, as shown in Figure 11-1. ●

The Six Steps of the Independent-Samples *t* Test

We can use the same six steps of hypothesis testing to conduct an independent-samples *t* test. Let's look at an example.

EXAMPLE 11.2

Does the price of a product influence how much you like it? If you're told that your sister's new television cost $3000, do you perceive the picture quality to be sharper than if you're told it cost $1200? If you think your friend's new shirt is from a high-end designer like Dolce & Gabbana, do you covet it more than if he tells you it's from a trendy but low-priced mass-retailer like Target?

Economics researchers from Northern California, not far from prime wine country, wondered whether enjoyment of wine is influenced by price (Plassmann, O'Doherty, Shiv, & Rangel, 2008). In part of their study, they randomly assigned some wine drinkers to taste wine that was said to cost $10 per bottle and others to taste *the same wine* at a supposed price of $90 per bottle. (Note that we're altering some aspects of the design and statistical analysis of this study for teaching purposes, but the results are similar.) The researchers asked participants to rate, on a scale from 1–5, how much they liked the wine; they also used functional magnetic resonance imaging (fMRI), a brain-scanning technique, to determine whether differences were evident in areas of the brain that are typically activated when people experience a stimulus as pleasant (e.g., the medial orbitofrontal cortex). Which do you think participants preferred, the wine priced at $10 or the same wine priced at $90?

We will conduct an independent-samples *t* test using the ratings of how much nine people like the wine they were randomly assigned to taste (four tasting wine from the "$10" bottle and five tasting wine from the "$90" bottle). Remember, everyone is actually tasting wine from the *same* bottle! Notice that we do not need to have the same number of participants in each sample, although it is best if the sample sizes are fairly similar.

Mean "liking ratings" of the wine

"$10" wine: 1.5 2.3 2.8 3.4

"$90" wine: 2.9 3.5 3.5 4.9 5.2

Price and Perception: Designer versus Knockoff Does the perceived price of a product influence how much you like it? The one on the right is the high-priced designer version. Quick—how much do you like it? OK, we lied; the one on the right is the knockoff. Did your perception of it change? If researchers ask some people to rate the designer version of Ray-Ban sunglasses and other people to rate the Ray-Ban knockoff version, we could conduct an independent-samples *t* test to determine if there is a statistically significant difference in the ratings.

> **STEP 1: Identify the populations, distribution, and assumptions.**

In terms of determining the populations, this step is similar to that for the paired-samples *t* test: There are two populations—those told they are drinking wine from a $10 bottle and those told they are drinking wine from a $90 bottle. The comparison distribution for an independent-samples *t* test, however, will be a distribution of differences between means (rather than a distribution of mean difference scores). Table 11-1 summarizes the distributions we have encountered with the hypothesis tests we have learned so far.

As usual, the comparison distribution is based on the null hypothesis. As with the paired-samples *t* test, the null hypothesis for the independent-samples *t* test posits no mean difference. So the mean of the comparison distribution would be 0; this reflects a mean difference between means of 0. We compare the difference between the sample means to a difference of 0, which is what there would be if there were no difference between groups. The assumptions for an independent-samples *t* test are the same as those for the single-sample *t* test and the paired-samples *t* test.

Summary: Population 1: People told they are drinking wine from a $10 bottle. Population 2: People told they are drinking wine from a $90 bottle.

The comparison distribution will be a distribution of differences between means based on the null hypothesis. The hypothesis test will be an independent-samples *t* test because we have two samples composed of different groups of participants. This study meets one of the three assumptions. (1) The dependent variable is a

---

TABLE 11-1   Hypothesis Tests and Their Distributions

We must consider the appropriate comparison distribution when we choose which hypothesis test to use.

Hypothesis Test	Number of Samples	Comparison Distribution
z test	One	Distribution of means
Single-sample *t* test	One	Distribution of means
Paired-samples *t* test	Two (same participants)	Distribution of mean difference scores
Independent-samples *t* test	Two (different participants)	Distribution of differences between means

rating on a liking measure, which can be considered a scale variable. (2) We do not know whether the population is normally distributed, and there are not at least 30 participants. However, the sample data do not suggest that the underlying population distribution is skewed. (3) The wine drinkers in this study were not randomly selected from among all wine drinkers, so we must be cautious with respect to generalizing these findings.

STEP 2: State the null and research hypotheses.

This step for an independent-samples *t* test is identical to that for the previous *t* tests.

Summary: Null hypothesis: On average, people drinking wine they were told was from a \$10 bottle give it the same rating as do people drinking wine they were told was from a \$90 bottle—$H_0: \mu_1 = \mu_2$. Research hypothesis: On average, people drinking wine they were told was from a \$10 bottle give it a different rating than do people drinking wine they were told was from a \$90 bottle—$H_1: \mu_1 \neq \mu_2$.

STEP 3: Determine the characteristics of the comparison distribution.

This step for an independent-samples *t* test is similar to that for previous *t* tests: We determine the appropriate mean and the appropriate standard error of the comparison distribution—the distribution based on the null hypothesis. According to the null hypothesis, no mean difference exists between the populations; that is, the difference between means is 0. So the mean of the comparison distribution is always 0, as long as the null hypothesis posits no mean difference.

Because we have two samples for an independent-samples *t* test, however, it is more complicated to calculate the appropriate measure of spread. There are five stages to this process. First, let's consider them in words; then we'll learn the calculations. These instructions are basic, and you'll understand them better when you do the calculations, but they'll help you to keep the overall framework in mind. (These verbal descriptions are keyed by letter to the calculation stages below.)

    a. Calculate the corrected variance for each sample. (Notice that we're working with variance, not standard deviation.)

    b. Pool the variances. Pooling the variances involves taking an average of the two sample variances while accounting for any differences in the sizes of the two samples. Pooled variance is an estimate of the common population variance.

    c. Convert the pooled variance from squared standard deviation (that is, variance) to squared standard error (another version of variance) by dividing the pooled variance by the sample size, first for one sample and then again for the second sample. These are the estimated variances for each sample's distribution of means.

    d. Add the two variances (*squared* standard errors), one for each distribution of sample means, to calculate the estimated variance of the distribution of differences between means.

    e. Calculate the square root of this form of variance (*squared* standard error) to get the estimated standard error of the distribution of differences between means.

Notice that stages (a) and (b) are an expanded version of the usual first calculation for a *t* test. Instead of calculating one corrected estimate of standard deviation, we're calculating two for an independent-samples *t* test—one for each sample. Also, for an independent-samples *t* test, we use variances instead of standard deviations. Because there are two calculations of variance, we combine them (i.e., the pooled variance). Stages (c) and (d) are an expanded version of the usual second calculation for a *t* test. Once again, we convert to standard error for each sample (only this time it is squared because we are working with variances) and combine the variances from each sample. In stage (e), we take the square root so that we have standard error. Let's examine the calculations.

a. We calculate corrected variance for each sample (corrected variance is the one we learned in Chapter 9 that uses $N - 1$ in the denominator). First, we calculate variance for X, the sample of people told they are drinking wine from a $10 bottle. Be sure to use the mean of the ratings of the $10 wine drinkers only, which we calculate to be 2.5. Notice that the symbol for this variance uses s^2, instead of SD^2 (just as the standard deviation used s instead of SD in the previous *t* tests). Also, we included the subscript X to indicate that this is variance for the first sample, whose scores are arbitrarily called X. (Remember, don't take the square root. We want variance, not standard deviation.)

X	$X - M$	$(X - M)^2$
1.5	−1.0	1.00
2.3	−0.2	0.04
2.8	0.3	0.09
3.4	0.9	0.81

$$s_X^2 = \frac{\Sigma(X - M)^2}{N - 1} = \frac{(1.00 + 0.04 + 0.09 + 0.81)}{4 - 1} = \frac{1.94}{3} = 0.647$$

Now we do the same for Y, the people told they are drinking wine from a $90 bottle. Remember to use the mean for Y; it's easy to forget and use the mean we calculated earlier for X. We calculate the mean for Y to be 4.0. The subscript Y indicates that this is the variance for the second sample, whose scores are arbitrarily called Y. (We could call these scores by any letter, but statisticians tend to call the scores in the first two samples X and Y.)

Y	$Y - M$	$(Y - M)^2$
2.9	−1.1	1.21
3.5	−0.5	0.25
3.5	−0.5	0.25
4.9	0.9	0.81
5.2	1.2	1.44

$$s_Y^2 = \frac{\Sigma(Y - M)^2}{N - 1} = \frac{(1.21 + 0.25 + 0.25 + 0.81 + 1.44)}{5 - 1} = \frac{3.96}{4} = 0.990$$

b. We pool the two estimates of variance. Because there are often different numbers of people in each sample, we cannot simply take their mean. We mentioned earlier in this book that estimates of spread taken from smaller samples tend to be less accurate. So we weight the estimate from the smaller sample a bit less and weight the estimate from the larger sample a bit more.

We do this by calculating the proportion of degrees of freedom represented by each sample. Each sample has degrees of freedom of $N - 1$. We also calculate a total degrees of freedom that sums the degrees of freedom for the two samples. Here are the calculations:

$$df_X = N - 1 = 4 - 1 = 3$$
$$df_Y = N - 1 = 5 - 1 = 4$$
$$df_{total} = df_X + df_Y = 3 + 4 = 7$$

Using these degrees of freedom, we calculate a sort of average variance. **Pooled variance** *is a weighted average of the two estimates of variance—one from each sample—that are calculated when conducting an independent-samples* t *test.* The estimate of variance from the larger sample counts for more in the pooled variance than does the estimate from the smaller sample because larger samples tend to lead to somewhat more accurate estimates than do smaller samples. Here's the formula for pooled variance, and the calculations for this example:

$$s_{pooled}^2 = \left(\frac{df_X}{df_{total}}\right)s_X^2 + \left(\frac{df_Y}{df_{total}}\right)s_Y^2 = \left(\frac{3}{7}\right)0.647 + \left(\frac{4}{7}\right)0.990 = 0.277 + 0.566 = 0.843$$

(*Note:* If we had exactly the same number of participants in each sample, this would be an unweighted average—that is, we could compute the average in the usual way by summing the two sample variances and dividing by 2.)

c. Now that we have pooled the variances, we have an estimate of spread. This is similar to the estimate of the standard deviation in the previous *t* tests, but now it's based on two samples (and is an estimate of variance rather than standard deviation). The next calculation in the previous *t* tests was dividing standard deviation by $\sqrt{N}$ to get standard error. In this case, we divide by N instead of $\sqrt{N}$. Why? Because we are dealing with variances, not standard deviations. Variance is the square of standard deviation, so we divide by the square of $\sqrt{N}$, which is simply N. We do this once for each sample, using pooled variance as the estimate of spread. We use pooled variance because an estimate based on two samples is better than an estimate based on one. The key here is to divide by the appropriate N: in this case, 4 for the first sample and 5 for the second sample.

$$s_{M_X}^2 = \frac{s_{pooled}^2}{N_X} = \frac{0.843}{4} = 0.211$$

$$s_{M_Y}^2 = \frac{s_{pooled}^2}{N_Y} = \frac{0.843}{5} = 0.169$$

d. In stage (c), we calculated the variance versions of standard error for each sample, but we want only one such measure of spread when we calculate the test statistic. So, we combine the two variances, similar to the way in which we combined the two estimates of variance in stage (b). This stage is even simpler, however. We merely add the two variances together. When we sum them, we get the variance of the distribution of differences between means, symbolized as $s_{difference}^2$. Here are the formula and the calculations for this example:

$$s_{difference}^2 = s_{M_X}^2 + s_{M_Y}^2 = 0.211 + 0.169 = 0.380$$

e. We now have paralleled the two calculations of the previous *t* tests by doing two things: (1) We calculated an estimate of spread (we made two calculations, one for each sample, then combined them), and (2) we then adjusted the estimate for the sample size (again, we made two calculations, one for each sample, then combined them). The main difference is that we have kept all calculations as variances rather than standard deviations. At this final stage, we convert from variance form to standard deviation form. Because standard deviation is the square root of variance, we do this by simply taking the square root:

$$s_{difference} = \sqrt{s^2_{difference}} = \sqrt{0.380} = 0.616$$

Summary: The mean of the distribution of differences between means is: $\mu_X - \mu_Y = 0$. The standard deviation of the distribution of differences between means is: $s_{difference} = 0.616$.

> **STEP 4: Determine critical values, or cutoffs.**

This step for the independent-samples *t* test is similar to those for previous *t* tests, but we use the total degrees of freedom, df_{total}.

Summary: The critical values, based on a two-tailed test, a *p* level of 0.05, and a df_{total} of 7, are −2.365 and 2.365 (as seen in the curve in Figure 11-2).

> **STEP 5: Calculate the test statistic.**

This step for the independent-samples *t* test is similar to the fifth step in previous *t* tests. Here we subtract the population difference between means based on the null hypothesis from the difference between means for the samples. The formula is:

$$t = \frac{(M_X - M_Y) - (\mu_X - \mu_Y)}{s_{difference}}$$

As in previous *t* tests, the test statistic is calculated by subtracting a number based on the populations from a number based on the samples, then dividing by a version of standard error. Because the population difference between means (according to the null hypothesis) is almost always 0, many statisticians choose to eliminate the latter part of the formula. So the formula for the test statistic for an independent-samples *t* test is often abbreviated as:

$$t = \frac{(M_X - M_Y)}{s_{difference}}$$

MASTERING THE FORMULA

11-4: To calculate the variance of the distribution of differences between means, we sum the variance versions of standard error that we calculated in the previous step: $s^2_{difference} = s^2_{M_X} + s^2_{M_Y}$.

MASTERING THE FORMULA

11-5: To calculate the standard deviation of the distribution of differences between means, we take the square root of the previous calculation, the variance of the distribution of differences between means. The formula is: $s_{difference} = \sqrt{s^2_{difference}}$.

● **Pooled variance** is a weighted average of the two estimates of variance—one from each sample—that are calculated when conducting an independent-samples *t* test.

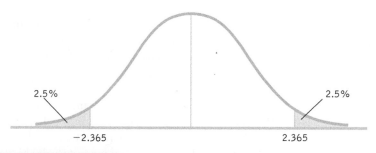

−2.365   2.365

2.5%   2.5%

FIGURE 11-2

Determining Cutoffs for an Independent-Samples *t* Test

To determine the critical values for an independent-samples *t* test, we use the total degrees of freedom, df_{total}. This is the sum of the degrees of freedom for each sample, which is *N* − 1 for each sample.

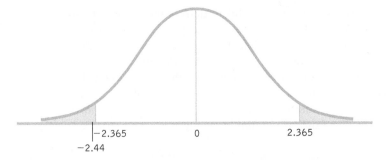

-2.365   0   2.365
-2.44

You might find it easier to use the first formula, however, as it reminds us that we are subtracting the population difference between means according to the null hypothesis (0) from the actual difference between the sample means. This format more closely parallels the formulas of the test statistics we calculated in Chapter 9.

Summary: $t = \dfrac{(2.5 - 4.0) - 0}{0.616} = -2.44$

STEP 6: Make a decision.

This step for the independent-samples *t* test is identical to that for the previous *t* tests. If we reject the null hypothesis, we need to examine the means of the two conditions so that we know the direction of the effect.

Summary: Reject the null hypothesis. It appears that those told they are drinking wine from a $10 bottle give it lower ratings, on average, than those told they are drinking from a $90 bottle (as shown by the curve in Figure 11-3).

This finding documents the fact that people report liking a more expensive wine better than a less expensive one—even when it's the same wine! The researchers documented a similar finding with a narrower gap between prices—$5 and $45. Naysayers might point out, however, that participants drinking an expensive wine may report liking it better than participants drinking an inexpensive wine simply because they are expected to say they like it better because of its price. However, the fMRI that was conducted, which is a more objective measure, yielded a similar finding. Those drinking the supposedly more expensive wines showed increased activation in brain areas such as the medial orbitofrontal cortex, essentially an indication in the brain that people are enjoying an experience. Expectations really do seem to influence us. ●

Reporting the Statistics

To report the statistics as they would appear in a journal article, follow standard APA format. Be sure to include the degrees of freedom, the value of the test statistic, and the *p* value associated with the test statistic. (Note that because the *t* table in Appendix B only includes the *p* values of 0.10, 0.05, and 0.01, we cannot use it to determine the actual *p* value for the test statistic. Unless we use software, we can only report whether or not the *p* value is less than the critical *p* level.) In the current example, the statistics would read:

$$t(7) = -2.44, p < 0.05$$

In addition to the results of hypothesis testing, we would also include the means and standard deviations for the two samples. We calculated the means in step 3 of hypothesis testing, and we also calculated the variances (0.647 for those told they were drinking from a $10 bottle and 0.990 for those told they were drinking from a $90 bottle). We can calculate the standard deviations by taking the square roots of the variances. The descriptive statistics can be reported in parentheses as:

($10 bottle: $M = 2.5$, $SD = 0.80$; $90 bottle: $M = 4.0$, $SD = 0.99$)

CHECK YOUR LEARNING

Reviewing the Concepts

> When we conduct an independent-samples *t* test, we cannot calculate individual difference scores. That is why we compare the mean of one sample with the mean of the other sample.

> The comparison distribution is a distribution of differences between means.

> We use the same six steps of hypothesis testing that we used with the *z* test and with the single-sample and paired-samples *t* tests.

> Conceptually, the *t* test for independent samples makes the same comparisons as the other *t* tests. However, the calculations are different, and the critical values are based on degrees of freedom from two samples.

Clarifying the Concepts **11-1** In what situation do we conduct a paired-samples *t* test? In what situation do we conduct an independent-samples *t* test?

11-2 What is pooled variance?

Calculating the Statistics **11-3** Imagine you have the following data from two independent groups:

Group 1: 3, 2, 4, 6, 1, 2

Group 2: 5, 4, 6, 2, 6

Compute each of the following calculations needed to complete the final calculation of the independent-samples *t* test.

a. Calculate the corrected variance for each group.

b. Calculate the degrees of freedom and pooled variance.

c. Calculate the variance version of standard error for each group.

d. Calculate the variance of the distribution of differences between means, then convert this number to standard deviation.

e. Calculate the test statistic.

Applying the Concepts **11-4** In the previous Check Your Learning exercise, you calculated several statistics; now let's consider a context for those numbers. Steele and Pinto (2006) examined whether people's level of trust in their direct supervisor affected their level of agreement with a policy supported by that leader. They found that the extent to which subordinates agreed with their supervisor was statistically significantly related to trust and showed no relation to gender, age, time on the job, or length of time working with the supervisor. We have presented fictional data to re-create these findings, where group 1 represents employees with low trust in their supervisor and group 2 represents the high-trust employees. The scores presented are the level of agreement with a decision made by a leader, from 1 (strongly disagree) to 7 (strongly agree).

Group 1 (low trust in leader): 3, 2, 4, 6, 1, 2

Group 2 (high trust in leader): 5, 4, 6, 2, 6

a. State the null and research hypotheses.

b. Identify the critical values and make a decision.

c. Write your conclusion in a formal sentence that includes presentation of the statistic in APA format.

Solutions to these Check Your Learning questions can be found in Appendix D.

d. Explain why your results are different from those in the original research, despite having a similar mean difference.

MASTERING THE CONCEPT

11-2: As we can with the *z* test, the single-sample *t* test, and the paired-samples *t* test, we can determine a confidence interval and calculate a measure of effect size—Cohen's *d*—when we conduct an independent-samples *t* test.

Beyond Hypothesis Testing

After working at Guinness, Stella Cunliffe was hired by the British government's criminology department. She noticed that adult male prisoners who had short prison sentences returned to prison at a very high rate—an apparent justification for longer prison sentences. The genius of Stella Cunliffe was that she always looked carefully at the source of the original numbers. This time she discovered that the returning prisoners behind these numbers were almost all older people with mental health problems; they were trapped in the prison system because the mental hospitals would not take them; so, these data did not justify long, harsh prison sentences. Good researchers insist on knowing what the numbers *really* mean.

Two ways that researchers can evaluate the findings of a hypothesis test are by calculating a confidence interval and an effect size.

Calculating a Confidence Interval for an Independent-Samples t Test

Confidence intervals for an independent-samples *t* test are centered around the *difference between means* (rather than the means themselves). So we use the difference between means for the samples and the standard error for the difference between means, $s_{difference}$, which we calculate in an identical manner to the one used in hypothesis testing.

We use the formula for the independent-samples *t* statistic when calculating the raw differences between means. To do this, we use algebra on the original formula for an independent-samples *t* test to isolate the upper and lower mean differences. Here is the original *t* statistic formula:

$$t = \frac{(M_X - M_Y) - (\mu_X - \mu_Y)}{s_{difference}}$$

We replace the population mean difference, $(\mu_X - \mu_Y)$, with the sample mean difference $(M_X - M_Y)_{sample}$, because this is what the confidence interval is centered around. We also indicate that the first mean difference in the numerator refers to the bounds of the confidence intervals, the upper bound in this case:

$$t_{upper} = \frac{(M_X - M_Y)_{upper} - (M_X - M_Y)_{sample}}{s_{difference}}$$

With algebra, we isolate the upper bound of the confidence interval to create the following formula:

$$(M_X - M_Y)_{upper} = t(s_{difference}) + (M_X - M_Y)_{sample}$$

We create the formula for the lower bound of the confidence interval in exactly the same way, using the negative version of the *t* statistic:

$$(M_X - M_Y)_{lower} = -t(s_{difference}) + (M_X - M_Y)_{sample}$$

MASTERING THE FORMULA

11-7: The formulas for the upper and lower bounds of the confidence interval are: $(M_X - M_Y)_{upper} = t(s_{difference}) + (M_X - M_Y)_{sample}$ and $(M_X - M_Y)_{lower} = -t(s_{difference}) + (M_X - M_Y)_{sample}$, respectively. In each case, we multiply the *t* statistic that marks off the tail by the standard error for the differences between means and add it to the difference between means in the sample. Remember that one of the *t* statistics is negative.

EXAMPLE 11.3

Let's calculate the confidence interval that parallels the hypothesis test we conducted earlier, comparing ratings of those who are told they are drinking wine from a $10 bottle and ratings of those told they are drinking wine from a $90 bottle

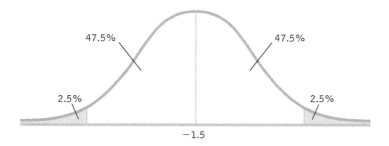

FIGURE 11-4

A 95% Confidence Interval for Differences Between Means, Part I

As with a confidence interval for a single-sample *t* test, we start the confidence interval for a difference between means by drawing a curve with the sample difference between means in the center.

(Plassmann et al., 2008). The difference between the means of these samples was calculated in the numerator of the *t* statistic. It is $2.5 - 4.0 = -1.5$. (Note that the order of subtraction in calculating the difference between means is irrelevant; we could just as easily have subtracted 2.5 from 4.0 and gotten a positive result, 1.5.) The standard error for the differences between means, $s_{difference}$, was calculated to be 0.616. The degrees of freedom were determined to be 7. Here are the five steps for determining a confidence interval for a difference between means:

> **STEP 1:** Draw a normal curve with the sample difference between means in the center (as shown in Figure 11-4).

> **STEP 2:** Indicate the bounds of the confidence interval on either end, and write the percentages under each segment of the curve (see Figure 11-4).

> **STEP 3:** Look up the *t* statistics for the lower and upper ends of the confidence interval in the *t* table.

Use a two-tailed test and a *p* level of 0.05 (which corresponds to a 95% confidence interval). Use the degrees of freedom—7—that we calculated earlier. The table indicates a *t* statistic of 2.365. Because the normal curve is symmetric, the bounds of the confidence interval fall at *t* statistics of −2.365 and 2.365. (Note that these cutoffs are identical to those used for the independent-samples *t* test because the *p* level of 0.05 corresponds to a confidence level of 95%.) We add those *t* statistics to the normal curve, as in Figure 11-5.

> **STEP 4:** Convert the *t* statistics to raw differences between means for the lower and upper ends of the confidence interval.

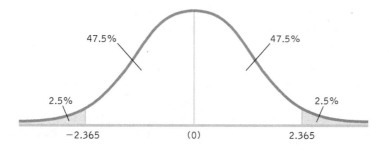

FIGURE 11-5

A 95% Confidence Interval for Differences Between Means, Part II

The next step in calculating a confidence interval is identifying the *t* statistics that indicate each end of the interval. Because the curve is symmetric, the *t* statistics have the same magnitude—one is negative and one is positive.

FIGURE 11-6

A 95% Confidence Interval for Differences Between Means, Part III

The final step in calculating a confidence interval is converting the *t* statistics that indicate each end of the interval into raw differences between means.

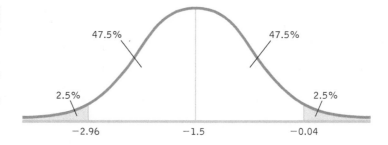

For the lower end, the formula is:

$$(M_X - M_Y)_{lower} = -t(s_{difference}) + (M_X - M_Y)_{sample}$$
$$= -2.365(0.616) + (-1.5) = -2.96$$

For the upper end, the formula is:

$$(M_X - M_Y)_{upper} = t(s_{difference}) + (M_X - M_Y)_{sample}$$
$$= 2.365(0.616) + (-1.5) = -0.04$$

The confidence interval is $[-2.96, -0.04]$, as shown in Figure 11-6.

> **STEP 5: Check your answer.**

Each end of the confidence interval should be exactly the same distance from the sample mean.

$$-2.96 - (-1.5) = -1.46$$
$$-0.04 - (-1.5) = 1.46$$

The interval checks out. The bounds of the confidence interval are calculated as the difference between sample means, plus or minus 1.46. Also, the confidence interval does not include 0; thus, it is not plausible that there is no difference between means. We can conclude that people told they are drinking wine from a $10 bottle give different ratings, on average, than those told they are drinking wine from a $90 bottle. When we conducted the independent-samples *t* test earlier, we rejected the null hypothesis and drew the same conclusion as we did with the confidence interval. But the confidence interval provides more information because it is an interval estimate rather than a point estimate. ●

Calculating Effect Size for an Independent-Samples *t* Test

As with all hypothesis tests, it is recommended that the results be supplemented with an effect size. For an independent-samples *t* test, as with other *t* tests, we can use Cohen's *d* as the measure of effect size.

EXAMPLE 11.4

The fictional data on which we conducted an independent-samples *t* test provided means of 2.5 for those told they were drinking wine from a $10 bottle and 4.0 for those told they were drinking wine from a $90 bottle (Plassmann et al., 2008).

Previously, we calculated a standard error for the difference between means, $s_{difference}$, of 0.616. Here are the calculations we performed:

Stage (a) (variance for each sample):

$$s_X^2 = \frac{\Sigma(X - M)^2}{N - 1} = 0.647$$

$$s_Y^2 = \frac{\Sigma(Y - M)^2}{N - 1} = 0.990$$

Stage (b) (combining variances):

$$s_{pooled}^2 = \left(\frac{df_X}{df_{total}}\right)s_X^2 + \left(\frac{df_Y}{df_{total}}\right)s_Y^2 = 0.843$$

Stage (c) (variance form of standard error for each sample):

$$s_{M_X}^2 = \frac{s_{pooled}^2}{N_X} = 0.211; \; s_{M_Y}^2 = \frac{s_{pooled}^2}{N_Y} = 0.169$$

Stage (d) (combining variance forms of standard error):

$$s_{difference}^2 = s_{M_X}^2 + s_{M_Y}^2 = 0.380$$

Stage (e) (converting the variance form of standard error to the standard deviation form of standard error):

$$s_{difference} = \sqrt{s_{difference}^2} = 0.616$$

Because the goal is to disregard the influence of sample size in order to calculate Cohen's d, we want to use the standard deviation, rather than the standard error, in the denominator. So we can ignore the last three stages, all of which contribute to the calculation of standard error. That leaves stages (a) and (b). It makes more sense to use the one that includes information from both samples, so we focus our attention on stage (b). Here is where many students make a mistake. What we have calculated in stage (b) is pooled *variance*, not pooled *standard deviation*. We must take the square root of the pooled variance to get the pooled standard deviation, the appropriate value for the denominator of Cohen's d.

$$s_{pooled} = \sqrt{s_{pooled}^2} = \sqrt{0.843} = 0.918$$

The test statistic that we calculated for this study was:

$$t = \frac{(M_X - M_Y) - (\mu_X - \mu_Y)}{s_{difference}} = \frac{(2.5 - 4.0) - (0)}{0.616} = -2.44$$

For Cohen's d, we simply replace the denominator with standard deviation, s_{pooled}, instead of standard error, $s_{difference}$.

$$\text{Cohen's } d = \frac{(M_X - M_Y) - (\mu_X - \mu_Y)}{s_{pooled}} = \frac{(2.5 - 4.0) - (0)}{0.918} = -1.63$$

For this study, the effect size is reported as: $d = 1.63$. The two sample means are 1.63 standard deviations apart. According to the conventions that we learned in Chapter 8 and are shown again in Table 11-2, this is a large effect. ●

TABLE 11-2	Cohen's Conventions for Effect Sizes: *d*

Jacob Cohen has published guidelines (or conventions), based on the overlap between two distributions, to help researchers determine whether an effect is small, medium, or large. These numbers are not cutoffs; they are merely rough guidelines to help researchers interpret results.

Effect Size	Convention	Overlap
Small	0.2	85%
Medium	0.5	67%
Large	0.8	53%

Next Steps — The Bayesian Approach to Data Analysis

Prior Beliefs about Pizza When we encounter new information in everyday life, we evaluate it in terms of what we already know. If your friend tells you your favorite pizza place is closing, and you were just there, you're not as likely to believe it as if you had not been by in months.

Some ideas just won't go away. One of them, Bayesian analysis, named for Thomas Bayes, is having a resurgence in the field of psychology. Bayes (1763) was a non-conformist minister whose statistical idea proposed that we should not just rely on the data at hand, but should also consider what we already know (Kruschke, 2010a). John Kruschke, a modern-day proponent of Bayesian analysis, points out that in real life we examine new data and determine "how much we should change our beliefs relative to our prior beliefs" (2011; p. 277; Gallistel, 2015b). Kruschke and other experts go so far to call this shift in thinking a revolution, noting that this way of statistical thinking is more intuitive and straightforward than hypothesis testing (2010b; Gallistel, 2015a).

Here's an example of how you already think in terms of Bayesian analysis in your own life. A friend mentions that your favorite pizza place is closing. But you say, "No, it can't be. I was there just last night and no one mentioned it." Your prior beliefs affect the likelihood that you believe your friend. Later that day, you walk by your pizza place and it is indeed closed, but you're still not convinced. Maybe they're just opening late today or doing renovations. However, this new information, coupled with your friend's comment, makes you start to believe that your pizza place might be closing for good. You check their Web site, and it's down—even more evidence to consider. Bayesian analysis is built on this logic: Each new piece of data is evaluated in terms of a growing set of prior beliefs (rather than in a vacuum).

So Bayesian statistics help us to take both prior beliefs—"priors" for short—and probabilities into account. We might respond, "Isn't that what statistics already do?" For the most part, the answer is "no." The traditional approach to statistical inference assumes that we never learn from prior experience—the comparison distribution is always some version of chance. For example, with an independent-samples *t* test, we typically analyze the data against a null hypothesis of no difference, regardless of what previous research has found. The issue here is that often we already know quite a bit from previous research. Bayesian analysis allows us to use these priors (Kruschke, 2010c).

John Kruschke offers an example of Bayesian thinking that leads to different conclusions based on two different priors—a strong prior belief and a weak prior belief (2010a). Imagine that a particular event occurs 535 out of 1000 times. How likely are you to believe that this is higher than chance, which would be 500 out of 1000 times? Let's say that the "event" that occurs is a coin flip that lands on heads. If it's a coin that you know to be real—that is, you know that it's an official coin rather than a trick one—you're not likely to conclude that it's a biased coin if it comes up heads 535 out of 1000 times. As Kruschke puts it, you have a "strong prior belief that the coin is fair" (p. 663). On the other hand, Kruschke asks us to imagine that we are "parachuted into a random foreign city where two candidates are running for mayor" (p. 663). In this case, we have no prior belief—or what Kruschke calls a weak prior belief—about the percentage of the population that is likely to vote for each of these candidates. So, if a poll indicates that 535 out of 1000 people here prefer one of the candidates, we might be pretty confident that this reflects the true underlying voting intentions of the population of this city.

It turns out that children are particularly good at thinking in this way—that is, in using prior probabilities from actual data. In one study, children between 19 and 24 months old watched a researcher do one of two things: (1) remove five green toy frogs from a box containing mostly toy frogs or (2) remove five toy frogs from a box containing mostly yellow toy ducks (Kushnir, Xu, & Wellman, 2010). (Some children experienced the opposite conditions—five toy *ducks* were removed from a box that contained either mostly toy frogs or mostly toy ducks. The findings for both versions were combined, but we'll focus on the toy frog version here.) Later, an assistant then gave the child two small bowls of toys—one all green frogs and one all yellow ducks. The researcher then asked the child to give her some toys and the researchers recorded which toy the child touched first and which they eventually offered to the researcher.

If the researcher removed the frogs from a box of mostly frogs, then the child was just as likely to touch a duck as a frog, and then give the duck to the researcher. However, if the researcher picked out the frogs from among the box of mostly ducks, the child was more likely to touch a frog, and then give the frog to the researcher. In this second case, the children seemed to guess that the researcher preferred frogs, given that she went out of her way to choose them. The children's prior beliefs about what the researcher wanted, which used data-based observations of probability, affected their behavior.

Kruschke and other researchers argue that Bayesian analysis should entirely replace hypothesis testing (Kruschke, 2011). And, eventually, it may just do that. For now, most statistics students still learn how to conduct hypothesis testing. But if you go on to graduate school and have the opportunity to take a course in Bayesian analysis, we strongly encourage you to do so. For now, the implications of Bayesian reasoning are just starting to hit behavioral statistics, and we can't definitively predict where Bayesian reasoning will take us next. But it's an impressive outcome for an obscure clergyman who was born at the beginning of the eighteenth century.

CHECK YOUR LEARNING

Reviewing the Concepts
> A confidence interval can be created with a *t* distribution around a difference between means.
> We can calculate an effect size, Cohen's *d*, for an independent-samples *t* test.
> Bayesian statistics approach statistical analysis in a different way from traditional hypothesis testing. The main difference is that they take both prior beliefs—"priors" for short—and probabilities into account, whereas traditional hypothesis testing is based just on probabilities.

Clarifying the Concepts   **11-5**   Why do we calculate confidence intervals?

11-6   How does considering the conclusions in terms of effect size help to prevent incorrect interpretations of the findings?

continued on next page

Calculating the Statistics **11-7**	Use the hypothetical data on level of agreement with a supervisor, as listed here, to calculate the following. We already made some of these calculations for Check Your Learning 11-3.

Group 1 (low trust in leader): 3, 2, 4, 6, 1, 2

Group 2 (high trust in leader): 5, 4, 6, 2, 6

a. Calculate the 95% confidence interval.

b. Calculate effect size using Cohen's *d*.

Applying the Concepts **11-8**	Explain what the confidence interval calculated in Check Your Learning 11-7 tells us. Why is this confidence interval superior to the hypothesis test that we conducted?
Solutions to these Check Your Learning questions can be found in Appendix D. **11-9**	Interpret the meaning of the effect size calculated in Check Your Learning 11-7. What does this add to the confidence interval and hypothesis test?

REVIEW OF CONCEPTS

Conducting an Independent-Samples t Test

We use *independent-samples* t *tests* when we have two samples and different participants are in each sample. Because the samples comprise different people, we cannot calculate difference scores, so the comparison distribution is a distribution of differences between means. Because we are working with two separate samples of scores (rather than one set of difference scores) when we conduct an independent-samples *t* test, we need additional steps to calculate an estimate of spread. As part of these steps, we calculate estimates of variance from each sample, and then combine them to create a *pooled variance*. We can present the statistics in APA style as we did with other hypothesis tests.

Beyond Hypothesis Testing

As with other forms of hypothesis testing, it is useful to replace or supplement the independent-samples *t* test with a confidence interval. A confidence interval can be created around a difference between means using a *t* distribution. To understand the importance of a finding, we must also calculate an effect size. With an independent-samples *t* test, as with other *t* tests, a common effect-size measure is Cohen's *d*.

Bayesian statistics approach statistical analysis in a different way from traditional hypothesis testing. The main difference is that they take both prior beliefs—"priors" for short—and probabilities into account, whereas traditional hypothesis testing is based just on probabilities.

SPSS®

We can conduct an independent-samples *t* test using SPSS for the wine-tasting data we presented earlier in this chapter. To begin, let's identify the variables included in the problem. First, there is the dependent variable: rating of the bottle of wine. Second, there is the independent variable: whether the participant was told it was a $10 bottle of wine or a $90 bottle of wine. This is a categorical variable that has two levels. We need to tell SPSS that this variable is categorical

as well as the different levels for each category. To do so, participants are given a "1" if they were told the wine was from a $10 bottle and a "2" if they were told that the wine was from a $90 bottle. We can then use the "Values" function in the Variable View to tell SPSS that 1 = $10 and 2 = $90. We also want to be sure to change the "Measures" function in the Variable View to "nominal" for this variable. For an independent-samples *t* test, the independent variable can either be a nominal variable or an ordinal variable. The dependent variable should always be a scale variable.

We place each participant's data in one row—an arbitrarily assigned ID number in the first column, a score for the stated cost of the wine in the second column, and a liking rating in the third column. Remember: generally speaking, it is a good rule of thumb to always give each participant an ID number. That way, we can always double-check any data that appear to be incorrect. We can now conduct the hypothesis test.

Note: When we are in Data View, we can switch between showing the actual value labels (i.e., $10 or $90 in this study) or the numbers assigned to each group (i.e., 1 or 2). Under the "view" menu at the top, we either check or uncheck the option "value labels" to turn the labels on or off. This does not change the data. This simply changes the way we see the data.

Select Analyze → Compare Means → Independent-Samples T Test. First, we choose the dependent variable, "Rating," by clicking it, then clicking the arrow in the upper center. We'll now see "Rating" in the box titled "Test Variable." Second, we choose the independent variable, "Cost," by clicking it, then clicking the arrow in the lower center. We'll now see "Cost" in the box titled "Grouping Variable." Again, we need to tell SPSS

what two groups we are comparing. To do so, we click the "Define Groups" button, then provide the values for each level of the independent variable. For example, we enter "1" for group 1 (aka the $10 group) and "2" for group 2 (aka the $90 group), and click "Continue." Then we click "OK."

The output is shown in the screenshot below. In the first table, "Group Statistics," we see means and standard deviations for each group: participants told they were drinking wine from a $10 bottle and participants told they were drinking wine from a $90 bottle. For example, the output tells us that the mean for those told they were drinking wine from a $10 bottle is 2.50, with a standard deviation of 0.80416.

In the second output table, "Independent-Samples Test," we focus our attention on the top line. We can see that the *t* statistic is −2.436, with a *p* value (under "Sig. (2-tailed)") of 0.045. The *t* statistic is the same as the one we calculated earlier, −2.44. We can also see the mean difference (the numerator used to calculate the *t* statistic), the standard error difference (the denominator used to calculate the *t* statistic), and the 95% confidence interval for the *t* statistic. These values should also match the previously calculated values presented in the example earlier.

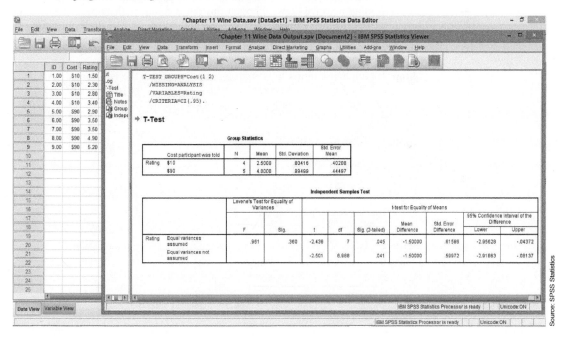

Source: SPSS Statistics

HOW IT WORKS

11.1 INDEPENDENT-SAMPLES *t* TEST

Who do you think have a better sense of humor—women or men? Researchers at Stanford University examined brain activity in women and men during exposure to humorous cartoons (Azim, Mobbs, Jo, Menon, & Reiss, 2005). Using fMRI (functional magnetic resonance imaging), researchers observed more activity in the reward centers of women's brains than men's, the same reward centers that respond when receiving money or feeling happy. The researchers suggested that this might be because women have lower expectations of humor than do men, so they find it more rewarding when something is actually funny.

However, the researchers were aware of other possible explanations for these findings. For example, they considered whether one gender is more likely to find humorous stimuli funny to begin with. In this study, men and women indicated the percentage of 30 cartoons that they perceived to be either "funny" or "unfunny." Below are fictional data for nine people (four women and five men); these fictional data have approximately the same means as in the original study.

Percentage of cartoons labeled as "funny"

Women: 84, 97, 58, 90
Men: 88, 90, 52, 97, 86

How can we conduct all six steps of hypothesis testing for an independent-samples *t* test for this scenario, using a two-tailed test with critical values based on a *p* level of 0.05? Here are the steps:

Step 1: Population 1: Women exposed to humorous cartoons. Population 2: Men exposed to humorous cartoons.

The comparison distribution will be a distribution of differences between means based on the null hypothesis. The hypothesis test will be an independent-samples *t* test because we have two samples composed of different groups of participants. This study meets only the first of the three assumptions. (1) The dependent variable is a percentage of cartoons categorized as "funny," which is a scale variable. (2) However, we do not know whether the population is normally distributed, and there are not at least 30 participants. Moreover, the data suggest some negative skew; although this test is robust with respect to this assumption, we must be cautious. (3) The men and women in this study were not randomly selected from among all men and women, so we must be cautious with respect to generalizing these findings.

Step 2: Null hypothesis: On average, women categorize the same percentage of cartoons as "funny" as men—H_0: $\mu_1 = \mu_2$. Research hypothesis: On average, women categorize a different percentage of cartoons as "funny" as compared with men—H_1: $\mu_1 \neq \mu_2$.

Step 3: $(\mu_1 - \mu_2) = 0$; $s_{difference} = 11.641$

Calculations:

a. $M_X = 82.25$

X	X − M	$(X - M)^2$
84	1.75	3.063
97	14.75	217.563
58	−24.25	588.063
90	7.75	60.063

$$s_X^2 = \frac{\Sigma(X - M)^2}{N - 1} = \frac{(3.063 + 217.563 + 588.063 + 60.063)}{4 - 1} = 289.584$$

$M_Y = 82.6$

Y	Y − M	$(Y - M)^2$
88	5.4	29.16
90	7.4	54.76
52	−30.6	936.36
97	14.4	207.36
86	3.4	11.56

$$s_Y^2 = \frac{\Sigma(Y - M)^2}{N - 1} = \frac{(29.16 + 54.76 + 936.36 + 207.36 + 11.56)}{5 - 1} = 309.800$$

b. $df_X = N - 1 = 4 - 1 = 3$

$df_Y = N - 1 = 5 - 1 = 4$

$df_{total} = df_X + df_Y = 3 + 4 = 7$

$s^2_{pooled} = \left(\dfrac{df_X}{df_{total}}\right)s^2_X + \left(\dfrac{df_Y}{df_{total}}\right)s^2_Y = \left(\dfrac{3}{7}\right)289.584 + \left(\dfrac{4}{7}\right)309.800 = 124.107 + 177.029 = 301.136$

c. $s^2_{M_X} = \dfrac{s^2_{pooled}}{N_X} = \dfrac{301.136}{4} = 75.284$

$s^2_{M_Y} = \dfrac{s^2_{pooled}}{N_Y} = \dfrac{301.136}{5} = 60.227$

d. $s^2_{difference} = s^2_{M_X} + s^2_{M_Y} = 75.284 + 60.227 = 135.511$

e. $s_{difference} = \sqrt{s^2_{difference}} = \sqrt{135.511} = 11.641$

Step 4: The critical values, based on a two-tailed test, a *p* level of 0.05, and a df_{total} of 7, are −2.365 and 2.365 (as seen in the curve in Figure 11-2 on page 281).

Step 5: $t = \dfrac{(82.25 - 82.6) - (0)}{11.641} = 0.03$

Step 6: Fail to reject the null hypothesis. We conclude that there is no evidence from this study to support the research hypothesis that either men or women are more likely than the opposite gender, on average, to find cartoons funny.

11.2 REPORTING THE STATISTICS IN A JOURNAL

How would we report the results of the hypothesis test described in How It Works 11.1? The statistics would appear in a journal article as: $t(7) = -0.03, p > 0.05$. In addition to the results of hypothesis testing, we would also include the means and standard deviations for the two samples. We calculated the means in step 3 of hypothesis testing, and we also calculated the variances. We can calculate the standard deviations by taking the square roots of the variances. The descriptive statistics can be reported in parentheses as:

(Women: $M = 82.25$, $SD = 17.02$; Men: $M = 82.60$, $SD = 17.60$)

11.3 CONFIDENCE INTERVALS FOR AN INDEPENDENT-SAMPLES *t* TEST

How would we calculate a 95% confidence interval for the independent-samples *t* test we conducted in How It Works 11.1? Previously, we calculated the difference between the means of these samples to be $82.25 - 82.6 = -0.35$; the standard error for the differences between means, $s_{difference}$, to be 11.641; and the degrees of freedom to be 7. (Note that the order of subtraction in calculating the difference between means is irrelevant; we could just as easily have subtracted 82.25 from 82.6 and gotten a positive result, 0.35.)

1. We draw a normal curve with the sample difference between means in the center.
2. We indicate the bounds of the 95% confidence interval on either end and write the percentages under each segment of the curve: 2.5% in each tail.
3. We look up the *t* statistics for the lower and upper ends of the confidence interval in the *t* table, based on a two-tailed test, a *p* level of 0.05 (which corresponds to a 95% confidence interval), and the degrees of freedom—7—that we calculated earlier. Because the normal curve is symmetric, the bounds of the confidence interval fall at *t* statistics of −2.365 and 2.365. We add those *t* statistics to the normal curve.
4. We convert the *t* statistics to raw differences between means for the lower and upper ends of the confidence interval.

$(M_X - M_Y)_{lower} = -t(s_{difference}) + (M_X - M_Y)_{sample} = -2.365(11.641) + (-0.35) = -27.88$

$(M_X - M_Y)_{upper} = t(s_{difference}) + (M_X - M_Y)_{sample} = 2.365(11.641) + (-0.35) = 27.18$

The confidence interval is $[-27.88, 27.18]$.

5. We check the answer; each end of the confidence interval should be exactly the same distance from the sample mean.

$$-27.88 - (-0.35) = -27.53$$
$$27.18 - (-0.35) = 27.53$$

The interval checks out, and we know that the margin of error is 27.53.

11.4 EFFECT SIZE FOR AN INDEPENDENT-SAMPLES *t* TEST

How can we calculate an effect size for the independent-samples *t* test we conducted in How It Works 11.1? In How It Works 11.1, we calculated means of 82.25 for women and 82.6 for men. Previously, we calculated a standard error for the difference between means, $s_{difference}$, of 11.641. This time, we'll take the square root of the pooled variance to get the pooled standard deviation, the appropriate value for the denominator of Cohen's *d*.

$$s_{pooled} = \sqrt{s_{pooled}^2} = \sqrt{301.136} = 17.353$$

For Cohen's *d*, we simply replace the denominator of the formula for the test statistic with the standard deviation, s_{pooled}, instead of the standard error, $s_{difference}$.

$$\text{Cohen's } d = \frac{(M_X - M_Y) - (\mu_X - \mu_Y)}{s_{pooled}} = \frac{(82.25 - 82.6) - (0)}{17.353} = -0.02$$

According to Cohen's conventions, this is not even near the level of a small effect.

EXERCISES

Clarifying the Concepts

11.1 When is it appropriate to use the independent-samples *t* test?

11.2 Explain random assignment and what it controls.

11.3 What are independent events?

11.4 Explain how the paired-samples *t* test helps us evaluate individual differences and the independent-samples *t* test helps us evaluate group differences.

11.5 As they relate to comparison distributions, what is the difference between *mean differences* and *differences between means*?

11.6 As measures of variability, what is the difference between standard deviation and variance?

11.7 What is the difference between s_X^2 and s_Y^2?

11.8 What is pooled variance?

11.9 Why would we want the variability estimate based on a larger sample to count more (to be more heavily weighted) than one based on a smaller sample?

11.10 Define the symbols in the following formula: $s_{difference}^2 = s_{M_X}^2 + s_{M_Y}^2$

11.11 How do confidence intervals relate to margin of error?

11.12 What is the difference between pooled variance and pooled standard deviation?

11.13 How does the size of the confidence interval relate to the precision of the prediction?

11.14 Why does the effect-size calculation use standard deviation rather than standard error?

11.15 Explain how we determine standard deviation (needed to calculate Cohen's *d*) from the several steps of calculations we made to determine standard error.

11.16 For an independent-samples *t* test, what is the difference between the formula for the *t* statistic and the formula for Cohen's *d*?

11.17 How do we interpret effect size using Cohen's *d*?

Calculating the Statistic

11.18 In the next column are several sample means. For each class, calculate the differences between the means for students who sit in the front versus the back of a classroom.

Mean Test Grades	Students in the Front	Students in the Back
Class 1	82	78
Class 2	79.5	77.41
Class 3	71.5	76
Class 4	72	71.3

11.19 Consider the following data from two independent groups:

Group 1: 97, 83, 105, 102, 92

Group 2: 111, 103, 96, 106

a. Calculate s^2 for group 1 and for group 2.

b. Calculate df_X, df_Y, and df_{total}.

c. Determine the critical values for *t*, assuming a two-tailed test with a *p* level of 0.05.

d. Calculate pooled variance, s^2_{pooled}.

e. Calculate the variance version of standard error for each group.

f. Calculate the variance and the standard deviation of the distribution of differences between means.

g. Calculate the *t* statistic.

h. Calculate the 95% confidence interval.

i. Calculate Cohen's *d*.

11.20 Consider the following data from two independent groups:

Liberals: 2, 1, 3, 2

Conservatives: 4, 3, 3, 5, 2, 4

a. Calculate s^2 for each group.

b. Calculate df_X, df_Y, and df_{total}.

c. Determine the critical values for *t*, assuming a two-tailed test with a *p* level of 0.05.

d. Calculate pooled variance, s^2_{pooled}.

e. Calculate the variance version of standard error for each group.

f. Calculate the variance and the standard deviation of the distribution of differences between means.

g. Calculate the *t* statistic.

h. Calculate the 95% confidence interval.

i. Calculate Cohen's *d*.

11.21 Find the critical *t* values for the following data sets:

a. Group 1 has 21 participants and group 2 has 16 participants. You are performing a two-tailed test with a *p* level of 0.05.

b. You studied 3-year-old children and 6-year-old children, with samples of 12 and 16, respectively. You are performing a two-tailed test with a *p* level of 0.01.

c. You have a total of 17 degrees of freedom for a two-tailed test and a *p* level of 0.10.

Applying the Concepts

11.22 **Making a decision:** Numeric results for several independent-samples *t* tests are presented here. Decide whether each test is statistically significant, and report each result in the standard APA format.

a. A total of 73 people were studied, 40 in one group and 33 in the other group. The test statistic was calculated as 2.13 for a two-tailed test with a *p* level of 0.05.

b. One group of 23 people was compared to another group of 18 people. The *t* statistic obtained for their data was 1.77. Assume you were performing a two-tailed test with a *p* level of 0.05.

c. One group of nine mice was compared to another group of six mice, using a two-tailed test at a *p* level of 0.01. The test statistic was calculated as 3.02.

11.23 **The independent-samples *t* test, hypnosis, and the Stroop effect:** Using data from Exercise 10.33 on the effects of posthypnotic suggestion on the Stroop effect (Raz, Fan, & Posner, 2005), let's conduct an independent-samples *t* test. For this test, we will pretend that two sets of people participated in the study, a between-groups design, whereas previously we considered data from a within-groups design. The first score for each original participant will be in the first sample—those not receiving a posthypnotic suggestion. The second score for each original participant will be in the second sample—those receiving a posthypnotic suggestion.

Sample 1: 12.6, 13.8, 11.6, 12.2, 12.1, 13.0

Sample 2: 8.5, 9.6, 10.0, 9.2, 8.9, 10.8

a. Conduct all six steps of an independent-samples *t* test. Be sure to label all six steps.

b. Report the statistics as you would in a journal article.

c. What happens to the test statistic when you switch from having all participants be in both samples to having two separate samples? Given the same numbers, is it easier to reject the null hypothesis with a within-groups design or with a between-groups design?

d. In your own words, why do you think it is easier to reject the null hypothesis in one of these situations than in the other?

e. Calculate the 95% confidence interval.

f. State in your own words what we learn from this confidence interval.

g. What information does the confidence interval give us that we also get from the hypothesis test?

h. What additional information does the confidence interval give us that we do not get from the hypothesis test?

i. Calculate the appropriate measure of effect size.

j. Based on Cohen's conventions, is this a small, medium, or large effect size?

k. Why is it useful to have this information in addition to the results of a hypothesis test?

11.24 **An independent-samples *t* test and getting ready for a date:** In an example we sometimes use in our statistics classes, several semesters' worth of male and female students were asked how long, in minutes, they spend getting ready for a date. The data reported below reflect the actual means and the approximate standard deviations for the actual data from 142 students.

Men: 28, 35, 52, 14

Women: 30, 82, 53, 61

a. Conduct all six steps of an independent-samples *t* test. Be sure to label all six steps.

b. Report the statistics as you would in a journal article.

c. Calculate the 95% confidence interval.

d. Calculate the 90% confidence interval.

e. How are the confidence intervals different from each other? Explain why they are different.

f. Calculate the appropriate measure of effect size.

g. Based on Cohen's conventions, is this a small, medium, or large effect size?

h. Why is it useful to have this information in addition to the results of a hypothesis test?

11.25 An independent-samples *t* test, gender, and talk-ativeness: "Are Women Really More Talkative Than Men?" is the title of an article that appeared in the journal *Science*. In the article, Mehl, Vazire, Ramirez-Esparza, Slatcher, & Pennebaker (2007) report the results of a study of 396 men and women. Each participant wore a microphone that recorded every word he or she uttered. The researchers counted the number of words uttered by men and women and compared them. The data below are fictional but they re-create the pattern that Mehl and colleagues observed:

Men: 16,345 17,222 15,646 14,889 16,701

Women: 17,345 15,593 16,624 16,696 14,200

a. Conduct all six steps of an independent-samples *t* test. Be sure to label all six steps.

b. Report the statistics as you would in a journal article.

c. Calculate the 95% confidence interval.

d. Express the confidence interval in writing, according to the format discussed in the chapter.

e. State in your own words what we learn from this confidence interval.

f. Calculate the appropriate measure of effect size.

g. Based on Cohen's conventions, is this a small, medium, or large effect size?

h. Why is it useful to have this information in addition to the results of a hypothesis test?

11.26 An independent-samples *t* test and getting people to turn off the light: Do you turn off the light when you leave the room? South Korean researchers wondered how they could increase the number of people who do (Ahn, Kim, & Aggarwal, 2013). They compared two poster campaigns. In one, an image of a light bulb was anthropomorphized by giving it eyes, nose, and a mouth, as well as adding the words, "I'm burning hot, turn me off when you leave!" (p. 225). In a second, there were no human features on the light bulb and the text simply said, "Our bulbs are burning hot, turn the lights off when you leave!" (p. 226). Participants were randomly assigned to view one of these posters

and then were asked to rate a series of items about how likely they would be to behave in an environmentally friendly manner. The scale went from 1 (very unlikely) to 9 (very likely). The summary statistics for the data below approximate the actual means and standard errors in the study.

Anthropomorphism	Nonanthropomorphism
7.2	5.3
8.1	6.2
7.5	6.5
6.9	7.0
6.6	5.6
7.4	6.8
6.5	6.2

a. Conduct all six steps of an independent-samples *t* test. Be sure to label all six steps.

b. Report the statistics as you would in a journal article.

c. Is there a shortcut you could or did use to compute your hypothesis test? (*Hint:* There are equal numbers of participants in the two groups.)

d. Calculate the 95% confidence interval.

e. State in your own words what we learn from this confidence interval.

f. Explain why interval estimates are better than point estimates.

g. Calculate the appropriate measure of effect size.

h. Based on Cohen's conventions, is this a small, medium, or large effect size?

i. Why is it useful to have this information in addition to the results of a hypothesis test?

11.27 An independent-samples *t* test, award-winning television, and the theory of mind: Does watching award-winning fiction on television help us to understand other people? Psychologists Jessica Black and Jennifer Barnes tested whether people who watched award-winning fictional television shows like *Mad Men* and *The West Wing* performed better on a test of theory of mind than people who watch documentaries like episodes from the series *Shark Week* and *How the Universe Works* (2015). After randomly watching either a high-quality fictional show or a documentary for about a half-hour, participants were asked to look at a series of 36 photos of people's eyes and decide if each person was jealous, panicked, arrogant, or hateful. Scores ranged from 0 (guessed no emotions correctly) to 36 (guessed every emotion correctly). The data below approximate the actual means and standard errors in the study.

TV Fiction	Documentary
28	27
30	26
31	28
27	29
29	29
29	28
31	27
27	26
29	

a. Conduct all six steps of an independent-samples *t* test. Be sure to label all six steps.

b. Report the statistics as you would in a journal article.

c. Calculate the 95% confidence interval.

d. State in your own words what we learn from this confidence interval.

e. Express the confidence interval, in a sentence, as a margin of error.

f. Calculate the appropriate measure of effect size.

g. Based on Cohen's conventions, is this a small, medium, or large effect size?

h. Why is it useful to have this information in addition to the results of a hypothesis test?

11.28 Choosing a hypothesis test: For each of the following three scenarios, state which hypothesis test you would use from among the four introduced so far: the *z* test, the single-sample *t* test, the paired-samples *t* test, and the independent-samples *t* test. (*Note:* In the actual studies described, the researchers did not always use one of these tests, often because the actual experiment had additional variables.) Explain your answer.

a. A study of 40 children who had survived a brain tumor revealed that the children were more likely to have behavioral and emotional difficulties than were children who had not experienced such a trauma (Upton & Eiser, 2006). Parents rated children's difficulties, and the ratings data were compared with known means from published population norms.

b. Talarico and Rubin (2003) recorded the memories of 54 students just after the terrorist attacks in the United States on September 11, 2001— some memories related to the terrorist attacks on that day (called *flashbulb memories* for their vividness and emotional content) and some everyday memories. They found that flashbulb memories were no more consistent over time than everyday memories, even though they were perceived to be more accurate.

c. The HOPE VI Panel Study (Popkin & Woodley, 2002) was initiated to test a U.S. program aimed at improving troubled public housing developments. Residents of five HOPE VI developments were examined at the beginning of the study so researchers could later ascertain whether their quality of life had improved. Means at the beginning of the study were compared to known national data sources (e.g., the U.S. Census, the American Housing Survey) that had summary statistics, including means and standard deviations.

11.29 Choosing a hypothesis test: For each of the following three scenarios, state which hypothesis test you would use from among the four introduced so far: the *z* test, the single-sample *t* test, the paired-samples *t* test, and the independent-samples *t* test. (*Note:* In the actual studies described, the researchers did not always use one of these tests, often because the actual experiment had additional variables.) Explain your answer.

a. Taylor and Ste-Marie (2001) studied eating disorders in 41 Canadian female figure skaters. They compared the figure skaters' data on the Eating Disorder Inventory to the means of known populations, including women with eating disorders. On average, the figure skaters were more similar to the population of women with eating disorders than to those without eating disorders.

b. In an article titled "A Fair and Balanced Look at the News: What Affects Memory for Controversial Arguments," Wiley (2005) found that people with a high level of previous knowledge about a given controversial topic (e.g., abortion, military intervention) had better average recall for arguments on both sides of that issue than did those with lower levels of knowledge.

c. Engle-Friedman and colleagues (2003) studied the effects of sleep deprivation. Fifty students were assigned to one night of sleep loss (students were required to call the laboratory every half-hour all night) and then one night of no sleep loss (normal sleep). The next day, students were offered a choice of math problems with differing levels of difficulty. Following sleep loss, students tended to choose less challenging problems.

11.30 Null and research hypotheses: Using the research studies described in the previous exercise, create null hypotheses and research hypotheses appropriate for the chosen statistical test:

a. Taylor and Ste-Marie (2001) studied eating disorders in 41 Canadian female figure skaters. They compared the figure skaters' data on the Eating Disorder Inventory to the means of known populations, including women with eating disorders. On average, the figure skaters were more similar to the population of women with eating disorders than to those without eating disorders.

b. In an article titled "A Fair and Balanced Look at the News: What Affects Memory for Controversial Arguments," Wiley (2005) found that people with a high level of previous knowledge about a given controversial topic (e.g., abortion, military intervention) had better average recall for arguments on both sides of that issue than did those with lower levels of knowledge.

c. Engle-Friedman and colleagues (2003) studied the effects of sleep deprivation. Fifty students were assigned to one night of sleep loss (students were required to call the laboratory every half-hour all night) and then one night of no sleep loss (normal sleep). The next day, students were offered a choice of math problems with differing levels of difficulty. Following sleep loss, students tended to choose less challenging problems.

11.31 Independent-samples *t* test and walking speed: The New York City Department of City Planning (2006) studied pedestrian walking speeds. The report stated that pedestrians who were en route to work walked a median of 4.41 feet per second, whereas tourist pedestrians walked a median of 3.79 feet per second. They did not report results of any hypothesis tests.

a. Why would an independent-samples *t* test be appropriate in this situation?

b. What would the null hypothesis and research hypothesis be in this situation?

11.32 Independent-sample *t* tests and the "fun theory": Volkswagen has created a series of videos based on its "fun theory," the idea that you can change behavior if you take an activity that is good for society and make it fun. (You can watch the videos at http://www.thefuntheory.com/.) For each of the following examples, state the independent variable (and its levels) as well as the dependent variable (and the types of variables that both of these are). Then, state whether you could use an independent-samples *t* test to analyze the data, and explain your answer.

a. A "Speed Camera Lottery"—in which an electronic sign told people how fast they were going so they could adjust their speed—was introduced. As people passed the electronic sign, a camera took a photo of their license plate. If they were speeding, they were mailed a ticket and had to pay a fine. If they were obeying the speed limit, they were entered into a lottery to win some of the money from those who paid speeding tickets. The average speed using the Speed Camera Lottery sign was 25 kilometers per hour, and the average speed with no lottery sign was 32 kilometers per hour.

b. At the exit of a subway station, stairs and an escalator were side by side. The stairs were turned into a piano, so that when you climbed them, you heard musical notes. While the Piano Staircase was in place, 66% more people took the stairs—rather than the escalator—than when the Piano Staircase was not in place.

c. A trash bin was designed so that when someone threw trash into it, there was a long whistling sound, followed by a thud, as if the trash were falling into an extremely deep bin. When the bin was used, an average of 72 kg of trash was disposed of in a day; when it was not used, an average of 31 kg of trash was disposed of in a day.

11.33 Cafeteria trays, food consumption, and an independent-samples *t* test: Kiho Kim and Stevia Morawski (2012) reported the following in the abstract (brief summary) of their published research study: "Here, we report on the results of an experiment to evaluate the effects of tray availability on food waste production and dish use in a university dining facility. We sampled 360 individual diners over a 6-day period and documented a 32% reduction in food waste and a 27% reduction in dish use when trays were unavailable."

a. What was the independent variable and what were its levels?

b. What were the dependent variables? How did the researchers likely operationalize their variables?

c. The researchers describe their study as an experiment. Explain what they mean by this.

d. Why would it be possible to use independent-samples *t* tests to analyze the data from their study?

11.34 Independent-sample *t* tests and "Blinded with Science": Researchers studied the effects of learning about the effectiveness of a new medication (Tal & Wansink, 2014). Some participants heard information about the medication; others heard the same information and saw a graph that depicted the data they had heard about. Thus, the two groups had identical information. Participants rated the effectiveness of the medication on a scale of 1–9, with 9 indicating a higher level of effectiveness. The researchers reported "Participants given graphs expressed greater belief in the claims, rating the medication as more effective (6.83 of 9) than did participants given verbal description only (6.12 of 9): $t(59) = -2.1, p = .04$" (p. 4). The researchers titled their paper "Blinded with Science" because the mere presence of a scientific cue—a graph—altered perceptions of the medication.

a. What kind of *t* test did the researchers use? Explain your answer.

b. How do we know this finding is statistically significant?

c. How many participants were in this experiment?

d. Identify the means of the two groups.

e. What additional statistics would it have been helpful for the researchers to include?

11.35 Independent-sample *t* tests and note-taking—laptop or longhand: Researchers explored whether there were mean differences between students who were randomly assigned to take notes longhand and students who were randomly assigned to take notes on their laptops (Mueller & Oppenheimer, 2014).

They had observed that students who took notes by hand performed better, on average, on conceptual questions—those that involved thinking beyond just recalling facts—than students who took notes on their laptops. To explore reasons for this difference, they examined the students' notes. The researchers "found that laptop notes contained an average of 14.6% verbatim overlap with the lecture ($SD = 7.3\%$), whereas longhand notes averaged only 8.8% ($SD = 4.8\%$), $t(63) = -3.77, p < .001, d = 0.94$" (p. 3). They concluded that when people took notes longhand, they were more likely to put ideas in their own words, which likely led to deeper processing and better learning of information.

a. What kind of *t* test did the researchers use? Explain your answer.

b. How do we know this finding is statistically significant?

c. How many participants were in this experiment?

d. Identify the means of the two groups.

e. What is the effect size for this finding? Interpret what that means in terms of Cohen's conventions.

Putting It All Together

11.36 Gender and number words: Chang, Sandhofer, and Brown (2011) wondered whether mothers used number words more, on average, with their preschool sons than with their preschool daughters. Each participating family included one mother and one child—either female or male. They speculated that early exposure to more number words might predispose children to like mathematics. They reported the following: "An independent-samples *t* test revealed statistically significant differences in the percentages of overall numeric speech used when interacting with boys compared with girls, $t(30) = 2.40, p < .05, d = .88$. That is, mothers used number terms with boys an average of 9.49% of utterances ($SD = 6.78\%$) compared with 4.64% of utterances with girls ($SD = 4.43\%$)" (pp. 444–445).

a. Is this a between-groups or within-groups design? Explain your answer.

b. What is the independent variable? What is the dependent variable?

c. How many children were in the total sample? Explain how you determined this.

d. Is the sample likely randomly selected? Is it likely that the researchers used random assignment?

e. Were the researchers able to reject the null hypothesis? Explain.

f. What can you say about the size of the effect?

g. Describe how you could design an experiment to test whether exposure to more number words in preschool leads children to like mathematics more when they enter school.

11.37 School lunches: Alice Waters, owner of the Berkeley, California, restaurant Chez Panisse, has long been an advocate for the use of simple, fresh, organic ingredients in home and restaurant cooking. She has also turned her considerable expertise to school cafeterias. Waters (2006) praised changes in school lunch menus that have expanded nutritious offerings, but she hypothesizes that students are likely to circumvent healthy lunches by avoiding vegetables and smuggling in banned junk food unless they receive accompanying nutrition education and hands-on involvement in their meals. She has spearheaded an Edible Schoolyard program in Berkeley, which involves public school students in the cultivation and preparation of fresh foods, and states that such interactive education is necessary to combat growing levels of childhood obesity. "Nothing less," Waters writes, "will change their behavior."

a. In your own words, what is Waters predicting? Citing the confirmation bias, explain why Waters' program, although intuitively appealing, should not be instituted nationwide without further study.

b. Describe a simple between-groups experiment with a nominal independent variable with two levels and a scale dependent variable to test Waters' hypothesis. Specifically identify the independent variable, its levels, and the dependent variable. State how you will operationalize the dependent variable.

c. Which hypothesis test would be used to analyze this experiment? Explain your answer.

d. Conduct step 1 of hypothesis testing.

e. Conduct step 2 of hypothesis testing.

f. State at least one other way you could operationalize the dependent variable.

g. Let's say, hypothetically, that Waters discounted the need for the research you propose by citing her own data that the Berkeley school in which she instituted the program has lower rates of obesity than other California schools. Describe the flaw in this argument by discussing the importance of random selection and random assignment.

11.38 Perception and portion sizes: Researchers at the Cornell University Food and Brand Lab conducted an experiment at a fitness camp for adolescents (Wansink & van Ittersum, 2003). Campers were given either a 22-ounce glass that was tall and thin or a 22-ounce glass that was short and wide. Campers with the short glasses tended to pour more soda, milk, or juice than campers with the tall glasses.

a. Is it likely that the researchers used random selection? Explain.

b. Is it likely that the researchers used random assignment? Explain.

c. What is the independent variable, and what are its levels?

d. What is the dependent variable?

e. Which hypothesis test would the researchers use? Explain.

f. Conduct step 1 of hypothesis testing.

g. Conduct step 2 of hypothesis testing.

h. How could the researchers redesign this study so that they could use a paired-samples *t* test?

11.39 Independent-samples *t* test and the perils of informal e-mail addresses: Is your e-mail address something like hotstuff@fake-mail.com? You may not want to use it when you apply for a job or e-mail your professors. Dutch psychologists studied the effect of using informal e-mail addresses on the likelihood of being hired (Toorenburg, Oostrom, & Pollet, 2015). The researchers asked employment recruiters to look at resumes that either had a formal e-mail address based on the user's name, like sannejong@hotmail.com, or an informal e-mail address, like luv_u_sanne@hotmail.com. Recruiters then rated the likelihood that they would hire the person whose résumés they looked at. The researchers reported that "hirability ratings regarding the résumés with informal e-mail addresses were significantly lower, ... $t(362) = 7.72, p < 0.001$, than the hirability ratings regarding résumés that featured a formal e-mail address (Cohen's $d = 0.81$). The effect of the e-mail address was as strong as the effect

of spelling errors, ...$t(362) = 7.66, p < 0.001$, Cohen's $d = 0.80$" (p. 137).

a. Explain why the researchers were able to test their hypotheses using independent-samples *t* tests.

b. For the first result described here, what is the independent variable and what are its levels? What is the dependent variable?

c. There is less information about the second result described here. For the information presented, what do you think the independent variable is and what are the likely levels? What is the dependent variable?

d. Is the sample likely randomly selected? Is it likely that the researchers used random assignment? Explain your answers.

e. The researchers assessed hirability by having recruiters rate four items on a scale of 1–6. For example, recruiters were asked to rate how likely they would be to interview the applicant. Describe one different way that the researchers might have operationalized hirability.

f. Explain why it would have been more helpful for the researchers to report confidence intervals instead of hypothesis tests.

g. Based on what information can the researchers say that "the effect of the e-mail address was as strong as the effect of spelling errors"? Explain your answer.

TERMS

independent-samples *t* test (p. 274)
pooled variance (p. 280)

FORMULAS

$df_{total} = df_X + df_Y$ (p. 280)

$s^2_{pooled} = \left(\frac{df_X}{df_{total}}\right)s^2_X + \left(\frac{df_Y}{df_{total}}\right)s^2_Y$ (p. 280)

$s^2_{M_X} = \frac{s^2_{pooled}}{N_X}$ (p. 280)

$s^2_{M_Y} = \frac{s^2_{pooled}}{N_Y}$ (p. 280)

$s^2_{difference} = s^2_{M_X} + s^2_{M_Y}$ (p. 281)

$s_{difference} = \sqrt{s^2_{difference}}$ (p. 281)

$t = \frac{(M_X - M_Y) - (\mu_X - \mu_Y)}{s_{difference}}$, often

abbreviated as: $t = \frac{(M_X - M_Y)}{s_{difference}}$ (p. 282)

$(M_X - M_Y)_{upper} = t(s_{difference}) + (M_X - M_Y)_{sample}$ (p. 284)

$(M_X - M_Y)_{lower} = -t(s_{difference}) + (M_X - M_Y)_{sample}$ (p. 284)

$s_{pooled} = \sqrt{s^2_{pooled}}$ (p. 287)

Cohen's $d = \frac{(M_X - M_Y) - (\mu_X - \mu_Y)}{s_{pooled}}$
for a difference between means (p. 287)

SYMBOLS

s^2_{pooled} (p. 280)
$s^2_{difference}$ (p. 280)
$s_{difference}$ (p. 281)

One-Way Between-Groups ANOVA

BEFORE YOU GO ON

■ You should understand the *z* distribution and the *t* distributions. You should also be able to differentiate among distributions of scores (Chapter 6), means (Chapter 6), and differences between means (Chapter 11).

■ You should know the six steps of hypothesis testing (Chapter 7).

■ You should understand what variance is (Chapter 4).

■ You should be able to differentiate between between-groups designs and within-groups designs (Chapter 1).

■ You should understand the concept of effect size (Chapter 8).

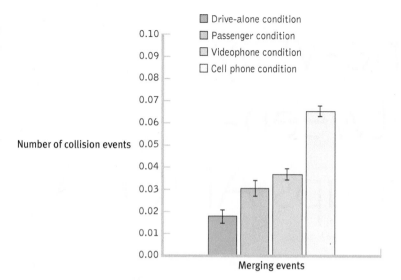

Comparing Three or More Groups

Researchers compared four groups in one study, which allowed them to discover that a conversation on a hands-free mobile phone was statistically significantly more dangerous than a conversation with a real passenger seated next to us, a conversation with a remote passenger using a videophone, or when driving alone (Gaspar et al., 2014).

Here's the bad news: You are not very good at multitasking. Here's some additional bad news: You probably think you're pretty good at multitasking—especially when it comes to using your mobile phone while driving.

Usually, nothing bad happens when you drive and talk on your mobile phone, so many people probably conclude that they are pretty good at multitasking while driving. But here's a simple research question: Are we worse drivers when we talk on a hands-free device or when we have a conversation with the person in the passenger seat? A simple, two-group design analyzed with a *t* test will answer that question. But reality is often more complicated than a simple two-group design and people drive while holding a conversation in a variety of ways.

To address the variety of conversations, researchers used a driving simulator with eight surrounding projection screens to create a series of dangerous driving situations, such as merging into traffic (Gaspar et al., 2014). There were four different experimental conditions: (1) driving alone, (2) driving and talking with a passenger seated next to them, (3) driving and talking on a videophone with a "remote passenger" in a separate room, and (4) driving and talking on a hands-free mobile phone. The third condition– with the videophone–used two projection screens that allowed the "remote passenger" to see both what the driver saw (the road ahead) and the driver's face—just like a real passenger. Which condition do you think was most dangerous (Figure 12-1)?

For researchers, a four-group ANOVA is a bargain: multiple experiments for the price of one! In this chapter, we will learn about (a) the distributions used with ANOVA (the *F* distributions); (b) how to conduct an ANOVA when we have a between-groups design; (c) the effect-size statistic used with between-groups ANOVA; and (d) how to conduct a post hoc (or follow-up) test to determine exactly which groups are different from one another.

Using the *F* Distributions with Three or More Samples

The talking-while-driving study demonstrated that talking on a hands-free mobile phone was the most dangerous out of the four conditions. Comparing three or more groups is slightly more complicated than comparing two groups, so it requires comparison distributions that can accommodate that complexity: the *F* distributions.

Type I Errors When Making Three or More Comparisons

When comparing three or more groups, it is tempting to conduct an easy-to-understand *t* test on each of the possible comparisons. Unfortunately, there's a big downside: You may not be able to believe your own results. Why? Conducting numerous *t* tests greatly increases the probability of a Type I error (a false positive: rejecting the null hypothesis when the null hypothesis is true). Statisticians use a curious expression to describe the problem of too many possible comparisons: *inflating alpha*. For example, a study with three groups compares:

> Group 1 with group 2
>
> Group 1 with group 3
>
> Group 2 with group 3

That's 3 comparisons. If there were four groups, there would be 6 comparisons. With five groups, there would be 10 comparisons, and so on. With only 1 comparison, there is a 0.05 chance of having a Type I error in any given analysis if the null hypothesis is true, and a 0.95 chance of not having a Type I error when the null hypothesis is true. Those are pretty good odds, and we would tend to believe the conclusions in that study. However, Table 12-1 shows what happens when we conduct more studies on the same sample. The chances of not having a Type I error on the first analysis *and* not having a Type I error on the second analysis are $(0.95)(0.95) = (0.95)^2 = 0.903$, or about 90%. This means that the chance of having a Type I error is almost 10%. With three analyses, the chance of not having a Type I error is $(0.95)(0.95)(0.95) = (0.95)^3 = 0.857$, or about 86%. This means that there is about a 14% chance of having at least one Type I error. And so on, as we see in Table 12-1. ANOVA is a more powerful approach because it lets us test differences among three or more groups in just one test.

The *F* Statistic as an Expansion of the *z* and *t* Statistics

We use *F* distributions because they allow us to conduct a single hypothesis test with multiple groups. *F* distributions are more conservative versions of the *z* distribution and the *t* distributions. Just as the *z* distribution is still part of the *t* distributions, the *t* distributions are also part of the *F* distributions—and they all rely on the characteristics of the normal bell-shaped curve. The distributions are like progressively more complex versions of the Swiss Army knife: The *z* distribution has just one blade; the *t* distributions add some more tools; and the versatile *F* distributions can do everything the *z* and the *t* can do—as well as many more complex statistical tasks.

TABLE 12-1	The Probability of a Type I Error Increases as the Number of Statistical Comparisons Increases

As the number of samples increases, the number of *t* tests necessary to compare every possible pair of means increases at an even greater rate. And with that, the probability of a Type I error quickly becomes far larger than 0.05.

Number of Means	Number of Comparisons	Probability of a Type I Error
2	1	0.050
3	3	0.143
4	6	0.265
5	10	0.401
6	15	0.537
7	21	0.659

z, t, and F Distributions
Statistical distributions are similar to the increasing complexity of ever-more sophisticated Swiss Army knives. Specifically, the *z*, *t*, and *F* distributions are three increasingly complex variations on one great idea: the normal curve.

© Simon Belcher/Alamy

Simple Stock Shots/IPNStock

© Nick Emm/Alamy

The hypothesis tests that we have learned so far—the z test and the three types of t tests—are calculated in similar ways. The numerator describes how far apart comparison groups are from each other (between-groups variability); the denominator describes other sources of variability, such as individual differences and chance (within-groups variability). For example, the average height of men is greater than the average height of women: between-groups variability. Yet not all men are the same height and not all women are the same height: within-groups variability. Many women are taller than many men, so there is considerable overlap between the two distributions. The F statistic calculates between-group variance and within-group variance to conduct the hypothesis test called *analysis of variance* (*ANOVA*; pronounced "ah-NO-vah"), *a hypothesis test typically used with one or more nominal (and sometimes ordinal) independent variables (with at least three groups overall) and a scale dependent variable.*

The F Distributions for Analyzing Variability to Compare Means

Comparing heights of men and women demonstrates that *the* **F** *statistic is a ratio of two measures of variance: (1) between-groups variance, which indicates differences among sample means, and (2) within-groups variance, the average of the sample variances.*

$$F = \frac{\text{between-groups variance}}{\text{within-groups variance}}$$

- **Analysis of variance (ANOVA)** is a hypothesis test typically used with one or more nominal (and sometimes ordinal) independent variables (with at least three groups overall) and a scale dependent variable.

- The **F statistic** is a ratio of two measures of variance: (1) between-groups variance, which indicates differences among sample means, and (2) within-groups variance, which is essentially an average of the sample variances.

- **Between-groups variance** is an estimate of the population variance, based on the differences among the means.

- **Within-groups variance** is an estimate of the population variance, based on the differences within each of the three (or more) sample distributions.

Let's begin with the numerator, called **between-groups variance** because it *is an estimate of the population variance, based on the differences among the means.* A big number in the numerator indicates a great deal of distance (or spread) between the means, suggesting that they come from different populations. A small number in the numerator indicates very little distance (or spread) between the means, suggesting that they come from the same population. With more than two means, we can't use simple subtraction to find a number that indicates how spread apart they are, so we calculate the variance among the sample means. For example, if we wanted to compare how fast people talk in Vancouver, Memphis, Chicago, and Toronto, then the number representing between-groups variance (in this case, the between-cities variance) is an estimate of the variability among the average number of words per minute spoken by the people representing each of those four cities.

The denominator of the F statistic is called the **within-groups variance**, *an estimate of the population variance, based on the differences within each of the three (or more) sample distributions.* For example, not everyone living in Vancouver, Memphis, Chicago, or Toronto speaks at the same pace. There are within-city differences in talking speeds, so within-groups variance refers to the average of the four variances.

To calculate the F statistic, we simply divide the between-groups variance by the within-groups variance. If the F statistic is a large number (when the between-groups variance is much larger than the within-groups variance), then we can infer that the sample means are different from one another. But we cannot make that inference when the F statistic is close to the number 1 (the between-groups variance is about the same as the within-groups variance).

To summarize, we can think of within-groups variance as reflecting the difference between means that we'd expect just by chance. There is variability within any population, so we would expect some difference among means just by chance. Between-groups variance reflects the difference between means that we found in the data. If this difference is much larger than the within-groups variance—what we'd expect by chance—then we can reject the null hypothesis and conclude that there is some difference between means.

TABLE 12-2	Connections Among Distributions

The z distribution is subsumed under the t distributions in certain specific circumstances, and both the z and t distributions are subsumed under the F distributions in certain specific circumstances.

	When Used	Links Among the Distributions
z	One sample; μ and σ are known	Subsumed under the t and F distributions
t	(1) One sample; only μ is known (2) Two samples	Same as z distribution if there is a sample size of infinity (∞), or a very large sample size
F	Three or more samples (but can be used with two samples)	Square of z distribution if there are only two samples and a sample size of infinity (∞), or a very large sample size; square of t distribution if there are only two samples

The *F* Table

The F table is an expansion of the t table. Just as there are many t distributions represented in the t table—one for each possible sample size—there are many F distributions. Both tables include a wide range of sample sizes (represented by degrees of freedom) but the F table adds a third factor: the number of samples. (The t statistic is limited to two samples.) There is an F distribution for every possible combination of sample size (represented by one type of degrees of freedom) and number of samples (represented by another type of degrees of freedom).

The F table for two samples can even be used as a t test; the numbers are the same except that the F is based on variance and the t on the square root of the variance, the standard deviation. For example, if we look in the F table under two samples for a sample size of infinity for the equivalent of the 95th percentile, we see 2.71. If we take the square root of this, we get 1.646. We can find 1.645 on the z table for the 95th percentile and on the t table for the 95th percentile with a sample size of infinity. (The slight differences are due only to rounding decisions.) The connections between the z, t, and F distributions are summarized in Table 12-2.

The Language and Assumptions for ANOVA

Here is a simple guide to the language that statisticians use to describe different kinds of ANOVAs (Landrum, 2005). The word *ANOVA* is almost always preceded by two adjectives that indicate: (1) the number of independent variables; and (2) the research design (between-groups or within-groups).

Study 1. What would you call an ANOVA with year in school as the only independent variable and ratings of students' attachment to their university as the dependent variable? Answer: A one-way between-groups ANOVA. *A **one-way** ANOVA is a hypothesis test that includes both one nominal independent variable with more than two levels and a scale dependent variable.* *A **between-groups** ANOVA is a hypothesis test in which there are more than two samples, and each sample is composed of different participants.*

Study 2. What if you wanted to test the same group of students every year? Answer: You would use a one-way within-groups ANOVA. *A **within-groups** ANOVA is a hypothesis test in which there are more than two samples, and each sample is composed of the same participants.* (This test is also called a *repeated-measures ANOVA*.)

Study 3. And what if you wanted to add gender to the first study, something we explore in Chapter 14? Now you have two independent variables: year in school *and* gender. Answer: You would use a two-way between-groups ANOVA.

- A **one-way ANOVA** is a hypothesis test that includes both one nominal independent variable with more than two levels and a scale dependent variable.

- A **between-groups ANOVA** is a hypothesis test in which there are more than two samples, and each sample is composed of different participants.

- A **within-groups ANOVA** is a hypothesis test in which there are more than two samples, and each sample is composed of the same participants; also called a *repeated-measures ANOVA*.

- **Homoscedastic** populations are those that have the same variance; homoscedasticity is also called *homogeneity of variance*.

- **Heteroscedastic** populations are those that have different variances.

All ANOVAs, regardless of type, share the same three assumptions that represent the optimal conditions for valid data analysis. (We'll learn about within-groups ANOVAs in Chapter 13 and two-way ANOVAs in Chapter 14.)

Assumption 1. *Random selection* is necessary if we want to generalize beyond a sample. Because of the difficulty of random sampling, researchers often substitute convenience sampling and then replicate their experiment with a new sample.

Assumption 2. A *normally distributed population* allows us to examine the distributions of the samples to get a sense of what the underlying population distribution might look like. This assumption becomes less important as the sample size increases.

Assumption 3. *Homoscedasticity* (also called *homogeneity of variance*) assumes that the samples all come from populations with the same variances. (*Heteroscedasticity* means that the populations do not all have the same variance.) **Homoscedastic** *populations are those that have the same variance.* **Heteroscedastic** *populations are those that have different variances.*

What if your study doesn't match these ideal conditions? You may have to throw away your data—but that is usually not necessary. You also can (a) report and justify your decision to violate those assumptions; or (b) conduct a more conservative non-parametric test (see Chapter 18).

CHECK YOUR LEARNING

Reviewing the Concepts

> The *F* statistic, used in analysis of variance (ANOVA), is essentially an expansion of the *z* statistic and the *t* statistic that can be used to compare more than two samples.

> Like the *z* statistic and the *t* statistic, the *F* statistic is a ratio of a difference between group means (in this case, using a measure of variability) to a measure of variability within samples.

> One-way between-groups ANOVA is an analysis in which there is one independent variable with at least three levels and in which different participants are in each level of the independent variable. A within-groups ANOVA differs in that all participants experience all levels of the independent variable.

> The assumptions for ANOVA are that participants are randomly selected, the populations from which the samples are drawn are normally distributed, and those populations have the same variance (an assumption known as homoscedasticity).

Clarifying the Concepts **12-1** The *F* statistic is a ratio of what two kinds of variance?

12-2 What are the two types of research designs for a one-way ANOVA?

Calculating the Statistics **12-3** Calculate the *F* statistic, writing the ratio accurately, for each of the following cases:

    a. Between-groups variance is 8.6 and within-groups variance is 3.7.

    b. Within-groups variance is 123.77 and between-groups variance is 102.4.

    c. Between-groups variance is 45.2 and within-groups variance is 32.1.

Applying the Concepts **12-4** Consider the research on multitasking that we explored in Chapter 9 (Mark, Gonzalez, & Harris, 2005). Let's say we compared three conditions to see which one would lead to the quickest resumption of a task following an interruption. In one condition, the control group, no changes were made to the working environment. In the second condition, a communication ban was instituted from 1:00 to 3:00 P.M.

In the third condition, a communication ban was instituted from 11:00 A.M. to 3:00 P.M. We recorded the time, in minutes, until work on an interrupted task was resumed.

a. What type of distribution would be used in this situation? Explain your answer.

b. In your own words, explain how we would calculate between-groups variance. Focus on the logic rather than on the calculations.

Solutions to these Check Your Learning questions can be found in Appendix D.

c. In your own words, explain how we would calculate within-groups variance. Focus on the logic rather than on the calculations.

One-Way Between-Groups ANOVA

The talking-while-driving study showed us that it's dangerous when the person on the other end of the conversation doesn't know when difficult driving conditions are developing. But we needed to analyze the data from four groups with an ANOVA to reach that conclusion. In this section, we use another four-group study to apply the principles of ANOVA to hypothesis testing with a between-groups research design.

Everything About ANOVA but the Calculations

To introduce the steps of hypothesis testing for a one-way between-groups ANOVA, we use an international study about whether the economic makeup of a society affects the degree to which people behave in a fair manner toward others (Henrich et al., 2010).

EXAMPLE 12.1

The researchers studied people in 15 societies from around the world. For teaching purposes, we'll look at data from four types of societies—foraging, farming, natural resources, and industrial.

1. *Foraging.* Several societies, including ones in Bolivia and Papua New Guinea, were categorized as foraging societies. They acquired most of their food through hunting and gathering.

2. *Farming.* Some societies, including ones in Kenya and Tanzania, primarily practiced farming and tended to grow their own food.

3. *Natural resources.* Other societies, such as in Colombia, built their economies by extracting natural resources, such as trees and fish. Most food was purchased.

4. *Industrial.* In industrial societies, which include the major city of Accra in Ghana as well as rural Missouri in the United States, most food was purchased.

The researchers wondered which groups would behave more or less fairly toward others—the first and second groups, which grew their own food, or the third and fourth groups, which depended on others for food. The researchers measured fairness through several games. In the Dictator Game, for example, two players were given a sum of money equal to approximately the daily minimum wage for that society. The first player (the dictator) could keep all of the money or give any portion of it to the other person. The proportion of money given to the second player constituted the measure of fairness. For example, it would be considered fairer to give the second player 40% of the money than to give him or her only 10% of the money.

This research design would be analyzed with a one-way between-groups ANOVA that uses the fairness measure, the proportion of money given to the second player, as the dependent variable. There is one independent variable (type of society) and it has four levels (foraging, farming, natural resources, and industrial). It is a between-groups

The Dictator Game Here a researcher introduces a fairness game to a woman from Papua New Guinea, one of the foraging societies. Using games, researchers were able to compare fairness behaviors among different types of societies—those that depend on foraging, farming, natural resources, or industry. Because there are four groups and each participant is in only one group, the results can be analyzed with a one-way between-groups ANOVA.

Courtesy of Dr. David Tracer

design because each player lived in one and only one of those societies. It is an ANOVA because it analyzes variance by estimating the variability among the different types of societies and dividing it by the variability within the types of societies. The fairness scores below are from 13 fictional people, but the groups have almost the same mean fairness scores that the researchers observed in their actual (much larger) data set.

Foraging: 28, 36, 38, 31

Farming: 32, 33, 40

Natural resources: 47, 43, 52

Industrial: 40, 47, 45

Let's begin by applying a familiar framework: the six steps of hypothesis testing. We will learn the calculations in the next section.

> **STEP 1:** Identify the populations, distribution, and assumptions.

The first step of hypothesis testing is to identify the populations to be compared, the comparison distribution, the appropriate test, and the assumptions of the test. Let's summarize the fairness study with respect to this first step of hypothesis testing.

Summary: *The populations to be compared:* Population 1: All people living in foraging societies. Population 2: All people living in farming societies. Population 3: All people living in societies that extract natural resources. Population 4: All people living in industrial societies.

The comparison distribution and hypothesis test: The comparison distribution will be an *F* distribution. The hypothesis test will be a one-way between-groups ANOVA.

Assumptions: (1) The data are not selected randomly, so we must generalize only with caution. (2) We do not know if the underlying population distributions are normal, but the sample data do not indicate severe skew. (3) We will test homoscedasticity when we calculate the test statistics by checking to see whether the largest variance is not more than twice the smallest. (*Note:* Don't forget this step just because it comes later in the analysis.)

> **STEP 2:** State the null and research hypotheses.

The second step is to state the null and research hypotheses. As usual, the null hypothesis posits no difference among the population means. The symbols are the same as before, but with more populations: H_0: $\mu_1 = \mu_2 = \mu_3 = \mu_4$. However, the research hypothesis is more complicated because we can reject the null hypothesis even if only one group is different, on average, from the others. The research hypothesis that $\mu_1 \neq \mu_2 \neq \mu_3 \neq \mu_4$ does not include all possible outcomes, such as the hypothesis that the mean fairness scores for groups 1 *and* 2 are greater than the mean fairness scores for groups 3 *and* 4. The research hypothesis is that at least one population mean is different from at least one other population mean, so H_1 is that at least one μ is different from another μ.

Summary: Null hypothesis: People living in societies based on foraging, farming, the extraction of natural resources, and industry all exhibit, on average, the same fairness behaviors—H_0: $\mu_1 = \mu_2 = \mu_3 = \mu_4$. Research hypothesis: People living in societies based on foraging, farming, the extraction of natural resources, and industry do not all exhibit the same fairness behaviors, on average.

> **STEP 3: Determine the characteristics of the comparison distribution.**

The third step is to explicitly state the relevant characteristics of the comparison distribution. This step is an easy one in ANOVA because most calculations are in step 5. Here we merely state that the comparison distribution is an F distribution and provide the appropriate degrees of freedom. As we discussed, the F statistic is a ratio of two independent estimates of the population variance, between-groups variance and within-groups variance (both of which we calculate in step 5). Each variance estimate has its own degrees of freedom. The sample between-groups variance estimates the population variance through the difference among the means of the samples—four, in this case. The degrees of freedom for the between-groups variance estimate is the number of samples minus 1:

$$df_{between} = N_{groups} - 1 = 4 - 1 = 3$$

Because there are four groups (foraging, farming, the extraction of natural resources, and industry), the between-groups degrees of freedom is 3.

The sample within-groups variance estimates the variance of the population by averaging the variances of the samples, without regard to differences among the sample means. We first must calculate the degrees of freedom for each sample. Because there are four participants in the first sample (farming), we would calculate:

$$df_1 = n_1 - 1 = 4 - 1 = 3$$

n represents the number of participants in the particular sample. We would then do this for the remaining samples. For this example, there are four samples, so the formula would be:

$$df_{within} = df_1 + df_2 + df_3 + df_4$$

For this example, the calculations would be:

$$df_1 = 4 - 1 = 3$$
$$df_2 = 3 - 1 = 2$$
$$df_3 = 3 - 1 = 2$$
$$df_4 = 3 - 1 = 2$$
$$df_{within} = 3 + 2 + 2 + 2 = 9$$

Summary: We would use the F distribution with 3 and 9 degrees of freedom.

MASTERING THE FORMULA

12-1: The formula for the between-groups degrees of freedom is: $df_{between} = N_{groups} - 1$. We subtract 1 from the number of groups in the study.

MASTERING THE FORMULA

12-2: The formula for the within-groups degrees of freedom for a one-way between-groups ANOVA conducted with four samples is: $df_{within} = df_1 + df_2 + df_3 + df_4$. We sum the degrees of freedom for each of the four groups. We calculate degrees of freedom for each group by subtracting 1 from the number of people in that sample. For example, for the first group, the formula is: $df_1 = n_1 - 1$.

<table>
<tr><td>**STEP 4: Determine the critical value, or cutoff.**</td></tr>
</table>

The fourth step is to determine a critical value, or cutoff, indicating how extreme the data must be to reject the null hypothesis. For ANOVA, we use an F statistic, for which the critical value on an F distribution will always be positive (because the F is based on estimates of variance and variances are always positive). We determine the critical value by examining the F table in Appendix B (excerpted in Table 12-3). The between-groups degrees of freedom are found in a row across the top of the table. Notice that, in the full table, this row only goes up to 6, as it is rare to have more than 7 conditions, or groups, in a study. The within-groups degrees of freedom are in a column along the left-hand side of the table. Because the number of participants in a study can range from a few to many, the column continues for several pages, with the same range of values of between-groups degrees of freedom on the top of each page.

Use the F table by first finding the appropriate within-groups degrees of freedom along the left-hand side of the page: 9. Then find the appropriate between-groups degrees of freedom along the top: 3. The place in the table where this row and this

---

TABLE 12-3 Excerpt from the F Table

We use the F table to determine a critical value for a given p level, based on the degrees of freedom in the numerator (between-groups degrees of freedom) and the degrees of freedom in the denominator (within-groups degrees of freedom). Note that critical values are in boldface for **0.01**, regular type for 0.05, and italics for *0.10*.

Within-Groups Degrees of Freedom: Denominator	*p* level	Between-Groups Degrees of Freedom: Numerator			
		1	2	3	4 . . .
9	**0.01**	**10.56**	**8.02**	**6.99**	**6.42**
	0.05	5.12	4.26	3.86	3.63
	0.10	*3.36*	*3.01*	*2.81*	*2.69*
10	**0.01**	**10.05**	**7.56**	**6.55**	**6.00**
	0.05	4.97	4.10	3.71	3.48
	0.10	*3.29*	*2.93*	*2.73*	*2.61*
11	**0.01**	**9.65**	**7.21**	**6.22**	**5.67**
	0.05	4.85	3.98	3.59	3.36
	0.10	*3.23*	*2.86*	*2.66*	*2.54*
12	**0.01**	**9.33**	**6.93**	**5.95**	**5.41**
	0.05	4.75	3.88	3.49	3.26
	0.10	*3.18*	*2.81*	*2.61*	*2.48*
13	**0.01**	**9.07**	**6.70**	**5.74**	**5.20**
	0.05	4.67	3.80	3.41	3.18
	0.10	*3.14*	*2.76*	*2.56*	*2.43*
14	**0.01**	**8.86**	**6.51**	**5.56**	**5.03**
	0.05	4.60	3.74	3.34	3.11
	0.10	*3.10*	*2.73*	*2.52*	*2.39*

column intersect contains three numbers: p levels for 0.01, 0.05, and 0.10. Researchers usually use the middle one, 0.05, which for this study is 3.86 (Figure 12-2).

Summary: The cutoff, or critical value, for the F statistic for a p level of 0.05 is 3.86, as displayed in the curve in Figure 12-2.

| STEP 5: Calculate the test statistic. | *In the fifth step, we calculate the test statistic.* We use the two |

estimates of the between-groups variance and the within-groups variance to calculate the F statistic. We compare the F statistic to the cutoff to determine whether to reject the null hypothesis. We will learn to do these calculations in the next section.

Summary: To be calculated in the next section.

| STEP 6: Make a decision. | *In the final step, we decide whether to reject or fail to reject the null hypothesis.* If the F statistic is |

beyond the critical value, then we know that it is in the most extreme 5% of possible test statistics *if* the null hypothesis is true. We can then reject the null hypothesis and conclude, "It seems that people exhibit different fairness behaviors, on average, depending on the type of society in which they live." ANOVA only tells us that at least one mean is significantly different from another; it does not tell us *which* societies are different.

If the test statistic is not beyond the critical value, then we must fail to reject the null hypothesis. The test statistic would not be very rare if the null hypothesis were true. In this circumstance, we report only that there is no evidence from the present study to support the research hypothesis.

Summary: Because the decision we will make must be evidence-based, we cannot make it until we complete step 5, in which we calculate the probabilities associated with that evidence. We will complete step 6 in the Making a Decision section on p. 319. ●

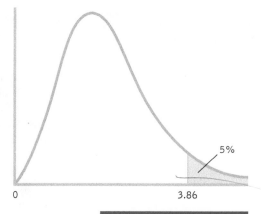

FIGURE 12-2

Determining Cutoffs for an F Distribution

We determine a single critical value on an F distribution. Because F is a squared version of a z (or t in some circumstances), we have only one cutoff for a two-tailed test.

MASTERING THE CONCEPT

12-2: When conducting an ANOVA, we use the same six steps of hypothesis testing that we've already learned. One of the differences from what we've learned is that we calculate an F statistic, the ratio of between-groups variance to within-groups variance.

The Logic and Calculations of the F Statistic

In this section, we first review the logic behind ANOVA's use of between-groups variance and within-groups variance. Then we apply the same six steps of hypothesis testing we have used in previous statistical tests to make a data-driven decision about what story the data are trying to tell us. Our goal in performing the calculations of ANOVA is to understand the *sources* of all the variability in a study.

As we noted before, grown men, on average, are slightly taller than grown women, on average. We call that "between-groups variability." We also noted that not all women are the same height and not all men are the same height. We call that "within-groups variability." The F statistic is simply an estimate of between-groups variability (in the numerator) divided by an estimate of within-groups variability (in the denominator).

$$F = \frac{\text{between-groups variability}}{\text{within-groups variability}}$$

Quantifying Overlap with ANOVA On average, men are taller than women; however, many women are taller than many men, so their distributions overlap. The amount of

Gender Differences in Height
Men, on average, are slightly taller than women (between-groups variance). However, neither men nor women are all the same height within their groups (within-groups variance). F is between-groups variability divided by within-groups variability.

overlap is influenced by the distance between the means (between-groups variability) and the amount of spread (within-groups variability). In Figure 12-3a, there is a great deal of overlap; the means are close together and the distributions are spread out. Distributions with a lot of overlap suggest that any differences among them are probably due to chance.

There is less overlap in the second set of distributions (see Figure 12-3b), but only because the means are farther apart; the within-groups variability remains the same. The F statistic is larger because the numerator is larger; the denominator has not changed. Distributions with little overlap are less likely to be drawn from the same population. It is less likely that any differences among them are due to chance.

There is even less overlap in the third set of distributions (see Figure 12-3c) because the numerator representing the between-groups variance is still large *and* the denominator representing the within-groups variance has gotten smaller. Both changes contributed to a larger F statistic. Distributions with very little overlap suggest that any differences are probably not due to chance. It would be difficult to convince someone that these three samples were drawn by chance from the very same population.

Two Ways to Estimate Population Variance Between-groups variability and within-groups variability estimate two different kinds of variance in the population. If those two estimates are the same, then the F statistic will be 1.0. For example, if the estimate of the between-groups variance is 32 and the estimate of the within-groups variance is also 32, then the F statistic is $32/32 = 1.0$. This is a bit different from the z and t tests, in which a z or t of 0 would mean no difference at all. Here, an F of 1 means no difference at all. As the sample means get farther apart, the between-groups variance (the numerator) increases, which means that the F statistic also increases.

● A **source table** presents the important calculations and final results of an ANOVA in a consistent and easy-to-read format.

Calculating the F Statistic with the Source Table The goal of any statistical analysis is to understand the *sources* of variability in a study. We achieve that in ANOVA by calculating many squared deviations from the mean and three sums of squares. We organize the results into *a **source table*** that *presents the important calculations and final results of an ANOVA in a consistent and easy-to-read format.* A source table is

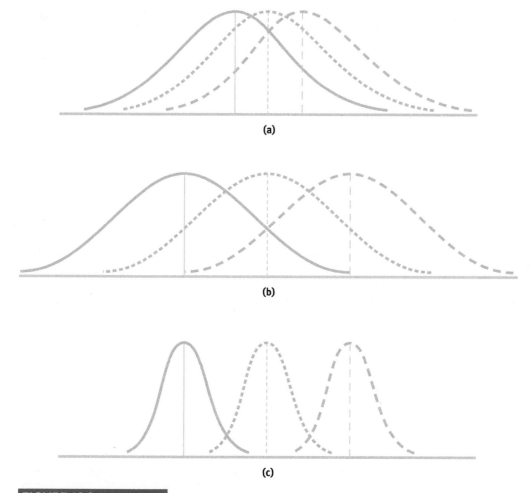

(a)

(b)

(c)

FIGURE 12-3

The Logic of ANOVA

Compare the top (a) and middle (b) sets of sample distributions. As the variability between means increases, the *F* statistic becomes larger. Compare the middle (b) and bottom (c) sets of sample distributions. As the variability within the samples themselves decreases, the *F* statistic becomes larger because there is less overlap between the three curves. Both the increased spread among the sample means and the decreased spread within each sample contribute to this increase in the *F* statistic.

shown in Table 12-4; the symbols in this table would be replaced by numbers in an actual source table. We're going to explain the source table displayed in Table 12-4 starting with column 1; we will then work backward from column 5 to column 4 to column 3 and finally to column 2.

Column 1: Source. One possible source of population variance comes from the spread *between* means; a second source comes from the spread *within* each sample. In this chapter, the row labeled "Total" allows us to check the calculations of the sum of squares (*SS*) and degrees of freedom (*df*). Now let's work backward through the source table to learn how it describes these two familiar sources of variability.

Column 5: F. We calculate *F* using simple division: between-groups variance divided by within-groups variance.

TABLE 12-4 The Source Table Organizes the ANOVA Calculations

A source table helps researchers organize the most important calculations necessary to conduct an ANOVA, as well as the final results of the ANOVA. The numbers 1–5 in the first row are used in this particular table only to help you understand the format of source tables; they would not be included in an actual source table.

1 Source	2 SS	3 df	4 MS	5 F
Between	$SS_{between}$	$df_{between}$	$MS_{between}$	F
Within	SS_{within}	df_{within}	MS_{within}	
Total	SS_{total}	df_{total}		

12-3: One formula for the total degrees of freedom for a one-way between-groups ANOVA is: $df_{total} = df_{between} + df_{within}$. We sum the between-groups degrees of freedom and the within-groups degrees of freedom. An alternate formula is: $df_{total} = N_{total} - 1$. We subtract 1 from the total number of people in the study—that is, from the number of people in all groups.

Column 4: MS. MS is the conventional symbol for variance in ANOVA. It stands for "mean square" because variance is the arithmetic mean of the squared deviations for between-groups variance ($MS_{between}$) and within-groups variance (MS_{within}). We divide $MS_{between}$ by MS_{within} to calculate F.

Column 3: df. We calculate the between-groups degrees of freedom ($df_{between}$) and the within-groups degrees of freedom (df_{within}), and then add the two together to calculate the total degrees of freedom:

$$df_{total} = df_{between} + df_{within}$$

In our version of the fairness study, $df_{total} = 3 + 9 = 12$. A second way to calculate df_{total} is:

$$df_{total} = N_{total} - 1$$

N_{total} refers to the total number of people in the entire study. In our abbreviated version of the fairness study, there were four groups, with 4, 3, 3, and 3 participants in the groups, and $4 + 3 + 3 + 3 = 13$. We calculate total degrees of freedom for this study as $df_{total} = 13 - 1 = 12$. If we calculate degrees of freedom both ways and the answers don't match up, then we know we have to go back and check the calculations.

Column 2: SS. We calculate three *sums of squares*. One SS represents between-groups variability ($SS_{between}$), a second represents within-groups variability (SS_{within}), and a third represents total variability (SS_{total}). The first two sums of squares add up to the third; calculate all three to be sure they match.

The source table is a convenient summary because it describes everything we have learned about the sources of numerical variability. Once we calculate the sums of squares for between-groups variance and within-groups variance, there are just two steps.

Step 1: Divide each sum of squares by the appropriate degrees of freedom—the appropriate version of $(N - 1)$. We divide the $SS_{between}$ by the $df_{between}$ and the SS_{within} by the df_{within}. We then have the two variance estimates ($MS_{between}$ and MS_{within}).

Step 2: Calculate the ratio of $MS_{between}$ and MS_{within} to get the F statistic. Once we have the sums of squared deviations, the rest of the calculation is simple division.

Sums of Squared Deviations Language Alert! The term "deviations" is another word used to describe variability. ANOVA analyzes three different types of statistical deviations: (1) deviations between groups, (2) deviations within groups, and (3) total deviations. We begin by calculating the sum of squares for each type of deviation, or source of variability: between, within, and total.

It is easiest to start with the total sum of squares, SS_{total}. Organize all the scores and place them in a single column with a horizontal line dividing each sample from the next. Use the data (from our version of the fairness study) in the column labeled "X" of Table 12-5 as a model; X stands for each of the 13 individual scores listed below. Each set of scores is next to its sample; the means are underneath the names of each respective sample. (We have included subscripts on each mean in the first column—e.g., *for* for foraging, *nr* for natural resources—to indicate its sample.)

To calculate the total sum of squares, subtract the overall mean from each score, including everyone in the study, regardless of sample. The mean of all the scores is called the *grand mean*, and its symbol is *GM*. The **grand mean** is the mean of every score in a study, regardless of which sample the score came from:

$$GM = \frac{\Sigma(X)}{N_{total}}$$

The grand mean of these scores is 39.385. (As usual, we write each number to three decimal places until we get to the final answer, *F*. We report the final answer to two decimal places.)

The third column in Table 12-5 shows the deviation of each score from the grand mean. The fourth column shows the squares of these deviations. For example, for the first score, 28, we subtract the grand mean:

$$28 - 39.385 = -11.385$$

Then we square the deviation:

$$(-11.385)^2 = 129.618$$

- The **grand mean** is the mean of every score in a study, regardless of which sample the score came from.

MASTERING THE FORMULA

12-4: The grand mean is the mean score of all people in a study, regardless of which sample the score came from. The formula is:

$$GM = \frac{\Sigma(X)}{N_{total}}.$$

We add up everyone's score, then divide by the total number of people in the study.

TABLE 12-5 Calculating the Total Sum of Squares

The total sum of squares is calculated by subtracting the overall mean, called the *grand mean*, from every score to create deviations, then squaring the deviations and summing the squared deviations.

Sample	X	$(X - GM)$	$(X - GM)^2$
Foraging	28	−11.385	129.618
	36	−3.385	11.458
$M_{for} = 33.250$	38	−1.385	1.918
	31	−8.385	70.308
Farming	32	−7.385	54.538
	33	−6.385	40.768
$M_{farm} = 35.000$	40	0.615	0.378
Natural resources	47	7.615	57.988
	43	3.615	13.068
$M_{nr} = 47.333$	52	12.615	159.138
Industrial	40	0.615	0.378
	47	7.615	57.988
$M_{ind} = 44.000$	45	5.615	31.528
$GM = 39.385$			$SS_{total} = $ **629.074**

MASTERING THE FORMULA

12-5: The total sum of squares in· an ANOVA is calculated using the following formula: $SS_{total} = \Sigma(X - GM)^2$. We subtract the grand mean from every score, then square these deviations. We then sum all the squared deviations.

Below the fourth column, we have summed the squared deviations: 629.074. This is the total sum of squares, SS_{total}. The formula for the total sum of squares is:

$$SS_{total} = \Sigma(X - GM)^2$$

The model for calculating the within-groups sum of squares is shown in Table 12-6. This time the deviations are around the mean of each particular group (separated by horizontal lines) instead of around the grand mean. For the four scores in the first sample, we subtract their sample mean, 33.25. For example, the calculation for the first score is:

$$(28 - 33.25)^2 = 27.563$$

For the three scores in the second sample, we subtract their sample mean, 35.0. And so on for all four samples. (*Note:* Don't forget to switch means when you get to each new sample!)

Once we have all the deviations, we square them and sum them to calculate the within-groups sum of squares, 167.419, the number below the fourth column. Because we subtract the sample mean, rather than the grand mean, from each score, the formula is:

$$SS_{within} = \Sigma(X - M)^2$$

MASTERING THE FORMULA

12-6: The within-groups sum of squares in a one-way between-groups ANOVA is calculated using the following formula: $SS_{within} = \Sigma(X - M)^2$. From each score, we subtract its group mean. We then square these deviations. We sum all the squared deviations for everyone in all groups.

Notice how the weighting for sample size is built into the calculation: The first sample has four scores and contributes four squared deviations to the total. The other samples have only three scores, so they only contribute three squared deviations.

TABLE 12-6   Calculating the Within-Groups Sum of Squares

The within-groups sum of squares is calculated by taking each score and subtracting the mean of the sample from which it comes—not the grand mean—to create deviations, then squaring the deviations and summing the squared deviations.

Sample	X	$(X - M)$	$(X - M)^2$
Foraging	28	−5.25	27.563
	36	2.75	7.563
$M_{for} = 33.250$	38	4.75	22.563
	31	−2.25	5.063
Farming	32	−3.000	9.000
	33	−2.000	4.000
$M_{farm} = 35.000$	40	5.000	25.000
Natural resources	47	−0.333	0.111
	43	−4.333	18.775
$M_{nr} = 47.333$	52	4.667	21.781
Industrial	40	24.000	16.000
	47	3.000	9.000
$M_{ind} = 44.000$	45	1.000	1.000
	$GM = 39.385$		$SS_{within} = $ **167.419**

TABLE 12-7	Calculating the Between-Groups Sum of Squares

The between-groups sum of squares is calculated by subtracting the grand mean from the sample mean for every score to create deviations, then squaring the deviations and summing the squared deviations. The individual scores themselves are not involved in any calculations.

Sample	X	(M − GM)	(M − GM)²
Foraging	28	−6.135	37.638
	36	−6.135	37.638
M_{for} = 33.250	38	−6.135	37.638
	31	−6.135	37.638
Farming	32	−4.385	19.228
	33	−4.385	19.228
M_{farm} = 35.000	40	−4.385	19.228
Natural resources	47	7.948	63.171
	43	7.948	63.171
M_{nr} = 47.333	52	7.948	63.171
Industrial	40	4.615	21.298
	47	4.615	21.298
M_{ind} = 44.000	45	4.615	21.298
	GM = 39.385		$SS_{between}$ = **461.643**

Finally, we calculate the between-groups sum of squares. Remember, the goal for this step is to estimate how much each *group*—not each *individual participant*—deviates from the overall grand mean, so we use means rather than individual scores in the calculations. For each of the 13 people in this study, we subtract the grand mean from the mean of the group to which that individual belongs.★

For example, the first person has a score of 28 and belongs to the group labeled "foraging," which has a mean score of 33.25. The grand mean is 39.385. We ignore this person's individual score and subtract 39.385 (the grand mean) from 33.25 (the group mean) to get the deviation score, −6.135. The next person, also in the group labeled "foraging," has a score of 36. The group mean of that sample is 33.25. Once again, we ignore that person's individual score and subtract 39.385 (the grand mean) from 33.25 (the group mean) to get the deviation score, also −6.135.

In fact, we subtract 39.385 from 33.25 for all four scores, as you can see in Table 12-7. When we get to the horizontal line between samples, we look for the next sample mean. For all three scores in the next sample, we subtract the grand mean, 39.385, from the sample mean, 35.0, and so on.

Notice that individual scores are *never* involved in the calculations, just the sample means and the grand mean. Also notice that the first group (foraging), with four participants, has more weight in the calculation than the other three groups, which each have

---

★There is a shortcut to the formula for the between-groups sum of squares, but it can only be used when there are equal numbers of participants in each group. In that case, we only need to subtract the grand mean from each mean once – not for every individual. After squaring and summing the deviations for each mean, we then multiply that sum of squares by the number of participants in each sample. The formula is:

$$SS_{between} = n[\Sigma(M - GM)^2]$$

where *n* is the number of participants in each sample.

MASTERING THE FORMULA

12-7: The between-groups sum of squares in an ANOVA is calculated using the following formula: $SS_{between} = \Sigma(M - GM)^2$. For each score, we subtract the grand mean from that score's group mean, and square this deviation. Note that we do not use the scores in any of these calculations. We sum all the squared deviations.

MASTERING THE FORMULA

12-8: We can also calculate the total sum of squares for a one-way between-groups ANOVA by adding the within-groups sum of squares and the between-groups sum of squares: $SS_{total} = SS_{within} + SS_{between}$. This is a useful check on the calculations.

only three participants. The third column of Table 12-7 includes the deviations and the fourth includes the squared deviations. The between-groups sum of squares, in bold under the fourth column, is 461.643. The formula for the between-groups sum of squares is:

$$SS_{between} = \Sigma(M - GM)^2$$

Now is the moment of arithmetic truth. Were the calculations correct? To find out, we add the within-groups sum of squares (167.419) to the between-groups sum of squares (461.643) to see if they equal the total sum of squares (629.074). Here's the formula:

$$SS_{total} = SS_{within} + SS_{between} = 629.062 = 167.419 + 461.643$$

Indeed, the total sum of squares, 629.074, is almost equal to the sum of the other two sums of squares, 167.419 and 461.643, which is 629.062. The calculations were correct (the slight difference is due to rounding decisions).

To recap (Table 12-8), for the total sum of squares, we subtract the *grand mean* from each individual *score* to get the deviations. For the within-groups sum of squares, we subtract the appropriate *sample mean* from every *score* to get the deviations. And for the between-groups sum of squares, we subtract the *grand mean* from the appropriate *sample mean*, once for each score, to get the deviations; for the between-groups sum of squares, the actual scores are never involved in any calculations.

Now we insert these numbers into the source table to calculate the F statistic. See Table 12-9 for the source table that lists all the formulas and Table 12-10 for the completed source table. We divide the between-groups sum of squares and the within-groups

TABLE 12-8 The Three Sums of Squares of ANOVA

The calculations in ANOVA are built on the foundation we learned in Chapter 4, sums of squared deviations. We calculate three types of sums of squares, one for between-groups variance, one for within-groups variance, and one for total variance. Once we have the three sums of squares, most of the remaining calculations involve simple division.

Sum of Squares	To Calculate the Deviations, Subtract the . . .	Formula
Between-groups	Grand mean from the sample mean (for each score)	$SS_{between} = \Sigma(M - GM)^2$
Within-groups	Sample mean from each score	$SS_{within} = \Sigma(X - M)^2$
Total	Grand mean from each score	$SS_{total} = \Sigma(X - GM)^2$

TABLE 12-9 A Source Table with Formulas

This table summarizes the formulas for calculating an F statistic.

Source	SS	df	MS	F
Between	$\Sigma(M - GM)^2$	$N_{groups} - 1$	$\dfrac{SS_{between}}{df_{between}}$	$\dfrac{MS_{between}}{MS_{within}}$
Within	$\Sigma(X - M)^2$	$df_1 + df_2 + \cdots + df_{last}$	$\dfrac{SS_{within}}{df_{within}}$	
Total	$\Sigma(X - GM)^2$	$N_{total} - 1$		

[Expanded formula: $df_{within} = (N_1 - 1) + (N_2 - 1) + \cdots + (N_{last} - 1)$]

TABLE 12-10	A Completed Source Table

Once we calculate the sums of squares and the degrees of freedom, the rest is just simple division. We use the first two columns of numbers to calculate the variances and the F statistic. We divide the between-groups sum of squares and within-groups sum of squares by their associated degrees of freedom to get the between-groups variance and within-groups variance. Then we divide the between-groups variance by the within-groups variance to get the F statistic, 8.27.

Source	SS	df	MS	F
Between-groups	461.643	3	153.881	**8.27**
Within-groups	167.419	9	18.602	
Total	629.074	12		

sum of squares by their associated degrees of freedom to get the between-groups variance and the within-groups variance. The formulas are:

$$MS_{between} = \frac{SS_{between}}{df_{between}} = \frac{461.643}{3} = 153.881$$

$$MS_{within} = \frac{SS_{within}}{df_{within}} = \frac{167.419}{9} = 18.602$$

We then divide the between-groups variance by the within-groups variance to calculate the F statistic. The formula, in bold in Table 12-9, is:

$$F = \frac{MS_{between}}{MS_{within}} = \frac{153.881}{18.602} = 8.27$$

Making a Decision

Now we have to come back to the six steps of hypothesis testing for ANOVA to fill in the gaps in steps 1 and 6. We finished steps 2 through 5 in the previous section.

Step 1: ANOVA assumes that participants were selected from populations with equal variances. Statistical software, such as SPSS, tests this assumption while analyzing the overall data. For now, we can use the last column from the within-groups sum of squares calculations in Table 12-6. Variance is computed by dividing the sum of squares by the sample size minus 1. We can add the squared deviations for each sample, then divide by the sample size minus 1. Table 12-11 shows the calculations for variance within each of the four samples. Because the largest variance, 20.917, is not more than twice the smallest variance, 13.0, we have met the assumption of equal variances.

Step 6: Now that we have the test statistic, we compare it with 3.86, the critical F value that we identified in step 4. The F statistic we calculated was 8.27, and Figure 12-4 demonstrates that the F statistic is beyond the critical value: We can reject the null hypothesis. It appears that people living in some types of societies are fairer, on average, than are people living in other types of societies. And congratulations on making your way through your first ANOVA! Statistical software will do all of these calculations for you, but understanding how the computer produces those numbers adds to your overall understanding.

The ANOVA, however, only allows us to conclude that at least one mean is different from at least one other mean. The next section describes how to determine which groups are different.

TABLE 12-11 Calculating Sample Variances

We calculate the variances of the samples by dividing each sum of squares by the sample size minus 1 to check one of the assumptions of ANOVA. For unequal sample sizes, as we have here, we want the largest variance (20.917 in this case) to be no more than twice the smallest (13.0 in this case). Two times 13.0 is 26.0, which is more than 20.917, so we meet this assumption.

Sample	Foraging	Farming	Natural Resources	Industrial
Squared deviations	27.563	9.000	0.111	16.000
	7.563	4.000	18.775	9.000
	22.563	25.000	21.781	1.000
	5.063			
Sum of squares:	62.752	38.000	40.667	26.000
$N - 1$:	3	2	2	2
Variance	**20.917**	**19.000**	**20.334**	**13.000**

FIGURE 12-4

Making a Decision with an F Distribution

We compare the F statistic that we calculated for the samples to a single cutoff, or critical value, on the appropriate F distribution. We can reject the null hypothesis if the test statistic is beyond—more to the right than—the cutoff. Here, the F statistic of 8.27 is beyond the cutoff of 3.86, so we can reject the null hypothesis.

Summary: We reject the null hypothesis. It appears that mean fairness levels differ based on the type of society in which a person lives. In a scientific journal, these statistics are presented in a similar way to the z and t statistics but with separate degrees of freedom in parentheses for between-groups and within-groups: $F(3, 9) = 8.27$, $p < 0.05$. (*Note:* Report the actual p value when analyzing ANOVA with statistical software.)

CHECK YOUR LEARNING

Reviewing the Concepts

> One-way between-groups ANOVA uses the same six steps of hypothesis testing that we learned in Chapter 7, but with a few minor changes in steps 3 and 5.

> In step 3, we merely state the comparison distribution and provide two different types of degrees of freedom, df for the between-groups variance and df for the within-groups variance.

> In step 5, we complete the calculations, using a source table to organize the results. First, we estimate population variance by considering the differences among means (between-groups variance). Second, we estimate population variance by calculating a weighted average of the variances within each sample (within-groups variance).

> The calculation of variability requires several means, including sample means and the grand mean, which is the mean of all scores, regardless of which sample the scores came from.

> We divide between-groups variance by within-groups variance to calculate the F statistic.

> Before making a decision based on the F statistic, we check to see whether the assumption of equal sample variances is met. This assumption is met when the largest sample variance is not more than twice the amount of the smallest variance.

Clarifying the Concepts	**12-5** If the F statistic is beyond the cutoff, what does that tell us? What doesn't that tell us?
	12-6 What is the primary subtraction that enters into the calculation of $SS_{between}$?

Calculating the Statistics 12-7   Calculate each type of degrees of freedom for the following data, assuming a between-groups design:

Group 1: 37, 30, 22, 29

Group 2: 49, 52, 41, 39

Group 3: 36, 49, 42

a. $df_{between} = N_{groups} - 1$

b. $df_{within} = df_1 + df_2 + \cdots + df_{last}$

c. $df_{total} = df_{between} + df_{within}$, or $df_{total} = N_{total} - 1$

12-8   Using the data in Check Your Learning 12-7, compute the grand mean.

12-9   Using the data in Check Your Learning 12-7, compute each type of sum of squares.

a.   Total sum of squares

b.   Within-groups sum of squares

c.   Between-groups sum of squares

12-10   Using all of your calculations in Check Your Learning 12-7 to 12-9, perform the simple division to complete an entire between-groups ANOVA source table for these data.

Applying the Concepts 12-11   Let's create a context for the data provided above. Hollon, Thase, and Markowitz (2002) reviewed the efficacy of different treatments for depression, including medications, electroconvulsive therapy, psychotherapy, and placebo treatments. These data re-create some of the basic findings the researchers present regarding psychotherapy. Each group is meant to represent people who received a different psychotherapy-based treatment, including psychodynamic therapy in group 1, interpersonal therapy in group 2, and cognitive-behavioral therapy in group 3. The scores presented here represent the extent to which someone responded to the treatment, with higher numbers indicating greater efficacy of treatment.

Group 1 (psychodynamic therapy): 37, 30, 22, 29

Group 2 (interpersonal therapy): 49, 52, 41, 39

Group 3 (cognitive-behavioral therapy): 36, 49, 42

a.   Write hypotheses, in words, for this research.

b.   Check the assumptions of ANOVA.

Solutions to these Check Your Learning questions can be found in Appendix D.

c.   Determine the critical value for F. Using your calculations from Check Your Learning 12-10, make a decision about the null hypothesis for these treatment options.

Beyond Hypothesis Testing for the One-Way Between-Groups ANOVA

Is driving while talking on a hands-free mobile phone really more dangerous than talking with a passenger sitting next to us? Do expectations for fairness differ across types of societies? Hypothesis testing is a good way to start answering such questions. We can obtain more specific answers by (1) calculating effect size (as we did with z tests and t tests), and (2) conducting post hoc tests to determine exactly which groups are significantly different from each other.

R^2, the Effect Size for ANOVA

In Chapter 8, we learned how to use Cohen's d to calculate effect size. However, Cohen's d only applies when subtracting one mean from another (as for a z test or a t test). With ANOVA, we calculate $\boldsymbol{R^2}$ (pronounced "r squared"), *the proportion of variance in the dependent variable that is accounted for by the independent variable.* We could also calculate a similar statistic called η^2 (pronounced "eta squared"). We can interpret η^2 exactly as we interpret R^2.

Like the F statistic, R^2 is a ratio. However, it calculates the proportion of variance accounted for by the independent variable out of all of the variance. Its numerator uses only the between-groups sum of squares, $SS_{between}$, to indicate variability among the means (ignoring the variability within each sample). The denominator uses total variability (both between-groups variance and within-groups variance), which is the total sum of squares: SS_{total}. The formula is:

$$R^2 = \frac{SS_{between}}{SS_{total}}$$

EXAMPLE 12.2

Let's apply this to the ANOVA we conducted on fairness across different types of societies. We can use the statistics in the source table we created earlier to calculate R^2:

$$R^2 = \frac{SS_{between}}{SS_{total}} = \frac{461.643}{629.074} = 0.73$$

Table 12-12 displays Jacob Cohen's conventions for R^2 that, like Cohen's d, indicate whether the effect size is small, medium, or large. This R^2 of 0.73 is large. This is not surprising; if we can reject the null hypothesis when the sample size is small, then the effect size must be large. We can also turn the proportion into the more familiar language of percentages by multiplying by 100.

- R^2 is the proportion of variance in the dependent variable that is accounted for by the independent variable.

- A **post hoc test** is a statistical procedure frequently carried out after the null hypothesis has been rejected in an analysis of variance; it allows us to make multiple comparisons among several means; often referred to as a *follow-up test.*

- The **Tukey *HSD* test** is a widely used post hoc test that determines the differences between means in terms of standard error; the *HSD* is compared to a critical value; sometimes called the *q test.*

TABLE 12-12 Cohen's Conventions for Effect Sizes: R^2

The following guidelines, called *conventions* by statisticians, are meant to help researchers decide how important an effect is. These numbers are not cutoffs; they are merely rough guidelines to help researchers interpret results.

Effect Size	Convention
Small	0.01
Medium	0.06
Large	0.14

We can then say that a specific percentage of the variance in the dependent variable is accounted for by the independent variable. In this case, we could say that 73% of the variability in sharing is due to the type of society. (Note that our overall pattern of results match those of the original study; however, the actual effect size was lower than this.) ●

Post Hoc Tests

The statistically significant F statistic means that some difference exists somewhere in the study. The R^2 tells us that the difference is large, but we still don't know which pairs of means are responsible for these effects. Here's an easy way to figure it out: Graph the data. The picture will suggest which means are different, but those differences still need to be confirmed with a post hoc test. *A **post hoc test** is a statistical procedure frequently carried out after the null hypothesis has been rejected in an analysis of variance; it allows us to make multiple comparisons among several means.* The name of the test, post hoc, means "after this" in Latin; these tests are often referred to as *follow-up tests.* (Post hoc tests are not conducted if we fail to reject the null hypothesis, because we already know that there are no statistically significant differences among means.)

For example, the fairness study produced the following mean scores: foraging, 33.25; farming, 35.0; industrial, 44.0; and natural resources, 47.333. The ANOVA told us to reject the null hypothesis, so something is going on in this data set. The Pareto chart (organized by highest to lowest) and a post hoc test will tell us "where the action is" in this statistically significant ANOVA.

The graph in Figure 12-5 helps us think through the possibilities. For example, people in industrial societies and in societies that extract natural resources might exhibit higher levels of fairness, on average, than people in foraging or farming societies (groups 1 and 2 versus groups 3 and 4). Or people in societies that extract natural resources might be higher, on average, only compared with those in foraging societies (group 1 versus group 4). Maybe all four groups are different from one another, on average. There are so many possibilities that we need a post hoc test to reach a statistically valid conclusion. There are many post hoc tests and most are named for their founders, almost exclusively people with fabulous names—for example, Bonferroni, Scheffé (pronounced "sheff-ay"), and Tukey (pronounced "tookee"). We will focus on the Tukey *HSD* test here.

Tukey *HSD*

*The **Tukey HSD test** is a widely used post hoc test that determines the differences between means in terms of standard error; the HSD is compared to a critical value.* The Tukey *HSD* test (also called the *q test*) stands for "*honestly significant difference*" because it allows us to make multiple comparisons to identify differences that are "honestly" there.

In the Tukey *HSD* test, we (1) calculate differences between each pair of means, (2) divide each difference by the standard error, and (3) compare the *HSD* for each pair of means to a critical value (a *q* value, found in Appendix B) to determine whether the means are different enough to reject the null hypothesis. The formula for the Tukey *HSD* test is a variant of the *z* test and *t* tests for any two sample means:

$$HSD = \frac{(M_1 - M_2)}{s_M}$$

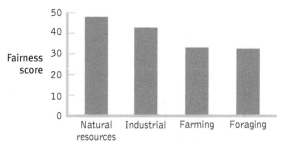

The formula for the standard error is:

$$s_M = \sqrt{\frac{MS_{within}}{N}}$$

N in this case is the sample size within each group, with the assumption that all samples have the same number of participants.

When samples are different sizes, as in the example of societies, we have to calculate a weighted sample size, also known as a *harmonic mean*, N' (pronounced "N prime") before we can calculate standard error:

$$N' = \frac{N_{groups}}{\Sigma(1/N)}$$

EXAMPLE 12.3

We calculate N' by dividing the number of groups (the numerator) by the sum of 1 divided by the sample size for every group (the denominator). For the example in which there were four participants in foraging societies and three in each of the other three types of societies, the formula is:

$$N' = \frac{4}{\left(\dfrac{1}{4} + \dfrac{1}{3} + \dfrac{1}{3} + \dfrac{1}{3}\right)} = \frac{4}{1.25} = 3.20$$

When sample sizes are not equal, we use a formula for s_M based on N' instead of N:

$$s_M = \sqrt{\frac{MS_{within}}{N'}} = \sqrt{\frac{18.602}{3.20}} = 2.411$$

Now we use simple subtraction to calculate *HSD* for each pair of means. Which comes first doesn't matter; for example, we could subtract the mean for foraging societies from the mean for farming societies, or vice versa. We can ignore the sign of the answer because it is contingent on the arbitrary decision of which mean to subtract from the other.

Foraging (33.250) versus farming (35.000):

$$HSD = \frac{(33.250 - 35.000)}{2.411} = -0.73$$

Foraging (33.250) versus natural resources (47.333):

$$HSD = \frac{(33.250 - 47.333)}{2.411} = -5.84$$

Foraging (33.250) versus industrial (44.000):

$$HSD = \frac{(33.250 - 44.000)}{2.411} = -4.46$$

Farming (35.000) versus natural resources (47.333):

$$HSD = \frac{(35.000 - 47.333)}{2.411} = -5.12$$

Farming (35.000) versus industrial (44.000):

$$HSD = \frac{(35.000 - 44.000)}{2.411} = -3.73$$

TABLE 12-13	Excerpt from the q Table

Like the *F* table, we use the *q* table to determine critical values for a given *p* level, based on the number of means being compared and the within-groups degrees of freedom. Note that critical values are in regular type for 0.05 and boldface for 0.01.

Within-Groups Degrees of Freedom	p level	k = Number of Treatments (levels)		
		. . . 3	4	5 . . .
⋮				
8	.05	4.04	4.53	4.89
	.01	**5.64**	**6.20**	**6.62**
9	.05	3.95	4.41	4.76
	.01	**5.43**	**5.96**	**6.35**
10	.05	3.88	4.33	4.65
⋮	**.01**	**5.27**	**5.77**	**6.14**

Natural resources (47.333) versus industrial (44.000):

$$HSD = \frac{(47.333 - 44.000)}{2.411} = -1.38$$

Now all we need is a critical value from the *q* table in Appendix B (excerpted in Table 12-13) to which we can compare the *HSD*s. The numbers of means being compared (levels of the independent variable) are in a row along the top of the *q* table, and the within-groups degrees of freedom are in a column along the left-hand side. We first look up the within-groups degrees of freedom for the test, 9, along the left column. We then go across from 9 to the numbers below the number of means being compared, 4. For a *p* level of 0.05, the cutoff *q* is 4.41. Again, the sign of the *HSD* does not matter. This is a two-tailed test, and any *HSD* above 4.41 or below −4.41 would be considered statistically significant.

The *q* table indicates three statistically significant differences whose *HSD*s are beyond the critical value of −4.41: −5.84, −4.46, and −5.12. It appears that people in foraging societies are less fair, on average, than people in societies that depend on natural resources and people in industrial societies. In addition, people in farming societies are less fair, on average, than are people in societies that depend on natural resources. We have not rejected the null hypothesis for any other pairs, so we can only conclude that there is not enough evidence to determine whether their means are different.

What might explain these differences? The researchers observed that people who purchase food routinely interact with other people in an economic market. They concluded that higher levels of market integration are associated with higher levels of fairness (Henrich et al., 2010). Social norms of fairness may develop in market societies that require cooperative interactions between people who do not know each other.

How much faith can we have in these findings? Cautious confidence and replication are recommended; researchers could not randomly assign people to live in particular societies, so some third variable may explain the relation between market integration and fairness. ●

Next Steps	The Bonferroni Test

For many researchers, the Tukey *HSD* test is the default post hoc test, and in many cases, it really is the best choice. But the wise researcher thinks about which test to choose before automatically conducting a Tukey *HSD* test. One other post hoc test that is often used is the Bonferroni test. It is more conservative than the Tukey *HSD* test, meaning that the test makes it more difficult to reject the null hypothesis. Also, the Bonferroni test is easy to implement.

*The **Bonferroni test** is a post hoc test that provides a more strict critical value for every comparison of means.* Normally, social scientists use a cutoff level of 0.05. With a Bonferroni test, sometimes called the *Dunn Multiple Comparison test*, we use a smaller critical region to make it more difficult to reject the null hypothesis. To use a Bonferroni test, we determine the number of comparisons we plan to make. Table 12-14 states the number of comparisons for two through seven means.

The Bonferroni test is straightforward. We merely divide the p level by the number of comparisons. For a p level of 0.05 and four means, as in the fairness study, we make six comparisons using a 0.008 p level (0.05/6) for each comparison. We then conduct a series of independent-samples t tests using the more extreme p level to determine the cutoffs. That is, the difference between means would have to be in the extremely narrow tails of a t distribution, at 0.008 (0.8%), before we would be willing to reject the null hypothesis.

For seven means, we would make 21 comparisons using the (0.05/21) = 0.002 p level for each comparison. The difference would have to be in the most extreme 0.2% of a t distribution before we would reject the null hypothesis!

In each case, the p levels for every comparison add up to 0.05, so we are still using a 0.05 p level overall. For example, when we make six comparisons at the 0.008 level, we have a (0.008 + 0.008 + 0.008 + 0.008 + 0.008 + 0.008) = 6(0.008) = 0.05 p level overall. Even though the overall p level remains at 0.05, the p levels for the individual comparisons rapidly become very extreme (see Table 12-14). The difference between two means must be quite extreme before we can reject the null hypothesis. We may fail to detect real differences that are not quite extreme enough, which is a Type II error.

● The **Bonferroni test** (also sometimes called the Dunn Multiple Comparison test) is a post hoc test that provides a more strict critical value for every comparison of means.

TABLE 12-14 The Bonferroni Test: Few Groups, Many Comparisons

Even with a few means, we must make many comparisons to account for every possible difference. Because we run the risk of incorrectly rejecting the null hypothesis just by chance if we run so many tests, it is a wise idea to use a more conservative procedure, such as the Bonferroni test, when comparing means. The Bonferroni test requires that we divide an overall p level, such as 0.05, by the number of comparisons we will make.

Number of Means	Number of Comparisons	Bonferroni p Level (overall $p = 0.05$)
2	1	0.05
3	3	0.017
4	6	0.008
5	10	0.005
6	15	0.003
7	21	0.002

In the fairness study, we conduct independent-samples t tests but use a critical value based on 0.008 p level. (In the t table, we could only look up the closest p level to 0.008, 0.01, although software can help us be more specific.) Using software, we conducted an independent-samples t test to compare the means for people in foraging societies and people in industrial societies, calculating a t statistic of -3.34. For a test of two groups with four and three participants, respectively, the total degrees of freedom is 5 (the sum of the degrees of freedom for each group, 3 and 2). The critical t values for a two-tailed independent-samples t test with 5 degrees of freedom at a p level of 0.01 (the closest to 0.008) are -4.032 and 4.032. This comparison is not statistically significant.

Unlike the Tukey HSD test, the Bonferroni test does not allow us to conclude that people in foraging societies are less fair, on average, than people in industrial societies. The test statistic is no longer beyond the critical value, because the critical value based on a Bonferroni test is more extreme than the critical value based on a Tukey HSD test.

CHECK YOUR LEARNING

Reviewing the Concepts

> As with other hypothesis tests, it is recommended that we calculate a measure of effect size when we have conducted an ANOVA. The most commonly reported effect size for ANOVA is R^2.

> If we are able to reject the null hypothesis with ANOVA, we're not finished. We must conduct a post hoc test, such as a Tukey HSD test, to determine exactly which pairs of means are significantly different from one another.

> When computing a post hoc Tukey HSD test on samples with unequal N's, we need to calculate a weighted sample size, called N'.

> The Bonferroni test is a more conservative post hoc test than the Tukey HSD test. It makes it more difficult to reject the null hypothesis.

Clarifying the Concepts

12-12   When do we conduct a post hoc test, such as a Tukey HSD test, and what does it tell us?

12-13   How is R^2 interpreted?

Calculating the Statistics

12-14   Assume that a researcher is interested in whether reaction time varies as a function of grade level. After measuring the reaction times of 10 children in fourth grade, 12 children in fifth grade, and 13 children in sixth grade, the researcher conducts an ANOVA and finds an $SS_{between}$ of 336.360 and an SS_{total} of 522.782.

   a.   Calculate R^2.

   b.   Write a sentence interpreting this R^2. Be sure to do so in terms of the independent and dependent variables described for this study.

12-15   If the researcher in the previous Check Your Learning exercise rejected the null hypothesis after performing the ANOVA and intended to perform Tukey HSD post hoc comparisons, what would the critical value of the q statistic be for the comparisons?

12-16   If the researcher in the previous Check Your Learning exercise were to conduct post hoc tests using the Bonferroni test, what would the adjusted p level be?

Applying the Concepts

12-17   Perform Tukey HSD post hoc comparisons on the data you analyzed in Check Your Learning 12-10. For which comparisons do you reject the null hypothesis?

Solutions to these Check Your Learning questions can be found in Appendix D.

12-18   Calculate the effect size for the data you analyzed in Check Your Learning 12-10 and interpret its meaning.

REVIEW OF CONCEPTS

Using the *F* Distribution with Three or More Samples

We use the *F statistic* when we want to compare three or more samples. As with the *z* and *t* statistics, the *F* statistic is calculated by dividing a measure of the differences among sample means (*between-groups variance*) by a measure of variability within the samples (*within-groups variance*). The hypothesis test based on the *F* statistic is called *analysis of variance (ANOVA)*.

ANOVA offers a solution to the problem of having to run multiple *t* tests, because it allows for multiple comparisons in just one statistical analysis. There are several different types of ANOVA, and each has two descriptors. One indicates the number of independent variables, such as *one-way ANOVA* for one independent variable. The other indicates whether participants are in only one condition (*between-groups ANOVA*) or in every condition (*within-groups ANOVA*). The major assumptions for ANOVA are random selection of participants, normally distributed underlying populations, and *homoscedasticity*, which means that all populations have the same variance (versus *heteroscedasticity*, which means that the populations do not all have the same variance). As with previous statistical tests, most real-life analyses do not meet all of these assumptions.

One-Way Between-Groups ANOVA

The one-way between-groups ANOVA uses the six steps of hypothesis testing that we have already learned, but with some modifications, particularly to steps 3 and 5. Step 3 is simpler than with *t* tests; we only have to state that the comparison distribution is an *F* distribution and provide the degrees of freedom. In step 5, we calculate the *F* statistic; a *source table* helps us to keep track of the calculations. The *F* statistic is a ratio of two different estimates of population variance, both of distributions of scores rather than distributions of means. The denominator, within-groups variance, is similar to the pooled variance of the independent-samples *t* test; it's basically a weighted average of the variance within each sample. The numerator, between-groups variance, is an estimate based on the difference between the sample means, but it is then inflated to represent a distribution of scores rather than a distribution of means. As part of the calculations of between-groups variance and within-groups variance, we need to calculate a *grand mean*, the mean score of every participant in the study.

A large between-groups variance and a small within-groups variance indicate a small degree of overlap among samples and likely a small degree of overlap among populations. A large between-groups variance divided by a small within-groups variance produces a large *F* statistic. If the *F* statistic is beyond a prescribed cutoff, or critical value, then we can reject the null hypothesis.

Beyond Hypothesis Testing for the One-Way Between-Groups ANOVA

It is also recommended, as with other hypothesis tests, that we calculate an effect size—usually R^2—when we conduct an ANOVA. In addition, when we reject the null hypothesis in an ANOVA, we only know that at least one of the means is different from at least one other mean. But we do not know exactly where the differences lie until we conduct a *post hoc test* such as the *Tukey HSD test*. The Bonferroni test is a more conservative post hoc test and is helpful to researchers who want to explore a data set while minimizing the probability of making a Type I error.

SPSS®

In this chapter, we conducted a one-way between-groups ANOVA to compare people in four different types of societies regarding how fairly they behaved in a game. The level of fair behavior was assessed by the proportion of money that they gave to a second player in that game. The type of society is a nominal independent variable, and the proportion of money that they gave to the second player is a scale dependent variable. To conduct a one-way between-groups ANOVA using SPSS, we enter the data so that all of the data for each participant is in a single row. For example, a person would have a score in the first column indicating the type of society in which he or she lives, perhaps a 1 for foraging or a 3 for natural resources. That person would also have a score in the second column indicating fairness level—the proportion of money he or she gave to a second player. The data as they should be entered are visible behind the output on the screenshot shown here. Remember: we can change how we view categorical data by selecting "View" and either checking or unchecking the box "value labels." In the screenshot, "value labels" is turned on.

Once the data have been entered, we can instruct SPSS to conduct the ANOVA by selecting Analyze → Compare Means → One-Way ANOVA. Now select the variables from the list. The independent variable named "Society" goes in the box marked "Factor," and the dependent variable named "Fairness" goes in the box labeled "Dependent List." To request a post hoc test to compare the means of the four groups, select "Post Hoc," then "Tukey," and then click "Continue." To request descriptive statistics—like the means and standard deviations for each group—select "Options," then "Descriptive," and then click "Continue." Click "OK" to run the ANOVA.

The SPSS output will provide four different tables. The first table (not included in the screenshot) includes the descriptive statistics for each level of the independent variable.

The second table is the source table. Notice that the sums of squares, degrees of freedom, mean squares, and F statistic match the ones we calculated earlier. Any slight differences are due to differences in rounding decisions. The last column, titled "Sig.," says .006. This number indicates that the actual p value of this test statistic is just 0.006, which is less than the 0.05 p level typically used in hypothesis testing and an indication that we can reject the null hypothesis.

Below the source table, we can see the output for the post hoc test (the table labeled "Multiple Comparisons"). Mean differences with an asterisk are statistically significant at a p level of 0.05. The output here matches the post hoc test we conducted earlier. Each line in the table indicates a comparison between two groups. For example, the first line compares the foraging and farming groups, and includes the mean difference and standard error for that comparison. The next column provides the p value for that comparison: .949. This p value is above the 0.05 standard, so there is not a statistically significant difference between these two means. When we look at the second line—the comparison between the foraging and natural resources groups—and we move across the row to the "Sig" column, we can see a p value of 0.009. This p value is lower than 0.05, and SPSS makes it easier to see this by including an asterisk next to the mean comparison value. Note that this table provides several redundant comparisons. For example, the first line compares foraging to farming, and the fourth line compares farming to foraging. These two comparisons are the same, just with a different order. Regardless of the order, the conclusion about the comparison is the same.

The Tukey post hoc test in SPSS provides an additional table after the Multiple Comparisons table (labeled "Homogeneous Subsets," shown next to the SPSS screenshot). The conclusions made using this table will be the same as the conclusions we make using the "Multiple

Source: SPSS Statistics

Comparisons" table and with the hand calculations we made earlier. This table provides the means for each level of the independent variable and provides us with two pieces of information. First, means found in the same column are not statistically significantly different from one another. Second, means found in different columns are statistically significantly different from each other. For example, the first column includes the means for the foraging and farming groups, so we can conclude that there is not a statistically significant difference between these groups. For the second column, we can see the means for the farming and industrial groups, so these two means also are not statistically significantly different from one another. The patterns in the column, therefore, allow us to determine visually which means are in the same column and are not statistically significantly different. Additionally, we can see what means are not in the same column and are statistically significantly different. For example, the mean for the foraging group and the mean for the industrial group are never in the same column. We can conclude, then, that the foraging and industrial groups are statistically significantly different from one another. We can also see that the mean for the foraging group and the mean for the natural

resources group are never in the same column. Again, we can conclude that the foraging and natural resources groups are statistically significantly different from one another. Regardless of which table we use to interpret the results of the post hoc tests, the conclusions will be the same.

Homogeneous Subsets

The proportion of money given to the second play

Tukey HSD[a,b]

Type of society	N	Subset for alpha = 0.05		
		1	2	3
Foraging	4	33.2500		
Farming	3	35.0000	35.0000	
Industrial	3		44.0000	44.0000
Natural resources	3			47.3333
Sig.		.954	.103	.765

Means for groups in homogeneous subsets are displayed.

a. Uses Harmonic Mean Sample Size = 3.200.

b. The group sizes are unequal. The harmonic mean of the group sizes is used. Type I error levels are not guaranteed.

HOW IT WORKS

12.1 CONDUCTING A ONE-WAY BETWEEN-GROUPS ANOVA

Who do you think is more outgoing, first-born or later-born siblings? Rohrer and colleagues (2015) used three nationally based data sets from the United States, Great Britain, and Germany to understand the relations between a person's birth-order position and his or her personality. Each national data set used a different measure of personality, but all measures were theoretically based on the Big Five personality traits: extroversion, emotional stability, agreeableness, conscientiousness, and openness. The researchers standardized scores from each personality measure so comparisons could be made among all participants. They used a method similar to z scores, but with a mean of 50 rather than 0. The researchers also adjusted the personality scores for age, as "changes in personality over time… are inherently confounded with birth order" (p. 5).

Here is an abbreviated version of this study with fictional data for the personality trait extroversion. The means of these data points, however, are the actual means of the study. The findings from this smaller, fictional data match the findings from the large, multi-national study. The data represent participants with two siblings (i.e., families with three children).

Oldest Sibling: 47.15, 51.25, 49.75, 52.45

Middle Sibling: 47.55, 49.7, 50.8, 53.75

Youngest Sibling: 47.97, 49.49, 50.21, 53.89

In this study, the independent variable was birth-order position, with three levels: oldest, middle, and youngest. The dependent variable was the standardized personality score for extroversion. So there is one ordinal independent variable with three between-groups levels and one scale dependent variable. How can we conduct a one-way between-groups ANOVA?

Summary of Step 1

Population 1: People who are the oldest child in a family of three siblings. Population 2: People who are the middle child in a family of three siblings. Population 3: People who are the youngest child in a family of three siblings.

The comparison distribution will be an F distribution. The hypothesis test will be a one-way between-groups ANOVA. The participants were unlikely to have been randomly selected from among all children in families in which there are three siblings, so we should be cautious when generalizing conclusions from this study. We do not know if the underlying population distributions are normal, and this fictional example does not have a sufficient sample size that we can assume normal distributions based on the central limit theorem. (The actual study, however, did have a large sample size, so this assumption would have been met.) To see if we meet the homoscedasticity assumption, we will check to see if the largest variance is no greater than twice the smallest variance. From the calculations below, we see that the largest variance, 6.66 for middle children, is not more than twice the smallest, 5.22 for the oldest children, so we have met the homoscedasticity assumption. (The following information is taken from the calculation of SS_{within}.)

Sample	Oldest	Middle	Youngest
Squared deviations	9.000	8.410	5.856
	1.210	0.563	0.810
	0.160	0.123	0.032
	5.290	10.890	12.250
Sun of Squares	15.660	19.986	18.948
$N - 1$	3	3	3
Variance	**5.220**	**6.662**	**6.316**

Summary of Step 2

Null hypothesis: Extroversion as a personality trait is the same, on average, regardless of a person's birth-order position—H_0: $\mu_1 = \mu_2 = \mu_3$. Research hypothesis: Extroversion as a personality trait is not the same, on average, for oldest children, middle children, and younger children—H_1 is that at least one μ is different from at least one other μ.

Summary of Step 3

$$df_{between} = N_{groups} - 1 = 3 - 1 = 2$$
$$df_1 = 4 - 1 = 3; df_2 = 4 - 1 = 3; df_3 = 4 - 1 = 3$$
$$df_{within} = 3 + 3 + 3 = 9$$

The comparison distribution will be an F distribution with 2 and 9 degrees of freedom.

Summary of Step 4

The critical F statistic based on a p level of 0.05 is 4.26.

Summary of Step 5

$$df_{total} = 2 + 9 = 11 \text{ or } df_{total} = 12 - 1 = 11$$
$$SS_{total} = \Sigma(X - GM)^2 = 54.794$$

Sample	X	(X − GM)	(X − GM)²
Oldest	47.15	−3.180	10.112
$M_{oldest} = 50.15$	51.25	0.920	0.846
	49.75	−0.580	0.336
	52.45	2.120	4.494
Middle	47.55	−2.780	7.728
$M_{middle} = 50.45$	49.70	−0.630	0.397
	50.80	0.470	0.221
	53.75	3.420	11.696
Youngest	47.97	−2.360	5.570
$M_{youngest} = 50.39$	49.49	−0.840	0.706
	50.21	−0.120	0.014
	53.89	3.560	12.674
	$GM = 50.33$		$SS_{total} = \textbf{54.794}$

$$SS_{within} = \Sigma(X - M)^2 = 54.594$$

Sample	X	(X − M)	(X − M)²
Oldest	47.15	−3.000	9.000
M_{oldest} = 50.15	51.25	1.100	1.210
	49.75	−0.400	0.160
	52.45	2.300	5.290
Middle	47.55	−2.900	8.410
M_{middle} = 50.45	49.70	−0.750	0.563
	50.80	0.350	0.123
	53.75	3.300	10.890
Youngest	47.97	−2.420	5.856
$M_{youngest}$ = 50.39	49.49	−0.900	0.810
	50.21	−0.180	0.032
	53.89	3.500	12.250
	GM = 50.33		SS_{within} = 54.594

$$SS_{between} = \Sigma(M - GM)^2 = 0.200$$

Sample	X	(M − GM)	(M − GM)²
Oldest	47.15	−0.18	0.032
M_{oldest} = 50.15	51.25	−0.18	0.032
	49.75	−0.18	0.032
	52.45	−0.18	0.032
Middle	47.55	0.12	0.014
M_{middle} = 50.45	49.70	0.12	0.014
	50.80	0.12	0.014
	53.75	0.12	0.014
Youngest	47.97	0.06	0.004
$M_{youngest}$ = 50.39	49.49	0.06	0.004
	50.21	0.06	0.004
	53.89	0.06	0.004
	GM = 50.33		$SS_{between}$ = 0.200

$$MS_{between} = \frac{SS_{between}}{df_{between}} = \frac{0.200}{2} = 0.100$$

$$MS_{within} = \frac{SS_{within}}{df_{within}} = \frac{54.594}{9} = 6.066$$

$$F = \frac{MS_{within}}{MS_{between}} = \frac{0.100}{6.066} = 0.016$$

Source	SS	df	MS	F
Between	0.20	2	0.10	0.02
Within	54.59	9	6.07	
Total	54.79	11		

Summary of Step 6

The F statistic, 0.016, is not beyond the cutoff of 4.26. We cannot reject the null hypothesis. There is no evidence that there is a mean difference in extroversion among oldest children, middle children, or youngest children. Post hoc tests are not completed because we cannot reject the null hypothesis. How It Works 12.2 demonstrates how to calculate the effect size for this example.

12.2 EFFECT SIZE FOR A ONE-WAY BETWEEN-GROUPS ANOVA

How would be calculate an effect size for the one-way between-groups ANOVA we conducted in How It Works 12.1?

$$R^2 = \frac{SS_{between}}{SS_{total}} = \frac{0.200}{54.594} = 0.004$$

According to Cohen's conventions for effect sizes (R^2), this is a very small effect.

EXERCISES

Clarifying the Concepts

12.1 What is an ANOVA?

12.2 What do the F distributions allow us to do that the t distributions do not?

12.3 The F statistic is a ratio of between-groups variance and within-groups variance. What are these two types of variance?

12.4 What is the difference between a within-groups (repeated-measures) ANOVA and a between-groups ANOVA?

12.5 What are the three assumptions for a between-groups ANOVA?

12.6 The null hypothesis for ANOVA posits no difference among population means, as in other hypothesis tests, but the research hypothesis in this case is a bit different. Why?

12.7 Why is the F statistic always positive?

12.8 Define the word *source* as you would use it in everyday conversation. Provide at least two different meanings that might be used. Then define the word as a statistician would use it.

12.9 Explain the concept of *sum of squares.*

12.10 The total sum of squares for a one-way between-groups ANOVA is found by adding which two statistics together?

12.11 What is the grand mean?

12.12 How do we calculate the between-groups sum of squares?

12.13 What do we typically use to measure effect size for a z test or a t test? What do we use to measure effect size for an ANOVA?

12.14 What are Cohen's conventions for interpreting effect size using R^2?

12.15 What does *post hoc* mean, and when are these tests needed with ANOVA?

12.16 Define the symbols in the following formula:

$$N' = \frac{N_{groups}}{\Sigma(1/N)}$$

12.17 Find the error in the statistics language in each of the following statements about z, t, or F distributions or their related tests. Explain why it is incorrect and provide the correct word.

a. The professor reported the mean and standard error for the final exam in the statistics class.

b. Before we can calculate a t statistic, we must know the population mean and the population standard deviation.

c. The researcher calculated the parameters for her three samples so that she could calculate an F statistic and conduct an ANOVA.

d. For her honors project, Evelyn calculated a z statistic so that she could compare the mean video game scores of a sample of students who had ingested caffeine with a sample of students who had not ingested caffeine.

12.18 Find the incorrectly used symbol or symbols in each of the following statements or formulas. For each statement or formula, (i) state which symbol(s) is/are used incorrectly, (ii) explain why the symbol(s) in the original statement is/are incorrect, and (iii) state which symbol(s) *should* be used.

a. When calculating an F statistic, the numerator includes the estimate for the between-groups variance, s.

b. $SS_{between} = (X - GM)^2$

12.19 Find the incorrectly used symbol or symbols in each of the following statements or formulas. For each statement or formula, (i) state which symbol(s) is/are used incorrectly, (ii) explain why the symbol(s) in the original statement is/are incorrect, and (iii) state which symbol(s) should be used.

a. $SS_{within} = (X - M)$

b. $F = \sqrt{t}$

12.20 What are the necessary steps for performing a Bonferroni post hoc comparison?

12.21 Explain what statisticians mean when they say that a Bonferroni post hoc comparison is more conservative than a Tukey HSD test.

Calculating the Statistics

12.22 For the following data, assuming a between-groups design, determine:

Group 1: 11, 17, 22, 15

Group 2: 21, 15, 16

Group 3: 7, 8, 3, 10, 6, 4

Group 4: 13, 6, 17, 27, 20

  a. $df_{between}$

  b. df_{within}

  c. df_{total}

  d. The critical value, assuming a p value of 0.05

  e. The mean for each group and the grand mean

  f. The total sum of squares

  g. The within-groups sum of squares

  h. The between-groups sum of squares

  i. The rest of the ANOVA source table for these data

  j. Tukey HSD values

12.23 For the following data, assuming a between-groups design, determine:

1990: 45, 211, 158, 74

2000: 92, 128, 382

2010: 273, 396, 178, 248, 374

  a. $df_{between}$

  b. df_{within}

  c. df_{total}

  d. The critical value, assuming a p value of 0.05

  e. The mean for each group and the grand mean

  f. The total sum of squares

  g. The within-groups sum of squares

  h. The between-groups sum of squares

  i. The rest of the ANOVA source table for these data

  j. The effect size and an indication of its size

12.24 Calculate the F statistic, writing the ratio accurately, for each of the following cases:

  a. Between-groups variance is 29.4 and within-groups variance is 19.1

  b. Within-groups variance is 0.27 and between-groups variance is 1.56

  c. Between-groups variance is 4595 and within-groups variance is 3972

12.25 Calculate the F statistic, writing the ratio accurately, for each of the following cases:

  a. Between-groups variance is 321.83 and within-groups variance is 177.24

  b. Between-groups variance is 2.79 and within-groups variance is 2.20

  c. Within-groups variance is 41.60 and between-groups variance is 34.45

12.26 An incomplete one-way between-groups ANOVA source table is shown below. Compute the missing values.

Source	SS	df	MS	F
Between	191.450	—	47.863	—
Within	104.720	32	—	
Total	—	36		

12.27 An incomplete one-way between-groups ANOVA source table is shown below. Compute the missing values.

Source	SS	df	MS	F
Between	—	2	—	—
Within	89	11	—	
Total	132	—		

12.28 Each of the following is a calculated F statistic with its degrees of freedom. Using the F table, estimate the level of significance for each. You can do this by indicating whether its likelihood of occurring is greater than or less than a p level shown on the table.

  a. $F = 4.11$, with 3 $df_{between}$ and 30 df_{within}

  b. $F = 1.12$, with 5 $df_{between}$ and 83 df_{within}

  c. $F = 2.28$, with 4 $df_{between}$ and 42 df_{within}

12.29 A researcher designs an experiment in which the single independent variable has four levels. If the researcher performed an ANOVA and rejected the null hypothesis, how many post hoc comparisons would she make (assuming she was making all possible comparisons)?

12.30 A researcher designs an experiment in which the single independent variable has five levels. If the researcher performed an ANOVA and rejected the null hypothesis, how many post hoc comparisons would he make (assuming he was making all possible comparisons)?

12.31 A researcher designs an experiment in which the single independent variable has seven levels. If the researcher performed an ANOVA and rejected the null hypothesis, how many post hoc comparisons would she make (assuming she was making all possible comparisons)?

12.32 Irwin and colleagues (2004) conducted a study on adherence to an exercise program. Participants were asked to attend a monthly group education program to help them change their exercise behavior. Attendance was taken and participants were divided into three categories: those who attended fewer than 5 sessions, those who attended between 5 and 8 sessions, and those who attended between 9 and 12 sessions. Assume that you plan to do Bonferroni post hoc comparisons if the ANOVA is statistically significant.

a. With a desired p level of 0.05 overall, what would the cutoff p value be for each comparison using a Bonferroni test?

b. With a desired p level of 0.01 overall, what would the cutoff p value be for each comparison using a Bonferroni test?

c. Using statistical software, we performed all of the possible pairwise independent-samples t tests on a subset of data that matches the sample means in the study (see exercise 12.39); the actual p values (listed in the Sig. column in SPSS) associated with each of those tests appears below. Assuming an overall p level of 0.05, decide whether to reject or fail to reject the null hypothesis for each comparison.

<5 versus 5–8: $p = 0.041$

<5 versus 9–12: $p = 0.001$

5–8 versus 9–12: $p = 0.060$

Applying the Concepts

12.33 **Comedy versus news and hypothesis testing:** Focusing on coverage of the U.S. presidential election, Julia R. Fox, a telecommunications professor at Indiana University, wondered whether *The Daily Show*, despite its comedy format, was a valid source of news. She coded a number of half-hour episodes of *The Daily Show* as well as a number of half-hour episodes of the network news (Indiana University Media Relations, 2006). Fox reported that the average amounts of "video and audio substance" were not statistically significantly different between the two types of shows. Her analyses are described as "second by second," so, for this exercise, assume that all outcome variables are measures of time.

a. As the study is described, what are the independent and dependent variables? For nominal variables, state the levels.

b. As the study is described, what type of hypothesis test would Fox use?

c. Now imagine that Fox added a third category, a cable news channel such as CNN. Based on this new information, state the independent variable or variables and the levels of any nominal independent variables. What hypothesis test would she use?

12.34 **The comparison distribution:** For each of the following situations, state whether the distribution of interest is the z distribution, a t distribution, or an F distribution. Explain your answer.

a. A city employee locates a U.S. Census report that includes the mean and standard deviation for income in the state of Wyoming and then takes a random sample of 100 residents of the city of Cheyenne. He wonders whether residents of Cheyenne earn more, on average, than Wyoming residents as a whole.

b. A researcher studies the effect of different contexts on work interruptions. Using discreet video cameras, she observes employees working in enclosed offices in the workplace, in open cubicles in the workplace, and in home offices.

c. An honors student wondered whether an education in statistics reduces the tendency to believe advertising that cites data. He compares social science majors who had taken statistics and social science majors who had not taken statistics with respect to their responses to an interactive advertising assessment.

12.35 **The comparison distribution:** For each of the following situations, state whether the distribution of interest is the z distribution, a t distribution, or an F distribution. Explain your answer.

a. A student reads in her *Introduction to Psychology* textbook that the mean IQ is 100. She asks 10 friends what their IQ scores are (they attend a university that assesses everyone's IQ score) to determine whether her friends are smarter than average.

b. Is the presence of books in the home a marker of a stable family? A social worker counted the number of books on view in the living rooms of all the families he visited over the course of one year. He categorized families into four groups: no books visible, only children's books visible, only adult books visible, and both children's and adult books visible. The department for which he worked had stability ratings for each family based on a number of measures.

c. Which television show leads to more learning? A researcher assessed the vocabularies of a sample of children randomly assigned to watch *Sesame Street* as much as they wanted for a year but to not watch *The Wiggles*. She also assessed the vocabularies of a sample of children randomly assigned to watch *The Wiggles* as much as they wanted for a year but not to watch *Sesame Street*. She compared the average vocabulary scores for the two groups.

12.36 **Links among distributions:** The z, t, and F distributions are closely linked. In fact, it is possible to use an F distribution in all cases in which a t or a z could be used.

a. If you calculated an F statistic of 4.22 but you could have used a t statistic (i.e., the situation met all criteria for using a t statistic), what would the t statistic have been? Explain your answer.

b. If you calculated an F statistic of 4.22 but you could have used a z statistic, what would the z statistic have been? Explain your answer.

c. If you calculated a t statistic of 0.67 but you could have used a z statistic, what would the z statistic have been? Explain your answer.

d. Cite at least one possible reason that all three types of distributions (i.e., z, t, and F) are still in use when we really only need an F distribution.

12.37 International students and type of ANOVA: Catherine Ruby, a doctoral student at New York University, conducted an online survey to ascertain the reasons that international students chose to attend graduate school in the United States. One of several dependent variables that she considered was reputation; students were asked to rate the importance in their decision of factors such as the reputation of the institution, the institution and program's academic accreditations, and the reputation of the faculty. Students rated factors on a 1–5 scale, and then all reputation ratings were averaged to form a summary score for each respondent. For each of the following scenarios, state the independent variable with its levels (the dependent variable is reputation in all cases). Then state what kind of an ANOVA she would use.

a. Ruby compared the importance of reputation among graduate students in different types of programs: arts and sciences, education, law, and business.

b. Imagine that Ruby followed these graduate students for 3 years and assessed their rating of reputation once a year.

c. Ruby compared international students working toward a master's, a doctoral, or a professional degree (e.g., MBA) on reputation.

d. Imagine that Ruby followed international students from their master's program to their doctoral program to their postdoctoral fellowship, assessing their ratings of reputation once at each level of their training.

12.38 Type of ANOVA in study of remembering names: Do people remember names better under different circumstances? In a fictional study, a cognitive psychologist studied memory for names after a group activity that lasted 20 minutes. Participants were not told that this was a study of memory. After the group activity, participants were asked to name the other group members. The researcher randomly assigned 120 participants to one of three conditions: (1) group members introduced themselves once (one introduction only), (2) group members were introduced by the experimenter and by themselves (two introductions), and (3) group members were introduced by the experimenter and themselves

and also wore name tags throughout the group activity (two introductions and name tags).

a. Identify the type of ANOVA that should be used to analyze the data from this study.

b. State what the researcher could do to redesign this study so it would be analyzed with a one-way within-groups ANOVA. Be specific.

12.39 Exercise and education programs: Irwin and colleagues (2004) conducted research on adherence to an exercise regimen. We give an overview of the study in exercise 12.32. Here are the data:

<5 sessions: 155, 120, 130

5–8 sessions: 199, 160, 184

9–12 sessions: 230, 214, 195, 209

a. What is the independent variable in this study? What are its levels?

b. What is the dependent variable in this study?

c. Use the six steps of hypothesis testing to conduct a one-way between-groups ANOVA.

12.40 Exercise and post hoc tests: Use the same data from Exercise 12.39 in this exercise.

a. Explain why it is necessary to conduct a post hoc test such as a Tukey *HSD* test when an ANOVA is statistically significant.

b. Conduct a Tukey *HSD* test. Show all calculations.

c. Explain why we cannot assume that two groups have the same means when we fail to reject the null hypothesis using a Tukey *HSD* test. Refer to the current example in your answer.

12.41 Grade point average and comparing the *t* and *F* distributions: Based on your knowledge of the relation of the t and F distributions, complete the software output tables on the next page. The table for the independent-samples t test and the table for the one-way between-groups ANOVA were calculated using the identical fictional data comparing grade point averages (GPAs).

a. What is the F statistic? Show your calculations. (*Hint:* The "Mean Square" column includes the two estimates of variance used to calculate the F statistic.)

b. What is the t statistic? Show your calculations. (*Hint:* Use the F statistic that you calculated in part (a).)

c. In statistical software output, "Sig." refers to the actual p level of the statistic. We can compare the actual p level to a cutoff p level such as 0.05 to decide whether to reject the null hypothesis. For the t test, what is the "Sig."? Explain how you determined this. (*Hint:* Would we expect the "Sig." for the independent-samples t test to be the same as or different from that for the one-way between-groups ANOVA?)

Independent Samples Test

				t-test for Equality of Means			95% Confidence Interval of the Difference	
	t	df	Sig. (2-tailed)	Mean Difference	Standard Error Difference			
							Lower	Upper
GPA		82		−.28251	.12194		−.52508	−.03993

ANOVA

GPA	Sum of Squares	df	Mean Square	F	Sig.
Between groups	4.623	1	4.623		.005
Within groups	42.804	82	.522		
Total	47.427	83			

12.42 Consideration of Future Consequences and two kinds of hypothesis testing: Two samples of students, one composed of social science majors and one composed of students with other majors, completed the Consideration of Future Consequences scale (CFC). The accompanying tables include the output from software for an independent-samples t test and a one-way between-groups ANOVA on these data.

a. Demonstrate that the results of the independent-samples t test and the one-way between-groups ANOVA are the same. (*Hint:* Find the t statistic for the t test and the F statistic for the ANOVA.)

b. In statistical software output, "Sig." refers to the actual p level of the statistic. We can compare the actual p level to a cutoff p level such as 0.05 to decide whether to reject the null hypothesis. What

Independent Samples Test

	t	df	Sig. (2-tailed)	Mean Difference	Standard Error Difference	95% Confidence Interval of the Difference	
						Lower	Upper
CFC scores	−.650	28	.521	−.17500	.26930	−.72664	.37664

ANOVA

CFC Scores

	Sum of Squares	df	Mean Square	F	Sig.
Between Groups	.204	1	.204	.422	.521
Within Groups	13.538	28	.483		
Total	13.742	29			

Group Statistics

Major		N	Mean	Standard Deviation	Standard Error Mean
CFC Scores	Other	10	3.2000	.88819	.28087
	Social Science	20	3.3750	.58208	.13016

are the "Sig." levels for the two tests here—the independent-samples t test and the one-way between-groups ANOVA? Are they the same or different? Explain why this is the case.

c. In the CFC ANOVA, the column titled "Mean Square" includes the estimates of variance. Show how the F statistic was calculated from two types of variance. (*Hint:* Look at the far-left column to determine which estimate of variance is which.)

d. Looking at the table titled "Group Statistics," how many participants were in each sample?

e. Looking at the table titled "Group Statistics," what is the mean CFC score for the social science majors?

12.43 Instructors on Facebook and one-way ANOVA: Researchers investigated whether the amount of self-disclosure on Facebook affected student perceptions of the instructor, the class, and the classroom environment (Mazer, Murphy, & Simonds, 2007). Students were randomly assigned to view one of three Facebook pages of an instructor. The pages were identical except that one instructor had high self-disclosure, one had medium self-disclosure, and one had low self-disclosure. Self-disclosure was "manipulated in photographs, biological information, and posts" (p. 6). The researchers reported that "Participants who accessed the Facebook website of a teacher high in self-disclosure anticipated higher levels of motivation and affective learning and a more positive classroom climate" (p. 1).

a. What is the independent variable, what kind of variable is it, and what are its levels?

b. What is the first dependent variable mentioned, and what kind of variable is this?

c. Is this a between-groups design or a within-groups design? Explain your answer.

d. Based on your answers to parts (a) through (c), what kind of ANOVA would the researchers use to analyze the data? Explain your answer.

e. Is this a true experiment? Explain your answer, and explain what this means for the researchers' conclusion.

12.44 Post hoc tests and p values: The most recent version of the *Publication Manual of the American Psychological Association* (2010) recommends reporting the exact p values for all statistical tests to two decimal places (previously, it recommended reporting $p < 0.05$ or $p > 0.05$). Explain how this reporting format allows a reader to more critically interpret the results of post hoc comparisons reported by an author.

12.45 Post hoc tests, bilingualism, and language skills: Researchers Raluca Barac and Ellen Bialystok (2012) conducted a study in which they compared the language skills of 104 six-year-old children who were in one of four groups. Some children spoke only English. Others were bilingual, speaking English along with Chinese, French, or Spanish. The children completed the Peabody Picture Vocabulary Test (PPVT) as a measure of their vocabulary. An excerpt from the results section of the published journal article follows: "A one-way ANOVA on PPVT scores showed a main effect of language group, $F(3, 100) = 8.27$, $p < .0001$. Post hoc Bonferroni contrasts indicated that the monolingual children and the Spanish-English bilingual children outperformed the other two bilingual groups who did not differ from each other."

a. What is the independent variable, what kind of variable is it, and what are its levels? What is the dependent variable and what kind of variable is it?

b. How do we know that this finding is statistically significant?

c. Why was the one-way ANOVA not sufficient to draw a conclusion from these data?

d. Explain what is meant here by the Bonferroni test.

e. Summarize this finding in your own words.

12.46 Romantic love and post hoc tests: Researchers who conducted a study of brain activation and romantic love divided their analyses into two groups (Aron et al., 2005). Some analyses—those for which they had developed specific hypotheses prior to data collection—used a p level of 0.05. The rest of the analyses used a p level of 0.001.

a. Explain why the researchers' plan to have different p levels for the two groups was a wise one.

b. Suggest one method by which the researchers could have come up with a p level of 0.001 as their cutoff.

Putting It All Together

12.47 Trust in leadership and one-way between-groups ANOVA: In Chapter 11, we introduced a study by Steele and Pinto (2006) that examined whether people's level of trust in their direct supervisor was related to their level of agreement with a policy supported by that leader. Steele and Pinto found that the extent to which subordinates agreed with their supervisor was related to trust and showed no relation to gender, age, time on the job, or length of time working with the supervisor. Let's assume we used a scale that sorted employees into three groups: low trust, moderate trust, and high trust in supervisors. Below are fictional data regarding level of agreement with a leader's decision for these three groups. The scores presented are the level of agreement with a decision made by a leader, from 1, the least agreement, to 40, the highest level of agreement.

Note: These fictional data are different from those presented in Chapter 11.

> Employees with low trust in their leader:
> 9, 14, 11, 18
>
> Employees with moderate trust in their leader:
> 14, 35, 23
>
> Employees with high trust in their leader:
> 27, 33, 21, 34

a. What is the independent variable? What are its levels?

b. What is the dependent variable?

c. Conduct all six steps of hypothesis testing for a one-way between-groups ANOVA.

d. How would you report the statistics in a journal article?

e. Conduct a Tukey *HSD* test. What did you learn?

f. Why is it not possible to conduct a *t* test in this situation?

g. Why is it not possible to use a within-groups design for this study?

12.48 Orthodontics and one-way between-groups ANOVA: Iranian researchers studied factors affecting patients' likelihood of wearing orthodontic appliances, noting that orthodontics is perhaps the area of health care with the highest need for patient cooperation (Behenam & Pooya, 2007). Among their analyses, they compared students in primary school, junior high school, and high school. The data that follow have almost exactly the same means as they found in their study, but with far smaller samples. The score for each student is his or her daily hours of wearing the orthodontic appliance.

> Primary school: 16, 13, 18
>
> Junior high school: 8, 13, 14, 12
>
> High school: 20, 15, 16, 18

a. What is the independent variable? What are its levels?

b. What is the dependent variable?

c. Conduct all six steps of hypothesis testing for a one-way between-groups ANOVA.

d. How would you report the statistics in a journal article?

e. Conduct a Tukey *HSD* test. What did you learn?

f. Calculate the appropriate measure of effect size for this sample.

g. Based on Cohen's conventions, is this a small, medium, or large effect size?

h. Why is it useful to know the effect size in addition to the results of a hypothesis test?

i. How could this study be conducted using a within-groups design?

12.49 ANOVA, award-winning television, and the theory of mind: Can watching high-quality television dramas improve our theory of mind—our ability to understand others? Psychologists Jessica Black and Jennifer Barnes explored this question in a study in which participants were randomly assigned to watch 42 minutes of an award-winning television drama like *The Good Wife,* 42 minutes of an award-winning television documentary such as an episode of *Through the Wormhole,* or no television at all (2015). (*Note:* Exercise 11.27 is about a different study reported in this same journal article.) Next, all participants were asked to look at a series of 36 photos of people's eyes and decide if each person was jealous, panicked, arrogant, or hateful. Scores ranged from 0 (guessed no emotions correctly) to 36 (guessed every emotion correctly). The researchers analyzed the data and found that the "mean . . . differed across the three groups, $F(2, 173) = 6.04$, $p = .003$, partial $= .065$." (Partial η^2 can be interpreted in the same way as R^2.) The means were 28.02 for the drama group, 26.55 for the documentary group, and 25.30 for the control group. They reported a significant difference only between the means for the drama group and control group.

a. What is the independent variable in this study? What are its levels?

b. What is the dependent variable in this study?

c. Is this an experiment or a correlational study? Explain your answer.

d. What statistical analysis did the researchers use? Explain your answer.

e. Explain the statistics reported in the research excerpt. What does each of these mean?

f. Explain what the researchers likely did to determine which means were significantly different from each other.

g. Explain the overall pattern of results in your own words.

h. The effect size is given in terms of partial η^2. What does this tell us about the effect size?

i. Let's say you prefer documentaries to dramas. You notice that the mean for documentaries is also higher than the mean for controls, and decide that documentaries are helpful, too. Why is this statement problematic from a statistical point of view?

j. If the one significant mean difference observed in this study is an incorrect conclusion, what kind of error is this? Explain your answer.

k. The researchers represented these research findings in a graph similar to the one shown here. Cite at least two ways you would revise the graph to fit with what you learned in Chapter 3.

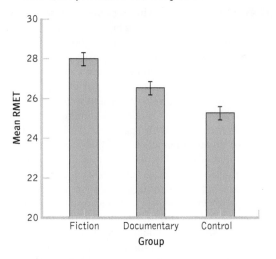

12.50 **ANOVA and taking notes:** Researchers studied the type of note taking that would lead to the best performance on conceptual questions on a test (Mueller & Oppenheimer, 2014). Conceptual questions are those in which students have to apply the material, rather than just answer fact-based questions. Students were randomly assigned to one of the following groups:

1. Take notes by hand (the longhand group)
2. Take notes on their laptops as usual (the laptop-nonintervention group)
3. Take notes on their laptops with instructions to try to put the notes in their own words (the laptop-intervention group)

Because people tend to take notes verbatim on their laptops, the researchers speculated that the laptop-nonintervention group would lead to less learning, on average, than the other two groups. The researchers reported that "results showed that on conceptual-application questions, longhand participants performed better (z-score $M = 0.28$, $SD = 1.04$) than laptop-nonintervention participants (z-score $M = -0.15$, $SD = 0.85$), $F(1, 89) = 11.98$, $p = .017$, $\eta_p^2 = .12$. Scores for laptop-intervention participants (z-score $M = -0.11$, $SD = 1.02$) did not significantly differ from those for either laptop-nonintervention ($p = .91$) or longhand ($p = .29$) participants" (p. 1162).

a. What is the independent variable in this study? What are its levels?

b. What is the dependent variable in this study?

c. Is this an experiment or a correlational study? Explain your answer.

d. The report of the statistics provides us with z-score M rather than M. Explain what these researchers are reporting here.

e. Which groups are significantly different from each other? Describe two ways that we know this.

f. The effect size is given in terms of η_p^2. What does this tell us about the effect size? (Note: The subscript p means "partial," and indicates that this effect size is just for this particular finding. You may ignore the p in your answer. Remember that η^2 is roughly equivalent to R^2).

g. A friend hears this finding and says, "I don't want to take notes longhand, but I'll think about typing the notes in my own words. The mean z-score of $-.11$ is higher than the mean z-score of $-.15$." Why is this statement problematic from a statistical point of view?

h. If the finding of no significant difference between the longhand group and the laptop-intervention group is wrong, what kind of error is this? Explain your answer.

TERMS

analysis of variance (ANOVA) (p. 304)
F statistic (p. 304)
between-groups variance (p. 304)
within-groups variance (p. 304)
one-way ANOVA (p. 305)

between-groups ANOVA (p. 305)
within-groups ANOVA (p. 305)
homoscedastic (p. 306)
heteroscedastic (p. 306)
source table (p. 312)

grand mean (p. 315)
R^2 (p. 322)
post hoc test (p. 323)
Tukey HSD test (p. 323)
Bonferroni test (p. 326)

FORMULAS

$df_{between} = N_{groups} - 1$ (p. 309)

$df_{within} = df_1 + df_2 + \cdots 1\ df_{last}$
(in which df_1, df_2, etc., are the degrees of freedom, $N - 1$, for

each sample) [formula for a one-way between-groups ANOVA]   (p. 309)

$df_{total} = df_{between} + df_{within}$
[formula for a one-way between-groups ANOVA]   (p. 314)

$df_{total} = N_{total} - 1$ (p. 314)

$$GM = \frac{\Sigma(X)}{N_{total}}$$ (p. 315)

$$SS_{total} = \Sigma(X - GM)^2$$ (p. 316)

$$SS_{within} = \Sigma(X - M)^2$$
[formula for a one-way between-groups ANOVA] (p. 316)

$$SS_{between} = \Sigma(M - GM)^2$$ (p. 318)

$$SS_{total} = SS_{within} + SS_{between}$$
[alternative formula for a one-way between-groups ANOVA] (p. 318)

$$MS_{between} = \frac{SS_{between}}{df_{between}}$$ (p. 319)

$$MS_{within} = \frac{SS_{within}}{df_{within}}$$ (p. 319)

$$F = \frac{MS_{between}}{MS_{within}}$$ (p. 319)

$$R^2 = \frac{SS_{between}}{SS_{total}}$$ [formula for a one-way between-groups ANOVA] (p. 322)

$$s_M = \sqrt{\frac{MS_{within}}{N}}, \text{ if equal}$$
sample sizes (p. 323)

$$HSD = \frac{(M_1 - M_2)}{s_M}, \text{ for any}$$
two sample means (p. 323)

$$N' = \frac{N_{groups}}{\Sigma(1/N)}$$ (p. 324)

$$s_M = \sqrt{\frac{MS_{within}}{N'}}, \text{ if unequal}$$
sample sizes (p. 324)

SYMBOLS

F	(p. 302)	df_{total}	(p. 314)	R^2	(p. 322)
$df_{between}$	(p. 309)	$SS_{between}$	(p. 314)	HSD	(p. 323)
df_{within}	(p. 309)	SS_{within}	(p. 314)	N'	(p. 324)
$MS_{between}$	(p. 314)	SS_{total}	(p. 314)		
MS_{within}	(p. 314)	GM	(p. 315)		

One-Way Within-Groups ANOVA

One-Way Within-Groups ANOVA
The Benefits of Within-Groups ANOVA
The Six Steps of Hypothesis Testing

Beyond Hypothesis Testing for the One-Way Within-Groups ANOVA
R^2, the Effect Size for ANOVA
Tukey *HSD*

Next Steps: Matched Groups

REUTERS/Jose Miguel Gomez

Within-Groups Design Whenever researchers have people provide ratings of several items—such as here, with different types of coffee—they are using a within-groups design. If the order of the flavors is varied for each person, the researcher is using counterbalancing.

"What's in a name?" Juliet asks Romeo. "That which we call a rose / By any other name would smell as sweet." A group of Canadian researchers decided to test Juliet's assertion (Djordjevic et al., 2007). They assigned names associated with positive, negative, or neutral odors to 15 different odors and then presented them to participants, who were asked to rate the pleasantness and the intensity of the aroma. Positive names for aromas included "cinnamon stick" and "jasmine tea." Negative names for odors included "rotten fish" and "dry vomit." Neutral names were 2-digit numbers such as "36."

The researchers used a within-groups design, which means that each participant smelled the same odor with a positive name, a negative name, and a neutral name. Having each participant experience each level of the independent variable is one of the advantages of using a within-groups design: Researchers require fewer participants. The research team found that participants generally rated aromas with positive names as more pleasant and odors with negative names as more intense.

This odor study also demonstrates why this chapter is divided into two parts. The first part discusses the one-way within-groups ANOVA, which shows how to determine the probability that any differences are real (such as the differences between odor ratings based on a positive, negative, or neutral name). The second part takes us beyond hypothesis testing and discusses how to calculate the size of those differences.

One-Way Within-Groups ANOVA

There is not much difference between chapters 12 and 13. Chapter 12 taught you how to conduct the multiple-group equivalent of an independent-samples *t* test, the one-way between-groups ANOVA. You also learned how to calculate effect size and conduct a post hoc test for a one-way between-groups ANOVA. Chapter 13 draws on the same ideas, but this time you will be learning how to conduct the multiple-group equivalent of a paired-samples *t* test, called a *one-way within-groups ANOVA* (also known as a *repeated-measures ANOVA*). Just as you did for the one-way between-groups ANOVA, you will learn how to calculate effect size and conduct a post hoc test for the one-way within-groups ANOVA. If you understand how a between-groups design differs from a within-groups design, then you already understand the key concept in this chapter.

EXAMPLE 13.1

Have you ever participated in a taste test? If you have, then you were probably a participant in a within-groups experiment. About a decade ago, when pricier microbrew beers were becoming popular in North America, the journalist James Fallows, who loves beer, found himself spending increasingly more on a bottle of beer. He began to wonder whether he was getting his money's worth for these more expensive beers. So, he recruited 12 colleagues, all self-professed beer snobs, to participate in a taste test to see whether they really could tell whether a beer was expensive or cheap (Fallows, 1999).

Fallows wanted to know whether his recruits could distinguish among widely available American beers that were categorized into three groups based on price— "high-end" beers like Sam Adams, "mid-range" beers like Budweiser, and "cheap" beers like Busch. All of these beers are lagers, a type of beer chosen because it can be found at every price point. Here are data—mean scores on a scale of 0–100 for each category of beer—for five of the participants. (*Note:* For teaching purposes, the means are slightly different and have been rounded to the nearest whole number; the take-home data story, however, remains the same.)

Participant	Cheap Beer	Mid-Range Beer	High-End Beer
1	40	30	53
2	42	45	65
3	30	38	64
4	37	32	43
5	23	28	38

The Benefits of Within-Groups ANOVA

Fallows only reported his overall findings. If he had conducted hypothesis testing, then he would have used a one-way within-groups ANOVA, the appropriate statistic when there is one nominal or ordinal independent variable (type of beer) that has more than two levels (cheap, mid-range, and high-end), a scale dependent variable (ratings of beers), and participants who experience every level of the independent variable (each participant tasted the beers in every category).

The beauty of the within-groups design is that it reduces errors that are due to differences between the groups, because each group includes exactly the same participants. The beer study could not be influenced by individual taste preferences, amount of alcohol typically consumed, tendency to be critical or lenient when rating, and so on. This enables us to reduce the within-groups variability associated with differences among the people in the study across groups. The lower within-groups variability means a smaller denominator for the F statistic and a larger F statistic that makes it easier to reject the null hypothesis.

The Six Steps of Hypothesis Testing

We'll use the data from the beer taste test to walk through the same six steps of hypothesis testing that we have used for every other statistical test.

EXAMPLE 13.2

STEP 1: Identify the populations, distribution, and assumptions.

The one-way within-groups ANOVA requires an additional assumption compared to the one-way between-groups ANOVA: We must be careful to avoid order effects. In the beer study, order may have influenced participants' judgments because all participants tasted the beers in the same order: a mid-range beer, followed by a high-end beer, followed by a cheap beer, followed by another cheap beer, and so on. Perhaps the first sip of beer tastes the best, no matter what kind of beer is being tasted. Ideally, Fallows would have used counterbalancing, so that participants tasted the beers in different orders.

Summary: Population 1: People who drink cheap beer. Population 2: People who drink mid-range beer. Population 3: People who drink high-end beer.

The comparison distribution and hypothesis test: The comparison distribution is an F distribution. The hypothesis test is a one-way within-groups ANOVA.

Assumptions: (1) The participants were not selected randomly, so we must generalize with caution. (2) We do not know if the underlying population distributions are normal, but the sample data do not indicate severe skew. (3) After we calculate the test statistic, we will test the homoscedasticity assumption by checking to see whether the largest variance is more than twice the smallest. (4) The experimenter did not counterbalance, so there may be order effects.

> **STEP 2: State the null and research hypotheses.**

This step is identical to that for a one-way between-groups ANOVA.

Summary: Null hypothesis: People who drink cheap, mid-range, and high-end beer rate their beverages the same, on average—$H_0: \mu_1 = \mu_2 = \mu_3$. Research hypothesis: People who drink cheap, mid-range, and high-end beer do not rate their beverages the same, on average—H_1 is that at least one μ is different from another μ.

13-2: The calculations for a one-way within-groups ANOVA are similar to those for a one-way between-groups ANOVA, but we now calculate a subjects sum of squares in addition to the between-groups, within-groups, and total sum of squares. The subjects sum of squares reduces the within-groups sum of squares by removing the variability associated with participants' differences across groups.

13-1: The formula for the subjects degrees of freedom is: $df_{subjects} = n - 1$. We subtract 1 from the number of participants in the study. We use the lowercase n to indicate that this is the number of data points in a single sample, even though we know that every participant is in all three groups.

13-2: The formula for the within-groups degrees of freedom for a one-way within-groups ANOVA is: $df_{within} = (df_{between})(df_{subjects})$. We multiply the between-groups degrees of freedom by the subjects degrees of freedom. This gives a lower number than we calculated for a one-way between-groups ANOVA because we want to exclude individual differences across groups from the within-groups sum of squares, and the degrees of freedom must reflect that.

> **STEP 3: Determine the characteristics of the comparison distribution.**

We state that the comparison distribution is an F distribution and determine the degrees of freedom. Instead of three, we now calculate four kinds of degrees of freedom—between-groups, subjects, within-groups, and total. The subjects degrees of freedom corresponds to a sum of squares for differences across participants: the *subjects sum of squares*, or $SS_{subjects}$. In a one-way within-groups ANOVA, we calculate between-groups degrees of freedom and subjects degrees of freedom first because we multiply these two together to calculate the within-groups degrees of freedom.

We calculate the between-groups degrees of freedom exactly as before:

$$df_{between} = N_{groups} - 1 = 3 - 1 = 2$$

We next calculate the degrees of freedom that pairs with $SS_{subjects}$. Called $df_{subjects}$, it is calculated by subtracting 1 from the actual number of subjects, not from the number of data points. We use a lowercase n to indicate that this is the number of participants in a single sample (even though they're all in every sample). The formula is:

$$df_{subjects} = n - 1 = 5 - 1 = 4$$

Once we know the between-groups degrees of freedom and the subjects degrees of freedom, we calculate the within-groups degrees of freedom by multiplying the first two:

$$df_{within} = (df_{between})(df_{subjects}) = (2)(4) = 8$$

Note that the within-groups degrees of freedom is smaller than we would have calculated for a one-way between-groups ANOVA. For a one-way between-groups ANOVA, we would have subtracted 1 from each sample ($5 - 1 = 4$) and summed them to get 12. The within-groups degrees of freedom is smaller because we exclude variability related to differences among the participants from the within-groups sum of squares, and the degrees of freedom must reflect that.

Finally, we calculate total degrees of freedom using either method we learned earlier. We can sum the other degrees of freedom:

$$df_{total} = df_{between} + df_{subjects} + df_{within} = 2 + 4 + 8 = 14$$

Alternatively, we can use the second formula we learned before, treating the total number of participants as every data point, rather than every person. We know, of course, that there are just five participants and that they participate in all three levels of the independent variable, but for this step, we count the 15 total data points:

$$df_{total} = N_{total} - 1 = 15 - 1 = 14$$

We have calculated the 4 degrees of freedom that we will include in the source table. However, we only report the between-groups and within-groups degrees of freedom at this step.

Summary: We use the F distribution with 2 and 8 degrees of freedom.

MASTERING THE FORMULA

13-3: We can calculate the total degrees of freedom for a one-way within-groups ANOVA in two ways. We can sum all of the other degrees of freedom: $df_{total} = df_{between} + df_{subjects} + df_{within}$. Or we can subtract 1 from the total number of observations in the study: $df_{total} = N_{total} - 1$.

STEP 4: Determine the critical values, or cutoffs.

The fourth step is identical to that for a one-way between-groups ANOVA. We use the between-groups degrees of freedom and within-groups degrees of freedom to look up a critical value on the F table in Appendix B.

Summary: The critical value for the F statistic for a p level of 0.05 and 2 and 8 degrees of freedom is 4.46.

STEP 5: Calculate the test statistic.

As before, we calculate the test statistic in the fifth step. To start, we calculate four sums of squares—one each for between-groups, subjects, within-groups, and total. For each sum of squares, we calculate deviations between two different types of means or scores, square the deviations, and then sum the squared differences. We calculate a squared deviation for *every* score; so for each sum of squares in this example, we sum 15 squared deviations.

As we did with the one-way between-groups ANOVA, let's start with the total sum of squares, SS_{total}. We calculate this exactly as we calculated it previously:

$$SS_{total} = \Sigma(X - GM)^2 = 2117.732$$

Type of Beer	Rating (X)	($X - GM$)	($X - GM$)^2
Cheap	40	−0.533	0.284
Cheap	42	1.467	2.152
Cheap	30	−10.533	110.944
Cheap	37	−3.533	12.482
Cheap	23	−17.533	307.406
Mid-range	30	−10.533	110.944
Mid-range	45	4.467	19.954
Mid-range	38	−2.533	6.416
Mid-range	32	−8.533	72.812
Mid-range	28	−12.533	157.076
High-end	53	12.467	155.426
High-end	65	24.467	598.634
High-end	64	23.467	550.700
High-end	43	2.467	6.086
High-end	38	−2.533	6.416
GM = 40.533			$\Sigma(X - GM)^2$ = 2117.732

Next, we calculate the between-groups sum of squares. It, too, is the same as for a one-way between-groups ANOVA:

$$SS_{between} = \Sigma(M - GM)^2 = 1092.130$$

Type of Beer	Rating (X)	Group Mean (M)	($M - GM$)	($M - GM$)^2
Cheap	40	34.4	−6.133	37.614
Cheap	42	34.4	−6.133	37.614
Cheap	30	34.4	−6.133	37.614
Cheap	37	34.4	−6.133	37.614
Cheap	23	34.4	−6.133	37.614
Mid-range	30	34.6	−5.933	35.200
Mid-range	45	34.6	−5.933	35.200
Mid-range	38	34.6	−5.933	35.200
Mid-range	32	34.6	−5.933	35.200
Mid-range	28	34.6	−5.933	35.200
High-end	53	52.6	12.067	145.612
High-end	65	52.6	12.067	145.612
High-end	64	52.6	12.067	145.612
High-end	43	52.6	12.067	145.612
High-end	38	52.6	12.067	145.612

$$GM = 40.533 \qquad \Sigma(M - GM)^2 = 1092.130$$

MASTERING THE FORMULA

13-4: The subjects sum of squares in a one-way within-groups ANOVA is calculated using the following formula: $SS_{subjects} = \Sigma(M_{participant} - GM)^2$. For each score, we subtract the grand mean from that participant's mean for all of his or her scores and square this deviation. Note that we do not use the scores in any of these calculations. We sum all the squared deviations.

So far, the calculations of the sums of squares for a one-way within-groups ANOVA have been the same as they were for a one-way between-groups ANOVA. We left the subjects sum of squares and within-groups sum of squares for last. Here is where we see some changes. We want to remove the variability caused by participant differences from the estimate of variability across conditions. So we calculate the subjects sum of squares separately from the within-groups sum of squares. To do that, we subtract the grand mean from each participant's mean *for all of his or her scores.* We first have to calculate a mean for each participant across the three conditions. For example, the first participant had ratings of 40 for cheap beers, 30 for mid-range beers, and 53 for high-end beers. This participant's mean is 41.

So the formula for the subjects sum of squares is:

$$SS_{subjects} = \Sigma(M_{participant} - GM)^2 = 729.738$$

Participant	Type of Beer	Rating (X)	Participant Mean ($M_{participant}$)	($M_{participant} - GM$)	($M_{participant} - GM$)^2
1	Cheap	40	41	0.467	0.218
2	Cheap	42	50.667	10.134	102.698
3	Cheap	30	44	3.467	12.02
4	Cheap	37	37.333	−3.2	10.24
5	Cheap	23	29.667	−10.866	118.07
1	Mid-range	30	41	0.467	0.218
2	Mid-range	45	50.667	10.134	102.698
3	Mid-range	38	44	3.467	12.02
4	Mid-range	32	37.333	−3.2	10.24
5	Mid-range	28	29.667	−10.866	118.07

Contiuned

Participant	Type of Beer	Rating (X)	Participant Mean $(M_{participant})$	$(M_{participant} - GM)$	$(M_{participant} - GM)^2$
1	High-end	53	41	0.467	0.218
2	High-end	65	50.667	10.134	102.698
3	High-end	64	44	3.467	12.02
4	High-end	43	37.333	−3.2	10.24
5	High-end	38	29.667	−10.866	118.07
		$GM = 40.533$			$\Sigma(M_{participant} - GM)^2 = 729.738$

We only have one sum of squares left to go. To calculate the within-groups sum of squares from which we've removed the subjects sum of squares, we take the total sum of squares and subtract the two others that we've calculated so far—the between-groups sum of squares and the subjects sum of squares. The formula is:

$$SS_{within} = SS_{total} - SS_{between} - SS_{subjects}$$
$$= 2117.732 - 1092.130 - 729.738 = 295.864$$

We now have enough information to fill in the first three columns of the source table—the source, SS, and df columns. We calculate the rest of the source table as we did for a one-way between-groups ANOVA. For each of the three sources—between-groups, subjects, and within-groups—we divide the sum of squares by the degrees of freedom to get its variance, MS.

$$MS_{between} = \frac{SS_{between}}{df_{between}} = \frac{1092.130}{2} = 546.065$$

$$MS_{subjects} = \frac{SS_{subjects}}{df_{subjects}} = \frac{729.738}{4} = 182.435$$

$$MS_{within} = \frac{SS_{within}}{df_{within}} = \frac{295.864}{8} = 36.981$$

We then calculate two F statistics—one for between-groups and one for subjects. For the between-groups F statistic, we divide its MS by the within-groups MS. For the subjects F statistic, we divide its MS by the within-groups MS.

$$F_{between} = \frac{MS_{between}}{MS_{within}} = \frac{546.065}{36.981} = 14.766$$

$$F_{subjects} = \frac{MS_{subjects}}{MS_{within}} = \frac{182.435}{36.981} = 4.933$$

The completed source table is shown here:

Source	SS	df	MS	F
Between-groups	1092.130	2	546.065	14.766
Subjects	729.738	4	182.435	4.933
Within-groups	295.864	8	36.981	
Total	2117.732	14		

MASTERING THE FORMULA

13-5: The within-groups sum of squares for a one-way within-groups ANOVA is calculated using the following formula: $SS_{within} = SS_{total} - SS_{between} - SS_{subjects}$. We subtract the between-groups sum of squares and the subjects sum of squares from the total sum of squares.

MASTERING THE FORMULA

13-6: We calculate the subjects mean square by dividing its associated sum of squares by its associated degrees of freedom:
$$MS_{subjects} = \frac{SS_{subjects}}{df_{subjects}}.$$

MASTERING THE FORMULA

13-7: The formula for the subjects F statistic is:
$$F_{subjects} = \frac{MS_{subjects}}{MS_{within}}.$$
We divide the subjects mean square by the within-groups mean square.

Here is a recap of the formulas used to calculate a one-way within-groups ANOVA:

Source	SS	df	MS	F
Between-groups	$\Sigma(M - GM)^2$	$N_{groups} - 1$	$\dfrac{SS_{between}}{df_{between}}$	$\dfrac{MS_{between}}{MS_{within}}$
Subjects	$\Sigma(M_{participant} - GM)^2$	$n - 1$	$\dfrac{SS_{subjects}}{df_{subjects}}$	$\dfrac{MS_{subjects}}{MS_{within}}$
Within-groups	$SS_{total} - SS_{between} - SS_{subjects}$	$(df_{between})(df_{subjects})$	$\dfrac{SS_{within}}{df_{within}}$	
Total	$\Sigma(X - GM)^2$	$N_{total} - 1$		

We calculated two F statistics, but we're really only interested in the between-groups F statistic, 14.766, that tells us whether there is a statistically significant difference between groups.

Summary: The F statistic associated with the between-groups difference is 14.77.

STEP 6: Make a decision

This step is identical to that for the one-way between-groups ANOVA.

Summary: The F statistic, 14.77, is beyond the critical value, 4.46. We reject the null hypothesis. It appears that mean ratings of beers differ based on the type of beer in terms of price category, although we cannot yet know exactly which means differ. We report the statistics in a journal article as $F(2,8) = 14.77, p < 0.05$. (*Note:* If we used software, we would report the exact p value.) ●

CHECK YOUR LEARNING

Reviewing the Concepts

> We use one-way within-groups ANOVA when we have a nominal or ordinal independent variable with at least three levels, a scale dependent variable, and participants who experience all levels of the independent variable.

> Because all participants experience all levels of the independent variable, we reduce the within-groups variability by reducing individual differences; each person serves as a control for him- or herself. A possible concern with this design is order effects.

> One-way within-groups ANOVA uses the same six steps of hypothesis testing that are used for one-way between-groups ANOVA—with one major exception. We calculate statistics for four sources rather than three. The fourth source, which is in addition to between-groups, within-groups, and total, is typically called "subjects."

Clarifying the Concepts   13-1   Why is the within-groups variability, or sum of squares, smaller for the within-groups ANOVA compared to the between-groups ANOVA?

Calculating the Statistics 13-2   Calculate the four degrees of freedom for the following groups, assuming a within-groups design:

	Participant 1	Participant 2	Participant 3
Group 1	7	9	8
Group 2	5	8	9
Group 3	6	4	6

a. $df_{between} = N_{groups} - 1$

b. $df_{subjects} = n - 1$

c. $df_{within} = (df_{between})(df_{subjects})$

d. $df_{total} = df_{between} + df_{subjects} + df_{within}$; or $df_{total} = N_{total} - 1$

13-3   Calculate the four sums of squares for the data in the previous Check Your Learning exercise:

a. $SS_{total} = \Sigma(X - GM)^2$

b. $SS_{between} = \Sigma(M - GM)^2$

c. $SS_{subjects} = \Sigma(M_{participant} - GM)^2$

d. $SS_{within} = SS_{total} - SS_{between} - SS_{subjects}$

13-4   Using all of your calculations in the two previous Check Your Learning exercises, perform the simple division to complete an ANOVA source table for these data.

Applying the Concepts   **13-5**   Let's create a context for the data presented in Check Your Learning 13-2. Suppose a car dealer wants to sell a car by having people test drive it and two other cars in the same class (e.g., midsize sedans). The data from these three groups might represent the ratings, ranging from 1 (low quality) to 10 (high quality), that drivers gave the driving experience after test-driving the cars. Using the F values you calculated above, complete the following:

a. Write hypotheses, in words, for this study.

b. How might you conduct this research such that you would satisfy the fourth assumption of the within-groups ANOVA?

Solutions to these Check Your Learning questions can be found in Appendix D.

c. Determine the critical value for F and make a decision about the outcome of this research.

Beyond Hypothesis Testing for the One-Way Within-Groups ANOVA

Hypothesis testing with a one-way within-groups ANOVA can tell us whether people can, on average, distinguish between types of beer based on price category—that is, whether people give beers different mean ratings based on price. Effect sizes help us figure out whether these differences are large enough to matter. The Tukey *HSD* test can tell us exactly which means are statistically significantly different from each other.

R^2, the Effect Size for ANOVA

The calculations for R^2 for a one-way within-groups ANOVA and a one-way between-groups ANOVA are similar. As before, the numerator is a measure of the variability that takes into account just the differences among means, $SS_{between}$. The denominator, however, takes into account the total variability, SS_{total}, but removes the variability caused by differences among participants, $SS_{subjects}$. This enables us to determine the variability explained only by between-groups differences. The formula is:

$$R^2 = \frac{SS_{between}}{(SS_{total} - SS_{subjects})}$$

MASTERING THE FORMULA

13-8: The formula for effect size for a one-way within-groups ANOVA is:

$$R^2 = \frac{SS_{between}}{(SS_{total} - SS_{subjects})}.$$

We divide the between-groups sum of squares by the difference between the total sum of squares and the subjects sum of squares. We remove the subjects sum of squares so we can determine the variability explained only by between-groups differences.

EXAMPLE 13.3

Let's apply this to the ANOVA we just conducted. We can use the statistics in the source table shown on page 349 to calculate R^2:

$$R^2 = \frac{SS_{between}}{(SS_{total} - SS_{subjects})} = \frac{1092.130}{(2117.732 - 729.738)} = 0.787$$

The conventions for R^2 are the same as those shown in Table 12-12 (see page 322). This effect size of 0.79 is a very large effect: 79% of the variability in ratings of beer is explained by price. ●

Tukey *HSD*

We use the same procedure that we used for a one-way between-groups ANOVA, the Tukey *HSD* test. Let's look at the calculations for the beer-tasting example.

EXAMPLE 13.4

We calculate an *HSD* for each pair of means by first calculating the standard error:

$$s_M = \sqrt{\frac{MS_{within}}{N}} = \sqrt{\frac{36.981}{5}} = 2.720$$

The standard error allows us to calculate *HSD* for each pair of means.
Cheap beer (34.4) versus mid-range beer (34.6):

$$HSD = \frac{(34.4 - 34.6)}{2.720} = -0.074$$

Cheap beer (34.4) versus high-end beer (52.6):

$$HSD = \frac{(34.4 - 52.6)}{2.720} = -6.691$$

Mid-range beer (34.6) versus high-end beer (52.6):

$$HSD = \frac{(34.6 - 52.6)}{2.720} = -6.618$$

Now we look up the critical value in the q table in Appendix B. For a comparison of three means with within-groups degrees of freedom of 8 and a p level of 0.05, the cutoff q is 4.04. As before, the sign of each *HSD* does not matter.

The q table indicates two statistically significant differences for which the *HSD*s are beyond the critical values: -6.691 and -6.618. It appears that high-end beers elicit higher average ratings than cheap beers; high-end beers also elicit higher average ratings than mid-range beers. No statistically significant difference is found between cheap beers and mid-range beers.

What might explain these differences? It's not surprising that expensive beers came out ahead of cheap and midrange beers, but Fallows was surprised that no observable average difference was found between cheap and mid-range beers, which led to this advice that he gave to his beer-drinking colleagues: Buy high-end beer "when [you] want an individual glass of lager to be as good as it can be," but buy cheap beer "at all other times, since it gives the maximum taste and social influence per dollar invested." The mid-range beers? Not worth the money.

Within-Groups Designs in Everyday Life We often use a within-groups design without even knowing it. A bride might use a within-groups design when she has all of her bridesmaids (the participants) try on several different possible dresses (the levels of the study). They would then choose the dress that is most flattering, on average, on the bridesmaids. We even have an intuitive understanding of order effects. A bride, for example, might ask her bridesmaids to try on the dress that she prefers either first or last (but not in the middle) so they'll remember it better and be more likely to prefer it!

How much faith can we have in these findings? As behavioral scientists, we critically examine the design and procedures. Did the darker color of Sam Adams (the beer that received the highest average ratings) give it away as a high-end beer? The beers were labeled with letters (Budweiser was labeled with F). Yet, in line with many academic grading systems, the letter A has a positive connotation and F has a negative one. Were there order effects? Did the testers get more lenient (or critical) with every swallow? The panel of tasters was mostly Microsoft employees and was all men. Would we get different results for non-tech employees or with female participants? Science is a slow but sure way of knowing that depends on replication of experiments. ●

Matched Groups

Next Steps

So far, we've learned two hypothesis tests that we can use with a within-groups design. In Chapter 10, we introduced the paired-samples *t* test, and in this chapter, we introduced the within-groups ANOVA. Previously, we stated that a within-groups design requires that every participant experience every level of the independent variable, but there is one important exception: A ***matched-groups design*** *is similar to a within-groups design; it has different people in each level of the independent variable, but they are similar (matched) on characteristics important to the study.* A matched design has more statistical power because it allows us to analyze the data as if the same people were in each group.

This research design is particularly useful when participants can't be in two groups at the same time. For example, a matched-groups design works when we want to learn whether psychology majors or history majors are more interested in current events. We can't randomly assign students to their majors, of course, and we want to control for confounding variables such as time spent reading online news sources that might differ systematically between psychology majors and history majors. We want to know that it is their major, not some other variable, that is associated with any mean difference in interest in current events, so we would match students on these other variables.

● A **matched-groups design** is similar to a within-groups design; it has different people in each level of the independent variable, but they are similar (matched) on characteristics important to the study.

Let's look at a published example in the social science literature. Researchers in Indiana compared depression levels of elderly Mexican American caregivers with elderly Mexican American noncaregivers (Hernandez & Bigatti, 2010). Sixty-five people who cared for individuals with Alzheimer's disease or a disability were matched with 65 noncaregivers on variables that the researchers knew to be related to depression—age, gender, socioeconomic status, physical health, and level of acculturation to the United States. For example, a caregiver who was female, 68 years old, healthy, and well-acculturated to the United States would be matched with a noncaregiver who shared these characteristics. In this way, the researchers could know that these matched variables were not responsible for any differences between groups, making it more likely that caregiver status caused any mean difference in depression between the two groups. In this study, the researchers found that caregivers were more likely to be depressed than noncaregivers, on average.

Using matched groups increases statistical power the same way that a within-groups design has more statistical power than a between-groups design. However, there are two main problems, and they may already have occurred to you. First, we might not be aware of all of the important variables of interest. For example, social support is related to depression, and caregivers may be so busy caring for others that they have little time to develop their own network of social support. If we did not match the groups on level of social support, then social support might account for any mean differences in the dependent variable.

Second, if one of the people in a matched pair decides not to complete the study, then we must discard the data for the match for this person. This makes for less-than-efficient research. In the study comparing caregivers and noncaregivers, data from 8 caregivers had to be discarded because they did not provide much of the data needed to complete the data set. Because of this, the researchers had to discard the data from the 8 noncaregivers who were matched to these participants, even though they had completed most of the measures. So only 57 of the 65 matched pairs remained in the final data set. If these problems can be addressed, however, matched groups can allow researchers to harness the increased statistical power of a within-groups design.

CHECK YOUR LEARNING

Reviewing the Concepts

> It is recommended, as it is for other hypothesis tests, that we calculate a measure of effect size, R^2, for a one-way within-groups ANOVA.

> As with one-way between-groups ANOVA, if we are able to reject the null hypothesis with a one-way within-groups ANOVA, we're not finished. We must conduct a post hoc test, such as a Tukey HSD test, to determine exactly which pairs of means are significantly different from one another.

> Matched pairs and matched groups allow us to use within-groups designs even if different participants experience each level of the independent variable. Rather than using the same participants, we match different participants on possible confounding variables.

Clarifying the Concepts

13-6 How does the calculation of the effect size R^2 differ between the one-way within-groups ANOVA and the one-way between-groups ANOVA?

13-7 How does the calculation of the Tukey HSD differ between the one-way within-groups ANOVA and the one-way between-groups ANOVA?

Calculating the Statistics **13-8** A researcher measured the reaction time of six participants at three different times and found the mean reaction time at time 1 ($M_1 = 155.833$), time 2 ($M_2 = 206.833$), and time 3 ($M_3 = 251.667$). The researcher rejected the null hypothesis after performing a one-way within-groups ANOVA. For the ANOVA, $df_{between} = 2$, $df_{within} = 10$, and $MS_{within} = 771.256$.

a. Calculate the HSD for each of the three mean comparisons.

b. What is the critical value of q for this Tukey HSD test?

c. For which comparisons do we reject the null hypothesis?

13-9 Use the following source table to calculate the effect size R^2 for the one-way within-groups ANOVA.

Source	SS	df	MS	F
Between	27,590.486	2	13,795.243	17.887
Subjects	16,812.189	5	3362.438	4.360
Within	7712.436	10	771.244	
Total	52,115.111	17		

Applying the Concepts **13-10** In Check Your Learning 13-4 and 13-5, we conducted an analysis of driver-experience ratings following test drives.

Solutions to these Check Your Learning questions can be found in Appendix D.

a. Calculate R^2 for this ANOVA, and state what size effect this is.

b. Which follow-up tests are needed for this ANOVA, if any?

REVIEW OF CONCEPTS

One-Way Within-Groups ANOVA

We use a one-way within-groups ANOVA (also called a *repeated-measures ANOVA*) when there is one nominal or ordinal variable with at least three levels and a scale dependent variable, and every participant experiences every level of the independent variable. We use the same six steps of hypothesis testing for one-way within-groups ANOVA as we do for one-way between-groups ANOVA, except that for the former, we calculate statistics for four sources instead of three. We still calculate statistics for the between-groups, within-groups, and total sources, but we also calculate statistics for a fourth source, "subjects." Although we calculate two F statistics, one for the between-groups variability and one for the subjects variability, we compare the between-groups F statistic to a critical value and either reject or fail to reject the null hypothesis.

Beyond Hypothesis Testing for the One-Way Within-Groups ANOVA

As we do with the one-way between-groups ANOVA, we calculate a measure of effect size, usually R^2, and we conduct a post hoc test, such as the Tukey HSD test, if we reject the null hypothesis. There is one exception to the requirement that the same participants experience every level of the independent variable if we want to use a paired-samples t test or within-groups ANOVA. If we match the participants in each group on all likely confounding variables, then we can treat the groups—in a statistical sense—as if they include the same participants.

SPSS®

To conduct a one-way within-groups ANOVA on SPSS using the beer-rating data from the chapter, we enter the data so that each participant has one row with all of his data. This results in a different format from that of the data entered for a one-way between-groups ANOVA. In that case, we had a score for each participant's level of the independent variable and a score for the dependent variable. For a within-groups ANOVA, each participant has multiple scores on the dependent variable. The levels of the independent variable are indicated in the titles for each of the three columns in SPSS. For example, as seen on the left of the SPSS screenshot, the first participant has scores of 40 for the cheap beer, 30 for the mid-range beer, and 53 for the high-end beer. Instruct SPSS to conduct the ANOVA by selecting Analyze → General Linear Model → Repeated Measures. (Remember that *repeated measures* is another way to say "within groups" when describing ANOVA.) Next, under "Within-Subject Factor Name," change the generic "factor1" to the actual name of the independent variable, such as "type_of_beer" (using underscores between words because SPSS doesn't recognize spaces in a variable name). Next to

"Number of Levels," type "3" to represent the number of levels of the independent variable in this study. Now click "Add," followed by "Define." Define the levels by clicking each of the three levels, then clicking the arrow button, in turn. You can see the entered data, and the box in which to define the levels, in the screenshot. To see the results of the ANOVA, click "OK."

The output includes more tables than in the between-groups ANOVA SPSS output. The one we want to pay attention to is titled "Tests of Within-Subjects Effects." This table provides four F values and four "Sig." values (the actual p values). There are several more advanced considerations that play into deciding which one to use; for the purposes of this introduction to SPSS, we simply note that the F values are all the same, and all match the F of 14.77 that we calculated previously. Moreover, all of the p values are less than the cutoff of 0.05. As we could when we conducted this one-way within-groups ANOVA by hand, we can reject the null hypothesis.

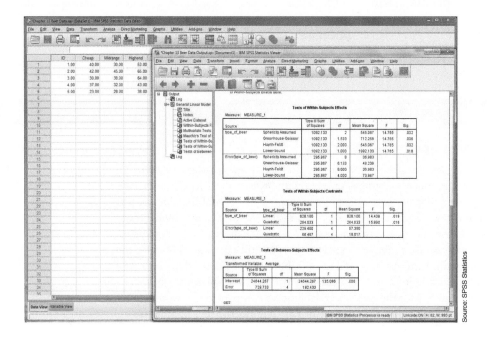

Source: SPSS Statistics

HOW IT WORKS

13.1 CONDUCTING A ONE-WAY WITHIN-GROUPS ANOVA

Researchers followed the progress of 42 people undergoing inpatient rehabilitation following a spinal cord injury (White, Driver, & Warren, 2010). They assessed the patients on a variety of measures on three separate occasions—when they were admitted to the rehabilitation facility, 3 weeks later, and at discharge. Below are data that reflect the patients' symptoms of depression on the Patient Health Questionnaire-9 (PHQ-9).

(The data for these three fictional patients have the same means as the actual larger data set, as well as the same outcome in terms of the decision in step 6 of the ANOVA below.)

	Admission	Three Weeks	Discharge
Patient 1	6.1	5.5	5.3
Patient 2	6.9	5.7	4.2
Patient 3	7.4	6.5	4.9

How can we use one-way within-groups ANOVA to determine whether depression levels changed as patients went through rehabilitation for spinal cord injury? We'll walk through all six steps of hypothesis testing for a one-way within-groups ANOVA.

Step 1: Population 1: People just admitted to an inpatient rehabilitation facility following a spinal cord injury. Population 2: People 3 weeks after they were admitted to an inpatient rehabilitation facility following a spinal cord injury. Population 3: People being discharged from an inpatient rehabilitation facility following spinal cord injury.

The comparison distribution will be an F distribution. The hypothesis test will be a one-way within-groups ANOVA. Regarding the assumptions: (1) The patients were not selected randomly (all were from the same hospital), so we must generalize with caution. (2) We do not know if the underlying population distributions are normal, but the sample data do not indicate severe skew. (3) To see if we meet the homoscedasticity assumption, we will check to see if the variances are similar (typically, when the largest variance is not more than twice the smallest) when we calculate the test statistic. (4) The experimenter could not counterbalance, so order effects might be present. With different levels of a time-related variable, it is not possible to assign someone to be measured at, for example, the final time point before the first time point.

Step 2: Null hypothesis: People in an inpatient rehabilitation hospital for a spinal cord injury have the same levels of depression, on average, at admission, 3 weeks later, and at discharge—H_0: $\mu_1 = \mu_2 = \mu_3$. Research hypothesis: People in an inpatient rehabilitation hospital for a spinal cord injury do not have the same levels of depression, on average, at admission, 3 weeks later, and at discharge—H_1 is that at least one μ is different from another μ.

Step 3: We use an F distribution with 2 and 4 degrees of freedom.

$$df_{between} = N_{groups} - 1 = 3 - 1 = 2$$
$$df_{subjects} = n - 1 = 3 - 1 = 2$$
$$df_{within} = (df_{between})(df_{subjects}) = (2)(2) = 4$$
$$df_{total} = df_{between} + df_{subjects} + df_{within} = 2 + 2 + 4 = 8$$
$$(\text{or } df_{total} = N_{total} - 1 = 9 - 1 = 8)$$

Step 4: The critical value for the F statistic for a p level of 0.05 and 2 and 4 degrees of freedom is 6.95.

Step 5: $SS_{total} = \Sigma(X - GM)^2 = 8.059$.

Time	X	X − GM	$(X - GM)^2$
Admission	6.1	0.267	0.071
Admission	6.9	1.067	1.138
Admission	7.4	1.567	2.455
Three weeks	5.5	−0.333	0.111
Three weeks	5.7	−0.133	0.018
Three weeks	6.5	0.667	0.445
Discharge	5.3	−0.533	0.284
Discharge	4.2	−1.633	2.667
Discharge	4.9	−0.933	0.87
	GM = 5.833		$\Sigma(X - GM)^2 = 8.059$

$$SS_{between} = \Sigma(M - GM)^2 = 6.018$$

Time	X	Group Mean (M)	M − GM	(M − GM)²
Admission	6.1	6.8	0.967	0.935
Admission	6.9	6.8	0.967	0.935
Admission	7.4	6.8	0.967	0.935
Three weeks	5.5	5.9	0.067	0.004
Three weeks	5.7	5.9	0.067	0.004
Three weeks	6.5	5.9	0.067	0.004
Discharge	5.3	4.8	−1.033	1.067
Discharge	4.2	4.8	−1.033	1.067
Discharge	4.9	4.8	−1.033	1.067
$GM = 5.833$				$\Sigma(M - GM)^2 = 6.018$

$$SS_{subjects} = \Sigma(M_{participant} - GM)^2 = 0.846$$

Participant	Time	X	Participant Mean ($M_{participant}$)	$M_{participant} - GM$	$(M_{participant} - GM)^2$
1	Admission	6.1	5.633	−0.2	0.040
2	Admission	6.9	5.6	−0.233	0.054
3	Admission	7.4	6.267	0.434	0.188
1	Three weeks	5.5	5.633	−0.2	0.040
2	Three weeks	5.7	5.6	−0.233	0.054
3	Three weeks	6.5	6.267	0.434	0.188
1	Discharge	5.3	5.633	−0.2	0.040
2	Discharge	4.2	5.6	−0.233	0.054
3	Discharge	4.9	6.267	0.434	0.188
	$GM = 5.833$			$\Sigma(M_{participant} - GM)^2 = 0.846$	

$$SS_{within} = SS_{total} - SS_{between} - SS_{subjects} = 8.059 - 6.018 - 0.846 = 1.195$$

We now have enough information to fill in the first three columns of the source table—the source, SS, and df columns—and to divide each sum of squares by the degrees of freedom to get variance, MS.

$$MS_{between} = \frac{SS_{between}}{df_{between}} = \frac{6.018}{2} = 3.009$$

$$MS_{subjects} = \frac{SS_{subjects}}{df_{subjects}} = \frac{0.846}{2} = 0.423$$

$$MS_{within} = \frac{SS_{within}}{df_{within}} = \frac{1.195}{4} = 0.299$$

We then calculate two F statistics—one for between-groups and one for subjects—by dividing each MS by the within-groups MS.

$$F_{between} = \frac{MS_{between}}{MS_{within}} = \frac{3.009}{0.299} = 10.06$$

$$F_{subjects} = \frac{MS_{subjects}}{MS_{within}} = \frac{0.423}{0.299} = 1.41$$

The completed source table is:

Source	SS	df	MS	F
Between	6.018	2	3.009	10.06
Subjects	0.846	2	0.423	1.41
Within	1.195	4	0.299	
Total	8.059	8		

We want to know if there's a statistically significant difference between groups, so we'll look at the between-groups F statistic, 10.06.

Step 6: The F statistic, 10.06, is beyond the critical value, 6.95. We can reject the null hypothesis. It appears that depression scores differ based on the time point during rehabilitation. A post hoc test is necessary to know exactly which pairs of means are significantly different.

13.2 CALCULATING THE EFFECT SIZE FOR A ONE-WAY WITHIN-GROUPS ANOVA

How can we calculate the effect size for these data?

The appropriate measure of effect size for a one-way within-groups ANOVA is R^2, which is calculated as:

$$R^2 = \frac{SS_{between}}{(SS_{total} - SS_{subjects})} = \frac{6.018}{(8.059 - 0.846)} = 0.834$$

Based on the conventions for R^2, this is a very large effect: 83% of the variability in depression scores is explained by the time during rehabilitation.

13.3 CALCULATING THE TUKEY *HSD* POST HOC TEST FOR A ONE-WAY WITHIN-GROUPS ANOVA

The F test calculated in How It Works 13.1 only tells us that there is a statistically significant difference, but we are unable to determine where those significant differences lie without conducting a post hoc test. How can we calculate the Tukey *HSD* test for a one-way within-groups ANOVA?

First, we must calculate the standard error:

$$s_M = \sqrt{\frac{MS_{within}}{N}} = \sqrt{\frac{0.299}{9}} = 0.182$$

Then, we calculate an *HSD* for each mean pair comparison:

To compare the mean depression rate at time of admission ($M = 6.8$) to the mean depression rate three weeks into rehabilitation ($M = 5.9$), we calculate:

$$HSD = \frac{6.8 - 5.9}{0.182} = 4.945$$

To compare the mean depression rate at time of admission ($M = 6.8$) to the mean depression rate at discharge ($M = 4.8$), we calculate:

$$HSD = \frac{6.8 - 4.8}{0.182} = 10.989$$

To compare the mean depression rate at three weeks into rehabilitation ($M = 5.9$) to the mean depression rate at discharge ($M = 4.8$), we calculate:

$$HSD = \frac{5.9 - 4.8}{0.182} = 6.044$$

The critical value in the q table for a comparison of three means with within-groups degrees of freedom of 4 and a p level of 0.05 is 5.04. Only two of the comparisons are statistically significant (comparisons where the HSD is beyond the critical value): the comparison of the mean depression rate at time of admission and time of discharge, and the comparison of the mean depression rate at three weeks into rehabilitation and time of discharge.

EXERCISES

Clarifying the Concepts

13.1 What are the four assumptions for a within-groups ANOVA?

13.2 What are order effects?

13.3 Explain the source of variability called "subjects."

13.4 What is the advantage of the design of the within-groups ANOVA over that of the between-groups ANOVA?

13.5 What is counterbalancing?

13.6 Why is it appropriate to counterbalance when using a within-groups design?

13.7 How do we calculate the sum of squares for subjects?

13.8 How is the calculation of df_{within} different in a between-groups ANOVA from the calculation in a within-groups ANOVA?

13.9 How could we turn a between-groups study into a within-groups study?

13.10 What are some situations in which it might be impossible—or not make sense—to turn a between-groups study into a within-groups study?

13.11 How is the calculation of effect size different for a one-way between-groups ANOVA versus a one-way within-groups ANOVA?

13.12 What is a matched-groups research design?

Calculating the Statistics

13.13 For the following data, assuming a within-groups design, determine:

	Person			
	1	2	3	4
Level 1 of the independent variable	7	16	3	9
Level 2 of the independent variable	15	18	18	13
Level 3 of the independent variable	22	28	26	29

   a. $df_{between} = N_{groups} - 1$
   b. $df_{subjects} = n - 1$
   c. $df_{within} = (df_{between})(df_{subjects})$
   d. $df_{total} = df_{between} + df_{subjects} + df_{within}$, or $df_{total} = N_{total} - 1$
   e. $SS_{total} = \Sigma(X - GM)^2$
   f. $SS_{between} = \Sigma(M - GM)^2$
   g. $SS_{subjects} = \Sigma(M_{participant} - GM)^2$

   h. $SS_{within} = SS_{total} - SS_{between} - SS_{subjects}$
   i. The rest of the ANOVA source table for these data
   j. The effect size
   k. The Tukey HSD statistic for the comparisons between level 1 and level 3

13.14 For the following data, assuming a within-groups design, determine:

	Person					
	1	2	3	4	5	6
Level 1	5	6	3	4	2	5
Level 2	6	8	4	7	3	7
Level 3	4	5	2	4	0	4

   a. $df_{between} = N_{groups} - 1$
   b. $df_{subjects} = n - 1$
   c. $df_{within} = (df_{between})(df_{subjects})$
   d. $df_{total} = df_{between} + df_{subjects} + df_{within}$, or $df_{total} = N_{total} - 1$
   e. $SS_{total} = \Sigma(X - GM)^2$
   f. $SS_{between} = \Sigma(M - GM)^2$
   g. $SS_{subjects} = \Sigma(M_{participant} - GM)^2$
   h. $SS_{within} = SS_{total} - SS_{between} - SS_{subjects}$
   i. The rest of the ANOVA source table for these data
   j. The critical F value and your decision about the null hypothesis
   k. If appropriate, the Tukey HSD statistic for all possible mean comparisons
   l. The critical q value; then, make a decision for each comparison in part (k)
   m. The effect size

13.15 For the following incomplete source table below for a one-way within-groups ANOVA:

Source	SS	df	MS	F
Between	941.102	2	—	—
Subjects	3807.322	—	—	—
Within	—	20	—	
Total	5674.502	—		

   a. Complete the missing information.
   b. Calculate R^2.

13.16 Assume that a researcher had 14 individuals participate in all three conditions of her experiment. Use this information to complete the source table below.

Source	SS	df	MS	F
Between	60	—	—	—
Subjects	—	—	—	—
Within	50	—	—	
Total	136	—		

13.17 An incomplete one-way between-groups ANOVA source table is shown below. Compute the missing values.

Source	SS	df	MS	F
Between	56.570	—	28.285	2.435
Subjects	83.865	—	10.483	—
Within	—	16		
Total	326.265	26		

13.18 An incomplete one-way between-groups ANOVA source table is shown below. There were 3 conditions and 6 participants. Compute the missing values.

Source	SS	df	MS	F
Between	0.588	—	—	—
Subjects	0.236	—	—	—
Within	0.126	—	—	
Total	—	—		

Applying the Concepts

13.19 Fear of dogs and one-way within-groups ANOVA: Imagine a researcher wanted to assess people's fear of dogs as a function of the size of the dog. He assessed fear among people who indicated they were afraid of dogs, using a 30-point scale from 0 (no fear) to 30 (extreme fear). The researcher exposed each participant to three different dogs, a small dog weighing 20 pounds, a medium-sized dog weighing 55 pounds, and a large dog weighing 110 pounds, and assessed the fear level after each exposure. Here are some hypothetical data; note that these are the data from Exercise 13.13, on which you have already calculated numerous statistics:

	Person			
	1	2	3	4
Small dog	7	16	3	9
Medium dog	15	18	18	13
Large dog	22	28	26	29

a. State the null and research hypotheses.

b. Determine whether the assumptions of random selection and order effects were met.

c. In Exercise 13.13, you calculated the effect size for these data. What does this statistic tell us about the effect of size of dog on fear levels?

d. In Exercise 13.13, you calculated a Tukey *HSD* test for the difference between levels 1 (small dog) and 3 (big dog). What can you conclude about the effect of size of dog on fear levels based on this statistic?

13.20 Chewing-gum commercials and one-way within-groups ANOVA: Commercials for chewing gum make claims about how long the flavor will last. In fact, some commercials claim that the flavor lasts too long, affecting sales and profit. Let's put these claims to a test. Imagine a student decides to compare four different gums using five participants. Each randomly selected participant was asked to chew a different piece of gum each day for 4 days, such that at the end of the 4 days, each participant had chewed all four types of gum. The order of the gums was randomly determined for each participant. After 2 hours of chewing, participants recorded the intensity of flavor from 1 (not intense) to 9 (very intense). Here are some hypothetical data:

	Person				
	1	2	3	4	5
Gum 1	4	6	3	4	4
Gum 2	8	6	9	9	8
Gum 3	5	6	7	4	5
Gum 4	2	2	3	2	1

a. Conduct all six steps of the hypothesis test.

b. Are any additional tests warranted? Explain your answer.

c. How could the researchers conduct this study with a matched-groups research design?

13.21 Pessimism and one-way within-groups ANOVA: Researchers Busseri, Choma, and Sadava (2009) asked a sample of individuals who scored as pessimists on a measure of life orientation about past, present, and projected future satisfaction with their lives. Higher scores on the life-satisfaction measure indicate higher satisfaction. The data below reproduce the pattern of means that the researchers observed in self-reported life satisfaction of the sample of pessimists for the three time points. Do pessimists predict a gloomy future for themselves?

	Person				
	1	2	3	4	5
Past	18	17.5	19	16	20
Present	18.5	19.5	20	17	18
Future	22	24	20	23.5	21

a. Perform steps 5 and 6 of hypothesis testing. Be sure to complete the source table when calculating the *F* ratio for step 5.

b. If appropriate, calculate the Tukey *HSD* for all possible mean comparisons. Find the critical value of *q* and make a decision regarding the null hypothesis for each of the mean comparisons.

c. Calculate the R^2 measure of effect size for this ANOVA.

13.22 Optimism and one-way within-groups ANOVA: The previous exercise describes a study conducted by Busseri and colleagues (2009) using a group of pessimists. These researchers asked the same question of a group of optimists: Optimists rated their past, present, and projected future satisfaction with their lives. Higher scores on the life-satisfaction measure indicate higher satisfaction. The data below reproduce the pattern of means that the researchers observed in self-reported life satisfaction of the sample of optimists for the three time points. Do optimists see a rosy future ahead?

| | Person | | | | |
	1	2	3	4	5
Past	22	23	25	24	26
Present	25	26	27	28	29
Future	24	27	26	28	29

a. Perform steps 5 and 6 of hypothesis testing. Be sure to complete the source table when calculating the *F* ratio for step 5.

b. If appropriate, calculate the Tukey *HSD* for all possible mean comparisons. Find the critical value of *q* and make a decision regarding the null hypothesis for each of the mean comparisons.

c. Calculate the R^2 measure of effect size for this ANOVA.

13.23 Wagging tails and one-way within-groups ANOVA: How does a dog's tail wag in response to seeing different people and other pets? Quaranta, Siniscalchi, and Vallortigara (2007) investigated the amplitude and direction of a dog's tail wagging in response to seeing its owner, an unfamiliar cat, and an unfamiliar dog. The fictional data below are measures of amplitude. These data reproduce the pattern of results in the study, averaging leftward tail wags and rightward tail wags. Use these data to construct the source table for a one-way within-groups ANOVA.

Dog Participant	Owner	Cat	Other Dog
1	69	28	45
2	72	32	43
3	65	30	47
4	75	29	45
5	70	31	44

13.24 Memory, post hoc tests, and effect size: Luo, Hendriks, and Craik (2007) were interested in whether people might better remember lists of words if the lists were paired with either pictures or sound effects. They asked participants to memorize lists of words under three different learning conditions. In the first condition, participants just saw a list of nouns that they were to remember (word-alone condition). In the second condition, the words were also accompanied by a picture of the object (picture condition). In the third condition, the words were accompanied by a sound effect matching the object (sound effect condition). The researchers measured the proportion of words participants got correct in a later recognition test. Fictional data from four participants produce results similar to those of the original study. The average proportion of words recognized was $M = 0.54$ in the word-alone condition, $M = 0.69$ in the picture condition, and $M = 0.838$ in the sound effect condition. The source table below depicts the results of the ANOVA on the data from the four fictional participants.

Source	SS	df	MS	F
Between	0.177	2	0.089	8.900
Subjects	0.002	3	0.001	0.100
Within	0.059	6	0.010	
Total	0.238	11		

a. Is it appropriate to perform post hoc comparisons on the data? Why or why not?

b. Use the information provided in the ANOVA table to calculate R^2. Interpret the effect size using Cohen's conventions. State what this R^2 means in terms of the independent and dependent variables used in this study.

13.25 Wagging tails, hypothesis-test decision making, and post hoc tests: Assume that we recruited a different sample of five dogs and attempted to replicate the Quaranta and colleagues (2007) study described in Exercise 13.23. The source table for our fictional replication appears below. Find the critical *F* value and make a decision regarding the null hypothesis. Based on this decision, is it appropriate to conduct post hoc comparisons? Why or why not?

Source	SS	df	MS	F
Between	58.133	2	29.067	0.066
Subjects	642.267	4	160.567	0.364
Within	532.533	8	441.567	
Total	4232.933	14		

13.26 Pilots' mental efforts and a one-way within-groups ANOVA: Researchers examined the amount of mental effort that participants felt they were expending on a cognitively complex task, piloting an unmanned air vehicle (UAV) (Ayaz, Shewokis, Bunce, Izzetoglu, Willems, & Onaral, 2012). The researchers used the Task Load Index (TLX), a measure that assesses participants' perception of their mental effort following a series of approach and landing tasks in simulated UAV tasks. They wondered whether expertise would have an effect on perceptions of mental effort. In the results section, the researchers reported the results of their analyses, a series of one-way repeated-measures ANOVA. "The results indicated a significant main effect of practice level (beginner/intermediate/advanced conditions) for mental demand ($F(2, 8) = 17.87, p < 0.01, \eta^2 = 0.817$), effort ($F(2, 8) = 16.32, p < 0.01, \eta^2 = 0.803$), and frustration ($F(2, 8) = 8.60, p < 0.01, \eta^2 = 0.682$)." They went on to explain that mental demand, effort, and frustration all tended to decrease with expertise.

a. What is the independent variable in this study?

b. What are the dependent variables in this study?

c. Explain why the researchers were able to use a one-way within-groups ANOVA in this situation.

d. η^2 is roughly equivalent to R^2. How large are each of these effects, based on Cohen's conventions?

e. The researchers drew a specific conclusion beyond that there was some difference, on average, in the dependent variables, depending on the particular levels of the independent variable. What additional test were they likely to have conducted? Explain your answer.

f. How could the researchers conduct this study with a matched-groups research design?

Putting It All Together

13.27 Eye glare, football, and one-way within-groups ANOVA: Does the black grease beneath football players' eyes really reduce glare or does it just make them look intimidating? In a variation of a study actually conducted at Yale University, 46 participants placed one of three substances below their eyes: black grease, black antiglare stickers, or petroleum jelly. The researchers assessed eye glare using a contrast chart for each participant that gives a value on a scale measure. Every participant was assessed with each of the three substances, one at a time. Black grease led to a reduction in glare compared with the two other conditions, antiglare stickers or petroleum jelly (DeBroff & Pahk, 2003).

Person	Black Grease	Antiglare Stickers	Petroleum Jelly
1	19.8	17.1	15.9
2	18.2	17.2	16.3
3	19.2	18.0	16.2
4	18.7	17.9	17.0

a. What is the independent variable? What are its levels?

b. What is the dependent variable?

c. What kind of ANOVA is this?

d. What is the first assumption for ANOVA? Is it likely that the researchers met this assumption? Explain your answer.

e. What is the second assumption for ANOVA? How could the researchers check to see if they had met this assumption? Be specific.

f. What is the third assumption for ANOVA? How could the researchers check to see if they had met this assumption? Be specific.

g. What is the fourth assumption, specific to the within-groups ANOVA? What would the researchers need to do to ensure that they meet this assumption?

h. Perform steps 5 and 6 of hypothesis testing. Be sure to complete the source table when calculating the F ratio for step 5.

i. If appropriate, calculate the Tukey HSD for all possible mean comparisons. Find the critical value of q and make a decision regarding the null hypothesis for each of the mean comparisons.

j. Calculate the R^2 measure of effect size for this ANOVA.

k. How could this study be conducted using a between-groups design?

l. How could this study be conducted using a matched-groups design?

13.28 ANOVA, athletes, and social support: Researchers examined differences among student-athletes' perceptions of different kinds of support related to their sports (Adams, Coffee, & Lavallee, 2015). Male athletes at a Scottish University who played one of seven sports—including cricket, basketball, and badminton—were surveyed about the level of support they received in four areas. Students provided ratings for each of these four areas, with higher scores indicating more support. The means for the four areas in this study were 8.47 for emotional support (mood-related), 8.42 for esteem support (encouragement), 7.63 for informational support (technical advice), and 6.66 for tangible support (help in planning, for example). Here is the description of the analyses from the researchers: "A one-way repeated measures analysis of variance (ANOVA) was conducted to determine the differences…. [Effect size] values were interpreted by following the guidelines proposed by Cohen" (p. 41). The researchers included the following statistics: $F(3,68) = 29.88, p < .001$. They also reported that: "Pairwise comparisons between all four types of social support indicated a significant difference between all support types except that between emotional support and esteem support

(95% CI = −0.342 − 0.428, p = 1.000)" (p. 42). Finally, the researchers reported an effect size of 0.57 for the statistically significant comparisons. (Note that they reported partial η^2 for effect size, which you may recall is interpreted like R^2.)

a. What is the independent variable in this study? What are its levels?

b. What is the dependent variable in this study? What type of variable is it?

c. Is this an experiment or a correlational study? Explain your answer.

d. The researchers explain that they used a one-way repeated-measures ANOVA, another way to say one-way within-groups ANOVA. Explain why they used this statistical analysis.

e. The researchers reported that they interpreted the effect size using Cohen's guidelines. Explain how they would have interpreted the effect size that they found.

f. Explain the statistics that the researchers reported. What does each of these mean? (Hint: For the pairwise comparisons, the researchers likely conducted paired-samples t tests. Also, "CI" refers to confidence interval.)

g. Explain the overall pattern of results in your own words.

h. If the one mean difference in this study that was *not* statistically significant is an incorrect conclusion, what kind of error is this? Explain your answer.

i. The researchers also reported that "a Bonferroni adjustment was used to adjust the p value from the initial .05 to .017 for the pairwise comparison of the results." Based on what you learned in the Next Steps section of Chapter 12, what does this mean? Why did the researchers make this adjustment?

j. Create a graph that depicts the differences among these means. Follow the graphing guidelines you learned in Chapter 3.

TERMS

matched groups (p. 353)

FORMULAS

$df_{subjects} = n - 1$ (p. 346)

$df_{within} = (df_{between})(df_{subjects})$
  [formula for a one-way
  within-groups ANOVA] (p. 346)

$df_{total} = df_{between} + df_{subjects} + df_{within}$
  [formula for a one-way
  within-groups ANOVA] (p. 347)

$SS_{subjects} = \Sigma(M_{participant} - GM)^2$ (p. 348)

$SS_{within} = SS_{total} - SS_{between} - SS_{subjects}$
  [formula for a one-way
  within-groups ANOVA] (p. 349)

$MS_{subjects} = \dfrac{SS_{subjects}}{df_{subjects}}$ (p. 349)

$F_{subjects} = \dfrac{MS_{subjects}}{MS_{within}}$ (p. 349)

$R^2 = \dfrac{SS_{between}}{(SS_{total} - SS_{subjects})}$
  [formula for a one-way
  within-groups ANOVA] (p. 351)

SYMBOLS

$df_{subjects}$ (p. 346)

$SS_{subjects}$ (p. 346)

$MS_{subjects}$ (p. 349)

$F_{subjects}$ (p. 349)

Two-Way Between-Groups ANOVA

BEFORE YOU GO ON

■ You should understand the six steps of
hypothesis testing (Chapter 7).

■ You should be able to conduct and
interpret a one-way between-groups ANOVA
(Chapter 12).

■ You should understand the concept of effect
size (Chapter 8) and the measure of effect
size for ANOVA, R^2 (Chapter 12).

FIGURE 14-1

Ski Bums Beware!

This bar graph tells a useful story for consumers about a statistically significant interaction. Ski resorts tend to exaggerate the amount of snowfall, especially snowfall on weekends.

● A statistical **interaction** occurs in a factorial design when two or more independent variables have an effect on the dependent variable in combination that neither independent variable has on its own.

Jonathan Zinman and Eric Zitzewitz are social science researchers and ski bums who live in New Hampshire. They had become annoyed when they hit the slopes only to find that snowfall reports had clearly been exaggerated. So they collected snowfall data both from ski resorts and the weather station for weekdays (when fewer people go skiing or snowboarding) and for the more profitable weekends. Figure 14-1 summarizes what they found: The ski resorts reported greater snowfall than weather stations did, an effect that was even more pronounced on weekends, when such an exaggeration was likely to draw more paying customers.

In the study by Zinman and Zitzewitz (2009), the dependent variable is the amount of snow reported, in inches. But there are two independent variables (source of the snow report and time of the week), and each one seems to have its own effect on the amount of snow reported. Ski resorts reported more snowfall, on average, when we disregard whether it fell on weekdays or weekends, than weather stations did. This is called a *main effect* of the source of the snow report. Figure 14-1 also shows that snow reports are higher on weekends than on weekdays when we disregard the source of the snow report. This is called a *main effect* of time of the week.

But there is a third finding, and it's the most interesting one: Only ski resorts, and not weather stations, bumped up their estimates even more on the weekend than they did during the week! So the variable for the source of the report interacted with the variable for the time of week, making its own unique impact on the reported amount of snowfall. This is called an *interaction* between the variables for the source of the snow report and the time of week.

Armed with empirical evidence of biased reporting, these researchers concluded that skiers and snowboarders could fight back. Zinman and Zitzewitz (2009) wrote: "Near the end of our sample period, a new iPhone application feature makes it easier for skiers to share information on ski conditions in real time. Exaggeration falls sharply, especially at resorts with better iPhone reception." It's a great reminder that we can question reported data, create new data, and take advantage of social media to share information in meaningful ways.

With two independent variables and one dependent variable, the experiment contains three comparisons that might influence a skier's decision about whether to hit the slopes: (1) the source of the snowfall report (ski resort versus weather station); (2) the time of week (weekday versus weekend); and (3) the combined effects of the source of snowfall report *and* the time of week. In this study, researchers discovered that the combined effects were the most important of the influences on the amount of snowfall reported. The effect of the source of the snowfall report on the amount of snow reported depended on whether it was a weekday or a weekend.

In this chapter, we examine a hypothesis test that checks for the presence of combined effects, also called *interactions*. *A statistical **interaction** occurs in a factorial design when two or more independent variables have an effect on the dependent variable in combination that neither independent variable has on its own.*

Crowdsourcing Snowfall Data Internet-savvy skiers can share information about conditions on the slopes in real time, foiling attempts by ski resorts to exaggerate snowfall amounts. This exaggeration had been exposed through a statistical interaction.

We learn about interactions in relation to a research design that has *two* nominal (or sometimes ordinal) independent variables, one scale dependent variable, and a between-groups design. We learn how the six steps of hypothesis testing apply to this statistical test, and how to calculate effect sizes for this test.

Two-Way ANOVA

Skiing-related decisions (and many other behaviors) are routinely influenced by multiple variables, so we need a way to measure the interactive effects of multiple variables.

A two-way ANOVA (analysis of variance) allows us to compare levels from two independent variables plus the joint effects of those two variables. *A **two-way ANOVA** is a hypothesis test that includes two nominal independent variables, regardless of their numbers of levels, and a scale dependent variable.* We can also have ANOVAs with more than two independent variables. As the number of independent variables increases, the number increases in the name of the ANOVA—three-way, four-way, five-way, and so on. Table 14-1 shows a range of possibilities for naming ANOVAs.

Regardless of the number of independent variables, we can use the research designs that we have already discussed. As with other hypothesis tests, a between-groups design is one in which every participant is in only one condition, and a within-groups design is one in which every participant is in all conditions. A mixed design is one in which one of the independent variables is between-groups and one is within-groups. In this chapter, we focus on the ANOVA that uses the second modifier from column 1 and the first modifier from column 2: the two-way between-groups ANOVA.

Language Alert! There is a catch-all phrase for two-way, three-way, and higher-order ANOVAs; any ANOVA with at least two independent variables can be called a ***factorial ANOVA***, *a statistical analysis used with one scale dependent variable and at least two nominal independent variables* (also called *factors*). This is also called a *multifactorial ANOVA*. ***Factor*** *is another word used to describe an independent variable in a study with more than one independent variable.*

In this section, we learn more about the situations in which we use a two-way ANOVA, as well as the language that is used in reference to this type of hypothesis test. Then we learn about the three outcomes we can examine with a two-way ANOVA.

Why We Use Two-Way ANOVA

Behavioral science researchers understand the benefits of the two-way ANOVA. Let's look at a study where the interaction tells a more interesting and more complete story

- A **two-way ANOVA** is a hypothesis test that includes two nominal independent variables, regardless of their numbers of levels, and a scale dependent variable.

- A **factorial ANOVA** is a statistical analysis used with one scale dependent variable and at least two nominal independent variables (also called *factors*); also called a *multifactorial ANOVA*.

- **Factor** is a term used to describe an independent variable in a study with more than one independent variable.

TABLE 14-1   How to Name an ANOVA

ANOVAs are typically described by two adjectives, one from the first column and one from the second. So, we could have a one-way between-groups ANOVA or a one-way within-groups ANOVA, a two-way between-groups ANOVA or a two-way within-groups ANOVA, and so on. If at least one independent variable is between-groups and at least one is within-groups, it is a mixed-design ANOVA.

Number of Independent Variables: Pick One	Participants in One or All Samples: Pick One	Always Follows Descriptors
One-way	Between-groups	ANOVA
Two-way	Within-groups	
Three-way	Mixed-design	

than the main effects. In recent years, there has been a great deal of research demonstrating gender discrimination in science, technology, engineering, and mathematics fields—the so-called STEM fields. In one experiment, for example, faculty members viewed an application for a laboratory manager position (Moss-Racusin, Dovidio, Brescoll, Graham, & Handelsman, 2012). The applications were identical, except half had a male name (John) and half had a female name (Jennifer). The faculty members rated John as more competent and more "hireable," on average, than Jennifer, and were more likely to offer John a higher salary and career mentoring. Remember, their applications were *identical*. Imagine that you read this summary. How much credibility would you give it?

EXAMPLE 14.1

Ian Handley and his research team based their own study on the lab manager experiment you just read about (Handley, Brown, Moss-Racusin, & Smith, 2015). They wondered about the effect of gender on perceptions of research on gender disparities in STEM: Would male faculty members be less open to this research, on average, than female faculty members? They also wondered about the effect of academic discipline: Would faculty members in STEM fields be less open to this research, on average, than faculty members in other fields?

To examine these hypotheses, the researchers could have conducted two studies—one comparing male and female faculty members and another comparing faculty members in STEM and non-STEM fields. But conducting separate studies is limiting. The researchers were actually even more interested in whether the pattern of gender differences would be different within STEM fields than it is outside of STEM fields.

Jennifer or John? Are you surprised that faculty members preferred an applicant named John over one named Jennifer for a lab manager position—even though they had identical applications (Moss-Racusin et al., 2012)? Your answer may be depend on your background. One study found that the likelihood that professors find this research credible depends on the interaction of two factors—their gender and their academic discipline (Handley et al., 2015). Two-way ANOVAs can help us to understand the interactions between multiple factors.

A single study simultaneously examining gender and academic discipline is more efficient than two studies examining each independent variable separately. Two-way ANOVAs allow researchers to examine both hypotheses with the resources, time, and energy of a single study. But a two-way ANOVA yields even more information than two separate experiments.

Specifically, a two-way ANOVA allows researchers to explore exactly what Handley and his colleagues wanted to explore: interactions. Does the effect of gender depend on the particular levels of another independent variable, academic discipline? A two-way ANOVA can examine (1) the effect of gender, (2) the effect of academic discipline, *and* (3) the ways in which gender and academic discipline might combine to create some entirely new, and often unexpected, effect. ●

The More Specific Vocabulary of Two-Way ANOVA

Every ANOVA, we learned, has two descriptors, one indicating the number of independent variables and one indicating the research design. Many researchers expand the first descriptor to provide even more information about the independent variables. Let's consider these expanded descriptors in the context of the study on people's perceptions of research on gender discrimination in STEM fields. Were Handley and his colleagues to conduct just one study that examined both gender and academic discipline, they would recruit both female and male faculty members in STEM fields

TABLE 14-2 Interactions in Perceptions of Gender Discrimination Research

A two-way ANOVA allows researchers to examine two independent variables (gender and academic discipline), as well as the ways in which they might interact, simultaneously.

	STEM fields (S)	Non-STEM fields (NS)
Women (W)	W & S	W & NS
Men (M)	M & S	M & NS

and female and male faculty members in non-STEM fields. This research design is shown in Table 14-2.

When we draw the design of a study, such as in Table 14-2, we call each box of the design a *cell*, *a box that depicts one unique combination of levels of the independent variables in a factorial design.* When cells contain numbers, they are usually means of the scores of all participants who were assigned to that combination of levels. Many social science researchers hope to have about 30 participants in each cell—that's why experiments can quickly become very expensive. In the study we're considering here, participants are included in one of four cells depending on their gender and academic discipline. Each participant is included in one of the two levels of the variable "gender" (women or men) listed in the rows of the table of cells.

Each participant is *also* included in one of the two levels of the variable "academic discipline" (STEM or non-STEM field) listed in the rows of the table of cells. A participant might be included in the female and STEM groups (upper-left cell), male and non-STEM groups (lower-right cell), or either of the other two combinations.

Language Alert! This leads us to the new ANOVA vocabulary. Instead of the descriptor *two-way*, many researchers refer to an ANOVA with this arrangement of cells as a *2 × 2 ANOVA* (pronounced "two by two," not "two times two"). As with the two-way descriptor, the ANOVA is described with a second modifier—usually *between-groups* or *within-groups*. Because participants would be categorized in only one gender and only one type of academic discipline, the hypothesis test could be called either a *two-way between-groups ANOVA* or a *2 × 2 between-groups ANOVA*. (An added benefit to the method of naming ANOVAs by the numbers of levels in each independent variable is the ease of calculating the total number of cells. Simply multiply the levels of the independent variables. In this case, the 2 × 2 ANOVA would have (2 × 2) = 4 cells.)

Two Main Effects and an Interaction

Two-way ANOVAs produce *three* F statistics: one for the first independent variable, one for the second independent variable, and one for the interaction between the two independent variables. The F statistics for each of the two independent variables describe *main effects*. *A **main effect** occurs in a factorial design when one of the independent variables has an influence on the dependent variable.* We evaluate whether there is a main effect by disregarding the influence of any other independent variables in the study—we temporarily pretend that the other variable doesn't exist.

So, with two independent variables, Handley and his colleagues would have two possibilities for a main effect. For example, after testing their participants in a two-way ANOVA, they might find a main effect of "gender," temporarily pretending that the variable "academic discipline" hadn't even been included in the study.

● A **cell** is a box that depicts one unique combination of levels of the independent variables in a factorial design.

● A **main effect** occurs in a factorial design when one of the independent variables has an influence on the dependent variable.

For example, male faculty members might be less receptive, on average, to the conclusions of the gender discrimination research than female faculty members. That's the first F statistic. They also might find a main effect of "academic discipline," temporarily pretending that the variable "gender" hadn't even been included in the study. For example, faculty members in STEM fields might be less receptive, on average, to the gender discrimination research than faculty members in non-STEM fields. That's the second F statistic.

14-1: In a two-way ANOVA, we test three different effects—two main effects (one for each independent variable), and one interaction (the joint effect of the two independent variables).

The third F statistic in a two-way ANOVA has the potential to be the most interesting because it is complicated by multiple, interacting variables. For example, the researchers might find a stronger gender difference among faculty members in STEM fields than among faculty members in non-STEM fields. In other words, the effect of gender on the perception of this research might be different among STEM faculty members than among non-STEM faculty members. Alternately, the researchers might find a stronger difference between STEM and non-STEM faculty members among men than among women. In other words, the effect of academic discipline on the perception of this research might be different depending on the gender of the faculty member.

Each of the three F statistics has its own between-groups sum of squares (SS), degrees of freedom (df), mean square (MS), and critical value, but they all share a within-groups mean square (MS_{within}). The source table is shown in Table 14-3. The symbols in the body of the table are replaced by the specific values of these statistics in an actual source table.

TABLE 14-3 An Expanded Source Table

This source table is the framework into which we place the calculations for the two-way between-groups ANOVA with independent variables of gender and academic discipline—here listed as "discipline" for short. It tells three stories: one each for the two main effects, which are listed first, and one for the interaction.

Source	SS	df	MS	F
Gender	SS_{gender}	df_{gender}	MS_{gender}	F_{gender}
Discipline	$SS_{discipline}$	$df_{discipline}$	$MS_{discipline}$	$F_{discipline}$
Gender × Discipline	$SS_{gender \times discipline}$	$df_{gender \times discipline}$	$MS_{gender \times discipline}$	$F_{gender \times discipline}$
Within	SS_{within}	df_{within}	MS_{within}	
Total	SS_{total}	df_{total}		

CHECK YOUR LEARNING

Reviewing the Concepts

> Factorial ANOVAs are used with multiple independent variables because they allow us to examine several hypotheses in a single study and explore interactions.

> Factorial ANOVAs are often referred to by the levels of their independent variables (e.g., 2 × 3) rather than the number of independent variables (e.g., two-way). Sometimes the independent variables are called *factors*.

> A two-way ANOVA can have two main effects (one for each independent variable) and one interaction (the combined influence of both variables). Each effect and interaction has its own set of statistics, including its own F statistic, which are displayed in an expanded source table.

Clarifying the Concepts	14-1	What is a factorial ANOVA?
	14-2	What is an interaction?

Calculating the Statistics	14-3	Determine how many factors are in each of the following designs:

    a. The effect of three diet programs and two exercise programs on weight loss.

    b. The effect of three diet programs, two exercise programs, and three different personal metabolism types on weight loss.

    c. The effect of gift certificate value ($15, $25, $50, and $100) on the amount people spend over that value.

    d. The effect of gift certificate value ($15, $25, $50, and $100) and store quality (low end versus high end) on consumer overspending.

Applying the Concepts	14-4	Adam Alter, a graduate student at Princeton University, and his advisor, Daniel Oppenheimer, studied whether names of stocks affected selling prices (Alter & Oppenheimer, 2006). They found that stocks with pronounceable ticker-code names, like "BAL," tended to sell at higher prices than did stocks with unpronounceable names, like "BDL." They examined this effect 1 day, 1 week, 6 months, and 1 year after the stock was offered for sale. The effect was strongest 1 day after the stocks were initially offered.

    a. What are the "participants" in this study?

    b. What are the independent variables and what are their levels?

    c. What is the dependent variable?

    d. Using the descriptors from Chapter 12, what would you call the hypothesis test that would be used?

    e. Using the new descriptors from *this* chapter, what would you call the hypothesis test that would be used?

Solutions to these Check Your Learning questions can be found in Appendix D.

    f. How many cells are there? Explain how you calculated this answer.

Understanding Interactions in ANOVA

A two-way ANOVA is like a "buy 1, get 3" clearance sale. We get three distinct findings by conducting just one study. The first finding by New Hampshire ski bums Jonathan Zinman and Eric Zitzewitz concerned the effect of the source of the snowfall reports. Their second finding concerned the effect of when the snowfall report was issued (time of week). The third finding related to the combined effects (the interaction) of the source of the snowfall reports *and* the time of week the snowfall reports were issued. The interaction informed us that the effect of the source of a snowfall report depended on when the report was issued (time of week). A statistical interaction occurs when any subgroup represents a significant exception in any direction to the general trend in the data.

In this section, we explore the concept of an interaction in a two-way ANOVA in more depth. We look at a real-life example of an interaction, then introduce two different types of interactions—quantitative and qualitative.

Interactions and Public Policy

Hurricane Katrina, which ravaged New Orleans in 2005, demonstrates the importance of understanding interactions. First, the hurricane itself was an interaction among sev-

- A **quantitative interaction** is an interaction in which the effect of one independent variable is strengthened or weakened at one or more levels of the other independent variable, but the direction of the initial effect does not change.

- A **qualitative interaction** is a particular type of quantitative interaction of two (or more) independent variables in which one independent variable reverses its effect depending on the level of the other independent variable.

eral weather variables. The devastating effects of the hurricane depended on particular levels of other variables, such as where it made landfall and the speed of its movement across the Gulf of Mexico.

Interactions were relevant for the people affected by Hurricane Katrina as well. For example, one would think that Hurricane Katrina would have been universally bad for the health of all those displaced people—a main effect of a hurricane on health care. However, there were exceptions to that rule, and three researchers from the Tulane University School of Public Health and Tropical Diseases in New Orleans proposed a startling interaction regarding the effects of the hurricane on health care for pregnant women (Buekens, Xiong, & Harville, 2006).

Some women gave birth in the squalor of the public shelter in New Orleans' Superdome sports stadium or in alleys while waiting for rescuers. When it comes to pregnant women, the first priority of disaster relief agencies is to provide obstetric and neonatal care. Massive relief efforts sometimes mean that access to care for pregnant women is actually improved in the aftermath of a disaster. Of course, the quality of health care certainly doesn't improve for everybody, which means that an interaction is involved. So the quality of health care improved for pregnant women in the aftermath of the disaster, whereas it became worse for almost everyone else. In the language of two-way ANOVA, the effect of a disaster (one independent variable with two levels: disaster versus no disaster) on the quality of health care (the dependent variable) depends on the type of health care needed (the second independent variable, also with two levels: obstetric/neonatal versus all other types of health care).

Interpreting Interactions

The two-way between-groups ANOVA allows us to separate between-groups variance into three finer categories: the two main effects and an interaction effect. The interaction effect is a blended effect resulting from the interaction between the two independent variables; it is not a separate individual variable. The interaction effect is like mixing chocolate syrup into a glass of milk; the two liquids blend into something familiar yet new.

MASTERING THE CONCEPT

14-2: Researchers often describe interactions with one of two terms—*quantitative* or *qualitative*. In a quantitative interaction, the effect of one independent variable is strengthened or weakened at one or more levels of the other independent variable, but the direction of the initial effect does not change. In a qualitative interaction, one independent variable actually reverses its effect depending on the level of the other independent variable.

Quantitative Interactions Two terms often used to describe interactions are *quantitative* and *qualitative* (e.g., Newton & Rudestam, 1999). *A **quantitative interaction** is an interaction in which the effect of one independent variable is strengthened or weakened at one or more levels of the other independent variable, but the direction of the initial effect does not change.* The researcher ski bums, Jonathan Zinman and Eric Zitzewitz, found a quantitative interaction when they discovered that resort snowfall reports were always exaggerated compared to weather reports, and especially on the weekends. More specifically, the effect of one independent variable is modified in the presence of another independent variable.

*A **qualitative interaction** is a particular type of quantitative interaction of two (or more) independent variables in which one independent variable reverses its effect depending on the level of the other independent variable.* In a qualitative interaction, the effect of one variable doesn't just become stronger or weaker; it actually reverses direction in the presence of another variable. Let's first examine a quantitative interaction.

AP Photo/Haraz N. Ghanbari

Disaster Relief and Pregnant Women This refugee from Hurricane Katrina and her newborn baby received care at a shelter in Louisiana. There was a surprising interaction after Hurricane Katrina: For some pregnant women, massive relief efforts actually *improved* their access to health care.

The gender discrimination in STEM fields example is a helpful illustration of a quantitative interaction. Let's examine what the researchers found. Male faculty members in STEM fields "evaluated the research less favorably" than did female faculty members in STEM fields. There was not a similar statistically significant difference between male and female faculty members in non-STEM fields. (Handley et al., 2015). So, there was a gender difference among STEM professors, but not among non-STEM professors. Let's look at the actual means from the study in Table 14-4. Higher scores indicate a more favorable view, on average, of the research. (For the purposes of this research, we will assume equal sample sizes across cells.)

First, we consider main effects; then we consider the overall pattern that constitutes the interaction. If there is a significant interaction, we ignore any significant main effects. The significant interaction supersedes any significant main effects.

Table 14-4 includes mean perception scores for the four cells of the study. It also includes numbers in the margins of the table, to the right of and below the cells; these numbers are also means, but are for every participant in a given row or in a given column. Each of these is called a ***marginal mean***, *the mean of a row or a column in a table that shows the cells of a study with a two-way ANOVA design.* In Table 14-4, for example, the mean across from the row for female, 4.67, is the mean perception score of every female faculty member in the study, regardless of her academic discipline. The mean below the column for STEM fields, 4.41, is the mean perception score of every faculty member in a STEM field in the study, regardless of his or her gender.

The easiest way to understand the main effects is to make a smaller table for each, with only the appropriate marginal means. Separate tables let us focus on one main effect at a time without being distracted by the means in the cells. For the main effect of gender, we construct a table with two cells, as shown in Table 14-5. The table makes it easy to see that women had more favorable views of the gender disparity research, on average, than did men.

EXAMPLE 14.2

TABLE 14-4   A Table of Means

We use a table to display the cell and marginal means so that we can interpret any main effects. Higher numbers indicate a more favorable view of the gender discrimination research.

	STEM	Non-STEM	
Women	4.80	4.54	4.67
Men	4.02	4.55	4.285
	4.41	4.545	

TABLE 14-5   The Main Effect of Gender

This table shows only the marginal means that demonstrate the main effect of gender. Because we have isolated these marginal means, we cannot get distracted or confused by the other means in the table.

Women	4.67
Men	4.285

TABLE 14-6   The Main Effect of Academic Discipline

This table shows only the marginal means that demonstrate the main effect of academic discipline. Because we have isolated these marginal means, we cannot get distracted or confused by the other means in the table.

STEM	Non-STEM
4.41	4.545

Let's now consider the second main effect, that for academic discipline. As before, we construct a table (such as Table 14-6) that shows only the means for academic discipline, as if gender were not included in the study. We kept the means for gender in rows and the means for academic discipline in columns, just as they were in the original table. You may, however, arrange them either way, using whichever order makes sense to you. Table 14-6 shows that views of gender disparity research for non-STEM fields were higher, on average, than for STEM fields. Both results would need to be verified with a hypothesis test, but we seem to have two main effects: (1) a main effect of gender (women, on average, had a more favorable view of the gender disparity research than men did), and (2) a main effect of academic discipline (faculty members in non-STEM fields had a more favorable view of the gender disparity research compared to faculty members in STEM fields).

But that's not the whole story. Here's where the interaction comes in. Now we ignore the marginal means and get back to the means in the cells themselves, seen again in Table 14-7. Here we can see the overall pattern by framing it in two different ways. We

● A **marginal mean** is the mean of a row or a column in a table that shows the cells of a study with a two-way ANOVA design.

TABLE 14-7	Examining the Overall Pattern of Means

A first step in understanding an interaction is examining the overall pattern of means in the cells.

	STEM	Non-STEM
Women	4.80	4.54
Men	4.02	4.55

can start by considering gender. Was there a gender difference in perceptions of the gender disparity research? It depends. Specifically, it depends on whether the faculty member was in a STEM field or a non-STEM field. The researchers report that the tiny gender difference among faculty members in non-STEM fields is *not* statistically significant (Handley et al., 2015). But the gender difference among faculty members in STEM fields *is* significantly different with a substantial effect size. The Cohen's *d* of 0.74 is close to Cohen's guideline of 0.8 for a large effect. So, men seemed to have a less favorable view of the gender disparity research than women did, but only if they were in STEM fields.

We can also frame the question by starting with academic discipline. Did academic discipline lead to different perceptions of the gender disparity research? It depends. Specifically, it depends on whether the faculty members were male or female. It seemed to make a difference for men; the difference between the means for men in STEM fields and men in non-STEM fields was statistically significant. The difference between the means for women in STEM fields and women in non-STEM fields, however, was not statistically significant. This is a quantitative interaction because the *strength* of the effect varies under certain conditions, but the *direction* does not (considering only the statistically significant findings as different).

People sometimes perceive an interaction where there is none. If men always had less favorable impressions of the gender disparity research than women, regardless of their academic discipline, there would be no interaction. On the other hand, there is an interaction in the example we have been considering because gender has a significant effect only among STEM faculty members. The tendency to see an interaction when there is none can be diminished by constructing a bar graph, as in Figure 14-2.

The bar graph helps us to see the overall pattern, but one more step is necessary: to connect each set of bars with a line. If the lines intersect (or would eventually intersect if they were extended), that is an indication that there may be an interaction. We have two choices that match the two ways we framed the interaction in words above: (1) As in Figure 14-3, we could connect the bars for one of the independent variables, academic discipline. We would connect the two bars for STEM fields and the two bars for non-STEM fields. (2) Alternatively, as in Figure 14-4, we could connect the bars for the two genders. We would connect the two bars for female faculty members and the two bars for male faculty members.

In Figure 14-3, notice that the lines do not intersect, but they're not parallel to one another either. If the lines were extended far enough, eventually those connecting the two bars for each type of academic discipline would intersect. Perfectly parallel lines indicate the likely absence of an interaction, but we almost never see perfectly parallel lines emerging from real-life data sets; real-life data are usually messy. Nonparallel lines may indicate a statistically significant interaction, but we have to conduct an ANOVA to be sure. Only if the lines are significantly different from parallel can we reject the null hypothesis that there is no interaction; and we only want to interpret an interaction if we reject the null hypothesis. In the case of this study, the researchers reported a statistically significant interaction with an effect size of 0.03 (using a measure similar to R^2). According to Cohen's conventions, this is a small-to-medium effect.

Some social scientists refer to an interaction as a significant difference in differences. In the context of the gender disparity study, there is a significant gender difference among

FIGURE 14-2

Bar Graphs and Interactions

Bar graphs help us determine if there really is an interaction. The bars in this graph help us to see that there seems to be a gender difference among faculty members in STEM fields but not among faculty members in non-STEM fields.

FIGURE 14-3

Are the Lines Parallel? Part I

We add lines to bar graphs to help us determine whether there really is an interaction. We draw a line connecting the bars for the male and female faculty members in STEM fields. We then draw a line connecting the bars for the male and female faculty members in non-STEM fields. Were the two lines to continue, they would eventually intersect, an indication of an interaction. The presence of a significant interaction was confirmed by the researchers who reported it in their publication (Handley et al., 2015).

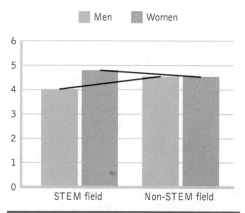

FIGURE 14-4

Are the Lines Parallel? Part II

There are always two ways to examine the pattern of the bar graphs. Here, we draw two lines, one connecting the two bars for the female faculty members and one connecting the two bars for the male faculty members. You can see that the lines are about to intersect, an indication of interaction. The presence of a significant interaction was confirmed by the researchers in their publication (Handley et al., 2015).

faculty members in STEM fields but not among faculty members in non-STEM fields. This is an example of a significant difference between differences. This interaction is represented graphically whenever the lines connecting the bars are significantly different from parallel.

However, if women had similarly higher perceptions of the gender disparity research, as compared to men, in non-STEM fields as in STEM fields, the graph would look like the one in Figure 14-5. In this case, there is still a gender difference, on average, in STEM fields, but there is also a gender difference, on average, in non-STEM fields, and there is likely no interaction. If these were the real data, then gender would have the same effect on perceptions of the gender disparity research, regardless of academic discipline. When in doubt about whether there is an interaction or just two main effects that add up to a greater effect, draw a graph and connect the bars with lines.

However, don't just draw lines and skip the step of creating the bar graph. Ali and Peebles (2012) found that line graphs were more frequently misinterpreted than bar graphs. In one of their experiments, students randomly assigned to interpret line graphs were significantly more likely than students randomly assigned to interpret bar graphs to ignore the variable on the *x*-axis. Those interpreting line graphs were more often also unable to explain the finding at all than were those interpreting bar graphs. In addition, Zacks and Tversky (1997) reported that some people view lines as indicating a continuous variable in a line graph. A participant in one of their experiments viewed a line graph and stated: "The more male a person is, the taller he/she is" (p. 148). A bar graph would likely have led that participant to perceive, accurately, that men are, on average, taller than women. ●

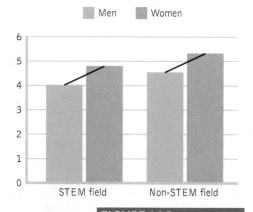

FIGURE 14-5

Parallel Lines

The two lines are exactly parallel. Were they to continue indefinitely, they would never intersect. Were this true among the population (not just this sample), there would be no interaction.

Qualitative Interactions Let's recall the definition of a qualitative interaction: a particular type of quantitative interaction in which the effect of one independent variable *reverses* its effect depending on the level of the other independent variable.

EXAMPLE 14.3

BJI / Blue Jean Images/Getty Images

Choosing the Best Car When making decisions, such as which car to buy, do we make better choices after conscious or unconscious deliberation? Research by Dijksterhuis and colleagues (2006) suggests that less complex decisions are typically better after conscious deliberation, whereas more complex decisions are typically better after unconscious deliberation.

Do you think that, on average, people make better decisions when they consciously focus on the decision? Or do they make better decisions when the decision-making process is unconscious (i.e., making the decision after being distracted by other tasks)? Researchers in the Netherlands conducted a series of studies in which participants were asked to decide between two options following either conscious or unconscious thinking about the choice. The studies were analyzed with two-way ANOVAs (Dijksterhuis, Bos, Nordgren, & van Baaren, 2006).

In one study, participants were asked to choose one of four cars. One car was objectively the best of the four, and one was objectively the worst. Some participants made a less complex decision; they were told 4 characteristics of each car. Some participants made a more complex decision; they were told 14 characteristics of each car. After learning about the cars, half the participants in each group were randomly assigned to think consciously about the cars for 4 minutes before making a decision. Half were randomly assigned to distract themselves for 4 minutes by solving anagrams before making a decision. The research design, with two independent variables, is shown in Table 14-8. The first independent variable is complexity, with two levels: less complex (4 attributes) and more complex (14 attributes). The second independent variable is type of decision making, with two levels: conscious thought and unconscious thought (distraction).

The researchers calculated a score for each participant that reflected his or her ability to differentiate between the objectively best and objectively worst cars in the group. This score represents the dependent variable, and higher numbers indicate a better ability to differentiate between the best and worst cars. Table 14-9 presents the cell means and marginal means for this experiment.

TABLE 14-8 A Two-Way Between-Groups ANOVA

Dutch researchers designed a study to examine what style of decision making led to the best choices in less complex and more complex situations. Would you predict an interaction? In other words, would the lines connecting bars on a graph be different from parallel? And if they are different from parallel, how are they different? If they are different just in strength, we are predicting a quantitative interaction. If the direction of effect actually reverses, we are predicting a qualitative interaction.

	Conscious thought	Unconscious thought (distraction)
Less complex (4 attributes of each car)	Less complex; conscious	Less complex; unconscious
More complex (14 attributes of each car)	More complex; conscious	More complex; unconscious

---

TABLE 14-9 Decision-Making Tactics

To understand the main effects and overall pattern of a two-way ANOVA, we start by examining the cell means and marginal means.

	Conscious thought	Unconscious thought (distraction)	
Less complex	5.5	2.3	3.9
More complex	0.6	5.0	2.8
	3.05	3.65	

For the teaching purposes of this example, note that (a) the cell means are approximate, (b) the marginal means assume the same number of participants in each cell, and (c) all the observed differences are statistically significant. (In a real research situation, we would conduct an ANOVA to determine statistical significance.)

Because there was an overall pattern—an interaction—the researchers did not pay attention to the main effects in this study; an interaction trumps any main effects. However, let's examine the main effects to get some practice. We'll create tables for each of the two main effects so that we can examine them independently (Tables 14-10 and 14-11). The marginal means indicate that when the type of decision making is ignored entirely, people make better decisions, on average, in less complex situations than in more complex situations. The marginal means also suggest that when complexity of decision is ignored, people make better decisions, on average, when the decision-making process is unconscious than when it is conscious.

However, if there is also a significant interaction, then these main effects don't tell the whole story. The interaction demonstrates that the effect of the decision-making method *depends* on the complexity of the decision. Conscious decision making tends to be better than unconscious decision making in less complex situations, but unconscious decision making tends to be better than conscious decision making in more complex situations. This reversal of direction is what makes this a qualitative interaction. It's not just the strength of the effect that changes, but the actual direction!

A bar graph, shown in Figure 14-6, makes the pattern of the data far clearer. We can actually see the qualitative interaction.

As we do with a quantitative interaction, we add lines to determine whether they are parallel (no matter how long the lines are) or intersect (or would do so if extended far enough), as in Figure 14-7. Here we see that the lines intersect without even having to extend them beyond the graph. This is likely an interaction. Type of decision making has an effect on differentiation between best cars and worst cars, but it depends on the complexity of the decision. Those making a less complex decision tend to make better choices if they use conscious thought. Those making a more complex decision tend to make better choices if they use unconscious thought. We would, as these researchers did, verify this finding by conducting a hypothesis test before rejecting the null hypothesis that there is no interaction.

TABLE 14-10	Main Effect of Complexity of Decision

These marginal means suggest that, overall, participants are better at making less complex decisions.

Less complex	3.9
More complex	2.8

TABLE 14-11	Main Effect of Type of Decision Making

These marginal means suggest that, overall, participants are better at making decisions when the decision making is unconscious—that is, when the participants are distracted.

Conscious	Unconscious
3.05	3.65

FIGURE 14-6

Graphing Decision-Making Methods

This bar graph displays the interaction far better than a table or words. We can see that it is a qualitative interaction; there is an actual reversal of direction of the effect of decision-making method in less complex situations versus more complex situations.

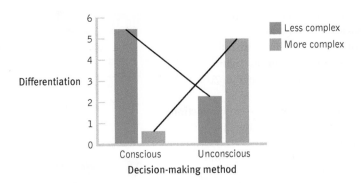

The Intersecting Lines of a Qualitative Interaction

When we draw two lines, one for the two bars that represent less complex situations and one for the two bars that represent more complex situations, we can easily see that they intersect. Lines that intersect, or would intersect if we extended them, indicate a possible interaction.

The qualitative interaction of decision-making method and complexity of situation was not likely to have been predicted by common sense. In such instances, we should be cautious before generalizing the findings. In this case, the research was carefully conducted and the researchers replicated their findings across several situations. For example, the researchers found similar effects in a real-life context when the less complex situation was shopping at a department store that sold clothing and kitchen products, and the more complex situation was purchasing furniture at IKEA. Such an intriguing finding would not have been possible without the inclusion of two independent variables in one study, which required that researchers use a two-way ANOVA capable of testing for an interaction.

So what do these findings mean for us as we approach the decisions we face every day? Which sunblock should we buy to best protect against UV rays? Should we go to graduate school or get a job following graduation? Should we consciously consider characteristics of sunblocks but "sleep on" graduate school–related factors? Research would suggest that the answer to the last question is yes (Dijksterhuis et al., 2006). Yet if the history of social science research is any indication, there are other factors (not included in these studies) that likely could affect the quality of our decisions. And so the research process continues. ●

CHECK YOUR LEARNING

Reviewing the Concepts

> A two-way ANOVA is represented by a grid in which cells represent each unique combination of independent variables. Means are calculated for cells, and are called cell means. Means are also computed for each level of an independent variable, by itself, regardless of the levels of the other independent variable. These means, found in the margins of the grid, are called marginal means.

> When there is a statistically significant interaction, the main effects are considered to be modified by an interaction. As a result, we focus only on the overall pattern of cell means that reveals the interaction.

> Two categories of interactions describe the overall pattern of cell means: quantitative and qualitative interactions.

> The most common interaction is a quantitative interaction, in which the effect of the first independent variable depends on the levels of the second independent variable, but the differences at each level vary only in the strength of the effect.

> Qualitative interactions are those in which the effect of the first independent variable depends on the levels of the second independent variable, but the direction of the effect actually reverses.

> There are three ways to identify a statistically significant interaction: (1) visually, whenever the lines connecting the means of each group are significantly different from parallel; (2) conceptually, when we need to use the idea of "it depends" to tell the data's story; and (3) statistically, when the p value associated with an interaction in a source table is < 0.05, as with other hypothesis tests. This last method, the statistical analysis, is the only objective way to assess the interaction.

Clarifying the Concepts

14-5 What is the difference between a quantitative interaction and a qualitative interaction?

14-6 Why are main effects ignored when there is an interaction? (We often say they are *trumped* by an interaction.)

Calculating the Statistics

14-7 Data are presented here for two hypothetical independent variables (IVs) and their combinations.

> IV 1, level A; IV 2, level A: 2, 1, 1, 3
>
> IV 1, level B; IV 2, level A: 5, 4, 3, 4
>
> IV 1, level A; IV 2, level B: 2, 3, 3, 3
>
> IV 1, level B; IV 2, level B: 3, 2, 2, 3

a. Figure out how many cells are in this study's table, and draw a grid to represent them.

b. Calculate cell means and write them in the cells of the grid.

c. Calculate marginal means and write them in the margins of the grid.

d. Draw a bar graph of these data.

Applying the Concepts

14-8 Researchers wondered whether students' genders and attractiveness influences their grades (Hernández-Julián & Peters, 2015). The researchers had a group of unbiased people rate the attractiveness of more than 5,000 male and female students based on their university photos. These students were divided into three categories of attractiveness: below average, average, and above average. The researchers also had access to students' grades on a grade point average (GPA) scale of 0 to 4. The results, as summarized in a news story about this research, indicated that "among similarly qualified female students—those who are physically attractive earn better grades than others. For male students, there is no significant relationship between attractiveness and grades" (Jaschik, 2016).

a. What are the independent variables in this study, and what are the levels of the independent variables?

b. What is the dependent variable in this study? What type of variable is it?

c. Based on your answers to (a) and (b), explain why it would be possible to conduct an ANOVA on these data. Using the language introduced in this chapter, what kind of ANOVA would it be?

d. Explain why the summary of the research indicates that there is an interaction.

e. Construct a table showing the cells. Include numbers in the cells that demonstrate the pattern of the interaction. (There are many possible specific numbers that would work.)

f. Is the interaction qualitative or quantitative? Explain your answer.

g. The researchers noted two possible explanations for these findings—that the more attractive women were simply smarter and that the professors were biased toward more attractive women. Explain why this presents a confound in this study. (The researchers conducted the same study in online courses where appearance is not a factor, and the attractiveness effect for women was not statistically significant, pointing to professor bias.)

Solutions to these Check Your Learning questions can be found in Appendix D.

Conducting a Two-Way Between-Groups ANOVA

Understanding interactions makes it easier to explain patterns in the data. For example, it is easy to understand why a ski resort would be tempted to exaggerate snowfall reports—especially right before a big, money-making weekend. Conducting a two-way ANOVA (with two independent variables) is the only way to test whether the effect of one independent variable *depends* on the levels of another independent variable.

Behavioral scientists explore interactions by using two-way ANOVAs. Fortunately, hypothesis testing for a two-way between-groups ANOVA uses the same logic as for a one-way between-groups ANOVA. For example, the null hypothesis is exactly the same: There are no mean differences between groups. Type I and Type II errors still pose the same threats to decision making. We compare an F statistic to a critical F value to make a decision. The main way that a two-way ANOVA differs from a one-way ANOVA is that three ideas are being tested and each idea is a separate source of variability.

The three ideas being tested in a two-way between-groups ANOVA are the main effect of the first independent variable, the main effect of the second independent variable, and the interaction effect of the two independent variables. A fourth source of variability in a two-way ANOVA is within-groups variance. Let's learn how to separate and measure these four sources of variance by evaluating a commonly used educational method to improve public health: myth busting.

The Six Steps of Two-Way ANOVA

Two-way ANOVAs use the same six hypothesis-testing steps that you already know. The main difference is that you essentially perform most of the steps three times—once for each main effect and once for the interaction. Let's look at an example.

EXAMPLE 14.4

Does myth busting really improve public health? Here are some myths and facts. From the Web site of the Canadian Mental Health Association (2016):

Myth: "People who experience mental illnesses can't work."
Fact: "Whether you realize it or not, workplaces are filled with people who have experienced mental illnesses. Mental illnesses don't mean that someone is no longer capable of working."

From the Web site for the World Health Organization (2016):

Myth: "Disasters bring out the worst in human behavior."
Fact: "Although isolated cases of antisocial behavior exist, the majority of people respond spontaneously and generously."

A group of Canadian researchers examined the effectiveness of myth busting (Skurnik, Yoon, Park, & Schwarz, 2005). They wondered whether the effectiveness of debunking false medical claims depends on the age of the person targeted by the message. In one study, they compared two groups of adults: younger adults, ages 18–25, and older adults, ages 71–86. Participants were presented with a series of claims and were told that each claim was either true or false. (In reality, all claims were true, partly because researchers did not want to run the risk that participants would

Do We Remember the Medical Myth or the Fact? Skurnik and colleagues (2005) studied the factors that influence the misremembering of false medical claims as facts. They asked: When a physician tells a patient a false claim, then debunks it with the facts, does the patient remember the false claim or the facts? A source table examines each factor in the study and tells us how much of the variability in the dependent variable is explained by that factor.

Don Smetzer/The Image Bank/Getty Images

misremember false claims as being true.) In some cases, the claim was presented once, and in other cases, it was repeated three times. In either case, the accurate information was presented after each "false" statement. (Note that for our teaching purposes, we have slightly altered the study's design.)

The two independent variables in this study were age, with two levels (younger, older), and number of repetitions, with two levels (once, three times). The dependent variable, proportion of responses that were wrong after a 3-day delay, was calculated for each participant. This was a two-way between-groups ANOVA—more specifically, a 2×2 between-groups ANOVA. From this name, we know that the table has four cells: $(2 \times 2) = 4$. There were 64 participants—16 in each cell. But here we use an example with 12 participants—3 in each cell. Here are the data that we'll use; they have similar means to those in the actual study, and the F statistics are similar as well.

Experimental Conditions	Proportion of Responses That Were Wrong	Mean
Younger, one repetition	0.25, 0.21, 0.14	0.20
Younger, three repetitions	0.07, 0.13, 0.16	0.12
Older, one repetition	0.27, 0.22, 0.17	0.22
Older, three repetitions	0.33, 0.31, 0.26	0.30

Let's consider the steps of hypothesis testing for a two-way between-groups ANOVA in the context of this example.

> **STEP 1: Identify the populations, distribution, and assumptions.**

The first step of hypothesis testing for a two-way between-groups ANOVA is very similar to that for a one-way between-groups ANOVA. First, we state the populations, but we specify that they are broken down into more than one category. In the current example, there are four populations, so there are four cells (as shown in Table 14-12). As we do the calculations, the first independent variable, age, appears in the rows of the table, and the second independent variable, number of repetitions, appears in the columns of the table.

There are four populations, each with labels representing the levels of the two independent variables to which they belong.

Population 1 (Y; 1): Younger adults who hear one repetition of a false claim
Population 2 (Y; 3): Younger adults who hear three repetitions of a false claim
Population 3 (O; 1): Older adults who hear one repetition of a false claim
Population 4 (O; 3): Older adults who hear three repetitions of a false claim

We next consider the characteristics of the data to determine the distributions to which we compare the sample. There are more than two groups, so we need to

---

TABLE 14-12 Studying the Memory of False Claims Using a Two-Way ANOVA

The study of memory for false claims has two independent variables: age (younger, older) and number of repetitions (one, three).

	One repetition (1)	Three repetitions (3)
Younger (Y)	Y; 1	Y; 3
Older (0)	O; 1	O; 3

consider variances to analyze differences among means. Therefore, we use F distributions. Finally, we list the hypothesis test that we use for those distributions and check the assumptions for that test. For F distributions, we use ANOVA—in this case, two-way between-groups ANOVA.

The assumptions are the same for all types of ANOVA: The sample should be selected randomly; the populations should be distributed normally; and the population variances should be equal. Let's explore that a bit further.

(1) These data were not randomly selected. Younger adults were recruited from a university, and older adults were recruited from the local community. Because random sampling was not used, we must be cautious when generalizing from these samples. (2) The researchers did not report whether they investigated the shapes of the distributions of their samples to assess the shapes of the underlying populations. (3) The researchers did not provide standard deviations of the samples as an indication of whether the population spreads might be approximately equal—the condition known as homoscedasticity, which we explored in Chapter 12. We typically explore these assumptions using the sample data.

Summary: Population 1 (Y; 1): Younger adults who hear one repetition of a false claim. Population 2 (Y; 3): Younger adults who hear three repetitions of a false claim. Population 3 (O; 1): Older adults who hear one repetition of a false claim. Population 4 (O; 3): Older adults who hear three repetitions of a false claim.

The comparison distributions will be F distributions. The hypothesis test will be a two-way between-groups ANOVA. Assumptions: (1) The data are not from random samples, so we must generalize only with caution. (2) From the published research report, we do not know if the underlying population distributions are normal. (3) We do not know if the population variances are approximately equal (homoscedasticity).

STEP 2: State the null and research hypotheses.

The second step, to state the null and research hypotheses, is similar to that for a one-way between-groups ANOVA, except that we now have three sets of hypotheses, one for each main effect and one for the interaction. Those for the two main effects are the same as those for the one effect of a one-way between-groups ANOVA (see the summary below). If there are only two levels, then we can simply say that the two levels are not equal; if there are only two levels and there is a statistically significant difference, the difference must be between those two levels. Note that because there are two independent variables, we clarify which variable we are referring to by using initial letters or abbreviations for the levels of each (e.g., Y for younger and O for older). If an independent variable has more than two levels, the research hypothesis would be that any two levels of the independent variable are not equal.

The hypotheses for the interaction are typically stated in words but not in symbols. The null hypothesis is that the effect of one independent variable is not dependent on the levels of the other independent variable. The research hypothesis is that the effect of one independent variable depends on the levels of the other independent variable. It does not matter which independent variable we list first (e.g., "The effect of age is not dependent…" or "The effect of number of repetitions is not dependent…"). Write the hypotheses in the way that makes the most sense to you.

Summary: The hypotheses for the main effect of the first independent variable, age, are as follows. Null hypothesis: On average, compared with older adults, younger adults have the same proportion of responses that are wrong when remembering which claims are myths—$H_0: \mu_Y = \mu_O$. Research hypothesis: On average, compared with older adults, younger adults have a different proportion of responses that are wrong when remembering which claims are myths—H_1: $\mu_Y \neq \mu_O$.

The hypotheses for the main effect of the second independent variable, number of repetitions, are as follows. Null hypothesis: On average, those who hear one repetition have the same proportion of responses that are wrong when remembering which claims are myths compared with those who hear three repetitions—H_0: $\mu_1 = \mu_3$. Research hypothesis: On average, those who hear one repetition have a different proportion of responses that are wrong when remembering which claims are myths compared with those who hear three repetitions—H_1: $\mu_1 \neq \mu_3$.

The hypotheses for the interaction of age and number of repetitions are as follows. Null hypothesis: The effect of number of repetitions is not dependent on the levels of age. Research hypothesis: The effect of number of repetitions depends on the levels of age.

> **STEP 3: Determine the characteristics of the comparison distribution.**

The third step is similar to that of a one-way between-groups ANOVA, except that there are three comparison distributions, all of them F distributions. We need to provide the appropriate degrees of freedom for each of these: two main effects and one interaction. As before, each F statistic is a ratio of between-groups variance and within-groups variance. Because there are three effects, there are three between-groups variance estimates, each with its own degrees of freedom. There is only one within-groups variance estimate, with its degrees of freedom for all three.

For each main effect, the between-groups degrees of freedom is calculated as for a one-way ANOVA: the number of groups minus 1. The first independent variable, age, is in the rows of the table of cells, so the between-groups degrees of freedom is:

$$df_{rows(age)} = N_{rows} - 1 = 2 - 1 = 1$$

The second independent variable, number of repetitions, is in the columns of the table of cells, so the between-groups degrees of freedom is:

$$df_{columns(reps)} = N_{columns} - 1 = 2 - 1 = 1$$

We now need a between-groups degrees of freedom for the interaction, which we calculate by multiplying the degrees of freedom for the two main effects:

$$df_{interaction} = (df_{rows(age)})(df_{columns(reps)}) = (1)(1) = 1$$

The within-groups degrees of freedom is calculated like that for a one-way between-groups ANOVA, the sum of the degrees of freedom in each of the cells. In the current example, there are three participants in each cell, so the within-groups degrees of freedom is calculated as follows, with N representing the number in each cell:

$$df_{Y,1} = N - 1 = 3 - 1 = 2$$
$$df_{Y,3} = N - 1 = 3 - 1 = 2$$
$$df_{O,1} = N - 1 = 3 - 1 = 2$$
$$df_{O,3} = N - 1 = 3 - 1 = 2$$
$$df_{within} = df_{Y,1} + df_{Y,3} + df_{O,1} + df_{O,3} = 2 + 2 + 2 + 2 = 8$$

For a check on our work, we calculate the total degrees of freedom just as we did for the one-way between-groups ANOVA. We subtract 1 from the total number of participants:

$$df_{total} = N_{total} - 1 = 12 - 1 = 11$$

> **MASTERING THE FORMULA**
>
> **14-1:** The formula for the between-groups degrees of freedom for the independent variable in the rows of the table of cells is:
> $$df_{rows} = N_{rows} - 1.$$
> We subtract 1 from the number of rows, representing levels, for that variable.

> **MASTERING THE FORMULA**
>
> **14-2:** The formula for the between-groups degrees of freedom for the independent variable in the columns of the table of cells is:
> $$df_{columns} = N_{columns} - 1.$$
> We subtract 1 from the number of columns, representing levels, for that variable.

> **MASTERING THE FORMULA**
>
> **14-3:** The formula for the between groups degrees of freedom for the interaction is:
> $$df_{interaction} = (df_{rows})(df_{columns}).$$
> We multiply the degrees of freedom for each of the independent variables.

> **MASTERING THE FORMULA**
>
> **14-4:** To calculate the within-groups degrees of freedom, we first calculate degrees of freedom for each cell; that is, we subtract one from the number of participants in each cell. We then sum the degrees of freedom for each cell. For a study in which there are four cells, we'd use this formula:
> $$df_{within} = df_{cell\ 1} + df_{cell\ 2} + df_{cell\ 3} + df_{cell\ 4}.$$

We now add up the three between-groups degrees of freedom and the within-groups degrees of freedom to see if they equal 11. We have a match:

$$11 = 1 + 1 + 1 + 8$$

Finally, for this step, we list the distributions with their degrees of freedom for the three effects. Note that, although the between-groups degrees of freedom for the three effects are the same in this case, they are often different. For example, if one independent variable had three levels and the other had four, the between-groups degrees of freedom for the main effects would be 2 and 3, respectively, and the between-groups degrees of freedom for the interaction would be 6.

Summary: Main effect of age: F distribution with 1 and 8 degrees of freedom. Main effect of number of repetitions: F distribution with 1 and 8 degrees of freedom. Interaction of age and number of repetitions: F distribution with 1 and 8 degrees of freedom. (*Note:* It is helpful to include all degrees of freedom calculations in this step.)

> **STEP 4: Determine the critical values, or cutoffs.**

Again, this step for the two-way between-groups ANOVA is just an expansion of that for the one-way version. We now need three critical values but we determine them just as we determined them before. We use the F table in Appendix B.

For each main effect and for the interaction, we look up the within-groups degrees of freedom, which is always the same for each effect, along the left-hand side and the appropriate between-groups degrees of freedom across the top of the table. The place on the grid where this row and this column intersect contains three numbers. From top to bottom, the table provides cutoffs for p levels of 0.01, 0.05, and 0.10. As usual, we typically use 0.05. In this instance, it happens that the critical value is the same for all three effects because the between-groups degrees of freedom is the same for all three. But when the between-groups degrees of freedom are different, there are different critical values. Here, we look up the between-groups degrees of freedom of 1, within-groups degrees of freedom of 8, and p level of 0.05. The cutoff for all three is 5.32, as seen in Figure 14-8.

Summary: There are three critical values (which in this case are all the same), as seen in the curve in Figure 14-8. The critical F value for the main effect of age is 5.32. The critical F value for the main effect of number of repetitions is 5.32. The critical F value for the interaction of age and number of repetitions is 5.32.

5%

0   5.32

FIGURE 14-8

Determining Cutoffs for an F Distribution

We determine the critical values for an *F* distribution for a two-way between-groups ANOVA just as we did for a one-way between-groups ANOVA, except that we calculate three cutoffs, one for each main effect and one for the interaction. In this case, the between-groups degrees of freedom are the same for all three, so the cutoffs are the same.

> **STEP 5: Calculate the test statistic.**

As with the one-way between-groups ANOVA, the fifth step for the two-way between-groups ANOVA is the most time consuming. As you might guess, it's similar to what we already learned, but we have to calculate three F statistics instead of one. We learn the logic and the specific calculations for this step in the next section.

> **STEP 6: Make a decision.**

This step is the same as for a one-way between-groups ANOVA, except that we compare each of the three F statistics to its appropriate cutoff F statistic. If the F statistic is beyond the critical value, then we know that it is in the most extreme 5% of possible test statistics *if* the null hypothesis is true. After making a decision for each F statistic, we present the results in one of three ways.

First, if we are able to reject the null hypothesis for the interaction, then we draw a specific conclusion with the help of a table and graph. Because we have more than two groups, we use a post hoc test, such as the one that we learned in Chapter 12. When there are three effects, post hoc tests are typically implemented separately for each main effect and for the interaction (Hays, 1994). If the interaction is statistically significant, then it might not matter whether the main effects are also significant; if they are also significant, then those findings are usually qualified by the interaction, and are not described separately. The overall pattern of cell means tells the whole story.

Second, if we are not able to reject the null hypothesis for the interaction, then we focus on any significant main effects, drawing a specific directional conclusion for each. In this study, each independent variable has only two levels, so there is no need for a post hoc test. If there were three or more levels, however, then each significant main effect would require a post hoc test to determine exactly where the differences lie.

Third, if we do not reject the null hypothesis for either main effect or the interaction, then we can only conclude that there is insufficient evidence from this study to support the research hypotheses. We will complete step 6 of hypothesis testing for this study in the next section, after we consider the calculations of the source table for a two-way between-groups ANOVA. ●

Identifying Four Sources of Variability in a Two-Way ANOVA

In this section, we complete step 5 for a two-way between-groups ANOVA. The calculations are similar to those for a one-way between-groups ANOVA, except that we calculate three F statistics. We use a source table with elements like those shown in Table 14-18 on page 389.

First, we calculate the total sum of squares (Table 14-13). We calculate this number in exactly the same way as we do for a one-way ANOVA. We subtract the grand mean,

TABLE 14-13   Calculating the Total Sum of Squares

The total sum of squares is calculated by subtracting the overall mean, called the *grand mean,* from every score to create deviations, then squaring the deviations and summing them: $\Sigma(X - GM)^2 = 0.0672$.

	X	$(X - GM)$	$(X - GM)^2$
Y, 1	0.25	$(0.25 - 0.21) = 0.04$	0.0016
	0.21	$(0.21 - 0.21) = 0.00$	0.0000
	0.14	$(0.14 - 0.21) = -0.07$	0.0049
Y, 3	0.07	$(0.07 - 0.21) = -0.14$	0.0196
	0.13	$(0.13 - 0.21) = -0.08$	0.0064
	0.16	$(0.16 - 0.21) = -0.05$	0.0025
0, 1	0.27	$(0.27 - 0.21) = 0.06$	0.0036
	0.22	$(0.22 - 0.21) = 0.01$	0.0001
	0.17	$(0.17 - 0.21) = -0.04$	0.0016
0, 3	0.33	$(0.33 - 0.21) = 0.12$	0.0144
	0.31	$(0.31 - 0.21) = 0.10$	0.0100
	0.26	$(0.26 - 0.21) = 0.05$	0.0025

MASTERING THE FORMULA

14-6: We calculate the total sum of squares using the following formula:

$$SS_{total} = \Sigma(X - GM)^2.$$

We subtract the grand mean from every score to create deviations, then square the deviations, and finally sum the squared deviations.

MASTERING THE FORMULA

14-7: We calculate the between-groups sum of squares for the first independent variable, that in the rows of the table of cells, using the following formula:

$$SS_{between(rows)} = \Sigma(M_{row} - GM)^2.$$

For every participant, we subtract the grand mean from the marginal mean for the appropriate row for that participant. We square these deviations and sum the squared deviations.

in this case 0.21, from every score to create deviations, then square the deviations, and finally sum the squared deviations:

$$SS_{total} = \Sigma(X - GM)^2 = 0.0672$$

We now calculate the between-groups sums of squares for the two main effects. Both are calculated similarly to the between-groups sum of squares for a one-way between-groups ANOVA. Table 14-14 shows the cell means, marginal means, and grand mean. The between-groups sum of squares for the main effect of the independent variable age would be the sum, for every score, of the marginal mean minus the grand mean, squared. We list all 12 scores in Table 14-15, marking the divisions among the cells. For each of the six younger participants, those in the top six rows of Table 14-15, we subtract the grand mean, 0.21, from the marginal mean, 0.16. For the six older participants, those in the bottom six rows, we subtract 0.21 from the marginal mean, 0.26. We square all of these deviations and then add them to calculate the sum of squares for the rows, the independent variable of age:

$$SS_{between(rows)} = \Sigma(M_{row(age)} - GM)^2 = 0.03$$

TABLE 14-14 Means for False Medical Claims Study

The study of the misremembering of false medical claims as true had two independent variables, age and number of repetitions. The cell means and marginal means for error rates are shown in the table. The grand mean is 0.21.

	One repetition (1)	Three repetitions (3)	
Younger (Y)	0.20	0.12	0.16
Older (O)	0.22	0.30	0.26
	0.21	0.21	0.21

TABLE 14-15 Calculating the Sum of Squares for the First Independent Variable

The sum of squares for the first independent variable is calculated by subtracting the overall mean (the grand mean) from the mean for each level of that variable—in this case, age—to create deviations, then squaring the deviations and summing them: $\Sigma(M_{row(age)} - GM)^2 = 0.03$.

	X	$(M_{row(age)} - GM)$	$(M_{row(age)} - GM)^2$
Y, 1	0.25	$(0.16 - 0.21) = -0.05$	0.0025
	0.21	$(0.16 - 0.21) = -0.05$	0.0025
	0.14	$(0.16 - 0.21) = -0.05$	0.0025
Y, 3	0.07	$(0.16 - 0.21) = -0.05$	0.0025
	0.13	$(0.16 - 0.21) = -0.05$	0.0025
	0.16	$(0.16 - 0.21) = -0.05$	0.0025
O, 1	0.27	$(0.26 - 0.21) = 0.05$	0.0025
	0.22	$(0.26 - 0.21) = 0.05$	0.0025
	0.17	$(0.26 - 0.21) = 0.05$	0.0025
O, 3	0.33	$(0.26 - 0.21) = 0.05$	0.0025
	0.31	$(0.26 - 0.21) = 0.05$	0.0025
	0.26	$(0.26 - 0.21) = 0.05$	0.0025

We repeat this process for the second possible main effect, that of the independent variable in the columns (Table 14-16). The between-groups sum of squares for number of repetitions, then, would be the sum, for every score, of the marginal mean minus the grand mean, squared. We again list all 12 scores, marking the divisions among the cells. For each of the six participants who had one repetition, those in the left-hand column of Table 14-14 and in rows 1–3 and 7–9 of Table 14-16, we subtract the grand mean, 0.21, from the marginal mean, 0.21. For each of the six participants who had three repetitions, those in the right-hand column of Table 14-14 and in rows 4–6 and 10–12 of Table 14-16, we subtract 0.21 from the marginal mean, 0.21. (*Note:* It is a coincidence that in this case the marginal means are exactly the same.) We square all of these deviations and add them to calculate the between-groups sum of squares for the columns, the independent variable of number of repetitions. Again, the calculations for the between-groups sum of squares for each main effect are just like the calculations for a one-way between-groups ANOVA:

$$SS_{between(columns)} = \Sigma(M_{columns(reps)} - GM)^2 = 0$$

The within-groups sum of squares is calculated in exactly the same way as for the one-way between-groups ANOVA (Table 14-17). The cell mean is subtracted from each of the 12 scores. The deviations are squared and summed:

$$SS_{within} = \Sigma(X - M_{cell})^2 = 0.018$$

All we need now is the between-groups sum of squares for the interaction. We calculate this by subtracting the other between-groups sums of squares (those for the two main effects) and the within-groups sum of squares from the total sum of squares. The between-groups sum of squares for the interaction is essentially what is left over when the main effects are accounted for. Mathematically, any variability that

MASTERING THE FORMULA

14-8: We calculate the between-groups sum of squares for the second independent variable, that in the columns of the table of cells, using the following formula: $SS_{between(columns)} = \Sigma(M_{column} - GM)^2$. For every participant, we subtract the grand mean from the marginal mean for the appropriate column for that participant. We square these deviations, and then sum the squared deviations.

MASTERING THE FORMULA

14-9: We calculate the within-groups sum of squares using the following formula: $SS_{within} = \Sigma(X - M_{cell})^2$. For every participant, we subtract the appropriate cell mean from that participant's score. We square these deviations and sum the squared deviations.

TABLE 14-16 Calculating the Sum of Squares for the Second Independent Variable

The sum of squares for the second independent variable is calculated by subtracting the overall mean (the grand mean) from the mean for each level of that variable—in this case, number of repetitions—to create deviations, then squaring the deviations and summing them: $\Sigma(M_{column(reps)} - GM)^2 = 0$.

	X	$(M_{column(reps)} - GM)$	$(M_{column(reps)} - GM)^2$
Y, 1	0.25	(0.21 − 0.21) = 0	0
	0.21	(0.21 − 0.21) = 0	0
	0.14	(0.21 − 0.21) = 0	0
Y, 3	0.07	(0.21 − 0.21) = 0	0
	0.13	(0.21 − 0.21) = 0	0
	0.16	(0.21 − 0.21) = 0	0
0, 1	0.27	(0.21 − 0.21) = 0	0
	0.22	(0.21 − 0.21) = 0	0
	0.17	(0.21 − 0.21) = 0	0
0, 3	0.33	(0.21 − 0.21) = 0	0
	0.31	(0.21 − 0.21) = 0	0
	0.26	(0.21 − 0.21) = 0	0

TABLE 14-17 Calculating the Within-Groups Sum of Squares

The within-groups sum of squares is calculated the same way for a two-way ANOVA as for a one-way ANOVA. We take each score and subtract the mean of the cell from which it comes—not the grand mean—to create deviations; then we square the deviations and sum them: $\Sigma(X - M_{cell})^2 = 0.018$.

	X	$\Sigma(X - M_{cell})$	$\Sigma(X - M_{cell})^2$
Y, 1	0.25	$(0.25 - 0.20) = 0.05$	0.0025
	0.21	$(0.21 - 0.20) = 0.01$	0.0001
	0.14	$(0.14 - 0.20) = -0.06$	0.0036
Y, 3	0.07	$(0.07 - 0.12) = -0.05$	0.0025
	0.13	$(0.13 - 0.12) = 0.01$	0.0001
	0.16	$(0.16 - 0.12) = 0.04$	0.0016
0, 1	0.27	$(0.27 - 0.22) = 0.05$	0.0025
	0.22	$(0.22 - 0.22) = 0.00$	0.0000
	0.17	$(0.17 - 0.22) = -0.05$	0.0025
0, 3	0.33	$(0.33 - 0.30) = 0.03$	0.0009
	0.31	$(0.31 - 0.30) = 0.01$	0.0001
	0.26	$(0.26 - 0.30) = -0.04$	0.0016

is predicted by these variables, but is not directly predicted by either independent variable on its own, is attributed to the interaction. The formula is:

$$SS_{between(interaction)} = SS_{total} - (SS_{between(rows)} + SS_{between(columns)} + SS_{within})$$

The calculations are:

$$SS_{between(interaction)} = 0.0672 - (0.03 + 0 + 0.018) = 0.0192$$

Now we complete step 6 of hypothesis testing by calculating the F statistics using the formulas in Table 14-18. The results are in the source table (Table 14-19). The main effect of age is statistically significant because the F statistic, 13.04, is larger than the critical value of 5.32. The means tell us that older participants tend to make more mistakes, remembering more medical myths as true, than do younger participants. The main effect of number of repetitions is not statistically significant, however, because the F statistic of 0.00 is not larger than the cutoff of 5.32. It is unusual to have an F statistic of 0.00. Even when there is no statistically significant effect, there is usually some difference among means due to random sampling. The interaction is also statistically significant because the F statistic of 8.35 is larger than the cutoff of 5.32. Therefore, we construct a bar graph of the cell means, as seen in Figure 14-9, to interpret the interaction.

In Figure 14-9, the lines are not parallel; in fact, they intersect without even having to extend them beyond the graph. We see that among younger participants, the proportion of responses that were incorrect was *lower*, on average, with three repetitions than with one repetition. Among older participants, the proportion of responses that were incorrect was *higher*, on average, with three repetitions than with one repetition. Does repetition help? It depends. It helps for younger people but is detrimental for older people. Specifically, repetition tends to help younger people distinguish between myth

TABLE 14-18	The Expanded Source Table and the Formulas

This source table includes all of the formulas for the calculations necessary to conduct a two-way between-groups ANOVA.

Source	SS	df	MS	F
Age (between/rows)	$\Sigma(M_{between(rows)} - GM)^2$	$N_{rows} - 1$	$\dfrac{SS_{between(rows)}}{df_{between(rows)}}$	$\dfrac{MS_{between(rows)}}{MS_{within}}$
Repetitions (between/columns)	$\Sigma(M_{between(columns)} - GM)^2$	$N_{columns} - 1$	$\dfrac{SS_{between(columns)}}{df_{between(columns)}}$	$\dfrac{MS_{between(columns)}}{MS_{within}}$
Age × repetitions (between/interaction)	$SS_{total} - (SS_{between(rows)} + SS_{between(columns)} + SS_{within})$	$(df_{rows})(df_{columns})$	$\dfrac{SS_{interaction}}{df_{interaction}}$	$\dfrac{MS_{interaction}}{MS_{within}}$
Within	$\Sigma(X - M_{cell})^2$	$df_{cell\ 1} + df_{cell\ 2} + df_{cell\ 3} + df_{cell\ 4}$ (and so on for any additional cells)	$\dfrac{SS_{within}}{df_{within}}$	
Total	$\Sigma(X - GM)^2$	$N_{total} - 1$		

TABLE 14-19	The Expanded Source Table and False Medical Claims

This expanded source table shows the actual sums of squares, degrees of freedom, mean squares, and F statistics for the study on false medical claims.

Source	SS	df	MS	F
Age (A)	0.0300	1	0.0300	13.04
Repetitions (R)	0.0000	1	0.0000	0.00
A × R	0.0192	1	0.0192	8.35
Within	0.0180	8	0.0023	
Total	0.0672	11		

MASTERING THE FORMULA

14-11: The formulas to calculate the four mean squares are in Table 14-18. There are three between-groups mean squares—one for each main effect and one for the interaction—and one within-groups mean square. For each mean square, we divide the appropriate sum of squares by its related degrees of freedom. The formulas for the three F statistics, one for each main effect and one for the interaction, are also in Table 14-18. For each of the three effects, we divide the appropriate between-groups mean square by the within-group mean square. The denominator is the same in all three cases.

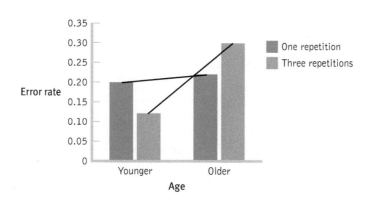

FIGURE 14-9

Interpreting the Interaction

The nonparallel lines demonstrate the interaction. The bars tell us that, on average, repetition decreases errors for younger people but increases them for older people. Because the direction reverses, this is a qualitative interaction.

and fact. But the mere repetition of a medical myth tends to lead older people to be more likely to view it as fact. The researchers speculate that older people remember that they are familiar with a statement but forget the context in which they heard it. This is a qualitative interaction because the direction of the effect of repetition *reverses* from one age group to another.

Effect Size for Two-Way ANOVA

With a two-way ANOVA, as with a one-way ANOVA, we calculate R^2 as the measure of effect size. As before, we use sums of squares as indicators of variability. For each of the three effects—the two main effects and the interaction—we divide the appropriate between-groups sum of squares by the total sum of squares minus the sums of squares for both of the other effects. We subtract the sums of squares for the other two effects from the total so that we isolate the effect size for a single effect at a time. For example, if we want to determine effect size for the main effect in the rows, we divide the sum of squares for the rows by the total sum of squares minus the sum of squares for the column and the sum of squares for the interaction.

For the first main effect, the one in the rows of the table of cells, the formula is:

$$R^2_{rows} = \frac{SS_{rows}}{(SS_{total} - SS_{columns} - SS_{interaction})}$$

For the second main effect, the one in the columns of the table of cells, the formula is:

$$R^2_{columns} = \frac{SS_{columns}}{(SS_{total} - SS_{rows} - SS_{interaction})}$$

For the interaction, the formula is:

$$R^2_{interaction} = \frac{SS_{interaction}}{(SS_{total} - SS_{rows} - SS_{columns})}$$

14-12: To calculate effect size for two-way ANOVA, we make three R^2 calculations, one for each main effect and one for the interaction. In each case, we divide the appropriate between-groups sum of squares by the total sum of squares minus the sums of squares for the other two effects. For example, the effect size for the interaction is calculated using this formula: $R^2_{interaction} = \frac{SS_{interaction}}{(SS_{total} - SS_{rows} - SS_{columns})}$.

EXAMPLE 14.5

Let's apply this to the ANOVA we just conducted. We use the statistics in the source table shown in Table 14-19 to calculate R^2 for each main effect and the interaction. Here are the calculations for the main effect for age:

$$R^2_{rows(age)} = \frac{SS_{rows(age)}}{(SS_{total} - SS_{columns(repetition)} - SS_{interaction})}$$

$$= \frac{0.0300}{(0.0672 - 0.000 - 0.0192)} = 0.625$$

Here are the calculations for the main effect for repetitions:

$$R^2_{columns(repetitions)} = \frac{SS_{columns(repetitions)}}{(SS_{total} - SS_{rows(age)} - SS_{interaction})}$$

$$= \frac{0.000}{(0.0672 - 0.0300 - 0.0192)} = 0.000$$

Here are the calculations for the interaction:

$$R^2_{interaction} = \frac{SS_{interaction}}{(SS_{total} - SS_{rows(age)} - SS_{columns(repetitions)})}$$

$$= \frac{0.0192}{0.0672 - 0.0300 - 0.0000} = 0.516$$

TABLE 14-20 Cohen's Conventions for Effect Sizes: R^2

The following guidelines, called *conventions* by statisticians, are meant to help researchers decide how important an effect is. These numbers are not cutoffs; they are merely rough guidelines to help researchers interpret results.

Effect Size	Convention
Small	0.01
Medium	0.06
Large	0.14

The conventions are the same as those presented in Chapter 12, shown again here in Table 14-20. From this table, we can see that the R^2 of 0.63 for the main effect of age and 0.52 for the interaction are very large. The R^2 of 0.00 for the main effect of repetitions indicates that there is no observable effect in this study.

Variations on ANOVA

Next Steps

We've already seen the flexibility that ANOVA offers in terms of both independent variables and research design. Yet ANOVA is even more flexible than we've seen so far in this and the previous two chapters. We described within-groups ANOVAs in which the participants experience all of the research conditions. Researchers also use four slightly more complicated designs.

1. *A **mixed-design ANOVA** is used to analyze the data from a study with at least two independent variables; at least one variable must be within-groups and at least one variable must be between-groups.* In other words, a mixed design includes both a between-groups variable and a within-groups variable.

2. *A **multivariate analysis of variance (MANOVA)** is a form of ANOVA in which there is more than one dependent variable.* The word *multivariate* refers to the number of dependent variables, not the number of independent variables. (Remember, a plain old ANOVA already can handle multiple independent variables.)

3. *Analysis of covariance (**ANCOVA**) is a type of ANOVA in which a covariate is included so that statistical findings reflect effects after a scale variable has been statistically removed.* Specifically, a **covariate** *is a scale variable that we suspect associates, or covaries, with the independent variable of interest.* So ANCOVA statistically subtracts the effect of a possible confounding variable.

4. We can also combine the features of a MANOVA and an ANCOVA. A **multivariate analysis of covariance (MANCOVA)** *is an ANOVA with multiple dependent variables and a covariate.* MANOVAs, ANCOVAs, and MANCOVAs can each have a between-groups design, a within-groups design, or even a mixed design. Table 14-21 shows variations on ANOVA.

Let's consider an example of a mixed-design ANOVA. Researchers explored the the effects of different types of e-mails on exam grades later in the course (Forsyth, Lawrence, Burnette, & Baumeister, 2007). There were three independent variables. The first independent variable was previous grade. There were two levels of this independent variable—students who had a grade of C on the first exam and those with a grade of D or F on the first exam. The second independent variable was type of email.

- A **mixed-design ANOVA** is used to analyze the data from a study with at least two independent variables; at least one variable must be within-groups and at least one variable must be between-groups.

- A **multivariate analysis of variance (MANOVA)** is a form of ANOVA in which there is more than one dependent variable.

- **Analysis of covariance (ANCOVA)** is a type of ANOVA in which a covariate is included so that statistical findings reflect effects after a scale variable has been statistically removed.

- A **covariate** is a scale variable that we suspect associates, or covaries, with the independent variable of interest.

- A **multivariate analysis of covariance (MANCOVA)** is an ANOVA with multiple dependent variables and a covariate.

TABLE 14-21 Variations on ANOVA

There are many variations on ANOVA that allow us to analyze a variety of research designs. A MANOVA allows us to include more than one dependent variable. An ANCOVA allows us to include covariates to correct for third variables that might influence our study. A MANCOVA allows us to include both more than one dependent variable and a covariate.

	Independent Variables	Dependent Variables	Covariate
ANOVA	Any number	Only one	None
MANOVA	Any number	More than one	None
ANCOVA	Any number	Only one	At least one
MANCOVA	Any number	More than one	At least one

There were three types of emails that students could receive over the semester: e-mails intended to bolster their self-esteem, e-mails intended to enhance their sense of control over their grades, and e-mails that just included review questions (control group).

The third independent variable was type of exam grade. The researchers assessed two types of exam grades; the second midterm exam grades and the final exam grades. Because every student took both exams, this third independent variable was within-groups. This means that the research design had two between-groups independent variables and one within-groups independent variable. This is an example of a three-way, mixed-design ANOVA. Specifically, this ANOVA would be referred to as a 2 (grade: C, D/F) × 3 (type of e-mail: control, self-esteem, take responsibility) × 2 (exam: midterm, final) mixed-design ANOVA.

Let's consider an example of a MANCOVA, an analysis that includes both (a) multiple dependent variables and (b) at least one covariate.

(a) We sometimes use a multivariate analysis when we have several similar dependent variables. Aside from the use of multiple dependent variables, multivariate analyses are not all that different from those with one dependent variable. Essentially, the calculations treat the group of dependent variables as one dependent variable. Although we can follow up a MANOVA by considering the different univariate (single dependent variable) ANOVAs embedded in the MANOVA, we often are most interested in the effect of the independent variables on the composite of dependent variables.

(b) There are often situations in which we suspect that a third variable might be affecting the dependent variable. In these cases, we might conduct an ANCOVA or MANCOVA. We might, for example, have level of education as one of the independent variables and worry that age, which is likely related to level of education, is actually what is influencing the dependent variable, not education. In this case, we could include age as a covariate.

The inclusion of a covariate means that the analysis will look at the effects of the independent variables on the dependent variables after statistically removing the effect of one or more third variables. At its most basic, conducting an ANCOVA is almost like conducting an ANOVA at each level of the covariate. If age were the covariate with level of education as the independent variable and income as the dependent variable, then we'd essentially be looking at a regular ANOVA for each age. We want to answer the question: Given a certain age, does education predict income? Of course, this is a simplified explanation, but that's the basic logic behind the procedure. If the calculations find that education has an effect on income among 33-year-olds, 58-year-olds, and every other age group, then we know that there is a main effect of education on income, over and above the effect of age.

Let's see how it works. Researchers conducted a MANCOVA to analyze the results of a study examining military service and marital status within the context of men's satisfaction within their romantic relationships (McLeland & Sutton, 2005). The independent variables were military service (military, nonmilitary) and marital status (married, unmarried). There were two dependent variables, both measures of relationship satisfaction: the Kansas Marital Satisfaction Scale (KMSS) and the ENRICH Marital Satisfaction Scale (EMS). The researchers also included the covariate of age.

Initial analyses also found that age was significantly associated with relationship satisfaction: Older men tended to be more satisfied than younger men. The researchers wanted to be certain that it was military status and marital status, not age, that affected relationship satisfaction, so they controlled for age as a covariate. The MANCOVA led to only one statistically significant finding: Military men were less satisfied than nonmilitary men with respect to their relationships, when controlling for the age of the men. That is, given a certain age, military men of that age are likely to be less satisfied with their relationships than are nonmilitary men of that age.

CHECK YOUR LEARNING

Reviewing the Concepts

> The six steps of hypothesis testing for a two-way between-groups ANOVA are similar to those for a one-way between-groups ANOVA.

> Because we have the possibility of two main effects and an interaction, each step is broken down into three parts, with three sets of hypotheses, comparison distributions, critical F values, F statistics, and conclusions.

> An expanded source table helps us to keep track of the calculations.

> Statistically significant F statistics require post hoc tests to determine where differences lie when there are more than two groups.

> We calculate a measure of effect size, R^2, for each main effect and for the interaction.

> Factorial ANOVAs can have a mixed design in addition to a between-groups design or within-groups design. In a mixed design, at least one of the independent variables is between-groups and at least one of the independent variables is within-groups.

> Researchers can also include multiple dependent variables, not just multiple independent variables, in a single study, analyzed with a MANOVA.

> Researchers can add a covariate to an ANOVA and conduct an ANCOVA, which allows us to control for the effect of a variable that is related to the independent variable.

> Researchers can include multiple dependent variables and one or more covariates in an analysis called a MANCOVA.

Clarifying the Concepts   14-9   What is the basic difference between the six steps of hypothesis testing for a two-way between-groups ANOVA and a one-way between-groups ANOVA?

    14-10   What are the four sources of variability in a two-way ANOVA?

Calculating the Statistics   14-11   Compute the three between-groups degrees of freedom (both main effects and the interaction), the within-groups degrees of freedom, and the total degrees of freedom for the following data: (Note: IV 1 refers to the first independent variable and IV 2 refers to the second independent variable.)

IV 1, level A; IV 2, level A: 2, 1, 1, 3

IV 1, level B; IV 2, level A: 5, 4, 3, 4

IV 1, level A; IV 2, level B: 2, 3, 3, 3

IV 1, level B; IV 2, level B: 3, 2, 2, 3

continued on next page

14-12 Using the degrees of freedom you calculated in the previous Check Your Learning exercise, determine critical values, or cutoffs, using a p level of 0.05, for the F statistics of the two main effects and the interaction.

Applying the Concepts 14-13 In the Next Steps section of this chapter, we considered an example of a mixed-design ANOVA. In that example, researchers studied the effect of e-mail messages on students' final exam grades (Forsyth & Kerr, 1999; Forsyth et al., 2007). Here, let's imagine that the researchers conducted a two-way, between-groups ANOVA (instead of a three-way, mixed-design ANOVA) using only the independent variables for previous grade (C or D/F) and type of email. Remember that participants were randomly assigned to receive several e-mails in one of three conditions: e-mails intended to bolster their self-esteem, e-mails intended to enhance their sense of control over their grades (the "take responsibility" group), and e-mails that just included review questions (control group). The accompanying table shows the cell means for the final exam grades (note that some of these are approximate, but all represent actual findings). For simplicity, assume there were 84 participants in the study evenly divided among cells.

	Self-esteem (SE)	Take responsibility (TR)	Control group (CG)
C	67.31	69.83	71.12
D/F	47.83	60.98	62.13

a. From step 1 of hypothesis testing, list the populations for this study.

b. Conduct step 2 of hypothesis testing.

c. Conduct step 3 of hypothesis testing.

d. Conduct step 4 of hypothesis testing.

Solutions to these Check Your Learning questions can be found in Appendix D.

e. The F statistics are 20.84 for the main effect of the independent variable of initial grade, 1.69 for the main effect of the independent variable of type of e-mail, and 3.02 for the interaction. Conduct step 6 of hypothesis testing.

REVIEW OF CONCEPTS

Two-Way ANOVA

Factorial ANOVAs (also called *multifactorial ANOVAs*), those with more than one independent variable (or *factor*), permit us to test more than one hypothesis in a single study. They also allow us to examine *interactions* between independent variables. Factorial ANOVAs are often named by referring to the levels of their independent variables (e.g., 2 × 2) rather than the number of independent variables (e.g., two-way). With a *two-way ANOVA*, we can examine two *main effects* (one for each independent variable) and one interaction (the way in which the two variables might work together to influence the dependent variable). Because we are examining three hypotheses, we calculate three sets of statistics for a two-way ANOVA.

Understanding Interactions in ANOVA

Researchers typically interpret interactions by examining the overall pattern of cell means. A *cell* is one condition in a study. We typically write the mean of a group in its cell. We write the *marginal means* for each row to the right of the cells and the marginal means for each column below the cells. If the main effect of one independent variable is stronger under certain conditions of the second independent variable, there is a *quantitative interaction*. If the direction of the main effect actually reverses under certain conditions of the second independent variable, there is a *qualitative interaction*.

Conducting a Two-Way Between-Groups ANOVA

A two-way between-groups ANOVA uses the same six steps of hypothesis testing that we used previously, with minor changes. Because we test for two main effects and one interaction, each step is broken down into three parts. Specifically, we have three sets of hypotheses, three comparison distributions, three critical F values, three F statistics, and three conclusions. We use an expanded source table to aid in the calculations of the F statistics. We also calculate a measure of effect size, R^2, for each of the main effects and for the interaction.

There are several ways to expand on ANOVA. A mixed-design ANOVA has at least one between-groups independent variable and at least one within-groups independent variable. We also can include multiple dependent variables, not just multiple independent variables, in a single study, analyzed with a multivariate analysis of variance (MANOVA). Alternately, we can add a covariate to the ANOVA and conduct an analysis of covariance (ANCOVA), which allows us to control for the effect of a variable that we believe might be related to our independent variable. Finally, we can include multiple dependent variables and a covariate in an analysis called a multivariate analysis of covariance (MANCOVA).

SPSS®

Let's use SPSS to conduct a two-way ANOVA for the data on myth busting that we used in this chapter. We enter the data in three columns—one for each participant's scores on each independent variable (age and number of repetitions) and one for each participant's score on the dependent variable (false memory).

We instruct SPSS to conduct the ANOVA by selecting Analyze → General Linear Model → Univariate and selecting the variables. (Even though there are two independent variables, we still choose univariate, which means one variable, instead of multivariate, which means many variables. That's because this choice refers to the dependent variable

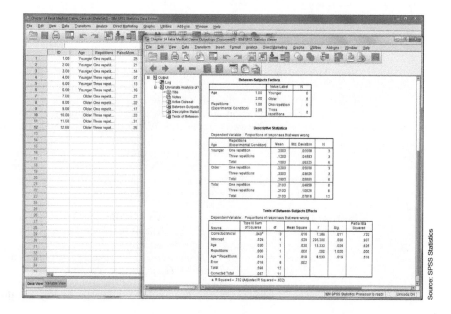

rather than the independent variable, and there's just one dependent variable, false memory.)

Select the dependent variable, false memory, by highlighting it and clicking the arrow next to "Dependent Variable." Select the independent variables (called "fixed factors" here), age and repetitions, by clicking each of them, then clicking the arrow next to "Fixed Factor(s)." To include specific descriptive statistics, as well as a measure of effect size, select "Options," then select "Descriptive statistics" and "Estimates of effect size." Then, select "Continue." Finally, click "OK" to run the analysis.

The output in the screenshot shown here includes the same statistics that we calculated earlier. The small differences are due only to rounding decisions. For example, we see that the F statistic for the main effect of age is 13.333. Its p value is found in the column headed "Sig." and is .006. This is well below the typical p level of 0.05, which tells us that this is a statistically significant effect. The effect size is found in the final column, "Partial Eta Squared," which can be interpreted as we learned to interpret R^2. The effect size of .625 indicates that this is a very large effect.

HOW IT WORKS

14.1 CONDUCTING A TWO-WAY BETWEEN-GROUPS ANOVA

The online dating Web site Match.com allows users to post personal ads to meet others. Each person is asked to specify a range from the youngest age that would be acceptable for a dating partner to the oldest acceptable age. The following data were randomly selected from the ads of 25-year-old people living in the New York City area. The scores represent the youngest acceptable ages listed by those in the sample. So, in the first line, the first of the five 25-year-old women who are seeking men states that she will not date a man younger than 26 years old.

25-year-old women seeking men: 26, 24, 25, 24, 25

25-year-old men seeking women: 18, 21, 22, 22, 18

25-year-old women seeking women: 22, 25, 22, 25, 25

25-year-old men seeking men: 23, 25, 24, 22, 20

There are two independent variables and one dependent variable. The first independent variable is gender of the seeker, and its levels are male and female. The second independent variable is gender of the person being sought, and its levels are men and women. The dependent variable is the youngest acceptable age of the person being sought. Based on these variables, how can we conduct a two-way between-groups ANOVA on these data? The cell means are:

	Female seekers	Male seekers
Men sought	24.8	22.8
Women sought	23.8	20.2

Here are the six steps of hypothesis testing for this example.

Step 1: Population 1 (female, men): Women seeking men. Population 2 (male, women): Men seeking women. Population 3 (female, women): Women seeking women. Population 4 (male, men): Men seeking men.

The comparison distributions will be F distributions. The hypothesis test will be a two-way between-groups ANOVA. Assumptions: The data are not from random samples, so we must generalize with caution. From these small sample sizes, it's hard to tell if the underlying population distributions are normal, so we should proceed with caution. The homogeneity of variance assumption is violated because the largest variance (3.70) is more than five times as large as the smallest variance (0.70). For the purposes of demonstration, we will proceed anyway.

Step 2: The hypotheses for the main effect of the first independent variable, gender of seeker, is as follows: Null hypothesis: On average, male and female seekers report the same youngest acceptable ages for their partners—H_0: $\mu_M = \mu_F$. Research hypothesis: On average, male and female seekers report different youngest acceptable ages for their partners—H_0: $\mu_M \neq \mu_F$.

The hypotheses for the main effect of the second independent variable, gender of person sought, is as follows: Null hypothesis: On average, those seeking men and those seeking women report the same youngest acceptable ages for their partners—$H_0: \mu_M = \mu_W$. Research hypothesis: On average, those seeking men and those seeking women report different youngest acceptable ages for their partners—$H_0: \mu_M \neq \mu_W$.

The hypotheses for the interaction of gender of seeker and gender of person sought are as follows: Null hypothesis: The effect of the gender of the seeker on youngest acceptable ages for their partners does not depend on the gender of the person sought. Research hypothesis: The effect of the gender of the seeker on youngest acceptable ages for their partners does depend on the gender of the person sought.

Step 3: $df_{columns(seeker)} = 2 - 1 = 1$

$df_{rows(sought)} = 2 - 1 = 1$

$df_{interaction} = (1)(1) = 1$

$df_{within} = df_{F,M} + df_{M,W} + df_{F,M} + df_{M,M} = 4 + 4 + 4 + 4 = 16$

Main effect of gender of seeker: F distribution with 1 and 16 degrees of freedom

Main effect of gender of sought: F distribution with 1 and 16 degrees of freedom

Interaction of seeker and sought: F distribution with 1 and 16 degrees of freedom

Step 4: Critical F for main effect of seeker: 4.49

Critical F for main effect of sought: 4.49

Critical F for interaction of seeker and sought: 4.49

Step 5: $SS_{total} = \Sigma(X - GM)^2 = 103.800$

$SS_{column(seeker)} = \Sigma(M_{column(seeker)} - GM)^2 = 39.200$

$SS_{row(sought)} = \Sigma(M_{row(sought)} - GM)^2 = 16.200$

$SS_{within} = \Sigma(X - M_{cell})^2 = 45.200$

$SS_{interaction} = SS_{total} - (SS_{row} + SS_{column} + SS_{within}) = 3.200$

Source	SS	df	MS	F
Seeker gender	39.200	1	39.200	13.876
Sought gender	16.200	1	16.200	5.735
Seeker 3 sought	3.200	1	3.200	1.133
Within	45.200	16	2.825	
Total	103.800	19		

Step 6: There is a significant main effect of gender of the seeker and a significant main effect of gender of the person being sought. We can reject the null hypotheses for both of these main effects. Male seekers are willing to accept younger partners, on average, than are female seekers. Those seeking women are willing to accept younger partners, on average, than are those seeking men. We cannot reject the null hypothesis for the interaction; we can only conclude that there is not sufficient evidence that the effect of the gender of the seeker on youngest acceptable age depends on the gender of the person sought.

14.2 CALCULATING EFFECT SIZE FOR A TWO-WAY BETWEEN-GROUPS ANOVA

How can we compute and interpret the effect sizes, R^2, for each main effect and the interaction for the ANOVA we conducted in How It Works 14.1? Here are the effect size calculations and interpretations, according to Cohen's conventions, for each of the three effects.

For the main effect of seeker gender:

$$R^2_{rows} = \frac{SS_{rows}}{(SS_{total} - SS_{columns} - SS_{interaction})} = \frac{39.2}{(103.8 - 16.2 - 3.2)} = 0.46$$

This is a large effect size.
For the main effect of sought gender:

$$R^2_{columns} = \frac{SS_{columns}}{(SS_{total} - SS_{rows} - SS_{interaction})} = \frac{16.2}{(103.8 - 39.2 - 3.2)} = 0.26$$

This is a large effect size.
For the interaction:

$$R^2_{interaction} = \frac{SS_{interaction}}{(SS_{total} - SS_{rows} - SS_{columns})} = \frac{3.2}{(103.8 - 39.2 - 16.2)} = 0.07$$

This is a medium effect size.

EXERCISES

Clarifying the Concepts

14.1 What is a two-way ANOVA?

14.2 What is a factor?

14.3 In your own words, define the word *cell*, first as you would use it in everyday conversation and then as a statistician would use it.

14.4 What is a four-way within-groups ANOVA?

14.5 What is the difference in information provided when we say *two-way ANOVA* versus *2 × 3 ANOVA*?

14.6 What are the three different *F* statistics in a two-way ANOVA?

14.7 What is a marginal mean?

14.8 What are the three ways to identify a statistically significant interaction?

14.9 How do bar graphs help us identify and interpret interactions? Explain how adding lines to the bar graph can help.

14.10 Why is a bar graph a better choice than a line graph for depicting the means of a two-way ANOVA?

14.11 In step 6 of hypothesis testing for a two-way between-groups ANOVA, we make a decision for each *F* statistic. What are the three possible outcomes with respect to the overall pattern of results?

14.12 When are post hoc tests needed for a two-way between-groups ANOVA?

14.13 Explain the following formula in your own words: $SS_{interaction} = SS_{total} - (SS_{rows} + SS_{columns} + SS_{within})$.

14.14 In your own words, define the word *interaction*, first as you would use it in everyday conversation and then as a statistician would use it.

14.15 What effect-size measure is used with two-way ANOVA?

14.16 What is a two-way mixed-design ANOVA?

14.17 How is an ANCOVA different from an ANOVA?

14.18 How is a MANOVA different from an ANOVA?

14.19 When might a researcher decide to use a MANOVA rather than an ANOVA?

14.20 When might a researcher decide to use an ANCOVA rather than an ANOVA?

14.21 What is a two-way mixed-design MANOVA?

Calculating the Statistics

14.22 For each of the following scenarios, what are two names for the ANOVA that would be conducted to analyze the data?

a. A researcher examined the effect of gender and pet ownership (no pets, one pet, more than one pet) on a measure of loneliness.

b. In a study on memory, participants completed a memory task once each week for 4 weeks—twice after sleeping 8 hours and twice after sleeping 4 hours. In each sleep condition, the participants completed the task after ingesting a caffeinated beverage and again, on another day, after ingesting a "placebo" beverage that they were told contained caffeine.

c. A study examined the impact of students' Instagram profiles on numbers of Instagram friends. The researchers were interested in the effect of 1) the profile photo—either an identifiable photo of the student or a photo of someone or something else (e.g., a dog)—and 2) bio length—either short (fewer than 75 characters) or long (75 characters or more).

14.23 Identify the factors and their levels in the following research designs.

a. Men and women's enjoyment of two different sporting events, Sport 1 and Sport 2, are compared using a 20-point enjoyment scale.

b. The amount of underage drinking, as documented in formal incident reports, is compared at "dry" college campuses (no alcohol at all) and "wet" campuses (those that enforce the legal age for possession of alcohol). Three different types of colleges are considered: state institutions, private schools, and schools with a religious affiliation.

c. The extent of contact with juvenile authorities is compared for youth across three age groups (12–13, 14–15, 16–17), considering both gender and family composition (two parents, single parent, or no identified authority figure).

14.24 State how many cells there should be for each of these studies. Then, create an empty grid to represent those cells.

a. Men and women's enjoyment of two different sporting events, Sport 1 and Sport 2, are compared using a 20-point enjoyment scale.

b. The amount of underage drinking, as documented in formal incident reports, is compared at "dry" college campuses (no alcohol at all) and "wet" campuses (those that enforce the legal age for possession of alcohol). Three different types of colleges are considered: state institutions, private schools, and schools with a religious affiliation.

c. The extent of contact with juvenile authorities is compared for youth across three age groups (12–13, 14–15, 16–17), considering both gender and family composition (two parents, single parent, or no identified authority figure).

14.25 Use these "enjoyment" data to perform the following:

	Ice hockey	Figure skating
Men	19, 17, 18, 17	6, 4, 8, 3
Women	13, 14, 18, 8	11, 7, 4, 14

a. Calculate the cell and marginal means.

b. Draw a bar graph.

c. Calculate the five different degrees of freedom, and indicate the critical F value based on each set of degrees of freedom, assuming the p level is 0.01.

d. Calculate the total sum of squares.

e. Calculate the between-groups sum of squares for the independent variable gender.

f. Calculate the between-groups sum of squares for the independent variable sporting event.

g. Calculate the within-groups sum of squares.

h. Calculate the sum of squares for the interaction.

i. Create a source table.

14.26 Use these data—incidents of reports of underage drinking—to perform the following:

"Dry" campus, state school: 47, 52, 27, 50

"Dry" campus, private school: 25, 33, 31

"Wet" campus, state school: 77, 61, 55, 48

"Wet" campus, private school: 52, 68, 60

a. Calculate the cell and marginal means. Notice the unequal Ns.

b. Draw a bar graph.

c. Calculate the five different degrees of freedom, and indicate the critical F value based on each set of degrees of freedom, assuming the p level is 0.05.

d. Calculate the total sum of squares.

e. Calculate the between-groups sum of squares for the independent variable campus.

f. Calculate the between-groups sum of squares for the independent variable school.

g. Calculate the within-groups sum of squares.

h. Calculate the sum of squares for the interaction.

i. Create a source table.

14.27 Using what you know about the expanded source table, fill in the missing values in the table shown here:

Source	SS	df	MS	F
Gender	248.25	1		
Parenting style	84.34	3		
Gender × style	33.60			
Within	1107.20	36		
Total				

14.28 Using the information in the source table provided here, compute R^2 values for each effect. Using Cohen's conventions, explain what these values mean.

Source	SS	df	MS	F
A (rows)	0.267	1	0.267	0.004
B (columns)	3534.008	2	1767.004	24.432
A × B	5.371	2	2.686	0.037
Within	1157.167	16	72.323	
Total	4696.813	21		

14.29 Using the information in the source table provided here, compute R^2 values for each effect. Using Cohen's conventions, explain what these values mean.

Source	SS	df	MS	F
A (rows)	30.006	1	30.006	0.511
B (columns)	33.482	1	33.482	0.570
A × B	1.720	1	1.720	0.029
Within	587.083	10	58.708	
Total	652.291	13		

Applying the Concepts

14.30 **Football, eye glare, and ANOVA:** In Exercise 13.27 (page 363), we described a Yale University study. Let's consider a redesign in which researchers randomly assigned 46 participants to place one of three substances below their eyes: black grease, black antiglare stickers, or petroleum jelly. They assessed eye glare using a contrast chart that gives a value for each participant, a scale measure. Black grease led to a reduction in glare compared with the two other conditions, antiglare stickers or petroleum jelly (DeBroff & Pahk, 2003). Imagine that every participant was tested twice, once in broad daylight and again under the artificial lights used at night.

a. What are the independent variables and their levels?

b. What kind of ANOVA would we use?

14.31 Health-related myths and the type of ANOVA: Consider the study we used as an example for a two-way between-groups ANOVA. Older and younger people were randomly assigned to hear either one repetition or three repetitions of a health-related myth, accompanied by the accurate information that "busted" the myth.

a. Explain why this study would be analyzed with a between-groups ANOVA.

b. How could this study be redesigned to use a within-groups ANOVA? (*Hint:* Think long term.)

14.32 Memory and choosing the type of ANOVA: In a fictional study, a cognitive psychologist studied memory for names after a group activity. The researcher randomly assigned 120 participants to one of three conditions: (1) group members introduced themselves once, (2) group members were introduced by the experimenter and by themselves, and (3) group members were introduced by the experimenter and themselves, and they wore name tags throughout the group activity.

a. How could the researcher redesign this study so it would be analyzed with a two-way between-groups ANOVA? Be specific. (*Note:* There are several possible ways that the researcher could do this.)

b. How could the researcher redesign this study so it would be analyzed with a two-way mixed-design ANOVA? Be specific. (*Note:* There are several possible ways the researcher could do this.)

14.33 Anger, culture, and choosing the type of ANOVA: Researchers explored the effect of the expression of anger on physical health in two cultures—the United States and Japan (Kitayama et al., 2015). They noted that previous research linked the expression of anger with health problems, but this research had been conducted in Western cultures. In their cross–cultural study, the researchers found that high levels of anger (compared with low levels of anger) led to worse health, including higher blood pressure, among American participants, but better health among Japanese participants. The researchers speculate that in the United States, anger tends to indicate that people have experienced negative events. On the other hand, the researchers believe

that, in Japan, anger tends to indicate that people feel "empowered and entitled," positive feelings that tend to occur only among people in Japan who have more control over their lives.

a. List any independent variables, along with the levels.

b. What is the dependent variable?

c. What kind of ANOVA would the researchers use?

d. Now name the ANOVA using the more specific language that enumerates the numbers of levels.

e. Use your answer to part (d) to calculate the number of cells. Explain how you made this calculation.

f. Draw a table that depicts the cells of this ANOVA.

g. Is this a quantitative or qualitative interaction? Explain your answer.

14.34 Racism, juries, and interactions: In a study of racism, Nail, Harton, and Decker (2003) had participants read a scenario in which a police officer assaulted a motorist. Half the participants read about a black officer who assaulted a white motorist, and half read about a white officer who assaulted a black motorist. Participants were categorized based on political orientation: liberal, moderate, or conservative. Participants were told that the officer was acquitted of assault charges in state court but was found guilty of violating the motorist's rights in federal court. Double jeopardy occurs when an individual is tried twice for the same crime. Participants were asked to rate, on a scale of 1–7, the degree to which the officer had been placed in double jeopardy by the second trial.

The researchers reported the interaction as $F(2, 58) = 10.93$, $p < 0.0001$. The means for the *liberal* participants were 3.18 for those who read about the black officer and 1.91 for those who read about the white officer. The means for the *moderate* participants were 3.50 for those who read about the black officer and 3.33 for those who read about the white officer. The means for the *conservative* participants were 1.25 for those who read about the black officer and 4.62 for those who read about the white officer.

a. Draw a table of cell means that includes the actual means for this study.

b. Do the reported statistics indicate that there is a significant interaction? If yes, describe the interaction in your own words.

c. Draw a bar graph that depicts the interaction. Include lines that connect the tops of the bars and show the pattern of the interaction.

d. Is this a quantitative or qualitative interaction? Explain.

e. Change the cell mean for the conservative participants who read about a black officer so that this is now a quantitative interaction.

f. Draw a bar graph that depicts the pattern that includes the new cell means.

g. Change the cell means for the moderate and conservative participants who read about a black officer so that there is now no interaction.

h. Draw a bar graph that depicts the pattern that includes the new cell means.

14.35 Self-interest, ANOVA, and interactions: Ratner and Miller (2001) wondered whether people are uncomfortable when they act in a way that's not obviously in their own self-interest. They randomly assigned 33 women and 32 men to read a fictional passage saying that government funding would soon be cut for research into a gastrointestinal illness that mostly affected either (1) women or (2) men. They were then asked to rate, on a 1–7 scale, how comfortable they would be "attending a meeting of concerned citizens who share your position" on this cause (p. 11). A higher rating indicates a greater degree of comfort. The journal article reported the statistics for the interaction as $F(1, 58) = 9.83$, $p < 0.01$. Women who read about women had a mean of 4.88, whereas those who read about men had a mean of 3.56. Men who read about women had a mean of 3.29, whereas those who read about men had a mean of 4.67.

a. What are the independent variables and their levels? What is the dependent variable?

b. What kind of ANOVA did the researchers conduct?

c. Do the reported statistics indicate that there is a significant interaction? Explain your answer.

d. Draw a table that includes the cells of the study. Include the cell means.

e. Draw a bar graph that depicts these findings.

f. Describe the pattern of the interaction in words. Is this a qualitative or a quantitative interaction? Explain your answer.

g. Draw a new table of cells, but change the means for male participants reading about women so that there is now a quantitative, rather than a qualitative, interaction.

h. Draw a bar graph of the means in part (g).

i. Draw a new table of cells, but change the means for male participants reading about women so that there is no interaction.

14.36 Gender, negotiating a salary, and an interaction: Eleanor Barkhorn (2012) reported in the *Atlantic* about differences in women's and men's negotiating styles. She first explained that researchers did not find a significant difference in how likely women and men are to negotiate salaries. But this did not tell the whole story. Barkhorn wrote: "Women are more likely to negotiate when an employer explicitly says that wages are negotiable. Men, on the other hand, are more likely to negotiate when the employer does not directly state that they can negotiate."

For each of the following, state whether the finding is a result of examining a main effect or examining an interaction. Explain your answer.

a. The finding that women and men do not significantly differ, on average, in their likelihood of negotiating.

b. The finding of a gender difference in the circumstances under which one will negotiate.

14.37 The cross-race effect, main effects, and interactions: Hugenberg, Miller, and Claypool (2007) conducted a study to better understand the cross-race effect, in which people have a difficult time recognizing members of different racial groups—colloquially known as the "they all look the same to me" effect. In a variation on this study, white participants viewed either 20 black faces or 20 white faces for 3 seconds each. Half the participants were told to pay particular attention to distinguishing features of the faces. Later, participants were shown 40 black faces or 40 white faces (the same race that they were shown in the prior stage of the experiment), 20 of which were new. Each participant received a score that measured his or her recognition accuracy.

The researchers reported two effects, one for the race of the people in the pictures, $F(1, 136) = 23.06$, $p < 0.001$, such that white faces were more easily recognized, on average, than black faces. There also was a significant interaction of the race of the people in the pictures and the instructions, $F(1, 136) = 5.27$, $p < 0.05$. When given no instructions, the mean recognition scores were 1.46 for white faces and 1.04 for black faces. When given instructions to pay attention to distinguishing features, the mean recognition scores were 1.38 for white faces and 1.23 for black faces.

a. What are the independent variables and their levels? What is the dependent variable?

b. What kind of ANOVA did the researchers conduct?

c. Do the reported statistics indicate that there is a significant main effect? If yes, describe it.

d. Why is the main effect not sufficient in this situation to understand the findings? Be specific about why the main effect is misleading by itself.

e. Do the reported statistics indicate that there is a significant interaction? Explain your answer.

f. Draw a table that includes the cells of the study and the cell means.

g. Draw a bar graph that depicts these findings.

h. Describe the pattern of the interaction in words. Is this a qualitative or a quantitative interaction? Explain your answer.

14.38 Grade point average, fraternities, sororities, and two-way between-groups ANOVA: A sample of students from our statistics classes reported their grade point averages (GPAs), indicated their genders, and stated whether they were in the university's Greek system (i.e., in a fraternity or sorority). Following are the GPAs for the different groups of students:

Men in a fraternity: 2.6, 2.4, 2.9, 3.0
Men not in a fraternity: 3.0, 2.9, 3.4, 3.7, 3.0
Women in a sorority: 3.1, 3.0, 3.2, 2.9
Women not in a sorority: 3.4, 3.0, 3.1, 3.1

a. What are the independent variables and their levels? What is the dependent variable?

b. Draw a table that lists the cells of the study design. Include the cell means.

c. Conduct all six steps of hypothesis testing.

d. Draw a bar graph for all statistically significant effects.

e. Is there a significant interaction? If yes, describe it in words and indicate whether it is a qualitative or a quantitative interaction. Explain.

f. Compute the effect sizes, R^2, for the main effects and interaction. Using Cohen's conventions, interpret the effect-size values.

14.39 Age, online dating, and two-way between-groups ANOVA: The data below were from the same 25-year-old participants described in How It Works 14.1, but now the scores represent the oldest age that would be acceptable in a dating partner.

25-year-old women seeking men: 40, 35, 29, 35, 35
25-year-old men seeking women: 26, 26, 28, 28, 28
25-year-old women seeking women: 35, 35, 30, 35, 45
25-year-old men seeking men: 33, 35, 35, 36, 38

a. What are the independent variables and their levels? What is the dependent variable?

b. Draw a table that lists the cells of the study design. Include the cell means.

c. Conduct all six steps of hypothesis testing.

d. Is there a significant interaction? If yes, describe it in words, indicate whether it is a quantitative or a qualitative interaction, and draw a bar graph.

e. Compute the effect sizes, R^2, for the main effects and interaction. Using Cohen's conventions, interpret the effect-size values.

14.40 Helping, payment, and two-way between-groups ANOVA: Heyman and Ariely (2004) were interested in whether effort and willingness to help were affected by the form and amount of payment offered in return for effort. They predicted that when money was used as payment, in what is called a *money market*, effort would increase as a function of payment level. On the other hand, if effort were performed out of altruism, in what is called a *social market,* the level of effort would be consistently high and unaffected by level of payment. In one of their studies, college students were asked to estimate another student's willingness to help load a sofa into a van in return for a cash payment or candy of equivalent value. Willingness to help was assessed using an 11-point scale ranging from "Not at all likely to help" to "Will help for sure." Data are presented here to re-create some of their findings.

Cash payment, low amount of $0.50: 4, 5, 6, 4
Cash payment, moderate amount of $5.00: 7, 8, 8, 7
Candy payment, low amount valued at $0.50: 6, 5, 7, 7
Candy payment, moderate amount valued at $5.00: 8, 6, 5, 5

a. What are the independent variables and their levels?

b. What is the dependent variable?

c. Draw a table that lists the cells of the study design. Include the cell and marginal means.

d. Create a bar graph.

e. Using this graph and the table of cell means, describe what effects you see in the pattern of the data.

f. Write the null and research hypotheses.

g. Complete all of the calculations and construct a full source table for these data.

h. Determine the critical value for each effect at a p level of 0.05.

i. Make your decisions. Is there a significant interaction? If yes, describe it in words and indicate whether it is a qualitative or a quantitative interaction. Explain.

j. Compute the effect sizes, R^2, for the main effects and interaction. Using Cohen's conventions, interpret the effect-size values.

14.41 Helping, payment, and interactions: Expanding on the work of Heyman and Ariely (2004) as described in the previous exercise, let's assume a higher level of payment was included and the following data were collected. (Notice that all data are the same as earlier, with the addition of new data under a high payment amount.)

Cash payment, low amount of $0.50: 4, 5, 6, 4
Cash payment, moderate amount of $5.00: 7, 8, 8, 7
Cash payment, high amount of $50.00: 9, 8, 7, 8
Candy payment, low amount, valued at $0.50: 6, 5, 7, 7
Candy payment, moderate amount, valued at $5.00: 8, 6, 5, 5
Candy payment, high amount, valued at $50.00: 6, 7, 7, 6

a. What are the independent variables and their levels? What is the dependent variable?

b. Draw a table that lists the cells of the study design. Include the cell and marginal means.

c. Create a new bar graph of these data.

d. Do you think there is a significant interaction? If yes, describe it in words.

e. Now that one independent variable has three levels, what additional analyses are needed? Explain what you would do and why. Based on the graph you created, where do you think there would be significant differences?

14.42 Exercise, well-being, and type of ANOVA: Cox, Thomas, Hinton, and Donahue (2006) studied the effects of exercise on well-being. There were three independent variables: age (18–20 years old, 35–45 years old), intensity of exercise (low, moderate, high), and time point (15, 20, 25, and 30 minutes). The dependent variable was positive well-being. Every participant was assessed at all intensity levels and all time points. (Generally, moderate-intensity exercise and high-intensity exercise led to higher levels of positive well-being than did low-intensity exercise.)

a. What type of ANOVA would the researchers conduct?

b. The researchers included two covariates related to the physical effects of exercise, measures of hemoglobin and serum ferritin. What statistical test would they use? Explain.

c. The researchers conducted separate analyses for three dependent variables: perceived fatigue, psychological distress, and positive well-being. If they wanted to include all three dependent variables in the analysis described in part (a), what statistical test would they use? Explain.

d. If the researchers wanted to use all three dependent variables in the analysis described in part (b), the analysis that included covariates, what statistical test would they use? Explain.

14.43 Body weight, salary, and the need for covariates: A nutritional software program called DietPower offers encouragement to its users when they sign in each day. In one instance, the program states that people at their ideal body weight tend to have higher salaries than do people who are overweight and then explicitly states that losing weight might lead to an increase in pay!

a. Why is this a problematic statement? List at least two confounding variables that might affect this finding.

b. Imagine that you were going to conduct a study that compared the salaries of two groups: people who were overweight and people who were at their ideal body weight. Why would it be useful to include one or more covariates? What scale variables might you include as covariates?

14.44 Math performance and type of ANOVA: Imagine that a college professor is interested in the effects of a new instructional method on the math performance of first-year college students. All students take a math pre-test and then are randomly assigned to a class in which

the new instructional method is used or a class in which the old method is used. At the end of the semester, the professor gives all students the same final exam and has all students complete a national standardized test that assesses math ability.

a. What is the independent variable and what are its levels?

b. What scale variable could the professor use as a covariate in the statistical analysis of this study?

c. What are the dependent variables assessed by the professor?

d. What type of ANOVA could be used to analyze the results of this study?

14.45 College students, anxiety, depression, and a MANOVA: Jason Nelson and Noel Gregg (2012) conducted a study of college students with disabilities. They reported that: "A 3 × 3 × 2 MANOVA was conducted to determine the effect of level of educational attainment (transitioning adolescents and college underclassmen—that is, freshmen and sophomores—and college upperclassmen—that is, juniors and seniors), disability status (dyslexia, ADHD, and ADHD/dyslexia), and gender on BDI-II and BAI scores" (p. 249). (The BDI is the Beck Depression Inventory, which assesses symptoms of depression; the BAI is the Beck Anxiety Inventory, which assesses symptoms of anxiety.)

a. What are the independent variables in this study and what are their levels?

b. What are the dependent variables in this study?

c. Based on these variables, explain why the researchers conducted a MANOVA.

d. The researchers report that there was only one significant effect in this MANOVA. Specifically, "Tukey's *HSD* post hoc tests indicated college underclassmen with disabilities had higher BAI ($M = 9.10$, $SD = 8.37$) and BDI-II scores ($M = 9.30$, $SD = 8.92$) than did transitioning adolescents with disabilities (BAI: $M = 5.18$, $SD = 6.18$; BDI-II: $M = 4.50$, $SD = 5.40$). The effect sizes for these group differences on the BAI ($d = .50$) and BDI-II ($d = .59$) were medium in magnitude."

i. Put these findings into plain English and in your own words.

ii. Explain why the researchers conducted Tukey *HSD* tests.

iii. Why did the researchers report Cohen's *d* when they conducted a form of ANOVA (i.e., MANOVA)? (*Hint:* Think about the number of means in their comparisons.)

14.46 Gender, pizza, and an interaction: Researchers examined whether men and women eat different amounts of food in the company of same-sex dining partners versus opposite-sex dining partners (Kniffin, Sigirci, & Wansink, 2016). From an evolutionary perspective, the researchers wondered which of the following two hypotheses would receive support: 1) Men—most of them presumably heterosexual—would show off by eating more in the presence of women to attract a mate; or 2) men would show off by eating more in the presence of other men in order to demonstrate status or dominance. Restaurant diners were observed eating lunch. Research assistants counted the number of pizza slices eaten by each diner in the study, along with the genders of their dining companions. The graph here depicts the results.

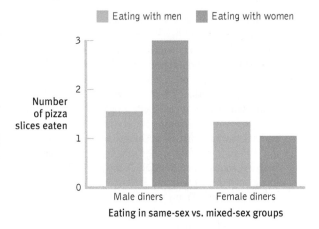

a. Based on this graph, what type of ANOVA did the researchers conduct?

b. Does it seem as if there is a main effect of the gender of the diner? If yes, explain the effect in your own words. If not, explain your answer.

c. Does it seem as if there is a main effect of type of the gender of the diner's lunch companion? If yes, explain the effect in your own words. If not, explain your answer.

d. Describe the interaction in your own words. Is this a quantitative interaction or a qualitative interaction? Explain your answer.

e. Which of the competing hypotheses received support from this study?

14.47 Negotiation, an interaction, and a graph: German psychologist David Loschelder and his colleagues conducted an experiment on negotiations (2014). They cited tennis player Andy Roddick's agent, who thought it was always detrimental to make an initial offer, saying "The first offer gives you an insight into [the other party's] thought process." The researchers wondered if this was always true. So, they conducted an experiment with two independent variables. One independent variable was the person's role in the negotiations—either the person starting the negotiation (the sender) or the person being targeted (the receiver). The second independent variable was the type of information in the initial offer—different or the same. That is, the sender

was either asking for something that is different from what the other partner wants or asking for something that the other person also wants. For example, if you are negotiating with a new employer, you might ask for five weeks of vacation and a higher salary than you think you can get. And maybe the employer was already prepared to give you five weeks vacation. So, the researchers thought the type of information that matches what the other person wants (like the information about vacation time) might give the receiver a bargaining chip. Knowing what the sender really wants might let you lowball on other aspects of the negotiation. So, the employer can then grant the vacation time, and perhaps not have to offer the higher salary. The graph here depicts the results of this experiment, in which success in the negotiation was measured in the percentage of a pool of money that could be earned.

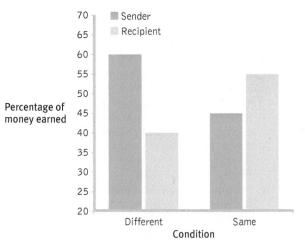

a. Based on this graph, what type of ANOVA did the researchers conduct?

b. Does it seem as if there's a main effect of role in the negotiations (sender or receiver)? If yes, explain the effect in your own words. If not, explain your answer.

c. Does it seem as if there's a main effect of type of information provided? If yes, explain the effect in your own words? If not, explain your answer.

d. Describe the interaction in your own words. Is this a quantitative interaction or a qualitative interaction? Explain your answer.

e. Based on what you learned about graphing in Chapter 3, explain an important problem with the y-axis.

Putting It All Together

14.48 Skepticism, self-interest, and two-way ANOVA: A study on motivated skepticism examined whether participants were more likely to be skeptical when it served their self-interest (Ditto & Lopez, 1992). Ninety-three participants completed a fictitious medical test that told them they had high levels of a certain enzyme, TAA. Participants were randomly assigned to be told either that high levels of TAA had potentially unhealthy consequences or potentially healthy consequences. They were also randomly assigned to complete a dependent measure before or after the TAA test. The dependent measure assessed their perception of the accuracy of the TAA test on a scale of 1 (very inaccurate) to 9 (very accurate). Ditto and Lopez found the following means for those who completed the dependent measure before taking the TAA test: unhealthy result, 6.6; healthy result, 6.9. They found the following means for those who completed the dependent measure after taking the TAA test: unhealthy result, 5.6; healthy result, 7.3. From their ANOVA, they reported statistics for two findings. For the main effect of test outcome, they reported the following statistic: $F(1,73) = 7.74, p < 0.01$. For the interaction of test outcome and timing of the dependent measure, they reported the following statistic: $F(1, 73) = 4.01, p < 0.05$.

a. State the independent variables and their levels. State the dependent variable.

b. What kind of ANOVA would be used to analyze these data? State the name using the original language as well as the more specific language.

c. Use the more specific language of ANOVA to calculate the number of cells in this research design.

d. Draw a table of cell means, marginal means, and the grand mean. Assume that equal numbers of participants were assigned to each cell (even though this was not the case in the actual study).

e. Describe the significant main effect in your own words.

f. Draw a bar graph that depicts the main effect.

g. Why is the main effect misleading by itself?

h. Is the main effect qualified by a statistically significant interaction? Explain. Describe the interaction in your own words.

i. Draw a bar graph that depicts the interaction. Include lines that connect the tops of the bars and show the pattern of the interaction.

j. Is this a quantitative or qualitative interaction? Explain.

k. Change the cell mean for the participants who had a healthy test outcome and completed the dependent measure before the TAA test so that this is now a qualitative interaction.

l. Draw a bar graph depicting the pattern that includes the new cell mean.

m. Change the cell mean for the participants who had a healthy test outcome and completed the dependent measure before the TAA test so that there is now no interaction.

n. Draw a bar graph that depicts the pattern that includes the new cell mean.

14.49 **Feedback and ANOVA:** Stacey Finkelstein and Ayelet Fishbach (2012) examined the impact of feedback in the learning process. The following is an excerpt from their abstract: "This article explores what feedback people seek and respond to. We predict and find a shift from positive to negative feedback as people gain expertise. We document this shift in a variety of domains, including feedback on language acquisition, pursuit of environmental causes, and use of consumer products. Across these domains, novices sought and responded to positive feedback, and experts sought and responded to negative feedback" (p. 22).

a. Based on the abstract, what are the independent variables and what are their levels?

b. What are possible dependent variables, based on the description in the abstract?

c. The researchers conducted several experiments, one of which examined students in beginning and advanced French classes. Here is the result of one analysis: "The analysis also yielded the predicted expertise × feedback interaction ($F(1,79) = 7.31, p < .01$)." Is this interaction statistically significant? Explain your answer.

d. What important statistic is missing from their report? Why would it be helpful to include this statistic?

e. The results in part (c) are represented by the graph below. We would, of course, have to conduct additional analyses to know exactly which bars are significantly different from each other. That said, what does the overall pattern seem to indicate for this analysis?

f. How would you redesign this graph in line with what you learned in Chapter 3? Give at least two specific suggestions.

TERMS

interaction (p. 366)
two-way ANOVA (p. 367)
factorial ANOVA (p. 367)
factor (p. 367)
cell (p. 369)
main effect (p. 369)

quantitative interaction (p. 372)
qualitative interaction (p. 372)
marginal mean (p. 373)
mixed-design ANOVA (p. 391)
multivariate analysis of variance
   (MANOVA) (p. 391)

analysis of covariance (ANCOVA) (p. 391)
covariate (p. 391)
multivariate analysis of covariance
   (MANCOVA) (p. 391)

FORMULAS

$df_{rows} = N_{rows} - 1$ (p. 383)

$df_{columns} = N_{columns} - 1$ (p. 383)

$df_{interaction} = (df_{rows})(df_{columns})$ (p. 383)

$df_{within} = df_{cell\ 1} + df_{cell\ 2}$
$\quad + df_{cell\ 3} \ldots + df_{cell\ last}$ (p. 383)

$df_{total} = N_{total} - 1$ (p. 384)

$SS_{total} = \Sigma(X - GM)^2$
   for each score   (p. 386)

$SS_{between(rows)} = \Sigma(M_{row} - GM)^2$
   for each score   (p. 386)

$SS_{between(columns)} = \Sigma(M_{column} - GM)^2$
   for each score   (p. 387)

$SS_{within} = \Sigma(X - M_{cell})^2$
   for each score   (p. 387)

$SS_{between(interaction)} = SS_{total} -$
   $(SS_{between(rows)} + SS_{between(columns)}$
   $+ SS_{within})$ (p. 388)

$R^2_{rows} = \dfrac{SS_{rows}}{(SS_{total} - SS_{columns} - SS_{interaction})}$
   (p. 390)

$R^2_{columns} = \dfrac{SS_{columns}}{(SS_{total} - SS_{rows} - SS_{interaction})}$
   (p. 398)

$R^2_{interaction} = \dfrac{SS_{interaction}}{(SS_{total} - SS_{rows} - SS_{columns})}$
   (p. 398)

Correlation

The Meaning of Correlation

The Characteristics of Correlation

Correlation Is Not Causation

The Pearson Correlation Coefficient

Calculating the Pearson
  Correlation Coefficient

Hypothesis Testing with the Pearson
  Correlation Coefficient

Applying Correlation in Psychometrics

Reliability

Validity

Next Steps: Partial Correlation

BEFORE YOU GO ON

- **You should know the difference between correlational research and experimental research (Chapter 1).**

- **You should understand how to calculate the deviations of scores from a mean (Chapter 4).**

- **You should understand the concept of sum of squares (Chapter 4).**

- **You should understand the six steps of hypothesis testing (Chapter 7).**

- **You should understand the concept of effect size (Chapter 8).**

Eric Audras/PhotoAlto/Alamy

A Correlation Between Cheating and Grades Does cheating lead to poorer grades? Researchers can't say whether cheating causes lower grades, but there is a negative correlation between cheating and final exam grade.

John Snow's map of the London cholera epidemic (Chapter 1) revealed a *correlation*, a systematic association (or relation) between two variables. Researchers from the Massachusetts Institute of Technology (MIT) used a correlation to reveal the dangers of academic cheating (Palazzo, Lee, Warnakulasooriya, & Pritchard, 2010). They compared the final exam scores of 428 physics students with how frequently they had copied computerized homework assignments from classmates. They assumed that the minority of students who finished their homework within a ridiculously short time—less than 10% of them—had cheated. You might expect cheating to boost grades—after all, that is the point of cheating, isn't it? But you'd be wrong. The more a student cheated during the semester (variable 1), the lower his or her final exam grade (variable 2).

What might be going on here? Students' preexisting abilities in math and physics were not correlated with cheating, so these were not weak students who were also incompetent at cheating. Their computerized homework revealed a correlation that suggested another possible answer: Cheaters procrastinated by starting their homework too late to complete it without cheating. Did they have outside jobs, suffer from anxiety, or have other commitments that cut into homework time? *Correlations can't tell us which explanation is right*, but they can force us to think about the possible explanations.

This chapter demonstrates how to (a) assess the direction and size of a correlation, (b) identify limitations of correlation, and (c) calculate the most common form of correlation: *r*, the Pearson correlation coefficient. We then use the six steps of hypothesis testing to determine whether a correlation is statistically significant.

The Meaning of Correlation

A correlation is exactly what its name suggests: a co-relation between two variables. Lots of everyday observations are co-related: junk food eaten and body fat, distance driven and the wear on tires, air conditioner usage and the electric bill. If you can measure any two variables, you can calculate the degree to which they are co-related.

The Characteristics of Correlation

A **correlation coefficient** *is a statistic that quantifies a relation between two variables.* In this chapter, we learn how to quantify a relation—that is, we learn to calculate a correlation coefficient—when the data are linearly related. A linear relation means that the data form an overall pattern through which it would make sense to draw a straight line—that is, the dots on a scatterplot are roughly clustered around a line, rather than, say, a curve. You can actually see—and understand—the data story with just a glance. There are three main characteristics of the correlation coefficient.

1. The correlation coefficient can be either positive or negative.
2. The correlation coefficient always falls between −1.00 and 1.00.
3. It is the strength (also called the *magnitude*) of the coefficient, not its sign, that indicates how large it is.

The first important characteristic of the correlation coefficient is that it can be either positive or negative. A positive correlation has a positive sign (e.g., +0.32, or

- A **correlation coefficient** is a statistic that quantifies a relation between two variables.

- A **positive correlation** is an association between two variables such that participants with high scores on one variable tend to have high scores on the other variable as well, and those with low scores on one variable tend to have low scores on the other variable.

- A **negative correlation** is an association between two variables in which participants with high scores on one variable tend to have low scores on the other variable.

more typically, just 0.32), and a negative correlation has a negative sign (e.g., −0.32). *A **positive correlation** is an association between two variables such that participants with high scores on one variable tend to have high scores on the other variable as well, and those with low scores on one variable tend to have low scores on the other variable.*

Contrary to what some people think, when participants with low scores on one variable tend to have low scores on the other, it is *not* a negative correlation. A positive correlation describes a situation in which participants tend to have *similar* scores, with respect to the mean and spread, on both variables—whether both scores are low, medium, or high. The line that summarizes a scatterplot with a positive correlation slopes upward and to the right.

MASTERING THE CONCEPT

15-1: The sign indicates the direction of the correlation, positive or negative. A positive correlation occurs when people who are high on one variable tend to be high on the other as well, and people who are low on one variable tend to be low on the other. A negative correlation occurs when people who are high on one variable tend to be low on the other.

EXAMPLE 15.1

The scatterplot in Figure 15.1 shows a positive correlation between the words infants hear and their vocabulary two years later. These data are based on actual findings by researcher Rochelle Newman and her colleagues (2015). (The means and standard deviations are similar, although the overall correlation is somewhat higher than in the original research.) The *x*-axis reflects the number of different words infants' mothers used during a 15-minute play session when their children were younger than 7 months. The *y*-axis reflects the child's vocabulary size at age 2.

For example, the dot in the green diamond indicates a child whose mother used only 91 different words when she or he was an infant and had a vocabulary of 132 words at age 2; this child was lower than average on both scores. The dot in the red diamond is for a child who heard 469 different words as an infant during the same 15-minute play session, and then had a vocabulary of 353 different words at age 2; this child is higher than average on both scores. This makes sense because a good deal of research indicates that children who hear more words from their parents develop better language skills, on average. ●

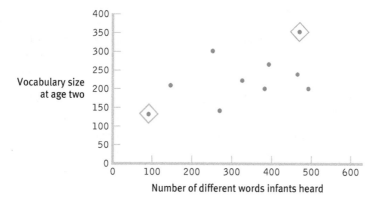

FIGURE 15-1

A Positive Correlation

These data points depict a positive correlation between the diversity of vocabulary infants hear from their mothers and their vocabulary at age two. Those who hear more different words at a very young age tend to have bigger vocabularies at age two, and those who hear fewer different words tend to have smaller vocabularies later on.

EXAMPLE 15.2

The scatterplot in Figure 15-2 shows the negative correlation of −0.43 between cheating and final exam grade for the MIT study. *A **negative correlation** is an association between two variables in which participants with high scores on one variable tend to have low scores on the other variable.* The line that summarizes a scatterplot with a negative correlation slopes downward and to the right. Each dot represents one person's values on both variables. The proportion of homework copied during the semester is on the horizontal

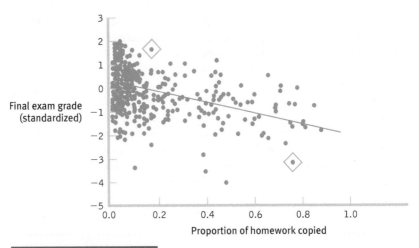

A Negative Correlation

In this negative correlation from the MIT study, those who cheat more tend to have a lower final grade; those who cheat less tend to have a higher final grade.

x-axis, and the final exam grade (converted to standardized *z* scores) is on the vertical *y*-axis. For example, the dot in the green diamond indicates a student who copied less than 0.2, or 20%, of the homework, and scored almost 2 standard deviations above the mean on the final exam. The dot in the red diamond indicates a student who copied almost 80% of the homework and scored more than 3 standard deviations below the mean on the final exam. Even though most dots are not as extreme as the pattern of the two students we just described, the overall trend is for students who copied more to perform more poorly on the final—a linear relation. ●

A second important characteristic of the correlation coefficient is that it always falls between −1.00 and 1.00. Both −1.00 and 1.00 are perfect correlations. If we calculate a coefficient that is outside this range, we have made a mistake in the calculations. A correlation coefficient of 1.00 indicates a perfect positive correlation; every point on the scatterplot falls on one line, as seen in the imaginary relation between absences and exam grades depicted in Figure 15-3. Higher scores on one variable are associated with higher scores on the other variable, and lower scores on one variable are associated with lower scores on the other variable. When a correlation coefficient is either −1.00 or 1.00, knowing somebody's score on one variable tells you exactly what that person's score is on the other variable. They are perfectly related.

15-2: A correlation coefficient always falls between −1.00 and 1.00. The size of the coefficient, not its sign, indicates how large it is.

A Perfect Positive Correlation

Every dot falls exactly on a straight line that moves up and to the right. This perfect, positive correlation is not real. More absences almost certainly don't lead to higher grades—and certainly they don't for every student.

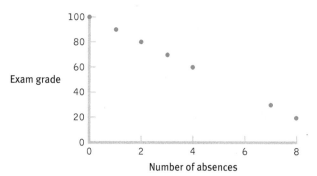

FIGURE 15-4

A Perfect Negative Correlation

When every pair of scores falls on the same line on a scatterplot and higher scores on one variable are associated with lower scores on the other variable, there is a perfect negative correlation of −1.00, a situation that almost never happens in real life.

A correlation coefficient of −1.00 indicates a perfect negative correlation. Every point on the scatterplot falls on one line, as seen in the imaginary relation between absences and exam grades depicted in Figure 15-4, but now higher scores on one variable go with lower scores on the other variable. As with a perfect positive correlation, knowing somebody's score on one variable tells you that person's exact score on the other variable. A correlation of 0.00 falls right in the middle of the two extremes and indicates no correlation—no association between the two variables.

The third useful characteristic of the correlation coefficient is that its sign—positive or negative—indicates only the direction of the association, not the strength or size of the association. So a correlation coefficient of −0.35 is the same size as one of 0.35. A correlation coefficient of −0.67 is larger than one of 0.55. Don't be fooled by a negative sign; the sign indicates the *direction* of the relation, not the *strength*.

The strength of the correlation is determined by how close to "perfect" the data points are. The closer the data points are to the imaginary line that one could draw through them, the closer the correlation is to being perfect (either −1.00 or 1.00), and the stronger the relation between the two variables. The farther the points are from this imaginary line, the farther the correlation is from being perfect (so, closer to 0.00), and the weaker the relation between the two variables.

The scores in a positive correlation move up and down together, the same way the mercury rises or falls in a thermometer as the temperature goes up or down. The scores in a negative correlation move up and down in opposition to each other, as though on a teeter-totter. Knowing the direction of a correlation allows us to use a person's score on one variable to predict his or her score on another variable. Fortunately, the correlation statistic lets us identify both the direction and the strength of the relation between two variables.

How big does a correlation coefficient have to be to be considered important? As he did for effect sizes, Jacob Cohen (1988) published standards, shown in Table 15-1, to help us interpret the correlation coefficient. Very few findings in the behavioral sciences have correlation coefficients of 0.50 or larger because any particular outcome—a student's exam grade, for example—is likely influenced by many variables. A student's exam grade is likely influenced by absences from class, attention level, hours of studying, interest in the subject matter, IQ, and many other variables. So, the correlation of −0.43 between cheating and exam grades found among MIT students is a large correlation for the behavioral sciences.

The Teeter-Tottering Negative Correlation When two variables are negatively correlated, a high score on one variable indicates a likely low score on the other variable—just like children on a teeter-totter.

TABLE 15-1 How Strong Is an Association?

Cohen (1988) published guidelines to help researchers determine the strength of a correlation from the correlation coefficient. In behavioral science research, however, it is extremely unusual to have a correlation as high as 0.50, and some researchers have disputed the utility of Cohen's conventions for many behavioral science contexts.

Size of the Correlation	Correlation Coefficient
Small	0.10
Medium	0.30
Large	0.50

FIGURE 15-5

Three Possible Causal Explanations for a Correlation

Any correlation can be explained in one of several ways. The first variable, (A), might cause the second variable, (B). Or the reverse could be true—the second variable, (B), could cause the first variable, (A). Finally, a third variable, (C), could cause both (A) and (B). In fact, there could be many "third" variables.

MASTERING THE CONCEPT

15-3: Just because two variables are related doesn't mean one causes the other. It could be that the first causes the second, the second causes the first, or a third variable causes both. Correlation does not indicate causation.

Correlation Is Not Causation

You need to understand what correlations do *not* reveal about the relation between variables. Correlations *only* provide clues to causality; they do *not* demonstrate or test for causality; they *only* quantify the strength and direction of the relation between variables. Your appreciation for what correlations do *not* reveal suggests that you are thinking scientifically. For example, we know that there was a strong negative correlation in the MIT study between cheating and final exam grade; it is not unreasonable to think that cheating causes bad grades. However, there are three possible reasons for this observed correlation.

First, variable A (cheating) could cause variable B (poor grades). Second, variable B (poor grades) could cause variable A (cheating). Third, variable C (some other influence) could be causing the correlation between variable A (cheating) and variable B (poor grades). You can think of these three possibilities as the A-B-C model (Figure 15-5).

Knowing that correlation does *not* imply causation coaxes our brains into thinking of alternate explanations. The researchers found that physics and math ability did not correlate with cheating; so that's an unlikely answer. But we also mentioned working, anxiety, and other time commitments. You can probably think of even more possibilities. Never confuse correlation with causation.

CHECK YOUR LEARNING

Reviewing the Concepts

> A correlation coefficient is a statistic that quantifies a relation between two variables.

> The correlation coefficient always falls between -1.00 and 1.00.

> When two variables are related such that people with high scores on one tend to have high scores on the other and people with low scores on one tend to have low scores on the other, we describe the variables as positively correlated.

> When two variables are related such that people with high scores on one tend to have low scores on the other, we describe the variables as negatively correlated.

> When two variables are not related, there is no correlation and they have a correlation coefficient close to 0.

> The strength of a correlation, captured by the number value of the coefficient, is independent of its sign. Cohen established standards for evaluating the strength of association.

> Correlation is not equivalent to causation. In fact, a correlation does not help us decide the merits of different causal explanations.

> When two variables are correlated, this association might occur because the first variable, (A), causes the second, (B); or because the second variable, (B), causes the first, (A). Alternately, a third variable, (C), could cause both of the correlated variables, (A) and (B).

Clarifying the Concepts	**15-1**	There are three main characteristics of the correlation coefficient. What are they?
	15-2	Why doesn't correlation indicate causation?

Calculating the Statistics	**15-3**	Use Cohen's guidelines to describe the strength of the following coefficients:

a. −0.60

b. 0.35

c. 0.04

15-4 Draw a hypothetical scatterplot to depict the following correlation coefficients:

a. −0.60

b. 0.35

c. 0.04

Applying the Concepts **15-5** A writer for *Runner's World* magazine debated the merits of running while listening to music (Seymour, 2006). The writer, an avid iPod user, interviewed a clinical psychologist, whose response to the debate about whether to listen to music while running was: "I like to do what the great ones do and try to emulate that. What are the Kenyans doing?"

Let's say a researcher conducted a study in which he determined the correlation between the percentage of a country's marathon runners who train while using a portable music device and the average marathon finishing time for that country's runners. (Note that in this case the participants are countries, not people.) Let's say the researcher finds a strong positive correlation. That is, the more of a country's runners who train with music, the longer the average marathon finishing time. Remember, in a marathon, a longer time is bad. So this fictional finding is that training with music is associated with slower marathon finishing times; the United States, for example, would have a higher percentage of music use and higher (slower) finishing times than Kenya.

Using the A-B-C model, provide three possible explanations for this finding.

Solutions to these Check Your Learning questions can be found in Appendix D.

The Pearson Correlation Coefficient

The most widely used correlation coefficient is the ***Pearson correlation coefficient***, *a statistic that quantifies a linear relation between two scale variables.* In other words, a single number is used to describe the direction and strength of the relation between two variables when their overall pattern indicates a straight-line relation. The Pearson correlation coefficient is symbolized by the italic letter *r* when it is a statistic based on sample data and by the Greek letter ρ (written as "rho" and pronounced "row," even though it looks a bit like the Latin letter *p*). We use ρ when we're referring to the population parameter for the correlation coefficient, such as when we're writing the hypotheses for significance testing.

Calculating the Pearson Correlation Coefficient

The correlation coefficient can be used as a descriptive statistic that describes the direction and strength of an association between two variables. However, it can also be used as an inferential statistic that relies on a hypothesis test to determine whether the

● The **Pearson correlation coefficient** is a statistic that quantifies a linear relation between two scale variables.

correlation coefficient is significantly different from 0 (no correlation). In this section, we construct a scatterplot from the data and learn how to calculate the correlation coefficient. Then we walk through the steps of hypothesis testing.

EXAMPLE 15.3

Every couple of semesters, we have a student who avows that she does not have to attend statistics classes regularly to do well because she can learn it all from the book. What do you think? Table 15-2 displays the data for 10 students in one of our statistics classes. The second column shows the number of absences over the semester (out of 29 classes total) for each student, and the third column shows each student's final exam grade.

Let's begin with a visual exploration of the scatterplot in Figure 15-6. The data, overall, have a pattern through which we could imagine drawing a straight line, so it makes sense to use the Pearson correlation coefficient. Look more closely at the scatterplot. Are the dots clustered closely around the imaginary line? If they are, then the correlation is probably close to 1.00 or −1.00; if they are not, then the correlation is probably closer to 0.00.

TABLE 15-2 Is Skipping Class Related to Statistics Exam Grades?

Here are the scores for 10 students on two scale variables: number of absences from class in one semester and exam grade.

Student	Absences	Exam Grade
1	4	82
2	2	98
3	2	76
4	3	68
5	1	84
6	0	99
7	4	67
8	8	58
9	7	50
10	3	78

FIGURE 15-6

Always Start with a Scatterplot

Let your eyes do the work! Look at the scatterplot *before* calculating a correlation coefficient. Do the dots appear to form a straight line? Do they flow up and to the right (positive) or down and to the right (negative)? The dots in this scatterplot cluster tightly around an imaginary straight line that goes down and to the right so the correlation will probably be fairly close to −1.00.

A positive correlation results when a high score (above the mean) on one variable tends to indicate a high score (also above the mean) on the other variable. A negative correlation results when a high score (above the mean) on one variable tends to indicate a low score (below the mean) on the other variable. We can determine whether an individual falls above or below the mean by calculating deviations from the mean for each score. If participants tend to have two positive deviations (both scores above the mean) or two negative deviations (both scores below the mean), then the two variables are likely to be positively correlated. If participants tend to have one positive deviation (above the mean) and one negative deviation (below the mean), then the two variables are likely to be negatively correlated. That's a big part of how the formula for the correlation coefficient does its work.

Think about why calculating deviations from the mean makes sense. With a positive correlation, high scores are above the mean and so would have positive deviations. The product of a pair of high scores would be positive. Low scores are below the mean and would have negative deviations. The product of a pair of low scores would also be positive. When we calculate a correlation coefficient, part of the process involves adding up the products of the deviations. If most of these are positive, we get a positive correlation coefficient.

Let's consider a negative correlation. High scores, which are above the mean, would have positive deviations. Low scores, which are below the mean, would have negative deviations. The product of one positive deviation and one negative deviation would be negative. If most of the products of the deviations are negative, we would get a negative correlation coefficient.

The process we just described is the calculation of the numerator of the correlation coefficient. Table 15-3 shows us the calculations. The first column has the number of absences for each student. The second column shows the deviations from the mean, 3.40. The third column has the exam grade for each student. The fourth column shows the deviations from the mean for that variable, 76.00. The fifth column shows the products of the deviations. Below the fifth column, we see the sum of the products of the deviations, -304.0.

As we see in Table 15-3, the pairs of scores tend to fall on either side of the mean—that is, for each student, a negative deviation on one score tends to indicate a positive

TABLE 15-3 Calculating the Numerator of the Correlation Coefficient

Absences (X)	($X - M_X$)	Exam Grade (Y)	($Y - M_Y$)	($X - M_X$)($Y - M_Y$)
4	0.6	82	6	3.6
2	-1.4	98	22	-30.8
2	-1.4	76	0	0.0
3	-0.4	68	-8	3.2
1	-2.4	84	8	-19.2
0	-3.4	99	23	-78.2
4	0.6	67	-9	-5.4
8	4.6	58	-18	-82.8
7	3.6	50	-26	-93.6
3	-0.4	78	2	-0.8

$M_X = 3.400$ $\qquad$ $M_Y = 76.000$ $\qquad$ $\Sigma[(X - M_X)(Y - M_Y)] = -304.0$

deviation on the other score. For example, student 6 was never absent, so she has a score of 0, which is well below the mean, and she got a 99 on the exam, well above the mean. On the other hand, student 9 was absent 7 times, well above the mean, and she only got a 50 on the exam, well below the mean. So most of the products of the deviations are negative, and when we sum the products, we get a negative total. This indicates a negative correlation.

You might have noticed that this number, -304.0, is not between -1.00 and 1.00. The problem is that this number is influenced by two factors—sample size and variability. First, the more people in the sample, the more deviations there are to contribute to the sum. Second, if the scores in the study were more variable, the deviations would be larger and so would the sum of the products. So we have to correct for these two factors in the denominator.

It makes sense that we would have to correct for variability. In Chapter 6, we learned that z scores provide an important function in statistics by allowing us to standardize. You may remember that the formula for the z score that we first learned was $z = \dfrac{(X - M)}{SD}$. In the calculations in the numerator for correlation, we already subtracted the mean from the scores when we created deviations, but we didn't divide by the standard deviation. If we correct for variability in the denominator, that takes care of one of the two factors for which we have to correct.

But we also have to correct for sample size. You may remember that when we calculate standard deviation, the last two steps are (1) dividing the sum of squared deviations by the sample size, N, to remove the influence of the sample size and to calculate variance; and (2) taking the square root of the variance to get the standard deviation. So to factor in sample size along with standard deviation (which we just mentioned allows us to factor in variability), we can go backward in the calculations. If we multiply variance by sample size, we get the sum of squared deviations, or sum of squares. Because of this, the denominator of the correlation coefficient is based on the sums of squares for both variables. To make the denominator match the numerator, we multiply the two sums of squares together, and then we take their square root, as we would with standard deviation. Table 15-4 shows the calculations for the sum of squares for the two variables, absences and exam grades.

TABLE 15-4 Calculating the Denominator of the Correlation Coefficient

Absences (X)	$(X - M_X)$	$(X - M_X)^2$	Exam Grade (Y)	$(Y - M_Y)$	$(Y - M_Y)^2$
4	0.6	0.36	82	6	36
2	−1.4	1.96	98	22	484
2	−1.4	1.96	76	0	0
3	−0.4	0.16	68	−8	64
1	−2.4	5.76	84	8	64
0	−3.4	11.56	99	23	529
4	0.6	0.36	67	−9	81
8	4.6	21.16	58	−18	324
7	3.6	12.96	50	−26	676
3	−0.4	0.16	78	2	4
		$\Sigma(X - M_X)^2 = 56.4$			$\Sigma(Y - M_Y)^2 = 2262$

We now have all of the ingredients necessary to calculate the correlation coefficient. Here's the formula:

$$r = \frac{\Sigma[(X - M_X)(Y - M_Y)]}{\sqrt{(SS_X)(SS_Y)}}$$

The numerator is the sum of the products of the deviations for each variable (see Table 15-3).

STEP 1: For each score, calculate the deviation from its mean.

STEP 2: For each participant, multiply the deviations for his or her two scores.

STEP 3: Sum the products of the deviations.

The denominator is the square root of the product of the two sums of squares. The sums of squares calculations are in Table 15-4.

STEP 1: Calculate a sum of squares for each variable.

STEP 2: Multiply the two sums of squares.

STEP 3: Take the square root of the product of the sums of squares.

Let's apply the formula for the correlation coefficient to the data:

$$r = \frac{\Sigma[(X - M_X)(Y - M_Y)]}{\sqrt{(SS_X)(SS_Y)}} = \frac{-304.0}{\sqrt{(56.4)(2262.0)}} = \frac{-304.0}{357.179} = -0.85$$

So the Pearson correlation coefficient, r, is -0.85. This is a very strong negative correlation. If we examine the scatterplot in Figure 15-6 carefully, we notice that there aren't any glaring individual exceptions to this rule. The data tell a consistent story. So what should our students learn from this result? Go to class! ●

Hypothesis Testing with the Pearson Correlation Coefficient

We said earlier that correlation could be used in two ways: (1) as a descriptive statistic to simply describe a relation between two variables *and* (2) as an inferential statistic.

• •

EXAMPLE 15.4

Here we outline the six steps for hypothesis testing with a correlation coefficient. Usually when we conduct hypothesis testing with correlation, we want to test whether a correlation is statistically significantly different from no correlation—an r of 0.

STEP 1: Identify the populations, distribution, and assumptions.

Population 1: Students like those whom we studied in Example 15.3. Population 2: Students for whom there is no correlation between number of absences and exam grade.

The comparison distribution is a distribution of correlations taken from the population, but with the characteristics of our study, such as a sample size of 10. In this case, it is a distribution of all possible correlations between the numbers of absences and exam grades when 10 students are considered.

The first two assumptions are like those for other parametric tests. (1) The data must be randomly selected, or external validity will be limited. In this case, we do not know how the data were selected, so we should generalize with caution. (2) The underlying population distributions for the two variables must be approximately normal. In our study, it's difficult to tell if the distribution is normal because we have so few data points.

The third assumption is specific to correlation: Each variable should vary equally, no matter the magnitude of the other variable. That is, number of absences should show the same amount of variability at each level of exam grade; conversely, exam grade should show the same amount of variability at each number of absences. You can get a sense of this by looking at the scatterplot in Figure 15-7. In our study, it's hard to determine whether the amount of variability is the same for each variable across all levels of the other variable because we have so few data points. But it seems as if there's variability of between 10 and 20 points on exam grade at each number of absences. The center of that variability decreases as we increase in number of absences, but the range stays roughly the same. It also seems that there's variability of between two and three absences at each exam grade. Again, the center of that variability decreases as exam grade increases, but the range stays roughly the same.

> **STEP 2: State the null and research hypotheses.**

Null hypothesis: There is no correlation between number of absences and exam grade—$H_0: \rho = 0$. Research hypothesis: There is a correlation between number of absences and exam grade—$H_1: \rho \neq 0$. (*Note:* We use the Greek letter rho because hypotheses are about population parameters.)

> **STEP 3: Determine the characteristics of the comparison distribution.**

The comparison distribution is an r distribution with degrees of freedom calculated by subtracting 2 from the sample size, which for Pearson correlation is the number of participants rather than the number of scores:

$$df_r = N - 2$$

In our study, degrees of freedom are calculated as follows:

$$df_r = N - 2 = 10 - 2 = 8$$

So the comparison distribution is an r distribution with 8 degrees of freedom.

FIGURE 15-7

Using a Scatterplot to Examine the Assumptions

We can use a scatterplot to see whether one variable varies equally at each level of the other variable. With only 10 data points, we can't be certain. But this scatterplot suggests a variability of between 10 and 20 points on exam grade at each number of absences and a variability of between two and three absences at each exam grade.

STEP 4: Determine the critical values, or cutoffs.

Now we can look up the critical values in the r table in Appendix B. Like the z table and the t table, the r table includes only positive values. For a two-tailed test, we take the negative and positive versions of the critical test statistic indicated in the table. The critical values for an r distribution with 8 degrees of freedom for a two-tailed test with a p level of 0.05 are -0.632 and 0.632.

STEP 5: Calculate the test statistic.

We already calculated the test statistic, r, in the preceding section. It is -0.85.

STEP 6: Make a decision.

The test statistic, $r = -0.85$, is larger in magnitude than the critical value of -0.632. We can reject the null hypothesis and conclude that number of absences and exam grade seem to be negatively correlated. ●

MASTERING THE FORMULA

15-2: When conducting hypothesis testing for the Pearson correlation coefficient, r, we calculate degrees of freedom by subtracting 2 from the sample size. For Pearson correlation, the sample size is the number of participants, not the number of scores. The formula is:

$$df_r = N - 2.$$

CHECK YOUR LEARNING

Reviewing the Concepts

> The Pearson correlation coefficient allows us to quantify the relations that we observe.

> Before we calculate a Pearson correlation coefficient, we should always construct a scatterplot to be sure the two variables are linearly related.

> The Pearson correlation coefficient is calculated in three basic steps. (1) Calculate the deviation of each score from its mean, multiply the two deviations for each person, and sum the products of the deviations. (2) Calculate a sum of squares for each variable, multiply the sums of squares, and take the square root. (3) Divide the sum from step 1 by the square root in step 2.

> We use the six steps of hypothesis testing to determine whether the correlation coefficient is statistically significantly different from 0 on an r distribution.

Clarifying the Concepts **15-6** Define the Pearson correlation coefficient.

15-7 The denominator of the correlation equation corrects for which two issues present in the calculation of the numerator?

Calculating the Statistics **15-8** Create a scatterplot for the following data:

Variable A	Variable B
8.0	14.0
7.0	13.0
6.0	10.0
5.0	9.5
4.0	8.0
5.5	9.0
6.0	12.0
8.0	11.0

15-9 Calculate the correlation coefficient for the data provided in the previous Check Your Learning exercise.

continued on next page

Solutions to these Check Your Learning questions can be found in Appendix D.

Applying the Concepts   15-10

According to social learning theory, children exposed to aggressive behavior, including family violence, are more likely to engage in aggressive behavior than are children who do not witness such violence. Let's assume the data you worked with in Check Your Learning 15-8 and 15-9 represent exposure to violence as the first variable, (A), and aggressive behavior as the second variable, (B). For both variables, higher values indicate higher levels, either of exposure to violence or of incidents of aggressive behavior. You computed the correlation coefficient, step 5 in hypothesis testing, in the previous Check Your Learning exercise. Now, complete steps 1, 2, 3, 4, and 6 of hypothesis testing.

- **Psychometrics** is the branch of statistics used in the development of tests and measures.

- **Psychometricians** are the statisticians and psychologists who develop tests and measures.

- **Test–retest reliability** refers to whether the scale being used provides consistent information every time the test is taken.

Applying Correlation in Psychometrics

Here's an in-demand career available to students of the behavioral sciences: *psychometrics, which is the branch of statistics used in the development of tests and measures.* Not surprisingly, *the statisticians and psychologists who develop tests and measures are called psychometricians.* Psychometricians use the statistical procedures referred to in this textbook, particularly those for which correlation forms the mathematical backbone. Psychometricians make sure that elections are fair, they test for cultural biases in standardized tests, they identify high-achieving employees, and they make a wide range of social contributions—and we don't have nearly enough of them. The *New York Times* reported (Herszenhorn, 2006) a "critical shortage" of such experts and intense competition for the few who are available—who are being offered U.S. salaries as high as $200,000 a year! Psychometricians use correlation to examine two important aspects of the development of measures—reliability and validity.

Reliability

In Chapter 1, we defined a reliable measure as one that is consistent. For example, if we measure shyness, then a reliable measure leads to nearly the same score every time a person takes the shyness test. One particular type of reliability is test–retest reliability. *Test–retest reliability refers to whether the scale being used provides consistent information every time the test is taken.* To calculate a measure's test–retest reliability, the measure is given twice to the *same sample*, typically with a delay between tests. The participants' scores for the first time they complete the measure are correlated with their scores for the second time they complete the measure. A large correlation indicates that the measure yields the same results consistently over time—that is, good test–retest reliability (Cortina, 1993).

Another way to measure the reliability of a test is by assessing its internal consistency in order to verify that all the items were measuring the same idea (DeVellis, 1991). Initially, researchers measured internal consistency via *split-half* reliability, correlating the odd-numbered items (1, 3, 5, etc.) with the even-numbered items (2, 4, 6, etc.). If this correlation coefficient is large, then the test has high internal consistency. The odd–even approach is easy to understand, but computers now allow researchers to take a more sophisticated approach. A computer can calculate the average of *every possible* split-half reliability.

Correlation and Reliability Correlation is used by psychometricians to help professional sports teams assess the reliability of athletic performance, such as how fast a pitcher can throw a baseball.

AP Photo/Michael Manning

Consider a 10-item measure. A computer can calculate correlations between the odd-numbered items and even-numbered items, between the first 5 items and the last 5 items, between items 1, 2, 4, 8, 10 and items 3, 5, 6, 7, 9, and so on for every combination of two groups of 5 items. The computer can then calculate what is essentially (although not always exactly) the average of all possible split-half correlations (Cortina, 1993). The average of these is called *coefficient alpha* (or *Cronbach's alpha*, in honor of the statistician who developed it). ***Coefficient alpha** (symbolized as α) is a commonly used estimate of a test or measure's reliability and is calculated by taking the average of all possible split-half correlations.* Coefficient alpha is used frequently across a wide range of fields, including psychology, education, sociology, political science, medicine, economics, criminology, and anthropology (Cortina, 1993). (Note that this alpha is different from the *p* level.)

When developing a new scale or measure, how high should its reliability be? It would not be worth using a scale in research if the scale's coefficient alpha is less than 0.80. However, if we are using a scale to make decisions about individuals—for example, if we are using a standardized academic test to place a child in the right class or a measure of depressive symptoms to determine treatment—we should aim for a coefficient alpha of 0.90 or even of 0.95 (Nunnally & Bernstein, 1994). We want high reliability when we are using a test that directly affects people's lives—but the test also needs to be valid.

Validity

In Chapter 1, we defined a valid measure as one that assesses what it was designed or intended to assess. Many researchers consider validity to be the most important concept in the field of psychometrics (e.g., Nunnally & Bernstein, 1994). It can be a great deal more work to measure validity than reliability, however, so that work is not always done. In fact, it is quite possible to have a reliable test, one that measures a variable, such as shyness, consistently over time and is internally consistent but is still not valid. Just because the items on a test all measure the same thing doesn't mean that they're measuring what we want them to measure or what we think they are measuring.

For example, *Cosmopolitan* magazine often has quizzes that claim to assess readers' relationships with their boyfriends. If you've ever taken one of these quizzes, you might wonder whether some of the quiz items actually measure what the quiz suggests. One quiz, titled "Is He Devoted to You?," asks "Be honest: Do you ever worry that he might cheat on you?" Does this item assess a man's devotion to his partner or his partner's jealousy? Another item asks: "When you introduced him to your closest friends, he said:" and then offers three options—(1) "I've heard so much about all of you! So, how'd you become friends?" (2) "'Hi,' then silence— he looked a bit bored." (3) "'Nice to meet you' with a big smile." Does this measure his devotion or his social skills? Such a quiz might be reliable (you'd consistently get the same score), but it might not be a valid measure of a man's devotion to his partner. Devotion, jealousy, and social skills are different concepts.

It takes a psychometrician who understands correlation to test the validity of such measures. Typically, a psychometrician finds other measures with which to correlate the new measure. For instance, a new scale to measure

● **Coefficient alpha**, symbolized as α, is a commonly used estimate of a test or measure's reliability and is calculated by taking the average of all possible split-half correlations; sometimes called *Cronbach's alpha*.

MASTERING THE CONCEPT

15-6: Correlation is used to calculate reliability either through test–retest reliability or through a measure of internal consistency such as coefficient alpha.

MASTERING THE CONCEPT

15-7: Correlation is used to calculate validity, often by correlating a new measure with existing measures known to assess the variable of interest.

Spencer Grant/PhotoEdit

Validity and Personality Quizzes
Correlation also can help establish the validity of a personality test—a more difficult task than establishing reliability. Magazine publishers and Web sites probably never check on the reliability or validity of the quizzes they develop. Think of them as mere entertainment.

anxiety might be correlated with an existing measure known to be valid, or with physiological measures of anxiety such as heart rate. If the new anxiety measure correlates with other measures, this is evidence of its validity.

Here's another example concerning validity. In a groundbreaking study on affirmative action in higher education, researchers studied the success of more than 35,000 black and white students who attended 1 of 28 highly selective universities (Bowen & Bok, 2000). When determining validity, it is important that we consider how we will operationalize the variable of interest—here, success.

In this study, the researchers first considered the obvious criteria to operationalize success: these students' future graduate education and career achievement. Their findings debunked the myth that black graduates of such institutions did not achieve the successes of their white counterparts. The researchers then went a step further and assessed a success-related criterion very important to the social fabric of a society: graduates' levels of civic and community participation, including political involvement and community service. They found that significantly more black graduates than white graduates of these top institutions were actively involved in their communities. Through an examination of validity, this research changed the nature of the debate on affirmative action—by widening the pool of criteria by which we operationalize success.

Next Steps | Partial Correlation

The higher levels of community participation by black college graduates compared to white college graduates demonstrates why it takes more than just two correlated variables to understand a complicated world. Fortunately, correlation also provides a helpful way—through using *partial correlation*—to think about the relative influence of multiple variables. **Partial correlation** *is a technique that quantifies the degree of association between two variables that remains when the correlations of these two variables with a third variable are mathematically eliminated.*

Earlier in this chapter, we explored the absences and exam grades of a subsample of 10 students from one class. In the entire sample of 26 students, taken from several classes, we found a correlation of −0.44. Students with more absences tended to have a lower exam grade; students with fewer absences tended to have a higher exam grade. We also discussed the many possible third variables that might influence this association. Here's another possibility: the completion of homework assignments. As expected, the correlation between the percentage of completed homework assignments and exam grades was 0.53. Students who completed a higher percentage of homework assignments tended to earn better grades; students who completed a lower percentage of homework assignments tended to earn poorer grades.

The introduction of this third variable also lets us ask about the correlation between the number of absences and the percentage of completed homework assignments. In fact, the correlation between number of absences and percentage of completed homework assignments was −0.51. Students who missed class more tended to have completed less homework; students who missed class less tended to have completed more homework.

MASTERING THE CONCEPT

15-8: Partial correlation allows us to quantify the relation between two variables, controlling for the correlation of each of these variables with a third related variable.

● **Partial correlation** is a technique that quantifies the degree of association between two variables that remains when the correlations of these two variables with a third variable are mathematically eliminated.

Partial correlation enables us to tease apart the relation between two variables when we suspect that there is a third variable at work. How is it done? First of all, we have to measure all three variables and make sure they are all scale variables. Then, we calculate a correlation coefficient that expresses the association between two variables, over and above the association of either of these variables with a third variable. We can let software do the number crunching. But it is important to understand that it is calculating a partial correlation by subtracting the influence of a third variable from the correlation coefficient.

The visual display in Figure 15-8 (called a Venn diagram) represents the three variables: number of absences, percentage of homework assignments completed, and exam grade. The circles overlap to the degree that the variables are associated. Each pair of variables is correlated to the degree to which the two circles that represent them overlap in the diagram. There is a portion of the diagram that represents the association among all three variables—the section where all three circles overlap.

Partial correlation quantifies the correlation between two variables by removing (or correcting for) the overlapping variability of each variable with the third. The idea is that we calculate a correlation of two variables, over and above each of their correlations with the third variable. That allows us to calculate the partial correlation of number of absences and grade, correcting for percentage of homework assignments completed.

Let's describe this same idea visually. In the Venn diagram in Figure 15-8, we calculate the association represented by the letter A—the part left over when B is removed (because that section accounts for the overlap among all three). The partial correlation is -0.23, smaller than the initial Pearson correlation, -0.44, but still fairly substantial.

We also can calculate the partial correlation of percentage of homework assignments and grade, correcting for number of absences. To do this, we calculate the association represented by C in the Venn diagram—the part left over when B is removed. The partial correlation is 0.40, smaller than the initial Pearson correlation coefficient, 0.53, but still substantial. The completion of homework assignments has a strong association with exam grade, even after we've removed the contribution of number of absences.

It appears that the variables of "number of absences" and "percentage of homework assignments completed" both have substantial correlations, independent of each other, with the variable of "exam grade." We can think of it this way: First, for any particular specific number of absences, there is a correlation between homework and grade. Second, for any particular number of completed homework assignments, there is a correlation between absences and grade, although it is not as strong as the first partial correlation (between homework and grade).

What's the message for the students in this class? Coming to class is associated with good exam grades, no matter how many of your homework assignments you complete. And doing homework is even more strongly associated with good exam grades, no matter how often you come to class. We can't know that these behaviors *cause* good exam grades (correlation can never tell us about causality), but these data do suggest that students who come to class and do their homework tend to get the best exam grades.

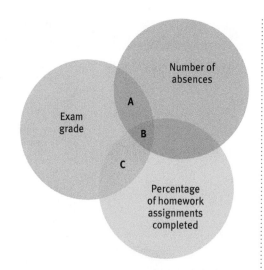

FIGURE 15-8

A Venn Diagram: Partial Correlation and Overlapping Variability

Partial correlation can help us understand the degree to which two variables are associated, independent of a third variable. We can, for example, assess the correlation between number of absences and exam grade, over and above the correlation of percentage of completed homework assignments with these variables.

Alan Fersht, Gonville and Caius College, Cambridge

A Venn Diagram in Stained Glass The beauty of John Venn's idea of a partial correlation is preserved in stained glass in the dining hall of Gonville & Caius College, University of Cambridge.

CHECK YOUR LEARNING

Reviewing the Concepts

> Correlation is a central part of psychometrics, the statistics of the construction of tests and measures.

> Psychometricians, the statisticians who practice psychometrics, use correlation to establish the reliability and the validity of a test.

> Test–retest reliability can be estimated by correlating the same participants' scores on the same test at two different time points.

> Coefficient alpha, now widely used to establish reliability, is essentially calculated by taking the average of all possible split-half correlations (i.e., not just the odds vs. the evens).

> A measure is valid when it assesses what it was designed or intended to assess.

> Partial correlation lets us quantify the association between two variables, over and above the association of a third variable with either of these variables.

Clarifying the Concepts

15-11 How does the field of psychometrics make use of correlation?

15-12 What does coefficient alpha measure and how is it calculated?

Calculating the Statistics

15-13 A researcher is assessing a diagnostic tool for determining whether students should be placed in a remedial reading program. The researcher calculates coefficient alpha and finds that it is 0.85.

  a. Does the test have sufficient reliability to be used as a diagnostic tool? Why or why not?

  b. Does the test have sufficient validity to be used as a diagnostic tool? Why or why not?

  c. What information would we need to appropriately assess the validity of the test?

Applying the Concepts

15-14 Remember the *Cosmopolitan* devotion quiz we referred to when discussing validity? Imagine that the magazine hired a psychometrician to assess the reliability and validity of its quizzes, and she administered this 10-item quiz to 100 readers of that magazine who had boyfriends.

  a. How could the psychometrician establish the reliability of the quiz? That is, which of the methods introduced in this chapter could she use in this case? Be specific, and cite at least two ways.

  b. How could the psychometrician establish the validity of the quiz? Be specific, and cite at least two ways.

  c. Choose one of your criteria from part (b) and explain why it might not actually measure the underlying variable of interest. That is, explain how your criterion itself might not be valid.

Solutions to these Check Your Learning questions can be found in Appendix D.

REVIEW OF CONCEPTS

The Meaning of Correlation

Correlation is an association between two variables and is quantified by a *correlation coefficient*. A *positive correlation* indicates that a participant who has a high score on one variable is likely to have a high score on the other variable, and someone with a low score on one variable is likely to have a low score on the other variable. A *negative correlation* indicates that someone with a high score on one variable is likely to have a low score on the other variable. All correlation coefficients must fall between -1.00 and 1.00. The strength of the correlation is independent of its sign.

Correlation coefficients are useful, but they can be misleading. When interpreting a correlation coefficient, we must be certain not to confuse correlation with causation. We cannot know the causal direction in which two variables are related from a correlation coefficient, nor can we know if there is a hidden third variable that causes the apparent relation.

The Pearson Correlation Coefficient

The *Pearson correlation coefficient* is used when two scale variables are linearly related, as determined from a scatterplot. Calculating a correlation coefficient involves three steps. (1) We calculate the deviation of each score from its mean, multiply the deviations on each variable for each participant, and sum the products of the deviations. (2) We multiply the sums of squares for each variable, then take the square root of the product. (3) We divide the sum of the products of the deviations (from step 1) by the square root of the product of the sums of squares (from step 2). We use the six steps of hypothesis testing to determine whether the correlation coefficient is statistically significantly different from 0 on the r distribution.

Applying Correlation in Psychometrics

Psychometrics is the statistics of the development of tests and measures. *Psychometricians* assess the reliability and validity of a test. Reliability is sometimes measured by *test–retest reliability*, whereby participants' scores on the same measure at two different points in time are correlated. With *coefficient alpha*, a computer essentially calculates the average of all possible split-half correlations (e.g., odd and even items, first and second halves of items). Validity is sometimes assessed by correlating a new measure with existing measures that have been shown to be valid.

With partial correlation, researchers quantify the degree of association between two variables that remains when the correlations of these two variables with a third variable are mathematically eliminated. Researchers use partial correlation when a third variable may be influencing the co-relation of the first two variables.

SPSS®

Enter the data for the example used to calculate the correlation coefficient in this chapter: numbers of absences and exam grades (Example 15.3 on p. 414). Be sure to put each student's two scores on the same row. Check that both are listed as scale variables.

To view a scatterplot, select: Graphs → Chart Builder → Gallery → Scatter/Dot. (*Note:* The first time you click "Chart Builder," you may have to then click "OK" to indicate that you have correctly listed the variables as scale, ordinal, or nominal.) Choose "Scatter/Dot" from the list of charts at the bottom. Select and drag the first scatterplot option to the large box on top. Then select the variables to be included in the scatterplot by dragging the independent variable, absences, to the x-axis and the dependent variable, grade, to the y-axis. Click "OK."

If the scatterplot indicates that we meet the assumptions for a Pearson correlation coefficient, we can analyze the data. Select: Analyze → Correlate → Bivariate. (*Note:* Bivariate means that you are analyzing two variables.) Then select the two variables to be analyzed, absences and grade, and move them into the Variables list. "Pearson" will already be checked as the type of correlation coefficient to be calculated. (*Note:* If more than two variables are selected, SPSS will build a correlation matrix of all possible pairs of variables.) Click "OK" to see the Output screen. The screenshot here shows the output for the Pearson correlation coefficient. Notice that the correlation coefficient is -0.851, the same as the coefficient that we calculated by hand earlier. The two asterisks indicate that it is statistically significant at a p level of less than 0.01. You can see under the correlation coefficient that the actual p value is 0.002.

HOW IT WORKS

15.1 UNDERSTANDING CORRELATION COEFFICIENTS

A researcher gathered data on psychology students' ratings of their likelihood of attending graduate school and the numbers of credits they had completed in their psychology major (Rajecki, Lauer, & Metzner, 1998). Imagine that each of the following numbers represents the Pearson correlation coefficient that quantifies the relation between these two variables. From each coefficient, what do we know about the relation between the two variables?

1. 1.00: This correlation coefficient reflects a perfect positive relation between students' ratings of the likelihood of attending graduate school and the number of psychology credits they completed. This correlation is the strongest correlation of the six options.

2. −0.001: This correlation coefficient reflects a lack of relation between students' ratings and the number of psychology credits they completed. This is the weakest correlation of the six options.

3. 0.56: This correlation coefficient reflects a large positive relation between students' ratings and the number of completed psychology credits.

4. −0.27: This coefficient reflects a medium negative relation between students' ratings and the number of completed psychology credits. (*Note:* This is the actual correlation between these variables found in the study.)

5. −0.98: This coefficient reflects a large (close to perfect) negative relation between students' ratings and the number of psychology credits they have completed.

6. 0.09: This coefficient reflects a small positive relation between students' ratings and the number of completed psychology credits.

15.2 CALCULATING THE PEARSON CORRELATION COEFFICIENT

Is age associated with how much people study? How can we calculate the Pearson correlation coefficient for the accompanying data (taken from students in some of our statistics classes)?

Student	Age	Number of Hours Studied per Week		Student	Age	Number of Hours Studied per Week
1	19	5		6	23	25
2	20	20		7	22	15
3	20	8		8	20	10
4	21	12		9	19	14
5	21	18		10	25	15

Step 1: First, construct a scatterplot:

We see from the scatterplot that the data, overall, have a pattern through which we could imagine drawing a straight line. So, it is safe to calculate the Pearson correlation coefficient.

Step 2: Next, calculate the numerator of the Pearson correlation coefficient. The numerator is the sum of the product of the deviations for each variable. The mean for age is 21, and the mean for hours studied is 14.2. We use these means to calculate each score's deviation from its mean. We then multiply the deviations for each student's two scores and sum the products of the deviations. Here are the calculations:

Age (X)	$(X - M_X)$	Hours studied (Y)	$(Y - M_Y)$	$(X - M_X)(Y - M_Y)$
19	−2	5	−9.2	18.4
20	−1	20	5.8	−5.8
20	−1	8	−6.2	6.2
21	0	12	−2.2	0
21	0	18	3.8	0
23	2	25	10.8	21.6
22	1	15	0.8	0.8
20	−1	10	−4.2	4.2
19	−2	14	−0.2	0.4
25	4	15	0.8	3.2
$M_X = 21$		$M_Y = 14.2$	$\Sigma[(X - M_X)(Y - M_Y)] = 49.0$	

The numerator is 49.0.

Step 3: Calculate the denominator of the Pearson correlation coefficient. The denominator is the square root of the product of the two sums of squares. We first calculate a sum of squares for each variable. The calculations are here:

Age (X)	$(X - M_X)$	$(X - M_X)^2$	Hours studied (Y)	$(Y - M_Y)$	$(Y - M_Y)^2$
19	−2	4	5	−9.2	84.64
20	−1	1	20	5.8	33.64
20	−1	1	8	−6.2	38.44
21	0	0	12	−2.2	4.84
21	0	0	18	3.8	14.44
23	2	4	25	10.8	116.64
22	1	1	15	0.8	0.64
20	−1	1	10	−4.2	17.64
19	−2	4	14	−0.2	0.04
25	4	16	15	0.8	0.64
$M_X = 21$		$\Sigma(X - M_X)^2 = 32$	$M_Y = 14.2$		$\Sigma(Y - M_Y)^2 = 311.6$

We now multiply the two sums of squares, then take the square root of the product of the sums of squares.

$$\sqrt{(SS_X)(SS_Y)} = \sqrt{(32)(311.6)} = 99.856$$

Step 4: Finally, we can put the numerator and denominator together to calculate the Pearson correlation coefficient:

$$r = \frac{\Sigma[(X - M_X)(Y - M_Y)]}{\sqrt{(SS_X)(SS_Y)}} = \frac{49.0}{99.856} = 0.49$$

Now that we have calculated the Pearson correlation coefficient (0.49), we determine what the statistic tells us about the direction and the strength of the association between the two variables (age and number of hours studied). This is a positive correlation. Higher ages tend to be associated with longer hours spent studying, and lower ages tend to be associated with fewer hours spent studying.

EXERCISES

Clarifying the Concepts

15.1 What is a correlation coefficient?

15.2 What is a linear relation?

15.3 Describe a perfect correlation, including its possible coefficients.

15.4 What is the difference between a *positive correlation* and a *negative correlation*?

15.5 What *magnitude* of a correlation coefficient is large enough to be considered important, or worth talking about?

15.6 When we have a straight-line relation between two variables, we use a Pearson correlation coefficient. What does this coefficient describe?

15.7 Explain how the correlation coefficient can be used as a descriptive or an inferential statistic.

15.8 How are deviation scores used in assessing the relation between variables?

15.9 Explain how the sum of the product of deviations determines the sign of the correlation.

15.10 What are the null and research hypotheses for correlations?

15.11 What are the three basic steps to calculate the Pearson correlation coefficient?

15.12 Describe the third assumption of hypothesis testing with correlation.

15.13 What is the difference between test–retest reliability and coefficient alpha?

15.14 Why is a correlation coefficient never greater than 1 (or less than −1)?

15.15 In your own words, briefly explain the difference between a Pearson correlation coefficient and a partial correlation coefficient.

15.16 How does partial correlation begin to address the third variable problem?

Calculating the Statistics

15.17 Determine whether the data in each of the graphs provided would result in a negative or positive correlation coefficient.

a.

b.

c.

15.18 Decide which of the three correlation coefficient values below goes with each of the scatterplots presented in Exercise 15.17.

a. 0.545

b. 0.018

c. −0.20

15.19 Use Cohen's guidelines to describe the strength of the following correlation coefficients:

a. −0.28

b. 0.79

c. 1.0

d. −0.015

15.20 For each of the pairs of correlation coefficients provided, determine which one indicates a stronger relation between variables:

a. −0.28 and −0.31

b. 0.79 and 0.61

c. 1.0 and −1.0

d. −0.15 and 0.13

15.21 Using the following data:

X	Y
0.13	645
0.27	486
0.49	435
0.57	689
0.84	137
0.64	167

a. Create a scatterplot.

b. Calculate deviation scores and products of the deviations for each individual, and then sum all products. This is the numerator of the correlation coefficient equation.

c. Calculate the sum of squares for each variable. Then compute the square root of the product of the sums of squares. This is the denominator of the correlation coefficient equation.

d. Divide the numerator by the denominator to compute the coefficient, r.

e. Calculate degrees of freedom.

f. Determine the critical values, or cutoffs, assuming a two-tailed test with a p level of 0.05.

15.22 Using the following data:

X	Y
394	25
972	75
349	25
349	65
593	35
276	40
254	45
156	20
248	75

a. Create a scatterplot.

b. Calculate deviation scores and products of the deviations for each individual, and then sum all products. This is the numerator of the correlation coefficient equation.

c. Calculate the sum of squares for each variable. Then compute the square root of the product of the sums of squares. This is the denominator of the correlation coefficient equation.

d. Divide the numerator by the denominator to compute the coefficient, r.

e. Calculate degrees of freedom.

f. Determine the critical values, or cutoffs, assuming a two-tailed test with a p level of 0.05.

15.23 Using the following data:

X	Y
40	60
45	55
20	30
75	25
15	20
35	40
65	30

a. Create a scatterplot.

b. Calculate deviation scores and products of the deviations for each individual, and then sum all products. This is the numerator of the correlation coefficient equation.

c. Calculate the sum of squares for each variable. Then compute the square root of the product of the sums of squares. This is the denominator of the correlation coefficient equation.

d. Divide the numerator by the denominator to compute the coefficient, r.

e. Calculate degrees of freedom.

f. Determine the critical values, or cutoffs, assuming a two-tailed test with a p level of 0.05.

15.24 Calculate the degrees of freedom and the critical values, or cutoffs, assuming a two-tailed test with a p level of 0.05, for each of the following designs:

a. Forty students were recruited for a study about the relation between knowledge regarding academic integrity and values held by students, with the idea that students with less knowledge would care less about the issue than students with more knowledge.

b. Twenty-seven couples are surveyed regarding their years together and their relationship satisfaction.

15.25 Calculate the degrees of freedom and the critical values, or cutoffs, assuming a two-tailed test with a p level of 0.05, for each of the following designs:

a. Data are collected to examine the relation between size of dog and rate of bone and joint health issues. Veterinarians from around the country contributed data on 3113 dogs.

b. Hours spent studying per week was correlated with credit-hour load for 72 students.

15.26 Which of the following is not a possible coefficient alpha: 1.67, 0.12, −0.88? Explain your answer.

15.27 A researcher is deciding among three diagnostic tools. The first has a coefficient alpha of 0.82, the second has one of 0.95, and the third has one of 0.91. Based on this information, which tool would you suggest she use and why?

15.28 There is a 0.86 correlation between variables A and B. The partial correlation between A and B, after controlling for a third variable, is 0.67. Does this third variable completely account for the relation between A and B? Explain your answer.

15.29 There is a 0.86 correlation between variables A and B. The partial correlation between A and B, after controlling for a third variable, is 0.86. Does this third variable completely account for the relation between A and B? Explain your answer.

Applying the Concepts

15.30 Quick thinking, smooth talking, and a correlation: Australian psychologist William von Hippel and his colleagues examined the premise that the ability to think quickly would be related to social skills in a paper titled "Quick Thinkers Are Smooth Talkers" (von Hippel, Ronay, Baker, Kjelsaas, & Murphy, 2016). They summarized their findings by saying: "Participants who were able to answer common-knowledge questions more rapidly and to respond more rapidly in general were evaluated by their peers as being more charismatic than participants who responded more slowly. These findings are consistent with the notion that mental speed facilitates social functioning" (p. 121). Are the researchers describing a positive correlation or a negative correlation? Explain your answer.

15.31 Grip strength, mortality, and correlation: An international team of researchers studied the association between grip strength (using a tool that measures the strength of participants' hands) and mortality among adults in 17 countries. They reported that "Low grip strength is associated with higher … fatality rates" (p. 271). Are the researchers describing a positive correlation or a negative correlation? Explain your answer.

15.32 Awe and correlation in the news: The *New York Times* reported on a study that examined the link between positive emotions and health. First citing previous research connecting negative moods with poor health, the reporter said: "Far less is known, however, about the health benefits of specific upbeat moods—whether contentment, say, might promote good health more robustly than joy or pride does. A new study singles out one surprising emotion as a potent medicine: awe" (Reynolds, 2015). What is awe? The reporter interviewed one of the researchers, Dacher Keltner, who said that awe is something that "will pass the goose-bumps test." Keltner explained that "Some people feel awe listening to music, others watching a sunset or attending a political rally or seeing kids play."

a. If this study were an experiment, how might the researchers have studied the emotion of awe as a medicine?

b. Why is it unlikely that the researchers conducted a true experiment?

c. The researchers actually conducted a correlational study (Stellar, John-Henderson, Anderson, Gordon, McNeil, & Keltner, 2015). They used elevated levels of interleukin-6 (IL-6), a measure of inflammation, as a marker of poorer health in their participants. They examined a number of positive emotions, and reported that "awe had the strongest relationship with IL-6 of any positive emotion." Is this relation likely to be positive or negative? Explain your answer.

d. Why can the researchers not conclude that awe causes a change in levels of inflammation?

e. Why should the reporter avoid the word "medicine" in her article?

15.33 Debunking astrology with correlation: The *New York Times* reported that an officer of the International Society for Astrological Research, Anne Massey, stated that a certain phase of the planet Mercury, the retrograde phase, leads to breakdowns in areas as wide-ranging as communication and travel (Newman, 2006). The *Times* reporter, Andy Newman, documented the likelihood of breakdown on a number of variables, and discovered that, contrary to Massey's hypothesis, New Jersey Transit commuter trains were less likely to be late, although by just 0.4%, during the retrograde phase. On the other hand, consistent with Massey's hypothesis, the rate of baggage complaints at LaGuardia airport increased a tiny amount during retrograde periods. Newman's findings were contradictory across all examined variables—rates of theft, computer crashes, traffic disruptions, delayed plane arrivals—with some variables backing Massey and others not. Transportation statistics expert Bruce Schaller said, "If all of this is due to randomness, that's the result you'd expect." Astrologer Massey counters that the pattern she predicts would only emerge across thousands of years of data.

a. Do reporter Newman's data suggest a correlation between Mercury's phase and breakdowns?

b. Why might astrologer Massey believe there is a correlation? Discuss the confirmation bias and illusory correlations (Chapter 5) in your answer.

c. How do transportation expert Schaller's statement and Newman's contradictory results relate to what you learned about probability in Chapter 5? Discuss expected relative-frequency probability in your answer.

d. If there were indeed a small correlation that one could observe only across thousands of years of data, how useful would that knowledge be in terms of predicting events in your own life?

e. Write a brief response to Massey's contention of a correlation between Mercury's phases and breakdowns in aspects of day-to-day living.

15.34 Obesity, age at death, and correlation: In a newspaper column, Paul Krugman (2006) mentioned obesity (as measured by body mass index) as a possible correlate of age at death.

a. Describe the implied correlation between these two variables. Is it likely to be positive or negative? Explain.

b. Draw a scatterplot that depicts the correlation you described in part (a).

15.35 Exercise, number of friends, and correlation: Does the amount that people exercise correlate with the number of friends they have? The accompanying table contains data collected in some of our statistics classes. The first and third columns show hours exercised per week and the second and fourth columns show the number of close friends reported by each participant.

Hours of Exercise	Number of Friends	Hours of Exercise	Number of Friends
1	4	8	4
0	3	2	4
1	2	10	4
6	6	5	7
1	3	4	5
6	5	2	6
2	4	7	5
3	5	1	5
5	6		

a. Create a scatterplot of these data. Be sure to label both axes.

b. What does the scatterplot suggest about the relation between these two variables?

c. Would it be appropriate to calculate a Pearson correlation coefficient? Explain your answer.

15.36 Externalizing behavior, anxiety, and correlation: As part of their study on the relation between rejection and depression in adolescents (Nolan, Flynn, & Garber, 2003), researchers collected data on externalizing behaviors (e.g., acting out in negative ways, such as causing fights) and anxiety. They wondered whether externalizing behaviors were related to feelings of anxiety. Some of the data are presented in the accompanying table.

Externalizing Behaviors	Anxiety	Externalizing Behaviors	Anxiety
9	37	6	33
7	23	2	26
7	26	6	35
3	21	6	23
11	42	9	28

a. Create a scatterplot of these data. Be sure to label both axes.

b. What does the scatterplot suggest about the relation between these two variables?

c. Would it be appropriate to calculate a Pearson correlation coefficient? Explain your answer.

d. Construct a second scatterplot, but this time add a participant who scored 1 on externalizing behaviors and 45 on anxiety. Would you expect the correlation coefficient to be positive or negative now? Small in magnitude or large in magnitude?

e. The Pearson correlation coefficient for the first set of data is 0.65; for the second set of data it is 0.12. Explain why the correlation changed so much with the addition of just one participant.

15.37 Externalizing behavior, anxiety, and hypothesis testing for correlation: Using the data in the previous exercise, perform all six steps of hypothesis testing to explore the relation between externalizing and anxiety.

15.38 Direction of a correlation: For each of the following pairs of variables, would you expect a positive correlation or a negative correlation between the two variables? Explain your answer.

a. How hard the rain is falling and your commuting time

b. How often you say no to dessert and your body fat

c. The amount of wine you consume with dinner and your alertness after dinner

15.39 Cats, mental health problems, and the direction of a correlation: You may be aware of the stereotype about the "crazy" person who owns a lot of cats. Have you wondered whether the stereotype is true? As a researcher, you decide to assess 100 people on two variables: (1) the number of cats they own, and (2) their level of mental health problems (a higher score indicates more problems).

a. Imagine that you found a positive relation between these two variables. What might you expect for someone who owns a lot of cats? Explain.

b. Imagine that you found a positive relation between these two variables. What might you expect for someone who owns no cats or just one cat? Explain.

c. Imagine that you found a negative relation between these two variables. What might you expect for someone who owns a lot of cats? Explain.

d. Imagine that you found a negative relation between these two variables. What might you expect for someone who owns no cats or just one cat? Explain.

15.40 Cats, mental health problems, and scatterplots: Consider the scenario in the previous exercise again. The two variables under consideration were (1) number of cats owned, and (2) level of mental health problems (with a higher score indicating more problems). Each possible relation between these variables would be represented by a different scatterplot. Using data for approximately 10 participants, draw a scatterplot that depicts a correlation between these variables for each of the following:

a. A weak positive correlation

b. A strong positive correlation

c. A perfect positive correlation

d. A weak negative correlation

e. A strong negative correlation

f. A perfect negative correlation

g. No (or almost no) correlation

15.41 Trauma, femininity, and correlation: Graduate student Angela Holiday (2007) conducted a study examining perceptions of combat veterans suffering from mental illness. Participants read a description of either a male or female soldier who had recently returned from combat in Iraq and who was suffering from depression. Participants rated the situation (combat in Iraq) with respect to how traumatic they believed it was; they also rated the combat veterans on a range of variables, including scales that assessed how masculine and how feminine they perceived the person to be. Among other analyses, Holiday examined the relation between the perception of the situation as traumatic and the perception of the veteran as being masculine or feminine. When the person was male, the perception of the situation as traumatic was strongly positively correlated with the perception of the man as feminine but was only weakly positively correlated with the perception of the man as masculine. What would you expect when the person was female? The accompanying table presents some of the data for the perception of the situation as traumatic (on a scale of 1–10, with 10 being the most traumatic) and the perception of the woman as feminine (on a scale of 1–10, with 10 being the most feminine).

Perceived Trauma	Perceived Femininity
5	6
6	5
4	6
5	6
7	4
8	5

a. Draw a scatterplot for these data. Does the scatterplot suggest that it is appropriate to calculate a Pearson correlation coefficient? Explain.

b. Calculate the Pearson correlation coefficient.

c. State what the Pearson correlation coefficient tells us about the relation between these two variables.

d. Explain why the pattern of pairs of deviation scores enables us to understand the relation between the two variables. (That is, consider whether pairs of deviations tend to have the same sign or opposite signs.)

15.42 Trauma, femininity, and hypothesis testing for correlation: Using the data and your work in the previous exercise, perform the remaining five steps of hypothesis testing to explore the relation between trauma and femininity. In step 6, be sure to evaluate the size of the correlation using Cohen's guidelines. [You completed step 5, the calculation of the correlation coefficient, in 15.41(b).]

15.43 Trauma, masculinity, and correlation: See the description of Holiday's experiment in Exercise 15.41. We calculated the correlation coefficient for the relation between the perception of a situation as traumatic and the perception of a woman's femininity. Now let's look at data to examine the relation between the perception of a situation as traumatic and the perception of a woman's masculinity (on a scale of 1–10, with 10 being the most masculine).

Perceived Trauma	Perceived Masculinity
5	3
6	3
4	2
5	2
7	4
8	3

a. Draw a scatterplot for these data. Does the scatterplot suggest that it is appropriate to calculate a Pearson correlation coefficient? Explain.

b. Calculate the Pearson correlation coefficient.

c. State what the Pearson correlation coefficient tells us about the relation between these two variables.

d. Explain why the pattern of pairs of deviation scores enables us to understand the relation between the two variables. (That is, consider whether pairs of deviation scores tend to share the same sign or to have opposite signs.)

e. Explain how the relations between the perception of a situation as traumatic and the perception of a woman as either masculine or feminine differ from those same relations with respect to men.

15.44 Trauma, masculinity, and hypothesis testing for correlation: Using the data and your work in the previous exercise, perform the remaining five steps of hypothesis testing to explore the relation between trauma and masculinity. In step 6, be sure to evaluate the size of the correlation using Cohen's guidelines. [You completed step 5, the calculation of the correlation coefficient, in 15.43(b).]

15.45 Traffic, running late, and bias: A friend tells you that there is a correlation between how late she's running and the amount of traffic. Whenever she's going somewhere and she's behind schedule, there's a lot of traffic. And when she has plenty of time, the traffic is sparser. She tells you that this happens no matter what time of day she's traveling or where she's going. She concludes that she's cursed with respect to traffic.

a. Explain to your friend how other phenomena, such as coincidence, superstition, and the confirmation bias (Chapter 5), might explain her conclusion.

b. How could she quantify the relation between these two variables: the degree to which she is late and the amount of traffic? In your answer, be sure to explain how you might operationalize these variables. Of course, these could be operationalized in many different ways.

15.46 IQ-boosting water and illusory correlation: The trashy tabloid *Weekly World News* published an article—"Water from Mountain Falls Can Make You a Genius"—stating that drinking water from a special waterfall in a secret location in Switzerland "boosts IQ by 14 points—in the blink of an eye!" Hans and Inger Thurlemann, two hikers lost in the woods, drank some of the water, noticed an improvement in their thinking, and instantly found their way out of the woods. The more water they drank, the smarter they seemed to get. They credited the "miracle water" with enhancing their IQs. They brought some of the water home to their friends, who also claimed to notice an improvement in their thinking. Explain how a reliance on anecdotes may have led the Thurlemanns to perceive an illusory correlation (Chapter 5).

15.47 Driving a convertible, correlation, and causality: How safe are convertibles? *USA Today* (Healey, 2006) examined the pros and cons of convertible automobiles. The Insurance Institute for Highway Safety determined that, depending on the model, 52 to 99 drivers of 1 million registered convertibles died in a car crash. The average rate of deaths for all passenger cars was 87. "Counter to conventional wisdom," the reporter wrote, "convertibles generally aren't unsafe."

a. What does the reporter suggest about the safety of convertibles?

b. Can you think of another explanation for the fairly low fatality rates? (*Hint:* The same article reported that convertibles "are often second or third cars.")

c. Given your explanation in part (b), suggest data that might make for a more appropriate comparison.

15.48 Standardized tests, correlation, and causality: A *New York Times* editorial ("Public vs. Private Schools," 2006) cited a finding by the U.S. Department of Education that standardized test scores were significantly higher among students in private schools than among students in public schools.

a. What are the researchers suggesting with respect to causality?

b. How could this correlation be explained by reversing the direction of hypothesized causality? Be specific.

c. How might a third variable account for this correlation? Be specific. Note that there are many possible "third" variables. (*Note:* In the actual study, the difference between types of school disappeared when the researchers statistically controlled for related third variables including race, gender, parents' education, and family income.)

15.49 Arts education, correlation, and causality: The Broadway musical *Annie* and the Entertainment Industry Foundation teamed up to promote arts education programs for underserved children. In an ad in the *New York Times*, they said, "Students in arts education programs perform better and stay in school longer."

a. What are the musical (*Annie*) and the foundation suggesting with respect to causality?

b. How could this correlation be explained by reversing the direction of hypothesized causality? Be specific.

c. How might a third variable account for this correlation? Be specific. Note that there are many possible "third" variables.

15.50 Facebook likes and correlation: Be careful what you "like." Researchers examined the relations between the number of Facebook "likes" a person has posted and the researchers' ability to correctly identify various characteristics of the person, including gender, age, sexual orientation, ethnicity, religion, political beliefs, personality traits, and intelligence (Kosinski, Stillwell, & Graepel, 2013). The graph below shows the relations between number of likes and accuracy of identifying gender, age, and the personality characteristic of openness, respectively.

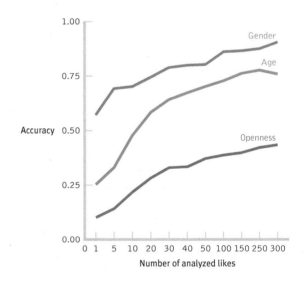

a. In your own words, what story is this graph telling?

b. Based on what you learned in Chapter 3 about graphs, explain why the *x*-axis is misleading, and describe how you would redesign the graph.

15.51 Swearing, vocabulary, and correlation: Psychology researchers set out to test the folk assumption that people swear a lot because their overall vocabulary is limited (Jay & Jay, 2015). They asked participants to name as many taboo words, described as "curse words or swear words" (p. 253), as they could in one minute. They then asked participants to repeat the task but with other categories of words, such as naming as many animals as they could in one minute. Below are fictional data that have the same overall pattern—similar means, standard deviations, and statistical significance of the correlation coefficient—as the data in the actual study.

Number of taboo words (X)	Number of animals (Y)
9	23
5	20
4	17
12	28
14	26
10	16
9	17
11	18
14	23
6	21
7	25
13	19

a. Create a scatterplot of these data and describe your impression of the relation between these variables based on the scatterplot.

b. Compute the Pearson correlation coefficient for these data.

c. Explain why the correlation coefficient you just computed is a descriptive statistic, not an inferential statistic. What would you need to do to make this an inferential statistic?

d. Perform the six steps of hypothesis testing.

e. Could the researchers have studied this phenomenon with an experiment rather than a correlational study? Explain your answer.

15.52 Romantic love, brain activation, and reliability: Aron and colleagues (2005) found a correlation between intense romantic love (as assessed by the Passionate Love Scale [PLS]) and activation in a specific region of the brain [as assessed by functional magnetic resonance imaging [fMRI]). The PLS (Hatfield & Sprecher, 1986) assessed the intensity of romantic love by asking people in romantic relationships to rate their agreement with a series of statements, such as "I want _____ physically, emotionally, and mentally" and "Sometimes I can't control my thoughts; they are obsessively on _____," replacing the blanks with the name of their partner.

a. How might we examine the reliability of this measure using test–retest reliability techniques? Be specific and explain the role of correlation.

b. Would test–retest reliability be appropriate for this measure? That is, is there likely to be a practice effect? Explain.

c. How could we examine the reliability of this measure using coefficient alpha? Be specific and explain the role of correlation.

d. Coefficient alpha in this study was 0.81. Based on coefficient alpha, was the use of this scale in this study warranted? Explain.

e. What is the idea that this measure is trying to assess?

f. What would it mean for this measure to be valid? Be specific.

15.53 A biased exam question, validity, and correlation: New York State's fourth-grade English exam led to an outcry from parents because of a question that was perceived to be an unfair measure of fourth graders' performance. Students read a story, "Why the Rooster Crows at Dawn," that described an arrogant rooster who claims to be king, and Brownie, "the kindest of all the cows," who eventually acts in a mean way toward the rooster. In the beginning the rooster does whatever he wants, but by the end, the cows, led by Brownie, have convinced him that as self-proclaimed king, he must be the first to wake up in the morning and the last to go to sleep. To the cows' delight, the arrogant rooster complies. Students were then asked to respond to several questions about the story, including one that asked: "What causes Brownie's behavior to change?" Several parents started a Web site, http://browniethecow.org, to point out problems with the test, particularly with this question. Students, they argued, were confused because it seemed that it was the rooster's behavior, not the cow's behavior, that changed. The correct answer, according to a quote on the Web site from an unnamed state official, was that the cow started out kind and ended up mean.

a. This test item was supposed to evaluate writing skills. According to the Web site, test items should lead to good student writing; be unambiguous; test for writing, not another skill; and allow for objective, reliable scoring. If students were marked down for talking about the rooster rather than the cow, as alleged by the Web site, would it meet these criteria? Explain. Does this seem to be a valid question? Explain.

b. The Web site states that New York City schools use the tests to, among other things, evaluate teachers and principals. The logic behind this, ostensibly, is that good teachers and administrators cause higher test performance. List at least two possible third variables that might lead to better performance in some schools than in other schools, other than the presence of good teachers and administrators.

15.54 Holiday weight gain, reliability, and validity: The *Wall Street Journal* reported on a study of holiday weight gain. Researchers assessed weight gain by asking people how much weight they typically gain in the fall and winter (Parker-Pope, 2005). The average answer was 2.3 kilograms. But a study of actual weight gain over this period found that people gained, on average, 0.48 kilograms.

a. Is the method of asking people about their weight gain likely to be reliable? Explain.

b. Is this method of asking people about their weight gain likely to be valid? Explain.

Putting It All Together

15.55 Health care spending, longevity, and correlation: *New York Times* columnist Paul Krugman (2006) used the idea of correlation in a newspaper column when he asked, "Is being an American bad for your health?" Krugman explained that the United States has higher per capita spending on health care than any country in the world and yet is surpassed by many countries in life expectancy [Krugman cited a study by Banks, Marmot, Oldfield, and Smith (2006), published in the *Journal of the American Medical Association*].

a. Name the "participants" in this study.

b. What are the two scale variables being studied, and how was each of them operationalized? Suggest at least one alternate way, other than life expectancy, to operationalize health.

c. What was the study finding, and why might this finding be surprising? If the finding described above holds true across countries, would this be a negative correlation or a positive correlation? Explain.

d. Some people thought race or income might be a third variable related to higher spending and lower life expectancy. But Krugman further reported that a comparison of non-Hispanic white people from America and from England (thus taking race out of the equation) yielded a surprising finding: The wealthiest third of Americans have poorer health than do even the *least* wealthy third of the English. What are some other possible third variables that might affect both of the variables in this study?

e. Why is this research considered a correlational study rather than a true experiment?

f. Why would it not be possible to conduct a true experiment to determine whether the amount of health care spending causes changes in health?

15.56 Availability of food, amount eaten, and correlation: Did you know that sometimes you eat more just because the food is in front of you? Geier, Rozin, and Doros (2006) studied how portion size affected the amount people consumed. They discovered interesting things such as that people eat more M&M's when the candies are dispensed using a big spoon as compared with when a small spoon is used. They investigated whether people eat more when more food is available. Hypothetical data are presented below for the amount of candy presented in a bowl for customers to take and the amount of candy taken by the end of each day of the study:

Number of Pieces Presented	Number of Pieces Taken
10	3
25	14
50	26
75	44
100	36
125	57
150	41

a. What are the two variables in this study? What type of variable is each?

b. Create a scatterplot of these data.

c. Describe your impression of the relation between these variables based on the scatterplot.

d. Compute the Pearson correlation coefficient for these data.

e. Summarize your findings using Cohen's guidelines.

f. Perform the remaining steps of hypothesis testing.

g. What limitations are there to the conclusions you can draw based on this correlation?

h. Use the A-B-C model to explain possible causes for the relation between these variables.

15.57 High school athletic participation and correlation: Researchers examined longitudinal data to explore the long-term effects of high school athletic participation (Lutz, Cornish, Gonnerman, Ralston, & Baker, 2009). They reported three findings. First, they found that high school athletic participation was related to a number of positive outcomes. These included increases in high school GPA, college completion, earnings as an adult, and various positive health behaviors. Second, they found that a number of other variables affected the relation between high school athletic participation and these positive outcomes; these other variables included race, gender, and type of school (e.g., public, private). Third, they found that high school athletic participation was related to several negative outcomes among male athletes; these included increases in alcohol consumption, sexist and homophobic attitudes, and violence.

a. How might high school athletic participation be operationalized as a nominal variable? Be specific.

b. How might high school athletic participation be operationalized as a scale variable? Be specific.

c. Why might correlation be a useful tool with data like those used in this study? (Assume the use of scale variables.)

d. Did the researchers report positive correlations? If yes, list at least two. Explain why these are positive correlations.

e. Did the researchers report negative correlations? If yes, list at least two. Explain why these are negative correlations.

f. Use the A-B-C model to offer three different causal explanations for the correlation between high school athletic participation and positive health behaviors.

g. Why might partial correlation be useful in this study? Give at least one specific example of how it might be useful.

15.58 Mental health and partial correlation: A study by Nolan and colleagues (2003) examined the relation between externalizing behaviors (acting out) and anxiety in adolescents. Depression has been shown to relate to both of these variables. What role might depression play in the observed positive relation between these variables? The correlation matrix below displays the Pearson correlation coefficients, as calculated by computer software, for each pair of the variables of interest: depression, externalizing, and anxiety. The Pearson correlation coefficients for each pair of variables are at the intersection in the chart of the two variables. For example, the correlation coefficient for the association between depression (top row) and externalizing (second column of correlations) is 0.635, a very strong positive correlation.

a. Given that the authors calculated correlation coefficients, what kind of variables are depression, anxiety, and externalizing? Explain your answer.

	Correlations		
	Depression	Externalizing	Anxiety
Depression			
Pearson Correlation	1	0.635(★★)	0.368(★★)
Sig. (2-tailed)		.000	.000
N	220	219	207
Externalizing			
Pearson Correlation	0.635(★★)	1	0.356(★★)
Sig. (2-tailed)	.000		.000
N	219	220	207
Anxiety			
Pearson Correlation	0.368(★★)	0.356(★★)	1
Sig. (2-tailed)	.000	.000	
N	207	207	207

★★Correlation is significant at the 0.01 level (2-tailed).

b. What is the correlation coefficient for the association between depression and anxiety? Explain what this correlation coefficient tells us about the relation between these variables.

c. What is the correlation coefficient for the association between anxiety and externalizing? Explain what this correlation coefficient tells us about the relation between these variables.

d. The partial correlation of anxiety and externalizing is 0.17, controlling for the variable of depression. How is this different from the original Pearson correlation coefficient between these two variables?

e. Why is the partial correlation coefficient different from the original Pearson correlation coefficient between these two variables? What did we learn by calculating a partial correlation?

f. Why can we not draw causal conclusions with respect to these findings?

TERMS

FORMULAS

$$r = \frac{\Sigma[(X - M_X)(Y - M_Y)]}{\sqrt{(SS_X)(SS_Y)}} \quad \text{(p. 417)}$$

$$df_r = N - 2 \qquad \text{(p. 419)}$$

SYMBOLS

r (p. 413)

ρ (p. 413)

α (p. 421)

Regression

Simple Linear Regression

Prediction versus Relation

Regression with z Scores

Determining the Regression Equation

The Standardized Regression Coefficient
and Hypothesis Testing with Regression

Interpretation and Prediction

Regression and Error

Applying the Lessons of Correlation to Regression

Regression to the Mean

Proportionate Reduction in Error

Multiple Regression

Understanding the Equation

Multiple Regression in Everyday Life

Next Steps: Structural Equation Modeling (SEM)

BEFORE YOU GO ON

- **You should understand the six steps of hypothesis testing (Chapter 7).**

- **You should understand the concept of effect size (Chapter 8).**

- **You should understand the concept of correlation (Chapter 15).**

- **You should be able to explain the limitations of correlation (Chapter 15).**

Facebook and Social Capital The prediction tools introduced in this chapter helped researchers determine that increased use of Facebook predicts higher levels of social capital.

In 2004, college student Mark Zuckerberg created the social networking site Facebook, which soon exploded in popularity across college campuses. By 2012, Facebook had raised $16 billion in a public stock offering. As of 2016, Facebook was starting to approach 2 billion active users. As Facebook use ballooned, researchers at Michigan State University (MSU) (Ellison, Steinfeld, & Lampe, 2007) wanted to understand what college students were getting out of their Facebook relationships—that is, what they were gaining in *social capital*.

One type of social capital the researchers studied was "bridging" social capital: the loose social connections we think of as acquaintances rather than friends. The researchers hypothesized that greater use of Facebook would predict more bridging social capital. They measured bridging social capital by asking students to rate several items, such as "I feel I am part of the MSU community" and "At MSU, I come into contact with new people all the time."

Obviously, the amount of time spent on Facebook is only one of many influences that determine how much social capital students get from Facebook. Clear answers to the research question are probably complicated by many different factors such as shyness, gender, and quality of Internet connections. The MSU Facebook study had to control for the influence of many variables, but the data still supported the researcher's hypothesis: the more students used Facebook, the higher they tended to score on a measure of social capital. But *how* did the researchers isolate the effect of time on Facebook from other variables?

The analytical methods we learn in this chapter build on correlation to help us to create prediction tools. We begin by learning how to use just one scale variable to predict the outcome on a second scale variable. Then we discuss the limitations of this method—limitations that are similar to those we encountered with correlation. Finally, we expand this analytical method to use multiple scale variables to predict the outcome on another scale variable.

Simple Linear Regression

Correlation is a marvelous tool because it allows us to know the direction and strength of a relation between two variables. We can also use a correlation coefficient to develop a *prediction tool*—an equation to predict a person's score on a scale dependent variable from his or her score on a scale independent variable. For instance, the MSU research team used the amount of time a student spends on Facebook to predict a high score on a measure of social capital.

Being able to predict the future is powerful stuff, but it's not magic—it's statistics. Of course, statistical prediction requires building in some margin of error. For example, many universities use variables such as high school grades and standardized test scores to predict the success of prospective students. They aren't perfect predictions, but they are much better than gazing into a crystal ball. Similarly, insurance companies input demographic data into an equation to predict the likelihood of a class of people (such as young male drivers) to submit a claim. Mark Zuckerberg, the founder of Facebook, is even alleged to have used data from Facebook users to predict breakups of romantic relationships! He used independent variables, such as the amount of time looking at others' Facebook profiles, changes in postings to others' Facebook walls, and photo-tagging patterns, to predict the dependent variable: the end of a relationship as evidenced by the user's Facebook relationship status. He was right about one-third of the time ("Can Facebook Predict Your Breakup?," 2010).

Prediction Versus Relation

The name for the prediction tool that we've been discussing is *regression*, a statistical technique that can provide specific quantitative information that predicts relations between variables. More specifically, **simple linear regression** *is a statistical tool that lets us predict a person's score on a dependent variable from his or her score on one independent variable.*

Simple linear regression allows us to calculate the equation for a straight line that describes the data. Once we can graph that line, we can look at any point on the *x*-axis and find its corresponding point on the *y*-axis. That corresponding point is what we predict for *y*. (*Note:* As with the Pearson correlation coefficient, we are not able to use simple linear regression if the data do not form the pattern of a straight line.) Let's consider an example of research that uses regression techniques, and then walk through the steps to develop a regression equation.

Christopher Ruhm, an economist, often uses regression in his research. In one study, he wanted to explore the reasons for his finding (Ruhm, 2000) that the death rate *decreases* when unemployment goes up—a surprising negative relation between the death rate and an economic indicator. He took this relation a step further, into the realm of prediction: He found that an increase of 1% in unemployment predicted a decrease in the death rate of 0.5%, on average. In other words, a *poorer* economy predicted *better* health!

To explore the reasons for this surprising finding, Ruhm (2006) conducted regression analyses for independent variables related to health (smoking, obesity, and physical activity) and dependent variables related to the economy (income, unemployment, and the length of the workweek). He analyzed data from a sample of nearly 1.5 million participants collected from telephone surveys over more than a decade. Among other things, Ruhm found that a decrease in working hours predicted decreases in smoking, obesity, and physical inactivity.

Regression can take us a step beyond correlation. Regression can provide specific quantitative predictions that more precisely explain relations among variables. For example, Ruhm reported that a decrease in the workweek of just 1 hour predicted a 1% decrease in physical inactivity. Ruhm suggested that shorter working hours free up time for physical activity—something he might not have thought of without the more specific quantitative information provided by regression. Let's now conduct a simple linear regression analysis using information that we're already familiar with: *z* scores.

Regression with *z* Scores

In Chapter 15, we calculated a Pearson correlation coefficient to quantify the relation between students' numbers of absences from statistics class and their statistics final exam grades; the data for the 10 students in the sample are shown in Table 16-1. Remember, the mean number of absences was 3.400; the standard deviation for these data is 2.375. The mean exam grade was 76.000; the standard deviation for these data is 15.040. The Pearson correlation coefficient that we calculated in Chapter 15 was −0.85, but simple linear regression can take us a step further. We can develop an equation to predict students' final exam grades from their numbers of absences.

Prediction and Box Office Success "Forget zombies. The data crunchers are invading Hollywood." So begins a *New York Times* article about Vinny Bruzzese, a former statistics professor turned script advisor (Barnes, 2013). Bruzzese uses data about the elements of past films to predict future success at the box office. The makers of *Oz the Great and Powerful* took Bruzzese's advice, and the film made hundreds of millions of dollars. On the other hand, the makers of *Abraham Lincoln: Vampire Hunter* ignored Bruzzese's advice, and they didn't even earn a quarter of what *Oz* pulled in. Two data points, however, are never enough to declare a pattern.

Walt Disney Pictures/The Kobal Collection

MASTERING THE CONCEPT

16-1: Simple linear regression allows us to determine an equation for a straight line that predicts a person's score on a dependent variable from his or her score on the independent variable. We can only use it when the data are approximately linearly related.

● **Simple linear regression** is a statistical tool that lets us predict a person's score on the dependent variable from his or her score on one independent variable.

> ### TABLE 16-1   Is Skipping Class Related to Exam Grades?
>
> Here are the scores for 10 students on two scale variables: number of absences from class in one semester and the final exam grade for that semester. The correlation between these variables is -0.85, but regression can take us a step further. We can develop a regression equation to assist with prediction.
>
> | Student | Absences | Exam Grade |
> |---------|----------|------------|
> | 1 | 4 | 82 |
> | 2 | 2 | 98 |
> | 3 | 2 | 76 |
> | 4 | 3 | 68 |
> | 5 | 1 | 84 |
> | 6 | 0 | 99 |
> | 7 | 4 | 67 |
> | 8 | 8 | 58 |
> | 9 | 7 | 50 |
> | 10 | 3 | 78 |

Let's say that a student (let's call him Skip) announces on the first day of class that he intends to skip five classes during the semester. We can refer to the size and direction of the correlation (-0.85) as a benchmark to predict his final exam grade. To predict his grade, we unite regression with a statistic we are more familiar with: z scores. If we know Skip's z score on one variable, we can multiply by the correlation coefficient to calculate his predicted z score on the second variable. Remember that z scores indicate how far a participant falls from the mean in terms of standard deviations. The formula, called the *standardized regression equation* because it uses z scores, is:

$$z_{\hat{Y}} = (r_{XY})(z_X)$$

16-1: The standardized regression equation predicts the z score of a dependent variable, Y, from the z score of an independent variable, X. We simply multiply the independent variable's z score by the Pearson correlation coefficient to get the predicted z score on the dependent variable:

$$z_{\hat{Y}} = (r_{XY})(z_X).$$

The subscripts in the formula indicate that the first z score is for the dependent variable, Y, and that the second z score is for the independent variable, X. The ^ symbol over the subscript Y, called a "hat" by statisticians, refers to the fact that this variable is predicted. This is the z score for "Y hat"—the z score for the *predicted* score on the dependent variable, not the actual score. We cannot, of course, predict the actual score, and the "hat" reminds us of this. When we refer to this score, we can either say "the predicted score for Y" (with no hat, because we have specified with words that it is predicted) or we can use the hat, $\hat{Y}$, to indicate that it is predicted. (We would not use both expressions because that would be redundant.) The subscripts X and Y for the Pearson correlation coefficient, r, indicate that this is the correlation between variables X and Y.

· ·

EXAMPLE 16.1

If Skip's projected number of absences were identical to the mean number of absences for the entire class, then he'd have a z score of 0. If we multiply that by the correlation coefficient, then he'd have a predicted z score of 0 for final exam grade:

$$z_{\hat{Y}} = (-0.85)(0) = 0$$

TABLE 16-2 Regression to the Mean

One reason that regression equations are so named is because they predict a z score on the dependent variable that is closer to the mean than is the z score on the independent variable. Scores regress, or go backwards, toward the mean. In fact, this phenomenon is often called *regression to the mean*. The following predicted z scores for the dependent variable, Y, were calculated by multiplying the z score for the independent variable, X, by the Pearson correlation coefficient of −0.85.

z Score for the Independent Variable, X	Predicted z Score for the Dependent Variable, Y
−2.0	1.70
−1.0	0.85
0.0	0.00
1.0	−0.85
2.0	−1.70

So if Skip's score is right at the mean on the independent variable, then we'd predict that he'd be right at the mean on the dependent variable.

If Skip missed more classes than average and had a z score of 1.0 on the independent variable (1 standard deviation above the mean), then his predicted score on the dependent variable would be −0.85 (that is, 0.85 standard deviation below the mean):

$$z_{\hat{Y}} = (-0.85)(1) = -0.85$$

If his z score were −2 (that is, if it were 2 standard deviations below the mean), his predicted z score on the dependent variable would be 1.7 (that is, 1.7 standard deviations above the mean):

$$z_{\hat{Y}} = (-0.85)(-2) = 1.70$$

Notice two things: First, because this is a negative correlation, a score above the mean on absences predicts a score below the mean on grade, and vice versa. Second, the predicted z score on the dependent variable is closer to its mean than is the z score for the independent variable. Table 16-2 illustrates this for several z scores.

This regressing of the dependent variable—the fact that it is closer to its mean—is called **regression to the mean**, *the tendency of scores that are particularly high or low to drift toward the mean over time.*

In the social sciences, many phenomena demonstrate regression to the mean. For example, parents who are very tall tend to have children who are somewhat shorter than they are, although probably still above average. And parents who are very short tend to have children who are somewhat taller than they are, although probably still below average. We explore this concept in more detail later in this chapter.

When we don't have a person's z score on the independent variable, we have to perform the additional step of converting his or her raw score to a z score. In addition, when we calculate a predicted z score on the dependent variable, we can use the formula that determines a raw score from a z score. Let's try it with the skipping class and exam grade example, using Skip as the subject. ●

● **Regression to the mean** is the tendency of scores that are particularly high or low to drift toward the mean over time.

EXAMPLE 16.2

We already know that Skip has announced his plans to skip five classes. What would we predict for his final exam grade?

| **STEP 1: Calculate the z score.** |

We first have to calculate Skip's z score on number of absences. Using the mean (3.400) and the standard deviation (2.375), we calculate:

$$z_X = \frac{(X - M_X)}{SD_X} = \frac{(5 - 3.400)}{2.375} = 0.674$$

| **STEP 2: Multiply the z score by the correlation coefficient.** |

We multiply this z score by the correlation coefficient to get his predicted z score on the dependent variable, final exam grade:

$$z_{\hat{Y}} = (r_{XY})(z_X) = (-0.85)(0.674) = -0.573$$

| **STEP 3: Convert the z score to a raw score.** |

We convert from the predicted z score on Y, -0.573, to a predicted raw score for Y:

$$\hat{Y} = z_Y(SD_Y) + M_Y = -.0573(15.040) + 76.00 = 67.38$$

If Skip skipped five classes, this number would reflect more classes than the typical student skipped, so we would expect him to earn a lower-than-average grade. And the formula makes this very prediction—that Skip's final exam grade would be 67.38, which is lower than the mean (76.00).

The admissions counselor, the insurance salesperson, and Mark Zuckerberg of Facebook, however, are unlikely to have the time or interest to do conversions from raw scores to z scores and back, so the z score regression equation is not useful in a practical sense for situations in which we must make ongoing predictions using the same variables. It is very useful, however, as a tool to help us develop a regression equation we can use with raw scores, a procedure we look at in the next section. ●

Determining the Regression Equation

You may remember the equation for a line that you learned in geometry class. The version you likely learned was: $y = m(x) + b$. (In this equation, b is the intercept and m is the slope.) In statistics, we use a slightly different version of this formula:

$$\hat{Y} = a + b(X)$$

In the regression formula, a is the **intercept,** *the predicted value for* Y *when* X *is equal to 0, which is the point at which the line crosses, or intercepts, the y-axis.* In Figure 16-1, the intercept is 5. b is the **slope,** *the amount that* Y *is predicted to increase for an increase of 1 in* X. In Figure 16-1, the slope is 2. As X increases from 3 to 4, for example, we see an increase in what we predict for a Y of 2: from 11 to 13. The equation, therefore, is: $\hat{Y} = 5 + 2(X)$. If the score on X is 6, for example, the predicted score for Y is: $\hat{Y} = 5 + 2(6) = 5 + 12 = 17$. We can verify this on the line in Figure 16-1. Here, we were given the regression equation and regression line, but usually we have to determine these from the data. In this section, we learn the process of calculating a regression equation from data.

Once we have the equation for a line, it's easy to input any value for X to determine the predicted value for Y. Let's imagine that one of Skip's classmates, Allie, anticipates

16-2: The simple linear regression equation uses the formula:

$$\hat{Y} = a + b(X).$$

In this formula, X is the raw score on the independent variable and $\hat{Y}$ is the predicted raw score on the dependent variable. a is the intercept of the line, and b is its slope.

● The **intercept** is the predicted value for **Y** when **X** is equal to 0, which is the point at which the line crosses, or intercepts, the *y*-axis.

● The **slope** is the amount that **Y** is predicted to increase for an increase of 1 in **X**.

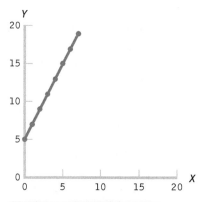

FIGURE 16-1

The Equation for a Line

The equation for a line includes the intercept, the point at which the line crosses the y-axis; here the intercept is 5. It also includes the slope, the amount that Y increases for an increase of 1 in X. Here, the slope is 2. The equation, therefore, is: $\hat{Y} = 5 + 2(X)$.

two absences this semester. If we had a regression equation, then we could input Allie's score of 2 on X and find her predicted score on Y. But first we have to develop the regression equation. Using the z score regression equation to find the intercept and slope enables us to "see" where these numbers come from in a way that makes sense (Aron & Aron, 2002). For this, we use the z score regression equation: $z_{\hat{Y}} = (r_{XY})(z_X)$.

We start by calculating a, the intercept, a process that takes three steps.

EXAMPLE 16.3

STEP 1: Find the z score for an X of 0. We know that the intercept is the point at which the line crosses the y-axis when X is equal to 0. So we start by finding the z score for an X of 0 using the formula:

$$z_X = \frac{(X - M_X)}{SD_X}.$$

$$z_X = \frac{(X - M_X)}{SD_X} = \frac{(0 - 3.400)}{2.375} = -1.432$$

STEP 2: Use the z score regression equation to calculate the predicted z score on Y. We use the z score regression equation $z_{\hat{Y}} = (r_{XY})(z_X)$, to calculate the predicted z score on Y for an X of 0.

$$z_{\hat{Y}} = (r_{XY})(z_X) = (-0.85)\,(-1.432) = 1.217$$

STEP 3: Convert the z score to its raw score. We convert the z score for $\hat{Y}$ to its raw score using the formula: $\hat{Y} = z_{\hat{Y}}(SD_Y) + M_Y$.

$$\hat{Y} = z_{\hat{Y}}(SD_Y) + M_Y = 1.217(15.040) + 76.000 = 94.30.$$

We have the intercept! When X is 0, $\hat{Y}$ is 94.30. That is, we would predict that someone who never misses class would earn a final exam grade of 94.30.

Next, we calculate b, the slope, a process that is similar to the one for calculating the intercept, but calculating the slope takes four steps. We know that the slope is the amount that $\hat{Y}$ increases when X increases by 1. So all we need to do is calculate what we would predict for an X of 1. We can then compare the $\hat{Y}$ increases for an X of 0 to the $\hat{Y}$ for an X of 1. The difference between the two is the slope.

STEP 1: Find the z score for an X of 1.

We find the z score for an X of 1, using the formula: $z_X = \dfrac{(X - M_X)}{SD_X}$.

$$z_X = \frac{(X - M_X)}{SD_X} = \frac{(1 - 3.400)}{2.375} = -1.011$$

STEP 2: Use the z score regression equation to calculate the predicted z score on Y

We use the z score regression equation, $z_{\hat{Y}} = (r_{XY})(z_X)$, to calculate the predicted z score on Y for an X of $z_{\hat{Y}} = (r_{XY})(z_X) = (-0.85)(-1.011) = 0.859$.

STEP 3: Convert the z score to its raw score.

We convert the z score for $\hat{Y}$ to its raw score, using the formula: $\hat{Y} = z_{\hat{Y}}(SD_Y) + M_Y$.

$$\hat{Y} = z_{\hat{Y}}(SD_Y) + M_Y = 0.859(15.040) + 76.000 = 88.919$$

STEP 4: Determine the slope.

The prediction is that a student who misses one class would have a final exam grade of 88.919. As X, number of absences, increased from 0 to 1, what happened to Y? First, ask yourself if it increased or decreased. An increase would mean a positive slope, and a decrease would mean a negative slope. Here, we see a decrease in exam grade as the number of absences increased. Next, determine how much it increased or decreased. In this case, the decrease is 5.385 (calculated as $94.304 - 88.919 = 5.385$). So, the slope here is -5.39.

We now have the intercept and the slope and can put them into the equation: $\hat{Y} = a + b(X)$, which becomes $\hat{Y} = 94.30 - 5.39(X)$. We can use this equation to predict Allie's final exam grade based on her number of absences, two.

$$\hat{Y} = 94.30 - 5.39(X) = 94.30 - 5.39(2) = 83.52$$

Based on the data from our statistics classes, we predict that Allie would earn a final exam grade of 83.52 if she skips two classes. We could have predicted this same grade for Allie using the z score regression equation. The difference is that now we can input any score into the raw-score regression equation, and it does all the work of converting for us. The admissions counselor, the insurance salesperson, and the Facebook founder have an easy formula and don't have to know z scores to use it.

We can also use the regression equation to draw the regression line and get a visual sense of what it looks like. We do this by calculating at least two points on the regression line, usually for one low score on X and one high score on X. We would always have $\hat{Y}$ for two scores, 0 and 1 (although in some cases these numbers won't make sense, such as for the variable of human body temperature; you'd never have a temperature that low!). Because these scores are low on the scale for number of absences, we would choose a high score as well; 8 is the highest score in the original data set, so we can use that:

$$\hat{Y} = 94.30 - 5.39(X) = 94.30 - 5.39(8) = 51.18$$

For someone who skipped eight classes, we predict a final exam grade of 51.18. We now have three points, as shown in Table 16-3. It's useful to have three points because the third point serves as a check on the other two. If the three points do not fall in a straight line, we have made an error.

We then draw a line through the dots, but it's not just any line. This line, which you can see in Figure 16-2, is the regression line, which has another name that is wonderfully intuitive: the line of best fit. If you have ever had some clothes tailored to fit your body, perhaps for a wedding or other special occasion, then you know that there really is such a thing as a "best fit."

In regression, the meaning of "the line of best fit" is the same as that characteristic in a tailored set of clothes. We couldn't make the line a little steeper, or raise or lower it, or manipulate it in any way that would make it represent those dots any better than it already does. When we look at the scatterplot around the line in Figure 16-3, we see that the line goes precisely through the middle of the data. Statistically, this is the line that leads to the least amount of error in prediction.

Language Alert! Notice that the line we just drew starts in the upper left of the graph and ends in the lower right, meaning that it has a negative slope. The word *slope* is often used when discussing, say, ski slopes. A negative slope means that the line looks like it's going downhill as we move from left to right. This makes sense because the calculations for the regression equation are based on the correlation coefficient, and the scatterplot associated with a negative correlation coefficient has dots that also go "downhill." If the slope were positive, the line would start in the lower left of the graph and end in the upper right. A positive slope means that the line looks like it's going uphill as we move from left to right. Again, this makes sense, because we base the calculations on a positive correlation coefficient, and the scatterplot associated with a positive correlation coefficient has dots that also go "uphill." ●

TABLE 16-3	Drawing a Regression Line

We calculate at least two, and preferably three, pairs of scores for X and $\hat{Y}$. Ideally, at least one is low on the scale for X and at least one is high.

X	$\hat{Y}$
0	94.30
1	88.92
8	51.18

BananaStock/Jupiter Images/Getty Images Plus

The Line of Best Fit The line of best fit in regression has the same characteristics as tailored clothes; there is nothing we could do to that line that would make it fit the data any better.

FIGURE 16-2

The Regression Line

To draw a regression line, we plot at least two, and preferably three, pairs of scores for X and $\hat{Y}$. We then draw a line through the dots.

FIGURE 16-3

The Line of Best Fit

The regression line is the line that best fits the points on the scatterplot. Statistically, the regression line is the line that leads to the least amount of error in prediction.

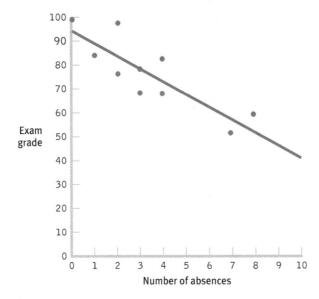

The Standardized Regression Coefficient and Hypothesis Testing with Regression

The steepness of the slope tells us the amount that the dependent variable changes as the independent variable increases by 1. So, for the skipping class and exam grades example, the slope of -5.39 tells us that for each additional class skipped, we can predict that the exam grade will be 5.39 points lower. Let's say that another professor uses skipped classes to predict the class grade on a grade point average (GPA) scale of 0–4. And let's say that we found a slope of -0.23 with these data. For each additional skipped class, we would predict that the grade, in terms of the 0–4 scale, would decrease by 0.23. The problem here is that we can't directly compare one professor's findings with another professor's findings. A decrease of 5.39 is larger than a decrease of 0.23, but they're not comparable because they're on different scales.

This problem might remind you of the problems we faced in comparing scores on different scales. To appropriately compare scores, we standardized them using the z statistic. We can standardize slopes in a similar way by calculating the standardized regression coefficient. The **standardized regression coefficient**, *a standardized version of the slope in a regression equation, is the predicted change in the dependent variable in terms of standard deviations for an increase of 1 standard deviation in the independent variable.* It is symbolized by β and is often called a *beta weight* because of its symbol (pronounced "beta"). It is calculated using the formula:

$$\beta = (b) \frac{\sqrt{SS_X}}{\sqrt{SS_Y}}$$

We calculated the slope, -5.39, earlier in this chapter. We calculated the sums of squares in Chapter 15. Table 16-4 repeats part of the calculations for the denominator of the correlation coefficient equation. At the bottom of the table, we can see that the sum of squares for the independent variable of classes skipped is 56.4 and the sum of squares for the dependent variable of exam grade is 2262. By inputting these numbers into the formula, we calculate:

MASTERING THE FORMULA

16-3: The standardized regression coefficient, β, is calculated by multiplying the slope of the regression equation by the quotient of the square root of the sum of squares for the independent variable by the square root of the sum of squares for the dependent variable:

$$\beta = (b) \frac{\sqrt{SS_X}}{\sqrt{SS_Y}}.$$

● The **standardized regression coefficient**, a standardized version of the slope in a regression equation, is the predicted change in the dependent variable in terms of standard deviations for an increase of 1 standard deviation in the independent variable; symbolized by β and often called *beta weight*.

$$\beta = (b) \frac{\sqrt{SS_X}}{\sqrt{SS_Y}} = (-5.39) \frac{\sqrt{56.4}}{\sqrt{2262}} = (-5.39) \frac{7.510}{47.560} = (-5.39)\, 0.158 = -0.85$$

TABLE 16-4	The Denominator of the Correlation Coefficient: The Calculations for Sums of Squares					
Absences (X)	$(X - M_X)$	$(X - M_X)^2$	Exam Grade (Y)	$(Y - M_Y)$	$(Y - M_Y)^2$
4	0.6	0.36	82	6	36
2	−1.4	1.96	98	22	484
2	−1.4	1.96	76	0	0
3	−0.4	0.16	68	−8	64
1	−2.4	5.76	84	8	64
0	−3.4	11.56	99	23	529
4	0.6	0.36	67	−9	81
8	4.6	21.16	58	−18	324
7	3.6	12.96	50	−26	676
3	−0.4	0.16	78	2	4
		$\Sigma(X - M_X)^2 = 56.4$			$\Sigma(Y - M_Y)^2 = 2262$

Notice that this result is the same as the Pearson correlation coefficient of −0.85. In fact, for simple linear regression, it is always exactly the same. Any difference would be due to rounding decisions for both calculations. Both the standardized regression coefficient and the correlation coefficient indicate the change in standard deviation that we expect when the independent variable increases by 1 standard deviation. Note that the correlation coefficient is *not* the same as the standardized regression coefficient when an equation includes more than one independent variable, a situation we'll encounter later in the section "Multiple Regression."

Because the standardized regression coefficient is the same as the correlation coefficient with simple linear regression, the outcome of hypothesis testing is also identical. The hypothesis-testing process that we used to test whether the correlation coefficient is statistically significantly different from 0 can also be used to test whether the standardized regression coefficient is statistically significantly different from 0. As you'll remember from Chapter 15, the Pearson correlation coefficient, $r = -0.85$, was larger in magnitude than the critical value of −0.632 (determined based on 8 degrees of freedom and a p level of 0.05). We rejected the null hypothesis and concluded that number of absences and exam grade seem to be negatively correlated.

> **MASTERING THE CONCEPT**
>
> **16-2:** A standardized regression coefficient is the standardized version of a slope, much like a z statistic is a standardized version of a raw score. For simple linear regression, the standardized regression coefficient is identical to the correlation coefficient. This means that when we conduct hypothesis testing and conclude that a correlation coefficient is statistically significantly different from 0, we can draw the same conclusion about the standardized regression coefficient.

CHECK YOUR LEARNING

Reviewing the Concepts

> Regression builds on correlation, enabling us not only to quantify the relation between two variables but also to predict a score on a dependent variable from a score on an independent variable.

> With the standardized regression equation, we simply multiply a person's z score on an independent variable by the Pearson correlation coefficient to predict that person's z score on a dependent variable.

> The raw-score regression equation is easier to use in that the equation itself does the transformations from raw score to z score and back.

continued on next page

> We use the standardized regression equation to build the regression equation that can predict a raw score on a dependent variable from a raw score on an independent variable.

> We can graph the regression line, $\hat{Y} = a + b(X)$, based on values for the y intercept, a; the predicted value on Y when X is 0; and the slope, b, which is the change in Y expected for a 1-unit increase in X.

> The slope, which captures the nature of the relation between the variables, can be standardized by calculating the standardized regression coefficient. The standardized regression coefficient tells us the predicted change in the dependent variable in terms of standard deviations for every increase of 1 standard deviation in the independent variable.

> With simple linear regression, the standardized regression coefficient is identical to the Pearson correlation coefficient.

Clarifying the Concepts   **16-1**   What is simple linear regression?

16-2   What purpose does the regression line serve?

Calculating the Statistics   **16-3**   Let's assume we know that women's heights and weights are correlated and the Pearson coefficient is 0.28. Let's also assume that we know the following descriptive statistics: For women's height, the mean is 5 feet 4 inches (64 inches), with a standard deviation of 2 inches; for women's weight, the mean is 155 pounds, with a standard deviation of 15 pounds. Sarah is 5 feet 7 inches tall. How much would you predict she weighs? To answer this question, complete the following steps:

a. Transform the raw score for the independent variable into a z score.

b. Calculate the predicted z score for the dependent variable.

c. Transform the z score for the dependent variable back into a predicted raw score.

16-4   Given the regression line $\hat{Y} = 12 + 0.67(X)$, make predictions for each of the following:

a. $X = 78$

b. $X = -14$

c. $X = 52$

Applying the Concepts   **16-5**   In Exercise 15.51, we explored the relation between number of taboo words said in one minute and the number of animal words said in one minute. We computed a correlation of 0.353 between these variables. The fictional data are presented below.

Number of taboo words (X)	Number of animals (Y)
9	23
5	20
4	17
12	28
14	26
10	16
9	17
11	18
14	23
6	21
7	25
13	19

a. What is the intercept?

b. What is the slope?

c. What is the regression equation?

d. Interpret both the *y* intercept and the slope in this regression equation.

e. Compute the standardized regression coefficient.

f. Explain what a strong correlation means for the predictive ability of the regression line.

Solutions to these Check Your Learning questions can be found in Appendix D.

g. What conclusion would you make if you performed a hypothesis test for this regression?

Interpretation and Prediction

In this section, we explore how the logic of regression is already a part of our everyday reasoning. Then we discuss why regression doesn't allow us to designate causation as we interpret data; for instance, MSU researchers could not say that spending more time on Facebook *caused* students to bridge more social capital with their online connections. This discussion of causation then leads us to a familiar warning about interpreting the meaning of regression, this time due to the process called *regression to the mean*. Finally, we learn how to calculate effect sizes so we can make interpretations about how well a regression equation predicts behavior.

Regression and Error

For many different reasons, predictions are full of errors, and that margin of error is factored into the regression analysis. For example, we might predict that a student would get a certain grade based on how many classes she skipped, but we could be wrong in our prediction. Other factors, such as her intelligence, the amount of sleep she got the night before, and the number of related classes she's taken all are likely to affect her grade as well. The number of skipped classes is highly unlikely to be a perfect predictor.

Errors in prediction lead to variability—and that is something we can measure. For *t* tests and ANOVAs, for example, we use standard deviation and standard error to calculate the variability around the mean. For regression, we calculate the variability around the line of best fit. Figure 16-4 illustrates that there is less variability—or error—when the data points are clustered tightly around the line of best fit. There is more variability—or error—when the data points are far away from the line of best fit.

The amount of error around the line of best fit can be quantified. The number that describes how far away, on average, the data points are from the line of best fit is called the **standard error of the estimate**, *a statistic that indicates the typical distance between a regression line and the actual data points.* The standard error of the estimate is essentially the standard deviation of the actual data points around the regression line. We usually get the standard error of the estimate using software, so its calculation is not covered here.

Applying the Lessons of Correlation to Regression

In addition to understanding the ways in which regression can help us, it is important to understand the limitations associated with using regression. It is extremely rare that the data analyzed in a regression equation are from a true experiment (one that used randomization to assign participants to conditions). Typically, we cannot randomly

● The **standard error of the estimate** is a statistic that indicates the typical distance between a regression line and the actual data points.

(a)

(b)

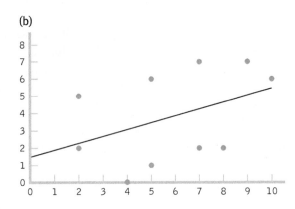

FIGURE 16-4

The Standard Error of the Estimate

Data points clustered closely around the line of best fit, as in graph (a), are described by a small standard error of the estimate. Data points clustered far away from the line of best fit, as in graph (b), are described by a large standard error of the estimate. We have a high level of confidence in the predictive ability of the independent variable when the data points are tightly clustered around the line of best fit, as in (a) (that is, there is much less error), and we have a low level of confidence in the predictive ability of the independent variable when the data points vary widely around the line of best fit, as in (b) (that is, there is much more error).

assign participants to conditions when the independent variable is a scale variable (rather than a nominal variable), as is usually the case with regression. So, the results are subject to the same limitations in interpretation that we discussed with respect to correlation.

In Chapter 15, we introduced the A-B-C model of understanding correlation. We noted that the correlation between number of absences and exam grade could be explained if skipping class (A) harmed one's grade (B); if a bad grade (B) led one to skip class more often (A) because of frustration; or if a third variable (C)—such as intelligence—led both to the awareness that going to class is a good thing (A) and to good grades (B). When drawing conclusions from regression, we must consider the same set of possible confounding variables that limited our confidence in the findings following a correlation.

In fact, regression, like correlation, can be wildly inaccurate in its predictions. As with the Pearson correlation coefficient, a good statistician questions causality *after* the statistical analysis (to identify potential confounding variables). But one more source of error can affect fair-minded interpretations of regression analyses: regression to the mean.

Regression to the Mean

In the study that we considered earlier in this chapter (Ruhm, 2006), economic factors predicted several indicators of health. The study also reported that "the drop in tobacco use disproportionately occurs among heavy smokers, the fall in body weight among the severely obese, and the increase in exercise among those who were completely inactive" (p. 2). What Ruhm describes captures the meaning of the word *regression*, as defined by its early proponents. Those who were most extreme on a given variable regressed (toward the mean). In other words, they became somewhat less extreme on that variable.

Francis Galton (Darwin's cousin) was the first to describe the phenomenon of regression to the mean, and he did so in a number of contexts (Bernstein, 1996). For example, Galton asked nine people—including Darwin—to plant sweet pea seeds in the widely scattered

MASTERING THE CONCEPT

16-3: Regression to the mean occurs because extreme scores tend to become less extreme—that is, they tend to regress toward the mean. Very tall parents tend to have tall children, but usually not as tall as they are, whereas very short parents tend to have short children, but usually not as short as they are.

locations in Britain where these people lived. Galton found that the variability among the seeds he sent out to be planted was larger than among the seeds that were produced by these plants. The largest seeds produced seeds smaller than they were. The smallest seeds produced seeds larger than they were.

Similarly, among people, Galton documented that, although tall parents tend to have taller-than-average children, their children tend to be a little shorter than they are. And although short parents tend to have shorter-than-average children, their children tend to be a little taller than they are. Galton noted that if regression to the mean did *not* occur, with tall people and large sweet peas producing offspring even taller or larger, and short people and small sweet peas producing offspring even shorter or smaller, "the world would consist of nothing but midgets and giants" (quoted in Bernstein, 1996, p. 167).

You can probably think of lots of additional examples of regression to the mean. Kevin Pemoulie, chef and co-owner of the now-closed Thirty Acres restaurant in Jersey City, wrote about regression to the mean in sports and upscale, foodie restaurants (2015). Pemoulie asked his readers, "Are you aware of the curse of John Madden? Each year, EA Sports puts out a John Madden football game, and the guy who's on the cover of the game almost inevitably gets hurt or costs his team a championship. . . . [Los Angeles restaurant] Alma is literally the John Madden problem: It was the No. 1 restaurant" on a highly respected list of the best newcomers to the restaurant scene in 2012, a list that Pemoulie's Thirty Acres was also on. Thirty Acres and Alma both closed in 2015.

An understanding of regression to the mean can help us make better choices in our daily lives. For example, regression to the mean is a particularly important concept to remember when we begin to save for retirement and have to choose the specific allocations of our savings. Table 16-5 shows data from *Morningstar*, an investment publication. The percentages represent the increase in that investment vehicle over two 5-year periods: 1984–1989 and 1989–1994 (Bernstein, 1996). As most descriptions of mutual funds remind potential investors, previous performance is not necessarily indicative of future performance. Consider regression to the mean in your own investment decisions. It might help you ride out a decrease in a mutual fund rather than panic and sell before the likely drift back toward the mean. And it might help you avoid buying into the fund that's been on top for several years, knowing that it stands a chance of sliding back toward the mean.

Regression to the Mean Tall parents tend to have children who are taller than average, but not as tall as they are. Similarly, short parents (like the older parents in this photograph) tend to have children who are shorter than average, but not as short as they are. Francis Galton was the first to document this phenomenon, which came to be called *regression to the mean*.

Jack Hollingsworth/Getty Images

TABLE 16-5	**Regression to the Mean: Investing**

Bernstein (1996) presented these data from *Morningstar*, an investment publication, demonstrating regression to the mean in action. Notice that the category that showed the highest performances during the first time period (international stocks) had declined by the second time period, whereas the category with the poorest performances in the first time period (aggressive growth) had improved by the second time period.

Five Years to Objective	1984–1989 (percent increase)	1989–1994 (percent increase)
International stocks	20.6	9.4
Income	14.3	11.2
Growth and income	14.2	11.9
Growth	13.3	13.9
Small company	10.3	15.9
Aggressive growth	8.9	16.1
Average	13.6	13.1

● The **proportionate reduction in error** is a statistic that quantifies how much more accurate predictions are when we use the regression line instead of the mean as a prediction tool; also called the *coefficient of determination*.

Proportionate Reduction in Error

In the previous section, we developed a regression equation to predict a final exam score from number of absences. Now we want to know: How good is this regression equation? Is it worth having students use this equation to predict their own final exam grades from the numbers of classes they plan to skip? To answer this question, we calculate a form of effect size, *the **proportionate reduction in error**—a statistic that quantifies how much more accurate predictions are when we use the regression line instead of the mean as a prediction tool.* (Note that the proportionate reduction in error is sometimes called the *coefficient of determination*.) More specifically, the proportionate reduction in error is a statistic that quantifies how much more accurate predictions are when scores are predicted using a specific regression equation rather than when the mean is just predicted for everyone.

Earlier in this chapter, we noted that if we did not have a regression equation, the best we could do is predict the mean for everyone, regardless of number of absences. The average final exam grade for students in this sample is 76. With no further information, we could only tell our students that our best guess for their statistics grade is a 76. There would obviously be a great deal of error if we predicted the mean for everyone. Using the mean to estimate scores is a reasonable way to proceed if that's all the information we have. But the regression line provides a more precise picture of the relation between variables, so using a regression equation reduces error.

Less error is the same thing as having a smaller standard error of the estimate—a smaller standard error of the estimate means that we'd be doing much better in our predictions than if we had a larger one; visually, this means that the actual scores are closer to the regression line. Conversely, with a larger standard error of the estimate, we'd be doing much worse in our predictions than if we had a smaller one; visually, the actual scores are farther away from the regression line.

But we can do more than just quantify the standard deviation around the regression line. We can determine how much better the regression equation is compared to the mean: We calculate the proportion of error that we eliminate by using the regression equation, rather than the mean, to make a prediction. (In this next section, we learn the long way to calculate this proportion in order to understand exactly what the proportion represents. Then we learn a shortcut.)

EXAMPLE 16.4

Using a sample, we can calculate the amount of error from using the mean as a predictive tool. We quantify that error by determining how far off a person's score on the dependent variable (final exam grade) is from the mean, as seen in the column labeled "Error $(Y - M_Y)$" in Table 16-6.

For example, for student 1, the error is $82 - 76 = 6$. We then square these errors for all 10 students and sum them. This is another type of sum of squares: the sum of squared errors. Here, the sum of squared errors is 2262 (the sum of the values in the "Squared Error" column). This is a measure of the error that would result if we predicted the mean for every person in the sample. We'll call this particular type of sum of squared errors the *sum of squares total*, SS_{total}, because it represents the worst-case scenario, the total error we would have if there were no regression equation. We can visualize this error on a graph that depicts a horizontal line for the mean, as seen in Figure 16-5. We can add the actual points, as we would in a scatterplot, and draw vertical lines from each point to the mean. These vertical lines give us a visual sense of the error that results from predicting the mean for everyone.

TABLE 16-6	Calculating Error When We Predict the Mean for Everyone

If we do not have a regression equation, the best we can do is predict the mean for Y for every participant. When we do that, we will of course have some error, because not everyone will have exactly the mean value on Y. This table presents the squared errors for each participant when we predict the mean for each of them. The sum is 2262.

Student	Grade (Y)	Mean for Y	Error ($Y - M_Y$)	Squared Error
1	82	76	6	36
2	98	76	22	484
3	76	76	0	0
4	68	76	−8	64
5	84	76	8	64
6	99	76	23	529
7	67	76	−9	81
8	58	76	−18	324
9	50	76	−26	676
10	78	76	2	4

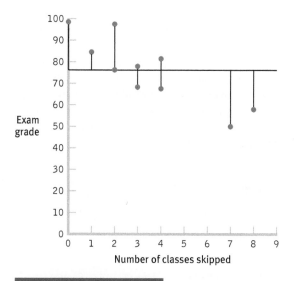

FIGURE 16-5

Visualizing Error

A graph with a horizontal line for the mean, 76, allows us to visualize the error that would result if we predicted the mean for everyone. We draw lines for each person's point on a scatterplot to the mean. Those lines are a visual representation of error.

The regression equation can't make the predictions any worse than they would be if we just predicted the mean for everyone. But it's not worth the time and effort to use a regression equation if it doesn't lead to a substantial improvement over just predicting the mean. As we can with the mean, we can calculate the amount of error from using the regression equation with the sample. We can then see how much better we do with the regression equation than with the mean.

First, we calculate what we would predict for each student if we used the regression equation. We do this by plugging each X into the regression equation. Here are the calculations using the equation $\hat{Y} = 94.30 - 5.39(X)$:

$$\hat{Y} = 94.30 - 5.39(4); \hat{Y} = 72.74$$
$$\hat{Y} = 94.30 - 5.39(2); \hat{Y} = 83.52$$
$$\hat{Y} = 94.30 - 5.39(2); \hat{Y} = 83.52$$
$$\hat{Y} = 94.30 - 5.39(3); \hat{Y} = 78.13$$
$$\hat{Y} = 94.30 - 5.39(1); \hat{Y} = 88.91$$
$$\hat{Y} = 94.30 - 5.39(0); \hat{Y} = 94.30$$
$$\hat{Y} = 94.30 - 5.39(4); \hat{Y} = 72.74$$
$$\hat{Y} = 94.30 - 5.39(8); \hat{Y} = 51.18$$
$$\hat{Y} = 94.30 - 5.39(7); \hat{Y} = 56.57$$
$$\hat{Y} = 94.30 - 5.39(3); \hat{Y} = 78.13$$

The $\hat{Y}$'s, or predicted scores for Y, that we just calculated are presented in Table 16-7, where the errors are calculated based on the predicted scores rather than the mean. For example, for student 1, the error is the actual score minus the predicted score: $82 - 72.74 = 9.26$. As before, we square the errors and sum them. The sum of squared errors based on the regression equation is 623.425. We call this the *sum of squared errors, SS_{error}* because it represents the error that we'd have if we predicted Y using the regression equation.

As before, we can visualize this error on a graph that includes the regression line, as seen in Figure 16-6. We again add the actual points, as in a scatterplot, and we draw vertical lines from each point to the regression line. These vertical lines give us a visual sense of the error that results from predicting Y for everyone using the regression equation. Notice that these vertical lines in Figure 16-6 tend to be shorter than those connecting each person's point with the mean in Figure 16-5.

TABLE 16-7 Calculating Error when We Use the Regression Equation to Predict

When we use a regression equation for prediction, as opposed to using the mean, we have less error. However, we still have some error because not every participant falls exactly on the regression line. This table presents the squared errors for each participant when we predict each one's score on Y using the regression equation. The sum is 623.425.

Student	Absences (X)	Grade (Y)	Predicted ($\hat{Y}$)	Error ($Y - \hat{Y}$)	Squared Error
1	4	82	72.74	9.26	85.748
2	2	98	83.52	14.48	209.670
3	2	76	83.52	−7.52	56.550
4	3	68	78.13	−10.13	102.617
5	1	84	88.91	−4.91	24.108
6	0	99	94.30	4.70	22.090
7	4	67	72.74	−5.74	32.948
8	8	58	51.18	6.82	46.512
9	7	50	56.57	−6.57	43.165
10	3	78	78.13	−0.13	0.017

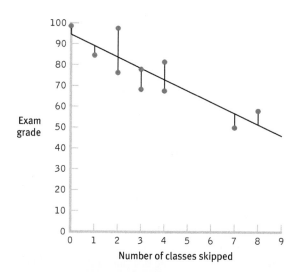

FIGURE 16-6

Visualizing Error

A graph that depicts the regression line allows us to visualize the error that would result if we predicted Y for everyone using the regression equation. We draw lines for each person's point on a scatterplot to the regression line. Those lines are a visual representation of error.

So how much better did we do? The error we predict by using the mean for everyone in this sample is 2262. The error we predict by using the regression equation for everyone in this sample is 623.425. Remember that the measure of how well the regression equation predicts is called the proportionate *reduction* in error. What we want to know is how much error we have gotten rid of—reduced—by using the regression equation instead of the mean. The amount of error we've reduced is $2262 - 623.425 = 1638.575$. But the word *proportionate* indicates that we want a proportion of the total error that we have reduced, so we set up a ratio to determine this. We have reduced 1638.575 of the original 2262, or $\dfrac{1638.575}{2262} = 0.724$.

We have reduced 0.724, or 72.4%, of the original error by using the regression equation versus using the mean to predict Y. This ratio can be calculated using an equation that represents what we just calculated: the proportionate reduction in error, symbolized as:

$$r^2 = \frac{(SS_{total} - SS_{error})}{SS_{total}} = \frac{(2262 - 623.425)}{2262} = 0.724$$

To recap, we simply have to do the following:

1. Determine the error associated with using the mean as the predictor.
2. Determine the error associated with using the regression equation as the predictor.
3. Subtract the error associated with the regression equation from the error associated with the mean.
4. Divide the difference (calculated in step 3) by the error associated with using the mean.

The proportionate reduction in error tells us how good the regression equation is. Here is another way to state it: The proportionate reduction in error is a measure of the amount of variance in the dependent variable that is explained by the independent variable. Did you notice the symbol for the proportionate reduction in error?

The symbol is r^2. Perhaps you see the connection with another number we have calculated. Yes, we could simply square the correlation coefficient!

The longer calculations are necessary, however, to see the difference between the error in prediction from using the regression equation and the error in prediction from simply predicting the mean for everyone. Once you have calculated the proportionate reduction in error the long way a few times, you'll have a good sense of exactly what you're calculating. In addition to the relation of the proportionate reduction in error to the correlation coefficient, it also is the same as another number we've calculated—the effect size for ANOVA, R^2. In both cases, this number represents the proportion of variance in the dependent variable that is explained by the independent variable.

Because the proportionate reduction in error can be calculated by squaring the correlation coefficient, we can have a sense of the amount of error that would be reduced simply by looking at the correlation coefficient. A correlation coefficient that is high in magnitude, whether negative or positive, indicates a strong relation between two variables. If two variables are highly related, it makes sense that one of them would be a good predictor of the other. And it makes sense that when we use one variable to predict the other, we're going to reduce error. ●

CHECK YOUR LEARNING

Reviewing the Concepts

> Findings from regression analyses are subject to the same types of limitations as correlation. Regression, like correlation, does not tell us about causation.

> People with extreme scores at one point in time tend to have less extreme scores (scores closer to the mean) at a later point in time, a phenomenon called *regression to the mean*.

> Error based on the mean is referred to as the sum of squares total (SS_{total}), whereas error based on the regression equation is referred to as the sum of squared error (SS_{error}).

> Proportionate reduction in error, r^2, is the amount of error we have eliminated by using a particular regression equation to predict a person's score on the dependent variable versus simply predicting the mean on the dependent variable for that person.

Clarifying the Concepts **16-6** Distinguish the standard error of the estimate around the line of best fit from the error of prediction around the mean.

16-7 Explain how, for regression, the strength of the correlation is related to the proportionate reduction in error.

Calculating the Statistics 16-8 Data are provided here with means, standard deviations, a correlation coefficient, and a regression equation: $r = -0.77$, $\hat{Y} = 7.846 - 0.431(X)$.

X	Y
5	6
6	5
4	6
5	6
7	4
8	5
$M_X = 5.833$	$M_Y = 5.333$
$SD_X = 1.344$	$SD_Y = 0.745$

a. Using this information, calculate the sum of squared error for the mean, SS_{total}.

b. Now, using the regression equation provided, calculate the sum of squared error for the regression equation, SS_{error}.

c. Using your work from parts (a) and (b), calculate the proportionate reduction in error for these data.

d. Check that this calculation of r^2 equals the square of the correlation coefficient.

Applying the Concepts   **16-9**   Earlier you read about regression to the mean in a football video game and in the world of high-end restaurants. Many athletes and sports fans believe that an appearance on the cover of *Sports Illustrated (SI)* is a curse. Shortly after appearing on the cover of *SI*, players or teams often have a particularly poor performance. This tendency is documented in the pages of (what else?) *Sports Illustrated* and even has a name, the "*SI* jinx" (Wolff, 2002). In fact, of 2456 covers, *SI* counted 913 "victims." And their potential victims have noticed: After the New England Patriots football team won their league championship, their coach at the time, Bill Parcells, called his daughter, then an *SI* staffer, and ordered: "No cover." Using your knowledge about the limitations of regression, what would you say to Coach Parcells?

Solutions to these Check Your Learning questions can be found in Appendix D.

Multiple Regression

In regression analysis, we explain more of the variability in the dependent variable if we can discover genuine predictors that are separate and distinct. This involves ***orthogonal variables,*** *independent variables that make separate and distinct contributions in the prediction of a dependent variable, as compared with the contributions of other variables.* Orthogonal variables do not overlap each other. For example, the study we discussed earlier explored whether the amount of Facebook use predicted social capital. It is likely that a person's personality also predicts social capital; for example, we would expect extroverted, or outgoing, people to be more likely to have this kind of social capital than introverted, or shy, people. It would be useful to separate the effects of the amount of Facebook use and extroversion on social capital.

The statistical technique we consider next is a way of quantifying (1) whether multiple pieces of evidence really are better than one, and (2) precisely how much better each additional piece of evidence actually is.

- An **orthogonal variable** is an independent variable that makes a separate and distinct contribution in the prediction of a dependent variable, as compared with the contributions of another variable.

- **Multiple regression** is a statistical technique that includes two or more predictor variables in a prediction equation.

Understanding the Equation

Just as a regression equation using one independent variable is a better predictor than the mean, a regression equation using more than one independent variable is likely to be an even better predictor. This makes sense in the same way that knowing a baseball player's historical batting average *plus* knowing that the player continues to suffer from a serious injury is likely to improve our ability to predict the player's future performance. So it is not surprising that multiple regression is far more common than simple linear regression. ***Multiple regression*** *is a statistical technique that includes two or more predictor variables in a prediction equation.*

Let's examine an equation that might be used to predict a final exam grade from two variables, number of absences *and* number of hours that students studied for the final exam. Table 16-8 repeats the data from Table 16-1, with the added variable of hours studied. (Note that although the scores on number of absences and final exam grade are real-life data from our statistics classes, the numbers of hours that students studied are fictional.)

> **MASTERING THE CONCEPT**
>
> **16-5:** Multiple regression predicts scores on a single dependent variable from scores on more than one independent variable. Because behavior tends to be influenced by many factors, multiple regression allows us to better predict a given outcome.

TABLE 16-8	Predicting Exam Grade from Two Variables

Multiple regression allows us to develop a regression equation that predicts a dependent variable from two or more independent variables. Here, we will use these data to develop a regression equation that predicts exam grade from number of absences *and* numbers of hours that students studied for the final exam.

Student	Absences	Hours Studied	Exam Grade
1	4	6	82
2	2	7.5	98
3	2	5	76
4	3	5	68
5	1	5.5	84
6	0	7	99
7	4	6	67
8	8	5	58
9	7	4.5	50
10	3	5.5	78

The computer gives us the printout seen in Figure 16-7. The column in which we're interested is the one labeled "B," under "Unstandardized Coefficients." The first number, across from "(Constant)," is the intercept. The intercept is called *constant* because it does not change; it is not multiplied by any value of an independent variable. The intercept here is 35.230. The second number is the slope for the independent variable, number of absences. Number of absences is negatively correlated with final exam grade, so the slope, −3.389, is negative. The third number in this column is the slope for the independent variable of number of hours studied for the exam. As we might guess, hours studied and final exam grade are positively correlated; a student who spends more time studying tends to have a higher final exam grade. So the slope, 9.174, is positive. We can put these numbers into a regression equation, with X_1 representing the first variable, absences, and X_2 representing the second variable, hours studied:

$$\hat{Y} = 35.230 - 3.389(X_1) + 9.174(X_2)$$

Coefficients[a]

Model		Unstandardized Coefficients		Standardized Cofficients	t	Sig.
		B	Std. Error	Beta		
1	(Constant)	35.230	13.802		2.553	.038
	Number of Absences	−3.389	.796	−.535	−4.256	.004
	Hours Studied	9.174	2.101	.549	4.366	.003

a. Dependent Variable: Final Exam Grade

FIGURE 16-7

Software Output for Regression

Computer software provides the information necessary for the multiple regression equation. All necessary coefficients are in column B under "Unstandardized Coefficients." The constant, 35.230, is the intercept; the number next to "Number of absences," −3.389, is the slope for that independent variable; and the number next to "Hours Studied," 9.174, is the slope for that independent variable.

Once we develop the multiple regression equation, we can input raw scores on number of absences and hours spent studying to determine a student's predicted score on Y. Imagine that our student, Allie, spent six hours studying. We already know she planned to miss two classes this semester. What would we predict her final exam grade to be?

$$\hat{Y} = 35.230 - 3.389(X_1) + 9.174(X_2)$$
$$= 35.230 - 3.389(2) + 9.174(6)$$
$$= 35.230 - 6.778 + 55.044 = 83.496$$

Multiple Independent Variables Researchers use multiple regression when they have measured at least two independent variables that they believe predict the dependent variable. For example, researchers might explore whether hours spent playing violent video games, scores on a personality measure, and numbers of close friends predict aggression levels in children.

Based on these two variables, we predict a final exam grade of 83.496 for Allie. How good is this multiple regression equation? From software, we calculated that the proportionate reduction in error for this equation is a whopping 0.926. By using a multiple regression equation with the independent variables of number of absences and number of hours studied, we have reduced 93% of the error that would result from predicting the mean of 76 for everyone.

When we calculate proportionate reduction in error for a multiple regression, the symbol changes slightly. The symbol is now R^2 instead of r^2. The capitalization of this statistic is an indication that the proportionate reduction in error is based on more than one independent variable.

Multiple Regression in Everyday Life

With the development of increasingly more powerful computers and the availability of ever-larger amounts of electronic data, tools based on multiple regression have proliferated. Now the general public can access many of them online (Darlin, 2006; Rosenbloom, 2015). Many apps and Web sites, including Flyr, Skypicker, Hopper, Kayak, and Google Flights, predict the price of an airline ticket for specific routes, travel dates, and, most important, purchase dates. Often using the same data available to travel agents, along with additional independent variables such as the weather and even which sports teams' fans might be traveling to a championship game, farecasting tools mimic the regression equations used by the airlines. Airlines predict how much money potential travelers are willing to pay on a given date for a given flight and use these predictions to adjust their fares so they can earn the most money.

Online farecasting tools are attempting an end run, using mathematical prediction tools, to help savvy airline consumers either beat or wait out the airlines' price hikes. In 2007, one early farecasting site claimed a 74.5% accuracy rate for its predictions. Zillow.com does for real estate what the farecasting sites do for airline tickets. Using archival land records, Zillow predicts U.S. housing prices and claims to be accurate to within 10% of the actual selling price of a given home.

Amazon.com is trying to take the prediction game to a new level. In 2014 they filed a patent for something called "anticipatory shipping" (Bensinger, 2014). Amazon could take advantage of their immense database of customer information to ship products to distribution centers closer to customers, or even load products onto trucks—all *before* customers make a purchase! Amazon indicated that it might base its shipping behavior on customers' searches, wish lists, and previous orders, as well as their online behavior, down to noticing the amount of time a customer spends with her cursor over a particular product.

What's interesting about prediction tools is that they all depend on the independent variables that the researchers choose. Different inputs lead to different predictions. Let's take just one example—the predictive tools that Amazon and Netflix use to determine what books, movies, or other media you might like. In describing the difference, a reporter asked readers to imagine they were in a brick-and-mortar store (Domingos, 2015). Based on their individual regression equations, "Amazon would be more likely to walk you over to shelves you've frequented previously; Netflix would take you to unfamiliar and seemingly odd sections of the store but lead you to stuff you'd end up loving." Is one better than the other? Perhaps not. You have to pay for each item you order from Amazon, so you may not be as likely to take risks. With Netflix, everything is included in your monthly subscription, so an offbeat recommendation is much less of a gamble. Prediction is not an exact science, but it is certainly an exciting one—and one that provides exciting opportunities for the statistically inclined. Like the future of visual displays of data, the future of the regression equation is limited only by the creativity of the rising generation of behavioral scientists and statisticians.

Next Steps   Structural Equation Modeling (SEM)

We're going to introduce an approach to data analysis that is infinitely more flexible and visually more expressive than multiple regression. It also is another technique that allows us to move away from the limitations of traditional hypothesis testing. *Structural equation modeling (SEM) is a statistical technique that quantifies how well sample data "fit" a theoretical model that hypothesizes a set of relations among multiple variables.* Here, we are discussing "fit" in much the same way you might try on some new clothes and say, "That's a good fit" or "That really doesn't fit!" Statisticians who use SEM refer to the "model" that they are testing. In this case, a *statistical (or theoretical) model is a hypothesized network of relations, often portrayed graphically, among multiple variables.*

Psychologist Joseph Lee Rodgers refers to the growing use of statistical modeling as a "quiet methodological revolution" (p. 1, 2010). Rodgers believes that thinking in terms of statistical models increases creativity among researchers because it focuses us on the driving force behind research, the hypotheses. Instead of testing data against a null hypothesis, Rodgers says, we should build and evaluate statistical models.

What's the difference between traditional hypothesis testing and statistical models? Instead of thinking of variables as "independent" variables or "dependent" variables, SEM encourages researchers to think of variables as a series of connections. Consider an independent variable such as the number of hours spent studying. What predicts how many hours a person will study? We can answer that by thinking of hours studying as a dependent variable with its own set of independent variables. But an independent variable in one study can become a dependent variable in another study. SEM quantifies a network of relations, so some of the variables are independent variables that predict other variables later in the network, as well as dependent variables that are predicted by other variables earlier in the network. This is why we will refer to variables without the usual adjectives of *independent* or *dependent* as we discuss SEM.

● **Structural equation modeling (SEM)** is a statistical technique that quantifies how well sample data "fit" a theoretical model that hypothesizes a set of relations among multiple variables.

● **A statistical (or theoretical) model** is a hypothesized network of relations, often portrayed graphically, among multiple variables.

Language Alert! In the historical development of SEM, the analyses based on this kind of diagram were called *path analyses* for the fairly obvious reason that the arrows represented "paths"—factors that lead to whatever the next variable in the model happened to be. ***Path*** *is the term that statisticians use to describe the connection between two variables in a statistical model.* ***Path analysis*** *is a statistical method that examines a hypothesized model, usually by conducting a series of regression analyses that quantify the paths at each succeeding step in the model.*

Path analysis is used rarely these days because the more powerful technique of SEM can better quantify the relations among variables in a model. But we still find the term *path* to be a more intuitive way to describe the flow of behavior through a network of variables, and the word *path* continues to be used in structural equation models. SEM uses a statistic much like the correlation coefficient to indicate the relation between any two variables. Like a path through a forest, a path could be small and barely discernible (close to 0) or large and easy to follow (closer to −1.00 or 1.00).

In SEM, we start with measurements called ***manifest variables,*** *the variables in a study that we can observe and that are measured.* We assess something that we can observe in an attempt to understand the underlying main idea in which we're interested. In SEM, these main idea variables are called ***latent variables,*** *the ideas that we want to research but cannot directly measure.* For example, we cannot actually see the latent variable we call "shyness," but we still try to measure shyness in the manifest variables using self-report scales, naturalistic observations, and reports by others about shy behavior. We use these manifest variables and latent variables to create a model that is depicted in a visual diagram of variables.

Let's examine one published SEM study. In a longitudinal study, researchers examined whether receiving good parenting at age 17 predicted emotional adjustment at age 26 (Dumas, Lawford, Tieu, & Pratt, 2009). They explored the relations among four latent variables in a sample of 100 adolescents in Ontario, Canada. The latent variables were the following:

1. *Positive parenting,* an estimate of whether an adolescent received good parenting as assessed by three self-report manifest variables at age 17
2. *Story ending* (a variable called *narrative coherent positive resolution* by the researchers), an estimate based on stories that participants were asked to tell at age 26 about their most difficult life experience and that included the manifest variables of the positivity of the story's ending, the negativity of the story's ending, whether the ending was coherent, and whether the story had a resolution
3. *Identity maturity* with respect to religion, politics, and career at age 26, quantified via the manifest variables of achievement (strong identity in these areas), moratorium (still deciding with respect to these areas), and diffusion (weak identity in these areas)
4. *Emotional adjustment,* assessed at age 26 by the manifest variables of optimism, depression, and general well-being

Note that higher scores on all four latent variables indicate a more positive outcome. Figure 16-8 depicts the researchers' model.

To understand the story of this model, we need to understand only three components—the four circles, the three or four squares attached to each circle, and the arrows linking the circles. The circles represent the underlying ideas of interest, the latent variables. These are latent variables because positive parenting cannot be directly measured, nor can emotional adjustment be directly "seen."

Path is the term that statisticians use to describe the connection between two variables in a statistical model.

Path analysis is a statistical method that examines a hypothesized model, usually by conducting a series of regression analyses that quantify the paths between variables at each succeeding step in the model.

Manifest variables are the variables in a study that we can observe and that are measured.

Latent variables are the ideas that we want to research but cannot directly measure.

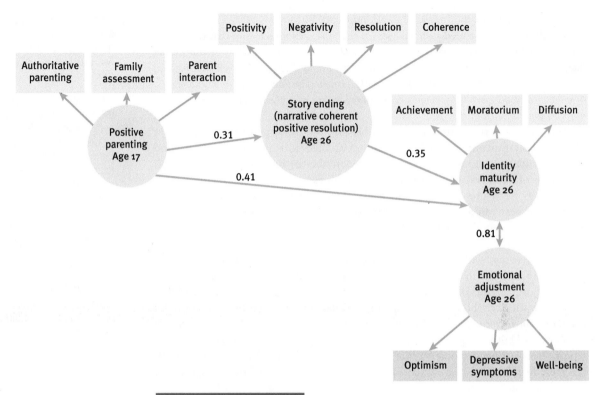

FIGURE 16-8

A SEM Diagram

This diagram depicts a structural equation model (SEM). By "reading" the numbers connecting variables, we can begin to understand the story this graph tells. For example, the path between the left-hand circle, "Positive Parenting," and the upper-right-hand circle, "Identity Maturity," has a coefficient of 0.41. This indicates a strong positive predictive relation between the type of parenting an adolescent received at age 17 and the maturity of her or his identity formation at age 26. As another example, the path between the two circles on the right, "Identity Maturity" and "Emotional Adjustment," has a coefficient of 0.81. This indicates a very strong positive relation between the maturity of one's identity formation and one's emotional adjustment at age 26. The two-headed arrow indicates that these constructs are theorized to predict each other.

The squares above or below each circle represent the measurement tools used to operationalize each latent variable. These are the manifest variables, the ones that can be observed. Let's look at "Story ending," the latent variable related to the stories that the 26-year-old participants told about their worst life experiences. There are four boxes above it: "Positivity," "Negativity," "Resolution," and "Coherence." These refer to the four different measures of the story's ending that we described above.

Once we understand the latent variables (as measured by the three or more manifest variables), all that's left for us to understand is the arrows that represent each path. The numbers on each path give us a sense of the relation between each pair of variables. Similar to correlation coefficients, the sign of the number indicates the direction of the relation, either negative or positive, and the value of the number indicates the strength of the relation. Although this is a simplification, these basic rules will allow you to "read" the story in the diagram of the model.

So how does this SEM diagram address the research question about the effects of good parenting? We'll start on the left and read across. Notice the two paths that lead from positive parenting to story ending and to identity maturity. The numbers are 0.31 and 0.41, respectively. These are fairly large positive numbers. They suggest that receiving positive parenting at age 17 leads to a healthier interpretation of a negative life experience and to a well-established identity at age 26. Characteristics of the narrative that participants told also positively predict identity maturity at a level of 0.35.

Now notice the two-headed vertical arrow between identity maturity and emotional adjustment at age 26 with the number 0.81. This shows that identity maturity and emotional adjustment are strong predictors of each other at age 26. Positive parenting does indeed seem to predict later emotional adjustment (through the variables of how participants interpret negative events in their lives and the degree of maturity in their identity formation). It seems that good parenting helps an adolescent to be more mature, which leads to good emotional adjustment.

When you encounter a model such as SEM, follow these basic steps: First, figure out what variables the researcher is studying. Then, look at the numbers to see which variables are related and look at the signs of the numbers to see the direction of the relation.

CHECK YOUR LEARNING

Reviewing the Concepts
> Multiple regression is used to predict a dependent variable from more than one independent variable. Ideally, these variables are distinct from one another in such a way that they contribute uniquely to the predictions.

> We can develop a multiple regression equation and input specific scores for each independent variable to determine the predicted score on the dependent variable.

> Multiple regression is the backbone of many online tools that we can use for predicting everyday variables such as home prices or traffic.

> Structural equation modeling (SEM) allows us to examine the "fit" of a sample's data to a hypothesized model of the relations among multiple variables, the latent variables that we hypothesize to exist but cannot see.

Clarifying the Concepts **16-10** What is multiple regression, and what are its benefits over simple linear regression?

Calculating the Statistics **16-11** Write the equation for the line of prediction using the following output from a multiple regression analysis:

Coefficients[a]

Model		Unstandardized Coefficients		Standardized Coefficients	t	Sig.
		B	Std. Error	Beta		
1	(Constant)	5.251	4.084		1.286	.225
	Variable A	.060	.107	.168	.562	.585
	Variable B	1.105	.437	.758	2.531	.028

a. Dependent Variable: Outcome variable

16-12 Use the equation for the line you created in Check Your Learning 16-11 to make predictions for each of the following:

a. $X_1 = 40, X_2 = 14$

b. $X_1 = 101, X_2 = 39$

c. $X_1 = 76, X_2 = 20$

continued on next page

Applying the Concepts   **16-13**   As regression analyses become more common in situations that we encounter every day, there are bound to be problems (Kirchner, 2015). Below are two examples of problematic regression equations. For each, state the likely independent variable or variables and the likely dependent variable or variables. Be as specific as you can. Based just on the information provided, is this an example of a simple linear regression or a multiple regression? Explain your answer.

     a. The *Wall Street Journal* (Valentino-Devries, Singer-Vine, & Soltani, 2012) reported that the office supply store Staples used a regression to determine prices for customers in different locations. Customers who lived farther away from office supply stores that are competitors to Staples were charged higher prices than those who lived closer to competitors. The problem? Customers living futher from competitors' stores were more likely to be living in poor or rural regions. The reporter pointed out that "it diminishes the Internet's role as an equalizer."

     b. A 2015 report examined the predictive equations used in sentencing those convicted of crimes in an attempt to predict the likelihood that an individual would become a repeat offender (Barry-Jester, Casselman, & Goldstein, 2015). Beyond the person's criminal record, they used information like age, job history, and patterns of crime within the person's family. The reporter asked "Is it fair to score people based on not only their own past criminal behavior, but on statistics about other people who fit the same profile?"

REVIEW OF CONCEPTS

Simple Linear Regression

Regression is an expansion of correlation in that it allows us not only to quantify a relation between two variables but also to quantify one variable's ability to predict another variable. We can predict a dependent variable's z score from an independent variable's z score, or we can do a bit more initial work and predict a dependent variable's raw score from an independent variable's raw score. The latter method uses the equation for a line with an *intercept* and a *slope*.

We use *simple linear regression* when we predict one dependent variable from one independent variable when the two variables are linearly related. We can graph this line using the regression equation, plugging in low and high values of X and plotting those values with their associated predicted values on Y, then connecting the dots to form the regression line.

Just as we can standardize a raw score by converting it to a z score, we can standardize a slope by converting it to a *standardized regression coefficient*. This number indicates the predicted change on the dependent variable in terms of standard deviation for every increase of 1 standard deviation in the independent variable. For simple linear regression, the standardized regression coefficient is the same as the Pearson correlation coefficient. Hypothesis testing that determines whether the correlation coefficient is statistically significantly different from 0 also indicates whether the standardized regression coefficient is statistically significantly different from 0.

Interpretation and Prediction

A regression equation is rarely a perfect predictor of scores on the dependent variable. There is always some prediction error, which can be quantified by the *standard error of the estimate*, the number that describes the typical amount that an observation falls from the regression line. In addition, regression suffers from the same drawbacks as correlation. For example, we cannot know if the predictive relation is causal; the posited direction could be the reverse (with Y causally predicting X), or there could be a third variable at work.

When we use regression, we must also be aware of the phenomenon called regression to the mean, in which extreme values tend to become less extreme over time.

When we use regression, we must consider the degree to which an independent variable predicts a dependent variable. To do this, we can calculate the *proportionate reduction in error*, symbolized as r^2. The proportionate reduction in error tells us how much better our prediction is with the regression equation than with the mean as the only predictive tool.

Multiple Regression

We use *multiple regression* when we have more than one independent variable, as is usual in most research in the behavioral sciences. Multiple regression is particularly useful when we have *orthogonal variables*, independent variables that make separate contributions to the prediction of a dependent variable. Multiple regression has led to the development of many Web-based prediction tools that allow us to make educated guesses about such outcomes as airplane ticket prices.

A number of more sophisticated statistical analyses, such as path analysis and its more complex counterpart, structural equation modeling (SEM), have been developed in recent years. These techniques allow us to see predictive relations among a number of variables as predicted by a statistical (or theoretical) model. SEM diagrams can be "read" with a basic understanding of a few concepts. Latent variables, represented by large circles, represent the constructs of interest that we cannot directly measure. We operationalize latent variables by measuring several manifest variables, represented by squares, that we believe represent the latent variable. Finally, we look at the numbers above the paths, represented by arrows, to determine the strength and direction of relations between variables.

SPSS®

The most common form of regression analysis in SPSS uses at least two scale variables: an independent variable (predictor) and a dependent variable (the variable being predicted). Let's use the number of absences and exam grade data as an example. Once again, begin by visualizing the data.

Request the scatterplot of the data by selecting: Graphs → Chart Builder → Gallery → Scatter/Dot. Drag the upper-left sample graph to the large box on top. Then select the variables to be included in the scatterplot by dragging the independent variable, "absences," to the x-axis, and the dependent variable, "grade," to the y-axis. Click "OK." Double-click on the graph to make changes using the Chart Editor. To add the regression line, click "Elements," then "Fit Line at Total." Close the Chart Editor by clicking the x in the upper right-hand corner.

To analyze the linear regression, select: Analyze → Regression → Linear. Select "absences" as the independent (predictor) variable and "grade" as the dependent variable being predicted.

As usual, click on "OK" to see the Output screen. Part of the output is shown in the screenshot here. In the box titled "Model Summary," we can see the correlation coefficient of .851 under "R" and the proportionate reduction of error, .724, under "R Square." In the box titled "Coefficients," we can look in the first column under "B" to determine the regression equation. The intercept, 94.326, is across from "(Constant)," and the slope, −5.390, is across from "Number of Absences." (Any slight differences from the numbers we calculated earlier are due to rounding decisions.)

HOW IT WORKS

16.1 REGRESSION WITH z SCORES

Shannon Callahan, a former student in the experimental psychology master's program at Seton Hall University, conducted a study that examined evaluations of faculty members on Ratemyprofessor.com. She wondered if professors who were rated high on "clarity" were more likely to be viewed as "easy." Callahan found a significant correlation of 0.267 between the average easiness rating a professor garnered and the average rating he or she received with respect to clarity of teaching.

If we know that a professor's z score on clarity is 2.2 (an indication that she is very clear), how could we predict her z score on easiness?

$$z_{\hat{Y}} = (r_{XY})(z_X) = (0.267)(2.2) = 0.59$$

When there's a positive correlation, we predict a z score above the mean when her original z score is above the mean.

And if a professor's z score on clarity is -1.8 (an indication that she's not very clear), how could we predict her z score on easiness?

$$z_{\hat{Y}} = (r_{XY})(z_X) = (0.267)(-1.8) = -0.48$$

When there's a positive correlation, we predict a z score below the mean when her original z score is below the mean.

16.2 REGRESSION WITH RAW SCORES

Using Shannon Callahan's data, how can we develop the regression equation so that we can work directly with raw scores? To do this, we need a little more information. For this data set, the mean clarity score is 3.673, with a standard deviation of 0.890; the mean easiness score is 2.843, with a standard deviation of 0.701. As noted before, the correlation between these variables is 0.267.

To calculate the regression equation, we need to find the intercept and the slope. We determine the *intercept* by calculating what we predict for Y (easiness) when X (clarity) equals 0. Given the means, the standard deviations, and the correlation calculated above, we first find z_X:

$$z_X = \frac{(X - M_X)}{SD_X} = \frac{(0 - 3.673)}{0.890} = -4.127$$

We then calculate the predicted z score for easiness:

$$z_{\hat{Y}} = (r_{XY})(z_X) = (0.267)(-4.127) = -1.102$$

Finally, we transform the predicted easiness z score into the predicted easiness raw score:

$$\hat{Y} = z_{\hat{Y}}(SD_Y) + M_Y = -1.102(0.701) + 2.843 = 2.070$$

The intercept, therefore, is 2.070.

To determine the *slope*, we calculate what we would predict for Y (easiness) when X (clarity) equals 1, and determine how much that differs from what we would predict when X equals 0. The z score for X corresponding to the raw score of 1 is:

$$z_X = \frac{(X - M_X)}{SD_X} = \frac{(1 - 3.673)}{0.890} = -3.003$$

We then calculate the predicted z score for easiness:

$$z_{\hat{Y}} = (r_{XY})(z_X) = (0.267)(-3.003) = -0.802$$

Finally, we transform the predicted easiness z score into the predicted easiness raw score:

$$\hat{Y} = z_{\hat{Y}}(SD_Y) + M_Y = -0.802(0.701) + 2.843 = 2.281$$

The difference between the predicted Y when X equals 1 (2.281) and that when X equals 0 (2.070) yields the slope, which is $2.281 - 2.070 = 0.211$. So the regression equation is:

$$\hat{Y} = 2.07 + 0.21(X)$$

We can then use this regression equation to calculate a professor's predicted easiness score from his or her clarity score. Let's say a professor has a clarity score of 3.2. We would use the regression equation to predict her easiness score as follows:

$$\hat{Y} = 2.07 + 0.21(X) = 2.07 + 0.21(3.2) = 2.74$$

This result makes sense because she is below the mean on clarity, so, given that there is a positive correlation, we predict her score to fall below the mean on easiness.

EXERCISES

Clarifying the Concepts

16.1 What does regression add above and beyond what we learn from correlation?

16.2 How does the regression line relate to the correlation of the two variables?

16.3 Is there any difference between $\hat{Y}$ and a predicted score for Y? Explain your answer.

16.4 What do each of the symbols stand for in the formula for the regression equation: $z_{\hat{Y}} = (r_{XY})(z_X)$?

16.5 The equation for a line is $\hat{Y} = a + b(X)$. Define the symbols a and b.

16.6 What are the three steps to calculate the intercept?

16.7 When is the intercept not meaningful or useful?

16.8 What does the slope tell us?

16.9 Why do we also call the regression line the line of best fit?

16.10 How are the sign of the correlation coefficient and the sign of the slope related?

16.11 What is the difference between a small standard error of the estimate and a large one?

16.12 Why are explanations of the causes behind relations explored with regression limited in the same way they are with correlation?

16.13 What is the connection between regression to the mean and the bell-shaped normal curve?

16.14 Explain why the regression equation is a better source of predictions than the mean.

16.15 What is the SS_{total}?

16.16 When drawing error lines between data points and the regression line, why is it important that these lines be perfectly vertical?

16.17 What are the basic steps to calculate the proportionate reduction in error?

16.18 What information does the proportionate reduction in error give us?

16.19 What is an orthogonal variable?

16.20 If you know the correlation coefficient, how can you determine the proportionate reduction in error?

16.21 Why is multiple regression often more useful than simple linear regression?

16.22 What is the difference between the symbol for the effect size for simple linear regression and the symbol for the effect size for multiple regression?

16.23 How does structural equation modeling (SEM) differ from multiple regression?

16.24 What is the difference between a latent variable and a manifest variable?

16.25 What are the three primary components that we need to understand an SEM diagram? Explain what each component means.

16.26 How are the numbers on the paths of a SEM diagram interpreted?

Calculating the Statistics

16.27 Using the following information, make a prediction for Y, given an X score of 2.9:

> Variable X: $M = 1.9$, $SD = 0.6$
>
> Variable Y: $M = 10$, $SD = 3.2$
>
> Pearson correlation of variables X and $Y = 0.31$

a. Transform the raw score for the independent variable to a z score.

b. Calculate the predicted z score for the dependent variable.

c. Transform the z score for the dependent variable back into a raw score.

16.28 Using the following information, make a prediction for Y, given an X score of 8:

> Variable X: $M = 12$, $SD = 3$
>
> Variable Y: $M = 74$, $SD = 18$
>
> Pearson correlation of variables X and $Y = 0.46$

a. Transform the raw score for the independent variable to a z score.

b. Calculate the predicted z score for the dependent variable.

c. Transform the z score for the dependent variable back into a raw score.

d. Calculate the y intercept, a.

e. Calculate the slope, b.

f. Write the equation for the line.

g. Draw the line on an empty scatterplot, basing the line on predicted Y values for X values of 0, 1, and 18.

16.29 Let's assume we know that age is related to bone density, with a Pearson correlation coefficient of -0.19. (Notice that the correlation is negative, indicating that bone density tends to be lower at older ages than at younger ages.) Assume we also know the following descriptive statistics:

> Age of people studied: 55 years on average, with a standard deviation of 12 years
>
> Bone density of people studied: 1000 mg/cm^2 on average, with a standard deviation of 95 mg/cm^2

Virginia is 76 years old. What would you predict her bone density to be? To answer this question, complete the following steps:

a. Transform the raw score for the independent variable to a z score.

b. Calculate the predicted z score for the dependent variable.

c. Transform the z score for the dependent variable back into a raw score.

d. Calculate the y intercept, a.

e. Calculate the slope, b.

f. Write the equation for the line.

g. Draw the line on an empty scatterplot, basing the line on predicted Y values for X values of 0, 1, and 18.

16.30 Given the regression line $\hat{Y} = -6 + 0.41(X)$, make predictions for each of the following:

a. $X = 25$

b. $X = 50$

c. $X = 75$

16.31 Given the regression line $\hat{Y} = 49 - 0.18(X)$, make predictions for each of the following:

a. $X = -31$

b. $X = 65$

c. $X = 14$

16.32 Data are provided here with descriptive statistics, a correlation coefficient, and a regression equation: $r = 0.426$, $\hat{Y} = 219.974 + 186.595(X)$.

X	Y
0.13	200.00
0.27	98.00
0.49	543.00
0.57	385.00
0.84	420.00
1.12	312.00

$M_X = 0.57 \quad M_Y = 326.333$
$SD_X = 0.333 \quad SD_Y = 145.752$

Using this information, compute the following estimates of prediction error:

a. Calculate the sum of squared error for the mean, SS_{total}.

b. Now, using the regression equation provided, calculate the sum of squared error for the regression equation, SS_{error}.

c. Using your work, calculate the proportionate reduction in error for these data.

d. Check that this calculation of r^2 equals the square of the correlation coefficient.

e. Compute the standardized regression coefficient.

16.33 Data are provided here with descriptive statistics, a correlation coefficient, and a regression equation: $r = 0.52$, $\hat{Y} = 2.643 + 0.469(X)$.

X	Y
4.00	6.00
6.00	3.00
7.00	7.00
8.00	5.00
9.00	4.00
10.00	12.00
12.00	9.00
14.00	8.00

$M_X = 8.75 \quad M_Y = 6.75$
$SD_X = 3.031 \quad SD_Y = 2.727$

Using this information, compute the following estimates of prediction error:

a. Calculate the sum of squared error for the mean, SS_{total}.

b. Now, using the regression equation provided, calculate the sum of squared error for the regression equation, SS_{error}.

c. Using your work, calculate the proportionate reduction in error for these data.

d. Check that this calculation of r^2 equals the square of the correlation coefficient.

e. Compute the standardized regression coefficient.

16.34 Use this output from a multiple regression analysis to answer the following questions:

Coefficients[a]

Model		Unstandardized Coefficients		Standardized Coefficients		
		B	Std. Error	Beta	t	Sig.
1	(Constant)	3.977	1.193		3.333	.001
	Variable 1	.414	.096	.458	4.313	.000
	Variable 2	-.019	.011	-.181	-1.704	.093

a. Dependent Variable: Outcome (Y)

a. Write the equation for the line of prediction.

b. Use the equation for part (a) to make predictions for: Variable 1 = 6, variable 2 = 60.

c. Use the equation for part (a) to make predictions for: Variable 1 = 9, variable 2 = 54.3.

d. Use the equation for part (a) to make predictions for: Variable 1 = 13, variable 2 = 44.8.

16.35 Use this output from a multiple regression analysis to answer the following questions:

Coefficients[a]

Model		Unstandardized Coefficients		Standardized Coefficients		
		B	Std. Error	Beta	t	Sig.
1	(Constant)	1.675	.563		2.972	.004
	SAT	.001	.000	.321	2.953	.004
	Rank	-.008	.003	-.279	-2.566	.012

a. Dependent Variable: GPA

a. Write the equation for the line of prediction.

b. Use the equation for part (a) to make predictions for: SAT = 1030, rank = 41.

c. Use the equation for part (a) to make predictions for: SAT = 860, rank = 22.

d. Use the equation for part (a) to make predictions for: SAT = 1060, rank = 8.

16.36 Researchers investigated the links among the ability to show compassion for oneself, problems controlling emotions, and stress levels among psychologists in Australia (Finlay-Jones, Rees, & Kane, 2015). The figure here represents just the latent variables of a SEM diagram. The asterisks indicate paths that are statistically significant. In your own words, describe how you would interpret the two statistically significant paths in this diagram.

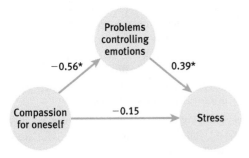

16.37 Refer to the structural equation model (SEM) depicted in Figure 16-8 to answer the following:

a. Which two variables are most strongly related to each other?

b. Is positive parenting at age 17 directly related to emotional adjustment at age 26? How do you know?

c. Is positive parenting at age 17 directly related to identity maturity at age 26? How do you know?

d. What is the difference between the variables represented in boxes and those represented in circles?

Applying the Concepts

16.38 Birth weight, blood pressure, and regression: A meta-analysis found a negative correlation between birth weight and blood pressure later in life (Mu et al., 2012).

a. Explain what is meant by a negative correlation between these two variables.

b. If you were to examine these two variables with simple linear regression instead of correlation, how would you frame the question? (*Hint:* The research question for correlation would be: Is birth weight related to blood pressure?)

c. What is the difference between simple linear regression and multiple regression?

d. If you were to conduct a multiple regression instead of a simple linear regression, what other independent variables might you include?

16.39 Predictive policing: The *New York Times* reported on predictive policing, a strategy based on formulas that "forecast" whether a particular person is likely to commit a crime (Elgion & Williams, 2015). What are the predictive data that the police consider? They look at personal connections—whether in real life or on social media—with victims of homicides, members of gangs, or people in prison. They also look at whether people are unemployed or have a history of drug or alcohol problems.

a. What are the independent variables in this example?

b. What is the dependent variable?

c. What other variables might predict this dependent variable? Name at least three.

d. The same article that described predictive policing also discussed critiques of this method. They noted that these tactics "legitimize the profiling of racial minorities who live in poor, high-crime neighborhoods, and prompted officers to enforce laws selectively." Based on this example, explain why regression is not a perfect science—why can regression lead to problems with prediction?

16.40 Age, hours studied, and prediction: In How It Works 15.2, we calculated the correlation coefficient between students' age and number of hours they study per week. The correlation between these two variables is 0.49.

a. Elif's z score for age is −0.82. What would we predict for the z score for the number of hours she studies per week?

b. John's z score for age is 1.2. What would we predict for the z score for the number of hours he studies per week?

c. Eugene's z score for age is 0. What would we predict for the z score for the number of hours he studies per week?

d. For part (c), explain why the concept of regression to the mean is not relevant (and why you didn't really need the formula).

16.41 Consideration of Future Consequences scale, z scores, and raw scores: A study of Consideration of Future Consequences (CFC) found a mean score of 3.51, with a standard deviation of 0.61, for the 664 students in the sample (Petrocelli, 2003).

a. Imagine that your z score on the CFC score was −1.2. What would your raw score be? Use symbolic notation and the formula. Explain why this answer makes sense.

b. Imagine that your z score on the CFC score was 0.66. What would your raw score be? Use symbolic notation and the formula. Explain why this answer makes sense.

16.42 IMDB, z scores, and raw scores: The 23,396 films on the Internet Movie Database (IMBD) have a mean of 6.2 and a standard deviation of 1.4 (Moertel, 2006). They are roughly normally distributed. (Note that this population includes all films that were reviewed by at least 100 people.)

a. Convert the following z scores to raw scores without using a formula: (i) −1.0, (ii) 1.0, (iii) 0.0

b. Now convert the same z scores to raw scores using symbolic notation and the formula: (i) −1.0, (ii) 1.0, (iii) 0.0

16.43 Hours studied, grade, and regression: A regression analysis of data from some of our statistics classes yielded the following regression equation for the independent variable (hours studied) and the dependent variable (grade point average [GPA]): $\hat{Y} = 2.96 + 0.02(X)$.

a. If you plan to study 8 hours per week, what would you predict your GPA will be?

b. If you plan to study 10 hours per week, what would you predict your GPA will be?

c. If you plan to study 11 hours per week, what would you predict your GPA will be?

d. Create a graph and draw the regression line based on these three pairs of scores.

e. Determine the number of hours you'd have to study to have a predicted GPA of the maximum possible, 4.0. Why is it misleading to make predictions for anyone who plans to study this many hours (or more)?

16.44 Precipitation, violence, and limitations of regression: Does the level of precipitation predict violence? Dubner and Levitt (2006b) reported on various studies that found links between rain and violence. They mentioned one study by Miguel, Satyanath, and Sergenti that found that decreased rain was linked with an increased likelihood of civil war across a number of African countries they examined. Referring to the study's authors, Dubner and Levitt state, "The causal effect of a drought, they argue, was frighteningly strong."

a. What is the independent variable in this study?

b. What is the dependent variable?

c. What possible third variables might play a role in this connection? Is it just the lack of rain that's causing violence, or is it something else? (*Hint:* Consider the likely economic base of many African countries.)

16.45 Cola consumption, bone mineral density, and limitations of regression: Does one's cola consumption predict one's bone mineral density? Using regression analyses, nutrition researchers found that older women who drank more cola (but not more of other carbonated drinks) tended to have lower bone mineral density, a risk factor for osteoporosis (Tucker, Morita, Qiao, Hannan, Cupples, & Kiel, 2006). Cola intake, therefore, does seem to predict bone mineral density.

a. Explain why we cannot conclude that cola intake causes a decrease in bone mineral density.

b. The researchers included a number of possible third variables in their regression analyses. Among the included variables were physical activity score, smoking, alcohol use, and calcium intake. They included the possible third variables first, and then added the bone density measure. Why would they have used multiple regression in this case? Explain.

c. How might physical activity play a role as a third variable? Discuss its possible relation to both bone density and cola consumption.

d. How might calcium intake play a role as a third variable? Discuss its possible relation to both bone density and cola consumption.

16.46 Tutoring, mathematics performance, and problems with regression: A researcher conducted a study in which children with problems learning mathematics were offered the opportunity to purchase time with special tutors. The number of weeks that children met with their tutors varied from 1 to 20. He found that the number of weeks of tutoring predicted these children's mathematics performance and recommended that parents of such children send them for tutoring.

a. List one problem with that interpretation. Explain your answer.

b. If you were to develop a study that uses a multiple regression equation instead of a simple linear regression equation, what additional variables might be good independent variables? List at least one variable that can be manipulated (e.g., weeks of tutoring) and at least one variable that cannot be manipulated (e.g., parents' years of education).

16.47 Anxiety, depression, and simple linear regression: We analyzed data from a larger data set that one of the authors used for previous research (Nolan, Flynn, & Garber, 2003). In the current analyses, we used regression to look at factors that predict anxiety over a 3-year period. Shown below is the output for the regression analysis examining whether depression at year 1 predicted anxiety at year 3.

Coefficients(a)

	Unstandardized Coefficients		Standardized Coefficients	t	Sig.
	B	Std. Error	Beta		
(Constant)	24.698	.566		43.665	.000
Depression Year 1	.161	.048	.235	3.333	.001

a. Dependent Variable: Anxiety Year 3

a. From this software output, write the regression equation.

b. As depression at year 1 increases by 1 point, what happens to the predicted anxiety level for year 3? Be specific.

c. If someone has a depression score of 10 at year 1, what would we predict for her anxiety score at year 3?

d. If someone has a depression score of 2 at year 1, what would we predict for his anxiety score at year 3?

16.48 Anxiety, depression, and multiple regression: We conducted a second regression analysis on the data from the previous exercise. In addition to depression at year 1, we included a second independent variable to predict anxiety at year 3. We also included anxiety at year 1. (We might expect that the best predictor of anxiety at a later point in time is one's anxiety at an earlier point in time.) Here is the output for that analysis.

Coefficients(a)

	Unstandardized Coefficients		Standardized Coefficients	t	Sig.
	B	Std. Error	Beta		
(Constant)	17.038	1.484		11.482	.000
Depression Year 1	-.013	.055	-.019	-.237	.813
Anxiety Year 1	.307	.056	.442	5.521	.000

a. Dependent Variable: Anxiety Year 3

a. From this software output, write the regression equation.

b. As the first independent variable, depression at year 1, increases by 1 point, what happens to the predicted score on anxiety at year 3?

c. As the second independent variable, anxiety at year 1, increases by 1 point, what happens to the predicted score on anxiety at year 3?

d. Compare the predictive utility of depression at year 1 using the regression equation in the previous exercise and using the regression equation you just wrote in part (a) of this exercise. In which regression equation is depression at year 1 a better predictor? Given that we're using the same sample, is depression at year 1 actually better at predicting anxiety at year 3 in one regression equation versus the other? Why do you think there's a difference?

e. The table below is the correlation matrix for the three variables. As you can see, all three are highly correlated with one another. If we look at the intersection of each pair of variables, the number next to "Pearson correlation" is the correlation coefficient. For example, the correlation between "Anxiety year 1" and "Depression year 1" is .549.
Which two variables show the strongest correlation? How might this explain the fact that depression at year 1 seems to be a better predictor when it's the only independent variable than when anxiety at year 1 also is included? What does this tell us about the importance of including third variables in the regression analyses when possible?

f. Let's say you want to add a fourth independent variable. You have to choose among three possible independent variables: (1) a variable highly correlated with both independent variables and the dependent variable, (2) a variable highly correlated with the dependent variable but not correlated with either independent variable, and (3) a variable not correlated with either of the independent variables or with the dependent variable. Which of the three variables is likely to make the multiple regression equation better? That is, which is likely to increase the proportionate reduction in error? Explain.

Correlations

		Depression Year 1	Anxiety Year 1	Anxiety Year 3
Depression Year 1	Pearson Correlation	1	.549(**)	.235(**)
	Sig. (2-tailed)		.000	.001
	N	240	240	192
Anxiety Year 1	Pearson Correlation	.549(**)	1	.432(**)
	Sig. (2-tailed)	.000		.000
	N	240	240	192
Anxiety Year 3	Pearson Correlation	.235(**)	.432(**)	1
	Sig. (2-tailed)	.001	.000	
	N	192	192	192

** Correlation is significant at the 0.01 level (2-tailed).

16.49 Cohabitation, divorce, and prediction: A study by the Institute for Fiscal Studies (Goodman & Greaves, 2010) found that parents' marital status when a child was born predicted the likelihood of the relationship's demise. Parents who were cohabiting when their child was born had a 27% chance of breaking up by the time the child was 5, whereas those who were married when their child was born had a 9% chance of breaking up by the time the child was 5—a difference of 18%. The researchers, however, reported that cohabiting parents tended to be younger, less affluent, less likely to own a home, less educated, and more likely to have an unplanned pregnancy. When the researchers statistically controlled for these variables, they found that there was just a 2% difference between cohabitating and married parents.

a. What are the independent and dependent variables used in this study?

b. Were the researchers likely to have used simple linear regression or multiple regression for their analyses? Explain your answer.

c. In your own words, explain why the ability of marital status at the time of a child's birth to predict divorce within 5 years almost disappeared when other variables were considered. Explain your answer.

d. Name at least one additional "third variable" that might have been at play in this situation. Explain your answer.

16.50 Google, the flu, and third variables: The *New York Times* reported: "Several years ago, Google, aware of how many of us were sneezing and coughing, created a fancy equation on its Web site to figure out just how many people had influenza. The math works like this: people's location + flu-related search queries on Google + some really smart algorithms = the number of people with the flu in the United States" (Bilton, 2013; http://bits.blogs.nytimes.com/2013/02/24/disruptions-google-flu-trends-shows-problems-of-big-data-without-context/).

a. A friend who knows you're taking statistics asks you to explain what this means in statistical terms. In your own words, what is it likely that the Google statisticians did?

b. The problem was that their "fancy equation" didn't work. It estimated that 11% of the U.S. population had the flu, but the real number was only 6%. The *New York Times* article warned against taking data out of context. What do you think may have gone wrong in this case? (*Hint:* Think about your own Google searches and the varied reasons you have for conducting those searches.)

16.51 Sugar, diabetes, and multiple regression: A *New York Times* reporter wrote: "A study published in the journal PLOS ONE links increased consumption of sugar with increased rates of diabetes by examining the data on sugar availability and the rate of diabetes in 175 countries over the past decade. And after accounting for many other factors, the researchers found that increased sugar in a population's food supply was linked to higher diabetes rates independent of rates of obesity" (Bittman, 2013).

a. Explain how the researchers may have used multiple regression to analyze these data.

b. Why did the reporter emphasize that the researchers accounted for many other factors?

c. List at least three other factors that the researchers may have included.

d. The reporter also wrote: "In other words, according to this study, obesity doesn't cause diabetes: sugar does. The study demonstrates this with the same level of confidence that linked cigarettes and lung cancer in the 1960s." Explain in your own words why Bittman likely feels justified in drawing a causal conclusion from correlational research.

16.52 The age of a country, the level of concern for the environment, and multiple regression: Researchers analyzed the impact of the age of a country on the overall level of concern for the environment (Hershfield, Bang, & Weber, 2014). They noted that some countries—Sweden, for example—are more likely to enact environmentally friendly legislation, whereas others, like India, are less likely to do so. They predicted that older countries—those with more of a history—would be more likely to be future-oriented and therefore develop environmentally friendly policies. So, they conducted a regression to examine whether a country's age predicted a country's score on a measure called the Environmental Performance Index (EPI). They controlled for wealth, as measured by a country's gross domestic product (GDP) and a scale that assessed a government's overall stability. They reported that, "even after controlling for these factors, however, we found that country age accounted for approximately 6% of the variation in country-level environmental performance." They reported a p value of 0.001.

a. Explain how you know researchers used multiple regression in this case.

b. What is the most likely reason that researchers controlled for wealth and stability in their multiple regression?

c. List at least one additional variable that the researchers might have considered controlling for.

16.53 Neighborhood social disorder and structural equation modeling: The attached figure is from a journal article entitled "Neighborhood Social Disorder as a Determinant of Drug Injection Behaviors: A Structural Equation Modeling Approach" (Latkin, Williams, Wang, & Curry, 2005).

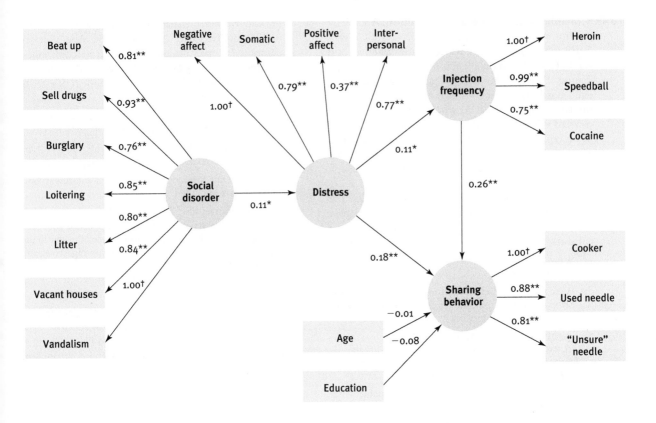

a. What are the four latent variables examined in this study?

b. What manifest variables were used to operationalize social disorder? Based on these manifest variables, explain in your own words what you think the authors mean by "social disorder."

c. Looking only at the latent variables, which two variables seem to be most strongly related to each other? What is the number on that path? Is it positive or negative, and what does the sign of the number indicate about the relation between these variables?

d. Looking only at the latent variables, what overall story is this model telling? (*Note:* Asterisks denote relations that inferential statistics indicate are likely "real," even if they are fairly small.)

16.54 Physical health around the world and structural equation modeling: The figure on the next page shows the latent variables of a structural equation model (Pressman, Gallagher, & Lopez, 2013). Researchers examined predictors of mental health in more than 150,000 people from 142 countries. Use the figure to answer the following questions.

a. Explain the relations of positive and negative emotions to physical health.

b. In the explanation of their structural equation model, the researchers stated about positive emotions and negative emotions: "Together, they accounted for almost half (46.1%) of the variance in health" (p. 1). From your understanding of variance, explain what the researchers mean by this statement.

c. A reporter in the Huffington Post wrote about this research: "Is the concept of emotions having an effect on health a "First World" problem? According to a new study, no, it is not—and in fact, the association may be even stronger in developing nations" (http://www.huffingtonpost.com/2013/03/25/positivity-and-good-health-lower-income-countries-emotions_n_2916288.html, 2013). What is the reporter implying by this statement in terms of causality?

d. Knowing only about the relations you described in part (a), list several third variables that might be responsible for the relation between emotions and physical health.

e. Food and shelter along with safety needs are included in the model. How does this make the relations you described in part (a) more convincing as explanations?

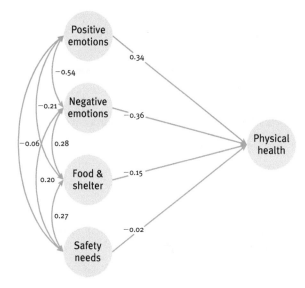

Putting It All Together

16.55 Age, hours studied, and regression: In *How It Works* 15.2, we calculated the correlation coefficient between students' age and the number of hours they study per week. The mean for age is 21, and the standard deviation is 1.789. The mean for hours studied is 14.2, and the standard deviation is 5.582. The correlation between these two variables is 0.49. Use the z score formula.

a. João is 24 years old. How many hours would we predict he studies per week?

b. Kimberly is 19 years old. How many hours would we predict she studies per week?

c. Seung is 45 years old. Why might it not be a good idea to predict how many hours per week he studies?

d. From a mathematical perspective, why is the word *regression* used? (*Hint:* Look at parts (a) and (b), and discuss the scores on the first variable with respect to their mean versus the predicted scores on the second variable with respect to their mean.)

e. Calculate the regression equation.

f. Use the regression equation to predict the number of hours studied for a 17-year-old student and for a 22-year-old student.

g. Using the four pairs of scores that you have (age and predicted hours studied from part (b), and the predicted scores for a score of 0 and 1 from calculating the regression equation), create a graph that includes the regression line.

h. Why is it misleading to include young ages such as 0 and 5 on the graph?

i. Construct a graph that includes both the scatterplot for these data and the regression line. Draw vertical lines to connect each dot on the scatterplot with the regression line.

j. Construct a second graph that includes both the scatterplot and a line for the mean for hours studied, 14.2. The line will be horizontal and will begin at 14.2 on the y-axis. Draw vertical lines to connect each dot on the scatterplot with the regression line.

k. Part (i) is a depiction of the error we make if we use the regression equation to predict hours studied. Part (j) is a depiction of the error we make if we use the mean to predict hours studied (i.e., if we predict that everyone has the mean of 16.2 on hours studied per week). Which one appears to have less error? Briefly explain why the error is less in one situation.

l. Calculate the proportionate reduction in error the long way.

m. Explain what the proportionate reduction in error that you calculated in part (l) tells us. Be specific about what it tells us about predicting using the regression equation versus predicting using the mean.

n. Demonstrate how the proportionate reduction in error could be calculated using the shortcut. Why does this make sense? That is, why does the correlation coefficient give us a sense of how useful the regression equation will be?

o. Compute the standardized regression coefficient.

p. How does this coefficient relate to other information you know?

q. Draw a conclusion about your analysis based on what you know about hypothesis testing with regression.

16.56 Corporate political contributions, profits, and regression: Researchers studied whether corporate political contributions predicted profits (Cooper, Gulen, & Ovtchinnikov, 2007). From archival data, they determined how many political candidates each company supported with financial contributions, as well as each company's profit in terms of a percentage. The accompanying table shows data for five companies. (*Note:* The data points are hypothetical but are based on averages for companies falling in the 2nd, 4th, 6th, and 8th deciles in terms of candidates supported. A decile is a range of 10%, so the 2nd decile includes those with percentiles between 10 and 19.9.)

Number of Candidates Supported	Profit (%)
6	12.37
17	12.91
39	12.59
62	13.43
98	13.42

a. Create the scatterplot for these scores.

b. Calculate the mean and standard deviation for the variable "number of candidates supported."

c. Calculate the mean and standard deviation for the variable "profit."

d. Calculate the correlation between number of candidates supported and profit.

e. Calculate the regression equation for the prediction of profit from number of candidates supported.

f. Create a graph and draw the regression line.

g. What do these data suggest about the political process?

h. What third variables might be at play here?

i. Compute the standardized regression coefficient.

j. How does this coefficient relate to other information you know?

k. Draw a conclusion about your analysis based on what you know about hypothesis testing with simple linear regression.

TERMS

simple linear regression (p. 441)

regression to the mean (p. 443)

intercept (p. 444)

slope (p. 444)

standardized regression coefficient (p. 448)

standard error of the estimate (p. 451)

proportionate reduction in error (p. 454)

orthogonal variable (p. 459)

multiple regression (p. 459)

structural equation modeling (SEM) (p. 462)

statistical (or theoretical) model (p. 462)

path (p. 463)

path analysis (p. 463)

manifest variables (p. 463)

latent variables (p. 463)

FORMULAS

$z_{\hat{Y}} = (r_{XY})(z_X)$ (p. 442)

$\hat{Y} = a + b(X)$ (p. 444)

$\beta = (b)\dfrac{\sqrt{SS_X}}{\sqrt{SS_Y}}$ (p. 448)

$r^2 = \dfrac{(SS_{total} - SS_{error})}{SS_{total}}$ (p. 457)

SYMBOLS

$\hat{Y}$ (p. 442)

a (p. 444)

b (p. 444)

β (p. 448)

SS_{total} (p. 454)

SS_{error} (p. 456)

r^2 (p. 457)

R^2 (p. 461)

Chi-Square Tests

17

Nonparametric Statistics
An Example of a Nonparametric Test
When to Use Nonparametric Tests

Chi-Square Tests
Chi-Square Test for Goodness of Fit
Chi-Square Test for Independence

Beyond Hypothesis Testing
Cramér's *V*, the Effect Size for Chi Square
Graphing Chi-Square Percentages
Relative Risk

Next Steps: Adjusted Standardized Residuals

BEFORE YOU GO ON

- You should be able to differentiate between a parametric and a nonparametric hypothesis test (Chapter 7).

- You should know the six steps of hypothesis testing (Chapter 7).

- You should understand the concept of effect size (Chapter 8).

Selfies and Gender Stereotypes Do we fall back on gender stereotypes when we pose for our selfies? Research suggests that we do (Döring, Reif, & Poeschl, 2016). Women are more likely than men to pose in a seductive manner, such as with "duckface," whereas men are more likely than women to pose showing off muscles.

Check out the last selfie you posted. What does it say about you? German researchers Nicola Döring, Anne Reif, and Sandra Poeschl conducted a study that suggested that, for many of us, our selfies reflect our gender (2016). They looked at 500 selfies—half of men and half of women—and counted how many times the photos met various gender stereotypes. They counted how often the people in the selfies exhibited stereotypically feminine behaviors or postures like lying down, looking away, or appearing seductive—such as what is sometimes called "duckface." They also counted stereotypically masculine behaviors such as showing off muscles.

How would you analyze data like this? We don't have a scale variable. The researchers are just counting behaviors in selfies; they're not giving the selfies some kind of a score. So, these are nominal data—you either exhibit a behavior—such as duckface—or you don't. As you may realize, we don't yet have the tools to handle a study with only nominal data. We've only learned parametric tests so far, the ones summarized in Table 17-1. In this chapter and the next, we'll learn about nonparametric tests, which allow us to analyze data when we don't have a scale dependent variable.

So what did Döring and her colleagues find? Using the nonparametric chi-square tests, they found that women and men did indeed fall back on gender stereotypes in their selfie poses. In fact, the gender stereotyping was even more pronounced than what we see in advertisements.

This chapter helps us to explore hypotheses about nonparametric data by teaching when to use a nonparametric test and by demonstrating how to use two nonparametric tests based on nominal data. In Chapter 18, we'll introduce four nonparametric tests used with ordinal data.

Nonparametric hypothesis tests allow us to distinguish between pattern and chance when observational data do not have a scale dependent variable. We use the chi-square statistic when all of the data are nominal variables—like in the selfie study. If we can count the frequency of any event and assign each frequency to one (and only one) category, then the chi-square statistic lets us test for the independence of those categories and estimate effect sizes.

TABLE 17-1 A Summary of Research Designs

We have encountered several research designs so far, most of which fall in one of two categories. Some designs—those listed in category I—include at least one scale independent variable and a scale dependent variable. Other designs—those listed in category II—include a nominal (or sometimes ordinal) independent variable and a scale dependent variable. Until now, we have not encountered a research design with a nominal independent variable and a nominal dependent variable, or a research design with an ordinal dependent variable.

I. Scale Independent Variable and Scale Dependent Variable	II. Nominal Independent Variable and Scale Dependent Variable
Correlation	*z* test
Regression	All kinds of *t* tests
	All kinds of ANOVAs

Nonparametric Statistics

Selfies are not just a place where gender stereotypes run wild. They can even be dangerous. The headline of a British newspaper warned us that "Selfies Are Killing More People Than Shark Attacks," with 12 people dying while taking selfies—from falls, for example—in the first half of the year but only 8 being killed by sharks (Sandhu, 2015). This is another example of a study based on nominal data—counts of people in categories—rather than scale data. Many studies, like the study on the dangers of selfies, violate parametric assumptions for hypothesis testing (especially the assumption that the data be drawn from a normally distributed population). The chi-square statistic provides a solution because it is a more conservative nonparametric statistic that is *not* based on critical assumptions about the population.

An Example of a Nonparametric Test

Nonparametric statistics are exciting because they expand the universe of things that we can study. For example, a team of Israeli physician-researchers, led by Dr. Shevach Friedler, a trained mime as well as a physician (Ryan, 2006), found that live entertainment by clowns—yes, clowns!—was associated with higher rates of conception during in vitro fertilization (IVF) (Rockwell, 2006). Friedler had a professional clown entertain 93 women during the 15 minutes after embryo transfer (Brinn, 2006); a comparison group of 93 women did not receive entertainment by a clown during IVF. Thirty-three who were entertained by a clown (35%) conceived, compared with 18 in the comparison group (19%). Is this real or just chance?

The hypothesis is that a woman becoming pregnant depends on whether or not she receives clown therapy. The independent variable is type of post-IVF treatment, with two levels (clown therapy versus no clown therapy). The dependent variable is outcome, with two levels (becomes pregnant versus does not become pregnant). This is a new statistical situation because pregnancy, of course, is not a scale variable. You can't be "just a little pregnant." Both the independent variable and the dependent variable are nominal. (We'll explore their results in more detail later.)

This new situation (two nominal variables) calls for a new statistic and a new hypothesis test: The chi-square statistic is symbolized as χ^2 (pronounced "kai square"—rhymes with *sky*) and relies on the chi-square distribution.

When to Use Nonparametric Tests

We use a nonparametric test when (1) the dependent variable is nominal, (2) the dependent variable is ordinal, or (3) the sample size is small and the population of interest may be skewed.

Situation 1 (a nominal dependent variable) occurs whenever we categorize the observations: pregnant or not pregnant, male or female, driver's license or no driver's license. We often think of our world in terms of categories.

Situation 2 (an ordinal dependent variable) describes rank, such as in athletic competitions, class position, or preferred flavor of ice cream. Top 10 lists and favorite nephews are also ordinal observations.

Situation 3 (a small sample size, usually of less than 30, and a potentially skewed population) occurs less frequently. It would be difficult to recruit enough participants to study the brain patterns among people who have won the Nobel Prize in literature, no matter how hard we tried or how much we paid people to participate.

Although nonparametric tests expand the range of variables available for research, they have two big problems: (1) confidence intervals and effect-size measures are not

> **MASTERING THE CONCEPT**
>
> **17-1:** We use nonparametric tests when
> (1) the dependent variable is nominal,
> (2) the dependent variable is ordinal, or
> (3) the sample size is small and we suspect that the underlying population distribution is not normal.

typically available for nominal or ordinal data; (2) nonparametric tests tend to have less statistical power than parametric tests. This increases the risk of a Type II error: We are less likely to reject the null hypothesis when we should reject it (that is, when there is a real difference between groups). Nonparametric tests are often the backup plan, not the go-to statistical tests.

CHECK YOUR LEARNING

Reviewing the Concepts

> We use a nonparametric test when we cannot meet the assumptions of a parametric test, primarily the assumptions of having a scale dependent variable and a normally distributed population.

> The most common situations in which we use a nonparametric test are when we have a nominal or ordinal dependent variable or a small sample in which the data for the dependent variable suggest that the underlying population distribution might be skewed.

Clarifying the Concepts 17-1 Distinguish a parametric test from a nonparametric test.

17-2 When do we use nonparametric tests?

Calculating the Statistics 17-3 For each of the following situations, identify the independent and dependent variables and how they are measured (nominal, ordinal, or scale).

a. Bernstein (1996) reported that Francis Galton created a "beauty map" in the early 1900s by recording the numbers of women he encountered in different cities in England who were either pretty or not so pretty. London women, he found, were the most likely to be pretty and Aberdeen women the least likely.

b. Imagine that Galton instead gave every woman a beauty score on a scale of 1–10 and then compared means for the women in each of five cities.

c. Galton was famous for discounting the intelligence of most women (Bernstein, 1996). Imagine that he assessed the intelligence of 50 women and then applied the beauty scale mentioned in part (b). Let's say he found that women with higher intelligence were more likely to be pretty, whereas women with lower intelligence were less likely to be pretty.

d. Imagine that Galton now ranked 50 women on their beauty and on their intelligence.

Applying the Concepts 17-4 For each of the situations listed in Check Your Learning 17-3, state the category (I or II) from Table 17-1 from which you would choose the appropriate hypothesis test. If you would not choose a test from either category I or II, simply list category III—other. Explain why you chose I, II, or III.

Solutions to these Check Your Learning questions can be found in Appendix D.

Chi-Square Tests

Selfie research is beginning to be a legitimate area of scholarship. Australian researchers recently presented their ideas on the rise of controversial selfies, such as selfies at funerals (Gibbs, Nansen, Carter, & Kohn, 2014). It might be interesting to explore the circumstances under which people take selfies at funerals. For example, are they more common at funerals of young people? Of those who died tragically in accidents? These are testable ideas, and this chapter describes what is being tested in two common kinds of chi-square statistical tests: (1) the ***chi-square test for goodness of fit***, *a nonparametric*

● The **chi-square test for goodness of fit** is a nonparametric hypothesis test that is used when there is one nominal variable.

hypothesis test that is used when there is one nominal variable; (2) the **chi-square test for independence**, *a nonparametric hypothesis test that is used when there are two nominal variables.* Both chi-square tests involve the by-now familiar six steps of hypothesis testing.

Both chi-square tests use the chi-square statistic: χ^2. The chi-square statistic is based on the chi-square distribution. As with t and F distributions, there are also several chi-square distributions, depending on the degrees of freedom. After we introduce chi-square tests, we'll introduce several ways of determining the size of a finding—by calculating an effect size, graphing the finding, or determining relative risk.

Chi-Square Test for Goodness of Fit

The chi-square test for goodness of fit calculates a statistic based on just one variable. There is no independent variable or dependent variable, just one categorical variable with two or more categories into which participants are placed. In fact, the chi-square test for goodness of fit received its name because it measures how good the fit is between the observed data in the various categories of a single nominal variable and the data we would expect according to the null hypothesis. If there's a really good fit with the null hypothesis, then we cannot reject the null hypothesis. If we hope to receive empirical support for the research hypothesis, then we're actually hoping for a *bad fit* between the observed data and what we expect according to the null hypothesis.

EXAMPLE 17.1

For example, researchers reported that the best youth soccer players in the world were more likely to have been born early in the year than later (Dubner & Levitt, 2006a). As one example, they reported that 52 elite youth players in Germany were born in January, February, or March, whereas only 4 players were born in October, November, or December. (Those born in other months were not included in this study.)

The null hypothesis predicts that when a person was born will not make any difference; the research hypothesis predicts that the month a person was born will matter when it comes to being an elite soccer player. Assuming that births in the general population are evenly distributed across months of the year, the null hypothesis posits that equal numbers of elite soccer players were born in the first 3 months and the last 3 months of the year. With 56 participants in the study (52 born in the first 3 months and 4 in the last 3 months), equal frequencies lead us to expect 28 players to have been born in the first 3 months and 28 in the last 3 months just by chance. The birth months don't appear to be evenly distributed, but is this a real pattern, or just chance?

Like previous hypothesis tests, the chi-square goodness of fit test uses the six steps of hypothesis testing.

STEP 1: Identify the populations, distribution, and assumptions.

There are always two populations involved in a chi-square test: one population that matches the frequencies of participants like those we observed and another population that matches the frequencies of participants like those we would expect according to the null hypothesis. In this case, there is a population of elite German youth soccer players with birth dates like those

Are Elite Soccer Players Born in the Early Months of the Year? Based on data for elite German youth soccer players, a chi-square test for goodness of fit showed a statistically significant effect: Players were more likely to be born in the first 3 months than in the last 3 months of the year (Dubner & Levitt, 2006a).

we observed and a population of elite German youth soccer players with birth dates like those in the general population. The comparison distribution is a chi-square distribution. There's just one nominal variable, birth months, so we'll conduct a chi-square test for goodness of fit.

The first assumption is that the variable (birth month) is nominal. The second assumption is that each observation is independent; no single participant can be in more than one category. The third assumption is that participants were randomly selected. If not, it may be unwise to confidently generalize beyond the sample. A fourth assumption is that there is a minimum number of expected participants in every category (also called a *cell*)—at least 5 and preferably more. An alternative guideline (Delucchi, 1983) is for there to be at least five times as many participants as cells. In any case, the chi-square tests seem robust to violations of this last assumption.

Summary: Population 1: Elite German youth soccer players with birth dates like those we observed. Population 2: Elite German youth soccer players with birth dates like those in the general population.

The comparison distribution is a chi-square distribution. The hypothesis test will be a chi-square test for goodness of fit because we have one nominal variable only, birth months. This study meets three of the four assumptions: (1) The one variable is nominal. (2) Every participant is in only one cell (you can't be born in both January and November). (3) This is not a randomly selected sample of all elite soccer players. The sample includes only German youth soccer players in the elite leagues. We must be cautious in generalizing beyond young German elite players. (4) There are more than five times as many participants as cells (the table has two cells, and $2 \times 5 = 10$). We have 56 participants, far more than the 10 necessary to meet this guideline.

> **STEP 2: State the null and research hypotheses.**

For chi-square tests, it's easiest to state the hypotheses in words only, rather than in both words and symbols.

Summary: Null hypothesis: Elite German youth soccer players have the same pattern of birth months as those in the general population. Research hypothesis: Elite German youth soccer players have a different pattern of birth months than those in the general population.

> **STEP 3: Determine the characteristics of the comparison distribution.**

The only task at this step is to determine the degrees of freedom. In most previous hypothesis tests, the degrees of freedom have been based on sample size. For the chi-square hypothesis tests, however, the degrees of freedom are based on the numbers of categories, or cells, in which participants can be counted. The degrees of freedom for a chi-square test for goodness of fit is the number of categories minus 1:

$$df_{\chi^2} = k - 1$$

Here, k is the symbol for the number of categories. The current example has only two categories: Each soccer player in this study was born in either the first 3 months of the year or the last 3 months of the year:

$$df_{\chi^2} = 2 - 1 = 1$$

Summary: The comparison distribution is a chi-square distribution, which has 1 degree of freedom: $df_{\chi^2} = 2 - 1 = 1$.

MASTERING THE FORMULA

17-1: We calculate the degrees of freedom for the chi-square test for goodness of fit by subtracting 1 from the number of categories, represented in the formula by k. The formula is:

$$df_{\chi^2} = k - 1.$$

TABLE 17-2 Excerpt from the χ^2 Table

We use the χ^2 table to determine critical values for a given p level, based on the degrees of freedom.

df	Proportion in Critical Region		
	0.10	0.05	0.01
1	2.706	3.841	6.635
2	4.605	5.992	9.211
3	6.252	7.815	11.345

STEP 4: Determine the critical value, or cutoff.

To determine the cutoff, or critical value, for the chi-square statistic, we use the chi-square table in Appendix B. χ^2 is based on squares and can never be negative, so there is just one critical value. An excerpt from Appendix B that applies to the soccer study is given in Table 17-2. We look under the p level, usually 0.05, and across from the appropriate degrees of freedom, in this case, 1. For this situation, the critical chi-square statistic is 3.841.

Summary: The critical χ^2, based on a p level of 0.05 and 1 degree of freedom, is 3.841, as seen in the curve in Figure 17-1.

STEP 5: Calculate the test statistic.

To calculate a chi-square statistic, we determine the observed frequencies and the expected frequencies, as seen in Table 17-3 and in the second and third columns of Table 17-4. The expected frequencies are determined from the information we have about the general population. In this case, we estimate that, in the general population, about half of all births (only, of course, among those born in the first or last 3 months of the year) occur in the first 3 months of the year, a proportion of 0.50:

$$(0.50)(56) = 28$$

Of the 56 elite German youth soccer players in the study, we would expect to find that 28 were born in the first 3 months of the year (versus the last 3 months of the year) if these youth soccer players are no different from the general population with respect to birth date. Similarly, we would expect a proportion of $1 - 0.50 = 0.50$ of these soccer players to be born in the last 3 months of the year:

$$(0.50)(56) = 28$$

These numbers are identical only because the proportions are 0.50 and 0.50. If the proportion expected for the first 3 months of the year, based on the general population,

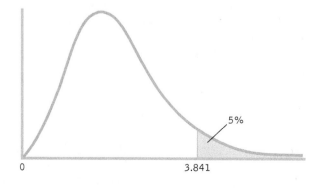

FIGURE 17-1

Determining the Cutoff for a Chi-Square Statistic

We look up the critical value for a chi-square statistic, based on a certain p level and degrees of freedom, in the chi-square table. Because the chi-square statistic is squared, it is never negative, so there is only one critical value.

TABLE 17-3	Observed Frequencies and Expected Frequencies

The first step in calculating the chi-square statistic is creating two tables, one with cells that display the observed frequencies of birth dates among elite German youth soccer players and one with cells that display the expected frequencies.

Observed (when elite players were born)	
First 3 Months of the Year	Last 3 Months of the Year
52	4

Expected (based on the general population)	
First 3 Months of the Year	Last 3 Months of the Year
28	28

TABLE 17-4	The Chi-Square Calculations

As with many other statistics, we calculate the chi-square statistic using columns to keep track of our work. We list the observed frequencies, then calculate the expected frequencies, the difference between the observed frequencies and the expected frequencies, then we square the differences and then divide each square by its appropriate expected frequency. Finally, we add up the numbers in the sixth column to find the chi-square statistic.

Column 1	2	3	4	5	6
Category	Observed (O)	Expected (E)	($O - E$)	$(O - E)^2$	$\dfrac{(O - E)^2}{E}$
First 3 months	52	28	24	576	20.571
Last 3 months	4	28	−24	576	20.571

were 0.60, then we would expect a proportion of $1 - 0.60 = 0.40$ for the last 3 months of the year.

The next step in calculating the chi-square statistic is to calculate a sort of sum of squared differences. We start by determining the difference between each observed frequency and its matching expected frequency. This is usually done in columns, so we use this format even though we have only two categories. The first three columns of Table 17-4 show us the categories, observed frequencies, and expected frequencies, respectively. The fourth column, using O for observed and E for expected, displays the differences. As in the other situations, if we sum the differences, we get 0; they cancel out because some are positive and some are negative. We solve this problem as we have others—by squaring the differences, as shown in the fifth column. Next, however, we have a step that we haven't seen before with squared differences. We divide each squared difference by the expected value for its cell, as seen in the sixth column. The numbers in the sixth column are the ones we sum.

As an example, here are the calculations for the category "first 3 months":

$$O - E = (52 - 28) = 24$$

$$(O - E)^2 = (24)^2 = 576$$

$$\frac{(O - E)^2}{E} = \frac{576}{28} = 20.571$$

Once we complete the table, the last step is easy. We just add up the numbers in the sixth column. In this case, the chi-square statistic is $20.571 + 20.571 = 41.14$. We can finish the formula by adding a summation sign to the formula in the sixth column. Note that we don't have to divide this sum by anything, as we've done with other statistics. We already did the dividing before we summed. This sum is the chi-square statistic. Here is the formula:

$$\chi^2 = \Sigma\left[\frac{(O - E)^2}{E}\right]$$

Summary: $\chi^2 = \Sigma\left[\dfrac{(O - E)^2}{E}\right] = 20.571 + 20.571 = 41.14$

MASTERING THE FORMULA

17-2: The formula for the chi-square statistic is:

$$\chi^2 = \Sigma\left[\frac{(O - E)^2}{E}\right].$$

For each cell, we subtract the expected count, E, from the observed count, O. Then we square each difference and divide the square by the expected count. Finally, we sum the calculations for each of the cells.

STEP 6: Make a decision.

This last step is identical to that of previous hypothesis tests. We reject the null hypothesis if the test statistic is beyond the critical value, and we fail to reject the null hypothesis if the test statistic is not beyond the critical value. In this case, the test statistic, 41.14, is far beyond the cutoff, 3.841, as seen in Figure 17-2. We reject the null hypothesis. Because there are only two categories, it's clear where the difference lies. It appears that elite German youth soccer players are more likely to have been born in the first 3 months of the year, and less likely to have been born in the last 3 months of the year, than members of the general population. (If we had failed to reject the null hypothesis, we could only have concluded that these data did not provide sufficient evidence to show that elite German youth soccer players have a different likelihood of being born in the first, versus last, 3 months of the year than those in the general population.)

Summary: Reject the null hypothesis; it appears that elite German youth soccer players are more likely to have been born in the first 3 months of the year, and less likely to have been born in the last 3 months of the year, than people in the general population.

We report these statistics in a journal article in almost the same format that we've seen previously. We report the degrees of freedom, the value of the test statistic, and whether the p value associated with the test statistic is less than or greater than the cutoff based on the p level of 0.05. (As usual, we would report the actual p level if we conducted this hypothesis test using software.) In addition, we report the sample size in parentheses with the degrees of freedom. In the current example, the statistics read:

$$\chi^2(1, N = 56) = 41.14, p < 0.05$$

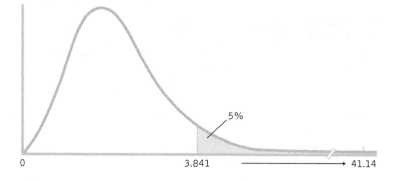

FIGURE 17-2

Making a Decision

As with other hypothesis tests, we make a decision with a chi-square test by comparing the test statistic to the cutoff, or critical value. We see here that 41.14 would be *far* to the right of 3.841.

Clown Therapy Israeli researchers tested whether entertainment by a clown led to higher pregnancy rates after in vitro fertilization treatment. Their study had two nominal variables—entertainment (clown, no clown) and pregnancy (pregnant, not pregnant)—and could have been analyzed with a chi-square test for independence.

The researchers who conducted this study imagined four possible explanations: "a) certain astrological signs confer superior soccer skills; b) winter-born babies tend to have higher oxygen capacity, which increases soccer stamina; c) soccer-mad parents are more likely to conceive children in springtime, at the annual peak of soccer mania; d) none of the above" (Dubner & Levitt, 2006a). What's your guess?

Dubner and Levitt (2006a) picked (d) and suggested another alternative. Participation in German youth soccer leagues has a strict cutoff date: December 31. Compared to those born in December, children born the previous January are likely to be more physically and emotionally mature, perceived as more talented, chosen for the best leagues, and given better coaching—a self-fulfilling prophecy. All this from a simple chi-square test for goodness of fit! ●

Chi-Square Test for Independence

The chi-square test for goodness of fit analyzes just one nominal variable. The chi-square test for independence analyzes *two* nominal variables.

Like the correlation coefficient, the chi-square test for independence does not require that we identify independent and dependent variables. However, specifying an independent variable and a dependent variable can help us articulate hypotheses. The chi-square test for independence is so named because it is used to determine whether the two variables—no matter which one is considered to be the independent variable—are independent of each other. Let's take a closer look at whether pregnancy rates are independent of (that is, depend on) whether one is entertained by a clown after IVF treatment.

EXAMPLE 17.2

In the clown study, as reported in the mass media (Ryan, 2006), 186 women were randomly assigned to receive IVF treatment only or to receive IVF treatment followed by 15 minutes of clown entertainment. Eighteen of the 93 who received only the IVF treatment became pregnant, whereas 33 of the 93 who received both IVF treatment and clown entertainment became pregnant. The cells for these observed frequencies can be seen in Table 17-5. The table of cells for a chi-square test for independence is called a *contingency table* because it helps us see if the outcome of one variable (e.g., becoming pregnant versus not becoming pregnant) is contingent on the other variable (clown versus no clown). Let's implement the six steps of hypothesis testing for a chi-square test for independence.

> **STEP 1: Identify the populations, distribution, and assumptions.**

Summary: Population 1: Women receiving IVF treatment like the women we observed. Population 2: Women receiving

TABLE 17-5 Observed Pregnancy Rates

This table depicts the cells and their frequencies for the study on whether entertainment by a clown is associated with pregnancy rates among women undergoing in vitro fertilization.

	Observed	
	Pregnant	Not Pregnant
Clown	33	60
No clown	18	75

IVF treatment for whom the presence of a clown is not associated with eventual pregnancy.

The comparison distribution is a chi-square distribution. The hypothesis test will be a chi-square test for independence because there are two nominal variables. This study meets three of the four assumptions: (1) The two variables are nominal. (2) Every participant is in only one cell. (3) The participants were not, however, randomly selected from the population of all women undergoing IVF treatment. We must be cautious in generalizing beyond the sample of Israeli women at this particular hospital. (4) There are more than five times as many participants as cells (186 participants and 4 cells; $4 \times 5 = 20$). We have far more participants, 186, than the 20 necessary to meet this guideline.

> **STEP 2: State the null and research hypotheses.**

Summary: Null hypothesis: Pregnancy rates are independent of whether one is entertained by a clown after IVF treatment. Research hypothesis: Pregnancy rates depend on whether one is entertained by a clown after IVF treatment.

> **STEP 3: Determine the characteristics of the comparison distribution.**

For a chi-square test for independence, we calculate degrees of freedom for each variable and then multiply the two to get the overall degrees of freedom. The degrees of freedom for the variable in the rows of the contingency table are:

$$df_{row} = k_{row} - 1$$

The degrees of freedom for the variable in the columns of the contingency table are:

$$df_{column} = k_{column} - 1$$

The overall degrees of freedom are:

$$df_{\chi^2} = (df_{row})(df_{column})$$

To expand this last formula, we write:

$$df_{\chi^2} = (k_{row} - 1)(k_{column} - 1)$$

So, the degrees of freedom for this chi-square test are:

$$df_{\chi^2} = (k_{row} - 1)(k_{column} - 1) = (2 - 1)(2 - 1) = 1$$

Summary: The comparison distribution is a chi-square distribution, which has 1 degree of freedom: $df_{\chi^2} = (k_{row} - 1)(k_{column} - 1) = (2 - 1)(2 - 1) = 1$.

MASTERING THE FORMULA

17-3: To calculate the degrees of freedom for the chi-square test for independence, we first have to calculate the degrees of freedom for each variable. For the variable in the rows, we subtract 1 from the number of categories in the rows: $df_{row} = k_{row} - 1$. For the variable in the columns, we subtract 1 from the number of categories in the columns: $df_{column} = k_{column} - 1$. We multiply these two numbers to get the overall degrees of freedom: $df_{\chi^2} = (df_{row})(df_{column})$. To combine all the calculations, we can use the following formula instead: $df_{\chi^2} = (k_{row} - 1)(k_{column} - 1)$.

> **STEP 4: Determine the critical values, or cutoffs.**

Summary: The critical value, or cutoff, for the chi-square statistic, based on a p level of 0.05 and 1 degree of freedom, is 3.841 (Figure 17-3).

> **STEP 5: Calculate the test statistic.**

The next step, determining the appropriate expected frequencies, is the most important in the calculation of the chi-square test for independence. Errors are often made in this step, and if the wrong expected frequencies are used, the chi-square statistic derived from them will also be wrong. Many students want to divide the total number of participants

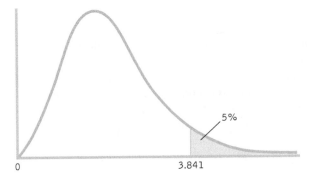

(here, 186) by the number of cells (here, 4) and place equivalent frequencies in all cells for the expected data. Here, that would mean that the expected frequencies would be 46.5.

But this would not make sense. Of the 186 women, only 51 became pregnant; $51/186 = 0.274$, or 27.4%, of these women became pregnant. If pregnancy rates do not depend on clown entertainment, then we would expect the same percentage of successful pregnancies, 27.4%, regardless of exposure to clowns. If we have expected frequencies of 46.5 in all four cells, then we have a 50%, not a 27.4%, pregnancy rate. We must always consider the specifics of the situation.

In the current study, we already calculated that 27.4% of all women in the study became pregnant. If pregnancy rates are independent of whether a woman is entertained by a clown, then we would expect 27.4% of the women who were entertained by a clown to become pregnant and 27.4% of women who were not entertained by a clown to become pregnant. Based on this percentage, $100 - 27.4 = 72.6\%$ of women in the study did not become pregnant. We would therefore expect 72.6% of women who were entertained by a clown to fail to become pregnant and 72.6% of women who were not entertained by a clown to fail to become pregnant. Again, we expect the same pregnancy and nonpregnancy rates in both groups—those who were and were not entertained by clowns.

Table 17-6 shows the observed data, and it also shows totals for each row, each column, and the whole table. From Table 17-6, we see that 93 women were entertained by a clown after IVF treatment. As we calculated above, we would expect 27.4% of them to become pregnant:

$$(0.274)(93) = 25.482$$

Of the 93 women who were not entertained by a clown, we would expect 27.4% to become pregnant if clown entertainment is independent of pregnancy rates:

$$(0.274)(93) = 25.482$$

TABLE 17-6 Observed Frequencies

This table depicts the cells and their frequencies for the study on whether entertainment by a clown is associated with pregnancy rates among women undergoing in vitro fertilization. It also includes row totals (93, 93), column totals (51, 135), and the grand total for the whole table (186).

	Observed		
	Pregnant	Not Pregnant	
Clown	33	60	93
No clown	18	75	93
	51	135	186

We now repeat the same procedure for not becoming pregnant. We would expect 72.6% of women in both groups to not become pregnant. For the women who were entertained by a clown, we would expect 72.6% of them to not become pregnant:

$$(0.726)(93) = 67.518$$

Of the women who were not entertained by a clown, we would expect 72.6% to not become pregnant:

$$(0.726)(93) = 67.518$$

(Note that the two expected frequencies for the first row are the same as the two expected frequencies for the second row, but only because the same number of people were in each clown condition, 93. If these two numbers were different, we would not see the same expected frequencies in the two rows.)

The method of calculating the expected frequencies that we described above is ideal because it is directly based on our own thinking about the frequencies in the rows and in the columns. Sometimes, however, our thinking can get muddled, particularly when the two (or more) row totals do not match and the two (or more) column totals do not match. For these situations, a simple set of rules leads to accurate expected frequencies. For each cell, we divide its column total ($Total_{column}$) by the grand total (N) and multiply that by the row total ($Total_{row}$):

$$\frac{Total_{column}}{N}(Total_{row})$$

As an example, the observed frequency of those who became pregnant and were entertained by a clown is 33. The row total for this cell is 93. The column total is 51. The grand total, N, is 186. The expected frequency, therefore, is:

$$\frac{Total_{column}}{N}(Total_{row}) = \frac{51}{186}(93) = (0.274)(93) = 25.482$$

Notice that this result is identical to what we calculated without a formula. The middle step above shows that, even with the formula, we actually did calculate the pregnancy rate overall, by dividing the column total (51) by the grand total (186). We then calculated how many in that row of 93 participants we would expect to become pregnant using this overall rate:

$$(0.274)(93) = 25.482$$

The formula follows the logic of the test and keeps us on track when there are multiple calculations.

As a final check on the calculations, shown in Table 17-7, we can add up the frequencies to be sure that they still match the row, column, and grand totals. For example, if we add the two numbers in the first column, 25.482 and 25.482, we get 50.964 (different from 51 only because of rounding decisions).* If we had made the mistake of dividing the 186 participants into cells by dividing by 4, we would have had 46.5 in each cell; then the total for the first column would have been $46.5 + 46.5 = 93$, which is not a match with 51. This final check ensures that we have the appropriate expected frequencies in the cells.

> **MASTERING THE FORMULA**
>
> **17-4:** When conducting a chi-square test for independence, we can calculate the expected frequencies in each cell by taking the total for the column that the cell is in, dividing it by the total in the study, and then multiplying by the total for the row that the cell is in:
>
> $$\frac{Total_{column}}{N}(Total_{row}).$$

---

*Because we started the calculations with the pregnancy rates, the expected frequencies are not exactly 50% of 51 and 135. If we had started the calculations with clown exposure, the rounding process would have led to different expected frequencies—25.5 for both frequencies in the "Pregnant" column and 67.5 for both frequencies in the "Not Pregnant" column.

TABLE 17-7 Expected Frequencies with Totals

This table includes the expected frequencies for each of the four cells. The expected frequencies should still add up to the row totals (93, 93), column totals (51, 135), and the grand total for the whole table (186). Note: See footnote on the previous page.

	Expected		
	Pregnant	Not Pregnant	
Clown	25.482	67.518	93
No clown	25.482	67.518	93
	51	135	186

TABLE 17-8 The Chi-Square Calculations

For the chi-square test for independence calculations, we use the same format as we did for the chi-square test for goodness of fit. We calculate the difference between each observed frequency and expected frequency, square the difference, then divide each square by its appropriate expected frequency. Finally, we add up the numbers in the last column, which gives us the chi-square statistic.

Category	Observed (O)	Expected (E)	($O - E$)	($O - E)^2$	$\dfrac{(O - E)^2}{E}$
Clown; pregnant	33	25.482	7.518	56.520	2.218
Clown; not pregnant	60	67.518	27.518	56.520	0.837
No clown; pregnant	18	25.482	27.482	55.980	2.197
No clown; not pregnant	75	67.518	7.482	55.980	0.829

The remainder of the fifth step is identical to that for a chi-square test for goodness of fit, as seen in Table 17-8. As before, we calculate the difference between each observed frequency and its matching expected frequency, square these differences, and divide each squared difference by the appropriate expected frequency. We add up the numbers in the final column of the table to calculate the chi-square statistic.

Summary: $\chi^2 = \Sigma \left[\dfrac{(O - E)^2}{E} \right] = 2.218 + 0.837 + 2.197 + 0.829 = 6.081$

STEP 6: Make a decision.

Summary: Reject the null hypothesis; it appears that pregnancy rates depend on whether a woman receives clown entertainment following IVF treatment (Figure 17-4).

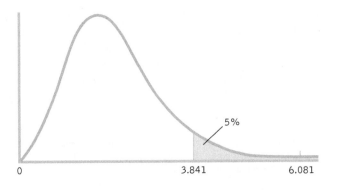

FIGURE 17-4

The Decision

Because the chi-square statistic, 6.081, is beyond the critical value, 3.841, we can reject the null hypothesis. It is unlikely that the pregnancy rates for those who received clown therapy versus those who did not were this different from each other just by chance.

The statistics, as reported in a journal article, would follow the format we learned for a chi-square test for goodness of fit as well as for other hypothesis tests in earlier chapters. We report the degrees of freedom and sample size, the value of the test statistic, and whether the p value associated with the test statistic is less than or greater than the critical value based on the p level of 0.05. (We would report the actual p level if we conducted this hypothesis test using software.) In the current example, the statistics would read:

$$\chi^2(1, N = 186) = 6.08, p < 0.05 \bullet$$

CHECK YOUR LEARNING

Reviewing the Concepts

> The chi-square tests are used when all variables are nominal.

> The chi-square test for goodness of fit is used with one nominal variable.

> The chi-square test for independence is used with two nominal variables; usually one can be thought of as the independent variable and one as the dependent variable.

> Both chi-square hypothesis tests use the same six steps of hypothesis testing with which we are familiar.

Clarifying the Concepts

17-5 When do we use chi-square tests?

17-6 What are observed frequencies and expected frequencies?

Calculating the Statistics

17-7 Imagine a town that boasts clear blue skies 80% of the time. You get to work in that town one summer for 78 days and record the following data. (*Note:* For each day you picked just one label.)

Clear blue skies: 59 days

Cloudy/hazy/gray skies: 19 days

a. Calculate degrees of freedom for this chi-square test for goodness of fit.

b. Determine the observed and expected frequencies.

c. Calculate the differences and squared differences between frequencies, and calculate the chi-square statistic. Use the six-column format provided here.

Category	Observed (O)	Expected (E)	O − E	(O − E)²	$\frac{(O - E)^2}{E}$
Clear blue skies					
Unclear skies					

Applying the Concepts

17-8 The Chicago Police Department conducted a study comparing two types of lineups for suspect identification: simultaneous lineups and sequential lineups (Mecklenburg, Malpass, & Ebbesen, 2006). In simultaneous lineups, witnesses saw the suspects all at once, either live or in photographs, and then made their selection. In sequential lineups, witnesses saw the people in the lineup one at a time, either live or in photographs, and said yes or no to suspects one at a time. After numerous high-profile cases in which DNA evidence exonerated people who had been convicted, including many on death row, many police departments shifted to sequential lineups in the hope of reducing incorrect identifications. Several previous studies had indicated the superiority of sequential lineups with respect to accuracy. Over one year, three jurisdictions in Illinois compared the two types of lineups. Of 319 simultaneous lineups, 191 led to identification of the suspect, 8 led to identification of another person in the lineup, and 120 led to no identification. Of 229 sequential lineups, 102 led to identification of

continued on next page

the suspect, 20 led to identification of another person in the lineup, and 107 led to no identification.

a. Who or what are the participants in this study? Identify the independent variable and its levels as well as the dependent variable and its levels.

b. Conduct all six steps of hypothesis testing.

c. Report the statistics as you would in a journal article.

d. Why is this study an example of the importance of using two-tailed rather than one-tailed hypothesis tests?

Solutions to these Check Your Learning questions can be found in Appendix D.

Beyond Hypothesis Testing

In the selfie study that introduced this chapter, Döring and her colleagues conducted a chi-square analysis that supported their hypothesis that women and men fall back on gender stereotypes in their selfie poses (2016). For a statistically significant finding like this, we would want to know more. For example, we might ask how large the gender difference was and we might want to see the difference in a graph.

Most nonparametric hypothesis tests do not have associated effect-size measures, but chi square does. Using the pregnancy and clown example, we'll introduce Cramér's V, the effect size for chi square, as one method to determine how large a finding is. We'll then show how to depict chi-square findings visually in a graph so that we can see how large the effect is. We'll also demonstrate how to calculate relative risk, another way to understand the size of an effect by quantifying the chances of a given outcome. Finally, we'll show how to conduct a type of post hoc test that can be used to determine exactly where any differences lie among the cells of a chi-square design.

- Cramér's V is the standard effect size used with the chi-square test for independence; also called *Cramér's phi*, symbolized as ϕ.

Cramér's V, the Effect Size for Chi Square

A hypothesis test tells us only that there is a likely effect—that it would be unlikely that the observed effect would have occurred merely by chance if the null hypothesis were true. But we have to calculate an additional statistic, an effect size, before we can make claims about the importance of a study's finding.

***Cramér's* V** *is the standard effect size used with the chi-square test for independence.* It is also called *Cramér's phi* (pronounced "fie"—rhymes with *fly*) and symbolized by ϕ. Once we have calculated the test statistic, it is easy to calculate Cramér's V by hand. The formula is:

$$\text{Cramér's } V = \sqrt{\frac{\chi^2}{(N)(df_{row/column})}}$$

χ^2 is the test statistic we just calculated, N is the total number of participants in the study (the lower-right number in the contingency table), and $df_{row/column}$ is the degrees of freedom for either the category in the rows or the category in the columns, whichever is smaller.

MASTERING THE FORMULA

17-5: The formula for Cramér's V, the effect size typically used with the chi-square statistic, is:

$$\text{Cramér's } V = \sqrt{\frac{\chi^2}{(N)(df_{row/column})}}.$$

The numerator is the chi-square statistic, χ^2. The denominator is the product of the sample size, N, and either the degrees of freedom for the rows or the degrees of freedom for the columns, whichever is smaller. We take the square root of this quotient to get Cramér's V.

EXAMPLE 17.3

For the clown example, we calculated a chi-square statistic of 6.081, there were 186 participants, and the degrees of freedom for both categories were 1. When neither degree of freedom is smaller than the other, of course, it doesn't matter which one we choose. The effect size for the clown study, therefore, is:

$$\text{Cramér's } V = \sqrt{\frac{\chi^2}{(N)(df_{row/column})}} = \sqrt{\frac{6.081}{(186)(1)}} = \sqrt{0.033} = 0.182$$

TABLE 17-9	Conventions for Determining Effect Size Based on Cramér's V

Jacob Cohen (1992) developed guidelines to determine whether particular effect sizes should be considered small, medium, or large. The effect-size guidelines vary depending on the size of the contingency table. There are different guidelines based on whether the smaller of the two degrees of freedom (row or column) is 1, 2, or 3.

Effect Size	When $df_{row/column} = 1$	When $df_{row/column} = 2$	When $df_{row/column} = 3$
Small	0.10	0.07	0.06
Medium	0.30	0.21	0.17
Large	0.50	0.35	0.29

Now that we have the effect size, we must ask what it means. As with other effect sizes, Jacob Cohen (1992) has developed guidelines, shown in Table 17-9, for determining whether a particular effect is small, medium, or large. The guidelines vary based on the size of the contingency table. When the smaller of the two degrees of freedom for the row and column is 1, we use the guidelines in the second column. When the smaller of the two degrees of freedom is 2, we use the guidelines in the third column. And when it is 3, we use the guidelines in the fourth column. As with the other guidelines for judging effect sizes, such as those for Cohen's d, the guidelines are not cutoffs. Rather, they are rough indicators to help researchers gauge a finding's importance.

The effect size for the clowning and pregnancy study was 0.18. The smaller of the two degrees of freedom, that for the row and that for the column, was 1 (in fact, both were 1). So we use the second column in Table 17-9. This Cramér's V falls about halfway between the effect-size guidelines for a small effect (0.10) and a medium effect (0.30). We would call this a small-to-medium effect. We can build on the report of the statistics by adding the Cramér's V to the end:

$$\chi^2(1, N = 186) = 6.08, p < 0.05, \text{Cramér's } V = 0.18 \bullet$$

Graphing Chi-Square Percentages

In addition to calculating Cramér's V, we can graph the data. A visual depiction of the pattern of results is an effective way to understand the size of the relation between two variables assessed using the chi-square statistic. We don't graph the frequencies, however. We graph proportions or percentages.

EXAMPLE 17.4

For the women entertained by a clown, we calculate the proportion who became pregnant and the proportion who did not. For the women not entertained by a clown, we again calculate the proportion who became pregnant and the proportion who did not. The calculations for the proportions are below.

In each case, we're dividing the number of a given outcome by the total number of women in that group. The proportions are called *conditional proportions* because we're not calculating the proportions out of all women in the study; we're calculating proportions for women in a certain condition. We calculate the proportion of women who became pregnant, for example, conditional on their having been entertained by a clown.

Entertained by a clown
    Became pregnant: 33/93 = 0.355
    Did not become pregnant: 60/93 = 0.645

● **Relative risk** is a measure created by making a ratio of two conditional proportions; also called *relative likelihood* or *relative chance*.

TABLE 17-10	Conditional Proportions		

To construct a graph depicting the results of a chi-square test for independence, we first calculate conditional proportions. For example, we calculate the proportions of women who got pregnant, conditional on having been entertained by a clown after in vitro fertilization: 33/93 = 0.355.

	Conditional Proportions		
	Pregnant	Not Pregnant	
Clown	0.355	0.645	1.00
No clown	0.194	0.806	1.00

Not entertained by a clown
Became pregnant: 18/93 = 0.194
Did not become pregnant: 75/93 = 0.806

We can put those proportions into a table (such as Table 17-10). For each category of entertainment (clown, no clown), the proportions should add up to 1.00; or if we used percentages, they should add up to 100%.

We can now graph the conditional proportions, as in Figure 17-5. Alternately, we could have simply graphed the two rates at which women got pregnant—0.355 and 0.194—given that the rates at which they did not become pregnant are based on these rates. This graph is depicted in Figure 17-6. In both cases, we include the scale of proportions on the *y*-axis from 0 to 1.0 so that the graph does not mislead the viewer into thinking that rates are higher than they are. ●

Relative Risk

Public health statisticians like John Snow (Chapter 1) are called epidemiologists. They often think about the size of an effect with chi square in terms of ***relative risk***, *a measure created by making a ratio of two conditional proportions*. It is also called *relative likelihood* or *relative chance*.

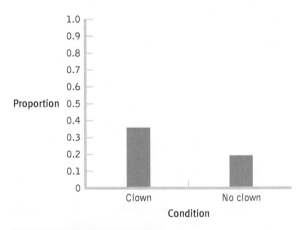

FIGURE 17-5

Graphing and Chi Square

When we graph the data for a chi-square test for independence, we graph conditional proportions rather than frequencies. The proportions allow us to compare the rates at which women became pregnant in the two conditions.

FIGURE 17-6

A Simpler Graph of Conditional Probabilities

Because the rates at which women did not become pregnant are based on the rates at which they did become pregnant, we can simply graph one set of rates. Here we see the rates at which women became pregnant in each of the two clown conditions.

EXAMPLE 17.5

As with Figure 17-5, we calculate the chance of getting pregnant with clown entertainment after IVF by dividing the number of pregnancies in this group by the total number of women entertained by clowns:

$$33/93 = 0.355$$

We then calculate the chance of getting pregnant with no clown entertainment after IVF by dividing the number of pregnancies in this group by the total number of women not entertained by clowns:

$$18/93 = 0.194$$

If we divide the chance of getting pregnant having been entertained by clowns by the chance of getting pregnant not having been entertained by clowns, then we get the relative likelihood:

$$0.355/0.194 = 1.830$$

Based on the relative risk calculation, the chance of getting pregnant when IVF is followed by clown entertainment is 1.83 times (or about twice) the chance of getting pregnant when IVF is not followed by clown entertainment. This matches the impression that we get from the graph.

Alternately, we can reverse the ratio, dividing the chance of becoming pregnant without clown entertainment, 0.194, by the chance of becoming pregnant following clown entertainment, 0.355. This is the relative likelihood for the reversed ratio:

$$0.194/0.355 = 0.546$$

This number gives us the same information in a different way. The chance of getting pregnant when IVF is followed by no entertainment is 0.55 (or about half) the chance of getting pregnant when IVF is followed by clown entertainment. Again, this matches the graph; one bar is about half that of the other.

Note: When this calculation is made with respect to diseases, it is referred to as *relative risk* (rather than relative likelihood). We should be careful when relative risks and relative likelihoods are reported, however. We must always be aware of base rates. If, for example, a certain disease occurs in just 0.01% of the population (that is, 1 in 10,000) and is twice as likely to occur among people who eat ice cream, then the rate is 0.02% (2 in 10,000) among those who eat ice cream. Relative risks and relative likelihoods can be used to scare the general public unnecessarily—which is one more reason why statistical reasoning is a healthy way to think. ●

> **MASTERING THE CONCEPT**
>
> **17-3:** We can quantify the size of an effect with chi square through relative risk, also called *relative likelihood*. By making a ratio of two conditional proportions, we can say, for example, that one group is twice as likely to show some outcome or, conversely, that the other group is one-half as likely to show that outcome.

Adjusted Standardized Residuals   **Next Steps**

Chi-square tests present a problem when there are more than two levels of one of the variables. A significant chi-square hypothesis test means only that at least some of the cells' observed frequencies are statistically significantly different from their corresponding expected frequencies. We cannot know how many cells or exactly which ones are significantly different without an additional step. That next step is the calculation of a statistic for each cell based on its residual.

A cell's residual is the difference between the expected frequency and the observed frequency for that cell, but we take it a step further. We calculate *an **adjusted standardized***

● **Adjusted standardized residual** is the difference between the observed frequency and the expected frequency for a cell in a chi-square research design, divided by the standard error; also called *adjusted residual*.

residual, *the difference between the observed frequency and the expected frequency for a cell in a chi-square research design, divided by the standard error*. In other words, an adjusted standardized residual (often called just *adjusted residual* by software) is a measure of the number of standard errors that an observed frequency falls from its associated expected frequency.

Does this sound familiar? The adjusted standardized frequency is kind of like a z statistic for each cell (Agresti & Franklin, 2006). A larger adjusted standardized residual indicates that an observed frequency is farther from its expected frequency than a smaller adjusted standardized residual indicates. And as with a z statistic, we're not concerned with the sign. A large positive adjusted standardized residual and a large negative adjusted standardized residual tell us the same thing. If it's large enough, then we're willing to conclude that the observed frequency really is different from what we would expect if the null hypothesis were true.

Also like a z statistic, any time a cell has an adjusted standardized residual that is at least 2 (whether the sign is positive or negative), we are willing to conclude that the cell's observed frequency is different from its expected frequency. Some statisticians prefer a more stringent criterion, drawing this conclusion only if an adjusted standardized residual is larger than 3 (again, whether the sign is positive or negative). Regardless of the criterion used, the method and logic for determining the probabilities of z statistics and determining adjusted standardized residuals are the same.

Adjusted standardized residuals are too complicated to calculate without the aid of a computer, but we'll show you a software printout of the adjusted standardized residuals for the clown therapy study. Figure 17-7 shows the printout from the SPSS software package. The row labeled "Count" includes the observed frequencies. The "Expected Count" row includes the expected frequencies. The "Adjusted Residual" row includes the adjusted standardized residuals. So, for example, the upper-left-hand cell has data about women who became pregnant following post-IVF entertainment by a clown; the observed frequency for this cell was 33, the expected frequency was 25.5, and the adjusted standardized residual was 2.5. Any adjusted standardized residual greater than 2 or less than -2 indicates that the observed frequency is farther from the expected frequency than we would expect if the two variables were independent of each other. In this case, all four adjusted standardized residuals are either 2.5 or -2.5, so we can conclude that all four observed frequencies are farther from their corresponding expected frequencies than would likely occur if the null hypothesis were true.

Type of Entertainment* Result of IVF Crosstabulation

			Result of IVF		Total
			Pregnant	Not Pregnant	
Type of Entertainment	Clown	Count	33	60	93
		Expected Count	25.5	67.5	93.0
		Adjusted Residual	2.5	−2.5	
	No Clown	Count	18	75	93
		Expected Count	25.5	67.5	93.0
		Adjusted Residual	−2.5	2.5	
Total		Count	51	135	186

FIGURE 17-7

Adjusted Standardized Residuals

Software calculates an adjusted standardized residual, called *adjusted residual* by most software packages, for each cell. It is calculated by taking the residual for each cell, calculating the difference between the observed frequency and expected frequency, and dividing by standard error. When an adjusted standardized residual is greater than 2 or less than −2, we typically conclude that the observed frequency is greater than the expected frequency.

CHECK YOUR LEARNING

Reviewing the Concepts
> The appropriate effect-size measure for the chi-square test for independence is Cramér's V.

> We can depict the effect size visually by calculating and graphing conditional proportions so that we can compare the rates of a certain outcome in each of two or more groups.

> Another way to consider the size of an effect is through relative risk, a ratio of conditional proportions for each of two groups.

> A statistically significant chi-square hypothesis test does not tell us exactly which cells are farther from their expected frequencies than would occur if the two variables were independent. We must calculate adjusted standardized residuals to identify these cells.

Clarifying the Concepts   17-9   What is the effect-size measure for chi-square tests and how is it calculated?

Calculating the Statistics 17-10   In the selfie research we discussed at the beginning of this chapter, we talked about gender stereotypes in people's poses and behaviors (Döring et al., 2016). Out of 250 women's selfies, 29 showed a "kissing pout," better known as duckface. Out of 250 men's selfies, 6 did. Calculate the relative likelihood of taking a duckface selfie if you're a woman as opposed to a man.

Applying the Concepts   17-11   In Check Your Learning 17-8, you were asked to conduct a chi-square test on a Chicago Police Department study comparing two types of lineups for suspect identification: simultaneous lineups and sequential lineups (Mecklenburg et al., 2006).

a.   Calculate the appropriate measure of effect size for this study.

b.   Create a graph of the conditional proportions for these data.

Solutions to these Check Your
Learning questions can be found
in Appendix D.

c.   Calculate the relative likelihood of a suspect being accurately identified in the simultaneous lineups versus the sequential lineups.

REVIEW OF CONCEPTS

Nonparametric Statistics

Nonparametric hypothesis tests are used when a study's design does not meet the assumptions of a parametric test. This often occurs when there is a nominal or ordinal dependent variable or a small sample in which the data suggest a skewed population distribution. Given the choice, we should use a parametric test because these tests tend to have more statistical power and because we can more frequently calculate confidence intervals and effect sizes for parametric hypothesis tests.

Chi-Square Tests

We use the *chi-square test for goodness of fit* when there is only one variable and it is nominal. We use the *chi-square test for independence* when there are two nominal variables; typically, for the purposes of articulating hypotheses, one variable is thought of as the independent variable and the other is thought of as the dependent variable. With both chi-square tests, we analyze whether the data that we observe match what we would expect according to the null hypothesis. Both tests use the same basic six steps of hypothesis testing that we learned previously.

Beyond Hypothesis Testing

We usually calculate an effect size as well; the most commonly calculated effect size with chi square is *Cramér's V*, also called *Cramér's phi*. We can also create a graph that depicts the conditional proportions of an outcome for each group. Alternately, we can calculate *relative risk (relative likelihood* or *relative chance*) to more easily compare the rates of certain outcomes in each of two groups. We can determine this by calculating adjusted standardized residuals, the distances of the observed frequencies from their corresponding expected frequencies in terms of standard errors.

SPSS®

In SPSS, we can conduct both a chi-square test for goodness of fit and a chi-square test for independence. Using data from the soccer player example, we enter the data for the one variable: whether or not a soccer player was born in the first three months. We enter the data as a nominal variable. Remember, with nominal and ordinal variables we have to tell SPSS the names for each category (see Chapter 11 for a refresher on how to enter nominal data in SPSS). In this example, we can use 1 to represent soccer players who were born in the first three months and 2 to represent soccer players who were born in the last three months.

To conduct a chi-square test for goodness of fit, select: Analyze → Nonparametric Tests → Legacy Dialogue → Chi-square. Select the variable of interest, in this example "birth," and move it into the Test Variable List. In this example, we hypothesize that soccer players have the sample patterns of birth months as those in the general population, meaning that we expect that all categories will be equal. If, however, we expect a different proportion (like in the How It Works 17.1 example), we would need to enter those proportions into the Expected Values. For now, we can keep the default selected, all categories equal. Click "OK" to run the analysis.

The accompanying output displays two tables. The first table provides the observed values for each level in the variable, the expected values, and the residual. The second table, "Test Statistics," provides the chi-square value, the degrees of freedom, and the *p* value (next to "Asymp, Sig."). The chi-square value of 41.193 and the degrees of freedom of 1 match what we calculated earlier in the chapter. The *p* value here is less than 0.05; therefore, we reject the null hypothesis. (Any slight differences we see in this table versus what we calculated earlier are due to rounding decisions.)

We can also conduct a chi-square test for independence using SPSS. To demonstrate how, we will use data from the pregnancy and clown example. Each participant gets a score on each variable: one for a woman's status with respect to entertainment by a clown (yes or no) and one for her pregnancy status (yes or no). We can use the numbers 0 to represent no and 1 to represent yes. Select: Analyze → Descriptive Statistics → Crosstabs. (Select a nominal variable for the row and a nominal variable for the column; we selected entertainment-by-clown status for the rows and pregnancy status for the columns, but it doesn't matter which we choose.) Click "Statistics" and select two boxes "Chi-Square" and "Phi & Cramér's *V*" (for effect sizes). Click "Continue." Select "Cells" and then click "Row" under percentages to get the percentage of women who became pregnant in each clown condition. Click "Continue," and then click "OK" to run the analysis.

Most of the output, along with a view of some of the data, can be seen in the accompanying screenshot. In the top box of the output, we can see the percentages of women who did or did not become pregnant in each condition. For example, 35.5% of women who were entertained by a clown became pregnant. We can also see that the chi-square statistic (in the box titled "Chi-Square Tests" in the row labeled "Pearson Chi-Square") is 6.078, the same as the one we calculated by hand earlier. In the box titled "Symmetric Measures," we can see the Cramér's *V* statistic of .181, also the same as we calculated earlier. (Again, any slight differences we see in this table versus what we calculated earlier are due to rounding decisions.)

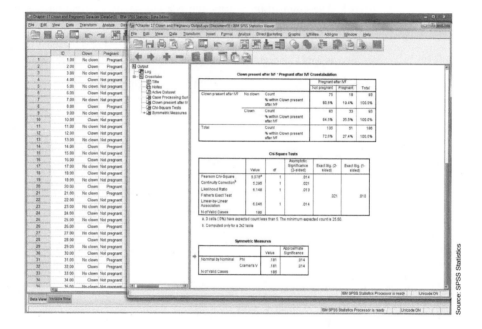

Source: SPSS Statistics

HOW IT WORKS

17.1 CONDUCTING A CHI-SQUARE TEST FOR GOODNESS OF FIT

Have you heard of the Bechdel Test? Allison Bechdel developed a simple rubric to determine if a movie (or other fictional work) was at least trying for gender equality. The test: You have to be able to answer "yes" to three questions: 1) Are there at least two women in the film? 2) Who talk to each other? 3) About something other than a man? It's surprisingly hard to find films that meet these criteria. Researchers examined the effect of the screenwriters' genders on films' gender equality (Friedman, Daniels, & Blinderman, 2016). Of high-earning films written entirely by men, 53% failed the Bechdel Test. What about similarly successful films with at least one female writer? In a sample of 61 top films that had at least one woman on the writing team, 23 failed the Bechdel Test and 38 passed. (For fun, check out the researchers' Bechdel Test simulator on http://poly-graph.co/bechdel/. You can see the likelihood that a film will pass the Bechdel Test given a particular director, producer, and writer. For example, a film directed by Tina Fey, produced by Judd Apatow, and written by Shonda Rimes would only have an 11% chance of failing.) How can we use the Bechdel Test to conduct the six steps of hypothesis testing for a chi-square test for goodness of fit?

Step 1: Population 1: High-earning films with at least one woman on the writing team. Population 2: High-earning films written entirely by men.

The comparison distribution is a chi-square distribution. The hypothesis test will be a chi-square test for goodness of fit because we have one nominal variable only. This study meets three of the four assumptions: (1) The one variable is nominal. (2) Every participant is in only one cell (either passing the Bechdel Test or not passing the test). (3) There are far more than five times as many participants as cells (there are 61 films included in the sample and only two cells). (4) We do not know how the 61 films (top films with at least one woman on the writing team) were selected, and therefore do not know if they were randomly selected. This limits our ability to generalize beyond the films in this sample.

Step 2: Null hypothesis: Films with at least one female writer will be just as likely to pass the Bechdel Test as films written entirely by men. Research hypothesis: Films with at least one woman writer will pass the Bechdel Test at a different rate than films written entirely by men.

Step 3: The comparison distribution is a chi-square distribution that has 1 degree of freedom: $df_{\chi^2} = 2 - 1 = 1$.

Step 4: The critical chi-square value, based on a p level of 0.05 and 1 degree of freedom, is 3.841, as seen in the curve in Figure 17-3.

Step 5: Observed (among films with at least 1 woman writer)

Pass	Fail
38	23

Expected (based on 53%—or 0.53—of films written entirely by men failing the test)

Pass	Fail
(0.47)(61) = 28.67	(0.53)(61) = 32.33

	Observed (O)	Expected (E)	O − E	(O − E)^2	$\dfrac{(O - E)^2}{E}$
Pass	38	28.67	9.33	87.049	3.036
Fail	23	32.33	−9.33	87.049	2.693

$$\chi^2 = \Sigma \left[\frac{(O - E)^2}{E} \right] = 3.036 + 2.693 = 5.729$$

Step 6: Reject the null hypothesis; it appears that films with at least one woman writer pass the Bechdel Test more often than do films written entirely by men.

The statistics, as reported in a journal article, would read:

$$\chi^2(1, N = 61) = 5.73, p < 0.05$$

17.2 CONDUCTING A CHI-SQUARE TEST FOR INDEPENDENCE

Do people who move far from their hometown have a more exciting life? Since 1972, the General Social Survey (GSS) has asked approximately 40,000 adults in the United States numerous questions about their lives. During several years of the GSS, participants were asked, "In general, do you find life exciting, pretty routine, or dull?" (a variable called LIFE) and "When you were 16 years old, were you living in the same (city/town/country)?" (a variable called MOBILE16). How can we use these data to conduct the six steps of hypothesis testing for a chi-square test for independence?

In this case, there are two nominal variables. The independent variable is where a person lives relative to when he or she was 16 years old (same city, or same state but different city, or different state). The dependent variable is how the person finds life (exciting, routine, dull). Here are the data:

	Exciting	Routine	Dull
Same city	4890	6010	637
Same state/different city	3368	3488	337
Different state	4604	4139	434

Step 1: Population 1: People like those in this sample. Population 2: People from a population in which a person's characterization of life as exciting, routine, or dull does not depend on where that person is living relative to when he or she was 16 years old.

The comparison distribution is a chi-square distribution. The hypothesis test will be a chi-square test for independence because there are two nominal variables. This study meets all four assumptions: (1) The two variables are nominal. (2) Every participant is in only one cell. (3) There are more than five times as many participants as there are cells (there are 27,907 participants and 9 cells). (4) The GSS sample uses a form of random selection.

Step 2: Null hypothesis: The proportion of people who find life to be exciting, routine, or dull does not depend on where they live relative to where they lived when they were 16 years old. Research hypothesis: The proportion of people who find life exciting, routine, or dull differs depending on where they live relative to where they lived when they were 16 years old.

Step 3: The comparison distribution is a chi-square distribution with 4 degrees of freedom:

$$df_{\chi^2} = (k_{row} - 1)(k_{column} - 1) = (3 - 1)(3 - 1) = (2)(2) = 4$$

Step 4: The critical chi-square statistic, based on a p level of 0.05 and 4 degrees of freedom, is 9.488.

Step 5:

	Observed (Expected in parentheses)			
	Exciting	**Routine**	**Dull**	
Same city	4890	6010	637	11,537
	(5317.264)	(5637.656)	(582.080)	
Same state/different city	3368	3488	337	7193
	(3315.167)	(3514.922)	(362.911)	
Different state	4604	4139	434	9177
	(4229.569)	(4484.421)	(463.010)	
	12,862	13,637	1408	27,907

$$\frac{Total_{column}}{N}(Total_{row}) = \frac{12,862}{27,907}(11,537) = 5317.264$$

$$\frac{Total_{column}}{N}(Total_{row}) = \frac{12,862}{27,907}(7193) = 3315.167$$

$$\frac{Total_{column}}{N}(Total_{row}) = \frac{12,862}{27,907}(9177) = 4229.569$$

$$\frac{Total_{column}}{N}(Total_{row}) = \frac{13,637}{27,907}(11,537) = 5637.656$$

$$\frac{Total_{column}}{N}(Total_{row}) = \frac{13,637}{27,907}(7193) = 3514.922$$

$$\frac{Total_{column}}{N}(Total_{row}) = \frac{13,637}{27,907}(9177) = 4484.421$$

$$\frac{Total_{column}}{N}(Total_{row}) = \frac{1408}{27,907}(11,537) = 582.080$$

$$\frac{Total_{column}}{N}(Total_{row}) = \frac{1408}{27,907}(7193) = 362.911$$

$$\frac{Total_{column}}{N}(Total_{row}) = \frac{1408}{27,907}(9177) = 463.010$$

Category	$(O - E)^2$	$\dfrac{(O - E)^2}{E}$
Same city; exciting	182,554.526	34.332
Same city; routine	138,640.054	24.592
Same city; dull	3016.206	5.182
Same state/different city; exciting	2791.326	0.842
Same state/different city; routine	724.794	0.206
Same state/different city; dull	671.38	1.850
Different state; exciting	140,198.574	33.147
Different state; routine	119,315.667	26.607
Different state; dull	841.580	1.818

$$\chi^2 = \Sigma\left[\frac{(O - E)^2}{E}\right] = 128.576$$

Step 6: Reject the null hypothesis. The calculated chi-square statistic exceeds the critical value. How exciting a person finds life does appear to vary with where the person lives relative to where he or she lived when he or she was 16 years old.

We would present these statistics in a journal article as: $\chi^2(4, N = 27,907) = 128.58, p < 0.05$.

17.3 CALCULATING CRAMÉR'S V

What is the effect size, Cramér's V, for the chi-square test for independence we conducted in How It Works 17.2?

$$V = \sqrt{\frac{\chi^2}{(N)(df_{row/column})}} = \sqrt{\frac{128.576}{(27,907)(2)}} = \sqrt{\frac{128.576}{55,814}} = 0.048$$

According to Cohen's conventions, this is a small effect size. With this piece of information, we'd present the statistics in a journal article as:

$$\chi^2(4, N = 27,907) = 128.58 < 0.05, \text{Cramér's } V = 0.05$$

EXERCISES

Clarifying the Concepts

17.1 Distinguish among nominal, ordinal, and scale data.

17.2 What are the three main situations in which we use a nonparametric test?

17.3 What is the difference between the chi-square test for goodness of fit and the chi-square test for independence?

17.4 What are the four assumptions for the chi-square tests?

17.5 List two ways in which statisticians use the word *independence* or *independent* with respect to concepts introduced earlier in this book. Then describe how

independence is used by statisticians with respect to chi square.

17.6 What are the hypotheses when conducting the chi-square test for goodness of fit?

17.7 How are the degrees of freedom for the chi-square hypothesis tests different from those of most other hypothesis tests?

17.8 Why is there just one critical value for a chi-square test, even when the hypothesis is a two-tailed test?

17.9 What information is presented in a contingency table in the chi-square test for independence?

17.10 What measure of effect size is used with chi square?

17.11 Define the symbols in the following formula:

$$\chi^2 = \Sigma\left[\frac{(O - E)^2}{E}\right]$$

17.12 What is the formula $\frac{Total_{column}}{N}(Total_{row})$ used for?

17.13 What information does the measure of relative likelihood provide?

17.14 In order to calculate relative likelihood, what must we first calculate?

17.15 What is the difference between relative likelihood and relative risk?

17.16 Why might relative likelihood be easier to understand as an effect size than Cramér's V?

17.17 Which graph is most useful for displaying the results of a chi-square test for independence?

17.18 How are adjusted standardized residuals calculated?

17.19 How are adjusted standardized residuals used as a post hoc test for chi-square tests?

Calculating the Statistics

17.20 For each of the following, (i) identify the incorrect symbol, (ii) state what the correct symbol should be, and (iii) explain why the initial symbol was incorrect.

a. For the chi-square test for goodness of fit: $df_{\chi^2} = N - 1$

b. For the chi-square test for independence: $df_{\chi^2} = (k_{row} - 1) + (k_{column} - 1)$

c. $\chi^2 = \Sigma\left[\frac{(M - E)^2}{E}\right]$

d. Cramér's $V = \sqrt{\dfrac{\chi^2}{(N)(k_{row/column})}}$

e. Expected frequency for each cell $= \dfrac{k_{column}}{(N)(k_{row})}$

17.21 For each of the following, identify the independent variable(s), the dependent variable(s), and the level of measurement (nominal, ordinal, scale).

a. The number of loads of laundry washed per month was tracked for women and men living in college dorms.

b. A researcher interested in people's need to maintain their social image collected data on the number of miles on someone's car and his or her rank for "need for approval" out of the 183 people studied.

c. A professor of social science was interested in whether involvement in campus life is significantly impacted by whether a student lives on or off campus.

Thirty-seven students living on campus and 37 students living off campus were asked whether they were an active member of a club.

17.22 Use this calculation table for the chi-square test for goodness of fit to complete this exercise.

Category	Observed (O)	Expected (E)	O − E	(O − E)²	$\frac{(O - E)^2}{E}$
1	48	60			
2	46	30			
3	6	10			

a. Calculate degrees of freedom for this chi-square test for goodness of fit.

b. Perform all of the calculations to complete this table.

c. Compute the chi-square statistic.

17.23 Use this calculation table for the chi-square test for goodness of fit to complete this exercise.

Category	Observed (O)	Expected (E)	O − E	(O − E)²	$\frac{(O - E)^2}{E}$
1	750	625			
2	650	625			
3	600	625			
4	500	625			

a. Calculate degrees of freedom for this chi-square test for goodness of fit.

b. Perform all of the calculations to complete this table.

c. Compute the chi-square statistic.

17.24 Below are some data to use in a chi-square test for independence.

	Observed		
	Accidents	No Accidents	
Rain	19	26	45
No rain	20	71	91
	39	97	136

a. Calculate the degrees of freedom for this test.

b. Complete this table of expected frequencies.

	Expected	
	Accidents	No Accidents
Rain		
No rain		

c. Calculate the test statistic.

d. Calculate the appropriate measure of effect size.

e. Calculate the relative likelihood of accidents, given that it is raining.

17.25 The data below are from a study of lung cancer patients in Turkey (Yilmaz et al., 2000). Use these data to calculate the relative likelihood of the patient being a smoker, given that a person is female rather than male.

	Nonsmoker	Smoker
Female	186	13
Male	182	723

17.26 The following table (output from SPSS) represents the observed frequencies for the data presented in Exercise 17.24 and the adjusted standardized residuals for each of the cells. Using this information and the criterion of 2, indicate for which of these cells there is a significant difference between the observed and the expected frequencies.

		Observed		
		Accident	No Accident	
Rain	Observed	19	26	45
	Adjusted Residual	2.5	−2.5	
No rain	Observed	20	71	91
	Adjusted Residual	−2.5	2.5	
		39	97	136

17.27 The following table represents the observed frequencies for hypothetical data on housing status and having a car. The table also includes the adjusted standardized residuals for each of the cells. Using this information and the criterion of 2, indicate for which of these cells there is a significant difference between the observed and the expected frequencies.

		Observed		
		No car	Car	
On campus	Observed	33	11	44
	Adjusted residual	4.7	−4.7	
Off campus	Observed	8	28	36
	Adjusted residual	−4.7	4.7	
		41	39	80

Applying the Concepts

17.28 A nonparametric test and gender differences in obeying bicycling laws: Students at Hunter College studied bicycle safety in New York City (Tuckel & Milczarski, 2014). They reported data on cyclists who were riding their own bikes and were not cycling as part of their job (they were not, for example, riding as

delivery workers). They reported that 28.4% of male cyclists stopped completely at a red light, whereas 38.3% of female cyclists did so. 30.9% of male cyclists and 35.4% of female cyclists paused but then rolled through the red light. And 40.7% of male cyclists and 26.3% of female cyclists just ran the light. What hypothesis test would the researchers conduct? Explain your answer.

17.29 Gender, salary negotiation, and chi square: Researchers investigated whether language in job postings affected the likelihood that women and men would negotiate regarding salary (Leibbrandt & List, 2012). Some job postings clearly indicated that the salary was negotiable, and others contained no such statement. The postings were otherwise identical. The researchers examined the behavior of almost 2500 applicants for one of the jobs in these advertisements. The graph shows the proportions of women and men who negotiated in response to either type of listing.

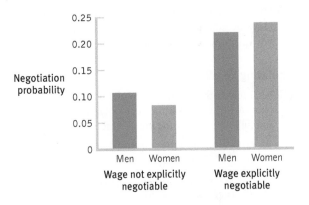

a. What are the variables in this study, what are their levels, and what types of variables are they?

b. Explain why the researchers would have been able to use chi square in this study. Which type of chi-square test would have been appropriate?

c. Based on the graph, explain in your own words what the researchers found.

17.30 Gender, the Oscars, and nonparametric tests: In 2010, Sandra Bullock won an Academy Award for best actress. Shortly thereafter, she discovered that her husband was cheating on her. Headlines erupted about a supposed Oscar curse that befalls women, and many in the media wondered whether ambitious women—whether actors or corporate leaders—are more likely than ambitious men to run the risk of ruining their family lives. Reporters breathlessly listed female actors who were divorced within a couple of years of winning an Oscar—Julia Roberts, Helen Hunt, Kate Winslet, Halle Berry, and Reese Witherspoon among them.

a. A good researcher always asks, "Compared to what?" In this case, what would be an appropriate comparison group to use to determine whether there really is a gender difference in likelihood of relationship breakups among Oscar winners? Explain your answer.

b. Kate Harding (2010) reported that many men—including Russell Crowe, William Hurt, Dustin Hoffman, Robert Duvall, and Clark Gable—experienced the same outcome. Indeed, Harding counted 15 best actor winners, compared with just 8 best actress winners, who divorced not long after winning an Oscar. If she wanted to conduct statistical analyses, what test would Harding use? Explain your answer.

c. Explain how an illusory correlation, bolstered by a confirmation bias, might have led to the headlines despite evidence to the contrary.

17.31 Parametric or nonparametric test? For each of the following research questions, state whether a parametric or nonparametric hypothesis test is more appropriate. Explain your answers.

a. Are women more or less likely than men to be economics majors?

b. At a small company with 15 staff and one top boss, do those with a college education tend to make a different amount of money than those without one?

c. At your high school, did athletes or nonathletes tend to have higher grade point averages?

d. At your high school, did athletes or nonathletes tend to have higher class ranks?

e. Compare car accidents in which the occupants were wearing seat belts with accidents in which the occupants were not wearing seat belts. Do seat belts seem to make a difference in the numbers of accidents that lead to no injuries, nonfatal injuries, and fatal injuries?

f. Compare car accidents in which the occupants were wearing seat belts with accidents in which the occupants were not wearing seat belts. Were those wearing seat belts driving at slower speeds, on average, than those not wearing seat belts?

17.32 Types of variables and student evaluations of professors: Weinberg, Fleisher, and Hashimoto (2007) studied almost 50,000 students' evaluations of their professors in nearly 400 economics courses at the Ohio State University over a 10-year period. For each of their findings, outlined below, state (i) the independent variable or variables, and, where appropriate, their levels; (ii) the dependent variable(s); and (iii) which category of research design is being used:

　I—Scale independent variable(s) and scale dependent variable

　II—Nominal independent variable(s) and scale dependent variable

　III—Only nominal variables

Explain your answer to part (iii).

a. The researchers found that students' ratings of their professors were predictive of grades in the class for which the professor was evaluated.

b. The researchers also found that students' ratings of their professors were not predictive of grades for other, related future classes. (The researchers stated that these first two findings suggest that student ratings of professors are tied to their current grades but not to learning—which would affect future grades.)

c. The researchers found that male professors received statistically significantly higher student ratings, on average, than did female professors.

d. The researchers reported, however, that average levels of students' learning (as assessed by grades in related future classes) were not statistically significantly different between those who had male professors and those who had female professors.

e. The researchers might have been interested in whether there were proportionally more female professors teaching upper-level than lower-level courses and proportionally more male professors teaching lower-level than upper-level courses (perhaps a reason for the lower average ratings of female professors).

f. The researchers found no statistically significant differences in average student evaluations among non-tenure-track lecturers, graduate student teaching associates, and tenure-track faculty members.

17.33 Grade inflation and types of variables: A *New York Times* article on grade inflation reported several findings related to a tendency for average grades to rise over the years and a tendency for the top-ranked institutions to give the highest average grades (Archibold, 1998). For each of the findings outlined below, state (i) the independent variable or variables, and, where appropriate, their levels; (ii) the dependent variable(s); and (iii) which category of research design is being used:

　I—Scale independent variable(s) and scale dependent variable

　II—Nominal independent variable(s) and scale dependent variable

　III—Only nominal variables

Explain your answer to part (iii).

a. In 1969, 7% of all grades were A's; in 1994, 25% of all grades were A's.

b. The average grade point average (GPA) for the graduating students of elite schools is 3.2, the average GPA for graduating students at selective schools (the level below elite schools) is 3.04, and the average GPA for graduating students at state colleges is 2.95.

c. At Dartmouth College, an elite university, SAT scores of incoming students have increased along with their subsequent college GPAs (perhaps an explanation for grade inflation).

17.34 Researching selfies and types of variables: Here are three ways to assess data related to selfies: (1) numbers of selfies taken in a month, (2) whether or not you took any selfies this past month, and (3) where you rank in terms of the number of selfies you took in the past month. For example, Abdul might have taken 11 selfies last month, which would mean he had taken selfies. He also may have been the 23rd most frequent selfie-taker over the last month.

a. Which of these variables could be considered a nominal variable? Explain.

b. Which of these variables is most clearly an ordinal variable? Explain.

c. Which of these variables is a scale variable? Explain.

d. Which of these variables gives us the most information about Abdul's selfie-taking?

e. If we were to use one of these variables in an analysis, which variable (as the dependent variable) would lead to the lowest chance of a Type II error? Explain why.

17.35 Immigration, crime, and research design: "Do Immigrants Make Us Safer?" asked the title of a *New York Times Magazine* article (Press, 2006). The article reported findings from several U.S.-based studies, including several conducted by Harvard sociologist Robert Sampson in Chicago. For each of the following findings, draw the table of cells that would comprise the research design. Include the labels for each row and column.

a. Mexican immigrants were more likely to be married (versus single) than either blacks or whites.

b. People living in immigrant neighborhoods were 15% less likely than were people living in nonimmigrant neighborhoods to commit crimes. This finding was true among both those living in households headed by a married couple and those living in households not headed by a married couple.

c. The crime rate was higher among second-generation than among first-generation immigrants; moreover, the crime rate was higher among third-generation than among second-generation immigrants.

17.36 Sex selection and hypothesis testing: Across all of India, there are only 933 girls for every 1000 boys (Lloyd, 2006), evidence of a bias that leads many parents to illegally select for boys or to kill their infant girls. (Note that this translates into a proportion of girls of 0.483.) In Punjab, a region of India in which residents tend to be more educated than in other regions, there are only 798 girls for every 1000 boys. Assume that you are a researcher interested in whether sex selection is more or less prevalent in educated regions of India, and that 1798 children from Punjab constitute the entire sample. (*Hint:* You will use the proportions from the national database for comparison.)

a. How many variables are there in this study? What are the levels of any variable you identified?

b. Which hypothesis test would be used to analyze these data? Justify your answer.

c. Conduct the six steps of hypothesis testing for this example. (*Note:* Be sure to use the correct proportions for the expected values, not the actual numbers for the population.)

d. Report the statistics as you would in a journal article.

17.37 Gender, op-ed writers, and hypothesis testing: Richards (2006) reported data from a study by the *American Prospect* on the genders of op-ed writers who addressed the topic of abortion in the *New York Times*. Over a 2-year period, the *American Prospect* counted 124 articles that discussed abortion (from a wide range of political and ideological perspectives). Of these, just 21 were written by women.

a. How many variables are there in this study? What are the levels of any variable you identified?

b. Which hypothesis test would be used to analyze these data? Justify your answer.

c. Conduct the six steps of hypothesis testing for this example.

d. Report the statistics as you would in a journal article.

17.38 Romantic music, behavior, chi square, and effect size: Guéguen, Jacob, and Lamy (2010) investigated whether exposure to romantic music affects dating behavior. The participants, young, single, heterosexual French women, waited for the experiment to start in a room in which songs with either romantic lyrics or neutral lyrics were playing. After a few minutes, each woman who participated completed a marketing survey administered by a young male confederate. During a break, the confederate asked the participant for her phone number. Of the women who listened to romantic music, 52.2% (23 out of 44) gave him her phone number, whereas 27.9% (12 out of 43) of the women who listened to neutral music did so. The researchers conducted a chi-square test for independence, and found the following results: $(\chi^2 (1, N = 83) = 5.37, p < .02)$.

a. Calculate Cramér's V. What size effect is this?

b. Calculate the relative likelihood of providing her phone number for women listening to romantic music versus neutral music. Explain what we learn from this relative likelihood.

17.39 The General Social Survey, an exciting life, and relative risk: In How It Works 17.2, we walked through a chi-square test for independence using two items from the General Social Survey (GSS)—LIFE and MOBILE16. Use these data to answer the following questions.

a. Construct a table that shows only the appropriate conditional proportions for this example. For example, the percentage of people who find life exciting, given that they live in the same city, is 42.4. The proportion, therefore, is 0.424.

b. Construct a graph that displays these conditional proportions.

c. Calculate the relative risk (or relative likelihood) of finding life exciting if one lives in a different state compared to if one lives in the same city as one did at 16.

17.40 Gender, ESPN, and chi square: Many of the numbers we see in the news could be analyzed with chi square. The feminist blog *Culturally Disoriented* examined the photos in the 2012 "body issue" of *ESPN The Magazine*—the publication's annual spread of photographs of nude athletes. The blogger reported: "Female athlete after female athlete was photographed not as a talented, powerful sportswoman, but as… eye candy" (http://culturallydisoriented.wordpress.com/2012/07/12/the-bodies-we-want-female-athletes-in-espn-magazines-body-issue/). The blogger reported that there were 19 photos of male athletes and 17 of female athletes. Of these, 15 of the men were in active poses and 9 of the women were in active poses. Active poses were typically those in which they were engaged in their sport, whereas the passive photos looked more like a modeling shoot—"where they're just looking hot for the camera," in the words of *Culturally Disoriented*.

a. Why is a chi-square statistical analysis a good choice for these data? Which kind of chi-square test should you use? Explain your answer.

b. Conduct the six steps of hypothesis testing for this example.

c. Calculate an effect size. Explain why there might be a fairly substantial effect size even though we were not able to reject the null hypothesis.

d. Report the statistics as you would in a journal article.

e. Construct a table that shows only the appropriate conditional proportions for this example—that is, the proportion of people in active poses given that they are men or women.

f. Construct a graph that displays these conditional proportions.

g. Calculate the relative likelihood of being photographed in an active pose if you are a male athlete compared to if you are a female athlete.

17.41 Premarital doubts, divorce, and chi square: In an article titled "Do Cold Feet Warn of Trouble Ahead?", researchers studied 464 married heterosexual spouses to determine whether or not doubts before marriage were predictive of marital troubles, and divorce, later on (Lavner, Karney, & Bradbury, 2012). The following is an excerpt

from the results section of their paper: "For husbands, 9% of those who reported not having premarital doubts divorced by four years ($n = 10$ of 117) compared with 14% of those who did report premarital doubts ($n = 15$ of 106); these groups did not differ significantly, χ^2 (1, $n = 223) = 1.76, p > .10$. Among wives, 8% of those who reported not having premarital doubts divorced by four years ($n = 11$ of 141) compared with 19% of those who did report premarital doubts ($n = 16$ of 84). Chi-square analyses indicated that these rates differed significantly, χ^2 (1, $n = 225) = 6.31, p < .05$."

a. What are the variables in this study, and what are their levels?

b. Explain why the researchers were able to use chi-square tests. Which kind of chi-square tests did they use?

c. What changes would the APA want to see in the reporting of these results?

d. Explain in your own words what the researchers found.

17.42 Police lineups, SPSS, and adjusted standardized residual: In Check Your Learning 17-8, we introduced the example of the Chicago Police Department's study of lineups. Below is a printout from SPSS software that depicts the data for the six cells.

a. For simultaneous lineups, what is the observed frequency for the identification of suspects?

b. For sequential lineups, what is the expected frequency for the identification of a person other than the suspect?

c. For simultaneous lineups, what is the adjusted standardized residual for cases in which there was no identification? What does this number indicate?

d. If you were to use an adjusted standardized residual criterion of 2 (regardless of the sign), for which cells would you conclude that the difference between observed frequency and expected frequency is greater than you would expect if the two variables were independent?

e. Repeat part (d) for an adjusted standardized residual criterion of 3 (regardless of the sign).

			Type of Lineup		Total
			Simultaneous	Sequential	
Identification	Suspect	Count	191	102	293
		Expected Count	170.6	122.4	293.0
		Adjusted Residual	3.5	-3.5	
	Another Person	Count	8	20	28
		Expected Count	16.3	11.7	28.0
		Adjusted Residual	-3.3	3.3	
	No Identification	Count	120	107	227
		Expected Count	132.1	94.9	227.0
		Adjusted Residual	-2.1	2.1	
Total		Count	319	229	548

Putting It All Together

17.43 Gender bias, poor growth, and hypothesis testing: Grimberg, Kutikov, and Cucchiara (2005) wondered whether gender biases were evident in referrals of children for poor growth. They believed that boys were more likely to be referred even when there was no problem—which is bad for boys because families of short boys might falsely view their height as a medical problem. They also believed that girls were less likely to be referred even when there was a problem—which is bad for girls because real problems might not be diagnosed and treated. They studied all new patients at the Children's Hospital of Philadelphia Diagnostic and Research Growth Center who were referred for potential problems related to short stature. Of the 182 boys who were referred, 27 had an underlying medical problem, 86 did not but were below norms for their age, and 69 were of normal height according to growth charts. Of the 96 girls who were referred, 39 had an underlying medical problem, 38 did not but were below norms for their age, and 19 were of normal height according to growth charts.

a. How many variables are there in this study? What are the levels of any variable you identified?

b. Which hypothesis test would be used to analyze these data? Justify your answer.

c. Conduct the six steps of hypothesis testing for this example.

d. Calculate the appropriate measure of effect size. According to Cohen's conventions, what size effect is this?

e. Report the statistics as you would in a journal article.

f. Draw a table that includes the conditional proportions for boys and for girls.

g. Create a graph with bars showing the proportions for all six conditions.

h. Among only children who are below height norms, calculate the relative risk of having an underlying medical condition if one is a boy as opposed to a girl. Show your calculations.

i. Explain what we learn from this relative risk.

j. Now calculate the relative risk of having an underlying medical condition if one is a girl. Show your calculations.

k. Explain what we learn from this relative risk.

l. Explain how the calculations in parts (h) and (j) provide us with the same information in two different ways.

m. Below is a printout from SPSS software that depicts the data for the six cells. For each cell, there is an observed frequency (count), expected frequency (expected count), and adjusted standardized residual (adjusted residual). For boys, what are the observed and expected frequencies for having an underlying medical condition?

n. For boys, what is the adjusted standardized residual for those with an underlying medical condition? What does this number indicate? If you used an adjusted standardized residual criterion of 2 (regardless of the sign), for which cells would you conclude that the difference between observed frequency and expected frequency is greater than you would expect if the two variables were independent? What if you used an adjusted standardized residual criterion of 3 (regardless of the sign)? Are the results different from those using a criterion of 2? If yes, explain how they're different.

Gender * Problem Crosstabulation

			Problem			
			Underlying medical condition	Below norms	Normal height	Total
Gender	Boy	Count	27	86	69	182
		Expected Count	43.2	81.2	57.6	182.0
		Adjusted Residual	-4.8	1.2	3.1	
	Girl	Count	39	38	19	96
		Expected Count	22.8	42.8	30.4	96.0
		Adjusted Residual	4.8	-1.2	-3.1	
Total		Count	66	124	88	278
		Expected Count	66.0	124.0	88.0	278.0

17.44 The prisoner's dilemma, cross-cultural research, and hypothesis testing: In a classic prisoner's dilemma game with money for prizes, players who cooperate with each other both earn good prizes. If, however, your opposing player cooperates but you do not (the term used is *defect*), you receive an even bigger payout and your opponent receives nothing. If you cooperate but your opposing player defects, he or she receives that bigger payout and you receive nothing. If you both defect, you each get a small prize. Because of this, most players of such games choose to defect, knowing that if they cooperate but their partners don't, they won't win anything. The strategies of U.S. and Chinese students were compared. The researchers hypothesized that those from the market economy (United States) would cooperate less (i.e., would defect more often) than would those from the nonmarket economy (China).

	Defect	Cooperate
China	31	36
United States	41	14

a. How many variables are there in this study? What are the levels of any variables you identified?

b. Which hypothesis test would be used to analyze these data? Justify your answer.

c. Conduct the six steps of hypothesis testing for this example, using the above data.

d. Calculate the appropriate measure of effect size. According to Cohen's conventions, what size effect is this?

e. Report the statistics as you would in a journal article.

f. Draw a table that includes the conditional proportions for participants from China and from the United States.

g. Create a graph with bars showing the proportions for all four conditions.

h. Create a graph with two bars showing just the proportions for the defections for each country.

i. Calculate the relative risk (or relative likelihood) of defecting, given that one is from China versus the United States. Show your calculations.

j. Explain what we learn from this relative risk.

k. Now calculate the relative risk of defecting, given that one is from the United States versus China. Show your calculations.

l. Explain what we learn from this relative risk.

m. Explain how the calculations in parts (i) and (k) provide us with the same information in two different ways.

TERMS

chi-square test for goodness of fit   (p. 482)
chi-square test for independence   (p. 483)

Cramér's V (p. 494)
relative risk   (p. 496)

adjusted standardized residual   (p. 497)

FORMULAS

$df_{\chi^2} = k - 1$ (degrees of freedom for chi-square test for goodness of fit)   (p. 484)

$\chi^2 = \Sigma\left[\dfrac{(O - E)^2}{E}\right]$ (p. 487)

$df_{\chi^2} = (k_{row} - 1)(k_{column} - 1)$ (degrees of freedom for chi-square test for independence) (p. 489)

Expected frequency for each cell $= \dfrac{Total_{column}}{N}(Total_{row})$, where we use the overall number of participants, N, along with the totals for the rows and columns for each particular cell   (p. 491)

Cramér's $V = \sqrt{\dfrac{\chi^2}{(N)df_{row/column}}}$ (p. 494)

SYMBOLS

χ^2 (p. 481)
k (p. 484)

Cramér's V (p. 494)
Cramér's ϕ (p. 494)

Nonparametric Tests with Ordinal Data

Ordinal Data and Correlation
When the Data Are Ordinal
The Spearman Rank-Order
Correlation Coefficient

Nonparametric Hypothesis Tests
The Wilcoxon Signed-Rank Test
The Mann-Whitney *U* Test
The Kruskal-Wallis *H* Test

Next Steps: Bootstrapping

BEFORE YOU GO ON

- You should be able to differentiate between a parametric and a nonparametric hypothesis test (Chapter 7).

- You should know the six steps of hypothesis testing (Chapter 7).

- You should understand the concept of correlation (Chapters 1 and 15)

- You should know when to use a paired-samples *t* test (Chapter 10), an independent-samples *t* test (Chapter 11), and a one-way between-groups ANOVA (Chapter 12).

Keeping Up with Your Friends With respect to money and material goods, we can't help but compare ourselves to others. And research suggests that we're happier when we have more money than others around us (Hagerty, 2000). So, even if you make a lot of money, you may not be happy if your friends make even more.

Would you be happy with an unexpected 10% raise in salary if you found out that a coworker received a 12% raise? If you answered no, then earning more money than somebody else (an ordinal observation) is more important to your happiness than the actual amount of money you earn (a scale observation). In studying a representative sample of more than 7000 U.S. citizens, a researcher found three statistical ideas that were important in gauging people's happiness when they were making income comparisons—(1) the sample, (2) the range, and (3) the shape of the distribution (Hagerty, 2000).

1. When it comes to income and happiness, people are concerned about the sample (who is in the comparison group). The sample is important because people find it more meaningful to compare themselves to other people in their own community than to people outside their community.

2. People also think about the range when they consider income and happiness, particularly the top income and the bottom income. This is because we can make two kinds of comparisons. Upward social comparisons can make us feel like failures compared to very wealthy people. Downward social comparisons can make us feel like successes compared to very poor people.

3. The shape of the distribution also matters. If you are "average" in a normal distribution, then there are just as many people above you as below you. But if you are "average" in a positively skewed distribution—one in which a few very wealthy people have pulled the average (as measured by the mean) much farther to the right—then there are many more people below you than above you. You're still "average" in one sense, but a positively skewed distribution places you in a more exclusive club.

The irrational ways in which we think about happiness and money are particularly important for this chapter (Airely, 2010). They suggest that irrational human thinking does not always match up with the rational assumptions we make about statistical tests. In this chapter, we'll cover nonparametric tests—tests that use data that do not meet the assumptions for a parametric test.

Ordinal Data and Correlation

The statistical tests we discuss in this section allow researchers to draw conclusions from data that do not meet the assumptions for a parametric test, such as when the data are rank ordered. In this section, we learn how to convert scale data to ordinal data. Then we examine four tests that can be used with ordinal data: nonparametric versions of the Pearson correlation coefficient (the Spearman rank-order correlation coefficient), the paired-samples t test (the Wilcoxon signed-rank test), the independent-samples t test (the Mann–Whitney U test), and the one-way between-groups ANOVA (the Kruskal-Wallis H test).

When the Data Are Ordinal

A University of Chicago News Office press release proclaimed, "Americans and Venezuelans Lead the World in National Pride." Researchers from the University of Chicago's National Opinion Research Center (NORC) surveyed citizens of 33 countries (Smith & Kim, 2006) and developed two different kinds of national pride scores: pride in specific accomplishments of their nations, like science or sports (which they called domain-specific national pride) and a more general national pride in which citizens responded to items such as, "People should support their country even if the country is in the wrong."

So, the researchers had two sets of national pride scores—accomplishment-related and general—for each country. They converted the scores to ranks, and when results on the two scales were merged, Venezuela and the United States were tied for first place. These findings suggest many hypotheses about what creates and inflates national pride. The authors noted that countries that were settled as colonies tend to rank higher than their "mother country," that formerly socialist countries tend to rank lower than other countries, and that countries in Asia tend to rank lower than those from other continents. The researchers also reported that there were increases in national pride among countries that had recently been subject to terrorist attacks.

National Pride University of Chicago researchers ranked 33 countries in terms of national pride. Venezuela, along with the United States, came out on top. Ordinal data such as these are analyzed using nonparametric statistics.

We wondered about other possible precursors of national pride, such as competitiveness. Because the researchers provided ordinal data, the only way we can explore these interesting hypotheses is by using nonparametric statistics. Parametric statistics are appropriate for scale data, but they are not appropriate for ordinal data. The very nature of an ordinal variable means that it will not meet the assumptions of a scale dependent variable and a normally distributed population. As we can see in Figure 18-1, the shape of a distribution of ordinal variables is rectangular because every participant has a different rank.

Fortunately, the logic of many nonparametric statistics will be familiar to students. This is because many of the nonparametric statistical tests are specific alternatives to parametric statistical tests. These nonparametric tests may be used whenever assumptions for a parametric test are not met. In this chapter, we'll consider four such tests (shown in Table 18-1): (1) a nonparametric equivalent for the Pearson correlation coefficient, the *Spearman rank-order correlation coefficient*; (2) a nonparametric equivalent for the paired-samples *t* test, the *Wilcoxon signed-rank test*; (3) a nonparametric equivalent for the independent-samples *t* test, the *Mann–Whitney U test*; and (4) a nonparametric equivalent for the one-way between-groups ANOVA, the *Kruskal–Wallis H test*. There is almost always an established nonparametric alterative to a parametric test. When researchers can't meet the assumptions of the parametric test they would like to conduct, they can choose the nonparametric test that is appropriate for their data.

FIGURE 18-1

A Histogram of Ordinal Data

When ordinal data are graphed in a histogram, the resulting distribution is rectangular. These are data for ranks 1–10. For each rank, there is one individual. Ordinal data are never normally distributed.

TABLE 18-1 | Parametric and Nonparametric Partners

Most parametric hypothesis tests have at least one equivalent nonparametric alternative. The parametric tests listed here all call for scale dependent variables, and their nonparametric counterparts all call for ordinal dependent variables.

Design	Parametric Test	Nonparametric Test
Association between two variables	Pearson correlation coefficient	Spearman rank-order correlation coefficient
Two groups; within-groups design	Paired-samples t test	Wilcoxon signed-rank test
Two groups; between-groups design	Independent-samples t test	Mann–Whitney U test
More than two groups; between-groups design	One-way between-groups ANOVA	Kruskal–Wallis H test

EXAMPLE 18.1

Nonparametric tests for ordinal data are typically used in one of two situations. First and most obviously, we use nonparametric tests when the sample data are ordinal. Second, we use nonparametric tests when the dependent variable suggests that the underlying population distribution is greatly skewed, a common situation when the sample size is small. This second reason is likely why the national pride researchers converted their data to ranks (Smith & Kim, 2006). Figure 18-2 shows a histogram of their full set of data for the variable accomplishment-related national pride—the variable that we will use for many examples in this chapter. The data appear to be

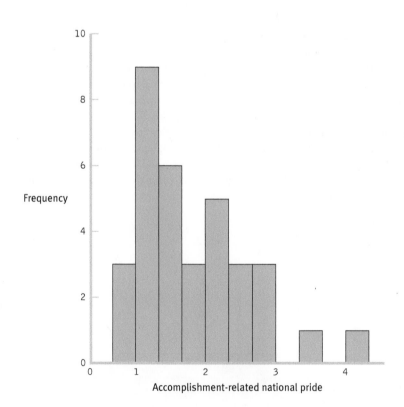

FIGURE 18-2

Skewed Data

The sample data for the variable, accomplishment-related national pride, are skewed. This indicates the possibility that the underlying population distribution is skewed. It is likely that the researchers chose to report their data as ranks for this reason (Smith & Kim, 2006).

positively skewed, most likely because two countries, Venezuela and the United States, appear to be outliers. Because of this, we have to transform the data from scale to ordinal.

It is appropriate to transform scale data to ordinal data whenever the data from a small sample are skewed. For example, look what happens to the following five data points for income when we change the data from scale to ordinal. In the first row, the one that includes the scale data, there is a severe outlier ($550,000) and the sample data suggest a skewed distribution. In the second row, the severe outlier merely becomes the last ranking. The ranked data do not have an outlier.

> Scale: $24,000 $27,000 $35,000 $46,000 $550,000
>
> Ordinal: 1 2 3 4 5

In the next section, we'll transform scale data to ordinal data so that we can calculate the Spearman rank-order correlation coefficient. ●

The Spearman Rank-Order Correlation Coefficient

Many everyday, automatic decisions are based on rank-ordered observations. For example, a person may prefer Chunky Monkey ice cream to Chubby Hubby ice cream but would not be able to specify that he liked it precisely twice as much. When we collect ranked data, we analyze it using nonparametric statistics. The **Spearman rank-order correlation coefficient** is a nonparametric statistic that quantifies the association between two ordinal variables.

EXAMPLE 18.2

To see how the Spearman rank-order correlation coefficient works, let's look at a study that uses two ordinal variables, one taken from the University of Chicago study on national pride (Smith & Kim, 2006). We wondered whether accomplishment-related national pride is related to the underlying trait of competitiveness. So, we randomly selected 10 countries from the university's list and compiled those countries' scores for accomplishment-related national pride. We also included rankings of competitiveness that had been compiled by an international business school (IMD International, 2001).

A correlation between these variables, if found, would be evidence that countries' levels of accomplishment-related national pride are tied to levels of competitiveness. The competitiveness variable we borrowed from the business school rankings was already ordinal. However, the accomplishment-related national pride variable was initially a scale variable. When even one of the variables is ordinal, we use the Spearman rank-order correlation coefficient (often called just the *Spearman correlation coefficient*, or *Spearman's rho*). Its symbol is almost like the one for the Pearson correlation coefficient, but it has a subscript S to indicate that it is Spearman's correlation coefficient: r_S.

To convert scale data to ordinal data, we simply organize the data from highest to lowest (or lowest to highest, if that makes more sense) and then rank them. Table 18-2 shows the conversion of accomplishment-related national pride from scale data to ordinal data. Sometimes, as seen for Austria and Canada, we have a tie. Both of these countries had an accomplishment-related national pride score of 2.40.

● The **Spearman rank-order correlation coefficient** is a nonparametric statistic that quantifies the association between two ordinal variables.

TABLE 18-2 Converting Pride Scores to Ranks

When we convert scale data to ordinal data, we simply arrange the data from highest to lowest (or lowest to highest, if that makes more sense) and then rank them. These are the original data for accomplishment-related national pride. In cases of ties, we average the two ranks that these participants—countries, in this case—would hold.

Country	Pride Score	Pride Rank
United States	4.0	1
South Africa	2.7	2
Austria	2.4	3.5
Canada	2.4	3.5
Chile	2.3	5
Japan	1.8	6
Hungary	1.6	7
France	1.5	8
Norway	1.3	9
Slovenia	1.1	10

When we rank the data, Austria and Canada take the third and fourth positions, but they must have the same rank because their scores are the same. So we take the average of the two ranks they would hold if the scores were different: $(3 + 4)/2 = 3.5$. Both of these countries receive the rank of 3.5.

Now that we have the ranks, we can compute the Spearman correlation coefficient. We first need to include both sets of ranks in the same table, as in the second and third columns in Table 18-3. We then calculate the difference (D) between each pair of ranks, as in the fourth column. The differences always add up to 0, so we must square the differences, as in the last column. As we have frequently done with squared differences in the past, we sum them—another variation on the concept of a sum of squares. The sum of these squared differences is:

$$\Sigma D^2 = (0 + 64 + 2.25 + 0.25 + 0 + 1 + 1 + 4 + 25 + 1) = 98.5$$

The formula for calculating the Spearman correlation coefficient includes the sum of the squared differences that we just calculated, 98.5. The formula is:

$$r_S = 1 - \frac{6(\Sigma D^2)}{N(N^2 - 1)}$$

Aside from the sum of squared differences, the only other information we need is the sample size, N, which is 10 in this example. (The number 6 is a constant; it is always included in the calculation of the Spearman correlation coefficient.) The Spearman correlation coefficient, therefore, is:

$$r_S = 1 - \frac{6(\Sigma D^2)}{N(N^2 - 1)} = 1 - \frac{6(98.5)}{10(10^2 - 1)} = 1 - \frac{591}{10(100 - 1)} = 1 - \frac{591}{10(99)}$$

$$= 1 - \frac{591}{990} = 1 - 0.597 = 0.403$$

The Spearman correlation coefficient is 0.40. ●

18-1: The formula for the Spearman correlation coefficient is:

$$r_S = 1 - \frac{6(\Sigma D^2)}{N(N^2 - 1)}.$$

The numerator includes a constant, 6, as well as the sum of the squared differences between ranks for each participant. The denominator is calculated by multiplying the sample size, N, by the square of the sample size minus 1.

| TABLE 18-3 | Calculating a Spearman Correlation Coefficient |

The first step in calculating a Spearman correlation coefficient is creating a table that includes the ranks for all participants—countries, in this case—on both variables of interest (accomplishment-related national pride and competitiveness). We then calculate differences for each participant (country, here) and square each difference.

Country	Pride Rank	Competitiveness Rank	Difference (D)	Squared Difference (D^2)
United States	1	1	0	0
South Africa	2	10	−8	64
Austria	3.5	2	1.5	2.25
Canada	3.5	3	0.5	0.25
Chile	5	5	0	0
Japan	6	7	−1	1
Hungary	7	8	−1	1
France	8	6	2	4
Norway	9	4	5	25
Slovenia	10	9	1	1

The interpretation of the Spearman correlation coefficient is identical to that for the Pearson correlation coefficient. The coefficient can range from −1, a perfect negative correlation, to 1, a perfect positive correlation. A correlation coefficient of 0 indicates no relation between the two variables. As with the Pearson correlation coefficient, it is not the sign of the Spearman correlation coefficient that indicates the strength of a relation. So, for example, a coefficient of −0.66 indicates a stronger association than does a coefficient of 0.23. Finally, as with the Pearson correlation coefficient, we can implement the six steps of hypothesis testing to determine whether the Spearman correlation coefficient is statistically significantly different from 0. If we do decide to conduct hypothesis testing, we can find the critical values for the Spearman correlation coefficient in Appendix B.7.

Like the Pearson correlation coefficient, the Spearman correlation coefficient does not tell us about causation. It is possible that there is a causal relation in one of two directions. The relation between competitiveness (variable A) and accomplishment-related national pride (variable B) is 0.40, a fairly strong positive correlation. It is possible that competitiveness (variable A) causes a country to feel prouder (variable B) of its accomplishments. On the other hand, it is also possible that accomplishment-related national pride (variable B) causes competitiveness (variable A). Finally, it is also possible that a third variable, C, causes both of the other two variables (A and B). For example, a high gross domestic product (variable C) might cause both a sense of competitiveness with other economic powerhouses (variable A) and a feeling of national pride at this economic accomplishment (variable B). A strong correlation indicates only a strong association; we can draw no conclusions about causation.

CHECK YOUR LEARNING

Reviewing the Concepts

> Nonparametric statistics are used when all variables are nominal, when the dependent variable is ordinal, and when the sample suggests both that the underlying population distribution is skewed and that the sample size is small.

> Nonparametric tests for ordinal data are used when the data are already ordinal or when it is clear that the assumptions are severely violated. In the latter case, the scale data must be converted to ordinal data.

> When we want to calculate a correlation between two ordinal variables, we calculate a Spearman rank-order correlation coefficient, which is interpreted in the same way as a Pearson correlation coefficient.

> As with the Pearson correlation coefficient, the Spearman correlation coefficient does not tell us about causation. It simply quantifies the magnitude and direction of association between two ordinal variables.

Clarifying the Concepts 18-1 Describe a common situation in which we use nonparametric tests other than chi-square tests.

Calculating the Statistics 18-2 Convert the following scale data to ordinal or ranked data, starting with a rank of 1 for the smallest data point.

Observation	Variable 1	Variable 2
1	1.30	54.39
2	1.80	50.11
3	1.20	53.39
4	1.06	44.89
5	1.80	48.50

18-3 Compute the Spearman correlation coefficient for the data listed in Check Your Learning 18-2.

Applying the Concepts 18-4 Reporter Ben Blatt conducted a textual analysis of three popular book series (2013). Specifically, using a computer, he counted the most common sentences used in Suzanne Collins' *Hunger Games* series, Stephenie Meyer's *Twilight* series, and J. K. Rowling's *Harry Potter* series. Below are the 10 most common full sentences used by each author, ordered from most common at the top of each column to least common at the bottom.

The Top Ten Sentences in Three Bestselling Book Series

Harry Potter	*Hunger Games*	*Twilight*
Nothing happened.	My name is Katniss Everdeen.	I sighed.
Harry looked around.	I don't know.	He sighed.
Harry stared.	I shake my head.	I shrugged.
He waited.	I am seventeen years old.	I frowned.
Harry said nothing.	My home is District 12.	He chuckled.
They looked at each other.	Now I wish I had.	I laughed.
Harry blinked.	I swallowed hard.	He shrugged.
He looked around.	He hesitates.	I flinched.
Something he didn't have last time.	I'm not really surprised.	I took a deep breath.
He stood up.	Something is wrong.	He didn't answer.

Data compiled by @BenBlatt of Slate.com
Source: Harry Potter Books 1-7, Hunger Games Books 1-3, Twilight Books 1-4

a. If you wanted to compare aspects of the most common sentences for these three authors, why might it be better to use a nonparametric test than a parametric test? (Hint: Think about the sample sizes and the likely distribution of the counts for each sentence.)

b. Explain how the author created these ranked lists from the original counts of how common each sentence was.

Solutions to these Check Your Learning questions can be found in Appendix D.

c. If there were outlier scores—that is, sentences that were extremely common—what would happen to these outliers when the scores were converted from a scale measure to an ordinal measure?

Nonparametric Hypothesis Tests

We sometimes want to compare groups with respect to a dependent variable that does not meet the criteria for a parametric test. Fortunately, there are several nonparametric hypothesis tests that can be used to answer important research questions—often based on nonnormal data—such as those raised about income and happiness (Hagerty, 2000). In this section, we'll learn how to conduct three of these hypothesis tests: the Wilcoxon signed-rank test, which is the nonparametric equivalent of the paired-samples t test; the Mann–Whitney U test, which is the nonparametric equivalent of the independent-samples t test; and the Kruskal–Wallis H test, which is the nonparametric equivalent for the one-way between-groups ANOVA. We will use these new statistics to test more hypotheses about the ranked data on national pride.

The Wilcoxon Signed-Rank Test

The Wilcoxon signed-rank test is the nonparametric version of the paired-samples t test, so it is useful whenever we are comparing changes in rank over time.

• •

For example, the national pride researchers provided data for two time periods, 1995–1996 and 2003–2004 (Smith & Kim, 2006). We examined the data from the six countries for which English is a primary language: the United States, Australia, Ireland, New Zealand, Canada, and Great Britain. We wondered whether the scores on accomplishment-related national pride were different in these two time periods. The scores for each time period are listed in Table 18-4, with the differences between the two time periods for each country. The differences are calculated by subtracting the first score from the second. So, for the United States, there was an increase of $4.00 - 3.11 = 0.89$. For Ireland, there was a decrease of $2.90 - 3.36 = -0.46$.

The independent variable for this analysis is time period, with two levels: 1995–1996 and 2003–2004. The dependent variable is accomplishment-related national pride. This is a within-groups design because every participant, or country, had a score for each level of the independent variable. If we used the scale scores on accomplishment-related national pride, we would use a paired-samples t test. Because these data are better analyzed as ordinal data than as scale data, we will use a nonparametric equivalent for the paired-samples t test, the *Wilcoxon signed-rank test* for matched pairs. The ***Wilcoxon signed-rank test*** *for matched pairs is a nonparametric hypothesis test used when there are two groups, a within-groups design, and an ordinal dependent variable.* The test statistic for this test is symbolized by T. Be sure to capitalize the T so that it is not mistaken for the test statistic in t tests.

For nonparametric tests, the six steps of hypothesis testing are similar to those for parametric tests. The good news is that these six steps for nonparametric hypothesis tests are usually easier to compute, and some of the steps, such as the one for assumptions,

EXAMPLE 18.3

● The **Wilcoxon signed-rank test** for matched pairs is a nonparametric hypothesis test used when there are two groups, a within-groups design, and an ordinal dependent variable.

TABLE 18-4	Accomplishment-Related National Pride Scores

Smith and Kim (2006) provided scores on accomplishment-related national pride for two periods, 1995–1996 and 2003–2004. Here are the data for the countries for which English is a primary language. For each country, there are scores for each time period, as well as a difference score.

Country	1995–1996	2003–2004	Difference
United States	3.11	4.00	0.89
Australia	2.10	2.90	0.80
Ireland	3.36	2.90	−0.46
New Zealand	2.62	2.60	−0.02
Canada	2.56	2.40	−0.16
Great Britain	2.09	2.20	0.11

are shorter. We will outline the six steps for hypothesis testing with the Wilcoxon signed-rank test for matched pairs using the example about accomplishment-related national pride rankings.

STEP 1: Identify the assumptions.

There are three assumptions. (1) The differences between pairs must be able to be ranked. (2) We should use random selection, or the ability to generalize will be limited. (3) The difference scores should come from a symmetric population distribution. This third assumption, combined with the fact that the paired-samples t test is robust with respect to violations of the assumption that the population distribution is normal, means that the t test is often the preferred choice. Only when the assumption of a normal population distribution is seriously questioned should researchers use the Wilcoxon signed-rank test for matched pairs.

Summary: We convert the data from scale to ordinal. The researchers did not indicate whether they used random selection to choose the countries in the sample, so we must be cautious when generalizing from these results. It is difficult to know from a small sample whether the difference scores come from a symmetric population distribution.

STEP 2: State the null and research hypotheses.

We state the null and research hypotheses only in words, not in symbols.

Summary: Null hypothesis: English-speaking countries in 1995–1996 did not differ in accomplishment-related national pride from English-speaking countries in 2003–2004. Research hypothesis: English-speaking countries in 1995–1996 differed in accomplishment-related national pride from English-speaking countries in 2003–2004.

STEP 3: Determine the characteristics of the comparison distribution.

We use the Wilcoxon signed-rank test for matched pairs to compare the T statistic to the T distribution. The main reason we determine the characteristics of the comparison distribution is to move on to later steps. In step 4, we determine a cutoff, or critical value. To do so, we need to (1) decide on the cutoff level (usually 0.05); (2) clarify whether we're using a one-tailed or a two-tailed test (usually two-tailed); and (3) determine the sample size. The sample size for this test is a bit different from the sample size for other tests; it is the number of difference scores that are *not* 0. For this example, none of the six observed difference scores is 0, so the sample size will be 6.

Summary: We use a p level of 0.05 and a two-tailed test. The sample size is 6.

> **STEP 4: Determine the critical values, or cutoffs.**

We use Table B.9 from Appendix B to determine the cutoff, or critical value, for the Wilcoxon signed-rank test for matched pairs. In the table, we find the sample size on the left and the appropriate number of tails and the p level across the top. There is an important difference between this critical value and those we considered with parametric tests. We reject the null hypothesis only if the test statistic is equal to or *less than* the critical value.

Summary: The cutoff for a Wilcoxon signed-rank test for matched pairs with $N = 6$, a p level of 0.05, and a two-tailed test is 0. This critical value of 0 suggests that the sample size is too small to have sufficient statistical power. We must be wary of the validity of the decision in this case.

> **STEP 5: Calculate the test statistic.**

We start the calculations by organizing the difference scores from highest to lowest in terms of absolute value, as seen in Table 18-5. Because we organize by absolute value, −0.46 is higher than 0.11, for example. We then rank the absolute values of the differences, as seen in the second column of numbers in Table 18-5. We separate the ranks into two columns, the fourth and fifth columns in the table. The fourth column includes only the ranks associated with positive differences, and the fifth column includes only the ranks associated with negative differences. (*Note:* We omit any difference scores of 0 from the ranking and from any further calculations.)

Table 18-5 also serves as a graph. We can determine by the pattern of the ranks in the last two columns whether there seems to be a difference. The pattern for these data suggests that there has been more of an increase than a decrease in accomplishment-related national pride among English-speaking countries. We can draw no conclusions, however, until we have compared the test statistic to the critical value.

TABLE 18-5 Organizing Data for a Wilcoxon Signed-Rank Test for Matched Pairs

To conduct a Wilcoxon signed-rank test for matched pairs, we first organize the data from highest to lowest in terms of absolute value. We rank the absolute values and then create two separate columns—one for ranks associated with positive scores and one for ranks associated with negative scores.

Country	Difference	Ranks	Ranks for Positive Differences	Ranks for Negative Differences
United States	0.89	1	1	
Australia	0.80	2	2	
Ireland	−0.46	3		3
Canada	−0.16	4		4
Great Britain	0.11	5	5	
New Zealand	−0.02	6		6

MASTERING THE FORMULA

18-2: The formula for the Wilcoxon signed-rank test for matched pairs is: $T = \Sigma R_{smaller}$. We sum the ranks for each group and then take the smaller sum as the T statistic.

- The **Mann–Whitney U test** is a nonparametric hypothesis test used when there are two groups, a between-groups design, and an ordinal dependent variable.

The final step in calculating the test statistic is to sum the ranks for the positive scores and, separately, sum the ranks for the negative scores.

$$\Sigma R_+ = (1 + 2 + 5) = 8$$
$$\Sigma R_- = (3 + 4 + 6) = 13$$

The work is done. The smaller of these is the test statistic, T. The formula is:

$$T = \Sigma R_{smaller}$$

In this case, $T = \Sigma R_+ = 8$.

Summary: $T = \Sigma R_{smaller} = 8$ (*Note:* Show all calculations in your summary.)

STEP 6: Make a decision.

The test statistic, 8, is not smaller than the critical value, 0, so we fail to reject the null hypothesis. We expected this from the very small critical value. We likely did not have sufficient statistical power to detect any real differences that might exist. We cannot conclude that the two groups are different with respect to accomplishment-related national pride rankings.

After completing the hypothesis test, we report the primary statistical information in a format similar to that used for parametric tests. In the write-up, we'll list the totals for positive ranks, 8, and negative ranks, 13. There are no degrees of freedom, so the test statistic is reported like this:

$$T = 8, p > 0.05$$

(*Note:* If we conduct the Wilcoxon signed-rank test using software, we report the actual p value associated with the test statistic.) ●

The Mann–Whitney U Test

As mentioned earlier, most parametric hypothesis tests have nonparametric equivalents. In this section, we learn how to conduct one of the most common of these tests—the Mann–Whitney U test, the nonparametric equivalent of the independent-samples t test. The ***Mann–Whitney U test*** *is a nonparametric hypothesis test used when there are two groups, a between-groups design, and an ordinal dependent variable.* The test statistic is symbolized as U. Let's use this new statistic to test more hypotheses about the ranked data on national pride.

MASTERING THE CONCEPT

18-2: We conduct a Mann–Whitney U test to compare two independent groups with respect to an ordinal dependent variable. It is the nonparametric equivalent of the independent-samples t test.

EXAMPLE 18.4

The researchers observed that countries with a recent communist past tended to have lower ranks on national pride (Smith & Kim, 2006). Let's choose 10 European countries, 5 of which were communist during part of the twentieth century. The independent variable is type of country, with two levels: formerly communist and not formerly communist. The dependent variable is rank on accomplishment-related national pride. As in previous situations, we may start with ordinal data, or we may convert scale data to ordinal data because we were far from meeting the assumptions of a parametric test. Table 18-6 shows the scores for the 10 countries.

As noted earlier, nonparametric tests use the same six steps of hypothesis testing as parametric tests but are usually easier to calculate.

TABLE 18-6	Comparing Two Groups

Here are the data for two samples: Formerly communist European countries and European countries that have not been communist. The data in this table are scale; because we do not meet the assumptions for a parametric test, we have to convert the data from scale to ordinal as one step of the calculations.

Country	Pride Score
Noncommunist	
Ireland	2.9
Austria	2.4
Spain	1.6
Portugal	1.6
Sweden	1.2
Communist	
Hungary	1.6
Czech Republic	1.3
Slovenia	1.1
Slovakia	1.1
Poland	0.9

STEP 1: Identify the assumptions.

There are three assumptions. (1) The data must be ordinal. (2) We should use random selection; otherwise, the ability to generalize will be limited. (3) Ideally, no ranks are tied. The Mann–Whitney U test is robust with respect to violations of the third assumption; if there are only a few ties, then it is usually safe to proceed.

Summary: (1) We need to convert the data from scale to ordinal. (2) The researchers did not indicate whether they used random selection to choose the European countries in the sample, so we must be cautious when generalizing from these results. (3) There are some ties, but we will assume that there are not so many as to render the results of the test invalid.

STEP 2: State the null and research hypotheses.

We state the null and research hypotheses only in words, not in symbols.

Summary: Null hypothesis: Formerly communist European countries and European countries that have not been communist do not tend to differ in accomplishment-related national pride. Research hypothesis: Formerly communist European countries and European countries that have not been communist tend to differ in accomplishment-related national pride.

STEP 3: Determine the characteristics of the comparison distribution.

The Mann–Whitney U test compares the two distributions—those represented by the two samples. There is no comparison distribution in the sense of a parametric test. To complete step 4 and find a cutoff, or critical value, we need two pieces of information: the sample size for the first group and the sample size for the second group.

Summary: There are five countries in the formerly communist group and five countries in the noncommunist group.

> **STEP 4: Determine the critical values, or cutoffs.**

There are two Mann–Whitney U tables. We use Table B.8A (for a one-tailed test) or Table B.8B (for a two-tailed test) from Appendix B to determine the cutoff, or critical value, for the Mann–Whitney U test. In the tables, we find the sample size for the first group across the top row and the sample size for the second group down the left-hand column. The table includes only critical values for a hypothesis test with a p level of 0.05. There are two differences between this critical value and those we considered with parametric tests. First, we calculate two test statistics, but we only compare the *smaller* one with the critical value. Second, we want the test statistic to be equal to or *smaller than* the critical value.

Summary: The cutoff, or critical value, for a Mann–Whitney U test with two groups of five participants (countries), a p level of 0.05, and a two-tailed test is 2. (*Note:* Remember that we want the *smaller* of the test statistics to be equal to or *smaller than* this critical value.)

> **STEP 5: Calculate the test statistic.**

As noted above, we calculate two test statistics for a Mann–Whitney U test, one for each group. We start the calculations by organizing the data by raw score from highest to lowest in one single column and then by rank in the next column, as shown in Table 18-7. For the two sets of tied scores, we take the average of the ranks they would have held and apply that rank to the tied scores. For example, Spain, Portugal, and Hungary all received scores of 1.6; they would have been ranked 3, 4, and 5, but because they are tied, they all received the average of these three scores, 4. (We have chosen to give the highest score a rank of 1, as did the researchers.) We include the group membership of each participant (country) next to its score and rank: C indicates a formerly communist country and NC represents a noncommunist country. The final two columns separate the ranks by group;

TABLE 18-7   Organizing Data for a Mann–Whitney U Test

To conduct a Mann–Whitney U test, we first organize the data. We organize the raw scores from highest to lowest in a single column, then rank them in an adjacent column. Notice that when scores are tied, we average the ranks of the two or three tied scores. The next column includes the group to which each country belongs—in this case, a recently communist country (C) or a noncommunist (NC) country. The last two columns separate the ranks by group.

Country	Pride Score	Pride Rank	Type of Country	NC Rank	C Rank
Ireland	2.9	1	NC	1	
Austria	2.4	2	NC	2	
Spain	1.6	4	NC	4	
Portugal	1.6	4	NC	4	
Hungary	1.6	4	C		4
Czech Republic	1.3	6	C		6
Sweden	1.2	7	NC	7	
Slovenia	1.1	8.5	C		8.5
Slovakia	1.1	8.5	C		8.5
Poland	0.9	10	C		10

from these columns we can easily see that the noncommunist countries tend to hold the higher ranks and the communist countries, the lower ranks.

Before we continue, we sum the ranks (R) for each group and add subscripts to indicate which group is which:

$$\Sigma R_{NC} = 1 + 2 + 4 + 4 + 7 = 18$$

$$\Sigma R_{C} = 4 + 6 + 8.5 + 8.5 + 10 = 37$$

The formula for the first group, with the n's referring to sample size in a particular group, is:

$$U_1 = (n_1)(n_2) + \frac{n_1(n_1 + 1)}{2} - \Sigma R_1 =$$

$$U_{NC} = (n_{NC})(n_C) + \frac{n_{NC}(n_{NC} + 1)}{2} - \Sigma R_{NC} = (5)(5) + \frac{5(5 + 1)}{2} - 18$$

$$= 25 + 15 - 18 = 22$$

The formula for the second group is:

$$U_2 = (n_1)(n_2) + \frac{n_2(n_2 + 1)}{2} - \Sigma R_2 =$$

$$U_C = (n_{NC})(n_C) + \frac{n_C(n_C + 1)}{2} - \Sigma R_C = (5)(5) + \frac{5(5 + 1)}{2} - 37$$

$$= 25 + 15 - 37 = 3$$

Summary: $U_{NC} = 22$; $U_C = 3$

STEP 6: Make a decision.

For a Mann–Whitney U test, we compare only the smaller test statistic, 3, with the critical value, 2. This test statistic is not smaller than the critical value, so we fail to reject the null hypothesis. We cannot conclude that the two groups are different with respect to accomplishment-related national pride rankings. The researchers concluded, however, that noncommunist countries tend to have more national pride—but remember, the researchers used more countries in their analyses than we did here, so they had more statistical power (Smith & Kim, 2006). We selected just 10 of the European countries on their list. As with parametric tests, increased sample sizes lead to increased statistical power.

Summary: The test statistic, 3, is not smaller than the critical value, 2. We cannot reject the null hypothesis. We conclude only that there is insufficient evidence to show that the two groups are different with respect to accomplishment-related national pride.

After completing the hypothesis test, we want to present the primary statistical information in a report. In the write-up, we list the two groups and their sample sizes, but there are no degrees of freedom. In addition, we report the smaller test statistic; because this is the standard, we do not include a subscript. The statistics read:

$$U = 3, p > 0.05$$

(*Note:* If we conduct the Mann–Whitney U test using software, we report the actual p value associated with the test statistic.) ●

> **MASTERING THE FORMULA**
>
> **18-3:** The formula for the first group in a Mann–Whitney U test is:
>
> $$U_1 = (n_1)(n_2) + \frac{n_1(n_1 + 1)}{2} - \Sigma R_1.$$
>
> The formula for the second group is:
>
> $$U_2 = (n_1)(n_2) + \frac{n_2(n_2 + 1)}{2} - \Sigma R_2.$$
>
> The symbol n refers to the sample size for a particular group. In these formulas, the first group is labeled 1 and the second group is labeled 2. ΣR refers to the sum of the ranks for a particular group.

The Kruskal–Wallis *H* Test

The Kruskal–Wallis *H* test is the nonparametric version of the one-way between-groups ANOVA, so it is useful whenever we are comparing the rankings between more than two groups.

EXAMPLE 18.5

For example, we can compare countries with high rankings on national pride. Do countries from different regions of the world have different levels of national pride? Specifically, we wondered whether Asian countries would have different levels of national pride than countries from other parts of the world (due to a tendency to think in terms of the community rather than the individual). We selected three Asian countries, three European countries, and three South American countries. Their levels of accomplishment-related national pride are in Table 18-8. The independent variable is region of the world, with three levels: Asia, Europe, and South America. The dependent variable is accomplishment-related national pride.

We want to convert the data from scale to ordinal during the calculations. This is similar to what we did when we used a Mann–Whitney *U* test, except now we have more than two levels of the independent variable. If we wanted to use the scale data, we would use a one-way between-groups ANOVA. Because we want to use ordinal data, we will use its nonparametric equivalent, the Kruskal–Wallis *H* test. *The **Kruskal–Wallis H test** is a nonparametric hypothesis test used when there are more than two groups, a between-groups design, and an ordinal dependent variable.* The Kruskal–Wallis *H* test statistic is symbolized with the capital letter *H*.

As with the other nonparametric hypothesis tests, we use the same six steps of hypothesis testing.

> **STEP 1: Identify the assumptions.**

There are two assumptions. (1) The data must be ordinal. (2) We should use random selection; otherwise, the ability to generalize will be limited.

Summary: We convert the data from scale to ordinal. The researchers did not indicate whether they used random selection to choose the countries in the sample, so we must be cautious when generalizing from these results.

> **STEP 2: State the null and research hypotheses.**

We will state the null and research hypotheses only in words, not in symbols.

Summary: Null hypothesis: The population distributions for accomplishment-related national pride scores for the Asian countries, European countries, and South American countries are the same. Research hypothesis: The population distributions for accomplishment-related national pride scores for the Asian countries, European countries, and South American countries are different.

● The **Kruskal–Wallis *H* test** is a nonparametric hypothesis test used when there are more than two groups, a between-groups design, and an ordinal dependent variable.

TABLE 18-8 Does the Region of the World Affect National Pride?

The table here includes accomplishment-related national pride scores for three countries from Asia, three from Europe, and three from South America.

Asia	Pride	Europe	Pride	South America	Pride
Japan	1.80	Finland	1.80	Venezuela	3.60
South Korea	1.00	Portugal	1.60	Chile	2.30
Taiwan	0.90	France	1.50	Uruguay	2.00

STEP 3: Determine the characteristics of the comparison distribution.

The Kruskal–Wallis H test compares the three distributions—those represented by the three samples. The distribution of the test statistic, H, is close enough to the chi-square distribution that we can use the chi-square table. To complete step 4 and find a cutoff, we need to know the p level that we plan to use and the degrees of freedom. The degrees of freedom are equal to the number of groups minus 1; here, $3 - 1 = 2$.

Summary: We use the chi-square distribution for a p level of 0.05 and 2 degrees of freedom.

STEP 4: Determine the critical values, or cutoffs.

We use the chi-square table. We look up the appropriate p level, 0.05, and degrees of freedom, 2. The cutoff, or critical value, is 5.992.

Summary: The cutoff for a Kruskal–Wallis H test, based on the chi-square distribution with a p level of 0.05 and 2 degrees of freedom, is 5.992.

STEP 5: Calculate the test statistic.

We start the calculations by organizing the data by raw score from highest to lowest in one single column, and then by rank in the next column. The scores for Finland and Japan are both 1.8. We deal with this tie by assigning them the average of the two ranks they would hold, 4 and 5. They both receive the average of these ranks, 4.5. We include the group membership of each participant (country) next to its score and rank. A indicates an Asian country; E represents a European country; S represents a South American country. Table 18-9 shows these data.

The final three columns of Table 18-9 separate the ranks by group. From these columns, we can easily see that the South American countries tend to hold the highest ranks. Of course, we want to conduct the hypothesis test before drawing any conclusions. Notice that the format of this table is the same as that for the Mann–Whitney U test. There are just more columns when the ranks are separated—one for each level of the independent variable.

TABLE 18-9 Organizing Data for a Kruskal–Wallis H Test

To conduct a Kruskal–Wallis H test, we first organize the data. We organize the raw scores from highest to lowest in a single column, then rank them in an adjacent column. Notice that when scores are tied, we average the ranks of the scores. The next column includes the group to which each country belongs. The last three columns separate the ranks by group.

Country	Pride Score	Pride Rank	Type of Country	A Ranks	E Ranks	S Ranks
Venezuela	3.6	1	S			1
Chile	2.3	2	S			2
Uruguay	2.0	3	S			3
Finland	1.8	4.5	E		4.5	
Japan	1.8	4.5	A	4.5		
Portugal	1.6	6	E		6	
France	1.5	7	E		7	
South Korea	1.0	8	A	8		
Taiwan	0.9	9	A	9		

Before we continue, we take the mean of the ranks for each group, including subscripts to indicate which group is which. Notice that we are taking the *mean* of the ranks, not the sum of the ranks as we did with the Mann–Whitney U test. There are some similarities to ANOVA because the calculation of the test statistic tells us whether these groups are different; by calculating the mean ranks of the three groups, we're able to get a sense of the between-groups variability. We also need the grand mean, the mean rank for every country in the study.

$$M_A = \frac{\Sigma R_A}{n} = \frac{(4.5 + 8 + 9)}{3} = 7.167$$

$$M_E = \frac{\Sigma R_E}{n} = \frac{(4.5 + 6 + 7)}{3} = 5.833$$

$$M_S = \frac{\Sigma R_S}{n} = \frac{(1 + 2 + 3)}{3} = 2$$

$$GM = \frac{\Sigma R}{N} = \frac{(1 + 2 + 3 + 4.5 + 4.5 + 6 + 7 + 8 + 9)}{9} = 5$$

The formula for the test statistic, H, is:

$$H = \left[\frac{12}{N(N+1)}\right]\left[\Sigma n(M - GM)^2\right]$$

The 12 is a constant; it is always in the equation. The uppercase N's in the first part of the equation refer to the sample size for the whole study, 9. The lowercase n refers to the sample size for each group. The second part of the equation tells us to make that calculation for each group using its sample size (n), mean rank (M), and the grand mean (GM; the mean rank for the whole study). The summation sign, Σ, tells us that we have to do this calculation for each group and then add them together.

If there were no differences, each group would have the same mean rank, which would be the same as the grand mean. If the mean rank for each group were exactly equal to the grand mean, the second part of the equation would be 0, which, when multiplied by the first part, would still be 0. So an H of 0 indicates no difference among mean ranks. Similarly, as the mean ranks for the individual samples get farther from the grand mean, the second part of the equation becomes larger, and the test statistic is larger.

$$H = \left[\frac{12}{N(N+1)}\right]\left[\Sigma n(M - GM)^2\right]$$

$$= \left[\frac{12}{9(9+1)}\right]\left[(3(7.167 - 5)^2) + (3(5.833 - 5)^2) + (3(2 - 5)^2)\right]$$

$$= \left[\frac{12}{9(10)}\right]\left[(3(2.167)^2) + (3(0.833)^2) + (3(-3)^2)\right]$$

$$= \left[\frac{12}{90}\right]\left[(3)(4.696) + (3)(0.694) + (3)(9)\right]$$

$$= [0.133][14.088 + 2.082 + 27]$$

$$= [0.133][43.170] = 5.742$$

$$H = 5.742$$

Summary: $H = 5.74$

> **STEP 6: Make a decision.**

For a Kruskal–Wallis H test, we compare the test statistic, 5.74, with the critical value, 5.992. This test statistic is not larger than the critical value, so we cannot reject the null hypothesis. Despite the very small sample size, however, the test statistic is almost as large as the critical value. This appears to be another case in which there is insufficient statistical power to detect any real differences. If we did find a statistically significant difference, then we would have the same problem we had with an ANOVA. We know only that there is a difference somewhere, but not specifically where that difference is. We would have to follow the Kruskal–Wallis H test with a post hoc test, often a series of Mann–Whitney U tests or Kruskal–Wallis H tests on each pair.

Summary: The test statistic, 5.74, is not larger than the critical value, 5.992. We cannot reject the null hypothesis. We can conclude only that there is insufficient evidence that there are differences among the countries based on region.

After completing the hypothesis test, we want to present the primary statistical information in a report. In the write-up, the statistics would read:

$$H = 5.742, p > 0.05.$$

(*Note*: If we conduct the Kruskal–Wallis H test using software, we report the actual p value associated with the test statistic.) ●

Bootstrapping

> **Next Steps**

We sometimes describe people as "pulling themselves up by their own bootstraps" when they create personal success with minimal resources. Statisticians borrowed the word when they had to maximize the information they could gain from only a few resources. ***Bootstrapping*** *is a statistical process in which the original sample data are used to represent the entire population and samples are repeatedly taken from the original sample data to form a confidence interval.*

When bootstrapping data, we use no information other than the sample data. But we treat the sample data as if they constitute the entire population. The secret to successful statistical bootstrapping is one clever technique: sampling with replacement. We first take the mean of the original sample, and then we continue to sample from the original sample. Specifically, we repeatedly take the same number of participants' scores from the sample (e.g., if there are eight participants in the sample, we keep drawing eight participants' scores from that pool) as if we're drawing from the population, then calculate the mean. In bootstrapping, we do this by replacing each participant, one by one, immediately after we select his or her score to be part of the sample.

Here's an example. If the eight scores are 1, 5, 6, 6, 8, 9, 12, and 13 (with a mean of 7.5), then we would repeatedly pull eight scores, one at a time. But after pulling each single score, we put it back, making it possible to pull that exact same score again—or even several times in a row. Based on this, we might draw the following sample: 1, 1, 1, 6, 8, 9, 12, and 13 (with a mean of 6.375). This sample includes the score of 1 several times because it got pulled more than once after being replaced. There also is one score, 5, that was not pulled at all in this sample, just by chance. Each time we draw a sample of eight, we calculate the mean. We do this over and over, thousands of times.

● **Bootstrapping** is a statistical process in which the original sample data are used to represent the entire population and samples are repeatedly taken from the original sample data to form a confidence interval.

TABLE 18-10	Bootstrapping

Bootstrapping is a statistical process whereby we have an original sample and then draw additional samples from that original sample as if the original sample represented the entire population. Here we have five possible samples, along with their means, drawn from the original sample of 1, 5, 6, 6, 8, 9, 12, and 13. All samples are drawn with replacement, so for each new sample, the same score might show up more than once and some scores might not be pulled at all.

Sample								Mean
5	6	6	6	8	12	13	13	8.625
1	5	5	6	9	9	12	13	7.500
1	1	6	6	8	8	12	13	6.875
1	5	5	6	6	6	9	12	6.250
1	5	6	8	8	9	12	13	7.750

Table 18-10 shows just a few possible samples from the original sample (all samples are arranged from lowest to highest, although it is unlikely that they would have been drawn in this order). Of course, doing this by hand would take a very long time, particularly with a sample much larger than eight, so we rely on the computer to do the work for us. So now we have the mean of the original sample of eight (which was 7.5) and thousands of means of samples of eight drawn from the original sample—with replacement.

Once we have these thousands of means from the thousands of samples drawn from this pool, we can create a 95% confidence interval around the original mean. The middle 95% of the means of the thousands of samples represents the 95% confidence interval. As the confidence interval, the middle 95% provides information about the precision of the mean of the original sample. A wide confidence interval indicates that the estimate for the mean is not very precise. A narrow confidence interval indicates a greater degree of precision.

The important thing to remember is that we only bootstrap when circumstances have constrained our choices and the information is potentially very important. Under those circumstances, bootstrapping is a fair way to gain the benefits of a larger sample than we actually have.

CHECK YOUR LEARNING

Reviewing the Concepts

> There are nonparametric hypothesis tests that can be used to replace the various parametric hypothesis tests when it seems clear that there are severe violations of the assumptions.

> We use the Wilcoxon signed-rank test in place of the paired-samples t test, the Mann–Whitney U test in place of the independent-samples t test, and the Kruskal–Wallis H test in place of the one-way between-groups ANOVA. Nonparametric hypothesis tests use the same six steps of hypothesis testing that are used for parametric tests, but the steps and the calculations tend to be simpler.

> A recent technique, popularized by the rise of extremely fast computers, is bootstrapping, which involves sampling with replacement from the original sample. We develop a 95% confidence interval by taking the middle 95% of the means from many samples.

Clarifying the Concepts	18-5	Why must scale data be transformed into ordinal data before any nonparametric tests are performed?

Calculating the Statistics	18-6	Calculate T, the statistic for the Wilcoxon signed-rank test, for the following set of data:

Person	Score 1	Score 2
A	2	5
B	7	2
C	4	5
D	10	3
E	5	1

Applying the Statistics	18-7	Researchers provided accomplishment-related national pride scores for a number of countries (Smith & Kim, 2006). We selected seven countries for which English is the primary language and seven countries for which it is not. We wondered whether English-speaking countries would be different on the variable of accomplishment-related national pride from non-English-speaking countries. The data are in the accompanying table. Conduct a Mann–Whitney U test on these data. Remember to organize the data in one column before starting.

English-Speaking Countries	Pride Score	Non-English-Speaking Countries	Pride Score
United States	4.00	Chile	2.30
Australia	2.90	Japan	1.80
Ireland	2.90	France	1.50
South Africa	2.70	Czech Republic	1.30
New Zealand	2.60	Norway	1.30
Canada	2.40	Slovenia	1.10
Great Britain	2.20	South Korea	1.00

Solutions to these Check Your Learning questions can be found in Appendix D.

REVIEW OF CONCEPTS

Ordinal Data and Correlation

Nonparametric hypothesis tests have been developed as replacements for most parametric tests for situations in which there are severe violations of assumptions. We use nonparametric tests primarily (1) when the dependent variable is ordinal and (2) when the data are skewed and the sample is small, in which case we convert scale data to ordinal data. The nonparametric parallel to the Pearson correlation coefficient is the *Spearman rank-order correlation coefficient*, a statistic that is interpreted just like its parametric cousin with respect to magnitude and direction.

Nonparametric Hypothesis Tests

The *Wilcoxon signed-rank test* is the nonparametric parallel of the paired-samples t test. The *Mann–Whitney U test* is the nonparametric parallel of the independent-samples *t* test. The *Kruskal–Wallis* H *test* is the nonparametric parallel of the one-way between-groups ANOVA. The same six steps of hypothesis testing are used for both parametric and nonparametric tests, but the steps and the calculations for the nonparametric tests tend to be simpler. In *bootstrapping*, we continually sample with replacement from the original sample. This technique allows us to develop a 95% confidence interval from the middle 95% of the means of the many samples.

SPSS®

Let's conduct a Mann–Whitney *U* test on the data we used when comparing communist and noncommunist countries on accomplishment-related pride. In SPSS, we may enter either scale data or ordinal data for the dependent variable. If the data are scale, SPSS automatically ranks the data when we conduct a statistical analysis for ordinal data. If the data are already ranked, SPSS makes no change to the values when conducting the analysis. We conduct a Mann–Whitney *U* test by selecting: Analyze → Nonparametric Tests → Legacy Dialogs → 2 Independent-Samples Tests. The dependent variable, rankings on accomplishment-related national pride, goes under "Test Variable List," and the independent

variable, political system (noncommunist versus communist), goes under "Grouping Variable." Define the groups by clicking "Define Groups" and telling SPSS the value assigned to each condition (e.g., 1 and 2 for noncommunist and communist, respectively). Select "Mann–Whitney *U*" as the test type. The output will provide the mean ranks for each group, as well as information on the test statistic. We can see from the output below that SPSS calculates the same value for the Mann–Whitney *U* statistic, 3, that we calculated earlier. The Asymp. Sig. (2-tailed) value is greater than 0.05, telling us to make the same conclusion: We do not have evidence for a difference in the rankings between the two groups.

HOW IT WORKS

18.1 CALCULATING THE SPEARMAN RANK-ORDER CORRELATION COEFFICIENT

The accompanying table includes ranks for accomplishment-related national pride, along with numbers of medals won at the 2000 Sydney Olympics for 10 countries. (Of course, this might not be the best way to operationalize the variable of Olympic performance; perhaps we should be ranking Olympic medals per capita.) How can we calculate the Spearman correlation coefficient for these two variables—seen in the first two columns of the accompanying table—pride rank and Olympic medals?

First, we have to convert the numbers of Olympic medals to ranks. Then we can calculate the correlation coefficient.

Country	Pride Rank	Olympic Medals	Medals Rank	Difference (D)	Squared Difference (D^2)
United States	1	97	1	0	0
South Africa	2	5	7	−5	25
Austria	3	3	8	−5	25
Canada	4	14	5	−1	1
Chile	5	1	10	−5	25
Japan	6	18	3	3	9
Hungary	7	17	4	3	9
France	8	38	2	6	36
Norway	9	10	6	3	9
Slovenia	10	2	9	1	1

$$\Sigma D^2 = (0 + 25 + 25 + 1 + 25 + 9 + 9 + 36 + 9 + 1) = 140$$

$$r_S = 1 - \frac{6(\Sigma D^2)}{N(N^2 - 1)} = 1 - \frac{6(140)}{10(10^2 - 1)} = 1 - \frac{840}{10(100 - 1)} = 1 - \frac{840}{990}$$

$$= 1 - 0.848 = 0.152$$

18.2 CONDUCTING THE WILCOXON SIGNED-RANK TEST

The Wilcoxon signed-rank test is the nonparametric version of the paired-samples t test. Did European countries fare better or worse at the 2012 Olympics in Beijing than they fared at the 2008 Olympics in London? We'll operationalize their performance as the numbers of gold medals won. The list below includes a random selection of 12 European countries that participated in both the 2008 and the 2012 Olympics (BBC, 2012a; 2012b).

How can we conduct a Wilcoxon signed-rank test for this example? The independent variable is time: 2008 Olympics in London and 2012 Olympics in Beijing. The dependent variable is the ranking of the difference of number of gold medals won.

	2008	2012	Difference
Bulgaria	1	0	−1
Croatia	0	3	3
France	7	11	4
Germany	16	11	−5
Great Britain and Northern Ireland	19	29	10
Hungary	3	8	5
Ireland	0	1	1
Italy	8	8	0
Lithuania	0	2	2
Slovakia	3	0	−3
Slovenia	1	1	0
Spain	5	3	−2

Step 1: This study meets the first two of the three assumptions: (1) The difference in number of medals won can be ranked. (2) This is a random selection of European countries. (3) We do not know if the difference scores come from a symmetric population.

Step 2: Null hypothesis: The number of gold medals won in 2008 did not differ from the number of gold medals won in 2012 for European countries. Research hypothesis: The number of gold medals won in 2008 did differ from the number of gold medals won in 2012 for European countries.

Step 3: The sample includes 12 countries.

Step 4: Using the Wilcoxon signed-rank test table, the critical value for a p level of 0.05, a two-tailed test, and a sample of 12 is 13.

Step 5: We rank the difference scores from highest to lowest for the absolute value for each difference.

	2008	2012	Difference	Absolute Value of Difference	Rank
Great Britain and Northern Ireland	19	29	10	10	1
Germany	16	11	−5	5	2.5
Hungary	3	8	5	5	2.5
France	7	11	4	4	4
Croatia	0	3	3	3	5.5
Slovakia	3	0	−3	3	5.5
Lithuania	0	2	2	2	7.5
Spain	5	3	−2	2	7.5
Bulgaria	1	0	−1	1	9.5
Ireland	0	1	1	1	9.5
Italy	8	8	0	0	—
Slovenia	1	1	0	0	—

The ranks are then separated into those ranks that are associated with positive differences and those ranks that are associated with negative differences. For countries with a tie, we take the average of the ranks. Note that any difference scores of 0 are not included in the analysis.

	2008	2012	Difference	Rank	Positive Rank	Negative Rank
Bulgaria	1	0	−1	9.5		9.5
Croatia	0	3	3	5.5	5.5	
France	7	11	4	4	4	
Germany	16	11	−5	2.5		2.5
Great Britain & Northern Ireland	19	29	10	1	1	
Hungary	3	8	5	2.5	2.5	
Ireland	0	1	1	9.5	9.5	
Italy	8	8	0	—		
Lithuania	0	2	2	7.5	7.5	
Slovakia	3	0	−3	5.5		5.5
Slovenia	1	1	0	—		
Spain	5	3	−2	7.5		7.5

Now we sum the ranks for the positive scores and for the negative scores:

$$\Sigma R_+ = 5.5 + 4 + 1 + 2.5 + 9.5 + 7.5 = 30$$

$$\Sigma R_- = 9.5 + 2.5 + 5.5 + 7.5 = 25$$

The smaller of the two test statistics is used for T: 25.

Step 6: The test statistic 25 is not smaller than the critical value, 13. We fail to reject the null hypothesis. The number of gold medals won in 2008 was not statistically significantly different from the number of gold medals won in 2012 for European countries. In a journal article, the statistics would read:

$$T = 25, p > 0.05$$

18.3 CONDUCTING THE MANN–WHITNEY *U* TEST

The Mann–Whitney *U* test is the nonparametric version of the independent-samples *t* test, so it is useful when comparing the rankings of two different groups. For example, we can use rankings to ask: In which of two world regions—Europe and the Americas (comprising North and South America)—can we find the best museums in the world? The museums below are the top 20 museums in the world, according to Tripadvisor's 2015 Traveler's Choice Awards.

Tripadvisor's 2015 Ranking	Museum	City	Country	Continent
1	The Metropolitan Museum of Art	New York	United States	North America
2	Musée D'Orsay	Paris	France	Europe
3	Art Institute of Chicago	Chicago	United States	North America
4	Prado National Museum	Madrid	Spain	Europe
5	Musée du Louvre	Paris	France	Europe
6	State Hermitage Museum and Winter Palace	St. Petersburg	Russia	Europe
7	National Gallery	London	United Kingdom	Europe
8	Rijksmuseum	Amsterdam	Netherlands	Europe
9	Vasa Museum	Stockholm	Sweden	Europe
10	National Museum of Anthropology	Mexico City	Mexico	North America
11	The Acropolis Museum	Athens	Greece	Europe
12	British Museum	London	United Kingdom	Europe
13	Van Gogh Museum	Amsterdam	Netherlands	Europe
14	Academia Gallery	Florence	Italy	Europe
15	The National WWII Museum	New Orleans	United States	North America
16	Pergamon Museum	Berlin	Germany	Europe
17	The Getty Center	Los Angeles	United States	North America
18	Smithsonian National Air and Space Museum	Washington, D.C.	United States	North America
19	Instituto Ricardo Brennand	Recife	Brazil	South America
20	Inhotim	Brumadinho	Brazil	South America

How can we conduct a Mann–Whitney *U* test for this example? The independent variable is region of the world, and its levels are Europe and the Americas (North America or South America). The dependent variable is Tripadvisor ranking.

Step 1: This study meets the first and third of the three assumptions: (1) The data are ordinal—the ranking of each museum according to tripadvisor. (2) The list of museums is not a random selection of museums. (3) There are no ties.

Step 2: Null hypothesis: Museums in Europe and those in the Americas (North America or South America) do not differ in Tripadvisor rankings. Research hypothesis: Museums in Europe and those in the Americas differ in Tripadvisor rankings.

Step 3: There are 8 museums in the Americas and 12 in Europe.

Step 4: The cutoff, or critical value, for a Mann–Whitney U test with one group of 8 museums and one group of 12 museums, a p level of 0.05, and a two-tailed test is 22.

Step 5: Before we continue, we sum the ranks for each group and add subscripts to indicate which group is which:

$$\Sigma R_E = (1 + 3 + 10 + 15 + 17 + 18 + 19 + 20) = 103$$

$$\Sigma R_M = (2 + 4 + 5 + 6 + 7 + 8 + 9 + 11 + 12 + 13 + 14 + 16) = 107$$

The formula for the first group is:

$$U_E = (n_E)(n_M) + \frac{n_E(n_E + 1)}{2} - \Sigma R_E = (8)(12) + \frac{8(8 + 1)}{2} - 103$$

$$= 96 + 36 - 103 = 29$$

The formula for the second group is:

$$U_M = (n_E)(n_M) + \frac{n_M(n_M + 1)}{2} - \Sigma R_M = (8)(12) + \frac{12(12 + 1)}{2} - 107$$

$$= 96 + 78 - 107 = 67$$

Step 6: For a Mann–Whitney U test, we compare only the smaller test statistic, 29, with the critical value, 22. This test statistic is not smaller than the critical value, so we fail to reject the null hypothesis. We cannot conclude that the continent-based groups—Europe versus the Americas—are different with respect to museum rankings. In a journal article, the statistics would read:

$$U = 29, p > 0.05$$

18.4 CONDUCTING THE KRUSKAL–WALLIS *H* TEST

The Kruskal–Wallis H test is the nonparametric version of the one-way between-groups ANOVA. Based on research by Filippo Lovato, The Economist Intelligence Unit at *The Economist* ranked cities around the world using an index based on green spaces, sprawl, natural assets, connectivity, isolation, and pollution as a measure of quality of life (2012). Below are the top 22 cities in the world using the Spatially Adjusted Liveability Index.

How can we conduct a Kruskal–Wallis H test for this example? The independent variable is the continent, and its levels are Asia/Oceania, Europe, and North America. The dependent variable is the Spatial Adjusted Liveability Index ranking.

City/Country	Spatial Adjusted Liveability Index Rank	Continent
Hong Kong	1	Asia/Oceania
Amsterdam	2	Europe
Osaka	3	Asia/Oceania
Paris	4	Europe
Sydney	5	Asia/Oceania
Stockholm	6	Europe
Berlin	7	Europe
Toronto	8	North America
Munich	9	Europe
Tokyo	10	Asia/Oceania
Rome	11	Europe
London	12	Europe
Madrid	13	Europe
Washington, D.C.	14	North America
Chicago	15	North America
New York	16	North America

Los Angeles	17	North America
San Francisco	18	North America
Boston	19	North America
Seoul	20	Asia/Oceania
Atlanta	21	North America
Singapore	22	Asia/Oceania

Step 1: This study meets the first and third of the three assumptions: (1) The data are ordinal—the ranking of each city according to the Spatial Adjusted Liveability Index. (2) The list of cities is not a random selection. (3) There are no ties.

Step 2: Null hypothesis: Cities in different continents do not differ in their rankings on the Spatial Adjusted Liveability Index. Research hypothesis: Cities in different continents do differ in their rankings on the Spatial Adjusted Liveability Index.

Step 3: There are three groups (Asia/Oceania, Europe, and North America).
$$df = 3 - 1 = 2$$

Step 4: Using the chi-square table, the critical value for a p level of 0.05 and 2 degrees of freedom is 5.992.

Step 5: First, we find the mean rank for every continent in the study:

$$M_A = \frac{\Sigma R_A}{n_A} = \frac{1 + 3 + 5 + 10 + 20 + 22}{6} = \frac{61}{6} = 10.167$$

$$M_E = \frac{\Sigma R_E}{n_E} = \frac{2 + 4 + 6 + 7 + 9 + 11 + 12 + 13}{8} = \frac{64}{8} = 8.0$$

$$M_{NA} = \frac{\Sigma R_{NA}}{n_{NA}} = \frac{8 + 14 + 15 + 16 + 17 + 18 + 19 + 21}{8} = \frac{128}{8} = 16.0$$

Next, we find the grand mean:

$$GM = \frac{\Sigma R}{N}$$

$$= \frac{1+2+3+4+5+6+7+8+9+10+11+12+13+14+15+16+17+18+19+20+21+22}{22}$$

$$= \frac{253}{22} = 11.5$$

Now we can calculate the test statistic, H:

$$H = \left[\frac{12}{N(N+1)}\right]\left[\Sigma n(M - GM)^2\right]$$

$$H = \left[\frac{12}{22(22+1)}\right]\left[6(10.167 - 11.5)^2 + 8(8 - 11.5)^2 + 8(16 - 11.5)^2\right]$$

$$H = \left[\frac{12}{506}\right]\left[6(-1.333)^2 + 8(-3.5)^2 + 8(4.5)^2\right]$$

$$H = \left[\frac{12}{506}\right]\left[6(1.777) + 8(12.25) + 8(20.25)\right]$$

$$H = \left[\frac{12}{506}\right]\left[10.662 + 98 + 162\right]$$

$$H = \left[\frac{12}{506}\right]\left[270.662\right] = 6.419$$

Step 6: For a Kruskal–Wallis H test, we compare the test statistic, 6.419, with the critical value, 5.992. This test statistic is larger than the critical value, so we reject the null hypothesis. We can conclude that the three continents are different with respect to the rankings of cities on the Spatial Adjusted Liveability Index. In a journal article, the statistics would read:

$$U = 6.26, p < 0.05$$

EXERCISES

Clarifying the Concepts

18.1 When do we convert scale data to ordinal data?

18.2 When the data on at least one variable are ordinal, the data on any scale variable must be converted from scale to ordinal. How do we convert a scale variable into an ordinal one?

18.3 How does the transformation of scale data to ordinal data solve the problem of outliers?

18.4 What does a histogram of rank-ordered data look like and why does it look that way?

18.5 Explain how the relation between ranks is the core of the Spearman rank-order correlation.

18.6 Define the symbols in the following term:

$$r_S = 1 - \frac{6(\Sigma D^2)}{N(N^2 - 1)}$$

18.7 What is the possible range of values for the Spearman rank-order correlation and how are these values interpreted?

18.8 How would you respond in a situation in which you are ranking a set of scale data and there are two numbers that are exactly the same?

18.9 When is it appropriate to use the Wilcoxon signed-rank test?

18.10 How is N determined for the Wilcoxon signed-rank test and how does this differ from the way N is typically determined for most statistical tests?

18.11 When conducting a Wilcoxon signed-rank test, why do we use absolute values when ranking the differences?

18.12 When do we use the Mann–Whitney U test?

18.13 What are the assumptions of the Mann–Whitney U test?

18.14 How are the critical values for the Mann–Whitney U test used differently than critical values for parametric tests?

18.15 When is it appropriate to use the Kruskal–Wallis H test?

18.16 Define and explain the symbols in the following equation: $H = \left[\dfrac{12}{N(N + 1)}\right]\left[\Sigma n(M - GM)^2\right]$

18.17 If the data meet the assumptions of the parametric test, why is it preferable to use the parametric test rather than the nonparametric alternative?

18.18 What is bootstrapping?

18.19 How can bootstrapping be used as an alternative to nonparametric tests when working with small sample sizes?

Calculating the Statistics

18.20 In order to compute statistics, we need to have working formulas. For the following, (i) identify the incorrect symbol, (ii) state what the correct symbol should be, and (iii) explain why the initial symbol was incorrect.

a. $U_1 = (n_1)(n_2) + \dfrac{n_1(n_1 + 1)}{2} - \Sigma R_1^2$

b. $r = 1 - \dfrac{6(\Sigma D^2)}{N(N^2 - 1)}$

c. $T = \Sigma R_{larger}$

d. $H = \left[\dfrac{12}{N(N^2 + 1)}\right]\left[\Sigma n(M - GM)^2\right]$

18.21 Consider the following scale data.

Participant	Variable X	Variable Y
1	134.5	64.00
2	186	60.00
3	157	61.50
4	129	66.25
5	147	65.50
6	133	62.00
7	141	62.50
8	147	62.00
9	136	63.00
10	147	65.50

a. Convert the data to ordinal or ranked data, starting with a rank of 1 for the smallest data point.

b. Compute the Spearman correlation coefficient.

18.22 Consider the following scale data.

Participant	Variable X	Variable Y
1	$1250	25
2	$1400	21
3	$1100	32
4	$1450	54
5	$1600	38
6	$2100	62
7	$3750	43
8	$1300	32

a. Convert the data to ordinal or ranked data, starting with a rank of 1 for the smallest data point.

b. Compute the Spearman correlation coefficient.

18.23 The following fictional data represent the finishing place for runners of a marathon and the number of hours they trained per week.

Race Rank	Hours Trained	Race Rank	Hours Trained
1	25	6	18
2	25	7	12
3	22	8	17
4	18	9	15
5	19	10	16

a. Calculate the Spearman correlation for this set of data.

b. Make a decision regarding the null hypothesis. Is there a significant correlation between a runner's finishing place and the amount the runner trained?

18.24 Imagine that a researcher measured a group of participants at two time points. Fictional scores for these two time points appear below. Are the scores different at time 1 and time 2?

Person	Time 1	Time 2
1	56	83
2	74	116
3	81	96
4	47	56
5	78	120
6	96	100
7	72	71

a. Compute the Wilcoxon signed-rank test statistic.

b. Make a decision regarding the null hypothesis.

18.25 Assume a group of students provides happiness ratings for how happy they feel during the school year and how happy they feel during the summer. Do happiness levels differ depending on the time of year? Fictional data appear below:

Student	School Year	Summer
1	7	4
2	4	6
3	5	5
4	3	4
5	4	8
6	5	7
7	3	2

a. Compute the Wilcoxon signed-rank test statistic.

b. Make a decision regarding the null hypothesis.

18.26 Compute the Wilcoxon signed-rank test statistic for the following set of data:

Person	Score 1	Score 2
1	6	6
2	5	3
3	4	2
4	3	5
5	2	1
6	1	4

18.27 Compute the Mann–Whitney U statistic for the following data. Each participant has been assigned a group and a participant number; these are shown in the "Group 1" and "Group 2" columns.

Group 1	Ordinal Dependent Variable	Group 2	Ordinal Dependent Variable
1	1	1	11
2	2.5	2	9
3	8	3	2.5
4	4	4	5
5	6	5	7
6	10	6	12

18.28 Compute the Mann–Whitney U statistic for the following data. Each participant has been assigned a group and a participant number; these are shown in the "Group 1" and "Group 2" columns.

Group 1	Scale Dependent Variable	Group 2	Scale Dependent Variable
1	8	9	3
2	5	10	4
3	5	11	2
4	7	12	1
5	10	13	1
6	14	14	5
7	9	15	6
8	11		

18.29 Are men or women more likely to be at the top of their class? The following table depicts fictional class standings for a group of men and women:

Student	Gender	Class Standing	Student	Gender	Class Standing
1	Male	98	7	Male	43
2	Female	72	8	Male	33
3	Male	15	9	Female	17
4	Female	3	10	Female	82
5	Female	102	11	Male	63
6	Female	8	12	Male	25

a. Compute the Mann–Whitney U test statistic.

b. Make a decision regarding the null hypothesis. Is there a significant difference in the class ranks of men and women?

18.30 Assume a researcher compared the performance of two independent groups of participants on an ordinal variable using the Mann–Whitney U test. The first group had 8 participants and the second group had 11 participants.

a. Using a p level of 0.05 and a two-tailed test, determine the critical value.

b. Assume the researcher calculated $U_1 = 22$ and $U_2 = 17$. Make a decision regarding the null hypothesis and explain that decision.

c. Assume the researcher calculated $U_1 = 24$ and $U_2 = 30$. Make a decision regarding the null hypothesis and explain that decision.

d. Assume the researcher calculated $U_1 = 13$ and $U_2 = 9$. Make a decision regarding the null hypothesis and explain that decision.

18.31 The following data set represents the scores of three independent groups of participants on a single scale dependent variable. Calculate the Kruskal–Wallis H statistic for this data set.

Group 1	Group 2	Group 3
0.22	1.03	0.52
0.55	0.89	0.67
1.20	0.74	2.83
0.83	1.86	3.20
1.01	2.21	2.75
0.86	0.94	1.74

18.32 The following data set represents the scores of three independent groups of participants on a single ordinal dependent variable. Calculate the Kruskal–Wallis H statistic for this data set.

Group 1	Group 2	Group 3
1	1	5
5	3	4
3	3	1
2	4	1
2	2	3

18.33 The following data set represents the scores of three independent groups of participants on a single scale dependent variable:

Group 1	Group 2	Group 3
15	38	12
27	22	72
16	56	84
	41	33

a. Calculate the Kruskal–Wallis H statistic for this data set.

b. Make a decision regarding the null hypothesis. Is there a significant difference among the groups?

Applying the Concepts

18.34 University students, cell phone bills, and ordinal data: Here are some monthly cell phone bills, in dollars, for university students:

```
100 60   35   50    50   50 60 65
   0 75 100   55    50   40 80
200 30   50 108   500 100 45
 40 45   50   40    40 100 80
```

a. Convert these data from scale to ordinal. (Don't forget to put them in order first.) What happens to an outlier when you convert these data to ordinal?

b. What approximate shape would the distribution of these data take? Would they likely be normally distributed? Explain why the distribution of ordinal data is never normal.

c. Why does it not matter if the ordinal variable is normally distributed? (*Hint:* Think about what kind of hypothesis test you would conduct.)

18.35 World cities, livability, and nonparametric hypothesis tests: CNN.com reported on a 2012 study that ranked the world's cities in terms of how livable they are (http://travel.cnn.com/explorations/life/worlds-most-livable-city-525619), using a range of criteria related to stability, health care, culture and environment, education, and infrastructure. The top 10, in order, were: Melbourne, Australia; Vienna, Austria; Vancouver, Toronto, and Calgary, all in Canada; Adelaide and Sydney, both in Australia; Helsinki, Finland; Perth, Australia; and Auckland, New Zealand. For each of the following research questions, state which nonparametric hypothesis test is appropriate: the Spearman rank-order correlation coefficient, the Wilcoxon signed-rank test, the Mann–Whitney *U* test, or the Kruskal–Wallis *H* test. Explain your answers and indicate the equivalent parametric test.

a. Which cities tend to receive higher rankings—those north of the equator or those south of the equator?

b. Did the top 10 cities tend to change rank relative to their position in a similar 2010 study?

c. Are the livability rankings related to a city's economic status?

d. On which continent do cities tend to have the highest rankings?

18.36 Fantasy baseball and the Spearman correlation coefficient: In fantasy baseball, groups of 12 league participants conduct a draft in which they can "buy" any baseball players from any teams across one of the two Major League Baseball (MLB) leagues (the American League and the National League). These makeshift teams are compared on the basis of the combined statistics of the individual baseball players. For example, statistics about home runs are transformed into points, and each fantasy team receives a total score of all combined points based on its baseball players, regardless of their real-life team. Many in the fantasy and real-life baseball worlds have wondered how success in fantasy leagues maps onto real MLB teams' success in terms of winning baseball games. Walker (2006) compared the fantasy league performances of the players for each American League team with their actual American League finishes for the 2004 season, the year the Boston Red Sox broke the legendary "curse" against them and won the World Series. The data, sorted from highest to lowest fantasy league score, are shown in the accompanying table.

Team	Fantasy League Points	Actual American League Finish
Boston	117.5	2
New York	109.5	1
Anaheim	108	3.5
Minnesota	97	3.5
Texas	85	6
Chicago	80	7
Cleveland	79	8
Oakland	77	5
Baltimore	74.5	9
Detroit	68.5	10
Seattle	51	13
Tampa Bay	47.5	11
Toronto	35.5	12
Kansas City	20	14

a. What are the two variables of interest? For each variable, state whether it's scale or ordinal.

b. Calculate the Spearman correlation coefficient for these two variables. Remember to convert any scale variables to ranks.

c. What does the coefficient tell us about the relation between these two variables?

d. Why couldn't we calculate a Pearson correlation coefficient for these data?

18.37 Test-taking speed, grade, and the Spearman correlation coefficient: Does speed in completing a test correlate with one's grade? Here are test scores for eight students in one of our statistics classes. They are arranged in order from the student who turned in the test first to the student who turned in the test last.

98 74 87 92 88 93 62 67

a. What are the two variables of interest? For each variable, state whether it's scale or ordinal.

b. Calculate the Spearman correlation coefficient for these two variables. Remember to convert any scale variables to ranks.

c. What does the coefficient tell us about the relation between these two variables?

d. Why couldn't we calculate a Pearson correlation coefficient for these data?

e. Does this Spearman correlation coefficient suggest that students should take their tests as quickly as possible? That is, does it indicate that taking the test quickly *causes* a good grade? Explain your answer.

f. What third variables might be responsible for this correlation? That is, what third variables might cause both speedy test taking and a good test grade?

g. Imagine that each of the following numbers represents the Spearman correlation coefficient that quantifies the relation between test grade and speed in taking the test:

$$1.00, -0.001, 0.52, -0.27, -0.98, 0.09$$

Specify which of these coefficients suggests the strongest relation between the two variables as well as which coefficient suggests the weakest relation between the two variables.

18.38 Online plane tickets and the Wilcoxon signed-rank test: Which Web site offers better fares—Cheap-Tickets or Expedia? We conducted searches in February 2007, for the cheapest fares for round-trip international flights during peak summer travel season (which was not all that far into the future): leaving on July 7, 2007, and returning on July 28, 2007. We conducted a search for each itinerary using both search engines.

Itinerary	CheapTickets	Expedia
Athens, GA, to Johannesburg, South Africa	$2403	$2580
Chicago to Chennai, India	1884	2044
Columbus, OH, to Belgrade, Serbia	1259	1436
Denver to Geneva, Switzerland	1392	1412
Montréal to Dublin, Ireland	1097	1152
New York City to Reykjavik, Iceland	935	931
San Antonio to Hong Kong	1407	1400
Toronto to Istanbul, Turkey	1261	1429
Tulsa to Guadalajara, Mexico	565	507
Vancouver to Melbourne, Australia	1621	1613

a. What is the independent variable and what are its levels? What is the dependent variable?

b. Is this a between-groups or a within-groups design? Explain.

c. Conduct all six steps of hypothesis testing for a Wilcoxon signed-rank test for matched pairs.

d. How would you present these statistics in a journal article?

18.39 Hockey wins and the Wilcoxon signed-rank test: Are Canadian professional hockey teams consistent over time? Here are the wins per season (out of 82 games) for the six Canadian teams in the National Hockey League (NHL). For comparison, in 1995–1996, the top team in the Eastern Conference was the Pittsburgh Penguins, with 49 wins, and the top team in the Western Conference was the Detroit Red Wings, with 62 wins. In 2005–2006, the top team in the Eastern Conference was the Ottawa Senators, with 52 wins, and the top team in

the Western Conference was, once again, Detroit, with 58 wins. (The Winnipeg Jets weren't in existence in the 2005–2006 season, so we didn't include them here.)

Team	1995–1996 Season	2005–2006 Season
Calgary Flames	34	46
Edmonton Oilers	30	41
Montréal Canadiens	40	42
Ottawa Senators	18	52
Toronto Maple Leafs	34	41
Vancouver Canucks	32	42

a. What is the independent variable and what are its levels? What is the dependent variable?

b. Is this a between-groups or a within-groups design? Explain.

c. Why might it be preferable to use a nonparametric hypothesis test for these data?

d. Conduct all six steps of hypothesis testing for a Wilcoxon signed-rank test for matched pairs.

e. How would you present these statistics in a journal article?

18.40 Nonparametric tests and a longitudinal study of mathematically gifted teenagers: Researchers studied male and female teenagers who had scored in the top 1% on mathematical reasoning measures (Lubinski, Benbow, & Kell, 2014). The researchers were able to follow the participants' progression over the next 40 years. They tracked two groups, or cohorts, of participants on a number of variables, including career-related variables. They reported "pronounced and significant sex differences in the percentage of participants who were working full time (Cohort 1: 89% of males and 69% of females; Cohort 2: 90% of males and 59% of females), $\chi^2(1, N = 1,131) = 67.56, p < .001$, and $\chi^2(1, N = 481) = 68.55, p < .001$." So, the researchers looked at income only among those who were employed full time. For example, for one cohort they reported median incomes of $150,000 for men and $101,000 for women. This gender difference was statistically significant for both groups: "Mann–Whitney U test, $zs \geq 5.09, ps < .001$."

a. Explain why the researchers conducted a chi-square test for their data on whether participants were working full time. (Think back to what you learned in Chapter 17.)

b. Explain the finding on full-time work in your own words.

c. Explain why the researchers conducted a Mann–Whitney U test for their data on incomes.

d. Explain the finding on incomes in your own words.

e. Why did the researchers report median income rather than mean income?

18.41 Public versus private universities and the Mann–Whitney *U* test: Do public or private universities tend to have better sociology graduate programs? *U.S. News & World Report* publishes online rankings of graduate schools across a range of disciplines. The table below includes the *Report's* 2013 list of the top 19 doctoral programs in sociology and notes whether the schools are public or private. Schools listed at the same rank are tied.

a. What is the independent variable, and what are its levels? What is the dependent variable?

b. Is this a between-groups or within-groups design? Explain.

c. Why do we have to use a nonparametric hypothesis test for these data?

d. Conduct all six steps of hypothesis testing for a Mann–Whitney *U* test.

e. How would you present these statistics in a journal article?

University	Rank	Type of School	Public Rank	Private Rank
Princeton University	2	Private		2
University of California, Berkeley	2	Public	2	
University of Wisconsin, Madison	2	Public	2	
Stanford University	4.5	Private		4.5
University of Michigan, Ann Arbor	4.5	Public	4.5	
Harvard University	7	Private		7
University of Chicago	7	Private		7
University of North Carolina, Chapel Hill	7	Public	7	
University of California, Los Angeles	9	Public	9	
Northwestern University	10.5	Private		10.5
University of Pennsylvania	10.5	Private		10.5
Columbia University	12.5	Private		12.5
Indiana University, Bloomington	12.5	Public	12.5	
Duke University	14.5	Private		14.5
University of Texas, Austin	14.5	Public	14.5	
New York University	16	Private		16
Cornell University	18	Private		18
Ohio State University	18	Public	18	
Pennsylvania State University, University Park	18	Public	18	

18.42 Gender, aggression, and the interpretation of a Mann–Whitney *U* test: Spanish researchers examining aggression in children's dreams reported the following: "Using the Mann–Whitney nonparametrical statistical test on the gender differences, we found a significant difference between boys and girls in Group 1 for overall [aggression] ($U = 44.00$, $p = 0.004$) and received aggression ($U = 48.00$, $p = 0.005$). So, in their dreams, younger boys not only had a higher level of general aggression but also received more *severe* aggressive acts than girls of the same age" (emphasis in original) (Oberst, Charles, & Chamarro, 2005, p. 175).

a. What is the independent variable, and what are its levels? What is the dependent variable?

b. Is this a between-groups or within-groups design?

c. Which hypothesis test did the researchers conduct? Why might they have chosen a nonparametric test?

Why do you think they chose this particular nonparametric test?

d. In your own words, describe what they found.

e. Can we conclude that gender caused a difference in levels of aggression in dreams? Explain. Provide at least two reasons why gender might not cause certain levels of aggression in dreams even though these variables are associated.

18.43 Cell phone bill, hours spent studying, and the shapes of distributions: The following figures display data that depict the relation between students' monthly cell phone bills and the number of hours they report that they study per week.

a. What does the accompanying scatterplot suggest about the shape of the distribution for hours studied per week? What does it suggest about the shape of the distribution for a monthly cell phone bill?

b. What does the accompanying grouped frequency histogram suggest about the shape of the distribution for a monthly cell phone bill?

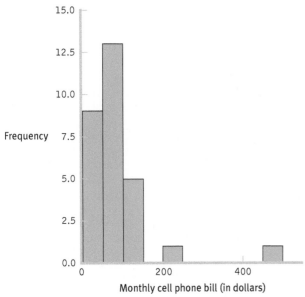

c. Is it a good idea to use a parametric hypothesis test for these data? Explain.

Putting It All Together

18.44 Stroke patients, treatment, and type of nonparametric test: A common situation faced by researchers working with special populations, such as neurologically impaired people or people with less common psychiatric conditions, is that the studies often have small sample sizes due to the relatively few number of patients. As a result, these researchers often turn to nonparametric statistical tests. For each of the following research descriptions, state which nonparametric hypothesis test is most appropriate: the Spearman rank-order correlation coefficient, the Wilcoxon signed-rank test, the Mann–Whitney U test, or the Kruskal–Wallis H test. Explain your answers.

a. People who have had a stroke often have whole or partial paralysis on the side of their body opposite the side of the brain damage. Leung, Ng, and Fong (2009) were interested in the effects of a treatment program for constrained movement on the recovery from paralysis. They compared the arm-movement ability of eight stroke patients before and after the treatment.

b. Leung and colleagues (2009) were also interested in whether the amount of improvement after the therapy was related to the number of months that had passed since the patient experienced the stroke.

c. Five of Leung and colleagues' (2009) patients were male and three were female. We could ask whether post-treatment movement performance was different between men and women.

d. For parts (a), (b), and (c), what tests would you use if you had 180 patients instead of 8? Explain your answers.

e. For parts (a), (b), and (c), what was the dependent variable in each case, and how might the researchers have operationalized this variable?

f. The researchers used a treatment program to help patients recover from a stroke. If the researchers had enough patients to randomly assign some to treatment and others to no treatment, would they have been able to have either a blind or a double-blind design? Explain your answer.

18.45 "Smart" states and the Kruskal–Wallis H test: The Morgan Quitno Press regularly ranks U.S. states on how "smart" they are, based on 21 criteria including per-student school expenditures, percent of population with high school degrees, high school dropout rate, average class size, and "percent of 4th graders whose parents have strict rules about getting homework done." Here are the rankings for all 50 states for 2004.

1. Massachusetts (NE)
2. Connecticut (NE)
3. Vermont (NE)
4. New Jersey (NE)
5. Wisconsin (MW)
6. New York (NE)
7. Minnesota (MW)
8. Iowa (MW)
9. Pennsylvania (NE)
10. Montana
11. Maine (NE)
12. Virginia (S)
13. Nebraska (MW)
14. New Hampshire (NE)
15. Kansas (MW)
16. Wyoming
17. Indiana (MW)
18. Maryland
19. North Dakota
20. Ohio (MW)
21. Colorado
22. South Dakota
23. Rhode Island (NE)
24. Illinois (MW)
25. North Carolina (S)
26. Missouri (MW)
27. Delaware
28. Utah
29. Idaho
30. Washington
31. Michigan (MW)
32. South Carolina (S)

33. Texas
34. West Virginia
35. Oregon
36. Arkansas (S)
37. Kentucky (S)
38. Georgia (S)
39. Florida (S)
40. Oklahoma
41. Tennessee (S)

42. Hawaii
43. California
44. Alabama (S)
45. Alaska
46. Louisiana (S)
47. Mississippi (S)
48. Arizona
49. Nevada
50. New Mexico

We marked states in the Northeast with an NE, in the Midwest with a MW, and in the South with an S. Do these regions tend to have different rankings from one another?

a. What is the independent variable and what are its levels? What is the dependent variable?

b. Is this a between-groups or within-groups design? Explain.

c. Why do we have to use a nonparametric hypothesis test for these data?

d. Conduct all six steps of hypothesis testing for a Kruskal–Wallis H test. Note that you have to rank just the states in this study, separate from the original ranking list.

e. How would you present these statistics in a journal article?

f. Explain why a statistically significant Kruskal–Wallis H statistic does not tell us exactly where the specific differences lie. If there is a statistically significant finding for this example, determine where the difference lies by calculating Kruskal–Wallis H statistics for each pair.

g. What test would you conduct if you had scale scores for the 50 states? Explain your answer.

h. If you were interested in the validity of the categorizing of states as "smart," how could you determine this? What criteria might you use? Be specific.

18.46 Common executive names and thinking about ordinal data: The ordinal data here can help us think about many of the concepts we've explored in this book. Below are the 10 most common female and male names among high-level U.S. executives, such as CEOs and presidents (Boyce, 2015). When considering these data, note that the author explains that "there are tremendously more male executives in the U.S. than female."

Rank	Women	Men
1	Mary	John
2	Susan	Robert
3	Karen	David
4	Linda	Michael
5	Elizabeth	James
6	Barbara	William
7	Lisa	Thomas
8	Patricia	Richard
9	Nancy	Mark
10	Kathleen	Paul

a. The author noted that there are more male than female top executives. What additional information would you need to know in order to use a nonparametric test to analyze whether women or men more commonly had these types of positions?

b. If you had the information you listed in part (a), what nonparametric test would you use to analyze these data? Explain your answer.

c. The author tells us, when naming our children, to "Select a timeless name here that commands respect—perhaps you'll select one based off a favorite innovator or leader." The author also reports that the typical American executive is 53.5 years old, so the typical person in this study was born in 1962. Based on the ages of the executives in this data set, why is her advice about how to name your children potentially problematic?

d. Add to your answer in part (c) about why this statement is problematic. Specifically, knowing what you know about correlation versus causation (from Chapter 15), explain why this logic is flawed.

e. Each of the names listed in this study is accompanied by a graph like the one below. This time plot shows the change in the rank of the name Susan over time.

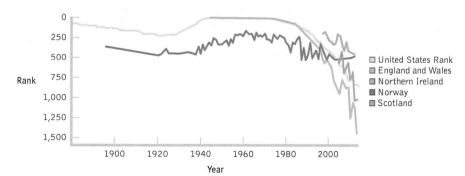

(Yes, both of your authors—Tom and Susan—are on this list of top executive names, and yes, we're probably older than you are!) Explain how this graph helps us understand why the high frequency of Susan as a top name for female executives is likely to decline in the future.

f. Explain why the advice to choose your baby's name from this list is also problematic from a sampling perspective. For example, the author reported top names for executives in the U.S. Is this likely to generalize to other countries? Explain how the graph helps us to see the problems in generalizing beyond a single sample. In your answer, discuss the specific countries that are depicted on this graph—all of which are countries in which Susan has been at least a somewhat popular name at some point.

TERMS

Spearman rank-order correlation coefficient (p. 517)

Wilcoxon signed-rank test (p. 521)

Mann–Whitney U test (p. 524)

Kruskal–Wallis H test (p. 528)

bootstrapping (p. 531)

FORMULAS

$$r_S = 1 - \frac{6(\Sigma D^2)}{N(N^2 - 1)} \quad \text{(p. 518)}$$

$$T = \Sigma R_{smaller} \quad \text{(p. 524)}$$

$$U_1 = (n_1)(n_2) + \frac{n_1(n_1 + 1)}{2} - \Sigma R_1 \quad \text{(p. 527)}$$

$$U_2 = (n_1)(n_2) + \frac{n_2(n_2 + 1)}{2} - \Sigma R_2 \quad \text{(p. 527)}$$

$$M_1 = \frac{\Sigma R_1}{n} \text{ [for the first group in a Kruskal–Wallis } H \text{ test]} \quad \text{(p. 530)}$$

$$GM = \frac{\Sigma R}{N} \quad \text{(p. 530)}$$

$$H = \left[\frac{12}{N(N + 1)}\right]\left[\Sigma n(M - GM)^2\right] \quad \text{(p. 530)}$$

SYMBOLS

r_S (p. 517)
T (p. 522)

U (p. 524)
H (p. 528)

A FINAL WORD

Hey! You've done it; congratulations. You have made your way through all (or most) of what, for many of you, is your first or second course in statistics. We know it wasn't easy, but we hope it has been inspiring. You now have the basic tools to quantify everyday observations, describe your observations in tables and graphs, and test how well whatever you discovered in your sample fits with a larger population.

And please, send us an email with any details that can make this textbook better. We will be sure to thank you in the next edition and you will have made life a little easier for the next generation of statistical thinkers.

Susan and Tom

Appendix A

REFERENCE FOR BASIC MATHEMATICS

This appendix serves as a reference for the basic mathematical operations that are used in the book. We provide quick reference tables to help you with symbols and notation; instruction on the order of operations; guidelines for converting fractions, decimals, and percentages; and examples of how to solve basic algebraic equations. Some of you will need a more extensive review than is presented in these pages. That review, which involves more detail and instruction, can be found on the book's companion Web site. Most of you will be familiar with much of this material. However, the inclusion of this reference can help you to solve problems throughout this book, particularly when you come across material that appears unfamiliar.

We include a diagnostic quiz for you to assess your current comfort level with the material. Following the diagnostic test, we provide instruction and reference tables for each section so that you can review the concepts, apply the concepts through worked problems, and review your skills with a brief self-quiz.

Section A.1   Diagnostic Test: Skills Evaluation
Section A.2   Symbols and Notation: Arithmetic Operations
Section A.3   Order of Operations
Section A.4   Proportions: Fractions, Decimals, and Percentages
Section A.5   Solving Equations with a Single Unknown Variable
Section A.6   Answers to Diagnostic Test and Self-Quizzes

A.1 Diagnostic Test: Skills Evaluation

This diagnostic test is divided into four parts that correspond to the sections of the basic mathematics review that follows. The purpose of the diagnostic test is to help you understand which areas you need to review prior to completing work in this book. (Answers to each of the questions can be found at the end of the review on page A-6.)

SECTION 1 (Symbols and Notation: Arithmetic Operations)

1. $8 + 2 + 14 + 4 =$ _____
2. $4 \times (-6) =$ _____
3. $22 - (-4) + 3 =$ _____
4. $8 \times 6 =$ _____
5. $36 \div (-9) =$ _____
6. $13 + (-2) + 8 =$ _____
7. $44 \div 11 =$ _____
8. $-6 \, (-3) =$ _____
9. $-6 - 8 =$ _____
10. $-14 \, / -2 =$ _____

SECTION 2 (Order of Operations)

1. $3 \times (6 + 4) - 30 =$ _____
2. $4 + 6(2 + 1) + 6 =$ _____
3. $(3 - 6) \times 2 + 5 =$ _____
4. $4 + 6 \times 2 =$ _____
5. $16 \, / \, 2 + 6(3 - 1) =$ _____
6. $2^2 \, (12 - 8) =$ _____
7. $5 - 3(4 - 1) =$ _____
8. $7 \times 2 - (9 - 3) \times 2 =$ _____
9. $15 \div 5 + (6 + 2) \, / \, 2 =$ _____
10. $15 - 3^2 + 5(2) =$ _____

SECTION 3 (Proportions: Fractions, Decimals, and Percentages)

1. Convert 0.42 into a fraction _____
2. Convert $\dfrac{6}{10}$ into a decimal _____
3. Convert $\dfrac{4}{5}$ into a percentage _____
4. $\dfrac{6}{13} + \dfrac{4}{13} =$ _____
5. $0.8 \times 0.42 =$ _____
6. 40% of 120 = _____
7. $\dfrac{2}{7} + \dfrac{2}{5} =$ _____
8. $\dfrac{2}{5} \times 80 =$ _____
9. $\dfrac{1}{4} \div \dfrac{1}{3} =$ _____
10. $\dfrac{4}{7} \times \dfrac{5}{9} =$ _____

SECTION 4 (Solving Equations with a Single Unknown Variable)

1. $5X - 13 = 7$ _____
2. $3(X - 2) = 9$ _____
3. $X \, / \, 3 + 2 = 10$ _____
4. $X(-3) + 2 = -16$ _____
5. $X(6 - 4) + 3 = 15$ _____

6. $X / 4 + 3 = 6$ _____

7. $3X + (-9) / (-3) = 24$ _____

8. $9 + X / 4 = 12$ _____

9. $4X - 5 = 19$ _____

10. $5 + (-2) + 3X = 9$ _____

A.2 Symbols and Notation: Arithmetic Operations

SYMBOLS AND NOTATION

The basic mathematical symbols used throughout this book are located in Table A.1. These include the most common arithmetic operations, and most of you will find that you are familiar with them. However, it is worth your time to review the reference table and material that outline the operations using positive and negative numbers. For those of you who have spent little time solving math equations recently, familiarizing yourselves with this material can help you avoid making common mistakes.

TABLE A-1	Symbols and Notations	
$+$	Addition	$8 + 3 = 11$
$-$	Subtraction	$14 - 6 = 8$
$\times, (\,)$	Multiplication	$4 \times 3 = 12, 4(3) = 12$
$\div, /$	Division	$12 \div 6 = 2, 12/6 = 2$
$>$	Greater than	$7 > 5$
$<$	Less than	$4 < 9$
$\geq$	Greater than or equal to	$7 \geq 5, 4 \geq 4$
$\leq$	Less than or equal to	$5 \leq 9, 6 \leq 6$
$\neq$	Not equal to	$5 \neq 3$

ARITHMETIC OPERATIONS: Worked Examples

Adding, Subtracting, Multiplying, and Dividing with Positive and Negative Numbers

1. Adding with positive numbers: Add the two (or series of) numbers to produce a sum.
   a. $4 + 7 = 11$
   b. $7 + 4 + 9 = 20$
   c. $4 + 6 + 7 + 2 = 19$

2. Adding with negative numbers: Sum the absolute values of each number and place a negative sign in front of the sum. (*Hint:* When a positive sign directly precedes a negative sign, change both signs to a single negative sign.)
   a. $-6 + (-4) = -10$
      $-6 - 4 = -10$
   b. $-3 + (-2) = -5$
      $-3 - 2 = -5$

3. Adding two numbers with opposite signs: Find the difference between the two numbers and assign the sign (positive or negative) of the larger number to the answer.
   a. $17 + (-9) = 8$
   b. $-16 + 10 = -6$

4. Subtracting one number from another number. (*Hint:* When subtracting a negative number from another number, two negative signs come in sequence, as in part (a). To solve the equations, change the two sequential negative signs into a single positive sign.)
   a. $5 - (-4) = 9$
      $5 + 4 = 9$
   b. $5 - 8 = -3$
   c. $-6 - 3 = -9$

5. Multiplying two positive numbers produces a positive result.
   a. $6 \times 9 = 54$
   b. $6(9) = 54$
   c. $4 \times 3 = 12$
   d. $4(3) = 12$

6. Multiplying two negative numbers produces a positive result.
   a. $-3 \times -9 = 27$
   b. $-3(-9) = 27$
   c. $-4 \times (-3) = 12$
   d. $-4(-3) = 12$

7. Multiplying one positive and one negative number produces a negative result.
   a. $-3 \times 9 = -27$
   b. $-3(9) = -27$
   c. $4 \times (-3) = -12$
   d. $4(-3) = -12$

8. Dividing two positive numbers produces a positive result.
   a. $12 \div 4 = 3$
   b. $12 / 4 = 3$
   c. $16 \div 8 = 2$
   d. $16 / 8 = 2$

9. Dividing two negative numbers produces a positive result.
   a. $-12 \div -4 = 3$
   b. $-12 / -4 = 3$
   c. $-16 \div (-8) = 2$
   d. $-16 / (-8) = 2$

10. Dividing a positive number by a negative number (or dividing a negative number by a positive number) produces a negative result.
    a. $-12 \div 4 = -3$
    b. $-12 / 4 = -3$
    c. $16 \div (-8) = -2$
    d. $16 / (-8) = -2$

SELF-QUIZ #1: Symbols and Notation: Arithmetic Operations

(Answers to this quiz can be found on page A-6.)

1. $4 \times 7 =$
2. $6 + 3 + 9 =$
3. $-6 - 3 =$
4. $-27 / 3 =$
5. $4(9) =$
6. $12 + (-5) =$
7. $16(-3) =$
8. $-24 / -3 =$
9. $75 \div 5 =$
10. $-7(-4) =$

A.3 Order of Operations

Equations and formulas often include a number of mathematical operations combining addition, subtraction, multiplication, and division. Some also include exponents and square roots. In complex equations with more than one operation, it is important to perform the operations in a specific sequence. Deviating from this sequence can produce a wrong answer. Table A.2 lists the order of operations for quick reference.

TABLE A-2   Order of Operations

Rule of Operation	Example
1. Complete any calculations within parentheses first.	1a. $(6 + 2) - 4 \times 3 / 2^2 + 6 =$ 1b. $8 - 4 \times 3 / 2^2 + 6 =$
2. Complete any squaring (or raising to another exponent) second.	2a. $8 - 4 \times 3 / 2^2 + 6 =$ 2b. $8 - 4 \times 3 / 4 + 6 =$
3. From left to right, complete all multiplication and division operations. This may require multiple steps.	3a. $8 - 4 \times 3 / 4 + 6 =$ 3b. $8 - 12 / 4 + 6 =$ 3c. $8 - 12 / 4 + 6 =$ 3d. $8 - 3 + 6 =$
4. Last, complete all the addition and subtraction operations.	4a. $8 - 3 + 6 =$ 4b. $5 + 6 =$ 4c. $11 = 11$

ORDER OF OPERATIONS:
Worked Examples

1. $-3 + 6(4) - 7 =$ Multiplication
   $-3 + 24 - 7 =$ Addition
   $21 - 7 =$ Subtraction
   $14 = 14$ Answer

2. $2(8) + 6 / 3 \times 8 =$ Multiplication
   $16 + 6 / 3 \times 8 =$ Division
   $16 + 2 \times 8 =$ Multiplication
   $16 + 16 =$ Addition
   $32 = 32$ Answer

3. $3^2 + 6 / 3 - 12(2) =$ Square (raise exponent)
   $9 + 6 / 3 - 12(2) =$ Division
   $9 + 2 - 12(2) =$ Multiplication
   $9 + 2 - 24 =$ Addition
   $11 - 24 =$ Subtraction
   $-13 = -13$ Answer

4. $(10 + 6) - 6^2 / 4 + 3(10) =$ Within parentheses
   $16 - 6^2 / 4 + 3(10) =$ Square (raise exponent)
   $16 - 36 / 4 + 3(10) =$ Division
   $16 - 9 + 3(10) =$ Multiplication
   $16 - 9 + 30 =$ Subtraction
   $7 + 30 =$ Addition
   $37 = 37$ Answer

5. $8 + (-4) + 3(12 - 8) =$ Within parentheses
   $8 + (-4) + 3(4) =$ Multiplication
   $8 + (-4) + 12 =$ Addition
   $4 + 12 =$ Addition
   $16 = 16$ Answer

SELF-QUIZ #2: Order of Operations
(Answers to this quiz can be found on page A-6.)

1. $3(7) - 12 / 3 + 2 =$
2. $4 / 2 + 6 - 2(3) =$
3. $-5(4) + 16 =$
4. $8 + (-16) / 4 =$
5. $6 - 3 + 5 - 3(5) + 10 =$
6. $4^2 / 8 - 4(3) + (8 - 3) =$
7. $(14 - 6) + 72 / 9 + 4 =$
8. $(54 - 18) / 4 + 7 \times 3 =$
9. $32 - 4(3 + 4) + 8 =$
10. $100 \times 3 - 87 =$

A.4 Proportions: Fractions, Decimals, and Percentages

A proportion is a part in relation to a whole. When we look at fractions, we understand the denominator (the bottom number) to be the number of equal parts that comprise the whole. The numerator represents the proportion of parts of that whole that are present. Fractions can be converted into decimals by dividing the numerator by the denominator. Decimals can then be converted into percentages by multiplying by 100 (Table A.3). It is important to use the percentage symbol (%) when differentiating decimals from percentages. Additionally, decimals are often rounded to the nearest hundredth before they are converted into a percentage.

TABLE A-3   Proportions: Converting Fractions to Decimals to Percentages

 $= 2/8$ $= 0.25$ $= 25\%$

 $= 5/8$ $= 0.625$ $= 62.5\%$ or 63%

 $= 10/20$ $= 0.50$ $= 50\%$

FRACTIONS

Equivalent Fractions

The same proportion can be expressed in a number of equivalent fractions. Equivalent fractions are found by multiplying both the numerator and the denominator by the same number.

$$\frac{1}{2} = \frac{2}{4} = \frac{6}{12} = \frac{30}{60}$$

In this case, we multiply each side of $\frac{1}{2}$ by 2 to reach the equivalent $\frac{2}{4}$, then by 3 to reach the equivalent $\frac{6}{12}$, then by 5 to reach the equivalent $\frac{30}{60}$. Or we could have multiplied the numerator and denominator of the original $\frac{1}{2}$ by 30 to reach our concluding $\frac{30}{60}$.

Fractions can also be reduced to a simpler form by dividing the numerator and denominator by the same number. Be sure to divide each by a number that will result in a whole number for both the numerator and the denominator.

$$\frac{25}{75} = \frac{5}{15} = \frac{1}{3}$$

By dividing each side by 5, the fraction was reduced from $\frac{25}{75}$ to $\frac{5}{15}$. By further dividing by 5, we reduce the fraction to its simplest form, $\frac{1}{3}$. Or we could have divided the numerator and denominator of the original $\frac{25}{75}$ by 25, resulting in the simplest expression of this fraction, $\frac{1}{3}$.

Adding and Subtracting Fractions with the Same Denominator

Finding equivalent fractions is essential to adding and subtracting two or more fractions. In order to add or subtract, each fraction must have the same denominator. If the two fractions already have the same denominator, add or subtract the numbers in the numerators only.

$$\frac{2}{7} + \frac{1}{7} = \frac{3}{7} \qquad \frac{4}{5} - \frac{3}{5} = \frac{1}{5}$$

In each of these instances, we are adding or subtracting from the same whole (or same pie, as in lines 1 and 2 of Table A.3). In the first equation, we are increasing our proportion of 2 by 1 to equal 3 pieces of the whole. In the second equation, we are reducing the number of proportions from 4 by 3 to equal just 1 piece of the whole.

Adding and Subtracting Fractions with Different Denominators

When adding or subtracting two proportions with different denominators, it is necessary to find a common denominator before performing the operation. It is often easiest to multiply each side (numerator and denominator) by the number equal to the denominator of the other fraction. This provides an easy route to finding a common denominator.

$$\frac{2}{5} + \frac{1}{6} =$$

Multiply the numerator and denominator of $\frac{2}{5}$ by 6, equaling $\frac{12}{30}$.
Multiply the numerator and denominator of $\frac{1}{6}$ by 5, equaling $\frac{5}{30}$.

$$\frac{12}{30} + \frac{5}{30} = \frac{17}{30}$$

Multiplying Fractions

When multiplying fractions, it is not necessary to find common denominators. Just multiply the two numerators in each fraction and the two denominators in each fraction.

$$\frac{4}{7} \times \frac{5}{8} = \frac{(4 \times 5)}{(7 \times 8)} = \frac{20}{56}$$

(*Note:* This fraction can be reduced to a simpler equivalent by dividing both the numerator and denominator by 4. The result is $\frac{5}{14}$.)

Dividing Fractions

When dividing a fraction by another fraction, invert the second fraction and multiply as above.

$$\frac{1}{3} \div \frac{2}{3} = \frac{1}{3} \times \frac{3}{2} = \frac{(1 \times 3)}{(3 \times 2)} = \frac{3}{6}$$

(*Note:* This can be reduced to a simpler equivalent by dividing both the numerator and denominator by 3. The result is one-half, $\frac{1}{2}$.)

SELF-QUIZ #3: Fractions

(Answers to this quiz can be found on page A-6.)

1. $\frac{2}{5} + \frac{1}{5} =$

2. $\frac{2}{7} \times \frac{4}{5} =$

3. $\frac{11}{15} - \frac{2}{5} =$

4. $\frac{3}{5} \div \frac{6}{8} =$

5. $\frac{3}{8} + \frac{1}{4} =$

6. $\frac{1}{8} \div \frac{4}{5} =$

7. $\frac{8}{9} - \frac{5}{9} + \frac{2}{9} =$

8. $\frac{2}{7} + \frac{1}{3} =$

9. $\frac{4}{15} \times \frac{3}{5} =$

10. $\frac{6}{7} - \frac{3}{4} =$

DECIMALS

Converting Decimals to Fractions

Decimals represent proportions of a whole, similar to fractions. Each decimal place represents a factor of 10. So the first decimal place represents a number over 10, the second decimal place represents a number over 100, the third decimal place represents a number over 1000, the fourth decimal place represents a number over 10,000, and so on.

To convert a decimal to a fraction, take the number as the numerator and place it over 10, 100, 1000, and so on based on how many numbers are to the right of the decimal point. For example:

$$0.6 = \frac{6}{10} \qquad 0.58 = \frac{58}{100}$$

$$0.926 = \frac{926}{1000} \qquad 0.7841 = \frac{7841}{10,000}$$

Adding and Subtracting Decimals

When adding or subtracting decimal points, it is necessary to keep the decimal points in a vertical line. Then add or subtract each vertical row as you normally would.

$$
\begin{array}{r}
3.83 \\
+1.358 \\
\hline
5.188
\end{array}
\qquad
\begin{array}{r}
4.4992 \\
-1.738 \\
\hline
2.7612
\end{array}
$$

Multiplying Decimals

Multiplying decimals requires two basic steps. First, multiply the two decimals just as you would any numbers, paying no concern to where the decimal point is located. Once you have completed that operation, add the number of places to the right of the decimal in each number and count off that many decimal points in the solution line. That is your answer, which you may round up to three decimal places (two for the final answer).

$$4.26 \text{ (two decimal places)}$$
$$\underline{\times\, 0.398} \text{ (three decimal places)}$$
$$3408$$
$$3834$$
$$\underline{1278}$$
$$1.69548 \text{ (five decimal places)}$$

$$0.532 \text{ (three decimal places)}$$
$$\underline{\times\, 0.8} \text{ (one decimal place)}$$
$$0.4256 \text{ (four decimal places)}$$

Dividing Decimals

When dividing decimals, it is easiest to multiply each decimal by the factor of 10 associated with the number of places to the right of the decimal point. So, if one of the numbers has two numbers to the right of the decimal point and the other number has one, each number should be multiplied by 100. For example:

$$0.7 \div 1.32 = \frac{0.7}{1.32}$$

Then multiply each side by the factor of 10 associated with the most spaces to the right of the decimal point in either number. In this case, that is 2, so we multiply each side by 100.

$$0.7 \times 100 = 70$$
$$1.32 \times 100 = 132$$

The new fraction is $\frac{70}{132}$, which we can solve: $70 \div 132 = 0.530$

SELF-QUIZ #4: Decimals

(Answers to this quiz can be found on page A-6.)

1. $1.83 \times 0.68 =$
2. $2.637 + 4.2 =$
3. $1.894 - 0.62 =$
4. $0.35 \div 0.7 =$
5. $3.419 \times 0.12 =$
6. $\dfrac{0.82}{1.74} =$
7. $0.125 \div 0.625 =$
8. $0.44 \times 0.163 =$
9. $0.8 + 1.239 =$
10. $13.288 - 4.46 =$

PERCENTAGES

Converting Percentages to Fractions or Decimals

Convert a percentage into a fraction by removing the percentage symbol and placing the number over a denominator of 100.

$$82\% = \frac{82}{100} \quad \text{or} \quad \frac{41}{50} \quad \text{or} \quad 0.82$$

$$20\% = \frac{20}{100} \quad \text{or} \quad \frac{1}{5} \quad \text{or} \quad 0.2$$

Multiplying with Percentages

In statistics, it is often necessary to determine the percentage of a whole number when analyzing data. To multiply with a percentage, convert the percentage to a decimal (see Table A.3) and solve the equation. To convert a percentage to a decimal, remove the percentage symbol and move the decimal point two places to the left.

$$80\% \text{ of } 45 = 80\% \times 45 = 0.80 \times 45 = 36$$
$$25\% \text{ of } 94 = 25\% \times 94 = 0.25 \times 94 = 23.5$$

SELF-QUIZ #5: Percentages

(Answers to this quiz can be found on page A-6.)

1. $45\% \times 100 =$
2. $22\% \text{ of } 80 =$
3. $35\% \text{ of } 90 =$
4. $80\% \times 23 =$
5. $58\% \times 60 =$
6. $32 \times 16\% =$
7. $125 \times 73\% =$
8. $24 \times 75\% =$
9. $69\% \text{ of } 224 =$
10. $51\% \times 37 =$

A.5 Solving Equations with a Single Unknown Variable

When solving equations with an unknown variable, isolate the unknown variable on one side of the equation. By isolating the variable, you free up the other side of the equation so you can solve it to a single number, which gives you the value of the variable.

To isolate the variable, add, subtract, multiply, or divide each side of the equation to solve the operations on the side of the equation that contains the variable (Table A.4).

TABLE A-4	Solving Equations with a Single Variable
Addition $$X + 7 = 18$$ $$X + 7 - 7 = 18 - 7$$ $$X = 11$$	Subtracting 7 from each side zeros the addition operation.
Subtraction $$X - 13 = 27$$ $$X - 13 + 13 = 27 + 13$$ $$X = 40$$	Adding 13 to each side zeros the subtraction operation.
Multiplication $$X \times 5 = 20$$ $$X \times 5 / 5 = 20 / 5$$ $$X = 4$$	Dividing each side by 5 zeros the multiplication operation.
Division $$X / 5 = 40$$ $$X / 5 \times 5 = 40 \times 5$$ $$X = 200$$	Multiplying each side by 5 zeros the division operation.
Multiple Operations $$4X + 6 = 18$$ $$4X + 6 - 6 = 18 - 6$$ $$4X = 12$$ $$4X / 4 = 12 / 4$$ $$X = 3$$	When isolating a variable, work *backward* through the order of operations (see Table A.2). Isolate addition and subtraction operations first. Then isolate operations for multiplication and division.

SOLVING EQUATIONS WITH A SINGLE UNKNOWN VARIABLE: Worked Examples

1.
$$X + 12 = 42$$
$$X + 12 - 12 = 42 - 12$$
$$X = 30$$

2.
$$X - 13 = -5$$
$$X - 13 + 13 = -5 + 13$$
$$X = 8$$

3.
$$(X - 3) / 6 = 2$$
$$(X - 3) / 6 \times 6 = 2 \times 6$$
$$X - 3 = 12$$
$$X - 3 + 3 = 12 + 3$$
$$X = 15$$

4.
$$(3X + 4) / 2 = 8$$
$$(3X + 4) / 2 \times 2 = 8 \times 2$$
$$3X + 4 = 16$$
$$3X + 4 - 4 = 16 - 4$$
$$3X = 12$$
$$3X / 3 = 12 / 3$$
$$X = 4$$

5.
$$(X - 2) / 3 = 7$$
$$(X - 2) / 3 \times 3 = 7 \times 3$$
$$X - 2 = 21$$
$$X - 2 + 2 = 21 + 2$$
$$X = 23$$

SELF-QUIZ #6: Solving Equations with a Single Unknown Variable

(Answers to this quiz can be found in the right column.)

1. $7X = 42$

$X =$

2. $87 - X + 16 = 57$

$X =$

3. $X - 17 = -6$

$X =$

4. $5X - 4 = 21$

$X =$

5. $X - 10 = -4$

$X =$

6. $X / 8 = 20$

$X =$

7. $(X + 17) / 3 = 10$

$X =$

8. $2(X + 4) = 24$

$X =$

9. $X(3 + 12) - 20 = 40$

$X =$

10. $34 - X / 6 = 27$

$X =$

A.6 Answers to Diagnostic Test and Self-Quizzes

Answers to Diagnostic Test

Section 1
1. 28;   **2.** −24;   **3.** 29;   **4.** 48;   **5.** −4;   **6.** 19;   **7.** 4;   **8.** 18;   **9.** −14;   **10.** 7

Section 2
1. 0;   **2.** 28;   **3.** −1;   **4.** 16;   **5.** 20;   **6.** 16;   **7.** −4;   **8.** 2;   **9.** 7;   **10.** 16

Section 3
1. $\dfrac{42}{100}$ or $\dfrac{21}{50}$;   **2.** 0.6;   **3.** 80%;   **4.** $\dfrac{10}{13}$;   **5.** 0.336;   **6.** 48;

7. $\dfrac{24}{35}$;   **8.** 32;   **9.** $\dfrac{3}{4}$;   **10.** $\dfrac{20}{63}$

Section 4
1. 4;   **2.** 5;   **3.** 24;   **4.** 6;   **5.** 6;   **6.** 12;   **7.** 7;   **8.** 12;   **9.** 6;   **10.** 2

Answers for Self-Quiz #1: Symbols and Notation
1. 28;   **2.** 18;   **3.** −9;   **4.** −9;   **5.** 36;   **6.** 7;   **7.** −48;   **8.** 8;   **9.** 15;   **10.** 28

Answers for Self-Quiz #2: Order of Operations
1. 19;   **2.** 2;   **3.** −4;   **4.** 4;   **5.** 3;   **6.** −5;   **7.** 20;   **8.** 30;   **9.** 12;   **10.** 213

Answers for Self-Quiz #3: Fractions
1. $\dfrac{3}{5}$;   **2.** $\dfrac{8}{35}$;   **3.** $\dfrac{1}{3}$ or $\dfrac{5}{15}$ or $\dfrac{25}{75}$;   **4.** $\dfrac{24}{30}$ or $\dfrac{4}{5}$;   **5.** $\dfrac{5}{8}$;

6. $\dfrac{5}{32}$;   **7.** $\dfrac{5}{9}$;   **8.** $\dfrac{13}{21}$;   **9.** $\dfrac{12}{75}$ or $\dfrac{4}{25}$;   **10.** $\dfrac{3}{28}$

Answers for Self-Quiz #4: Decimals
1. 1.244;   **2.** 6.837;   **3.** 1.274;   **4.** $\dfrac{35}{70}$ or $\dfrac{1}{2}$ or 0.5;   **5.** 0.41028;

6. $\dfrac{82}{174}$ or $\dfrac{41}{87}$ or 0.47;   **7.** $\dfrac{125}{625}$ or $\dfrac{1}{5}$ or 0.2;   **8.** 0.07172;   **9.** 2.039;   **10.** 8.828

Answers for Self-Quiz #5: Percentages
1. 45;   **2.** 17.6;   **3.** 31.5;   **4.** 18.4;   **5.** 34.8;   **6.** 5.12;   **7.** 91.25;   **8.** 18;   **9.** 154.56;   **10.** 18.87

Answers for Self-Quiz #6: Solving Equations with a Single Unknown Variable
1. 6;   **2.** 46;   **3.** 11;   **4.** 5;   **5.** 6;   **6.** 160;   **7.** 13;   **8.** 8;   **9.** 4;   **10.** 42

Appendix B

STATISTICAL TABLES

TABLE B-I	The z Distribution

Normal curve columns represent percentages between the mean and the z scores and percentages beyond the z scores in the tail.

z	% Mean to z	% in Tail	z	% Mean to z	% in Tail
0.00	0.00	50.00	0.25	9.87	40.13
0.01	0.40	49.60	0.26	10.26	39.74
0.02	0.80	49.20	0.27	10.64	39.36
0.03	1.20	48.80	0.28	11.03	38.97
0.04	1.60	48.40	0.29	11.41	38.59
0.05	1.99	48.01	0.30	11.79	38.21
0.06	2.39	47.61	0.31	12.17	37.83
0.07	2.79	47.21	0.32	12.55	37.45
0.08	3.19	46.81	0.33	12.93	37.07
0.09	3.59	46.41	0.34	13.31	36.69
0.10	3.98	46.02	0.35	13.68	36.32
0.11	4.38	45.62	0.36	14.06	35.94
0.12	4.78	45.22	0.37	14.43	35.57
0.13	5.17	44.83	0.38	14.80	35.20
0.14	5.57	44.43	0.39	15.17	34.83
0.15	5.96	44.04	0.40	15.54	34.46
0.16	6.36	43.64	0.41	15.91	34.09
0.17	6.75	43.25	0.42	16.28	33.72
0.18	7.14	42.86	0.43	16.64	33.36
0.19	7.53	42.47	0.44	17.00	33.00
0.20	7.93	42.07	0.45	17.36	32.64
0.21	8.32	41.68	0.46	17.72	32.28
0.22	8.71	41.29	0.47	18.08	31.92
0.23	9.10	40.90	0.48	18.44	31.56
0.24	9.48	40.52	0.49	18.79	31.21

z	% Mean to z	% in Tail	z	% Mean to z	% in Tail
0.50	19.15	30.85	0.90	31.59	18.41
0.51	19.50	30.50	0.91	31.86	18.14
0.52	19.85	30.15	0.92	32.12	17.88
0.53	20.19	29.81	0.93	32.38	17.62
0.54	20.54	29.46	0.94	32.64	17.36
0.55	20.88	29.12	0.95	32.89	17.11
0.56	21.23	28.77	0.96	33.15	16.85
0.57	21.57	28.43	0.97	33.40	16.60
0.58	21.90	28.10	0.98	33.65	16.35
0.59	22.24	27.76	0.99	33.89	16.11
0.60	22.57	27.43	1.00	34.13	15.87
0.61	22.91	27.09	1.01	34.38	15.62
0.62	23.24	26.76	1.02	34.61	15.39
0.63	23.57	26.43	1.03	34.85	15.15
0.64	23.89	26.11	1.04	35.08	14.92
0.65	24.22	25.78	1.05	35.31	14.69
0.66	24.54	25.46	1.06	35.54	14.46
0.67	24.86	25.14	1.07	35.77	14.23
0.68	25.17	24.83	1.08	35.99	14.01
0.69	25.49	24.51	1.09	36.21	13.79
0.70	25.80	24.20	1.10	36.43	13.57
0.71	26.11	23.89	1.11	36.65	13.35
0.72	26.42	23.58	1.12	36.86	13.14
0.73	26.73	23.27	1.13	37.08	12.92
0.74	27.04	22.96	1.14	37.29	12.71
0.75	27.34	22.66	1.15	37.49	12.51
0.76	27.64	22.36	1.16	37.70	12.30
0.77	27.94	22.06	1.17	37.90	12.10
0.78	28.23	21.77	1.18	38.10	11.90
0.79	28.52	21.48	1.19	38.30	11.70
0.80	28.81	21.19	1.20	38.49	11.51
0.81	29.10	20.90	1.21	38.69	11.31
0.82	29.39	20.61	1.22	38.88	11.12
0.83	29.67	20.33	1.23	39.07	10.93
0.84	29.95	20.05	1.24	39.25	10.75
0.85	30.23	19.77	1.25	39.44	10.56
0.86	30.51	19.49	1.26	39.62	10.38
0.87	30.78	19.22	1.27	39.80	10.20
0.88	31.06	18.94	1.28	39.97	10.03
0.89	31.33	18.67	1.29	40.15	9.85

z	% Mean to z	% in Tail	z	% Mean to z	% in Tail
1.30	40.32	9.68	1.70	45.54	4.46
1.31	40.49	9.51	1.71	45.64	4.36
1.32	40.66	9.34	1.72	45.73	4.27
1.33	40.82	9.18	1.73	45.82	4.18
1.34	40.99	9.01	1.74	45.91	4.09
1.35	41.15	8.85	1.75	45.99	4.01
1.36	41.31	8.69	1.76	46.08	3.92
1.37	41.47	8.53	1.77	46.16	3.84
1.38	41.62	8.38	1.78	46.25	3.75
1.39	41.77	8.23	1.79	46.33	3.67
1.40	41.92	8.08	1.80	46.41	3.59
1.41	42.07	7.93	1.81	46.49	3.51
1.42	42.22	7.78	1.82	46.56	3.44
1.43	42.36	7.64	1.83	46.64	3.36
1.44	42.51	7.49	1.84	46.71	3.29
1.45	42.65	7.35	1.85	46.78	3.22
1.46	42.79	7.21	1.86	46.86	3.14
1.47	42.92	7.08	1.87	46.93	3.07
1.48	43.06	6.94	1.88	46.99	3.01
1.49	43.19	6.81	1.89	47.06	2.94
1.50	43.32	6.68	1.90	47.13	2.87
1.51	43.45	6.55	1.91	47.19	2.81
1.52	43.57	6.43	1.92	47.26	2.74
1.53	43.70	6.30	1.93	47.32	2.68
1.54	43.82	6.18	1.94	47.38	2.62
1.55	43.94	6.06	1.95	47.44	2.56
1.56	44.06	5.94	1.96	47.50	2.50
1.57	44.18	5.82	1.97	47.56	2.44
1.58	44.29	5.71	1.98	47.61	2.39
1.59	44.41	5.59	1.99	47.67	2.33
1.60	44.52	5.48	2.00	47.72	2.28
1.61	44.63	5.37	2.01	47.78	2.22
1.62	44.74	5.26	2.02	47.83	2.17
1.63	44.84	5.16	2.03	47.88	2.12
1.64	44.95	5.05	2.04	47.93	2.07
1.65	45.05	4.95	2.05	47.98	2.02
1.66	45.15	4.85	2.06	48.03	1.97
1.67	45.25	4.75	2.07	48.08	1.92
1.68	45.35	4.65	2.08	48.12	1.88
1.69	45.45	4.55	2.09	48.17	1.83

z	% Mean to z	% in Tail	z	% Mean to z	% in Tail
2.10	48.21	1.79	2.50	49.38	0.62
2.11	48.26	1.74	2.51	49.40	0.60
2.12	48.30	1.70	2.52	49.41	0.59
2.13	48.34	1.66	2.53	49.43	0.57
2.14	48.38	1.62	2.54	49.45	0.55
2.15	48.42	1.58	2.55	49.46	0.54
2.16	48.46	1.54	2.56	49.48	0.52
2.17	48.50	1.50	2.57	49.49	0.51
2.18	48.54	1.46	2.58	49.51	0.49
2.19	48.57	1.43	2.59	49.52	0.48
2.20	48.61	1.39	2.60	49.53	0.47
2.21	48.64	1.36	2.61	49.55	0.45
2.22	48.68	1.32	2.62	49.56	0.44
2.23	48.71	1.29	2.63	49.57	0.43
2.24	48.75	1.25	2.64	49.59	0.41
2.25	48.78	1.22	2.65	49.60	0.40
2.26	48.81	1.19	2.66	49.61	0.39
2.27	48.84	1.16	2.67	49.62	0.38
2.28	48.87	1.13	2.68	49.63	0.37
2.29	48.90	1.10	2.69	49.64	0.36
2.30	48.93	1.07	2.70	49.65	0.35
2.31	48.96	1.04	2.71	49.66	0.34
2.32	48.98	1.02	2.72	49.67	0.33
2.33	49.01	0.99	2.73	49.68	0.32
2.34	49.04	0.96	2.74	49.69	0.31
2.35	49.06	0.94	2.75	49.70	0.30
2.36	49.09	0.91	2.76	49.71	0.29
2.37	49.11	0.89	2.77	49.72	0.28
2.38	49.13	0.87	2.78	49.73	0.27
2.39	49.16	0.84	2.79	49.74	0.26
2.40	49.18	0.82	2.80	49.74	0.26
2.41	49.20	0.80	2.81	49.75	0.25
2.42	49.22	0.78	2.82	49.76	0.24
2.43	49.25	0.75	2.83	49.77	0.23
2.44	49.27	0.73	2.84	49.77	0.23
2.45	49.29	0.71	2.85	49.78	0.22
2.46	49.31	0.69	2.86	49.79	0.21
2.47	49.32	0.68	2.87	49.79	0.21
2.48	49.34	0.66	2.88	49.80	0.20
2.49	49.36	0.64	2.89	49.81	0.19

TABLE B-1 continued

z	% Mean to z	% in Tail	z	% Mean to z	% in Tail
2.90	49.81	0.19	2.97	49.85	0.15
2.91	49.82	0.18	2.98	49.86	0.14
2.92	49.82	0.18	2.99	49.86	0.14
2.93	49.83	0.17	3.00	49.87	0.13
2.94	49.84	0.16	3.50	49.98	0.02
2.95	49.84	0.16	4.00	50.00	0.00
2.96	49.85	0.15	4.50	50.00	0.00

TABLE B-2 The *t* Distributions

 or

	One-Tailed Tests p level			Two-Tailed Tests p level		
df	0.10	0.05	0.01	0.10	0.05	0.01
1	3.078	6.314	31.821	6.314	12.706	63.657
2	1.886	2.920	6.965	2.920	4.303	9.925
3	1.638	2.353	4.541	2.353	3.182	5.841
4	1.533	2.132	3.747	2.132	2.776	4.604
5	1.476	2.015	3.365	2.015	2.571	4.032
6	1.440	1.943	3.143	1.943	2.447	3.708
7	1.415	1.895	2.998	1.895	2.365	3.500
8	1.397	1.860	2.897	1.860	2.306	3.356
9	1.383	1.833	2.822	1.833	2.262	3.250
10	1.372	1.813	2.764	1.813	2.228	3.170
11	1.364	1.796	2.718	1.796	2.201	3.106
12	1.356	1.783	2.681	1.783	2.179	3.055
13	1.350	1.771	2.651	1.771	2.161	3.013
14	1.345	1.762	2.625	1.762	2.145	2.977
15	1.341	1.753	2.603	1.753	2.132	2.947
16	1.337	1.746	2.584	1.746	2.120	2.921
17	1.334	1.740	2.567	1.740	2.110	2.898
18	1.331	1.734	2.553	1.734	2.101	2.879
19	1.328	1.729	2.540	1.729	2.093	2.861
20	1.326	1.725	2.528	1.725	2.086	2.846

TABLE B-2 continued

df	One-Tailed Tests p level			Two-Tailed Tests p level		
	0.10	0.05	0.01	0.10	0.05	0.01
21	1.323	1.721	2.518	1.721	2.080	2.832
22	1.321	1.717	2.509	1.717	2.074	2.819
23	1.320	1.714	2.500	1.714	2.069	2.808
24	1.318	1.711	2.492	1.711	2.064	2.797
25	1.317	1.708	2.485	1.708	2.060	2.788
26	1.315	1.706	2.479	1.706	2.056	2.779
27	1.314	1.704`	2.473	1.704	2.052	2.771
28	1.313	1.701	2.467	1.701	2.049	2.764
29	1.312	1.699	2.462	1.699	2.045	2.757
30	1.311	1.698	2.458	1.698	2.043	2.750
35	1.306	1.690	2.438	1.690	2.030	2.724
40	1.303	1.684	2.424	1.684	2.021	2.705
60	1.296	1.671	2.390	1.671	2.001	2.661
80	1.292	1.664	2.374	1.664	1.990	2.639
100	1.290	1.660	2.364	1.660	1.984	2.626
120	1.289	1.658	2.358	1.658	1.980	2.617
∞	1.282	1.645	2.327	1.645	1.960	2.576

TABLE B-3 The *F* Distributions

Within-Groups df	Significance (p) Level	Between-Groups Degrees of Freedom					
		1	2	3	4	5	6
1	0.01	4052	5000	5404	5625	5764	5859
	0.05	162	200	216	225	230	234
	0.10	*39.9*	*49.5*	*53.6*	*55.8*	*57.2*	*58.2*
2	0.01	98.50	99.00	99.17	99.25	99.30	99.33
	0.05	18.51	19.00	19.17	19.25	19.30	19.33
	0.10	*8.53*	*9.00*	*9.16*	*9.24*	*9.29*	*9.33*
3	0.01	34.12	30.82	29.46	28.71	28.24	27.91
	0.05	10.13	9.55	9.28	9.12	9.01	8.94
	0.10	*5.54*	*5.46*	*5.39*	*5.34*	*5.31*	*5.28*

Within-Groups df	Significance (p) Level	Between-Groups Degrees of Freedom					
		1	2	3	4	5	6
4	0.01	21.20	18.00	16.70	15.98	15.52	15.21
	0.05	7.71	6.95	6.59	6.39	6.26	6.16
	0.10	4.55	4.33	4.19	4.11	4.05	4.01
5	0.01	16.26	13.27	12.06	11.39	10.97	10.67
	0.05	6.61	5.79	5.41	5.19	5.05	4.95
	0.10	4.06	3.78	3.62	3.52	3.45	3.41
6	0.01	13.75	10.93	9.78	9.15	8.75	8.47
	0.05	5.99	5.14	4.76	4.53	4.39	4.28
	0.10	3.78	3.46	3.29	3.18	3.11	3.06
7	0.01	12.25	9.55	8.45	7.85	7.46	7.19
	0.05	5.59	4.74	4.35	4.12	3.97	3.87
	0.10	3.59	3.26	3.08	2.96	2.88	2.83
8	0.01	11.26	8.65	7.59	7.01	6.63	6.37
	0.05	5.32	4.46	4.07	3.84	3.69	3.58
	0.10	3.46	3.11	2.92	2.81	2.73	2.67
9	0.01	10.56	8.02	6.99	6.42	6.06	5.80
	0.05	5.12	4.26	3.86	3.63	3.48	3.37
	0.10	3.36	3.01	2.81	2.69	2.61	2.55
10	0.01	10.05	7.56	6.55	6.00	5.64	5.39
	0.05	4.97	4.10	3.71	3.48	3.33	3.22
	0.10	3.29	2.93	2.73	2.61	2.52	2.46
11	0.01	9.65	7.21	6.22	5.67	5.32	5.07
	0.05	4.85	3.98	3.59	3.36	3.20	3.10
	0.10	3.23	2.86	2.66	2.54	2.45	2.39
12	0.01	9.33	6.93	5.95	5.41	5.07	4.82
	0.05	4.75	3.89	3.49	3.26	3.11	3.00
	0.10	3.18	2.81	2.61	2.48	2.40	2.33
13	0.01	9.07	6.70	5.74	5.21	4.86	4.62
	0.05	4.67	3.81	3.41	3.18	3.03	2.92
	0.10	3.14	2.76	2.56	2.43	2.35	2.28
14	0.01	8.86	6.52	5.56	5.04	4.70	4.46
	0.05	4.60	3.74	3.34	3.11	2.96	2.85
	0.10	3.10	2.73	2.52	2.40	2.31	2.24

Within-Groups df	Significance (p) Level	Between-Groups Degrees of Freedom					
		1	2	3	4	5	6
15	0.01	8.68	6.36	5.42	4.89	4.56	4.32
	0.05	4.54	3.68	3.29	3.06	2.90	2.79
	0.10	3.07	2.70	2.49	2.36	2.27	2.21
16	0.01	8.53	6.23	5.29	4.77	4.44	4.20
	0.05	4.49	3.63	3.24	3.01	2.85	2.74
	0.10	3.05	2.67	2.46	2.33	2.24	2.18
17	0.01	8.40	6.11	5.19	4.67	4.34	4.10
	0.05	4.45	3.59	3.20	2.97	2.81	2.70
	0.10	3.03	2.65	2.44	2.31	2.22	2.15
18	0.01	8.29	6.01	5.09	4.58	4.25	4.02
	0.05	4.41	3.56	3.16	2.93	2.77	2.66
	0.10	3.01	2.62	2.42	2.29	2.20	2.13
19	0.01	8.19	5.93	5.01	4.50	4.17	3.94
	0.05	4.38	3.52	3.13	2.90	2.74	2.63
	0.10	2.99	2.61	2.40	2.27	2.18	2.11
20	0.01	8.10	5.85	4.94	4.43	4.10	3.87
	0.05	4.35	3.49	3.10	2.87	2.71	2.60
	0.10	2.98	2.59	2.38	2.25	2.16	2.09
21	0.01	8.02	5.78	4.88	4.37	4.04	3.81
	0.05	4.33	3.47	3.07	2.84	2.69	2.57
	0.10	2.96	2.58	2.37	2.23	2.14	2.08
22	0.01	7.95	5.72	4.82	4.31	3.99	3.76
	0.05	4.30	3.44	3.05	2.82	2.66	2.55
	0.10	2.95	2.56	2.35	2.22	2.13	2.06
23	0.01	7.88	5.66	4.77	4.26	3.94	3.71
	0.05	4.28	3.42	3.03	2.80	2.64	2.53
	0.10	2.94	2.55	2.34	2.21	2.12	2.05
24	0.01	7.82	5.61	4.72	4.22	3.90	3.67
	0.05	4.26	3.40	3.01	2.78	2.62	2.51
	0.10	2.93	2.54	2.33	2.20	2.10	2.04
25	0.01	7.77	5.57	4.68	4.18	3.86	3.63
	0.05	4.24	3.39	2.99	2.76	2.60	2.49
	0.10	2.92	2.53	2.32	2.19	2.09	2.03

Within-Groups df	Significance (p) Level	Between-Groups Degrees of Freedom					
		1	2	3	4	5	6
26	0.01	7.72	5.53	4.64	4.14	3.82	3.59
	0.05	4.23	3.37	2.98	2.74	2.59	2.48
	0.10	2.91	2.52	2.31	2.18	2.08	2.01
27	0.01	7.68	5.49	4.60	4.11	3.79	3.56
	0.05	4.21	3.36	2.96	2.73	2.57	2.46
	0.10	2.90	2.51	2.30	2.17	2.07	2.01
28	0.01	7.64	5.45	4.57	4.08	3.75	3.53
	0.05	4.20	3.34	2.95	2.72	2.56	2.45
	0.10	2.89	2.50	2.29	2.16	2.07	2.00
29	0.01	7.60	5.42	4.54	4.05	3.73	3.50
	0.05	4.18	3.33	2.94	2.70	2.55	2.43
	0.10	2.89	2.50	2.28	2.15	2.06	1.99
30	0.01	7.56	5.39	4.51	4.02	3.70	3.47
	0.05	4.17	3.32	2.92	2.69	2.53	2.42
	0.10	2.88	2.49	2.28	2.14	2.05	1.98
35	0.01	7.42	5.27	4.40	3.91	3.59	3.37
	0.05	4.12	3.27	2.88	2.64	2.49	2.37
	0.10	2.86	2.46	2.25	2.11	2.02	1.95
40	0.01	7.32	5.18	4.31	3.83	3.51	3.29
	0.05	4.09	3.23	2.84	2.61	2.45	2.34
	0.10	2.84	2.44	2.23	2.09	2.00	1.93
45	0.01	7.23	5.11	4.25	3.77	3.46	3.23
	0.05	4.06	3.21	2.81	2.58	2.42	2.31
	0.10	2.82	2.43	2.21	2.08	1.98	1.91
50	0.01	7.17	5.06	4.20	3.72	3.41	3.19
	0.05	4.04	3.18	2.79	2.56	2.40	2.29
	0.10	2.81	2.41	2.20	2.06	1.97	1.90
55	0.01	7.12	5.01	4.16	3.68	3.37	3.15
	0.05	4.02	3.17	2.77	2.54	2.38	2.27
	0.10	2.80	2.40	2.19	2.05	1.96	1.89
60	0.01	7.08	4.98	4.13	3.65	3.34	3.12
	0.05	4.00	3.15	2.76	2.53	2.37	2.26
	0.10	2.79	2.39	2.18	2.04	1.95	1.88

Within-Groups df	Significance (p) Level	Between-Groups Degrees of Freedom					
		1	2	3	4	5	6
65	0.01	7.04	4.95	4.10	3.62	3.31	3.09
	0.05	3.99	3.14	2.75	2.51	2.36	2.24
	0.10	2.79	2.39	2.17	2.03	1.94	1.87
70	0.01	7.01	4.92	4.08	3.60	3.29	3.07
	0.05	3.98	3.13	2.74	2.50	2.35	2.23
	0.10	2.78	2.38	2.16	2.03	1.93	1.86
75	0.01	6.99	4.90	4.06	3.58	3.27	3.05
	0.05	3.97	3.12	2.73	2.49	2.34	2.22
	0.10	2.77	2.38	2.16	2.02	1.93	1.86
80	0.01	6.96	4.88	4.04	3.56	3.26	3.04
	0.05	3.96	3.11	2.72	2.49	2.33	2.22
	0.10	2.77	2.37	2.15	2.02	1.92	1.85
85	0.01	6.94	4.86	4.02	3.55	3.24	3.02
	0.05	3.95	3.10	2.71	2.48	2.32	2.21
	0.10	2.77	2.37	2.15	2.01	1.92	1.85
90	0.01	6.93	4.85	4.01	3.54	3.23	3.01
	0.05	3.95	3.10	2.71	2.47	2.32	2.20
	0.10	2.76	2.36	2.15	2.01	1.91	1.84
95	0.01	6.91	4.84	4.00	3.52	3.22	3.00
	0.05	3.94	3.09	2.70	2.47	2.31	2.20
	0.10	2.76	2.36	2.14	2.01	1.91	1.84
100	0.01	6.90	4.82	3.98	3.51	3.21	2.99
	0.05	3.94	3.09	2.70	2.46	2.31	2.19
	0.10	2.76	2.36	2.14	2.00	1.91	1.83
200	0.01	6.76	4.71	3.88	3.41	3.11	2.89
	0.05	3.89	3.04	2.65	2.42	2.26	2.14
	0.10	2.73	2.33	2.11	1.97	1.88	1.80
1000	0.01	6.66	4.63	3.80	3.34	3.04	2.82
	0.05	3.85	3.00	2.61	2.38	2.22	2.11
	0.10	2.71	2.31	2.09	1.95	1.85	1.78
∞	0.01	6.64	4.61	3.78	3.32	3.02	2.80
	0.05	3.84	3.00	2.61	2.37	2.22	2.10
	0.10	2.71	2.30	2.08	1.95	1.85	1.78

TABLE B-4   The Chi-Square Distributions

df	Significance (p) Level		
	0.10	0.05	0.01
1	2.706	3.841	6.635
2	4.605	5.992	9.211
3	6.252	7.815	11.345
4	7.780	9.488	13.277
5	9.237	11.071	15.087
6	10.645	12.592	16.812
7	12.017	14.067	18.475
8	13.362	15.507	20.090
9	14.684	16.919	21.666
10	15.987	18.307	23.209

TABLE B-5   The q Statistic (Tukey HSD Test)

Within-Groups df	Significance (p) Level	k = Number of Treatments (Levels)										
		2	3	4	5	6	7	8	9	10	11	12
4	0.05	3.93	5.04	5.76	6.29	6.71	7.05	7.35	7.60	7.83	8.03	8.21
	0.01	6.51	8.12	9.17	9.96	10.58	11.10	11.54	11.92	12.26	12.57	12.84
5	0.05	3.64	4.60	5.22	5.67	6.03	6.33	6.58	6.80	6.99	7.17	7.32
	0.01	5.70	6.98	7.80	8.42	8.91	9.32	9.67	9.97	10.24	10.48	10.70
6	0.05	3.46	4.34	4.90	5.30	5.63	5.90	6.12	6.32	6.49	6.65	6.79
	0.01	5.24	6.33	7.03	7.56	7.97	8.32	8.61	8.87	9.10	9.30	9.48
7	0.05	3.34	4.16	4.68	5.06	5.36	5.61	5.82	6.00	6.16	6.30	6.43
	0.01	4.95	5.92	6.54	7.01	7.37	7.68	7.94	8.17	8.37	8.55	8.71
8	0.05	3.26	4.04	4.53	4.89	5.17	5.40	5.60	5.77	5.92	6.05	6.18
	0.01	4.75	5.64	6.20	6.62	6.96	7.24	7.47	7.68	7.86	8.03	8.18
9	0.05	3.20	3.95	4.41	4.76	5.02	5.24	5.43	5.59	5.74	5.87	5.98
	0.01	4.60	5.43	5.96	6.35	6.66	6.91	7.13	7.33	7.49	7.65	7.78
10	0.05	3.15	3.88	4.33	4.65	4.91	5.12	5.30	5.46	5.60	5.72	5.83
	0.01	4.48	5.27	5.77	6.14	6.43	6.67	6.87	7.05	7.21	7.36	7.49
11	0.05	3.11	3.82	4.26	4.57	4.82	5.03	5.20	5.35	5.49	5.61	5.71
	0.01	4.39	5.15	5.62	5.97	6.25	6.48	6.67	6.84	6.99	7.13	7.25

Within-Groups df	Signif-icance (p) Level	k = Number of Treatments (Levels)										
		2	3	4	5	6	7	8	9	10	11	12
12	0.05	3.08	3.77	4.20	4.51	4.75	4.95	5.12	5.27	5.39	5.51	5.61
	0.01	4.32	5.05	5.50	5.84	6.10	6.32	6.51	6.67	6.81	6.94	7.06
13	0.05	3.06	3.73	4.15	4.45	4.69	4.88	5.05	5.19	5.32	5.43	5.53
	0.01	4.26	4.96	5.40	5.73	5.98	6.19	6.37	6.53	6.67	6.79	6.90
14	0.05	3.03	3.70	4.11	4.41	4.64	4.83	4.99	5.13	5.25	5.36	5.46
	0.01	4.21	4.89	5.32	5.63	5.88	6.08	6.26	6.41	6.54	6.66	6.77
15	0.05	3.01	3.67	4.08	4.37	4.59	4.78	4.94	5.08	5.20	5.31	5.40
	0.01	4.17	4.84	5.25	5.56	5.80	5.99	6.16	6.31	6.44	6.55	6.66
16	0.05	3.00	3.65	4.05	4.33	4.56	4.74	4.90	5.03	5.15	5.26	5.35
	0.01	4.13	4.79	5.19	5.49	5.72	5.92	6.08	6.22	6.35	6.46	6.56
17	0.05	2.98	3.63	4.02	4.30	4.52	4.70	4.86	4.99	5.11	5.21	5.31
	0.01	4.10	4.74	5.14	5.43	5.66	5.85	6.01	6.15	6.27	6.38	6.48
18	0.05	2.97	3.61	4.00	4.28	4.49	4.67	4.82	4.96	5.07	5.17	5.27
	0.01	4.07	4.70	5.09	5.38	5.60	5.79	5.94	6.08	6.20	6.31	6.41
19	0.05	2.96	3.59	3.98	4.25	4.47	4.65	4.79	4.92	5.04	5.14	5.23
	0.01	4.05	4.67	5.05	5.33	5.55	5.73	5.89	6.02	6.14	6.25	6.34
20	0.05	2.95	3.58	3.96	4.23	4.45	4.62	4.77	4.90	5.01	5.11	5.20
	0.01	4.02	4.64	5.02	5.29	5.51	5.69	5.84	5.97	6.09	6.19	6.28
24	0.05	2.92	3.53	3.90	4.17	4.37	4.54	4.68	4.81	4.92	5.01	5.10
	0.01	3.96	4.55	4.91	5.17	5.37	5.54	5.69	5.81	5.92	6.02	6.11
30	0.05	2.89	3.49	3.85	4.10	4.30	4.46	4.60	4.72	4.82	4.92	5.00
	0.01	3.89	4.45	4.80	5.05	5.24	5.40	5.54	5.65	5.76	5.85	5.93
40	0.05	2.86	3.44	3.79	4.04	4.23	4.39	4.52	4.63	4.73	4.82	4.90
	0.01	3.82	4.37	4.70	4.93	5.11	5.26	5.39	5.50	5.60	5.69	5.76
60	0.05	2.83	3.40	3.74	3.98	4.16	4.31	4.44	4.55	4.65	4.73	4.81
	0.01	3.76	4.28	4.59	4.82	4.99	5.13	5.25	5.36	5.45	5.53	5.60
120	0.05	2.80	3.36	3.68	3.92	4.10	4.24	4.36	4.47	4.56	4.64	4.71
	0.01	3.70	4.20	4.50	4.71	4.87	5.01	5.12	5.21	5.30	5.37	5.44
∞	0.05	2.77	3.31	3.63	3.86	4.03	4.17	4.28	4.39	4.47	4.55	4.62
	0.01	3.64	4.12	4.40	4.60	4.76	4.88	4.99	5.08	5.16	5.23	5.29

TABLE B-6 The Pearson Correlation Coefficient

To be significant, the sample correlation coefficient, r, must be greater than or equal to the critical value in the table.

df = N − 2	Level of Significance for One-Tailed Test p level 0.05	0.01	df = N − 2	Level of Significance for Two-Tailed Test p level 0.05	0.01
1	0.988	0.9995	1	0.997	0.9999
2	0.900	0.980	2	0.950	0.990
3	0.805	0.934	3	0.878	0.959
4	0.729	0.882	4	0.811	0.917
5	0.669	0.833	5	0.754	0.874
6	0.622	0.789	6	0.707	0.834
7	0.582	0.750	7	0.666	0.798
8	0.549	0.716	8	0.632	0.765
9	0.521	0.685	9	0.602	0.735
10	0.497	0.658	10	0.576	0.708
11	0.476	0.634	11	0.553	0.684
12	0.458	0.612	12	0.532	0.661
13	0.441	0.592	13	0.514	0.641
14	0.426	0.574	14	0.497	0.623
15	0.412	0.558	15	0.482	0.606
16	0.400	0.542	16	0.468	0.590
17	0.389	0.528	17	0.456	0.575
18	0.378	0.516	18	0.444	0.561
19	0.369	0.503	19	0.433	0.549
20	0.360	0.492	20	0.423	0.537
21	0.352	0.482	21	0.413	0.526
22	0.344	0.472	22	0.404	0.515
23	0.337	0.462	23	0.396	0.505
24	0.330	0.453	24	0.388	0.496
25	0.323	0.445	25	0.381	0.487
26	0.317	0.437	26	0.374	0.479
27	0.311	0.430	27	0.367	0.471
28	0.306	0.423	28	0.361	0.463
29	0.301	0.416	29	0.355	0.456
30	0.296	0.409	30	0.349	0.449
35	0.275	0.381	35	0.325	0.418
40	0.257	0.358	40	0.304	0.393
45	0.243	0.338	45	0.288	0.372
50	0.231	0.322	50	0.273	0.354
60	0.211	0.295	60	0.250	0.325

TABLE B-6 continued

df = N − 2	Level of Significance for One-Tailed Test *p* Level		df = N − 2	Level of Significance for Two-Tailed Test *p* level	
	0.05	0.01		0.05	0.01
70	0.195	0.274	70	0.232	0.302
80	0.183	0.256	80	0.217	0.283
90	0.173	0.242	90	0.205	0.267
100	0.164	0.230	100	0.195	0.254

TABLE B-7 The Spearman Correlation Coefficient

To be significant, the sample correlation coefficient, r_s, must be greater than or equal to the critical value in the table.

N	Level of Significance for One-Tailed Test *p* level		N	Level of Significance for Two-Tailed Test *p* level	
	0.05	0.01		0.05	0.01
4	1.000	—	4	—	—
5	0.900	1.000	5	1.000	—
6	0.829	0.943	6	0.886	1.000
7	0.714	0.893	7	0.786	0.929
8	0.643	0.833	8	0.738	0.881
9	0.600	0.783	9	0.700	0.833
10	0.564	0.745	10	0.648	0.794
11	0.536	0.709	11	0.618	0.755
12	0.503	0.671	12	0.587	0.727
13	0.484	0.648	13	0.560	0.703
14	0.464	0.622	14	0.538	0.675
15	0.443	0.604	15	0.521	0.654
16	0.429	0.582	16	0.503	0.635
17	0.414	0.566	17	0.485	0.615
18	0.401	0.550	18	0.472	0.600
19	0.391	0.535	19	0.460	0.584
20	0.380	0.520	20	0.447	0.570
21	0.370	0.508	21	0.435	0.556
22	0.361	0.496	22	0.425	0.544
23	0.353	0.486	23	0.415	0.532
24	0.344	0.476	24	0.406	0.521
25	0.337	0.466	25	0.398	0.511
26	0.331	0.457	26	0.390	0.501
27	0.324	0.448	27	0.382	0.491
28	0.317	0.440	28	0.375	0.483

N	Level of Significance for One-Tailed Test p level 0.05	0.01	N	Level of Significance for Two-Tailed Test p level 0.05	0.01
29	0.312	0.433	29	0.368	0.475
30	0.306	0.425	30	0.362	0.467
35	0.283	0.394	35	0.335	0.433
40	0.264	0.368	40	0.313	0.405
45	0.248	0.347	45	0.294	0.382
50	0.235	0.329	50	0.279	0.363
60	0.214	0.300	60	0.255	0.331
70	0.190	0.278	70	0.235	0.307
80	0.185	0.260	80	0.220	0.287
90	0.174	0.245	90	0.207	0.271
100	0.165	0.233	100	0.197	0.257

TABLE B-8A Mann–Whitney U for a p Level of .05 for a One-Tailed Test

To be statistically significant, the smaller U must be equal to or less than the value in the table.

N_A/N_B	1	2	3	4	5	6	7	8	9	10	11	12	13	14	15	16	17	18	19	20
1	—	—	—	—	—	—	—	—	—	—	—	—	—	—	—	—	—	—	0	0
2	—	—	—	—	0	0	0	1	1	1	1	2	2	2	3	3	3	4	4	4
3	—	—	0	0	1	2	2	3	3	4	5	5	6	7	7	8	9	9	10	11
4	—	—	0	1	2	3	4	5	6	7	8	9	10	11	12	14	15	16	17	18
5	—	0	1	2	4	5	6	8	9	11	12	13	15	16	18	19	20	22	23	25
6	—	0	2	3	5	7	8	10	12	14	16	17	19	21	23	25	26	28	30	32
7	—	0	2	4	6	8	11	13	15	17	19	21	24	26	28	30	33	35	37	39
8	—	1	3	5	8	10	13	15	18	20	23	26	28	31	33	36	39	41	44	47
9	—	1	3	6	9	12	15	18	21	24	27	30	33	36	39	42	45	48	51	54
10	—	1	4	7	11	14	17	20	24	27	31	34	37	41	44	48	51	55	58	62
11	—	1	5	8	12	16	19	23	27	31	34	38	42	46	50	54	57	61	65	69
12	—	2	5	9	13	17	21	26	30	34	38	42	47	51	55	60	64	68	72	77
13	—	2	6	10	15	19	24	28	33	37	42	47	51	56	61	65	70	75	80	84
14	—	2	7	11	16	21	26	31	36	41	46	51	56	61	66	71	77	82	87	92
15	—	3	7	12	18	23	28	33	39	44	50	55	61	66	72	77	83	88	94	100
16	—	3	8	14	19	25	30	36	42	48	54	60	65	71	77	83	89	95	101	107
17	—	3	9	15	20	26	33	39	45	51	57	64	70	77	83	89	96	102	109	115
18	—	4	9	16	22	28	35	41	48	55	61	68	75	82	88	95	102	109	116	123
19	0	4	10	17	23	30	37	44	51	58	65	72	80	87	94	101	109	116	123	130
20	0	4	11	18	25	32	39	47	54	62	69	77	84	92	100	107	115	123	130	138

TABLE B-8B   Mann–Whitney U for a p Level of .05 for a Two-Tailed Test

To be statistically significant, the smaller U must be equal to or less than the value in the table.

N_A/N_B	1	2	3	4	5	6	7	8	9	10	11	12	13	14	15	16	17	18	19	20
1	—	—	—	—	—	—	—	—	—	—	—	—	—	—	—	—	—	—	—	—
2	—	—	—	—	—	—	—	0	0	0	0	1	1	1	1	1	2	2	2	2
3	—	—	—	—	0	1	1	2	2	3	3	4	4	5	5	6	6	7	7	8
4	—	—	—	0	1	2	3	4	4	5	6	7	8	9	10	11	11	12	13	13
5	—	—	0	1	2	3	5	6	7	8	9	11	12	13	14	15	17	18	19	20
6	—	—	1	2	3	5	6	8	10	11	13	14	16	17	19	21	22	24	25	27
7	—	—	1	3	5	6	8	10	12	14	16	18	20	22	24	26	28	30	32	34
8	—	0	2	4	6	8	10	13	15	17	19	22	24	26	29	31	34	36	38	41
9	—	0	2	4	7	10	12	15	17	20	23	26	28	31	34	37	39	42	45	48
10	—	0	3	5	8	11	14	17	20	23	26	29	33	36	39	42	45	48	52	55
11	—	0	3	6	9	13	16	19	23	26	30	33	37	40	44	47	51	55	58	62
12	—	1	4	7	11	14	18	22	26	29	33	37	41	45	49	53	57	61	65	69
13	—	1	4	8	12	16	20	24	28	33	37	41	45	50	54	59	63	67	72	76
14	—	1	5	9	13	17	22	26	31	36	40	45	50	55	59	64	67	74	78	83
15	—	1	5	10	14	19	24	29	34	39	44	49	54	59	64	70	75	80	85	90
16	—	1	6	11	15	21	26	31	37	42	47	53	59	64	70	75	81	86	92	98
17	—	2	6	11	17	22	28	34	39	45	51	57	63	67	75	81	87	93	99	105
18	—	2	7	12	18	24	30	36	42	48	55	61	67	74	80	86	93	99	106	112
19	—	2	7	13	19	25	32	38	45	52	58	65	72	78	85	92	99	106	113	119
20	—	2	8	13	20	27	34	41	48	55	62	69	76	83	90	98	105	112	119	127

TABLE B-9	Wilcoxon Signed-Ranks Test for Matched Pairs (T)

	Level of Significance (p level) for One-Tailed Test			Level of Significance (p level) for Two-Tailed Test	
N	0.05	0.01	N	0.05	0.01
5	0	—	5	—	—
6	2	—	6	0	—
7	3	0	7	2	—
8	5	1	8	3	0
9	8	3	9	5	1
10	10	5	10	8	3
11	13	7	11	10	5
12	17	9	12	13	7
13	21	12	13	17	9
14	25	15	14	21	12
15	30	19	15	25	15
16	35	23	16	29	19
17	41	27	17	34	23
18	47	32	18	40	27
19	53	37	19	46	32
20	60	43	20	52	37
21	67	49	21	58	42
22	75	55	22	65	48
23	83	62	23	73	54
24	91	69	24	81	61
25	100	76	25	89	68
26	110	84	26	98	75
27	119	92	27	107	83
28	130	101	28	116	91
29	140	110	29	126	100
30	151	120	30	137	109
31	163	130	31	147	118
32	175	140	32	159	128
33	187	151	33	170	138
34	200	162	34	182	148
35	213	173	35	195	159
36	227	185	36	208	171
37	241	198	37	221	182
38	256	211	38	235	194
39	271	224	39	249	207
40	286	238	40	264	220
41	302	252	41	279	233

TABLE B-9 continued

	Level of Significance (p level) for One-Tailed Test			Level of Significance (p level) for Two-Tailed Test	
N	0.05	0.01	N	0.05	0.01
42	319	266	42	294	247
43	336	281	43	310	261
44	353	296	44	327	276
45	371	312	45	343	291
46	389	328	46	361	307
47	407	345	47	378	322
48	426	362	48	396	339
49	446	379	49	415	355
50	466	397	50	434	373

TABLE B-10 Random Digits

19223	95034	05756	28713	96409	12531	42544	82853
73676	47150	99400	01927	27754	42648	82425	36290
45467	71709	77558	00095	32863	29485	82226	90056
52711	38889	93074	60227	40011	85848	48767	52573
95592	94007	69971	91481	60779	53791	17297	59335
68417	35013	15529	72765	85089	57067	50211	47487
82739	57890	20807	47511	81676	55300	94383	14893
60940	72024	17868	24943	61790	90656	87964	18883
36009	19365	15412	39638	85453	46816	83485	41979
38448	48789	18338	24697	39364	42006	76688	08708
81486	69487	60513	09297	00412	71238	27649	39950
59636	88804	04634	71197	19352	73089	84898	45785
62568	70206	40325	03699	71080	22553	11486	11776
45149	32992	75730	66280	03819	56202	02938	70915
61041	77684	94322	24709	73698	14526	31893	32592
14459	26056	31424	80371	65103	62253	50490	61181
38167	98532	62183	70632	23417	26185	41448	75532
73190	32533	04470	29669	84407	90785	65956	86382
95857	07118	87664	92099	58806	66979	98624	84826
35476	55972	39421	65850	04266	35435	43742	11937
71487	09984	29077	14863	61683	47052	62224	51025
13873	81598	95052	90908	73592	75186	87136	95761
54580	81507	27102	56027	55892	33063	41842	81868
71035	09001	43367	49497	72719	96758	27611	91596
96746	12149	37823	71868	18442	35119	62103	39244

96927	19931	36809	74192	77567	88741	48409	41903
43909	99477	25330	64359	40085	16925	85117	36071
15689	14227	06565	14374	13352	49367	81982	87209
36759	58984	68288	22913	18638	54303	00795	08727
69051	64817	87174	09517	84534	06489	87201	97245
05007	16632	81194	14873	04197	85576	45195	96565
68732	55259	84292	08796	43165	93739	31685	97150
45740	41807	65561	33302	07051	93623	18132	09547
27816	78416	18329	21337	35213	37741	04312	68508
66925	55658	39100	78458	11206	19876	87151	31260
08421	44753	77377	28744	75592	08563	79140	92454
53645	66812	61421	47836	12609	15373	98481	14592
66831	68908	40772	21558	47781	33586	79177	06928
55588	99404	70708	41098	43563	56934	48394	51719
12975	13258	13048	45144	72321	81940	00360	02428
96767	35964	23822	96012	94591	65194	50842	53372
72829	50232	97892	63408	77919	44575	24870	04178
88565	42628	17797	49376	61762	16953	88604	12724
62964	88145	83083	69453	46109	59505	69680	00900
19687	12633	57857	95806	09931	02150	43163	58636
37609	59057	66967	83401	60705	02384	90597	93600
54973	86278	88737	74351	47500	84552	19909	67181
00694	05977	19664	65441	20903	62371	22725	53340
71546	05233	53946	68743	72460	27601	45403	88692
07511	88915	41267	16853	84569	79367	32337	03316

Appendix C

SOLUTIONS TO END-OF-CHAPTER PROBLEMS

Chapter 1

1-1 Descriptive statistics organize, summarize, and communicate a group of numerical observations. Inferential statistics use sample data to make general estimates about the larger population.

1-3 The four types of variables are nominal, ordinal, interval, and ratio. A nominal variable is used for observations that have categories, or names, as their values. An ordinal variable is used for observations that have rankings (i.e., 1st, 2nd, 3rd) as their values. An interval variable has numbers as its values; the distance (or interval) between pairs of consecutive numbers is assumed to be equal. A ratio variable meets the criteria for interval variables but also has a meaningful zero point. Interval and ratio variables are both often referred to as scale variables.

1-5 Discrete variables can only be represented by specific numbers, usually whole numbers; continuous variables can take on any values, including those with great decimal precision (e.g., 1.597).

1-7 A confounding variable (also called a *confound*) is any variable that systematically varies with the independent variable so that we cannot logically determine which variable affects the dependent variable. Researchers attempt to control confounding variables in experiments by randomly assigning participants to conditions. The hope with random assignment is that the confounding variable will be spread equally across the different conditions of the study, thus neutralizing its effects.

1-9 An operational definition specifies the operations or procedures used to measure or manipulate an independent or dependent variable.

1-11 When conducting experiments, the researcher randomly assigns participants to conditions or levels of the independent variable. When random assignment is not possible, such as when studying something like gender or marital status, correlational research is used. Correlational research allows us to examine how variables are related to each other; experimental research allows us to make assertions about how an independent variable causes an effect in a dependent variable.

1-13 **a.** "This was an experiment." (not "This was a correlational study.")

b. "the independent variable of caffeine" (not "the dependent variable of caffeine")

c. "A university assessed the validity" (not "A university assessed the reliability")

d. "In a between-groups experiment" (not "In a within-groups experiment")

1-15 An outlier is a participant or observation that is very different from other observations in the study.

1-17 The sample is the 2500 Canadians who work out every week. The population is all Canadians.

1-19 The sample is the 100 customers who completed the survey. The population is all of the customers at the grocery store.

1-21 **a.** 73 people

b. All people who shop in grocery stores similar to the one where data were collected

c. Inferential statistic

d. Answer may vary, but here is one way that the amount of fruit and vegetable items purchased could be operationalized as a nominal variable: People could be labeled as having a "healthy diet" or an "unhealthy diet."

e. Answers may vary, but one way is to rank people according to how many fruits and vegetables they purchased, so that the person who purchased the most is ranked 1, the person who purchased the second most is ranked 2, and so on.

f. Answers may vary, but the number of items could be counted or weighed.

1-23 **a.** The independent variables are physical distance and emotional distance. The dependent variable is accuracy of memory.

b. There are two levels of physical distance (within 100 miles and 100 miles or farther) and three levels of emotional distance (knowing no one who was affected, knowing people who were affected but lived, and knowing someone who died).

c. Answers may vary, but accuracy of memory could be operationalized as the number of facts correctly recalled.

1-25 Both Miguel Induráin and Lance Armstrong could be considered outliers because their scores (number of consecutive wins) are extreme compared to the typical number of consecutive wins by Tour de France winners.

1-27 **a.** The average weight for a 10-year-old girl was 77.4 pounds in 1963 and nearly 88 pounds in 2002.

b. No; the CDC would not be able to weigh every single girl in the United States because it would be too expensive and time consuming.

c. It is a descriptive statistic because it is a numerical summary of a sample. It is an inferential statistic because the researchers drew conclusions about the population's average weight based on this information from a sample.

1-29 a. Ordinal

b. Scale

c. Nominal

1-31 a. Discrete

b. Continuous

c. Discrete

d. Discrete

1-33 a. The independent variables are temperature and rainfall. Both are continuous scale variables.

b. The dependent variable is experts' ratings. This is a discrete scale variable.

c. The researchers wanted to know if the wine experts are consistent in their ratings—that is, if they're reliable.

d. This observation would suggest that Robert Parker's judgments are valid. His ratings seem to be measuring what they intend to measure—wine quality.

1-35 a. *Forbes* is operationalizing earnings as all of a comedian's pretax gross income from all sources, provided that he earned the majority of his money from live performances.

b. Erin Gloria Ryan likely has a problem with this definition because not all comedians perform live as their primary source of income. In her article, she explains: "The *Forbes* list isn't a brofest because men 100% dominate the top echelons of comedy… [It] employs an outdated definition of what comedy is and who is earning money from it that is always going to skew male. The game is rigged."

c. *Forbes* could operationalize the earnings of comedians as pretax gross income, as they are already doing, *but* they could include all comedians, whether they earned most of their money from concerts, TV or Internet shows, movies, books, MP3 sales, or any other comedy-related source. This would remove the restriction that most income must come from concert sales. According to Ryan, this broader definition would have put Ellen DeGeneres in first place; she earned $53 million in 2013. Other female comedians who would have leaped onto this list include Sofia Vergara, Tina Fey, Amy Poehler, and Chelsea Handler.

1-37 a. An experiment requires random assignment to conditions. It would not be ethical to randomly assign some people to smoke and some people not to smoke, so this research had to be correlational.

b. Other unhealthy behaviors have been associated with smoking, such as poor diet and infrequent exercise. These other unhealthy behaviors might be confounded with smoking.

c. The tobacco industry could claim it was not the smoking that was harming people, but rather the other activities in which smokers tend to engage or fail to engage.

d. You could randomly assign people to either a smoking group or a nonsmoking group and assess their health over time.

1-39 a. Answers may vary, but one hypothesis could be "Charging for plastic bags increases the likelihood that a customer will bring his or her own bags."

b. You could observe the number of customers who bring their own bags at stores that do not charge for plastic bags and at other stores that do charge for plastic bags. You could

then determine the percentages of customers who bring their own bags in each situation.

c. You could randomly assign certain days of the week to charge for plastic bags, and other days to not charge for plastic bags. As in part (b), you could then determine the percentages of customers who bring their own bags in each situation.

1-41 a. The person who took 3 minutes would be considered an outlier because the person's response time was much more extreme than any of the response times exhibited by the other participants.

b. In this case, the researcher might look to see if the participant was slow on other experimental tasks as well or if there was some other independent evidence that the participant did not take the experimental task seriously.

1-43 a. Researchers could have randomly assigned some people who are HIV-positive to take the oral vaccine and other people who are HIV-positive not to take the oral vaccine. The second group would likely take a placebo.

b. This would have been a between-groups experiment because the people who are HIV-positive would have been in only one group: either vaccine or no vaccine.

c. This limits the researchers' ability to draw causal conclusions because the participants who received the vaccine may have been different in some way from those who did not receive the vaccine. There may have been a confounding variable that led to these findings. For example, those who received the vaccine might have had better access to health care and better sanitary conditions to begin with, making them less likely to contract cholera regardless of the vaccine's effectiveness.

d. The researchers might not have used random assignment because it would have meant recruiting participants, likely immunizing half, then following up with all of them. The researchers likely did not want to deny the vaccine to people who were HIV-positive because they might have contracted cholera and died without it.

1-45 a. A "good charity" is operationally defined as one that spends more of its money for the cause it is supporting and less for fundraising or administration.

b. The rating is a scale variable, as it has a meaningful zero point, has equal distance between intervals, and is continuous.

c. The tier is an ordinal variable, as it involves ranking the organizations into categories (1st, 2nd, 3rd, 4th, or 5th tier) and it is discrete.

d. The type of charity is a nominal variable, as it uses names or categories to classify the values (e.g., health and medical needs) and it is discrete.

e. Measuring finances is more objective and easier to measure than some of the criteria mentioned by Ord, such as importance of the problem and competency and honesty.

f. Charity Navigator's ratings are more likely to be reliable than GiveWell's ratings because they are based on an objective measure. It is more likely that different assessors would come up with the same rating for Charity Navigator than for GiveWell.

g. GiveWell's ratings are likely to be more valid than Charity Navigator's, provided that they can attain some level of reliability. GiveWell's more comprehensive rating system incorporates a better-rounded assessment of a charity.

h. This would be a correlational study because donation funds, the independent variable, would not be randomly assigned based on country but measured as they naturally occur.

i. This would be an experiment because the levels of donation funds, the independent variable, are randomly assigned to different regions to determine the effect on death rate.

Chapter 2

2-1 Raw scores are the original data, to which nothing has been done.

2-3 A frequency table is a visual depiction of data that shows how often each value occurred; that is, it shows how many scores are at each value. Values are listed in one column, and the numbers of individuals with scores at that value are listed in the second column. A grouped frequency table is a visual depiction of data that reports the frequency within each given interval, rather than the frequency for each specific value.

2-5 Bar graphs typically provide scores for nominal data, whereas histograms typically provide frequencies for scale data. Also, the categories in bar graphs do not need to be arranged in a particular order and the bars should not touch, whereas the intervals in histograms are arranged in a meaningful order (lowest to highest) and the bars should touch each other.

2-7 A histogram looks like a bar graph but is usually used to depict scale data, with the values (or midpoints of intervals) of the variable on the x-axis and the frequencies on the y-axis. A frequency polygon is a line graph, with the x-axis representing values (or midpoints of intervals) and the y-axis representing frequencies; a dot is placed at the frequency for each value (or midpoint), and the points are connected.

2-9 In everyday conversation, you might use the word *distribution* in a number of different contexts, from the distribution of food to a marketing distribution. A statistician would use *distribution* only to describe the way that a set of scores, such as a set of grades, is distributed. A statistician is looking at the overall pattern of the data—what the shape is, where the data tend to cluster, and how they trail off.

2-11 With positively skewed data, the distribution's tail extends to the right, in a positive direction, and with negatively skewed data, the distribution's tail extends to the left, in a negative direction.

2-13 A ceiling effect occurs when there are no scores above a certain value; a ceiling effect leads to a negatively skewed distribution because the upper part of the distribution is constrained.

2-15 A stem-and-leaf plot is much like a histogram in that it conveys how often different values in a data set occur. Also, when a stem-and-leaf plot is turned on its side, it has the same shape as a histogram of the same data set.

2-17 17.95% and 40.67%

2-19 0.10% and 96.77%

2-21 0.04, 198.22, and 17.89

2-23 The full range of data is 68 minus 2, plus 1, or 67. The range (67) divided by the desired seven intervals gives us an interval size of 9.57, or 10 when rounded. The seven intervals are: 0–9, 10–19, 20–29, 30–39, 40–49, 50–59, and 60–69.

2-25 Four countries had at least 30 volcanoes.

2-27 Serial killers would create positive skew, adding high numbers of murders to the data that are clustered around 1.

2-29 **a.** For the college population, the range of ages extends farther to the right (with a larger number of years) than to the left, creating positive skew.

b. The fact that youthful prodigies have limited access to college creates a sort of floor effect that makes low scores less possible.

2-31 **a.** The lines for each stem number need to be combined so that the new stem-and-leaf plot looks like this (the leaves for both 3s, 2s, 1s, and 0s need to be combined):

3 001333444455568888

2 003445778889

1 03688

0 15

b. This stem-and-leaf plot depicts a negatively skewed distribution.

2-33 **a.**

Percentage	Frequency	Percentage
10	1	5.26
9	0	0.00
8	0	0.00
7	0	0.00
6	0	0.00
5	2	10.53
4	2	10.53
3	4	21.05
2	4	21.05
1	5	26.32
0	1	5.26

b. In 10.53% of these schools, exactly 4% of the students reported that they wrote between 5 and 10 twenty-page papers that year.

c. This is not a random sample. It includes schools that chose to participate in this survey and opted to have their results made public.

d.

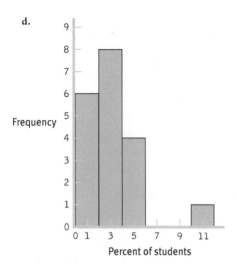

Percent of students

e. One

f. The data are clustered around 1% to 4%, with a high outlier, 10%.

2-35 a.

Interval	Frequency
80–84	7
75–79	9
70–74	5
65–69	3
60–64	3
55–59	2
50–54	1

b. There are many possible answers. One research hypothesis might be that the economic status of different regions of the world predicts life expectancies.

c.

Life expectancies

d.

Life expectancies

e. The data presented here demonstrate a negatively skewed distribution. There are more countries that have a life expectancy on the higher end—longer than 70 years—than there are in the rest of the distribution.

2-37 a. Extroversion scores are most likely to have a normal distribution. Most people would fall toward the middle, with some people having higher levels and some having lower levels.

b. The distribution of finishing times for a marathon is likely to be positively skewed. The floor is the fastest possible time, a little over 2 hours; however, some runners take as long as 6 hours or more. Unfortunately for the very, very slow but unbelievably dedicated runners, many marathons shut down the finish line 6 hours after the start of the race.

c. The distribution of numbers of meals eaten in a dining hall in a semester on a three-meal-a-day plan is likely to be negatively skewed. The ceiling is three times per day, multiplied by the number of days; most people who choose to pay for the full plan would eat many of these meals. A few would hardly ever eat in the dining hall, pulling the tail in a negative direction.

2-39

Numbers of television sets

2-41 a. A frequency polygon based on these data is likely to be negatively skewed. The scale is 1–10 and most films are rated above the midpoint. Very few are as low as *Gunday*.

b. There is more likely to be a ceiling effect. With most films earning high ratings, it seems that the limiting factor is the top score of 10. No film earned the lowest possible score of 1, and few were as low as *Gunday's* 1.4. So, there doesn't seem to be a floor effect of 1.

c. IMDb ratings don't seem to be a good way to operationalize movie quality. Audience ratings may be based on something other than how good the film is. In this case, many of those who rated *Gunday* based their scores on politics rather than on the qualities of the film itself. Another way to operationalize movie quality is a rating based on critics' reviews, such as the system used by rottentomatoes.com. This site provides an average rating from critics, based on published reviews, in addition to one by movie audiences. Critics are unlikely to rate a movie simply based on politics.

2-43 The stem-and-leaf plot is depicted below:

```
6 0
5 01367
4 002234489
3 13779
2 33567999
1 89
```

2-45 a.

Months	Frequency	Percentage
12	1	5
11	0	0
10	1	5
9	1	5
8	0	0
7	1	5
6	1	5
5	0	0
4	1	5
3	4	20
2	2	10
1	3	15
0	5	25

b.

c.

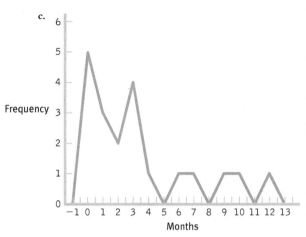

d.

Interval	Frequency
10–14 months	2
5–9 months	3
0–4 months	15

e.

f.

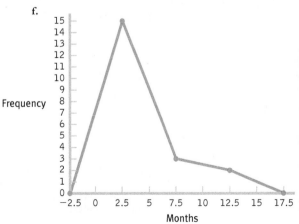

g. These data are centered around the 3-month period, with positive skew extending the data out to the 12-month period.

h. The bulk of the data would need to be shifted from the 3-month period to approximately 12 months, so the women who have breast-fed for 3 months so far might be the focus of attention. Perhaps early contact at the hospital and at follow-up visits after birth would help encourage mothers to breast-feed, and to breast-feed longer. One could also consider studying the women who create the positive skew to learn what unique characteristics or knowledge they have that influenced their behavior.

2-47 a.

Former Students Now in Top Jobs	Frequency	Percentage
13	1	1.85
12	0	0.00
11	0	0.00
10	0	0.00
9	1	1.85
8	3	5.56
7	4	7.41
6	5	9.26
5	9	16.67
4	8	14.81
3	23	42.59

b.

c.

d. This distribution is positively skewed.

e. The researchers operationalized the variable of mentoring success as numbers of students placed into top professorial positions. There are many other ways this variable could have been operationalized. For example, the researchers might have counted numbers of student publications while in graduate school or might have asked graduates to rate their satisfaction with their graduate mentoring experiences.

f. The students might have attained their positions as professors because of the prestige of their advisor, not because of his mentoring.

g. There are many possible answers to this question. For example, the attainment of a top professorial position might be predicted by the prestige of the institution, the number of publications while in graduate school, or the graduate student's academic ability.

Chapter 3

3-1 The five techniques for misleading with graphs are the biased scale lie, the sneaky sample lie, the interpolation lie, the extrapolation lie, and the inaccurate values lie.

3-3 Each dot on a scatterplot represents an individual's scores on two scale variables. It falls above the individual's score on the *x*-axis and across from the individual's score on the *y*-axis.

3-5 With scale data, a scatterplot allows for a helpful visual analysis of the relation between two variables. If the data points appear to fall approximately along a straight line, the variables may have a linear relation. If the data form a line that changes direction along its path, the variables may have a nonlinear relation. If the data points show no particular relation, it is possible that the two variables are not related.

3-7 A bar graph is a visual depiction of data in which the independent variable is nominal or ordinal and the dependent variable is scale. Each bar typically represents the mean value of the dependent variable for each category. A Pareto chart is a specific type of bar graph in which the categories along the *x*-axis are ordered from highest bar on the left to lowest bar on the right.

3-9 A pictorial graph is a visual depiction of data typically used for a nominal independent variable with very few levels (categories) and a scale dependent variable. Each level uses a picture or symbol to represent its value on the scale dependent variable. A pie chart is a graph in the shape of a circle, with a slice for every level. The size of each slice represents the proportion (or percentage) of each category. In most cases, a bar graph is preferable to a pictorial graph or a pie chart.

3-11 The independent variable typically goes on the horizontal *x*-axis and the dependent variable goes on the vertical *y*-axis.

3-13 Moiré vibrations are any visual patterns that create a distracting impression of vibration and movement. A grid is a background pattern, almost like graph paper, on which the data representations, such as bars, are superimposed. Ducks are features of the data that have been dressed up to be something other than merely data.

3-15 Like a traditional scatterplot, the locations of the points on the bubble graph simultaneously represent the values that a single case (or country) has on two scale variables. The graph as a whole depicts the relation between these two variables.

3-17 Total dollars donated per year is scale data. A time plot would nicely show how donations varied across years.

3-19 a. The independent variable is gender and the dependent variable is video game score.

b. Nominal

c. Scale

d. The best graph for these data would be a bar graph because there is a nominal independent variable and a scale dependent variable.

3-21 Linear, because the data could be fit with a line drawn from the upper-left to the lower-right corner of the graph.

3-23 a. Bar graph

b. Line graph; more specifically, a time plot

c. The y-axis should go down to 0.

d. The lines in the background are grids, and the three-dimensional effect is a type of duck.

e. 3.20%, 3.22%, 2.80%

f. If the y-axis started at 0, all of the bars would appear to be about the same height. The differences would be minimized.

3-25 The minimum value is 0.04 and the maximum is 0.36, so the axis could be labeled from 0.00 to 0.40. We might choose to mark every 0.05 value:

0.00 0.05 0.10 0.15 0.20 0.25 0.30 0.35 0.40

3-27 The relation between physical health and positive emotions seems to be positive, with the data fitting a line moving from the lower-left to the upper-right corner of the graph. As positive emotions increase, self-reported physical health also tends to increase.

3-29 a. For this study, the independent and dependent variables are scale because a numerical value represents each variable. For example, international representation is measured by how many countries are represented by the different authors for each journal article; impact score is measured using a scale that ranges from 0–30.

b. This graph is a scatterplot. A scatterplot is appropriate for this data because there are two scale variables of interest.

c. This graph demonstrates that there is a positive relation between impact score and the number of countries represented by the different authors, such that the more countries represented the higher the impact score. This graph demonstrates that there is linear relationship between the two variables.

3-31 a. The independent variable is country and the dependent variable is male suicide rate.

b. Country is a nominal variable and suicide rate is a scale variable.

c. The best graph for these data would be a bar graph or a Pareto chart. Because there are six categories or countries to list along the x-axis, it may be best to arrange them in order from highest to lowest using a Pareto chart.

d. A time series plot could show year on the x-axis and suicide rate on the y-axis. Each country would be represented by a different color line.

3-33 a.

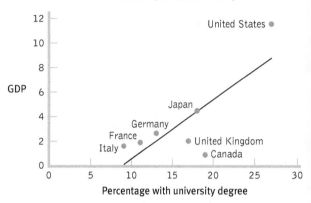

Relation Between Percentage with University Degree and GDP (in trillions of USD)

b. The percentage of residents with a university degree appears to be related to GDP. As the percentage with a university degree increases, so does GDP.

c. It is possible that an educated populace has the skills to make that country productive and profitable. Conversely, it is possible that a productive and profitable country has the money needed for the populace to be educated.

3-35 a. The independent variable is the subfield in psychology. The independent variable is a nominal variable because there are unique categories or levels. There are 10 different levels for the independent variable: clinical psychology, cognitive psychology, counseling psychology, developmental psychology, experimental psychology, industrial/organizational psychology, neuroscience, school psychology, social psychology, and other applied psychology.

b. The dependent variable is the overall acceptance rate. The dependent variable is a scale variable because there are numbers as the values. The units for the dependent variable is the percentage of number of people accepted into a specific doctoral program. The minimum value is 7% and the maximum value is 29%.

c. The default will differ, depending on which software is used. Here is one example.

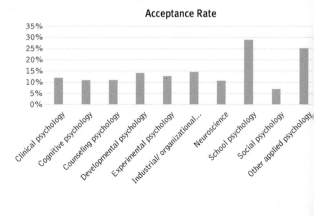

Acceptance Rate

d. The redesign will differ, depending on which software is used. In this example, we updated chart title, added the *x*-axis label, added to the *y*-axis label, rotated the *y*-axis label to read horizontally, removed the unnecessary lines in the background, added tick marks to the *y*-axis, and enlarged the *x*-axis so that "Industrial/organizational psychology" was not cut off.

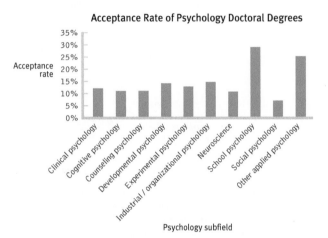

Acceptance Rate of Psychology Doctoral Degrees

e. Answers may vary. Here are some examples of potential follow-up research questions. What are the graduation rates for each subfield? How likely are graduates to get a job within each subfield? On average, how many years does each program take to complete? Are there differences in the number of credits, internship hours, and other requirements for each subfield? Are there gender differences in the applicant pool for each subfield?

f. Pictures could be used instead of bars. For example, using the Greek letter ψ (Psi) would be appropriate considering the data is about psychology doctoral programs and ψ is often used as a symbol for psychology.

g. If ψ becomes wider as it gets taller (to represent a higher acceptance rate), the overall size would be proportionally larger than the increase in donation rate it is meant to represent. A bar graph is not subject to this problem because graphmakers are not likely to make bars wider as they get taller.

3-37 a. One independent variable is time frame; it has two levels: 1945–1950 and 1996–1998. The other independent variable is type of graduate program; it also has two levels: clinical psychology and experimental psychology.

b. The dependent variable is percentage of graduates who had a mentor while in graduate school.

c.

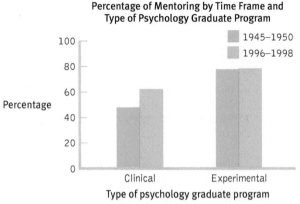

Percentage of Mentoring by Time Frame and Type of Psychology Graduate Program

d. These data suggest that clinical psychology graduate students were more likely to have been mentored if they were in school in the 1996–1998 time frame than if they were in school during the 1945–1950 time frame. There does not appear to be such a difference among experimental psychology students.

e. This was not a true experiment. Students were not randomly assigned to time period or type of graduate program.

f. A time series plot would be inappropriate with so few data points. It would suggest that we could interpolate between these data points. It would suggest a continual increase in the likelihood of being mentored among clinical psychology students, as well as a stable trend, albeit at a high level, among experimental psychology students.

g. The story based on two time points might be falsely interpreted as a continual increase of mentoring rates for the clinical psychology students and a plateau for the experimental psychology students. The expanded data set suggests that the rates of mentoring have fluctuated over the years. Without the four time points, we might be seduced by interpolation into thinking that the two scores represent the end points of a linear trend. We cannot draw conclusions about time points for which we have no data—especially when we have only two points, but even when we have more points.

3-39 a. The details will differ, depending on the software used. Here is one example.

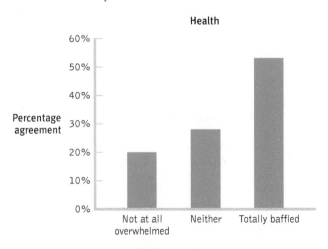

Health

b. The default options that students choose to override will differ. For the bar graph shown here, we changed the default settings by (1) adding a chart title, (2) adding a y-axis label, (3) rotating the y-axis label to read horizontally, (4) eliminating lines in the background, and (5) adding tick marks for the y-axis.

3-41 a. The graph is a scatterplot: individual points are identified for two scale variables—academic standing and "hotness."

b. The variables are academic standing and "hotness."

c. The graph could be redesigned to get rid of moiré vibrations, such as the colored background; the grid (the background pattern of graph paper); and the duck (the woman in the background image). In addition, the scoring on the x-axis could be reversed so that 0 indicated the lowest academic score and 100 indicated the highest academic score. It's more intuitive for a low number to match a low score, and for a high number to match a high score.

3-43 Each student's advice will differ. The following are examples of advice.

a. Business and women: Eliminate all the pictures, including the woman, piggy banks, the dollar signs in the background, and the icons to the right (e.g., house). The two bars near the top could mislead us into thinking they indicated quantities, even though they are the same length for two different median wages. Either eliminate the bars or size them so that they are appropriate to the dollars they represent. Ideally, the two median wages would be presented in a bar graph. Eliminate unnecessary words (e.g., "The Mothers of Business Invention").

b. Workforce participation: Eliminate all the pictures. A falling line in the art shown indicates an *increase* in percentage; notice that 40% is at the top and 80% is at the bottom. Make the y-axis go from highest to lowest, starting from 0. Make the lines easier to compare by eliminating the three-dimensional effect. Make it clear where the data point for each year falls by including a tick mark for each number on the x-axis.

3-45 a. The graph proposes that Type I regrets of action are initially intense but decline over the years, while Type II regrets of inaction are initially mild but become more intense over the years.

b. There are two independent variables: type of regret (a nominal variable) and age (a scale variable). There is one dependent variable: intensity of regrets (also a scale variable).

c. This is a graph of a theory. No data have been collected, so there are no statistics of any kind.

d. The story that this theoretical relation suggests is that regrets over things a person has done are intense shortly after the actual behavior but decline over the years. In contrast, regrets over things a person has not done but wishes they had are initially low in intensity but become more intense as the years go by.

3-47 a. These data tell us that most domestic Canadian students—59%—strongly agreed or somewhat agreed that international students have improved their universities' reputations. Far fewer—15%—strongly disagreed or somewhat disagreed with this statement, and 27% reserved judgment for some reason.

b. To understand this pie chart, we have to look back and forth between the label and each "pie slice" that it describes. We

then need to mentally compare the various percentages in the graph. A bar graph would allow for easier comparisons among the possible responses.

c.

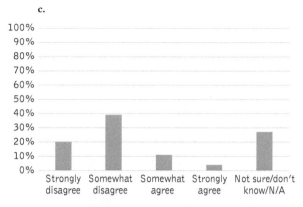

d. In this case, it makes sense to keep the possible responses in order from most negative to most positive (with the catch-all "other" category at the end). If we arranged the bars in order of height—somewhat disagree, not sure/don't know/N/A, strongly disagree, somewhat agree, and strongly agree—the story is not as easy to understand. This graph allows us to "see" that Canadian students tend to hold positive opinions toward the effect of international students on their universities' reputations.

3-49 a. The primary flaw in this graph is that it is very misleading. It looks like murders went down after "Stand Your Ground" but they actually went up. The y-axis is rotated 180 degrees, so that 0 is at the top of the graph, and 1,000 is at the bottom of the graph where the y-axis intersects with the x-axis.

b. Answers to this question should include revising the chart so that the y-axis begins with 0 at the point of intersection with the x-axis, adding a y-axis label, and reducing clutter by including fewer years along the x-axis.

3-51 a. Using the word cloud, we can see that "social life," "activities," and "health" are three top areas perceived to be related to well-being for participants. *Social life* is the largest word, and can be interpreted as the most frequently used term. "Activities" and "health" follow as the second and third most frequently discussed areas of well-being. Older adults want to have fun in addition to being healthy.

b. Based on this word cloud, further research questions might focus on specific elements of social life, such as activities. Additionally, further research might consider the importance of health in the context of well-being for communities of older adults.

3-53 a. The independent variable is song type, with two levels: romantic song and nonromantic song.

b. The dependent variable is dating behavior.

c. This is a between-groups study because each participant is exposed to only one level or condition of the independent variable.

d. Dating behavior was operationalized by giving one's phone number to an attractive person of the opposite sex. This may not be a valid measure of dating behavior, as we do not know if the participant actually intended to go on a date with the researcher. Giving one's phone number might not necessarily indicate an intention to date.

e. We would use a bar graph because there is one nominal independent variable and one scale dependent variable.

f. The default graph will differ, depending on which software is used. Here is one example:

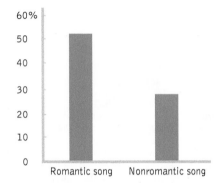

g. The default options that students choose to override will differ. Here is one example:

Percentage of Women Who Gave Phone Number Based on Song Type

Chapter 4

4-1 The mean is the arithmetic average of a group of scores; it is calculated by summing all the scores and dividing by the total number of scores. The median is the middle score of all the scores when a group of scores is arranged in ascending order. If there is no single middle score, the median is the mean of the two middle scores. The mode is the most common score of all the scores in a group of scores.

4-3 The mean takes into account the actual numeric value of each score. The mean is the mathematic center of the data. It is the center balance point in the data, such that the sum of the deviations (rather than the number of deviations) below the mean equals the sum of deviations above the mean.

4-5 The mean might not be useful in a bimodal or multimodal distribution because in these distributions the mathematical center of the distribution is not the number that describes what is typical or most representative of that distribution.

4-7 The mean is affected by outliers because the numeric value of the outlier is used in the computation of the mean. The median typically is not affected by outliers because its computation is based on the data in the middle of the distribution, and outliers lie at the extremes of the distribution.

4-9 The standard deviation is the typical amount each score in a distribution varies from the mean of the distribution.

4-11 The standard deviation is a measure of variability in terms of the values of the measure used to assess the variable, whereas the variance is squared values. Squared values simply don't make intuitive sense to us, so we take the square root of the variance and report this value, the standard deviation.

4-13 The range is the difference between the highest score and the lowest score in the data set. Thus, the range is completely driven by the most extreme scores in the data set and is susceptible to the effects of outliers. The interquartile range is based on the middle 50% of the data. Unlike the range, it is not affected by outliers.

4-15 The first quartile is the 25th percentile.

4-17 a. The mean is calculated:

$$M = \frac{\Sigma X}{N} = \frac{(15 + 34 + 32 + 46 + 22 + 36 + 34 + 28 + 52 + 28)}{10}$$
$$= \frac{327}{10} = 32.70$$

The median is found by arranging the scores in numeric order—15, 22, 28, 28, 32, 34, 34, 36, 46, 52—then dividing the number of scores, 10, by 2 and adding 1/2 to get 5.5. The mean of the 5th and 6th score in the ordered list of scores is the median—(32 + 34)/2 = 33—so 33 is the median.

The mode is the most common score. In these data, two scores appear twice, so we have two modes, 28 and 34.

b. Adding the value of 112 to the data changes the calculation of the mean in the following way:

(15 + 34 + 32 + 46 + 22 + 36 + 34 + 28 + 52 + 28 + 112)/11 = 439/11 = 39.91

The mean gets larger with this outlier.

There are now 11 data points, so the median is the 6th value in the ordered list, which is 34.

The modes are unchanged at 28 and 34.

This outlier increases the mean by approximately 7 values; it increases the median by 1; and it does not affect the mode at all.

c. The range is: $X_{highest} - X_{lowest} = 52 - 15 = 37$

The variance is: $SD^2 = \dfrac{\Sigma(X - M)^2}{N}$

We start by calculating the mean, which is 32.70. We then calculate the deviation of each score from the mean and the square of that deviation.

$$SD^2 = \frac{\Sigma(X - M)^2}{N} = \frac{1036.10}{10} = 103.61$$

X	X − M	(X − M)²
15	−17.70	313.29
34	1.30	1.69
32	−0.70	0.49
46	13.30	176.89
22	−10.70	114.49
36	3.30	10.89
34	1.30	1.69
28	−4.70	22.09
52	19.30	372.49
28	−4.70	22.09

The standard deviation is: $SD = \sqrt{SD^2}$ or

$$SD = \sqrt{\frac{\Sigma(X - M)^2}{N}} = \sqrt{103.61} = 10.18$$

4-19 a. The mean is calculated as:

$$M = \frac{\Sigma X}{N} = \frac{[-3.7 + (-1.7) + 5.9 + 16.4 + 29.5 + \ldots + 1.7]}{12}$$

$$= \frac{244.2}{12} = 20.35°F$$

The median is found by arranging the temperatures in numeric order:

$-3.7, -1.7, 1.7, 5.9, 13.6, 16.4, 24, 29.5, 34.6, 38.5, 42.1, 43.3$

There are 12 data points, so the mean of the 6th and 7th data points gives us the median: $(16.4 + 24)/2 = 20.20°F$.

b. The mean is calculated as:

$$M = \frac{\Sigma X}{N} = \frac{[47 + (-46) + (-38) + (-20) + \ldots + 46]}{12}$$

$$= \frac{-163}{12} = -13.58°F$$

The median is found by arranging the temperatures in numeric order:

$-47, -46, -46, -38, -20, -20, -5, -2, 8, 9, 20, 24$

There are 12 data points, so the mean of the 6th and 7th data points gives us the median: $[-20 + (-5)]/2 = -25/2 = -12.50°F$.

There are two modes: both −46 and −20 were recorded twice.

c. The mean is calculated as:

$$M = \frac{\Sigma X}{N} = \frac{[173 + 166 + 180 + \ldots + 178]}{12} = \frac{2022}{12}$$

$$= 168.50 \text{ mph}$$

The median is found by arranging the wind gusts in numeric order:

136, 142, 154, 161, 163, 164, 166, 173, 174, 178, 180, 231

There are 12 data points, so the mean of the 6th and 7th data points gives us the median: $(164 + 166)/2 = 165$ mph.

There is no mode among these wind gusts.

d. For the wind gust data, we could create 10 mph intervals and calculate the mode as the interval that occurs most often. There are four recorded gusts in the 160–169 mph interval, three in the 170–179 interval, and only one in the other intervals. So, the 160–169 mph interval could be presented as the mode.

e. The range is: $X_{highest} - X_{lowest} = 43.3 - (-3.7) = 47°F$

The variance is: $SD^2 = \dfrac{\Sigma(X - M)^2}{N}$

X	X − M	(X − M)²
−3.7	−24.05	578.403
−1.7	−22.05	486.203
5.9	−14.45	208.803
16.4	−3.95	15.603
29.5	9.15	83.723
38.5	18.15	329.423
43.3	22.95	526.703
42.1	21.75	473.063
34.6	14.25	203.063
24	3.65	13.323
13.6	−6.75	45.563
1.7	−18.65	347.823

We start by calculating the mean, which is 20.35°F. We then calculate the deviation of each score from the mean and the square of that deviation.

The variance is: $SD^2 = \dfrac{\Sigma(X - M)^2}{N} = \dfrac{3311.696}{12} = 275.975$

The standard deviation is: $SD = \sqrt{SD^2}$ or

$$SD = \sqrt{\frac{\Sigma(X - M)^2}{N}} = \sqrt{275.975} = 16.61°F$$

f. The range is $X_{highest} - X_{lowest} = 24 - (-47) = 71°F$

The variance is: $SD^2 = \dfrac{\Sigma(X - M)^2}{N}$

We already calculated the mean, $-13.583°F$. We now calculate the deviation of each score from the mean and the square of that deviation.

The variance is: $SD^2 = \dfrac{\Sigma(X-M)^2}{N} = \dfrac{7620.018}{12}$

$$= 635.077$$

X	$X-M$	$(X-M)^2$
-47	-33.417	1116.696
-46	-32.417	1050.862
-38	-24.417	596.190
-20	-6.417	41.178
-2	11.583	134.166
8	21.583	465.826
24	37.583	1412.482
20	33.583	1127.818
9	22.583	509.992
-5	8.583	73.668
-20	-6.417	41.178
-46	-32.417	1050.862

The standard deviation is: $SD = \sqrt{SD^2}$ or

$$SD = \sqrt{\dfrac{\Sigma(X-M)^2}{N}} = \sqrt{635.077} = 25.20°F$$

g. For the peak wind gust data, the range is $X_{highest} - X_{lowest} = 231 - 136 = 95$ mph

The variance is: $SD^2 = \dfrac{\Sigma(X-M)^2}{N}$

We start by calculating the mean, which is 168.50 mph. We then calculate the deviation of each score from the mean and the square of that deviation.

X	$X-M$	$(X-M)^2$
173	4.50	20.25
166	-2.50	6.25
180	11.50	132.25
231	62.50	3906.25
164	-4.50	20.25
136	-32.50	1056.25
154	-14.50	210.25
142	-26.50	702.25
174	5.50	30.25
161	-7.50	56.25
163	-5.50	30.25
178	9.50	90.25

The variance is: $SD^2 = \dfrac{\Sigma(X-M)^2}{N} = \dfrac{6261}{12} = 521.75$

The standard deviation is: $SD = \sqrt{SD^2}$ or

$$SD = \sqrt{\dfrac{\Sigma(X-M)^2}{N}} = \sqrt{520.75} = 22.82 \text{ mph}$$

4-21 Calculating the interquartile range requires that we order the observations from lowest to highest, find the first and third quartiles, and subtract the first from the third. Here are the data sorted from lowest to highest:

1 1 1 2 2 2 2 3 3 3 3 3 4 4 5 6 7 7 8 12

Q1 is the median of the first half of the observations, which is 2. Q3 is the median of the second half of the observations, which is 5.50. The IQR = Q3 − Q1, or IQR = 5.50 − 2 = 3.50.

4-23 The interquartile range of 18.50 is so much smaller than the range of 95 because there is an outlier of 231 mph in the wind gust data. This outlier affects the range but not the interquartile range.

4-25 The mean for salary is often greater than the median for salary because the high salaries of top management inflate the mean but not the median. If we are trying to attract people to our company, we may want to present the typical salary as whichever value is higher—in most cases, the mean. However, if we are going to offer someone a low salary, presenting the median might make them feel better about that amount!

4-27 There are few participants in this study (only seven) so a single extreme score would influence the mean more than it would influence the median. The median is a more trustworthy indicator than the mean when there is only a handful of scores.

4-29 In April 1934, a wind gust of 231 mph was recorded. This data point is rather far from the next closest record of 180 mph. If this extreme score were excluded from analyses of central tendency, the mean would be lower, the median would change only slightly, and the mode would be unaffected.

4-31 There are many possible answers to this question. All answers will include a distribution that is skewed, perhaps one that has outliers. A skewed distribution would affect the mean but not the median. One example would be the variable of number of foreign countries visited; the few jet-setters who have been to many countries would pull the mean higher. The median is more representative of the typical score.

4-33 a. These ads are likely presenting outlier data.

b. To capture the experience of the typical individual who uses the product, the ad could include the mean result and the standard deviation. If the distribution of outcomes is skewed, it would be best to present the median result.

4-35 a. $M = \dfrac{\Sigma X}{N} = \dfrac{(0+5+3\ldots+5)}{19} = \dfrac{53}{19} = 2.789$

b. The formula for variance is $SD^2 = \dfrac{\Sigma(X-M)^2}{N}$

We start by creating three columns: one for the scores, one for the deviations of the scores from the mean, and one for the squares of the deviations.

We can now calculate variance:

$$SD^2 = \frac{\Sigma(X - M)^2}{N}$$

$$= \frac{(7.779 + 4.889 + 0.045 + 0.045 + \cdots + 0.045 + 4.889)}{19}$$

$$= \frac{91.167}{19} = 4.798$$

X	X − M	(X − M)²
0	−2.789	7.779
5	2.211	4.889
3	0.211	0.045
3	0.211	0.045
1	−1.789	3.201
10	7.211	51.999
2	−0.789	0.623
2	−0.789	0.623
3	0.211	0.045
1	−1.789	3.201
2	−0.789	0.623
4	1.211	1.467
2	−0.789	0.623
1	−0.789	3.201
1	−0.789	3.201
1	−0.789	3.201
4	1.211	1.467
3	0.211	0.045
5	2.211	4.889

  c. We calculate standard deviation the same way we calculate variance, but we then take the square root:

$$SD = \sqrt{\frac{\Sigma(X - M)^2}{N}} = \sqrt{4.798} = 2.19$$

  d. The typical score is around 2.79, and the typical deviation from 2.79 is around 2.19.

4-37 There are many possible answers to these questions. The following are only examples.

  a. 70, 70. There is no skew; the mean is not pulled away from the median.

  b. 80, 70. There is positive skew; the mean is pulled up, but the median is unaffected.

  c. 60, 70. There is negative skew; the mean is pulled down, but the median is unaffected.

4-39 a. Because the policy for which violations were issued changed during this time frame, we cannot make accurate comparisons before and after Hurricane Sandy. The conditions for issuing violations were not constant; thus, the policy change would be a likely explanation for a change in the data.

  b. The removal of violations in Zone A, which appears to have been most affected by infestations after the hurricane, would result in eliminating an otherwise extreme number, or outlier, of issued violations. This would lead to inaccurate data as it does not accurately portray the number of rat violations, only the number of rat violations issued under the current policy.

4-41 It would probably be appropriate to use the mean because the data are scale; we would assume we have a large number of data points available to us; and the mean is the most commonly used measure of central tendency. Because of the large amount of data available, the effect of outliers is minimized. All of these factors would support the use of the mean for presenting information about the heights or weights of large numbers of people.

4-43 We cannot directly compare the mean ages reported by Canada with the median ages reported by the United States because it is likely that there were some older outliers in both Canada and the United States, and these outliers would affect the means reported by Canada much more than they would affect the medians reported by the United States.

4-45 a. The researchers reported an increase in early literacy among students in the intervention group (those whose parents received the text messages) as compared with the students who were not in the intervention group (those whose parents did *not* receive texts). The intervention seemed to work. That is, those in the intervention group as a whole ended up higher in literacy skills as compared with the mean for the nonintervention group. The increase was between 0.21 and 0.34 deviations. We know that the standard deviation indicates the difference of a typical student from the mean. So, the shift for the group as a whole is *not* as big as the amount that the typical student differs from the mean. It's just part of a standard deviation.

  b. The researchers used a between-groups design because each student could only be in one group—either the group in which parents received the text messages or the group in which the parents did not receive the text messages.

4-47 a.

Interval	Frequency
60–69	1
50–59	5
40–49	9
30–39	5
20–29	8
10–19	2

b.

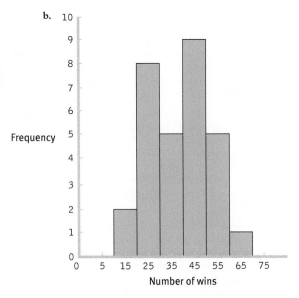

c. $M = \dfrac{\Sigma X}{N} = \dfrac{[60 + 44 + 39 + 29 + \ldots + 23]}{30}$

$\quad = \dfrac{1144}{30} = 38.133$

With 30 scores, the median would be between the 15th and 16th scores: (30/2) + 0.5 + 15.5. The 15th and 16th scores are 39 and 40, respectively, so the median is 39.50. The mode is 29; there are three scores of 29.

d. Software reports that the range is 42 and the standard deviation is 11.59.

e. The summary will differ for each student but should include the following information: The data appear to be roughly symmetric and unimodal, maybe a bit negatively skewed. There are no glaring outliers.

f. Answers will vary. One example is whether number of wins is related to the average age of a team's players.

Chapter 5

5-1 It is rare to have access to an entire population. That is why we study samples and use inferential statistics to estimate what is happening in the population.

5-3 Generalizability refers to the ability of researchers to apply findings from one sample or in one context to other samples or contexts.

5-5 Random sampling means that every member of a population has an equal chance of being selected to participate in a study. Random assignment means that each selected participant has an equal chance of being in any of the experimental conditions.

5-7 Random assignment is a process in which every participant (regardless of how he or she was selected) has an equal chance of being in any of the experimental conditions. This avoids bias across experimental conditions.

5-9 An illusory correlation is a belief that two events are associated when in fact they are not.

5-11 Students' answers will vary. Personal probability is a person's belief about the probability of an event occurring: for example, someone's belief about the likelihood that she or he will complete a particular task.

5-13 In reference to probability, the term *trial* refers to each occasion that a given procedure is carried out. For example, each time we flip a coin, it is a trial. *Outcome* refers to the result of a trial. For coin-flip trials, the outcome is either heads or tails. *Success* refers to the outcome for which we're trying to determine the probability. If we are testing for the probability of heads, then success is heads.

5-15 The independent variable is the variable the researcher manipulates. Independent trials or events are those that do not affect each other; the flip of a coin is independent of another flip of a coin because the two events do not affect each other.

5-17 A null hypothesis is a statement that postulates that there is no mean difference between populations or that the mean difference is in a direction opposite of that anticipated by the researcher. A research hypothesis, also called an alternative hypothesis, is a statement that postulates that there is a mean difference between populations or sometimes, more specifically, that there is a mean difference in a certain direction, positive or negative.

5-19 We commit a Type I error when we reject the null hypothesis but the null hypothesis is true. We commit a Type II error when we fail to reject the null hypothesis but the null hypothesis is false.

5-21 In each of the six groups of 10 passengers that go through the checkpoint, we would check the ninth, ninth, tenth, first, tenth, and eighth passengers, respectively.

5-23 Only recording the numbers 1 to 5, the sequence appears as 5, 3, 5, 5, 2, 2, and 2. So, the first person is assigned to the fifth condition, the second person to the third condition, and so on.

5-25 Illusory correlation is particularly dangerous because people might perceive there to be an association between two variables that does not in fact exist. Because we often make decisions based on associations, it is important that those associations be real and be based on objective evidence. For example, a parent might perceive an illusory correlation between body piercings and trustworthiness, believing that a person with a large number of body piercings is untrustworthy. This illusory correlation might lead the parent to unfairly eliminate anyone with a body piercing from consideration when choosing babysitters.

5-27 The probability of winning is estimated as the number of people who have already won out of the total number of contestants, or 8/266 = 0.03.

5-29 a. 0.627
b. 0.003
c. 0.042

5-31 a. Expected relative-frequency probability
b. Personal probability
c. Personal probability
d. Expected relative-frequency probability

5-33 Most of us believe we can think randomly. However, it is extremely difficult for us to come up with a string of four numbers in which we determined each of the numbers completely independently. We may choose numbers with some meaning for us, perhaps without even realizing we are doing so. We also tend to consider the previous numbers when we come up with each new one. As the BBC article reported, people are lazy when it comes to choosing PINs and passwords. "They use birthdays, wedding days, the names of siblings or children or pets. They use their house number, street name or pick on a favourite pop star" (Ward, 2013). So, the best advice would be to let a random numbers table choose your PIN.

5-35 **a.** The independent variable is type of news information, with two levels: information about an improving job market and information about a declining job market.

b. The dependent variable is psychologists' attitudes toward their careers.

c. The null hypothesis would be that, on average, the psychologists who received the positive article about the job market have the same attitude toward their career as those who read a negative article about the job market. The research hypothesis would be that a difference, on average, exists between the two groups.

5-37 Although we all believe we can think randomly if we want to, we do not, in fact, generate numbers independently of the ones that came before. We tend to glance at the preceding numbers in order to make the next ones "random." Yet once we do this, the numbers are not independent and therefore are not random. Moreover, even if we can keep ourselves from looking at the previous numbers, the numbers we generate are not likely to be random. For example, if we were born on the sixth of the month, then we may be more likely to choose 6's than other digits. Humans just don't think randomly.

5-39 **a.** The typical study volunteer is likely someone who cares deeply about U.S. college football. Moreover, it is particularly the fans of the top ACC teams, who themselves are likely extremely biased, who are most likely to vote.

b. External validity refers to the ability to generalize beyond the current sample. In this case, it is likely that fans of the top ACC teams are voting and that the poll results do not reflect the opinions of U.S. college football fans at large.

c. There are several possible answers to this question. As one example, only eight options were provided. Even though one of these options was "other," this limited the range of possible answers that respondents would be likely to provide. The sample is also biased in favor of those who know about and would spend time at the *USA Today* Web site in the first place.

5-41 **a.** It is unlikely the journalist's results would be representative of the U.S. population. Instead, participants who complete the survey are more likely to be representative of people who subscribe to or frequently read the Gizmodo blog *Throb*. This sample would likely include only people who use the Internet and read this specific blog. Not everyone in the U.S. population uses the Internet and reads the blog *Throb*.

b. Those most likely to volunteer are those who have stumbled across, or searched for, this particular blog.

c. The journalist's perspective seems to be that teens primarily either are misinformed or have incorrect information about sex. However, her interpretation of the forums she reviewed could be framed as a positive opportunity where misinformation about sex is discussed and corrected. Additionally, it is possible that teenagers who are well informed about sex do not frequent online forums about sex. Her perspective— that most teenagers are misinformed about sex—might attract readers who are actively seeking out clarifications about sex using the Internet and ultimately reading her contributions to the blog *Throb*. But inviting people to participate in this manner often leads to a confirmation bias in research. This method of sampling involves convenience and volunteer sampling (as opposed to random sampling), where the sample is likely to reflect a specific population of individuals who read the blog *Throb*, which endorses a specific perspective about teenagers' knowledge about sex.

d. It does not matter how large a sample is if it is not representative. With respect to external validity, it would be far preferable to have a smaller but representative sample than a very large but unrepresentative sample.

5-43 If a depressed person has negative thoughts about himself or herself and about the world, confirmation bias may make it difficult to change those thoughts because confirmation bias would lead this person to pay more attention to and better remember negative events than positive events. For example, he or she might remember the one friend who slighted him or her at a party but not the many friends who were excited to see him or her.

5-45 **a.** *Probability* refers to the proportion of Waldos that we expect to see in these two 1.5-inch bands in the long run. In the long run, given 53% of Waldos falling in these bands, we would expect the proportion of Waldos to be 0.53.

b. *Proportion* refers to the observed fraction of Waldos in these bands—the number of successes (Waldo in one of these bands) divided by the number of trials (total Waldo illustrations used). In this case, the proportion of Waldos in one of these bands is 0.53.

c. *Percentage* refers to the proportion multiplied by 100: 0.53(100) = 53%, as reported by Blatt in this case. The media often report percentage versions of probabilities.

d. Although it is improbable that this pattern would occur just by chance, Blatt did not analyze every *Where's Waldo?* illustration that exists. It does seem that this is more than coincidence, but we might expect a fluctuation in the short run. We can't know for certain that the *Where's Waldo?* game has a bias.

5-47 These polls could be considered independent trials if they were conducted for each state individually, and if the state currently being polled did not have any information about the polling results from other states. However, these are not truly independent trials, as state-by-state polls are often presented in the media as they take place, thus potentially influencing voters in states that have not yet been polled.

5-49 **a.** The null hypothesis is that the average tendency to develop false memories is either unchanged or is lowered by the repetition of false information. The research hypothesis is that false memories are higher, on average, when false information is repeated than when it is not.

b. The null hypothesis is that the average outcome is the same or worse whether or not structured assessments are used. The research hypothesis is that the average outcome is better when structured assessments are used than when they are not used.

c. The null hypothesis is that average employee morale is the same whether employees work in enclosed offices or in cubicles. The research hypothesis is that average employee morale is different when employees work in enclosed offices versus in cubicles.

d. The null hypothesis is that ability to speak one's native language is the same, on average, whether or not a second language is taught from birth. The research hypothesis is that the ability to speak one's native language is different, on average, when a second language is taught from birth than when no second language is taught.

5-51 a. If this conclusion is incorrect, the researcher has made a Type I error. The researcher rejected the null hypothesis when the null hypothesis is really true. (Of course, he or she never knows whether there has been an error! She or he just has to acknowledge the possibility.)

b. If this conclusion is incorrect, the researcher has made a Type I error. She has rejected the null hypothesis when the null hypothesis is really true.

c. If this conclusion is incorrect, the researcher has made a Type II error. He has failed to reject the null hypothesis when the null hypothesis is not true.

d. If this conclusion is incorrect, the researcher has made a Type II error. She has failed to reject the null hypothesis when the null hypothesis is not true.

5-53 a. Confirmation bias has guided his logic in that he looked for specific events that occurred during the day to fit the horoscope but ignored the events that did not fit the prediction.

b. If this conclusion is incorrect, they have made a Type I error. Dean and Kelly would have failed to reject the null hypothesis when the null hypothesis is not true.

c. If an event occurs regularly or a research finding is replicated many times and by other researchers and in a range of contexts, then it is likely the event or finding is not occurring in error or by chance alone.

5-55 a. The population in which you would be interested is all people who already had read *Harry Potter and the Half-Blood Prince*.

b. The sample would be just bel 78. It is dangerous to rely on just one review, bel 78's testimonial. She clearly felt strongly about the book if she spent the time to post her review. She is not likely to be representative of the typical reader of this book.

c. This is a large sample, but it is not likely representative of those who had read this book. Not only does this sample consist solely of Amazon users, but it consists of readers who chose to post a review. It is likely that those who took the time to write and post a review were those who felt more strongly about the book than did the typical reader.

d. In this case, the population of interest would be all Amazon users who had read this book. We would need Amazon to generate a list of everyone who bought the book (something that they would not do because of ethical considerations), and we would have to randomly select a sample from this population. We would then have to identify the people who actually read the book (who may not be the buyers) and elicit the ratings from the randomly selected sample.

e. We could explain that testimonials are typically written by those who feel most strongly about a book. The sample of reviewers, therefore, is unlikely to be representative of the population of readers.

5-57 a. The population of interest is male students with alcohol problems. The sample is the 64 students who were ordered to meet with a school counselor.

b. Random selection was not used. The sample comprised 64 male students who had been ordered to meet with a school counselor; they were not chosen out of all male students with alcohol problems.

c. Random assignment was used. Each participant had an equal chance of being assigned to either of the two conditions.

d. The independent variable is type of counseling. It has two levels: BMI and AE. The dependent variable is number of alcohol-related problems at follow-up.

e. The null hypothesis is that the mean number of alcohol-related problems at follow-up is the same, regardless of type of counseling (BMI or AE). The research hypothesis is that students who undergo a BMI have different mean numbers of alcohol-related problems at follow-up than do students who participate in AE.

f. The researchers rejected the null hypothesis.

g. If the researchers were incorrect in their decision, then they made a Type I error, rejecting the null hypothesis when the null hypothesis is true. The consequences of this type of error are that a new treatment that is no better, on average, than the standard treatment would be implemented. This might lead to unnecessary costs to train counselors to implement the new treatment.

Chapter 6

6-1 In everyday conversation, the word *normal* is used to refer to events or objects that are common or that typically occur. Statisticians use the word to refer to distributions that conform to a specific bell-shaped curve, with a peak in the middle where most of the observations lie, and symmetric areas underneath the curve on either side of the midpoint. This normal curve represents the pattern of occurrence of many different kinds of events.

6-3 The distribution of sample scores approaches normal as the sample size increases, assuming the population is normally distributed.

6-5 A z score is a way to standardize data; it expresses how far a data point is from the mean of its distribution in terms of standard deviations.

6-7 The mean is 0 and the standard deviation is 1.0.

6-9 The symbol μ_M stands for the mean of the distribution of means. The μ indicates that it is the mean of a *population*, and the subscript M indicates that the population is composed of *sample means*—the means of all possible samples of a given size from a particular population of individual scores.

6-11 Standard deviation is the measure of spread for a distribution of scores in a single sample or in a population of scores. Standard error is the standard deviation (or measure of spread) in a distribution of means of all possible samples of a given size from a particular population of individual scores.

6-13 The z statistic tells us how many standard errors a sample mean is from the population mean.

6-15 a.

b.

c.

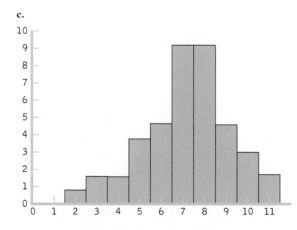

d. As the sample size increases, the distribution approaches the shape of the normal curve.

6-17 a. $z = \dfrac{(X - \mu)}{\sigma} = \dfrac{1000 - 1179}{164} = -1.09$

b. $z = \dfrac{721 - 1179}{164} = -2.79$

c. $z = \dfrac{1531 - 1179}{164} = 2.15$

d. $z = \dfrac{1184 - 1179}{164} = 0.03$

6-19 $z = \dfrac{203 - 250}{47} = -1.0$

$z = \dfrac{(297 - 250)}{47} = 1.0$

Each of these scores is 47 points away from the mean, which is the value of the standard deviation. The z scores of -1.0 and 1.0 express that the first score, 203, is 1 standard deviation below the mean, whereas the other score, 297, is 1 standard deviation above the mean.

6-21 a. $X = z(\sigma) + \mu = -0.23(164) + 1179 = 1141.28$

b. $X = 1.41(164) + 1179 = 1410.24$

c. $X = 2.06(164) + 1179 = 1516.84$

d. $X = 0.03(164) + 1179 = 1183.92$

6-23 a. $X = z(\sigma) + \mu = 1.5(100) + 500 = 650$

b. $X = z(\sigma) + \mu = -0.5(100) + 500 = 450$

c. $X = z(\sigma) + \mu = -2.0(100) + 500 = 300$

6-25 a. $z = \dfrac{45 - 51}{4} = -1.5$

$z = \dfrac{732 - 765}{23} = -1.43$

b. Both of these scores fall below the means of their distributions, resulting in negative z scores. One score (45) is a little farther below its mean than the other (732).

6-27 a. 50%

b. 82% (34 + 34 + 14)

c. 4% (2 + 2)

d. 48% (34 + 14)

e. 100% or nearly 100%

6-29 a. $\mu_M = \mu = 55$, and $\sigma_M = \dfrac{8}{\sqrt{30}} = 1.46$

b. $\mu_M = \mu = 55$, and $\sigma_M = \dfrac{8}{\sqrt{300}} = 0.46$

c. $\mu_M = \mu = 55$, and $\sigma_M = \dfrac{8}{\sqrt{3000}} = 0.15$

6-31 a. $z = \dfrac{(M - \mu_M)}{\dfrac{\sigma}{\sqrt{N}}} = \dfrac{85 - 80}{\dfrac{20}{\sqrt{100}}} = \dfrac{5}{\dfrac{20}{10}} = \dfrac{5}{2} = 2.50$

$z = \dfrac{(M - \mu_M)}{\dfrac{\sigma}{\sqrt{N}}} = \dfrac{17 - 15}{\dfrac{5}{\sqrt{100}}} = \dfrac{2}{\dfrac{5}{10}} = \dfrac{2}{0.50} = 4.00$

b. The first sample had a mean that was 2.50 standard deviations above the population mean, whereas the second sample had a mean that was 4 standard deviations above the mean. Compared to the population mean (as measured by this scale), both samples are extreme scores; however, a z score of 4.0 is even more extreme than a z score of 2.5.

6-33 a. Histogram for the 10 scores:

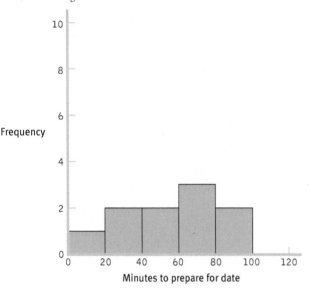

Minutes to prepare for date

b. Histogram for the 40 scores:

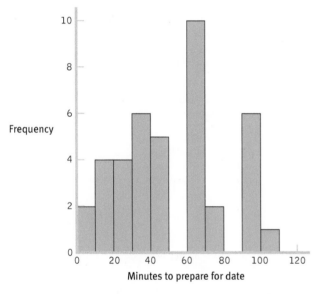

Minutes to prepare for date

c. The shape of the distribution became more normal as the number of scores increased. If we added more scores, the distribution would become more and more normal. This happens because many physical, psychological, and behavioral variables are normally distributed. With smaller samples, this might not be clear. But as the sample size approaches the size of the population, the shape of the sample distribution approaches that of the population.

d. These are distributions of scores, as each individual score is represented in the histograms on its own, not as part of a mean.

e. There are several possible answers to this question. For example, instead of using retrospective self-reports, we could have had students call a number or send an e-mail as they began to get ready; they would then have called the same number or sent another e-mail when they were ready. This would have led to scores that would be closer to the actual time it took the students to get ready.

f. There are several possible answers to this question. For example, we could examine whether there was a mean gender difference in time spent getting ready for a date.

6-35 a. The mean of the z distribution is always 0.

b. $z = \dfrac{(X - \mu)}{\sigma} = \dfrac{(6.65 - 6.65)}{1.24} = 0$

c. The standard deviation of the z distribution is always 1.

d. A student 1 standard deviation above the mean would have a score of $6.65 + 1.24 = 7.89$. This person's z score would be: $z = \dfrac{(X - \mu)}{\sigma} = \dfrac{(7.89 - 6.65)}{1.24} = 1$

e. The answer will differ for each student but will involve substituting one's own score for X in this equation:

$$z = \dfrac{(X - 6.65)}{1.24}$$

6-37 a. It would not make sense to compare the mean of this sample to the distribution of individual scores because, in a sample of means, the occasional extreme individual score is balanced by less extreme scores that are also part of the sample. Thus, there is less variability.

b. The null hypothesis would state that the population from which the sample was drawn has a mean of 3.20. The research hypothesis would state that the mean for the population from which our sample was drawn is not 3.20.

c. $\mu_M = \mu = 3.20$

$\sigma_M = \dfrac{\sigma}{\sqrt{N}} = \dfrac{0.70}{\sqrt{40}} = 0.111$

d. $z = \dfrac{(M - \mu_M)}{\sigma_M} = \dfrac{(3.62 - 3.20)}{0.111} = 3.78$

6-39 a. Yes, the distribution of the number of movies college students watch in a year would likely approximate a normal curve. You can imagine that a small number of students watch an enormous number of movies and that a small number watch very few but that most watch a moderate number of movies between these two extremes.

b. Yes, the number of full-page advertisements in magazines is likely to approximate a normal curve. We could find magazines that have no or just one or two full-page advertisements and some that are chock full of them, but most magazines have some intermediate number of full-page advertisements.

c. Yes, human birth weights in Canada could be expected to approximate a normal curve. Few infants would weigh in at the extremes of very light or very heavy, and the weight of most infants would cluster around some intermediate value.

6-41 Household income is positively skewed. Most households cluster around a relatively low central tendency, but the 1-percenters—the Mark Zuckerbergs and Lady Gagas of the world—pull the tail of the distribution in a positive direction.

6-43 a. $z = \dfrac{(X - \mu)}{\sigma} = \dfrac{(94.00 - 81.00)}{11.733} = 1.11$

b. $z = \dfrac{(X - \mu)}{\sigma} = \dfrac{(13.00 - 7.969)}{3.036} = 1.66$

c. According to these data, the Falcons had a better regular season (they had a higher z score) than did the Braves.

d. The Braves would have had to have won 101 regular season games to have a slightly higher z score than the Falcons:

$$z = \dfrac{(X - \mu)}{\sigma} = \dfrac{(101.00 - 81.00)}{11.733} = 1.70$$

e. There are several possible answers to this question. For example, we could have summed the teams' scores for every game (as compared to other teams' scores within their leagues).

6-45 a. $X = z(\sigma) + \mu = -1.705(11.733) + 81.00 = 61$ games (rounded to a whole number)

b. $X = z(\sigma) + \mu = -0.319(3.036) + 7.969 = 7$ games (rounded to a whole number)

c. Fifty percent of scores fall below the mean, so 34% $(84 - 50 = 34)$ fall between the mean and the Colts' score. We know that 34% of scores fall between the mean and a z score of 1.0, so the Colts have a z score of 1.0. $X = z(\sigma) + \mu = 1(3.036) + 7.969 = 11$ games (rounded to a whole number).

d. We can examine our answers to be sure that negative z scores match up with answers that are below the mean and positive z scores match up with answers that are above the mean.

6-47 a. $\mu = 50; \sigma = 10$

b. $\mu_M = \mu = 50; \sigma_M = \dfrac{\sigma}{\sqrt{N}} = \dfrac{10}{\sqrt{95}} = 1.03$

c. When we calculate the mean of the scores for 95 individuals, the most extreme MMPI-2 depression scores will likely be balanced by scores toward the middle. It would be rare to have an extreme mean of the scores for 95 individuals. Thus, the spread is smaller than is the spread for all of the individual MMPI-2 depression scores.

6-49 a. These are the data for a distribution of scores rather than means because they have been obtained by entering each individual score into the analysis.

b. Comparing the sizes of the mean and the standard deviation suggests that there is positive skew. A person can't have fewer than zero friends, so the distribution would have to extend in a positive direction to have a standard deviation larger than the mean.

c. Because the mean is larger than either the median or the mode, it suggests that the distribution is positively skewed. There are extreme scores in the positive end of the distribution that are causing the mean to be more extreme than the median or mode.

d. You would compare this person to a distribution of scores. When making a comparison of an individual score, we must use a distribution of scores.

e. You would compare this sample to a distribution of means. When making a comparison involving a sample mean, we must use a distribution of means because it has a different pattern of variability from a distribution of scores (it has less variability).

f. $\mu_M = \mu = 7.44$. The number of individuals in the sample is 80. Substituting 80 in the standard error equation yields

$$\sigma_M = \dfrac{\sigma}{\sqrt{N}} = \dfrac{10.98}{\sqrt{80}} = 1.23$$

g. The distribution of means is likely to be a normal curve. Because the sample of 80 is well above the 30 recommended to see the central limit theorem at work, we expect that the distribution of the sample means will approximate a normal distribution.

6-51 a. You would compare this sample mean to a distribution of means. When we are making a comparison involving a sample mean, we need to use a distribution of means because it is this distribution that indicates the variability we are likely to see in sample means.

b. $z = \dfrac{(M - \mu_M)}{\sigma_M} = \dfrac{(8.7 - 7.44)}{1.228} = 1.03$

This z statistic of 1.03 is approximately 1 standard deviation above the mean. Because 50% of the sample are below the mean and 34% are between the mean and 1 standard deviation above it, this sample would be at approximately the 84th percentile.

c. It does make sense to calculate a percentile for this sample. Given the central limit theorem and the size of the sample used to calculate the mean (80), we would expect the distribution of the sample means to be approximately normal.

6-53 z scores can help us to compare scores that come from different distributions. In this example, the number of heart surgeries conducted per doctor might have a different distribution compared to the number of hip surgeries conducted per doctor. By converting raw scores (i.e., number of surgeries for each doctor) in each distribution to a z score, we can see if this specific cardiologist is particularly high on the national distribution for numbers of heart surgeries and compare this to the level of hip surgeries in Munster with respect to the national distribution for numbers of hip surgeries.

6-55 a. The population is all patients treated for blocked coronary arteries in the United States. The sample is Medicare patients in Elyria, Ohio, who received angioplasty.

b. Medicare and the commercial insurer compared the angioplasty rate in Elyria to that in other towns. Given that the rate was so far above that of other towns, they decided that such a high angioplasty rate was unlikely to happen just by chance. Thus, they used probability to make a decision to investigate.

c. Medicare and the commercial insurer could look at the z distribution of angioplasty rates in cities from all over the country. Locating the rate of Elyria within that distribution would indicate exactly how extreme or unlikely its angioplasty rates are.

d. The error made would be a Type I error, as they would be rejecting the null hypothesis that there is no difference among the various towns in rates of angioplasty, and concluding that there is a difference, when there really is no difference.

e. Elyria's extremely high rates do not necessarily mean the doctors are committing fraud. One could imagine that an area with a population composed mostly of retirees (that is, more elderly people) would have a higher rate of angioplasty. Conversely, perhaps Elyria has a talented set of surgeons who are renowned for their angioplasty skills and people from all over the country come there to have angioplasty.

6-57 a. The researchers are operationally defining cheating as the change in standardized test score for a given classroom. This variable is a scale variable.

b. Researchers could establish a cut-off z statistic at which those who had a mean change larger than that z statistic would be considered "suspicious." For example, a classroom with a z statistic of 2 or more may have cheated on this year's test.

c. A histogram or frequency polygon would provide an easy visual to see where a given classroom falls on the distribution. A researcher could even draw lines indicating the cutoffs and see which classrooms fall beyond them.

d. They would be committing a Type I error, because they would be rejecting the null hypothesis that there is no difference in a classroom's test scores from one year to the next when there really is no difference and they should have failed to reject the null hypothesis.

Chapter 7

7-1 A percentile is the percentage of scores that fall below a certain point on a distribution.

7-3 We add the percentage between the mean and the positive z score to 50%, which is the percentage of scores below the mean (50% of scores are on each side of the mean).

7-5 In statistics, *assumptions* are the characteristics we ideally require the population from which we are sampling to have so that we can make accurate inferences.

7-7 *Parametric tests* are statistical analyses based on a set of assumptions about the population. By contrast, *nonparametric tests* are statistical analyses that are not based on assumptions about the population.

7-9 *Critical values*, often simply called *cutoffs*, are the test statistic values beyond which we reject the null hypothesis. The *critical region* refers to the area in the tails of the distribution in which the null hypothesis will be rejected if the test statistic falls there.

7-11 A *statistically significant* finding is one in which we have rejected the null hypothesis because the pattern in the data differed from what we would expect by chance. The word *significant* has a particular meaning in statistics. "Statistical significance" does *not* mean that the finding is necessarily important or meaningful. Statistical significance only means that we are justified in believing that the pattern in the data is likely to reoccur; that is, the pattern is likely genuine.

7-13 *Critical region* may have been chosen because values of a test statistic describe the area beneath the normal curve that represents a statistically significant result.

7-15 For a one-tailed test, the critical region (usually 5%, or a p level of 0.05) is placed in only one tail of the distribution; for a two-tailed test, the critical region must be split in half and shared between both tails (usually 2.5%, or 0.025, in each tail).

7-17 The following are the two options for one-tailed test hypotheses.
1) Null hypothesis: $H_0: \mu_1 \geq \mu_2$
   Research hypothesis: $H_1: \mu_1 < \mu_2$
2) Null hypothesis: $H_0: \mu_1 \leq \mu_1$
   Research hypothesis: $H_1: \mu_1 > \mu_2$

7-19 The failure to replicate a finding can potentially mean a few things. The conclusion from the original study may have been a Type I error (an incorrect rejection of the null hypothesis that led the researcher to state that there is a statistically significant finding). Or the failure to replicate may be a Type II error (an incorrect failure to reject the null hypothesis). Differences in findings might also reflect differences in the research context, perhaps because of differences between laboratories, samples, or researchers. Or perhaps the phenomenon itself has changed over the time that passed between replications. There are potentially other explanations, especially if there is even the smallest shift in methodology, but these are often the primary explanations.

7-21 a. If 22.96% are beyond this z score (in the tail), then 77.04% are below it (100% − 22.96%).

b. If 22.96% are beyond this z score, then 27.04% are between it and the mean (50% − 22.96%).

c. Because the curve is symmetric, the area beyond a z score of −0.74 is the same as that beyond 0.74. Expressed as a proportion, 22.96% appears as 0.2296.

7-23 a. The percentage above is the percentage in the tail, 4.36%.

b. The percentage below is calculated by adding the area below the mean, 50%, and the area between the mean and this z score, 45.64%, to get 95.64%.

c. The percentage at least as extreme is computed by doubling the amount beyond the z score, 4.36%, to get 8.72%.

7-25 a. 19%

b. 4%

c. 92%

7-27 a. 2.5% in each tail

b. 5% in each tail

c. 0.5% in each tail

7-29 $\mu_M = \mu = 500$

$$\sigma_M = \frac{\sigma}{\sqrt{N}} = \frac{100}{\sqrt{50}} = 14.14$$

7-31 a. Fail to reject the null hypothesis because 1.06 does not exceed the cutoff of 1.96.

b. Reject the null hypothesis because −2.06 is more extreme than −1.96.

c. Fail to reject the null hypothesis because a z statistic with 7% of the data in the tail occurs between ±1.48 and ±1.47, which are not more extreme than ±1.96.

7-33 a. Fail to reject the null hypothesis because 0.95 does not exceed 1.65.

   b. Reject the null hypothesis because -1.77 is more extreme than -1.65.

   c. Reject the null hypothesis because the critical value resulting in 2% in the tail falls within the 5% cutoff region in each tail.

7-35 a. $z = \dfrac{(X - \mu)}{\sigma} = \dfrac{5.4 - 7}{1.85} = \dfrac{-1.6}{1.85} = -0.86$

   The percentage below is 19.49%.

   b. $z = \dfrac{(X - \mu)}{\sigma} = \dfrac{8.5 - 7}{1.85} = \dfrac{1.5}{1.85} = 0.81$

   The percentage below is 50% + 29.10% = 79.10%.

   c. $z = \dfrac{(X - \mu)}{\sigma} = \dfrac{8.9 - 7}{1.85} = \dfrac{1.9}{1.85} = 1.03$

   The percentage below is 50% + 34.85% = 84.85%.

   d. $z = \dfrac{(X - \mu)}{\sigma} = \dfrac{6.5 - 7}{1.85} = \dfrac{-0.5}{1.85} = -0.27$

   The percentage below is 39.36%.

7-37 a. $z = \dfrac{(X - \mu)}{\sigma} = \dfrac{72 - 67}{3.19} = 1.57$

   b. 44.18% of scores are between this z score and the mean. We need to add this to the area below the mean, 50%, to get the percentile score of 94.18%.

   c. 94.18% of boys are shorter than Kona at this age.

   d. If 94.18% of boys are shorter than Kona, that leaves 5.82% in the tail. To compute how many scores are at least as extreme, we double this to get 11.64%.

   e. We look at the z table to find a critical value that puts 30% of scores in the tail, or as close as we can get to 30%. A z score of -0.52 puts 30.15% in the tail. We can use that z score to compute the raw score for height:

$$X = -0.52(3.19) + 67 = 65.34 \text{ inches}$$

   At 72 inches tall, Kona is 6.66 inches taller than Ian.

7-39 a. $z = \dfrac{(M - \mu_M)}{\sigma_M} = \dfrac{69.5 - 67}{\dfrac{3.19}{\sqrt{13}}} = 2.83$

   b. The z statistic indicates that this sample mean is 2.83 standard deviations above the expected mean for samples of size 13. In other words, this sample of boys is, on average, exceptionally tall.

   c. The percentile rank is 99.77%, meaning that 99.77% of sample means would be of lesser value than the one obtained for this sample.

7-41 a. $\mu_M = \mu = 63.8$

$$\sigma_M = \dfrac{\sigma}{\sqrt{N}} = \dfrac{2.66}{\sqrt{14}} = 0.711$$

   b. $z = \dfrac{(M - \mu_M)}{\sigma_M} = \dfrac{62.4 - 63.8}{0.711} = -1.97$

   c. 2.44% of sample means would be shorter than this mean.

   d. We double 2.44% to account for both tails, so we get 4.88% of the time.

   e. The average height of this group of 15-year-old females is rare, or statistically significant.

7-43 a. This is a nondirectional hypothesis because the researcher is predicting that it will alter skin moisture, not just decrease it or increase it.

   b. This is a directional hypothesis because better grades are expected.

   c. This hypothesis is nondirectional because any change is of interest, not just a decrease or an increase in closeness of relationships.

7-45 a.

	X	$(X - \mu)$	$(X - \mu)^2$
January	4.41	0.257	0.066
February	8.24	4.087	16.704
March	4.69	0.537	0.288
April	3.31	−0.843	0.711
May	4.07	−0.083	0.007
June	2.52	−1.633	2.667
July	10.65	6.497	42.211
August	3.77	−0.383	0.147
September	4.07	−0.083	0.007
October	0.04	−4.113	16.917
November	0.75	−3.403	11.580
December	3.32	−0.833	0.694

$\mu = 4.153$; $SS = \Sigma(X - \mu)^2 = 91.999$;

$$\sigma^2 = \dfrac{\Sigma(X - \mu)^2}{N} = \dfrac{(91.999)}{12} = 7.667$$

$$\sigma = \sqrt{\sigma^2} = \sqrt{7.667} = 2.769$$

August: $X = 3.77$

$$z = \dfrac{(X - \mu)}{\sigma} = \dfrac{(3.77 - 4.153)}{2.769} = -0.14$$

   b. The table tells us that 44.43% of scores fall in the tail beyond a z score of -0.14. So, the percentile for August is 44.43%. This is surprising because it is below the mean, and it was the month in which a devastating hurricane hit New Orleans. (*Note:* It is helpful to draw a picture of the curve when calculating this answer.)

   c. Paragraphs will be different for each student but will include the fact that a monthly total based on missing data is inaccurate. The mean and the standard deviation based on this population, therefore, are inaccurate. Moreover, even if we had these data points, they would likely be large and would increase the total precipitation for August; August would likely be an outlier, skewing the overall mean. The median would be a more accurate measure of central tendency than the mean under these circumstances.

   d. We would look up the z score that has 10% in the tail. The closest z score is 1.28, so the cutoffs are -1.28 and 1.28. (*Note:* It is helpful to draw a picture of the curve that includes these z scores.) We can then convert these z scores to raw scores. $X = z(\sigma) + \mu = -1.28(2.769) + 4.153 = 0.61$; $X = z(\sigma) + \mu = 1.28(2.769) + 4.153 = 7.70$. Only October (0.04) is below 0.61. Only February

(8.24) and July (10.65) are above 7.70. These data are likely inaccurate, however, because the mean and the standard deviation of the population are based on an inaccurate mean from August. Moreover, it is quite likely that August would have been in the most extreme upper 10% if there were complete data for this month.

7-47 Because we have a population mean and a population standard deviation, we can use a z test. To conduct this study, we would need a sample of red-haired women. Ideally, we would recruit at least 30 women so that we could be assured that the underlying population distribution was normal (based on the central limit theorem). Each participant would create a password, and we would rate the strength of her password using Kuo's scoring system. We would take the mean of all of the password scores. We would then conduct all six steps of hypothesis testing to determine whether the sample mean for red-haired women was statistically significantly higher than the population mean of 15.7.

7-49 a. The independent variable is whether a patient received the video with information about orthodontics. One group received the video; the other group did not. The dependent variable is the number of hours per day patients wore their appliances.

b. The researcher did not use random selection when choosing his sample. He selected the next 15 patients to come into his clinic.

c. *Step 1:* Population 1 is patients who did not receive the video. Population 2 is patients who received the video. The comparison distribution will be a distribution of means. The hypothesis test will be a z test because we have only one sample and we know the population mean and the standard deviation. This study meets the assumption that the dependent variable is a scale measure. We might expect the distribution of number of hours per day people wear their appliances to be normally distributed, but from the information provided it is not possible to tell for sure. Additionally, the sample includes fewer than 30 participants, so the central limit theorem may not apply here. The distribution of sample means may not approach normality. Finally, the participants were not randomly selected. Therefore, we may not want to generalize the results beyond this sample.

Step 2: Null hypothesis: Patients who received the video do not wear their appliances a different mean number of hours per day than patients who did not receive the video: $H_0: \mu_1 = \mu_2$.

Research hypothesis: Patients who received the video wear their appliances a different mean number of hours per day than patients who did not receive the video: $H_1: \mu_1 \neq \mu_2$.

Step 3: $\mu_M = \mu = 14.78; \sigma_M = \dfrac{\sigma}{\sqrt{N}} = \dfrac{5.31}{\sqrt{15}} = 1.371$

Step 4: The cutoff z statistics, based on a p level of 0.05 and a two-tailed test, are -1.96 and 1.96. (*Note:* It is helpful to draw a picture of the normal curve and include these z statistics on it.)

Step 5: $z = \dfrac{(X - \mu_M)}{\sigma_M} = \dfrac{(17 - 14.78)}{1.371} = 1.62$

(*Note:* It is helpful to add this z statistic to your drawing of the normal curve that includes the cutoff z statistics.)

Step 6: Fail to reject the null hypothesis. We cannot conclude that receiving the video improves average patient compliance.

d. The researcher would have made a Type II error. He would have failed to reject the null hypothesis when a mean difference actually existed between the two populations.

e. Replication studies help increase our confidence in a particular finding. If this finding is replicated, we have more confidence that watching the video helps increase the number of hours orthodontic appliances are worn. Without a replication study, this finding might be limited to this specific sample, or this specific dental clinic.

f. Failure to replicate may be a reflection of the research context, such as cultural values around dental care (or more broadly, health care). Participating patients in Iran may have different priorities when it comes to dental and health care compared to other communities.

Chapter 8

8-1 There may be a statistically significant difference between group means, but the difference might not be meaningful or have a real-life application.

8-3 Confidence intervals add details to the hypothesis test. Specifically, they tell us a range within which the population mean would fall 95% of the time if we were to conduct repeated hypothesis tests using samples of the same size from the same population.

8-5 In everyday language, we use the word *effect* to refer to the outcome of some event. Statisticians use the word in a similar way when they look at effect sizes. They want to assess a given outcome. For statisticians, the outcome is any change in a dependent variable, and the event creating the outcome is an independent variable. When statisticians calculate an effect size, they are calculating the size of an outcome.

8-7 If two distributions overlap a lot, then we would probably find a small effect size and not be willing to conclude that the distributions are necessarily different. If the distributions do not overlap much, this would be evidence for a larger effect or a meaningful difference between them.

8-9 According to Cohen's guidelines for interpreting the d statistic, a small effect is around 0.2, a medium effect is around 0.5, and a large effect is around 0.8.

8-11 In everyday language, we use the word *power* to mean either an ability to get something done or an ability to make others do things. Statisticians use the word *power* to refer to the ability to detect an effect, given that one exists.

8-13 80%

8-15 A researcher could increase statistical power by (1) increasing the alpha level; (2) performing a one-tailed test instead of a two-tailed test; (3) increasing the sample size; (4) maximizing the difference in the levels of the independent variable (e.g., giving a larger dose of a medication); (5) decreasing variability in the distributions by using, for example, reliable measures and homogeneous samples. Researchers want statistical power in their studies, and each of these techniques increases the probability of discovering an effect that genuinely exists. In many instances, the most practical way to increase statistical power is to increase the sample size.

8-17 The goal of a meta-analysis is to find the mean of the effect sizes from many different studies that all manipulated the same independent variable and measured the same dependent variable.

8-19 The file drawer analysis allows us to calculate the number of studies with null results that would have to exist so that a mean effect size would no longer be statistically significant. If it would take many studies (e.g., hundreds) in order to render the effect nonsignificant, then a statistically significant meta-analysis finding would be more persuasive. Specifically, we would be more convinced that a mean effect size really is statistically significantly different from zero.

8-21 (i) σ_M is incorrect. (ii) The correct symbol is σ. (iii) Because we are calculating Cohen's d, a measure of effect size, we divide by the standard deviation, σ, not the standard error of the mean. We use standard deviation rather than standard error because effect size is independent of sample size.

8-23 18.5% to 25.5% of respondents were suspicious of steroid use among swimmers.

8-25 **a.** 20%

   b. 15%

   c. 1%

8-27 **a.** A z of 0.84 leaves 19.77% in the tail.

   b. A z of 1.04 leaves 14.92% in the tail.

   c. A z of 2.33 leaves 0.99% in the tail.

8-29 We know that the cutoffs for the 95% confidence interval are $z = \pm 1.96$. The standard error is calculated as:

$$\sigma_M = \frac{\sigma}{\sqrt{N}} = \frac{1.3}{\sqrt{78}} = 0.147$$

Now we can calculate the lower and upper bounds of the confidence interval.

$M_{lower} = -z(\sigma_M) + M_{sample} = -1.96(0.147) + 4.1 = 3.812$ hours

$M_{upper} = z(\sigma_M) + M_{sample} = 1.96(0.147) + 4.1 = 4.388$ hours

The 95% confidence interval can be expressed as [3.81, 4.39].

8-31 z values of ± 2.58 put 0.49% in each tail, without going over, so we will use those as the critical values for the 99% confidence interval. The standard error is calculated as:

$$\sigma_M = \frac{\sigma}{\sqrt{N}} = \frac{1.3}{\sqrt{78}} = 0.147$$

Now we can calculate the lower and upper bounds of the confidence interval.

$M_{lower} = -z(\sigma_M) + M_{sample} = -2.58(0.147) + 4.1 = 3.721$ hours

$M_{upper} = z(\sigma_M) + M_{sample} = 2.58(0.147) + 4.1 = 4.479$ hours

The 99% confidence interval can be expressed as [3.72, 4.48].

8-33 **a.** $\sigma_M = \frac{\sigma}{\sqrt{N}} = \frac{136}{\sqrt{12}} = 39.261$

$$z = \frac{(M - \mu_M)}{\sigma_M} = \frac{1057 - 1014}{39.261} = 1.10$$

b. $\sigma_M = \frac{\sigma}{\sqrt{N}} = \frac{136}{\sqrt{39}} = 21.777$

$$z = \frac{1057 - 1014}{21.777} = 1.97$$

c. $\sigma_M = \frac{\sigma}{\sqrt{N}} = \frac{136}{\sqrt{188}} = 9.919$

$$z = \frac{1057 - 1014}{9.919} = 4.34$$

8-35 **a.** Cohen's $d = \frac{(M - \mu)}{\sigma} = \frac{(480 - 500)}{100} = -0.20$

b. Cohen's $d = \frac{(M - \mu)}{\sigma} = \frac{(520 - 500)}{100} = 0.20$

c. Cohen's $d = \frac{(M - \mu)}{\sigma} = \frac{(610 - 500)}{100} = 1.10$

8-37 **a.** Large

   b. Medium

   c. Small

   d. No effect (very close to zero)

8-39 **a.** The percentage beyond the z statistic of 2.23 is 1.29%. Doubled to take into account both tails, this is 2.58%. Converted to a proportion by dividing by 100, we get a p value of 0.0258, or 0.03.

   b. For -1.82, the percentage in the tail is 3.44%. Doubled, it is 6.88%. As a proportion, it is 0.0688, or 0.07.

   c. For 0.33, the percentage in the tail is 37.07%. Doubled, it is 74.14%. As a proportion, it is 0.7414, or 0.74.

8-41 We would fail to reject the null hypothesis because the confidence interval around the mean effect size includes 0.

8-43 **a.** The mean effect size is $d = 0.91$.

   b. This is a large effect size.

8-45 Your friend is not considering the fact that the two distributions, that of IQ scores of Burakumin and that of IQ scores of other Japanese, will have a great deal of overlap. The fact that one mean is higher than another does not imply that all members of one group have higher IQ scores than all members of another group. Any individual member of either group, such as your friend's former student, might fall well above the mean for his or her group (and the other group) or well below the mean for his or her group (and the other group). Research reports that do not give an indication of the overlap between two distributions risk misleading their audience.

8-47 **a.** *Step 3:*

$$\mu_M = \mu = 20.4; \sigma_M = \frac{\sigma}{\sqrt{N}} = \frac{3.2}{\sqrt{3}} = 1.848$$

Step 4: The cutoff z statistics are -1.96 and 1.96.

Step 5:

$$z = \frac{(M - \mu_M)}{\sigma_M} = \frac{(17.5 - 20.4)}{1.848} = -1.57$$

Step 6: Fail to reject the null hypothesis; we can conclude only that there is not sufficient evidence that Canadian adults have different average GNT scores from English adults. The conclusion has changed, but the actual difference between groups has not. The smaller sample size led to a larger standard error and a smaller test statistic. This makes sense because an extreme mean based on just a few participants is more likely to have occurred by chance than is an extreme mean based on many participants.

b. *Step 3:*

$$\mu_M = \mu = 20.4; \sigma_M = \frac{\sigma}{\sqrt{N}} = \frac{3.2}{\sqrt{100}} = 0.32$$

Step 5:

$$z = \frac{(M - \mu_M)}{\sigma_M} = \frac{(17.5 - 20.4)}{0.32} = -9.06$$

Step 6: Reject the null hypothesis. It appears that Canadian adults have lower average GNT scores than English adults. The test statistic has increased along with the increase in sample size.

c. *Step 3:*

$$\mu_M = \mu = 20.4; \sigma_M = \frac{\sigma}{\sqrt{N}} = \frac{3.2}{\sqrt{20,000}} = 0.023$$

Step 5:

$$z = \frac{(M - \mu_M)}{\sigma_M} = \frac{(17.5 - 20.4)}{0.023} = -126.09$$

The test statistic is now even larger, as the sample size has grown even larger. Step 6 is the same as in part (b).

d. As sample size increases, the test statistic increases. A mean difference based on a very small sample could have occurred just by chance. Based on a very large sample, that same mean difference is less likely to have occurred just by chance.

e. The underlying difference between groups has not changed. This might pose a problem for hypothesis testing because the same mean difference is statistically significant under some circumstances but not others. A very large test statistic might not indicate a very large difference between means; therefore, a statistically significant difference might not be an important difference.

8-49 a. No, we cannot tell which student will do better on the TOEFL. It is likely that the distributions of TOEFL scores for people from Serbia and people from Portugal have a great deal of overlap. Just because one group, on average, does better than another group does not mean that everyone in one group does better than everyone in another group.

b. Answers to this will vary, but the two distributions should overlap and the mean of the distribution for people whose first language is Serbian should be farther to the right (i.e., higher) than the mean for people whose first language is Portuguese. The figure here shows one example.

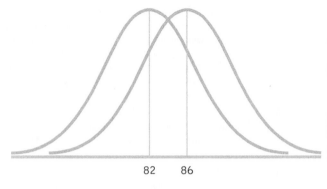

82   86

8-51 a. Given $\mu = 6.00$, $\sigma = 1.30$, and $N = 63$,

we calculate $\sigma_M = \frac{\sigma}{\sqrt{N}} = \frac{1.30}{\sqrt{63}} = 0.16$. To calculate the 95% confidence interval, we find the z values that mark off the most extreme 0.025 in each tail, which are -1.96 and 1.96. We calculate the lower end of the interval as $M_{lower} = -z(\sigma_M) + M_{sample} = -1.96(0.16) + 7.087 = 6.766$ and the upper end of the interval as $M_{upper} = z(\sigma_M) + M_{sample} = 1.96(0.16) + 7.087 = 7.408$. The confidence interval around the mean of 7.087 is [6.77, 7.41] when rounded to two decimal places for the final answer.

b. Because 6.00, the null-hypothesized value of the population mean, does not fall within this confidence interval, it is not plausible that the scores of the 63 international students at the University of Melbourne are the same, on average, as the scores for the population of students who completed this listening module of the IELTS. One explanation for the difference is that the sample may come from a different population.

c. Because the confidence interval does not include the hypothesized population mean of 6.00, we would reject the null hypothesis if we conducted a hypothesis test. It is plausible that the sample came from a different population.

d. In addition to letting us know that it is unlikely that the sample of University of Melbourne international students came from the same population as the IELTS test-takers, the confidence interval tells us a range of plausible values for the IELTS for international students at the University of Melbourne.

8-53 a. The appropriate measure of effect size for a z statistic is Cohen's d, which is calculated as:

$$d = \frac{(M - \mu)}{\sigma} = \frac{7.087 - 6.00}{1.30} = 0.836$$

b. Based on Cohen's conventions, this is a large effect size.

c. The hypothesis test tells us only whether a sample mean is likely to have been obtained by chance, whereas the effect size gives us the additional information of how much overlap there is between the distributions. Cohen's d, in particular, tells us how far apart two means are in terms of standard deviation. Because it's based on standard deviation, not standard error, Cohen's d is independent of sample size and therefore has the added benefit of allowing us to compare across studies. In summary, effect size tells us the magnitude of the effect, giving us a sense of how important or practical this finding is, and allows us to standardize the results of the study. Here, we know that there's a large effect.

8-55 a. We know that the cutoffs for the 95% confidence interval are $z = \pm 1.96$. Standard error is calculated as:

$$\sigma_M = \frac{\sigma}{\sqrt{N}} = \frac{16}{\sqrt{18}} = 3.771$$

Now we can calculate the lower and upper bounds of the confidence interval.

$$M_{lower} = -z(\sigma_M) + M_{sample} = -1.96(3.771) + 38 = \$30.61$$

$$M_{upper} = z(\sigma_M) + M_{sample} = 1.96(3.771) + 38 = \$45.39$$

The 95% confidence interval can be expressed as [\$30.61, \$45.39].

b. Standard error is now calculated as:

$$\sigma_M = \frac{\sigma}{\sqrt{N}} = \frac{16}{\sqrt{180}} = 1.193$$

Now we can calculate the lower and upper bounds of the confidence interval.

$$M_{lower} = -z(\sigma_M) + M_{sample} = -1.96(1.193) + 38 = \$35.66$$

$$M_{upper} = z(\sigma_M) + M_{sample} = 1.96(1.193) + 38 = \$40.34$$

The 95% confidence interval can be expressed as [\$35.66, \$40.34].

c. The null-hypothesized mean of \$45 falls in the 95% confidence interval when N is 18. Because of this, we cannot claim that things were lower in 2009 than what we would normally expect. When N is increased to 180, the confidence interval becomes narrower because standard error is reduced. As a result, the mean of \$45 no longer falls within the interval, and we can now conclude that Valentine's Day spending was different in 2009 from what was expected based on previous population data.

d. Cohen's $d = \frac{(M - \mu)}{\sigma} = \frac{(38 - 45)}{16} = -0.44$, just around a medium effect size.

8-57 a. Standard error is calculated as:

$$\sigma_M = \frac{\sigma}{\sqrt{N}} = \frac{12}{\sqrt{26}} = 2.353$$

Now we can calculate the lower and upper bounds of the confidence interval.

$$M_{lower} = -z(\sigma_M) + M_{sample} = -1.96(2.353) + 123$$
$$= 118.39 \text{ mph}$$

$$M_{upper} = z(\sigma_M) + M_{sample} = 1.96(2.353) + 123$$
$$= 127.61 \text{ mph}$$

The 95% confidence interval can be expressed as [118.39, 127.61].

Because the population mean of 118 mph does not fall within the confidence interval around the new mean, we can conclude that the program had an impact. In fact, we can conclude that the program seemed to increase the average speed of women's serves.

b. Cohen's $d = \frac{(M - \mu)}{\sigma} = \frac{(123 - 118)}{12} = 0.42$, a medium effect.

c. Because standard error, which utilizes sample size in its calculation, is part of the calculations for confidence interval, the interval becomes narrower as the sample size increases; however, because sample size is eliminated from the calculation of effect size, the effect size does not change.

8-59 a. *Step 1:* We know the following about population 2: $\mu = 118$ mph and $\sigma = 12$ mph. We know the following about population 1: $N = 26$ and $M = 123$ mph. Standard error is calculated as:

$$\sigma_M = \frac{\sigma}{\sqrt{N}} = \frac{12}{\sqrt{26}} = 2.353$$

Step 2: Because we are testing whether the sample hits a tennis ball faster, we will conduct a one-tailed test focused on the high end of the distribution.

We need to find the cutoff that marks where 5% of the data fall in the tail of population 2. We know that the critical z value for a one-tailed test is $+1.64$. Using that z, we can calculate a raw score.

$$M = z(\sigma_M) + \mu_M = +1.64(2.353) + 118 = 121.859 \text{ mph}$$

This mean of 121.859 mph marks the point beyond which 5% of all means based on samples of 26 observations will fall, assuming that population 2 is true.

Step 3: For the second distribution, centered around 123 mph, we need to calculate how often means of 121.859 (the cutoff) and more occur. We do this by calculating the z statistic for the raw mean of 121.859 with respect to the sample mean of 123.

$$z = \frac{121.859 - 123}{2.353} = -0.48$$

We now look up this z statistic on the table and find that 18.44% falls between this negative z and the mean. We add this to the 50% that falls between the mean and the high tail to get our power of 68.44%.

b. At an alpha of 10%, the critical value moves to $+1.28$. This changes the following calculations:

$$M = z(\sigma_M) + \mu_M = +1.28(2.353) + 118 = 121.012 \text{ mph}$$

This new mean of 121.012 mph marks the point beyond which 10% of all means based on samples of 26 observations will fall, assuming that population 2 is true.

For the second distribution, centered around 123 mph, we need to calculate how often means of 121.012 (the cutoff) or larger occur. We do this by calculating the z statistic for the raw mean of 121.012 with respect to the sample mean of 123.

$$z = \frac{121.012 - 123}{2.353} = -0.84$$

We look up this z statistic on the table and find that 29.95% falls between this negative z and the mean. We add this to the 50% that falls between the mean and the high tail to get power of 79.95%.

c. Power has moved from 68.44% at alpha of 0.05 to 79.95% at alpha of 0.10. As alpha increased, so did power.

8-61 a. The topic is the effectiveness of culturally adapted therapies.

b. The researchers used Cohen's d as a measure of effect size for each study in the analysis.

c. The mean effect size they found was 0.45. According to Cohen's conventions, this is a medium effect.

d. The researchers could use the group means and standard deviations to calculate a measure of effect size.

8-63 *Step 1:* The authors of the article first selected a topic of interest: gender differences in mathematical performance. They identified the necessary statistical information: Cohen's d. The authors likely wanted to include journal articles that compared men and women on mathematical tasks. Any study that did not fit this criterion was likely to have not been included. Additionally, they probably only included studies that had similar research designs.

Step 2: After identifying the criteria, the authors attempted to locate every relevant study. Because the authors note that they included only published studies, it is likely that they did not include (or perhaps even search for) unpublished studies on gender differences and mathematical performance.

Step 3: The authors then either identified or calculated an effect size for every study that met the inclusion criteria.

Step 4: Last, the authors calculated summary statistics ($d = 0.05$, variance ratio $= 1.08$). It is likely the authors included a visual display of the effect sizes.

8-65 a. A statistically significant difference just indicates that the difference between the means is unlikely to be due to chance. It does not tell us that there is *no* overlap in the distributions of the two populations we are considering. It is likely that there is overlap between the distributions and that some players with three children actually perform better than some players with two or fewer children. The drawings of distributions will vary; the two curves will overlap, but the mean of the distribution representing two or fewer children should be farther to the right than the mean of the distribution representing three or more children. However, the X for the player who had a third child should be to the right of the Y for the player who had a first or second child.

b. A difference can be statistically significant even if it is very small. In fact, if there are enough observations in a sample, even a tiny difference will approach statistical significance. Statistical significance does not indicate the importance or size of an effect—we need measures of effect size, which are not influenced by sample size, to understand the importance of an effect. These measures of effect size allow us to compare different predictors of performance. For example, in this case, it is likely that other aspects of a player's stats are more strongly associated with his performance and therefore would have a larger effect size. We could make the decision about whom to include in the fantasy team on the basis of the largest predictors of performance.

c. Even if the association is true, we cannot conclude that having a third child causes a decline in baseball performance. There are a number of possible causal explanations

for this relation. It could be the reverse; perhaps those players who are not performing as well in their careers end up devoting more time to family, so not playing well could lead to having more children. Alternatively, a third variable could explain both (a) having three children, and (b) poorer baseball performance. For example, perhaps less competitive or more laid-back players have more children and also perform more poorly.

d. The sample size for this analysis is likely small, so the statistical power to detect an effect is likely small as well.

8-67 a. The sample is the group of low-income students utilized for the study by Hoxby and Turner (2013). The population is low-income students applying to college.

b. The independent variable is intervention, with two levels—no intervention and intervention.

c. The dependent variable is number of applications submitted.

d. Just because a finding is statistically significant, it does not mean that it is practically significant. Justification for the impact of using the intervention based on a cost-benefit analysis may be needed.

e. The effect size for number of applications submitted was 0.247. This is a small effect size, according to Cohen's conventions.

f. Effect sizes demonstrate the difference between two means in terms of standard deviations. Thus, for the number of applications submitted, the means for the two groups were 0.247 standard deviations apart.

g. The intervention increased the average number of applications submitted by 19%.

Chapter 9

9-1 We should use a t distribution when we do not know the population standard deviation and are comparing two groups.

9-3 For both tests, standard error is calculated as the standard deviation divided by the square root of N. For the z test, the population standard deviation is calculated with N in the denominator. For the t test, the population standard deviation is estimated by dividing the sum of squared deviations by $N - 1$.

9-5 t stands for the t statistic, M is the sample mean, μ_M is the mean of the distribution of means, and s_M is the standard error as estimated from a sample.

9-7 *Free to vary* refers to the number of scores that can take on different values if a given parameter is known.

9-9 As the sample size increases, we can feel more confident in the estimate of the variability in the population. Remember, this estimate of variability (s) is calculated with $N - 1$ in the denominator in order to inflate the estimate somewhat. As the sample increases from 10 to 100, for example, and then up to 1000, subtracting 1 from N has less of an impact on the overall calculation. As this happens, the t distributions approach the z distribution, where we in fact knew the population standard deviation and did not need to estimate it.

9-11 The confidence interval gives us more information—an interval estimate, not just a point estimate.

9-13 A Cohen's d of 0.5 always indicates a medium effect, whether it accompanies a single-sample t test or any other hypothesis test.

9-15 A dot plot can depict the individual data points for two samples, one above the other, so we can easily compare the two distributions.

9-17 a. First we need to calculate the mean:

$$M = \frac{\Sigma X}{N} = \frac{93 + 97 + 91 + 88 + 103 + 94 + 97}{7} = \frac{663}{7} = 94.714$$

We then calculate the deviation of each score from the mean and the square of that deviation.

X	X − M	(X − M)²
93	−1.714	2.938
97	2.286	5.226
91	−3.714	13.794
88	−6.714	45.078
103	8.286	68.658
94	−0.714	0.510
97	2.286	5.226

Numerator: $\Sigma(X - M)^2 = 141.430$

The standard deviation is:

$$SD = \sqrt{\frac{\Sigma(X - M)^2}{N}} = \sqrt{\frac{141.430}{7}} = \sqrt{20.204} = 4.49$$

b. When estimating the population variability, we calculate s:

$$s = \sqrt{\frac{\Sigma(X - M)^2}{N - 1}} = \sqrt{\frac{141.430}{7 - 1}} = \sqrt{23.572} = 4.855$$

c. $s_M = \dfrac{s}{\sqrt{N}} = \dfrac{4.855}{\sqrt{7}} = 1.835$

d. $t = \dfrac{(M - \mu)}{s_M} = \dfrac{(94.714 - 96)}{1.835} = -0.70$

9-19 a. Because 73 df is not on the table, we go to 60 df (we do not go to the closest value, which would be 80, because we want to be conservative and go to the next-lowest value for df) to find the critical value of 1.296 in the upper tail. If we are looking in the lower tail, the critical value is −1.296.

b. ±1.984

c. Either −2.438 or 2.438

9-21 a. This is a two-tailed test with $df = 25$, so the critical t values are ±2.060.

b. $df = 17$, so the critical t value is 2.567, assuming you're anticipating an increase in marital satisfaction.

c. $df = 33$, so the critical t values are ±2.043.

9-23 a. $t = \dfrac{(M - \mu_M)}{s_M} = \dfrac{(8.5 - 7)}{\left(\dfrac{2.1}{\sqrt{41}}\right)} = 4.57$

b. $M_{lower} = -t(s_M) + M_{sample} = -2.705(0.328) + 8.5 = 7.61$

$M_{upper} = t(s_M) + M_{sample} = 2.705(0.328) + 8.5 = 9.39$

c. $d = \dfrac{(M - \mu)}{s} = \dfrac{(8.5 - 7)}{2.1} = 0.71$

9-25 a. The critical value for the test would be 2.624. The df is 14. It is a one-tailed test, with a p level of .01.

b. The critical values for the test would be −2.021 or 2.021. The df is 43, but the table only includes critical t values for $df = 40$ and $df = 50$. We use the more conservative critical t values, which would be for a df of 40. It is a two-tailed test, with a p level of .05.

c. The critical value for the test would be 1.310. The df is 30. It is a one-tailed test, with a p level of .10.

9-27 a. ±1.96

b. Either −2.33 or +2.33, depending on the tail of interest

c. ±1.96

9-29 a. *Step 1:* Population 1 is male U.S. Marines following a month-long training exercise. Population 2 is college men. The comparison distribution will be a distribution of means. The hypothesis test will be a single-sample t test because we have only one sample and we know the population mean but not the standard deviation. This study meets one of the three assumptions and may meet another. The dependent variable, anger, appears to be scale. The data were not likely randomly selected, so we must be cautious with respect to generalizing to all Marines who complete this training. We do not know whether the population is normally distributed, and there are not at least 30 participants. However, the data from the sample do not suggest a skewed distribution.

Step 2: Null hypothesis: Male U.S. Marines after a month-long training exercise have the same average anger levels as college men: $H_0: \mu_1 = \mu_2$.

Research hypothesis: Male U.S. Marines after a month-long training exercise have different average anger levels than college men: $H_1: \mu_1 \neq \mu_2$.

Step 3: $\mu_M = \mu = 8.90$; $s_M = 0.494$

X	X − M	(X − M)²
14	0.667	0.445
12	−1.333	1.777
13	−0.333	0.111
12	−1.333	1.777
14	0.667	0.445
15	1.667	2.779

$M = 13.333$

$SS = \Sigma(X - M)^2 = \Sigma(0.445 + 1.777 + 0.111 + 1.777 + 0.445 + 2.779) = 7.334$

$$s = \sqrt{\frac{\Sigma(X - M)^2}{N - 1}} = \sqrt{\frac{SS}{(N - 1)}} = \sqrt{\frac{7.334}{6 - 1}} = \sqrt{1.467} = 1.211$$

$$s_M = \frac{s}{\sqrt{N}} = \frac{1.211}{\sqrt{6}} = 0.494$$

Step 4: $df = N - 1 = 6 - 1 = 5$; the critical values, based on 5 degrees of freedom, a p level of 0.05, and a two-tailed test, are -2.571 and 2.571. (*Note:* It is helpful to draw a curve that includes these cutoffs.)

Step 5: $t = \dfrac{(M - \mu_M)}{s_M} = \dfrac{(13.333 - 8.90)}{0.494} = 8.97$

(*Note:* It is helpful to add this t statistic to the curve that you drew in step 4.)

Step 6: Reject the null hypothesis. It appears that male U.S. Marines just after a month-long training exercise have higher average anger levels than college men have; $t(5) = 8.97, p < 0.05$.

b. $t = \dfrac{(M - \mu_M)}{s_M} = \dfrac{(13.333 - 9.20)}{0.494} = 8.37$; reject the null

hypothesis; it appears that male U.S. Marines just after a month-long training exercise have higher average anger levels than adult men; $t(5) = 8.37, p < 0.05$.

c. $t = \dfrac{(M - \mu_M)}{s_M} = \dfrac{(13.333 - 13.5)}{0.494} = -0.34$. Fail to reject

the null hypothesis; we conclude that there is no evidence from this study to support the research hypothesis; $t(5) = -0.34, p > 0.05$.

d. We can conclude that Marines' anger scores just after high-altitude, cold-weather training are, on average, higher than those of college men and adult men. We cannot conclude, however, that they are different, on average, from those of male psychiatric outpatients. With respect to the latter difference, we can only conclude that there is no evidence to support that there is a difference between Marines' mean anger scores and those of male psychiatric outpatients.

9-31 a.

b. The distributions are similar in that 0 is the modal amount of credit card debt for both women and men. The majority of participants in this study reported no credit card debt. Both distributions are positively skewed, particularly the distribution for women. Moreover, the distribution for women shows a potential outlier.

9-33 a. A single-sample t test is the appropriate hypothesis test because we are comparing a sample to a population. We have only one sample and we know the population mean, but we do not know the population standard deviation.

b. Step 1: Population 1: The number of mosquitos that chose to enter a chamber with a hand in it with no perfume or insect repellent (control condition).

Population 2: The number of mosquitos that chose to enter a chamber with a hand in it sprayed with a high concentration of Victoria's Secret Bombshell perfume.

The comparison distribution will be a distribution of means. The hypothesis test will be a single-sample t test because we have only one sample and we know the population mean, but we do not know the population standard deviation. This study meets at least one of the three assumptions: The dependent variable is scale. It is not likely that the five hands were randomly selected from all hands in the population. Last, there are fewer than 5 participants (i.e., hands with perfume).

Step 2: Null hypothesis: The percentage of mosquitos that approached a hand with perfume is the same as the percentage of mosquitos that approached the hand with no perfume (or insect repellent)—$H_0: \mu_1 = \mu_2$.

Research hypothesis: A different percentage of mosquitos approached a hand with perfume compared to mosquitos that approached the hand with no perfume (or insect repellent)—$H_1: \mu_1 \neq \mu_2$.

Step 3:

$$\mu_M = \mu = 61\%$$

$$s_M = \frac{s}{\sqrt{N}} = \frac{12.052}{\sqrt{5}} = 5.390$$

Step 4: $df = N - 1 = 5 - 1 = 4$

The critical values, based on 4 degrees of freedom with a p level of 0.05 and a two-tailed test, are -2.776 and 2.776.

Step 5:

$$t = \frac{(M - \mu_M)}{s_M} = \frac{17\% - 61\%}{5.390} = -8.163$$

Step 6: Reject the null hypothesis. It appears that significantly fewer mosquitos approached the hand with perfume compared to mosquitos that experienced the control condition, no perfume. The statistics, as presented in a journal article, would read: $t(4) = -8.163, p < 0.05$

c. Cohen's $d = t = \dfrac{(M - \mu)}{s} = \dfrac{17\% - 61\%}{12.052} = -3.65$

Based on Cohen's conventions, this is a huge effect size. (Cohen considered 0.8 to be a large effect.)

d. Calculate the confidence interval for the sample mean for the perfume.

Given $M = 17\%$ and $s = 12.052$, standard error is:

$$s_M = \frac{s}{\sqrt{N}} = \frac{12.052}{\sqrt{5}} = 5.390$$

$M_{lower} = -t(s_M) + M_{sample} = -2.776(5.390) + 17\% = 2.037\%$

We calculate the upper end of the interval as:

$M_{upper} = t(s_M) + M_{sample} = 2.776(5.390) + 17\% = 31.963\%$

The 95% confidence interval around the mean of 17% is [2.04%, 31.96%].

e. The population mean, 61%, does not fall within the 95% confidence interval for a sample mean of 17%. We can conclude that the sample of perfumed hands placed in the chamber with the mosquitoes came from a different population than the mosquitoes who experienced the control condition. The confidence interval allows us to make the same conclusion as the t test, but it gives us more information with an interval estimate as opposed to a point estimate.

9-35 a. The appropriate mean: $\mu_M = \mu = 11.72$

The calculations for the appropriate standard deviation (in this case, standard error, s_M) are:

$$M = \frac{\Sigma X}{N} = \frac{(25.62 + 13.09 + 8.74 + 17.63 + 2.80 + 4.42)}{6} = 12.05$$

X	$X - M$	$(X - M)^2$
25.62	13.57	184.145
13.09	1.04	1.082
8.74	−3.31	10.956
17.63	5.58	31.136
2.80	−9.25	85.563
4.42	−7.63	58.217

Numerator: $\Sigma(X - M)^2 = \Sigma(184.145 + 1.082 + 10.956 + 31.136 + 85.563 + 58.217) = 371.099$

$$s = \sqrt{\frac{\Sigma(X - M)^2}{(N - 1)}} = \sqrt{\frac{371.099}{(6 - 1)}} = \sqrt{74.220} = 8.615$$

$$s_M = \frac{s}{\sqrt{N}} = \frac{8.615}{\sqrt{6}} = 3.517$$

b. $t = \frac{(M - \mu_M)}{s_M} = \frac{(12.05 - 11.72)}{3.517} = 0.09$

c. There are several possible answers to this question. Among the hypotheses that could be examined are whether the length of stay on death row depends on gender, race, or age. Specifically, given prior evidence of a racial bias in the implementation of the death penalty, we might hypothesize that black and Hispanic prisoners have shorter times to execution than do prisoners overall.

d. We would need to know the population standard deviation. If we were really interested in this, we could calculate the standard deviation from the entire online execution list.

e. The null hypothesis states that the average time spent on death row in recent years is equal to what it has been historically (no change): $H_0: \mu_1 = \mu_2$. The research hypothesis is that there has been a change in the average time spent on death row: $H_1: \mu_1 \neq \mu_2$.

f. The t statistic we calculated was 0.09. The critical t values for a two-tailed test, alpha or p of 0.05 and df of 5, are ±2.571. We fail to reject the null hypothesis and conclude that we do not have sufficient evidence to indicate a change in time spent on death row.

g. $M_{lower} = -t(s_M) + M_{sample} = -2.571(3.517) + 12.05 = 3.01$ years

$M_{upper} = t(s_M) + M_{sample} = 2.571(3.517) + 12.05 = 21.09$ years

The 95% confidence interval around the mean of 12.05 is [3.01, 21.09].

h. Because the population mean of 11.72 years is within the very large range of the confidence interval, we fail to reject the null hypothesis. This confidence interval is so large that it is not useful. The large size of the confidence interval is due to the large variability in the sample (s_M) and the small sample size (resulting in a large critical t value).

i. $d = \frac{(M - \mu)}{s} = \frac{(12.05 - 11.72)}{8.615} = 0.04$

j. This is a small effect.

Chapter 10

10-1 We can understand the meaning of a distribution of mean differences by reviewing how the distribution is created in the first place. A distribution of mean differences is constructed by measuring the difference scores for a sample of individuals and then averaging those differences. This process is performed repeatedly, using the same population and samples of the same size. Once a collection of mean differences is gathered, they can be displayed on a graph (in most cases, they form a bell-shaped curve).

10-3 The term *paired samples* is used to describe a test that compares an individual's scores in both conditions; it is also called a *paired-samples* t test. *Independent samples* refer to groups that do not overlap in any way, including membership; the observations made in one group in no way relate to or depend on the observations made in another group.

10-5 Unlike a single-sample t test, in the paired-samples t test we have two scores for every participant; we take the difference between these scores before calculating the sample mean difference that will be used in the t test.

10-7 If the confidence interval around the mean difference score includes the value of 0, then 0 is a plausible mean difference. If we conduct a hypothesis test for these data, we would fail to reject the null hypothesis.

10-9 As with other hypothesis tests, the conclusions from both the single-sample t test or paired-samples t test and the confidence interval are the same, but the confidence interval gives us more information—an interval estimate, not just a point estimate.

10-11 Order effects occur when performance on a task changes because the dependent variable is being presented for a second time.

10-13 Because order effects result in a change in the dependent variable that is not directly the result of the independent variable of interest, the researcher may decide to use a between-groups design, particularly when counterbalancing is not possible. For example, a researcher may be interested in how the amount of practice affects the acquisition of a new language. It would not be possible for the same participants to be in both a group that has small amounts of practice and a group that has large amounts of practice.

10-15 a. $df = 17$, so the critical t value is 2.567, assuming you're anticipating an increase in marital satisfaction.

b. $df = 63$, so the critical t values are ±2.001.

10-17 a.

Difference (D)	D − M	(D − M)²
−8	−9.25	85.563
8	6.75	45.563
2	0.75	0.563
5	3.75	14.063
−5	−6.25	39.063
4	2.75	7.563
−2	−3.25	10.563
6	4.75	22.563

$M_{difference} = 1.25$

$SS = \Sigma(D - M)^2 = 225.504$

$s = \sqrt{\dfrac{SS}{N-1}} = \sqrt{\dfrac{225.504}{7}} = 5.676$

$s_M = \dfrac{s}{\sqrt{N}} = \dfrac{5.676}{\sqrt{8}} = 2.007$

$t = \dfrac{(M - \mu_M)}{s_M} = \dfrac{(1.25 - 0)}{2.007} = 0.62$

b. With $df = 7$, the critical t values are ± 2.365. The calculated t statistic of 0.62 does not exceed the critical value. Therefore, we fail to reject the null hypothesis.

c. When increasing N to 1000, we need to recalculate s_M and the t test.

$s_M = \dfrac{s}{\sqrt{N}} = \dfrac{5.676}{\sqrt{1000}} = 0.179$

$t = \dfrac{(1.25 - 0)}{0.179} = 6.98$

The critical values with $df = 999$ are $t = \pm 1.98$. Because the calculated t exceeds one of the t critical values, we reject the null hypothesis.

d. Increasing the sample size increased the value of the t statistic and decreased the critical t values, making it easier for us to reject the null hypothesis.

10-19 a.

Difference (D)	D − M	(D − M)²
17	5.429	29.474
22	10.429	108.764
18	6.429	41.332
3	−8.571	73.462
11	−0.571	0.326
5	−6.571	43.178
5	−6.571	43.178

$M_{difference} = 11.571$

$SS = \Sigma(D - M)^2 = 339.714$

$s = \sqrt{\dfrac{SS}{N-1}} = \sqrt{\dfrac{339.714}{6}} = 7.525$

$s_M = \dfrac{s}{\sqrt{N}} = \dfrac{7.525}{\sqrt{7}} = 2.844$

$t = \dfrac{(M - \mu_M)}{s_M} = \dfrac{(11.571 - 0)}{2.844} = 4.07$

b. With $N = 7$, $df = 6$, $t = \pm 2.447$:

$M_{lower} = -t(s_M) + M_{sample} = -2.447(2.844) + 11.571 = 4.61$

$M_{upper} = t(s_M) + M_{sample} = 2.447(2.844) + 11.571 = 18.53$

c. $d = \dfrac{(M - \mu_M)}{s} = \dfrac{(11.571 - 0)}{7.525} = 1.54$

10-21 a. $s_M = \dfrac{s}{\sqrt{N}} = \dfrac{1.42}{\sqrt{13}} = 0.394$

$t = \dfrac{(-0.77 - 0)}{0.394} = -1.95$

b. $M_{lower} = -t(s_M) + M_{sample} = -2.179(0.394) + (-0.77) = -1.63$

$M_{upper} = t(s_M) + M_{sample} = 2.179(0.394) + (-0.77) = 0.09$

c. $d = \dfrac{(M - \mu)}{s} = \dfrac{(-0.77 - 0)}{1.42} = -0.54$

10-23 A study using a paired-samples t test design would compare people before and after training using the program of mental exercises designed by PowerBrainRx. Population 1 would be people before the mental exercises training. Population 2 would be people after the mental exercises training.

The comparison distribution is a distribution of mean differences. The participants receiving mental exercises training are the same in both samples. So, we would calculate a difference score for each participant and a mean difference score for the study. The mean difference score would be compared to a distribution of all possible mean difference scores for a sample of this size and based on the null hypothesis. In this case, the mean difference score would be compared to 0. Because we have two samples and all participants are in both samples, we would use a paired-samples t test.

10-25 a. *Step 1:* Population 1 is the Devils players in the 2007–2008 season. Population 2 is the Devils players in the 2008–2009 season. The comparison distribution is a distribution of mean differences. We meet one assumption: The dependent variable, goals, is scale. We do not, however, meet the assumption that the participants are randomly selected from the population. We may also not meet the assumption that the population distribution of scores is normally distributed (the scores do not appear normally distributed and we do not have an N of at least 30).

Step 2: Null hypothesis: The team performed no differently, on average, between the 2007–2008 and 2008–2009 seasons: $H_0: \mu_1 = \mu_2$.

Research hypothesis: The team performed differently, on average, between the 2007–2008 and 2008–2009 seasons: $H_1: \mu_1 \neq \mu_2$.

Step 3: $\mu = 0$ and $s_M = 3.682$

Difference (D)	D − M	(D − M)²
11	4.833	23.358
6	−0.167	0.028
−7	−13.167	173.370
16	9.833	96.688
−2	−8.167	66.670
13	6.833	46.690

$M_{difference} = 6.167$

$SS = \Sigma(D - M)^2 = 406.834$

$s = \sqrt{\dfrac{SS}{N-1}} = \sqrt{\dfrac{406.834}{5}} = 9.020$

$s_M = \dfrac{s}{\sqrt{N}} = \dfrac{9.020}{\sqrt{6}} = 3.682$

Step 4: The critical t values with a two-tailed test, a p level of 0.05, and 5 degrees of freedom, are ±2.571.

Step 5: $t = \dfrac{(M - \mu_M)}{s_M} = \dfrac{(6.167 - 0)}{3.682} = 1.67$

Step 6: Fail to reject the null hypothesis because the calculated t statistic of 1.67 does not exceed the critical t value.

b. $t(5) = 1.67$, $p > 0.05$ (*Note:* If we had used software, we would provide the actual p value.)

c. $M_{lower} = -t(s_M) + M_{sample} = -2.571(3.682) - 6.167 = -3.30$

$M_{upper} = t(s_M) + M_{sample} = 2.571(3.682) + 6.167 = 15.63$

Because the confidence interval includes 0, we fail to reject the null hypothesis. This is consistent with the results of the hypothesis test conducted in part (a).

d. $d = \dfrac{(M - \mu)}{s} = \dfrac{(6.167 - 0)}{9.020} = 0.68$

10-27 a. The professor would use a paired-samples t-test.

b. No. A change or a difference in mean score might not be statistically significant, particularly with a small sample.

c. It would be easier to reject the null hypothesis for a given mean difference with the class with 700 students than with the class with 7 students because the t value would be higher with the larger sample.

10-29 a. The independent variable is type of classroom. It has two levels—decorated and undecorated (or sparse).

b. The dependent variable is percentage correct on a science test.

c. The researchers used a paired-samples t test because they had two scores for each student—one in the sparse classroom and one in the decorated classroom. All students participated in both conditions.

d. Twenty-three students participated. We know this because the degrees of freedom is 22, and degrees of freedom is calculated as the number of participants minus 1.

e. We know the result is statistically significant because the p value of .007 is less than .05.

f. Students who learned science in an undecorated classroom got an average of 55% of questions correct on a test. The

same students learning science in a decorated classroom got only an average of 42% correct. This difference is statistically significant, which means it was unlikely to have occurred just by chance.

g. The researchers reported the effect size so that readers would have a sense of how large, or important, this finding is.

10-31 a. A paired-samples t test was appropriate in this situation because this is a within-group design; the dependent measure (checking e-mail) is measured twice with the same sample of participants. During one of the two weeks of the study, participants were instructed to check their e-mail only three times a day, and during the other week, participants were instructed to check their e-mail as often as they wanted to.

b. Confidence intervals provide an interval for the sample statistic, as opposed to a point estimate. Confidence intervals provide more information than a point estimate.

c. Effect sizes tell us the strength of the effect of the independent variable, in this case the specific instructions on how frequently participants should check their e-mail.

d. If all participants were told in the first week to only check their e-mail three times a day, they may have become accustomed to checking their e-mail three times a day by the end of the week. This has the potential to influence their e-mail checking behaviors in the following week, where they would be instructed to check their e-mail as often as they would like. Similarly, if participants were first instructed to check their e-mail as often as they would like in the first week, they may have had a difficult time shifting to only checking their e-mail three times a day in the second week. The potential difference in the actual number of times participants checked e-mail might not have been due to the instructions given, but instead due to an order effect. In order to address order effects in within-subject design, counterbalancing is necessary. Counterbalancing is when the order of treatments is altered between subjects.

e. This manipulation check—ensuring that participants were doing as they were instructed—confirmed that when participants were instructed to check their e-mail only three times a day they actually checked their e-mail significantly less often compared to the unlimited condition. This was true regardless of when they received the instruction to check their e-mail less either in the first week or the second week. The researchers also examined whether there was a statistically significant effect of the instructions on how many e-mails were received and on how many e-mails participants responded to. This allowed the researchers to ensure that any effects on stress were due to the frequency of checking e-mail rather than the numbers of e-mails that participants managed.

10-33 a. The independent variable is presence of posthypnotic suggestion, with two levels: suggestion or no suggestion. The dependent variable is Stroop reaction time in seconds.

b. *Step 1:* Population 1 is highly hypnotizable individuals who receive a posthypnotic suggestion. Population 2 is highly hypnotizable individuals who do not receive a posthypnotic suggestion. The comparison distribution will be a distribution of mean differences. The hypothesis test will be a paired-samples t test because we have two samples and all participants are in both samples. This study meets one of the three assumptions and may meet another. The dependent variable, reaction time in seconds, is scale. The data were not likely randomly selected, so we should be cautious when generalizing beyond the sample. We do not know whether the population is normally distributed and there are not at least 30 participants, but the sample data do not suggest skew.

Step 2: Null hypothesis: Highly hypnotizable individuals who receive a posthypnotic suggestion will have the same average Stroop reaction times as highly hypnotizable individuals who receive no posthypnotic suggestion: $H_0: \mu_1 = \mu_2$.

Research hypothesis: Highly hypnotizable individuals who receive a posthypnotic suggestion will have different average Stroop reaction times than will highly hypnotizable individuals who receive no posthypnotic suggestion: $H_1: \mu_1 \neq \mu_2$.

Step 3: $\mu_M = 1 = 0; s_M = 0.420$

(*Note:* Remember to cross out the original scores once you have created the difference scores so you won't be tempted to use them in your calculations.)

Difference (D)	D − M	(D − M)²
−4.1	−1.05	1.103
−4.2	−1.15	1.323
−1.6	1.45	2.103
−3.0	0.05	0.003
−3.2	−0.15	0.023
−2.2	0.85	0.723

$M_{difference} = -3.05$

$SS = \Sigma(D - M)^2 = \Sigma(1.103 + 1.323 + 2.103 + 0.003 + 0.023 + 0.723) = 5.278$

$s = \sqrt{\dfrac{\Sigma(D - M)^2}{(N - 1)}} = \sqrt{\dfrac{SS}{(N - 1)}}$

$= \sqrt{\dfrac{5.278}{(6 - 1)}} = \sqrt{1.056} = 1.$

$s_M = \dfrac{s}{\sqrt{N}} = \dfrac{1.028}{\sqrt{6}} = 0.420$

Step 4: $df = N - 1 = 6 - 1 = 5$; the critical values, based on 5 degrees of freedom, a p level of 0.05, and a two-tailed test, are −2.571 and 2.571.

Step 5: $t = \dfrac{(M_{difference} - \mu_{difference})}{s_M} = \dfrac{(-3.05 - 0)}{0.420} = -7.26$

Step 6: Reject the null hypothesis; it appears that highly hypnotizable people have faster Stroop reaction times when they receive a posthypnotic suggestion than when they do not.

c. $t(5) = -7.26, p < 0.05$

d. *Step 2:* Null hypothesis: The average Stroop reaction time of highly hypnotizable individuals who receive a posthypnotic suggestion is greater than or equal to that of highly hypnotizable individuals who receive no posthypnotic suggestion: $H_0: \mu_1 \geq \mu_2$.

Research hypothesis: Highly hypnotizable individuals who receive a posthypnotic suggestion will have faster (i.e., lower number) average Stroop reaction times than highly hypnotizable individuals who receive no posthypnotic suggestion: $H_1: \mu_1 < \mu_2$.

Step 4: $df = N - 1 = 6 - 1 = 5$; the critical value, based on 5 degrees of freedom, a p level of 0.05, and a one-tailed test, is −2.015. (*Note:* It is helpful to draw a curve that includes this cutoff.)

Step 6: Reject the null hypothesis; it appears that highly hypnotizable people have faster Stroop reaction times when they receive a posthypnotic suggestion than when they do not.

It is easier to reject the null hypothesis with a one-tailed test. Although we rejected the null hypothesis under both conditions, the critical t value is less extreme with a one-tailed test because the entire 0.05 (5%) critical region is in one tail instead of divided between two.

The difference between the means of the samples is identical, as is the test statistic. The only aspect that is affected is the critical value.

e. *Step 4:* $df = N - 1 = 6 - 1 = 5$; the critical values, based on 5 degrees of freedom, a p level of 0.01, and a two-tailed test, are −4.032 and 4.032. (*Note:* It is helpful to draw a curve that includes these cutoffs.)

Step 6: Reject the null hypothesis; it appears that highly hypnotizable people have faster mean Stroop reaction times when they receive a posthypnotic suggestion than when they do not.

A p level of 0.01 leads to more extreme critical values than a p level of 0.05. When the tails are limited to 1% versus 5%, the tails beyond the cutoffs are smaller and the cutoffs are more extreme. So it is easier to reject the null hypothesis with a p level of .05 than the null hypothesis with a p level of .01.

The difference between the means of the samples is identical, as is the test statistic. The only aspect that is affected is the critical value.

f. *Step 3:* $\mu_M = 0; s_M = 0.850$

(*Note:* Remember to cross out the original scores once you have created the difference scores so you won't be tempted to use them in your calculations.)

Difference (D)	D − M	(D − M)²
−4.1	−0.8	0.64
−4.2	−0.9	0.81
−1.6	1.7	2.89

$M_{difference} = -3.3$

$SS = \Sigma(D - M)^2 = \Sigma(0.64 + 0.81 + 2.89) = 4.34$

$s = \sqrt{\dfrac{\Sigma(D - M)^2}{(N - 1)}} = \sqrt{\dfrac{SS}{(N - 1)}}$

$= \sqrt{\dfrac{4.34}{(3 - 1)}} = \sqrt{2.17} = 1.473$

$s_M = \dfrac{s}{\sqrt{N}} = \dfrac{1.473}{\sqrt{3}} = 0.850$

Step 4: df = $N - 1 = 3 - 1 = 2$; the critical values, based on 2 degrees of freedom, a *p* level of 0.05, and a two-tailed test, are -4.303 and 4.303. (*Note:* It is helpful to draw a curve that includes these cutoffs.)

Step 5: $t = \dfrac{(M_{difference} - \mu_{difference})}{s_M} = \dfrac{(-3.3 - 0)}{0.850} = -3.88$

(*Note:* It is helpful to add this *t* statistic to the curve that you drew in step 4.)

This test statistic is no longer beyond the critical value. Reducing the sample size makes it more difficult to reject the null hypothesis because it results in a larger standard error and therefore a smaller test statistic. It also results in more extreme critical values.

g. Participants might get faster at completing the Stroop test as a result of practice with it. If so, their reaction times would be faster the second time they complete the task regardless of whether they had the posthypnotic suggestion.

h. The researchers could not use counterbalancing because this was a pre–post design. However, one way to get rid of possible order effects would be to use a between-groups design in which some participants are given the posthypnotic suggestion but others are not, and then compare.

Chapter 11

11-1 An independent-samples *t* test is used when we do not know the population parameters and are comparing two groups that are composed of unrelated participants or observations.

11-3 Independent events are things that do not affect each other. For example, the lunch you buy today does not impact the hours of sleep the authors of this book will get tonight.

11-5 The comparison distribution for the paired-samples *t* test is made up of *mean differences*—the average of many difference scores. The comparison distribution for the independent-samples *t* test is made up of *differences between means*, or the differences we can expect to see between group means if the null hypothesis is true.

11-7 Both of these represent corrected variance within a group (s^2), but one is for the *X* variable and the other is for the *Y* variable. Because these are corrected measures of variance, $N - 1$ is in the denominator of the equations.

11-9 We assume that larger samples do a better job of estimating the population than smaller samples do, so we would want the variability measure based on the larger sample to count more.

11-11 We can take the confidence interval's upper bound and lower bound, compare those to the point estimate in the numerator, and get the margin of error. So, if we predict a score of 7 with a confidence interval of [4.3, 9.7], we can also express this as a margin of error of 2.7 points (7 ± 2.7). Confidence interval and margin of error are simply two ways to say the same thing.

11-13 Larger ranges mean less precision in making predictions, just as widening the goal posts in rugby or in American football mean that you can be less precise when trying to kick the ball

between the posts. Smaller ranges indicate we are doing a better job of predicting the phenomenon within the population. For example, a 95% confidence interval that spans a range from 2 to 12 is larger than a 95% confidence interval from 5 to 6. Although the percentage range has stayed the same, the width of the distribution has changed.

11-15 We would take several steps back from the final calculation of standard error to the step in which we calculated pooled variance. Pooled variance is the variance version, or squared version, of standard deviation. To convert pooled variance to the pooled standard deviation, we take its square root.

11-17 Guidelines for interpreting the size of an effect based on Cohen's *d* were presented in Table 11-2. Those guidelines state that 0.2 is a small effect, 0.5 is a medium effect, and 0.8 is a large effect.

11-19 a. Group 1 is treated as the *X* variable; $M_X = 95.8$.

X	X − M	(X − M)²
97	1.2	1.44
83	−12.8	163.84
105	9.2	84.64
102	6.2	38.44
92	−3.8	14.44

$s_X^2 = \dfrac{\Sigma(X - M)^2}{N - 1} = \dfrac{(1.44 + 163.84 + 84.64 + 24.44 + 14.44)}{5 - 1}$
$= 75.7$

Group 2 is treated as the *Y* variable; $M_Y = 104$.

Y	Y − M	(Y − M)²
111	7	49
103	−1	1
96	−8	64
106	2	4

$s_Y^2 = \dfrac{\Sigma(Y - M)^2}{N - 1} = \dfrac{(49 + 1 + 64 + 4)}{4 - 1} = 39.333$

b. Treating group 1 as *X* and group 2 as *Y*, $df_X = N - 1 = 5 - 1 = 4$, $df_Y = 4 - 1 = 3$, and $df_{total} = df_X + df_Y = 4 + 3 = 7$.

c. -2.365, 2.365

d. $s_{pooled}^2 = \left(\dfrac{df_X}{df_{total}}\right)s_X^2 + \left(\dfrac{df_Y}{df_{total}}\right)s_Y^2 = \left(\dfrac{4}{7}\right)75.7 + \left(\dfrac{3}{7}\right)39.333$
$= 43.257 + 16.857 = 60.114$

e. For group 1: $s_{M_X}^2 = \dfrac{s_{pooled}^2}{N_X} = \dfrac{60.114}{5} = 12.023$

For group 2: $s_{M_Y}^2 = \dfrac{s_{pooled}^2}{N_Y} = \dfrac{60.114}{4} = 15.029$

f. $s_{difference}^2 = s_{M_Y}^2 = 12.023 + 15.029 = 27.052$

The standard deviation of the distribution of differences between means is:

$s_{difference} = \sqrt{s_{difference}^2} = \sqrt{27.052} = 5.201$

g. $t = \dfrac{(M_X - M_Y)}{s_{difference}} = \dfrac{(95.8 - 104) - (0)}{5.201} = -1.58$

h. The critical t values for the 95% confidence interval for a df of 7 are -2.365 and 2.365.

$(M_X - M_Y)_{lower} = -t(s_{difference}) + (M_X - M_Y)_{sample}$
$\qquad = -2.365(5.201) + (-8.2) = -20.50$

$(M_X - M_Y)_{upper} = t(s_{difference}) + (M_X - M_Y)_{sample}$
$\qquad = 2.365(5.201) + (-8.2) = 4.10$

The confidence interval is $[-20.50, 4.10]$.

i. To calculate Cohen's d, we need to calculate the pooled standard deviation for the data:

$s_{pooled} = \sqrt{s_{pooled}^2} = \sqrt{60.114} = 7.753$

Cohen's $d =$
$\dfrac{(M_X - M_Y) - (\mu_X - \mu_Y)}{s_{pooled}} = \dfrac{(95.8 - 104) - (0)}{7.753} = -1.06$

11-21 a. df_{total} is 35, and the cutoffs are -2.030 and 2.030.

b. df_{total} is 26, and the cutoffs are -2.779 and 2.779.

c. -1.740 and 1.740

11-23 a. *Step 1:* Population 1 is highly hypnotizable people who receive a posthypnotic suggestion. Population 2 is highly hypnotizable people who do not receive a posthypnotic suggestion. The comparison distribution will be a distribution of differences between means. The hypothesis test will be an independent-samples t test because there are two samples and every participant is in only one sample. This study meets one of the three assumptions and may meet another. The dependent variable, reaction time in seconds, is scale. The data were not likely randomly selected, so we should be cautious when generalizing beyond the sample. We do not know whether the population is normally distributed, and there are fewer than 30 participants, but the sample data do not suggest skew.

Step 2: Null hypothesis: Highly hypnotizable individuals who receive a posthypnotic suggestion have the same average Stroop reaction times as highly hypnotizable individuals who receive no posthypnotic suggestion—$H_0: \mu_1 = \mu_2$.
Research hypothesis: Highly hypnotizable individuals who receive a posthypnotic suggestion have different average Stroop reaction times than highly hypnotizable individuals who receive no posthypnotic suggestion—$H_1: \mu_1 \neq \mu_2$.

Step 3: $(\mu_1 - \mu_2) = 0$; $s_{difference} = 0.463$
Calculations:

$M_X = 12.55$

X	$X - M$	$(X - M)^2$
12.6	0.05	0.003
13.8	1.25	1.563
11.6	-0.95	0.903
12.2	-0.35	0.123
12.1	-0.45	0.203
13.0	0.45	0.203

$s_X^2 = \dfrac{\Sigma(X - M)^2}{N - 1}$

$\qquad = \dfrac{(0.003 + 1.563 + 0.903 + 0.123 + 0.203 + 0.203)}{6 - 1}$

$\qquad = 0.600$

$M_Y = 9.50$

Y	$Y - M$	$(Y - M)^2$
8.5	-1.0	1.000
9.6	0.1	0.010
10.0	0.5	0.250
9.2	-0.3	0.090
8.9	-0.6	0.360
10.8	1.3	1.690

$s_Y^2 = \dfrac{\Sigma(Y - M)^2}{N - 1}$

$\qquad = \dfrac{(1.0 + 0.01 + 0.25 + 0.09 + 0.36 + 1.69)}{6 - 1}$

$\qquad = 0.680$

$df_X = N - 1 = 6 - 1 = 5$
$df_Y = N - 1 = 6 - 1 = 5$
$df_{total} = df_X + df_Y = 5 + 5 = 10$

$s_{pooled}^2 = \left(\dfrac{df_X}{df_{total}}\right)s_X^2 + \left(\dfrac{df_Y}{df_{total}}\right)s_Y^2 = \left(\dfrac{5}{10}\right)0.600 + \left(\dfrac{5}{10}\right)0.680$
$\qquad = 0.300 + 0.340 = 0.640$

$s_{M_X}^2 = \dfrac{s_{pooled}^2}{N} = \dfrac{0.640}{6} = 0.107$

$s_{M_Y}^2 = \dfrac{s_{pooled}^2}{N} = \dfrac{0.640}{6} = 0.107$

$s_{difference}^2 = s_{M_X}^2 + s_{M_Y}^2 = 0.107 + 0.107 = 0.214$

$s_{difference} = \sqrt{s_{difference}^2} = \sqrt{0.214} = 0.463$

Step 4: The critical values, based on a two-tailed test, a p level of 0.05, and df_{total} of 10, are -2.228 and 2.228. (*Note:* It is helpful to draw a curve that includes these cutoffs.)

Step 5: $t = \dfrac{(12.55 - 9.50) - (0)}{0.463} = \dfrac{3.05}{0.463} = 6.59$

(*Note:* It is helpful to add this t statistic to the curve that you drew in step 4.)

Step 6: Reject the null hypothesis; it appears that highly hypnotizable people have faster Stroop reaction times when they receive a posthypnotic suggestion than when they do not.

b. $t(10) = 6.59, p < 0.05$. (*Note:* If we used software to conduct the t test, we would report the actual p value associated with this test statistic.)

c. When there are two separate samples, the t statistic becomes smaller. Thus, it becomes more difficult to reject the null hypothesis with a between-groups design than with a within-groups design.

d. In the within-groups design and the calculation of the paired-samples t test, we create a set of difference scores and conduct a t test on that set of difference scores. This means that any overall differences that participants have on the dependent variable are subtracted out and do not go into the measure of overall variability that is in the denominator of the t statistic.

e. To calculate the 95% confidence interval, first calculate:

$$s_{difference} = \sqrt{s^2_{difference}} = \sqrt{s^2_{M_X} + s^2_{M_Y}}$$

$$= \sqrt{\frac{s^2_{pooled}}{N_X} + \frac{s^2_{pooled}}{N_Y}}$$

$$= \sqrt{\frac{0.640}{6} + \frac{0.640}{6}} = \sqrt{0.214} = 0.463$$

The critical t statistics for a distribution with $df = 10$ that correspond to a p level of 0.05—that is, the values that mark off the most extreme 0.025 in each tail—are -2.228 and 2.228.

Then calculate:

$$(M_X - M_Y)_{lower} = -t(s_{difference}) + (M_X - M_Y)_{sample} = -2.228$$
$$(0.463) + (12.55 - 9.5) = -1.032 + 3.05 = 2.02$$

$$(M_X - M_Y)_{upper} = t(s_{difference}) + (M_X - M_Y)_{sample} =$$
$$2.228(0.463) + (12.55 - 9.5) = 1.032 + 3.05 = 4.08$$

The 95% confidence interval around the difference between means of 3.05 is [2.02, 4.08].

f. Were we to draw repeated samples (of the same sizes) from these two populations, 95% of the time the confidence interval would contain the true population parameter.

g. Because the confidence interval does not include 0, it is not plausible that there is no difference between means. Were we to conduct a hypothesis test, we would be able to reject the null hypothesis and could conclude that the means of the two samples are different.

h. In addition to determining statistical significance, the confidence interval allows us to determine a range of plausible differences between means. An interval estimate gives us a better sense than does a point estimate of how precisely we can estimate from this study.

i. The appropriate measure of effect size for a t statistic is Cohen's d, which is calculated as:

$$d = \frac{(M_X - M_Y) - (\mu_X - \mu_Y)}{s_{pooled}} = \frac{(12.55 - 9.5) - (0)}{\sqrt{0.640}} = 3.81$$

j. Based on Cohen's conventions, this is a large effect size.

k. It is useful to have effect-size information because the hypothesis test tells us only whether we were likely to have obtained our sample mean by chance. The effect size tells us the magnitude of the effect, giving us a sense of how important or practical this finding is, and allows us to standardize the results of the study so that we can compare across studies. Here, we know that there's a large effect.

11-25 a. *Step 1:* Population 1 consists of men. Population 2 consists of women. The comparison distribution is a distribution of differences between means. We will use an independent-samples t test because men and women cannot be in both conditions, and we have two groups. Of the three assumptions,

we meet one because the dependent variable, number of words uttered, is a scale variable. We do not know whether the data were randomly selected or whether the population is normally distributed, and there is a small N, so we should be cautious in drawing conclusions.

Step 2: Null hypothesis: There is no mean difference in the number of words uttered by men and women—$H_0: \mu_1 = \mu_2$.

Research hypothesis: Men and women utter a different number of words, on average—$H_1: \mu_1 \neq \mu_2$.

Step 3: $(\mu_1 - \mu_2) = 0$; $s_{difference} = 612.565$

Calculations (treating women as X and men as Y):

$$M_X = 16,091.600$$

X	$X - M$	$(X - M)^2$
17,345	1253.400	1,571,011.560
15,593	−498.600	248,601.960
16,624	532.400	283,499.760
16,696	604.400	365,299.360
14,200	−1891.600	3,578,150.560

$$s^2_X = \frac{\Sigma(X - M)^2}{N - 1} = \frac{(6,046,513.200)}{5 - 1} = 1,511,628.300$$

$$M_Y = 16,160.600$$

Y	$Y - M$	$(Y - M)^2$
16,345	184.400	34,003.360
17,222	1061.400	1,126,569.960
15,646	−514.600	264,813.160
14,889	−1271.600	1,616,966.560
16,701	540.400	292,032.160

$$s^2_Y = \frac{\Sigma(Y - M)^2}{N - 1} = \frac{(3,334,385.200)}{5 - 1} = 833,596.300$$

$$df_X = N - 1 = 5 - 1 = 4$$
$$df_Y = N - 1 = 5 - 1 = 4$$
$$df_{total} = df_X + df_Y = 8$$

$$s^2_{pooled} = \left(\frac{df_X}{df_{total}}\right)s^2_X + \left(\frac{df_Y}{df_{total}}\right)s^2_Y$$

$$= \left(\frac{4}{10}\right)1,511,628.300 + \left(\frac{4}{10}\right)833,596.300$$

$$= 938,089.84$$

$$s^2_{M_X} = \frac{s^2_{pooled}}{N_X} = \frac{938,089.84}{5} = 187,617.968$$

$$s^2_{M_Y} = \frac{s^2_{pooled}}{N_Y} = \frac{938,089.84}{5} = 187,617.968$$

$$s^2_{difference} = s^2_{M_X} + s^2_{M_Y} = 187,617.968 + 187,617.968$$
$$= 375,235.936$$

$$s_{difference} = \sqrt{s^2_{difference}} = \sqrt{375,235.936} = 612.565$$

Step 4: The critical values, based on a two-tailed test, a p level of 0.05, and a df_{total} of 8, are -2.306 and 2.306.

Step 5: $t = \dfrac{(16{,}091.600 - 16{,}160.600) - (0)}{612.565} = -0.11$

Step 6: We fail to reject the null hypothesis. The calculated t statistic of -0.11 is not more extreme than the critical t values.

b. $t(8) = -0.11$, $p > 0.05$. (*Note:* If we used software to conduct the t test, we would report the actual p value associated with this test statistic.)

c. $(M_X - M_Y)_{lower} = -t(s_{difference}) + (M_X - M_Y)_{sample}$

$\qquad = -2.306(612.565) + (-69.000)$

$\qquad = -1481.575$

$(M_X - M_Y)_{upper} = t(s_{difference}) + (M_X - M_Y)_{sample}$

$\qquad = 2.306(612.565) + (-69.000)$

$\qquad = 1343.575$

d. The 95% confidence interval around the observed mean difference of -69.00 is $[-1481.58, 1343.58]$.

e. The confidence interval does not include 0 (the hypothesized mean difference if the two samples had the same mean). The conclusion about the null hypothesis is the same for both the hypothesis test and the confidence interval.

f. First, we need the appropriate measure of variability. In this case, we calculate pooled standard deviation by taking the square root of the pooled variance:

$s_{pooled} = \sqrt{s^2_{pooled}} = \sqrt{938{,}089.84} = 968.550$

Now we can calculate Cohen's d:

$d = \dfrac{(M_X - M_Y)}{s} = \dfrac{(16{,}091.600 - 16{,}160.600) - (0)}{968.550}$

$\quad = -0.07$

g. This is a small effect.

h. Effect size tells us how big the difference we observed between means was, uninfluenced by sample size. Often, this measure will help us understand whether we want to continue along our current research lines; that is, if a strong effect is indicated but we fail to reject the null hypothesis, we might want to replicate the study with more statistical power. In this case, however, the failure to reject the null hypothesis is accompanied by a small effect.

11–27 a. *Step 1:* Population 1 is people who watch TV fictional shows. Population 2 is people who watch documentaries. The hypothesis test will be an independent-samples t test because there are two samples and every participant is in only one sample. This study meets two of the three assumptions and may meet another. The dependent variable, number of pictures in which the participant correctly identified the emotion (a measure of theory of mind), is a scale variable. Participants were not likely to have been randomly selected, so we must generalize with caution. In addition, we do not know whether the population is normally distributed, and there are fewer than 30 participants. Thus, we should be cautious in drawing conclusions from these data.

Step 2: Null hypothesis: The mean number of correctly identified emotions will not differ between people who watch TV fiction compared to people who watch documentaries—H_0: $\mu_1 = \mu_2$.

Research hypothesis: People who watch TV fiction will correctly identify a different number of emotions, on average, than people who watch documentaries—H_1: $\mu_1 \neq \mu_2$.

Step 3: $(\mu_1 - \mu_2) = 0$; $s_{difference} = 0.664$

Calculations:

$$M_X = 29$$

TV Fiction		
28	-1	1
30	1	1
31	2	4
27	-2	4
29	0	0
29	0	0
31	2	4
27	-2	4
29	0	0

$s^2_X = \dfrac{\Sigma(X - M)^2}{N - 1} = \dfrac{18}{9 - 1} = 2.250$

$$M_Y = 27.5$$

Documentary		
27	-0.5	0.25
26	-1.5	2.25
28	0.5	0.25
29	1.5	2.25
29	1.5	2.25
28	0.5	0.25
27	-0.5	0.25
26	-1.5	2.25

$s^2_x = \dfrac{\Sigma(X - M)^2}{N - 1} = \dfrac{10}{8 - 1} = 1.429$

$df_X = N - 1 = 9 - 1 = 8$

$df_Y = N - 1 = 8 - 1 = 7$

$df_{total} = df_X + df_Y = 8 + 7 = 15$

$s^2_{pooled} = \left(\dfrac{df_X}{df_{total}}\right)s^2_x + \left(\dfrac{df_Y}{df_{total}}\right)s^2_y = \left(\dfrac{8}{15}\right)2.250$

$\qquad + \left(\dfrac{7}{15}\right)1.429 = 1.200 + 0.667 = 1.867$

$s^2_{M_X} = \dfrac{s^2_{pooled}}{N_X} = \dfrac{1.867}{9} = 0.207$

$s^2_{M_Y} = \dfrac{s^2_{pooled}}{N_Y} = \dfrac{1.867}{8} = 0.233$

$s^2_{difference} = s^2_{M_X} + s^2_{M_Y} = 0.207 + 0.233 = 0.440$

$s_{difference} = \sqrt{s^2_{difference}} = \sqrt{0.440} = 0.663$

Step 4: The critical values, based on a two-tailed test, a *p* level of 0.05, and df_{total} of 15, are −2.132 and 2.132. (Note: It is helpful to draw a curve that includes these cutoffs.)

Step 5:

$$t = \frac{(M_X - M_Y)}{s_{difference}} = \frac{(29 - 27.5)}{0.663} = \frac{1.5}{0.663} = 2.262$$

(Note: It is helpful to add this *t* statistic to the curve that you drew in step 4.)

Step 6: Reject the null hypothesis; we conclude that there is evidence from this study to support the research hypothesis. It appears that people who view TV fiction are better, on average, at identifying others' emotions than are people who view documentaries.

b. $t(15) = 2.26$, $p < 0.05$ (Note: If we used software to conduct the *t* test, we would report the actual *p* value associated with this test statistic.)

c. To calculate the 95% confidence interval, we find the *t* statistics that correspond to a *p* level of 0.05 that we identified earlier, −2.132 and 2.132. We calculate the lower end of the interval as:

$(M_X - M_Y)_{lower} = -t(s_{difference}) + (M_X - M_Y)_{sample} = -2.132(0.663) + 1.5 = 0.086$

We calculate the upper end of the interval as:

$(M_X - M_Y)_{upper} = t(s_{difference}) + (M_X - M_Y)_{sample} = 2.132(0.663) + 1.5 = 2.914$

The 95% confidence interval around the difference between means of 1.5 is [0.09, 2.91].

d. The confidence interval does not include 0 (the hypothetical mean difference if the two samples had the same mean). The conclusion about the null hypothesis is the same for both the hypothesis test and the confidence interval. It appears that there is a mean difference between the two groups.

e. The margin of error is 1.415, and each end of the confidence interval should be exactly the same distance from the sample mean difference.

$$0.085 - (1.5) = -1.415$$
$$2.915 - (1.5) = 1.415$$

f. The appropriate measure of effect size is:

$$\text{Cohen's } d = \frac{(M_X - M_Y) - (\mu_X - \mu_Y)}{S_{pooled}} = \frac{1.5}{1.366} = 1.098$$

g. Based on Cohen's conventions, this is a large effect.

h. The effect size supplements the point estimate of the *t* test, and the confidence interval. A statistically significant finding may not be a large or important one. The effect size tells us how big of an effect watching fictional TV has on a test of theory of mind—a large effect, in fact.

11-29 a. We would use a single-sample *t* test because there is one sample of figure skaters and are comparing that sample to a population (women with eating disorders) for which we know the mean.

b. We would use an independent-samples *t* test because there are two samples, and no participant can be in both samples. One cannot have both a high level and a low level of knowledge about a topic.

c. We would use a paired-samples *t* test because there are two samples, but every student is assigned to both samples—one night of sleep loss and one night of no sleep loss.

11-31 a. We would use an independent-samples *t* test because there are two samples, and no participant can be in both samples. One cannot be a pedestrian en route to work and a tourist pedestrian at the same time.

b. Null hypothesis: People en route to work tend to walk at the same pace, on average, as people who are tourists—H_0: $\mu_1 = \mu_2$.

Research hypothesis: People en route to work tend to walk at a different pace, on average, than do those who are tourists—H_1: $\mu_1 \neq \mu_2$.

11-33 a. The independent variable is the tray availability with levels of not available and available.

b. The dependent variables are food waste and dish use. Food waste was likely operationalized by weight or volume of food disposed, whereas dish use was likely operationalized by number of dishes used or dirtied.

c. This study is an experiment because the environment was manipulated or controlled by the researchers. It assumes that the individuals were randomly sampled from the population and randomly assigned to one of the two levels of the independent variable.

d. We would use an independent-samples *t* test because there is a scale dependent variable, there are two samples, and no participant can be in both samples. One cannot have trays available and not available at the same time.

11-35 a. The researchers used an independent-samples *t* test. We know this because there were two separate groups, so this was a between-groups design. The researchers were comparing the difference between means.

b. We know that the finding is statistically significant because we are told that the *p* value is less than 0.001. Researchers often report very small *p* values this way rather than saying, for example, $p = 0.0000054$.

c. There were 65 participants. There were 63 total degrees of freedom. This would have been calculated by summing the degrees of freedom for each group. The degrees of freedom for each group was the sample size minus 1.

d. There was a mean of 14.6% verbatim overlap with the lecture for students taking notes on laptops, and a mean of 8.8% verbatim overlap with the lecture for students taking notes longhand.

e. The effect size is 0.94. This is a large effect, according to Cohen's conventions.

11-37 a. Waters is predicting lower levels of obesity among children who are in the Edible Schoolyard program than among children who are not in the program. Waters and others who believe in her program are likely to notice successes and overlook failures. Solid research is necessary before instituting such a program nationally, even though it sounds extremely promising.

b. Students could be randomly assigned to participate in the Edible Schoolyard program or to continue with their usual lunch plan. The independent variable is the program, with two levels (Edible Schoolyard, control), and the dependent variable could be weight. Weight is easily operationalized by weighing children, perhaps after one year in the program.

c. We would use an independent-samples t test because there are two samples and no student is in both samples.

d. *Step 1:* Population 1 is all students who participated in the Edible Schoolyard program. Population 2 is all students who did not participate in the Edible Schoolyard program. The comparison distribution will be a distribution of differences between means. The hypothesis test will be an independent-samples t test. This study meets all three assumptions. The dependent variable, weight, is scale. The data would be collected using a form of random selection. In addition, there would be more than 30 participants in the sample, indicating that the comparison distribution would likely be normal.

e. *Step 2:* Null hypothesis: Students who participate in the Edible Schoolyard program weigh the same, on average, as students who do not participate—$H_0: \mu_1 = \mu_2$.

Research hypothesis: Students who participate in the Edible Schoolyard program have different weights, on average, than students who do not participate—$H_1: \mu_1 \neq \mu_2$.

f. The dependent variable could be nutrition knowledge, as assessed by a test, or body mass index (BMI).

g. There are many possible confounds when we do not conduct a controlled experiment. For example, the Berkeley school might be different to begin with. After all, the school allowed Waters to begin the program, and perhaps it had already emphasized nutrition. Random selection allows us to have faith in the ability to generalize beyond our sample. Random assignment allows us to eliminate confounds, other variables that may explain any differences between groups.

11-39 a. This study used a between-groups design. Recruiters looked at one of two résumés: one with a formal email address or one with an informal email address. This makes two separate samples, where means could easily be compared. In addition, the dependent variable, hirability ratings, was scale.

b. The independent variable is the type of résumé looked at. This variable has two levels: formal email address or informal email address. The dependent variable is a rating of hirability.

c. The independent variable is likely the same: type of résumé, with two levels. However, the two levels might have to do with spelling errors. One résumé may have had many spelling errors and the other résumé may have had no spelling errors. The dependent variable is likely the same: a rating of hirability.

d. Yes, it is possible that the sample was a random selection of recruiters. They may have had access to a full list of recruiters from a professional organization in which case they could have randomly selected their participants. And it is likely that the researchers used random assignment when sending emails to recruiters in their sample.

e. Answers will vary. One possible way to measure hirability is to ask a yes or no question: based on this résumé, is this person hirable? A second possible way is for recruiters to review multiple resumes and have them rank the resumes, with 1 being the most hirable.

f. Confidence intervals provide a range of possible estimates, as opposed to the point estimate identified in the hypothesis test.

g. Cohen's d measures effect size. The reported Cohen's d for email address on hirability is 0.81, and the reported Cohen's d for spelling errors on hirability is 0.80. Both of these effects are equally large, suggesting that résumés with an informal email address and/or many spelling errors are more likely to be viewed negatively than those with formal email addresses or no spelling errors.

Chapter 12

12-1 An ANOVA is a hypothesis test with at least one nominal or ordinal independent variable (with at least three total groups) and a scale dependent variable.

12-3 Between-groups variance is an estimate of the population variance based on the differences among the means; within-groups variance is an estimate of the population variance based on the differences within each of the three (or more) sample distributions.

12-5 The three assumptions are that the participants were randomly selected, the underlying populations are normally distributed, and the underlying variances of the different conditions are similar, or *homoscedastic*.

12-7 The F statistic is calculated as the ratio of two variances. Variability, and the variance measure of it, is always positive—it always exists. Variance is calculated as the sum of squared deviations, and squaring both positive and negative values makes them positive.

12-9 With sums of squares, we add up all the squared values. Deviations from the mean always sum to 0. By squaring these deviations, we can sum them and they will not sum to 0. Sums of squares are measures of variability of scores from the mean.

12-11 The grand mean is the mean of every score in a study, regardless of which sample the score came from.

12-13 Cohen's d; R^2

12-15 *Post hoc* means "after this." These tests are needed when an ANOVA is significant and we want to discover where significant differences exist between the groups.

12-17 a. *Standard error* is wrong. The professor is reporting the spread for a distribution of scores, the *standard deviation*.

b. *t statistic* is wrong. We do not use the population standard deviation to calculate a t statistic. The sentence should say *z statistic* instead.

c. *Parameters* is wrong. Parameters are numbers that describe populations, not samples. The researcher calculated *statistics*.

d. *z statistic* is wrong. Evelyn is comparing two means; thus, she would have calculated a *t statistic*.

12-19 a. (i) The formula is missing the summation symbol, Σ, and it is missing the squared term. (ii) When calculating SS_{within}, you must square the deviation of each score from its own group mean and then sum those deviation scores. (iii) The formula should read $SS_{within} = \Sigma(X - M)^2$.

b. (i) The square root symbol is on the wrong side of the equation. (ii) F is a term based on variance, which means it is a squared term. t is the square root of F. (iii) The formula should read $t = \sqrt{F}$.

12-21 When statisticians state that one test is more conservative than another, they are saying that there is a lower risk of a Type I error but a higher risk of Type II error. That is, it sets the bar to reject the null hypothesis higher.

12-23 a. $df_{between} = N_{groups} - 1 = 3 - 1 = 2$

b. $df_{within} = df_1 + df_2 + \cdots + df_{last} = (4 - 1) + (3 - 1) + (5 - 1) = 3 + 2 + 4 = 9$

c. $df_{total} = df_{between} + df_{within} = 2 + 9 = 11$

d. The critical value for a between-groups degrees of freedom of 2 and a within-groups degrees of freedom of 9 at a p level of 0.05 is 4.26.

e. $M_{1990} = \dfrac{\Sigma(X)}{N} = \dfrac{45 + 211 + 158 + 74}{4} = 122$

$M_{2000} = \dfrac{\Sigma(X)}{N} = \dfrac{92 + 128 + 382}{3} = 200.667$

$M_{2010} = \dfrac{\Sigma(X)}{N} = \dfrac{273 + 396 + 178 + 248 + 374}{5} = 293.80$

$GM = \dfrac{\Sigma(X)}{N_{total}} = \dfrac{\left(\begin{array}{c} 45 + 211 + 158 + 74 + 92 + 128 + \\ 382 + 273 + 396 + 178 + 248 + 374 \end{array}\right)}{12}$

$= 213.25$

f. (*Note:* The total sum of squares may not exactly equal the sum of the between-groups and within-groups sums of squares because of rounding decisions.)

The total sum of squares is calculated here as $SS_{total} = \Sigma(X - GM)^2$:

Sample	X	$(X - GM)$	$(X - GM)^2$
1990	45	−168.25	28,308.063
$M_{1990} = 122$	211	−2.25	5.063
	158	−55.25	3052.563
	74	−139.25	19,390.563
2000	92	−121.25	14,701.563
$M_{2000} = 200.667$	128	−85.25	7267.563
	382	168.75	28,476.563
2010	273	59.75	3570.063
$M_{2010} = 293.8$	396	182.75	33,397.563
	178	−35.25	1242.563
	248	34.75	1207.563
	374	160.75	25,840.563
$GM = 213.25$			$SS_{total} = \mathbf{166,460.256}$

g. The within-groups sum of squares is calculated here as $SS_{within} = \Sigma(X - M)^2$:

Sample	X	$(X - M)$	$(X - M)^2$
1990	45	−77	5929.00
$M_{1990} = 122$	211	89	7921.00
	158	36	1296.00
	74	−48	2304.00
2000	92	−108.667	11,808.517
$M_{2000} = 200.667$	128	−72.667	5280.493
	382	181.333	32,881.657
2010	273	−20.8	432.64
$M_{2010} = 293.8$	396	102.2	10,444.84
	178	−115.8	13,409.64
	248	−45.8	2097.64
	374	80.2	6432.04
$GM = 213.25$			$SS_{within} = \mathbf{100,237.467}$

h. The between-groups sum of squares is calculated here as $SS_{between} = \Sigma(M - GM)^2$:

Sample	X	$(M - GM)$	$(M - GM)^2$
1990	45	−91.25	8326.563
$M_{1990} = 122$	211	−91.25	8326.563
	158	−91.25	8326.563
	74	−91.25	8326.563
2000	92	−12.583	158.332
$M_{2000} = 200.667$	128	−12.583	158.332
	382	−12.583	158.332
2010	273	80.55	6488.303
$M_{2010} = 293.8$	396	80.55	6488.303
	178	80.55	6488.303
	248	80.55	6488.303
	374	80.55	6488.303
$GM = 213.25$			$SS_{between} = \mathbf{66,222.763}$

i. $MS_{between} = \dfrac{SS_{between}}{df_{between}} = \dfrac{66,222.763}{2} = 33,111.382$

$MS_{within} = \dfrac{SS_{within}}{df_{within}} = \dfrac{100,237.467}{9} = 11,137.496$

$F = \dfrac{MS_{between}}{MS_{within}} = \dfrac{33,111.382}{11,137.496} = 2.97$

Source	SS	df	MS	F
Between	66,222.763	2	33,111.382	2.97
Within	100,237.467	9	11,137.496	
Total	166,460.256	11		

j. Effect size is calculated as $R^2 = \dfrac{SS_{between}}{SS_{total}} = \dfrac{66,222.763}{166,460.256} =$

0.40. According to Cohen's conventions for R^2, this is a very large effect.

12-25 a. $F = \dfrac{\text{between-groups variance}}{\text{within-groups variance}} = \dfrac{321.83}{177.24} = 1.82$

b. $F = \dfrac{2.79}{2.20} = 1.27$

c. $F = \dfrac{34.45}{41.60} = 0.83$

12-27

Source	SS	df	MS	F
Between	43	2	21.500	2.66
Within	89	11	8.091	
Total	132	13		

12-29 With four groups, there would be a total of six different comparisons.

12-31 With seven groups, there would be a total of 21 different comparisons. The first group would be compared with groups 2, 3, 4, 5, 6, and 7. The second group would be compared with groups 3, 4, 5, 6, and 7. The third group would be compared with groups 4, 5, 6, and 7. The fourth group would be compared with groups 5, 6, and 7. The fifth group would be compared with groups 6 and 7. And the sixth group would be compared with group 7.

12-33 a. The independent variable is type of program. The levels are *The Daily Show* and network news. The dependent variable is the number of seconds of substantive video and audio reporting.

b. The hypothesis test that Fox would use is an independent-samples *t* test.

c. The independent variable is still type of program, but now the levels are *The Daily Show*, network news, and cable news. The hypothesis test would be a one-way between-groups ANOVA.

12-35 a. A *t* distribution; we are comparing the mean IQ of a sample of 10 to the population mean of 100; this student knows only the population mean—she doesn't know the population standard deviation.

b. An *F* distribution; we are comparing the mean ratings of four samples—families with no books visible, with only children's books visible, with only adult books visible, and with both types of books visible.

c. A *t* distribution; we are comparing the average vocabulary scores of two groups.

12-37 a. The independent variable in this case is the type of program in which students are enrolled; the levels are arts and sciences, education, law, and business. Because every student is enrolled in only one program, Ruby would use a one-way between-groups ANOVA.

b. Now the independent variable is year, with levels of first, second, or third. Because the same participants are repeatedly measured, Ruby would use a one-way within-groups ANOVA.

c. The independent variable in this case is type of degree, and its levels are master's, doctoral, and professional. Because

every student is in only one type of degree program, Ruby would use a one-way between-groups ANOVA.

d. The independent variable in this case is stage of training, and its levels are master's, doctoral, and postdoctoral. Because the same students are repeatedly measured, Ruby would use a one-way within-groups ANOVA.

12-39 a. In this study, the independent variable was attendance, with three levels: <5 sessions, 5–8 sessions, and 9–12 sessions.

b. The dependent variable was number of minutes of exercise per week.

c. Summary of Step 1
Population 1: Postmenopausal women who attended fewer than 5 sessions of a group exercise-education program. Population 2: Postmenopausal women who attended 5–8 sessions of a group exercise-education program. Population 3: Postmenopausal women who attended 9–12 sessions of a group exercise-education program.

The comparison distribution will be an *F* distribution. The hypothesis test will be a one-way between-groups ANOVA. The data were not selected randomly, so we must generalize only with caution. We do not know if the underlying population distributions are normal, but the sample data do not indicate severe skew. To see if we meet the homoscedasticity assumption, we will check to see if the largest variance is no greater than twice the smallest variance. From the calculations below, we see that the largest variance, 387, is not more than twice the smallest, 208.67, so we have met the homoscedasticity assumption. (The following information is taken from the calculation of SS_{within}.)

Sample	<5	5–8	9–12
Squared deviations	400	324	324
	225	441	4
	25	9	289
			9
Sum of squares	650	774	626
$N-1$	2	2	3
Variance	325	387	208.67

Summary of Step 2
Null hypothesis: Postmenopausal women in different categories of attendance at a group exercise-education program exercise the same average number of minutes per week—H_0: $\mu_1 = \mu_2 = \mu_3$. Research hypothesis: Postmenopausal women in different categories of attendance at a group exercise-education program do not exercise the same average number of minutes per week—H_1 is that at least one μ is different from another μ.

Summary of Step 3
$df_{between} = N_{groups} - 1 = 3 - 1 = 2$
$df_1 = 3 - 1 = 2; df_2 = 3 - 1 = 2; df_3 = 4 - 1 = 3$
$df_{within} = 2 + 2 + 3 = 7$

The comparison distribution will be the *F* distribution with 2 and 7 degrees of freedom.

Summary of Step 4
The critical *F* statistic based on a *p* level of 0.05 is 4.74.

Summary of Step 5

$df_{total} = 2 + 7 = 9$ or $df_{total} = 10 - 1 = 9$

$SS_{total} = \Sigma(X - GM)^2 = 12,222.40$

Sample	X	$(X - GM)$	$(X - GM)^2$
<5	155	−24.6	605.16
$M_{>5} = 135$	120	−59.6	3552.16
	130	−49.6	2460.16
5–8	199	19.4	376.36
$M_{5-8} = 181$	160	−19.6	384.16
	184	4.4	19.36
9–12	230	50.4	2540.16
$M_{9-12} = 212$	214	34.4	1183.36
	195	15.4	237.16
	209	29.4	864.36
$GM = 179.60$		$SS_{total} =$	**12,222.40**

$SS_{within} = \Sigma(X - M)^2 = 2050.00$

Sample	X	$(X - M)$	$(X - M)^2$
<5	155	20	400
$M_{>5} = 135$	120	−15	225
	130	−5	25
5–8	199	18	324
$M_{5-8} = 181$	160	−21	441
	184	3	9
9–12	230	18	324
$M_{9-12} = 212$	214	2	4
	195	−17	289
	209	−3	9
$GM = 179.60$		$SS_{within} =$	**2050.00**

$SS_{between} = \Sigma(M - GM)^2 = 10,172.40$

Sample	X	$(M - GM)$	$(M - GM)^2$
<5	155	−44.6	1989.16
$M_{>5} = 135$	120	−44.6	1989.16
	130	−44.6	1989.16
5–8	199	1.4	1.96
$M_{5-8} = 181$	160	1.4	1.96
	184	1.4	1.96
9–12	230	32.4	1049.76
$M_{9-12} = 212$	214	32.4	1049.76
	195	32.4	1049.76
	209	32.4	1049.76
$GM = 179.60$		$SS_{between} =$	**10,172.40**

$SS_{total} = SS_{within} + SS_{between} = 12,222.40 = 2050.00 + 10,172.40$

$$MS_{between} = \frac{SS_{between}}{df_{between}} = \frac{10,172.40}{2} = 5086.20$$

$$MS_{within} = \frac{SS_{within}}{df_{within}} = \frac{2050.00}{7} = 292.857$$

$$F = \frac{MS_{between}}{MS_{within}} = \frac{5086.20}{292.857} = 17.37$$

Source	SS	df	MS	F
Between	10,172.40	2	5,086.200	17.37
Within	2,050.00	7	292.857	
Total	12,222.40	9		

Summary of Step 6

The F statistic, 17.37, is beyond the cutoff of 4.74. We can reject the null hypothesis. It appears that postmenopausal women in different categories of attendance at a group exercise-education program do exercise a different average number of minutes per week. However, the results from this ANOVA do not tell us where specific differences lie. The ANOVA tells us only that there is at least one difference between means. We must calculate a post hoc test to determine exactly which pairs of means are different.

12-41 a. $F = \dfrac{MS_{between}}{MS_{within}} = \dfrac{4.623}{0.522} = 8.856$

b. $t = \sqrt{F} = \sqrt{8.856} = 2.98$

c. The "Sig." for t is the same as that for the ANOVA, 0.005, because the F distribution reduces to the t distribution when we are dealing with two groups.

12-43 a. The independent variable is instructor self-disclosure, which is a nominal variable with three levels—high, medium, and low self-disclosure.

b. The first dependent variable mentioned is levels of motivation, which is a scale variable.

c. This is a between-groups design because students are only exposed to one of the three types of instructor self-disclosure via the Facebook pages.

d. A one-way between-subjects ANOVA would be used to analyze the data.

e. This is a true experiment as participants were randomly assigned to levels of a manipulated independent variable. This means that the researchers can draw a causal conclusion. That is, they can conclude that high self-disclosure causes "higher levels of motivation and affective learning and a more positive classroom climate," as compared with low and medium levels of self-disclosure.

12-45 a. The independent variable is languages spoken, which is a nominal variable with four levels—monolingual (English), bilingual (Spanish-English), bilingual (French-English), and bilingual (Chinese-English). The dependent variable is vocabulary skills as assessed by the PPVT, a scale variable.

b. We know that the finding is statistically significant because the p value of 0.0001 is less than the typical cutoff p level of 0.05.

c. The findings from the one-way ANOVA only tell us that there is at least one difference among the groups but not which specific groups are statistically significantly different from each other.

d. The Bonferroni test is a more conservative post hoc test. It is used to determine a critical value that is stricter than that based on a p level of .05. We can use this more conservative critical value to determine whether we can reject the null hypothesis when comparing the four levels of the independent variable.

e. Statistically significant mean differences between mean vocabulary scores exist between the monolingual children and the bilingual (Chinese-English) children and between the monolingual children and the bilingual (French-English) children. They also exist between the bilingual (Spanish-English) children and the bilingual (Chinese-English) children and between the bilingual (Spanish-English) children and the bilingual (French-English) children. However, the monolingual children and bilingual (Spanish-English) children did not statistically significantly differ from each other, on average, nor did the bilingual (Chinese-English) and bilingual (French-English) children statistically significantly differ from each other, on average.

12-47 a. Level of trust in the leader is the independent variable. It has three levels: low, moderate, and high.

b. The dependent variable is level of agreement with a policy supported by the leader or supervisor.

c. *Step 1:* Population 1 is employees with low trust in their leader. Population 2 is employees with moderate trust in their leader. Population 3 is employees with high trust in their leader. The comparison distribution will be an F distribution. The hypothesis test will be a one-way between-groups ANOVA. We do not know if employees were randomly selected. We also do not know if the underlying distributions are normal, and the sample sizes are small so we must proceed with caution. To check the final assumption, that we have homoscedastic variances, we will calculate variance for each group.

Sample	Low Trust	Moderate Trust	High Trust
Squared deviations	16	100	3.063
	1	121	18.063
	4	1	60.063
	25		27.563
Sum of squares	46	222	108.752
$N - 1$	3	2	3
Variance	15.33	111	36.25

Because the largest variance, 111, is much more than twice as large as the smallest variance, we can conclude we have heteroscedastic variances. Violation of this third assumption of homoscedastic samples means we should proceed with caution. Because these data are intended to give you practice calculating statistics, proceed with your analyses. When conducting real research, we would want to have much larger sample sizes and to more carefully consider meeting the assumptions.

Step 2: Null hypothesis: There are no mean differences between these three groups: The mean level of agreement with a policy does not vary across the three trust levels— $H_0: \mu_1 = \mu_2 = \mu_3$.

Research hypothesis: There are mean differences between some or all of these groups: The mean level of agreement depends on trust.

Step 3: $df_{between} = N_{groups} - 1 = 3 - 1 = 2$

$df_{within} = df_1 + df_2 + \cdots + df_{last} = (4 - 1) + (3 - 1) + (4 - 1) = 3 + 2 + 3 = 8$

$df_{total} = df_{between} + df_{within} = 2 + 8 = 10$

The comparison distribution will be an F distribution with 2 and 8 degrees of freedom.

Step 4: The critical value for the F statistic based on a p level of 0.05 is 4.46.

Step 5: $GM = 21.727$

Total sum of squares is calculated here as $SS_{total} = \Sigma(X - GM)^2$:

Sample	X	$(X - GM)$	$(X - GM)^2$
Low trust	9	−12.727	161.977
$M_{low} = 13$	14	−7.727	59.707
	11	−10.727	115.069
	18	−3.727	13.891
Moderate trust	14	−7.727	59.707
$M_{mod} = 24$	35	13.273	176.173
	23	1.273	1.621
High trust	27	5.273	27.805
$M_{high} = 28.75$	33	11.273	127.081
	21	−0.727	0.529
	34	12.273	150.627
$GM = 21.727$			$SS_{total} = \mathbf{894.187}$

Within-groups sum of squares is calculated here as $SS_{within} = \Sigma(X - M)^2$:

Sample	X	$(X - M)$	$(X - M)^2$
Low trust	9	−4	16.00
$M_{low} = 13$	14	1	1.00
	11	−2	4.00
	18	5	25.00
Moderate trust	14	−10	100.00
$M_{mod} = 24$	35	11	121.00
	23	−1	1.00
High trust	27	−1.75	3.063
$M_{high} = 28.75$	33	4.25	18.063
	21	−7.75	60.063
	34	5.25	27.563
$GM = 21.727$			$SS_{within} = 376.752$

Between-groups sum of squares is calculated here as $SS_{between} = \Sigma(M - GM)^2$:

Sample	X	$(M - GM)$	$(M - GM)^2$
Low trust	9	−8.727	76.161
$M_{low} = 13$	14	−8.727	76.161
	11	−8.727	76.161
	18	−8.727	76.161
Moderate trust	14	2.273	5.167
$M_{mod} = 24$	35	2.273	5.167
	23	2.273	5.167
High trust	27	7.023	49.323
$M_{high} = 28.75$	33	7.023	49.323
	21	7.023	49.323
	34	7.023	49.323
GM = 21.727			$SS_{between}$ = 517.437

$$MS_{between} = \frac{SS_{between}}{df_{between}} = \frac{517.437}{2} = 258.719$$

$$MS_{within} = \frac{SS_{within}}{df_{within}} = \frac{376.752}{8} = 47.094$$

$$F = \frac{MS_{between}}{MS_{within}} = \frac{258.719}{47.094} = 5.49$$

Source	SS	df	MS	F
Between	517.437	2	258.719	5.49
Within	376.752	8	47.094	
Total	894.187	10		

Step 6: The F statistic, 5.49, is beyond the cutoff of 4.46, so we can reject the null hypothesis. The mean level of agreement with a policy supported by a supervisor varies across level of trust in that supervisor. Remember, the research design and data did not meet the three assumptions of this statistical test, so we should be careful in interpreting this finding.

d. $F(2,8) = 5.49, p < 0.05$. (Note: We would include the actual p value if we used software to conduct this analysis).

e. Because there are unequal sample sizes, we must calculate a weighted sample size.

$$N' = \frac{N_{groups}}{\Sigma\left(\frac{1}{N}\right)} = \frac{3}{\left(\frac{1}{4} + \frac{1}{3} + \frac{1}{4}\right)} = \frac{3}{0.25 + 0.333 + 0.25}$$

$$= \frac{3}{0.833} = 3.601$$

$$s_M = \sqrt{\frac{MS_{within}}{N'}} = \sqrt{\frac{47.094}{3.601}} = 3.616$$

Now we can compare the three groups.

Low trust ($M = 13$) versus moderate trust ($M = 24$):

$$HSD = \frac{13 - 24}{3.616} = -3.04$$

Low trust ($M = 13$) versus high trust ($M = 28.75$):

$$HSD = \frac{13 - 28.75}{3.616} = -4.36$$

Moderate trust ($M = 24$) versus high trust ($M = 28.75$):

$$HSD = \frac{24 - 28.75}{3.616} = -1.31$$

According to the q table, the critical value is 4.04 for a p level of 0.05 when we are comparing three groups and have within-groups degrees of freedom of 8. We obtained one q value (−4.36) that exceeds this cutoff. Based on the calculations, there is a statistically significant difference between the mean level of agreement by employees with low trust in their supervisors compared to those with high trust. Because the sample sizes here were so small and we did not meet the three assumptions of ANOVA, we should be careful in making strong statements about this finding. In fact, these preliminary findings would encourage additional research.

f. It is not possible to conduct a t test in this situation because there are more than two groups or levels of the independent variable.

g. It is not possible to conduct this study with a within-groups design because participants cannot be in more than one of the groups or levels of the independent variable. In other words, an employee has only one level of trust in his or her supervisor.

12-49 a. The independent variable in this study is the type of television show watched. There are three levels: watching a drama, watching a documentary, or watching no television.

b. The dependent variable in this study is the number of emotions guessed correctly. It is a scale variable.

c. This is an experiment. We know this because the researchers manipulated the independent variable—type of television show watched—and randomly assigned participants to levels of the independent variable.

d. The researchers conducted a one-way between-groups ANOVA. We know this because the analysis included a categorical independent variable that had more than two levels and a dependent variable that was scale. Additionally, an F statistic is reported in the findings.

e. The values in the parentheses tell us that there are two between-groups degrees of freedom and 173 within-groups degrees of freedom. If we add 1 to the first number, we know that the analysis included 3 different groups. If we then add the two numbers in the parentheses together (2 + 173), we get 175, which is the degrees of freedom for the total sample. If we add 1 to the total degrees of freedom, we then know the sample size: 176 participants. The third number presented (6.04) is the test statistic: the calculated or observed F value. The fourth number presented, .003, is the p value. The p value is less than the standard of 0.05, which means that there is a statistically significant difference. The last number presented, .065, is the effect size. According to Cohen's conventions for R^2 (which we can use to interpret partial η^2), this is a medium effect.

f. An F statistic only demonstrates there is a statistically significant mean difference among at least two different levels of the independent variable; it does not indicate where those specific differences lie. It is likely the researchers conducted a post-hoc test, such as a Tukey HSD test, to determine which means were significantly different from each other.

g. Participants who watched a drama television show accurately identified significantly more emotions, on average, compared to the control group (people who did not watch any television prior to making judgments about emotions in pictures). However, there were no statistically significant mean differences between the drama group and the documentary group. Similarly, there were no statistically significant mean differences between the documentary group and the control group. We can only conclude that watching a drama series seems to increase accuracy, on average, compared to not watching TV.

h. According to Cohen's conventions for R^2 (which we can use to interpret partial η^2), this is a medium effect.

i. Although the mean for documentaries is higher than the mean for the control group, this comparison is not statistically significantly different. Documentaries might be helpful, but we do not have supporting evidence from this study.

j. This would be considered a Type I error: when we incorrectly reject the null hypothesis.

k. The label for the y-axis should be horizontal. The y-axis should begin at 0, not 20. The y-axis and x-axis should be labeled appropriately (e.g., "Mean score correct emotion identification" for y-axis, and "Condition" for x-axis).

Chapter 13

13-1 The four assumptions are that (1) the data are randomly selected; (2) the underlying population distributions are normal; (3) the variability is similar across groups, known as homoscedasticity; and (4) there are no order effects.

13-3 The "subjects" variability is noise in the data caused by each participant's personal variability compared with the other participants. It is calculated by comparing each person's mean response across all levels of the independent variable with the grand mean, which is the overall mean response across all levels of the independent variable.

13-5 Counterbalancing involves exposing participants to the different levels of the independent variable in different orders.

13-7 To calculate the sum of squares for subjects, we first calculate an average of each participant's scores across the levels of the independent variable. Then we subtract the grand mean from each participant's mean. We repeat this subtraction for each score the participant has—that is, for as many times as there are levels of the independent variable. Once we have the deviation scores, we square each of them and then sum the squared deviations to get the sum of squares for participants.

13-9 If we have a between-groups study in which different people are participating in the different conditions, then we can turn it into a within-groups study by having all the people in the sample participate in all the conditions.

13-11 The calculations for R^2 for a one-way within-groups ANOVA and a one-way between-groups ANOVA are similar. In both one-way ANOVAs, the numerator is a measure of the variability that takes into account just the differences among means, $SS_{between}$. The denominator, however, is different for the within-groups ANOVA, as it takes into account the total variability, SS_{total}, similarly to the between-groups ANOVA, but removes the variability due to differences among participants, $SS_{subjects}$. This enables the researcher to determine the variability explained only by between-groups differences.

13-13 a. $df_{between} = N_{groups} - 1 = 3 - 1 = 2$

b. $df_{subjects} = n - 1 = 4 - 1 = 3$

c. $df_{within} = (df_{between})(df_{subjects}) = (2)(3) = 6$

d. $df_{total} = df_{between} + df_{subjects} + df_{within} = 2 + 3 + 6 = 11$, or we can calculate it as $df_{total} = N_{total} - 1 = 12 - 1 = 11$

e. $SS_{total} = \Sigma(X - GM)^2 = 754$

Level	(X)	$X - GM$	$(X - GM)^2$
1	7	−10	100
1	16	−1	1
1	3	−14	196
1	9	−8	64
2	15	−2	4
2	18	1	1
2	18	1	1
2	13	−4	16
3	22	5	25
3	28	11	121
3	26	9	81
3	29	12	144

$GM = 17$ $\quad$ $\Sigma(X - GM)^2 = 754$

f. $SS_{between} = \Sigma(M - GM)^2 = 618.504$

Level	Rating (X)	Group Mean (M)	$M - GM$	$(M - GM)^2$
1	7	8.75	−8.25	68.063
1	16	8.75	−8.25	68.063
1	3	8.75	−8.25	68.063
1	9	8.75	−8.25	68.063
2	15	16	−1	1.000
2	18	16	−1	1.000
2	18	16	−1	1.000
2	13	16	−1	1.000
3	22	26.25	9.25	85.563
3	28	26.25	9.25	85.563
3	26	26.25	9.25	85.563
3	29	26.25	9.25	85.563

$GM = 17$ $\quad$ $\Sigma(M - GM)^2 = 618.504$

g. $SS_{subjects} = \Sigma(M_{participant} - GM)^2 = 62.001$

Participant	Level	Rating (X)	Participant Mean ($M_{participant}$)	$M_{participant} - GM$	$(M_{participant} - GM)^2$
1	1	7	14.667	−2.333	5.443
2	1	16	20.667	3.667	13.447
3	1	3	15.667	−1.333	1.777
4	1	9	17	0	0
1	2	15	14.667	−2.333	5.443
2	2	18	20.667	3.667	13.447
3	2	18	15.667	−1.333	1.777
4	2	13	17	0	0
1	3	22	14.667	−2.333	5.443
2	3	28	20.667	3.667	13.447
3	3	26	15.667	−1.333	1.777
4	3	29	17	0	0
			GM = 17		$\Sigma(M_{participant} - GM)^2 = 62.001$

h. $SS_{within} = SS_{total} - SS_{between} - SS_{subjects} = 754 - 618.504 - 62.001 = 73.495$

i. $MS_{between} = \dfrac{SS_{between}}{df_{between}} = \dfrac{618.504}{2} = 309.252$

$MS_{subjects} = \dfrac{SS_{subjects}}{df_{subjects}} = \dfrac{62.001}{3} = 20.667$

$MS_{within} = \dfrac{SS_{within}}{df_{within}} = \dfrac{73.495}{6} = 12.249$

$F_{between} = \dfrac{MS_{between}}{MS_{within}} = \dfrac{309.252}{12.249} = 25.247$

$F_{subjects} = \dfrac{MS_{subjects}}{MS_{within}} = \dfrac{20.667}{12.249} = 1.687$

Source	SS	df	MS	F
Between-groups	618.504	2	309.252	25.25
Subjects	62.001	3	20.667	1.69
Within-groups	73.495	6	12.249	
Total	754	11		

j. $R^2 = \dfrac{SS_{between}}{(SS_{total} - SS_{subjects})} = \dfrac{618.504}{(754 - 62.001)} = 0.89$

k. $s_M = \sqrt{\dfrac{MS_{within}}{N}} = \sqrt{\dfrac{12.249}{4}} = 1.750$

The Tukey HSD statistic comparing level 1 and level 3 would be:

$HSD = \dfrac{M_{level\ 1} - M_{level\ 3}}{S_M} = \dfrac{8.75 - 26.25}{1.750} = -10$

13-15 a.

Source	SS	df	MS	F
Between	941.102	2	470.551	10.16
Subjects	3807.322	10	380.732	8.22
Within	926.078	20	46.304	
Total	5674.502	32		

b.

$R^2 = \dfrac{SS_{between}}{(SS_{total} - SS_{subjects})} = \dfrac{941.102}{(5674.502 - 3807.322)} = -0.50$

13-17

Source	SS	df	MS	F
Between	56.570	2	28.285	2.435
Subjects	83.865	8	10.483	0.903
Within	185.830	16	11.614	
Total	326.265	26		

13-19 a. Null hypothesis: People experience the same mean amount of fear across all three levels of dog size—H_0: $\mu_1 = \mu_2 = \mu_3$.

Research hypothesis: People do not experience the same mean amount of fear across all three levels of dog size.

b. We do not know how the participants were selected, so the first assumption of random selection might not be met. We do not know how the dogs were presented to the participants, so we cannot assess whether order effects are present.

c. The effect size was 0.89, which is a large effect. This indicates that the effect might be important, meaning the size of a dog might have a large impact on the amount of fear people experience.

d. The Tukey HSD test statistic for the difference between groups 1 and 3 was −10. According to the q statistic table, the critical value for the Tukey HSD when there are 6 within-groups degrees of freedom and three treatment levels is 4.34. We can conclude that the mean difference in fear when a small versus large dog is presented is statistically significant, with the large dog evoking greater fear.

13-21 a. *Step 5:* We must first calculate df and SS to fill in the source table.

$df_{between} = N_{groups} - 1 = 2$

$df_{subjects} = n - 1 = 4$

$df_{within} = (df_{between})(df_{subjects}) = 8$

$df_{total} = N_{total} - 1 = 14$

For the total sum of squares: $SS_{total} = \Sigma(X - GM)^2 = 73.6$

Time	X	X − GM	(X − GM)²
Past	18	−1.6	2.56
Past	17.5	−2.1	4.41
Past	19	−0.6	0.36
Past	16	−3.6	12.96
Past	20	0.4	0.16
Present	18.5	−1.1	1.21
Present	19.5	−0.1	0.01
Present	20	0.4	0.16
Present	17	−2.6	6.76
Present	18	−1.6	2.56
Future	22	2.4	5.76
Future	24	4.4	19.36
Future	20	0.4	0.16
Future	23.5	3.9	15.21
Future	21	1.4	1.96

$GM = 19.6$ $SS_{total} = 73.6$

For sum of squares between: $SS_{between} = \Sigma(M - GM)^2 = 47.5$

Time	X	Group Mean (M)	M − GM	(M − GM)²
Past	18	18.1	−1.5	2.25
Past	17.5	18.1	−1.5	2.25
Past	19	18.1	−1.5	2.25
Past	16	18.1	−1.5	2.25
Past	20	18.1	−1.5	2.25
Present	18.5	18.6	−1	1
Present	19.5	18.6	−1	1
Present	20	18.6	−1	1
Present	17	18.6	−1	1
Present	18	18.6	−1	1
Future	22	22.1	2.5	6.25
Future	24	22.1	2.5	6.25
Future	20	22.1	2.5	6.25
Future	23.5	22.1	2.5	6.25
Future	21	22.1	2.5	6.25

$GM = 19.6$ $SS_{between} = 47.5$

For sum of squares subjects: $SS_{subjects} = \Sigma(M_{participant} - GM)^2 = 3.429$

Participant	Time	X	Participant Mean ($M_{participant}$)	$M_{participant} - GM$	$(M_{participant} - GM)^2$
1	Past	18	19.500	−0.100	0.010
2	Past	17.5	20.333	0.733	0.537
3	Past	19	19.667	0.067	0.004
4	Past	16	18.833	−0.767	0.588
5	Past	20	19.667	0.067	0.004
1	Present	18.5	19.500	−0.100	0.010
2	Present	19.5	20.333	0.733	0.537
3	Present	20	19.667	0.067	0.004
4	Present	17	18.833	−0.767	0.588
5	Present	18	19.667	0.067	0.004
1	Future	22	19.500	−0.100	0.010
2	Future	24	20.333	0.733	0.537
3	Future	20	19.667	0.067	0.004
4	Future	23.5	18.833	−0.767	0.588
5	Future	21	19.667	0.067	0.004

$GM = 19.6$ $SS_{subjects} = 3.429$

$SS_{within} = SS_{total} - SS_{between} - SS_{subjects} = 22.671$

Source	SS	df	MS	F
Between	47.5	2	23.750	8.38
Subjects	3.429	4	0.857	0.30
Within	22.671	8	2.834	
Total	73.6	14		

Step 6: The F statistic, 8.38, is beyond 4.46, the critical F value at a p level of 0.05. We would reject the null hypothesis. There is at least one difference, on average, among the past, present, and future self-reported life satisfaction of pessimists.

b. First, we calculate s_M: $s_M = \sqrt{\dfrac{MS_{within}}{N}} = \sqrt{\dfrac{2.834}{5}} = 0.753$

Next, we calculate HSD for each pair of means.

For past versus present: $HSD = \dfrac{(18.1 - 18.6)}{0.753} = -0.66$

For past versus future: $HSD = \dfrac{(18.1 - 22.1)}{0.753} = -5.31$

For present versus future: $HSD = \dfrac{(18.6 - 22.1)}{0.753} = -4.65$

The critical value of q at a p level of 0.05 is 4.04. Thus, we reject the null hypothesis for the past versus future comparison and for the present versus future comparison, but not for the past versus present comparison. These results indicate that the mean self-reported life satisfaction of pessimists is not significantly different for their past and present, but they expect to have greater life satisfaction in the future, on average.

c. $R^2 = \dfrac{SS_{between}}{(SS_{total} - SS_{subjects})} = \dfrac{47.5}{(73.6 - 3.429)} = 0.68$

13-23
$df_{between} = N_{groups} - 1 = 2$
$df_{subjects} = n - 1 = 4$
$df_{within} = (df_{between})(df_{subjects}) = 8$
$df_{total} = N_{total} - 1 = 14$
For the total sum of squares: $SS_{total} = \Sigma(X - GM)^2 = 4207.335$

Stimulus	X	X − GM	(X − GM)²
Owner	69	20.667	427.125
Owner	72	23.667	560.127
Owner	65	16.667	277.789
Owner	75	26.667	711.129
Owner	70	21.667	469.459
Cat	28	−20.333	413.431
Cat	32	−16.333	266.767
Cat	30	−18.333	336.099
Cat	29	−19.333	373.765
Cat	31	−17.333	300.433
Dog	45	−3.333	11.109
Dog	43	−5.333	28.441
Dog	47	−1.333	1.777
Dog	45	−3.333	11.109
Dog	44	−4.333	18.775

$GM = 48.333 \qquad SS_{total} = 4207.335$

For sum of squares between: $SS_{between} - \Sigma(M - GM)^2 = 4133.735$

Stimulus	X	Group Mean (M)	M − GM	(M − GM)²
Owner	69	70.2	21.867	478.166
Owner	72	70.2	21.867	478.166
Owner	65	70.2	21.867	478.166
Owner	75	70.2	21.867	478.166
Owner	70	70.2	21.867	478.166
Cat	28	30	−18.333	336.099
Cat	32	30	−18.333	336.099
Cat	30	30	−18.333	336.099
Cat	29	30	−18.333	336.099
Cat	31	30	−18.333	336.099
Dog	45	44.8	−3.533	12.482
Dog	43	44.8	−3.533	12.482
Dog	47	44.8	−3.533	12.482
Dog	45	44.8	−3.533	12.482
Dog	44	44.8	−3.533	12.482

$GM = 48.333 \qquad SS_{between} = 4133.735$

For sum of squares subjects: $SS_{subjects} = \Sigma(M_{participant} - GM)^2 = 12.675$

Stimulus	X	Participant Mean (M_participant)	M_participant − GM	(M_participant − GM)²
Owner	69	47.333	−1.000	1.000
Owner	72	49.000	0.667	0.445
Owner	65	47.333	−1.000	1.000
Owner	75	49.667	1.334	1.780
Owner	70	48.333	0.000	0.000
Cat	28	47.333	−1.000	1.000
Cat	32	49.000	0.667	0.445
Cat	30	47.333	−1.000	1.000
Cat	29	49.667	1.334	1.780
Cat	31	48.333	0.000	0.000
Dog	45	47.333	−1.000	1.000
Dog	43	49.000	0.667	0.445
Dog	47	47.333	−1.000	1.000
Dog	45	49.667	1.334	1.780
Dog	44	48.333	0.000	0.000

$GM = 48.333 \qquad SS_{subjects} = 12.675$

$SS_{within} = SS_{total} - SS_{between} - SS_{subjects} = 60.925$

Source	SS	df	MS	F
Between	4133.735	2	2066.868	271.38
Subjects	12.675	4	3.169	0.42
Within	60.925	8	7.616	
Total	4207.335	14		

13.25 At a p level of 0.05, the critical F value is 4.46. Because the calculated F statistic does not exceed the critical F value, we would fail to reject the null hypothesis. Because we failed to reject the null hypothesis, it would not be appropriate to perform post hoc comparisons.

13-27 a. The independent variable is the type of substance placed beneath the eyes, and its levels are black grease, black antiglare stickers, and petroleum jelly.

b. The dependent variable is eye glare.

c. This is a one-way within-groups ANOVA.

d. The first assumption of ANOVA is that the samples are randomly selected from their populations. It is unlikely that the researchers met this assumption. The study description indicates that the researchers were from Yale University and does not mention any techniques the researchers might have used to obtain participants from across the nation. So, it is likely that the Yale researchers used a sample of participants from their local area.

e. The second assumption is that the population distribution is normal. Although we do not know the exact distribution of the population of scores, there are more than 30 participants in the study. When there are at least 30 participants in a sample, the distribution of sample means will be approximately normal even if the underlying distribution of scores is not. So it is likely that the distribution of sample means is normal and that this assumption was met.

f. The third assumption is homoscedasticity—that the samples come from populations with equal variances. Based on the description of the study, it is not possible to tell whether this assumption was met. The researchers could assess whether this assumption was met by comparing the variance of each of the three treatment groups to ensure that the largest variance is no larger than two times the smallest variance.

g. The fourth assumption that is specific to the within-groups ANOVA is that there are no order effects. To protect against order effects, the researcher would want to have counterbalanced the order in which the participants experienced the treatment conditions.

h. *Step 5:* We must first calculate df and SS to fill in the source table.

$df_{between} = N_{groups} - 1 = 2$

$df_{subjects} = n - 1 = 3$

$df_{within} = (df_{between})(df_{subjects}) = 6$

$df_{total} = N_{total} - 1 = 11$

For the total sum of squares: $SS_{total} = \Sigma(X - GM)^2 = 16.527$

Condition	X	X − GM	(X − GM)²
Black grease	19.8	2.175	4.731
Black grease	18.2	0.575	0.331
Black grease	19.2	1.575	2.481
Black grease	18.7	1.075	1.156
Antiglare stickers	17.1	−0.525	0.276
Antiglare stickers	17.2	−0.425	0.181
Antiglare stickers	18	0.375	0.141
Antiglare stickers	17.9	0.275	0.076
Petroleum jelly	15.9	−1.725	2.976
Petroleum jelly	16.3	−1.325	1.756
Petroleum jelly	16.2	−1.425	2.031
Petroleum jelly	17	−0.625	0.391

$GM = 17.625$ $SS_{total} = 16.527$

For the sum of squares between: $SS_{between} = \Sigma(M - GM)^2 = 13.820$

Condition	X	Group Mean (M)	M − GM	(M − GM)²
Black grease	19.8	18.975	1.35	1.823
Black grease	18.2	18.975	1.35	1.823
Black grease	19.2	18.975	1.35	1.823
Black grease	18.7	18.975	1.35	1.823
Antiglare stickers	17.1	17.55	−0.075	0.006
Antiglare stickers	17.2	17.55	−0.075	0.006
Antiglare stickers	18	17.55	−0.075	0.006
Antiglare stickers	17.9	17.55	−0.075	0.006
Petroleum jelly	15.9	16.35	−1.275	1.626
Petroleum jelly	16.3	16.35	−1.275	1.626
Petroleum jelly	16.2	16.35	−1.275	1.626
Petroleum jelly	17	16.35	−1.275	1.626

$GM = 17.625$ $SS_{between} = 13.820$

For the sum of squares subjects: $SS_{subjects} = \Sigma(M_{participant} - GM)^2 = 0.735$

Participant	Condition	X	Participant Mean ($M_{participant}$)	$M_{participant} - GM$	$(M_{participant} - GM)^2$
1	Black grease	19.8	17.600	−0.025	0.001
2	Black grease	18.2	17.233	−0.392	0.154
3	Black grease	19.2	17.800	0.175	0.031
4	Black grease	18.7	17.867	0.242	0.059
1	Antiglare stickers	17.1	17.600	−0.025	0.001
2	Antiglare stickers	17.2	17.233	−0.392	0.154
3	Antiglare stickers	18	17.800	0.175	0.031
4	Antiglare stickers	17.9	17.867	0.242	0.059
1	Petroleum jelly	15.9	17.600	−0.025	0.001
2	Petroleum jelly	16.3	17.233	−0.392	0.154
3	Petroleum jelly	16.2	17.800	0.175	0.031
4	Petroleum jelly	17	17.867	0.242	0.059

$GM = 17.625$ $SS_{subjects} = 0.735$

$$SS_{within} = SS_{total} - SS_{between} - SS_{subjects} = 1.972$$

Source	SS	df	MS	F
Between	13.820	2	6.91	21.00
Subjects	0.735	3	0.245	0.74
Within	1.972	6	0.329	
Total	16.527	11		

Step 6: The *F* statistic, 21.00, is beyond 5.14, the critical *F* value at a *p* level of 0.05. We would reject the null hypothesis. There is a difference, on average, in the visual acuity of participants while wearing different substances beneath their eyes.

i. First, we calculate s_M: $s_M = \sqrt{\dfrac{MS_{within}}{N}} = \sqrt{\dfrac{0.329}{4}} = 0.287$

Next, we calculate *HSD* for each pair of means.

For grease versus stickers:

$$HSD = \frac{(18.975 - 17.550)}{0.287} = 4.97$$

For grease versus jelly:

$$HSD = \frac{(18.975 - 16.35)}{0.287} = 9.15$$

For stickers versus jelly:

$$HSD = \frac{(17.55 - 16.35)}{0.287} = 4.18$$

The critical value of *q* at a *p* level of 0.05 is 4.34. Thus, we reject the null hypothesis for the grease versus stickers comparison and for the grease versus jelly comparison, but not for the stickers versus jelly comparison. These results indicate that black grease beneath the eyes leads to better visual acuity, on average, than either antiglare stickers or petroleum jelly.

j. $R^2 = \dfrac{SS_{between}}{(SS_{total} - SS_{subjects})} = \dfrac{13.820}{(16.527 - 0.735)} = 0.88$

k. This study could be conducted using a between-groups design if football players were assigned to only one of the three conditions; thus, they would be exposed to the black grease, the antiglare stickers, or the petroleum jelly, rather than all three.

l. The study could be conducted using a matched-groups design if the participants in each condition were not the same but were matched on possible confounding variables. In this example, we may want to control for variables related to vision such as color blindness, nearsightedness or farsightedness, or reaction time to a visual stimuli by matching participants based on their scores on these variables. Any variable that might explain differences between groups should be accounted for in a matched-group design.

Chapter 14

14.1 A two-way ANOVA is a hypothesis test that includes two nominal (or sometimes ordinal) independent variables and a scale dependent variable.

14.3 In everyday conversation, the word *cell* conjures up images of a prison or a small room in which someone is forced to stay, or of one of the building blocks of a plant or animal. In statistics, the word *cell* refers to a single condition in a factorial ANOVA that is characterized by its values on each of the independent variables.

14.5 A two-way ANOVA has two independent variables. When we express that as a 2 × 3 ANOVA, we get added detail: the first number tells us that the first independent variable has two levels, and the second number tells us that the other independent variable has three levels.

14.7 A marginal mean is the mean of a row or a column in a table that shows the cells of a study with a two-way ANOVA design.

14.9 Bar graphs allow us to visually depict the relative changes across the different levels of each independent variable. By adding lines that connect the bars within each series, we can assess whether the lines appear parallel, significantly different from parallel, or intersecting. Intersecting and significantly nonparallel lines are indications of interactions.

14.11 First, we may be able to reject the null hypothesis for the interaction. (If the interaction is statistically significant, then it might not matter whether the main effects are significant; if they are also significant, then those findings are usually qualified by the interaction and they are not described separately. The overall pattern of cell means can tell the whole story.) Second, if we are not able to reject the null hypothesis for the interaction, then we focus on any significant main effects, drawing a specific directional conclusion for each. Third, if we do not reject the null hypothesis for either main effect or the interaction, then we can only conclude that there is insufficient evidence from this study to support the research hypotheses.

14.13 This is the formula for the between-groups sum of squares for the interaction; we can calculate this by subtracting the other between-groups sums of squares (those for the two main effects) and the within-groups sum of squares from the total sum of squares. (The between-groups sum of squares for the interaction is essentially what is left over when the main effects are accounted for.)

14.15 We can use R^2 to calculate effect size similarly to how we did for a one-way ANOVA according to Cohen's conventions. An effect size can be calculated for each main effect and for the interaction.

14.17 An ANCOVA and an ANOVA both have one or more nominal (or sometimes ordinal) independent variables and a single scale dependent variable, but an ANCOVA uses another scale variable as a covariate. Any variability in the dependent variable that is associated with this covariate is removed so that the effects of the independent variables can be observed without being contaminated by differences on the covariate.

14.19 If a researcher used multiple scale dependent variables that all assessed similar constructs, the researcher should use a MANOVA.

14.21 A two-way mixed-design MANOVA is an analysis used for a study in which there are at least two independent variables, and each participant experiences all levels of at least one independent variable, but only one level of at least one other independent variable. That is, at least one variable is between-groups and at least one variable is within-groups. In addition, there are multiple (at least 2) dependent variables that are being measured for each participant.

14.23 a. There are two independent variables or factors: gender and sporting event. Gender has two levels, male and female, and sporting event has two levels, Sport 1 and Sport 2.

b. Type of campus is one factor that has two levels: dry and wet. The second factor is type of college, which has three levels: state, private, and religious.

c. Age group is the first factor, with three levels: 12–13, 14–15, and 16–17. Gender is a second factor, with two levels: female and male. Family composition is the last factor, with three levels: two parents, single parent, no identified authority figure.

14.25 a.

	Ice hockey	Figure skating	
Men	$M = (19 + 17 + 18 + 17)/4 = 17.75$	$M = (6 + 4 + 8 + 3)/4 = 5.25$	$(17.75 + 5.25)/2 = 11.50$
Women	$M = (13 + 14 + 18 + 8)/4 = 13.25$	$M = (11 + 7 + 4 + 14)/4 = 9$	$(13.25 + 9)/2 + 11.125$
	$(17.75 + 13.25)/2 = 15.5$	$(5.25 + 9)/2 = 7.125$	

b.

c. $df_{rows(gender)} = N_{rows} - 1 = 2 - 1 = 1$
$df_{columns(sport)} = N_{columns} - 1 = 2 - 1 = 1$
$df_{interaction} = (df_{rows})(df_{columns}) = (1)(1) = 1$
$df_{within} = df_{M,H} + df_{M,S} + df_{W,H} + df_{W,S} = 3 + 3 + 3 + 3 = 12$
$df_{total} = N_{total} - 1 = 16 - 1 = 15$

We can also check that this answer is correct by adding all of the other degrees of freedom together:

$$1 + 1 + 1 + 12 = 15$$

The critical value for an F distribution with 1 and 12 degrees of freedom, at a p level of 0.01, is 9.33.

d. $GM = 11.313$
$SS_{total} = \Sigma(X - GM)^2$ for each score $= 475.438$

	X	$X - GM$	$(X - GM)^2$
Men, hockey	19	7.687	59.090
	17	5.687	32.342
	18	6.687	44.716
	17	5.687	32.342
Men, skating	6	−5.313	28.228
	4	−7.313	53.480
	8	−3.313	10.976
	3	−8.313	69.106
Women, hockey	13	1.687	2.846
	14	2.687	7.220
	18	6.687	44.716
	8	−3.313	10.976
Women, skating	11	−0.313	0.098
	7	−4.313	18.602
	4	−7.313	53.480
	14	2.687	7.220

$\Sigma = 475.438$

e. Sum of squares for gender: $SS_{between(rows)} = \Sigma(M_{row} - GM)^2$ for each score $= 0.560$

	X	$(M_{row} - GM)$	$(M_{row} - GM)^2$
Men, hockey	19	0.187	0.035
	17	0.187	0.035
	18	0.187	0.035
	17	0.187	0.035
Men, skating	6	0.187	0.035
	4	0.187	0.035
	8	0.187	0.035
	3	0.187	0.035
Women, hockey	13	−0.188	0.035
	14	−0.188	0.035
	18	−0.188	0.035
	8	−0.188	0.035
Women, skating	11	−0.188	0.035
	7	−0.188	0.035
	4	−0.188	0.035
	14	−0.188	0.035

$\Sigma = 0.560$

f. Sum of squares for sporting event: $SS_{between(columns)} = \Sigma(M_{column} - GM)^2$ for each score $= 280.560$

	X	$(M_{column} - GM)$	$(M_{column} - GM)^2$
Men, hockey	19	4.187	17.531
	17	4.187	17.531
	18	4.187	17.531
	17	4.187	17.531
Men, skating	6	−4.188	17.539
	4	−4.188	17.539
	8	−4.188	17.539
	3	−4.188	17.539
Women, hockey	13	4.187	17.531
	14	4.187	17.531
	18	4.187	17.531
	8	4.187	17.531
Women, skating	11	−4.188	17.539
	7	−4.188	17.539
	4	−4.188	17.539
	14	−4.188	17.539

$\Sigma = 280.560$

g. $SS_{within} = \Sigma(X - M_{cell})^2$ for each score $= 126.256$

	X	$(X - M_{cell})$	$(X - M_{cell})^2$
Men, hockey	19	1.25	1.563
	17	−0.75	0.563
	18	0.25	0.063
	17	−0.75	0.563
Men, skating	6	0.75	0.563
	4	−1.25	1.563
	8	2.75	7.563
	3	−2.25	5.063
Women, hockey	13	−0.25	0.063
	14	0.75	0.563
	18	4.75	22.563
	8	−5.25	27.563
Women, skating	11	2	4.000
	7	−2	4.000
	4	−5	25.000
	14	5	25.000

$\Sigma = 126.256$

h. We use subtraction to find the sum of squares for the interaction. We subtract all other sources from the total sum of squares, and the remaining amount is the sum of squares for the interaction.

$SS_{gender \times sport} = SS_{total} - (SS_{gender} + SS_{sport} + SS_{within})$

$SS_{gender \times sport} = 475.438 - (0.560 + 280.560 + 126.256)$
$= 68.062$

i.

Source	SS	df	MS	F
Gender	0.560	1	0.560	0.05
Sporting event	280.560	1	280.560	26.67
Gender × sport	68.062	1	68.062	6.47
Within	126.256	12	10.521	
Total	475.438	15		

14.27

Source	SS	df	MS	F
Gender	248.25	1	248.25	8.07
Parenting style	84.34	3	28.113	0.91
Gender × style	33.60	3	11.20	0.36
Within	1107.20	36	30.756	
Total	1473.39	43		

14.29 For the main effect A:

$$R^2_{rows} = \frac{SS_{rows}}{(SS_{total} - SS_{columns} - SS_{interaction})}$$

$$= \frac{30.006}{(652.291 - 33.482 - 1.720)} = 0.049$$

According to Cohen's conventions, this is approaching a medium effect size.

For the main effect B:

$$R^2_{columns} = \frac{SS_{columns}}{(SS_{total} - SS_{rows} - SS_{interaction})}$$

$$= \frac{33.482}{(652.291 - 30.006 - 1.720)} = 0.054$$

According to Cohen's conventions, this is approaching a medium effect size.

For the interaction:

$$R^2_{interaction} = \frac{SS_{interaction}}{(SS_{total} - SS_{rows} - SS_{columns})}$$

$$= \frac{1.720}{(652.291 - 30.006 - 33.482)} = 0.003$$

According to Cohen's conventions, this is smaller than a small effect size.

14.31 a. This study would be analyzed with a between-groups ANOVA because different groups of participants were assigned to the different treatment conditions.

b. This study could be redesigned to use a within-groups ANOVA by testing the same group of participants on some myths repeated once and some repeated three times both when the participants are young and then again when they are old.

14.33 a. There are two independent variables: country and anger. Country has two levels: Japan and the United States. Anger has two levels: low or high.

b. The dependent variable is health outcomes.

c. There are two independent variables and one dependent variable for these data. A two-way ANOVA would be the appropriate hypothesis test because it allows us to compare levels from two independent variables, as well as explore the combined effects of the two independent variables, on the dependent variable.

d. A 2 × 2 between-groups ANOVA would be the appropriate test to use.

e. There are two variables, each with two levels. By multiplying the number of levels for each variable (two multiplied by two), we know that we need four cells.

f.

	Low levels of anger	High levels of anger
Japan		
United States		

g. This is a quantitative interaction because the direction of the effect of one independent variable, level of anger, among people in Japan is opposite of the direction of the effect among people in the United States.

14.35 a. The first independent variable is the gender said to be most affected by the illness, and its levels are men and women. The second independent variable is the gender of the participant, and its levels are male and female. The dependent variable is level of comfort, on a scale of 1–7.

b. The researchers conducted a two-way between-groups ANOVA.

c. The reported statistics do indicate that there is a significant interaction because the probability associated with the F statistic for the interaction is less than 0.05.

d.

	Female participants	Male participants
Illness affects woman	4.88	3.29
Illness affects men	3.56	4.67

e. Bar graph for the interaction:

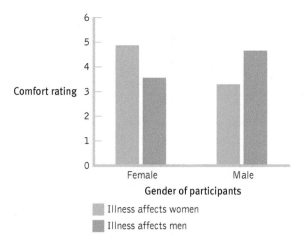

f. This is a qualitative interaction. Female participants indicated greater average comfort about attending a meeting regarding an illness that affects women than about attending a meeting regarding an illness that affects men. Male participants had the opposite pattern of results; male participants indicated greater average comfort about attending a meeting regarding an illness that affects men as opposed to one that affects women.

g.

	Female participants	Male participants
Illness affects women	4.88	**4.80**
Illness affects men	3.56	4.67

Note: There are several cell means that would work.

h. Bar graph for the new means:

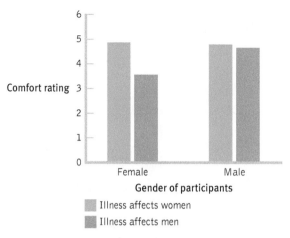

i.

	Female participants	Male participants
Illness affects women	4.88	**5.99**
Illness affects men	3.56	4.67

14.37 a. The first independent variable is the race of the face, and its levels are white and black. The second independent variable is the type of instruction given to the participants, and its levels are no instruction and instruction to attend to distinguishing features. The dependent variable is the measure of recognition accuracy.

   b. The researchers conducted a two-way between-groups ANOVA.

   c. The reported statistics indicate that there is a significant main effect of race. On average, the white participants who saw white faces had higher recognition scores than did white participants who saw black faces.

   d. The main effect is misleading because those who received instructions to attend to distinguishing features actually had lower mean recognition scores for the white faces than did those who received no instruction, whereas those who received instructions to attend to distinguishing features had higher mean recognition scores for the black faces than did those who received no instruction.

   e. The reported statistics do indicate that there is a significant interaction because the probability associated with the F statistic for the interaction is less than 0.05.

   f.

	Black face	White face
No instruction	1.04	1.46
Distinguishing features instruction	1.23	1.38

g. Bar graph of findings:

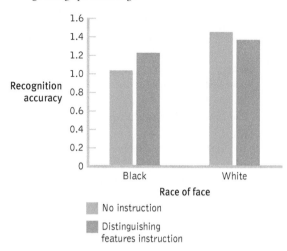

h. When given instructions to pay attention to distinguishing features of the faces, participants' average recognition of the black faces was higher than when given no instructions, whereas their average recognition of the white faces was worse than when given no instruction. This is a qualitative interaction because the direction of the effect changes between black and white.

14.39 a. The first independent variable is gender of the seeker, and its levels are men and women. The second independent variable is gender of the person being sought, and its levels are men and women. The dependent variable is the oldest acceptable age of the person being sought.

   b.

	Women seekers	Men seekers
Men sought	34.80	35.40
Women sought	36.00	27.20

   c. *Step 1:* Population 1 (women, men) is women seeking men. Population 2 (men, women) is men seeking women. Population 3 (women, women) is women seeking women. Population 4 (men, men) is men seeking men. The comparison distributions will be F distributions. The hypothesis test will be a two-way between-groups ANOVA.

   Assumptions: The data are not from random samples, so we must generalize with caution. From the small samples sizes, it's difficult to know if the underlying population distributions are normally distributed, so we must proceed with caution. The assumption of homogeneity of variance is violated because the largest variance (29.998) is much larger than the smallest variance (1.188). For the purposes of this exercise, however, we will conduct this ANOVA.

   Step 2: Main effect of first independent variable—gender of seeker:

   Null hypothesis: On average, men and women report the same oldest acceptable ages for a partner—$\mu_M = \mu_W$.

   Research hypothesis: On average, men and women report different oldest acceptable ages for a partner—$\mu_M \neq \mu_W$.

Main effect of second independent variable—gender of person sought:

Null hypothesis: On average, those seeking men and those seeking women report the same oldest acceptable ages for a partner—$\mu_M = \mu_W$.

Research hypothesis: On average, those seeking men and those seeking women report different oldest acceptable ages for a partner—$\mu_M \neq \mu_W$.

Interaction: Seeker × sought:

Null hypothesis: The effect of the gender of the seeker does not depend on the gender of the person sought.

Research hypothesis: The effect of the gender of the seeker does depend on the gender of the person sought.

Step 3: $df_{columns(seeker)} = 2 - 1 = 1$

$df_{rows(sought)} = 2 - 1 = 1$

$df_{interaction} = (1)(1) = 1$

$df_{within} = df_{W,M} + df_{M,W} + df_{W,W} + df_{M,M}$
$= 4 + 4 + 4 + 4 = 16$

Main effect of gender of seeker: F distribution with 1 and 16 degrees of freedom

Main effect of gender of sought: F distribution with 1 and 16 degrees of freedom

Interaction of seeker and sought: F distribution with 1 and 16 degrees of freedom

Step 4: Cutoff F for main effect of seeker: 4.49

Cutoff F for main effect of sought: 4.49

Cutoff F for interaction of seeker and sought: 4.49

Step 5: $SS_{total} = \Sigma(X - GM)^2 = 454.559$

$SS_{column(seeker)} = \Sigma(M_{column(seeker)} - GM)^2 = 84.050$

$SS_{row(sought)} = \Sigma(M_{row(sought)} - GM)^2 = 61.260$

$SS_{within} = \Sigma(X - M_{cell})^2 = 198.800$

$SS_{interaction} = SS_{total} - (SS_{row} + SS_{column} + SS_{within}) = 110.449$

Source	SS	df	MS	F
Seeker gender	84.050	1	84.050	6.76
Sought gender	61.260	1	61.260	4.93
Seeker × sought	110.449	1	110.449	8.89
Within	198.800	16	12.425	
Total	454.559	19		

Step 6: There is a significant main effect of gender of the seeker; it appears that women are willing to accept older dating partners, on average, than are men. There is also a significant main effect of gender of the person being sought; it appears that those seeking men are willing to accept older dating partners, on average, than are those seeking women. Additionally, there is a significant interaction between the gender of the seeker and the gender of the person being sought. Because there is a significant interaction, we ignore the main effects and report only the interaction.

d. There is a significant quantitative interaction because there is a difference for male seekers, but not for female seekers. We are not seeing a reversal of direction necessary for a qualitative interaction.

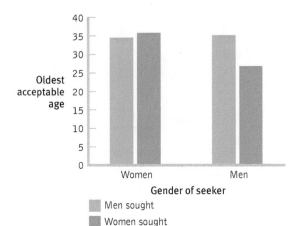

e. For the main effect of seeker gender:

$$R^2_{seeker} = \frac{SS_{seeker}}{(SS_{total} - SS_{sought} - SS_{interaction})}$$

$$= \frac{84.05}{454.559 - 61.26 - 110.449} = 0.30$$

According to Cohen's conventions, this is a large effect size. For the main effect of sought gender:

$$R^2_{sought} = \frac{SS_{sought}}{(SS_{total} - SS_{seeker} - SS_{interaction})}$$

$$= \frac{61.26}{454.559 - 84.05 - 110.449} = 0.24$$

According to Cohen's conventions, this is a large effect size. For the interaction:

$$R^2_{seeker} = \frac{SS_{interaction}}{(SS_{total} - SS_{seeker} - SS_{sought})}$$

$$= \frac{110.449}{454.559 - 84.05 - 61.26} = 0.36$$

According to Cohen's conventions, this is a large effect size.

14.41 a. The independent variables are type of payment, still with two levels, and level of payment, now with three levels (low, moderate, and high). The dependent variable is still willingness to help, as assessed with the 11-point scale.

b.

	Low amount	Moderate amount	High amount	
Cash payment	4.75	7.50	8.00	6.75
Candy payment	6.25	6.00	6.50	6.25
	5.50	6.75	7.25	

c.

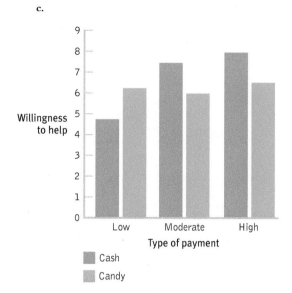

d. There does still seem to be the same qualitative interaction, such that the effect of the level of payment depends on the type of payment. When candy payments are used, the level seems to have no mean impact. However, when cash payments are used, a low level leads to a lower willingness to help, on average, than when candy is used, and a moderate or high level leads to a higher willingness to help, on average, than when candy is used.

e. Post hoc tests would be needed. Specifically, we would need to compare the three levels of payment to see where specific significant differences exist. Based on the graph we created, it appears as if willingness to help in the low payment condition is significantly lower, on average, than in the moderate and high conditions for payments.

14.43 a. This is problematic because it suggests a causal relation for correlational data. There are many possible confounds. It could be that people with high energy are more likely both to exercise (and lose weight) and to work long hours (and make more money). It could be that education level is associated with both weight and income. The act of losing weight might not cause one's income to change at all.

b. If you can include covariates, you can eliminate alternative explanations. There are several possible scale variables that could be included as covariates. For example, if you include education level as a covariate and there is still a link between weight and income, you can eliminate education level as a possible confound.

14.45 a. The independent variables are educational attainment (levels: transitioning adolescents, college underclassmen, college upperclassmen), disability status (levels: dyslexia, ADHD, ADHD/dyslexia), and gender (levels: male, female).

b. The dependent variables are depression as assessed by the BDI-II and anxiety as assessed by the BAI.

c. The researchers conducted a MANOVA because multiple dependent variables were being analyzed at the same time.

d. i. Upperclassmen with disabilities have higher levels of depression and anxiety, on average, than do transitioning adolescents with disabilities.

ii. Tukey *HSD* tests were likely conducted because statistically significant effects were found for the main effect of educational attainment. Because there were three levels, the researchers would not have known from a statistically significant effect which pairs of the three means were statistically significantly different from each other. The Tukey *HSD* tests allowed the researchers to test each pair of educational attainment levels for mean differences in anxiety and for mean differences in depression.

iii. Usually the appropriate effect size with ANOVA and its various forms, including MANOVA, is R^2. However, in this case, the researchers reported Cohen's *d* because the Tukey *HSD* tests assess the difference between pairs of means, and Cohen's *d* reports the differences in terms of standard deviation between pairs of means.

14.47 a. The researchers conducted a two-way between-groups ANOVA.

b. By averaging the percentages for each pair of bars, we can estimate that the mean for sender is around 52 or 53, and the mean for receiver is around 47 or 48. So, there does appear to be a main effect of role in the negotiations. Senders—the people who kick off the negotiations—end up doing better, on average, than do receivers.

c. It does not seem that there is a main effect of type of information provided. The mean of the two bars for each is around 50.

d. There seems to be a qualitative interaction. It seems to be better to be the sender (the one initiating the negotiation if the sender is *not* providing information about areas in which she or he is willing to acquiesce, whereas it seems better to be the receiver if the sender *is* providing information about what she or he will settle for.

e. The *y*-axis should begin at 0. Otherwise, the graph would exaggerate the differences between groups.

14.49 a. The independent variables are type of feedback (levels: positive, negative), level of expertise (levels: novice, expert), and domain (level: feedback on language acquisition, pursuit of environmental causes, use of consumer products).

b. The dependent variable appears to be levels of seeking behavior and response behavior.

c. This interaction is statistically significant, as the *p* value is less than 0.05.

d. The statistic missing from this report is a measure of effect size, such as R^2. The effect size helps us figure out whether something that is statistically significant is also practically important.

e. The bar graph illustrates what appears to be a qualitative interaction. Experts sought and responded more to negative feedback than to positive feedback; novices sought and responded more to positive feedback than to negative feedback.

f. Suggestions may vary. The graph needs a clear, specific title; the *y*-axis should go down to 0; and the label on the *y*-axis should be rotated so that it reads left to right.

Chapter 15

15-1 A correlation coefficient is a statistic that quantifies the relation between two variables.

15-3 A perfect relation occurs when the data points fall exactly on the line we fit through the data. A perfect relation results in a correlation coefficient of −1.0 or 1.0.

15-5 According to Cohen (1988), a correlation coefficient of 0.50 is a large correlation, and 0.30 is a medium one. However, it is unusual in social science research to have a correlation as high as 0.50. The decision of whether a correlation is worth talking about is sometimes based on whether it is statistically significant, as well as what practical effect a correlation of a certain size indicates.

15-7 When used to capture the relation between two variables, the correlation coefficient is a descriptive statistic. When used to draw conclusions about the greater population, such as with hypothesis testing, the coefficient serves as an inferential statistic.

15-9 Positive products of deviations, indicating a positive correlation, occur when both members of a pair of scores tend to result in a positive deviation or when both members tend to result in a negative deviation. Negative products of deviations, indicating a negative correlation, occur when members of a pair of scores tend to result in opposite-valued deviations (one negative and the other positive).

15-11 (1) We calculate the deviation of each score from its mean, multiply the two deviations for each participant, and sum the products of the deviations. (2) We calculate a sum of squares for each variable, multiply the two sums of squares, and take the square root of the product of the sums of squares. (3) We divide the sum from step 1 by the square root in step 2.

15-13 Test–retest reliability involves giving the same group of people the exact same test with some amount of time (perhaps a week) between the two administrations of the test. Test–retest reliability is then calculated as the correlation between their scores on the two administrations of the test. Calculation of coefficient alpha does not require giving the same test two times. Rather, coefficient alpha is based on correlations between different halves of the test items from a single administration of the test.

15-15 The difference between a Pearson correlation coefficient and a partial correlation coefficient is that the partial correlation coefficient has factored out the influence of one or more additional variables; thus, it is a better representation of the relation between the two variables because it controls for other related variables.

15-17 a. These data appear to be negatively correlated.
   b. These data appear to be positively correlated.
   c. Neither; these data appear to have a very small correlation, if any.

15-19 a. −0.28 is a medium correlation.
   b. 0.79 is a large correlation.
   c. 1.0 is a perfect correlation.
   d. −0.015 is almost no correlation.

15-21 a.

b.

X	$(X - M_X)$	Y	$(Y - M_Y)$	$(X - M_X)(Y - M_Y)$
0.13	−0.36	645	218.50	−78.660
0.27	−0.22	486	59.50	−13.090
0.49	0.00	435	8.50	0.000
0.57	0.08	689	262.50	21.000
0.84	0.35	137	−289.50	−101.325
0.64	0.13	167	−259.50	−38.925

$M_X = 0.49$ $\qquad M_Y = 426.5$ $\qquad \Sigma[(X - M_X)(Y - M_Y)] = -211.0$

c.

X	$(X - M_X)$	$(X - M_X)^2$	Y	$(Y - M_Y)$	$(Y - M_Y)^2$
0.13	−0.36	0.130	645	218.50	47,742.25
0.27	−0.22	0.048	486	59.50	3540.25
0.49	0.00	0.000	435	8.50	72.25
0.57	0.08	0.006	689	262.50	68,906.25
0.84	0.35	0.123	137	−289.50	83,810.25
0.64	0.13	0.023	167	−259.50	67,340.25

$\Sigma(X - M_X)^2 = 0.330$ $\qquad \Sigma(Y - M_Y)^2 = 271,411.50$

$$\sqrt{(SS_X)(SS_Y)} = \sqrt{(0.330)(271,411.50)} = \sqrt{89,565.795} = 299.275$$

d. $r = \dfrac{\Sigma[(X - M_X)(Y - M_Y)]}{\sqrt{(SS_X)(SS_Y)}} = \dfrac{-211.0}{299.275} = -0.71$

e. $df_r = N - 2 = 6 - 2 = 4$

f. −0.811 and 0.811

15-23 a.

Scatterplot with Y axis (0 to 60) and X axis (0 to 80).

b.

X	$(X - M_X)$	Y	$(Y - M_Y)$	$(X - M_X)(Y - M_Y)$
40	−2.143	60	22.857	−48.983
45	2.857	55	17.857	51.017
20	−22.143	30	−7.143	158.167
75	32.857	25	−12.143	−398.983
15	−27.143	20	−17.143	465.312
35	−7.143	40	2.857	−20.408
65	22.857	30	−7.143	163.268

$M_X = 42.143$ $M_Y = 37.143$ $\Sigma[(X - M_X)(Y - M_Y)] = 42.854$

c.

X	$(X - M_X)$	$(X - M_X)^2$	Y	$(Y - M_Y)$	$(Y - M_Y)^2$
40	−2.143	4.592	60	22.857	522.442
45	2.857	8.162	55	17.857	318.872
20	−22.143	490.312	30	−7.143	51.022
75	32.857	1079.582	25	−12.143	147.452
15	−27.143	736.742	20	−17.143	293.882
35	−7.143	51.022	40	2.857	8.162
65	22.857	522.442	30	−7.143	51.022

$\Sigma(X - M_X)^2 = 2892.854$ $\Sigma(Y - M_Y)^2 = 1392.854$

$$\sqrt{(SS_X)(SS_Y)} = \sqrt{(2892.854)(1392.854)}$$
$$= \sqrt{4,029,323.265} = 2007.317$$

d. $r = \dfrac{\Sigma[(X - M_X)(Y - M_Y)]}{\sqrt{(SS_X)(SS_Y)}} = \dfrac{42.854}{2007.317} = 0.02$

e. $df_r = N - 2 = 7 - 2 = 5$

f. −0.754 and 0.754

15-25 a. $df_r = N - 2 = 3113 - 2 = 3111$. The highest degrees of freedom listed on the table is 100, with cutoffs of −0.195 and 0.195.

b. $df_r = N - 2 = 72 - 2 = 70$; −0.232 and 0.232

15-27 When using a measure to diagnose individuals, having a reliability of at least 0.90 is important—and the more reliable the test, the better. So, based on reliability information alone, we would recommend she use the test with 0.95 reliability.

15-29 The third variable does not account for any of the correlation between A and B. The partial correlation, taking into account the third variable, is exactly the same as the original correlation between A and B.

15-31 The researchers are describing a negative relation. As grip strength increases, fatality rates decrease; when grip strength decreases, there are higher fatality rates.

15-33 a. Newman's data do not suggest a correlation between Mercury's phases and breakdowns. There was no consistency in the report of breakdowns during one of the phases.

b. Massey may observe a correlation because she already believes that there is a relation between astrological events and human events. As you learned in Chapter 5, the confirmation bias refers to the tendency to pay attention to those events that confirm our prior beliefs. The confirmation bias may lead Massey to observe an illusory correlation (i.e., she perceives a correlation that does not actually exist) because she attends only to those events that confirm her prior belief that the phase of Mercury is related to breakdowns.

c. Given that there are two phases of Mercury (and assuming they're equal in length), half of the breakdowns that occur would be expected to occur during the retrograde phase and the other half during the nonretrograde phase, just by chance. Expected relative-frequency probability refers to the expected frequency of events. So in this example we would expect 50% of breakdowns to occur during the retrograde phase and 50% during the nonretrograde phase. If we base our conclusions on only a small number of observations of breakdowns, the observed relative-frequency probability is more likely to differ from the expected relative-frequency probability because we are less likely to have a representative sample of breakdowns.

d. This correlation would not be useful in predicting events in your own life because no relation would be observed in this limited time span.

e. Available data do not support the idea that a correlation exists between Mercury's phases and breakdowns.

15-35 a. The accompanying scatterplot depicts the relation between hours of exercise and number of friends. Note that you could have chosen to put hours of exercise along the y-axis and number of friends along the x-axis.

Scatterplot: Number of friends (y-axis, 0 to 8) vs Hours of exercise (x-axis, 0 to 12).

b. The scatterplot suggests that as the number of hours of exercise each week increases from 0 to 5, there is an increase in the number of friends, but as the hours of exercise continue to increase past 5, there is a decrease in the number of friends.

c. It would not be appropriate to calculate a Pearson correlation coefficient with this set of data. The scatterplot suggests a nonlinear relation between exercise and number of friends, and the Pearson correlation coefficient measures only the extent of linear relation between two variables.

15-37 *Step 1:* Population 1: Adolescents like those we studied. Population 2: Adolescents for whom there is no relation between externalizing behavior and anxiety. The comparison distribution is made up of correlation coefficients based on many, many samples of our size, 10 people, randomly selected from the population.

We do not know if the data were randomly selected (first assumption), so we must be cautious when generalizing the findings. We also do not know if the underlying population distribution for externalizing behaviors and anxiety in adolescents is normally distributed (second assumption). The sample size is too small to make any conclusions about this assumption, so we should proceed with caution. The third assumption, unique to correlation, is that the variability of one variable is equal across the levels of the other variable. Because we have such a small data set, it is difficult to evaluate this. However, we can see from the scatterplot that the data are somewhat consistently variable.

Step 2: Null hypothesis: There is no correlation between externalizing behavior and anxiety among adolescents— $H_0: \rho = 0$.

Research hypothesis: There is a correlation between externalizing behavior and anxiety among adolescents— $H_1: \rho \neq 0$.

Step 3: The comparison distribution is a distribution of Pearson correlations, r, with the following degrees of freedom: $df_r = N - 2 = 10 - 2 = 8$.

Step 4: The critical values for an r distribution with 8 degrees of freedom for a two-tailed test with a p level of 0.05 are -0.632 and 0.632.

Step 5: The Pearson correlation coefficient is calculated in three steps. First, we calculate the numerator:

X	$(X - M_X)$	Y	$(Y - M_Y)$	$(X - M_X)(Y - M_Y)$
9	2.40	37	7.60	18.24
7	0.40	23	−6.40	−2.56
7	0.40	26	−3.40	−1.36
3	−3.60	21	−8.40	30.24
11	4.40	42	12.60	55.44
6	−0.60	33	3.60	−2.16
2	−4.60	26	−3.40	15.64
6	−0.60	35	5.60	−3.36
6	−0.60	23	−6.40	3.84
9	2.40	28	−1.40	−3.36

$M_X = 6.60 \qquad M_Y = 29.40 \qquad \Sigma[(X - M_X)(Y - M_Y)] = 110.60$

Second, we calculate the denominator:

X	$(X - M_X)$	$(X - M_X)^2$	Y	$(Y - M_Y)$	$(Y - M_Y)^2$
9	2.40	5.76	37	7.60	57.76
7	0.40	0.16	23	−6.40	40.96
7	0.40	0.16	26	−3.40	11.56
3	−3.60	12.96	21	−8.40	70.56
11	4.40	19.36	42	12.60	158.76
6	−0.60	0.36	33	3.60	12.96
2	−4.60	21.16	26	−3.40	11.56
6	−0.60	0.36	35	5.60	31.36
6	−0.60	0.36	23	−6.40	40.96
9	2.40	5.76	28	−1.40	1.96

$\Sigma(X - M_X)^2 = 66.40 \qquad\qquad \Sigma(Y - M_Y)^2 = 438.40$

$$\sqrt{(SS_X)(SS_Y)} = \sqrt{(66.40)(438.40)} = \sqrt{29,109.76} = 170.616$$

Finally, we compute r:

$$r = \frac{\Sigma[(X - M_X)(Y - M_Y)]}{\sqrt{(SS_X)(SS_Y)}} = \frac{110.60}{170.616} = 0.65$$

The test statistic, $r = 0.65$, is larger in magnitude than the critical value of 0.632. We can reject the null hypothesis and conclude that there is a strong positive correlation between the level of externalizing behaviors performed by adolescents and their level of anxiety.

15-39 a. You might expect a person who owns a lot of cats to tend to have many mental health problems. Because the two variables are positively correlated, as cat ownership increases, the number of mental health problems tends to increase.

b. You might expect a person who owns no cats or just one cat to tend to have few mental health problems. Because the variables are positively correlated, people who have a low score on one variable are also likely to have a low score on the other variable.

c. You might expect a person who owns a lot of cats to tend to have few mental health problems. Because the two variables are negatively related, as one variable increases, the other variable tends to decrease. This means a person who owns a lot of cats would likely have a low score on the mental health variable.

d. You might expect a person who owns no cats or just one cat to tend to have many mental health problems. Because the two variables are negatively related, as one variable decreases, the other variable tends to increase, which means that a person with fewer cats would likely have more mental health problems.

15-41 a. The accompanying scatterplot depicts a negative linear relation between perceived femininity and perceived trauma. Because the relation appears linear, it is appropriate to calculate the Pearson correlation coefficient for these data. (*Note:* The number (2) indicates that two participants share that pair of scores.)

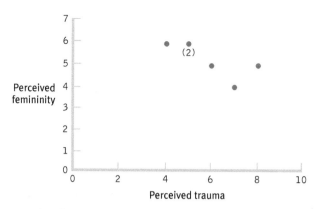

Perceived femininity (y-axis), Perceived trauma (x-axis)

b. The Pearson correlation coefficient is calculated in three steps. Step 1 is calculating the numerator:

X	$(X - M_X)$	Y	$(Y - M_Y)$	$(X - M_X)(Y - M_Y)$
5	−0.833	6	0.667	−0.556
6	0.167	5	−0.333	−0.056
4	−1.833	6	0.667	−1.223
5	−0.833	6	0.667	−0.556
7	1.167	4	−1.333	−1.556
8	2.167	5	−0.333	−0.722

$M_X = 5.833$ $M_Y = 5.333$ $\Sigma[(X - M_X)(Y - M_Y)] = -4.669$

Step 2 is calculating the denominator:

X	$(X - M_X)$	$(X - M_X)^2$	Y	$(Y - M_Y)$	$(Y - M_Y)^2$
5	−0.833	0.694	6	0.667	0.445
6	0.167	0.028	5	−0.333	0.111
4	−1.833	3.360	6	0.667	0.445
5	−0.833	0.694	6	0.667	0.445
7	1.167	1.362	4	−1.333	1.777
8	2.167	4.696	5	−0.333	0.111

$\Sigma[(X - M_X)^2 = 10.834$ $\Sigma(Y - M_Y)^2 = 3.334$

$$\sqrt{(SS_X)(SS_Y)} = \sqrt{(10.834)(3.334)} = \sqrt{36.121} = 6.010$$

Step 3 is computing r:

$$r = \frac{\Sigma[(X - M_X)(Y - M_Y)]}{\sqrt{(SS_X)(SS_Y)}} = \frac{-4.669}{6.010} = -0.78$$

c. The correlation coefficient reveals a strong negative relation between perceived femininity and perceived trauma; as trauma increases, perceived femininity tends to decrease.

d. Those participants who had positive deviation scores on trauma tended to have negative deviation scores on femininity (and vice versa), meaning that when a person's score on one variable was above the mean for that variable (positive deviation), his or her score on the second variable was typically below the mean for that variable (negative deviation). So, having a high score on one variable was associated with having a low score on the other, which is a negative correlation.

15-43 a. The accompanying scatterplot depicts a positive linear relation between perceived trauma and perceived masculinity. The data appear to be linearly related; therefore, it is appropriate to calculate a Pearson correlation coefficient.

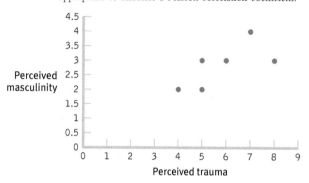

Perceived masculinity (y-axis), Perceived trauma (x-axis)

b. The Pearson correlation coefficient is calculated in three steps. Step 1 is calculating the numerator:

X	$(X - M_X)$	Y	$(Y - M_Y)$	$(X - M_X)(Y - M_Y)$
5	−0.833	3	0.167	−0.139
6	0.167	3	0.167	0.028
4	−1.833	2	−0.833	1.527
5	−0.833	2	−0.833	0.694
7	1.167	4	1.167	1.362
8	2.167	3	0.167	0.362

$M_X = 5.833$ $M_Y = 2.833$ $\Sigma[(X - M_X)(Y - M_Y)] = 3.834$

Step 2 is calculating the denominator:

X	$(X - M_X)$	$(X - M_X)^2$	Y	$(Y - M_Y)$	$(Y - M_Y)^2$
5	−0.833	0.694	3	0.167	0.028
6	0.167	0.028	3	0.167	0.028
4	−1.833	3.360	2	−0.833	0.694
5	−0.833	0.694	2	−0.833	0.694
7	1.167	1.362	4	1.167	1.362
8	2.167	4.696	3	0.167	0.028

$\Sigma[(X - M_X)^2 = 10.834$ $\Sigma(Y - M_Y)^2 = 2.834$

$$\sqrt{(SS_X)(SS_Y)} = \sqrt{(10.834)(2.834)} = \sqrt{30.704} = 5.541$$

Step 3 is computing r:

$$r = \frac{\Sigma[(X - M_X)(Y - M_Y)]}{\sqrt{(SS_X)(SS_Y)}} = \frac{3.834}{5.541} = 0.69$$

c. The correlation coefficient is large and positive. This means that as ratings of trauma increased, ratings of masculinity tended to increase as well.

d. For most of the participants, the sign of the deviation for the traumatic variable is the same as that for the masculinity variable, which indicates that those participants scoring above the mean on one variable also tended to score above the mean on the second variable (and likewise for the lowest scores). Because the scores for each participant tend to fall on the same side of the mean, this is a positive relation.

e. When the soldier was a woman, the perception of the situation as traumatic was strongly negatively correlated with the perception of the woman as feminine. This relation is opposite that observed when the soldier was a man. When the soldier was a man, the perception of the situation as traumatic was strongly positively correlated with the perception of the man as feminine. Regardless of whether the soldier was a man or a woman, there was a positive correlation between the perception of the situation as traumatic and the perception of masculinity, but the observed correlation was stronger for the perceptions of women than for the perceptions of men.

15-45 a. Because your friend is running late, she is likely more concerned about traffic than she otherwise would be. Thus, she may take note of traffic only when she is running late, leading her to believe that the amount of traffic correlates with how late she is. Furthermore, having this belief, in the future she may think only of cases that confirm her belief that a relation exists between how late she is and traffic conditions, reflecting a confirmation bias. Alternatively, traffic conditions might be worse when your friend is running late, but that could be a coincidence. A more systematic study of the relation between your friend's behavior and traffic conditions would be required before she could conclude that a relation exists.

b. There are a number of possible answers to this question. For example, we could operationalize the degree to which she is late as the number of minutes past her intended departure time that she gets in the car. We could operationalize the amount of traffic as the number of minutes the car is being driven at less than the speed limit (given that your friend would normally drive right at the speed limit).

15-47 a. The reporter suggests that convertibles are not generally less safe than other cars.

b. Convertibles may be driven less often than other cars, as they may be considered primarily a recreational vehicle. If they are driven less, owners have fewer chances to get into accidents while driving them.

c. A more appropriate comparison may be to determine the number of fatalities that occur per every 100 hours driven in various kinds of cars.

15-49 a. The researchers are suggesting that participation in arts education programs causes students to tend to perform better and stay in school longer.

b. It could be that those students who perform better and stay in school longer are more likely to be interested in, and therefore participate in, arts education programs.

c. There are many possible answers. For example, the socioeconomic status of the students' families may be associated with performance in school, years of schooling, and participation in arts education programs, with higher socioeconomic status tending to lead to improved performance, staying in school longer, and higher participation in arts education programs.

15-51 a.

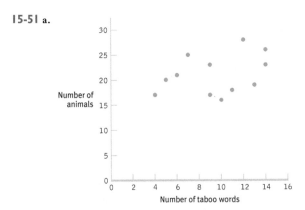

b. Step 1 is calculating the numerator:

Number of taboo words (X)	$(X - M_X)$	Number of animals (Y)	$(Y - M_Y)$	$(X - M_X)(Y - M_Y)$
9	−0.5	23	1.917	−0.959
5	−4.5	20	−1.083	4.874
4	−5.5	17	−4.083	22.457
12	2.5	28	6.917	17.293
14	4.5	26	4.917	22.127
10	0.5	16	−5.083	−2.542
9	−0.5	17	−4.083	2.042
11	1.5	18	−3.083	−4.625
14	4.5	23	1.917	8.627
6	−3.5	21	−0.083	0.291
7	−2.5	25	3.917	−9.793
13	3.5	19	−2.083	−7.291
$M_X = 9.5$		$M_Y = 21.083$		$\Sigma[(X - M_X)(Y - M_Y)] = 52.501$

Step 2 is calculating the denominator:

Number of taboo words (X)	$(X - M_X)$	$(X - M_X)^2$	Number of animals (Y)	$(Y - M_Y)$	$(Y - M_Y)^2$
9	−0.5	0.25	23	1.917	3.675
5	−4.5	20.25	20	−1.083	1.173
4	−5.5	30.25	17	−4.083	16.671
12	2.5	6.25	28	6.917	47.845
14	4.5	20.25	26	4.917	24.177
10	0.5	0.25	16	−5.083	25.837
9	−0.5	0.25	17	−4.083	16.671
11	1.5	2.25	18	−3.083	9.505
14	4.5	20.25	23	1.917	3.675
6	−3.5	12.25	21	−0.083	0.007
7	−2.5	6.25	25	3.917	15.343
13	3.5	12.25	19	−2.083	4.339
		$\Sigma(X - M_X)^2 = SS_X = 131$			$\Sigma(Y - M_Y)^2 = SS_Y = 168.918$

$$r = \frac{\Sigma[(X - M_X)(Y - M_Y)]}{\sqrt{(SS_X)(SS_Y)}} = \frac{52.501}{\sqrt{(131)(168.918)}} = \frac{52.501}{148.756} = 0.353$$

c. The correlation coefficient we just computed is a descriptive statistic because we can only use it to describe this particular sample. In order to make this correlation coefficient into an inferential statistic, we would need to conduct a hypothesis test. The hypothesis test will determine if the correlation coefficient is significantly different from zero.

d. *Step 1:* Population 1: Participants like those Jay and Jay (2015) studied. Population 2: Participants for whom there is no relation between the number of taboo words and the number of animal words that they could list in a minute. The comparison distribution is made up of correlation coefficients based on samples of this size (12 people) selected from the population. We do not know if these data were randomly selected, so we must be cautious when generalizing the findings. We also do not know if the underlying population distributions are normally distributed. The sample size is too small to make any conclusions about this assumption, so we should proceed with caution. Additionally, because we have such a small data set, it is difficult to evaluate whether the variability of the number of taboo words listed is equal across all levels of the second variable, the number of animal words listed. Similarly, we cannot easily evaluate whether the variability of the number of animal words listed is similar across all levels of the number of taboo words listed.

Step 2: Null hypothesis: There is no correlation between the number of taboo words said and the number of animal words said—H_0: $\rho = 0$.

Research hypothesis: There is a correlation between the number of taboo words said and the number of animal words said—H_1: $\rho \neq 0$.

Step 3: The comparison distribution is a distribution of Pearson correlation coefficients, r, with the following degrees of freedom: $df_r = N - 2 = 12 - 2 = 10$.

Step 4: The critical values for an r distribution with 10 degrees of freedom for a two-tailed test with a p level of 0.05 are -0.576 and 0.576.

Step 5: (same as the solution for 15.51b):

$M_X = 9.5$

$M_Y = 21.083$

$\Sigma[(X - M_X)(Y - M_Y)] = 52.501$

$\Sigma(X - M_X)^2 = SS_X = 131$

$\Sigma(Y - M_Y)^2 = SS_Y = 168.918$

$$r = \frac{\Sigma[(X - M_X)(Y - M_Y)]}{\sqrt{(SS_X)(SS_Y)}} = \frac{52.501}{\sqrt{(131)(168.918)}} = \frac{52.501}{148.756} = .353$$

Step 6: The test statistic, $r = .35$, is not larger in magnitude than the critical value of .576, so we fail to reject the null hypothesis. We cannot conclude that there is a relation between the number of taboo words said and the number of animal words said. Because the sample size is rather small and we calculated such a strong correlation with this small sample, we would be encouraged to replicate the study with a larger sample to increase statistical power so that we may more fully explore this relation. In fact, the researchers who conducted this study did find that this correlation was statistically significant, but they had many more participants than in our fictional example.

e. It is unlikely you could study this phenomenon using an experimental design because it would be difficult to manipulate a person's vocabulary size.

15-53 a. If students were marked down for talking about the rooster rather than the cow, the reading test would not meet the established criteria. The question asked on the test is ambiguous because the information regarding what caused the cow's behavior to change is not explicitly stated in the story. Furthermore, the correct answer to the question provided on the Web site is not actually an answer to the question itself. The question states, "What caused Brownie's behavior to change?" The answer that the cow started out kind and ended up mean is a description of *how* her behavior changed, not what caused her behavior to change. This question does not appear to be a valid question because it does not appear to provide an accurate assessment of students' *writing* ability.

b. One possible third variable that could lead to better performance in some schools over others is the average socioeconomic status of the families whose children attend the school. Schools in wealthier areas or counties would have students of higher socioeconomic status, who might be expected to perform better on a test of writing skill. A second possible third variable that could lead to better performance in some schools over others is the type of reading and writing curriculum implemented in the school. Different ways of teaching the material may be more effective than others, regardless of the effectiveness of the teachers who are actually presenting the material.

15-55 a. The participants in the study are the various countries on which rates were obtained.

b. The two variables are health care spending and health, as assessed by life expectancy. Health care spending was operationalized as the amount spent per capita on health care, whereas life expectancy is the average age at death. Another way to operationalize health could be rates of various diseases, such as heart disease, or obesity via body mass index (BMI).

c. The study finding was that there is a negative correlation between health care spending and life expectancy, in which countries, such as the United States, that have higher rates of spending on health care per capita have lower life expectancies. One would suspect the opposite to be true, that the more a country spends on health care, the healthier the population would be, thus resulting in higher life expectancy.

d. Other possible third variables could be the typical body weight in a country, the typical exercise levels in a country, accident rates, access to health care, access or knowledge of preventative health measures, stereotypes, or a country's typical diet.

e. This study is a correlational study, not a true experiment, because countries were not assigned to certain levels of health care spending, and then assessed for life expectancy. The data were obtained from naturally occurring events.

f. It would not be possible to conduct a true experiment on this topic as this would require a manipulation in the health care spending for various countries for the entire population for a long period of time, which would not be realistic, practical, or ethical to implement.

15-57 a. High school athletic participation might be operationalized as a nominal variable by indicating whether a student participates in athletics (levels: yes or no), or by categorizing each student according to the type of athletics (levels: none, football, baseball, etc.) in which they participate.

b. High school athletic participation might be operationalized as a scale variable by counting the number of sports in which a student participates (e.g., 0, 1, 2), or by counting the number of days on which a student participates in sports annually.

c. Correlation is a useful tool to quantify the relation between two scale variables, especially when manipulation of either variable does not or cannot occur, and measuring either variable on a nominal or ordinal level would result in information being lost.

d. The researchers reported the following positive correlations: high school athletic participation and high school GPA; high school athletic participation and college completion; high school athletic participation and earnings as an adult; and high school athletic participation and various positive health behaviors. There are several other positive correlations among only male students; they include the following: high school athletic performance and alcohol consumption; high school athletic performance and sexist attitudes; high school athletic performance and homophobic attitudes; and high school athletic performance and violence. These are all positive correlations because as high school athletic participation increases, so does each of these variables.

e. There are no negative correlations reported; in all cases, an increase in one variable tended to accompany an increase in the other variable.

f. One possible causal explanation is that high school athletic participation (A) tends to cause positive health behaviors (B). A second possible causal explanation is that positive health behaviors (B) tend to cause high school athletic participation (A). A third possible causal explanation is that some other variable, such as socioeconomic status (C), could tend to affect both high school athletic participation and positive health behaviors.

g. Partial correlation might be useful in this study because it would allow us to factor out, or control for, the contribution of a third (or fourth) variable to a relation between two variables. For example, we could calculate the partial correlation between high school athletic participation and college completion, controlling for high school or college GPA.

Chapter 16

16-1 Regression allows us to make predictions based on the relation established in the correlation. Regression also allows us to consider the contributions of several variables.

16-3 There is no difference between these two terms. They are two ways to express the same thing.

16-5 a is the intercept, the predicted value for Y when X is equal to 0, which is the point at which the line crosses, or intercepts, the y-axis. b is the slope, the amount that Y is predicted to increase for an increase of 1 in X.

16-7 The intercept is not meaningful or useful when it is impossible to observe a value of 0 for X. If height is being used to predict weight, it would not make sense to talk about the weight of someone with no height.

16-9 The line of best fit in regression means that we couldn't make the line a little steeper, or raise or lower it, in any way that would allow it to represent those dots any better than it already does. This is why we can look at the scatterplot around this line and observe that the line goes precisely through the middle of the dots. Statistically, this is the line that leads to the least amount of error in prediction.

16-11 Data points clustered closely around the line of best fit are described by a small standard error of the estimate; this allows us to have a high level of confidence in the predictive ability of the independent variable. Data points clustered far away from the line of best fit are described by a large standard error of the estimate, and result in our having a low level of confidence in the predictive ability of the independent variable.

16-13 If regression to the mean did not occur, every distribution would look bimodal, like a valley. Instead, the end result of the phenomenon of regression to the mean is that things look unimodal, like a hill or what we call the normal, bell-shaped curve. Remember that the center of the bell-shaped curve is the mean, and this is where the bulk of data cluster, thanks to regression to the mean.

16-15 The sum of squares total, SS_{total}, represents the worst-case scenario, the total error we would have in the predictions if there were no regression equation and we had to predict the mean for everybody.

16-17 The basic steps to calculate the proportionate reduction in error are: (1) Determine the error associated with using the mean as the predictor. (2) Determine the error associated with using the regression equation as the predictor. (3) Subtract the error associated with the regression equation from the error associated with the mean. (4) Divide the difference (calculated in step 3) by the error associated with using the mean.

16-19 An orthogonal variable is an independent variable that makes a separate and distinct contribution in the prediction of a dependent variable, as compared with the contributions of another independent variable.

16-21 Multiple regression is often more useful than simple linear regression because it allows us to take into account the contribution of multiple independent variables, or predictors, and increase the accuracy of prediction of the dependent variable, thus reducing the prediction error. Because behaviors are complex and tend to be influenced by many factors, multiple regression allows us to better predict a given outcome.

16-23 In multiple regression, the researcher assesses how well multiple independent variables predict a dependent variable. In multiple regression, all these variables must be explicitly measured by the researcher. Structural equation modeling (SEM) allows the researcher to look at relations among many variables all at once (without differentiating between independent and dependent variables). In SEM, variables include manifest variables, which are explicitly measured, as well as latent variables, or underlying constructs, that the researcher may ultimately be most interested in.

16-25 The three primary components needed to understand a SEM diagram are: (1) manifest variables—identified by squares in the diagram, these variables are the ones that are observed and measured; (2) latent variables—identified by circles in the diagram, these variables are the ideas or concepts we want to research but cannot directly measure; and (3) paths—identified by lines and arrows in the diagram, these represent the relations between pairs of variables and the direction of the relations.

16-27 a. $z_X = \dfrac{X - M_X}{SD_X} = \dfrac{2.9 - 1.9}{0.6} = 1.667$

b. $z_{\hat{Y}} = (r_{XY})(z_X) = (0.31)(1.667) = 0.517$

c. $\hat{Y} = z_{\hat{Y}}(SD_Y) + M_Y = (0.517)(3.2) + 10 = 11.65$

16-29 a. $z_X = \dfrac{X - M_X}{SD_X} = \dfrac{76 - 55}{12} = 1.75$

b. $z_{\hat{Y}} = (r_{XY})(z_X) = (-0.19)(1.75) = -0.333$

c. $\hat{Y} = z_{\hat{Y}}(SD_Y) + M_Y = (-0.333)(95) + 1000 = 968.37$

d. The y intercept occurs when X is equal to 0. We start by finding a z score:

$$z_X = \frac{X - M_X}{SD_X} = \frac{0 - 55}{12} = -4.583$$

This is the z score for an X of 0. Now we need to figure out the predicted z score on Y for this X value:

$$z_{\hat{Y}} = (r_{XY})(z_X) = (-0.19)(-4.583) = 0.871$$

The final step is to convert the predicted z score on this predicted Y to a raw score:

$$\hat{Y} = z_{\hat{Y}}(SD_Y) + M_Y = (0.871)(95) + 1000 = 1082.745$$

This is the y intercept.

e. The slope can be found by comparing the predicted Y value for an X value of 0 (the intercept) and an X value of 1. Using the same steps as in part (a), we can compute the predicted Y score for an X value of 1.

$$z_X = \frac{X - M_X}{SD_X} = \frac{1 - 55}{12} = -4.5$$

This is the z score for an X of 1. Now we need to figure out the predicted z score on Y for this X value:

$$z_{\hat{Y}} = (r_{XY})(z_X) = (-0.19)(-4.5) = 0.855$$

The final step is to convert the predicted z score on this predicted Y to a raw score:

$$\hat{Y} = z_{\hat{Y}}(SD_Y) + M_Y = (0.855)(95) + 1000 = 1081.225$$

We compute the slope by measuring the change in Y with this 1-unit increase in X:

$$1081.225 - 1082.745 = -1.52$$

This is the slope.

f. $\hat{Y} = 1082.745 - 1.52(X)$

g. In order to draw the line, we have one more $\hat{Y}$ value to compute. This time we can use the regression equation to make the prediction:

$$\hat{Y} = 1082.745 - 1.52(48) = 1009.785$$

Now we can draw the regression line.

16-31 a. $\hat{Y} = 49 + (-0.18)(X) = 49 + (-0.18)(-31) = 54.58$

b. $\hat{Y} = 49 + (-0.18)(65) = 37.3$

c. $\hat{Y} = 49 + (-0.18)(14) = 46.48$

16-33 a. The sum of squared error for the mean, SS_{total}:

X	Y	M_Y	Error	Squared Error
4	6	6.75	−0.75	0.563
6	3	6.75	−3.75	14.063
7	7	6.75	0.25	0.063
8	5	6.75	−1.75	3.063
9	4	6.75	−2.75	7.563
10	12	6.75	5.25	27.563
12	9	6.75	2.25	5.063
14	8	6.75	1.25	1.563

$$SS_{total} = \Sigma(Y - M_Y)^2 = 59.504$$

b. The sum of squared error for the regression equation, SS_{error}:

X	Y	Regression Equation	Y	Error $(Y - \hat{Y})$	Squared Error
4	6	$\hat{Y} = 2.643 + 0.469(4)$	= 4.519	1.481	2.193
6	3	$\hat{Y} = 2.643 + 0.469(6)$	= 5.457	−2.457	6.037
7	7	$\hat{Y} = 2.643 + 0.469(7)$	= 5.926	1.074	1.153
8	5	$\hat{Y} = 2.643 + 0.469(8)$	= 6.395	−1.395	1.946
9	4	$\hat{Y} = 2.643 + 0.469(9)$	= 6.864	−2.864	8.202
10	12	$\hat{Y} = 2.643 + 0.469(10)$	= 7.333	4.667	21.781
12	9	$\hat{Y} = 2.643 + 0.469(12)$	= 8.271	0.729	0.531
14	8	$\hat{Y} = 2.643 + 0.469(14)$	= 9.209	−1.209	1.462

$$SS_{error} = \Sigma(Y - \hat{Y})^2 = 43.305$$

c. The proportionate reduction in error for these data:

$$\hat{r}^2 = \frac{(SS_{total} - SS_{error})}{SS_{total}} = \frac{(59.504 - 43.305)}{59.504} = 0.272$$

d. This calculation of $\hat{r}^2$, 0.272, equals the square of the correlation coefficient, $r^2 = (0.52)(0.52) = 0.270$. These numbers are slightly different due to rounding decisions.

e. The standardized regression coefficient is equal to the correlation coefficient for simple linear regression, 0.52. We can also check that this is correct by computing β:

X	$(X - M_X)$	$(X - M_X)^2$	Y	$(Y - M_Y)$	$(Y - M_Y)^2$
4	−4.75	22.563	6	−0.75	0.563
6	−2.75	7.563	3	−3.75	14.063
7	−1.75	3.063	7	0.25	0.063
8	−0.75	0.563	5	−1.75	3.063
9	0.25	0.063	4	−2.75	7.563
10	1.25	1.563	12	5.25	27.563
12	3.25	10.563	9	2.25	5.063
14	5.25	27.563	8	1.25	1.563

$$\Sigma(X - M_X)^2 = 73.504 \qquad \Sigma(Y - M_Y)^2 = 59.504$$

$$\beta = (b)\frac{\sqrt{SS_X}}{\sqrt{SS_Y}} = (0.469)\frac{\sqrt{73.504}}{\sqrt{59.504}} = (0.469)\frac{8.573}{7.714} = 0.521$$

16-35 a. $\hat{Y} = 1.675 + (0.001)(X_{SAT}) + (-0.008)(X_{rank})$; or
$\hat{Y} = 1.675 + 0.001(X_{SAT}) - 0.008(X_{rank})$

b. $\hat{Y} = 1.675 + (0.001)(1030) - 0.008(41)$
$= 1.675 + 1.03 - 0.328 = 2.377$

c. $\hat{Y} = 1.675 + (0.001)(860) - 0.008(22)$
$= 1.675 + 0.86 - 0.176 = 2.359$

d. $\hat{Y} = 1.675 + (0.001)(1060) - 0.008(8)$
$= 1.675 + 1.06 - 0.064 = 2.671$

16-37 a. The strongest relation depicted in the model is between identity maturity at age 26 and emotional adjustment at age 26. The strength of the path between the two is 0.81.

b. Positive parenting at age 17 is not directly related to emotional adjustment at age 26 because the two variables are not connected by a link in the model.

c. Positive parenting at age 17 is directly related to identity maturity at age 26 because the two variables are connected by a direct link in the model.

d. The variables in boxes are those that were explicitly measured—the manifest variables. The variables in circles are latent variables—variables that were not explicitly measured but are underlying constructs that the manifest variables are thought to reflect.

16-39 a. The independent variables include personal connections with victims, personal connections with gang members, personal connections with people in prison, unemployment, and history of drug or alcohol problems.

b. The dependent variable is the likelihood of committing a crime.

c. Several other variables might predict a person's likelihood of committing a crime. Some examples might include their level of education, their current criminal record, the level of poverty in the community in which they live, and their positive connections to the community such as membership in a church or participation with a volunteer organization.

d. Regressions can lead to problems with prediction because predictions can have unforeseen consequences. There may be hidden confounding variables that may mean that regression-based decisions are not fair or accurate ones. Therefore, it is important to consider confounding variables when developing a regression model. Additionally, regressions are unable to make statements about causality. Only experimental studies (i.e., methodologically controlled studies) can demonstrate causality. And, last, regression toward the mean where extreme scores tend to become less extreme makes regression models problematic with respect to making accurate predictions.

In this example, there are many possible confounding variables that might predict crime. When including variables in a regression model, it is important to consider whether the independent variables are related. For example, quality public education and access to public transportation might be related as they are both services provided by the government. It is important to consider whether variables are orthogonal when developing regression models.

Similarly, for this example, using a regression model to make predictions can lead to the confusion of correlation and causation. Having a personal connection with an imprisoned person might predict crime, but we have no evidence that this connection causes crime. Data that are not based on an experimental design should be interpreted cautiously.

16-41 a. $X = z(\sigma) + \mu = -1.2(0.61) + 3.51 = 2.778$. This answer makes sense because the raw score of 2.778 is a bit more than 1 standard deviation below the mean of 3.51.

b. $X = z(\sigma) + \mu = 0.66(0.61) + 3.51 = 3.913$. This answer makes sense because the raw score of 3.913 is slightly more than 0.5 standard deviation above the mean of 3.51.

16-43 a. 3.12

b. 3.16

c. 3.18

d. The accompanying graph depicts the regression line for GPA and hours studied.

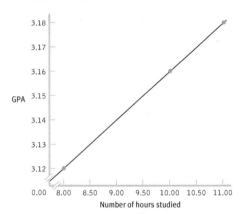

e. We can calculate the number of hours one would need to study in order to earn a 4.0 by substituting 4.0 for $\hat{Y}$ in the regression equation and solving for X: $4.0 = 2.96 + 0.02(X)$. To isolate the X, we subtract 2.96 from the left side of the equation and divide by 0.02: $X = (4.0 - 2.96)/0.02 = 52$. This regression equation predicts that we would have to study 52 hours per week in order to earn a 4.0. It is misleading to make predictions about what will happen when a person studies this many hours because the regression equation for prediction is almost certainly based on a sample that studied far fewer hours. Even though the relation between hours studied and GPA was linear within the range of studied scores, outside of that range it may have a different slope or no longer be linear, or the relation may not even exist.

16-45 a. We cannot conclude that cola consumption causes a decrease in bone mineral density because there are a number of different kinds of causal relations that could lead to the predictive relation observed by Tucker and colleagues. There may be some characteristic about these older women that both causes them to drink cola and leads to a decrease in bone mineral density. For example, perhaps overall poorer health habits lead to an increased consumption of cola and a decrease in bone mineral density.

b. Multiple regression allows us to assess the contributions of more than one independent variable to the outcome, the dependent variable. Performing this multiple regression allowed the researchers to explore the unique contributions of a third variable, such as physical activity, in addition to bone density.

c. Physical activity might produce an increase in bone mineral density, as exercise is known to increase bone density. Conversely, it is possible that physical activity might produce a decrease in cola consumption because people who exercise more might instead drink beverages that are more likely to keep them hydrated (such as water or sports drinks).

d. Calcium intake should produce an increase in bone mineral density, thereby producing a positive relation between calcium intake and bone density. It is possible that consumption of cola means less consumption of beverages with calcium in them, such as milk, producing a negative relation between cola consumption and bone density.

16-47 a. $\hat{Y} = 24.698 + 0.161(X)$, or predicted year 3 anxiety $= 24.698 + 0.161$ (year 1 depression)

b. As depression at year 1 increases by 1 point, predicted anxiety at year 3 increases, on average, by the slope of the regression equation, which is 0.161.

c. We would predict that her year 3 anxiety score would be 26.31.

d. We would predict that his year 3 anxiety score would be 25.02.

16-49 a. The independent variable in this study was marital status, and the dependent variable was chance of breaking up.

b. It appears that the researchers initially conducted a simple linear regression and then conducted a multiple regression analysis to account for the other variables (e.g., age, financial status) that may have been confounded with marital status in predicting the dependent variable.

c. Answers will differ, but the focus should be on the statistically significant contribution these other variables had in predicting the dependent variable, which appear to be more important than, and perhaps explain, the relation between marital status and the break-up of the relationship.

d. Another "third variable" in this study could have been length of relationship before the child was born. Married couples may have been together longer than cohabitating couples, and it may be that those who were together longer before the birth of the child, regardless of their marital status, are more likely to stay together than those who had only been together for a short period of time prior to the birth.

16-51 a. Multiple regression may have been used to predict countries' diabetes rates based on consumption of sugar while controlling for rates of obesity and other variables.

b. Accounting for other factors allowed the reporter to exclude the impact of potentially confounding variables. This is important as there are other variables, such as rates of obesity, that could have contributed to the relation between sugar consumption and rates of diabetes across countries. Factoring out other variables allows us to eliminate these potential confounds as explanations for a relation.

c. Numerous other factors may have been included. For example, the researchers may have controlled for countries' gross domestic product, median educational attainment, health care spending, unemployment rates, and so on.

d. Let's consider the A-B-C model of understanding possible causal explanations within correlation to understand why it is most likely that A (sugar consumption) causes B (rates of diabetes). First, it doesn't make sense that B (rates of diabetes) causes A (increased sugar consumption). Second, although it's still possible that one or more additional variables (C) account for the relation between A (sugar consumption) and B (diabetes rates), this explanation is not likely because the researchers controlled for most of the obvious possible confounding variables.

16-53 a. The four latent variables are social disorder, distress, injection frequency, and sharing behavior.

b. There are seven manifest variables: beat up, sell drugs, burglary, loitering, litter, vacant houses, and vandalism. By "social disorder," it appears that the authors are referring to physical or crime-related factors that lead a neighborhood to be chaotic.

c. Among the latent variables, injection frequency and sharing behavior seem to be most strongly related to each other. The number on this path, 0.26, is positive, an indication that as the frequency of injection increases, the frequency of sharing behaviors also tends to increase.

d. The overall story seems to be that social disorder increases the level of distress in a community. Distress in turn increases the frequency of both injection and sharing behavior. The frequency of injection also leads to an increase in sharing behavior. Ultimately, social disorder seems to lead to dangerous drug use behaviors.

16-55 a. To predict the number of hours João studies per week, we use the formula $z_{\hat{Y}} = (r_{XY})(z_X)$ to find the predicted z score for the number of hours he studies; then we can transform the predicted z score into his raw score. First, translate his predicted raw score for age into a z score for age: $z_X = \frac{(X - M_X)}{SD_X} = \frac{(24 - 21)}{1.789} = 1.677$. Then calculate his predicted z score for number of hours studied: $z_{\hat{Y}} = (r_{XY})(z_X) = (0.49)(1.677) = 0.82$. Finally, translate the z score for hours studied into the raw score for hours studied: $\hat{Y} = 0.82(5.582) + 14.2 = 18.777$.

b. First, translate Kimberly's age raw score into an age z score: $z_X = \frac{(X - M_X)}{SD_X} = \frac{(19 - 21)}{1.789} = -1.118$. Then calculate the predicted z score for hours studied: $z_{\hat{Y}} = (r_{XY})(z_X) = (0.49)(-1.118) = -0.548$. Finally, translate the z score for hours studied into the raw score for hours studied: $\hat{Y} = -0.548(5.582) + 14.2 = 11.141$.

c. Seung's age is well above the mean age of the students sampled. The relation that exists for traditional-aged students may not exist for students who are much older. Extrapolating beyond the range of the observed data may lead to erroneous conclusions.

d. From a mathematical perspective, the word *regression* refers to a tendency for extreme scores to drift toward the mean. In the calculation of regression, the predicted score is closer to its mean (i.e., less extreme) than the score used for prediction. For example, in part (a) the z score used for predicting was 1.677 and the predicted z score was 0.82, a less extreme score. Similarly, in part (b) the z score used for predicting was -1.118 and the predicted z score was -0.548, which is again a less extreme score.

e. First, we calculate what we would predict for Y when X equals 0; that number, -17.908, is the intercept.

$$z_X = \frac{(X - M_X)}{SD_X} = \frac{(0 - 21)}{1.789} = -11.738$$

$$z_{\hat{Y}} = (r_{XY})(z_X) = (0.49)(-11.738) = -5.752$$

$$\hat{Y} = z_{\hat{Y}}(SD_Y) + M_Y = -5.752(5.582) + 14.2 = -17.908$$

Note that the reason this prediction is negative (it doesn't make sense to have a negative number of hours) is that the number for age, 0, is not a number that would actually be used in this situation—it's another example of the dangers of extrapolation, but it still is necessary to determine the regression equation.

Then we calculate what we would predict for Y when X equals 1: the amount that that number, -16.378, differs from the prediction when X equals 0 is the slope.

$$z_X = \frac{(X - M_X)}{SD_X} = \frac{(1 - 21)}{1.789} = -11.179$$

$$z_{\hat{Y}} = (r_{XY})(z_X) = (0.49)(-11.179) = -5.478$$

$$\hat{Y} = z_{\hat{Y}}(SD_Y) + M_Y = -5.478(5.582) + 14.2 = -16.378$$

When X equals 0, -17.908 is the prediction for Y. When X equals 1, -16.378 is the prediction for Y. The latter number is 1.530 higher $[-16.378 - (-17.908) = 1.530]$—that is, more positive—than the former. Remember when you're calculating the difference to consider whether the prediction for Y was more positive or more negative when X increased from 0 to 1.

Thus, the regression equation is: $\hat{Y} = -17.91 + 1.53(X)$.

f. Substituting 17 for X in the regression equation for part (e) yields 8.1. Substituting 22 for X in the regression equation yields 15.75. We would predict that a 17-year-old would study 8.1 hours and a 22-year-old would study 15.75 hours.

g. The accompanying graph depicts the regression line for predicting hours studied per week from a person's age.

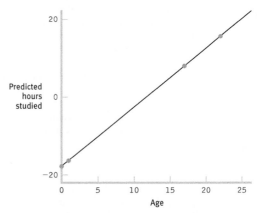

h. It is misleading to include young ages such as 0 and 5 on the graph because people of that age would never be college students.

i. The accompanying graph shows the scatterplot and regression line relating age and number of hours studied. Vertical lines from each observed data point are drawn to the regression line to represent the error prediction from the regression equation.

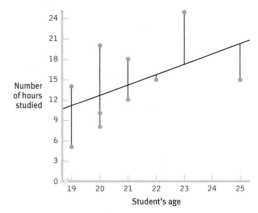

j. The accompanying scatterplot relating age and number of hours studied includes a horizontal line at the mean number of hours studied. Vertical lines between the observed data points and the mean represent the amount of error in predicting from the mean.

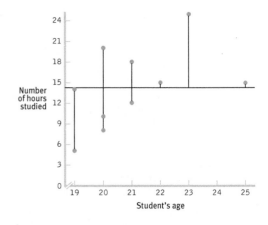

k. There appears to be less error in part (i), where the regression line is used to predict hours studied. This occurs because the regression line is the line that minimizes the distance between the observed scores and the line drawn through them. That is, the regression line is the *one* line that can be drawn through the data that produces the minimum error.

l. To calculate the proportionate reduction in error the long way, we first calculate the predicted Y scores (3rd column) for each of the observed X scores in the data set and determine how much those predicted Y scores differ from the observed Y scores (4th column), and then we square them (5th column).

Age	Observed Hours Studied	Predicted Hours Studied	Observed– Predicted	Square of Observed– Predicted	Observed– Mean	Square of Observed– Mean
19	5	11.16	−6.16	37.946	−9.2	84.64
20	20	12.69	7.31	53.436	5.8	33.64
20	8	12.69	−4.69	21.996	−6.2	38.44
21	12	14.22	−2.22	4.928	−2.2	4.84
21	18	14.22	3.78	14.288	3.8	14.44
23	25	17.28	7.72	59.598	10.8	116.64
22	15	15.75	−0.75	0.563	0.8	0.64
20	10	12.69	−2.69	7.236	−4.2	17.64
19	14	11.16	2.84	8.066	−0.2	0.04
25	15	20.34	−5.34	28.516	0.8	0.64

We then calculate SS_{error}, which is the sum of the squared error when using the regression equation as the basis of prediction. This sum, calculated by adding the numbers in column 5, is 236.573. We then subtract the mean from each score (column 6), and square these differences (column 7). Next, we calculate SS_{total}, which is the sum of the squared error when using the mean as the basis of prediction. This sum is 311.6. Finally, we calculate the proportionate reduction in error as $r^2 = \frac{(SS_{total} - SS_{error})}{SS_{total}} = 0.24$.

m. The r^2 calculated in part (l) indicates that 24% of the variability in hours studied is accounted for by a student's age. By using the regression equation, we have reduced the error of the prediction by 24% as compared with using the mean.

n. To calculate the proportionate reduction in error the short way, we would square the correlation coefficient. The correlation between age and hours studied is 0.49. Squaring 0.49 yields 0.24. It makes sense that the correlation coefficient could be used to determine how useful the regression equation will be because the correlation coefficient is a measure of the strength of association between two variables. If two variables are strongly related, we are better able to use one of the variables to predict the values of the other.

o. Here are the computations needed to compute β:

X	$(X - M_X)$	$(X - M_X)^2$	Y	$(Y - M_Y)$	$(Y - M_Y)^2$
19	−2	4	5	−9.2	84.64
20	−1	1	20	5.8	33.64
20	−1	1	8	−6.2	38.44
21	0	0	12	−2.2	4.84
21	0	0	18	3.8	14.44
23	2	4	25	10.8	116.64
22	1	1	15	0.8	0.64
20	−1	1	10	−4.2	17.64
19	−2	4	14	−0.2	0.04
25	4	16	15	0.8	0.64

$$\Sigma(X - M_X)^2 = 32 \qquad \Sigma(Y - M_Y)^2 = 311.6$$

$$\beta = (b)\frac{\sqrt{SS_X}}{\sqrt{SS_Y}} = (1.53)\frac{\sqrt{32}}{\sqrt{311.6}} = 0.490$$

p. The standardized regression coefficient is equal to the correlation coefficient, 0.49, for simple linear regression.

q. The hypothesis test for regression is the same as that for correlation. The critical values for r with 8 degrees of freedom at a p level of 0.05 are −0.632 and 0.632. With a correlation of 0.49, we fail to exceed the cutoff and therefore fail to reject the null hypothesis. The same is true then for the regression equation. We do not have a statistically significant regression and should be careful not to claim that the slope is different from 0.

Chapter 17

17-1 Nominal data are those that are categorical in nature; they cannot be ordered in any meaningful way, and they are often thought of as simply named. Ordinal data can be ordered, but we cannot assume even distances between points of equal separation. For example, the difference between the second and third scores may not be the same as the difference between the seventh and the eighth. Scale data are measured on either the interval or ratio level; we can assume equal intervals between points along these measures.

17-3 The chi-square test for goodness of fit is a nonparametric hypothesis test used with one nominal variable. The chi-square test for independence is a nonparametric test used with two nominal variables.

17-5 Throughout the book, we have referred to independent variables, those variables that we hypothesize to have an effect on the dependent variable. We also described how statisticians refer to observations that are independent of one another, such as a between-groups research design requiring that observations be taken from independent samples. Here, with regard to chi square, *independence* takes on a similar meaning. We are testing whether the effect of one variable is independent of the other—that the proportion of cases across the levels of one variable does not depend on the levels of the other variable.

17-7 In most previous hypothesis tests, the degrees of freedom have been based on sample size. For the chi-square hypothesis tests, however, the degrees of freedom are based on the numbers of categories, or cells, in which participants can be counted. For example, the degrees of freedom for the chi-square test for goodness of fit is the number of categories minus 1: $df_{\chi 2} = k - 1$. Here, k is the symbol for the number of categories.

17-9 The contingency table presents the observed frequencies for each cell in the study.

17-11 This is the formula to calculate the chi-square statistic. The symbols represent the sum, for each cell, of the squared difference between each observed frequency and its matching expected frequency, divided by the expected value for its cell.

17-13 Relative likelihood indicates the relative chance of an outcome (i.e., how many times more likely the outcome is, given the group membership of an observation). For example, we might determine the relative likelihood that a person would be a victim of bullying, given that the person is a boy versus a girl.

17-15 Relative likelihood and relative risk are exactly the same measure, but relative likelihood is typically called *relative risk* when it comes to health and medical situations because it describes a person's risk for a disease or health outcome.

17-17 The most useful graph for displaying the results of a chi-square test of independence is a bar graph that uses the conditional proportions rather than the frequencies, thus allowing us to compare the rates across the various levels of each variable.

17-19 If a researcher obtains a significant chi-square value but one of the variables has more than two levels, the researcher can determine which cells of the table differ from expectations by comparing the value of the adjusted standardized residual for that cell to a criterion. The criterion adopted by many researchers is 2, such that if the adjusted standardized residual is greater than 2, the observed values for that cell differ significantly from the expected values.

17-21 a. The independent variable is gender, which is nominal (men or women). The dependent variable is number of loads of laundry, which is scale.

b. The independent variable is need for approval, which is ordinal (rank). The dependent variable is miles on a car, which is scale.

c. The independent variable is place of residence, which is nominal (on or off campus). The dependent variable is whether the student is an active member of a club, which is also nominal (active or not active).

17-23 a. $df_{\chi 2} = k - 1 = 4 - 1 = 3$

b.

Category	Observed (O)	Expected (E)	$O - E$	$(O - E)^2$	$\dfrac{(O - E)^2}{E}$
1	750	625	$750 - 625 = 125$	15,625	25
2	650	625	$650 - 625 = 25$	625	1
3	600	625	$600 - 625 = -25$	625	1
4	500	625	$500 - 625 = -125$	15,625	25

c. $\chi^2 = \left[\dfrac{(O - E)^2}{E} \right] = 25 + 1 + 1 + 25 = 52$

17-25 The conditional probability of being a smoker, given that a person is female, is $\dfrac{13}{199} = 0.065$, and the conditional probability of being a smoker, given that a person is male, is $\dfrac{723}{905} = 0.799$. The relative likelihood of being a smoker given that one is female rather than male is $\dfrac{0.065}{0.799} = 0.08$. These Turkish women with lung cancer were less than one-tenth as likely to be smokers as were the male lung cancer patients.

17-27 All four adjusted residuals are greater than 2 or less than -2. We can conclude that all four observed frequencies are further from their corresponding expected frequencies than would likely occur if the null hypothesis were true.

17-29 a. The first variable is gender, which is nominal (male or female). The second variable is salary negotiation, which also is nominal (wage not explicitly negotiable or wage explicitly negotiable).

b. A chi-square test for independence would be appropriate because both variables are nominal.

c. The researchers found that both genders seemed to be more likely to negotiate when the ad stated that the wage was negotiable than when that was not stated; however, when the job posting stated that the wage was negotiable, women seemed to be somewhat more likely than men to negotiate, whereas, when wage was not explicitly mentioned as negotiable in the job posting, men seemed to be more likely than women to negotiate.

17-31 a. A nonparametric test would be appropriate because both of the variables are nominal: gender and major.

b. A nonparametric test is more appropriate because the sample size is small and the data are unlikely to be normal; the "top boss" is likely to have a much higher income than the other employees. This outlier would lead to a nonnormal distribution.

c. A parametric test would be appropriate because the independent variable (type of student: athlete versus nonathlete) is nominal and the dependent variable (grade point average) is scale.

d. A nonparametric test would be appropriate because the independent variable (athlete versus nonathlete) is nominal and the dependent variable (class rank) is ordinal.

e. A nonparametric test would be appropriate because the research question is about the relation between two nominal variables: seat-belt wearing and degree of injuries.

f. A parametric test would be appropriate because the independent variable (seat-belt use: no seat belt versus seat belt) is nominal and the dependent variable (speed) is scale.

17-33 a. (i) Year. (ii) Grades received. (iii) This is a category III research design because the independent variable, year, is nominal and the dependent variable, grade (A or not), could also be considered nominal.

b. (i) Type of school. (ii) Average GPA of graduating students. (iii) This is a category II research design because the independent variable, type of school, is nominal and the dependent variable, GPA, is scale.

c. (i) SAT scores of incoming students. (ii) College GPA. (iii) This is a category I research design because both the independent variable and the dependent variable are scale.

17-35 a.

	Mexican	White	Black
Married			
Single			

b.

	Married Head of Household	
	Immigrant Neighborhood	Nonimmigrant Neighborhood
Committed crime		
No crime		

	Unmarried Head Of Household	
	Immigrant Neighborhood	Nonimmigrant Neighborhood
Committed crime		
No crime		

c.

	First Generation	Second Generation	Third Generation
Committed crime			
No crime			

17-37 a. There is one variable, the gender of the op-ed writers. Its levels are men and women.

b. A chi-square test for goodness of fit would be used because we have data on a single nominal variable from one sample.

c. *Step 1:* Population 1 is op-ed contributors, in proportions of men and women that are like those in our sample. Population 2 is op-ed contributors, in proportions of men and women that are like those in the general population. The comparison distribution is a chi-square distribution. The hypothesis test will be a chi-square test for goodness of fit because we have only one nominal variable. This study meets three of the four assumptions: (1) The variable under study is nominal. (2) Each observation is independent of all the others. (3) There are more than five times as many participants as there are cells (there are 124 op-ed articles and only two cells). (4) This is not, however, a randomly selected sample of op-eds, so we must generalize with caution; specifically, we should not generalize beyond the *New York Times.*

Step 2: Null hypothesis: The proportions of male and female op-ed contributors are the same as those in the population as a whole.

Research hypothesis: The proportions of male and female op-ed contributors are different from those in the population as a whole.

Step 3: The comparison distribution is a chi-square distribution with 1 degree of freedom: $df_{\chi 2} = 2 - 1 = 1$.

Step 4: The critical χ^2, based on a p level of 0.05 and 1 degree of freedom, is 3.841.

Step 5:

Observed (Proportions of Men and Women)	
Men	Women
103	21

Expected (Based on the General Population)	
Men	Women
62	62

Category	Observed (O)	Expected (E)	$O - E$	$(O - E)^2$	$\dfrac{(O - E)^2}{E}$
Men	103	62	41	1681	27.113
Women	21	62	−41	1681	27.113

$$\chi^2 = \Sigma\left[\frac{(O - E)^2}{E}\right] = 27.113 + 27.113 = 54.226$$

Step 6: Reject the null hypothesis. The calculated chi-square statistic exceeds the critical value. It appears that the proportion of op-eds written by women versus men is not the same as the proportion of men and women in the population. Specifically, there are fewer women than in the general population.

d. $\chi^2(1, N = 124) = 54.23, p < 0.05$

17-39 a. The accompanying table shows the conditional proportions.

	Exciting	Routine	Dull	
Same city	0.424	0.521	0.055	1.00
Same state/different city	0.468	0.485	0.047	1.00
Different state	0.502	0.451	0.047	1.00

b. The accompanying graph shows these conditional proportions.

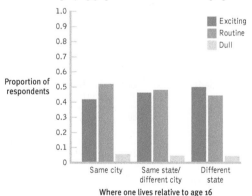

c. The relative likelihood of finding life exciting if one lives in a different state as opposed to the same city is $\dfrac{0.502}{0.424} = 1.18$.

17-41 a. There are two nominal variables—premarital doubts (yes or no) and divorced by 4 years (yes or no).

b. Chi-square tests for independence were used because there were two nominal variables. These tests were conducted for husbands and wives separately.

c. n should be reported as N. The specific p values for each hypothesis test should be provided. An effect size—Cramér's V in these cases—should be reported for each hypothesis test.

d. The researchers could not conclude that the likelihood of husbands being divorced by 4 years was dependent on premarital doubts. However, premarital doubts did seem to be related to being divorced by 4 years for wives.

17-43 a. There are two variables in this study. The independent variable is the referred child's gender (boy, girl) and the dependent variable is the diagnosis (problem, no problem but below norms, no problem and normal height).

b. A chi-square test for independence would be used because we have data on two nominal variables.

c. *Step 1:* Population 1 is referred children like those in this sample. Population 2 is referred children from a population in which growth problems do not depend on the child's gender. The comparison distribution is a chi-square distribution. The hypothesis test will be a chi-square test for independence because we have two nominal variables. This study meets three of the four assumptions. (1) The two variables are nominal. (2) Every participant is in only one cell. (3) There are more than five times as many participants as there are cells (there are 278 participants and six cells). (4) The sample, however, was not randomly selected, so we must use caution when generalizing.

Step 2: Null hypothesis: The proportion of boys in each diagnostic category is the same as the proportion of girls in each category.

Research hypothesis: The proportion of boys in each diagnostic category is different from the proportion of girls in each category.

Step 3: The comparison distribution is a chi-square distribution that has 2 degrees of freedom:

$$df_{\chi 2} = (k_{row} - 1)(k_{column} - 1) = (2 - 1)(3 - 1) = 2.$$

Step 4: The critical χ^2, based on a p level of 0.05 and 2 degrees of freedom, is 5.99.

Step 5:

	Observed		
	Medical Problem	No Problem/ Below Norm	No Problem/ Normal Height	
Boys	27	86	69	182
Girls	39	38	19	96
	66	124	88	278

$$\frac{Total_{column}}{N}(Total_{row}) = \frac{66}{278}(182) = 43.134$$

$$\frac{Total_{column}}{N}(Total_{row}) = \frac{66}{278}(96) = 22.752$$

$$\frac{Total_{column}}{N}(Total_{row}) = \frac{124}{278}(182) = 81.172$$

$$\frac{Total_{column}}{N}(Total_{row}) = \frac{124}{278}(96) = 42.816$$

$$\frac{Total_{column}}{N}(Total_{row}) = \frac{88}{278}(182) = 57.694$$

$$\frac{Total_{column}}{N}(Total_{row}) = \frac{88}{278}(96) = 30.432$$

	Expected		
	Medical Problem	No Problem/ Below Norm	No Problem/ Normal Height	
Boys	43.134	81.172	57.694	182
Girls	22.752	42.816	30.432	96
	65.886	123.988	88.126	278

Category	Observed (O)	Expected (E)	O − E	(O − E)²	$\frac{(O-E)^2}{E}$
Boy; med prob	27	43.134	−16.134	260.306	6.035
Boy; no prob/below	86	81.172	4.828	23.31	0.287
Boy; no prob/norm	69	57.694	11.306	127.826	2.216
Girl; med prob	39	22.752	16.248	263.998	11.603
Girl; no prob/below	38	42.816	−4.816	23.194	0.542
Girl; no prob/norm	19	30.432	−11.432	130.691	4.295

$$\chi^2 = \Sigma\left[\frac{(O-E)^2}{E}\right] = 6.035 + 0.287 + 2.216 + 11.603$$
$$+ 0.542 + 4.295 = 24.978$$

Step 6: Reject the null hypothesis. The calculated chi-square value exceeds the critical value. It appears that the proportion of boys in each diagnostic category is not the same as the proportion of girls in each category.

d. Cramér's $V = \sqrt{\dfrac{\chi^2}{df_{row/column}}} = \sqrt{\dfrac{24.978}{(278)(1)}} = 0.300$

According to Cohen's conventions, this is a medium effect size.

e. $\chi^2(1, N = 278) = 24.98, p < 0.05$, Cramér's $V = 0.30$

f. The accompanying table shows the conditional proportions.

	Observed		
	Medical Problem	No Problem/ Below Norm	No Problem/ Normal Height	
Boys	0.148	0.473	0.379	1.00
Girls	0.406	0.396	0.198	1.00

g. The accompanying graph shows all six conditions.

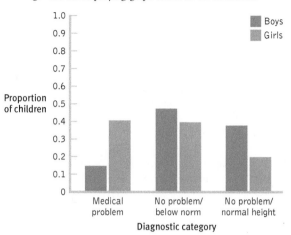

h. Of the 113 boys below normal height, 27 were diagnosed with a medical problem. Of the 77 girls below normal height, 39 were diagnosed with a medical problem. The conditional proportion for boys is 0.239 and for girls is 0.506. This makes the relative risk for having a medical condition, given that one is a boy as opposed to a girl $\frac{0.239}{0.506} = 0.472$.

i. Referred boys below normal height are about half as likely to have a medical condition as are referred girls below normal height.

j. If referred for short stature, the relative risk for having a medical condition, given that one is a girl, is $\frac{0.506}{0.239} = 2.117$.

k. If referred for short stature, girls below normal height are about twice as likely to have a medical condition as are boys below normal height.

l. The two relative risks give us complementary information. Saying that boys are half as likely to have a medical condition implies that girls are twice as likely to have a medical condition.

m. The observed frequency is 27. The expected frequency is 43.2.

n. The adjusted standardized residual for boys is -4.8. This number indicates that the observed frequency for boys is 4.8 standard errors below the expected frequency for boys. The cells for boys and for girls with an underlying medical condition exceed the criterion of 2, as do the cells for both boys and girls who are of normal height. Using the new criterion of 3 does not change the conclusion regarding which cells have observed frequencies significantly different from expected.

Chapter 18

18.1 When we are concerned about meeting the assumptions of a parametric test, we can convert scale data to ordinal data and use a nonparametric test.

18.3 When transforming scale data to ordinal data, the scale data are rank ordered. This means that even a very extreme scale score will have a rank that makes it continuous with the rest of the data when rank ordered.

18.5 In all correlations, we assess the relative position of a score on one variable with its position on the other variable. In the case of the Spearman rank-order correlation, we examine how ranks on one variable relate to ranks on the other variable. For example, with a positive correlation, scores that rank low on one variable tend to rank low on the other, and scores that rank high on one variable tend to rank high on the other. For a negative correlation, low ranks on one variable tend to be associated with high ranks on the other.

18.7 Values for the Spearman rank-order correlation coefficient range from -1.00 to $+1.00$, just like they do for its parametric equivalent, the Pearson correlation coefficient. Similarly, the conventions for interpreting the magnitude of the Pearson correlation coefficient can also be applied to the Spearman correlation coefficient (small is roughly 0.10, medium 0.30, and large 0.50).

18.9 The Wilcoxon signed-rank test is appropriate to use when comparing two sets of dependent observations (scores from the same participants) and the dependent variable is either ordinal or does not meet the assumptions required by the paired-samples t test.

18.11 We use absolute values when ranking the differences because what is important is the magnitude of each difference, not its direction. We take into account the directions of the differences when we rank the positive differences versus the negative differences.

18.13 The assumptions of the Mann–Whitney U test are that (1) the data are ordinal, (2) random selection was used, and (3) no ranks are tied.

18.15 The Kruskal–Wallis H test is appropriate to use when comparing three or more groups of independent observations (i.e., the independent variable has three or more levels) and the dependent variable is ordinal or does not meet the assumptions of the parametric test.

18.17 If the data meet the assumptions of the parametric test, then using the parametric test gives us more power to detect a significant effect than does the nonparametric equivalent. Transforming the scale data required for the parametric test into the ordinal data required for the nonparametric test results in a loss of precision of information (i.e., we know that one observation is greater than another, but we don't know how much greater it is).

18.19 Using the bootstrapping method of repeatedly sampling with replacement allows for the estimation of confidence intervals around the original observed sample mean. These confidence intervals can be used to establish likely ranges for the population mean. This method allows the researcher to extrapolate information about population parameters.

18.21 a.

Participant	Variable X	Rank X	Variable Y	Rank Y
1	134.5	3	64.00	7
2	186	10	60.00	1
3	157	9	61.50	2
4	129	1	66.25	10
5	147	7	65.50	8.5
6	133	2	62.00	3.5
7	141	5	62.50	5
8	147	7	62.00	3.5
9	136	4	63.00	6
10	147	7	65.50	8.5

b.

Participant	Rank X	Rank Y	Difference	Squared Difference
1	3	7	−4	16
2	10	1	9	81
3	9	2	7	49
4	1	10	−9	81
5	7	8.5	−1.5	2.25
6	2	3.5	−1.5	2.25
7	5	5	0	0
8	7	3.5	3.5	12.25
9	4	6	−2	4
10	7	8.5	−1.5	2.25

$$r_S = 1 - \frac{6(\Sigma D^2)}{N(N^2 - 1)} = 1 - \frac{6(250)}{10(100 - 1)} = 1 - \frac{1500}{990}$$

$$= 1 - 1.515 = -0.515$$

18.23 a. When calculating the Spearman correlation coefficient, we must first transform the variable "hours trained" into a rank-ordered variable. We then take the difference between the two ranks and square those differences:

Race Rank	Hours Trained	Hours Rank	Difference	Squared Difference
1	25	1.5	−0.5	0.25
2	25	1.5	0.5	0.25
3	22	3	0	0
4	18	5.5	−1.5	2.25
5	19	4	1	1
6	18	5.5	0.5	0.25
7	12	10	−3	9
8	17	7	1	1
9	15	9	0	0
10	16	8	2	4

We calculate the Spearman correlation coefficient as:

$$r_S = 1 - \frac{6(\Sigma D^2)}{N(N^2 - 1)} = 1 - \frac{6(18)}{10(10^2 - 1)}$$

$$= 1 - \frac{108}{990} = 1 - 0.109 = 0.891$$

b. The critical r_S with an N of 10, a p level of 0.05, and a two-tailed test is 0.648. The calculated r_S is 0.89, which exceeds the critical value. So we reject the null hypothesis. Finishing place was positively associated with the number of hours spent training.

18.25 a. To calculate the Wilcoxon signed-rank test, we first calculate difference scores for each student and then rank those difference scores. (To calculate difference scores, we subtract the first score from the second.) Next, we separately sum the ranks associated with the positive and negative difference scores.

Student	School Year	Summer	Difference	Rank	Rank for Negative Differences	Rank for Positive Differences
1	7	4	−3	2.0	2.0	
2	4	6	2	3.5		3.5
3	5	5	0			
4	3	4	1	5.5		5.5
5	4	8	4	1.0		1.0
6	5	7	2	3.5		3.5
7	3	2	−1	5.5	5.5	

The sum of the ranks for the negative differences is $\Sigma R_- = 2.0 + 5.5 = 7.5$.

The sum of the ranks for the positive differences is $\Sigma R_+ = 3.5 + 5.5 + 1.0 + 3.5 = 13.5$.

T is equal to the smaller of these two sums:

$T = \Sigma R_{smaller} = 7.5$.

b. For this data set, $N = 6$. Although there are 7 participants, there are only 6 nonzero difference scores, and it is the number of nonzero difference scores that determines N for the Wilcoxon signed-rank test. The critical value for a Wilcoxon signed-rank test with $N = 6$, a p level of 0.05, and a two-tailed test is 0. Because the calculated T is not smaller than the critical value of 0, we fail to reject the null hypothesis. We do not have evidence that there is a difference between happiness levels during the school year and summer.

18.27 $\Sigma R_{group1} = 1 + 2.5 + 8 + 4 + 6 + 10 = 31.5$

$\Sigma R_{group2} = 11 + 9 + 2.5 + 5 + 7 + 12 = 46.5$

The formula for the first group is:

$$U_{group1} = (n_{group1})(n_{group2}) + \frac{n_{group1}(n_{group1} + 1)}{2} - \Sigma R_{group1}$$

$$= (6)(6) + \frac{6(6 + 1)}{2} - 31.5 = 36 + 21 - 31.5 = 25.5$$

The formula for the second group is:

$$U_{group2} = (n_{group1})(n_{group2}) + \frac{n_{group2}(n_{group2} + 1)}{2} - \Sigma R_{group2}$$

$$= (6)(6) + \frac{6(6 + 1)}{2} - 46.5 = 36 + 21 - 46.5 = 10.5$$

18.29 a. To conduct the Mann–Whitney U test, we first obtain the rank of every person in the data set. We then separately sum the ranks of the two groups, men and women:

Student	Gender	Class Standing	Rank	Male Rank	Female Rank
1	Male	98	11	11	
2	Female	72	9		9
3	Male	15	3	3	
4	Female	3	1		1
5	Female	102	12		12
6	Female	8	2		2
7	Male	43	7	7	
8	Male	33	6	6	
9	Female	17	4		4
10	Female	82	10		10
11	Male	63	8	8	
12	Male	25	5	5	

We sum the ranks for the men:

$\Sigma R_m = 11 + 3 + 7 + 6 + 8 + 5 = 40$

We sum the ranks for the women:

$\Sigma R_w = 9 + 1 + 12 + 2 + 4 + 10 = 38$

We calculate U for the men:

$U_m = (n_m)(n_w) + \dfrac{n_m(n_m + 1)}{2} - \Sigma R_m$

$= (6)(6) + \left(\dfrac{6(6 + 1)}{2}\right) - 40 = 17$

We calculate U for the women:

$U_w = (n_m)(n_w) + \dfrac{n_w(n_w + 1)}{2} - \Sigma R_w$

$= (6)(6) + \left(\dfrac{6(6 + 1)}{2}\right) - 38 = 19$

b. The critical value for the Mann–Whitney U test with two samples of size 6, a p level of 0.05, and a two-tailed test is 5. We compare the smaller of the two U values to the critical value and reject the null hypothesis if it is smaller than the critical value. Because the smaller U of 17 is not less than 5, we fail to reject the null hypothesis. There is no evidence for a difference in the class standing of men and women.

18.31 To conduct the Kruskal–Wallis H test, we first rank each participant on the dependent variable and then sort the ranks by group. We then calculate the mean rank for each group (M) and for the whole data set (GM):

Group	Scale DV	Rank	Group 1 Rank	Group 2 Rank	Group 3 Rank
Group 1	1.20	7	7		
Group 1	1.01	9	9		
Group 1	0.86	12	12		
Group 1	0.83	13	13		
Group 1	0.55	16	16		
Group 1	0.22	18	18		
Group 2	2.21	4		4	
Group 2	1.86	5		5	
Group 2	1.03	8		8	
Group 2	0.94	10		10	
Group 2	0.89	11		11	
Group 2	0.74	14		14	
Group 3	3.20	1			1
Group 3	2.83	2			2
Group 3	2.75	3			3
Group 3	1.74	6			6
Group 3	0.67	15			15
Group 3	0.52	17			17
Mean rank		9.5	12.5	8.667	7.333

$H = \left[\dfrac{12}{N(N + 1)}\right]\left[\Sigma n(M - GM)^2\right]$

$= \left[\dfrac{12}{18(18 + 1)}\right]\left[(6(12.5 - 9.5)^2) + (6(8.667 - 9.5)^2)\right.$

$\left. + (6(7.333 - 9.5)^2)\right] = (0.035)(54 + 4.164 + 28.176)$

$= (0.035)(86.34) = 3.022$

18.33 a. To conduct the Kruskal–Wallis H test, we first rank each participant on the dependent variable and then sort the ranks by group. We then calculate the mean rank for each group (M) and for the whole data set (GM):

Group	Ordinal DV	Rank	Group 1 Rank	Group 2 Rank	Group 3 Rank
Group 1	27	7	7		
Group 1	16	9	9		
Group 1	15	10	10		
Group 2	56	3		3	
Group 2	41	4		4	
Group 2	38	5		5	
Group 2	22	8		8	
Group 3	84	1			1
Group 3	72	2			2
Group 3	33	6			6
Group 3	12	11			11
Mean rank		6	8.667	5	5

$$H = \left[\frac{12}{N(N+1)}\right]\left[\Sigma n(M - GM)^2\right]$$

$$= \left[\frac{12}{11(11+1)}\right]\left[(3(8.667 - 6)^2) + (4(5 - 6)^2) + (4(5 - 6)^2)\right]$$

$$= (0.091)(21.339 + 4 + 4) = (0.091)(29.339) = 2.670$$

b. The critical value for the Kruskal–Wallis H test is found using the table for chi square. The df is the number of groups minus 1, which in this case is 2. For $df = 2$, a p level of 0.05, and a two-tailed test, the critical value is 5.992. We fail to reject the null hypothesis because the calculated H does not exceed this critical value.

18.35 a. The Mann–Whitney U test would be most appropriate because it is a nonparametric equivalent to the independent-samples t test. It is used when there is a nominal independent variable with two levels (north and south of the equator), a between-groups research design, and an ordinal dependent variable (the ranking of the city).

b. The Wilcoxon signed-rank test would be most appropriate because there is a nominal independent variable with two levels (the time of the previous study versus 2012), a within-groups research design, and an ordinal dependent variable (ranking). The Wilcoxon signed-rank test is the nonparametric equivalent to the paired-samples t test.

c. The Spearman rank-order correlation would be most appropriate because this is a question about the relation between two ordinal variables. The Spearman rank-order correlation is the nonparametric equivalent to the Pearson correlation.

d. The Kruskal–Wallis H test would be most appropriate because it is a nonparametric equivalent to the one-way between-groups ANOVA. It is used when there is a nominal independent variable with three or more levels (the various continents, in this case), a between-groups research design, and an ordinal dependent variable (the ranking of the city).

18.37 a. The first variable of interest is test grade, which is a scale variable. The second variable of interest is the order in which students completed the test, which is an ordinal variable.

b. The accompanying table shows test grade converted to ranks, difference scores, and squared differences.

Grade Percentage	Grade Speed	Rank	D	D²
98	1	1	0	0
93	6	2	4	16
92	4	3	1	1
88	5	4	1	1
87	3	5	−2	4
74	2	6	−4	16
67	8	7	1	1
62	7	8	−1	1

We calculate the Spearman correlation coefficient as:

$$r_S = 1 - \frac{6(\Sigma D^2)}{N(N^2 - 1)} = 1 - \frac{6(40)}{8(64 - 1)} = 1 - \frac{240}{504} = 0.524$$

c. The coefficient tells us that there is a rather large positive relation between the two variables. Students who completed the test more quickly also tended to score higher.

d. We could not have calculated a Pearson correlation coefficient because one of the variables, order in which students turned in the test, is ordinal.

e. This correlation does not indicate that students should attempt to take their tests as quickly as possible. Correlation does not provide evidence for a particular causal relation. A number of underlying causal relations could produce this observed correlation.

f. A third variable that might cause both speedy test taking and a good test grade is knowledge of the material. Students with better knowledge of and more practice with the material would be able to get through the test more quickly and get a better grade.

g. 1.00 is the strongest correlation and −0.001 is the weakest correlation.

18.39 a. The independent variable is the season, and its levels are 1995–1996 and 2005–2006. The dependent variable is the number of wins per season.

b. This is a within-groups design because the same teams are being assessed at two different time points.

c. It would be preferable to conduct a nonparametric test because there is a very small sample size and the dependent variable, number of wins, is not likely to be normally distributed in the population.

d. *Step 1:* We will convert the scale data into ordinal data. It is difficult to know from this small sample whether the difference scores come from a symmetric population distribution. (*Note:* These were all of the Canadian NHL teams that existed in those two seasons, so the assumption of random selection is irrelevant.)

Step 2: Null hypothesis: There is no difference between the teams' performance rankings in the 1995–1996 season and those in the 2005–2006 season.

Research hypothesis: There is a difference between the teams' performance rankings in the 1995–1996 season and those in the 2005–2006 season.

Step 3: The comparison distribution will be a T distribution. We will use a p level of 0.05 and a two-tailed test. The sample size is 6.

Step 4: The critical T value is 0. The calculated T value must be less than or equal to 0 to be statistically significant.

Step 5: (*Note:* The difference scores are positive because they reflect an increase in wins.)

Team	1995–1996 Season	2005–2006 Season	D	D Rank	Positive Difference	Negative Difference
Calgary Flames	34	46	12	2	2	
Edmonton Oilers	30	41	11	3	3	
Montréal Canadiens	40	42	2	6	6	
Ottawa Senators	18	52	34	1	1	
Toronto Maple Leafs	34	41	7	5	5	
Vancouver Canucks	32	42	10	4	4	

$\Sigma R_- = 0$

$\Sigma R_+ = (2 + 3 + 6 + 1 + 5 + 4) = 21$

$T = \Sigma R_{smaller} = 0$

Step 6: The test statistic, 0, is equal to the critical value, so we reject the null hypothesis. Canadian teams had more wins in the 2005–2006 season than in the 1995–1996 season.

  e. $T = 0, p = 0.05$

18.41 a. The independent variable is the type of institution and its levels are public and private. The dependent variable is *U.S. News & World Report* ranking.

  b. This is a between-groups design because the institutions are either public or private; they cannot be both.

  c. We have to use a nonparametric test for these data because the dependent measure is ordinal.

  d. *Step 1:* The data are ordinal. The schools on the list have not been randomly selected but were systematically selected (they are the top 19 programs in the United States). Finally, a number of schools have tied ranks. The results of the Mann–Whitney U test may not be valid.

  Step 2: Null hypothesis: There will be no difference between the rankings of public and private schools.

  Research hypothesis: There will be a difference between the rankings of public and private schools.

  Step 3: There are 9 public universities and 10 private universities listed.

  Step 4: The critical value for a Mann–Whitney U test with one group of 9 and one group of 10, a p level of 0.05, and a two-tailed test is 20. The calculated statistic will need to be less than or equal to this critical value to be considered statistically significant.

  Step 5:

$\Sigma R_{public} = 2 + 2 + 4.5 + 7 + 9 + 12.5 + 14.5 + 18 + 18 = 87.5$

$\Sigma R_{private} = 2 + 4.5 + 7 + 7 + 10.5 + 10.5 + 12.5 + 14.5 + 16 + 18 = 102.5$

$U_{public} = (n_{public})(n_{private}) + \dfrac{n_{public}(n_{public} + 1)}{2} - \Sigma R_{public}$

$= (9)(10) + \dfrac{9(9 + 1)}{2} - 87.5 = 90 + 45 - 87.5 = 47.5$

$U_{private} = (n_{public})(n_{private}) + \dfrac{n_{private}(n_{private} + 1)}{2} - \Sigma R_{private}$

$= (9)(10) + \dfrac{10(10 + 1)}{2} - 102.5 = 90 + 55 - 102.5$

$= 42.5$

Step 6: The smaller U statistic, 42.5, is not smaller than the critical value of 20, so we fail to reject the null hypothesis.

  e. $U = 42.5, p > 0.05$

18.43 a. Hours studied per week appears to be roughly normal, with observations across the range of values—from 0 through 20. Monthly cell phone bill appears to be positively skewed, with one observation much higher than all the others.

  b. The histogram confirms the impression that the monthly cell phone bill is positively skewed. It appears that there is an outlier in the distribution.

  c. Parametric tests assume that the underlying population data are normally distributed or that there is a large enough sample size that the sampling distribution will be normal anyway. These data seem to indicate that the underlying distribution is not normally distributed; moreover, there is a fairly small sample size ($N = 29$). We would not want to use a parametric test.

18.45 a. The independent variable is region of the country, and its levels are Northeast, Midwest, and South. The dependent variable is "smart" ranking.

  b. This is a between-groups design because a state is in only one region of the country.

  c. We need to use a nonparametric test because the dependent measure is ordinal.

  d. *Step 1:* The data are ordinal. (This list includes all states in the regions of interest, so the assumption of random selection is not relevant.)

  Step 2: Null hypothesis: The "smart" ranking of a state does not tend to vary with the state's geographical region. Research hypothesis: The "smart" ranking of a state does tend to vary with the state's geographical region.

  Step 3: We will use the chi-square distribution as the comparison distribution with degrees of freedom of $3 - 1 = 2$.

  Step 4: The critical value with a *df* of 2 and p level of 0.05 is 5.992. The calculated statistic will need to be larger than this critical value to be considered statistically significant.

Step 5:

State	Rank	NE Rank	MW Rank	S Rank
Massachusetts	1	1		
Connecticut	2	2		
Vermont	3	3		
New Jersey	4	4		
Wisconsin	5		5	
New York	6	6		
Minnesota	7		7	
Iowa	8		8	
Pennsylvania	9	9		
Maine	10	10		
Virginia	11			11
Nebraska	12		12	
New Hampshire	13	13		
Kansas	14		14	
Indiana	15		15	
Ohio	16		16	
Rhode Island	17	17		
Illinois	18		18	
North Carolina	19			19
Missouri	20		20	
Michigan	21		21	
South Carolina	22			22
Arkansas	23			23
Kentucky	24			24
Georgia	25			25
Florida	26			26
Tennessee	27			27
Alabama	28			28
Louisiana	29			29
Mississippi	30			30

$$M_{NE} = \frac{\Sigma R_{NE}}{n} = \frac{65}{9} = 7.222$$

$$M_{MW} = \frac{\Sigma R_{MW}}{n} = \frac{136}{10} = 13.60$$

$$M_S = \frac{\Sigma R_s}{n} = \frac{264}{11} = 24.00$$

$$GM = \frac{\Sigma R}{N} = \frac{465}{30} = 15.50$$

$$H = \left[\frac{12}{N(N+1)}\right]\left[\Sigma n(M = GM)^2\right]$$

$$= \left[\frac{12}{30(30+1)}\right]\left[9(7.222 - 15.5)^2 \right.$$
$$\left. + (10(13.6 - 15.5)^2) + (11(24 - 15.5)^2)\right]$$

$$= (0.013)(1447.575) = 18.818$$

Step 6: The calculated statistic, 18.818, exceeds the critical value of 5.992, so we reject the null hypothesis. The "smart" ranking for a state does tend to vary with the geographical location of that state.

e. $H = 18.82, p < 0.05$

f. Like a one-way between-groups ANOVA, the Kruskal–Wallis H statistic when used with more than two groups just indicates that there is a difference among the groups, but it does not indicate where that difference is. Separate Kruskal–Wallis H tests for each group comparison in the current example appear below. For each test, the *df* is 1 and the critical value, given a p level of 0.05, is 3.84.

Northeast versus South: $H = 13.02, p < 0.05$

Northeast versus Midwest: $H = 4.86, p < 0.05$

Midwest versus South: $H = 10.49, p < 0.05$

All regions are statistically significantly different from each other. The states in the Northeast tend to have the highest rankings, followed by those in the Midwest, and then by those in the South.

g. If there were scale scores for the 50 states, we could conduct a parametric test—specifically a one-way between-groups ANOVA—to determine differences among the three levels, or groups, of states.

h. Intelligence could be operationally defined as the state average on IQ or other intelligence tests, or in the percentage of people with various levels of education.

Appendix D

CHECK YOUR LEARNING SOLUTIONS

Chapter 1

1-1 Data from samples are used in inferential statistics to make an inference about the larger population.

1-2 **a.** The average grade for your statistics class would be a descriptive statistic because it's being used only to describe the tendency of people in your class with respect to a statistics grade.

b. In this case, the average grade would be an inferential statistic because it is being used to estimate the results of a population of students taking statistics.

1-3 **a.** 1500 Americans

b. All Americans

c. The 1500 Americans in the sample know 600 people, on average.

d. The entire population of Americans has many acquaintances, on average. The sample mean, 600, is an estimate of the unknown population mean.

1-4 Discrete observations can take on only specific values, usually whole numbers; continuous observations can take on a full range of values.

1-5 **a.** These data are continuous because they can take on a full range of values.

b. The variable is a ratio observation because there is a true zero point.

c. On an ordinal scale, Lorna's score would be 2 (or 2nd).

1-6 **a.** This variable is a scale variable because it meets the criteria for an interval variable (the distance between pairs of consecutive numbers is assumed to be equal).

b. This variable is a nominal variable because there are categories (received a warning or not) that have no specific order.

c. This variable is a scale variable because it meets the criteria for a ratio variable (there is a meaningful zero; there can be zero hours spent logged into the Uber app).

d. This variable is an ordinal variable because drivers are ranked.

e. This variable is a nominal variable because there are categories (taken the class or not) that have no specific order.

1-7 Independent; dependent

1-8 **a.** There are two independent variables: beverage and subject to be remembered. The dependent variable is memory.

b. Beverage has two levels: caffeine and no caffeine. The subject to be remembered has three levels: numbers, word lists, and aspects of a story.

1-9 **a.** Whether or not trays were available

b. Trays were available; trays were not available

c. Food waste; food waste could have been measured via volume or weight as it was thrown away.

d. The measure of food waste would be consistent over time.

e. The measure of food waste was actually measuring how much food was wasted.

1-10 Experimental research involves random assignment to conditions; correlational research examines associations where random assignment is not possible and variables are not manipulated.

1-11 Random assignment helps to distribute the levels of confounding variables evenly across all conditions so that the levels of the independent variable are what truly vary across groups or conditions.

1-12 **a.** Answers may vary; operational definitions explicitly define ways to measure a variable of interest. Uber is identifying ways to measure performance of their drivers. Two examples of operational definitions that Uber used are rankings of top drivers and whether drivers have received a warning.

b. Answers may vary; cancellation rate may not be a good operational definition to measure performance because there are potentially thoughtful reasons for why a driver may cancel a ride, such as traffic that would delay a pick-up longer than would be expected or receiving a rude message from a potential passenger.

1-13 **a.** Researchers could randomly assign a certain number of women to be told about a gender difference on the test and randomly assign a certain number of other women to be told that no gender difference existed on this test.

b. If researchers did not use random assignment, any gender differences might be due to confounding variables. The women in the two groups might be different in some way (e.g., in math ability or belief in stereotypes) to begin with.

c. There are many possible confounds. Women who already believed the stereotype might do so because they had always performed poorly in mathematics, whereas those who did not believe the stereotype might be those who always did particularly well in math. Women who believed the stereotype might be those who were discouraged from studying math because "girls can't do math," whereas those who did not believe the stereotype might be those who were encouraged to study math because "girls are just as good as boys in math."

d. Math performance is operationalized as scores on a math test.

e. Researchers could have two math tests that are similar in difficulty. All women would take the first test after being told that women tend not to do as well as men on this test. After taking that test, they would be given the second test after being told that women tend to do as well as men on this test.

Chapter 2

2-1 Frequency tables, grouped frequency tables, histograms, and frequency polygons

2-2 A frequency is a count of how many times a score appears. A grouped frequency is a count for a defined interval, or group, of scores.

2-3 **a.**

Interval	Frequency
100–104	4
95–99	14
90–94	6
85–89	4
80–84	2
75–79	6
70–74	6
65–69	3
60–64	5

b.

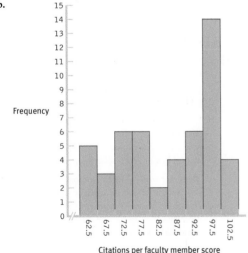

Citations per faculty member score

c.

Citations per faculty member score

2-4 **a.** We can now get a sense of the overall pattern of the data.

b. Schools in different academic systems may place different emphases on faculty conducting independent research and getting published, as well as have varying ranges of funding or financial resources to assist faculty research and publication.

2-5 A normal distribution is a specific distribution that is symmetric around a center high point: It looks like a bell. A skewed distribution is asymmetric or lopsided to the left or to the right, with a long tail of data to one side.

2-6 Negative; positive

2-7 This distribution is negatively skewed due to the data trailing off to the left and the bulk of the data clustering together on the right.

2-8 **a.** Early-onset Alzheimer's disease would create negative skew in the distribution for age of onset.

b. Because all humans eventually die, there is a sort of ceiling effect.

2-9 Being aware of these exceptional early-onset cases allows medical practitioners to be open to such surprising diagnoses. In addition, exceptional cases like these often give us great insight into the underlying mechanisms of disease.

Chapter 3

3-1 The purpose of a graph is to reveal and clarify relations between variables.

3-2 There were 43,405 nurses in 2010–2011 and 46,573 in 2011–2012. The difference is 46,573 − 43,405 = 3,168. This is a graphing lie because the graph appears to show a spike of many multiples of the total number of nurses that there were in 2010–2011. But in reality, this is about a 7% increase.

3-3 The graph on the left is misleading. It shows a sharp decline in annual traffic deaths in Connecticut from 1955 to 1956, but we cannot draw valid conclusions from just two data points. The graph on the right is a more accurate and complete depiction of the data. It includes nine, rather than two, data points and suggests that the sharp 1-year decline was the beginning of a clear downward trend in traffic fatalities that extended through 1959. It also shows that there had been previous 1-year declines of similar magnitude—from 1951 to 1952 and from 1953 to 1954. Also, the *y*-axis does not go down to 0, which exaggerates any differences.

3-4 Scatterplots and line graphs both depict the relation between two scale variables.

3-5 We should typically avoid using pictorial graphs and pie charts because the data can almost always be presented more clearly in a table or in a bar graph.

3-6 The line graph known as a time plot, or time series plot, allows us to calculate or evaluate how a variable changes over time.

3-7 **a.** A scatterplot is the best graph choice to depict the relation between two scale variables such as depression and stress.

b. A time plot, or time series plot, is the best graph choice to depict the change in a scale variable, such as the rise or decline in the number of facilities over time.

c. For one scale variable, such as number of siblings, the best graph choice would be either a frequency histogram or frequency polygon.

d. In this case, there is a nominal variable (region of the United States) and a scale variable (years of education). The best choice would be a bar graph, with one bar depicting the mean years of education for each region. In a Pareto chart, the bars would be arranged from highest to lowest, allowing for easier comparisons.

e. Calories and hours are both scale variables, and the question is about prediction rather than relation. In this case, we would calculate and graph a line of best fit.

3-8 Chartjunk is any unnecessary information or feature in a graph that detracts from the viewer's understanding.

3-9 **a.** Scatterplot or line graph

b. Bar graph

c. Scatterplot or line graph

3-10

The Effect of Sunlight on IQ Scores

The accompanying graph improves on the chartjunk graph in several ways. First, it has a clear, specific title. Second, all axes are labeled left to right. Third, there are no abbreviations. The units of measurement, IQ and hours of sunlight

per day, are included. The *y*-axis has 0 as its minimum, the colors are simple and muted, and all chartjunk has been eliminated. This graph wasn't as much fun to create, but it offers a far clearer presentation of the data! (*Note:* We are treating hours as an ordinal variable.)

Chapter 4

4-1 Statistics are calculated for samples; they are usually symbolized by Latin letters (e.g., *M*). Parameters are calculated for populations; they are usually symbolized by Greek letters (e.g., μ).

4-2 An outlier has the greatest effect on the mean, because the calculation of the mean takes into account the numeric value of each data point, including that outlier.

4-3 **a.** $M = \dfrac{\Sigma X}{N}$

$$= (10 + 8 + 22 + 5 + 6 + 1 + 19 + 8 + 13 + 12 + 8)/11$$

$$= 112/11 = 10.18$$

The median is found by arranging the scores in numeric order—1, 5, 6, 8, 8, 8, 10, 12, 13, 19, 22—then dividing the total number of scores, 11, by 2 and adding 1/2 to get 6. The 6th score in our ordered list of scores is the median, and in this case the 6th score is the number 8.

The mode is the most common score. In these data, the score 8 occurs most often (three times), so 8 is our mode.

b. $M = \dfrac{\Sigma X}{N}$

$$= (122.5 + 123.8 + 121.2 + 125.8 + 120.2 + 123.8$$
$$+ 120.5 + 119.8 + 126.3 + 123.6)/10$$

$$= 122.7/10 = 122.75$$

The data ordered are: 119.8, 120.2, 120.5, 121.2, 122.5, 123.6, 123.8, 123.8, 125.8, 126.3. Again, we find the median by ordering the data and then dividing the number of scores (here there are 10 scores) by 2 and adding 1/2. In this case, we get 5.5, so the mean of the 5th and 6th data points is the median. The median is (122.5 + 123.6)/2 = 123.05.

The mode is 123.8, which occurs twice in these data.

c. $M = \dfrac{\Sigma X}{N}$

$$= (0.100 + 0.866 + 0.781 + 0.555 + 0.222 + 0.245$$
$$+ 0.234)/7$$

$$= 3.003/7 = 0.429.$$

Note that three decimal places are included here (rather than the standard two places used throughout this book) because the data are carried out to three decimal places.

The median is found by first ordering the data: 0.100, 0.222, 0.234, 0.245, 0.555, 0.781, 0.866. Then the total number of scores, 7, is divided by 2 to get 3.5, to which 1/2 is added to get 4. So, the 4th score, 0.245, is the median. There is no mode in these data. All scores occur once.

4-4 **a.** $M = \dfrac{\Sigma X}{N}$

$$= (1 + 0 + 1 + 2 + 5 + ...4 + 6)/20 = 50/20 = 2.50$$

b. In this case, the scores would comprise a sample taken from the whole population, and this mean would be a statistic. The symbol, therefore, would be either M or $\overline{X}$.

c. In this case, the scores would constitute the entire population of interest, and the mean would be a parameter. Thus, the symbol would be μ.

d. To find the median, we would arrange the scores in order: 0, 0, 1, 1, 1, 1, 2, 2, 2, 2, 2, 2, 3, 3, 3, 3, 4, 5, 6, 7. We would then divide the total number of scores, 20, by 2 and add 1/2, which is 10.5. The median, therefore, is the mean of the 10th and 11th scores. Both of these scores are 2; therefore, the median is 2.

e. The mode is the most common score—in this case, there are six 2's, so the mode is 2.

f. The mean is a little higher than the median. This indicates that there are potential outliers pulling the mean higher; outliers would not affect the median.

4-5 By incorrectly labeling the debate as a regular edition of the newsmagazine program, the mean number of viewers for the show would be much higher as a result of the outlier from this special programming event, thus resulting in more advertising dollars for NBC.

4-6 Variability is the concept of variety in data, often measured as deviation around some center.

4-7 The range tells us the span of the data, from highest to lowest score. It is based on just two scores. The standard deviation tells us how far the typical score falls from the mean. The standard deviation takes every score into account.

4-8 **a.** The range is: $X_{highest} - X_{lowest} = 22 - 1 = 21$

The variance is:

$$SD^2 = \frac{\Sigma(X - M)^2}{N}$$

We start by calculating the mean, which is 10.182. We then calculate the deviation of each score from the mean and the square of that deviation.

X	X − M	(X − M)²
10	−0.182	0.033
8	−2.182	4.761
22	11.818	139.665
5	−5.182	26.853
6	−4.182	17.489
1	−9.182	84.309
19	8.818	77.757
8	−2.182	4.761
13	2.818	7.941
12	1.818	3.305
8	−2.182	4.761

$$SD^2 = \frac{\Sigma(X - M)^2}{N} = \frac{371.635}{11} = 33.785$$

The standard deviation is: $SD = \sqrt{SD^2}$ or

$$SD = \sqrt{\frac{\Sigma(X - M)^2}{N}} = \sqrt{33.785} = 5.81$$

b. The range is: $X_{highest} - X_{lowest} = 126.3 - 119.8 = 6.5$

The variance is:

$$SD^2 = \frac{\Sigma(X - M)^2}{N}$$

We start by calculating the mean, which is 122.750. We then calculate the deviation of each score from the mean and the square of that deviation.

X	X − M	(X − M)²
122.500	−0.250	0.063
123.800	1.050	1.103
121.200	−1.550	2.403
125.800	3.050	9.303
120.200	−2.550	6.503
123.800	1.050	1.103
120.500	−2.250	5.063
119.800	−2.950	8.703
126.300	3.550	12.603
123.600	0.850	0.723

$$SD^2 = \frac{\Sigma(X - M)^2}{N} = \frac{47.570}{10} = 4.757$$

The standard deviation is: $SD = \sqrt{SD^2}$

$$SD = \sqrt{\frac{\Sigma(X - M)^2}{N}} = \sqrt{4.757} = 2.18$$

c. The range is: $X_{highest} - X_{lowest} = 0.866 - 0.100 = 0.766$

The variance is:

$$SD^2 = \frac{\Sigma(X - M)^2}{N}$$

We start by calculating the mean, which is 0.429. We then calculate the deviation of each score from the mean and the square of that deviation.

X	X − M	(X − M)²
0.100	−0.329	0.108
0.866	0.437	0.191
0.781	0.352	0.124
0.555	0.126	0.016
0.222	−0.207	0.043
0.245	−0.184	0.034
0.234	−0.195	0.038

$$SD^2 = \frac{\Sigma(X - M)^2}{N} = \frac{0.554}{7} = 0.079$$

The standard deviation is: $SD = \sqrt{SD^2}$ or

$$SD = \sqrt{\frac{\Sigma(X - M)^2}{N}} = \sqrt{0.079} = 0.28$$

4-9 **a.** range $= X_{highest} - X_{lowest} = 1460 - 450 = 1010$

b. We do not know whether scores cluster at some point in the distribution—for example, near one end of the distribution—or whether the scores are more evenly spread out.

c. The formula for variance is:

$$SD^2 = \frac{\Sigma(X - M)^2}{N}$$

The first step is to calculate the mean, which is 927.500. We then create three columns: one for the scores, one for the deviations of the scores from the mean, and one for the squares of the deviations.

X	X − M	(X − M)²
450	−477.50	228,006.25
670	−257.50	66,306.25
1130	202.50	41,006.25
1460	532.50	283,556.25

We can now calculate variance:

$$SD^2 = \frac{\Sigma(X - M)^2}{N}$$

$$= (228,006.25 + 66,306.25 + 41,006.25 + 283,556.25)/4$$

$$= 618,875/4 = 154,718.75.$$

d. We calculate standard deviation the same way we calculate variance, but we then take the square root.

$$SD = \sqrt{\frac{\Sigma(X - M)^2}{N}} = \sqrt{154,718.75} = 393.34$$

e. If the researcher were interested only in these four students, these scores would represent the entire population of interest, and the variance and standard deviation would be parameters. Therefore, the symbols would be σ^2 and σ, respectively.

f. If the researcher hoped to generalize from these four students to all students at the university, these scores would represent a sample, and the variance and standard deviation would be statistics. Therefore, the symbols would be SD^2, s^2, or MS for variance and SD or s for standard deviation.

Chapter 5

5-1 The risks of sampling are that we might not have a representative sample, and sometimes it is difficult to know whether the sample is representative. If we didn't realize that the sample was not representative, then we might draw conclusions about the population that are inaccurate.

5-2 The numbers in the fourth row, reading across, are 59808 08391 45427 26842 83609 49700 46058. Each person is assigned a number from 01 to 80. We then read the numbers from the table as two-digit numbers: 59, 80, 80, 83, 91, 45, 42, 72, 68, and so on. We ignore repeat numbers (e.g., 80) and numbers that exceed the sample of 80. So, the six people chosen would have the assigned numbers: 59, 80, 45, 42, 72, and 68.

5-3 Reading down from the first column, then the second, and so on, noting only the appearance of 0's and 1's, we see the numbers 0, 0, 0, 0, 1, and 0 (ending in the sixth column). Using these numbers, we could assign the first through the fourth people and the sixth person to the group designated as 0, and the fifth person to the group designated as 1. If we want an equal number of people in each of the two groups, we would assign the first three people to the 0 group and the last three to the 1 group, because we pulled three 0's first.

5-4 **a.** The likely population is all patients who will undergo surgery; the researcher would not be able to access this population, and therefore random selection could not be used. Random assignment, however, could be used. The psychologist could randomly assign half of the patients to counseling and half to a control group.

b. The population is all children in this school system; the psychologist could identify all of these children and thus could use random selection. The psychologist could also use random assignment. She could randomly assign half the children to the interactive online textbook and half to the printed textbook.

c. The population is patients in therapy; because the whole population could not be identified, random selection could not be used. Moreover, random assignment could not be used. It is not possible to assign people to either have or not have a diagnosed personality disorder.

5-5 We regularly make personal assessments about how probable we think an event is, but we base these evaluations on our opinions about things rather than on systematically collected data. Statisticians are interested in objective probabilities that are based on unbiased research.

5-6 **a.** probability $=$ successes/trials $= 5/100 = 0.05$

b. $8/50 = 0.16$

c. $130/1044 = 0.12$

5-7 **a.** In the short run, we might see a wide range of numbers of successes. It would not be surprising to have several in a row or none in a row. In the short run, the observations seem almost like chaos.

b. Given the assumptions listed for this problem, in the long run, we'd expect 0.50, or 50%, to be women, although there would likely be strings of men and of women along the way.

5-8 When we reject the null hypothesis, we are saying we reject the idea that there is no mean difference in the dependent variable across the levels of our independent variable. Rejecting the null hypothesis means we can support the research hypothesis that there is a mean difference.

5-9 The null hypothesis assumes that no mean difference would be observed, so the mean difference in grades would be zero.

5-10 a. The null hypothesis is that a decrease in temperature does not affect mean academic performance (or does not decrease mean academic performance).

b. The research hypothesis is that a decrease in temperature does affect mean academic performance (or decreases mean academic performance).

c. The researchers would reject the null hypothesis.

d. The researchers would fail to reject the null hypothesis.

5-11 We make a Type I error when we reject the null hypothesis but the null hypothesis is correct. We make a Type II error when we fail to reject the null hypothesis but the null hypothesis is false.

5-12 In this scenario, a Type I error would be imprisoning a person who is really innocent, and 7 convictions out of 280 innocent people calculates to be 0.025, or 2.5%.

5-13 In this scenario, a Type II error would be failing to convict a guilty person, and 11 acquittals for every 35 guilty people calculates to be 0.314, or 31.4%.

5-14 a. If the virtual-reality glasses really don't have any effect, this is a Type I error, which is made when the null hypothesis is rejected but is really true.

b. If the virtual-reality glasses really do have an effect, this is a Type II error, which is made when the researchers fail to reject the null hypothesis but the null hypothesis is not true.

Chapter 6

6-1 Unimodal means there is one mode or high point to the curve. Symmetric means the left and right sides of the curve have the same shape and are mirror images of each other.

6-2 a.

b.

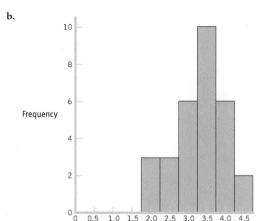

6-3 The shape of the distribution becomes more normal as the size of the sample increases (although the larger sample appears to be somewhat negatively skewed).

6-4 In standardization, we convert individual scores to standardized scores for which we know the percentiles.

6-5 The numeric value tells us how many standard deviations a score is from the mean of the distribution. The sign tells us whether the score is above or below the mean.

6-6 a. $z = \dfrac{(X - \mu)}{\sigma} = \dfrac{11.5 - 14}{2.5} = -1.0$

b. $z = \dfrac{(X - \mu)}{\sigma} = \dfrac{18 - 14}{2.5} = 1.6$

6-7 a. $X = z(\sigma) + \mu = 2(2.5) + 14 = 19$

b. $X = z(\sigma) + \mu = -1.4(2.5) + 14 = 10.5$

6-8 a. $z = \dfrac{(X - \mu)}{\sigma} = \dfrac{2.50 - 3.20}{0.70} = -1.00$;

approximately 16% of students have a CFC score of 2.5 or less.

b. $z = \dfrac{(X - \mu)}{\sigma} = \dfrac{4.60 - 3.20}{0.70} = 2.00$; this score is at approximately the 98th percentile.

c. This student has a z score of 1.

d. $X = z(\sigma) + \mu = 1(0.70) + 3.20 = 3.90$; this answer makes sense because 3.90 is above the mean of 3.20, as a z score of 1 would indicate.

6-9 a. Nicole is in better health because her score is above the mean for her measure, whereas Samantha's score is below the mean.

b. Samantha's z score is $z = \dfrac{(X - \mu)}{\sigma} = \dfrac{84 - 93}{4.5} = -2.0$

Nicole's z score is

$$z = \frac{(X - \mu)}{\sigma} = \frac{332 - 312}{20} = 1.0$$

Nicole is in better health, being 1 standard deviation above the mean, whereas Samantha is 2 standard deviations below the mean.

c. We can conclude that approximately 98% of the population is in better health than Samantha, who is 2 standard deviations below the mean. We can conclude that approximately 16% of the population is in better health than Nicole, who is 1 standard deviation above the mean.

6-10 The central limit theorem asserts that a distribution of sample means approaches the shape of the normal curve as sample size increases. It also asserts that the spread of the distribution of sample means gets smaller as the sample size gets larger.

6-11 A distribution of means is composed of many means that are calculated from all possible samples of a particular size from the same population.

6-12 $\sigma_M = \dfrac{\sigma}{\sqrt{N}} = \dfrac{11}{\sqrt{35}} = 1.86$

6-13 a. The scores range from 2.0 to 4.5, which gives us a range of $4.5 - 2.0 = 2.5$.

b. The means are 3.4 for the first row, 3.4 for the second row, and 3.15 for the third row [e.g., for the first row, $M = (3.5 + 3.5 + 3.0 + 4.0 + 2.0 + 4.0 + 2.0 + 4.0 + 3.5 + 4.5)/10 = 3.4$]. These three means range from 3.15 to 3.40, which gives us a range of $3.40 - 3.15 = 0.25$.

c. The range is smaller for the means of samples of 10 scores than for the individual scores because the more extreme scores are balanced by lower scores when samples of 10 are taken. Individual scores are not attenuated in that way.

d. The mean of the distribution of means will be the same as the mean of the individual scores: $\mu_M = \mu = 3.32$. The standard error will be smaller than the standard deviation; we must divide by the square root of the sample size of 10:

$$\sigma_M = \frac{\sigma}{\sqrt{N}} = \frac{0.69}{\sqrt{10}} = 0.22$$

Chapter 7

7-1 We need to know the mean, μ, and the standard deviation, σ, of the population.

7-2 Raw scores are used to compute z scores, and z scores are used to determine what percentage of scores fall below and above that particular position on the distribution. A z score can also be used to compute a raw score.

7-3 Because the curve is symmetric, the same percentage of scores (41.47%) lies between the mean and a z score of -1.37 as between the mean and a z score of 1.37.

7-4 Fifty percent of scores fall below the mean, and 12.93% fall between the mean and a z score of 0.33.

$50\% + 12.93\% = 62.93\%$

7-5 a. $\mu_M = \mu = 156.8$

$$\sigma_M = \frac{\sigma}{\sqrt{N}} = \frac{14.6}{\sqrt{36}} = 2.433$$

$$z = \frac{(M - \mu_M)}{\sigma_M} = \frac{(164.6 - 156.8)}{2.433} = 3.21$$

50% below the mean; 49.87% between the mean and this score; $50 + 49.87 = 99.87$th percentile

b. $100 - 99.87 = 0.13\%$ of samples of this size scored higher than the students at Baylor.

c. At the 99.87th percentile, these 36 students from Baylor are truly outstanding. If these students are representative of their majors, clearly these results reflect positively on Baylor's psychology and neuroscience department.

7-6 For most parametric hypothesis tests, we assume that (1) the dependent variable is assessed on a scale measure—that is, equal changes are reflected by equal distances on the measure; (2) the participants are randomly selected, meaning everyone has the same chance of being selected; and (3) the distribution of the population of interest is approximately normal.

7-7 If a test statistic is more extreme than the critical value, then the null hypothesis is rejected. If a test statistic is less extreme than the critical value, then we fail to reject the null hypothesis.

7-8 If the null hypothesis is true, he will reject it 8% of the time.

7-9 a. 0.15
b. 0.03
c. 0.055

7-10 a. (1) The dependent variable—diagnosis (correct versus incorrect)—is nominal, not scale, so this assumption is not met. Based only on this, we should not proceed with a hypothesis test based on a z distribution. (2) The samples include only outpatients seen over 2 specific months and only those at one community mental health center. The sample is not randomly selected, so we must be cautious about generalizing from it. (3) The populations are not normally distributed because the dependent variable is nominal.

b. (1) The dependent variable, health score, is likely scale. (2) The participants were randomly selected; all wild cats in zoos in North America had an equal chance of being selected for this study. (3) The data are not normally distributed; we are told that a few animals had very high scores, so the data are likely positively skewed. Moreover, there are fewer than 30 participants in this study. It is probably not a good idea to proceed with a hypothesis test based on a z distribution.

7-11 A directional test indicates that either a mean increase or a mean decrease in the dependent variable is hypothesized, but not both. A nondirectional test does not indicate a direction of mean difference for the research hypothesis, just that there is a mean difference.

7-12 $\mu_M = \mu = 1090$

$$\sigma_M = \frac{\sigma}{\sqrt{N}} = \frac{87}{\sqrt{53}} = 11.95$$

7-13 $z = \dfrac{(M - \mu_M)}{\sigma_M} = \dfrac{(1094 - 1090)}{11.95} = 0.33$

7-14 *Step 1:* Population 1 is coffee drinkers who spend the day in coffee shops. Population 2 is all coffee drinkers in the United States. The comparison distribution will be a distribution of means. The hypothesis test will be a z test because we have only one sample and we know the population mean and standard deviation. This study meets two of the three assumptions and may meet the third. The dependent variable, the number of cups coffee drinkers drank, is scale. In addition, there are more than 30 participants in the sample, indicating that the comparison distribution is normal. The data were not randomly selected, however, so we must be cautious when generalizing.

Step 2: The null hypothesis is that people who spend the day working in the coffee shop drink the same amount of coffee, on average, as those in the general U.S. population: $H_0: \mu_1 = \mu_2$.

The research hypothesis is that people who spend the day in coffee shops drink a different amount of coffee, on average, than those in the general U.S. population: $H_1: \mu_1 \neq \mu_2$.

Step 3: $\mu_M = \mu = 3.10$

$$\sigma_M = \frac{\sigma}{\sqrt{N}} = \frac{0.9}{\sqrt{34}} = 0.154$$

Step 4: The cutoff z statistics are -1.96 and 1.96.

Step 5: $z = \frac{(M - \mu_M)}{\sigma_M} = \frac{(3.17 - 3.10)}{0.154} = 0.45$

Step 6: Because the z statistic does not exceed the cutoffs, we fail to reject the null hypothesis. We did not find any evidence that the sample was different from what was expected according to the null hypothesis.

Chapter 8

8-1 Interval estimates provide a range of scores in which we have some confidence the population statistic will fall, whereas point estimates use just a single value to describe the population.

8-2 The interval estimate is 17% to 25% (21% − 4% = 17% and 21% + 4% = 25%); the point estimate is 21%.

8-3 **a.** First, we draw a normal curve with the sample mean, 3.20, in the center. Then we put the bounds of the 95% confidence interval on either end, writing the appropriate percentages under the segments of the curve: 2.5% beyond the cutoffs on either end and 47.5% between the mean and each cutoff. Now we look up the z statistics for these cutoffs; the z statistic associated with 47.5%, the percentage between the mean and the z statistic, is 1.96. Thus, the cutoffs are −1.96 and 1.96. Next, we calculate standard error so that we can convert these z statistics to raw means:

$$\sigma_M = \frac{\sigma}{\sqrt{N}} = \frac{0.70}{\sqrt{45}} = 0.104$$

$$M_{lower} = -z(\sigma_M) + M_{sample} = -1.96(0.104) + 3.45 = 3.25$$

$$M_{upper} = z(\sigma_M) + M_{sample} = 1.96(0.104) + 3.45 = 3.65$$

Finally, we check to be sure the answer makes sense by demonstrating that each end of the confidence interval is the same distance from the mean: $3.25 - 3.45 = -0.20$ and $3.65 - 3.45 = 0.20$. The confidence interval is [3.25, 3.65].

b. If we were to conduct this study over and over, with the same sample size, we would expect the population mean to fall in that interval 95% of the time. Thus, it provides a range of plausible values for the population mean. Because the null-hypothesized population mean of 3.20 is not a plausible value, we can conclude that those who attended the discussion group seem to have higher mean CFC scores than those who did not. This conclusion matches that of the hypothesis test, in which we rejected the null hypothesis.

c. The confidence interval is superior to the hypothesis test because not only does it lead to the same conclusion but it also gives us an interval estimate, rather than a point estimate, of the population mean.

8-4 Statistical significance means that the observation meets the standard for special events, typically something that occurs less than 5% of the time. Practical importance means that the outcome really matters.

8-5 Effect size is a standardized value that indicates the size of a difference with respect to a measure of spread but is not affected by sample size.

8-6 Cohen's $d = \frac{(M - \mu)}{\sigma} = \frac{(105 - 100)}{15} = 0.33$

8-7 **a.** We calculate Cohen's d, the effect size appropriate for data analyzed with a z test. We use standard deviation in the denominator, rather than standard error, because effect sizes are for distributions of scores rather than distributions of means.

$$\text{Cohen's } d = \frac{(M - \mu)}{\sigma} = \frac{(3.45 - 3.20)}{0.70} = 0.36$$

b. Cohen's conventions indicate that 0.2 is a small effect and 0.5 is a medium effect. This effect size, therefore, would be considered a small-to-medium effect.

c. If the career discussion group is easily implemented in terms of time and money, the small-to-medium effect might be worth the effort. For university students, a higher mean level of Consideration of Future Consequences might translate into a higher mean level of readiness for life after graduation, a premise that we could study.

8-8 Three ways to increase power are to increase alpha, to conduct a one-tailed test rather than a two-tailed test, and to increase N. All three of these techniques serve to increase the chance of rejecting the null hypothesis. (We could also increase the difference between means, or decrease variability, but these are more difficult.)

8-9 *Step 1:* We know the following about population 2: $\mu = 3.20$, $\sigma = 0.70$. We assume the following about population 1 based on the information from the sample: $N = 45$, $M = 3.45$. We need to calculate standard error based on the standard deviation for population 2 and the size of the sample:

$$\sigma_M = \frac{\sigma}{\sqrt{N}} = \frac{0.70}{\sqrt{45}} = 0.104$$

Step 2: Because the sample mean is higher than the population mean, we will conduct this one-tailed test by examining only the high end of the distribution. We need to find the cutoff that marks where 5% of the data fall in the tail. We know that the z cutoff for a one-tailed test is 1.64. Using that z statistic, we can calculate a raw score.

$$M = z(\sigma_M) + \mu_M = 1.64(0.104) + 3.20 = 3.371$$

This mean of 3.371 marks the point beyond which 5% of all means based on samples of 45 observations will fall.

Step 3: For the distribution based on population 1, centered around 3.45, we need to calculate how often means of 3.371 (the cutoff) and greater occur. We do this by calculating the z statistic for the raw mean of 3.371 with respect to the sample mean of 3.45.

$$z = \frac{3.371 - 3.45}{0.104} = -0.76$$

We now look up this z statistic on the table and find that 22.36% falls toward the tail and 27.64% falls between this z statistic and the mean. We calculate power as the proportion of observations between this z statistic and the tail of interest, which is at the high end. So we would add 27.64% and 50% to get statistical power of 77.64%.

8-10 a. The statistical power calculation means that, if population 1 really does exist, we have a 77.64% chance of observing a sample mean, based on 45 observations, that will allow us to reject the null hypothesis. We fall just short of the desired 80% statistical power.

b. We can increase statistical power by increasing the sample size, extending or enhancing the career discussion group such that we create a bigger effect, or by changing alpha.

Chapter 9

9-1 The t statistic indicates the distance of a sample mean from a population mean in terms of the estimated standard error.

9-2 First, we need to calculate the mean:

$$M = \frac{\Sigma X}{N} = (6 + 3 + 7 + 6 + 4 + 5)/6 = 31/6 = 5.167$$

We then calculate the deviation of each score from the mean and the square of that deviation.

X	$X - M$	$(X - M)^2$
6	0.833	0.694
3	−2.167	4.696
7	1.833	3.360
6	0.833	0.694
4	−1.167	1.362
5	−0.167	0.028

Numerator: $\Sigma(X - M)^2 = (0.694 + 4.696 + 3.360 + 0.694 + 1.362 + 0.028)^2 = 10.834$

The standard deviation is:

$$SD = \sqrt{\frac{\Sigma(X - M)^2}{N}} = \sqrt{\frac{10.834}{6}} = \sqrt{1.806} = 1.344$$

When estimating the population variability, we calculate s:

$$s = \sqrt{\frac{\Sigma(X - M)^2}{N - 1}} = \sqrt{\frac{10.834}{6 - 1}} = \sqrt{2.167} = 1.472$$

9-3 $s_M = \dfrac{s}{\sqrt{N}} = \dfrac{1.472}{\sqrt{6}} = 0.601$

9-4 a. We would use a distribution of means, specifically a t distribution. It is a distribution of means because we have a sample consisting of more than one individual. It is a t distribution because we are comparing one sample to a population, but we know only the population mean, not its standard deviation.

b. The appropriate mean: $\mu_M = \mu = 25$. The calculations for the appropriate standard deviation (in this case, standard error, s_M):

$$M = \frac{\Sigma X}{N} = (20 + 19 + 27 + 24 + 18)/5$$
$$= 108/5 = 21.6$$

X	$X - M$	$(X - M)^2$
20	−1.6	2.56
19	−2.6	6.76
27	5.4	29.16
24	2.4	5.76
18	−3.6	12.96

Numerator: $\Sigma(X - M)^2 = (2.56 + 6.76 + 29.16 + 5.76 + 12.96)^2$
$$= 57.2$$

$$s = \sqrt{\frac{\Sigma(X - M)^2}{(N - 1)}} = \sqrt{\frac{57.2}{5 - 1}} = \sqrt{14.3} = 3.782$$

$$s_M = \frac{s}{\sqrt{N}} = \frac{3.782}{\sqrt{5}} = 1.691$$

c. $t = \dfrac{(M - \mu_M)}{s_M} = \dfrac{(21.6 - 25)}{1.691} = -2.01$

9-5 *Degrees of freedom* is the number of scores that are free to vary, or take on any value, when a population parameter is estimated from a sample.

9-6 A single-sample t test is more useful than a z test because it requires only that we know the population mean (not the population standard deviation).

9-7 a. $df = N - 1 = 35 - 1 = 34$

b. $df = N - 1 = 14 - 1 = 13$

9-8 a. ± 2.201

b. Either -2.584 or $+2.584$, depending on the tail of interest

9-9 *Step 1:* Population 1 is statistics students. Population 2 is all university students.

The distribution will be a distribution of means, and we will use a single-sample t test. We meet the assumption that the dependent variable is scale. We do not know if the sample was randomly selected, and we do not know if the population variable was normally distributed. Some caution should be exercised when drawing conclusions from these data.

Step 2: The null hypothesis is H_0: $\mu_1 = \mu_2$; that is, statistics students miss the same number of classes, on average, as the general population.

The research hypothesis is H_1: $\mu_1 \neq \mu_2$; that is, statistics students miss a different number of classes, on average, than the general population.

Step 3: $\mu_M = \mu = 3.7$

$$M = \frac{\Sigma X}{N} = (6 + 3 + 7 + 6 + 4 + 5)/6 = 31/6 = 5.167$$

$$s = \sqrt{\frac{\Sigma(X - M)^2}{N - 1}} = \sqrt{\frac{10.834}{6 - 1}} = \sqrt{2.167} = 1.472$$

$$s_M = \frac{s}{\sqrt{N}} = \frac{1.472}{\sqrt{6}} = 0.601$$

Step 4: $df = N - 1 = 6 - 1 = 5$

For a two-tailed test with a p level of 0.05 and 5 degrees of freedom, the cutoffs are ± 2.571.

Step 5: $t = \dfrac{(M - \mu_M)}{s_M} = \dfrac{(5.167 - 3.7)}{0.601} = 2.441$

Step 6: Because the calculated t value falls short of the critical values, we fail to reject the null hypothesis.

Chapter 10

10-1 For a paired-samples t test, we calculate a difference score for every individual. We then compare the average difference observed to the average difference we would expect based on the null hypothesis. If there is no difference, then all difference scores should average to 0.

10-2 An individual difference score is a calculation of change or difference for each participant. For example, we might subtract weight before the holiday break from weight after the break to evaluate how many pounds an individual lost or gained.

10-3 We want to subtract the before-lunch energy level from the after-lunch energy level to get values that reflect loss of energy as a negative value and an increase of energy with food as a positive value. The mean of these differences is -1.4.

Before Lunch	After Lunch	After − Before
6	3	$3 - 6 = -3$
5	2	$2 - 5 = -3$
4	6	$6 - 4 = 2$
5	4	$4 - 5 = -1$
7	5	$5 - 7 = -2$

10-4 a. *Step 1:* Population 1 is students for whom we're measuring energy levels before lunch. Population 2 is students for whom we're measuring energy levels after lunch.

The comparison distribution is a distribution of mean difference scores. We use the paired-samples t test because each participant contributes a score to each of the two samples we are comparing.

We meet the assumption that the dependent variable is a scale measurement. However, we do not know whether the participants were randomly selected or if the population is normally distributed, and the sample is less than 30.

Step 2: The null hypothesis is that there is no difference in mean energy levels before and after lunch—H_0: $\mu_1 = \mu_2$.

The research hypothesis is that there is a mean difference in energy levels—H_1: $\mu_1 \neq \mu_2$.

Step 3:

Difference (D)	($D - M$)	($D - M$)^2
-3	-1.6	2.56
-3	-1.6	2.56
2	3.4	11.56
-1	0.4	0.16
-2	-0.6	0.36

$M_{difference} = -1.4$

$$s = \sqrt{\frac{\Sigma(X - M)^2}{(N - 1)}} = \sqrt{\frac{17.2}{(5 - 1)}} = \sqrt{4.3} = 2.074$$

$$s_M = \frac{s}{\sqrt{N}} = \frac{2.074}{\sqrt{5}} = 0.928$$

$\mu_M = 0$, $s_M = 0.928$

Step 4: The degrees of freedom are $5 - 1 = 4$, and the cutoffs, based on a two-tailed test and a p level of 0.05, are ± 2.776.

Step 5: $t = \dfrac{(-1.4 - 0)}{0.928} = -1.51$

Step 6: Because the test statistic, -1.51, did not exceed the critical value of -2.776, we fail to reject the null hypothesis.

10-5 The null hypothesis for the paired-samples t test is that the mean difference score is 0—that is, $\mu_M = 0$. Therefore, if the confidence interval around the mean difference does not include 0, we know that the sample mean is unlikely to have come from a distribution with a mean of 0 and we can reject the null hypothesis.

10-6 We calculate Cohen's d by subtracting 0 (the population mean based on the null hypothesis) from the sample mean and dividing by the standard deviation of the difference scores.

10-7 a. We first find the t values associated with a two-tailed hypothesis test and alpha of 0.05. These are ± 2.776. We then calculate s_M by dividing s by the square root of the sample size, which results in $s_M = 0.548$.

$M_{lower} = -t(s_M) + M_{sample} = -2.776(0.548) + 1.0 = -0.52$

$M_{upper} = t(s_M) + M_{sample} = 2.776(0.548) + 1.0 = 2.52$

The confidence interval can be written as $[-0.52, 2.52]$. Because this confidence interval includes 0, we would fail to reject the null hypothesis. Zero is one of the likely mean differences we would get when repeatedly sampling from a population with a mean difference score of 1.

b. We calculate Cohen's d as:

$$d = \frac{(M - \mu)}{s} = \frac{(1 - 0)}{1.225} = 0.82$$

This is a large effect size.

10-8 a. $M_{lower} = -t(s_M) + M_{sample} = -2.776(0.928) + (-1.4) = -3.98$

$M_{upper} = t(s_M) + M_{sample} = 2.776(0.928) + (-1.4) = 1.18$

The confidence interval can be written as $[-3.98, 1.18]$. Notice that the confidence interval spans 0, the null-hypothesized difference between mean energy levels before and after lunch. Because the null value is within the confidence interval, we fail to reject the null hypothesis.

b. $d = \dfrac{(M - \mu)}{s} = \dfrac{(-1.4 - 0)}{2.074} = -0.68$

This is a medium-to-large effect size, according to Cohen's guidelines.

Chapter 11

11-1 When the data we are comparing are collected using the same participants in both conditions, we use a paired-samples t test; each participant contributes two values to the analysis. When we are comparing two independent groups and no participant is in more than one condition, we use an independent-samples t test.

11-2 Pooled variance is a weighted combination of the variability in both groups in an independent-samples t test.

11-3 a. Group 1 is treated as the X variable; its mean is 3.0.

X	$X - M$	$(X - M)^2$
3	0	0
2	−1	1
4	1	1
6	3	9
1	−2	4
2	−1	1

$$s_X^2 = \dfrac{\Sigma(X - M)^2}{N - 1} = \dfrac{(0 + 1 + 1 + 9 + 4 + 1)}{6 - 1} = 3.2$$

Group 2 is treated as the Y variable; its mean is 4.6.

Y	$Y - M$	$(Y - M)^2$
5	0.4	0.16
4	−0.6	0.36
6	1.4	1.96
2	−2.6	6.76
6	1.4	1.96

$$s_Y^2 = \dfrac{\Sigma(Y - M)^2}{N - 1} = \dfrac{(0.16 + 0.36 + 1.96 + 6.76 + 1.96)}{5 - 1}$$
$$= 2.8$$

b. $df_X = N - 1 = 6 - 1 = 5$

$df_Y = N - 1 = 5 - 1 = 4$

$df_{total} = df_X + df_Y = 5 + 4 = 9$

$s_{pooled}^2 = \left(\dfrac{df_X}{df_{total}}\right)s_X^2 + \left(\dfrac{df_Y}{df_{total}}\right)s_Y^2 = \left(\dfrac{5}{9}\right)3.2 + \left(\dfrac{4}{9}\right)2.8$

$= 1.778 + 1.244 = 3.022$

c. The variance version of standard error is calculated for each sample as:

$$s_{M_X}^2 = \dfrac{s_{pooled}^2}{N_X} = \dfrac{3.022}{6} = 0.504$$

$$s_{M_Y}^2 = \dfrac{s_{pooled}^2}{N_Y} = \dfrac{3.022}{5} = 0.604$$

d. The variance of the distribution of differences between means is:

$$s_{difference}^2 = s_{M_X}^2 + s_{M_Y}^2 = 0.504 + 0.604 = 1.108$$

This can be converted to standard deviation units by taking the square root:

$$s_{difference} = \sqrt{s_{difference}^2} = \sqrt{1.108} = 1.053$$

e. $t = \dfrac{(M_X - M_Y) - (\mu_X - \mu_Y)}{s_{difference}} = \dfrac{(3 - 4.6) - (0)}{1.053} = -1.52$

11-4 a. The null hypothesis asserts that there is no average between-group difference; employees with low trust in their leader show the same mean level of agreement with decisions as those with high trust in their leader. Symbolically, this would be written $H_0: \mu_1 = \mu_2$.

The research hypothesis asserts that mean level of agreement is different between the two groups—$H_1: \mu_1 \neq \mu_2$.

b. The critical values, based on a two-tailed test, a p level of 0.05, and df_{total} of 9, are -2.262 and 2.262.

The t value we calculated, -1.519, does not exceed the cutoff of -2.262, so we fail to reject the null hypothesis.

c. Based on these results, we did not find evidence that mean level of agreement with a decision is different across the two levels of trust, $t(9) = -1.519, p > 0.05$.

d. Despite having similar means for the two groups, we failed to reject the null hypothesis, whereas the original researchers rejected the null hypothesis. The failure to reject the null hypothesis is likely due to the low statistical power from the small samples we used.

11-5 We calculate confidence intervals to determine a range of plausible values for the population parameter, based on the data.

11-6 Effect size tells us how large or small the difference we observed is, regardless of sample size. Even when a result is statistically significant, it might not be important. Effect size helps us evaluate practical significance.

11-7 a. The upper and lower bounds of the confidence interval are calculated as:

$(M_X - M_Y)_{lower} = -t(s_{difference}) + (M_X - M_Y)_{sample}$
$= -2.262(1.053) + (-1.6) = -3.98$

$(M_X - M_Y)_{upper} = t(s_{difference}) + (M_X - M_Y)_{sample}$
$= 2.262(1.053) + (-1.6) = 0.78$

The confidence interval is $[-3.98, 0.78]$.

b. To calculate Cohen's d, we need to calculate the pooled standard deviation for the data:

$s_{pooled} = \sqrt{s_{pooled}^2} = \sqrt{3.022} = 1.738$

$$\text{Cohen's } d = \frac{(M_X - M_Y) - (\mu_X - \mu_Y)}{s_{pooled}} = \frac{(3 - 4.6) - (0)}{1.738}$$

$$= -0.92$$

11-8 The confidence interval provides us with a range of differences between means in which we could expect the population mean difference to fall 95% of the time, based on samples of this size. Whereas the hypothesis test evaluates the point estimate of the difference between means—$(3 - 4.6)$, or -1.6, in this case—the confidence interval gives us a range, or interval estimate, of $[-3.98, 0.78]$.

11-9 The effect size we calculated, Cohen's d of -0.92, is a large effect according to Cohen's guidelines. Beyond the hypothesis test and confidence interval, which both lead us to fail to reject the null hypothesis, the size of the effect indicates that we might be on to a real effect here. We might want to replicate the study with more statistical power in an effort to better test this hypothesis.

Chapter 12

12-1 The F statistic is a ratio of between-groups variance and within-groups variance.

12-2 The two types of research design for a one-way ANOVA are a within-groups design and a between-groups design.

12-3 a. $F = \dfrac{\text{between-groups variance}}{\text{within-groups variance}} = \dfrac{8.6}{3.7} = 2.324$

b. $F = \dfrac{102.4}{123.77} = 0.827$

c. $F = \dfrac{45.2}{32.1} = 1.408$

12-4 a. We would use an F distribution because there are more than two groups.

b. We would determine the variance among the three sample means—the means for those in the control group, for those in the 2-hour communication ban, and for those in the 4-hour communication ban.

c. We would determine the variance within each of the three samples, and we would take a weighted average of the three variances.

12-5 If the F statistic is beyond the cutoff, then we can reject the null hypothesis—meaning that there is a significant mean difference (or differences) somewhere in the data, but we do not know where the difference lies.

12-6 When calculating $SS_{between}$, we subtract the grand mean (GM) from the mean of each group (M). We do this for every score.

12-7 a. $df_{between} = N_{groups} - 1 = 3 - 1 = 2$

b. $df_{within} = df_1 + df_2 + \ldots + df_{last} = (4 - 1) + (4 - 1) + (3 - 1)$
$= 3 + 3 + 2 = 8$

c. $df_{total} = df_{between} + df_{within} = 2 + 8 = 10$

12-8 $GM = \dfrac{\Sigma(X)}{N_{total}}$

$= \dfrac{(37 + 30 + 22 + 29 + 49 + 52 + 41 + 39 + 36 + 49 + 42)}{11}$

$= 38.727$

12-9 a. Total sum of squares is calculated here as $SS_{total} = \Sigma(X - GM)^2$:

Sample	X	(X − GM)	(X − GM)²
Group 1	37	−1.727	2.983
$M_1 = 29.5$	30	−8.727	76.161
	22	−16.727	279.793
	29	−9.727	94.615
Group 2	49	10.273	105.535
$M_2 = 45.25$	52	13.273	176.173
	41	2.273	5.167
	39	0.273	0.075
Group 3	36	−2.727	7.437
$M_3 = 42.333$	49	10.273	105.535
	42	3.273	10.713
$GM = 38.73$			$SS_{total} = 864.187$

b. Within-groups sum of squares is calculated here as $SS_{within} = \Sigma(X - M)^2$.

Sample	X	(X − M)	(X − M)²
Group 1	37	7.500	56.250
$M_1 = 29.5$	30	0.500	0.250
	22	−7.500	56.250
	29	−0.500	0.250
Group 2	49	3.750	14.063
$M_2 = 45.25$	52	6.750	45.563
	41	−4.250	18.063
	39	−6.250	39.063
Group 3	36	−6.333	40.107
$M_3 = 42.333$	49	6.667	44.449
	42	−0.333	0.111
$GM = 38.73$			$SS_{within} = 314.419$

c. Between-groups sum of squares is calculated here as $SS_{between} = \Sigma(M - GM)^2$:

Sample	X	(M − GM)	(M − GM)²
Group 1	37	−9.227	85.138
$M_1 = 29.5$	30	−9.227	85.138
	22	−9.227	85.138
	29	−9.227	85.138
Group 2	49	6.523	42.550
$M_2 = 45.25$	52	6.523	42.550
	41	6.523	42.550
	39	6.523	42.550
Group 3	36	3.606	13.003
$M_3 = 42.333$	49	3.606	13.003
	42	3.606	13.003
$GM = 38.73$			$SS_{between} = 549.761$

12-10 $MS_{between} = \dfrac{SS_{between}}{df_{between}} = \dfrac{549.761}{2} = 274.881$

$MS_{within} = \dfrac{SS_{within}}{df_{within}} = \dfrac{314.419}{8} = 39.302$

$F = \dfrac{SS_{between}}{df_{within}} = \dfrac{274.881}{39.302} = 6.99$

Source	SS	df	MS	F
Between	549.761	2	274.881	6.99
Within	314.419	8	39.302	
Total	864.187	10		

12-11 a. According to the null hypothesis, there are no mean differences in efficacy among these three treatment conditions; they would all come from one underlying distribution. The research hypothesis states that there are mean differences in efficacy across some or all of these treatment conditions.

b. There are three assumptions: that the participants were selected randomly, that the underlying populations are normally distributed, and that the underlying populations have similar variances. Although we can't say much about the first two assumptions, we can assess the last one using the sample data.

Sample	Group 1	Group 2	Group 3
Squared deviations of scores from sample means	56.25	14.063	40.107
	0.25	45.563	44.449
	56.25	18.063	0.111
	0.25	39.063	
Sum of squares	113	116.752	84.667
$N - 1$	3	3	2
Variance	37.67	38.92	42.33

Because these variances are all close together, with the biggest being no more than twice as large as the smallest, we can conclude that we meet the third assumption of homoscedastic samples.

c. The critical value for F with a p value of 0.05, two between-groups degrees of freedom, and 8 within-groups degrees of freedom, is 4.46. The F statistic exceeds this cutoff, so we can reject the null hypothesis. There are mean differences between these three groups, but we do not know where.

12-12 If we are able to reject the null hypothesis when conducting an ANOVA, then we must also conduct a post hoc test, such as a Tukey HSD test, to determine which pairs of means are significantly different from one another.

12-13 R^2 tells us the proportion of variance in the dependent variable that is accounted for by the independent variable.

12-14 a. $R^2 = \dfrac{SS_{between}}{SS_{total}} = \dfrac{336.360}{522.782} = 0.64$

b. Children's grade level accounted for 64% of the variability in reaction time. This is a large effect.

12-15 The number of levels of the independent variable is 3 and df_{within} is 32. At a p level of 0.05, the critical values of the q statistic are -3.49 and 3.49.

12-16 The adjusted p level is the p level for the experiment divided by the number of comparisons being made, which in this case is $\dfrac{0.05}{3} = 0.017$.

12-17 Because we have unequal sample sizes, we must calculate a weighted sample size.

$$N = \dfrac{N_{groups}}{\sum\left(\dfrac{1}{N}\right)} = \dfrac{3}{\left(\dfrac{1}{4} + \dfrac{1}{4} + \dfrac{1}{3}\right)}$$

$$= \dfrac{3}{0.25 + 0.25 + 0.333} = \dfrac{3}{0.833} = 3.601$$

$s_M = \sqrt{\dfrac{MS_{within}}{N'}}$, then equals $\sqrt{\dfrac{39.302}{3.601}} = 3.304$

Now we can compare the three treatment groups.

Psychodynamic therapy ($M = 29.50$) versus interpersonal therapy ($M = 45.25$):

$$HSD = \dfrac{29.50 - 45.25}{3.304} = -4.77$$

Psychodynamic therapy ($M = 29.5$) versus cognitive-behavioral therapy ($M = 42.333$):

$$HSD = \dfrac{29.50 - 42.333}{3.304} = -3.88$$

Interpersonal therapy ($M = 45.25$) versus cognitive-behavioral therapy ($M = 42.333$):

$$HSD = \dfrac{45.25 - 42.333}{3.304} = 0.88$$

We look up the critical value for this post hoc test on the q table. We look in the row for 8 within-groups degrees of freedom, and then in the column for 3 treatment groups. At a p level of 0.05, the value in the q table is 4.04, so the cutoffs are -4.04 and 4.04.

We have just one significant difference, which is between psychodynamic therapy and interpersonal therapy: Tukey $HSD = -4.77$. Specifically, clients responded at statistically significantly higher rates to interpersonal therapy than to psychodynamic therapy, with a difference between means of 15.75 points on this scale.

12-18 Effect size is calculated as

$$R^2 = \dfrac{SS_{between}}{SS_{total}} = \dfrac{549.761}{864.187} = 0.64$$

According to Cohen's conventions for R^2, this is a very large effect.

Chapter 13

13-1 For the one-way between-groups ANOVA, we calculate one kind of variability that occurs within groups: within-groups variability. But for the one-way within-groups ANOVA, the variability that occurs within groups is divided into two types: subjects variability and within-groups variability. Subjects variability assesses how much each person's overall mean differs from the others', assessed by comparing each person's mean score to the grand mean. We can remove this from the within-groups variability because we have the same people in each group, and they would be the same across levels of the independent variable on many variables that may affect the dependent variable. This makes the within-groups variability smaller.

13-2 a. $df_{between} = N_{groups} - 1 = 3 - 1 = 2$

b. $df_{subjects} = n - 1 = 3 - 1 = 2$

c. $df_{within} = (df_{between})(df_{subjects}) = (2)(2) = 4$

d. $df_{total} = df_{between} + df_{subjects} + df_{within} = 2 + 2 + 4 = 8$; or we can calculate it as $df_{total} = N_{total} - 1 = 9 - 1 = 8$

13-3 a. $SS_{total} = \Sigma(X - GM)^2 = 24.886$

Group	Rating (X)	X − GM	(X − GM)²
1	7	0.111	0.012
1	9	2.111	4.456
1	8	1.111	1.234
2	5	−1.889	3.568
2	8	1.111	1.234
2	9	2.111	4.456
3	6	−0.889	0.790
3	4	−2.889	8.346
3	6	−0.889	0.790

$GM = 6.889$ $\quad\quad \Sigma(X - GM)^2 = 24.886$

b. $SS_{between} = \Sigma(M - GM)^2 = 11.556$

Group	Rating (X)	Group Mean (M)	M − GM	(M − GM)²
1	7	8	1.111	1.234
1	9	8	1.111	1.234
1	8	8	1.111	1.234
2	5	7.333	0.444	0.197
2	8	7.333	0.444	0.197
2	9	7.333	0.444	0.197
3	6	5.333	−1.556	2.421
3	4	5.333	−1.556	2.421
3	6	5.333	−1.556	2.421

$GM = 6.889$ $\quad\quad \Sigma(M - GM)^2 = 11.556$

c. $SS_{subject} = \Sigma(M_{participant} - GM)^2 = 4.221$

Participant	Group	Rating (X)	Participant Mean ($M_{participant}$)	$M_{participant} - GM$	$(M_{participant} - GM)^2$
1	1	7	6	−0.889	0.790
2	1	9	7	0.111	0.012
3	1	8	7.667	0.778	0.605
1	2	5	6	−0.889	0.790
2	2	8	7	0.111	0.012
3	2	9	7.667	0.778	0.605
1	3	6	6	−0.889	0.790
2	3	4	7	0.111	0.012
3	3	6	7.667	0.778	0.605

$GM = 6.889$ $\quad\quad \Sigma(M_{participant} - GM)^2 = 4.221$

d. $SS_{within} = SS_{total} - SS_{between} - SS_{subjects}$
$= 24.886 - 11.556 - 4.221 = 9.109$

13-4 $MS_{between} = \dfrac{SS_{between}}{df_{between}} = \dfrac{11.556}{2} = 5.778$

$MS_{subjects} = \dfrac{SS_{subjects}}{df_{subjects}} = \dfrac{4.221}{2} = 2.111$

$MS_{within} = \dfrac{SS_{within}}{df_{within}} = \dfrac{9.109}{4} = 2.277$

$F_{between} = \dfrac{SS_{between}}{df_{within}} = \dfrac{5.778}{2.277} = 2.538$

$F_{subjects} = \dfrac{SS_{subjects}}{df_{within}} = \dfrac{2.111}{2.277} = 0.927$

Source	SS	df	MS	F
Between-groups	11.556	2	5.778	2.54
Subjects	4.221	2	2.111	0.93
Within-groups	9.109	4	2.277	
Total	24.886	8		

13-5 a. Null hypothesis: People rate the driving experience of these three cars the same, on average—H_0: $\mu_1 = \mu_2 = \mu_3$. Research hypothesis: People do not rate the driving experience of these three cars the same, on average.

b. Order effects are addressed by counterbalancing. We could create a list of random orders of the three cars to be driven. Then, as a new customer arrives, we would assign him or her to the next random order on the list. With a large enough sample size (much larger than the three participants we used in this example), we could feel confident that this assumption would be met using this approach.

c. The critical value for the F statistic for a p level of 0.05 and 2 and 4 degrees of freedom is 6.95. The between-groups

F statistic of 2.54 does not exceed this critical value. We cannot reject the null hypothesis, so we cannot conclude that there are differences among mean ratings of cars.

13-6 In both cases, the numerator in the ratio is $SS_{between}$, but the denominators differ in the two cases. For the between-groups ANOVA, the denominator of the R^2 calculation is SS_{total}. For the within-groups ANOVA, the denominator of the R^2 calculation is $SS_{total} - SS_{subjects}$, which takes into account the fact that we are subtracting out the variability caused by differences among participants (subjects sum of square) from the measure of error.

13-7 There are no differences in the way that the Tukey HSD is calculated. The formula for the calculation of the Tukey HSD is exactly the same for both the between-groups ANOVA and the within-groups ANOVA.

13-8 a. First, we calculate s_M:

$$s_M = \sqrt{\frac{MS_{within}}{N}} = \sqrt{\frac{771.256}{6}} = 11.338$$

Next, we calculate HSD for each pair of means.

For time 1 versus time 2:

$$HSD = \frac{(155.833 - 206.833)}{11.338} = -4.498$$

For time 1 versus time 3:

$$HSD = \frac{(155.833 - 251.667)}{11.338} = -8.452$$

For time 2 versus time 3:

$$HSD = \frac{(206.833 - 251.667)}{11.338} = -3.954$$

b. We have an independent variable with three levels and $df_{within} = 10$, so the q cutoff value at a p level of 0.05 is 3.88. Because we are performing a two-tailed test, the cutoff values are 3.88 and -3.88.

c. We reject the null hypothesis for all three of the mean comparisons because all of the HSD calculations exceed the critical value of -3.88. This tells us that all three of the group means are statistically significantly different from one another.

13-9 $R^2 = \dfrac{SS_{between}}{SS_{total} - SS_{subjects}} = \dfrac{27{,}590.486}{(52{,}115.111 - 16{,}812.189)} = 0.78$

13-10 a. $R^2 = \dfrac{SS_{between}}{(SS_{total} - SS_{subjects})} = \dfrac{11.556}{(24.886 - 4.221)} = 0.56$

This is a large effect size.

b. Because the F statistic did not exceed the critical value, we failed to reject the null hypothesis. As a result, Tukey HSD tests are not necessary.

Chapter 14

14-1 A factorial ANOVA is a statistical analysis used with one scale dependent variable and at least two nominal (or sometimes ordinal) independent variables (also called factors).

14-2 A statistical interaction occurs in a factorial design when the two independent variables have an effect in combination that we do not see when we examine each independent variable on its own.

14-3 a. There are two factors: diet programs and exercise programs.

b. There are three factors: diet programs, exercise programs, and metabolism type.

c. There is one factor: gift certificate value.

d. There are two factors: gift certificate value and store quality.

14-4 a. The participants are the stocks themselves.

b. One independent variable is the type of ticker-code name, with two levels: pronounceable and unpronounceable. The second independent variable is time lapsed since the stock was initially offered, with four levels: 1 day, 1 week, 6 months, and 1 year.

c. The dependent variable is the stocks' selling price.

d. This would be a two-way mixed-design ANOVA.

e. This would be a 2×4 mixed-design ANOVA.

f. This study would have eight cells: $2 \times 4 = 8$. We multiplied the numbers of levels of each of the two independent variables.

14-5 A *quantitative interaction* is an interaction in which one independent variable exhibits a strengthening or weakening of its effect at one or more levels of the other independent variable, but the direction of the initial effect does not change. More specifically, the effect of one independent variable is modified in the presence of another independent variable. A *qualitative interaction* is a particular type of quantitative interaction of two (or more) independent variables in which one independent variable reverses its effect depending on the level of the other independent variable. In a qualitative interaction, the effect of one variable doesn't just become stronger or weaker; it actually reverses direction in the presence of another variable.

14-6 An interaction indicates that the effect of one independent variable depends on the level of the other independent variable(s). The main effect alone cannot be interpreted because the effect of that one variable depends on another.

14-7 a. There are four cells.

		IV 2	
		Level A	Level B
IV 1	Level A		
	Level B		

b.

		IV 2	
		Level A	Level B
IV 1	Level A	$M = (2 + 1 + 1 + 3)/4$ $= 1.75$	$M = (2 + 3 + 3 + 3)/4$ $= 2.75$
	Level B	$M = (5 + 4 + 3 + 4)/4$ $= 4$	$M = (3 + 2 + 2 + 3)/4$ $= 2.5$

c. Because the sample size is the same for each cell, we can compute marginal means as simply the average between cell means.

		IV 2		Marginal means
		Level A	Level B	
IV I	Level A	1.75	2.75	2.25
	Level B	4	2.5	3.25
	Marginal means	2.875	2.625	

d.

14-8 a. The independent variables are gender and attractiveness. For gender, there are two levels: male and female. For attractiveness, there are three levels: below average, average, and above average.

b. The dependent variable is GPA. GPA is a scale variable.

c. There are two independent variables and one dependent variable for these data. The two independent variables are nominal (or, in the case of attractiveness, ordinal, but can be interpreted as nominal) and the dependent variable is continuous. A two-way between-groups ANOVA would be the appropriate hypothesis test because it allows us to compare the levels from two independent variables. Additionally, a two-way between-groups ANOVA allows us to compare the combined effects of these two variables on the dependent variable. In this example, a two-way between-groups ANOVA allows us to compare the combined effect of gender and attractiveness on GPA instead of simply looking at each independent variable separately.

d. The results indicate that there is a significant interaction because the effect of attractiveness only holds true for female students. Female students who were more attractive had higher GPA scores. However, this pattern did not hold true for male students. For men, there were not statistically significant differences in their GPAs, on average, based on ratings of attractiveness.

e. Here is one possible solution.

	Level of attractiveness		
	Below average	Average	Above average
Men	3.3	3.2	3.35
Women	3.0	3.25	3.55

f. The results suggest that this is a quantitative interaction: among women, grades were higher as they had increasingly higher levels of attractiveness, whereas there were not significant differences among the men at different levels of attractiveness. If the reverse had happened among male students—a decrease in grades associated with higher levels of attractiveness—this would be considered a qualitative interaction.

g. We don't necessarily know why attractive women receive better grades. It is possible that attractive women receive better grades because of professor bias. But it also is possible that prettier women are simply brighter. This second possibility has the potential to be a confound in the study—an alternative explanation for the finding. The second study eliminated the potential for professors to see a student's physical appearance because the study included online courses, so professors likely could not see a student's physical appearance. However, students were still ranked as below average, average, and above average as in the original study. When this potential confound (attractiveness bias from professors) was eliminated, the attractiveness effect on GPA for women was no longer statistically significant. The second study eliminated the possible confounding variable of intelligence. Attractive women are not necessarily smarter, but they do tend to receive higher grades as a result of their attractiveness. So, it seems as if there is professor bias toward attractive female students.

14-9 Hypothesis testing for a one-way between-groups ANOVA evaluates only one idea. However, hypothesis testing for a two-way between-groups ANOVA evaluates three ideas: two main effects and an interaction. So, the two-way ANOVA requires three hypotheses, three comparison distributions, three critical F values, three F statistics, and three conclusions.

14-10 Variability is associated with the two main effects, the interaction, and the within-groups component.

14-11 $df_{IV1} = df_{rows} = N_{rows} - 1 = 2 - 1 = 1$

$df_{IV2} = df_{columns} = N_{columns} - 1 = 2 - 1 = 1$

$df_{interaction} = (df_{rows})(df_{columns}) = (1)(1) = 1$

$df_{within} = df_{1A,2A} + df_{1A,2B} + df_{1B,2A} + df_{1B,2B} = 3 + 3 + 3 + 3 = 12$

$df_{total} = N_{total} - 1 = 16 - 1 = 15$

We can also verify that this calculation is correct by adding all of the other degrees of freedom together: $1 + 1 + 1 + 12 = 15$.

14-12 The critical value for the main effect of the first independent variable, based on a between-groups degrees of freedom of 1 and a within-groups degrees of freedom of 12, is 4.75. The critical value for the main effect of the second independent variable, based on 1 and 12 degrees of freedom, is 4.75. The critical value for the interaction, based on 1 and 12 degrees of freedom, is 4.75.

14-13 a. Population 1 is students who received an initial grade of C who received e-mail messages aimed at bolstering self-esteem. Population 2 is students who received an initial grade of C who received e-mail messages aimed at bolstering their sense of control over their grades. Population 3 is students who received an initial grade of C who received e-mails with just review questions. Population 4 is students who received an initial grade of D or F who received e-mail messages aimed at bolstering self-esteem. Population 5 is students who received an initial grade of D or F who received e-mail messages aimed at bolstering their sense of control over their grades. Population 6 is students who received an initial grade of D or F who received emails with just review questions.

b. *Step 2:* Main effect of first independent variable—initial grade:

Null hypothesis: The mean final exam grade of students with an initial grade of C is the same as that of students with an initial grade of D or F. H_0: $\mu_C = \mu_{D/F}$.

Research hypothesis: The mean final exam grade of students with an initial grade of C is not the same as that of students with an initial grade of D or F. H_1: $\mu_C \neq \mu_{D/F}$.

Main effect of second independent variable—type of email:

Null hypothesis: On average, the mean exam grades among those receiving different types of e-mails are the same—H_0: $\mu_{SE} = \mu_{CG} = \mu_{TR}$.

Research hypothesis: On average, the mean exam grades among those receiving different types of e-mails are not the same.

Interaction: Initial grade $\times$ type of e-mail:

Null hypothesis: The effect of type of e-mail is not dependent on the levels of initial grade.

Research hypothesis: The effect of type of e-mail depends on the levels of initial grade.

c. Step 3: $df_{between/grade} + N_{groups} - 1 = 2 - 1 = 1$

$df_{between/e\text{-}mail} = N_{groups} - 1 = 3 - 1 = 2$

$df_{interaction} = (df_{between/grade})(df_{between/e\text{-}mail}) = (1)(2) = 2$

$df_{C,SE} = N - 1 = 14 - 1 = 13$

$df_{C,C} = N - 1 = 14 - 1 = 13$

$df_{C,TR} = N - 1 = 14 - 1 = 13$

$df_{D/F,SE} = N - 1 = 14 - 1 = 13$

$df_{D/F,C} = N - 1 = 14 - 1 = 13$

$df_{D/F,TR} = N - 1 = 14 - 1 = 13$

$df_{within} = df_{C,SE} + df_{C,C} + df_{C,TR} + df_{D/F,SE} + df_{D/F,C} + df_{D/F,TR} = 13 + 13 + 13 + 13 + 13 + 13 = 78$

Main effect of initial grade: F distribution with 1 and 78 degrees of freedom

Main effect of type of e-mail: F distribution with 2 and 78 degrees of freedom

Main effect of interaction of initial grade and type of e-mail: F distribution with 2 and 78 degrees of freedom

d. *Step 4:* Note that when the specific degrees of freedom is not in the F table, you should choose the more conservative—that is, larger—cutoff. In this case, go with the cutoffs for a within-groups degrees of freedom of 75 rather than 80. The three cutoffs are:

Main effect of initial grade: 3.97

Main effect of type of e-mail: 3.12

Interaction of initial grade and type of e-mail: 3.12

e. *Step 6:* There is a significant main effect of initial grade because the F statistic, 20.84, is larger than the critical value of 3.97. The marginal means, seen in the accompanying table, tell us that students who earned a C on the initial exam have higher scores on the final exam, on average, than do students who earned a D or an F on the initial exam. There is no statistically significant main effect of type of e-mail, however. The F statistic of 1.69 is not larger than the critical value of 3.12. Had this main effect been significant, we would have conducted a post hoc test to determine where the differences were. There also is not a significant interaction. The F statistic of 3.02 is not larger than the critical value of 3.12. (Had we used a cutoff based on a p level of 0.10, we would have rejected the null hypothesis for the interaction. The cutoff for a p level of 0.10 is 2.38.) If we had rejected the null hypothesis for the interaction, we would have examined the cell means in tabular and graph form.

	Self-esteem	Take responsibility	Control group	Marginal means
C	67.31	69.83	71.12	69.42
D/F	47.83	60.98	62.13	56.98
Marginal means	57.57	65.41	66.63	

Chapter 15

15-1 (1) The correlation coefficient can be either positive or negative. (2) The correlation coefficient always falls between -1.00 and 1.00. (3) It is the strength, also called the *magnitude*, of the coefficient, not its sign, that indicates how large it is.

15-2 When two variables are correlated, there can be multiple explanations for that association. The first variable can cause the second variable; the second variable can cause the first variable; or a third variable can cause both the first and second variables. In fact, there may be more than one "third" variable causing both the first and second variables.

15-3 a. According to Cohen, this is a large (strong) correlation. Note that the sign (negative in this case) is not related to the assessment of strength.

b. This is just above a medium correlation.

c. This is lower than the guideline for a small correlation, 0.10.

15-4 Students will draw a variety of different scatterplots. The important thing to note is the closeness of data points to an imaginary line drawn through the data.

a. A scatterplot for a correlation coefficient of −0.60 might look like this:

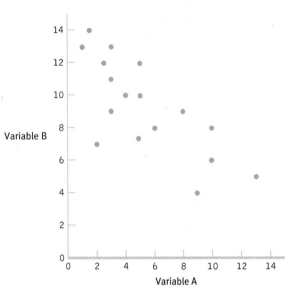

b. A scatterplot for a correlation coefficient of 0.35 might look like this:

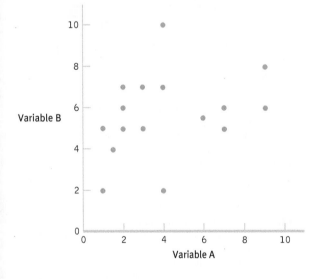

c. A scatterplot for a correlation coefficient of 0.04 might look like this:

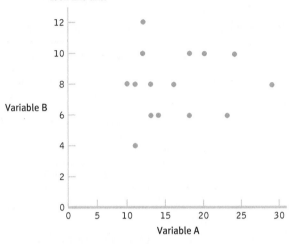

15-5 It is possible that training while listening to music (A) causes an increase in a country's average finishing time (B), perhaps because music decreases one's focus on running. It is also possible that high average finishing times (B) cause an increase in the percentage of marathon runners in a country who train while listening to music (A), perhaps because slow runners tend to get bored and need music to get through their runs. It also is possible that a third variable, such as a country's level of wealth (C), causes a higher percentage of runners who train while listening to music (because of the higher presence of technology in wealthy countries) (A) and also causes higher (slower) finishing times (perhaps because long-distance running is a less popular sport in wealthy countries with access to so many sport and entertainment options) (B). Without a true experiment, we cannot know the direction of causality.

15-6 The Pearson correlation coefficient is a statistic that quantifies a linear relation between two scale variables. Specifically, it describes the direction and strength of the relation between the variables.

15-7 The two issues are variability and sample size.

15-8

15-9 Step 1 is calculating the numerator:

Variable A (X)	(X − M_x)	Variable B (Y)	(Y − M_y)	(X − M_x) (Y − M_y)
8	1.812	14	3.187	5.775
7	0.812	13	2.187	1.776
6	−0.188	10	−0.813	0.153
5	−1.188	9.5	−1.313	1.56
4	−2.188	8	−2.813	6.155
5.5	−0.688	9	−1.813	1.247
6	−0.188	12	1.187	−0.223
8	1.812	11	0.187	0.339

$M_X = 6.118$ $M_Y = 10.813$ $\Sigma[(X − M_X)(Y − M_Y)] = 16.782$

Step 2 is calculating the denominator:

Variable A (X)	(X − M_x)	(X − M_x)²	Variable B (Y)	(Y − M_Y)	(Y − M_Y)²
8	1.812	3.283	14	3.187	10.157
7	0.812	0.659	13	2.187	4.783
6	−0.188	0.035	10	−0.813	0.661
5	−1.188	1.411	9.5	−1.313	1.724
4	−2.188	4.787	8	−2.813	7.913
5.5	−0.688	0.473	9	−1.813	3.287
6	−0.188	0.035	12	1.187	1.409
8	1.812	3.283	11	0.187	0.035

$\Sigma(X − M_X)^2 = 13.966$ $\Sigma(Y − M_Y)^2 = 29.969$

$$\sqrt{(SS_X)(SS_Y)} = \sqrt{(13.966)(29.969)} = \sqrt{418.547} = 20.458$$

Step 3 is computing r:

$$r = \frac{\Sigma[(X − M_X)(Y − M_Y)]}{\sqrt{(SS_X)(SS_Y)}} = \frac{16.782}{20.458} = 0.82$$

15-10 Step 1: Population 1: Children like those we studied. Population 2: Children for whom there is no relation between observed and performed acts of aggression. The comparison distribution is made up of correlations based on samples of this size, 8 people, selected from the population.

We do not know if the data were randomly selected, the first assumption, so we must be cautious when generalizing the findings. We also do not know if the underlying population distributions for witnessed aggression and performed acts of aggression by children are normally distributed. The sample size is too small to make any conclusions about this assumption, so we should proceed with caution. The third assumption, unique to correlation, is that the variability of one variable is equal across the levels of the other variable. Because we have such a small data set, it is difficult to evaluate this. However,

we can see from the scatterplot that the data are somewhat consistently variable.

Step 2: Null hypothesis: There is no correlation between the levels of witnessed and performed acts of aggression among children—$H_0: \rho = 0$. Research hypothesis: There is a correlation between the levels of witnessed and performed acts of aggression among children—$H_1: \rho \neq 0$.

Step 3: The comparison distribution is a distribution of Pearson correlations, r, with the following degrees of freedom: $df_r = N − 2 = 8 − 2 = 6$.

Step 4: The critical values for an r distribution with 6 degrees of freedom for a two-tailed test with a p level of 0.05 are −0.707 and 0.707.

Step 5: This was computed in the previous exercise.

Step 6: The test statistic, $r = 0.82$, is larger in magnitude than the critical value of 0.707. We can reject the null hypothesis and conclude that a strong positive correlation exists between the number of witnessed acts of aggression and the number of acts of aggression performed by children.

15-11 Psychometricians calculate correlations when assessing the reliability and validity of measures and tests.

15-12 Coefficient alpha is a measure of reliability. To calculate coefficient alpha, we take, in essence, the average of all split-half correlations. That is, the items on a test are split in half and the correlation of those two halves is calculated. This process is done repeatedly for all possible "halves" of the test, and then the average of those correlations is obtained.

15-13 a. The test does not have sufficient reliability to be used as a diagnostic tool. As stated in the chapter, when using tests to diagnose or make statements about the ability of individuals, a reliability of at least 0.90 is necessary.

b. We do not have enough information to determine whether the test is valid. The coefficient alpha tells us only about the reliability of the test.

c. To assess the validity of the test, we would need the correlation between this measure and other measures of reading ability or between this measure and students' grades in the nonremedial class (i.e., do students who perform very poorly in the nonremedial reading class also perform poorly on this measure?).

15-14 a. The psychometrician could assess test–retest reliability by administering the quiz to 100 readers who have boyfriends, and then one week later readministering the test to the same 100 readers. If their scores at the two times are highly correlated, the test would have high test–retest reliability. She also could calculate a coefficient alpha using computer software. The computer would essentially calculate correlations for every possible two groups of five items and then calculate the average of all of these split-half correlations.

b. The psychometrician could assess validity by choosing criteria that she believed assessed the underlying construct of interest, a boyfriend's devotion to his partner. There are many possible criteria. For example, she could correlate the quiz scores with the amount of money each participant's boyfriend spent on his partner's most recent birthday, the number of minutes the participant spent on the phone with his or her boyfriend today, or the number of months the relationship ends up lasting.

c. Of course, we assume that these other measures actually assess the underlying construct of a boyfriend's devotion, which may or may not be true! For example, the amount of money that the boyfriend spent on the participant's last birthday might be a measure of his income, not his devotion.

Chapter 16

16-1 Simple linear regression is a statistical tool that lets statisticians predict the score on a scale dependent variable from the score on a scale independent variable.

16-2 The regression line allows us to make predictions about one variable based on what we know about another variable. It gives us a visual representation of what we believe is the underlying relation between the variables, based on the data we have available to us.

16-3 a. $z_X = \dfrac{X - M_X}{SD_X} = \dfrac{67 - 64}{2} = 1.5$

b. $z_{\hat{Y}} = (r_{XY})(z_X) = (0.28)(1.5) = 0.42$

c. $\hat{Y} = z_{\hat{Y}}(SD_Y) + M_Y = (0.42)(15) + 155 = 161.3$ pounds

16-4 a. $\hat{Y} = 12 + 0.67\,(X) = 12 + 0.67\,(78) = 64.26$

b. $\hat{Y} = 12 + 0.67\,(-14) = 2.62$

c. $\hat{Y} = 12 + 0.67\,(52) = 46.84$

16-5 a. $z_X = \dfrac{(X - M_X)}{SD_X} = \dfrac{(0 - 9.5)}{3.304} = -2.875$

$z_{\hat{Y}} = (r_{XY})(z_X) = 0.353(-2.875) = -1.015$

$\hat{Y} = z_Y(SD_Y) + M_Y = -1.015(3.752) + 21.083 = 17.275$

b. $z_X = \dfrac{(X - M_X)}{SD_X} = \dfrac{(1 - 9.5)}{3.304} = -2.573$

$z_{\hat{Y}} = (r_{XY})(z_X) = 0.353(-2.573) = -0.908$

$\hat{Y} = z_Y(SD_Y) + M_Y = -0.908(3.752) + 21.083 = 17.676$

$b = 17.676 - 17.275 = 0.401$

c. The regression equation for these data is:

$\hat{Y} = 17.28 + 0.40(X)$.

d. The y intercept tells us what the value of $\hat{Y}$ is when X is 0. In this example, when X is 0, $\hat{Y}$ is 17.28. This means that when someone says zero taboo words in one minute, they will, on average, say 17.28 animal words in one minute.

The slope tells us how much $\hat{Y}$ changes with every one unit increase in X. In this example, for each additional taboo word a person says, we would expect them to say about 0.4 more animal words.

e. $\beta = (b)\dfrac{\sqrt{SS_X}}{\sqrt{SS_Y}} = 0.4\dfrac{\sqrt{131}}{\sqrt{168.918}} = 0.353$

f. A stronger correlation means that the predictions made from the regression line will be more accurate.

g. The steps for a hypothesis test of a standardized regression coefficient are the same for a correlation coefficient. In Exercise 15.51, we failed to reject the null hypothesis: the test statistic, $r = .35$, is not larger in magnitude than the critical value of .576. We can conclude the same if we were to complete a hypothesis test for the standardized regression coefficient.

16-6 The standard error of the estimate is a statistic that indicates the typical distance between a regression line and the actual data points. When we do not have enough information to compute a regression equation, we often use the mean as the "best guess." The error of prediction when the mean is used is typically greater than the standard error of the estimate.

16-7 Strong correlations mean highly accurate predictions with regression. This translates into a large proportionate reduction in error.

16-8 a.

X	Y	Mean For Y (M_Y)	Error ($Y - M_Y$)	Squared Error ($Y - M_Y)^2$
5	6	5.333	0.667	0.445
6	5	5.333	−0.333	0.111
4	6	5.333	0.667	0.445
5	6	5.333	0.667	0.445
7	4	5.333	−1.333	1.777
8	5	5.333	−0.333	0.111

$$SS_{total} = \Sigma(Y - M_Y)^2 = 3.334$$

b.

X	Y	Regression Equation	$\hat{Y}$	Error $(Y - \hat{Y})$	Squared Error
5	6	$\hat{Y} = 7.846 - 0.431\,(5) =$	5.691	0.309	0.095
6	5	$\hat{Y} = 7.846 - 0.431\,(6) =$	5.260	−0.260	0.068
4	6	$\hat{Y} = 7.846 - 0.431\,(4) =$	6.122	−0.122	0.015
5	6	$\hat{Y} = 7.846 - 0.431\,(5) =$	5.691	0.309	0.095
7	4	$\hat{Y} = 7.846 - 0.431\,(7) =$	4.829	−0.829	0.687
8	5	$\hat{Y} = 7.846 - 0.431\,(8) =$	4.398	0.602	0.362

$$SS_{error} = \Sigma(Y - \hat{Y})^2 = 1.322$$

c. We have reduced error from 3.334 to 1.322, which is a reduction of 2.012. Now we calculate this reduction as a proportion of the total error:

$$\dfrac{2.012}{3.334} = 0.603$$

This can also be written as:

$$r^2 = \dfrac{(SS_{total} - SS_{error})}{SS_{total}} = \dfrac{(3.334 - 1.322)}{3.334} = 0.603$$

We have reduced 0.603, or 60.3%, of error using the regression equation as an improvement over the use of the mean as our predictor.

d. $r^2 = (-0.77)(-0.77) = 0.593$, which closely matches our calculation of r^2 above, 0.603. These numbers are slightly different due to rounding decisions.

16-9 Tell Coach Parcells that prediction suffers from the same limitations as correlation. First, just because two variables are associated doesn't mean one causes the other. This is not a true experiment, and if we didn't randomly assign athletes to appear on a *Sports Illustrated* cover or not, then we cannot determine whether a cover appearance causes sporting failure. Moreover, we have a limited range; by definition, those lauded on the cover are the best in sports. Would the association be different among those with a wider range of athletic ability? Finally, and most important, there is the very strong possibility of regression to the mean. Those chosen for a cover appearance are at the very top of their game. There is nowhere to go but down, so it is not surprising that those who merit a cover appearance would soon thereafter experience a decline. There's likely no need to avoid that cover, Coach.

16-10 Multiple regression is a statistical tool that predicts a dependent variable by using two or more independent variables as predictors. It is an improvement over simple linear regression, which only allows one independent variable to inform predictions.

16-11 $\hat{Y} = 5.251 + 0.06(X_1) + 1.105(X_2)$

16-12 a. $\hat{Y} = 5.251 + 0.06(40) + 1.105(14) = 23.12$

b. $\hat{Y} = 5.251 + 0.06(101) + 1.105(39) = 54.41$

c. $\hat{Y} = 5.251 + 0.06(76) + 1.105(20) = 31.91$

16-13 a. The independent variable is how far a customer lives from an office supply store that is a competitor to Staples. The dependent variable is the price of various items at Staples. Distance to a store predicts the price of a product, such that people who live farther from a competitor are being charged higher prices at Staples. This an example of a simple linear regression because there is only one predictor variable.

b. There are several independent variables in this example: criminal record, age, job history, and patterns of crime within the person's family. The dependent variable is the likelihood that an individual would become a repeat offender. This is an example of a multiple regression because there are several independent variables predicting the dependent variable, likelihood that an individual would become a repeat offender.

Chapter 17

17-1 A parametric test is based on a set of assumptions about the population, whereas a nonparametric test is a statistical analysis that is not based on assumptions about the population.

17-2 We use nonparametric tests when the data violate the assumptions about the population that parametric tests make. The three most common situations that call for nonparametric tests are (1) having a nominal dependent variable, (2) having an ordinal dependent variable, and (3) having a small sample size with possible skew.

17-3 a. The independent variable is city, a nominal variable. The dependent variable is whether a woman is pretty or not so pretty, an ordinal variable.

b. The independent variable is city, a nominal variable. The dependent variable is beauty, assessed on a scale of 1–10. This is a scale variable.

c. The independent variable is intelligence, likely a scale variable. The dependent variable is beauty, assessed on a scale of 1–10. This is a scale variable.

d. The independent variable is ranking on intelligence, an ordinal variable. The dependent variable is ranking on beauty, also an ordinal variable.

17-4 a. We'd choose a hypothesis test from category III. We'd use a nonparametric test because the dependent variable is not scale and would not meet the primary assumption of a normally distributed dependent variable, even with a large sample.

b. We'd choose a test from category II because the independent variable is nominal and the dependent variable is scale. (In fact, we'd use a one-way between-groups ANOVA because there is only one independent variable and it has more than two levels.)

c. We'd choose a hypothesis test from category I because we have a scale independent variable and a scale dependent variable. (If we were assessing the relation between these variables, we'd use the Pearson correlation coefficient. If we wondered whether intelligence predicted beauty, we'd use simple linear regression.)

d. We'd choose a hypothesis test from category III because both the independent and dependent variables are ordinal. We would not meet the assumption of having a normal distribution of the dependent variable, even if we had a large sample.

17-5 We use chi-square tests when all variables are nominal.

17-6 Observed frequencies indicate how often something actually happens in a given category based on the data we collected. Expected frequencies indicate how often we expect something to happen in a given category based on what is known about the population according to the null hypothesis.

17-7 a. $df_{\chi^2} = k - 1 = 2 - 1 = 1$

b. Observed:

Clear Blue Skies	Unclear Skies
59 days	19 days

Expected:

Clear Blue Skies	Unclear Skies
$(78)(0.80) = 62.4$ days	$(78)(0.20) = 15.6$ days

c.

Category	Observed (O)	Expected (E)	O − E	(O − E)²	$\frac{(O-E)^2}{E}$
Clear blue skies	59	62.4	−3.4	11.56	0.185
Unclear skies	19	15.6	3.4	11.56	0.741

$$\chi^2 = \Sigma\left[\frac{(O-E)^2}{E}\right] = 0.185 + 0.741 = 0.93$$

17-8 a. The participants are the lineups. The independent variable is type of lineup (simultaneous, sequential), and the dependent variable is outcome of the lineup (suspect identification, other identification, no identification).

b. *Step 1:* Population 1 is police lineups like those we observed. Population 2 is police lineups for which type of lineup and outcome are independent. The comparison distribution is a chi-square distribution. The hypothesis test is a chi-square test for independence because we have two nominal variables. This study meets three of the four assumptions. The two variables are nominal; every participant (lineup) is in only one cell; and there are more than five times as many participants as cells (8 participants and 6 cells).

Step 2: Null hypothesis: Lineup outcome is independent of type of lineup.

Research hypothesis: Lineup outcome depends on type of lineup.

Step 3: The comparison distribution is a chi-square distribution with 2 degrees of freedom:

$$df_{\chi2} = (k_{row} - 1)(k_{column} - 1) = (2 - 1)(3 - 1) = (1)(2) = 2$$

Step 4: The cutoff chi-square statistic, based on a *p* level of 0.05 and 2 degrees of freedom, is 5.992. (*Note:* It is helpful to include a drawing of the chi-square distribution with the cutoff.)

Step 5:

	Observed		
	Suspect ID	Other ID	No ID
Simultaneous	191	8	120	319
Sequential	102	20	107	229
	293	28	227	548

We can calculate the expected frequencies in one of two ways. First, we can think about it. Out of the total of 548 lineups, 293 led to identification of the suspect, an identification rate of 293/548 = 0.535, or 53.5%. If identification were independent of type of lineup, we would expect the same rate for each type of lineup. For example, for the 319 simultaneous lineups, we would expect: (0.535)(319) = 170.665. For the 229 sequential lineups, we would expect: (0.535)(229) = 122.515. Or we can use the formula; for these same two cells (the column labeled "Suspect ID"), we calculate:

$$\frac{Total_{column}}{N}(Total_{row}) = \frac{293}{548}(319) = (0.535)(319) = 170.665$$

$$\frac{Total_{column}}{N}(Total_{row}) = \frac{293}{548}(229) = (0.535)(229) = 122.515$$

For the column labeled "Other ID":

$$\frac{Total_{column}}{N}(Total_{row}) = \frac{28}{548}(319) = (0.051)(319) = 16.269$$

$$\frac{Total_{column}}{N}(Total_{row}) = \frac{28}{548}(229) = (0.051)(229) = 11.679$$

For the column labeled "No ID":

$$\frac{Total_{column}}{N}(Total_{row}) = \frac{227}{548}(319) = (0.414)(319) = 132.066$$

$$\frac{Total_{column}}{N}(Total_{row}) = \frac{227}{548}(229) = (0.414)(229) = 94.806$$

	Expected		
	Suspect ID	Other ID	No ID
Simultaneous	170.665	16.269	132.066	319
Sequential	122.515	11.679	94.806	229
	293	28	227	548

Category	Observed (O)	Expected (E)	O − E	(O − E)²	$\frac{(O-E)^2}{E}$
Sim; suspect	191	170.665	20.335	413.512	2.423
Sim; other	8	16.269	−8.269	68.376	4.203
Sim; no	120	132.066	−12.066	145.588	1.102
Seq; suspect	102	122.515	−20.515	420.865	3.435
Seq; other	20	11.679	8.321	69.239	5.929
Seq; no	107	94.806	12.194	148.694	1.568

$$\chi^2 = \left(\frac{(O-E)^2}{E}\right) = (2.423 + 4.203 + 1.102 + 3.435 + 5.929 + 1.568)$$

$$= 18.660$$

Step 6: Reject the null hypothesis. It appears that the outcome of a lineup depends on the type of lineup. In general, simultaneous lineups tend to lead to a higher rate than expected of suspect identification, lower rates than expected of identification of other members of the lineup, and lower rates than expected of no identification at all. (*Note:* It is helpful to add the test statistic to the drawing that included the cutoff).

c. $\chi^2(1, N = 548) = 18.66, p < 0.05$

d. The findings of this study were the opposite of what had been expected by the investigators; the report of results noted that, prior to this study, police departments believed that the sequential lineup led to more accurate identification of suspects. This situation occurs frequently in behavioral research, a reminder of the importance of conducting two-tailed hypothesis tests. (Of course, the fact that this study produced different results doesn't end the debate. Future researchers should explore why there are different findings in different contexts in an effort to target the best lineup procedures for specific situations.)

17-9 The measure of effect size for chi square is Cramér's V. It is calculated by first multiplying the total N by the degrees of freedom for either the rows or columns (whichever is smaller) and then dividing the calculated chi-square value by this number. We then take the square root, which is Cramér's V.

17-10 To calculate the relative likelihood, we first need to calculate two conditional probabilities: the conditional probability of showing a "kissing pout" or duckface in a selfie for women which is $\frac{29}{250} = 0.116$, and the conditional probability of showing a "kissing pout" or duckface in a selfie for men, which is $\frac{6}{250} = 0.024$. Now we divide the conditional probability of showing a duckface given that one is a woman by the conditional probability of showing a duckface given that one is a man: $\frac{0.116}{0.024} = 4.833$. The relative likelihood of showing a duckface in a selfie for a woman as opposed to a man is 4.83.

17-11 a. Cramér's $V = \sqrt{\dfrac{\chi^2}{(N)(df_{row/column})}} = \sqrt{\dfrac{18.660}{(548)(1)}} = 0.185$.

This is a small-to-medium effect.

b. For simultaneous lineups:

Suspect identified: 191/319 = 0.599

Other person identified: 8/319 = 0.025

No person identified: 120/319 = 0.376

For sequential lineups:

Suspect identified: 102/229 = 0.445

Other person identified: 20/229 = 0.087

No person identified: 107/229 = 0.467

Conditional Proportions

	Suspect ID	Other ID	No ID	
Simultaneous	0.599	0.025	0.376	1.000
Sequential	0.445	0.087	0.467	0.999

Note: The bottom row adds up to 0.999 instead of 1.000 due to rounding.

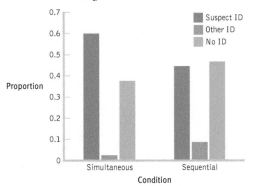

c. For simultaneous lineups:

Suspect identified: 191/319 = 0.599

For sequential lineups:

Suspect identified: 102/229 = 0.445

0.599/0.445 = 1.346

Based on this relative likelihood calculation, the chance of a suspect being accurately identified in a simultaneous lineup is 1.35 times that of a suspect being identified in a sequential lineup.

Chapter 18

18-1 We use such tests when we have an ordinal dependent variable.

18-2

	Variable 1		Variable 2	
Observation	Score	Rank	Score	Rank
1	1.30	3	54.39	5
2	1.80	4.5	50.11	3
3	1.20	2	53.39	4
4	1.06	1	44.89	1
5	1.80	4.5	48.50	2

18-3

Observation	Variable 1 Rank	Variable 2 Rank	Difference	Squared Difference
1	3	5	−2	4
2	4.5	3	1.5	2.25
3	2	4	−2	4
4	1	1	0	0
5	4.5	2	2.5	6.25

$$r_s = 1 - \frac{6(\Sigma D^2)}{N(N^2 - 1)} = 1 - \frac{6(16.5)}{5(5^2 - 1)} = 1 - \frac{99}{5(25 - 1)}$$

$$= 1 - \frac{99}{5(24)} = 1 - \frac{99}{120} = 1 - 0.825 = 0.175$$

18-4 a. It is possible that some of these sentences might be more common than others. Ranking sentences does not assume that the difference from 1st spot to the 2nd spot is equally the same from the 2nd spot to the 3rd spot, so one of these sentences might be an outlier compared to the others. Because of that, these lists are not likely to be normally distributed. Moreover, the sample sizes are small, so we cannot rely on the central limit theorem to achieve a normal distribution.

b. The authors ordered the sentences from most common to least common based on their frequency within each series. The authors then assigned a rank of 1 to the most common, 2 to the second most common, and so on.

c. Extremely common sentences would be included in the ranking at the top of the ordinal variable at rank 1. The next sentence might be far less common, but would be assigned the rank of 2. So, two very different numbers for sentence frequency would be transformed into ranks 1 and 2 when ordinal.

18-5 Nonparametric tests are performed on ordinal data, so any data that are scale must be converted to ordinal before we compute the nonparametric test.

18-6 To calculate T, we first take the difference between each person's two scores. (To calculate T, we first take the difference between each person's two scores, subtracting the first score from the second.) We then rank these differences and separately sum the ranks associated with positive and negative difference scores. The table shows the organized data:

Person	Score 1	Score 2	Difference	Ranks	Rank for Negative Differences	Rank for Positive Differences
A	2	5	3	4		4
B	7	2	−5	2	2	
C	4	5	1	5		5
D	10	3	−7	1	1	
E	5	1	−4	3	3	

The sum of the ranks for the negative differences is $\Sigma R_- = (2 + 1 + 3) = 6$.

The sum of the ranks for the positive differences is $\Sigma R_+ = (4 + 5) = 9$.

T is equal to the smaller of these two sums: $T = \Sigma R_{smaller} = 6$.

18-7 *Step 1:* We convert the data from scale to ordinal. The researchers did not indicate whether they used random selection to choose the countries in the sample, so we must be cautious when generalizing from these results. There are some ties, but we will assume that there are not so many as to render the results of the test invalid.

Step 2: Null hypothesis: Countries in which English is a primary language and countries in which English is not a primary language do not differ in accomplishment-related national pride.

Research hypothesis: Countries in which English is a primary language and countries in which English is not a primary language differ in accomplishment-related national pride.

Step 3: There are seven countries in the English-speaking group and seven countries in the non-English-speaking group.

Step 4: The cutoff, or critical value, for a Mann–Whitney U test with two groups of seven participants (countries), a p level of 0.05, and a two-tailed test is 8.

Step 5: (*Note:* "E" stands for English-speaking, and "NE" stands for non-English-speaking.)

Country	Pride Score	Pride Rank	English Language	E Rank	NE Rank
United States	4.00	1	E	1	
Australia	2.90	2.5	E	2.5	
Ireland	2.90	2.5	E	2.5	
South Africa	2.70	4	E	4	
New Zealand	2.60	5	E	5	
Canada	2.40	6	E	6	
Chile	2.30	7	NE		7
Great Britain	2.20	8	E	8	
Japan	1.80	9	NE		9
France	1.50	10	NE		10
Czech Republic	1.30	11.5	NE		11.5
Norway	1.30	11.5	NE		11.5
Slovenia	1.10	13	NE		13
South Korea	1.00	14	NE		14

$$\Sigma R_E = 1 + 2.5 + 2.5 + 4 + 5 + 6 + 8 = 29$$
$$\Sigma R_{NE} = 7 + 9 + 10 + 11.5 + 11.5 + 13 + 14 = 76$$

$$U_E = (n_E)(n_{NE}) + \frac{n_E(n_E + 1)}{2} - \Sigma R_E$$

$$= (7)(7) + \frac{7(7 + 1)}{2} - 29 = 49 + 28 - 29 = 48$$

$$U_{NE} = (n_E)(n_{NE}) + \frac{n_{NE}(n_{NE} + 1)}{2} - \Sigma R_{NE}$$

$$= (7)(7) + \frac{7(7 + 1)}{2} - 76 = 49 + 28 - 76 = 1$$

Step 6: The smaller test statistic, 1, is smaller than the critical value, 8. We can reject the null hypothesis; it appears that English-speaking countries tend to have higher accomplishment-related national pride than do non-English-speaking countries.

Appendix E

CHOOSING THE APPROPRIATE STATISTICAL TEST

We have learned four categories of statistical tests:

1. Statistical tests in which all variables are scale
2. Statistical tests in which the independent variable (or variables) is nominal, but the dependent variable is scale
3. Statistical tests in which all variables are nominal
4. Statistical tests in which any variable is ordinal

Category 1: Two Scale Variables

If we have a research design with only scale variables, we have two choices about how to analyze the data. The only question we have to answer is: Does the research question pertain to an association (or relation) between two variables or does it pertain to the degree to which one variable predicts the other? If the research question is about association, then we choose the Pearson correlation coefficient. If it is about prediction, then we choose regression. The decisions for category 1 are represented in **Table E-1**. (Note that the relation must be linear.)

TABLE E-1 Category 1 Statistics

When both the independent variable and the dependent variable are scale, we calculate either a Pearson correlation coefficient or a regression equation.

Research Question: Association (Relation)	Research Question: Prediction
Pearson correlation coefficient	Regression equation

Category 2: Nominal Independent Variable(s) and a Scale Dependent Variable

If the research design includes one or more nominal independent variables and a scale dependent variable, then we have several choices. The next question pertains to the number of independent variables.

1. If there is *just one independent variable*, then we ask ourselves how many levels it has.

   a. If there are *two levels, but just one sample*—that is, one level is represented by the sample and one level by the population—then we use either a z test or a single-sample t test. It is unusual to know enough about a population that we only need to collect data from a single sample. If this is the case, however, and we know *both* the population mean and the population standard deviation, then we can use a z test. If this is the case and we know *only* the population mean (but not the population standard deviation), then we use the single-sample t test.

   b. If there are *two levels, each represented by a sample* (either a single sample in which everyone participates in both levels or two different samples, one for each level), then we use either a paired-samples t test (if all participants are in both levels of the independent variable) or an independent-samples t test (if participants are in only one level of the independent variable).

   c. If there are three or more levels, then we use a form of a one-way ANOVA. We examine the research design to determine whether it is a between-groups ANOVA (participants are in just one level of the independent variable) or a within-groups ANOVA (participants are in all levels of the independent variable).

2. If there are *at least two independent variables*, we must use a form of ANOVA. Remember, we name ANOVAs according to the number of independent variables (one-way, two-way, three-way) and the research design (between-groups, within-groups).

The decisions about data that fall into category 2 and have one independent variable are summarized in **Table E-2**. For those with two or more independent variables, see Table 14-1 (page 367).

Category 3: One or Two Nominal Variables

If we have a design with only nominal variables—that is, counts, not means, in the cells—then we have two options, both of which are nonparametric tests. The only question we have to ask ourselves is whether there are one or two nominal variables. If there is one nominal variable, then we choose the chi-square test for goodness of fit. If there are two nominal variables, then we choose the chi-square test for independence. The decision for category 3 is represented in **Table E-3**.

TABLE E-2 Category 2 Statistics

When there are one or more nominal independent variables and a scale dependent variable, examine the data to see which test is appropriate to use. Begin by determining the number of independent variables. If there is just one independent variable, use the accompanying chart. (When there are two or more independent variables, we use a form of ANOVA; see Table 14-1, page 367.) The first two columns in the chart identify the number of levels of the independent variable and the number of samples. For two levels but one sample, choose either the z test and single-sample t test, depending on whether you know the population standard deviation; for two levels and two samples, choose either the paired-samples t test or the independent-samples t test, depending on the research design. For three or more levels (and the matching number of samples), choose either a one-way within-groups ANOVA or a one-way between-groups ANOVA, again basing your decision on the research design.

Number of Levels of Independent Variable	Number of Samples	Information About Population	Research Design	Hypothesis Test
Two	One (compared with the population)	Mean and standard deviation	—	z test
Two	One (compared with the population)	Mean only	—	Single-sample t test
Two	Two	—	Within-groups	Paired-samples t test
Two	Two	—	Between-groups	Independent-samples t test
Three (or more)	Three (or more)	—	Between-groups	One-way between-groups ANOVA
Three (or more)	Three (or more)	—	Within-groups	One-way within-groups ANOVA

TABLE E-3 Category 3 Statistics

When we have only nominal variables, then we choose one of the two chi-square tests.

One Nominal Variable	Two Nominal Variables
Chi-square test for goodness of fit	Chi-square test for independence

Category 4: At Least One Ordinal Variable

If we have a design with even one ordinal variable or a design in which it makes sense to convert the data from scale to ordinal, then we have several choices, as seen in **Table E-4**. All these choices have parallel parametric hypothesis tests, as seen in **Table E-5**. For situations in which we want to investigate the relation between two ordinal variables, we use the Spearman rank-order correlation coefficient. For situations in which we have a within-groups research design and two groups, we use the Wilcoxon signed-rank test. When we have a between-groups design with two groups, we use a Mann–Whitney U test. And when we have a between-groups design with more than two groups, we use a Kruskal–Wallis H test.

The decisions we've outlined are summarized in **Figure E-1**.

TABLE E-4 Category 4 Statistics

When at least one variable is ordinal, we have several choices. If both variables are ordinal, or can be converted to ordinal, and we are interested in quantifying the relation between them, we use the Spearman rank-order correlation coefficient. If the independent variable is nominal and the dependent variable is ordinal, we choose the correct nonparametric test based on the research design and the number of levels of the independent variable.

Type of Independent Variable (and number of levels, if applicable)	Research Design	Question to Be Answered	Hypothesis Test
Ordinal	Correlation	Are two variables related?	Spearman rank-order correlation coefficient
Nominal (two levels)	Within-groups	Are two groups different?	Wilcoxon signed-rank test
Nominal (two levels)	Between-groups	Are two groups different?	Mann–Whitney U test
Nominal (three or more levels)	Between-groups	Are three or more groups different?	Kruskal–Wallis H test

| TABLE E-5 | Nonparametric Statistics and Their Parametric Counterparts |

Every parametric hypothesis test has at least one nonparametric counterpart. If the data are far from meeting the assumptions for a parametric test or at least one variable is ordinal, we should use the appropriate nonparametric test instead of a parametric test.

Design	Parametric Test	Nonparametric Test
Association between two variables	Pearson correlation coefficient	Spearman rank-order correlation coefficient
Two groups; within-groups design	Paired-samples t test	Wilcoxon signed-rank test
Two groups; between-groups design	Independent-samples t test	Mann–Whitney U test
More than two groups; between-groups design	One-way between-groups ANOVA	Kruskal–Wallis H test

FIGURE E-1

Choosing the Appropriate Hypothesis Test

By asking the right questions about our variables and research design, we can choose the appropriate hypothesis test for our research.

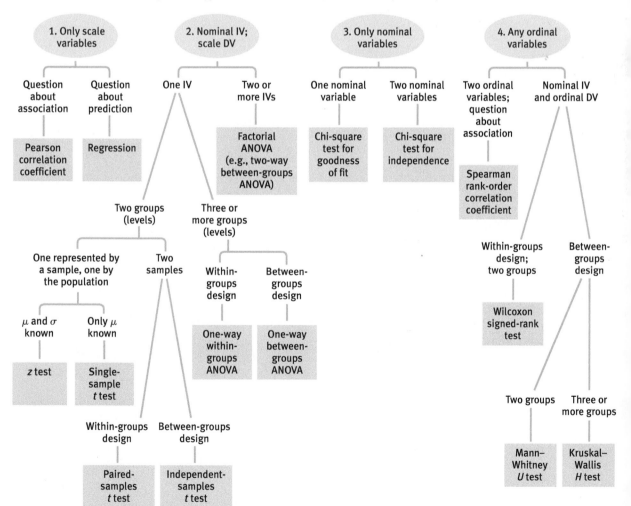

Four Categories of Hypothesis Tests (IV = independent variable; DV = dependent variable)

Appendix F

REPORTING STATISTICS

Overview of Reporting Statistics

In Chapter 11, How It Works 11.1, we described a study about gender differences in humor (Azim, Mobbs, Jo, Menon, & Reiss, 2005). Let's recap the results of the analyses and then use this information to report statistics in the Methods and Results sections of a paper written in the style of the American Psychological Association (APA). In the analyses of the humor data, we used fictional data that had the same means as the actual study by Azim and colleagues. We used the following raw data:

Percentage of cartoons labeled as "funny"
Women: 84, 97, 58, 90
Men: 88, 90, 52, 97, 86

We conducted an independent-samples t test on these data and found a test statistic, t, of -0.03. This test statistic was not beyond the cutoff, so we failed to reject the null hypothesis. We *cannot* conclude that men and women, on average, find different percentages of the cartoons to be funny; we can only conclude that this study did not provide evidence that women and men are different on this variable.

The statistics for this test, as reported in a journal article, would include the symbol for the statistic, the degrees of freedom, the value of the test statistic, and, for statistics calculated by hand, whether the p value associated with the test statistic was less than or greater than the cutoff p level of 0.05. In the humor example, the statistics would read:

$$t(7) = -0.03, p > 0.05$$

(Note that when we conducted this hypothesis test using SPSS, we got an exact p value of 0.977, so we would say $p = 0.98$ instead of $p > 0.05$ if we had used software.) In addition to the statistics, we also would report the means and standard deviations for the two samples:

Women: $M = 82.25$, $SD = 17.02$; Men: $M = 82.60$, $SD = 18.13$

We can also calculate that the percentage difference between women and men is $82.25 - 82.60 = -0.35$. There is just a 0.35% difference between women and men.

In How It Works 11.3, we calculated a confidence interval for these data. The 95% confidence interval, centered around the difference between means of $82.25 - 82.60 = -0.35$, is $[-27.88, 27.18]$.

In How It Works 11.4, we calculated the effect size for this study, a Cohen's d of -0.02. We now have sufficient information to write up these findings.

There are three topics to consider when reporting statistics, all covered in various sections of the *Publication Manual of the American Psychological Association* (APA, 2010):

1. In the Methods section, we justify the study by including information about the statistical power, reliability, and validity of any measures we used.
2. In the Results section, we report the traditional statistics, which include any relevant descriptive statistics and often the results of hypothesis testing.
3. In the Results section, we also report the newer statistics that are now required by the APA, including effect sizes and confidence intervals (APA, 2010).

Justifying the Study

To justify the study, we first report the results of the statistical power analyses that were conducted before the data were collected. Then we report any information related to the reliability and validity of the measured variables. This information usually goes in the Methods section of the paper.

To summarize this aspect of the findings, we include in the Methods section:

- Statistical power analyses
- Psychometric data for each scale used (reliability and validity information)

Reporting Traditional Statistics

The Results section should include any relevant summary statistics. For analyses with a scale dependent variable, include means, standard deviations, and sample sizes for each cell in the research design. For analyses with a nominal dependent variable (chi-square analyses), include the frequencies (counts) for each cell; there won't be means or standard deviations because there are no scores on a scale measure.

Summary statistics are sometimes presented first in a Results section but are more typically presented after a description of each hypothesis test. If there are only two or three cells, then the summary statistics are typically presented in the text; if there are more cells, then these statistics should be displayed in a table or figure.

Reports of hypothesis tests typically begin by reiterating the hypothesis to be tested and then describing the test that was conducted, including the independent and dependent variables. The results of the hypothesis test are then presented, usually including the symbol for the statistic, the degrees of freedom, the actual value of the statistic, and,

TABLE F-1	The Format for the Results of a Hypothesis Test

There is a general format for reporting the results of hypothesis tests. The symbol for the statistic is followed by the degrees of freedom in parentheses, then the value of the test statistic, and finally the exact p value associated with that test statistic. This table presents the way that format would be implemented for several of the test statistics discussed in this text. (Note that we will only have the exact p value if we use software. If we conduct a test by hand, we may report whether the p value is greater than or less than 0.05.)

Symbol	Degrees of Freedom	Value of the Test Statistic	Information About the Cutoff	Effect Size	Example
z	(df)	= XX,	$p = 0.XX$	$d = XX$	$z(54) = 0.60, p = 0.45, d = 0.08$
t	(df)	= XX,	$p = 0.XX$	$d = XX$	$t(146) = 2.29, p = 0.024, d = 0.50$
F	$(df_{between}, df_{within})$	= XX,	$p = 0.XX$	$R^2 = XX$	$F(2, 142) = 6.63, p = 0.002, R^2 = 0.09$
χ^2	$(df, N = XX)$	= XX,	$p = 0.XX$	$V = XX$	$\chi^2(1, N = 147) = 0.58, p = 0.447, V = 0.06$
T	None	= XX,	$p = 0.XX$	None	$T = 7, p = 0.04$
U	None	= XX,	$p = 0.XX$	None	$U = 19, p = 0.14$

if using software, the actual p value associated with that statistic. The format for reporting this information is included after each hypothesis test in this text and is presented again in Table F-1.

After the statistics are presented, a brief statement summarizes the results, indicating the direction of any effects. This brief statement does not draw conclusions beyond the actual finding. In the Results section, researchers do not discuss the finding in terms of the general theories in the field or in terms of its potential implications or applications (which go, appropriately enough, in the Discussion section). Researchers should present the results of all hypothesis tests that they conducted, even those in which they failed to reject the null hypothesis.

To summarize this aspect of Results sections:

- Include summary statistics: means, standard deviations, and either sample sizes for each cell (when the dependent variable is scale) or frequencies (counts) for each cell (when the dependent variable is nominal). These are often included after each hypothesis test.
- For each hypothesis test conducted:
  - Include a brief summary of the hypotheses and hypothesis test.
  - Report the results of hypothesis testing: the symbol for the statistic used, the degrees of freedom, the actual value of the statistic, and the p value associated with this statistic (if using software).
  - Provide a statement that summarizes the results of the hypothesis testing.
  - Use tables and figures to clarify patterns in the findings.
- Include all results, even for findings that are not statistically significant.

The statistics for the study from How It Works in Chapter 11 that compared the mean percentages of cartoons that women and men found funny might be reported as follows:

> To examine the hypothesis that women and men, on average, find different percentages of cartoons funny, we conducted an independent-samples t test. The independent variable was gender, with two levels: female and male. The dependent variable was the percentage of cartoons deemed funny. There was

not a statistically significant effect of gender, $t(7) = -0.03$, $p = 0.98$; this study does not provide evidence that women ($M = 82.25, SD = 17.02$) and men ($M = 82.60, SD = 18.13$) deem, on average, different percentages of cartoons to be funny. The difference between the mean percentages for women and men is just 0.35%.

Reporting the "New Statistics"

It is no longer enough to simply present the descriptive statistics and the results of the hypothesis test. As you learned in Chapter 8, effect sizes and confidence intervals should be included when relevant. The effect-size estimate is often included as part of the report of the statistics, just after the p value. There is often a statement that indicates the size of the effect in words, not just in numbers. The confidence interval can be presented after the effect size, abbreviated as "95% CI" with the actual interval in brackets. Note that nonparametric tests often do not have associated measures of effect size or confidence intervals. In these cases, researchers should provide enough descriptive information for readers to interpret the findings.

To summarize this aspect of the Results sections, we include:

- Effect size, along with a statement about the size of the effect.
- Confidence intervals when possible, along with a statement interpreting the confidence interval in the context of the study.

For the study on humor, we might report the effect size as part of the traditional statistics that we described above: There was not a statistically significant effect of gender, $t(7) = -0.03$, $p = 0.98$, $d = -0.02$, 95% CI $[-28.37, 27.67]$; this was a small, almost nonexistent, effect. In fact, there is only a 0.35% difference between the mean percentages for women and men. This study does not provide evidence that men and women, on average, rate different percentages of cartoons as funny.

For the humor study, we can now pull the parts together. Here is how the results would be reported:

> To examine the hypothesis that women and men, on average, find different percentages of cartoons funny, we conducted

an independent-samples t test. The independent variable was gender, with two levels: female and male. The dependent variable was the percentage of cartoons deemed funny. There was not a statistically significant effect of gender, $t(7) = -0.03$, $p = 0.98$, $d = -0.02$, 95% CI $[-28.37, 27.67]$; this was a small, almost nonexistent, effect.

Based on the hypothesis test and the confidence interval, this study does not provide evidence that women ($M = 82.25$, $SD = 17.02$) and men ($M = 82.60$, $SD = 18.13$) deem, on average, different percentages of cartoons to be funny. In fact, there is only a very small difference between the mean percentages for women and men, just 0.35%.

Appendix G

BUILDING BETTER GRAPHS USING EXCEL

In terms of default settings, there is no graphing software that adheres specifically to all of the APA guidelines; however, you can learn to use software to adapt the default graph into a clear and useful visualization of data. For example, Microsoft Excel is a program that is used in many settings to create graphs. Like other graphing software, Excel software changes with every application revision, so you might encounter slight variations from the instructions that follow.

This appendix demonstrates how to create a simple, clean-looking graph using the snowfall data from the opening example in Chapter 14. You may recall that ski resorts reported greater mean snowfall amounts than weather stations did, an effect that was even more pronounced on weekends. This effect is likely due to the benefit ski resorts receive when people think there is more snow.

Remember, the purpose of a graph is to *let the data speak*. You can introduce insight (rather than confusion) into an Excel graph by following the specific dos and don'ts in Chapter 3. In APA style, various kinds of visual displays of data are all referred to as "Figures." For example, Figure G-1 displays two nominal independent variables and the means for one scale dependent variable in a spreadsheet that Excel refers to as a "workbook."

FIGURE G-1

Summary Data in an Excel Spreadsheet

To transform these summary data in an Excel spreadsheet into an APA-style figure, first highlight all nine cells (A1 through C3) and then select the kind of chart you wish to create.

Step 1. Identify the independent and dependent variables and determine which type of observation each is. In the snowfall example, the dependent variable is a scale variable, and the

independent variables are nominal variables. Specifically, snowfall in inches is the scale dependent variable; the source of the snow report (levels: ski resort, weather station) is a nominal independent variable; and time of the week (levels: weekdays, weekends) is a second independent variable. (Think of these particular independent variables as predictor variables because they cannot be manipulated by the experimenter.)

Step 2. Enter the summary data (the averages of the dependent variable within each cell) in the Excel spreadsheet, as shown in Figure G-1. Then highlight the data and labels and select the type of figure you want to create. To do this, click "Insert," "Column," and under "2-D Column," select the left-most graph icon, called "Clustered Column." Do not select a 3-D graph because it will introduce chartjunk. Figure G-2 shows what the graph will look like at this point.

FIGURE G-2

The Default Graph Created by Excel

Step 3. Change the defaults so that the graph adheres to the graphing checklist from Chapter 3. If you click on the graph and then look at "Chart Tools" along the top of the Excel toolbar, you'll see a number of options for changing the graph. We modified the chart by using the tools in the "Layout" menu and by entering information directly into the text boxes that are part of the chart. For instance, in Step 2, we had selected a chart that included a title; we then put the cursor in the title box and retitled the chart to what you can see in Figure G-3 is "Biased reporting: Snowfall reports based on time of week and source of report." We then used the "Horizontal Title" option in the "Axis Titles" menu to add the *y*-axis label—"Snowfall (in inches)"—and set the orientation of the title.

A Graph Created in Excel That Has Been Altered to Adhere to the Graphing Guidelines

Notice that the bars are two-dimensional and that the label for the *y*-axis is turned horizontally so that it is easy to read.

Biased reporting: Snowfall reports based on time of week and source of report

We right-clicked on each of the data bars to change its color using the "Shape Fill" tool so that we could set the colors of the bars as variations on a single color. We wanted to reduce the chartjunk, so we first made the grid lines lighter by using the "Line Color" tool under the "Layout > Gridlines" menu to increase the solid line transparency; then we used the same "Gridlines" menu to display only major gridlines for the horizontal axis. Figure G-3 shows our choices.

Know your audience. A figure designed for submission to a scholarly journal will look a little different than a PowerPoint presentation to a class, just as a presentation at a sales meeting will look different than a research report submitted to your boss. Focus on clarity rather than gimmicks. Remember: *Let the data speak*.

GLOSSARY

A

adjusted standardized residual The difference between the observed frequency and the expected frequency for a cell in a chi-square research design, divided by the standard error. Also called *adjusted residual*.

alpha The chance of making a Type I error and another name for the *p* level; symbolized as α.

analysis of covariance (ANCOVA) A type of ANOVA in which a covariate is included so that statistical findings reflect effects after a scale variable has been statistically removed.

analysis of variance (ANOVA) A hypothesis test typically used with one or more nominal and sometimes ordinal independent variables (with at least three groups overall) and a scale dependent variable.

assumption A characteristic that we ideally require the population from which we are sampling to have so that we can make accurate inferences.

B

bar graph A visual depiction of data when the independent variable is nominal or ordinal and the dependent variable is scale. The height of each bar typically represents the average value of the dependent variable for each category.

between-groups ANOVA A hypothesis test in which there are more than two samples, and each sample is composed of different participants.

between-groups research design An experimental design in which participants experience one, and only one, level of the independent variable.

between-groups variance An estimate of the population variance based on the differences among the means.

bimodal A term describing a distribution that has two modes, or most common scores.

Bonferroni test A post hoc test that provides a more strict critical value for every comparison of means; sometimes called the *Dunn Multiple Comparison test*.

bootstrapping A statistical process in which the original sample data are used to represent the entire population, and samples are repeatedly taken from the original sample data to form a confidence interval.

C

ceiling effect A situation in which a constraint prevents a variable from taking on values above a given number.

cell A box that depicts one unique combination of levels of the independent variables in a factorial design.

central limit theorem The idea that a distribution of sample means is a more normal distribution than a distribution of scores, even when the population distribution is not normal.

central tendency A descriptive statistic that best represents the center of a data set, the particular value that all the other data seem to be gathering around.

chartjunk Any unnecessary information or feature in a graph that distracts from a viewer's ability to understand the data.

chi-square test for goodness-of-fit A nonparametric hypothesis test used when there is one nominal variable.

chi-square test for independence A nonparametric hypothesis test used when there are two nominal variables.

coefficient alpha A commonly used estimate of a test's or measure's reliability calculated by taking the average of all possible split-half correlations; symbolized as α; sometimes called *Cronbach's alpha*.

Cohen's *d* A measure of effect size that assesses the difference between two means in terms of standard deviation, not standard error.

confidence interval An interval estimate, based on the sample statistic, that includes the population mean a certain percentage of the time if we sampled from the same population repeatedly.

confirmation bias Our usually unintentional tendency to pay attention to evidence that confirms what we already believe and to ignore evidence that would disconfirm our beliefs. Confirmation biases closely follow illusory correlations.

confounding variable A variable that systematically varies with the independent variable so that we cannot logically determine which variable is at work; also called a *confound*.

continuous observation Observed data point that can take on a full range of values (e.g., numbers out to many decimal points); an infinite number of potential values exists.

control group A level of the independent variable that is designed to match the experimental group in all ways but the experimental manipulation itself.

convenience sample A subset of a population whose members are chosen strictly because they are readily available.

correlation An association between two or more variables.

correlation coefficient A statistic that quantifies a relation between two variables.

counterbalancing The minimization of order effects by varying the order of presentation of different levels of the independent variable from one participant to the next.

covariate A scale variable that we suspect associates, or covaries, with the independent variable of interest.

Cramér's *V* The standard effect size used with the chi-square test for independence; also called *Cramer's phi*, symbolized as Φ.

critical region The area in the tails of the comparison distribution in which we reject the null hypothesis if our test statistic falls there.

critical value A test statistic value beyond which we reject the null hypothesis; often called a *cutoff*.

D

defaults The options that a software designer has preselected. These are the built-in decisions that the software will implement if you do not instruct it otherwise.

degrees of freedom The number of scores that are free to vary when estimating a population parameter from a sample.

dependent variable The outcome variable that we hypothesize to be related to, or caused by, changes in the independent variable.

descriptive statistic Statistical technique used to organize, summarize, and communicate a group of numerical observations.

deviation from the mean The amount that a score in a sample differs from the mean of the sample; also called *deviation*.

discrete observation Observed data point that can take on only specific values (e.g., whole numbers); no other values can exist between these numbers.

distribution of means A distribution composed of many means that are calculated from all possible samples of a given size, all taken from the same population.

dot plot A graph that displays all the data points in a sample, with the range of scores along the *x*-axis and a dot for each data point above the appropriate value.

duck A form of chartjunk in which a feature of the data has been dressed up in a graph to be something other than merely data.

E

effect size A standardized value that indicates the size of a difference and is unaffected by sample size.

expected relative-frequency probability The likelihood of an event occurring based on the actual outcome of many, many trials.

experiment A study in which participants are randomly assigned to a condition or level of one or more independent variables.

experimental group A level of the independent variable that receives the treatment or intervention of interest in an experiment.

F

F **statistic** A ratio of two measures of variance: (1) between-groups variance, which indicates differences among sample means, and (2) within-groups variance, which is essentially an average of the sample variances.

factor A term used to describe an independent variable in a study with more than one independent variable.

factorial ANOVA A statistical analysis used with one scale dependent variable and at least two nominal independent variables (also called *factors*); also called a *multifactorial ANOVA*.

file drawer analysis A statistical calculation, following a meta-analysis, of the number of studies with null results that would have to exist so that a mean effect size would no longer be statistically significant.

first quartile The 25th percentile of a data set.

floor effect A situation in which a constraint prevents a variable from taking values below a certain point.

frequency distribution A distribution that describes the pattern of a set of numbers by displaying a count or proportion for each possible value of a variable.

frequency polygon A line graph with the *x*-axis representing values (or midpoints of intervals) and the *y*-axis representing frequencies. A dot is placed at the frequency for each value (or midpoint), and the dots are connected.

frequency table A visual depiction of data that shows how often each value occurred; that is, how many scores were at each value. Values are listed in one column, and the numbers of individuals with scores at that value are listed in the second column.

G

generalizability Researchers' ability to apply findings from one sample or in one context to other samples or contexts; also called *external validity*.

grand mean The mean of every score in a study, regardless of which sample the score came from.

grid A form of chartjunk that takes the form of a background pattern, almost like graph paper, on which the data representations, such as bars, are superimposed.

grouped frequency table A visual depiction of data that reports the frequencies within a given interval rather than the frequencies for a specific value.

H

heteroscedastic A term given to populations that have different variances.

hierarchical multiple regression A type of multiple regression in which the researcher adds independent variables into the equation in an order determined by theory.

histogram A graph that looks like a bar graph but depicts just one variable, usually based on scale data, with the values of the variable on the *x*-axis and the frequencies on the *y*-axis.

homoscedastic A term given to populations that have the same variance; also called *homogeneity of variance*.

hypothesis testing The process of drawing conclusions about whether a particular relation between variables is supported by the evidence.

I

illusory correlation The phenomenon of believing that one sees an association between variables when no such association exists.

independent variable A variable that we either manipulate or observe to determine its effects on the dependent variable.

independent-samples *t* test A hypothesis test used to compare two means for a between-groups design, a situation in which each participant is assigned to only one condition.

inferential statistic Statistical technique that uses sample data to make estimates about the larger population.

interaction The statistical result achieved in a factorial design when two or more independent variables have an effect on the dependent variable in combination that neither independent variable has on its own.

intercept The predicted value for Y when X is equal to 0, the point at which the line crosses, or intercepts, the y-axis.

interquartile range A measure of the difference between the first and third quartiles of a data set.

interval estimate An estimate based on a sample statistic, providing a range of plausible values for the population parameter.

interval variable A variable used for observations that have numbers as their values; the distance (or interval) between pairs of consecutive numbers is assumed to be equal.

K

Kruskal–Wallis *H* test A nonparametric hypothesis test used when there are more than two groups, a between-groups design, and an ordinal dependent variable.

L

latent variables The ideas that we want to research but cannot directly measure.

level A discrete value or condition that a variable can take on.

line graph A graph used to illustrate the relation between two scale variables; sometimes the line represents the predicted y scores for each x value, and sometimes the line represents change in a variable over time.

linear relation A relation between two variables best described by a straight line.

M

main effect A result occurring in a factorial design when one of the independent variables has an influence on the dependent variable.

manifest variables The variables in a study that we can observe and that are measured.

Mann–Whitney *U* test A nonparametric hypothesis test used when there are two groups, a between-groups design, and an ordinal dependent variable.

marginal mean The mean of a row or a column in a table that shows the cells of a study with a two-way ANOVA design.

matched groups A matched-groups design is similar to a within-groups design; it has different people in each level of the independent variable, but they are similar (matched) on characteristics important to the study.

mean The arithmetic average of a group of scores. It is calculated by summing all the scores and dividing by the total number of scores.

median The middle score of all the scores in a sample when the scores are arranged in ascending order. If there is no single middle score, the median is the mean of the two middle scores.

meta-analysis A study that involves the calculation of a mean effect size from the individual effect sizes of more than one study.

mixed-design ANOVA A hypothesis test used to analyze the data from a study with at least two independent variables; at least one variable must be within-groups and at least one variable must be between-groups.

mode The most common score of all the scores in a sample.

moiré vibrations Any patterns that create a distracting impression of vibration and movement.

multimodal A term for a distribution that has more than two modes, or most common scores.

multiple regression A statistical technique that includes two or more predictor variables in a prediction equation.

multivariate analysis of covariance (MANCOVA) An ANOVA with multiple dependent variables and the inclusion of a covariate.

multivariate analysis of variance (MANOVA) A form of ANOVA in which there is more than one dependent variable.

N

negative correlation An association between two variables in which participants with high scores on one variable tend to have low scores on the other variable.

negatively skewed data An asymmetric distribution whose tail extends to the left, in a negative direction.

nominal variable A variable used for observations that have categories, or names, as their values.

nonlinear relation A relation between variables best described by a line that breaks or curves in some way.

nonparametric test An inferential statistical analysis that is not based on a set of assumptions about the population.

normal curve A specific bell-shaped curve that is unimodal, symmetric, and defined mathematically.

normal distribution A specific frequency distribution in the shape of a bell-shaped, symmetric, unimodal curve.

null hypothesis A statement that postulates that there is no difference between populations or that the difference is in a direction opposite of that anticipated by the researcher.

O

one-tailed test A hypothesis test in which the research hypothesis is directional, positing either a mean decrease or a mean increase in the dependent variable, but not both, as a result of the independent variable.

one-way ANOVA A hypothesis test that includes one nominal independent variable with more than two levels and a scale dependent variable.

operational definition The operations or procedures used to measure or manipulate a variable.

order effects The effects produced when a participant's behavior changes when the dependent variable is presented for a second time; also called *practice effects*.

ordinal variable A variable used for observations that have rankings (i.e., 1st, 2nd, 3rd, . . .) as their values.

orthogonal variable An independent variable that makes a separate and distinct contribution to the prediction of a dependent variable, as compared with the contributions of another variable.

outcome In reference to probability, the result of a trial.

outlier An extreme score that is either very high or very low in comparison with the rest of the scores in a sample.

outlier analysis Studies that examine observations that do not fit the overall pattern of the data in an effort to understand the factors that influence the dependent variable.

P

p level The probability used to determine the critical values, or cutoffs, in hypothesis testing; often called *alpha*.

paired-samples *t* test A test used to compare two means for a within-groups design, a situation in which every participant is in both samples; also called a *dependent-samples* t *test*.

parameter A number based on the whole population; it is usually symbolized by a Greek letter.

parametric test An inferential statistical analysis based on a set of assumptions about the population.

Pareto chart A type of bar graph in which the categories along the *x*-axis are ordered from highest bar on the left to lowest bar on the right.

partial correlation A technique that quantifies the degree of association between two variables that remains when the correlations of these two variables with a third variable are mathematically eliminated.

path The term statisticians use to describe the connection between two variables in a statistical model.

path analysis A statistical method that examines a hypothesized model, usually by conducting a series of regression analyses that quantify the paths at each succeeding step in the model.

Pearson correlation coefficient A statistic that quantifies a linear relation between two scale variables.

personal probability A person's own judgment about the likelihood that an event will occur; also called *subjective probability*.

pictorial graph A visual depiction of data typically used for an independent variable with very few levels (categories) and a scale dependent variable. Each level uses a picture or symbol to represent its value on the scale dependent variable.

pie chart A graph in the shape of a circle with a slice for every level (category). The size of each slice represents the proportion (or percentage) of each level.

planned comparison A test conducted when there are multiple groups of scores but specific comparisons have been specified prior to data collection; also called an *a priori* comparison.

point estimate A summary statistic from a sample that is just one number used as an estimate of the population parameter.

pooled variance A weighted average of the two estimates of variance— one from each sample—that are calculated when conducting an independent-samples *t* test.

population All possible observations about which we'd like to know something.

positive correlation An association between two variables such that participants with high scores on one variable tend to have high scores on the other variable as well, and those with low scores on one variable tend to have low scores on the other variable.

positively skewed data An asymmetric data distribution whose tail extends to the right, in a positive direction.

post hoc test A statistical procedure frequently carried out after the null hypothesis has been rejected in an analysis of variance; it allows us to make multiple comparisons among several means; often referred to as a *follow-up test*.

probability The likelihood that a certain outcome will occur out of all possible outcomes.

proportionate reduction in error A statistic that quantifies how much more accurate predictions are when we use the regression line instead of the mean as a prediction tool; also called *coefficient of determination*.

psychometricians The statisticians and psychologists who develop tests and measures.

psychometrics The branch of statistics used in the development of tests and measures.

Q

qualitative interaction A particular type of quantitative interaction of two (or more) independent variables in which one independent variable reverses its effect depending on the level of the other independent variable.

quantitative interaction An interaction in which the effect of one independent variable is strengthened or weakened at one or more levels of the other independent variable, but the direction of the initial effect does not change.

R

R^2 The proportion of variance in the dependent variable that is accounted for by the independent variable.

random assignment The protocol established for an experiment whereby every participant in a study has an equal chance of being assigned to any of the groups, or experimental conditions, in the study.

random sample A subset of a population selected using a method that ensures that every member of the population has an equal chance of being selected into the study.

range A measure of variability calculated by subtracting the lowest score (the minimum) from the highest score (the maximum).

ratio variable A variable that meets the criteria for an interval variable but also has a meaningful zero point.

raw score A data point that has not yet been transformed or analyzed.

regression to the mean The tendency of scores that are particularly high or low to drift toward the mean over time.

relative risk A measure created by making a ratio of two conditional proportions; also called *relative likelihood* or *relative chance.*

reliability The consistency of a measure.

replication The duplication of scientific results, ideally in a different context or with a sample that has different characteristics.

research hypothesis A statement that postulates that there is a difference between populations or sometimes, more specifically, that there is a difference in a certain direction, positive or negative; also called an *alternative hypothesis.*

robust A term given to a hypothesis test that produces fairly accurate results even when the data suggest that the population might not meet some of the assumptions.

S

sample A set of observations drawn from the population of interest.

scale variable A variable that meets the criteria for an interval variable or a ratio variable.

scatterplot A graph that depicts the relation between two scale variables. The values of each variable are marked along the two axes, and a mark is made to indicate the intersection of the two scores for each participant.

simple linear regression A statistical tool that lets us predict a person's score on a dependent variable from his or her score on one independent variable.

single-sample *t* test A hypothesis test in which we compare a sample from which we collect data to a population for which we know the mean but not the standard deviation.

skewed distribution A distribution in which one of the tails of the distribution is pulled away from the center.

slope The amount that Y is predicted to increase for an increase of 1 in X.

source table A table that presents the important calculations and final results of an ANOVA in a consistent and easy-to-read format.

Spearman rank-order correlation coefficient A nonparametric statistic that quantifies the association between two ordinal variables.

square root transformation A transformation that reduces skew by compressing both the negative and positive sides of a skewed distribution.

standard deviation The square root of the average of the squared deviations from the mean; the typical amount that each score varies, or deviates, from the mean.

standard error The name for the standard deviation of a distribution of means.

standard error of the estimate A statistic indicating the typical distance between a regression line and the actual data points.

standard normal distribution A normal distribution of z scores.

standardization A way to convert individual scores from different normal distributions to a shared normal distribution with a known mean, standard deviation, and percentiles.

standardized regression coefficient A standardized version of the slope in a regression equation, it is the predicted change in the dependent variable in terms of standard deviations for an increase of 1 standard deviation in the independent variable; symbolized by β and often called the *beta weight.*

statistic A number based on a sample taken from a population; it is usually symbolized by a Latin letter.

statistical (or theoretical) model A hypothesized network of relations, often portrayed graphically, among multiple variables.

statistically significant A term for a finding in which the data differ from what we would expect by chance if there were, in fact, no actual difference.

statistical power A measure of the likelihood that we will reject the null hypothesis given that the null hypothesis is false.

stem-and-leaf plot A graph that displays all the data points of a variable (or of two levels of a variable) both numerically and visually.

stepwise multiple regression A type of multiple regression in which a computer program determines the order in which independent variables are included in the equation.

structural equation modeling (SEM) A statistical technique that quantifies how well sample data "fit" a theoretical model that hypothesizes a set of relations among multiple variables.

success In reference to probability, the outcome for which we're trying to determine the probability.

sum of squares The sum of each score's squared deviation from the mean. Symbolized as *SS.*

T

***t* statistic** A statistic that indicates the distance of a sample mean from a population mean in terms of the standard error.

test–retest reliability A term that refers to whether the scale being used provides consistent information every time the test is taken.

third quartile The 75th percentile of a data set.

time plot or **time series plot** A graph that plots a scale variable on the y-axis as it changes over an increment of time (e.g., second, day, century) labeled on the x-axis.

trial In reference to probability, each occasion that a given procedure is carried out.

Tukey *HSD* test A widely used post hoc test that determines the differences between means in terms of standard error; the *HSD* is compared to a critical value; sometimes called the *q test.*

two-tailed test A hypothesis test in which the research hypothesis does not indicate a direction of the mean difference or change in the dependent variable, but merely indicates that there will be a mean difference.

two-way ANOVA A hypothesis test that includes two nominal independent variables, regardless of their numbers of levels, and a scale dependent variable.

Type I error The result of rejecting the null hypothesis when the null hypothesis is correct.

Type II error The result of failing to reject the null hypothesis when the null hypothesis is false.

U

unimodal A term for a distribution that has one mode, or most common score.

V

validity The extent to which a test actually measures what it was intended to measure.

variability A numerical way of describing how much spread there is in a distribution.

variable Any observation of a physical, attitudinal, or behavioral characteristic that can take on different values.

variance The average of the squared deviations from the mean.

volunteer sample A special kind of convenience sample in which participants actively choose to participate in a study; also called a *self-selected sample.*

W

Wilcoxon signed-rank test A nonparametric hypothesis test for matched pairs used when there are two groups, a within-groups design, and an ordinal dependent variable.

within-groups ANOVA A hypothesis test in which there are more than two samples, and each sample is composed of the same participants; also called a *repeated-measures ANOVA.*

within-groups research design An experimental design in which all participants in the study experience the different levels of the independent variable; also called a *repeated-measures design.*

within-groups variance An estimate of the population variance based on the differences within each of the three (or more) sample distributions.

Z

z distribution A normal distribution of standardized scores.

z score The number of standard deviations a particular score is from the mean.

REFERENCES

Abumrad, J., & Krulwich, R. (Hosts). (2009, September 11). Stochasticity [Radio series episode]. In Wheeler, S., & Abumrad, J. (Producers), *Radiolab*. New York: WNYC.

Acerbi, A., Lampos, V., Garnett, P., & Bentley, R. A. (2013). The expression of emotions in 20th century books. *PLOS ONE, 8*, e59030.

Adams, J. (2012). Consideration of immediate and future consequences, smoking status, and body mass index. *Health Psychology, 31*, 260–263.

Agresti, A. & Franklin, C. (2006). *Statistics: The art and science of learning from data.* Upper Saddle River, NJ: Prentice Hall.

Airely, D. (2010). *Predictably irrational.* New York: HarperCollins.

Alter, A., & Oppenheimer, D. (2006). Predicting short-term stock fluctuations by using processing fluency. *Proceedings of the National Academy of Sciences of the United States of America, 103*, 9369–9372.

American Academy of Physician Assistants. (2005). Income reported by PAs who graduated in 2004. *American Academy of Physician Assistants.* Retrieved November 20, 2006, from http://www .aapa.org/research/05newgrad-income.pdf.

American Psychological Association (APA). (2010). *Publication manual of the American Psychological Association* (6th ed.). Washington, DC: Author.

American Psychological Association. (2014). Crowdsourcing with Mobile Apps Brings 'Big Data' To Psychological Research. American Psychological Association Press Release. Retrieved from www.apa.org.

Anderson, C. J., Bahník, Š., Barnett-Cowan, M., Bosco, F. A., Chandler, J., Chartier, C. R., … & Zuni, K. (2016). Response to Comment on "Estimating the reproducibility of psychological science." *Science, 351*, 1037-c.

Aneja, A., & Ross, A. (2015, June 23). These are the 5 elements of a viral video. *Time.* Retrieved from http://www.time.com/.

Archibold, R. C. (1998, February 18). Just because the grades are up, are Princeton students smarter? *New York Times.* Retrieved November 14, 2006, from http://www.nytimes.com.

Arcidiacono, P., Bayer, P., & Hizmo, A. (2008). Beyond signaling and human capital (NBER Working Paper No. 13591). Cambridge, MA: *National Bureau of Economic Research.* Retrieved March 4, 2013, from http://www.nber.org/papers/w13951.

Aron, A., & Aron, E. N. (2002). *Statistics for psychology* (3rd ed.). Upper Saddle River, NJ: Pearson Education.

Aron, A., Fisher, H., Mashek, D. J., Strong, G., Li, H., & Brown, L. L. (2005). Reward, motivation, and emotion systems associated with early-stage intense romantic love. *Journal of Neurophysiology, 94*, 327–337.

Association for Psychological Science. (2014). Business not as usual. *Psychological Science, 25*, 3–6.

Ayaz, H., Shewokis, P. A., Bunce, S., Izzetoglu, K., Willems, B., & Onaral, B. (2012). Optical brain monitoring for operator training and mental workload assessment. *Neuroimage, 59*, 36–47.

Azim, E., Mobbs, D., Jo, B., Menon, V., & Reiss, A. L. (2005). Sex differences in brain activation elicited by humor. *Proceedings of the National Academy of Sciences, 102*, 16496–16501. Retrieved February 10, 2006, from http://www.pnas.org/cgi/doi/10.1073/pnas.0408456102.

Bailey, D. G., & Dresser, G. K. (2004). Natural products and adverse drug interactions. *Canadian Medical Association Journal, 170*, 1531–1532.

Balzar, J. (1998, September 5). A world unzipped is unthinkable. *Los Angeles Times.* Retrieved from http://articles.latimes.com/1998/sep/05/news/mn-19744/2.

Banks, J., Marmot, M., Oldfield, Z., & Smith, J. P. (2006). Disease and disadvantage in the United States and England. *Journal of the American Medical Association, 295*, 2037–2045.

Barac, R., & Bialystok, E. (2012). Bilingual effects on cognitive and linguistic development: Role of language, cultural background, and education. *Child Development, 83*, 413–422.

Baranski, E. (2015, January 22). It's all happening—the future of crowdsourcing science. *Open Science Collaboration.* Retrieved from http://osc.centerforopenscience.org/2015/01/22/crowdsourcing -science/.

Bardwell, W. A., Ensign, W. Y., & Mills, P. J. (2005). Negative mood endures after completion of high-altitude military training. *Annals of Behavioral Medicine, 29*, 64–69.

Barkhorn, E. (2012). The word that gets women negotiating their salaries: Negotiate. *The Atlantic.* Retrieved July 1, 2013, from http://www .theatlantic.com/sexes/archive/2012/11/the-word-that-gets-women -negotiating-their-salaries-negotiate/264567/.

Barnes, B. (2013). Solving equation of a hit film script, with data. *The New York Times.* Retrieved on May 5, 2013 from http://www .nytimes.com/2013/05/06/business/media/solving-equation-of-a-hit -film-script-with-data.html.

Barrett, L. F. (2015, September 1). Psychology is not in crisis. *The New York Times.* Retrieved from www.nytimes.com.

Barry-Jester, A. M., Casselman, B., & Goldstein, D. (2015, August 4). The new science of sentencing: Should prison sentences be based on crimes that haven't been committed yet? *The Marshall Project.* Retrieved from www.themarshallproject.com.

Bartlett, T. (2014, June 23). Replication crisis in psychology research turns ugly and odd. *The Chronicle of Higher Education.* Retrieved from http://chronicle.com/.

Bartlett, C. P., Harris, R. J., & Bruey, C. (2008). The effect of the amount of blood in a violent video game on aggression, hostility, and arousal. *Journal of Experimental Social Psychology, 44*, 539–546.

Bayes, T. (1763). A letter from the late Reverend Mr. Thomas Bayes, FRS to John Canton, MA and FRS. *Philosophical transactions (1683– 1775), 53*, 269–271.

BBC. (2012a). Beijing 2008 medal table. *BBC.* Retrieved from http://www.bbc.com.

BBC. (2012b). London 2012 medal table. *BBC.* Retrieved from http://www.bbc.com.

Begg, C. B. (1994). Publication bias. In H. Cooper & L. V. Hedges (Eds.), *The handbook of research synthesis* (pp. 399–409). New York: Russell Sage Foundation.

Behenam, M., & Pooya, O. (2006). Factors affecting patients cooperation during orthodontic treatment. *The Orthodontic CYBER Journal.* Retrieved November 21, 2006, from http://www.oc-j.com/nov06/cooperation.htm.

Bellosta, S., Paoletti, R., & Corsini, A. (2004). Safety of statins: Focus on clinical pharmacokinetics and drug interactions. *Circulation, 109,* III-50–III-57.

Belluck, P. (2005). What it means to be human. *Princeton Alumni Weekly Online.* Retrieved October 13, 2005, from http://www.princeton.edu/~paw/archive_new/PAW04-05/15-0608/features1.html.

Benbow, C. P., & Stanley, J. C. (1980). Sex differences in math ability: Fact or artifact? *Science, 210,* 1262–1264.

Bennhold, K. (2015, October 9). London police 'super recognizer' walks beat with a Facebook of the mind. *The New York Times.* Retrieved from www.nytimes.com.

Berger, J., & Fitzsimons, G. (2008). Dogs on the street, Pumas on your feet: How cues in the environment influence product evaluation and choice. *Journal of Marketing Research, XLV,* 1–14.

Bernstein, P. L. (1996). *Against the gods: The remarkable story of risk.* New York: Wiley.

Bilton, N. (2013) Disruptions: Data without context tells a misleading story. *The New York Times.* Retrieved on May 5, 2013 from http://bits.blogs.nytimes.com/2013/02/24/disruptions-google-flu-trends-shows-problems-of-big-data-without-context/.

Blatt, B. (2013, November 20). A textual analysis of *The Hunger Games. Slate.* Retrieved from http://www.slate.com.

Bollinger, B., Leslie, P., & Sorensen, A. (2010). *Calorie posting in chain restaurants* (NBER Working Paper No. 15648). Cambridge: MA: National Bureau of Economic Research. Retrieved May 31, 2010, from http://www.gsb.stanford.edu/news/StarbucksCaloriePostingStudy.pdf.

Boone, D. E. (1992). WAIS-R scatter with psychiatric inpatients: I. Intrasubtest scatter. *Psychological Reports, 71,* 483–487.

Borsari, B., & Carey, K. B. (2005). Two brief alcohol interventions for mandated college students. *Psychology of Addictive Behaviors, 19,* 296–302.

Bowen, W. G., & Bok, D. (2000). *The shape of the river: Long-term consequences of considering race in college and university admissions.* Princeton, NJ: Princeton University Press.

Box, J. (1978). *R. A. Fisher: The life of a scientist.* New York: Wiley.

Boyce, T. (2015, November 10). 25 baby names that spell career success. *Moose Roots.* Retrieved from http://names.mooseroots.com/stories/7338/names-spell-career-success.

Brinn, D. (2006, June 25). Israeli "clown therapy" boosts fertility treatment birthrate. *Health.* Retrieved April 6, 2007, from http://www.Israel21c.org.

Buckley, C. (2013, February 6). Storm's toll creeps inland, 4 tiny feet at a time. *The New York Times.* Retrieved February 8, 2013, from http://www.nytimes.com/2013/02/07/nyregion/after-storm-rats-creep-inland.html.

Buekens, P., Xiong, X., & Harville, E. (2006). Hurricanes and pregnancy. *Birth, 33,* 91–93.

Buhrmester, M., Kwang, T., & Gosling, S. D. (2011). Amazon's Mechanical Turk a new source of inexpensive, yet high-quality, data. *Perspectives on Psychological Science, 6*(1), 3–5.

Busseri, M. A., Choma, B. L., & Sadava, S. W. (2009). "As good as it gets" or "the best is yet to come"? How optimists and pessimists view their past, present, and anticipated future life satisfaction. *Personality and Individual Differences, 47,* 352–356. doi:10.1016/j.paid.209.04.002.

Can Facebook predict your breakup? (2010). *The Week.* Retrieved June 8, 2010, from http://theweek.com/article/index/203122/can-facebook-predict-your-breakup.

Canadian Institute for Health Information (CIHI). (2011). Canadian organ replacement register annual report: Treatment of end-stage organ failure. Retrieved February 5, 2014 from https://secure.cihi.ca/free_products/2011_CORR_Annua_Report_EN.pdf.

Carey, B. (2011). Journal's paper on ESP expected to prompt outrage. *The New York Times.* Retrieved from www.nytimes.com.

Carey, B. (2011). You might already know this. *The New York Times.* Retrieved from www.nytimes.com.

Carey, B. (2015, August 29). Psychologists welcome analysis casting doubt on their work. *The New York Times.* Retrieved from http://www.nytimes.com/2015/08/29/science/psychologists-welcome-analysis-casting-doubt-on-their-work.html.

Carroll, R. (2014). Hawaiian volcano lava on verge of consuming homes on Big Island. *The Guardian.* Retrieved from http://www.theguardian.com/us-news/2014/oct/28/hawaiian-volcano-lava-consuming-homes-big-island.

Carter, B. (2012, February 1). In networks' race for ratings, chicanery is on the schedule. *The New York Times.* Retrieved February 17, 2012, from http://www.nytimes.com/2012/02/02/business/media/networks-resort-to-trickery-in-an-attempt-to-lift-ratings.html.

Centers for Disease Control (CDC). (2004). *Americans slightly taller, much heavier than four decades ago.* Retrieved May 26, 2005, from http://www.cdc.gov/nchs/pressroom/04news/americans.htm.

Chang, A., Sandhofer, C. M., & Brown, C. S. (2011). Gender biases in early number exposure to preschool-aged children. *Journal of Language and Social Psychology, 30,* 440–450. doi: 10.1177/0261927X11416207.

Clark, C., & Stoner, J. B. (2008). An investigation of the spelling skills of Braille readers. *Journal of Visual Impairment & Blindness, 102,* 553–563.

Cohen, J. (1988). *Statistical power analysis for the behavioral sciences* (2nd ed.). Hillsdale, NJ: Erlbaum.

Cohen, J. (1990). Things I have learned (so far). *American Psychologist, 45,* 1304–1312.

Cohen, J. (1992). A power primer. *Psychological Bulletin, 112,* 155–159.

Cohen, J. (1994). The earth is round ($p < .05$). *American Psychologist, 49,* 997–1003.

Conn, V. S., Valentine, J. C., Cooper, H. M., & Rantz, M. J. (2003). Grey literature in meta-analyses. *Nursing Research, 52,* 256–261.

Cooper, M. J., Gulen, H., & Ovtchinnikov, A. V. (2007). *Corporate political contributions and stock returns.* Available at SSRN: http://ssrn.com/abstract-940790.

Corsi, A., & Ashenfelter, O. (2001, April). *Wine quality: Experts' ratings and weather determinants* [Electronic version]. Poster session presented at the annual meeting of the European Association of Agricultural Economists, Zaragoza, Spain.

Cortina, J. M. (1993). What is coefficient alpha? An examination of theory and applications. *Journal of Applied Psychology, 78,* 98–104.

Coulson, M., Healey, M., Fidler, F., & Cumming, G. (2010). Confidence intervals permit, but do not guarantee, better inference than statistical significance testing. *Frontiers in Psychology: Quantitative Psychology and Measurement, 1,* 1–9. doi: 10.3389/fpsyg.2010.00026

Cox, R. H., Thomas, T. R., Hinton, P. S., & Donahue, W. M. (2006). Effects of acute bouts of aerobic exercise of varied intensity on subjective mood experiences in women of different age groups across time. *Journal of Sport Behavior, 29,* 40–59.

Cresswell, J. (2015, October 17). A small Indiana town scarred by a trusted doctor. *The New York Times.* Retrieved from www.nytimes.com.

Cumming, G. (2012). *Understanding the new statistics: Effect sizes, confidence intervals, and meta-analysis.* New York, NY: Routledge.

Cunliffe, S. (1976). Interaction. *Journal of the Royal Statistical Society, A, 139,* 1–19.

Czerwinski, M., Smith, G., Regan, T., Meyers, B., Robertson, G., & Starkweather, G. (2003). Toward characterizing the productivity benefits of very large displays. In M. Rauterberg et al. (Eds.), *Human-computer interaction: INTERACT '03* (pp. 9–16). Amsterdam, Netherlands: IOS Press.

Darlin, D. (2006, July 1). Air fare made easy (or easier). *The New York Times.* Retrieved July 1, 2006, from http://www.nytimes.com.

Das, A. & Biller, D. (2015, February 26). 11 most useless and misleading infographics on the internet. *io9.com.* Retrieved from http://io9.gizmodo.com/.

Dean, G., & Kelly, I. W. (2003). Is astrology relevant to consciousness and PSI? *Journal of Consciousness Studies, 10,* 175–198.

DeBroff, B. M., & Pahk, P. J. (2003). The ability of periorbitally applied antiglare products to improve contrast sensitivity in conditions of sunlight exposure. *Archives of Ophthalmology, 121,* 997–1001.

Delucchi, K. L. (1983). The use and misuse of chi square: Lewis and Burke revisited. *Psychological Bulletin, 94,* 166–176.

DeVellis, R. F. (1991). *Scale development: Theory and applications.* Newbury Park, CA: Sage.

Diamond, M. & Stone, M. (1981). Nightingale on Quetelet. I: The passionate statistician, II: The marginalia, III. Essay in memoriam. *Journal of the Royal Statistical Society, A,* 144, 66–79, 176–213, 332–351.

Diener, E., & Diener-Biswas, R. (n.d.). The replication crisis in psychology. *Noba Project.* Retrieved from http://nobaproject.com/modules/the-replication-crisis-in-psychology.

Dijksterhuis, A., Bos, M. W., Nordgren, L. F., & van Baaren, R. B. (2006). On making the right choice: The deliberation-without-attention effect. *Science, 311,* 1005–1007.

Ditto, P. H., & Lopez, D. L. (1992). Motivated skepticism: Use of differential decision criteria for preferred and nonpreferred conclusions. *Journal of Personality and Social Psychology, 63,* 568–584.

Djordjevic, J., Lundstrom, J. N., Clement, F., Boyle, J. A., Pouliot, S., & Jones-Gotman, M. (2007). A rose by any other name: Would it smell as sweet? *Journal of Neurophysiology, 99,* 386–393.

Döring, N., Reif, A., & Poeschl, S. (2016). How gender-stereotypical are selfies? A content analysis and comparison with magazine adverts. *Computers in Human Behavior, 55,* 955–962.

Douma, L., Steverink, N., Hutter, I., & Meijering, L. (2015). Exploring subjective well-being in older age by using participant-generated word clouds. *The Gerontologist,* 1-11, gnv119. doi:10.1093/geront/gnv119.

Dubner, S. J., & Levitt, S. D. (2006a, May 7). A star is made: The birth-month soccer anomaly. *The New York Times.* Retrieved May 7, 2006, from http://www.nytimes.com.

Dubner, S. J., & Levitt, S. D. (2006b, November 5). The way we live now: Freakonomics; The price of climate change. *The New York Times.* Retrieved March 7, 2007 from http://www.nytimes.com.

Dumas, T. M., Lawford, H., Tieu, T.-T., & Pratt, M. W. (2009). Positive parenting in adolescence and its relation to low point narration and identity status in emerging aduthood: A longitudinal analysis. *Developmental Psychology, 45,* 1531–1544.

Duggan, M., & Levitt, S. (2002). Winning isn't everything: Corruption in sumo wrestling. *American Economic Review, 92,* 1594-1605.

Economist Intelligence Unit, The. (2012). Best cities ranking and report. Retrieved from http://pages.eiu.com/rs/eiu2/images/EIU_BestCities.pdf.

Educational Testing Services. (2015). Test and Score Data Summary for TOEFL iBT® Tests: January 2014–December 2014 Test Data. Retrieved from https://www.ets.org/s/toefl/pdf/94227_unlweb.pdf.

Ellison, N. B., Steinfeld, C., & Lampe, C. (2007). The benefits of Facebook "friends": Social capital and college students' use of online social network sites. *Journal of Computer-Mediated Communication, 12,* at http://jcmc.indiana.edu/vol12/issue4/ellison.html.

Engle-Friedman, M., Riela, S., Golan, R., Ventuneac, A. M., Davis, C. M., Jefferson, A. D., & Major, D. (2003). The effect of sleep loss on next day effort. *Journal of Sleep Research, 12,* 113–124.

Erdfelder, E., Faul, F., & Buchner, A. (1996). G*Power: A general power analysis program. *Behavior Research Methods, Instruments, and Computers, 28,* 1–11.

Fackler, M. (2012, January 21). Japanese struggle to protect their food supply. *The New York Times.* Retrieved February 9, 2012, from http://www.nytimes.com/2012/01/22/world/asia/wary-japanesetake-food-safety-into-their-own-hands.html?_r=2&sq=radiation%20levels%20in%20japan&st=cse&scp=1&pagewanted=all.

Fallows, J. (1999). Booze you can use: Getting the best beer for your money. *Slate* online magazine. http://www.slate.com/33771/.

Feng, J., Spence, I., & Pratt, J. (2007). Playing an action video game reduces gender differences in spatial cognition. *Psychological Science, 18,* 850–855.

Finkelstein, S. R., & Fishbach, A. (2012). Tell me what I did wrong: Experts seek and respond to negative feedback. *Journal of Consumer Research, 39,* 22–38.

Finlay-Jones, A. L., Rees, C. S., & Kane, R. T. (2015). Self-compassion, emotion regulation and stress among Australian psychologists: Testing an emotion regulation model of self-compassion using structural equation modeling. *PLOS ONE, 10(7),* e0133481.

Forsyth, D. R., & Kerr, N. A. (1999, August). *Are adaptive illusions adaptive?* Poster presented at the annual meeting of the American Psychological Association, Boston, MA.

Forsyth, D. R., Lawrence, N. K., Burnette, J. L., & Baumeister, R. F. (2007). *Attempting to improve the academic performance of struggling college students by bolstering their self-esteem: An intervention that backfired.* Unpublished manuscript.

Fosse, E., Gross, N., & Ma, J. (2011). *Political bias in the graduate admissions process: A field experiment* (Working Paper). Retrieved April 9, 2013, from https://www10.arts.ubc.ca/fileadmin/template/main/images/departments/soci/faculty/gross/audit_paper_march_3.pdf.

Friedman, L., Daniels, M., & Blinderman, I. (2016, January). Hollywood's gender divide and its effect on films. *Polygraph.* Retrieved from http://polygraph.cool/bechdel/.

Friendly, M. (2005). Gallery of data visualization. Retrieved July 21, 2005, from http://www.math.yorku.ca/SCS/Gallery/.

Gallagher, R. P. (2009). National survey of counseling center directors. *Monographs of the International Association of Counseling Services, Inc.* (Monograph Series No. 8R). Alexandria, VA: International Association of Counseling Services.

Gallistel, C. R. (2015a). Bayes for beginners 2: The prior. *Observer.* Retrieved from http://www.psychologicalscience.org/index.php/publications/observer/2015/october-15/bayes-for-beginners-2-the-prior.html.

Gallistel, C. R. (2015b). Bayes for beginners: Probability and likelihood. *Observer.* Retrieved from http://www.psychologicalscience.org/index.php/publications/observer/2015/september-15/bayes-for-beginners-probability-and-likelihood.html.

Geier, A. B., Rozin, P., & Doros, G. (2006). Unit bias: A new heuristic that helps explain the effect of portion size on food intake. *Psychological Science, 17,* 521–525.

Georgiou, C. C., Betts, N. M., Hoerr, S. L., Keim, K., Peters, P. K., Stewart, B., & Voichick, J. (1997). Among young adults, college students and graduates practiced more healthful habits and made more healthful food choices than did nonstudents. *Journal of the American Dietetic Association, 97,* 754–759.

Gerber, A., & Malhotra, N. (2006). Can political science literatures be believed? A study of publication bias in the *APSR* and the *AJPS.* Retrieved March 23, 2007, from http://www.jspure.org/news2.htm.

Gibbs, M., Nansen, B., Carter, M., & Kohn, T. (2014). Selfies at funerals: Remediating rituals of mourning. *Selected Papers of Internet Research, 4.* Retrieved from https://minerva-access.unimelb.edu.au/bitstream/handle/11343/52809/Selfies%20at%20Funerals%20AoIR%202014-v9.doc?sequence=1.

Gilbert, D. T., King, G., Pettigrew, S., & Wilson, T. D. (2016). Comment on "Estimating the reproducibility of psychological science." *Science, 351,* 1037-b.

Gill, G. (2005). *Nightingales: The extraordinary upbringing and curious life of Miss Florence Nightingale.* New York: Random House.

Gilovich, T. (1991). *How we know what isn't so: The fallibility of human reason in everyday life.* New York: Free Press.

Gilovich, T., & Medvec, V. H. (1995). The experience of regret: What, when, and why. *Psychological Review, 102,* 379–395.

Gilovich, T., Vallone, R., & Tversky, A. (1985). The hot hand in basketball: On the misperception of random sequences. *Cognitive Psychology, 17,* 295–314.

Goldacre, B. (2013). Health care's trick coin. *The New York Times.* Retrieved February 4, 2013, from http://www.nytimes.com/2013/02/02/opinion/health-cares-trick-coin.html.

Golder, S. A., & Macy, M. W. (2011). Diurnal and seasonal mood vary with work, sleep, and daylength across diverse cultures. *Science, 333,* 1878–1881. doi:10.1126/science.1202775

Goodman, A., & Greaves, E. (2010). *Cohabitation, marriage and relationship stability (IFS Briefing Note BN107).* London: Institute for Fiscal Studies.

Gossett, W. S. (1908). The probable error of a mean. *Biometrics, 6,* 1–24.

Gossett, W. S. (1942). *"Student's" collected papers* (E. S. Pearson & J. Wishart, Eds). Cambridge, UK: Cambridge University Press.

Grimberg, A., Kutikov, J. K., & Cucchiara, A. J. (2005). Sex differences in patients referred for evaluation of poor growth. *Journal of Pediatrics, 146,* 212–216.

Griner, D., & Smith, T. B. (2006). Culturally adapted mental health intervention: A meta-analytic review. *Psychotherapy: Research, Practice, Training, 43,* 531–548.

Grosz, D. (2015). 6 tricks to get 86% more Chipotle burrito (for free!). *Apartment list RENTONOMICS.* Retrieved from https://www.apartmentlist.com/rentonomics/6-techniques-to-get-more-chipotle-burrito-for-free/.

Guéguen, N., Jacob, C., & Lamy, L. (2010). 'Love is in the air': Effects of songs with romantic lyrics on compliance with a courtship request. *Psychology of Music, 38,* 303–307.

Hagerty, M. R. (2000). Social comparisons of income in one's community: Evidence from national surveys of income and happiness. *Journal of Personality and Social Psychology, 78,* 764–771.

Handley, I. M., Brown, E. R., Moss-Racusin, C. A., & Smith, J. L. (2015). Quality of evidence revealing subtle gender biases in science is in the eye of the beholder. *Proceedings of the National Academy of Sciences, 112*(43), 13201–13206.

Hanrahan, F., Field, A. P., Jones, F. W., & Davey, G. C. L. (2013). A meta-analysis of cognitive therapy for worry in generalized anxiety disorder. *Clinical Psychology Review, 33,* 120–132.

Hatchett, G. T. (2003). Does psychopathology predict counseling duration? *Psychological Reports, 93,* 175–185.

Hatfield, E., & Sprecher, S. (1986). Measuring passionate love in intimate relationships. *Journal of Adolescence, 9,* 383–410.

Haug, T. T., Mykletun, A., & Dahl, A. A. (2002). Are anxiety and depression related to gastrointestinal symptoms in the general population? *Scandinavian Journal of Gastroenterology, 37*(3), 294-298.

Hays, W. L. (1994). *Statistics* (5th ed.). Fort Worth, TX: Harcourt Brace College Publishers.

Headquarters Counseling Center. (2005). Myths and facts about suicide. Retrieved February 12, 2007, from http://www.hqcc.lawrence.ks.us/suicide_prevention/myths_facts.html.

Healey, J. R. (2006, October 13). Driving the hard(top) way. *USA Today,* Page 1B.

Healy, J. (1990). *Endangered minds: Why our children don't think.* New York: Simon & Schuster.

Henrich, J., Ensminger, J., McElreath, R., Barr, A., Barrett, C., Bolyanatz, A., ... Ziker, J. (2010). Markets, religion, community size, and the evolution of fairness and punishment. *Science, 327,* 1480–1484, and supporting online material retrieved from http: // www.sciencemag.org/content/327/5972/1480.

Hernandez, A., & Bigatti, S. (2010). Depression among older Mexican American caregivers. *Cultural Diversity and Ethnic Minority Psychology, 16*(1), 50–58. doi:10.1037/a0015867.

Hernández-Julián, R., & Peters, C. (2015). Student appearance and academic performance. Retrieved from https://www.aeaweb.org/aea/2016conference/program/retrieve.php?pdfid=280.

Herszenhorn, D. M. (2006, May 5). As test-taking grows, test-makers grow rarer. *The New York Times.* Retrieved May 5, 2006, from http://www.nytimes.com.

Heyman, J., & Ariely, D. (2004). Effort for payment. *Psychological Science, 15,* 787– 793.

Hickey, W. (2015, November 18). The 20 Most Extreme Cases of "The Book Was Better Than The Movie." *FiveThirtyEight.* Retrieved from www.fivethirtyeight.com.

Highfield, R. (2005). Eurovision voting bias exposed. *Telegraph.* Retrieved December 17, 2012, from http://www.telegraph.co.uk/news/uknews/1490194/Eurovision-voting-bias-exposed.html.

Hockenbury, D. H., & Hockenbury, S. E. (2013). *Psychology* (6th ed.). New York: Worth.

Holiday, A. (2007). *Perceptions of depression based on etiology and gender.* Unpublished manuscript.

Hollon, S. D., Thase, M. E., & Markowitz, J. C. (2002). Treatment and prevention of depression. *Psychological Science in the Public Interest, 3,* 39–77.

Holm-Denoma, J. M., Joiner, T. E., Vohs, K. D., & Heatherton, T. F. (2008). The "freshman fifteen" (the "freshman five" actually): Predictions and possible explanations. *Health Psychology, 27,* s3–s9.

Howard, K. I., Moras, K., Brill, P. L., Martinovich, Z., & Lutz, W. (1996). Efficacy, effectiveness, and patient progress. *American Psychologist, 51,* 1059–1064.

Hoxby, C., & Turner, S. (2013). *Expanding college opportunities for high-achieving, low-income students* (SIEPR Discussion Paper No. 12-014.) Stanford, CA: Stanford Institute for Economic Policy Research.

Hsiehchen, D., Espinoza, M., & Hsieh, A. (2015). Multinational teams and diseconomies of scale in collaborative research. *Science Advances, 1*(8), e1500211.

Hugenberg, K., Miller, J., & Claypool, H. (2007). Categorization and individuation in the cross-race recognition deficit: Toward a solution to an insidious problem. *Journal of Experimental Social Psychology, 43,* 334–340.

Hughes, S. M., & Miller, N. E. (October 23, 2015). What sounds beautiful looks beautiful stereotype: The matching of attractiveness of voices and faces. *Journal of Social and Personal Relationships,* 1–14.

Hull, H. R., Radley, D., Dinger, M. K., & Fields, D. A. (2006). The effect of the Thanksgiving holiday on weight gain. *Nutrition Journal, 21,* 29–34.

Hyde, J. S. (2005). The gender similarities hypothesis. *American Psychologist, 60,* 581–592.

Hyde, J. S., Fennema, E., & Lamon, S. J. (1990). Gender differences in mathematics performance: A meta-analysis. *Psychological Bulletin, 107,* 139–155.

IMD International (2001). Competitiveness rankings as of April 2001. Retrieved June 29, 2006, from http://www. photius.com/wfb1999/rankings/competitiveness.html.

Indiana University Media Relations. (2006). It's no joke: IU study finds *The Daily Show* with Jon Stewart to be as substantive as network news. Retrieved December 10, 2006, from http://newsinfo.iu.edu/news/page/normal/4159.html.

Ingraham, C. (2015, May 27). An unprecedented death toll in Qatar. *The Washington Post.* In Rios, E. (2015, May 27). This Chart Shows the Staggering Human Cost of Staging a World Cup in Qatar. *Mother Jones.* Motherjones.com.

International English Language Test System (IELTS). (2013). Test performance 2013. Retrieved from http://www.ielts.org/researchers/analysis_of_test_data/test_performance_2013.aspx.

Irwin, M. L., Tworoger, S. S., Yasui, Y., Rajan, B., McVarish, L., LaCroix, K., ... McTiernan, A. (2004). Influence of demographic, physiologic, and psychosocial variables on adherence to a year-long moderate-intensity exercise trial in postmenopausal women. *Preventive Medicine, 39,* 1080–1086.

Jacob, J. E., & Eccles, J. (1982). Science and the media: Benbow and Stanley revisited. Report funded by the National Institute of Education, Washington, D.C. ERIC #ED235925.

Jacob, J. E., & Eccles, J. (1986). Social forces shape math attitudes and performance. *Signs, 11,* 367–380.

Jacobs, T. (2010). Ink on skin doesn't necessarily indicate sin. *PS Magazine.* Retrieved February 5, 2014, from http://www.psmag.com/navigation/books-and-culture/ink-on-skin-doesn-t-necessarily-indicate-sin-7068/.

Jakovcevic, A., Steg, L., Mazzeo, N., Caballero, R., Franco, P., Putrino, N., & Favara, J. (2014). Charges for plastic bags: Motivational and behavioral effects. *Journal of Environmental Psychology, 40,* 372-380. doi: 10.1016/j.jenvp.2014.09.004.

Jaschik, S. (2016, January 5). Graded on looks. *Inside Higher Ed.* Retrieved from www.insidehighered.com.

Jay, K. L., & Jay, T. B. (2015). Taboo word fluency and knowledge of slurs and general pejoratives: Deconstructing the poverty-of-vocabulary myth. *Language Sciences, 52,* 251–259.

Johnson, D. J., Cheung, F., & Donnellan, M. B. (2014a). Does cleanliness influence moral judgments? A direct replication of Schnall, Benton, and Harvey (2008). *Social Psychology, 45,* 209–215.

Johnson, D. J., Cheung, F., & Donnellan, M. B. (2014b). Hunting for artifacts: The perils of dismissing inconsistent replication results. *Social Psychology, 45,* 318-320.

Johnson, L. F., Mossong, J., Dorrington, R. E., Schomaker, M., Hoffmann, C. J., Keiser, O., ... Boulle, A. (2013). Life expectancies of South African adults starting antiretroviral treatment: Collaborative analysis of cohort studies. *PLOS Medicine, 10*(4), 1–11. doi:10.1371/journal.pmed.1001418

Johnson, W. B., Koch, C., Fallow, G. O., & Huwe, J. M. (2000). Prevalence of mentoring in clinical versus experimental doctoral programs: Survey findings, implications, and recommendations. *Psychotherapy: Theory, Research, Practice, Training, 37,* 325–334.

Kida, T. (2006). *Don't believe everything you think.* Amherst, NY: Prometheus Books.

Kim, K., & Morawski, S. (2012). Quantifying the impact of going trayless in a university dining hall. *Journal of Hunger and Environmental Nutrition, 7,* 482–486. http://dx.doi.org/10.1080/19320248.2012 .732918

Kirchner, L. (2015, November 3). What we know about the computer formulas making decisions in your life. *Pacific Standard.* Retrieved from http://www.psmag.com.

Kitayama, S., Park, J., Boylan, J. M., Miyamoto, Y., Levine, C. S., Markus, H. R., et al. (2015). Expression of anger and ill health in two cultures: An examination of inflammation and cardiovascular risk. *Psychological Science, 26*(2), 211–220.

Kniffin, K. M., Sigirci, O., & Wansink, B. (2016). Eating heavily: Men eat more in the company of women. *Evolutionary Psychological Science, 2,* 38–46.

Koch, J. R., Roberts, A. E., Armstrong, M. L., & Owens, D. C. (2010). Body art, deviance, and American college students. *The Social Science Journal, 47,* 151–161.

Koehler, J. J., & Conley, C. A. (2003). The "hot hand" myth in professional basketball. *Journal of Sport & Exercise Psychology, 25,* 253–259.

Kolata, G. (2001, June 5). On research frontier, basic questions. *The New York Times,* pp. F1, F9.

Kosinski, M., Stillwell, D., & Graepel, T. (2013). Private traits and attributes are predictable from digital records of human behavior. *Proceedings of the National Academy of Sciences, 110,* 5802–5805.

Krugman, P. (2006, May 5). Our sick society. *The New York Times.* Retrieved May 5, 2006, from http://www.nytimes.com.

Kruschke, J. K. (2010a). An open letter to editors of journals, chairs of departments, directors of funding programs, directors of graduate training, reviewers of grants and manuscripts, researchers, teachers, and students. Retrieved from http://www.indiana.edu/~kruschke/ AnOpenLetter.htm.

Kruschke, J. K. (2010b). Bayesian data analysis. Wiley Interdisciplinary Reviews: *Cognitive Science, 1*(5), 658–676.

Kruschke, J. K. (2010c). What to believe: Bayesian methods for data analysis. *Trends in Cognitive Sciences, 14*(7), 293–300.

Kruschke, J. K. (2011). *Doing Bayesian data analysis: A tutorial with R and BUGS.* Burlington, MA: Academic Press, Elsevier.

Kuper, S., & Szymanski, S. (2009). *Soccernomics: Why England loses, why Germany and Brazil win, and why the U.S., Japan, Australia, Turkey—and even Iraq—are destined to become the kings of the world's most popular sport.* New York: Nation Books.

Kushlev, K., & Dunn, E. W. (2015). Checking email less frequently reduces stress. *Computers in Human Behavior, 43,* 220–228.

Kushnir, T., Xu, F., & Wellman, H. M. (2010). Young children use statistical sampling to infer the preferences of other people. *Psychological Science, 21,* 1134–1140.

Lam, R. W., & Kennedy, S. H. (2005). Using meta-analysis to evaluate evidence: Practical tips and traps. *Canadian Journal of Psychiatry, 50,* 167–174.

Landrum, E. (2005). Core terms in undergraduate statistics. *Teaching of Psychology, 32,* 249–251.

Larzelere, R. E., Cox, R. B., & Swindle, T. M. (2015). Many replications do not causal inferences make: The need for critical replications to test competing explanations of nonrandomized studies. *Perspectives on Psychological Science, 10*(3), 380–389.

Latkin, C. A., Williams, C. T., Wang, J., & Curry, A. D. (2005). Neighborhood social disorder as a determinant of drug injection behaviors: A structural equation modeling approach. *Health Psychology, 24,* 96–100.

Lavner, J. A., Karney, B. R., & Bradbury, T. N. (2012). Do cold feet warn of trouble ahead? Premarital uncertainty and 4-year marital outcomes. *Journal of Family Psychology, 26,* 1012–1017.

Leibbrandt, A., & List, J. A. (2012). *Do women avoid salary negotiations? Evidence from a large scale natural field experiment* (NBER Working Paper No. 18511). Cambridge, MA: National Bureau of Economic Research.

Leong, D. P., Teo, K. K., Rangarajan, S., Lopez-Jaramillo, P., Avezum, A., Orlandini, A., et al. (2015). Prognostic value of grip strength: Findings from the Prospective Urban Rural Epidemiology (PURE) study. *The Lancet, 386*(9990), 266–273.

Leung, D. P. K., Ng, A. K. Y., & Fong, K. N. K. (2009). Effect of small group treatment of the modified constraint induced movement therapy for clients with chronic stroke in a community setting. *Human Movement Science, 28,* 798–808.

Levitt, S. D., & Dubner, S. J. (2009). *Freakonomics: A rogue economist explores the hidden side of everything.* New York: Morrow.

Lexis, W. (1903). *Abhandlungen zur theorie der bevolkerungs- Und moralstatistik.* Jena: Gustav Fisher. Treatises to the theory of population statistics and morality statistics. Kostock, Germany.

Lifestyle education reduced both 2-h plasma glucose and relative risk. (2006, March 6). *Health and Medicine Week.* Retrieved July 9, 2006, from http://www.newsrx.com.

Lindberg, S. M., Hyde, J. S., Petersen, J. L., & Linn, M. C. (2010). New trends in gender and mathematics performance: A meta-analysis. *Psychological Bulletin, 136,* 1123–1135.

Lloyd, C. (2006, December 14). Saved, or sacrificed? *Salon.com.* Retrieved February 26, 2007, from http://www.salon.com/mwt/broadsheet/2006/12/14/selection/index.html.

Lucas, M. E. S., Deen, J. L., von Seidlein, L., Wang, X., Ampuero, J., Puri, M., ... Clemens, J. D. (2005). Effectiveness of mass oral cholera vaccination in Beira, Mozambique. *New England Journal of Medicine, 352,* 757–767.

Lull, R. B., & Bushman, B. J. (2015). Do sex and violence sell? A meta-analytic review of the effects of sexual and violent media and ad content on memory, attitudes, and buying intentions. *Psychological Bulletin, 141,* 1022-1048. http://dx.doi.org/10.1037/bul0000018

Luo, L., Hendriks, T., & Craik, F. (2007). Age differences in recollection: Three patterns of enhanced encoding. *Psychology and Aging, 22,* 269–280.

Lusher, L., Campbell, D., and Carrell, S. (2015). TAs like me: Racial interactions between graduate teaching assistants and undergraduates. National Bureau of Economic Research Working Paper 21568. Retrieved from http://www.nber.org/papers/w21568.

Lutz, G. M., Cornish, D. L., Gonnerman Jr., M. E., Ralston, M., & Baker, P. (2009). Impacts of participation in high school extracurricular activities on early adult life experiences: A study of Iowa graduates. Cedar Falls, IA: University of Northern Iowa, Center for Social and Behavioral Research.

Maks, P. (2013, September 1). Handling momentum shifts key to success. Retrieved from http://ohiostate.rivals.com/content .asp?CID=1543712.

Maner, J. K., Miller, S. L., Rouby, D. A., & Gailliot, M. T. (2009). Intrasex vigilance: The implicit cognition of romantic rivalry. *Journal of Personality and Social Psychology, 97,* 74–87.

Mark, G., Gonzalez, V. M., & Harris, J. (2005, April). No task left behind? Examining the nature of fragmented work. *Proceedings of the Association for Computing Machinery Conference on Human Factors in Computing Systems* (ACM CHI 2005), Portland, OR, 321–330. New York: ACM Press.

Markoff, J. (2005, July 18). Marrying maps to data for a new web service. *The New York Times.* Retrieved July 18, 2005, from http://www .nytimes.com.

Mazer, J. P., Murphy, R. E., & Simonds, C. J. (2007). I'll see you on "Facebook": The effects of computer-mediated teacher self-disclosure on student motivation, affective learning, and classroom climate. *Communication Education, 56*(1), 1–17.

McCollum, J. F., & Bryant, J. (2003). Pacing in children's television programming. *Mass Communication and Society, 6,* 115–136.

McKee, S. (2014). Using word clouds to present your qualitative data. *surveygizmo* blog. Retrieved from https://www.surveygizmo .com/survey-blog/what-you-need-to-know-when-using-word-clouds -to-present-your-qualitative-data/.

McLeland, K. C., & Sutton, G. W. (2005). Military service, marital status, and men's relationship satisfaction. *Individual Difference Research, 3,* 177–182.

Mecklenburg, S. H., Malpass, R. S., & Ebbesen, E. (2006, March 17). Report to the legislature of the State of Illinois: The Illinois Pilot Program on Sequential Double-Blind Identification Procedures. Retrieved April 19, 2006, from http://eyewitness.utep.edu.

Mehl, M. R., Vazire, S., Ramirez-Esparza, N., Slatcher, R. B., & Pennebaker, J. W. (2007). Are women really more talkative than men? *Science, 317,* 82. doi:10.1126/science.1139940

Micceri, T. (1989). The unicorn, the normal curve, and other improbable creatures. *Psychological Bulletin, 105,* 156–166.

Miller, G. (1956). The magical number seven, plus or minus two: Some limits on our capacity for processing information. *Psychological Review, 63,* 81–97.

Ministry of Health New South Wales (2013, March). The NSW health system is… Recruiting more nurses. Retrieved from http://static.guim.co.uk/sys-images/Guardian/Pix/ pictures/2013/8/1/1375343461201/misleading.jpg.

Mitchell, P. (1999). Grapefruit juice found to cause havoc with drug uptake. *Lancet, 353,* 1355.

Mitroff, S. R., Biggs, A. T., Adamo, S. H., Dowd, E. W., Winkle, J., & Clark, K. (2015). What can 1 Billion trials tell us about visual search. *Journal of Experimental Psychology: Human Perception and Performance, 41,* 1–5.

Moertel, T. (2006, January 17). Mining gold from the Internet Movie Database, part 1: Decoding user ratings. *Tom Moertel's Blog.* Retrieved from http://blog.moertel.com/posts/2006-01-17-mining-gold-from -the-internet-movie-database-part-1.html.

Moller, A. P. (1995). Bumblebee preference for symmetrical flowers. *Proceedings of the National Academy of Science, USA, 92,* 2288–2292.

Möller, I., & Krahé, B. (2009). Exposure to violent video games and aggression in German adolescents: A longitudinal analysis. *Aggressive Behavior, 35,* 75–89.

Moss-Racusin, C. A., Dovidio, J. F., Brescoll, V. L., Graham, M. J., & Handelsman, J. (2012). Science faculty's subtle gender biases favor male students. *Proceedings of the National Academy of Sciences, 109,* 16474–16479.

Murphy, K. R., & Myors, B. (2004). *Statistical power analysis: A simple and general model for traditional and modern hypothesis tests.* Mahwah, NJ: Erlbaum.

Myers, D. G., & Diener, E. (1995). Who is happy? *Psychological Science, 6,* 10–19.

Nail, P. R., Harton, H. C., & Decker, B. P. (2003). Political orientation and modern versus aversive racism: Tests of Dovidio and Gaertner's (1998) integrated model. *Journal of Personality and Social Psychology, 84,* 754–770.

National Center for Health Statistics. (2000). *National Health and Nutrition Examination Survey, CDC growth charts: United States.* Retrieved January 6, 2006, from http://www.cdc.gov/nchs/about/ major/nhanes/growthcharts/charts.htm.

National Sleep Foundation (2015). Teens and sleep. Retrieved from https://sleepfoundation.org/sleep-topics/teens-and-sleep.

NDTV Sports. (2014). FIFA World Cup 2014: Nelly the Elephant, the fortune-teller. *NDTV.* Retrieved from http://sports.ndtv.com/ fifa-world-cup-2014/news/225158-fifa-world-cup-2014-nelly-the -elephant-the-fortune-teller.

Neighbors, L., & Sobal, J. (2008). Weight and weddings: Women's weight ideals and weight management behaviors for their wedding day. *Appetite, 50*(2–3), 550–554.

Nelson, J. M., & Gregg, N. (2012). Depression and anxiety among transitioning adolescents and college students with ADHD, dyslexia, or comorbid ADHD/dyslexia. *Journal of Attention Disorders, 16,* 244–254.

Newman, A. (2006, November 11). Missed the train? Lost a wallet? Maybe it was all Mercury's fault. *The New York Times,* p. B3.

Newton, R. R., & Rudestam, K. E. (1999). *Your statistical consultant: Answers to your data analysis questions.* Thousand Oaks, CA: Sage.

Noel, J., Forsyth, D. R., & Kelley, K. (1987). Improving the performance of failing students by overcoming their self-serving attributional biases. *Basic and Applied Social Psychology, 8,* 151–162.

Nolan, S. A., Flynn, C., & Garber, J. (2003). Prospective relations between rejection and depression in young adolescents. *Journal of Personality and Social Psychology, 85,* 745–755.

Norris, F. H., Stevens, S. P., Pfefferbaum, B., Wyche, K. F., & Pfefferbaum, R. L. (2008). Community resilience as a metaphor, theory, set of capacities, and strategy for disaster readiness. *American Journal of Community Psychology, 41,* 127–150.

Nunnally, J. C., & Bernstein, I. H. (1994). *Psychometric theory* (3rd ed.). New York: McGraw-Hill.

Nuzzo, R. (2014). Statistical errors. *Nature, 506,* 150–152.

Oberst, U., Charles, C., & Chamarro, A. (2005). Influence of gender and age in aggressive dream content of Spanish children and adolescents. *Dreaming, 15,* 170–177.

Odgaard, E. C., & Fowler, R. L. (2010). Confidence intervals for effect sizes: Compliance and clinical significance in the *Journal of Consulting and Clinical Psychology. Journal of Consulting and Clinical Psychology, 78,* 287–297.

Ogbu, J. U. (1986). The consequences of the American caste system. In U. Neisser (Ed.), *The school achievement of minority children: New perspectives* (pp. 19–56). Hillsdale, NJ: Erlbaum.

O'Loughlin, K., & Arkoudis, S. (2009). Investigating IELTS exit score gains in higher education. *IELTS Research Report, 10,* 95–180. Retrieved from https://www.ielts.org/pdf/Vol10_Report3.pdf.

Open Science Collaboration (2015). Open science framework. Retrieved from https://osf.io/vmrgu/wiki/home/.

Palazzo, D. J., Lee, Y-J, Warnakulasooriya, R., & Pritchard, D. E. (2010). Patterns, correlates, and reduction of homework copying. *Physical Review Special Topics—Physics Education Research, 6.* Retrieved June 4, 2012, from http://prst-per.aps.org/pdf/PRSTPER/v6/i1/e010104. doi: 10.1103/PhysRevSTPER.6.010104.

Pandey, A. V., Rall, K., Satterthwaite, M. L., Nov, O., & Bertini, E. (2015). How deceptive are deceptive visualizations?: An empirical analysis of common distortion techniques. In *Proceedings of the ACM Conference on Human Factors in Computing Systems;* NYU School of Law, Public Law Research Paper No. 15-03. Retrieved from SSRN: http://ssrn.com/abstract=2566968.

Parker-Pope, T. (2005, December 13). A weight guessing game: Holiday gains fall short of estimates, but pounds hang on. *The Wall Street Journal,* p. 31.

Petrocelli, J. V. (2003). Factor validation of the Consideration of Future Consequences Scale: Evidence for a shorter version. *Journal of Social Psychology, 143,* 405–413.

Plassman, H., O'Doherty, J., Shiv, B., & Rangel, A. (2008). Marketing actions can modulate neural representations of experienced pleasantness. *Proceedings of the National Academy of Sciences, 105,* 1050–1054. doi:10.1073/pnas.0706929105

Popkin, S. J., & Woodley, W. (2002). *Hope VI Panel Study.* Urban Institute: Washington, D.C.

Postman, N. (1985). *Amusing ourselves to death.* New York: Penguin Books.

Press, E. (2006, December 3). Do immigrants make us safer? *The New York Times Magazine,* pp. 20–24.

Pressman, S. D., Gallagher, M. W., & Lopez, S. J. (2013). Is the emotion-health connection a "first-world problem"? *Psychological Science, 24,* 544–549. doi:10.1177/0956797612457382

Psi Chi. (2015). The reproducibility project: A national project for Psi Chi in partnership with the Open Science Collaboration. Retrieved from http://c.ymcdn.com/sites/www.psichi.org/resource/resmgr/pdfs/psichiprojectosc.pdf?hhSearchTerms=%22reproducibility%22.

Public vs. private schools [Editorial]. (2006, July 19). *The New York Times.* Retrieved July 19, 2006, from http://www.nytimes.com.

Quaranta, A., Siniscalchi, M., & Vallortigara, G. (2007). Asymmetric tail-wagging responses by dogs to different emotive stimuli. *Current Biology, 17,* 199–201.

Raggi, A., Leonardi, M., Giovannetti, A., Curone, M., Bussone, G., & D'Amico, D. (2011). A longitudinal evaluation of changes in disability and quality of life in a sample of women with migraine. *Neurological Sciences, 32,* S189–S191.

Rajecki, D. W., Lauer, J. B., & Metzner, B. S. (1998). Early graduate school plans: Uninformed expectations. *Journal of College Student Development, 39,* 629–632.

Ratner, R. K., & Miller, D. T. (2001). The norm of self-interest and its effects on social action. *Journal of Personality and Social Psychology, 81,* 5–16.

Raz, A., Fan, J., & Posner, M. I. (2005). Hypnotic suggestion reduces conflict in the human brain. *Proceedings of the National Academy of Sciences, 102,* 9978–9983.

Reuters. (2014). FIFA World Cup 2014: Animals no longer able to predict World Cup correctly after Paul the Octopus' death. Retrieved from http://www.dnaindia.com/sport/fifa-world-cup-2014/report-fifa-world-cup-2014-animals-no-longer-able-to-predict-world-cup-correctly-after-paul-the-octopus-death-1997142.

Rhodes, G., Yoshikawa, S., Clark, A., Lee, K., McKay, R. & Akamatsu, A. (2001). Attractiveness of facial averageness and symmetry in non-Western cultures: In search of biologically based standards of beauty. *Perception, 30,* 611–625.

Richards, S. E. (2006, March 22). Women silent on abortion on NYT op-ed page. *Salon.com.* Retrieved March 22, 2006, from http://www.salon.com.

Richardson, M., & Reischman, D. (2011). The magical number 7. *Teaching Statistics, 33,* 17–19.

Roberts, P. M. (2003). Performance of Canadian adults on the Graded Naming Test. *Aphasiology, 17,* 933–946.

Roberts, S. B., & Mayer, J. (2000). Holiday weight gain: Fact or fiction? *Nutrition Review, 58,* 378–379.

Rockwell, P. (2006, June 23). Send in the clowns: No joke: "Medical clowning" seems to help women conceive. *Salon.com.* Retrieved June 25, 2006, from http://www.salon.com.

Rodriguez, S. D., Drake, L. L., Price, D. P., Hammond, J. I., & Hansen, I. A. (2015). The efficacy of some commercially available insect repellents for Aedes aegypti (Diptera: Culicidae) and Aedes albopictus (Diptera: Culicidae). *Journal of Insect Science, 15,* 140–144.

Rogers, S. (2013, February 1). Car, bike, train, or walk: How people get to work mapped. *The Guardian: Data Blog.* Retrieved May 19, 2013, from http://www.guardian.co.uk/news/datablog/interactive/2013/feb/01/cycle-drive-work-map-census-2011.

Rohrer, J. M., Egloff, B., & Schmukle, S. C. (2015). Examining the effects of birth order on personality. *Proceedings of the National Academy of Sciences, 112,* 14224–14229.

Rosenblat, A. (September 10, 2015). The future of work: For Uber drivers, data is the boss. Pacific Standard. http://www.psmag.com/.business-economics/the-future-of-work-for-uber-drivers-data-is-the-boss.

Rosenthal, R. (1991). *Meta-analytic procedures for social research.* Newbury Park, CA: Sage.

Rosenthal, R. (1995). Writing meta-analytic reviews. *Psychological Bulletin, 118,* 183–192.

Rosser, J. C., Lynch, P. J., Cuddihy, L., Gentile, D. A., Klonsky, J., & Merrell, R. (2007). The impact of video games on training surgeons in the 21st century. *Archives of Surgery, 142,* 181–186.

Ruby, C. (2006). *Coming to America: An examination of the factors that influence international students' graduate school choices.* Draft of dissertation.

Rudder, C. (2009, November 17). Your looks and your inbox. *Oktrends.* Retrieved from http://blog.okcupid.com/index.php/your-looks-and-online-dating/.

Ruhm, C. J. (2000). Are recessions good for your health? *Quarterly Journal of Economics, 115,* 617–650.

Ruhm, C. J. (2006). *Healthy living in hard times* (NBER Working Paper No. 9468). Cambridge, MA: National Bureau of Economic Research. Retrieved May 30, 2006, from http://www.nber.org/papers/w9468.

Ryan, C. (2006, June 21). "Therapeutic clowning" boosts IVF. *BBC News.* Retrieved June 25, 2006, from http://news.bbc.co.uk.

Samarrai, F. (2015, August 28). Massive collaboration testing reproducibility of psychology studies publishes findings. *University of Virginia.* Retrieved from http://as.virginia.edu/news/massive-collaboration-testing-reproducibility-psychology-studies-publishes-findings.

Sandhu, S. (2015, September 22). Selfies are killing more people than shark attacks. *Independent.* Retrieved from http://www.independent.co.uk/arts-entertainment/photography/selfies-are-killing-more-people-than-shark-attacks-10512449.html.

San Diego Supercomputer Center. Lillian Moller Gilbreth: Mother of modern management. Retrieved June 6, 2013, from http://www.sdsc.edu/ScienceWomen/gilbreth.html.

Sandberg, D. E., Bukowski, W. M., Fung, C. M., & Noll, R. B. (2004). Height and social adjustment: Are extremes a cause for concern and action? *Pediatrics, 114,* 744–750.

Schmidt, M. E., & Vandewater, E. A. (2008). Media and attention, cognition, and school achievement. *Future of Children, 18,* 39–61.

Schnall, S., Benton, J., & Harvey, S. (2008). With a clean conscience cleanliness reduces the severity of moral judgments. *Psychological Science, 19*(12), 1219–1222.

Schnall, S. (2014). Commentary and rejoinder on Johnson, Cheung, and Donnellan (2014a): Clean data: Statistical artifacts wash out replication efforts. *Social Psychology, 45,* 315–318.

Schulz, K. (2015, July 20). The really big one: An earthquake will destroy a sizable portion of the coastal Northwest. The question is when. *The New Yorker.* Retrieved from http://www.newyorker.com/.

Seymour, C. (2006). Listen while you run. *Runner's World.* Retrieved May 24, 2006, from http://msn.runnersworld.com.

Shenker, S. (2010). What are the chances Paul the Octopus is right? *BBC News.* Retrieved May 29, 2013, from http://www.bbc.co.uk/news/10567712.

Sherman, J. D., Honegger, S. D., & McGivern, J. L. (2003). *Comparative indicators of education in the United States and other G-8 countries: 2002,* NCES 2003-026. Washington, D.C.: U.S. Department of Education, National Center for Health Statistics. Retrieved from http://scsvt.org/resource/global_ed_compare2002.pdf.

Silberzahn, R., & Uhlmann, E. L. (2015). Many hands make tight work. *Nature, 526,* 189–191.

Silver, N. (2012). Oct. 21: Uncertainty clouds polling, but Obama remains Electoral College favorite. *The New York Times.* Retrieved October 14, 2012, from http://fivethirtyeight.blogs.nytimes.com/2012/10/22/oct-21-uncertainty-clouds-polling-but-obama-remains-electoral-college-favorite/.

Skurnik, I., Yoon, C., Park, D. C., & Schwarz, N. (2005). How warnings about false claims become recommendations. *Journal of Consumer Research, 31,* 713–724.

Smith, T. W., & Kim, S. (2006). National pride in cross-national and temporal perspective. *International Journal of Public Opinion Research, 18,* 127–136.

Spencer, S. J., Steele, C. M., & Quinn, D. M. (1999). Stereotype threat and women's math performance. *Journal of Experimental Social Psychology, 35,* 1–28.

Stampone, E. (1993). *Effects of gender of rater and a woman's hair length on the perceived likelihood of being sexually harassed.* Paper presented at the 46th Annual Undergraduate Psychology Conference, Mount Holyoke College, South Hadley, MA.

Stanford, E. (2015, October 30). Music to cats' ears. *The New York Times.* Retrieved from www.nytimes.com.

Stedman, L. (2011). A critical analysis of Atlanta's performance on the national assessment of educational progress. *Critical Education, 2*(9). Retrieved May 6, 2013, from http://prophet.library.ubc.ca/ojs/index.php/criticaled/article/viewFile/182354/182392.

Steele, C. M. (2011). Whistling Vivaldi: How Stereotypes Affect Us and What We Can Do. NY: Norton.

Steele, J. P., & Pinto, J. N. (2006). Influences of leader trust on policy agreement. *Psi Chi Journal of Undergraduate Research, 11,* 21–26.

Steinman, G. (2006). Mechanisms of twinning: VII. Effect of diet and heredity on human twinning rate. *Journal of Reproductive Medicine, 51,* 405–410.

Sterne, J. A. C., & Smith, G. D. (2001). Sifting the evidence—what's wrong with significance tests? *British Medical Journal, 322,* 226–231.

Stigler, S. M. (1986). *The history of statistics: The measurement of uncertainty before 1900.* Cambridge, MA: Belknap Press of Harvard University Press.

Stigler, S. M. (1999). *Statistics on the table: The history of statistical concepts and methods.* Cambridge, MA: Harvard University Press.

Suicide Prevention Action Network. (2004). National Strategy for Suicide Prevention Benchmark Survey. Retrieved July 7, 2005, from http://www.spanusa.org.pdf/NSSP_Benchmark_Survey_Results.pdf.

Talarico, J. M., & Rubin, D. C. (2003). Confidence, not consistency, characterizes flashbulb memories. *Psychological Science, 14,* 455–461.

Taylor, G. M., & Ste-Marie, D. M. (2001). Eating disorders symptoms in Canadian female pair and dance figure skaters. *International Journal of Sports Psychology, 32,* 21–28.

Tierney, J. (2008a). Health halo can hide the calories. *The New York Times.* Retrieved December 7, 2008, from http://www.nytimes.com/2008/12/02/science/02tier.html.

Tierney, J. (2008b). The perils of "healthy" food. *The New York Times.* Retrieved December 7, 2008, from http://tierneylab.blogs.nytimes.com.

Tishgart, Sierra. (2015, October 6). Another acclaimed, ambitious restaurant is closing—Here's why. *Grub Street.* Retrieved from http://www.grubstreet.com/2015/10/thirty-acres-closing.html#.

Tough, P. (2014, May 15). Who gets to graduate? *The New York Times.* Retrieved from http://www.nytimes.com.

Trafimow, D., & Marks, M. (2015). Editorial. *Basic and Applied Social Psychology, 37,* 1–2.

Trajectory Group (2013). Fitbit healthy futures report. Retrieved from http://www.trajectorypartnership.com/wp-content/uploads/2014/02/Fitbit-Healthy-Futures-Report-September-2013.pdf.

Tripadvisor.com. (n.d.). Top 25 museums—World. Retrieved from https://www.tripadvisor.com/TravelersChoice-Museums-g1-a_Mode.expanded.

Tucker, K. L., Morita, K., Qiao, N., Hannan, M. T., Cupples, A., & Kiel, D. P. (2006). Colas, but not other carbonated beverages, are associated with low bone mineral density in older women: The Framingham Osteoporosis Study. *American Journal of Clinical Nutrition, 84,* 936–942.

Tufte, E. R. (2005). *Visual explanations* (2nd ed.). Cheshire, CT: Graphics Press. (Original work published 1997)

Tufte, E. R. (2006a). *Beautiful evidence.* Cheshire, CT: Graphics Press.

Tufte, E. R. (2006b). *The visual display of quantitative information* (2nd ed.). (Original work published 2001) Cheshire, CT: Graphics Press.

Turner, L. (2015, September 23). Is Lake Kivu set to explode? *Pacific Standard.* Retrieved from http://www.psmag.com/.

Twenge, J., & Campbell, W. K. (2001). Age and birth cohort differences in self-esteem: A cross-temporal meta-analysis. *Personality and Social Psychology Review, 5,* 321–344.

United Nations Development Programme (2015a). Human development report 2015: Work for human development. Retrieved from http://hdr.undp.org/sites/default/files/2015_human_development_report.pdf.

United Nations Development Programme (2015b). Human development reports: Cartagena Data Festival. Retrieved from http://www.cartagenadatafest2015.org/.

U.S. News & World Report. (2013). National university rankings. Retrieved from http://colleges.usnews.rankingsandreviews.com/best-colleges/rankings/national-universities/data.

U.S. News & World Report. (2013). World's best universities top 400. Retrieved from http://www.usnews.com/education/worlds-best-universities-rankings/top-400-universities-in-the-world.

Upton, P, & Eiser, C. (2006). School experiences after treatment for a brain tumour. *Child: Care, Health and Development, 32,* 9–17.

Valentino-Devries, J., Singer-Vine, J., & Soltani, A. (2012, December 24). Websites vary prices, deals based on users' information. *The Wall Street Journal.* Retrieved from http://www.wsj.com.

van Toorenburg, M., Oostrom, J. K., & Pollet, T. V. (2015). What a Difference Your E-Mail Makes: Effects of Informal E-Mail Addresses in Online Résumé Screening. *Cyberpsychology, Behavior, and Social Networking, 18,* 135–140.

Vergin, R. C. (2000). Winning streaks in sports and the misperception of momentum. *Journal of Sports Behavior, 23,* 181–197.

Vevea, J. L., & Woods, C. M. (2005). Publication bias in research synthesis: Sensitivity analysis using a priori weight functions. *Psychological Methods, 10,* 428–443.

Vinten-Johansen, P., Brody, H., Paneth, N., Rachman, S., & Rip, M. (2003). *Cholera, chloroform, and the science of medicine: A life of John Snow.* Oxford University Press, New York.

Volcanoes by country (2016). Retrieved from http://volcano.oregonstate.edu/volcanoes_by_country.

von Hippel, W., Ronay, R., Baker, E., Kjelsaas, K., & Murphy, S. C. (2016). Quick thinkers are smooth talkers mental speed facilitates charisma. *Psychological Science, 27,* 119–122.

Voss, J. L., Federmeier, K. D., & Paller, K. A. (2012). The potato chip really does look like Elvis! Neural hallmarks of conceptual processing associated with finding novel shapes subjectively meaningful. *Cerebral Cortex, 22,* 2354–2364.

Walker, S. (2006). *Fantasyland: A season on baseball's lunatic fringe.* New York: Penguin.

Wansink, B., & van Ittersum, K. (2003). Bottoms up! The influence of elongation and pouring on consumption volume. *Journal of Consumer Research, 30,* 455–463.

Wasserstein, R. L. (Ed.) (2016). ASA Statement on Statistical Significance and p-values. *The American Statistician.*

Wasserstein, R. L., & Lazar, N. A. (2016): The ASA's statement on p-values: context, process, and purpose, *The American Statistician,* DOI: 10.1080/00031305.2016.1154108

Waters, A. (2006, February 24). Eating for credit. *The New York Times.* Retrieved February 24, 2006 from http://www.nytimes.com.

Weinberg, B. A., Fleisher, B. M., & Hashimoto, M. (2007). *Evaluating methods for evaluating instruction: The case of higher education* (NBER Working Paper No. 12844). Cambridge, MA: National Bureau of Economic Research.

West, T. (2011). Going viral: Factors that lead videos to become internet phenomena. *The Elon Journal of Undergraduate Research in Communications, 2,* 76–84.

Westfall, J., Judd, C. M., & Kenny, D. A. (2015). Replicating studies in which samples of participants respond to samples of stimuli. *Perspectives on Psychological Science, 10*(3), 390–399.

White, M. (2014, July 11). Is social media saving science? *Pacific Standard.* Retrieved from http://www.psmag.com/nature-and-technology/academic-publishing-social-media-saving-science-85733.

White, B., Driver, S., & Warren, A. (2010). Resilience and indicators of adjustment during rehabilitation from a spinal cord injury. *Rehabilitation Psychology, 55*(1), 23–32. doi:10.1037/a0018451

Wiley, J. (2005). A fair and balanced look at the news: What affects memory for controversial arguments. *Journal of Memory and Language, 53,* 95–109.

Wolff, A. (2002). Is the SI jinx for real? *Sports Illustrated,* January 21.

Wood, J. M., Nezworski, M. T., Lilienfeld, S. O., & Garb, H. N. (Eds.) (2003). *What's wrong with the Rorschach? Science confronts the controversial inkblot test.* San Francisco: Jossey-Bass.

World Health Organization. (2007). Myths and realities in disaster situations. Retrieved February 12, 2007, from http://www.who.int/hac/techguidance/ems/myths/en/index.html.

Yanovski, J. A., Yanovski, S. Z., Sovik, K. N., Nouven, T. T., O'Neil, P. M., & Sebring, N. G. A. (2000). A prospective study of holiday weight gain. *New England Journal of Medicine, 23,* 861–867.

Yilmaz, A., Baran, R., Bayramgürler, B., Karahalli, E., Unutmaz, S., & Üskül, T. B. (2000). Lung cancer in non-smokers. *Turkish Respiratory Journal, 2,* 13–15.

YKK. (2015). The cycle of goodness. Retrieved from http://ykkamerica.com/corp_philosophy.html.

Yong, E. (May, 2012). Replication studies: Bad copy. *Nature.* Retrieved from http://www.nature.com/news/replication-studies-bad-copy-1.10634.

YouTube's 50 Best Videos. (2015, September 25). *Time.* Retrieved from http://content.time.com/time/specials/packages/completelist/0,29569,1974961,00.html.

Zacks, J., & Tversky, B. (1997). Bars and lines: A study of graphic communication. AAAI Technical Report FS-97-03.

Zarate, C. A. (2006). A randomized trial of an N-methyl-D-aspartate antagonist in treatment-resistant major depression. *Archives of General Psychiatry, 63,* 856-864.

INDEX